Louis Kronenberger is the author of

Kings and Desperate Men:
Life in 18th Century England

The Thread of Laughter:
English Stage Comedy from Jonson to Maugham

Grand Right and Left

and the editor of many anthologies.

Cavalcade of Comedy

21 BRILLIANT COMEDIES

FROM JONSON AND WYCHERLEY

TO THURBER AND COWARD

Edited with Introductions
by Louis Kronenberger

Simon and Schuster, New York

COPYRIGHT, 1953, BY SIMON AND SCHUSTER, INC.

FIRST PRINTING

MANUFACTURED IN THE UNITED STATES OF AMERICA
BY THE HADDON CRAFTSMEN, SCRANTON, PA.

PUBLISHED SIMULTANEOUSLY IN CANADA

LIBRARY OF CONGRESS CATALOG CARD NUMBER 53-9696

CONTENTS

5837

CONTENTS

Because comedy is the form that most frankly sets out to entertain us and whose invocation of laughter most frequently brings delight, we are perhaps given to belittling its importance. The Puritan in us would characterize and even condemn it as frivolous. The solid citizen in us would speak well of it as a form of relaxation, but grant it no place in the major scheme, or even the Monday morning, of life. And the august philosopher in us, thinking thoughts that do often lie too deep for tears, would make light of those that are induced by laughter. At the level of laughter, moreover, our greatest playwright himself leaves something to be desired—for of all Shakespeare's comic characters, only Falstaff belongs in the company of Iago, Cleopatra, Coriolanus, Lear.

Yet neither Puritan theory nor Shakespearean practice is of decisive argument; nor, to be frank, are many of us habitually given to such thoughts as do lie too deep for tears. Indeed, if we took much thought of any kind, we might perceive how profound is our need for laughter, and to what depths within us it can pierce; how much it expresses that words can never state, how much that is sad can underlie its gaiety, or humane be woven into its mischievousness. We are all aware of what can be said, or suggested, or left unsaid by a joke; how frequently a joke can catch, better than a dozen treatises, the essence of a people, a period, an entire civilization. The world's collective wisdom, we might fairly contend, is compressed into its jokes, which are teeming granaries of human folly and conceit, credulity and presumption. But jokes, and even brilliant epigrams and repartees, are the merest small change of comedy: comedy in the end is, indeed, no form of joshing people or making sport of attitudes, but a trenchant and consistent way of regarding life. And since, in the theater, we require action, complication, conflict, in the theater comedy becomes, equally with regarding life, a way of portraying it.

Often enough this means portraying life as funny, as a series of ridiculous posturings, absurd misunderstandings, hilarious contretemps. We see men making fools of themselves or of one another: betraying themselves through an excess of caution, contradicting themselves from an excess of zeal, falling into traps through laying them for others, jubilantly escaping through one door to find the next one locked. And though comedy is infinitely more than the things that make us laugh out loud, it is essentially rooted in them; it is essentially rooted in human inconsistency and vanity and self-seeking; is almost altogether rooted in what *is* human—all too sadly human—about us. It is a way of surveying life *as it is*, in contrast to what we paint it to be, or ourselves pretend to being. It is a way of maintaining proportion and perspective— almost through showing how seldom men do any such things themselves; a way of preserving truthfulness by revealing man's great gift for self-deception; a way of skepticism, and yet of being skeptical about skepticism itself. For men have at times just as dubious motives for raising their eyebrows as for crossing their hearts or clenching their fists. Comedy is a kind of thermostat that regulates and corrects the emotional, ethical, intellectual temperatures at which we live: it looks with the same keen eye at our noble vows and our defensive pleas; it appraises that part of us that would play the god along with the part that reveals the beast. It keeps things life-sized, examines their workmanship, notes their flaws. Of human weakness and honest blundering it is altogether tolerant; but it is merciless toward pretense.

This manner of viewing life in the broad light of day, at sea level, in the temperate zone, has the greatest possible critical and corrective value. And it has something more, besides: just what, we can better judge if we first consider that form with which comedy is always contrasted—I mean, of course, tragedy. In all tragedy worth the name, the attitude toward life, the enactment and presentation of it, rises above the merely human; becomes more idealistic or affirmative or passionate; shows how grandly man can aspire, how godlike he can become; and achieves a peculiar beauty from man's ultimate defeat. What distinguishes the finest tragedy from the finest comedy is a sort of glowing paradox: in tragedy we are left with the sense of how noble is man in failure; in comedy we see how petty, or at any rate unheroic, he is in success.

This final difference—reduced to copybook language—is that in life the dream counts for far more than the reality, the aspiration far surpasses the achievement. It is the difference too, in a sense, between those who die splendidly, to ominous drumbeats and against dark skies, and those who live on, as respectably, as ignobly, as ourselves. Where tragedy exacts of us tears of homage, comedy evokes a sad fraternal smile of recognition. Comedy can be by far the sadder thing, just for being so unheroic and unexultant; and it is just such sadness that underlies what is best called high comedy—where life has first been raised to an exalted level, only to be played out at an increasingly mean one. In high comedy, the devoted lovers do not die selflessly in each other's arms, but—all passion spent—grow old and querulous and resentful. In high comedy, the fearless visionary or fiery leader is not slain or martyred, to seem more glorious in defeat than he ever could in victory; but grows smug, crotchety, unreasonable, a fatuous sage or bumbling armchair general. There is no more melancholy strain that that which runs through high comedy, too ironic for either tears or laughter, proclaiming how not just the feet, but the legs, and then the arms, and finally the whole body turns to clay.

For myself, comedy and tragedy are the only finally valid and artistic theater forms for portraying life; the only ones that can give an extra dimension to their subject matter. The naturalistic drama, for example, only gives an extra vividness to it, and bases its effect on a curious maneuver. It combines, that is to say, the grayest sort of material with the purplest sort of treatment; it makes use of the greatest number of scars and wrinkles, but also of the greatest amount of rouge and trick lighting. Everything is thus externalized, there is no inwardness or subsurface: only the flat fact and the flashbulb method. We are made to feel a quick, facile apprehension or pity, the thing we feel for what disturbs us in the newspaper or confronts us in the house across the street. But we get no true release or illumination; there is a want of that perspective that we derive from comedy, or of the enlargement that tragedy bestows.

In contrast to much that is merely earnest, dogged, documentary, comedy is a truly serious form of expression and treatment of life. As with every such form, it goes without saying that those who practice it must show a certain scruple about standards, as well as talent and knowledge. I suspect that no form is more frequently practiced without scruple. Among playwrights who write drama, even the hacks who reduce it to the merest formula exhibit a momentary sense of purpose or passion, an almost involuntary sincerity. But among writers of comedy, at even a pretty high level of skill, there is apt to be not the faintest indication of an artistic conscience; there is nothing, absolutely nothing, but a fanatically crass desire to get the audience, at whatever cost, by whatever means, to laugh. Some fairly "representative" comedy writers —which is to say, some pretty impressive Broadway names—have, on this score, appalling plays to their discredit. And where one is not appalled, one is yet—in play after play—disheartened by the insistent pandering, by the slickness and brassiness that assure success. The lengths to which men will go in order to succeed is a staple theme for comedy; and nowhere is it better exemplified than in the methods of certain comedy writers themselves.

But where writers do show scruples, do maintain standards, no form can be more serious than comedy. Laughter, equally with tears, can provide a full release or catharsis; laughter and tears must become, in fact, intermingled, all but indistinguishable; and wherever they are, as most immortally perhaps in *Don Quixote*, they constitute the very summits of art. Comedy can no less— from portraying human vanity and folly—achieve as genuine and as germane and as incisive criticism as the most realistic analysis. The truly insane (because utterly unsound) theory that what is amusing must be less significant than what is ponderous or grim; or that what is witty must be more superficial than what is sententious or sober; or that what is fanciful contains less truth than what is factual—all this is part of an age-old conspiracy whereby those who plod rather than leap, who ponder instead of react, seek to discredit their betters. It was one such plodder, I feel pretty sure, who first circulated the fable of the hare and the tortoise.

And especially in the theater, comedy stands forth a serious and valuable form; for, there, wit, sharpness, pungency are not only fine initial virtues; they are also notable preservatives. In the English-speaking theater, comedy is the only *prose* form that has managed, for even so long as two or three generations, to keep alive. In the theater, tragedy and drama seem to need for survival the leverage of verse rhythm and poetic speech: only so can emotion be at once sufficiently channeled and sufficiently liberated to take hold of later generations. What English prose drama from past centuries exists—outside the textbooks—today? How much more alive is even *The Second Mrs. Tanqueray*, after some sixty years, than *The London Merchant* after some two hundred? Indeed, for want of sufficient leverage—so fiberless and merely approximate is most of his writing—a Eugene O'Neill must all too soon almost surely perish. Thanks to rhythmic and poetic gifts that withstand prose form, the Irish playwrights—the Synge of *Riders to the Sea*, the O'Casey of *The Plough and the Stars*—will very likely endure.

But for comedy we need feel no qualms. While no prose drama written in English before the present century is an unquestioned part of today's living theater, prose comedy can boast, from the past three hundred years, such classics as *The Country Wife, The Way of the World, She Stoops to Conquer,*

The School for Scandal, The Importance of Being Earnest, and half a dozen, or maybe a full dozen, plays by Shaw. To be sure, there are fashions in wit no less than in weeping, and there is much that today we deprecate and dislike in, for example, Restoration comedy. After reading virtually any Restoration comedy, we must deplore the often nasty emphasis it puts on sex; after reading many Restoration comedies, we can only feel genuine revulsion. But in a dozen of the finest ones no one can deny the presence of much witty comment, sharp observation, brilliant writing—where, in the very best prose drama of the past, no one can avoid much hifalutin language, or hollow characterization, or maudlin sentiment. It is worth noting that during the hundred years between Sheridan and Wilde when comedy also foundered, it was wrecked by taboos and hypocrisies that everywhere assailed the stage. In a way, most forms of drama are always on nodding terms, if not indeed in cahoots, with hypocrisy—to the extent that proud *gestes* and gallantries, and noble conflicts and confrontations, have tremendous value as sheer "theater." But so soon as comedy shuts its eyes to the true nature of things, and fails to expose fraud or exhibit folly, it must well-nigh cease to be comedy.

In the theater, comedy also enjoys the advantage of being able to make all sorts of pleasant alliances. It can mingle humor and pathos; or fantasy and farce; or fantasy and satire; and though it seldom can mate with realism, it frequently can with melodrama. Again, by its irreverence it manages to make history oftener seem alive, and far oftener seem lively, than drama does. It runs a whole gamut; exhibits as many colors as a spectrum. And it can mix those colors almost at will. Theoretically, such mixing damages the "tone"; and where the tone is one of high breeding—as in very elegant drawing-room comedy—intrusions of farce or broad satire can be calamitous. A drawing room must not suddenly turn into a smoking car or shooting gallery; and though characters may insult one another—and in fact tend to do so consistently—they must do so as artists and not as boors or fishwives. But even in formal drawing-room comedy, the windows may now and then be left open, to admit muffled sounds from the street; or rugs may be taken up for dancing, or chairs brought in from the hall.

And in other types of comedy a *prevailing* atmosphere is sounder than a pedantic purity of tone. Much good straight comedy is helpfully splashed with farce; much good straight farce is pleasantly streaked with satire; much satire is the better for gaily spilling over into nonsense. We are much given to talk —or to expatiating in the textbooks—about the many types of comedy: comedy of character, or of situation, or of humors, or of manners, or of ideas; high comedy, drawing-room comedy, domestic or sardonic or romantic or philosophic comedy; farce, satire, extravaganza, burlesque. But in truth most successful stage comedy is a blend. Is *Life with Father* satire, or domestic comedy, or comedy of character, or comedy of manners? Is *Blithe Spirit* domestic comedy, or comedy of manners, or fantasy, or farce? Is *Volpone* sardonic comedy, or comedy of humors, or satire—or not comedy at all? If this book provides, among its examples, one relatively solid body of comedy, it is the comedy of manners; but even what is always so labeled, say *The Country Wife,* has far more in common with farce, satire, and the comedy of humors. The whole matter of labels is largely academic; the whole question of blending only matters when the varieties don't blend but clash—as in George Farquhar's *The Beaux' Stratagem*, where sex is at loggerheads with sentiment, and witty artifice with conventional romance.

If the comedy of manners rather predominates here, it is from tending to predominate at the higher levels of the stage itself. Since social life treats of foibles and fashions, of ambitions and subterfuges and intrigues, it particularly calls for wit, lightness, subtlety, finesse. And demanding, as it does, sharp characterization and polished dialogue rather more than movement and action, it relies on effects that are almost as rewarding in the library as in the theater. A mere romp like *Charley's Aunt* dies as soon as it vacates the stage. Comedy of situation, from being most farcical, can—when acted—be the most spontaneously funny; but it is not often hilarious in print.

But if the comedy of manners tends to predominate here, it is present in a variety of forms; while in two of the three playwrights that—from their pre-eminence—I have granted double representation, the comedy of manners scarcely figures at all. Ben Jonson is essentially a satirist, Bernard Shaw a master of the comedy of ideas. Goldsmith, again, is represented here by something very close to farce; Wilde and Coward by urbane nonsense; Maugham by genuine high comedy; Synge by something so happily compounded it defies labeling; Edwin Justus Mayer mates Jonson with Congreve; we are given romantic comedy in Mr. van Druten and domestic comedy by Mr. Osborn. It would be hard to conceive of two plays less alike than *The School for Scandal* and *The Show-Off*; of weightier comedy than *Volpone*, or frothier than *Blithe Spirit*; of comedy with more elegance than *The Way of the World*, or with less than *Juno and the Paycock*. I am glad to find such diversity as I do, but I must confess that I did nothing to insure it. It seemed best to choose plays on their individual merits; and indeed I consciously passed up certain "types" that might have made for a more representative, though I think less rewarding, anthology. This is a cavalcade, not a cross section; more a survival of the fittest than a mere Noah's Ark. There are no slam-bang farces like *Twentieth Century* because I think that off the stage they fall short. There are no gag farces or comedies because even on the stage I seldom find them amusing. There are no comedies of the Kaufman & Hart kind because, while often funny and even witty, their wit has been superimposed, not integrated; they lack temperament, inner life, a sense of the whole playwright. To my regret, there are also absent two or three plays for which permission was refused.

Obviously the table of contents could have been much different. But anthologies should, I think, be matters of personal taste—should seem like individual choices from a large menu, not something pedagogically devised as a sound and "balanced" diet. Of course, one could have started earlier than Jonson, or used something by Dryden or Farquhar, or S. N. Behrman or Sherwood; and of course there is the question of Shakespeare. But on the last score, even a rather immodest editor might assume that the Works of Shakespeare would be waiting on any shelves where this anthology might arrive.

L.K.

CAVALCADE OF COMEDY

The Alchemist

by BEN JONSON
(1572–1637)

With Ben Jonson begins the modern tradition of English comedy—even though no playwright could seem, in one way, more old-fashioned and, indeed, obsolete. His use of the Comedy of Humors, though it has been exaggerated in terms of his work and is largely extraneous to their success, has stamped his plays both queer and quaint. These walking manias—theatrically suggestive of the morality play, physiologically reminiscent of medieval medical theory*—have a gargoyle look; and indeed Ben Jonson must be accounted a great master of the grotesque, a direct ancestor of Dickens and Browning. His, however, is a world not simply of crotchets but of intensities; of fierce cravings and harsh methods; and though, at times, his people seem less human than animal and Aesopian, there is something all too humanly recognizable about their motives. In their single-minded, old-fashioned way (they have very little social veneer; at this point the English stage itself had little), they scheme to outwit the crafty, or fleece the credulous: what they want above all is money. In a different sense, the question d'argent as much actuates Jonson's world as Balzac's. And though his schemers are often monsters of greed, we can't quite write them off as mere stage types: they distort without ever denying reality. They know to what extent money governs—indeed even fashions—society; to what extent it haunts men's thinking and controls their lives; and that even such men as are not brutalized by the love of money, are debased by the need for it. And the love of money can as much corrupt men's reason as their morals, make even worse gulls of them than knaves.

Gulls or knaves—one or the other, and sometimes both—Jonson's characters overwhelmingly are; and it is this worldly, if in places too obsessive, basis of his plotting, this nakedly realistic approach to life, that makes Jonson the forefather of our more serious stage comedy. Also, beyond being worldly, he is

citified: his scene is no Forest of Arden or Illyrian seacoast, but London or Venice—a fact that further links him with the future. He is, again, a master of form; and he is finally a master of rhetoric which, however splendid or glowing, has about it something more solid and specific than poetry. Jonson, in a sense, is everything that his contemporary Shakespeare was not; and his virtual eclipse and consistent unpopularity has largely come about, I think, less because he is inferior to Shakespeare than because he is antithetical to him. Where Shakespeare is tragic and poetic, now soaring now profound, Jonson is cold, harsh, satirical. Where Shakespeare triumphs over stagecraft, Jonson triumphs through it; and though Shakespeare be the greatest dramatist who ever lived, Jonson was yet, in a strict sense, far and away the best playwright of his time.

His two finest plays—The Alchemist and Volpone—are at once greatly alike and decidedly different. In both, we have greedy men preying on their no less greedy fellows; in both, we have men turned witless by their greed. In both, we are fascinated by the wiliness of the plotting, the turns and twists of the plot, the credulousness that goes arm-in-arm with the cunning. In both, for that matter, there are passages of sumptuous rhetoric: though much fewer such in The Alchemist. And it is with this greatly lessened sense of grandeur—which applies to Jonson's villains no less than to his verse—that we can begin to differentiate the two plays. Indeed, there are no villains, no evildoers for mere evil's sake, in The Alchemist: there are only self-seeking crooks who function with wholehearted professional zeal, but with no personal malignity. Hence, though Jonson has introduced some vivid and, in the case of Sir Epicure Mammon, even towering characters, it is much less they than their schemes and counter-schemes that absorb us. There was never a more skilful interplay of forces, or a more graphic exposé of motive, or a finer demonstration of knavish method; hence there is nowhere in English a better managed or, satirically, a sharper-edged comedy of intrigue. Since fleecers and fleeced are alike in their craving for money and their lack of scruples about getting it, there is no need, morally, to take sides; having morally condemned them all, we can intellectually enjoy them all, in this sovereign stage demonstration of cheating cheaters.

*The old medical theory argued that each human body contained four "humors"—choler, melancholy, phlegm, and blood—and that, depending on which one dominated, a person was phlegmatic, sanguine, &c. by temperament. Applying this metaphorically, the Comedy of Humors trafficked in characters almost wholly actuated by a single obsession—greed, say, or gluttony or misogyny.

BEN JONSON

The Alchemist

THE PERSONS OF THE PLAY

SUBTLE, *the alchemist*

FACE, *the housekeeper*

DOLL COMMON, *their colleague*

DAPPER, *a clerk*

DRUGGER, *a tobacco-man*

SIR EPICURE MAMMON, *a knight*

PERTINAX SURLY, *a gamester*

TRIBULATION WHOLESOME, *a pastor of Amsterdam*

ANANIAS, *a deacon there*

KASTRIL, *the angry boy*

DAME PLIANT, *his sister, a widow*

LOVEWIT, *master of the house*

PARSON

NEIGHBOURS, OFFICERS, MUTES, &c.

THE SCENE: *London*

The Argument

T he sickness hot, a master quit, for fear,
H is house in town, and left one servant there.
E ase him corrupted, and gave means to know

A cheater and his punk; who, now brought low,
L eaving their narrow practice, were become
C oz'ners at large; and, only wanting some
H ouse to set up, with him they here contract,
E ach for a share, and all begin to act.
M uch company they draw, and much abuse,
I n casting figures, telling fortunes, news,
S elling of flies, flat bawdry, with the Stone—
T ill it, and they, and all in fume are gone.

Prologue

Fortune, that favours fools, these two short hours
We wish away, both for your sakes and ours,
Judging spectators; and desire, in place,
To th' author justice, to ourselves but grace.

Our scene is London, 'cause we would make known,
No country's mirth is better than our own.
No clime breeds better matter for your whore,
Bawd, squire, impostor, many persons more,
Whose manners, now called humours, feed the stage;
And which have still been subject for the rage
Or spleen of comic writers. Though this pen
Did never aim to grieve, but better men;
Howe'er the age he lives in doth endure
The vices that she breeds, above their cure.
But when the wholesome remedies are sweet,
And in their working gain and profit meet,
He hopes to find no spirit so much diseased,
But will with such fair correctives be pleased.
For here he doth not fear who can apply.
If there be any that will sit so nigh
Unto the stream, to look what it doth run,
They shall find things they'd think or wish were done;
They are so natural follies, but so shown,
As even the doers may see, and yet not own.

Act I

Lovewit's house

Enter Face, Subtle, and Doll.

FACE: Believe 't, I will.

SUBTLE: Thy worst. I fart at thee.

DOLL: Ha' you your wits? Why, gentlemen! for
    love——

FACE: Sirrah, I'll strip you——

SUBTLE: What to do? lick figs
    Out at my—

FACE: Rogue, rogue!—out of all your sleights.

DOLL: Nay, look ye! Sovereign, General, are you mad-
    men?

SUBTLE: O, let the wild sheep loose. I'll gum your
    silks.
    With good strong water, an you come.

DOLL: Will you have
    The neighbours hear you? will you betray all?
    Hark! I hear somebody.

FACE: Sirrah——

SUBTLE: I shall mar
    All that the tailor has made, if you approach.

FACE: You most notorious whelp, you insolent slave,
    Dare you do this?

SUBTLE: Yes, faith; yes, faith.

2

FACE: Why, who
Am I, mongrel, who am I?
SUBTLE: I'll tell you,
Since you know not yourself—
FACE: Speak lower, rogue.
SUBTLE: Yes, you were once—time's not long past—
    the good,
Honest, plain livery-three-pound-thrum, that kept
Your master's worship's house, here in the friars,
For the vacations——
FACE: Will you be so loud?
SUBTLE: Since, by my means, translated suburb-
    captain.
FACE: By your means, Doctor Dog!
SUBTLE: Within man's memory,
All this I speak of.
FACE: Why, I pray you, have I
Been countenanced by you? or you by me?
Do but collect, sir, where I met you first.
SUBTLE: I do not hear well.
FACE: Not of this, I think it.
But I shall put you in mind, sir,—at Pie Corner,
Taking your meal of steam in, from cooks' stalls,
Where, like the father of hunger, you did walk
Piteously costive, with your pinched horn-nose,
And your complexion of the Roman wash
Stuck full of black and melancholic worms,
Like powder-corns shot at th' artillery-yard.
SUBTLE: I wish you could advance your voice a little.
FACE: When you went pinned up in the several rags
You'd raked and picked from dunghills before day,
Your feet in mouldy slippers for your kibes,
A felt of rug, and a thin threaden cloak,
That scarce would cover your no-buttocks——
SUBTLE: So, sir!
FACE: When all your alchemy, and your algebra,
Your minerals, vegetals, and animals,
Your conjuring, coz'ning, and your dozen of trades,
Could not relieve your corpse with so much linen
Would make you tinder, but to see a fire;
I ga' you count'nance, credit for your coals,
Your stills, your glasses, your materials;
Built you a furnace, drew you customers,
Advanced all your black arts; lent you, beside,
A house to practise in——
SUBTLE: Your master's house!
FACE: Where you have studied the more thriving
    skill
Of bawdry, since.
SUBTLE: Yes, in your master's house;
You and the rats here kept possession.
Make it not strange. I know y' were one could keep
The butt'ry-hatch still locked, and save the chip-
    pings,
Sell the dole-beer to aqua-vitae men,
The which, together with your Christmas vails
At post-and-pair, your letting out of counters,
Made you a pretty stock, some twenty marks,
And gave you credit to converse with cobwebs

Here, since your mistress' death hath broke up
    house.
FACE: You might talk softlier, rascal.
SUBTLE: No, you scarab,
I'll thunder you in pieces. I will teach you
How to beware to tempt a fury again
That carries tempest in his hand and voice.
FACE: The place has made you valiant.
SUBTLE: No, your clothes.
Thou vermin, have I ta'en thee out of dung,
So poor, so wretched, when no living thing
Would keep thee company, but a spider, or worse?
Raised thee from brooms and dust and wat'ring-
    pots?
Sublimed thee, and exalted thee, and fixed thee
I' the third region, called our state of grace?
Wrought thee to spirit, to quintessence, with pains
Would twice have won me the Philosophers'
    Work?
Put thee in words and fashion, made thee fit
For more than ordinary fellowships?
Giv'n thee thy oaths, thy quarrelling dimensions,
Thy rules to cheat at horse-race, cockpit, cards,
Dice, or whatever gallant tincture else?
Made thee a second in mine own great art?
And have I this for thanks! Do you rebel,
Do you fly out i' the projection?
Would you be gone now?
DOLL: Gentlemen, what mean you?
Will you mar all?
SUBTLE: Slave, thou hadst had no name——
DOLL: Will you undo yourselves with civil war?
SUBTLE: Never been known, past Equi Clibanum,
The heat of horse-dung, underground in cellars,
Or an ale-house darker than Deaf John's; been lost
To all mankind, but laundresses and tapsters,
Had not I been.
DOLL: D'you know who hears you, Sovereign?
FACE: Sirrah——
DOLL: Nay, General, I thought you were civil.
FACE: I shall turn desperate, if you grow thus loud.
SUBTLE: And hang thyself, I care not.
FACE: Hang thee, collier,
And all thy pots and pans, in picture, I will,
Since thou hast moved me——
DOLL: O, this'll o'erthrow all.
FACE: Write thee up bawd in Paul's, have all thy
    tricks
Of coz'ning with a hollow coal, dust, scrapings,
Searching for things lost, with a sieve and shears,
Erecting figures in your rows of houses,
And taking in of shadows with a glass,
Told in red letters; and a face cut for thee,
Worse than Gamaliel Ratsey's.
DOLL: Are you sound?
Ha' you your senses, masters?
FACE: I will have
A book but barely reckoning thy impostures,
Shall prove a true Philosophers' Stone to printers.

SUBTLE: Away, you trencher-rascal!
FACE: Out, you dog-leech!
The vomit of all prisons——
DOLL: Will you be
Your own destructions, gentlemen?
FACE: Still spewed out
For lying too heavy o' the basket.
SUBTLE: Cheater!
FACE: Bawd!
SUBTLE: Cowherd!
FACE: Conjurer!
SUBTLE: Cutpurse!
FACE: Witch!
DOLL: O me,
We are ruined! lost! Ha' you no more regard
To your reputations? Where's your judgment?
'Slight,
Have yet some care of me, o' your republic——
FACE: Away, this brach! I'll bring thee, rogue, within
The statute of sorcery, Tricesimo Tertio
Of Harry the Eighth; ay, and perhaps thy neck
Within a noose, for laund'ring gold and barbing it.
DOLL: You'll bring your head within a coxcomb, will
   you? [Catches out Face's sword and breaks
   Subtle's glass]
And you, sir, with your menstrue—gather it up.
'Sdeath, you abominable pair of stinkards,
Leave off your barking, and grow one again,
Or, by the light that shines, I'll cut your throats.
I'll not be made a prey unto the Marshal
For ne'er a snarling dog-bolt o' you both.
Ha' you together cozened all this while,
And all the world, and shall it now be said,
You've made most courteous shift to cozen your-
selves?——
You will accuse him! You will bring him in
Within the statute! Who shall take your word?
A whoreson, upstart, apocryphal captain,
Whom not a Puritan in Blackfriars will trust
So much as for a feather!—And you, too,
Will give the cause, forsooth! You will insult,
And claim a primacy in the divisions!
You must be chief! as if you only, had
The powder to project with? and the work
Were not begun out of equality?
The venture tripartite? all things in common?
Without priority? 'Sdeath! you perpetual curs,
Fall to your couples again, and cozen kindly,
And heartily, and lovingly, as you should;
And loose not the beginning of a term,
Or, by this hand, I shall grow factious, too,
And take my part, and quit you.
FACE: 'Tis his fault;
He ever murmurs, and objects his pains,
And says, the weight of all lies upon him.
SUBTLE: Why, so it does.
DOLL: How does it? do not we
Sustain our parts?
SUBTLE: Yes, but they are not equal.

DOLL: Why, if your part exceed today, I hope
Ours may tomorrow match it.
SUBTLE: Ay, they may.
DOLL: May, murmuring mastiff! Ay, and do. God's
will!
Help me to throttle him.
SUBTLE: Dorothy! Mistress Dorothy!
'Ods precious, I'll do anything. What do you mean?
DOLL: Because o' your fermentation and cibation!
SUBTLE: Not I, by Heaven——
DOLL: Your Sol and Luna—Help me.
SUBTLE: Would I were hanged then! I'll conform my-
self.
DOLL: Will you, sir? Do so then, and quickly! Swear.
SUBTLE: What should I swear?
DOLL: To leave your faction, sir,
And labour kindly in the common work.
SUBTLE: Let me not breathe if I meant aught beside.
I only used those speeches as a spur
To him.
DOLL: I hope we need no spurs, sir. Do we?
FACE: 'Slid, prove today who shall shark best.
SUBTLE: Agreed.
DOLL: Yes, and work close and friendly.
SUBTLE: 'Slight, the knot
Shall grow the stronger, for this breach, with me.
DOLL: Why, so, my good baboons! Shall we go make
A sort of sober, scurvy, precise neighbours,
That scarce have smiled twice since the King came
in,
A feast of laughter at our follies? rascals,
Would run themselves from breath, to see me ride,
Or you t' have but a hole to thrust your heads in,
For which you should pay ear-rent! No, agree.
And may Don Provost ride a-feasting long,
In his old velvet jerkin and stained scarfs,
My noble Sovereign, and worthy General,
Ere we contribute a new crewel garter
To his most worsted worship.
SUBTLE: Royal Doll!
Spoken like Claridiana, and thyself.
FACE: For which at supper, thou shalt sit in triumph,
And not be styled Doll Common, but Doll Proper,
Doll Singular; the longest cut at night,
Shall draw thee for his Doll Particular.
                          [Bell rings without]
SUBTLE: Who's that? one rings. To the window, Doll.
   —Pray Heaven,
The Master do not trouble us this quarter.
FACE: O, fear not him. While there dies one a week
O' the plague, he's safe from thinking toward Lon-
don;
Beside, he's busy at his hop-yards now—
I had a letter from him. If he do,
He'll send such word, for airing o' the house,
As you shall have sufficient time to quit it;
Though we break up a fortnight, 'tis no matter.
SUBTLE: Who is it, Doll?
DOLL: A fine young quodling.

FACE: O,
My lawyer's clerk I lighted on last night,
In Holborn, at the Dagger. He would have——
I told you of him—a familiar,
To rifle with, at horses, and win cups.

DOLL: O, let him in.

SUBTLE: Stay. Who shall do't?

FACE: Get you
Your robes on. I will meet him, as going out.

DOLL: And what shall I do?

FACE: Not be seen; away!
                                          [*Exit* Doll]
Seem you very reserved.

SUBTLE: Enough.   [*Exit*]

FACE: God b'w'you, sir!
I pray you let him know that I was here.
His name is Dapper. I would gladly have stayed,
but——

Enter Dapper.

DAPPER: Captain, I am here.

FACE: Who's that? He's come, I think, Doctor.—
Good faith, sir, I was going away.

DAPPER: In truth,
I'm very sorry, Captain.

FACE: But I thought
Sure I should meet you.

DAPPER: Ay, I'm very glad
I had a scurvy writ or two to make,
And I had lent my watch last night to one
That dines today at the Sheriff's, and so was robbed
Of my pass-time.

Re-enter Subtle *in his robes.*
                          Is this the cunning-man?

FACE: This is his worship.

DAPPER: Is he a doctor?

FACE: Yes.

DAPPER: And ha' you broke with him, Captain?

FACE: Ay.

DAPPER: And how?

FACE: Faith, he does make the matter, sir, so dainty,
I know not what to say.

DAPPER: Not so, good Captain.

FACE: Would I were fairly rid on't, believe me.

DAPPER: Nay, now you grieve me, sir. Why should
     you wish so?
I dare assure you I'll not be ungrateful.

FACE: I cannot think you will, sir. But the law
Is such a thing—— And then he says, Read's
     matter
Falling so lately——

DAPPER: Read! he was an ass,
And dealt, sir, with a fool.

FACE: It was a clerk, sir.

DAPPER: A clerk!

FACE: Nay, hear me, sir, you know the law
Better, I think——

DAPPER: I should, sir, and the danger.
You know I showed the statute to you.

FACE: You did so.

DAPPER: And will I tell, then? By this hand of flesh,
Would it might never write good court-hand more,
If I discover. What do you think of me,
That I am a chouse?

FACE: What's that?

DAPPER: The Turk was, here——
As one would say, do you think I am a Turk?

FACE: I'll tell the Doctor so.

DAPPER: Do, good sweet Captain.

FACE: Come, noble Doctor, pray thee let's prevail;
This is the gentleman, and he is no chouse.

SUBTLE: Captain, I have returned you all my an-
     swer.
I would do much, sir, for your love—— But this
I neither may, nor can.

FACE: Tut, do not say so.
You deal now with a noble fellow, Doctor,
One that will thank you richly; and he's no chouse.
Let that, sir, move you.

SUBTLE: Pray you, forbear——

FACE: He has
Four angels here——

SUBTLE: You do me wrong, good sir.

FACE: Doctor, wherein? To tempt you with these
     spirits?

SUBTLE: To tempt my art and love, sir, to my peril.
'Fore Heav'n, I scarce can think you are my friend,
That so would draw me to apparent danger.

FACE: I draw you? A horse draw you, and a halter,
You and your flies together——

DAPPER: Nay, good Captain.

FACE: That knows no difference of men!

SUBTLE: Good words, sir.

FACE: Good deeds, sir, Doctor Dogs'-meat. 'Slight,
     I bring you
No cheating Clim-o'-the-Cloughs, or Claribels,
That look as big as five-and-fifty, and flush,
And spit out secrets like hot custard——

DAPPER: Captain!

FACE: Nor any melancholic under-scribe,
Shall tell the Vicar; but a special gentle,
That is the heir to forty marks a year,
Consorts with the small poets of the time,
Is the sole hope of his old grandmother;
That knows the law, and writes you six fair hands,
Is a fine clerk, and has his ciph'ring perfect,
Will take his oath o' the Greek Testament,
If need be, in his pocket; and can court
His mistress out of Ovid.

DAPPER: Nay, dear Captain——

FACE: Did you not tell me so?

DAPPER: Yes, but I'd ha' you
Use Master Doctor with some more respect.

FACE: Hang him, proud stag, with his broad velvet
     head!
But for your sake, I'd choke ere I would change
An article of breath with such a puckfist!
Come, let's be gone.

SUBTLE: Pray you le' me speak with you.
DAPPER: His worship calls you, Captain.
FACE: I am sorry
I e'er embarked myself in such a business.
DAPPER: Nay, good sir, he did call you.
FACE: Will he take, then?
SUBTLE: First, hear me——
FACE: Not a syllable, 'less you take.
SUBTLE: Pray ye, sir——
FACE: Upon no terms but an assumpsit.
SUBTLE: Your humour must be law.
                                        [*Takes the money*]
FACE: Why now, sir, talk;
Now I dare hear you with mine honour. Speak;
So may this gentleman too.
SUBTLE: Why, sir——
FACE: No whisp'ring.
SUBTLE: 'Fore Heav'n, you do not apprehend the loss
You do yourself in this.
FACE: Wherein? For what?
SUBTLE: Marry, to be so importunate for one
That, when he has it, will undo you all.
He'll win up all the money i' the town.
FACE: How?
SUBTLE: Yes, and blow up gamester after gamester,
As they do crackers in a puppet-play.
If I do give him a familiar,
Give you him all you play for; never set him;
For he will have it.
FACE: You're mistaken, Doctor.
Why, he does ask one but for cups and horses,
A rifling fly—none o' your great familiars.
DAPPER: Yes, Captain, I would have it for all games.
SUBTLE: I told you so.
FACE: 'Slight, that's a new business!—
I understood you, a tame bird, to fly
Twice in a term, or so, on Friday nights,
When you had left the office, for a nag
Of forty or fifty shillings.
DAPPER: Ay, 'tis true, sir,
But I do think now I shall leave the law,
And therefore——
FACE: Why, this changes quite the case.
D'you think that I dare move him?
DAPPER: If you please, sir,
All's one to him, I see.
FACE: What! for that money?
I cannot, with my conscience; nor should you
Make the request, methinks.
DAPPER: No, sir, I mean
To add consideration.
FACE: Why then, sir,
I'll try.— Say that it were for all games, Doctor?
SUBTLE: I say then, not a mouth shall eat for him
At any ordinary, but o' the score,
That is a gaming mouth, conceive me.
FACE: Indeed!
SUBTLE: He'll draw you all the treasure of the realm,
If it be set him.

FACE: Speak you this from art?
SUBTLE: Ay, sir, and reason too, the ground of art.
He's o' the only best complexion,
The Queen of Faery loves.
FACE: What! is he?
SUBTLE: Peace,
He'll overhear you. Sir, should she but see him——
FACE: What?
SUBTLE: Do not you tell him.
FACE: Will he win at cards too?
SUBTLE: The spirits of dead Holland, living Isaac,
You'd swear were in him; such a vigorous luck
As cannot be resisted. 'Slight, he'll put
Six o' your gallants to a cloak, indeed.
FACE: A strange success, that some men shall be born
    to!
SUBTLE: He hears you, man——
DAPPER: Sir, I'll not be ungrateful.
FACE: Faith, I have confidence in his good nature.
You hear, he says he will not be ungrateful.
SUBTLE: Why, as you please, my venture follows
    yours.
FACE: Troth, do it, Doctor. Think him trusty, and
    make him.
He may make us both happy in an hour;
Win some five thousand pound, and send us two
    on't.
DAPPER: Believe it, and I will, sir.
FACE: And you shall, sir.
                                        [*Takes him aside*]
You have heard all?
DAPPER: No, what was't? Nothing, I, sir.
FACE: Nothing!
DAPPER: A little, sir.
FACE: Well, a rare star
Reigned at your birth.
DAPPER: At mine, sir! No.
FACE: The Doctor
Swears that you are——
SUBTLE: Nay, Captain, you'll tell all now.
FACE: Allied to the Queen of Faery.
DAPPER: Who? that I am?
Believe it, no such matter——
FACE: Yes, and that
Y' were born with a caul o' your head.
DAPPER: Who says so?
FACE: Come,
You know it well enough, though you dissemble it.
DAPPER: I' fac, I do not. You are mistaken.
FACE: How!
Swear by your fac, and in a thing so known
Unto the Doctor? How shall we, sir, trust you
I' the other matter? Can we ever think,
When you have won five or six thousand pound,
You'll send us shares in't, by this rate?
DAPPER: By Gad, sir,
I'll win ten thousand pound, and send you half.
I' fac's no oath.
SUBTLE: No, no, he did but jest.

FACE: Go to. Go thank the Doctor. He's your friend
   To take it so.

DAPPER: I thank his worship.

FACE: So!—
   Another angel.

DAPPER: Must I?

FACE: Must you! 'Slight,
   What else is thanks? Will you be trivial?—Doctor,
   When must he come for his familiar?

DAPPER: Shall I not ha' it with me?

SUBTLE: O, good sir!
   There must a world of ceremonies pass;
   You must be bathed and fumigated first.
   Besides, the Queen of Faery does not rise
   Till it be noon.

FACE: Not if she danced tonight.

SUBTLE: And she must bless it.

FACE: Did you never see
   Her royal Grace yet?

DAPPER: Whom?

FACE: Your aunt of Faery?

SUBTLE: Not since she kissed him in the cradle, Captain;
   I can resolve you that.

FACE: Well, see her Grace,
   Whate'er it cost you, for a thing that I know!
   It will be somewhat hard to compass, but
   However, see her. You are made, believe it,
   If you can see her. Her Grace is a lone woman,
   And very rich; and if she take a fancy,
   She will do strange things. See her, at any hand.
   'Slid, she may hap to leave you all she has!
   It is the Doctor's fear.

DAPPER: How will't be done, then?

FACE: Let me alone, take you no thought. Do you
   But say to me, 'Captain, I'll see her Grace.'

DAPPER: Captain, I'll see her Grace.

FACE: Enough.
              [One knocks without]

SUBTLE: Who's there?
   Anon.—Conduct him forth by the back way.—
   Sir, against one o'clock prepare yourself;
   Till when, you must be fasting; only take
   Three drops of vinegar in at your nose,
   Two at your mouth, and one at either ear;
   Then bathe your fingers' ends and wash your
      eyes,
   To sharpen your five senses; and cry 'hum'
   Thrice, and then 'buzz' as often; and then, come.

FACE: Can you remember this?

DAPPER: I warrant you.

FACE: Well then, away. 'T is but your bestowing
   Some twenty nobles 'mong her Grace's servants;
   And put on a clean shirt. You do not know
   What grace her Grace may do you in clean linen.
             [Exeunt Face and Dapper]

SUBTLE: Come in!—Goodwives, I pray you forbear
   me now.
   Troth, I can do you no good till afternoon——

Enter Drugger.
   What is your name, say you, Abel Drugger?

DRUGGER: Yes, sir.

SUBTLE: A seller of tobacco?

DRUGGER: Yes, sir.

SUBTLE: Hmh!
   Free of the grocers?

DRUGGER: Ay, an't please you.

SUBTLE: Well——
   Your business, Abel?

DRUGGER: This, an't please your worship:
   I am a young beginner, and am building
   Of a new shop, an't like your worship, just
   At corner of a street,—here's the plot on't——
   And I would know by art, sir, of your worship,
   Which way I should make my door, by necro-
      mancy;
   And where my shelves; and which should be for
      boxes,
   And which for pots. I would be glad to thrive, sir.
   And I was wished to your worship by a gentleman,
   One Captain Face, that says you know men's
      planets,
   And their good angels and their bad.

SUBTLE: I do,
   If I do see 'em——

Re-enter Face.

FACE: What! my honest Abel?
   Thou art well met here.

DRUGGER: Troth, sir, I was speaking,
   Just as your worship came here, of your worship.
   I pray you speak for me to Master Doctor.

FACE: He shall do anything. Doctor, do you hear?
   This is my friend Abel, an honest fellow;
   He lets me have good tobacco, and he does not
   Sophisticate it with sack-lees or oil,
   Nor washes it in muscadel and grains,
   Nor buries it in gravel underground,
   Wrapped up in greasy leather, or pissed clouts;
   But keeps it in fine lily-pots that, opened,
   Smell like conserve of roses, or French beans.
   He has his maple block, his silver tongs,
   Winchester pipes, and fire of juniper—
   A neat, spruce, honest fellow, and no goldsmith.

SUBTLE: He's a fortunate fellow, that I am sure on,—

FACE: Already, sir, ha' you found it? Lo thee, Abel!

SUBTLE: And in right way toward riches.

FACE: Sir!

SUBTLE: This summer
   He will be of the clothing of his company,
   And next spring called to the scarlet; spend what
      he can.

FACE: What, and so little beard?

SUBTLE: Sir, you must think,
   He may have a receipt to make hair come.
   But he'll be wise—preserve his youth—and fine
      for 't;
   His fortune looks for him another way.

FACE: 'Slid, Doctor, how canst thou know this so
    soon?
    I am amused at that!

SUBTLE: By a rule, Captain,
    In metoposcopy, which I do work by;
    A certain star i' the forehead, which you see not.
    Your chestnut or your olive-coloured face
    Does never fail, and your long ear doth promise.
    I knew't, by certain spots, too, in his teeth,
    And on the nail of his mercurial finger.

FACE: Which finger's that?

SUBTLE: His little finger. Look.—
    Y' were born upon a Wednesday?

DRUGGER: Yes indeed, sir.

SUBTLE: The thumb, in chiromancy, we give Venus,
    The forefinger to Jove, the midst to Saturn,
    The ring to Sol, the least to Mercury,
    Who was the lord, sir, of his horoscope,
    His house of life being Libra; which foreshowed
    He should be a merchant, and should trade with
    balance.

FACE: Why, this is strange! Is not, honest Nab?

SUBTLE: There is a ship now coming from Ormus,
    That shall yield him such a commodity
    Of drugs—— This is the west, and this the south?

DRUGGER: Yes, sir.

SUBTLE: And those are your two sides?

DRUGGER: Ay, sir.

SUBTLE: Make me your door then south, your broad
    side west;
    And on the east side of your shop, aloft,
    Write Mathlai, Tarmiel, and Baraborat;
    Upon the north part, Rael, Velel, Thiel.
    They are the names of those mercurial spirits
    That do fright flies from boxes.

DRUGGER: Yes, sir.

SUBTLE: And
    Beneath your threshold, bury me a loadstone
    To draw in gallants that wear spurs. The rest,
    They'll seem to follow.

FACE: That's a secret, Nab!

SUBTLE: And, on your stall, a puppet, with a vice,
    And a court-fucus to call City dames.
    You shall deal much with minerals.

DRUGGER: Sir, I have,
    At home, already——

SUBTLE: Ay, I know you've ars'nic,
    Vitriol, sal-tartar, argol, alkali,
    Cinoper; I know all. This fellow, Captain,
    Will come, in time, to be a great distiller,
    And give a say—I will not say directly,
    But very fair—at the Philosophers' Stone.

FACE: Why, how now, Abel! Is this true?

DRUGGER: ——Good Captain,
    What must I give?

FACE: Nay, I'll not counsel thee.
    Thou hear'st what wealth he says—spend what
        thou canst—
    Thou'rt like to come to.

DRUGGER: I would gi' him a crown.

FACE: A crown! and toward such a fortune? Heart,
    Thou shalt rather gi' him thy shop. No gold about
        thee?

DRUGGER: Yes, I have a portague, I ha' kept this half-
    year.

FACE: Out on thee, Nab! 'Slight, there was such an
    offer——
    Shalt keep't no longer, I'll gi'it him for thee.—
        Doctor,
    Nab prays your worship to drink this, and swears
    He will appear more grateful, as your skill
    Does raise him in the world.

DRUGGER: I would entreat
    Another favour of his worship.

FACE: What is't, Nab?

DRUGGER: But to look over, sir, my almanac,
    And cross out my ill days, that I may neither
    Bargain nor trust upon them.

FACE: That he shall, Nab.
    Leave it, it shall be done, 'gainst afternoon.

SUBTLE: And a direction for his shelves.

FACE: Now, Nab
    Art thou well pleased, Nab?

DRUGGER: Thank, sir, both your worships.

FACE: Away.
                    [Exit Drugger]
    Why, now, you smoky persecutor of nature!
    Now do you see that something's to be done,
    Beside your beech-coal, and your corsive waters,
    Your crosslets, crucibles, and cucurbites?
    You must have stuff, brought home to you, to work
        on!
    And yet you think I am at no expense
    In searching out these veins, then following 'em,
    Then trying 'em out. 'Fore God, my intelligence
    Costs me more money than my share oft comes to,
    In these rare works.

SUBTLE: You're pleasant sir.

Re-enter Doll.

                    How now!
    What says my dainty Dolkin?

DOLL: Yonder fishwife
    Will not away. And there's your giantess,
    The bawd of Lambeth.

SUBTLE: Heart, I cannot speak with 'em.

DOLL: Not afore night, I have told 'em, in a voice,
    Thorough the trunk, like one of your familiars.
    But I have spied Sir Epicure Mammon——

SUBTLE: Where?

DOLL: Coming along, at far end of the lane,
    Slow of his feet, but earnest of his tongue
    To one that's with him.

SUBTLE: Face, go you and shift.
                    [Exit Face]
    Doll, you must presently make ready too.

DOLL: Why, what's the matter?

SUBTLE: O, I did look for him

With the sun's rising; marvel he could sleep!
This is the day I am to perfect for him
The magisterium, our great work, the Stone;
And yield it, made, into his hands; of which
He has, this month, talked as he were possessed.
And now he's dealing pieces on't away.
Methinks I see him ent'ring ordinaries,
Dispensing for the pox; and plaguy houses,
Reaching his dose; walking Moorfields for lepers;
And off'ring citizens' wives pomander bracelets,
As his preservative, made of the elixir;
Searching the Spittle, to make old bawds young;
And the highways, for beggars, to make rich.
I see no end of his labours. He will make
Nature ashamed of her long sleep; when Art,
Who's but a step-dame, shall do more than she,
In her best love to mankind, ever could.
If his dream last, he'll turn the age to gold.

                                        [*Exeunt*]

Act II

Lovewit's house

Enter Sir Epicure Mammon *and* Surly.

MAMMON: Come on, sir. Now you set your foot on shore
In Novo Orbe; here's the rich Peru,
And there within, sir, are the golden mines,
Great Solomon's Ophir! He was sailing to't
Three years, but we have reached it in ten months.
This is the day wherein, to all my friends,
I will pronounce the happy word, 'Be rich!'
This day you shall be spectatissimi.
You shall no more deal with the hollow die
Or the frail card. No more be at charge of keeping
The livery-punk for the young heir, that must
Seal, at all hours, in his shirt; no more,
If he deny, ha' him beaten to't, as he is
That brings him the commodity. No more
Shall thirst of satin, or the covetous hunger
Of velvet entrails for a rude-spun cloak,
To be displayed at Madam Augusta's, make
The sons of sword and hazard fall before
The golden calf, and on their knees, whole nights,
Commit idolatry with wine and trumpets;
Or go a-feasting after drum and ensign.
No more of this. You shall start up young viceroys,
And have your punks and punketees, my Surly.
And unto thee I speak it first: 'Be rich!'
Where is my Subtle, there? Within, ho!

FACE: [*Within*]   Sir,
He'll come to you by and by.

MAMMON: That's his fire-drake,
His lungs, his Zephyrus, he that puffs his coals
Till he firk nature up, in her own centre.
You are not faithful, sir. This night I'll change
All that is metal in my house to gold.

And early in the morning will I send
To all the plumbers and the pewterers,
And buy their tin and lead up; and to Lothbury,
For all the copper.

SURLY: What, and turn that, too?

MAMMON: Yes, and I'll purchase Devonshire and Cornwall,
And make them perfect Indies! You admire now?

SURLY: No, faith.

MAMMON: But when you see th' effects of the great med'cine,
Of which one part, projected on a hundred
Of Mercury, or Venus, on the moon,
Shall turn it to as many of the sun—
Nay, to a thousand—so, ad infinitum;
You will believe me.

SURLY: Yes, when I see't, I will.
But if my eyes do cozen me so, and I
Giving 'em no occasion, sure I'll have
A whore, shall piss 'em out next day.

MAMMON: Ha! Why?
Do you think I fable with you? I assure you,
He that has once the flower of the sun,
The perfect ruby, which we call elixir,
Not only can do that, but by its virtue,
Can confer honour, love, respect, long life;
Give safety, valour, yea, and victory,
To whom he will. In eight and twenty days,
I'll make an old man of fourscore a child.

SURLY: No doubt, he's that already.

MAMMON: Nay, I mean,
Restore his years; renew him, like an eagle,
To the fifth age; make him get sons and daughters,
Young giants, as our philosophers have done,—
The ancient patriarchs afore the flood—
But taking, once a week, on a knife's point,
The quantity of a grain of mustard of it;
Becomes stout Marses, and beget young Cupids.

SURLY: The decayed vestals of Picthatch would thank you,
That keep the fire alive there.

MAMMON: 'Tis the secret
Of nature, naturized 'gainst all infections;
Cures all diseases coming of all causes,
A month's grief in a day, a year's in twelve,
And, of what age soever, in a month;
Past all the doses of your drugging doctors.
I'll undertake, withal, to fright the plague
Out o' the kingdom in three months.

SURLY: And I'll
Be bound, the players shall sing your praises then,
Without their poets.

MAMMON: Sir, I'll do't. Meantime,
I'll give away so much, unto my man,
Shall serve th' whole city with preservative
Weekly, each house his dose, and at the rate—

SURLY: As he that built the waterwork does with water?

MAMMON: You are incredulous.

SURLY: Faith, I have a humour,
  I would not willingly be gulled. Your Stone
  Cannot transmute me.
MAMMON: Pertinax, my Surly,
  Will you believe antiquity? records?
  I'll show you a book where Moses, and his sister,
  And Solomon have written of the art;
  Ay, and a treatise penned by Adam——
SURLY: How!
MAMMON: O' the Philosophers' Stone, and in High
    Dutch.
SURLY: Did Adam write, sir, in High Dutch?
MAMMON: He did;
  Which proves it was the primitive tongue.
SURLY: What paper?
MAMMON: On cedar board.
SURLY: O, that indeed, they say,
  Will last 'gainst worms.
MAMMON: 'Tis like your Irish wood,
  'Gainst cobwebs. I have a piece of Jason's fleece
    too,
  Which was no other than a book of alchemy,
  Writ in large sheepskin, a good fat ram-vellum.
  Such was Pythagoras' thigh, Pandora's tub,
  And all that fable of Medea's charms,
  The manner of our work: the bulls, our furnace,
  Still breathing fire; our argent-vive, the dragon;
  The dragon's teeth, mercury sublimate,
  That keeps the whiteness, hardness, and the bit-
    ing;
  And they are gathered into Jason's helm,
  Th' alembic, and then sowed in Mars's field,
  And thence sublimed so often, till they are fixed.
  Both this, th' Hesperian garden, Cadmus' story,
  Jove's shower, the boon of Midas, Argus' eyes,
  Boccace's Demogorgon, thousands more,
  All abstract riddles of our Stone.

Enter Face *as a servant.*
                    How now!
  Do we succeed? Is our day come? and holds it?
FACE: The evening will set red upon you, sir;
  You have colour for it, crimson; the red ferment
  Has done his office. Three hours hence prepare you
  To see projection.
MAMMON: Pertinax, my Surly,
  Again I say to thee aloud, 'Be rich!'
  This day thou shalt have ingots, and tomorrow
  Give lords th' affront.—Is it, my Zephyrus, right?
  Blushes the bolt's-head?
FACE: Like a wench with child, sir,
  That were but now discovered to her master.
MAMMON: Excellent, witty Lungs! My only care is
  Where to get stuff enough now, to project on;
  This town will not half serve me.
FACE: No, sir? Buy
  The covering off o' churches.
MAMMON: That's true.
FACE: Yes.

Let 'em stand bare, as do their auditory;
Or cap 'em new with shingles.
MAMMON: No, good thatch—
  Thatch will lie light upo' the rafters, Lungs.
  Lungs, I will manumit thee from the furnace;
  I will restore thee thy complexion, Puff,
  Lost in the embers; and repair this brain,
  Hurt wi' the fume o' the metals.
FACE: I have blown, sir,
  Hard, for your worship; thrown by many a coal,
  When 'twas not beech; weighed those I put in just,
  To keep your heat still even. These bleared eyes
  Have waked to read your several colours, sir,
  Of the Pale Citron, the Green Lion, the Crow,
  The Peacock's Tail, the Plumèd Swan.
MAMMON: And lastly,
  Thou hast described the flower, the Sanguis Agni?
FACE: Yes, sir.
MAMMON: Where's Master?
FACE: At's prayers, sir, he;
  Good man, he's doing his devotions
  For the success.
MAMMON: Lungs, I will set a period
  To all thy labours: thou shalt be the master
  Of my seraglio.
FACE: Good, sir.
MAMMON: But do you hear?
  I'll geld you, Lungs.
FACE: Yes, sir.
MAMMON: For I do mean
  To have a list of wives and concubines
  Equal with Solomon, who had the Stone
  Alike with me; and I will make me a back,
  With the elixir, that shall be as tough
  As Hercules, to encounter fifty a night.
  Th' art sure thou saw'st it blood?
FACE: Both blood and spirit, sir.
MAMMON: I will have all my beds blown up, not
    stuffed—
  Down is too hard. And then, mine oval room
  Filled with such pictures as Tiberius took
  From Elephantis, and dull Aretine
  But coldly imitated. Then, my glasses
  Cut in more subtle angles, to disperse
  And multiply the figures, as I walk
  Naked between my succubae. My mists
  I'll have of perfume, vapoured 'bout the room,
  To lose ourselves in; and my baths, like pits
  To fall into, from whence we will come forth,
  And roll us dry in gossamer and roses.—
  Is it arrived at ruby?—— Where I spy
  A wealthy citizen, or rich lawyer,
  Have a sublimed, pure wife, unto that fellow
  I'll send a thousand pound to be my cuckold.
FACE: And I shall carry it?
MAMMON: No. I'll ha' no bawds
  But fathers and mothers—they will do it best,
  Best of all others. And my flatterers
  Shall be the pure and gravest of divines

That I can get for money. My mere fools
Eloquent burgesses, and then my poets
The same that writ so subtly of the fart,
Whom I will entertain still for that subject.
The few that would give out themselves to be
Court- and town-stallions, and eachwhere bely
Ladies who are known most innocent for them,
Those will I beg, to make me eunuchs of;
And they shall fan me with ten estrich tails
Apiece, made in a plume to gather wind.
We will be brave, Puff, now we ha' the med'cine.
My meat shall all come in, in Indian shells,
Dishes of agate, set in gold, and studded
With emeralds, sapphires, hyacinths, and rubies.
The tongues of carps, dormice, and camels' heels,
Boiled i' the spirit of Sol, and dissolved pearls,—
Apicius' diet, 'gainst the epilepsy—
And I will eat these broths with spoons of amber,
Headed with diamond and carbuncle.
My footboy shall eat pheasants, calvered salmons,
Knots, godwits, lampreys; I myself will have
The beards of barbels served, instead of salads;
Oiled mushrooms; and the swelling, unctuous paps
Of a fat, pregnant sow, newly cut off,
Dressed with an exquisite and poignant sauce,
For which I'll say unto my cook, 'There's gold;
Go forth, and be a knight!'

FACE: Sir, I'll go look
A little, how it heightens.   [Exit]

MAMMON: Do.—My shirts
I'll have of taffeta-sarsnet, soft and light
As cobwebs; and for all my other raiment,
It shall be such as might provoke the Persian,
Were he to teach the world riot anew.
My gloves of fishes' and birds' skins, perfumed
With gums of paradise, and eastern air——

SURLY: And do you think to have the Stone with this?

MAMMON: No, I do think t' have all this with the
    Stone.

SURLY: Why, I have heard he must be homo frugi,
A pious, holy, and religious man,
One free from mortal sin, a very virgin.

MAMMON: That makes it, sir, he is so. But I buy it;
My venture brings it me. He, honest wretch,
A notable, superstitious, good soul,
Has worn his knees bare, and his slippers bald,
With prayer and fasting for it. And, sir, let him
Do it alone, for me, still. Here he comes.
Not a profane word afore him; 'tis poison.

Enter Subtle.
Good morrow, father.

SUBTLE: Gentle son, good morrow,
And to your friend there. What is he, is with you?

MAMMON: An heretic, that I did bring along,
In hope, sir, to convert him.

SUBTLE: Son, I doubt
You're covetous, that thus you meet your time
I' the just point; prevent your day at morning.

This argues something worthy of a fear
Of importune and carnal appetite.
Take heed you do not cause the blessing leave you,
With your ungoverned haste. I should be sorry
To see my labours, now e'en at perfection,
Got by long watching and large patience,
Not prosper where my love and zeal hath placed
    'em.
Which—Heaven I call to witness, with yourself,
To whom I have poured my thoughts—in all my
    ends,
Have looked no way, but unto public good,
To pious uses, and dear charity,
Now grown a prodigy with men. Wherein
If you, my son, should now prevaricate,
And to your own particular lusts employ
So great and catholic a bliss, be sure
A curse will follow, yea, and overtake
Your subtle and most secret ways.

MAMMON: I know, sir,
You shall not need to fear me. I but come
To ha' you confute this gentleman.

SURLY: Who is,
Indeed, sir, somewhat costive of belief
Toward your Stone; would not be gulled.

SUBTLE: Well, son,
All that I can convince him in, is this:
The work is done; bright Sol is in his robe.
We have a med'cine of the triple soul,
The glorifièd spirit. Thanks be to Heaven,
And make us worthy of it!—Eulenspiegel!

FACE: Anon, sir.

SUBTLE: Look well to the register.
And let your heat still lessen by degrees,
To the aludels.

FACE: Yes, sir.

SUBTLE: Did you look
O' the bolt's-head yet?

FACE: Which? on D., sir?

SUBTLE: Ay,
What's the complexion?

FACE: Whitish.

SUBTLE: Infuse vinegar,
To draw his volatile substance and his tincture;
And let the water in glass E. be filtered,
And put into the Gripe's Egg. Lute him well,
And leave him closed in balneo.

FACE: I will, sir.

SURLY: What a brave language here is! next to
    canting!

SUBTLE: I have another work you never saw, son,
That, three days since, passed the Philosophers'
    Wheel,
In the lent heat of Athanor, and's become
Sulphur o' Nature.

MAMMON: But 'tis for me?

SUBTLE: What need you?
You have enough in that is perfect.

MAMMON: O, but——

SUBTLE: Why, this is covetise!

MAMMON: No, I assure you,
I shall employ it all in pious uses,
Founding of colleges and grammar-schools,
Marrying young virgins, building hospitals,
And now and then a church.

Re-enter Face.

SUBTLE: How now!

FACE: Sir, please you,
Shall I not change the filter?

SUBTLE: Marry, yes,
And bring me the complexion of glass B.
                                   [*Exit* Face]

MAMMON: Ha' you another?

SUBTLE: Yes, son, were I assured
Your piety were firm, we would not want
The means to glorify it. But I hope the best.
I mean to tinct C. in sand-heat tomorrow,
And give him imbibition.

MAMMON: Of white oil?

SUBTLE: No, sir, of red. F. is come over the helm,
   too,—
I thank my Maker—in Saint Mary's bath,
And shows Lac Virginis. Blessèd be Heaven!
I sent you of his faeces there calcined.
Out of that calx, I ha' won the salt of mercury.

MAMMON: By pouring on your rectifièd water?

SUBTLE: Yes, and reverberating in Athanor.

Re-enter Face.
How now! what colour says it?

FACE: The ground black, sir.

MAMMON: That's your crow's-head.

SURLY: —Your coxcomb's, is it not?

SUBTLE: No, 'tis not perfect. Would it were the
   Crow!
That work wants something.

SURLY: —O, I looked for this.
The hay is a-pitching.

SUBTLE: Are you sure you loosed 'em
I' their own menstrue?

FACE: Yes, sir, and then married 'em;
And put 'em in a bolt's-head, nipped to digestion,
According as you bade me, when I set
The liquor of Mars to circulation
In the same heat.

SUBTLE: The process then was right.

FACE: Yes, by the token, sir, the retort brake,
And what was saved was put into the Pelican,
And signed with Hermes' seal.

SUBTLE: I think 'twas so.
We should have a new amalgama.

SURLY: —O, this ferret
Is rank as any polecat.

SUBTLE: But I care not.
Let him e'en die; we have enough beside,
In embryon. H. has his white shirt on?

FACE: Yes, sir,
He's ripe for inceration; he stands warm,

In his ash-fire. I would not you should let
Any die now, if I might counsel, sir,
For luck's sake to the rest. It is not good.

MAMMON: He says right.

SURLY: —Ay, are you bolted?

FACE: Nay, I know't, sir,
I've seen th' ill fortune. What is some three ounces
Of fresh materials?

MAMMON: Is't no more?

FACE: No more, sir,
Of gold, t' amalgam with some six of mercury.

MAMMON: Away, here's money. What will serve?

FACE: Ask him, sir.

MAMMON: How much?

SUBTLE: Give him nine pound—you may gi'
   him ten.

SURLY: Yes, twenty, and be cozened, do.

MAMMON: There 'tis.

SUBTLE: This needs not, but that you will have it so,
To see conclusions of all; for two
Of our inferior works are at fixation,
A third is in ascension.—Go your ways.
Ha' you set the oil of Luna in chymia?

FACE: Yes, sir.

SUBTLE: And the Philosophers' Vinegar?

FACE: Ay. [*Exit*]

SURLY: We shall have a salad!

MAMMON: When do you make projection?

SUBTLE: Son, be not hasty. I exalt our med'cine,
By hanging him in balneo vaporoso,
And giving him solution; then congeal him;
And then dissolve him; then again congeal him.
For look, how oft I iterate the work,
So many times I add unto his virtue.
As, if at first, one ounce convert a hundred,
After his second loose, he'll turn a thousand;
His third solution, ten; his fourth, a hundred;
After his fifth, a thousand thousand ounces
Of any imperfect metal, into pure
Silver or gold, in all examinations,
As good as any of the natural mine.
Get you your stuff here, against afternoon,
Your brass, your pewter, and your andirons.

MAMMON: Not those of iron?

SUBTLE: Yes, you may bring them too;
We'll change all metals.

SURLY: I believe you in that.

MAMMON: Then I may send my spits?

SUBTLE: Yes, and your racks.

SURLY: And dripping-pans, and pot-hangers, and
   hooks?
Shall he not?

SUBTLE: If he please.

SURLY: To be an ass.

SUBTLE: How, sir!

MAMMON: This gent'man you must bear withal.
I told you he had no faith.

SURLY: And little hope, sir,
But much less charity, should I gull myself.

SUBTLE: Why, what have you observed, sir, in our art,
    Seems so impossible?

SURLY: But your whole work, no more:
    That you should hatch gold in a furnace, sir,
    As they do eggs in Egypt!

SUBTLE: Sir, do you
    Believe that eggs are hatched so?

SURLY: If I should?

SUBTLE: Why, I think that the greater miracle.
    No egg but differs from a chicken more
    Than metals in themselves.

SURLY: That cannot be.
    The egg's ordained by nature to that end,
    And is a chicken in potentia.

SUBTLE: The same we say of lead, and other metals,
    Which would be gold if they had time.

MAMMON: And that
    Our art doth further.

SUBTLE: Ay, for 'twere absurd
    To think that nature, in the earth, bred gold
    Perfect, i' the instant. Something went before.
    There must be remote matter.

SURLY: Ay, what is that?

SUBTLE: Marry, we say——

MAMMON: Ay, now it heats! Stand, father,
    Pound him to dust.

SUBTLE: It is, of the one part,
    A humid exhalation, which we call
    Materia liquida, or the unctuous water;
    On th' other part, a certain crass and viscous
    Portion of earth; both which, concorporate,
    Do make the elementary matter of gold;
    Which is not yet propria materia,
    But common to all metals and all stones.
    For, where it is forsaken of that moisture,
    And hath more dryness, it becomes a stone;
    Where it retains more of the humid fatness,
    It turns to sulphur, or to quicksilver,
    Who are the parents of all other metals.
    Nor can this remote matter suddenly
    Progress so from extreme unto extreme,
    As to grow gold, and leap o'er all the means.
    Nature doth first beget th' imperfect, then
    Proceeds she to the perfect. Of that airy
    And oily water, mercury is engendered;
    Sulphur o' the fat and earthy part——the one
    Which is the last, supplying the place of male;
    The other, of the female, in all metals.
    Some do believe hermaphrodeity,
    That both do act and suffer. But these two
    Make the rest ductile, malleable, extensive.
    And even in gold they are, for we do find
    Seeds of them by our fire, and gold in them;
    And can produce the species of each metal
    More perfect thence, than nature doth in earth.
    Beside, who doth not see, in daily practice,
    Art can beget bees, hornets, beetles, wasps,
    Out of the carcases and dung of creatures;
    Yea, scorpions of an herb, being rightly placed?

And these are living creatures, far more perfect
    And excellent than metals.

MAMMON: Well said, father!——
    Nay, if he take you in hand, sir, with an argument,
    He'll bray you in a mortar.

SURLY: Pray you, sir, stay.
    Rather than I'll be brayed, sir, I'll believe
    That alchemy is a pretty kind of game,
    Somewhat like tricks o' the cards, to cheat a man
    With charming.

SUBTLE: Sir?

SURLY: What else are all your terms,
    Whereon no one o' your writers 'grees with other?
    Of your elixir, your Lac Virginis,
    Your Stone, your med'cine, and your chrysosperm,
    Your sal, your sulphur, and your mercury,
    Your oil of height, your Tree of Life, your blood,
    Your marcasite, your tutie, your magnesia,
    Your Toad, your Crow, your Dragon, and your
        Panther,
    Your sun, your moon, your firmament, your adrop,
    Your lato, azoch, zarnich, kibrit, heautarit,
    And then your Red Man, and your White Woman,
    With all your broths, your menstrues, and mate-
        rials
    Of piss and egg-shells, women's terms, man's blood,
    Hair o' the head, burnt clouts, chalk, merds, and
        clay,
    Powder of bones, scalings of iron, glass,
    And worlds of other strange ingredients,
    Would burst a man to name?

SUBTLE: And all these named,
    Intending but one thing; which art our writers
    Used to obscure their art.

MAMMON: Sir, so I told him——
    Because the simple idiot should not learn it,
    And make it vulgar.

SUBTLE: Was not all the knowledge
    Of the Egyptians writ in mystic symbols?
    Speak not the scriptures oft in parables?
    Are not the choicest fables of the poets,
    That were the fountains and first springs of wis-
        dom,
    Wrapped in perplexèd allegories?

MAMMON: I urged that,
    And cleared to him, that Sisyphus was damned
    To roll the ceaseless stone, only because
    He would have made ours common. [Doll *is seen*]
    Who is this?

SUBTLE: God's precious! What do you mean? Go in,
    good lady,
    Let me entreat you.——Where's this varlet?

Re-enter Face.

FACE: Sir.

SUBTLE: You very knave! do you use me thus?

FACE: Wherein, sir?

SUBTLE: Go in and see, you traitor. Go! [*Exit* Face]

MAMMON: Who is it, sir?

SUBTLE: Nothing, sir; nothing.

MAMMON: What's the matter, good sir?
I have not seen you thus distempered. Who is't?

SUBTLE: All arts have still had, sir, their adversaries,
But ours the most ignorant.

Re-enter Face.

                                   What now?

FACE: 'Twas not my fault, sir, she would speak with
you.

SUBTLE: Would she, sir? Follow me.   [*Exit*]

MAMMON: Stay, Lungs.

FACE: I dare not, sir.

MAMMON: Stay, man; what is she?

FACE: A lord's sister, sir.

MAMMON: How! pray thee, stay.

FACE: She's mad, sir, and sent hither——
He'll be mad, too.

MAMMON: I warrant thee. Why sent hither?

FACE: Sir, to be cured.

SUBTLE: Why, rascal!

FACE: Lo you—Here, sir!
                                          [*Exit*]

MAMMON: 'Fore God, a Bradamante, a brave piece!

SURLY: Heart, this is a bawdy-house! I'll be burnt else.

MAMMON: O, by this light, no. Do not wrong him.
He's
Too scrupulous that way. It is his vice.
No, he's a rare physician, do him right,
An excellent Paracelsian; and has done
Strange cures with mineral physic. He deals all
With spirits, he. He will not hear a word
Of Galen, or his tedious recipes.

Re-enter Face.
How now, Lungs!

FACE: Softly, sir, speak softly. I meant
To ha' told your worship all.—This must not hear.

MAMMON: No, he will not be gulled; let him alone.

FACE: You're very right, sir, she is a most rare scholar,
And is gone mad with studying Broughton's works.
If you but name a word touching the Hebrew,
She falls into her fit, and will discourse
So learnedly of genealogies,
As you would run mad, too, to hear her, sir.

MAMMON: How might one do t' have conference with
her, Lungs?

FACE: O, divers have run mad upon the conference;
I do not know, sir. I am sent in haste
To fetch a vial.

SURLY: Be not gulled, Sir Mammon.

MAMMON: Wherein? Pray ye, be patient.

SURLY: Yes, as you are;
And trust confederate knaves and bawds and
whores.

MAMMON: You are too foul, believe it.—Come here,
Eulen,
One word.

FACE: I dare not, in good faith.

MAMMON: Stay, knave.

FACE: He's extreme angry that you saw her, sir.

MAMMON: Drink that. [*Gives him money*] What is
she when she's out of her fit?

FACE: O, the most affablest creature, sir! so merry!
So pleasant! She'll mount you up, like quicksilver
Over the helm, and circulate like oil,
A very vegetal; discourse of state,
Of mathematics, bawdry, anything——

MAMMON: Is she no way accessible? no means,
No trick to give a man a taste of her——
Wit—— or so?

SUBTLE: Eulen!

FACE: I'll come to you again, sir. [*Exit*]

MAMMON: Surly, I did not think one o' your breeding
Would traduce personages of worth.

SURLY: Sir Epicure,
Your friend to use; yet still loath to be gulled.
I do not like your philosophical bawds.
Their Stone is lechery enough to pay for,
Without this bait.

MAMMON: Heart, you abuse yourself.
I know the lady, and her friends, and means,
The original of this disaster. Her brother
Has told me all.

SURLY: And yet you ne'er saw her
Till now?

MAMMON: O yes, but I forgot. I have—believe it—
One o' the treacherous't memories, I do think,
Of all mankind.

SURLY: What call you her—brother?

MAMMON: My Lord——
He wi' not have his name known, now I think on't.

SURLY: A very treacherous memory!

MAMMON: O' my faith——

SURLY: Tut, if you have it not about you, pass it,
Till we meet next.

MAMMON: Nay, by this hand, 'tis true.
He's one I honour, and my noble friend,
And I respect his house.

SURLY: Heart! can it be
That a grave sir, a rich, that has no need,
A wise sir, too, at other times, should thus,
With his own oaths and arguments, make hard
mean
To gull himself? An this be your elixir,
Your lapis mineralis, and your lunary,
Give me your honest trick yet at primero,
Or gleek; and take your lutum sapientis,
Your menstruum simplex! I'll have gold before you,
And with less danger of the quicksilver,
Or the hot sulphur.

Re-enter Face.

FACE: [*To Surly*] Here's one from Captain Face, sir.
Desires you meet him i' the Temple Church,
Some half-hour hence, and upon earnest business.
                                   [*Whispers* Mammon]
Sir, if you please to quit us now, and come
Again within two hours, you shall have

My master busy examining o' the works;
And I will steal you in, unto the party,
That you may see her converse.—Sir, shall I say
You'll meet the Captain's worship?
SURLY: Sir, I will.—
But, by attorney, and to a second purpose.
Now I am sure it is a bawdy-house;
I'll swear it, were the Marshal here to thank me!
The naming this commander doth confirm it.
Don Face! Why, he's the most authentic dealer
I' these commodities, the superintendent
To all the quainter traffickers in town!
He is their visitor, and does appoint
Who lies with whom, and at what hour, what
     price,
Which gown, and in what smock, what fall, what
     tire.
Him will I prove, by a third person, to find
The subtleties of this dark labyrinth;
Which if I do discover, dear Sir Mammon,
You'll give your poor friend leave, though no phi-
     losopher,
To laugh; for you that are, 'tis thought, shall weep.
FACE: Sir, he does pray you'll not forget.
SURLY: I will not, sir.
Sir Epicure, I shall leave you.   [Exit]
MAMMON: I follow you straight.
FACE: But do so, good sir, to avoid suspicion.
This gent'man has a parlous head.
MAMMON: But wilt thou, Eulen,
Be constant to thy promise?
FACE: As my life, sir.
MAMMON: And wilt thou insinuate what I am, and
     praise me,
And say I am a noble fellow?
FACE: O, what else, sir?
And that you'll make her royal with the Stone,
An empress; and yourself King of Bantam.
MAMMON: Wilt thou do this?
FACE: Will I, sir?
MAMMON: Lungs, my Lungs!
I love thee.
FACE: Send your stuff, sir, that my master
May busy himself about projection.
MAMMON: Th' ast witched me, rogue. Take, go.
FACE: Your jack, and all, sir.
MAMMON: Thou art a villain—I will send my jack,
And the weights too. Slave, I could bite thine ear.
Away, thou dost not care for me.
FACE: Not I, sir?
MAMMON: Come, I was born to make thee, my good
     weasel;
Set thee on a bench, and ha' thee twirl a chain
With the best lord's vermin of 'em all.
FACE: Away, sir.
MAMMON: A count, nay, a count palatine——
FACE: Good sir, go.
MAMMON: Shall not advance thee better; no, nor
     faster.   [Exit]

Re-enter Subtle and Doll.
SUBTLE: Has he bit? has he bit?
FACE: And swallowed, too, my Subtle.
I ha' giv'n him line, and now he plays, i' faith.
SUBTLE: And shall we twitch him?
FACE: Through both the gills.
A wench is a rare bait, with which a man
No sooner's taken, but he straight firks mad.
SUBTLE: Doll, my Lord Whatchum's sister, you must
     now
Bear yourself statelich.
DOLL: O, let me alone.
I'll not forget my race, I warrant you.
I'll keep my distance, laugh and talk aloud;
Have all the tricks of a proud, scurvy lady,
And be as rude's her woman.
FACE: Well said, Sanguine!
SUBTLE: But will he send his andirons?
FACE: His jack, too,
And's iron shoeing-horn. I ha' spoke to him. Well,
I must not lose my wary gamester yonder.
SUBTLE: O, Monsieur Caution, that will not be
     gulled?
FACE: Ay, if I can strike a fine hook into him now,
The Temple Church, there I have cast mine angle.
Well, pray for me. I'll about it.   [One knocks]
SUBTLE: What, more gudgeons!
Doll, scout, scout!—Stay, Face, you must go to the
     door.
Pray God it be my Anabaptist—Who is't, Doll?
DOLL: I know him not. He looks like a gold-end man.
SUBTLE: God's so'! 'tis he; he said he would send.
What call you him,
The sanctifièd elder, that should deal
For Mammon's jack and andirons? Let him in.
Stay, help me off, first, with my gown. [Exit Face]
     Away,
Madam, to your withdrawing chamber. [Exit Doll]
     Now,
In a new tune, new gesture, but old language.
This fellow is sent from one negotiates with me
About the Stone, too, for the holy Brethren
Of Amsterdam, the exiled Saints, that hope
To raise their discipline by it. I must use him
In some strange fashion now, to make him admire
     me.

Enter Ananias.
Where is my drudge?

Re-enter Face.
FACE: Sir!
SUBTLE: Take away the recipient,
And rectify your menstrue from the phlegma.
Then pour it o' the Sol, in the cucurbite,
And let 'em macerate together.
FACE: Yes, sir.
And save the ground?
SUBTLE: No. Terra damnata

Must not have entrance in the work.—Who are
    you?
ANANIAS: A faithful Brother, if it please you.
SUBTLE: What's that?
    A Lullianist? a Ripley? Filius artis?
    Can you sublime and dulcify? calcine?
    Know you the sapor pontic? sapor styptic?
    Or what is homogene or heterogene?
ANANIAS: I understand no heathen language, truly.
SUBTLE: Heathen? you Knipperdoling! is Ars Sacra,
    Or chrysopoeia, or spagyrica,
    Or the pamphysic, or panarchic knowledge,
    A heathen language?
ANANIAS: Heathen Greek, I take it.
SUBTLE: How! heathen Greek?
ANANIAS: All's heathen but the Hebrew.
SUBTLE: Sirrah my varlet, stand you forth and speak
    to him
    Like a philosopher. Answer i' the language.
    Name the vexations and the martyrizations
    Of metals in the work.
FACE: Sir, putrefaction,
    Solution, ablution, sublimation,
    Cohobation, calcination, ceration, and
    Fixation.
SUBTLE: This is heathen Greek to you now?—
    And when comes vivification?
FACE: After mortification.
SUBTLE: What's cohobation?
FACE: 'Tis the pouring on
    Your Aqua Regis, and then drawing him off,
    To the trine circle of the Seven Spheres.
SUBTLE: What's the proper passion of metals?
FACE: Malleation.
SUBTLE: What's your ultimum supplicium auri?
FACE: Antimonium.
SUBTLE: This's heathen Greek to you?—And what's
    your mercury?
FACE: A very fugitive, he will be gone, sir.
SUBTLE: How know you him?
FACE: By his viscosity,
    His oleosity, and his suscitability.
SUBTLE: How do you sublime him?
FACE: With the calx of egg-shells,
    White marble, talc.
SUBTLE: Your magisterium now,
    What's that?
FACE: Shifting, sir, your elements,
    Dry into cold, cold into moist, moist in-
    To hot, hot into dry.
SUBTLE: This's heathen Greek to you still?—
    Your Lapis Philosophicus?
FACE: 'Tis a stone
    And not a stone, a spirit, a soul, and a body;
    Which if you do dissolve, it is dissolved;
    If you coagulate, it is coagulated;
    If you make it to fly, it flieth.
SUBTLE: Enough. [Exit Face]
    This's heathen Greek to you? What are you, sir?

ANANIAS: Please you, a servant of the exiled Brethren,
    That deal with widows' and with orphans' goods,
    And make a just account unto the Saints—
    A deacon.
SUBTLE: O, you are sent from Master Wholesome,
    Your teacher?
ANANIAS: From Tribulation Wholesome,
    Our very zealous pastor.
SUBTLE: Good! I have
    Some orphans' goods to come here.
ANANIAS: Of what kind, sir?
SUBTLE: Pewter and brass, andirons and kitchenware,
    Metals that we must use our med'cine on;
    Wherein the Brethren may have a penn'orth
    For ready money.
ANANIAS: Were the orphans' parents
    Sincere professors?
SUBTLE: Why do you ask?
ANANIAS: Because
    We then are to deal justly, and give, in truth,
    Their utmost value.
SUBTLE: 'Slid, you'd cozen else,
    And if their parents were not of the faithful!
    I will not trust you, now I think on it,
    Till I ha' talked with your pastor. Ha' you brought
    money
    To buy more coals?
ANANIAS: No, surely.
SUBTLE: No! How so?
ANANIAS: The Brethren bid me say unto you, sir,
    Surely, they will not venture any more
    Till they may see projection.
SUBTLE: How!
ANANIAS: You've had,
    For the instruments, as bricks and loam and glasses,
    Already thirty pound; and for materials,
    They say, some ninety more; and they have heard
    since,
    That one at Heidelberg made it of an egg
    And a small paper of pin-dust.
SUBTLE: What's your name?
ANANIAS: My name is Ananias.
SUBTLE: Out, the varlet
    That cozened the Apostles! Hence, away!
    Flee, mischief! Had your holy consistory
    No name to send me of another sound,
    Than wicked Ananias? Send your elders
    Hither, to make atonement for you, quickly,
    And gi' me satisfaction; or out goes
    The fire, and down th' alembics and the furnace,
    Piger Henricus, or what not. Thou wretch!
    Both sericon and bufo shall be lost,
    Tell 'em. All hope of rooting out the bishops
    Or th' Antichristian hierarchy, shall perish,
    If they stay threescore minutes. The aqueity,
    Terreity, and sulphureity
    Shall run together again, and all be annulled,
    Thou wicked Ananias! [Exit Ananias] This will
    fetch 'em,

And make 'em haste towards their gulling more.
A man must deal like a rough nurse, and fright
Those that are froward, to an appetite.

Re-enter Face *in his uniform, followed by* Drugger.

FACE: He's busy with his spirits, but we'll upon
    him.
SUBTLE: How now! what mates, what Bayards ha' we
    here?
FACE: I told you he would be furious.—Sir, here's
    Nab
Has brought y' another piece of gold to look on.—
We must appease him. Give it me.—And prays
    you,
You would devise—what is it, Nab?
DRUGGER: A sign, sir.
FACE: Ay, a good lucky one, a thriving sign, Doctor.
SUBTLE: I was devising now.
FACE: —'Slight, do not say so,
He will repent he ga' you any more.—
What say you to his constellation, Doctor,
The Balance?
SUBTLE: No, that way is stale and common.
A townsman, born in Taurus, gives the bull,
Or the bull's head; in Aries, the ram.
A poor device! No, I will have his name
Formed in some mystic character, whose radii,
Striking the senses of the passers-by,
Shall, by a virtual influence, breed affections
That may result upon the party owns it;
As thus——
FACE: Nab!
SUBTLE: He shall have a bell, that's 'Abel';
And by it standing one whose name is Dee,
In a rug gown, there's D. and rug, that's 'Drug';
And right anenst him a dog snarling 'Er';
There's 'Drugger,' 'Abel Drugger.' That's his sign;
And here's now mystery and hieroglyphic!
FACE: Abel, thou art made.
DRUGGER: Sir, I do thank his worship.
FACE: Six o' thy legs more will not do it, Nab.—
He has brought you a pipe of tobacco, Doctor.
DRUGGER: Yes, sir.
I have another thing I would impart——
FACE: Out with it, Nab.
DRUGGER: Sir, there is lodged, hard by me,
A rich young widow——
FACE: Good! a bona roba?
DRUGGER: But nineteen, at the most.
FACE: Very good, Abel.
DRUGGER: Marry, she's not in fashion yet; she wears
A hood, but't stands a-cop.
FACE: No matter, Abel.
DRUGGER: And I do now and then give her a
    fucus——
FACE: What! dost thou deal, Nab?
SUBTLE: I did tell you, Captain.
DRUGGER: And physic too, sometime, sir; for which
    she trusts me

With all her mind. She's come up here of purpose
To learn the fashion.
FACE: Good—his match too!—On, Nab.
DRUGGER: And she does strangely long to know her
    fortune.
FACE: God's lid, Nab! send her to the Doctor, hither.
DRUGGER: Yes, I have spoke to her of his worship
    already;
But she's afraid it will be blown abroad,
And hurt her marriage.
FACE: Hurt it! 'tis the way
To heal it, if 'twere hurt; to make it more
Followed and sought. Nab, thou shalt tell her this:
She'll be more known, more talked of; and your
    widows
Are ne'er of any price till they be famous.
Their honour is their multitude of suitors.
Send her, it may be thy good fortune. What!
Thou dost not know?
DRUGGER: No, sir, she'll never marry
Under a knight. Her brother has made a vow.
FACE: What! and dost thou despair, my little Nab,
Knowing what the Doctor has set down for thee,
And seeing so many o' the City dubbed?
One glass o' thy water, with a madam I know,
Will have it done, Nab. What's her brother, a
    knight?
DRUGGER: No, sir, a gentleman, newly warm in's land,
    sir,
Scarce cold in his one-and-twenty, that does govern
His sister here; and is a man himself
Of some three thousand a year, and is come up
To learn to quarrel, and to live by his wits,
And will go down again, and die i' the country.
FACE: How! to quarrel?
DRUGGER: Yes, sir, to carry quarrels
As gallants do, and manage 'em by line.
FACE: 'Slid, Nab, the Doctor is the only man
In Christendom for him! He has made a table,
With mathematical demonstrations,
Touching the art of quarrels. He will give him
An instrument to quarrel by. Go, bring 'em both,
Him and his sister. And, for thee, with her
The Doctor haply may persuade. Go to.
Shalt give his worship a new damask suit
Upon the premises.
SUBTLE: O, good Captain!
FACE: He shall,
He is the honestest fellow, Doctor.—Stay not,
No offers; bring the damask, and the parties.
DRUGGER: I'll try my power, sir.
FACE: And thy will too, Nab.
SUBTLE: 'Tis good tobacco, this! What is't an ounce?
FACE: He'll send you a pound, Doctor.
SUBTLE: O, no.
FACE: He will do't.
It is the goodest soul.—Abel, about it.
Thou shalt know more anon. Away, be gone.
                                  [*Exit* Drugger]

A miserable rogue, and lives with cheese,
And has the worms. That was the cause, indeed,
Why he came now. He dealt with me in private,
To get a med'cine for 'em.
SUBTLE: And shall, sir. This works.
FACE: A wife, a wife for one of us, my dear Subtle!
We'll e'en draw lots, and he that fails shall have
The more in goods, the other has in tail.
SUBTLE: Rather the less, for she may be so light
She may want grains.
FACE: Ay, or be such a burden,
A man would scarce endure her for the whole.
SUBTLE: Faith, best let's see her first, and then de-
termine.
FACE: Content. But Doll must ha' no breath on't.
SUBTLE: Mum.
Away! you to your Surly yonder, catch him.
FACE: Pray God, I ha' not stayed too long.
SUBTLE: I fear it.
                                                    [Exeunt]

Act III

SCENE 1: *Before Lovewit's house*

Enter Tribulation Wholesome *and* Ananias.
TRIBULATION: These chastisements are common to
the Saints,
And such rebukes we of the Separation
Must bear with willing shoulders, as the trials
Sent forth to tempt our frailties.
ANANIAS: In pure zeal,
I do not like the man. He is a heathen,
And speaks the language of Canaan, truly.
TRIBULATION: I think him a profane person indeed.
ANANIAS: He bears
The visible mark of the Beast in his forehead.
And for his Stone, it is a work of darkness,
And with philosophy blinds the eyes of man.
TRIBULATION: Good Brother, we must bend unto all
means
That may give furtherance to the Holy Cause.
ANANIAS: Which his cannot. The sanctified Cause
Should have a sanctified course.
TRIBULATION: Not always necessary.
The children of perdition are oft-times
Made instruments even of the greatest works.
Beside, we should give somewhat to man's nature,
The place he lives in, still about the fire
And fume of metals, that intoxicate
The brain of man, and make him prone to passion.
Where have you greater atheists than your cooks?
Or more profane, or choleric, than your glass-men?
More Antichristian than your bell-founders?
What makes the devil so devilish, I would ask you,
Satan, our common enemy, but his being
Perpetually about the fire, and boiling
Brimstone and ars'nic? We must give, I say,

Unto the motives, and the stirrers up
Of humours in the blood. It may be so,
Whenas the work is done, the Stone is made,
This heat of his may turn into a zeal,
And stand up for the beauteous discipline,
Against the menstruous cloth and rag of Rome.
We must await his calling, and the coming
Of the good spirit. You did fault, t' upbraid him
With the Brethren's blessing of Heidelberg, weigh-
ing
What need we have to hasten on the work
For the restoring of the silenced Saints,
Which ne'er will be, but by the Philosophers'
Stone.
And so a learnèd elder, one of Scotland,
Assured me; aurum potabile being
The only med'cine for the civil magistrate,
T' incline him to a feeling of the Cause;
And must be daily used in the disease.
ANANIAS: I have not edified more, truly, by man,
Not since the beautiful light first shone on me;
And I am sad my zeal hath so offended.
TRIBULATION: Let us call on him then.
ANANIAS: The motion's good,
And of the spirit; I will knock first.—Peace be
within!   [*They enter*]

SCENE 2: *Within Lovewit's house*

Enter Subtle, *followed by* Tribulation *and* Ananias.
SUBTLE: O, are you come? 'Twas time. Your three-
score minutes
Were at last thread, you see; and down had gone
Furnus acediae, turris circulatorius;
'Lembic, bolt's-head, retort, and Pelican
Had all been cinders. Wicked Ananias!
Art thou returned? Nay, then it goes down yet.
TRIBULATION: Sir, be appeasèd; he is come to humble
Himself in spirit, and to ask your patience,
If too much zeal hath carried him aside
From the due path.
SUBTLE: Why, this doth qualify!
TRIBULATION: The Brethren had no purpose, verily,
To give you the least grievance, but are ready
To lend their willing hands to any project
The spirit and you direct.
SUBTLE: This qualifies more!
TRIBULATION: And for the orphans' goods, let them
be valued,
Or what is needful else; to the holy work
It shall be numbered. Here, by me, the Saints
Throw down their purse before you.
SUBTLE: This qualifies most!
Why, thus it should be, now you understand.
Have I discoursed so unto you of our Stone,
And of the good that it shall bring your cause?
Showed you—beside the main of hiring forces
Abroad, drawing the Hollanders, your friends,

From th' Indies, to serve you, with all their fleet—
That even the med'cinal use shall make you a fac-
    tion
And party in the realm? As, put the case,
That some great man in state, he have the gout;
Why, you but send three drops of your elixir,
You help him straight. There you have made a
    friend.
Another has the palsy, or the dropsy;
He takes of your incombustible stuff,
He's young again. There you have made a friend.
A lady that is past the feat of body,
Though not of mind, and hath her face decayed
Beyond all cure of paintings, you restore,
With the oil of talc. There you have made a friend,
And all her friends. A lord that is a leper,
A knight that has the bone-ache, or a squire
That hath both these, you make 'em smooth and
    sound,
With a bare fricace of your med'cine. Still
You increase your friends.

TRIBULATION: Ay, 'tis very pregnant.

SUBTLE: And then the turning of this lawyer's pewter
To plate at Christmas——

ANANIAS: Christ-tide, I pray you.

SUBTLE: Yet, Ananias?

ANANIAS: I have done.

SUBTLE: Or changing
His parcel gilt to massy gold. You cannot
But raise you friends. Withal, to be of power
To pay an army in the field, to buy
The King of France out of his realms, or Spain
Out of his Indies—what can you not do
Against lords spiritual or temporal,
That shall oppone you?

TRIBULATION: Verily, 'tis true.
We may be temporal lords ourselves, I take it.

SUBTLE: You may be anything, and leave off to make
Long-winded exercises, or suck up
Your 'ha' and 'hum' in a tune. I not deny
But such as are not gracèd in a state,
May, for their ends, be adverse in religion,
And get a tune to call the flock together.
For, to say sooth, a tune does much with women,
And other phlegmatic people; it is your bell.

ANANIAS: Bells are profane; a tune may be religious.

SUBTLE: No warning with you? Then farewell my
    patience.
'Slight, it shall down! I will not be thus tortured.

TRIBULATION: I pray you, sir.

SUBTLE: All shall perish. I have spoke it.

TRIBULATION: Let me find grace, sir, in your eyes.
    The man
He stands corrected. Neither did his zeal,
But as yourself, allow a tune somewhere;
Which now, being toward the Stone, we shall not
    need.

SUBTLE: No, nor your holy vizard, to win widows
To give you legacies, or make zealous wives

To rob their husbands for the common cause;
Nor take the start of bonds, broke but one day,
And say they were forfeited by providence.
Nor shall you need o'ernight to eat huge meals,
To celebrate your next day's fast the better;
The whilst the Brethren and the Sisters, hum-
    bled,
Abate the stiffness of the flesh. Nor cast
Before your hungry hearers scrupulous bones:
As whether a Christian may hawk or hunt,
Or whether matrons of the holy assembly
May lay their hair out, or wear doublets,
Or have that idol, Starch, about their linen.

ANANIAS: It is indeed an idol.

TRIBULATION: Mind him not, sir.—
I do command thee, spirit of zeal, but trouble,
To peace within him!—Pray you, sir, go on.

SUBTLE: Nor shall you need to libel 'gainst the prel-
    ates,
And shorten so your ears, against the hearing
Of the next wire-drawn grace. Nor of necessity
Rail against plays, to please the alderman
Whose daily custard you devour; nor lie
With zealous rage till you are hoarse; not one
Of these so singular arts. Nor call yourselves
By names of Tribulation, Persecution,
Restraint, Long Patience, and suchlike, affected
By the whole family or wood of you,
Only for glory, and to catch the ear
Of the disciple.

TRIBULATION: Truly, sir, they are
Ways that the godly Brethren have invented,
For propagation of the glorious Cause,
As very notable means, and whereby, also,
Themselves grow soon and profitably famous.

SUBTLE: O, but the Stone, all's idle to it! nothing!
The art of angels, nature's miracle,
The divine secret that doth fly in clouds
From east to west, and whose tradition
Is not from men, but spirits!

ANANIAS: I hate traditions!
I do not trust them——

TRIBULATION: Peace!

ANANIAS: They are popish all.
I will not peace. I will not——

TRIBULATION: Ananias!

ANANIAS: Please the profane to grieve the godly, I may
    not.

SUBTLE: Well, Ananias, thou shalt overcome.

TRIBULATION: It is an ignorant zeal that haunts him,
    sir;
But truly else, a very faithful Brother,
A botcher, and a man, by revelation,
That hath a competent knowledge of the truth.

SUBTLE: Has he a competent sum there, i' the bag,
To buy the goods within? I am made guardian,
And must, for charity and conscience' sake,
Now see the most be made for my poor orphan;
Though I desire the Brethren, too, good gainers.

There they are, within. When you have viewed and
   bought 'em,
And ta'en the inventory of what they are,
They are ready for projection; there's no more
To do. Cast on the med'cine so much silver
As there is tin there, so much gold as brass,
I'll gi'it you in, by weight.

TRIBULATION: But how long time,
   Sir, must the Saints expect yet?

SUBTLE: Let me see,
   How's the moon now? Eight, nine, ten days hence,
   He will be silver potate; then, three days,
   Before he citronize. Some fifteen days,
   The magisterium will be perfected.

ANANIAS: About the second day of the third week,
   In the ninth month?

SUBTLE: Yes, my good Ananias.

TRIBULATION: What will the orphans' goods arise to,
   think you?

SUBTLE: Some hundred marks, as much as filled three
   cars
   Unladed now. You'll make six millions of 'em.
   But I must ha' more coals laid in.

TRIBULATION: How!

SUBTLE: Another load,
   And then we ha' finished. We must now increase
   Our fire to ignis ardens; we are past
   Fimus equinus, balnei, cineris,
   And all those lenter heats. If the holy purse
   Should with this draught fall low, and that the
   Saints
   Do need a present sum, I have a trick
   To melt the pewter you shall buy now, instantly,
   And with a tincture make you as good Dutch dol-
   lars
   As any are in Holland.

TRIBULATION: Can you so?

SUBTLE: Ay, and shall bide the third examination.

ANANIAS: It will be joyful tidings to the Brethren.

SUBTLE: But you must carry it secret.

TRIBULATION: Ay, but stay,
   This act of coining, is it lawful?

ANANIAS: Lawful!
   We know no magistrate; or, if we did,
   This's foreign coin.

SUBTLE: It is no coining, sir,
   It is but casting.

TRIBULATION: Ha! you distinguish well.
   Casting of money may be lawful.

ANANIAS: 'Tis, sir.

TRIBULATION: Truly, I take it so.

SUBTLE: There is no scruple,
   Sir, to be made of it, believe Ananias.
   This case of conscience he is studied in.

TRIBULATION: I'll make a question of it to the
   Brethren.

ANANIAS: The Brethren shall approve it lawful, doubt
   not.
   Where shall it be done?   [Knock without]

SUBTLE: For that we'll talk anon.
   There's some to speak with me. Go in, I pray you,
   And view the parcels. That's the inventory.
   I'll come to you straight.

[Exeunt Tribulation *and* Ananias]
              Who is it? Face! appear.

Enter Face *in his uniform.*
   How now! Good prize?

FACE: Good pox! Yon costive cheater
   Never came on.

SUBTLE: How then?

FACE: I ha' walked the round
   Till now, and no such thing.

SUBTLE: And have you quit him?

FACE: Quit him! an Hell would quit him, too, he
   were happy.
   'Slight! would you have me stalk like a mill-jade
   All day, for one that will not yield us grains?
   I know him of old.

SUBTLE: O, but to ha' gulled him
   Had been a mast'ry.

FACE: Let him go, black boy,
   And turn thee, that some fresh news may possess
   thee:
   A noble count, a Don of Spain,—my dear,
   Delicious compeer, and my party-bawd—
   Who is come hither private, for his conscience,
   And brought munition with him, six great slops,
   Bigger than three Dutch hoys, beside round trunks,
   Furnished with pistolets, and pieces of eight,
   Will straight be here, my rogue, to have thy
   bath—
   That is the colour—and to make his batt'ry
   Upon our Doll, our castle, our Cinque Port,
   Our Dover Pier, our what thou wilt. Where is
   she?
   She must prepare perfumes, delicate linen,
   The bath in chief, a banquet, and her wit,
   For she must milk his epididymis.
   Where is the doxy?

SUBTLE: I'll send her to thee;
   And but dispatch my brace of little John Leydens,
   And come again myself.

FACE: Are they within, then?

SUBTLE: Numb'ring the sum.

FACE: How much?

SUBTLE: A hundred marks, boy.
                      [Exit]

FACE: Why, this's a lucky day. Ten pounds of Mam-
   mon!
   Three o' my clerk! a portague o' my grocer!
   This o' the Brethren! beside reversions
   And states to come i' the widow, and my count!
   My share today will not be bought for forty——

Enter Doll.

DOLL: What?

FACE: Pounds, dainty Dorothy! art thou so near?

DOLL: Yes. Say, Lord General, how fares our camp?

FACE: As with the few that had entrenched them-
selves
Safe, by their discipline, against a world, Doll;
And laughed within those trenches, and grew fat
With thinking on the booties, Doll, brought in
Daily by their small parties. This dear hour,
A doughty Don is taken with my Doll;
And thou mayst make his ransom what thou wilt,
My Dousabel. He shall be brought here, fettered
With thy fair looks, before he sees thee; and
thrown
In a down-bed, as dark as any dungeon;
Where thou shalt keep him waking with thy
drum—
Thy drum, my Doll, thy drum—till he be tame
As the poor blackbirds were i' the great frost,
Or bees are with a basin; and so hive him
I' the swan-skin coverlet and cambric sheets,
Till he work honey and wax, my little God's-
Gift.
DOLL: What is he, General?
FACE: An Adelantado,
A grandee, girl. Was not my Dapper here yet?
DOLL: No.
FACE: Nor my Drugger?
DOLL: Neither.
FACE: A pox on 'em,
They are so long a-furnishing! Such stinkards
Would not be seen upon these festival days.

Re-enter Subtle.
How now! ha' you done?
SUBTLE: Done. They are gone. The sum
Is here in bank, my Face. I would we knew
Another chapman now, would buy 'em outright.
FACE: 'Slid, Nab shall do't, against he have the
widow,
To furnish household.
SUBTLE: Excellent, well thought on!
Pray God he come!
FACE: I pray he keep away
Till our new business be o'erpassed.
SUBTLE: But, Face,
How cam'st thou by this secret Don?
FACE: A spirit
Brought me th' intelligence, in a paper here,
As I was conjuring yonder in my circle
For Surly. I ha' my flies abroad. Your bath
Is famous, Subtle, by my means. Sweet Doll,
You must go tune your virginal, no losing
O' the least time. And, do you hear? good action.
Firk like a flounder; kiss like a scallop, close;
And tickle him with thy mother-tongue. His great
Verdugoship has not a jot of language—
So much the easier to be cozened, my Dolly.
He will come here in a hired coach, obscure,
And our own coachman, whom I have sent as
guide,
No creature else. [*One knocks*] Who's that?

SUBTLE: It i' not he?
[*Exit* Doll]
FACE: O no, not yet this hour.

Re-enter Doll
SUBTLE: Who is't?
DOLL: Dapper,
Your clerk.
FACE: God's will then, Queen of Faëry,
On with your tire. [*Exit* Doll] And, Doctor, with
your robes.
Let's dispatch him, for God's sake.
SUBTLE: 'Twill be long.
FACE: I warrant you, take but the cues I give you,
It shall be brief enough.—'Slight, here are more!
Abel, and I think the angry boy, the heir,
That fain would quarrel.
SUBTLE: And the widow?
FACE: No,
Not that I see. Away! [*Exit* Subtle]

Enter Dapper.
                              O sir, you are welcome.
The Doctor is within, a-moving for you;
I have had the most ado to win him to it
He swears you'll be the darling o' the dice;
He never heard her Highness dote till now.
Your aunt has giv'n you the most gracious words
That can be thought on.
DAPPER: Shall I see her Grace?
FACE: See her, and kiss her too.

Enter Drugger, *followed by* Kastril.
                              What! honest Nab?
Hast brought the damask?
NAB: No, sir, here's tobacco.
FACE: 'Tis well done, Nab. Thou'lt bring the damask
too?
DRUGGER: Yes. Here's the gentleman, Captain, Mas-
ter Kastril,
I have brought to see the Doctor.
FACE: Where's the widow?
DRUGGER: Sir, as he likes, his sister—he says—shall
come.
FACE: O, is it so? Good time. Is your name Kastril,
sir?
KASTRIL: Ay, and the best o' the Kastrils, I'd be sorry
else,
By fifteen hundred a year. Where is this doctor?
My mad tobacco-boy here tells me of one
That can do things. Has he any skill?
FACE: Wherein, sir?
KASTRIL: To carry a business, manage a quarrel fairly,
Upon fit terms.
FACE: It seems, sir, you're but young
About the town, that can make that a question!
KASTRIL: Sir, not so young but I have heard some
speech
Of the angry boys, and seen 'em take tobacco,

And in his shop; and I can take it, too.
And I would fain be one of 'em, and go down
And practise i' the country.

FACE: Sir, for the duello,
The Doctor, I assure you, shall inform you,
To the least shadow of a hair; and show you
An instrument he has, of his own making,
Wherewith no sooner shall you make report
Of any quarrel, but he will take the height on't
Most instantly, and tell in what degree
Of safety it lies in, or mortality;
And how it may be borne, whether in a right line
Or a half-circle; or may else be cast
Into an angle blunt, if not acute;
And this he will demonstrate. And then, rules
To give and take the lie by.

KASTRIL: How! to take it?

FACE: Yes, in oblique, he'll show you, or in circle;
But never in diameter. The whole town
Study his theorems, and dispute them ordinarily
At the eating academies.

KASTRIL: But does he teach
Living by the wits, too?

FACE: Anything whatever.
You cannot think that subtlety, but he reads it.
He made me a captain. I was a stark pimp,
Just o' your standing, 'fore I met with him;
It i' not two months since. I'll tell you his method:
First, he will enter you at some ordinary.

KASTRIL: No, I'll not come there. You shall pardon
   me.

FACE: For why, sir?

KASTRIL: There's gaming there, and tricks.

FACE: Why, would you be
A gallant, and not game?

KASTRIL: Ay, 'twill spend a man.

FACE: Spend you! it will repair you when you are
   spent.
How do they live by their wits there, that have
   vented
Six times your fortunes?

KASTRIL: What, three thousand a year!

FACE: Ay, forty thousand.

KASTRIL: Are there such?

FACE: Ay, sir,
And gallants yet. Here's a young gentleman
Is born to nothing—forty marks a year,
Which I count nothing. He's to be initiated,
And have a fly o' the Doctor. He will win you
By unresistible luck, within this fortnight,
Enough to buy a barony. They will set him
Upmost, at the groom-porter's, all the Christmas!
And, for the whole year through, at every place
Where there is play, present him with the chair;
The best attendance, the best drink, sometimes
Two glasses of Canary, and pay nothing;
The purest linen and the sharpest knife,
The partridge next his trencher; and somewhere
The dainty bed, in private, with the dainty.

You shall ha' your ordinaries bid for him,
As playhouses for a poet; and the master
Pray him aloud to name what dish he affects,
Which must be buttered shrimps; and those that
   drink
To no mouth else, will drink to his, as being
The goodly president-mouth of all the board.

KASTRIL: Do you not gull one?

FACE: God's my life! do you think it?
You shall have a cast commander—can but get
In credit with a glover, or a spurrier,
For some two pair of either's ware aforehand—
Will, by most swift posts, dealing with him,
Arrive at competent means to keep himself,
His punk, and naked boy, in excellent fashion;
And be admired for't.

KASTRIL: Will the Doctor teach this?

FACE: He will do more, sir: when your land is gone,—
As men of spirit hate to keep earth long—
In a vacation, when small money is stirring,
And ordinaries suspended till the term,
He'll show a perspective, where on one side
You shall behold the faces and the persons
Of all sufficient young heirs in town,
Whose bonds are current for commodity;
On th' other side, the merchants' forms, and others
That, without help of any second broker,—
Who would expect a share—will trust such parcels;
In the third square, the very street and sign
Where the commodity dwells, and does but wait
To be delivered, be it pepper, soap,
Hops, or tobacco, oatmeal, wood, or cheeses.
All which you may so handle, to enjoy
To your own use, and never stand obliged.

KASTRIL: I' faith! is he such a fellow?

FACE: Why, Nab here knows him.
And then for making matches for rich widows,
Young gentlewomen, heirs, the fortunat'st man!
He's sent to, far and near, all over England,
To have his counsel, and to know their fortunes.

KASTRIL: God's will, my suster shall see him!

FACE: I'll tell you, sir,
What he did tell me of Nab. It's a strange thing!—
By the way, you must eat no cheese, Nab; it breeds
   melancholy,
And that same melancholy breeds worms. But pass
   it.—
He told me honest Nab here was ne'er at tavern
But once in 's life.

DRUGGER: Truth, and no more I was not.

FACE: And then he was so sick——

DRUGGER: Could he tell you that too?

FACE: How should I know it?

DRUGGER: In troth, we had been a-shooting,
And had a piece of fat ram-mutton to supper,
That lay so heavy o' my stomach——

FACE: And he has no head
To bear any wine; for, what with the noise o' the
   fiddlers,

And care of his shop, for he dares keep no servants——

DRUGGER: My head did so ache——

FACE: As he was fain to be brought home,
The Doctor told me. And then a good old
woman——

DRUGGER: Yes, faith, she dwells in Seacoal Lane—did
cure me,
With sodden ale, and pellitory o' the wall—
Cost me but twopence. I had another sickness
Was worse than that.

FACE: Ay, that was with the grief
Thou took'st for being cessed at eighteenpence,
For the waterwork.

DRUGGER: In truth, and it was like
T' have cost me almost my life.

FACE: Thy hair went off?

DRUGGER: Yes, sir, 'twas done for spite.

FACE: Nay, so says the Doctor.

KASTRIL: Pray thee, tobacco-boy, go fetch my suster.
I'll see this learnèd boy before I go,
And so shall she.

FACE: Sir, he is busy now.
But, if you have a sister to fetch hither,
Perhaps your own pains may command her sooner;
And he by that time will be free.

KASTRIL: I go.   [Exit]

FACE: Drugger, she's thine! The damask. [Exit Abel]
Subtle and I
Must wrestle for her.—Come on, Master Dapper,
You see how I turn clients here away,
To give your cause dispatch. Ha' you performed
The ceremonies were enjoined you?

DAPPER: Yes, o' the vinegar,
And the clean shirt.

FACE: 'Tis well, that shirt may do you
More worship than you think. Your aunt's afire,
But that she will not show it, t' have a sight on
you.
Ha' you provided for her Grace's servants?

DAPPER: Yes, here are six score Edward shillings.

FACE: Good.

DAPPER: And an old Harry's sovereign.

FACE: Very good.

DAPPER: And three James shillings, and an Elizabeth
groat;
Just twenty nobles.

FACE: O, you are too just.
I would you had had the other noble in Maries.

DAPPER: I have some Philip and Maries.

FACE: Ay, those same
Are best of all. Where are they? Hark, the Doctor.

Enter Subtle, *disguised like a priest of Faery.*

SUBTLE: Is yet her Grace's cousin come?

FACE: He is come.

SUBTLE: And is he fasting?

FACE: Yes.

SUBTLE: And hath cried 'hum'?

FACE: —Thrice, you must answer.

DAPPER: Thrice.

SUBTLE: And as oft 'buzz'?

FACE: —If you have, say.

DAPPER: I have.

SUBTLE: Then, to her coz,
Hoping that he hath vinegared his senses,
As he was bid, the Faery Queen dispenses,
By me, this robe, the petticoat of Fortune;
Which that he straight put on, she doth impor-
tune.
And though to Fortune near be her petticoat,
Yet nearer is her smock, the Queen doth note.
And therefore, even of that a piece she hath sent,
Which, being a child, to wrap him in, was rent;
And prays him for a scarf he now will wear it,
With as much love as then her Grace did tear it,
About his eyes, to show he is fortunate. [*They
blind* Dapper *with a rag*]
And, trusting unto her to make his state,
He'll throw away all worldly pelf about him;
Which that he will perform, she doth not doubt
him.

FACE: She need not doubt him, sir. Alas, he has noth-
ing
But what he will part withal as willingly,
Upon her Grace's word,—Throw away your purse—
As she would ask it.—Handkerchiefs and all—
She cannot bid that thing but he'll obey.—
If you have a ring about you, cast it off,
Or a silver seal at your wrist. Her Grace will send
Her fairies here to search you, therefore deal
Directly with her Highness. If they find
That you conceal a mite, you are undone.
          [Dapper *throws away, as they bid him*]

DAPPER: Truly, there's all.

FACE: All what?

DAPPER: My money, truly.

FACE: Keep nothing that is transitory about you.—
Bid Doll play music. [Doll *plays on a cittern*] Look,
the elves are come.
To pinch you, if you tell not truth. Advise you.
                      [*They pinch him*]

DAPPER: O! I have a paper with a spur-royal in't.

FACE: 'Ti, ti.'
They knew't, they say.

SUBTLE: 'Ti-ti-ti-ti.' He has more yet.

FACE: 'Ti-ti-ti-ti.' I' the tother pocket?

SUBTLE: 'Titi-titi-titi-titi.'
They must pinch him or he will never confess, they
say.

DAPPER: O, O!

FACE: Nay, pray you hold. He is her Grace's
nephew.—
'Ti, ti, ti?'—What care you? Good faith, you shall
care.—
Deal plainly, sir, and shame the fairies. Show
You are an innocent.

DAPPER: By this good light, I ha' nothing.

SUBTLE: 'Ti-ti-ti-ti-to-ta.' He does equivocate, she
    says—
    'Ti-ti-do-ti, ti-ti-do-ti, da'—and swears by the light,
    when he is blinded.
DAPPER: By this good dark, I ha' nothing but a half-
    crown
    Of gold, about my wrist, that my love gave me;
    And a leaden heart I wore sin' she forsook me.
FACE: I thought 'twas something. And would you
    incur
    Your aunt's displeasure for these trifles? Come,
    I had rather you had thrown away twenty half-
    crowns.
    You may wear your leaden heart still.

Enter Doll.

                                        How now!
SUBTLE: What news, Doll?
DOLL: Yonder's your knight, Sir
    Mammon.
FACE: God's lid, we never thought of him till now!
    Where is he?
DOLL: Here hard by, he's at the door.
SUBTLE: And you are not ready now! Doll, get his
    suit.   [*Exit* Doll]
    He must not be sent back.
FACE: O, by no means.
    What shall we do with this same puffin here,
    Now he's o' the spit?
SUBTLE: Why, lay him back awhile,
    With some device.—'Ti, ti-ti, ti-ti-ti.' Would her
    Grace speak with me?
    I come.—Help, Doll!   [*Re-enter* Doll]
FACE: [*Speaks through the keyhole,* Mammon *knock-
    ing*] Who's there? Sir Epicure,
    My master's i' the way. Please you to walk
    Three or four turns, but till his back be turned,
    And I am for you.—Quickly, Doll!
SUBTLE: Her Grace
    Commends her kindly to you, Master Dapper.
DAPPER: I long to see her Grace.
SUBTLE: She now is set
    At dinner in her bed; and she has sent you,
    From her own private trencher, a dead mouse,
    And a piece of gingerbread, to be merry withal,
    And stay your stomach, lest you faint with fasting.
    Yet if you could hold out till she saw you, she says,
    It would be better for you.
FACE: Sir, he shall
    Hold out, an 'twere this two hours, for her High-
    ness;
    I can assure you that. We will not lose
    All we ha' done.
SUBTLE: He must not see, nor speak
    To anybody, till then.
FACE: For that we'll put, sir,
    A stay in's mouth.
SUBTLE: Of what?
FACE: Of gingerbread.

Make you it fit. He that hath pleased her Grace
Thus far, shall not now crinkle for a little.——
Gape, sir, and let him fit you.
SUBTLE: Where shall we now
Bestow him?
DOLL: I' the privy.
SUBTLE: Come along, sir,
I now must show you Fortune's privy lodgings.
FACE: Are they perfumed, and his bath ready?
SUBTLE: All.
Only the fumigation's somewhat strong.
FACE: Sir Epicure, I am yours, sir, by and by.
                                [*Exeunt with* Dapper]

Act IV

SCENE 1:   *Lovewit's house*

Enter Face *and* Mammon.
FACE: O, sir, you're come i' the only finest time——
MAMMON: Where's Master?
FACE: Now preparing for projection, sir.
    Your stuff will be all changed shortly.
MAMMON: Into gold?
FACE: To gold and silver, sir.
MAMMON: Silver I care not for.
FACE: Yes, sir, a little to give beggars.
MAMMON: Where's the lady?
FACE: At hand here. I ha' told her such brave things
    of you,
    Touching your bounty and your noble spirit——
MAMMON: Hast thou?
FACE: As she is almost in her fit to see you.
    But, good sir, no divinity i' your conference,
    For fear of putting her in rage.
MAMMON: I warrant thee.
FACE: Six men will not hold her down. And then,
    If the old man should hear or see you——
MAMMON: Fear not.
FACE: The very house, sir, would run mad. You know
    it,
    How scrupulous he is, and violent,
    'Gainst the least act of sin. Physic or mathematics,
    Poetry, state, or bawdry, as I told you,
    She will endure, and never startle; but
    No word of controversy.
MAMMON: I am schooled, good Eulen.
FACE: And you must praise her house, remember that,
    And her nobility.
MAMMON: Let me alone.
    No herald, no, nor antiquary, Lungs,
    Shall do it better. Go.
FACE: —Why, this is yet
    A kind of modern happiness, to have
    Doll Common for a great lady.   [*Exit*]
MAMMON: Now, Epicure,
    Heighten thyself, talk to her all in gold;
    Rain her as many showers as Jove did drops

Unto his Danaë; show the god a miser,
Compared with Mammon. What! the Stone will
 do't.
She shall feel gold, taste gold, hear gold, sleep
 gold—
Nay, we will concumberè gold. I will be puissant
And mighty in my talk to her!

Re-enter Face *with* Doll *richly dressed.*
                              Here she comes.

FACE: To him, Doll, suckle him.—This is the noble
 knight
I told your ladyship——

MAMMON: Madam, with your pardon,
 I kiss your vesture.

DOLL: Sir, I were uncivil
If I would suffer that; my lip to you, sir.

MAMMON: I hope my Lord your brother be in health,
 lady?

DOLL: My Lord my brother is, though I no lady, sir.

FACE: —Well said, my guinea-bird.

MAMMON: Right noble madam——

FACE: —O, we shall have most fierce idolatry.

MAMMON: 'Tis your prerogative.

DOLL: Rather your courtesy.

MAMMON: Were there nought else t' enlarge your
 virtues to me,
These answers speak your breeding and your blood.

DOLL: Blood we boast none, sir, a poor baron's daughter.

MAMMON: Poor! and gat you? Profane not. Had your
 father
Slept all the happy remnant of his life
After that act, lain but there still, and panted,
He'd done enough to make himself, his issue,
And his posterity noble.

DOLL: Sir, although
We may be said to want the gilt and trappings,
The dress of honour, yet we strive to keep
The seeds and the materials.

MAMMON: I do see
The old ingredient, virtue, was not lost,
Nor the drug, money, used to make your com-
 pound.
There is a strange nobility i' your eye,
This lip, that chin! Methinks you do resemble
One o' the Austriac princes.

FACE: —Very like!
Her father was an Irish costermonger.

MAMMON: The house of Valois just had such a nose,
And such a forehead yet the Medici
Of Florence boast.

DOLL: Troth, and I have been likened
To all these princes.

FACE: —I'll be sworn, I heard it.

MAMMON: I know not how; it is not any one,
But e'en the very choice of all their features.

FACE: —I'll in, and laugh.   [*Exit*]

MAMMON: A certain touch, or air,

That sparkles a divinity beyond
An earthly beauty!

DOLL: O, you play the courtier.

MAMMON: Good lady, gi' me leave——

DOLL: In faith, I may not,
To mock me, sir.

MAMMON: To burn i' this sweet flame.
The phoenix never knew a nobler death.

DOLL: Nay, now you court the courtier, and destroy
What you would build. This art, sir, i' your words,
Calls your whole faith in question.

MAMMON: By my soul——

DOLL: Nay, oaths are made o' the same air, sir.

MAMMON: Nature
Never bestowed upon mortality
A more unblamed, a more harmonious feature.
She played the step-dame in all faces else.
Sweet madam, le' me be particular——

DOLL: Particular, sir! I pray you know your distance.

MAMMON: In no ill sense, sweet lady, but to ask
How your fair graces pass the hours? I see
You're lodged here i' the house of a rare man,
An excellent artist; but what's that to you?

DOLL: Yes, sir. I study here the mathematics,
And distillation.

MAMMON: O, I cry your pardon.
He's a divine instructor! can extract
The souls of all things by his art; call all
The virtues, and the miracles of the sun,
Into a temperate furnace; teach dull nature
What her own forces are. A man the Emp'ror
Has courted above Kelly; sent his medals
And chains, t' invite him.

DOLL: Ay, and for his physic, sir——

MAMMON: Above the art of Aesculapius,
That drew the envy of the Thunderer!
I know all this, and more.

DOLL: Troth, I am taken, sir,
Whole with these studies, that contemplate nature.

MAMMON: It is a noble humour. But this form
Was not intended to so dark a use.
Had you been crooked, foul, of some coarse mould,
A cloister had done well; but such a feature,
That might stand up the glory of a kingdom,
To live recluse, is a mere solecism,
Though in a nunnery. It must not be!
I muse my Lord your brother will permit it!
You should spend half my land first, were I he.
Does not this diamond better on my finger
Than i' the quarry?

DOLL: Yes.

MAMMON: Why, you are like it.
You were created, lady, for the light.
Here, you shall wear it; take it, the first pledge
Of what I speak, to bind you to believe me.

DOLL: In chains of adamant?

MAMMON: Yes, the strongest bands.
And take a secret, too: here, by your side,
Doth stand this hour the happiest man in Europe.

DOLL: You are contented, sir?

MAMMON: Nay, in true being,
The envy of princes and the fear of states.

DOLL: Say you so, Sir Epicure?

MAMMON: Yes, and thou shalt prove it,
Daughter of honour. I have cast mine eye
Upon thy form, and I will rear this beauty
Above all styles.

DOLL: You mean no treason, sir?

MAMMON: No, I will take away that jealousy.
I am the lord of the Philosophers' Stone,
And thou the lady.

DOLL: How, sir! ha' you that?

MAMMON: I am the master of the mastery.
This day the good old wretch here o' the house
Has made it for us. Now he's at projection.
Think therefore thy first wish now, let me hear it;
And it shall rain into thy lap no shower,
But floods of gold, whole cataracts, a deluge,
To get a nation on thee!

DOLL: You are pleased, sir,
To work on the ambition of our sex.

MAMMON: I'm pleased the glory of her sex should
    know
This nook, here, of the Friars, is no climate
For her to live obscurely in, to learn
Physic and surgery, for the constable's wife
Of some odd hundred in Essex; but come forth,
And taste the air of palaces; eat, drink
The toils of emp'rics, and their boasted practice;
Tincture of pearl and coral, gold and amber;
Be seen at feasts and triumphs; have it asked
What miracle she is? set all the eyes
Of court afire, like a burning-glass,
And work 'em into cinders, when the jewels
Of twenty states adorn thee, and the light
Strikes out the stars; that, when thy name is mem-
    tioned,
Queens may look pale; and, we but showing our
    love,
Nero's Poppaea may be lost in story!
Thus will we have it.

DOLL: I could well consent, sir.
But in a monarchy, how will this be?
The Prince will soon take notice, and both seize
You and your Stone, it being a wealth unfit
For any private subject.

MAMMON: If he knew it.

DOLL: Yourself do boast it, sir.

MAMMON: To thee, my life.

DOLL: O, but beware, sir! You may come to end
The remnant of your days in a loathed prison,
By speaking of it.

MAMMON: 'Tis no idle fear!
We'll therefore go withal, my girl, and live
In a free state, where we will eat our mullets
Soused in High Country wines, sup pheasants'
    eggs,
And have our cockles boiled in silver shells;

Our shrimps to swim again, as when they lived,
In a rare butter made of dolphins' milk,
Whose cream does look like opals; and with these
Delicate meats, set ourselves high for pleasure,
And take us down again, and then renew
Our youth and strength with drinking the elixir,
And so enjoy a perpetuity
Of life and lust. And thou shalt ha' thy wardrobe
Richer than Nature's, still to change thyself,
And vary oftener, for thy pride, than she,
Or Art, her wise and almost equal servant.

Re-enter Face.

FACE: Sir, you are too loud. I hear you, every word,
Into the laboratory. Some fitter place:
The garden, or great chamber above. How like you
    her?

MAMMON: Excellent, Lungs! There's for thee.

FACE: But do you hear?
Good sir, beware, no mention of the rabbins.

MAMMON: We think not on 'em.
                    [*Exeunt* Mammon *and* Doll]

FACE: O, it is well, sir. Subtle!

Enter Subtle.
Dost thou not laugh?

SUBTLE: Yes. Are they gone?

FACE: All's clear.

SUBTLE: The widow is come.

FACE: And your quarrelling disciple?

SUBTLE: Ay.

FACE: I must to my captainship again then.

SUBTLE: Stay, bring 'em in first.

FACE: So I meant. What is she,
A bonnibel?

SUBTLE: I know not.

FACE: We'll draw lots,
You'll stand to that?

SUBTLE: What else?

FACE: O, for a suit
To fall now, like a curtain, flap!

SUBTLE: To th' door, man.

FACE: You'll ha' the first kiss, 'cause I am not ready.

SUBTLE: Yes, and perhaps hit you through both the
    nostrils.

Enter Kastril, *followed by* Dame Pliant.

FACE: Who would you speak with?

KASTRIL: Where's the Captain?

FACE: Gone, sir,
About some business.

KASTRIL: Gone?

FACE: He'll return straight.
But, Master Doctor, his lieutenant, is here. [*Exit*]

SUBTLE: Come near, my worshipful boy, my terrae
    fili,
That is, my boy of land; make thy approaches.
Welcome, I know thy lusts and thy desires,
And I will serve and satisfy 'em. Begin,

Charge me from thence, or thence, or in this line.
  Here is my centre; ground thy quarrel.
KASTRIL: You lie.
SUBTLE: How, child of wrath and anger! the loud lie?
  For what, my sudden boy?
KASTRIL: Nay, that look you to,
  I am aforehand.
SUBTLE: O, this 's no true grammar,
  And as ill logic! You must render causes, child,
  Your first and second intentions; know your canons
  And your divisions, moods, degrees, and differences;
  Your predicaments, substance and accident,
  Series extern and intern, with their causes,
  Efficient, material, formal, final;
  And have your elements perfect——
KASTRIL: What is this!
  The angry tongue he talks in?
SUBTLE: That false precept
  Of being aforehand, has deceived a number,
  And made 'em enter quarrels oftentimes
  Before they were aware; and afterward,
  Against their wills.
KASTRIL: How must I do then, sir?
SUBTLE: I cry this lady mercy. She should first
  Have been saluted. [Kisses her] I do call you lady,
  Because you are to be one ere t' be long,
  My soft and buxom widow.
KASTRIL: Is she, i' faith?
SUBTLE: Yes, or my art is an egregious liar.
KASTRIL: How know you?
SUBTLE: By inspection on her forehead,
  And subtlety of her lip, which must be tasted
  Often to make a judgment. [Kisses her again]
    'Slight, she melts
  Like a myrobalan!—Here is yet a line,
  In rivo frontis, tells me he is no knight.
DAME PLIANT: What is he then, sir?
SUBTLE: Let me see your hand.
  O, your linea Fortunae makes it plain;
  And stella, here, in monte Veneris;
  But, most of all, junctura annularis.
  He is a soldier, or a man of art, lady,
  But shall have some great honour shortly.
DAME PLIANT: Brother,
  He's a rare man, believe me!

  Re-enter Face, *in his uniform.*
KASTRIL: Hold your peace.
  Here comes the tother rare man.—Save you, Cap-
  tain.
FACE: Good Master Kastril! Is this your sister?
KASTRIL: Ay, sir.
  Please you to kuss her, and be proud to know her?
FACE: I shall be proud to know you, lady. [Kisses her]
DAME PLIANT: Brother,
  He calls me lady too.
KASTRIL: Ay, peace. I heard it.
FACE:—The Count is come.
SUBTLE: Where is he?

FACE: At the door.
SUBTLE: Why, you must entertain him.
FACE: What 'll you do
  With these the while?
SUBTLE: Why, have 'em up, and show 'em
  Some fustian book, or the dark glass.
FACE: 'Fore God,
  She is a delicate dabchick! I must have her. [Exit]
SUBTLE: Must you! ay, if your fortune will, you
  must.—
  Come, sir, the Captain will come to us presently.
  I'll ha' you to my chamber of demonstrations,
  Where I'll show you both the grammar and logic
  And rhetoric of quarrelling, my whole method
  Drawn out in tables; and my instrument,
  That hath the several scale upon't, shall make you
  Able to quarrel, at a straw's breadth, by moonlight.
  And, lady, I'll have you look in a glass,
  Some half an hour, but to clear your eyesight,
  Against you see your fortune; which is greater
  Than I may judge upon the sudden, trust me.
        [Exit, followed by Kastril and Dame Pliant]

  Re-enter Face.
FACE: Where are you, Doctor?
SUBTLE: I'll come to you presently.
FACE: I will ha' this same widow, now I ha' seen her,
  On any composition.

  Re-enter Subtle.
SUBTLE: What do you say?
FACE: Ha' you disposed of them?
SUBTLE: I ha' sent 'em up.
FACE: Subtle, in troth, I needs must have this widow.
SUBTLE: Is that the matter?
FACE: Nay, but hear me.
SUBTLE: Go to,
  If you rebel once, Doll shall know it all.
  Therefore be quiet, and obey your chance.
FACE: Nay, thou art so violent now. Do but conceive,
  Thou art old, and canst not serve——
SUBTLE: Who? cannot I?
  'Slight, I will serve her with thee, for a——
FACE: Nay,
  But understand: I'll gi' you composition.
SUBTLE: I will not treat with thee. What! sell my for-
  tune?
  'Tis better than my birthright. Do not murmur;
  Win her, and carry her. If you grumble, Doll
  Knows it directly.
FACE: Well, sir, I am silent.
  Will you go help to fetch in Don, in state? [Exit]
SUBTLE: I follow you, sir. We must keep Face in awe,
  Or he will overlook us like a tyrant.

  Re-enter Face, *with* Surly *like a Spaniard.*
  Brain of a tailor! Who comes here? Don John!
SURLY: Señores, beso las manos a vuestras mercedes.
SUBTLE: Would you had stooped a little, and kissed
  our anos!

FACE: Peace, Subtle.

SUBTLE: Stab me, I shall never hold, man!
He looks, in that deep ruff, like a head in a platter,
Served in by a short cloak upon two trestles.

FACE: Or what do you say to a collar of brawn, cut
     down
Beneath the souse, and wriggled with a knife?

SUBTLE: 'Slud, he does look too fat to be a Spaniard.

FACE: Perhaps some Fleming or some Hollander got
     him
In D'Alva's time; Count Egmont's bastard.

SUBTLE: Don,
Your scurvy, yellow, Madrid face is welcome.

SURLY: Gratia.

SUBTLE: He speaks out of a fortification.
Pray God he has no squibs in those deep sets.

SURLY: Por Dios, señores, muy linda casa!

SUBTLE: What says he?

FACE: Praises the house, I think;
I know no more but 's action.

SUBTLE: Yes, the casa,
My precious Diego, will prove fair enough
To cozen you in. Do you mark? You shall
Be cozened, Diego.

FACE: Cozened, do you see?
My worthy Donzel, cozened.

SURLY: Entiendo.

SUBTLE: Do you intend it? So do we, dear Don.
Have you brought pistolets, or portagues,
My solemn Don?—Dost thou feel any?

FACE: [Feels his pockets]   Full.

SUBTLE: You shall be emptied, Don, pumpèd and
     drawn
Dry, as they say.

FACE: Milkèd, in troth, sweet Don.

SUBTLE: See all the monsters, the great lion of all,
     Don.

SURLY: Con licencia, se puede ver a esta señora?

SUBTLE: What talks he now?

FACE: O' the señora.

SUBTLE: O, Don,
This is the lioness, which you shall see
Also, my Don.

FACE: 'Slid, Subtle, how shall we do?

SUBTLE: For what?

FACE: Why, Doll's employed, you know.

SUBTLE: That's true!
'Fore Heav'n, I know not. He must stay, that's all.

FACE: Stay! that he must not, by no means.

SUBTLE: No! why?

FACE: Unless you'll mar all. 'Slight, he'll suspect it;
And then he will not pay, not half so well.
This is a travelled punk-master, and does know
All the delays; a notable hot rascal,
And looks already rampant.

SUBTLE: 'Sdeath, and Mammon
Must not be troubled.

FACE: Mammon? in no case!

SUBTLE: What shall we do then?

FACE: Think; you must be sudden.

SURLY: Entiendo que la señora es tan hermosa, que
     codicio tan a verla, como la bien aventuranza
     de mi vida.

FACE: Mi vida? 'Slid, Subtle, he puts me in mind o'
     the widow.
What dost thou say to draw her to it, ha?
And tell her 'tis her fortune? All our venture
Now lies upon 't. It is but one man more,
Which on 's chance to have her; and beside,
There is no maidenhead to be feared or lost.
What dost thou think on 't, Subtle?

SUBTLE: Who, I? Why——

FACE: The credit of our house, too, is engaged.

SUBTLE: You make me an offer for my share erewhile.
What wilt thou gi' me, i' faith?

FACE: O, by that light,
I'll not buy now. You know your doom to me.
E'en take your lot, obey your chance, sir; win her,
And wear her out for me.

SUBTLE: 'Slight, I'll not work her then.

FACE: It is the common cause; therefore bethink
     you.
Doll else must know it, as you said.

SUBTLE: I care not.

SURLY: Señores, por qué se tarda tanto?

SUBTLE: Faith, I am not fit, I am old.

FACE: That's now no reason, sir.

SURLY: Puede ser de hacer burla de mi amor?

FACE: You hear the Don, too? By this air I call,
And loose the hinges. Doll!

SUBTLE: A plague of Hell——

FACE: Will you then do?

SUBTLE: You're a terrible rogue!
I'll think of this. Will you, sir, call the widow?

FACE: Yes, and I'll take her, too, with all her faults,
Now I do think on 't better.

SUBTLE: With all my heart, sir.
Am I discharged o' the lot?

FACE: As you please.

SUBTLE: Hands.

FACE: Remember now, that upon any change,
You never claim her.

SUBTLE: Much good joy and health to you, sir.
Marry a whore! Fate, let me wed a witch first.

SURLY: Por estas honradas barbas——

SUBTLE: He swears by his beard.
Dispatch, and call the brother too.   [Exit Face]

SURLY: Tengo duda, señores,
Que no me hagan alguna traición.

SUBTLE: How, issue on? Yes, presto, señor. Please you
Enthratha the chambratha, worthy Don;
Where if it please the fates, in your bathada,
You shall be soaked and stroked, and tubbed and
     rubbed,
And scrubbed and fubbed, dear Don, before you
     go.
You shall, in faith, my scurvy baboon Don,
Be curried, clawed, and flawed, and tawed, indeed.

I will the heartlier go about it now,
And make the widow a punk so much the sooner,
To be revenged on this impetuous Face.
The quickly doing of it is the grace.

[*Exit* Subtle *with* Surly]

SCENE 2: *Subtle's chamber*

Enter Face, Kastril, *and* Dame Pliant.

FACE: Come, lady, I knew the Doctor would not
leave
Till he had found the very nick of her fortune.

KASTRIL: To be a countess, say you, a Spanish
countess, sir?

DAME PLIANT: Why, is that better than an English
countess?

FACE: Better! 'Slight, make you that a question,
lady?

KASTRIL: Nay, she is a fool, Captain, you must pardon her.

FACE: Ask from your courtier to your inns-of-court
man,
To your mere milliner. They will tell you all,
Your Spanish jennet is the best horse; your Spanish
Stoop is the best garb; your Spanish beard
Is the best cut; your Spanish ruffs are the best
Wear; your Spanish pavan the best dance;
Your Spanish titillation in a glove
The best perfume. And for your Spanish pike
And Spanish blade, let your poor Captain speak.
Here comes the Doctor.

Enter Subtle.

SUBTLE: My most honoured lady,—
For so I am now to style you, having found,
By this my scheme, you are to undergo
An honourable fortune very shortly—
What will you say now, if some——

FACE: I ha' told her all, sir,
And her right worshipful brother here, that she
shall be
A countess,—do not delay 'em, sir—a Spanish
countess.

SUBTLE: Still, my scarce worshipful Captain, you can
keep
No secret! Well, since he has told you, madam,
Do you forgive him, and I do.

KASTRIL: She shall do that, sir;
I'll look to't, 'tis my charge.

SUBTLE: Well then, naught rests
But that she fit her love now to her fortune.

DAME PLIANT: Truly, I shall never brook a Spaniard.

SUBTLE: No?

DAME PLIANT: Never sin' 'eighty-eight, could I abide
'em,
And that was some three years afore I was born, in
truth.

SUBTLE: Come, you must love him, or be miserable;
Choose which you will.

FACE: By this good rush, persuade her,
She will cry strawberries else, within this twelvemonth.

SUBTLE: Nay, shads and mackerel, which is worse.

FACE: Indeed, sir?

KASTRIL: God's lid, you shall love him, or I'll kick you!

DAME PLIANT: Why,
I'll do as you will ha' me, brother.

KASTRIL: Do,
Or by this hand I'll maul you.

FACE: Nay, good sir,
Be not so fierce.

SUBTLE: No, my enragèd child;
She will be ruled. What, when she comes to taste
The pleasures of a countess! to be courted——

FACE: And kissed, and ruffled!

SUBTLE: Ay, behind the hangings.

FACE: And then come forth in pomp!

SUBTLE: And know her state!

FACE: Of keeping all th' idolaters o' the chamber
Barer to her, than at their prayers!

SUBTLE: Is served
Upon the knee!

FACE: And has her pages, ushers,
Footmen, and coaches——

SUBTLE: Her six mares——

FACE: Nay, eight!

SUBTLE: To hurry her through London to th' Exchange,
Bedlam, the china-houses——

FACE: Yes, and have
The citizens gape at her, and praise her tires,
And my Lord's goose-turd bands, that ride with
her!

KASTRIL: Most brave! By this hand, you are not my
suster
If you refuse.

DAME PLIANT: I will not refuse, brother.

Enter Surly.

SURLY: Qué es esto, señores, que no se venga?
Esta tardanza me mata!

FACE: It is the Count come!
The Doctor knew he would be here, by his art.

SUBTLE: En gallanta madama, Don! gallantissima!

SURLY: Por todos los dioses, la más acabada
Hermosura, que he visto en mi vida!

FACE: Is't not a gallant language that they speak?

KASTRIL: An admirable language! Is't not French?

FACE: No, Spanish, sir.

KASTRIL: It goes like law-French,
And that, they say, is the court-liest language.

FACE: List, sir.

SURLY: El sol ha perdido su lumbre, con el
Resplandor que trae esta dama. Válgame Dios!

FACE: H' admires your sister.

KASTRIL: Must not she make curtsy?

SUBTLE: God's will, she must go to him, man, and
kiss him!

It is the Spanish fashion, for the women
To make first court.

FACE: 'Tis true he tells you, sir,
His art knows all.

SURLY: Por qué no se acude?

KASTRIL: He speaks to her, I think.

FACE: That he does, sir.

SURLY: Por el amor de Dios, qué es esto, qué se
tarda?

KASTRIL: Nay, see, she will not understand him! Gull,
Noddy.

DAME PLIANT: What say you, brother?

KASTRIL: Ass, my suster,
Go kuss him, as the cunning-man would have you,
I'll thrust a pin i' your buttocks else.

FACE: O no, sir.

SURLY: Señora mía, mi persona muy indigna está
Allegar a tanta hermosura.

FACE: Does he not use her bravely?

KASTRIL: Bravely, i' faith!

FACE: Nay, he will use her better.

KASTRIL: Do you think so?

SURLY: Señora, si será servida, entremos.
    [Exit with Dame Pliant]

KASTRIL: Where does he carry her?

FACE: Into the garden, sir;
Take you no thought. I must interpret for her.

SUBTLE: Give Doll the word. [Exit Face] Come, my
fierce child, advance,
We'll to our quarrelling lesson again.

KASTRIL: Agreed.
I love a Spanish boy, with all my heart.

SUBTLE: Nay, and by this means, sir, you shall be
brother
To a great count.

KASTRIL: Ay, I knew that at first.
This match will advance the house of the Kastrils.

SUBTLE: Pray God your sister prove but pliant!

KASTRIL: Why,
Her name is so, by her other husband.

SUBTLE: How!

KASTRIL: The Widow Pliant. Knew you not that?

SUBTLE: No, faith, sir,
Yet, by erection of her figure, I guessed it.
Come, let's go practise.

KASTRIL: Yes, but do you think, Doctor,
I e'er shall quarrel well?

SUBTLE: I warrant you. [Exeunt]

SCENE 3: The chamber above

Enter Doll in her fit of talking, followed by Mammon.

DOLL: For after Alexander's death——

MAMMON: Good lady——

DOLL: That Perdiccas and Antigonus were slain,
The two that stood, Seleuc' and Ptolemy——

MAMMON: Madam——

DOLL: Made up the two legs, and
the fourth beast.
That was Gog-North and Egypt-South; which after
Was called Gog-Iron-Leg and South-Iron-Leg——

MAMMON: Lady——

DOLL: And then Gog-Hornèd. So was Egypt, too.
Then Egypt-Clay-Leg, and Gog-Clay-Leg——

MAMMON: Sweet madam——

DOLL: And last Gog-Dust, and Egypt-Dust, which
fall
In the last link of the fourth chain. And these
Be stars in story, which none see or look at——

MAMMON: What shall I do?

DOLL: For, as he says, except
We call the rabbins, and the heathen Greeks——

MAMMON: Dear lady——

DOLL: To come from Salem, and
from Athens,
And teach the people of Great Britain——

Enter Face, in his servant's dress.

FACE: What's the matter, sir?

DOLL: To speak the tongue of Eber and Javan——

MAMMON: O,
She's in her fit.

DOLL: We shall know nothing——

FACE: Death, sir,
We are undone!

DOLL: Where then a learned linguist
Shall see the ancient used communion
Of vowels and consonants——

FACE: My master will hear!

DOLL: A wisdom, which Pythagoras held most
high——

MAMMON: Sweet honourable lady!

DOLL: To comprise
All sounds of voices, in few marks of letters——

FACE: Nay, you must never hope to lay her now.

    [They speak together]

DOLL: And so we may arrive, by Talmud skill
And profane Greek, to raise the building up
Of Helen's house against the Ishmaelite,
King of Togarmah, and his habergeons
Brimstony, blue, and fiery; and the force
Of king Abaddon, and the beast of Cittim,
Which Rabbi David Kimchi, Onkelos,
And Aben Ezra do interpret Rome.

FACE: How did you put her into't?

MAMMON: Alas, I talked
Of a Fifth Monarchy I would erect
With the Philosophers' Stone, by chance, and she
Falls on the other four straight.

FACE: Out of Broughton!
I told you so. 'Slid, stop her mouth.

MAMMON: Is't best?

FACE: She'll never leave else.
If the old man hear her,
We are but faeces, ashes.

SUBTLE: What's to do there?

FACE: O, we are lost! Now she hears him, she is
quiet.

    [Exit with Doll]

Enter Subtle.

MAMMON: Where shall I hide me!

SUBTLE: How! what sight is here?
Close deeds of darkness, and that shun the light!
Bring him again. Who is he? What, my son!
O, I have lived too long.

MAMMON: Nay, good, dear Father,
There was no unchaste purpose.

SUBTLE: Not! and flee me,
When I come in?

MAMMON: That was my error.

SUBTLE: Error!
Guilt, guilt, my son. Give it the right name. No
    marvel,
If I found check in our great work within,
When such affairs as these were managing!

MAMMON: Why, have you so?

SUBTLE: It has stood still this half hour;
And all the rest of our less works gone back.
Where is the instrument of wickedness,
My lewd, false drudge?

MAMMON: Nay, good sir, blame not him;
Believe me, 'twas against his will or knowledge——
I saw her by chance.

SUBTLE: Will you commit more sin,
T'excuse a varlet?

MAMMON: By my hope, 'tis true, sir.

SUBTLE: Nay, then I wonder less, if you, for whom
The blessing was prepared, would so tempt Heaven,
And lose your fortunes.

MAMMON: Why, sir?

SUBTLE: This'll retard
The work a month at least.

MAMMON: Why, if it do,
What remedy? But think it not, good Father:
Our purposes were honest.

SUBTLE: As they were,
So the reward will prove.
              [*A great crack and noise within*]
                    How now! Ay me,
God and all saints be good to us.

Re-enter Face.

                          What's that?

FACE: O sir, we are defeated! All the works
Are flown in fumo, every glass is burst;
Furnace and all rent down, as if a bolt
Of thunder had been driven through the house!
Retorts, receivers, Pelicans, bolt-heads,
All struck in shivers!
              [Subtle *falls down, as in a swoon*]
                    Help, good sir! Alas,
Coldness and death invades him. Nay, Sir Mam-
    mon,
Do the fair offices of a man! You stand
As you were readier to depart than he.
                          [*One knocks*]
Who's there? My Lord her brother is come.

MAMMON: Ha, Lungs?

FACE: His coach is at the door. Avoid his sight,
For he's as furious as his sister's mad.

MAMMON: Alas!

FACE: My brain is quite undone with the
    fume, sir,
I ne'er must hope to be mine own man again.

MAMMON: Is all lost, Lungs? Will nothing be pre-
    served
Of all our cost?

FACE: Faith, very little, sir,
A peck of coals or so, which is cold comfort, sir.

MAMMON: O my voluptuous mind! I am justly pun-
    ished.

FACE: And so am I, sir.

MAMMON: Cast from all my hopes——

FACE: Nay, certainties, sir.

MAMMON: By mine own base affections.

SUBTLE: [*Seeming to come to himself*] O, the curst
    fruits of vice and lust!

MAMMON: Good father,
It was my sin. Forgive it.

SUBTLE: Hangs my roof
Over us still, and will not fall, O Justice,
Upon us, for this wicked man!

FACE: Nay, look, sir,
You grieve him now with staying in his sight.
Good sir, the nobleman will come too, and take
    you,
And that may breed a tragedy.

MAMMON: I'll go.

FACE: Ay, and repent at home, sir. It may be,
For some good penance you may ha' it yet;
A hundred pound to the box at Bedlam——

MAMMON: Yes.

FACE: For the restoring such as ha' their wits.

MAMMON: I'll do't.

FACE: I'll send one to you to receive it.

MAMMON: Do.
Is no projection left?

FACE: All flown, or stinks, sir.

MAMMON: Will nought be saved that's good for
    med'cine, think'st thou?

FACE: I cannot tell, sir. There will be perhaps
Something, about the scraping of the shards,
Will cure the itch—though not your itch of mind,
    sir.
It shall be saved for you, and sent home. Good sir,
This way for fear the Lord should meet you.
                          [*Exit* Mammon]

SUBTLE: Face!

FACE: Ay.

SUBTLE: Is he gone?

FACE: Yes, and as heavily
As all the gold he hoped for were in his blood.
Let us be light though.

SUBTLE: Ay, as balls, and bound,
And hit our heads against the roof for joy!
There's so much of our care now cast away.

FACE: Now to our Don.

SUBTLE: Yes, your young widow by this time
Is made a countess, Face. She's been in travail
Of a young heir for you.

FACE: Good, sir.

SUBTLE: Off with your case,
And greet her kindly, as a bridegroom should,
After these common hazards.

FACE: Very well, sir.
Will you go fetch Don Diego off the while?

SUBTLE: And fetch him over, too, if you'll be pleased,
sir.
Would Doll were in her place, to pick his pockets
now!

FACE: Why, you can do't as well, if you would set
to't.
I pray you prove your virtue.

SUBTLE: For your sake, sir.
[Exeunt]

SCENE 4: *The garden*

Enter Surly *and* Dame Pliant.

SURLY: Lady, you see into what hands you are fall'n;
'Mongst what a nest of villains! and how near
Your honour was t'have catched a certain clap,
Through your credulity, had I but been
So punctually forward, as place, time,
And other circumstance would ha' made a man—
For you're a handsome woman; would y' were wise,
too!
I am a gentleman, come here disguised,
Only to find the knaveries of this citadel;
And where I might have wronged your honour, and
have not,
I claim some interest in your love. You are,
They say, a widow rich, and I'm a bachelor
Worth nought. Your fortunes may make me a man,
As mine ha' preserved you a woman. Think upon
it,
And whether I have deserved you or no.

DAME PLIANT: I will, sir.

SURLY: And for these household-rogues, let me alone
To treat with them.

Enter Subtle.

SUBTLE: How doth my noble Diego,
And my dear madam Countess? Hath the Count
Been courteous, lady, liberal and open?
Donzel, methinks you look melancholic,
After your coitum, and scurvy! Truly,
I do not like the dulness of your eye;
It hath a heavy cast, 'tis upsea Dutch,
And says you are a lumpish whoremaster.
Be lighter; I will make your pockets so.
[*Falls to picking* Surly's *pockets*]

SURLY: Will you, Don Bawd and Pickpurse? How
now! reel you?
Stand up, sir, you shall find, since I am so heavy,
I'll gi' you equal weight.

SUBTLE: Help! murder!

SURLY: No, sir,
There's no such thing intended. A good cart
And a clean whip shall ease you of that fear.
I am the Spanish Don, that should be cozened,
Do you see? cozened! Where's your Captain Face,
That parcel-broker and whole-bawd, all rascal?

Enter Face *in his uniform.*

FACE: How, Surly!

SURLY: O, make your approach, good Captain.
I've found from whence your copper rings and
spoons
Come, now, wherewith you cheat abroad in tav-
erns.
'Twas here you learned t'anoint your boot with
brimstone,
Then rub men's gold on't, for a kind of touch,
And say 'twas naught, when you had changed the
colour,
That you might ha't for nothing. And this doctor,
Your sooty, smoky-bearded compeer, he
Will close you so much gold, in a bolt's-head,
And, on a turn, convey i' the stead another
With sublimed mercury, that shall burst i' the
heat,
And fly out all in fumo! Then weeps Mammon;
Then swoons his worship. Or, he is the Faustus,
That casteth figures and can conjure, cures
Plagues, piles, and pox, by the Ephemerides,
And holds intelligence with all the bawds
And midwives of three shires; while you send
in—— [*Exit* Face]
Captain!—What! is he gone?—damsels with child,
Wives that are barren, or the waiting-maid
With the greensickness.—Nay, sir, you must tarry,
Though he be 'scaped; and answer by the ears, sir.

Re-enter Face *with* Kastril.

FACE: Why, now's the time, if ever you will quarrel
Well, as they say, and be a true-born child.
The Doctor and your sister both are abused.

KASTRIL: Where is he? Which is he? He is a slave,
Whate'er he is, and the son of a whore.—Are you
The man, sir, I would know?

SURLY: I should be loath, sir,
To confess so much.

KASTRIL: Then you lie i' your throat.

SURLY: How!

FACE: ——A very arrant rogue, sir, and a cheater,
Employed here by another conjurer
That does not love the Doctor, and would cross
him
If he knew how——

SURLY: Sir, you are abused.

KASTRIL: You lie,
And 'tis no matter.

FACE: Well said, sir! He is
The impudent'st rascal——

SURLY: You are, indeed.—Will you hear me, sir?
FACE: By no means; bid him be gone.
KASTRIL: Begone, sir, quickly.
SURLY: This's strange!—Lady, do you inform your
    brother.
FACE: There is not such a foist in all the town,
    The Doctor had him presently; and finds yet
    The Spanish Count will come here.—Bear up,
    Subtle.
SUBTLE: Yes, sir, he must appear within this hour.
FACE: And yet this rogue would come in a disguise,
    By the temptation of another spirit,
    To trouble our art, though he could not hurt it!
KASTRIL: Ay,
    I know.—Away, you talk like a foolish mauther.
SURLY: Sir, all is truth she says.
FACE: Do not believe him, sir,
    He is the lying'st swabber! Come your ways, sir.
SURLY: You are valiant out of company!
KASTRIL: Yes, how then, sir?

    Enter Drugger.
FACE: Nay, here's an honest fellow, too, that knows
    him,
    And all his tricks.—Make good what I say, Abel.
    This cheater would ha' cozened thee o' the
    widow.—
    He owes this honest Drugger here seven pound,
    He has had on him in twopenny'orths of tobacco.
DRUGGER: Yes, sir. And he's damned himself three
    terms to pay me.
FACE: And what does he owe for lotion?
DRUGGER: Thirty shillings, sir,
    And for six syringes.
SURLY: Hydra of villainy!
FACE: —Nay, sir, you must quarrel him out o' the
    house.
KASTRIL: I will.
    —Sir, if you get not out o' doors, you lie;
    And you are a pimp.
SURLY: Why, this is madness, sir,
    Not valour in you. I must laugh at this.
KASTRIL: It is my humour: you are a pimp and a trig,
    And an Amadis de Gaul, or a Don Quixote.
DRUGGER: Or a knight o' the curious coxcomb, do you
    see?

    Enter Ananias.
ANANIAS: Peace to the household!
KASTRIL: I'll keep peace for no man.
ANANIAS: Casting of dollars is concluded lawful.
KASTRIL: Is he the Constable?
SUBTLE: Peace, Ananias.
FACE: No, sir.
KASTRIL: Then you are an otter, and a shad, a
    whit,
    A very tim.
SURLY: You'll hear me, sir?
KASTRIL: I will not.

ANANIAS: What is the motive?
SUBTLE: Zeal in the young gentleman,
    Against his Spanish slops.
ANANIAS: They are profane,
    Lewd, superstitious, and idolatrous breeches.
SURLY: New rascals!
KASTRIL: Will you be gone, sir?
ANANIAS: Avoid, Satan!
    Thou art not of the light. That ruff of pride,
    About thy neck, betrays thee; and is the same
    With that which the unclean birds, in 'seventy-
    seven,
    Were seen to prank it with, on divers coasts.
    Thou look'st like Antichrist in that lewd hat.
SURLY: I must give way.
KASTRIL: Begone, sir.
SURLY: But I'll take
    A course with you,——
ANANIAS: Depart, proud Spanish fiend!
SURLY: Captain, and Doctor,——
ANANIAS: Child of perdition!
KASTRIL: Hence, sir!
                       [*Exit* Surly]
    Did I not quarrel bravely?
FACE: Yes, indeed, sir.
KASTRIL: Nay, an I give my mind to't, I shall do't.
FACE: O, you must follow, sir, and threaten him
    tame.
    He'll turn again else.
KASTRIL: I'll re-turn him then. [*Exit*]
FACE: —Drugger, this rogue prevented us, for thee.
    We had determined that thou should'st ha' come
    In a Spanish suit, and ha' carried her so; and he
    A brokerly slave, goes, puts it on himself!
    Hast brought the damask?
DRUGGER: Yes, sir.
FACE: Thou must borrow
    A Spanish suit. Hast thou no credit with the
    players?
DRUGGER: Yes, sir, did you never see me play the fool?
FACE: I know not, Nab.—Thou shalt, if I can help
    it.—
    Hieronimo's old cloak, ruff, and hat will serve;
                     [*Exit* Drugger]
    I'll tell thee more when thou bring'st 'em.
ANANIAS: [*Having whispered with* Subtle *this while*]
                          Sir, I know
    The Spaniard hates the Brethren, and hath spies
    Upon their actions; and that this was one
    I make no scruple. But the Holy Synod
    Have been in prayer and meditation for it;
    And 'tis revealed no less to them than me,
    That casting of money is most lawful.
SUBTLE: True.
    But here I cannot do it; if the house
    Should chance to be suspected, all would out,
    And we be locked up in the Tower forever,
    To make gold there for th' state, never come out;
    And then are you defeated.

ANANIAS: I will tell
  This to the elders and the weaker Brethren,
  That the whole company of the Separation
  May join in humble prayer again.
SUBTLE: —And fasting.
ANANIAS: Yea, for some fitter place. The peace of
    mind
  Rest with these walls!   [*Exit*]
SUBTLE: Thanks, courteous Ananias.
FACE: What did he come for?
SUBTLE: About casting dollars
  Presently, out of hand. And so I told him
  A Spanish minister came here to spy
  Against the faithful——
FACE: I conceive. Come, Subtle,
  Thou art so down upon the least disaster!
  How wouldst th' ha' done, if I had not helped thee
    out?
SUBTLE: I thank thee, Face, for the angry boy, i' faith.
FACE: Who would ha' looked it should ha' been that
    rascal
  Surly? He had dyed his beard and all. Well, sir,
  Here's damask come, to make you a suit.
SUBTLE: Where's Drugger?
FACE: He is gone to borrow me a Spanish habit;
  I'll be the Count now.
SUBTLE: But where's the widow?
FACE: Within, with my Lord's sister; Madam Doll
  Is entertaining her.
SUBTLE: By your favour, Face,
  Now she is honest, I will stand again.
FACE: You will not offer it?
SUBTLE: Why?
FACE: Stand to your word,
  Or—here comes Doll—she knows——
SUBTLE: You're tyrannous still.

  Enter Doll.
FACE: Strict for my right.—How now, Doll! Hast told
    her
  The Spanish Count will come?
DOLL: Yes, but another is come,
  You little looked for!
FACE: Who is that?
DOLL: Your master,
  The master of the house.
SUBTLE: How, Doll!
FACE: She lies,
  This is some trick. Come, leave your quibblings,
    Dorothy.
DOLL: Look out and see.
SUBTLE: Art thou in earnest?
DOLL: 'Slight,
  Forty o' the neighbours are about him, talking.
FACE: 'Tis he, by this good day!
DOLL: 'Twill prove ill day
  For some on us.
FACE: We are undone, and taken!
DOLL: Lost, I'm afraid.

SUBTLE: You said he would not come,
  While there died one a week within the liberties.
FACE: No, 'twas within the walls.
SUBTLE: Was't so! Cry you mercy,
  I thought the liberties. What shall we do now,
    Face?
FACE: Be silent; not a word, if he call or knock.
  I'll into mine old shape again, and meet him,
  Of Jeremy, the butler. I' the meantime,
  Do you two pack up all the goods and purchase,
  That we can carry i' the two trunks. I'll keep him
  Off for today, if I cannot longer; and then
  At night, I'll ship you both away to Ratcliffe,
  Where we will meet tomorrow; and there we'll
    share.
  Let Mammon's brass and pewter keep the cellar;
  We'll have another time for that. But, Doll,
  Prithee go heat a little water quickly;
  Subtle must shave me. All my captain's beard
  Must off, to make me appear smooth Jeremy.
  You'll do't?
SUBTLE: Yes, I'll shave you, as well as I can.
FACE: And not cut my throat, but trim me?
SUBTLE: You shall see, sir.
                                        [*Exeunt*]

Act V

SCENE 1:   *Before Lovewit's door*

  Enter Lovewit, *with* Neighbours.
LOVEWIT: Has there been such resort, say you?
1ST NEIGHBOUR: Daily, sir.
2ND NEIGHBOUR: And nightly, too.
3RD NEIGHBOUR: Ay, some as brave as lords.
4TH NEIGHBOUR: Ladies and gentlewomen.
5TH NEIGHBOUR: Citizens' wives.
1ST NEIGHBOUR: And knights.
6TH NEIGHBOUR: In coaches.
2ND NEIGHBOUR: Yes, and oyster-women.
1ST NEIGHBOUR: Beside other gallants.
3RD NEIGHBOUR: Sailors' wives.
4TH NEIGHBOUR: Tobacco-men.
5TH NEIGHBOUR: Another Pimlico!
LOVEWIT: What should my knave advance,
  To draw this company? He hung out no banners
  Of a strange calf with five legs, to be seen,
  Or a huge lobster with six claws?
6TH NEIGHBOUR: No, sir.
3RD NEIGHBOUR: We had gone in then, sir.
LOVEWIT: He has no gift
  Of teaching i' the nose, that e'er I knew of.
  You saw no bills set up that promised cure
  Of agues, or the toothache?
2ND NEIGHBOUR: No such thing, sir!
LOVEWIT: Nor heard a drum struck, for baboons or
    puppets?
5TH NEIGHBOUR: Neither, sir.

LOVEWIT: What device should he
  bring forth now?
I love a teeming wit as I love my nourishment.
Pray God he ha' not kept such open house,
That he hath sold my hangings and my bedding!
I left him nothing else. If he have eat 'em,
A plague o' the moth, say I! Sure he has got
Some bawdy pictures to call all this ging;
The Friar and the Nun, or the new motion
Of the knight's courser covering the parson's mare;
The boy of six year old with the great thing.
Or 't may be, he has the fleas that run at tilt
Upon a table, or some dog to dance.
When saw you him?

1ST NEIGHBOUR: Who, sir, Jeremy?

2ND NEIGHBOUR: Jeremy butler?
  We saw him not this month.

LOVEWIT: How!

4TH NEIGHBOUR: Not these five weeks, sir.

1ST NEIGHBOUR: These six weeks at the least.

LOVEWIT: Y'amaze me, neighbours!

5TH NEIGHBOUR: Sure, if your worship know not
  where he is,
He's slipped away.

6TH NEIGHBOUR: Pray God he be not made away!

LOVEWIT: Ha! it's no time to question, then.
                                        [Knocks]

6TH NEIGHBOUR: About
Some three weeks since, I heard a doleful cry,
As I sat up a-mending my wife's stockings.

LOVEWIT: 'Tis strange that none will answer! Did'st
  thou hear
A cry, sayst thou?

6TH NEIGHBOUR: Yes, sir, like unto a man
That had been strangled an hour, and could not
  speak.

2ND NEIGHBOUR: I heard it too, just this day three
  weeks, at two o'clock
Next morning.

LOVEWIT: These be miracles, or you make 'em
  so!
A man an hour strangled, and could not speak,
And both you heard him cry?

3RD NEIGHBOUR: Yes, downward, sir.

LOVEWIT: Thou art a wise fellow. Give me thy hand,
  I pray thee.
What trade art thou on?

3RD NEIGHBOUR: A smith, an't please your
  worship.

LOVEWIT: A smith! then lend me thy help to get this
  door open.

3RD NEIGHBOUR: That I will presently, sir, but fetch
  my tools——   [Exit]

1ST NEIGHBOUR: Sir, best to knock again, afore you
  break it.

LOVEWIT: I will.

Enter Face *in his butler's livery.*

FACE: What mean you, sir?

1ST, 2ND, 4TH NEIGHBOURS: O, here's Jeremy!

FACE: Good sir, come from the door.

LOVEWIT: Why, what's the matter?

FACE: Yet farther, you are too near yet.

LOVEWIT: I' the name of wonder,
  What means the fellow?

FACE: The house, sir, has been visited.

LOVEWIT: What, with the plague? Stand thou then
  farther.

FACE: No, sir,
I had it not.

LOVEWIT: Who had it then? I left
None else but thee i' the house.

FACE: Yes, sir. My fellow,
The cat that kept the butt'ry, had it on her
A week, before I spied it; but I got her
Conveyed away i' the night. And so I shut
The house up for a month——

LOVEWIT: How!

FACE: Purposing then, sir,
T' have burnt rose-vinegar, treacle, and tar,
And ha' made it sweet, that you should ne'er ha'
  known it;
Because I knew the news would but afflict you,
  sir.

LOVEWIT: Breathe less, and farther off! Why this is
  stranger!
The neighbours tell me all here, that the doors
Have still been open——

FACE: How, sir!

LOVEWIT: Gallants, men and women,
And of all sorts, tag-rag, been seen to flock here
In threaves, these ten weeks, as to a second Hogs-
  den,
In days of Pimlico and Eyebright.

FACE: Sir,
Their wisdoms will not say so!

LOVEWIT: Today they speak
Of coaches and gallants. One in a French hood
Went in, they tell me; and another was seen
In a velvet gown at the window. Divers more
Pass in and out.

FACE: They did pass through the doors then,
Or walls, I assure their eyesights and their specta-
  cles.
For here, sir, are the keys, and here have been,
In this my pocket, now above twenty days;
And for before, I kept the fort alone there.
But that 'tis yet not deep i' the afternoon,
I should believe my neighbours had seen double
Through the black pot, and made these appari-
  tions!
For, on my faith to your worship, for these three
  weeks
And upwards, the door has not been opened.

LOVEWIT: Strange!

1ST NEIGHBOUR: Good faith, I think I saw a coach.

2ND NEIGHBOUR: And I, too,
I'd ha' been sworn.

LOVEWIT: Do you but think it now?
And but one coach?
4TH NEIGHBOUR: We cannot tell, sir. Jeremy
Is a very honest fellow.
FACE: Did you see me at all?
1ST NEIGHBOUR: No, that we are sure on.
2ND NEIGHBOUR: I'll be sworn o' that.
LOVEWIT: Fine rogues to have your testimonies built
    on!

Re-enter 3rd Neighbour.

3RD NEIGHBOUR: Is Jeremy come?
1ST NEIGHBOUR: O yes, you may leave your tools.
We were deceived, he says.
2ND NEIGHBOUR: He's had the keys,
And the door has been shut these three weeks.
3RD NEIGHBOUR: Like enough.
LOVEWIT: Peace, and get hence, you changelings.

Enter Surly *and* Mammon.

FACE: —Surly come!
And Mammon made acquainted! They'll tell all.
How shall I beat them off? What shall I do?
Nothing's more wretched than a guilty conscience.
SURLY: No, sir, he was a great physician. This,
    It was no bawdy-house, but a mere chancel!
    You knew the Lord and his sister.
MAMMON: Nay, good Surly,——
SURLY: The happy word, 'Be rich,'——
MAMMON: Play not the tyrant—
SURLY: Should be today pronounced to all your
    friends.
And where be your andirons now, and your brass
    pots,
That should ha' been golden flagons, and great
    wedges?
MAMMON: Let me but breathe. [*They knock*] What?
    They ha' shut their doors,
Methinks!
SURLY: Ay, now 'tis holiday with them.
MAMMON: Rogues,
Cozeners, impostors, bawds!
FACE: What mean you, sir?
MAMMON: To enter if we can.
FACE: Another man's house!
Here is the owner, sir. Turn you to him,
And speak your business.
MAMMON: Are you, sir, the owner?
LOVEWIT: Yes, sir.
MAMMON: And are those knaves, within, your
    cheaters?
LOVEWIT: What knaves? What cheaters?
MAMMON: Subtle and his Lungs.
FACE: The gentleman is distracted, sir! No lungs
Nor lights ha' been seen here these three weeks,
    sir,
Within these doors, upon my word!
SURLY: Your word,
Groom arrogant!

FACE: Yes, sir, I am the housekeeper,
And know the keys ha' not been out o' my hands.
SURLY: This's a new Face.
FACE: You do mistake the house, sir.
What sign was't at?
SURLY: You rascal! This is one
O' the confederacy. Come, let's get officers,
And force the door.
LOVEWIT: Pray you stay, gentlemen.
SURLY: No, sir, we'll come with warrant.
MAMMON: Ay, and then
We shall ha' your doors open.
                      [*Exeunt* Mammon *and* Surly]
LOVEWIT: What means this?
FACE: I cannot tell, sir.
1ST NEIGHBOUR: These are two o' the gallants
That we do think we saw.
FACE: Two o' the fools!
You talk as idly as they. Good faith, sir,
I think the moon has crazed 'em all.

Enter Kastril.

                             —O me,
The angry boy come too! He'll make a noise,
And ne'er away till he have betrayed us all.
KASTRIL: [*Knocks*] What, rogues, bawds, slaves, you'll
    open the door, anon!
Punk, cockatrice, my suster! By this light,
I'll fetch the Marshal to you. You are a whore,
To keep your castle——
FACE: Who would you speak with, sir?
KASTRIL: The bawdy Doctor, and the cozening Cap-
    tain,
And Puss, my suster.
LOVEWIT: This is something, sure.
FACE: Upon my trust, the doors were never open, sir.
KASTRIL: I have heard all their tricks told me twice
    over,
By the fat knight and the lean gentleman.
LOVEWIT: Here comes another.

Enter Ananias *and* Tribulation.

FACE: Ananias, too!
And his pastor!
TRIBULATION: [*Beating at the door*] The doors are
    shut against us.
ANANIAS: Come forth, you seed of sulphur, sons of
    fire!
Your stench it is broke forth; abomination
Is in the house.
KASTRIL: Ay, my suster's there.
ANANIAS: The place,
It is become a cage of unclean birds.
KASTRIL: Yes, I will fetch the Scavenger, and the
    Constable.
TRIBULATION: You shall do well.
ANANIAS: We'll join, to weed them out.
KASTRIL: You will not come then, punk-device, my
    suster?

ANANIAS: Call her not sister. She is a harlot verily.

KASTRIL: I'll raise the street.

LOVEWIT: Good gentlemen, a word.

ANANIAS: Satan, avoid, and hinder not our zeal!
    [*Exeunt* Ananias, Tribulation, *and* Kastril]

LOVEWIT: The world's turned Bedlam.

FACE: These are all broke loose,
    Out of Saint Katherine's, where they use, to keep
    The better sort of mad-folks.

1ST NEIGHBOUR: All these persons
    We saw go in and out here.

2ND NEIGHBOUR: Yes, indeed, sir.

3RD NEIGHBOUR: These were the parties.

FACE: Peace, you drunkards! Sir,
    I wonder at it! Please you to give me leave
    To touch the door, I'll try an the lock be changed.

LOVEWIT: It amazes me!

FACE: Good faith, sir, I believe
    There's no such thing. 'Tis all deceptio visus.—
    Would I could get him away!

DAPPER: [*Cries out within*] Master Captain! Master
    Doctor!

LOVEWIT: Who's that?

FACE: —Our clerk within, that I for-
    got!—I know not, sir.

DAPPER: For God's sake, when will her Grace be at
    leisure?

FACE: Ha!
    Illusions, some spirit 'o the air!—His gag is melted,
    And now he sets out the throat.

DAPPER: I am almost stifled——

FACE: —Would you were altogether.

LOVEWIT: 'Tis in the house.
    Ha, list!

FACE: Believe it, sir, i' the air.

LOVEWIT: Peace, you——

DAPPER: Mine aunt's Grace does not use me well.

SUBTLE: You fool,
    Peace, you'll mar all.

FACE: —Or you will else, you rogue.

LOVEWIT: O, is it so? Then you converse with spirits!
    Come, sir. No more o' your tricks, good Jeremy;
    The truth, the shortest way.

FACE: Dismiss this rabble, sir.—
    What shall I do? I am catched.

LOVEWIT: Good neighbours,
    I thank you all. You may depart. [*Exeunt* Neigh-
    bours] Come, sir,
    You know that I am an indulgent master;
    And therefore conceal nothing. What's your med'-
    cine,
    To draw so many several sorts of wildfowl?

FACE: Sir, you were wont to affect mirth and wit——
    But here's no place to talk on't i' the street.
    Give me but leave to make the best of my fortune,
    And only pardon me th' abuse of your house.
    It's all I beg. I'll help you to a widow,
    In recompense, that you shall gi' me thanks for,
    Will make you seven years younger, and a rich one.

'Tis but your putting on a Spanish cloak;
    I have her within. You need not fear the house,
    It was not visited.

LOVEWIT: But by me, who came
    Sooner than you expected.

FACE: It is true, sir.
    Pray you forgive me.

LOVEWIT: Well—let's see your widow.
                    [*Exeunt*]

SCENE 2: *Lovewit's house*

Enter Subtle *with* Dapper.

SUBTLE: How! ha' you eaten your gag?

DAPPER: Yes, faith, it crumbled
    Away i' my mouth.

SUBTLE: You ha' spoiled all then.

DAPPER: No!
    I hope my aunt of Faery will forgive me.

SUBTLE: Your aunt's a gracious lady, but in troth
    You were to blame.

DAPPER: The fume did overcome me,
    And I did do't to stay my stomach. Pray you
    So satisfy her Grace. Here comes the Captain.

Enter Face *in his uniform.*

FACE: How now! is his mouth down?

SUBTLE: Ay, he has spoken!

FACE: A pox, I heard him, and you too!—He's un-
    done then.—
    I have been fain to say the house is haunted
    With spirits, to keep churl back.

SUBTLE: And hast thou done it?

FACE: Sure, for this night.

SUBTLE: Why, then triumph and sing
    Of Face so famous, the precious king
    Of present wits.

FACE: Did you not hear the coil
    About the door?

SUBTLE: Yes, and I dwindled with it.

FACE: Show him his aunt, and let him be dispatched.
    I'll send her to you.   [*Exit* Face]

SUBTLE: Well, sir, your aunt, her Grace,
    Will give you audience presently, on my suit,
    And the Captain's word that you did not eat your
    gag
    In any contempt of her Highness.

DAPPER: Not I, in troth, sir.

Enter Doll *like the Queen of Faery.*

SUBTLE: Here she is come. Down o' your knees and
    wriggle.
    She has a stately presence.—Good! Yet nearer,
    And bid, 'God save you!'

DAPPER: Madam!

SUBTLE: And your aunt.

DAPPER: And my most gracious aunt, God save your
    Grace.

DOLL: Nephew, we thought to have been angry with
    you;

But that sweet face of yours hath turned the tide,
And made it flow with joy, that ebbed of love.
Arise, and touch our velvet gown.

SUBTLE: —The skirts,
And kiss 'em. So!

DOLL: Let me now stroke that head:
'Much, nephew, shalt thou win, much shalt thou
    spend,
Much shalt thou give away, much shalt thou lend.'

SUBTLE: Ay, much, indeed!—Why do you not thank
    her Grace?

DAPPER: I cannot speak for joy.

SUBTLE: See, the kind wretch!
Your Grace's kinsman right.

DOLL: Give me the bird.
Here is your fly in a purse, about your neck, cousin;
Wear it, and feed it about this day sev'night
On your right wrist——

SUBTLE: Open a vein with a pin,
And let it suck but once a week. Till then,
You must not look on't.

DOLL: No; and, kinsman,
Bear yourself worthy of the blood you come on.

SUBTLE: Her Grace would ha' you eat no more Wool-
    sack pies,
No Dagger frumenty.

DOLL: Nor break his fast
In Heaven and Hell.

SUBTLE: She's with you everywhere!
Nor play with costermongers, at mumchance, tray-
    trip,
God-make-you-rich,—whenas your aunt has done
    it—but keep
The gallant'st company, and the best games——

DAPPER: Yes, sir.

SUBTLE: Gleek and primero; and what you get, be
    true to us.

DAPPER: By this hand, I will.

SUBTLE: You may bring 's a thousand pound
Before tomorrow night, if but three thousand
Be stirring, an you will.

DAPPER: I swear I will then.

SUBTLE: Your fly will learn you all games.

FACE: Ha' you done there?

SUBTLE: Your Grace will command him no more
    duties?

DOLL: No,
But come and see me often. I may chance
To leave him three or four hundred chests of
    treasure,
And some twelve thousand acres of Fairyland,
If he game well and comely with good gamesters.

SUBTLE: There's a kind aunt! Kiss her departing part.
But you must sell your forty mark a year now.

DAPPER: Ay, sir, I mean.

SUBTLE: Or gi't away, pox on't!

DAPPER: I'll gi't mine aunt. I'll go and fetch the writ-
    ings.   [Exit]

SUBTLE: 'Tis well, away!

Re-enter Face.

FACE: Where's Subtle?

SUBTLE: Here. What news?

FACE: Drugger is at the door; go take his suit,
And bid him fetch a parson presently;
Say he shall marry the widow. Thou shalt spend
A hundred pound by the service!   [Exit Subtle]
                          Now, Queen Doll,
Ha' you packed up all?

DOLL: Yes.

FACE: And how do you like
The Lady Pliant?

DOLL: A good, dull innocent.

Re-enter Subtle.

SUBTLE: Here's your Hieronimo's cloak and hat.

FACE: Give me 'em.

SUBTLE: And the ruff too?

FACE: Yes; I'll come to you presently.
                                      [Exit]

SUBTLE: Now he is gone about his project, Doll,
I told you of, for the widow.

DOLL: 'Tis direct
Against our articles.

SUBTLE: Well, we'll fit him, wench.
Hast thou gulled her of her jewels or her bracelets?

DOLL: No, but I will do 't.

SUBTLE: Soon at night, my Dolly,
When we are shipped, and all our goods aboard,
Eastward for Ratcliffe; we will turn our course
To Brainford, westward, if thou sayst the word,
And take our leaves of this o'erweening rascal,
This peremptory Face.

DOLL: Content, I'm weary of him.

SUBTLE: Th'ast cause, when the slave will run awiv-
    ing, Doll,
Against the instrument that was drawn between us.

DOLL: I'll pluck his bird as bare as I can.

SUBTLE: Yes, tell her
She must, by any means, address some present
To th' cunning-man; make him amends for wrong-
    ing
His art with her suspicion; send a ring,
Or chain of pearl. She will be tortured else
Extremely in her sleep, say; and ha' strange things
Come to her. Wilt thou?

DOLL: Yes.

SUBTLE: My fine flittermouse,
My bird o' the night! we'll tickle it at the Pigeons,
When we have all, and may unlock the trunks,
And say, this 's mine, and thine; and thine, and
    mine——   [They kiss]

Re-enter Face.

FACE: What now! a-billing?

SUBTLE: Yes, a little exalted
In the good passage of our stock-affairs.

FACE: Drugger has brought his parson; take him in,
    Subtle,
And send Nab back again to wash his face.

SUBTLE: I will; and shave himself?   [Exit]

FACE: If you can get him.

DOLL: You are hot upon it, Face, whate'er it is!

FACE: A trick that Doll shall spend ten pound a month by.

Re-enter Subtle.

Is he gone?

SUBTLE: The chaplain waits you in the hall, sir.

FACE: I'll go bestow him.   [Exit]

DOLL: He'll now marry her instantly.

SUBTLE: He cannot yet; he is not ready. Dear Doll,
Cozen her of all thou canst. To deceive him
Is no deceit, but justice, that would break
Such an inextricable tie as ours was.

DOLL: Let me alone to fit him.

Re-enter Face.

FACE: Come, my venturers,
You ha' packed up all? Where be the trunks?
Bring forth.

SUBTLE: Here.

FACE: Let's see 'em. Where's the money?

SUBTLE: Here,
In this.

FACE: Mammon's ten pound; eight score before;
The Brethren's money this; Drugger's, and Dap-
per's—
What paper's that?

DOLL: The jewel of the waiting-maid's,
That stole it from her lady, to know certain——

FACE: If she should have precedence of her mistress?

DOLL: Yes.

FACE: What box is that?

SUBTLE: The fishwife's rings, I think,
And th' alewife's single money. Is't not, Doll?

DOLL: Yes, and the whistle that the sailor's wife
Brought you, to know an her husband were with
Ward.

FACE: We'll wet it tomorrow; and our silver beakers
And tavern cups. Where be the French petticoats,
And girdles and hangers?

SUBTLE: Here, i' the trunk,
And the bolts of lawn.

FACE: Is Drugger's damask there,
And the tobacco?

SUBTLE: Yes.

FACE: Give me the keys.

DOLL: Why you the keys?

SUBTLE: No matter, Doll, because
We shall not open 'em before he comes.

FACE: 'Tis true, you shall not open them, indeed;
Nor have 'em forth, do you see? not forth, Doll.

DOLL: No!

FACE: No, my smock-rampant. The right is, my master
Knows all, has pardoned me, and he will keep 'em.
Doctor, 'tis true,—you look—for all your figures!
I sent for him, indeed. Wherefore, good partners,

Both he and she, be satisfied; for here
Determines the indenture tripartite
'Twixt Subtle, Doll, and Face. All I can do
Is to help you over the wall, o' the back-side,
Or lend you a sheet to save your velvet gown, Doll.
Here will be officers presently. Bethink you
Of some course suddenly to 'scape the dock,
For thither you will come else. Hark you, thunder.
                                      [Some knock]

SUBTLE: You are a precious fiend!

OFFICERS: Open the door.

FACE: Doll, I am sorry for thee i' faith. But hear'st
thou?
It shall go hard, but I will place thee somewhere;
Thou shalt ha' my letter to Mistress Amo——

DOLL: Hang you—

FACE: Or Madam Caesarean.

DOLL: Pox upon you, rogue,
Would I had but time to beat thee!

FACE: Subtle,
Let's know where you set up next; I'll send you
A customer, now and then, for old acquaintance.
What new course have you?

SUBTLE: Rogue, I'll hang myself;
That I may walk a greater devil than thou,
And haunt thee i' the flock-bed and the buttery.
                                  [Exit with Doll]

SCENE 3: *Within Lovewit's door*

Enter Lovewit *in the Spanish dress, with a* Parson.

LOVEWIT: What do you mean, my masters?

MAMMON: [*Knocking without*]   Open your door,
Cheaters, bawds, conjurers.

OFFICER: Or we'll break it open.

LOVEWIT: What warrant have you?

OFFICER: Warrant enough, sir, doubt not,
If you'll not open it.

LOVEWIT: Is there an officer there?

OFFICER: Yes, two or three for failing.

LOVEWIT: Have but patience,
And I will open it straight.

Enter Face *as butler*.

FACE: Sir, ha' you done?
Is it a marriage? perfect?

LOVEWIT: Yes, my brain.

FACE: Off with your ruff and cloak then; be yourself,
sir.

SURLY: Down with the door!

KASTRIL: 'Slight, ding it open!

LOVEWIT: Hold,
Hold, gentlemen, what means this violence?

Enter Mammon, Surly, Kastril, Ananias, Tribulation, *and* Officers.

MAMMON: Where is this collier?

SURLY: And my Captain Face?

MAMMON: These day-owls.

SURLY: That are birding in men's purses.

MAMMON: Madam Suppository.

KASTRIL: Doxy, my suster.

ANANIAS: Locusts

Of the foul pit.

TRIBULATION: Profane as Bel and the Dragon.

ANANIAS: Worse than the grasshoppers, or the lice of
   Egypt.

LOVEWIT: Good gentlemen, hear me.—Are you officers,

And cannot stay this violence?

1ST OFFICER: Keep the peace!

LOVEWIT: Gentlemen, what is the matter? Whom do
   you seek?

MAMMON: The chemical cozener.

SURLY: And the captain pander.

KASTRIL: The nun, my suster.

MAMMON: Madam Rabbi.

ANANIAS: Scorpions

And caterpillars.

LOVEWIT: Fewer at once, I pray you.

1ST OFFICER: One after another, gentlemen, I charge
   you,

By virtue of my staff——

ANANIAS: They are the vessels

Of pride, lust, and the cart.

LOVEWIT: Good zeal, lie still

A little while.

TRIBULATION: Peace, Deacon Ananias.

LOVEWIT: The house is mine here, and the doors are
   open.

If there be any such persons as you seek for,

Use your authority, search on, o' God's name.

I am but newly come to town, and finding

This tumult 'bout my door, to tell you true,

It somewhat 'mazed me; till my man here, fearing

My more displeasure, told me he had done

Somewhat an insolent part, let out my house—

Belike presuming on my known aversion

From any air o' the town, while there was sickness—

To a doctor and a captain. Who, what they are,

Or where they be, he knows not.

MAMMON: Are they gone?

LOVEWIT: You may go in and search, sir. [Exeunt
   Mammon, Ananias, and Tribulation] Here, I
   find

The empty walls, worse than I left 'em, smoked;

A few cracked pots and glasses, and a furnace;

The ceiling filled with poesies of the candle;

And madam with a dildo writ o' the walls.

Only one gentlewoman I met here,

That is within, that said she was a widow——

KASTRIL: Ay, that's my suster. I'll go thump her.
   Where is she?   [Exit]

LOVEWIT: And should ha' married a Spanish count,
   but he,

When he came to't, neglected her so grossly,

That I, a widower, am gone through with her.

SURLY: How! have I lost her then?

LOVEWIT: Were you the Don, sir?

Good faith, now she does blame y' extremely, and
   says

You swore, and told her you had ta'en the pains

To dye your beard, and umber o'er your face;

Borrowed a suit and ruff, all for her love;

And then did nothing. What an oversight,

And want of putting forward, sir, was this!

Well fare an old harquebusier yet,

Could prime his powder, and give fire, and hit,

All in a twinkling!

Re-enter Mammon.

MAMMON: The whole nest are fled!

LOVEWIT: What sort of birds were they?

MAMMON: A kind of choughs,

Or thievish daws, sir, that have picked my purse

Of eight score and ten pounds within these five
   weeks,

Beside my first materials; and my goods,

That lie i' the cellar, which I am glad they ha' left,

I may have home yet.

LOVEWIT: Think you so, sir?

MAMMON: Ay.

LOVEWIT: By order of law, sir, but not otherwise.

MAMMON: Not mine own stuff!

LOVEWIT: Sir, I can take no knowledge

That they are yours, but by public means.

If you can bring certificate that you were gulled
   of 'em,

Or any formal writ, out of a court,

That you did cozen yourself, I will not hold them.

MAMMON: I'll rather lose 'em.

LOVEWIT: That you shall not, sir,

By me, in troth. Upon these terms, they 're yours.

What should they ha' been, sir? turned into gold
   all?

MAMMON: No.

I cannot tell—it may be they should. What then?

LOVEWIT: What a great loss in hope have you sustained!

MAMMON: Not I, the commonwealth has.

FACE: Ay, he would ha' built

The city new; and made a ditch about it

Of silver, should have run with cream from Hogs-
   den;

That every Sunday, in Moorfields, the younkers,

And tits, and tom-boys should have fed on, gratis.

MAMMON: I will go mount a turnip-cart, and preach

The end o' the world within these two months.
   Surly,

What! in a dream?

SURLY: Must I needs cheat myself

With that same foolish vice of honesty!

Come, let us go and hearken out the rogues.

That Face I'll mark for mine, if e'er I meet him.

FACE: If I can hear of him, sir, I'll bring you word

Unto your lodging. For in troth, they were
   strangers

To me; I thought 'em honest as myself, sir.

                        [*Exeunt* Mammon *and* Surly]

Re-enter Ananias *and* Tribulation.

TRIBULATION: 'Tis well, the Saints shall not lose all yet. Go
And get some carts——

LOVEWIT: For what, my zealous friends?

ANANIAS: To bear away the portion of the righteous
Out of this den of thieves.

LOVEWIT: What is that portion?

ANANIAS: The goods, sometimes the orphans', that the Brethren
Bought with their silver pence.

LOVEWIT: What, those i' the cellar,
The knight Sir Mammon claims?

ANANIAS: I do defy
The wicked Mammon; so do all the Brethren,
Thou profane man! I ask thee with what conscience
Thou canst advance that idol, against us
That have the seal? Were not the shillings numbered
That made the pounds? Were not the pounds told out
Upon the second day of the fourth week,
In the eighth month, upon the table dormant,
The year of the last patience of the Saints,
Six hundred and ten?

LOVEWIT: Mine earnest, vehement botcher,
And deacon also, I cannot dispute with you;
But if you get you not away the sooner,
I shall confute you with a cudgel.

ANANIAS: Sir!

TRIBULATION: Be patient, Ananias.

ANANIAS: I am strong,
And will stand up, well girt, against an host
That threaten Gad in exile.

LOVEWIT: I shall send you
To Amsterdam, to your cellar.

ANANIAS: I will pray there,
Against thy house: may dogs defile thy walls,
And wasps and hornets breed beneath thy roof,
This seat of falsehood, and this cave of cozenage!

              [*Exeunt* Ananias *and* Tribulation]

Enter Drugger.

LOVEWIT: Another, too?

DRUGGER: Not I, sir, I am no Brother.

LOVEWIT: [*Beats* Drugger *away*] Away, you Harry Nicholas! do you talk?

FACE: No, this was Abel Drugger. [*To the* Parson]
Good sir, go,
And satisfy him; tell him all is done.
He strayed too long a-washing of his face.
The Doctor, he shall hear of him at Westchester;
And of the Captain, tell him, at Yarmouth, or
Some good port-town else, lying for a wind.

                   [*Exit* Parson]

If you can get off the angry child now, sir——

Enter Kastril *with* Dame Pliant.

KASTRIL: Come on, you ewe, you have matched most sweetly, ha' you not?
Did not I say, I would never ha' you tupped
But by a dubbed boy, to make you a lady-tom?
'Slight, you are a mammet! O, I could touse you now.
Death, mun you marry with a pox?

LOVEWIT: You lie, boy!
As sound as you; and I am aforehand with you.

KASTRIL: Anon?

LOVEWIT: Come, will you quarrel? I will feeze you, sirrah.
Why do you not buckle to your tools?

KASTRIL: God's light,
This is a fine old boy as e'er I saw!

LOVEWIT: What, do you change your copy now? Proceed,
Here stands my dove; stoop at her if you dare.

KASTRIL: 'Slight, I must love him! I cannot choose, i' faith,
An I should be hanged for't! Suster, I protest,
I honour thee for this match.

LOVEWIT: O, do you so, sir?

KASTRIL: Yes, an thou canst take tobacco and drink, old boy,
I'll give her five hundred pound more to her marriage,
Than her own state.

LOVEWIT: Fill a pipe-full, Jeremy.

FACE: Yes, but go in and take it, sir.

LOVEWIT: We will.
I will be ruled by thee in anything, Jeremy.

KASTRIL: 'Slight, thou art not hide-bound! thou art a jovy boy!
Come, let's in, I pray thee, and take our whiffs.

LOVEWIT: Whiff in with your sister, brother boy.
      [*Exeunt* Kastril *and* Dame Pliant] That master
That had received such happiness by a servant,
In such a widow, and with so much wealth,
Were very ungrateful, if he would not be
A little indulgent to that servant's wit,
And help his fortune, though with some small strain
Of his own candour. Therefore, gentlemen,
And kind spectators, if I have outstripped
An old man's gravity, or strict canon, think
What a young wife and a good brain may do:
Stretch age's truth sometimes, and crack it too.——
Speak for thyself, knave.

FACE: So I will, sir.—Gentlemen,
My part a little fell in this last scene,
Yet 'twas decorum. And though I am clean
Got off from Subtle, Surly, Mammon, Doll,
Hot Ananias, Dapper, Drugger, all
With whom I traded; yet I put myself
On you, that are my country; and this pelf,
Which I have got, if you do quit me, rests
To feast you often, and invite new guests.

                       [*Exeunt*]

Volpone

by BEN JONSON

In The Alchemist we have—among people greedy for gold—a brilliantly adroit matching of wits and hatching of wiles. Character traits count for little except as they advance the plot; except as people are vain enough to be credulous, surly enough to be suspicious, smooth-spoken enough to carry conviction. We might almost say that, beyond their wanting money and not caring how they get it, there is no harm in these people. They don't plot against one another from resentment, or betray one another from malice, or even quarrel with one another out of personal dislike. It is the absence of anything menacing and dark that gives The Alchemist its fine exhilaration, its purely comic élan. Volpone is not so much of a piece, nor, as a result, so perfect a play. In Volpone we are no longer in a sunny world of mere crookedness, we are in one of large shadows and black sulphurous stains, a world where the actors work on the grand scale and their activities are satanic and malevolent. Volpone himself inhabits a world, and exhibits a wickedness, undreamed of in The Alchemist's burgher London. He is a Venetian grandee, coveting sumptuous splendor; but his lust for possessions is rather the initial than the ultimate motive for his plots and stratagems. Gradually, as he perceives to what lengths men will go in their own lust for gold, as, at the bidding of his brilliant parasite Mosca, they prepare to disinherit their children and dishonor their wives, Volpone abandons Midas for Mephistopheles, cares more about flaying his victims than fleecing them, would rather give pain to others

than gain pleasure for himself—though he is most delighted if he can do both at once.

But from desiring power, Volpone becomes drunk with it; from hatching plots, he becomes obsessed with hatching them; grows reckless of consequences, turns treacherous toward his own accomplice, and is at length exposed and brought low. It is the accomplice, Mosca, so full of mettle, so skilful of manner, so deft at involving others and extricating himself, who gives to Volpone its gay, glittering criminality. And if Mosca has a love of maneuver, he has also—unlike his master—a genuine need of money. But Mosca's master, in this world of flies and crows and ravens, is more than a fox, is closer to a fiend; and his malevolence darkens the whole picture, and creates a character and at length a series of situations where the Comic Spirit must feel uneasy, and even quite out of place. For Ben Jonson, as for Volpone, things—in turning so grandiosely sinister—also get out of hand. Jonson has let his hero go too far, has made him a creature of real evil whose harsh punishment by the State seems called for. And yet, in comedy, punishment so harsh must be a mistake. And Volpone, indeed, at once violates the laws of comedy, and exceeds the limits. The Alchemist is the better play, The Alchemist is much the more truly comic one. But Volpone, for all that, is a greater work of literature. It mounts higher, a monument of grand-style rhetoric; it pierces deeper; it has, what The Alchemist wholly lacks, a true intensity. And at least in Mosca, a very Mercury of evil-doing, it surpasses The Alchemist for comic brilliance.

BEN JONSON

Volpone
or, the Fox

THE PERSONS OF THE PLAY

VOLPONE, *a magnifico*

MOSCA, *his parasite*

VOLTORE, *an advocate*

CORBACCIO, *an old gentleman*

CORVINO, *a merchant*

BONARIO, *son to* CORBACCIO

SIR POLITIC WOULDBE

PEREGRINE, *a gentleman traveller*

NANO, *a dwarf*

CASTRONE, *an eunuch*

ANDROGYNO, *an hermaphrodite*

GREGE, *or mob*

COMMENDATORI, *officers of justice*

MERCATORI, *three merchants*

AVOCATORI, *four magistrates*

NOTARIO, *the register*

LADY WOULDBE, SIR POLITIC'S *wife*

CELIA, CORVINO'S *wife*

SERVITORI, WOMEN, &C.

THE SCENE: *Venice*

The Argument

V olpone, childless, rich, feigns sick, despairs,

O ffers his state to hopes of several heirs,

L ies languishing. His parasite receives

P resents of all, assures, deludes, then weaves

O ther cross-plots, which ope themselves, are told.

N ew tricks for safety are sought; they thrive; when, bold,

E ach tempts the other again, and all are sold.

Prologue

Now luck God send us, and a little **wit**
    Will serve to make our play a hit;
According to the palates of the season,
    Here is rhyme not empty of reason.
This we were bid to credit from our poet,
    Whose true scope, if you would know it,
In all his poems still hath been this measure,
    To mix profit with your pleasure;
And not as some, whose throats their envy failing,
    Cry hoarsely, all he writes is railing;
And when his plays come forth, think they can flout them
    With saying he was a year about them.
To these there needs no lie but this his creature,
    Which was two months since no feature.
And though he dares give them five lives to mend it,
    'Tis known, five weeks fully penned it,
From his own hand, without a coadjutor,
    Novice, journeyman, or tutor.
Yet thus much I can give you as a token
    Of his play's worth: no eggs are broken,
Nor quaking custards with fierce teeth affrighted,
    Wherewith your rout are so delighted;
Nor hales he in a gull, old ends reciting,
    To stop gaps in his loose writing;
With such a deal of monstrous and forced action,
    As might make Bedlam a faction.
Nor made he his play for jests stol'n from each table,
    But makes jests to fit his fable;
And so presents quick comedy, refined
    As best critics have designed.
The laws of time, place, persons he observeth;
    From no needful rule he swerveth.
All gall and copperas from his ink he draineth;
    Only a little salt remaineth,
Wherewith he'll rub your cheeks till, red with laughter,
    They shall look fresh a week after.

Act I

Volpone's house

Enter Volpone *and* Mosca.

VOLPONE: Good morning to the day; and next, my
    gold!—
  Open the shrine, that I may see my saint.—
  Hail the world's soul, and mine! More glad than is
  The teeming earth to see the longèd-for sun
  Peep through the horns of the celestial ram,
  Am I, to view thy splendour darkening his;
  That lying here, amongst my other hoards,
  Show'st like a flame by night, or like the day
  Struck out of chaos, when all darkness fled
  Unto the centre. O thou son of Sol,
  But brighter than thy father, let me kiss,
  With adoration, thee, and every relic
  Of sacred treasure in this blessèd room,
  Well did wise poets, by thy glorious name,
  Title that age which they would have the best;
  Thou being the best of things; and far transcending
  All style of joy in children, parents, friends,
  Or any other waking dream on earth.
  Thy looks when they to Venus did ascribe,
  They should have giv'n her twenty thousand
    Cupids;
  Such are thy beauties and our loves! Dear saint,
  Riches, the dumb god, that giv'st all men tongues!
  That canst do nought, and yet mak'st men do all
    things.
  The price of souls! even hell, with thee to boot,
  Is made worth heaven! Thou art virtue, fame,
  Honour, and all things else. Who can get thee,
  He shall be noble, valiant, honest, wise——

MOSCA: And what he will, sir. Riches are in fortune
  A greater good than wisdom is in nature.

VOLPONE: True, my beloved Mosca. Yet I glory
  More in the cunning purchase of my wealth,
  Than in the glad possession, since I gain
  No common way. I use no trade, no venture;
  I wound no earth with ploughshares, fat no beasts
  To feed the shambles; have no mills for iron,
  Oil, corn, or men, to grind 'em into powder;
  I blow no subtle glass, expose no ships
  To threat'nings of the furrow-facèd sea;
  I turn no monies in the public bank,
  Nor usure private——

MOSCA: No sir, nor devour
  Soft prodigals. You shall ha' some will swallow
  A melting heir as glibly as your Dutch
  Will pills of butter, and ne'er purge for 't;
  Tear forth the fathers of poor families
  Out of their beds, and coffin them alive
  In some kind, clasping prison, where their bones
  May be forthcoming when the flesh is rotten.
  But your sweet nature doth abhor these courses;
  You loathe the widow's or the orphan's tears

Should wash your pavements, or their piteous cries
  Ring in your roofs, and beat the air for vengeance.

VOLPONE: Right, Mosca, I do loathe it.

MOSCA: And, besides, sir,
  You are not like the thresher that doth stand
  With a huge flail, watching a heap of corn,
  And, hungry, dares not taste the smallest grain,
  But feeds on mallows and such bitter herbs;
  Nor like the merchant who hath filled his vaults
  With Romagnía, and rich Candian wines,
  Yet drinks the lees of Lombard's vinegar.
  You will not lie in straw, whilst moths and worms
  Feed on your sumptuous hangings and soft beds.
  You know the use of riches, and dare give now
  From that bright heap, to me, your poor observer,
  Or to your dwarf, or your hermaphrodite,
  Your eunuch, or what other household trifle
  Your pleasure allows maint'nance——

VOLPONE: Hold thee, Mosca,
  Take of my hand; thou strik'st on truth in all,
  And they are envious term thee parasite.
  Call forth my dwarf, my eunuch, and my fool,
  And let 'em make me sport! [*Exit* Mosca] What
    should I do
  But cocker up my genius, and live free
  To all delights my fortune calls me to?
  I have no wife, no parent, child, ally,
  To give my substance to; but whom I make
  Must be my heir, and this makes men observe me.
  This draws new clients daily to my house,
  Women and men of every sex and age,
  That bring me presents, send me plate, coin, jewels,
  With hope that when I die—which they expect
  Each greedy minute—it shall then return
  Tenfold upon them; whilst some, covetous
  Above the rest, seek to engross me whole,
  And counter-work the one unto the other,
  Contend in gifts, as they would seem, in love.
  All which I suffer, playing with their hopes,
  And am content to coin 'em into profit,
  And look upon their kindness, and take more,
  And look on that; still bearing them in hand,
  Letting the cherry knock against their lips,
  And draw it by their mouths, and back again.—
  How now!

Re-enter Mosca *with* Nano, Androgyno, *and* Castrone.

NANO: 'Now, room for fresh gamesters, who do will
  you to know,
  They do bring you neither play nor university show;
  And therefore do entreat you that whatsoever they
    rehearse
  May not fare a whit the worse for the false pace of
    the verse.
  If you wonder at this, you will wonder more ere we
    pass,
  For know, here is enclosed the soul of Pythagoras,
  That juggler divine, as hereafter shall follow:

Which soul, fast and loose, sir, came first from
    Apollo,
And was breathed into Aethalides, Mercurius's son,
Where it had the gift to remember all that ever
    was done.
From thence it fled forth, and made quick trans-
    migration
To goldy-locked Euphorbus, who was killed in
    good fashion
At the siege of old Troy, by the cuckold of Sparta.
Hermotimus was next—I find it in my charta—
To whom it did pass, where no sooner it was miss-
    ing,
But with one Pyrrhus of Delos it learned to go
    a-fishing;
And thence did it enter the Sophist of Greece.
From Pythagore, she went into a beautiful piece,
Hight Aspasia the Meretrix; and the next toss of
    her
Was again of a whore she became a philosopher,
Crates the Cynic, as itself doth relate it.
Since, kings, knights, and beggars, knaves, lords,
    and fools gat it,
Besides ox and ass, camel, mule, goat, and brock,
In all which it hath spoke, as in the cobbler's cock.
But I come not here to discourse of that matter,
Or his one, two, or three, or his great oath, "By
    Quater!"
His musics, his trigon, his golden thigh,
Or his telling how elements shift. But I
Would ask how of late thou hast suffered transla-
    tion,
And shifted thy coat in these days of reformation?'
ANDROGYNO: 'Like one of the reformèd, a fool, as you
    see,
    Counting all old doctrine heresy.'
NANO: 'But not on thine own forbid meats hast thou
    ventured?'
ANDROGYNO: 'On fish, when first a Carthusian I en-
    tered.'
NANO: 'Why, then thy dogmatical silence hath left
    thee?'
ANDROGYNO: 'Of that an obstreperous lawyer bereft
    me.'
NANO: 'O wonderful change! When Sir Lawyer for-
    sook thee,
    For Pythagore's sake, what body then took thee?'
ANDROGYNO: 'A good dull mule.'
NANO: 'And how! by that means
    Thou wert brought to allow of the eating of beans?'
ANDROGYNO: 'Yes.'
NANO: 'But from the mule into whom didst thou
    pass?'
ANDROGYNO: 'Into a very strange beast, by some
    writers called an ass;
    By others a precise, pure, illuminate brother,
    Of those devour flesh, and sometimes one another;
    And will drop you forth a libel, or a sanctified lie,
    Betwixt every spoonful of a nativity-pie.'

NANO: 'Now quit thee, 'fore Heaven, of that profane
    nation,
    And gently report thy next transmigration.'
ANDROGYNO: 'To the same that I am.'
NANO: 'A creature of delight,
    And, what is more than a fool, an hermaphrodite!
    Now, pr'ythee, sweet soul, in all thy variation,
    Which body wouldst thou choose to take up thy
    station?'
ANDROGYNO: 'Troth, this I am in; even here would I
    tarry.'
NANO: ' 'Cause here the delight of each sex thou canst
    vary?'
ANDROGYNO: 'Alas, those pleasures be stale and for-
    saken.
    No, 'tis your fool wherewith I am so taken,
    The only one creature that I can call blessèd;
    For all other forms I have proved most distressèd.'
NANO: 'Spoke true as thou wert in Pythagoras still.
    This learned opinion we celebrate will,
    Fellow eunuch, as behoves us, with all our wit and
    art,
    To dignify that whereof ourselves are so great and
    special a part.'
VOLPONE: Now, very, very pretty! Mosca, this
    Was thy invention?
MOSCA: If it please my patron,
    Not else.
VOLPONE: It doth, good Mosca.
MOSCA: Then it was, sir.

    SONG

'Fools they are the only nation
Worth men's envy or admiration,
Free from care or sorrow taking,
Selves and others merry making.
All they speak or do is sterling.
Your fool he is your great man's darling,
And your ladies' sport and pleasure;
Tongue and bauble are his treasure.
E'en his face begetteth laughter,
And he speaks truth free from slaughter.
He's the grace of every feast,
And sometimes the chiefest guest;
Hath his trencher and his stool,
When wit waits upon the fool.
    O, who would not be
    He, he, he?'

                          [One knocks without]
VOLPONE: Who's that? Away!—Look, Mosca.—Fool,
begone!
          [Exeunt Nano, Castrone, and Androgyno]
MOSCA: 'Tis Signior Voltore, the advocate;
    I know him by his knock.
VOLPONE: Fetch me my gown,
    My furs, and nightcaps; say my couch is changing;
    And let him entertain himself a while
    Without i' th' gallery. [Exit Mosca] Now, now my
    clients

Begin their visitation! Vulture, kite,
Raven, and gorcrow, all my birds of prey,
That think me turning carcase, now they come.
I am not for 'em yet. [*Re-enter* Mosca] How now!
  the news?
MOSCA: A piece of plate, sir.
VOLPONE: Of what bigness?
MOSCA: Huge,
Massy, and antique, with your name inscribed
And arms engraven.
VOLPONE: Good! and not a fox
Stretched on the earth, with fine delusive sleights,
Mocking a gaping crow? ha, Mosca?
MOSCA: Sharp, sir.
VOLPONE: Give me my furs. Why dost thou laugh so,
  man?
MOSCA: I cannot choose, sir, when I apprehend
What thoughts he has, without, now as he walks:
That this might be the last gift he should give;
That this would fetch you; if you died today,
And gave him all, what he should be tomorrow;
What large return would come of all his ventures;
How he should worshipped be, and reverenced;
Ride with his furs and foot-cloths, waited on
By herds of fools and clients; have clear way
Made for his mule, as lettered as himself;
Be called the great and learned advocate;
And then concludes there's nought impossible.
VOLPONE: Yes, to be learnèd, Mosca.
MOSCA: O no, rich
Implies it. Hood an ass with reverend purple,
So you can hide his two ambitious ears,
And he shall pass for a cathedral doctor.
VOLPONE: My caps, my caps, good Mosca. Fetch him
  in.
MOSCA: Stay, sir, your ointment for your eyes.
VOLPONE: That's true;
Dispatch, dispatch. I long to have possession
Of my new present.
MOSCA: That and thousands more
I hope to see you lord of.
VOLPONE: Thanks, kind Mosca.
MOSCA: And that, when I am lost in blended dust,
And hundred such as I am, in succession——
VOLPONE: Nay, that were too much, Mosca.
MOSCA: You shall live
Still to delude these harpies.
VOLPONE: Loving Mosca!
'Tis well; my pillow now, and let him enter.
                                      [*Exit* Mosca]
Now, my feigned cough, my phthisic, and my gout,
My apoplexy, palsy, and catarrhs,
Help, with your forcèd functions, this my posture,
Wherein this three year I have milked their hopes.
He comes; I hear him—Uh! uh! uh! uh! O!

Re-enter Mosca *with* Voltore.
MOSCA: You still are what you were, sir. Only you,
Of all the rest, are he, commands his love;

And you do wisely to preserve it thus
With early visitation, and kind notes
Of your good meaning to him, which, I know,
Cannot but come most grateful.—Patron! sir!
Here's Signior Voltore is come——
VOLPONE: What say you?
MOSCA: Sir, Signior Voltore is come this morning
To visit you.
VOLPONE: I thank him.
MOSCA: And hath brought
A piece of antique plate, bought of Saint Mark,
With which he here presents you.
VOLPONE: He is welcome.
Pray him to come more often.
MOSCA: Yes.
VOLTORE: What says he?
MOSCA: He thanks you, and desires you see him often.
VOLPONE: Mosca.
MOSCA: My patron!
VOLPONE: Bring him near; where is he?
I long to feel his hand.
MOSCA: The plate is here, sir.
VOLTORE: How fare you, sir?
VOLPONE: I thank you, Signior Voltore.
Where is the plate? mine eyes are bad.
VOLTORE: I'm sorry
To see you still thus weak.
MOSCA: —That he is not weaker.
VOLPONE: You are too munificent.
VOLTORE: No, sir, would to Heaven,
I could as well give health to you, as that plate!
VOLPONE: You give, sir, what you can. I thank you.
  Your love
Hath taste in this, and shall not be unanswered.
I pray you see me often.
VOLTORE: Yes, I shall, sir.
VOLPONE: Be not far from me.
MOSCA: Do you observe that, sir?
VOLPONE: Hearken unto me still. It will concern you.
MOSCA: You are a happy man, sir; know your good.
VOLPONE: I cannot now last long——
MOSCA: —You are his heir, sir.
VOLTORE: Am I?
VOLPONE: I feel me going—Uh! uh! uh! uh!
I'm sailing to my port—Uh! uh! uh! uh!
And I am glad I am so near my haven.
MOSCA: Alas, kind gentleman! Well, we must all
  go——
VOLTORE: But, Mosca——
MOSCA: Age will conquer.
VOLTORE: Pray thee, hear me.
Am I inscribed his heir for certain?
MOSCA: Are you!
I do beseech you, sir, you will vouchsafe
To write me i' your family. All my hopes
Depend upon your worship. I am lost,
Except the rising sun do shine on me.
VOLTORE: It shall both shine and warm thee, Mosca.
MOSCA: Sir,

I am a man that hath not done your love
All the worst offices: here I wear your keys,
See all your coffers and your caskets locked,
Keep the poor inventory of your jewels,
Your plate, and monies; am your steward, sir,
Husband your goods here.

VOLTORE: But am I sole heir?

MOSCA: Without a partner, sir, confirmed this morning;
The wax is warm yet, and the ink scarce dry
Upon the parchment.

VOLTORE: Happy, happy me!
By what good chance, sweet Mosca?

MOSCA: Your desert, sir;
I know no second cause.

VOLTORE: Thy modesty
Is loath to know it; well, we shall requite it.

MOSCA: He ever liked your course, sir; that first took
him.
I oft have heard him say how he admired
Men of your large profession, that could speak
To every cause, and things mere contraries,
Till they were hoarse again, yet all be law;
That, with most quick agility, could turn
And re-turn, make knots and undo them,
Give forkèd counsel, take provoking gold
On either hand, and put it up. These men,
He knew, would thrive with their humility.
And, for his part, he thought he should be blest
To have his heir of such a suffering spirit,
So wise, so grave, of so perplexed a tongue,
And loud withal, that would not wag, nor scarce
Lie still, without a fee; when every word
Your worship but lets fall, is a sequine!
                                    [Another knocks]
—Who's that? One knocks; I would not have you
seen, sir.
And yet—pretend you came and went in haste;
I'll fashion an excuse. And, gentle sir,
When you do come to swim in golden lard,
Up to the arms in honey, that your chin
Is borne up stiff with fatness of the flood,
Think on your vassal; but remember me.
I ha' not been your worst of clients.

VOLTORE: Mosca—

MOSCA: When will you have your inventory brought,
sir?
Or see a copy of the will?—Anon!—
I'll bring 'em to you, sir. Away, begone,
Put business i' your face.   [Exit Voltore]

VOLPONE: Excellent, Mosca!
Come hither, let me kiss thee.

MOSCA: Keep you still, sir.
Here is Corbaccio.

VOLPONE: Set the plate away.
The vulture's gone, and the old raven's come.

MOSCA: Betake you to your silence, and your sleep.—
Stand there and multiply.—Now we shall see
A wretch who is indeed more impotent

Than this can feign to be, yet hopes to hop
Over his grave.

Enter Corbaccio.
                          Signior Corbaccio!
You're very welcome, sir.

CORBACCIO: How does your patron?

MOSCA: Troth, as he did, sir; no amends.

CORBACCIO: What! mends he?

MOSCA: No, sir, he is rather worse.

CORBACCIO: That's well. Where is he?

MOSCA: Upon his couch, sir, newly fall'n asleep.

CORBACCIO: Does he sleep well?

MOSCA: No wink, sir, all this night
Nor yesterday, but slumbers.

CORBACCIO: Good! he should take
Some counsel of physicians: I have brought him
An opiate here, from mine own doctor.

MOSCA: He will not hear of drugs.

CORBACCIO: Why? I myself
Stood by while't was made, saw all th' ingredients;
And know it cannot but most gently work.
My life for his, 'tis but to make him sleep.

VOLPONE: —Ay, his last sleep, if he would take it.

MOSCA: Sir,
He has no faith in physic.

CORBACCIO: Say you? say you?

MOSCA: He has no faith in physic; he does think
Most of your doctors are the greater danger,
And worse disease, t' escape. I often have
Heard him protest that your physician
Should never be his heir.

CORBACCIO: Not I his heir?

MOSCA: Not your physician, sir.

CORBACCIO: O no, no, no.
I do not mean it.

MOSCA: No, sir, nor their fees
He cannot brook; he says they flay a man
Before they kill him.

CORBACCIO: Right, I do conceive you.

MOSCA: And then, they do it by experiment;
For which the law not only doth absolve 'em,
But gives them great reward; and he is loath
To hire his death so.

CORBACCIO: It is true, they kill
With as much licence as a judge.

MOSCA: Nay, more;
For he but kills, sir, where the law condemns,
And these can kill him too.

CORBACCIO: Ay, or me,
Or any man. How does his apoplex?
Is that strong on him still?

MOSCA: Most violent.
His speech is broken and his eyes are set,
His face drawn longer than 'twas wont——

CORBACCIO: How? how?
Stronger than he was wont?

MOSCA: No, sir; his face
Drawn longer than 'twas wont.

CORBACCIO: O, good!
MOSCA: His mouth
Is ever gaping, and his eyelids hang.
CORBACCIO: Good.
MOSCA: A freezing numbness stiffens all his joints,
And makes the colour of his flesh like lead.
CORBACCIO: 'Tis good.
MOSCA: His pulse beats slow and dull.
CORBACCIO: Good symptoms still.
MOSCA: And from his brain——
CORBACCIO: Ha! how? not from his brain?
MOSCA: Yes, sir, and from his brain——
CORBACCIO: I conceive you; good.
MOSCA: Flows a cold sweat, with a continual rheum,
Forth the resolvèd corners of his eyes.
CORBACCIO: Is't possible? Yet I am better, ha!
How does he with the swimming of his head?
MOSCA: O, sir, 'tis past the scotomy; he now
Hath lost his feeling, and hath left to snort.
You hardly can perceive him, that he breathes.
CORBACCIO: Excellent, excellent! sure I shall outlast
him!
This makes me young again a score of years.
MOSCA: I was a-coming for you, sir.
CORBACCIO: Has he made his will?
What has he giv'n me?
MOSCA: No, sir.
CORBACCIO: Nothing! ha?
MOSCA: He has not made his will, sir.
CORBACCIO: Oh, oh, oh.
What then did Voltore, the lawyer, here?
MOSCA: He smelt a carcase, sir, when he but heard
My master was about his testament;
As I did urge him to it, for your good——
CORBACCIO: He came unto him, did he? I thought
so.
MOSCA: Yes, and presented him this piece of plate.
CORBACCIO: To be his heir?
MOSCA: I do not know, sir.
CORBACCIO: True,
I know it too.
MOSCA: By your own scale, sir.
CORBACCIO: Well,
I shall prevent him yet. See, Mosca, look,
Here I have brought a bag of bright sequines,
Will quite weigh down his plate.
MOSCA: Yea, marry, sir,
This is true physic, this your sacred medicine!
No talk of opiates to this great elixir!
CORBACCIO: 'Tis aurum palpabile, if not potabile.
MOSCA: It shall be ministered to him in his bowl.
CORBACCIO: Ay, do, do, do.
MOSCA: Most blessed cordial!
This will recover him.
CORBACCIO: Yes, do, do, do.
MOSCA: I think it were not best, sir.
CORBACCIO: What?
MOSCA: To recover him.
CORBACCIO: O no, no, no, by no means.

MOSCA: Why, sir, this
Will work some strange effect, if he but feel it.
CORBACCIO: 'Tis true, therefore forbear; I'll take my
venture.
Give me 't again.
MOSCA: At no hand, pardon me;
You shall not do yourself that wrong, sir. I
Will so advise you, you shall have it all.
CORBACCIO: How?
MOSCA: All, sir, 'tis your right, your own; no man
Can claim a part. 'Tis yours without a rival,
Decreed by destiny.
CORBACCIO: How, how, good Mosca?
MOSCA: I'll tell you, sir. This fit he shall recover—
CORBACCIO: I do conceive you.
MOSCA: And on first advantage
Of his gained sense, will I re-importune him
Unto the making of his testament;
And show him this.
CORBACCIO: Good, good.
MOSCA: 'Tis better yet,
If you will hear, sir.
CORBACCIO: Yes, with all my heart.
MOSCA: Now would I counsel you, make home with
speed;
There, frame a will, whereto you shall inscribe
My master your sole heir.
CORBACCIO: And disinherit
My son?
MOSCA: O, sir, the better; for that colour
Shall make it much more taking.
CORBACCIO: O, but colour?
MOSCA: This will, sir, you shall send it unto me.
Now, when I come to enforce, as I will do,
Your cares, your watchings, and your many prayers,
Your more than many gifts, your this day's present;
And last, produce your will, where, without
thought
Or least regard unto your proper issue,
A son so brave and highly meriting,
The stream of your diverted love hath thrown you
Upon my master, and made him your heir;
He cannot be so stupid, or stone-dead,
But out of conscience and mere gratitude——
CORBACCIO: He must pronounce me his?
MOSCA: 'Tis true.
CORBACCIO: This plot
Did I think on before.
MOSCA: I do believe it.
CORBACCIO: Do you not believe it?
MOSCA: Yes, sir.
CORBACCIO: Mine own project.
MOSCA: Which, when he hath done, sir——
CORBACCIO: Published me his heir?
MOSCA: And you so certain to survive him——
CORBACCIO: Ay.
MOSCA: Being so lusty a man——
CORBACCIO: 'Tis true.
MOSCA: Yes, sir——

CORBACCIO: I thought on that, too. See, how he
    should be
The very organ to express my thoughts!
MOSCA: You have not only done yourself a good——
CORBACCIO: But multiplied it on my son!
MOSCA: 'Tis right, sir.
CORBACCIO: Still my invention.
MOSCA: 'Las, sir! Heaven knows,
It hath been all my study, all my care,——
I e'en grow gray withal—how to work things——
CORBACCIO: I do conceive, sweet Mosca.
MOSCA: You are he
For whom I labour here.
CORBACCIO: Ay, do, do, do!
I'll straight about it.
MOSCA: Rook go with you, raven!
CORBACCIO: I know thee honest.
MOSCA: You do lie, sir!
CORBACCIO: And——
MOSCA: Your knowledge is no better than your ears,
    sir.
CORBACCIO: I do not doubt to be a father to thee.
MOSCA: Nor I to gull my brother of his blessing.
CORBACCIO: I may ha' my youth restored to me, why
    not?
MOSCA: Your worship is a precious ass!
CORBACCIO: What sayest thou?
MOSCA: I do desire your worship to make haste,
    sir.
CORBACCIO: 'Tis done, 'tis done, I go.   [Exit]
VOLPONE: O, I shall burst!
Let out my sides, let out my sides——
MOSCA: Contain
Your flux of laughter, sir. You know this hope
Is such a bait, it covers any hook.
VOLPONE: O, but thy working and thy placing it!
I cannot hold; good rascal, let me kiss thee!
I never knew thee in so rare a humour.
MOSCA: Alas, sir, I but do as I am taught;
Follow your grave instructions; give 'em words;
Pour oil into their ears, and send them hence.
VOLPONE: 'Tis true, 'tis true. What a rare punish-
    ment.
Is avarice to itself!
MOSCA: Ay, with our help, sir.
VOLPONE: So many cares, so many maladies,
So many fears attending on old age,
Yea, death so often called on, as no wish
Can be more frequent with 'em, their limbs faint,
Their senses dull, their seeing, hearing, going,
All dead before them; yea, their very teeth,
Their instruments of eating, failing them;
Yet this is reckoned life! Nay, here was one,
Is now gone home, that wishes to live longer!
Feels not his gout, nor palsy; feigns himself
Younger by scores of years, flatters his age
With confident belying it, hopes he may
With charms, like Aeson, have his youth restored;
And with these thoughts so battens, as if fate

Would be as easily cheated on as he,
And all turns air! [Another knocks] Who's that
    there, now? a third?
MOSCA: Close, to your couch again. I hear his voice.
It is Corvino, our spruce merchant.
VOLPONE: Dead.
MOSCA: Another bout, sir, with your eyes.—Who's
    there?

Enter Corvino.
Signior Corvino! come most wished for! O,
How happy were you, if you know it, now!
CORVINO: Why, what? wherein?
MOSCA: The tardy hour is come, sir.
CORVINO: He is not dead?
MOSCA: Not dead, sir, but as good;
He knows no man.
CORVINO: How shall I do, then?
MOSCA: Why, sir?
CORVINO: I have brought him here a pearl.
MOSCA: Perhaps he has
So much remembrance left as to know you, sir;
He still calls on you; nothing but your name
Is in his mouth. Is your pearl orient, sir?
CORVINO: Venice was never owner of the like.
VOLPONE: Signior Corvino!
MOSCA: Hark.
VOLPONE: Signior Corvino!
MOSCA: He calls you; step and give it him.—He's
    here, sir,
And he has brought you a rich pearl.
CORVINO: How do you, sir?—
Tell him it doubles the twelfth carat.
MOSCA: Sir,
He cannot understand; his hearing's gone;
And yet it comforts him to see you——
CORVINO: Say
I have a diamond for him, too.
MOSCA: Best show't, sir,
Put it into his hand; 'tis only there
He apprehends. He has his feeling yet.
See how he grasps it!
CORVINO: 'Las, good gentleman!
How pitiful the sight is!
MOSCA: Tut, forget, sir.
The weeping of an heir should still be laughter
Under a visor.
CORVINO: Why, am I his heir?
MOSCA: Sir, I am sworn, I may not show the will
Till he be dead; but here has been Corbaccio,
Here has been Voltore, here were others too,
I cannot number 'em, they were so many,
All gaping here for legacies; but I,
Taking the vantage of his naming you,
'Signior Corvino,' 'Signior Corvino,' took
Paper and pen and ink, and there I asked him
Whom he would have his heir? 'Corvino!' Who
Should be executor? 'Corvino!' And
To any question he was silent to,

I still interpreted the nods he made,
Through weakness, for consent; and sent home th'
    others,
Nothing bequeathed them but to cry and curse.

CORVINO: O my dear Mosca! [*They embrace*] Does
    he not perceive us?

MOSCA: No more than a blind harper. He knows no
    man,
No face of friend nor name of any servant,
Who 'twas that fed him last or gave him drink;
Not those he hath begotten or brought up
Can he remember.

CORVINO: Has he children?

MOSCA: Bastards,
Some dozen, or more, that he begot on beggars,
Gipsies, and Jews, and black-moors, when he was
    drunk.
Knew you not that, sir? 'Tis the common fable.
The dwarf, the fool, the eunuch, are all his;
He's the true father of his family,
In all save me—but he has giv'n 'em nothing.

CORVINO: That's well, that's well! Art sure he does
    not hear us?

MOSCA: Sure, sir? why, look you, credit your own
    sense.—
The pox approach, and add to your diseases,
If it would send you hence the sooner, sir!
For your incontinence it hath deserved it
Throughly and throughly, and the plague to
    boot!—
You may come near, sir.—Would you would once
    close
Those filthy eyes of yours, that flow with slime,
Like two frog-pits; and those same hanging cheeks,
Covered with hide instead of skin—nay, help,
    sir.—
That look like frozen dish-clouts set on end!

CORVINO: Or like an old smoked wall, on which the
    rain
Ran down in streaks!

MOSCA: Excellent, sir! speak out;
You may be louder yet. A culverin
Discharged in his ear would hardly bore it.

CORVINO: His nose is like a common sewer, still run-
    ning.

MOSCA: 'Tis good! And what his mouth!

CORVINO: A very draught.

MOSCA: O, stop it up——

CORVINO: By no means.

MOSCA: Pray you let me.
Faith, I could stifle him rarely with a pillow,
As well as any woman that should keep him.

CORVINO: Do as you will, but I'll be gone.

MOSCA: Be so;
It is your presence makes him last so long.

CORVINO: I pray you use no violence.

MOSCA: No, sir! why?
Why should you be thus scrupulous, pray you, sir?

CORVINO: Nay, at your discretion.

MOSCA: Well, good sir, begone.

CORVINO: I will not trouble him now to take my
    pearl.

MOSCA: Pooh! nor your diamond. What a needless
    care
Is this afflicts you? Is not all here yours?
Am not I here, whom you have made your crea-
    ture,
That owe my being to you?

CORVINO: Grateful Mosca!
Thou art my friend, my fellow, my companion,
My partner, and shalt share in all my fortunes.

MOSCA: Excepting one.

CORVINO: What's that?

MOSCA: Your gallant wife, sir.
                                        [*Exit* Corvino]
Now he is gone. We had no other means
To shoot him hence, but this.

VOLPONE: My divine Mosca!
Thou hast today outdone thyself. [*Another knocks*]
    Who's there?
I will be troubled with no more. Prepare
Me music, dances, banquets, all delights;
The Turk is not more sensual in his pleasures
Than will Volpone. Let me see, a pearl!
A diamond! plate! sequines! Good morning's pur-
    chase.
Why, this is better than rob churches yet!
Or fat, by eating once a month a man——
Who is't?

MOSCA: The beauteous Lady Wouldbe, sir,
Wife to the English knight, Sir Politic Would-
    be,—
This is the style, sir, is directed me—
Hath sent to know how you have slept tonight,
And if you would be visited?

VOLPONE: Not now.
Some three hours hence——

MOSCA: I told the squire so much.

VOLPONE: When I am high with mirth and wine,
    then, then!
'Fore Heaven, I wonder at the desperate valour
Of the bold English, that they dare let loose
Their wives to all encounters!

MOSCA: Sir, this knight
Had not his name for nothing; he is politic,
And knows, howe'er his wife affect strange airs,
She hath not yet the face to be dishonest.
But had she Signior Corvino's wife's face——

VOLPONE: Has she so rare a face?

MOSCA: O, sir, the wonder,
The blazing star of Italy! a wench
O' the first year! a beauty ripe as harvest!
Whose skin is whiter than a swan all over!
Than silver, snow, or lilies! a soft lip,
Would tempt you to eternity of kissing!
And flesh that melteth in the touch to blood!
Bright as your gold, and lovely as your gold!

VOLPONE: Why had not I known this before?

MOSCA: Alas, sir,
   Myself but yesterday discovered it.
VOLPONE: How might I see her?
MOSCA: O, not possible.
   She's kept as warily as is your gold;
   Never does come abroad, never takes air
   But at a window. All her looks are sweet
   As the first grapes or cherries, and are watched
   As near as they are.
VOLPONE: I must see her!
MOSCA: Sir,
   There is a guard of ten spies thick upon her—
   All his whole household—each of which is set
   Upon his fellow, and have all their charge,
   When he goes out, when he comes in, examined.
VOLPONE: I will go see her, though but at her win-
   dow.
MOSCA: In some disguise, then.
VOLPONE: That is true. I must
   Maintain mine own shape still the same. We'll
   think.   [Exeunt]

Act II

SCENE 1: *Before Corvino's house, off the Piazza
of Saint Mark*

Enter Sir Politic Wouldbe *and* Peregrine.
SIR POLITIC: Sir, to a wise man, all the world's his soil.
   It is not Italy, nor France, nor Europe,
   That must bound me, if my fates call me forth.
   Yet I protest, it is no salt desire
   Of seeing countries, shifting a religion,
   Nor any disaffection to the state
   Where I was bred, and unto which I owe
   My dearest plots, hath brought me out; much less
   That idle, antique, stale, grey-headed project
   Of knowing men's minds and manners, with
   Ulysses;
   But a peculiar humour of my wife's,
   Laid for this height of Venice, to observe,
   To quote, to learn the language, and so forth——
   I hope you travel, sir, with licence?
PEREGRINE: Yes.
SIR POLITIC: I dare the safelier converse—— How
   long, sir,
   Since you left England?
PEREGRINE: Seven weeks.
SIR POLITIC: So lately!
   You ha' not been with my Lord Ambassador?
PEREGRINE: Not yet, sir.
SIR POLITIC: Pray you, what news, sir,
   vents our climate?
   I heard last night a most strange thing reported
   By some of my Lord's followers, and I long
   To hear how 'twill be seconded!
PEREGRINE: What was 't, sir?

SIR POLITIC: Marry, sir, of a raven that should build
   In a ship royal of the King's.
PEREGRINE: —This fellow,
   Does he gull me, trow, or is gulled?—Your name,
   sir?
SIR POLITIC: My name is Politic Wouldbe.
PEREGRINE: —O, that speaks him.—
   A knight, sir?
SIR POLITIC: A poor knight, sir.
PEREGRINE: Your lady
   Lies here in Venice, for intelligence
   Of tires and fashions and behaviour
   Among the courtesans? the fine Lady Would-
   be?
SIR POLITIC: Yes, sir, the spider and the bee ofttimes
   Suck from one flower.
PEREGRINE: Good Sir Politic,
   I cry you mercy! I have heard much of you.
   'Tis true, sir, of your raven.
SIR POLITIC: On your knowledge?
PEREGRINE: Yes, and your lion's whelping in the
   Tower.
SIR POLITIC: Another whelp?
PEREGRINE: Another, sir.
SIR POLITIC: Now, Heaven!
   What prodigies be these? The fires at Berwick!
   And the new star! these things concurring, strange
   And full of omen! Saw you those meteors?
PEREGRINE: I did, sir.
SIR POLITIC: Fearful! Pray you, sir, confirm
   me,
   Were there three porpoises seen above the bridge,
   As they give out?
PEREGRINE: Six, and a sturgeon, sir.
SIR POLITIC: I am astonished!
PEREGRINE: Nay, sir, be not so;
   I'll tell you a greater prodigy than these——
SIR POLITIC: What should these things portend?
PEREGRINE: The very day—
   Let me be sure—that I put forth from London,
   There was a whale discovered in the river,
   As high as Woolwich, that had waited there,
   Few know how many months, for the subversion
   Of the Stode fleet.
SIR POLITIC: Is't possible? Believe it,
   'Twas either sent from Spain, or the Archduke's!
   Spinola's whale, upon my life, my credit!
   Will they not leave these projects? Worthy sir,
   Some other news.
PEREGRINE: Faith, Stone the fool is dead,
   And they do lack a tavern-fool extremely.
SIR POLITIC: Is Mas' Stone dead?
PEREGRINE: He's dead, sir; why, I hope
   You thought him not immortal?—O, this knight,
   Were he well known, would be a precious thing
   To fit our English stage. He that should write
   But such a fellow, should be thought to feign
   Extremely, if not maliciously.
SIR POLITIC: Stone dead!

PEREGRINE: Dead. Lord, how deeply, sir, you appre-
hend it!
He was no kinsman to you?
SIR POLITIC: That I know of.
Well, that same fellow was an unknown fool.
PEREGRINE: And yet you knew him, it seems?
SIR POLITIC: I did so. Sir,
I knew him one of the most dangerous heads
Living within the state, and so I held him.
PEREGRINE: Indeed, sir?
SIR POLITIC: While he lived, in action.
He has received weekly intelligence,
Upon my knowledge, out of the Low Countries,
For all parts of the world, in cabbages;
And those dispensed again t'ambassadors,
In oranges, muskmelons, apricots,
Lemons, pomecitrons, and suchlike; sometimes
In Colchester oysters, and your Selsey cockles.
PEREGRINE: You make me wonder!
SIR POLITIC: Sir, upon my knowledge.
Nay, I have observed him, at your public ordinary,
Take his advertisement from a traveller—
A concealed statesman—in a trencher of meat;
And instantly, before the meal was done,
Convey an answer in a toothpick.
PEREGRINE: Strange!
How could this be, sir?
SIR POLITIC: Why, the meat was cut
So like his character, and so laid, as he
Must easily read the cipher.
PEREGRINE: I have heard
He could not read, sir.
SIR POLITIC: So 'twas given out,
In policy, by those that did employ him.
But he could read, and had your languages,
And to 't, as sound a noddle——
PEREGRINE: I have heard, sir,
That your baboons were spies, and that they were
A kind of subtle nation near to China.
SIR POLITIC: Ay, ay, your Mamaluchi. Faith, they
had
Their hand in a French plot or two; but they
Were so extremely given to women, as
They made discovery of all. Yet I
Had my advices here, on Wednesday last,
From one of their own coat, they were returned,
Made their relations, as the fashion is,
And now stand fair for fresh employment.
PEREGRINE: —Heart!
This Sir Poll will be ignorant of nothing.—
It seems, sir, you know all.
SIR POLITIC: Not all, sir, but
I have some general notions. I do love
To note and to observe. Though I live out,
Free from the active torrent, yet I'd mark
The currents and the passages of things,
For mine own private use; and know the ebbs
And flows of state.
PEREGRINE: Believe it, sir, I hold

Myself in no small tie unto my fortunes,
For casting me thus luckily upon you;
Whose knowledge, if your bounty equal it,
May do me great assistance, in instruction
For my behaviour and my bearing, which
Is yet so rude and raw——
SIR POLITIC: Why? came you forth
Empty of rules for travel?
PEREGRINE: Faith, I had
Some common ones, from out that vulgar gram-
mar,
Which he that cried Italian to me, taught me.
SIR POLITIC: Why, this it is that spoils all our brave
bloods:
Trusting our hopeful gentry unto pedants,
Fellows of outside, and mere bark. You seem
To be a gentleman of ingenuous race——
I not profess it, but my fate hath been
To be where I have been consulted with,
In this high kind, touching some great men's sons,
Persons of blood and honour——

Enter Mosca *and* Nano *disguised, followed by*
Grege.
PEREGRINE: Who be these, sir?
MOSCA: Under that window, there 't must be. The
same.
SIR POLITIC: Fellows to mount a bank! Did your in-
structor
In the dear tongues never discourse to you
Of the Italian mountebanks?
PEREGRINE: Yes, sir.
SIR POLITIC: Why,
Here you shall see one.
PEREGRINE: They are quacksalvers,
Fellows that live by venting oils and drugs.
SIR POLITIC: Was that the character he gave you of
them?
PEREGRINE: As I remember.
SIR POLITIC: Pity his ignorance.
They are the only knowing men of Europe!
Great general scholars, excellent physicians,
Most admired statesmen, professed favourites,
And cabinet counsellors to the greatest princes!
The only languaged men of all the world!
PEREGRINE: And, I have heard they are most lewd
impostors,
Made all of terms and shreds; no less beliers
Of great men's favours, than their own vile
med'cines;
Which they will utter, upon monstrous oaths,
Selling that drug for twopence, ere they part,
Which they have valued at twelve crowns before.
SIR POLITIC: Sir, calumnies are answered best with
silence.
Yourself shall judge.—Who is it mounts, my
friends?
MOSCA: Scoto of Mantua, sir.
SIR POLITIC: Is't he? Nay, then

I'll proudly promise, sir, you shall behold
Another man than has been fancied to you.
I wonder yet that he should mount his bank
Here in this nook, that has been wont t' appear
In face of the Piazza. Here he comes!

Enter Volpone *disguised as a mountebank.*

VOLPONE: Mount, zany.

GREGE: Follow, follow, follow, follow, follow!

SIR POLITIC: See how the people follow him! he's a man
  May write ten thousand crowns in bank here. Note,
  Mark but his gesture. I do use to observe
  The state he keeps in getting up.

PEREGRINE: 'Tis worth it, sir.

VOLPONE: 'Most noble gentlemen, and my worthy
  patrons: It may seem strange that I, your Scoto
  Mantuano, who was ever wont to fix my bank in
  face of the public Piazza, near the shelter of the
  portico to the Procuratia, should now, after eight
  months' absence from this illustrious city of
  Venice, humbly retire myself into an obscure nook
  of the Piazza.'

SIR POLITIC: Did not I now object the same?

PEREGRINE: Peace, sir.

VOLPONE: 'Let me tell you: I am not—as your Lombard proverb saith—cold on my feet, or content to
  part with my commodities at a cheaper rate than
  I accustomed; look not for it. Nor that the calum-
  nious reports of that impudent detractor and
  shame to our profession—Alessandro Buttone, I
  mean—who gave out in public, I was condemned
  a sforzato to the galleys, for poisoning the Cardinal Bembo's—cook, hath at all attached, much less
  dejected me. No, no, worthy gentlemen, to tell you
  true, I cannot endure to see the rabble of these
  ground ciarlatani, that spread their cloaks on the
  pavement as if they meant to do feats of activity,
  and then come in lamely, with their moudy tales
  out of Boccaccio, like stale Tabarine, the fabulist;
  some of them discoursing their travels, and of their
  tedious captivity in the Turk's galleys, when indeed
  —were the truth known—they were the Christian's galleys, where very temperately they eat
  bread and drunk water, as a wholesome penance,
  enjoined them by their confessors, for base pil-
  feries.'

SIR POLITIC: Note but his bearing, and contempt of
  these.

VOLPONE: 'These turdy-facy-nasty-paty-lousy-fartical
  rogues, with one poor groatsworth of unprepared
  antimony, finely wrapped up in several scartoccios,
  are able very well to kill their twenty a week, and
  play. Yet these meagre, starved spirits, who have
  half stopped the organs of their minds with earthy
  oppilations, want not their favourers among your
  shrivelled, salad-eating artisans, who are overjoyed
  that they may have their half-pe'rth of physic;

though it purge 'em into another world, 't makes
no matter.'

SIR POLITIC: Excellent! ha' you heard better language, sir?

VOLPONE: 'Well, let 'em go. And, gentlemen, honourable gentlemen, know that for this time our
  bank, being thus removed from the clamours of
  the canaglia, shall be the scene of pleasure and delight; for I have nothing to sell, little or nothing to
  sell.'

SIR POLITIC: I told you, sir, his end.

PEREGRINE: You did so, sir.

VOLPONE: 'I protest, I and my six servants are not
  able to make of this precious liquor, so fast as it
  is fetched away from my lodging by gentlemen of
  your city, strangers of the Terra Firma, worshipful merchants, ay, and senators too; who, ever since
  my arrival, have detained me to their uses, by their
  splendidous liberalities. And worthily, for what
  avails your rich man to have his magazines stuffed
  with moscadelli, or of the purest grape, when his
  physicians prescribe him, on pain of death, to drink
  nothing but water cocted with aniseeds? O health,
  health! the blessing of the rich! the riches of the
  poor! who can buy thee at too dear a rate, since
  there is no enjoying this world without thee? Be
  not then so sparing of your purses, honourable
  gentlemen, as to abridge the natural course of
  life——'

PEREGRINE: You see his end?

SIR POLITIC: Ay, is't not good?

VOLPONE: 'For when a humid flux, or catarrh, by the
  mutability of air, falls from your head into an arm,
  or shoulder, or any other part; take you a ducat, or
  your sequine of gold, and apply to the place
  affected; see what good effect it can work. No, no,
  'tis this blessed unguento, this rare extraction, that
  hath only power to disperse all malignant humours,
  that proceed either of hot, cold, moist, or windy
  causes——'

PEREGRINE: I would he had put in dry, too.

SIR POLITIC: Pray you observe.

VOLPONE: 'To fortify the most indigest and crude
  stomach, ay, were it of one that, through extreme
  weakness, vomited blood, applying only a warm
  napkin to the place, after the unction and fricace;
  for the vertigine in the head, putting but a drop
  into your nostrils, likewise behind the ears, a most
  sovereign and approved remedy; the Mal Caduco,
  cramps, convulsions, paralyses, epilepsies, Tremor
  Cordia, retired nerves, ill vapours of the spleen,
  stoppings of the liver, the stone, the stranguary,
  Hernia Ventosa, Iliaca Passio; stops a Dysenteria
  immediately; easeth the torsion of the small guts;
  and cures Melancholia Hypocondriaca, being
  taken and applied, according to my printed receipt.
  [*Pointing to his bill and his glass*] For this is the
  physician, this the medicine; this counsels, this
  cures; this gives the direction, this works the effect;

and, in sum, both together may be termed an abstract of the theoric and practic in the Aesculapian
art. 'Twill cost you eight crowns.—And, Zan
Fritada, pray thee sing a verse extempore in honour
of it.'

SIR POLITIC: How do you like him, sir?

PEREGRINE: Most strangely, I!

SIR POLITIC: Is not his language rare?

PEREGRINE: But alchemy,
I never heard the like; or Broughton's books.

SONG

'Had old Hippocrates or Galen,
That to their books put med'cines all in,
But known this secret, they had never—
Of which they will be guilty ever—
Been murderers of so much paper,
Or wasted many a hurtless taper.
No Indian drug had e'er been famèd,
Tobacco, sassafras not namèd;
Ne yet of guacum one small stick, sir,
Nor Raymund Lully's great elixir.
Ne had been known the Danish gonswart,
Or Paracelsus, with his long-sword.'

PEREGRINE: All this yet will not do; eight crowns is
high.

VOLPONE: 'No more.—Gentlemen, if I had but time
to discourse to you the miraculous effects of this
my oil, surnamed Oglio del Scoto; with the countless catalogue of those I have cured of th' aforesaid
and many more diseases; the patents and privileges
of all the princes and commonwealths of Christendom; or but the depositions of those that appeared
on my part, before the signiory of the Sanita and
most learned college of physicians; where I was
authorized, upon notice taken of the admirable virtues of my medicaments, and mine own excellency
in matter of rare and unknown secrets, not only to
disperse them publicly in this famous city, but in
all the territories that happily joy under the government of the most pious and magnificent state
of Italy. But may some other gallant fellow say,
"O, there be divers that make profession to have as
good and as experimented receipts as yours." Indeed, very many have assayed, like apes, in imitation of that which is really and essentially in me,
to make of this oil; bestowed great cost in fur-
naces, stills, alembics, continual fires, and preparation of the ingredients,—as indeed there goes to it
six hundred several simples, besides some quantity
of human fat, for the conglutination, which we buy
of the anatomists—but when these practitioners
come to the last decoction: blow, blow, puff, puff,
and all flies in fumo. Ha, ha, ha! Poor wretches! I
rather pity their folly and indiscretion, than their
loss of time and money; for those may be recovered
by industry, but to be a fool born is a disease incurable. For myself, I always from my youth have

endeavoured to get the rarest secrets, and book
them, either in exchange or for money. I spared
nor cost nor labour, where anything was worthy to
be learned. And gentlemen, honourable gentlemen,
I will undertake, by virtue of chemical art, out of
the honourable hat that covers your head, to extract the four elements: that is to say, the fire, air,
water, and earth, and return you your felt without
burn or stain. For whilst others have been at the
balloo, I have been at my book; and am now past
the craggy paths of study, and come to the flowery
plains of honour and reputation.'

SIR POLITIC: I do assure you, sir, that is his aim.

VOLPONE: 'But to our price——'

PEREGRINE: And that withal, Sir Poll.

VOLPONE: 'You all know, honourable gentlemen, I
never valued this ampulla, or vial, at less than eight
crowns; but for this time, I am content to be deprived of it for six. Six crowns is the price, and
less, in courtesy, I know you cannot offer me. Take
it or leave it, howsoever, both it and I am at your
service. I ask you not as the value of the thing, for
then I should demand of you a thousand crowns;
so the Cardinals Montalto, Farnese, the Great
Duke of Tuscany, my gossip, with divers other
princes, have given me, but I despise money. Only
to show my affection to you, honourable gentlemen, and your illustrious state here, I have neglected the messages of these princes, mine own
offices; framed my journey hither only to present
you with the fruits of my travels.—Tune your
voices once more to the touch of your instruments,
and give the honourable assembly some delightful
recreation.'

PEREGRINE: What monstrous and most painful circumstance
Is here, to get some three or four gazettes,
Some threepence i' the whole! for that 'twill come
to.

SONG

'You that would last long, list to my song,
Make no more coil, but buy of this oil.
Would you be ever fair and young?
Stout of teeth and strong of tongue?
Tart of palate? quick of ear?
Sharp of sight? of nostril clear?
Moist of hand and light of foot?
Or I will come nearer to't—
Would you live free from all diseases?
Do the act your mistress pleases,
Yet fright all aches from your bones?
Here's a med'cine for the nones.'

VOLPONE: 'Well, I am in a humour at this time to
make a present of the small quantity my coffer contains; to the rich, in courtesy, and to the poor, for
God's sake. Wherefore now mark: I asked you six
crowns, and six crowns, at other times, you have

paid me. You shall not give me six crowns, nor five, nor four, nor three, nor two, nor one; nor half a ducat; no, nor a moccenigo! Sixpence it will cost you, or six hundred pound—expect no lower price, for by the banner of my front, I will not bate a bagatine; that I will have, only, a pledge of your loves, to carry something from amongst you, to show I am not contemned by you. Therefore now, toss your handkerchiefs, cheerfully, cheerfully; and be advertised that the first heroic spirit that deigns to grace me with a handkerchief, I will give it a little remembrance of something beside, shall please it better than if I had presented it with a double pistolet.'

PEREGRINE: Will you be that heroic spark, Sir Poll?
    [Celia, *at the window, throws down her handker-chief*]

O, see, the window has prevented you!

VOLPONE: 'Lady, I kiss your bounty; and for this timely grace you have done your poor Scoto of Mantua, I will return you, over and above my oil, a secret of that high and inestimable nature, shall make you forever enamoured on that minute wherein your eye first descended on so mean, yet not altogether to be despised, an object. Here is a powder concealed in this paper, of which, if I should speak to the worth, nine thousand volumes were but as one page, that page as a line, that line as a word; so short is this pilgrimage of man, which some call life, to the expressing of it. Would I reflect on the price? why, the whole world were but as an empire, that empire as a province, that province as a bank, that bank as a private purse, to the purchase of it. I will only tell you: it is the powder that made Venus a goddess,—given her by Apollo—that kept her perpetually young, cleared her wrinkles, firmed her gums, filled her skin, coloured her hair; from her derived to Helen, and at the sack of Troy unfortunately lost; till now, in this our age, it was as happily recovered, by a studious antiquary, out of some ruins of Asia; who sent a moiety of it to the court of France—but much sophisticated—wherewith the ladies there now colour their hair. The rest, at this present, remains with me; extracted to a quintessence, so that, wherever it but touches, in youth it perpetually preserves, in age restores the complexion; seats your teeth, did they dance like virginal jacks, firm as a wall; makes them white as ivory, that were black as——'

Enter Corvino.

CORVINO: Spite o' the devil, and my shame! come down, here,
    Come down! No house but mine to make your scene?
    Signior Flaminio, will you down, sir? down?
    What, is my wife your Franciscina, sir?
    No windows on the whole Piazza here,

To make your properties, but mine? but mine?
    [*He beats away* Volpone, Mosca, Nano, *and* Grege]
    Heart! ere tomorrow I shall be new christened,
    And called the Pantalone di Bisognosi
    About the town.

PEREGRINE: What should this mean, Sir Poll?

SIR POLITIC: Some trick of state, believe it. I will home.

PEREGRINE: It may be some design on you.

SIR POLITIC: I know not.
    I'll stand upon my guard.

PEREGRINE: It is your best, sir.

SIR POLITIC: This three weeks, all my advices, all my letters,
    They have been intercepted.

PEREGRINE: Indeed, sir?
    Best have a care.

SIR POLITIC: Nay, so I will.

PEREGRINE: This knight,
    I may not lose him, for my mirth, till night.
                    [*Exeunt*]

SCENE 2:   *A street*

Enter Volpone *and* Mosca.

VOLPONE: O, I am wounded!

MOSCA: Where, sir?

VOLPONE: Not without;
    Those blows were nothing. I could bear them ever.
    But angry Cupid, bolting from her eyes,
    Hath shot himself into me like a flame;
    Where now he flings about his burning heat,
    As in a furnace an ambitious fire,
    Whose vent is stopped. The fight is all within me.
    I cannot live, except thou help me, Mosca.
    My liver melts, and I, without the hope
    Of some soft air from her refreshing breath,
    Am but a heap of cinders.

MOSCA: 'Las, good sir,
    Would you had never seen her!

VOLPONE: Nay, would thou
    Hadst never told me of her!

MOSCA: Sir, 'tis true;
    I do confess I was unfortunate,
    And you unhappy; but I'm bound in conscience,
    No less than duty, to effect my best
    To your release of torment, and I will, sir.

VOLPONE: Dear Mosca, shall I hope?

MOSCA: Sir, more than dear,
    I will not bid you to despair of aught
    Within a human compass.

VOLPONE: O, there spoke
    My better angel. Mosca, take my keys,
    Gold, plate, and jewels—all's at thy devotion.
    Employ them how thou wilt; nay, coin me, too—
    So thou in this but crown my longings, Mosca.

MOSCA: Use but your patience.

VOLPONE: So I have.

MOSCA: I doubt not
To bring success to your desires.
VOLPONE: Nay, then,
I not repent me of my late disguise.
MOSCA: If you can horn him, sir, you need not.
VOLPONE: True.
Besides, I never meant him for my heir.
Is not the colour o' my beard and eyebrows
To make me known?
MOSCA: No jot.
VOLPONE: I did it well.
MOSCA: So well, would I could follow you in mine,
With half the happiness! and yet I would
Escape your epilogue.
VOLPONE: But were they gulled
With a belief that I was Scoto?
MOSCA: Sir,
Scoto himself could hardly have distinguished!
I have not time to flatter you now, we'll part;
And as I prosper, so applaud my art.   [Exeunt]

SCENE 3: *Corvino's house*

Enter Corvino *with* Celia.
CORVINO: Death of mine honour, with the city's fool!
A juggling, tooth-drawing, prating mountebank!
And at a public window! where, whilst he,
With his strained action, and his dole of faces,
To his drug-lecture draws your itching ears,
A crew of old, unmarried, noted lechers
Stood leering up like satyrs; and you smile
Most graciously, and fan your favours forth,
To give your hot spectators satisfaction!
What, was your mountebank their call? their
   whistle?
Or were y' enamoured on his copper rings?
His saffron jewel with the toad-stone in't?
Or his embroidered suit, with the cope-stitch,
Made of a hearse-cloth? or his old tilt-feather?
Or his starched beard? Well, you shall have him,
   yes!
He shall come home, and minister unto you
The fricace for the mother. Or, let me see,
I think you'd rather mount; would you not mount?
Why, if you'll mount, you may; yes, truly, you may!
And so you may be seen, down to th' foot.
Get you a cittern, Lady Vanity,
And be a dealer with the virtuous man;
Make one. I'll but protest myself a cuckold,
And save your dowry. I'm a Dutchman, I!
For if you thought me an Italian,
You would be damned ere you did this, you whore!
Thou'dst tremble to imagine that the murder
Of father, mother, brother, all thy race,
Should follow, as the subject of my justice!
CELIA: Good, sir, have patience.
CORVINO: What couldst thou propose
Less to thyself than, in this heat of wrath,

And stung with my dishonour, I should strike
This steel into thee, with as many stabs
As thou wert gazed upon with goatish eyes?
CELIA: Alas, sir, be appeased! I could not think
My being at the window should more now
Move your impatience than at other times.
CORVINO: No? not to seek and entertain a parley,
With a known knave, before a multitude!
You were an actor, with your handkerchief,
Which he most sweetly kissed in the receipt,
And, might, no doubt, return it with a letter,
And 'point the place where you might meet—your
   sister's,
Your mother's, or your aunt's might serve the turn.
CELIA: Why, dear sir, when do I make these excuses,
Or ever stir abroad, but to the church?
And that so seldom——
CORVINO: Well, it shall be less;
And thy restraint before was liberty,
To what I now decree. And therefore mark me:
First, I will have this bawdy light dammed up;
And till't be done, some two or three yards off,
I'll chalk a line, o'er which if thou but chance
To set thy desp'rate foot, more hell, more horror,
More wild remorseless rage shall seize on thee,
Than on a conjuror that had heedless left
His circle's safety ere his devil was laid.
Then, here's a lock which I will hang upon thee;
And, now I think on't, I will keep thee backwards;
Thy lodging shall be backwards, thy walks back-
   wards,
Thy prospect all be backwards, and no pleasure,
That thou shalt know, but backwards. Nay, since
   you force
My honest nature, know it is your own
Being too open, makes me use you thus;
Since you will not contain your subtle nostrils
In a sweet room, but they must snuff the air
Of rank and sweaty passengers.   [*Knock within*]
   One knocks.
Away, and be not seen, pain of thy life;
Nor look toward the window; if thou dost—
Nay, stay, hear this—let me not prosper, whore,
But I will make thee an anatomy,
Dissect thee mine own self, and read a lecture
Upon thee to the city, and in public.
Away!—   [*Exit* Celia]

Enter Servitore.
            Who's there?
SERVITORE: 'Tis Signior Mosca, sir.
CORVINO: Let him come in. [*Exit* Servitore] His mas-
   ter's dead! There's yet
Some good to help the bad.

Enter Mosca.
                My Mosca, welcome!
I guess your news.
MOSCA: I fear you cannot, sir.
CORVINO: Is't not his death?

MOSCA: Rather the contrary.
CORVINO: Not his recovery?
MOSCA: Yes, sir.
CORVINO: I am cursed,
  I am bewitched, my crosses meet to vex me!
  How? how? how? how?
MOSCA: Why, sir, with Scoto's oil!
  Corbaccio and Voltore brought of it,
  Whilst I was busy in an inner room——
CORVINO: Death! that damned mountebank! but for
  the law
  Now, I could kill the rascal; 't cannot be
  His oil should have that virtue. Ha' not I
  Known him, a common rogue, come fiddling in
  To th' ostería, with a tumbling whore,
  And, when he has done all his forced tricks, been
    glad
  Of a poor spoonful of dead wine, with flies in't?
  It cannot be. All his ingredients
  Are a sheep's gall, a roasted bitch's marrow,
  Some few sod earwigs, pounded caterpillars,
  A little capon's grease, and fasting spittle.
  I know 'em to a dram.
MOSCA: I know not, sir,
  But some on't there they poured into his ears,
  Some in his nostrils, and recovered him,
  Applying but the fricace!
CORVINO: Pox o' that fricace!
MOSCA: And since, to seem the more officious,
  And flatt'ring of his health, there they have had,
  At extreme fees, the college of physicians
  Consulting on him, how they might restore him;
  Where one would have a cataplasm of spices,
  Another a flayed ape clapped to his breast,
  A third would ha' it a dog, a fourth an oil,
  With wild cats' skins; at last, they all resolved
  That, to preserve him, was no other means
  But some young woman must be straight sought
    out,
  Lusty and full of juice, to sleep by him.
  And to this service, most unhappily,
  And most unwillingly, am I now employed;
  Which here I thought to pre-acquaint you with,
  For your advice, since it concerns you most,
  Because I would not do that thing might cross
  Your ends, on whom I have my whole dependence,
    sir,
  Yet, if I do it not, they may delate
  My slackness to my patron, work me out
  Of his opinion; and there all your hopes,
  Ventures, or whatsoever, are all frustrate.
  I do but tell you, sir. Besides, they are all
  Now striving who shall first present him. There-
    fore—
  I could entreat you, briefly, conclude somewhat;
  Prevent 'em if you can!
CORVINO: Death to my hopes,
  This is my villainous fortune! Best to hire
  Some common courtesan.

MOSCA: Ay, I thought on that, sir;
  But they are all so subtle, full of art;
  And age again doting and flexible,
  So as—I cannot tell—we may perchance
  Light on a quean may cheat us all.
CORVINO: 'Tis true.
MOSCA: No, no. It must be one that has no tricks, sir,
  Some simple thing, a creature made unto it;
  Some wench you may command. Ha' you no kins-
    woman?
  God's so'—Think, think, think, think, think,
    think, think, sir.
  One o' the doctors offered there his daughter.
CORVINO: How!
MOSCA: Yes, Signior Lupo, the physician.
CORVINO: His daughter!
MOSCA: And a virgin, sir. Why, alas,
  He knows the state of's body, what it is;
  That nought can warm his blood, sir, but a fever;
  Nor any incantation raise his spirit—
  A long forgetfulness hath seized that part.
  Besides, sir, who shall know it? some one or two—
CORVINO: I pray thee give me leave.—If any man
  But I had had this luck—The thing in'tself,
  I know, is nothing—Wherefore should not I
  As well command my blood and my affections
  As this dull doctor? In the point of honour,
  The cases are all one, of wife and daughter.
MOSCA: —I hear him coming.
CORVINO: She shall do't. 'Tis done.
  'Slight! if this doctor, who is not engaged,
  Unless 't be for his counsel, which is nothing,
  Offer his daughter, what should I, that am
  So deeply in? I will prevent him. Wretch!
  Covetous wretch!—Mosca, I have determined.
MOSCA: How, sir?
CORVINO: We'll make all sure. The party you
  wot of
  Shall be mine own wife, Mosca.
MOSCA: Sir, the thing,
  But that I would not seem to counsel you,
  I should have motioned to you at the first;
  And, make your count, you have cut all their
    throats.
  Why, 'tis directly taking a possession!
  And in his next fit, we may let him go.
  'Tis but to pull the pillow from his head,
  And he is throttled; 't had been done before,
  But for your scrupulous doubts.
CORVINO: Ay, a plague on't,
  My conscience fools my wit! Well, I'll be brief,
  And so be thou, lest they should be before us.
  Go home, prepare him, tell him with what zeal
  And willingness I do it. Swear it was
  On the first hearing—as thou mayst do, truly—
  Mine own free motion.
MOSCA: Sir, I warrant you,
  I'll so possess him with it, that the rest
  Of his starved clients shall be banished all,

And only you received. But come not, sir,
Until I send, for I have something else
To ripen for your good; you must not know't.

CORVINO: But do not you forget to send now.

MOSCA: Fear not.
                                 [*Exit*]

CORVINO: Where are you, wife? my Celia! wife!

Re-enter Celia.
                       What, blubbering?
Come, dry those tears. I think thou thought'st me
   in earnest!
Ha! by this light, I talked so but to try thee.
Methinks the lightness of the occasion
Should ha' confirmed thee. Come, I am not jeal-
   ous.

CELIA: No?

CORVINO: Faith I am not, I, nor never was;
It is a poor, unprofitable humour.
Do not I know, if women have a will,
They'll do 'gainst all the watches o' the world?
And that the fiercest spies are tamed with gold?
Tut, I am confident in thee, thou shalt see't;
And see, I'll give thee cause, too, to believe it.
Come kiss me. Go, and make thee ready straight,
In all thy best attire, thy choicest jewels,
Put 'em all on, and, with 'em, thy best looks.
We are invited to a solemn feast
At old Volpone's, where it shall appear
How far I am free from jealousy or fear.   [*Exeunt*]

Act III

SCENE 1: *A street*

Enter Mosca.

MOSCA: I fear I shall begin to grow in love
With my dear self, and my most prosp'rous parts,
They do so spring and burgeon! I can feel
A whimsy i' my blood; I know not how,
Success hath made me wanton. I could skip
Out of my skin now, like a subtle snake,
I am so limber. O! your parasite
Is a most precious thing, dropped from above,
Not bred 'mongst clods and clodpoles here on
   earth.
I muse the mystery was not made a science,
It is so liberally professed! Almost
All the wise world is little else, in nature,
But parasites or sub-parasites. And yet
I mean not those that have your bare town-art,
To know who's fit to feed 'em; have no house,
No family, no care, and therefore mould
Tales for men's ears, to bait that sense; or get
Kitchen-invention, and some stale receipts
To please the belly and the groin; nor those,
With their court-dog tricks, that can fawn and fleer,

Make their revènue out of legs and faces,
Echo my lord, and lick away a moth;
But your fine, elegant rascal, that can rise
And stoop, almost together, like an arrow;
Shoot through the air as nimbly as a star;
Turn short as doth a swallow; and be here,
And there, and here, and yonder, all at once;
Present to any humour all occasion,
And change a visor swifter than a thought!
This is the creature had the art born with him;
Toils not to learn it, but doth practise it
Out of most excellent nature; and such sparks
Are the true parasites, others but their zanies.

Enter Bonario.
Who's this? Bonario, old Corbaccio's son?
The person I was bound to seek.—Fair sir,
You are happ'ly met.

BONARIO: That cannot be by thee.

MOSCA: Why, sir?

BONARIO: Nay, pray thee know thy way, and
   leave me.
I would be loath to interchange discourse
With such a mate as thou art.

MOSCA: Courteous sir,
Scorn not my poverty.

BONARIO: Not I, by Heaven!
But thou shalt give me leave to hate thy baseness.

MOSCA: Baseness?

BONARIO: Ay, answer me, is not thy sloth
Sufficient argument? thy flattery?
Thy means of feeding?

MOSCA: Heaven be good to me!
These imputations are too common, sir,
And eas'ly stuck on virtue when she's poor;
You are unequal to me, and howe'er
Your sentence may be righteous, yet you are not,
That, ere you know me, thus proceed in censure.
Saint Mark bear witness 'gainst you, 'tis inhuman!

BONARIO: —What! does he weep? the sign is soft and
   good.
I do repent me that I was so harsh.

MOSCA: 'Tis true that, swayed by strong necessity,
I am enforced to eat my careful bread
With too much obsequy. 'Tis true, beside,
That I am fain to spin mine own poor raiment
Out of my mere observance, being not born
To a free fortune. But that I have done
Base offices, in rending friends asunder,
Dividing families, betraying counsels,
Whispering false lies, or mining men with praises,
Trained their credulity with perjuries,
Corrupted chastity, or am in love
With mine own tender ease; but would not rather
Prove the most rugged and laborious course
That might redeem my present estimation,
Let me here perish, in all hope of goodness!

BONARIO: This cannot be a personated passion.—
I was to blame, so to mistake thy nature

Pray thee forgive me, and speak out thy business.
MOSCA: Sir, it concerns you; and though I may seem
    At first to make a main offence in manners,
    And in my gratitude unto my master,
    Yet for the pure love which I bear all right,
    And hatred of the wrong, I must reveal it.
    This very hour your father is in purpose
    To disinherit you——
BONARIO: How!
MOSCA: And thrust you forth,
    As a mere stranger to his blood; 'tis true, sir!
    The work no way engageth me, but as
    I claim an interest in the general state
    Of goodness and true virtue, which I hear
    T' abound in you; and for which mere respect,
    Without a second aim, sir, I have done it.
BONARIO: This tale hath lost thee much of the late
    trust
    Thou hadst with me; it is impossible.
    I know not how to lend it any thought,
    My father should be so unnatural.
MOSCA: It is a confidence that well becomes
    Your piety; and formed, no doubt, it is
    From your own simple innocence; which makes
    Your wrong more monstrous and abhorred. But,
    sir,
    I now will tell you more: this very minute
    It is, or will be, doing; and if you
    Shall be but pleased to go with me, I'll bring you——
    I dare not say where you shall see—but where
    Your ear shall be a witness of the deed;
    Hear yourself written bastard, and professed
    The common issue of the earth.
BONARIO: I'm 'mazed!
MOSCA: Sir, if I do it not, draw your just sword,
    And score your vengeance on my front and face;
    Mark me your villain. You have too much wrong,
    And I do suffer for you, sir. My heart
    Weeps blood in anguish——
BONARIO: Lead. I follow thee.
                          [Exeunt]

SCENE 2:   *Volpone's house*

Enter Volpone.
VOLPONE: Mosca stays long, methinks.—Bring forth
    your sports,
    And help to make the wretched time more sweet.

Enter Nano, Androgyno, *and* Castrone.
NANO: 'Dwarf, fool, and eunuch, well met here we be.
    A question it were now, whether of us three,
    Being all the known delicates of a rich man,
    In pleasing him, claim the precedency can?'
CASTRONE: 'I claim for myself.'
ANDROGYNO: 'And so doth the fool.'
NANO: ''Tis foolish indeed. Let me set you both to
    school:
    First, for your dwarf, he's little and witty,

And everything, as it is little, is pretty;
    Else why do men say to a creature of my shape,
    So soon as they see him, "It's a pretty little ape"?
    And why a pretty ape, but for pleasing imitation
    Of greater men's actions, in a ridiculous fashion?
    Beside, this feat body of mine doth not crave
    Half the meat, drink, and cloth one of your bulks
    will have.
    Admit your fool's face be the mother of laughter,
    Yet, for his brain, it must always come after;
    And though that do feed him, it's a pitiful case,
    His body is beholden to such a bad face.'
                          [One knocks]
VOLPONE: Who's there? my couch! Away! Look!
    Nano, see! [Exeunt Androgyno and Castrone]
    Give me my caps first—go, inquire.   [Exit Nano]
    Now, Cupid
    Send it be Mosca, and with fair return!
NANO: It is the beauteous Madam—
VOLPONE: Wouldbe—is it?
NANO: The same.
VOLPONE: Now torment on me! Squire her in;
    For she will enter, or dwell here forever.
    Nay, quickly, that my fit were past. I fear
    A second hell, too, that my loathing this
    Will quite expel my appetite to the other.
    Would she were taking now her tedious leave.
    Lord, how it threats me, what I am to suffer!

Re-enter Nano *with* Lady Wouldbe.
LADY WOULDBE: I thank you, good sir. Pray you
    signify
    Unto your patron I am here.—This band
    Shows not my neck enough.—I trouble you, sir,
    Let me request you bid one of my women
    Come hither to me. In good faith, I am dressed
    Most favourably today! It is no matter;
    'Tis well enough.

Enter 1st Woman.
                  Look, see these petulant things!
    How they have done this!
VOLPONE: —I do feel the fever
    Ent'ring in at mine ears. O for a charm
    To fright it hence!
LADY WOULDBE: Come nearer. Is this curl
    In his right place, or this? Why is this higher
    Than all the rest? You ha' not washed your eyes
    yet!
    Or do they not stand even i' your head?
    Where is your fellow? call her.   [Exit 1st Woman]
NANO: —Now, Saint Mark
    Deliver us! anon she'll beat her women,
    Because her nose is red.

Re-enter 1st Woman *with* 2nd Woman.
LADY WOULDBE: I pray you, view
    This tire, forsooth; are all things apt, or no?
1st WOMAN: One hair a little here sticks out, for-
    sooth.

LADY WOULDBE: Does't so, forsooth? and where was your dear sight,
When it did so, forsooth? What now! bird-eyed?
And you, too? Pray you both approach and mend it.
Now, by that light, I muse you're not ashamed!
I, that have preached these things so oft unto you,
Read you the principles, argued all the grounds,
Disputed every fitness, every grace,
Called you to counsel of so frequent dressings——

NANO: —More carefully than of your fame or honour.

LADY WOULDBE: Made you acquainted what an ample dowry
The knowledge of these things would be unto you,
Able alone to get you noble husbands
At your return; and you thus to neglect it!
Besides, you seeing what a curious nation
Th' Italians are, what will they say of me?
'The English lady cannot dress herself.'
Here's a fine imputation to our country!
Well, go your ways, and stay i' the next room.
This fucus was too coarse, too; it's no matter.—
Good sir, you'll give 'em entertainment?

[*Exit* Nano *with* Women]

VOLPONE: —The storm comes toward me.

LADY WOULDBE: How does my Volpone?

VOLPONE: Troubled with noise, I cannot sleep; I dreamt
That a strange fury entered now my house,
And, with the dreadful tempest of her breath,
Did cleave my roof asunder.

LADY WOULDBE: Believe me, and I
Had the most fearful dream, could I remember't——

VOLPONE: —Out on my fate! I ha' giv'n her the occasion
How to torment me: she will tell me hers.

LADY WOULDBE: Methought the golden mediocrity,
Polite and delicate——

VOLPONE: O, if you do love me
No more! I sweat and suffer at the mention
Of any dream. Feel how I tremble yet.

LADY WOULDBE: Alas, good soul! the passion of the heart.
Seed-pearl were good now, boiled with syrup of apples,
Tincture of gold, and coral, citron pills,
Your elecampane root, myrobalanes——

VOLPONE: —Ay me, I have ta'en a grasshopper by the wing!

LADY WOULDBE: Burnt silk and amber; you have muscadel
Good i' the house——

VOLPONE: You will not drink, and part?

LADY WOULDBE: No, fear not that. I doubt we shall not get
Some English saffron,—half a dram would serve—
Your sixteen cloves, a little musk, dried mints,
Bugloss, and barley-meal——

VOLPONE: —She's in again!
Before, I feigned diseases; now I have one.

LADY WOULDBE: And these applied with a right scarlet cloth.

VOLPONE: —Another flood of words! a very torrent!

LADY WOULDBE: Shall I, sir, make you a poultice?

VOLPONE: No, no, no!
I'm very well; you need prescribe no more.

LADY WOULDBE: I have a little studied physic; but now
I'm all for music, save, i' the forenoons,
An hour or two for painting. I would have
A lady, indeed, t' have all, letters and arts,
Be able to discourse, to write, to paint;
But principal—as Plato holds—your music—
And so does wise Pythagoras, I take it—
Is your true rapture; when there is consent
In face, in voice, and clothes; and is, indeed,
Our sex's chiefest ornament.

VOLPONE: The poet
As old in time as Plato, and as knowing,
Says that your highest female grace is silence.

LADY WOULDBE: Which o' your poets? Petrarch, or Tasso, or Dante?
Guarini? Ariosto? Aretine?
Cieco di Hadria? I have read them all.

VOLPONE: —Is everything a cause to my destruction?

LADY WOULDBE: I think I ha' two or three of 'em about me.

VOLPONE: —The sun, the sea, will sooner both stand still
Than her eternal tongue! nothing can 'scape it.

LADY WOULDBE: Here's 'Pastor Fido'——

VOLPONE: —Profess obstinate silence,
That's now my safest.

LADY WOULDBE: All our English writers,
I mean such as are happy in th' Italian,
Will deign to steal out of this author mainly,
Almost as much as from Montagnié.
He has so modern and facile a vein,
Fitting the time, and catching the court ear.
Your Petrarch is more passionate, yet he,
In days of sonnetting, trusted 'em with much.
Dante is hard, and few can understand him.
But, for a desperate wit, there's Aretine!
Only his pictures are a little obscene——
You mark me not.

VOLPONE: Alas, my mind's perturbed.

LADY WOULDBE: Why, in such cases, we must cure ourselves.
Make use of our philosophy——

VOLPONE: O 'y me!

LADY WOULDBE: And as we find our passions do rebel,
Encounter 'em with reason, or divert 'em,
By giving scope unto some other humour
Of lesser danger; as, in politic bodies,
There's nothing more doth overwhelm the judgment
And clouds the understanding, than too much

Settling and fixing and, as 'twere, subsiding
Upon one object. For the incorporating
Of these same outward things into that part
Which we call mental, leaves some certain faeces
That stop the organs, and, as Plato says,
Assassinates our knowledge.
VOLPONE: —Now, the spirit
Of patience help me!
LADY WOULDBE: Come, in faith, I must
Visit you more a-days, and make you well.
Laugh and be lusty!
VOLPONE: —My good angel save me!
LADY WOULDBE: There was but one sole man in all
  the world
With whom I e'er could sympathize; and he
Would lie you often three, four hours together,
To hear me speak; and be sometime so rapt,
As he would answer me quite from the purpose,
Like you, and you are like him, just. I'll discourse,
An't be but only, sir, to bring you asleep,
How we did spend our time and loves together,
For some six years.
VOLPONE: O, O, O, O, O, O!
LADY WOULDBE: For we were coaetanei, and brought
  up——
VOLPONE: Some power, some fate, some fortune
  rescue me!

Enter Mosca.
MOSCA: God save you, madam!
LADY WOULDBE: Good sir.
VOLPONE: —Mosca! welcome,
Welcome to my redemption.
MOSCA: Why, sir?
VOLPONE: O,
Rid me of this my torture, quickly, there,
My madam with the everlasting voice!
The bells, in time of pestilence, ne'er made
Like noise, or were in that perpetual motion;
The cock-pit comes not near it. All my house,
But now, steamed like a bath with her thick
  breath;
A lawyer could not have been heard; nor scarce
Another woman, such a hail of words
She has let fall. For Hell's sake, rid her hence.
MOSCA: Has she presented?
VOLPONE: O, I do not care!
I'll take her absence upon any price,
With any loss.
MOSCA: Madam——
LADY WOULDBE: I ha' brought your patron
A toy, a cap here, of mine own work——
MOSCA: 'Tis well.
I had forgot to tell you I saw your knight,
Where you'd little think it——
LADY WOULDBE: Where?
MOSCA: Marry,
Where yet, if you make haste, you may appre-
  hend him;

Rowing upon the water in a gondole,
With the most cunning courtesan of Venice.
LADY WOULDBE: Is't true?
MOSCA: Pursue 'em, and believe your eyes.
Leave me to make your gift.—I knew 'twould
  take.
For lightly, they that use themselves most licence,
Are still most jealous.
VOLPONE: Mosca, hearty thanks
For thy quick fiction, and delivery of me.
Now to my hopes, what sayst thou?
LADY WOULDBE: But do you hear, sir?——
VOLPONE: —Again! I fear a paroxysm.
LADY WOULDBE: Which way
Rowed they together?
MOSCA: Toward the Rialto.
LADY WOULDBE: I pray you lend me your dwarf.
MOSCA: I pray you take him.
                                [*Exit* Lady Wouldbe]
Your hopes, sir, are like happy blossoms fair,
And promise timely fruit, if you will stay
But the maturing. Keep you at your couch;
Corbaccio will arrive straight, with the will.
When he is gone, I'll tell you more.   [*Exit*]
VOLPONE: My blood,
My spirits are returned; I am alive!
And, like your wanton gamester at primero,
Whose thought had whispered to him, not go less,
Methinks I lie, and draw——for an encounter.

Enter Mosca *with* Bonario.
MOSCA: Sir, here concealed, you may hear all. But
  pray you
Have patience, sir. [*One knocks*] The same's your
  father knocks.
I am compelled to leave you.
BONARIO: Do so.—Yet
Cannot my thought imagine this a truth.

Mosca *leaves* Bonario, *and admits* Corvino, *fol-
lowed by* Celia.
MOSCA: Death on me! you are come too soon, what
  meant you?
Did not I say I would send?
CORVINO: Yes, but I feared
You might forget it, and then they prevent us.
MOSCA: —Prevent! Did e'er man haste so for his
  horns?
A courtier would not ply it so for a place.—
Well, now there's no helping it, stay here;
I'll presently return.
CORVINO: Where are you, Celia?
You know not wherefore I have brought you
  hither?
CELIA: Not well, except you told me.
CORVINO: Now I will:
Hark hither.   [*Whispers to her*]
MOSCA: [*To Bonario*] Sir, your father hath sent word,
It will be half an hour ere he come.
And therefore, if you please to walk the while

Into that gallery—at the upper end
There are some books to entertain the time—
And I'll take care no man shall come unto you, sir.
BONARIO: Yes, I will stay there.—I do doubt this fel-
low.
MOSCA: There, he is far enough; he can hear nothing;
And for his father, I can keep him off.
                    [*Withdraws to* Volpone's *couch*]
CORVINO: Nay, now there is no starting back, and
    therefore
Resolve upon it; I have so decreed.
It must be done. Nor would I move't afore,
Because I would avoid all shifts and tricks
That might deny me.
CELIA: Sir, let me beseech you,
Affect not these strange trials. If you doubt
My chastity, why, lock me up forever;
Make me the heir of darkness. Let me live
Where I may please your fears, if not your trust.
CORVINO: Believe it, I have no such humour, I.
All that I speak I mean; yet I'm not mad,
Not horn-mad, see you? Go to, show yourself
Obedient, and a wife.
CELIA: O Heaven!
CORVINO: I say it,
Do so.
CELIA: Was this the train?
CORVINO: I've told you reasons:
What the physicians have set down, how much
It may concern me, what my engagements are,
My means, and the necessity of those means
For my recovery. Wherefore, if you be
Loyal, and mine, be won, respect my venture.
CELIA: Before your honour?
CORVINO: Honour! tut, a breath;
There's no such thing in nature: a mere term
Invented to awe fools. What is my gold
The worse for touching? clothes for being looked
    on?
Why, this 's no more. An old, decrepit wretch,
That has no sense, no sinew; takes his meat
With others' fingers; only knows to gape
When you do scald his gums; a voice, a shadow;
And what can this man hurt you?
CELIA: Lord! what spirit
Is this hath entered him?
CORVINO: And for your fame,
That's such a jig; as if I would go tell it,
Cry it on the Piazza! Who shall know it
But he that cannot speak it, and this fellow,
Whose lips are i' my pocket? Save yourself—
If you'll proclaim't, you may. I know no other
Should come to know it.
CELIA: Are heaven and saints then nothing?
Will they be blind or stupid?
CORVINO: How?
CELIA: Good sir,
Be jealous still, emulate them; and think
What hate they burn with toward every sin.

CORVINO: I grant you. If I thought it were a sin,
I would not urge you. Should I offer this
To some young Frenchman, or hot Tuscan blood,
That had read Aretine, conned all his prints,
Knew every quirk within lust's labyrinth,
And were professed critic in lechery;
And I would look upon him, and applaud him—
This were a sin. But here 'tis contrary:
A pious work, mere charity, for physic,
And honest policy, to assure mine own.
CELIA: O Heaven! canst thou suffer such a change?
VOLPONE: —Thou art mine honour, Mosca, and my
    pride,
My joy, my tickling, my delight! Go bring 'em.
MOSCA: Please you draw near, sir.
CORVINO: Come on, what——
You will not be rebellious? by that light——
MOSCA: Sir, Signior Corvino, here, is come to see you.
VOLPONE: Oh!
MOSCA: And hearing of the consultation had,
So lately, for your health, is come to offer,
Or rather, sir, to prostitute——
CORVINO: Thanks, sweet Mosca.
MOSCA: Freely, unasked, or unentreated——
CORVINO: Well!
MOSCA: As the true, fervent instance of his love,
His own most fair and proper wife, the beauty
Only of price in Venice——
CORVINO: 'Tis well urged.
MOSCA: To be your comfortress, and to preserve
    you.
VOLPONE: Alas, I'm past, already! Pray you thank 'im
For his good care and promptness; but for that,
'Tis a vain labour e'en to fight 'gainst heaven,
Applying fire to stone,—uh, uh, uh, uh!—
Making a dead leaf grow again. I take
His wishes gently, though; and you may tell him
What I've done for him. Marry, my state is hope-
    less!
Will him to pray for me, and t' use his fortune
With reverence when he comes to 't.
MOSCA: Do you hear, sir?
Go to him with your wife.
CORVINO: Heart of my father!
Wilt thou persist thus? Come, I pray thee, come.
Thou seest 'tis nothing, Celia. By this hand,
I shall grow violent. Come, do't, I say.
CELIA: Sir, kill me, rather. I will take down poison,
Eat burning coals, do anything——
CORVINO: Be damned!
Heart, I will drag thee hence home by the hair,
Cry thee a strumpet through the streets, rip up
Thy mouth unto thine ears, and slit thy nose
Like a raw rochet—Do not tempt me, come!
Yield, I am loath—Death! I will buy some slave,
Whom I will kill, and bind thee to him alive,
And at my window hang you forth; devising
Some monstrous crime, which I, in capital letters,
Will eat into thy flesh with aquafortis

And burning corsives, on this stubborn breast.
Now, by the blood thou hast incensed, I'll do it!
CELIA: Sir, what you please, you may; I am your
  martyr.
CORVINO: Be not thus obstinate; I ha' not deserved it.
  Think who it is entreats you. Pray thee, sweet—
  Good faith, thou shalt have jewels, gowns, attires,
  What thou wilt think, and ask. Do but go kiss
  him.
  Or touch him but. For my sake—At my suit—
  This once—No? not? I shall remember this!
  Will you disgrace me thus? D'you thirst my un-
  doing?
MOSCA: Nay, gentle lady, be advised.
CORVINO: No, no.
  She has watched her time. God's precious, this is
  scurvy,
  'Tis very scurvy; and you are——
MOSCA: Nay, good sir.
CORVINO: An arrant locust, by Heaven, a locust!
  Whore,
  Crocodile, that hast thy tears prepared,
  Expecting how thou'lt bid 'em flow——
MOSCA: Nay, pray you, sir,
  She will consider.
CELIA: Would my life would serve
  To satisfy!
CORVINO: 'Sdeath! if she would but speak to him,
  And save my reputation, it were somewhat;
  But spitefully to affect my utter ruin!
MOSCA: Ay, now you've put your fortune in her
  hands.
  Why, i'faith, it is her modesty; I must quit her.
  If you were absent, she would be more coming;
  I know it, and dare undertake for her.
  What woman can before her husband? Pray you,
  Let us depart, and leave her here.
CORVINO: Sweet Celia,
  Thou mayst redeem all yet; I'll say no more.
  If not, esteem yourself as lost. Nay, stay there.
                          [Exit with Mosca]
CELIA: O God and his good angels! Whither, whither
  Is shame fled human breasts, that with such ease,
  Men dare put off your honours, and their own?
  Is that which ever was a cause of life
  Now placed beneath the basest circumstance,
  And modesty an exile made, for money?
VOLPONE: [Leaps off from his couch] Ay, in Corvino,
  and such earth-fed minds,
  That never tasted the true heav'n of love.
  Assure thee, Celia, he that would sell thee,
  Only for hope of gain, and that uncertain,
  He would have sold his part of paradise
  For ready money, had he met a cope-man.
  Why art thou 'mazed to see me thus revived?
  Rather applaud thy beauty's miracle;
  'Tis thy great work, that hath, not now alone,
  But sundry times raised me in several shapes,
  And, but this morning, like a mountebank,

To see thee at thy window. Ay, before
I would have left my practice for thy love,
In varying figures, I would have contended
With the blue Proteus, or the hornèd flood.
Now art thou welcome.
CELIA: Sir!
VOLPONE: Nay, fly me not.
  Nor let thy false imagination
  That I was bed-rid, make thee think I am so.
  Thou shalt not find it. I am now as fresh,
  As hot, as high, and in as jovial plight,
  As when, in that so celebrated scene,
  At recitation of our comedy
  For entertainment of the great Valois,
  I acted young Antinous; and attracted
  The eyes and ears of all the ladies present,
  T' admire each graceful gesture, note, and footing.

        SONG

  'Come, my Celia, let us prove,
  While we can, the sports of love.
  Time will not be ours forever,
  He at length our good will sever;
  Spend not then his gifts in vain.
  Suns that set may rise again;
  But if once we lose this light,
  'Tis with us perpetual night.
  Why should we defer our joys?
  Fame and rumour are but toys.
  Cannot we delude the eyes
  Of a few poor household spies?
  Or his easier ears beguile,
  Thus removèd by our wile?
  'Tis no sin love's fruits to steal,
  But the sweet thefts to reveal:
  To be taken, to be seen,
  These have crimes accounted been.'

CELIA: Some sèrene blast me, or dire lightning strike
  This my offending face!
VOLPONE: Why droops my Celia?
  Thou hast, in place of a base husband, found
  A worthy lover; use thy fortune well,
  With secrecy and pleasure. See, behold
  What thou art queen of, not in expectation—
  As I feed others—but possessed and crowned.
  See, here, a rope of pearl, and each more orient
  Than that the brave Egyptian queen caroused—
  Dissolve and drink 'em. See, a carbuncle,
  May put out both the eyes of our Saint Mark;
  A diamond would have bought Lollia Paulina,
  When she came in like starlight, hid with jewels
  That were the spoils of provinces—take these
  And wear, and lose 'em; yet remains an earring
  To purchase them again, and this whole state.
  A gem but worth a private patrimony,
  Is nothing; we will eat such at a meal.
  The heads of parrots, tongues of nightingales,
  The brains of peacocks, and of estriches,

Shall be our food; and, could we get the phoenix,
Though nature lost her kind, she were our dish.
CELIA: Good sir, these things might move a mind
       affected
With such delights; but I, whose innocence
Is all I can think wealthy, or worth th' enjoying,
And which, once lost, I have nought to lose beyond
       it,
Cannot be taken with these sensual baits.
If you have conscience——
VOLPONE: 'Tis the beggar's virtue.
If thou hast wisdom, hear me, Celia.
Thy baths shall be the juice of gillyflowers,
Spirit of roses, and of violets,
The milk of unicorns, and panthers' breath
Gathered in bags, and mixed with Cretan wines.
Our drink shall be preparèd gold and amber,
Which we will take until my roof whirl round
With the vertigo; and my dwarf shall dance,
My eunuch sing, my fool make up the antic.
Whilst we, in changèd shapes, act Ovid's tales,
Thou like Europa now, and I like Jove,
Then I like Mars, and thou like Erycine;
So of the rest, till we have quite run through,
And wearied all the fables of the gods.
Then will I have thee in more modern forms,
Attirèd like some sprightly dame of France,
Brave Tuscan lady, or proud Spanish beauty;
Sometimes unto the Persian Sophy's wife,
Or the Grand Signior's mistress; and for change,
To one of our most artful courtesans,
Or some quick Negro, or cold Russian.
And I will meet thee in as many shapes;
Where we may so transfuse our wand'ring souls
Out at our lips, and score up sums of pleasures,

'That the curious shall not know
How to tell them as they flow;
And the envious, when they find
What their number is, be pined.'

CELIA: If you have ears that will be pierced, or eyes
That can be opened, a heart may be touched,
Or any part that yet sounds man above you;
If you have touch of holy saints, or heaven,
Do me the grace to let me 'scape. If not,
Be bountiful and kill me. You do know
I am a creature hither ill betrayed,
By one whose shame I would forget it were.
If you will deign me neither of these graces,
Yet feed your wrath, sir, rather than your lust,—
It is a vice comes nearer manliness—
And punish that unhappy crime of nature
Which you miscall my beauty. Flay my face,
Or poison it with ointments, for seducing
Your blood to this rebellion. Rub these hands
With what may cause an eating leprosy,
E'en to my bones and marrow—anything

That may disfavour me, save in my honour.
And I will kneel to you, pray for you, pay down
A thousand hourly vows, sir, for your health;
Report and think you virtuous——
VOLPONE: Think me cold,
Frozen, and impotent, and so report me?
That I had Nestor's hernia thou wouldst think.
I do degenerate, and abuse my nation,
To play with opportunity thus long.
I should have done the act, and then have
       parleyed.
Yield, or I'll force thee.
CELIA: O! just God!
VOLPONE: In vain——
BONARIO: [Leaps out from where Mosca had placed
       him] Forbear, foul ravisher! libidinous swine!
Free the forced lady or thou diest, impostor.
But that I am loath to snatch thy punishment
Out of the hand of justice, thou shouldst yet
Be made the timely sacrifice of vengeance,
Before this altar, and this dross, thy idol.—
Lady, let's quit the place; it is the den
Of villainy. Fear nought, you have a guard;
And he ere long shall meet his just reward.
                          [Exeunt Bonario and Celia]
VOLPONE: Fall on me, roof, and bury me in ruin!
Become my grave, that wert my shelter! O!
I am unmasked, unspirited, undone,
Betrayed to beggary, to infamy——

Enter Mosca.
MOSCA: Where shall I run, most wretched shame of
       men,
To beat out my unlucky brains?
VOLPONE: Here, here.
What! dost thou bleed?
MOSCA: O that his well-driv'n sword
Had been so courteous to have cleft me down
Unto the navel, ere I lived to see
My life, my hopes, my spirits, my patron, all
Thus desperately engagèd by my error!
VOLPONE: Woe on thy fortune!
MOSCA: And my follies, sir.
VOLPONE: Th'ast made me miserable.
MOSCA: And myself, sir.
Who would have thought he would have heark-
       ened so?
VOLPONE: What shall we do?
MOSCA: I know not; if my heart
Could expiate the mischance, I'd pluck it out.
Will you be pleased to hang me, or cut my throat?
And I'll requite you, sir. Let's die like Romans,
Since we have lived like Grecians.
                          [They knock without]
VOLPONE: Hark! who's there?
I hear some footing; officers, the Saffi,
Come to apprehend us! I do feel the brand
Hissing already at my forehead; now
Mine ears are boring.

MOSCA: To your couch, sir; you
  Make that place good, however. Guilty men
  Suspect what they deserve still. Signior Corbaccio!

   Enter Corbaccio.
CORBACCIO: Why, how now, Mosca?
MOSCA: O, undone, amazed, sir!
  Your son,—I know not by what accident—
  Acquainted with your purpose to my patron,
  Touching your will, and making him your heir;
  Entered our house with violence, his sword drawn,
  Sought for you, called you wretch, unnatural,
  Vowed he would kill you.
CORBACCIO: Me?
MOSCA: Yes, and my patron.
CORBACCIO: This act shall disinherit him indeed!
  Here is the will.
MOSCA: 'Tis well, sir.
CORBACCIO: Right and well.
  Be you as careful now for me.

   Enter Voltore, *behind.*
MOSCA: My life, sir,
  Is not more tendered; I am only yours.
CORBACCIO: How does he? will he die shortly, think'st
  thou?
MOSCA: I fear
  He'll outlast May.
CORBACCIO: Today?
MOSCA: No, last out May, sir.
CORBACCIO: Couldst thou not gi' him a dram?
MOSCA: O, by no means, sir.
CORBACCIO: Nay, I'll not bid you.
VOLTORE: This is a knave, I see.
MOSCA: —How! Signior Voltore! did he hear me?
VOLTORE: Parasite!
MOSCA: Who's that?—O sir, most timely welcome—
VOLTORE: Scarce,
  To the discovery of your tricks, I fear.
  You are his only? And mine also, are you not?
MOSCA: Who? I, sir!
VOLTORE: You, sir. What device is this
  About a will?
MOSCA: A plot for you, sir.
VOLTORE: Come,
  Put not your foists upon me; I shall scent 'em.
MOSCA: Did you not hear it?
VOLTORE: Yes, I hear Corbaccio
  Hath made your patron there his heir.
MOSCA: 'Tis true;
  By my device, drawn to it by my plot,
  With hope——
VOLTORE: Your patron should reciprocate?
  And you have promised?
MOSCA: For your good I did, sir.
  Nay more, I told his son, brought, hid him here,
  Where he might hear his father pass the deed;
  Being persuaded to it by this thought, sir:
  That the unnaturalness, first, of the act,

And then his father's oft disclaiming in him—
Which I did mean t'help on—would sure enrage
  him
To do some violence upon his parent;
On which the law should take sufficient hold,
And you be stated in a double hope.
Truth be my comfort, and my conscience,
My only aim was to dig you a fortune
Out of these two old, rotten sepulchres——
VOLTORE: I cry thee mercy, Mosca.
MOSCA: Worth your patience,
  And your great merit, sir. And see the change!
VOLTORE: Why, what success?
MOSCA: Most hapless! you must help, sir.
  Whilst we expected th' old raven, in comes
  Corvino's wife, sent hither by her husband——
VOLTORE: What, with a present?
MOSCA: No, sir, on visitation,—
  I'll tell you how anon—and staying long,
  The youth he grows impatient, rushes forth,
  Seizeth the lady, wounds me, makes her swear—
  Or he would murder her, that was his vow—
  T' affirm my patron to have done her rape;
  Which how unlike it is, you see! And hence
  With that pretext he's gone, t' accuse his father,
  Defame my patron, defeat you——
VOLTORE: Where's her husband?
  Let him be sent for straight.
MOSCA: Sir, I'll go fetch him.
VOLTORE: Bring him to the Scrutineo.
MOSCA: Sir, I will.
VOLTORE: This must be stopped.
MOSCA: O, you do nobly, sir.
  Alas, 'twas laboured all, sir, for your good;
  Nor was there want of counsel in the plot.
  But fortune can, at any time, o'erthrow
  The projects of a hundred learned clerks, sir.
CORBACCIO: What's that?
VOLTORE: Will't please you, sir, to go along?
        [*Exit* Voltore, *followed by* Corbaccio]
MOSCA: Patron, go in, and pray for our success.
VOLPONE: Need makes devotion. Heaven your labour
  bless!   [*Exeunt*]

Act IV

SCENE 1: *A street*

   Enter Sir Politic Wouldbe *and* Peregrine.
SIR POLITIC: I told you, sir, it was a plot. You see
  What observation is. You mentioned me
  For some instructions: I will tell you, sir,
  Since we are met here in this height of Venice,
  Some few particulars I have set down,
  Only for this meridian, fit to be known
  Of your crude traveller; and they are these.
  I will not touch, sir, at your phrase, or clothes,
  For they are old.

PEREGRINE: Sir, I have better.
SIR POLITIC: Pardon,
  I meant, as they are themes.
PEREGRINE: O sir, proceed.
  I'll slander you no more of wit, good sir.
SIR POLITIC: First, for your garb, it must be grave and
    serious,
  Very reserved and locked; not tell a secret
  On any terms, not to your father; scarce
  A fable, but with caution; make sure choice
  Both of your company and discourse; beware
  You never speak a truth——
PEREGRINE: How!
SIR POLITIC: Not to strangers,
  For those be they you must converse with most;
  Others I would not know, sir, but at distance,
  So as I still might be a saver in 'em;
  You shall have tricks else passed upon you hourly.
  And then, for your religion, profess none,
  But wonder at the diversity of all;
  And, for your part, protest, were there no other
  But simply the laws o' th' land, you could content
    you.
  Nick Machiavel and Monsieur Bodin both
  Were of this mind. Then must you learn the use
  And handling of your silver fork at meals,
  The metal of your glass,—these are main matters
  With your Italian—and to know the hour
  When you must eat your melons and your figs.
PEREGRINE: Is that a point of state, too?
SIR POLITIC: Here it is.
  For your Venetian, if he see a man
  Preposterous in the least, he has him straight.
  He has; he strips him. I'll acquaint you, sir,
  I now have lived here 'tis some fourteen months;
  Within the first week of my landing here,
  And took me for a citizen of Venice.
  I knew the forms so well——
PEREGRINE: —And nothing else.
SIR POLITIC: I had read Contarene, took me a house,
  Dealt with my Jews to furnish it with movables—
  Well, if I could but find one man, one man
  To mine own heart, whom I durst trust, I
    would——
PEREGRINE: What, what, sir?
SIR POLITIC: Make him rich; make
    him a fortune.
  He should not think again. I would command
    it.
PEREGRINE: As how?
SIR POLITIC: With certain projects that I have,
  Which I may not discover.
PEREGRINE: —If I had
  But one to wager with, I would lay odds now,
  He tells me instantly.
SIR POLITIC: One is—and that
  I care not greatly who knows—to serve the state
  Of Venice with red herrings for three years,
  And at a certain rate, from Rotterdam,

Where I have correspondence. There's a letter,
  Sent me from one o' th' States, and to that pur-
    pose.
  He cannot write his name, but that's his mark.
PEREGRINE: He is a chandler?
SIR POLITIC: No, a cheesemonger.
  There are some other two with whom I treat
  About the same negotiation;
  And I will undertake it. For 'tis thus:
  I'll do't with ease, I've cast it all. Your hoy
  Carries but three men in her, and a boy,
  And she shall make me three returns a year;
  So if there come but one of three, I save;
  If two, I can defalc. But this is now,
  If my main project fail.
PEREGRINE: Then you have others?
SIR POLITIC: I should be loath to draw the subtle air
  Of such a place, without my thousand aims.
  I'll not dissemble, sir, where'er I come,
  I love to be considerative; and 'tis true
  I have at my free hours thought upon
  Some certain goods unto the state of Venice,
  Which I do call my cautions; and, sir, which
  I mean, in hope of pension, to propound
  To the Great Council, then unto the Forty,
  So to the Ten. My means are made already——
PEREGRINE: By whom?
SIR POLITIC: Sir, one that though his place
    be obscure,
  Yet he can sway, and they will hear him. He's
  A commendatore.
PEREGRINE: What! a common sergeant?
SIR POLITIC: Sir, such as they are, put it in their
    mouths,
  What they should say, sometimes, as well as
    greater.
  I think I have my notes to show you——
PEREGRINE: Good, sir.
SIR POLITIC: But you shall swear unto me, on your
    gentry,
  Not to anticipate——
PEREGRINE: I, sir?
SIR POLITIC: Nor reveal
  A circumstance——My paper is not with me.
PEREGRINE: O, but you can remember, sir.
SIR POLITIC: My first is
  Concerning tinder-boxes. You must know,
  No family is here without its box.
  Now, sir, it being so portable a thing,
  Put case that you or I were ill affected
  Unto the state; sir, with it in our pockets,
  Might not I go into the Arsenale?
  Or you? come out again? and none the wiser?
PEREGRINE: Except yourself, sir.
SIR POLITIC: Go to, then. I therefore
  Advertise to the state, how fit it were
  That none but such as were known patriots,
  Sound lovers of their country, should be suffered
  T' enjoy them in their houses; and even those

Sealed at some office, and at such a bigness
As might not lurk in pockets.
PEREGRINE: Admirable!
SIR POLITIC: My next is, how t' inquire, and be re-
    solved
By present demonstration, whether a ship,
Newly arrived from Syria, or from
Any suspected part of all the Levant,
Be guilty of the plague. And, where they use
To lie out forty, fifty days, sometimes,
About the Lazaretto, for their trial;
I'll save that charge and loss unto the merchant,
And in an hour clear the doubt.
PEREGRINE: Indeed, sir!
SIR POLITIC: Or——I will lose my labour.
PEREGRINE: My faith, that's much.
SIR POLITIC: Nay, sir, conceive me. 'Twill cost me, in
    onions,
Some thirty livres——
PEREGRINE: Which is one pound sterling.
SIR POLITIC: Beside my waterworks. For this I do, sir:
First, I bring in your ship 'twixt two brick walls——
But those the state shall venture. On the one
I strain me a fair tarpaulin, and in that
I stick my onions, cut in halves; the other
Is full of loopholes, out at which I thrust
The noses of my bellows; and those bellows
I keep, with waterworks, in perpetual motion,
Which is the easiest matter of a hundred.
Now, sir, your onion, which doth naturally
Attract th' infection, and your bellows blowing
The air upon him, will show instantly,
By his changed colour, if there be contagion;
Or else remain as fair as at the first.
Now 'tis known, 'tis nothing.
PEREGRINE: You are right, sir.
SIR POLITIC: I would I had my note.
PEREGRINE: Faith, so would I.—
But you ha' done well for once, sir.
SIR POLITIC: Were I false,
Or would be made so, I could show you reasons
How I could sell this state now to the Turk,
Spite of their galleys, or their——
PEREGRINE: Pray you, Sir Poll.
SIR POLITIC: I have 'em not about me.
PEREGRINE: That I feared.
They 're there, sir?
SIR POLITIC: No, this is my diary,
Wherein I note my actions of the day.
PEREGRINE: Pray you let's see, sir. What is here?—
'Notandum,
A rat had gnawn my spur-leathers; notwithstand-
    ing,
I put on new, and did go forth; but first
I threw three beans over the threshold. Item,
I went and bought two toothpicks, whereof one
I burst immediately, in a discourse
With a Dutch merchant, 'bout Ragion del Stato.
From him I went and paid a moccenigo

For piecing my silk stockings; by the way
I cheapened sprats; and at Saint Mark's I urined.'
Faith these are politic notes!
SIR POLITIC: Sir, I do slip
No action of my life, thus, but I quote it.
PEREGRINE: Believe me, it is wise!
SIR POLITIC: Nay, sir, read forth.

Enter Lady Wouldbe, Nano, *and two* Women.
LADY WOULDBE: Where should this loose knight be,
    trow? Sure, he's housed.
NANO: Why, then he's fast.
LADY WOULDBE: Ay, he plays both with me!
I pray you stay.—This heat will do more harm
To my complexion than his heart is worth.
I do not care to hinder, but to take him.
How it comes off!
1ST WOMAN: My master's yonder.
LADY WOULDBE: Where?
2ND WOMAN: With a young gentleman.
LADY WOULDBE: That same's the party,
In man's apparel!—Pray you, sir, jog my knight.
I will be tender to his reputation,
However he demerit.
SIR POLITIC: —My lady!
PEREGRINE: Where?
SIR POLITIC: 'Tis she indeed, sir, you shall know her.
    She is,
Were she not mine, a lady of that merit,
For fashion and behaviour; and for beauty
I durst compare——
PEREGRINE: It seems you are not jealous,
That dare commend her.
SIR POLITIC: Nay, and for discourse——
PEREGRINE: Being your wife, she cannot miss that.
SIR POLITIC: Madam,
Here is a gentleman, pray you, use him fairly;
He seems a youth, but he is——
LADY WOULDBE: None.
SIR POLITIC: Yes, one
Has put his face as soon into the world——
LADY WOULDBE: You mean, as early? but today?
SIR POLITIC: How's this?
LADY WOULDBE: Why, in this habit, sir, you appre-
    hend me.
Well, Master Wouldbe, this doth not become you.
I had thought the odour, sir, of your good name
Had been more precious to you; that you would not
Have done this dire massacre on your honour;
One of your gravity, and rank besides!
But knights, I see, care little for the oath
They make to ladies, chiefly their own ladies.
SIR POLITIC: Now, by my spurs, the symbol of my
    knighthood——
PEREGRINE: —Lord, how his brain is humbled for an
    oath!
SIR POLITIC: I reach you not.
LADY WOULDBE: Right, sir, your policy
May bear it through thus.—Sir, a word with you.

I would be loath to contest publicly
With any gentlewoman, or to seem
Froward, or violent, as the courtier says—
It comes too near rusticity in a lady,
Which I would shun by all means. And, however
I may deserve from Master Wouldbe, yet
T' have one fair gentlewoman thus be made
Th' unkind instrument to wrong another,
And one she knows not, ay, and to persever;
In my poor judgment, is not warranted
From being a solecism in our sex,
If not in manners.

PEREGRINE: How is this!

SIR POLITIC: Sweet madam,
Come nearer to your aim.

LADY WOULDBE: Marry, and will, sir.
Since you provoke me with your impudence,
And laughter of your light land-siren here,
Your Sporus, your hermaphrodite——

PEREGRINE: What's here?
Poetic fury and historic storms!

SIR POLITIC: The gentleman, believe it, is of worth,
And of our nation.

LADY WOULDBE: Ay, your Whitefriars nation!
Come, I blush for you, Master Wouldbe, I;
And am ashamed you should ha' no more forehead,
Than thus to be the patron, or Saint George,
To a lewd harlot, a base fricatrice,
A female devil in a male outside.

SIR POLITIC: Nay,
An you be such a one, I must bid adieu
To your delights. The case appears too liquid.
                                              [Exit]

LADY WOULDBE: Ay, you may carry't clear, with you
    state-face!
But for your carnival concupiscence,
Who here is fled for liberty of conscience,
From furious persecution of the Marshal,
Her will I disc'ple.

PEREGRINE: This is fine, i' faith!
And do you use this often? Is this part
Of your wit's exercise, 'gainst you have occasion?
Madam——

LADY WOULDBE: Go to, sir.

PEREGRINE: Do you hear me, lady?
Why, if your knight have set you to beg shirts,
Or to invite me home, you might have done it
A nearer way by far.

LADY WOULDBE: This cannot work you
Out of my snare.

PEREGRINE: Why, am I in it, then?
Indeed your husband told me you were fair,
And so you are; only your nose inclines—
That side that's next the sun—to the queen-apple.

LADY WOULDBE: This cannot be endured by any pa-
    tience.

Enter Mosca.

MOSCA: What's the matter, madam?

LADY WOULDBE: If the Senate
Right not my quest in this, I will protest 'em
To all the world no aristocracy.

MOSCA: What is the injury, lady?

LADY WOULDBE: Why, the callet
You told me of, here I have ta'en disguised.

MOSCA: Who? this! what means your ladyship? The
    creature
I mentioned to you is apprehended now
Before the Senate, you shall see her——

LADY WOULDBE: Where?

MOSCA: I'll bring you to her. This young gentleman,
I saw him land this morning at the port.

LADY WOULDBE: Is't possible? how has my judgment
    wandered!
Sir, I must, blushing, say to you I have erred,
And plead your pardon.

PEREGRINE: What, more changes yet?

LADY WOULDBE: I hope y' ha' not the malice to re-
    member
A gentlewoman's passion. If you stay
In Venice here, please you to use me, sir——

MOSCA: Will you go, madam?

LADY WOULDBE: Pray you, sir, use me. In faith,
The more you see me, the more I shall conceive
You have forgot our quarrel.
            [*Exeunt* Lady Wouldbe, Mosca, Nano, *and*
                  Women]

PEREGRINE: This is rare!
Sir Politic Wouldbe? no, Sir Politic Bawd,
To bring me thus acquainted with his wife!
Well, wise Sir Poll, since you have practised thus
Upon my freshmanship, I'll try your salt-head,
What proof it is against a counter-plot.   [*Exit*]

SCENE 2:   *The Scrutineo*

Enter Voltore, Corbaccio, Corvino, *and* Mosca.

VOLTORE: Well, now you know the carriage of the
    business,
Your constancy is all that is required
Unto the safety of it.

MOSCA: Is the lie
Safely conveyed amongst us? is that sure?
Knows every man his burden?

CORVINO: Yes.

MOSCA: Then shrink not.

CORVINO: —But knows the advocate the truth?

MOSCA: O sir,
By no means. I devised a formal tale,
That salved your reputation. But be valiant, sir.

CORVINO: I fear no one but him, that this his pleading
Should make him stand for a co-heir——

MOSCA: Co-halter!
Hang him, we will but use his tongue, his noise,
As we do Croaker's here.

CORVINO: Ay, what shall he do?

MOSCA: When we have done, you mean?

CORVINO: Yes.
MOSCA: Why, we'll think:
  Sell him for mummia; he's half dust already. [*To
    Voltore*]
  Do you not smile to see this buffalo,
  How he doth sport it with his head?—I should,
  If all were well and past. [*To Corbaccio*] Sir, only
    you
  Are he that shall enjoy the crop of all,
  And these not know for whom they toil.
CORBACCIO: Ay, peace.
MOSCA: [*To Corvino*] But you shall eat it.—Much!—
  [*To Voltore*] Worshipful sir,
  Mercury sit upon your thund'ring tongue,
  Or the French Hercules, and make your language
  As conquering as his club, to beat along,
  As with a tempest, flat, our adversaries;
  But much more yours, sir.
VOLTORE: Here they come, ha' done.
MOSCA: I have another witness, if you need, sir,
  I can produce.
VOLTORE: **Who is it?**
MOSCA: Sir, I have her.

Enter four Avocatori, Bonario, Celia, Notario,
   Commendatori, &c.

1ST AVOCATORE: The like of this the Senate never
  heard of.
2ND AVOCATORE: 'Twill come most strange to them,
  when we report it.
4TH AVOCATORE: The gentlewoman has been ever
  held
  Of unreprovèd name.
3RD AVOCATORE: So the young man.
4TH AVOCATORE: The more unnatural part that of his
  father.
2ND AVOCATORE: More of the husband.
1ST AVOCATORE: I not know to give
  His act a name, it is so monstrous!
4TH AVOCATORE: But the impostor, he is a thing
  created
  T' exceed example!
1ST AVOCATORE: And all after-times!
2ND AVOCATORE: I never heard a true voluptuary
  Described, but him.
3RD AVOCATORE: Appear yet those were cited?
NOTARIO: All but the old magnifico, Volpone.
1ST AVOCATORE: Why is not he here?
MOSCA: Please your fatherhoods,
  Here is his advocate. Himself's so weak,
  So feeble——
4TH AVOCATORE: Who are you?
BONARIO: His parasite,
  His knave, his pander! I beseech the court
  He may be forced to come, that your grave eyes
  May bear strong witness of his strange impostures.
VOLTORE: Upon my faith and credit with your virtues,
  He is not able to endure the air.
2ND AVOCATORE: Bring him, however.

3RD AVOCATORE: We will see him.
4TH AVOCATORE: Fetch him.   [*Exeunt* Officers]
VOLTORE: Your fatherhoods' fit pleasures be obeyed,
  But sure the sight will rather move your pities
  Than indignation. May it please the court,
  In the meantime, he may be heard in me:
  I know this place most void of prejudice,
  And therefore crave it, since we have no reason
  To fear our truth should hurt our cause.
3RD AVOCATORE: Speak free.
VOLTORE: Then know, most honoured fathers, I must
    now
  Discover to your strangely abusèd ears
  The most prodigious and most frontless piece
  Of solid impudence and treachery,
  That ever vicious nature yet brought forth
  To shame the state of Venice. This lewd woman,
  That wants no artificial looks or tears
  To help the visor she has now put on,
  Hath long been known a close adulteress
  To that lascivious youth there; not suspected,
  I say, but known, and taken in the act
  With him; and by this man, the easy husband,
  Pardoned; whose timeless bounty makes him now
  Stand here, the most unhappy, innocent person
  That ever man's own goodness made accused.
  For these, not knowing how to owe a gift
  Of that dear grace, but with their shame; being
    placed
  So above all powers of their gratitude,
  Began to hate the benefit; and in place
  Of thanks, devise t' extirp the memory
  Of such an act. Wherein, I pray your fatherhoods
  To observe the malice, yea, the rage of creatures
  Discovered in their evils; and what heart
  Such take, even from their crimes. But that anon
  Will more appear. This gentleman, the father,
  Hearing of this foul fact, with many others,
  Which daily struck at his too tender ears,
  And grieved in nothing more than that he could
    not
  Preserve himself a parent,—his son's ills
  Growing to that strange flood—at last decreed
  To disinherit him.
1ST AVOCATORE: These be strange turns!
2ND AVOCATORE: The young man's fame was ever fair
  and honest.
VOLTORE: So much more full of danger is his vice,
  That can beguile so, under shade of virtue.
  But, as I said, my honoured sires, his father
  Having this settled purpose,—by what means
  To him betrayed, we know not—and this day
  Appointed for the deed; that parricide,
  I cannot style him better, by confederacy
  Preparing this his paramour to be there,
  Entered Volpone's house,—who was the man,
  Your fatherhoods must understand, designed
  For the inheritance—there sought his father.
  But with what purpose sought he him, my lords?

I tremble to pronounce it, that a son
Unto a father, and to such a father,
Should have so foul, felonious intent:
It was to murder him! When, being prevented
By his more happy absence, what then did he?
Not check his wicked thoughts; no, now new
    deeds,—
Mischief doth never end where it begins—
An act of horror, fathers! he dragged forth
The aged gentleman that had there lain bed-rid
Three years and more, out off his innocent couch,
Naked, upon the floor, there left him; wounded
His servant in the face; and with this strumpet,
The stale to his forged practice, who was glad
To be so active,—I shall here desire
Your fatherhoods to note but my recollections,
As most remarkable—thought at once to stop
His father's ends, discredit his free choice
In the old gentleman, redeem themselves
By laying infamy upon this man,
To whom, with blushing, they should owe their
    lives.

1ST AVOCATORE: What proofs have you of this?
BONARIO: Most honoured fathers,
    I humbly crave there be no credit given
    To this man's mercenary tongue.
2ND AVOCATORE: Forbear.
BONARIO: His soul moves in his fee.
3RD AVOCATORE: O, sir!
BONARIO: This fellow,
    For six sols more would plead against his Maker.
1ST AVOCATORE: You do forget yourself.
VOLTORE: Nay, nay, grave fathers,
    Let him have scope. Can any man imagine
    That he will spare 's accuser, that would not
    Have spared his parent?
1ST AVOCATORE: Well, produce your proofs.
CELIA: —I would I could forget I were a creature!
VOLTORE: Signior Corbaccio!
4TH AVOCATORE: What is he?
VOLTORE: The father.
2ND AVOCATORE: Has he had an oath?
NOTARIO: Yes.
CORBACCIO: What must I do now?
NOTARIO: Your testimony's craved.
CORBACCIO: Speak to the knave?
    I'll ha' my mouth first stopped with earth. My
        heart
    Abhors his knowledge. I disclaim in him.
1ST AVOCATORE: But for what cause?
CORBACCIO: The mere portent of nature.
    He is an utter stranger to my loins.
BONARIO: Have they made you to this?
CORBACCIO: I will not hear thee,
    Monster of men, swine, goat, wolf, parricide!
    Speak not, thou viper.
BONARIO: Sir, I will sit down,
    And rather wish my innocence should suffer,
    Than I resist the authority of a father.

VOLTORE: Signior Corvino!
2ND AVOCATORE: This is strange.
1ST AVOCATORE: Who's this?
NOTARIO: The husband.
4TH AVOCATORE: Is he sworn?
NOTARIO: He is.
3RD AVOCATORE: Speak, then.
CORVINO: This woman, please your fatherhoods, is a
        whore
    Of most hot exercise, more than a partridge,
    Upon record——
1ST AVOCATORE: No more.
CORVINO: Neighs like a jennet.
NOTARIO: Preserve the honour of the court.
CORVINO: I shall,
    And modesty of your most reverend ears.
    And yet I hope that I may say these eyes
    Have seen her glued unto that piece of cedar,
    That fine, well-timbered gallant; and that here
    The letters may be read, thorough the horn,
    That make the story perfect.
MOSCA: —Excellent, sir!
CORVINO: —There is no shame in this now, is there?
MOSCA: None.
CORVINO: Or if I said, I hoped that she were onward
    To her damnation, if there be a hell
    Greater than whore and woman; a good Catholic
    May make the doubt.
3RD AVOCATORE: His grief hath made him frantic.
1ST AVOCATORE: Remove him hence.   [Celia swoons]
2ND AVOCATORE: Look to the woman.
CORVINO: Rare!
    Prettily feigned again!
4TH AVOCATORE: Stand from about her.
1ST AVOCATORE: Give her the air.
3RD AVOCATORE: What can you say?
MOSCA: My wound,
    May it please your wisdoms, speaks for me, re-
        ceived
    In aid of my good patron, when he missed
    His sought-for father, when that well-taught dame
    Had her cue given her to cry out a rape.
BONARIO: O most laid impudence! Fathers—
3RD AVOCATORE: Sir, be silent;
    You had your hearing frce, so must they theirs.
2ND AVOCATORE: I do begin to doubt th' imposture
        here.
4TH AVOCATORE: This woman has too many moods.
VOLTORE: Grave fathers,
    She is a creature of a most professed
    And prostituted lewdness.
CORVINO: Most impetuous,
    Unsatisfied, grave fathers!
VOLTORE: May her feignings
    Not take your wisdoms; but this day she baited
    A stranger, a grave knight, with her loose eyes
    And more lascivious kisses. This man saw 'em
    Together on the water in a gondola.
MOSCA: Here is the lady herself, that saw 'em too,

Without; who then had in the open streets
Pursued them, but for saving her knight's honour.
1ST AVOCATORE: Produce that lady.
2ND AVOCATORE: Let her come. [*Exit* Mosca]
4TH AVOCATORE: These things,
They strike with wonder!
3RD AVOCATORE: I am turned a stone!

Re-enter Mosca *with* Lady Wouldbe.
MOSCA: Be resolute, madam.
LADY WOULDBE: Ay, this same is she.—
Out, thou chameleon harlot! now thine eyes
Vie tears with the hyena. Dar'st thou look
Upon my wrongèd face?—I cry your pardons.
I fear I have forgettingly transgressed
Against the dignity of the court——
2ND AVOCATORE: No, madam,
LADY WOULDBE: And been exorbitant——
4TH AVOCATORE: You have not, lady,
These proofs are strong.
LADY WOULDBE: Surely, I had no purpose
To scandalize your honours, or my sex's.
3RD AVOCATORE: We do believe it.
LADY WOULDBE: Surely you may believe it.
2ND AVOCATORE: Madam, we do.
LADY WOULDBE: Indeed you may, my breeding
Is not so coarse——
4TH AVOCATORE: We know it.
LADY WOULDBE: To offend
With pertinacy——
3RD AVOCATORE: Lady——
LADY WOULDBE: Such a presence!
No surely.
1ST AVOCATORE: We well think it.
LADY WOULDBE: You may think it.
1ST AVOCATORE: Let her o'ercome.—What witnesses
have you,
To make good your report?
BONARIO: Our consciences.
CELIA: And Heaven, that never fails the innocent.
4TH AVOCATORE: These are no testimonies.
BONARIO: Not in your courts,
Where multitude and clamour overcomes.
1ST AVOCATORE: Nay, then you do wax insolent.

Volpone *is brought in, as impotent.*
VOLTORE: Here, here,
The testimony comes that will convince,
And put to utter dumbness their bold tongues!
See here, grave fathers, here's the ravisher,
The rider on men's wives, the great impostor,
The grand voluptuary! Do you not think
These limbs should affect venery? or these eyes
Covet a concubine? Pray you mark these hands;
Are they not fit to stroke a lady's breasts?
Perhaps he doth dissemble!
BONARIO: So he does.
VOLTORE: Would you ha' him tortured?
BONARIO: I would have him proved.

VOLTORE: Best try him then with goads, or burning
irons;
Put him to the strappado. I have heard
The rack hath cured the gout—faith, give it him,
And help him of a malady; be courteous.
I'll undertake, before these honoured fathers,
He shall have yet as many left diseases,
As she has known adulterers, or thou strumpets.
O my most equal hearers, if these deeds,
Acts of this bold and most exorbitant strain,
May pass with sufferance, what one citizen
But owes the forfeit of his life, yea, fame,
To him that dares traduce him? Which of you
Are safe, my honoured fathers? I would ask,
With leave of your grave fatherhoods, if their plot
Have any face or colour like to truth?
Or if, unto the dullest nostril here,
It smell not rank, and most abhorrèd slander?
I crave your care of this good gentleman,
Whose life is much endangered by their fable;
And as for them, I will conclude with this:
That vicious persons, when they're hot, and fleshed
In impious acts, their constancy abounds.
Damned deeds are done with greatest confidence.
1ST AVOCATORE: Take 'em to custody, and sever them.
2ND AVOCATORE: 'Tis pity two such prodigies should
live.
1ST AVOCATORE: Let the old gentleman be returned
with care.   [*Exeunt* Officers *with* Volpone]
I'm sorry our credulity hath wronged him.
4TH AVOCATORE: These are two creatures!
3RD AVOCATORE: I have an earthquake in me!
2ND AVOCATORE: Their shame, even in their cradles,
fled their faces.
4TH AVOCATORE: You've done a worthy service to the
state, sir,
In their discovery.
1ST AVOCATORE: You shall hear ere night
What punishment the court decrees upon 'em.
[*Exeunt* Avocatori, Notario, *and* Commendatori
with Bonario *and* Celia]
VOLTORE: We thank your fatherhoods.—How like
you it?
MOSCA: Rare.
I'd ha' your tongue, sir, tipped with gold for this;
I'd ha' you be the heir to the whole city;
The earth I'd have want men, ere you want living.
They're bound to erect your statue in Saint
Mark's.—
Signior Corvino, I would have you go
And show yourself, that you have conquered.
CORVINO: Yes.
MOSCA: It was much better that you should profess
Yourself a cuckold thus, than that the other
Should have been proved.
CORVINO: Nay, I considered that.
Now it is her fault.
MOSCA: Then it had been yours.
CORVINO: True. I do doubt this advocate still.

MOSCA: I' faith,
You need not; I dare ease you of that care.
CORVINO: I trust thee, Mosca.   [*Exit*]
MOSCA: As your own soul, sir.
CORBACCIO: Mosca!
MOSCA: Now for your business, sir.
CORBACCIO: How! ha' you business?
MOSCA: Yes, yours, sir.
CORBACCIO: O, none else.
MOSCA: None else, not I.
CORBACCIO: Be careful, then.
MOSCA: Rest you with both your eyes, sir.
CORBACCIO: Dispatch it.
MOSCA: Instantly.
CORBACCIO: And look that all
  Whatever be put in, jewels, plate, moneys,
  Household stuff, bedding, curtains.
MOSCA: Curtain-rings, sir;
  Only the advocate's fee must be deducted.
CORBACCIO: I'll pay him now; you'll be too prodigal.
MOSCA: Sir, I must tender it.
CORBACCIO: Two sequines is well?
MOSCA: No, six, sir.
CORBACCIO: 'Tis too much.
MOSCA: He talked a great while,
  You must consider that, sir.
CORBACCIO: Well, there's three——
MOSCA: I'll give it him.
CORBACCIO: Do so, and there's for thee.
                                             [*Exit*]
MOSCA: Bountiful bones! What horrid, strange of-
    fence
  Did he commit 'gainst nature, in his youth,
  Worthy this age?—You see, sir, how I work
  Unto your ends; take you no notice.
VOLTORE: No,
  I'll leave you.   [*Exit*]
MOSCA: All is yours, the devil and all,
  Good advocate!—Madam, I'll bring you home.
LADY WOULDBE: No, I'll go see your patron.
MOSCA: That you shall not.
  I'll tell you why: my purpose is to urge
  My patron to reform his will, and for
  The zeal you've shown today, whereas before
  You were but third or fourth, you shall be now
  Put in the first; which would appear as begged
  If you were present. Therefore——
LADY WOULDBE: You shall sway me.
                                          [*Exeunt*]

Act V

SCENE 1: *Volpone's house*

Enter Volpone.
VOLPONE: Well, I am here, and all this brunt is past.
  I ne'er was in dislike with my disguise
  Till this fled moment. Here 'twas good, in private;

But in your public—Cavè, whilst I breathe.
'Fore God, my left leg 'gan to have the cramp,
And I apprehended straight some power had struck
    me
With a dead palsy. Well, I must be merry,
And shake it off. A many of these fears
Would put me into some villainous disease,
Should they come thick upon me. I'll prevent 'em.
Give me a bowl of lusty wine, to fright
This humour from my heart. [*Drinks*] Hum, hum,
    hum!
'Tis almost gone already; I shall conquer.
Any device, now, of rare, ingenious knavery,
That would possess me with a violent laughter,
Would make me up again. [*Drinks again*] So, so,
    so, so!
This heat is life; 'tis blood by this time!—Mosca!

Enter Mosca.
MOSCA: How now, sir! does the day look clear again?
  Are we recovered, and wrought out of error,
  Into our way, to see our path before us?
  Is our trade free once more?
VOLPONE: Exquisite Mosca!
MOSCA: Was it not carried learnedly?
VOLPONE: And stoutly.
  Good wits are greatest in extremities.
MOSCA: It were a folly beyond thought, to trust
  Any grand act unto a cowardly spirit.
  You are not taken with it enough, methinks.
VOLPONE: O, more than if I had enjoyed the wench.
  The pleasure of all womankind's not like it.
MOSCA: Why, now you speak, sir! We must here be
    fixed;
  Here we must rest. This is our masterpiece;
  We cannot think to go beyond this.
VOLPONE: True,
  Th'ast played thy prize, my precious Mosca.
MOSCA: Nay, sir,
  To gull the court——
VOLPONE: And quite divert the torrent
  Upon the innocent.
MOSCA: Yes, and to make
  So rare a music out of discords——
VOLPONE: Right.
  That yet to me's the strangest; how th'ast borne it!
  That these, being so divided 'mongst themselves,
  Should not scent somewhat, or in me or thee,
  Or doubt their own side.
MOSCA: True, they will not see't.
  Too much light blinds 'em, I think. Each of 'em
  Is so possessed and stuffed with his own hopes
  That anything unto the contrary,
  Never so true, or never so apparent,
  Never so palpable, they will resist it——
VOLPONE: Like a temptation of the devil.
MOSCA: Right, sir.
  Merchants may talk of trade, and your great
    signiors

Of land that yields well; but if Italy
Have any glebe more fruitful than these fellows,
I am deceived. Did not your advocate rare?
VOLPONE: O—'My most honoured fathers, my grave
  fathers,
Under correction of your fatherhoods,
What face of truth is here? If these strange deeds
May pass, most honoured fathers'—I had much
 ado
To forbear laughing.
MOSCA: 'T seemed to me you sweat, sir.
VOLPONE: In troth, I did a little.
MOSCA: But confess, sir,
Were you not daunted?
VOLPONE: In good faith, I was
A little in a mist, but not dejected;
Never, but still myself.
MOSCA: I think it, sir.
Now, so truth help me, I must needs say this, sir,
And out of conscience for your advocate:
He 's taken pains, in faith, sir, and deserved,
In my poor judgment, I speak it under favour,
Not to contrary you, sir, very richly—
Well—to be cozened.
VOLPONE: Troth, and I think so too,
By that I heard him in the latter end.
MOSCA: O, but before, sir, had you heard him first
Draw it to certain heads, then aggravate,
Then use his vehement figures—I looked still
When he would shift a shirt; and doing this
Out of pure love, no hope of gain——
VOLPONE: 'Tis right.
I cannot answer him, Mosca, as I would,
Not yet; but for thy sake, at thy entreaty,
I will begin ev'n now—to vex 'em all,
This very instant.
MOSCA: Good, sir.
VOLPONE: Call the dwarf
And eunuch forth.
MOSCA: Castrone! Nano!

Enter Castrone *and* Nano.
NANO: Here.
VOLPONE: Shall we have a jig now?
MOSCA: What you please, sir.
VOLPONE: Go,
Straight give out about the streets, you two,
That I am dead; do it with constancy,
Sadly, do you hear? Impute it to the grief
Of this late slander. [*Exeunt* Castrone *and* Nano]
MOSCA: What do you mean, sir?
VOLPONE: O,
I shall have instantly my vulture, crow,
Raven, come flying hither, on the news,
To peck for carrion, my she-wolf and all,
Greedy and full of expectation——
MOSCA: And then to have it ravished from their
  mouths?
VOLPONE: 'Tis true. I will ha' thee put on a gown,

And take upon thee as thou wert mine heir;
Show 'em a will. Open that chest, and reach
Forth one of those that has the blanks. I'll straight
Put in thy name.
MOSCA: It will be rare, sir.
VOLPONE: Ay,
When they e'en gape, and find themselves de-
 luded——
MOSCA: Yes.
VOLPONE: And thou use them scurvily! Dispatch,
Get on thy gown.
MOSCA: But what, sir, if they ask
After the body?
VOLPONE: Say it was corrupted.
MOSCA: I'll say it stunk, sir; and was fain t' have it
Coffined up instantly, and sent away.
VOLPONE: Anything, what thou wilt. Hold, here's my
 will.
Get thee a cap, a count-book, pen and ink,
Papers afore thee; sit as thou wert taking
An inventory of parcels. I'll get up
Behind the curtain, on a stool, and hearken;
Sometime peep over, see how they do look,
With what degrees their blood doth leave their
 faces.
O, 'twill afford me a rare meal of laughter!
MOSCA: Your advocate will turn stark dull upon it.
VOLPONE: It will take off his oratory's edge.
MOSCA: But your clarissimo, old round-back, he
Will crump you like a hog-louse with the touch.
VOLPONE: And what Corvino?
MOSCA: O sir, look for him
Tomorrow morning, with a rope and dagger,
To visit all the streets; he must run mad.
My lady too, that came into the court,
To bear false witness for your worship——
VOLPONE: Yes,
And kissed me 'fore the fathers, when my face
Flowed all with oils——
MOSCA: And sweat, sir. Why, your gold
Is such another med'cine, it dries up
All those offensive savours! It transforms
The most deformèd, and restores 'em lovely
As 'twere the strange poetical girl. Jove
Could not invent t' himself a shroud more subtle
To pass Acrisius' guards. It is the thing
Makes all the world her grace, her youth, her
 beauty.
VOLPONE: I think she loves me.
MOSCA: Who? the lady, sir?
She's jealous of you.
VOLPONE: Dost thou say so?
MOSCA: Hark,
There's some already.
VOLPONE: Look.
MOSCA: It is the vulture;
He has the quickest scent.
VOLPONE: I'll to my place,
Thou to thy posture.

MOSCA: I am set.
VOLPONE: But, Mosca,
Play the artificer, now. torture 'em rarely.

Enter Voltore.

VOLPONE: How now, my Mosca?
MOSCA [*Writing*]   'Turkey carpets, nine——'
VOLTORE: Taking an inventory? that is well.
MOSCA: 'Two suits of bedding, tissue——'
VOLTORE: Where's the will?
Let me read that the while.

Enter Servitori *with* Corbaccio *in a chair.*

CORBACCIO: So, set me down,
And get you home.   [*Exeunt* Servitori]
VOLTORE: Is he come now, to trouble us?
MOSCA: 'Of cloth of gold, two more——'
CORBACCIO: Is it done, Mosca?
MOSCA: 'Of several velvets, eight——'
VOLTORE: I like his care.
CORBACCIO: Dost thou not hear?

Enter Corvino.

CORVINO: Ha! is the hour come, Mosca?
VOLPONE. [*Peeps from behind a traverse*] Ay, now
they muster.
CORVINO: What does the advocate here,
Or this Corbaccio?
CORBACCIO: What do these here?

Enter Lady Wouldbe.

LADY WOULDBE: Mosca!
Is his thread spun?
MOSCA: 'Eight chests of linen——'
VOLPONE: —O,
My fine Dame Wouldbe, too!
CORVINO: Mosca, the will,
That I may show it these, and rid 'em hence.
MOSCA: 'Six chests of diaper, four of damask—'
There.
CORBACCIO: Is that the will?
MOSCA: 'Down-beds, and bolsters——'
VOLPONE: —Rare!
Be busy still. Now they begin to flutter;
They never think of me. Look, see, see, see!
How their swift eyes run over the long deed,
Unto the name, and to the legacies,
What is bequeathed them there——
MOSCA: 'Ten suits of hangings——'
VOLPONE: —Ay, i' their garters, Mosca. Now their
hopes
Are at the gasp.
VOLTORE: Mosca the heir!
CORBACCIO: What's that?
VOLPONE: —My advocate is dumb; look to my mer-
chant,
He has heard of some strange storm, a ship is lost,
He faints; my lady will swoon. Old glazen-eyes
He hath not reached his despair yet.

CORBACCIO: All these
Are out of hope; I'm sure the man.
CORVINO: But, Mosca——
MOSCA: 'Two cabinets——'
CORVINO: Is this in earnest?
MOSCA: 'One
Of ebony——'
CORVINO: Or do you but delude me?
MOSCA: 'The other, mother of pearl'—I am very busy.
Good faith, it is a fortune thrown upon me——
'Item, one salt of agate'—not my seeking.
LADY WOULDBE: Do you hear, sir?
MOSCA: 'A perfumed box'—Pray you forbear,
You see I'm troubled—'made of an onyx——'
LADY WOULDBE: How!
MOSCA: Tomorrow or next day, I shall be at leisure
To talk with you all.
CORVINO: Is this my large hope's issue?
LADY WOULDBE: Sir, I must have a fairer answer.
MOSCA: Madam!
Marry, and shall: pray you, fairly quit my house.
Nay, raise no tempest with your looks; but hark
you,
Remember what your ladyship offered me
To put you in an heir; go to, think on 't;
And what you said e'en your best madams did
For maintenance, and why not you? Enough.
Go home, and use the poor Sir Poll, your knight,
well,
For fear I tell some riddles. Go, be melancholic.
                              [*Exit* Lady Wouldbe]
VOLPONE: —O my fine devil!
CORVINO: Mosca, pray you a word.
MOSCA: Lord! will not you take your dispatch hence
yet?
Methinks of all you should have been th' example.
Why should you stay here? with what thought?
what promise?
Hear you, do you not know I know you an ass,
And that you would most fain have been a wit-
tol
If fortune would have let you? that you are
A declared cuckold, on good terms? This pearl,
You'll say, was yours? right. This diamond?
I'll not deny't, but thank you. Much here else?
It may be so. Why, think that these good works
May help to hide your bad. I'll not betray you,
Although you be but extraordinary,
And have it only in title, it sufficeth.
Go home, be melancholic too, or mad.
                              [*Exit* Corvino]
VOLPONE: —Rare Mosca! how his villainy becomes
him!
VOLTORE: Certain, he doth delude all these for me.
CORBACCIO: Mosca the heir?
VOLPONE: O, his four eyes have found it!
CORBACCIO: I am cozened, cheated, by a parasite
slave!
Harlot, th'ast gulled me.

MOSCA: Yes, sir. Stop your mouth,
  Or I shall draw the only tooth is left.
  Are not you he, that filthy, covetous wretch,
  With the three legs, that here, in hope of prey,
  Have, any time this three year, snuffed about,
  With your most grov'ling nose; and would have
      hired
  Me to the pois'ning of my patron, sir?
  Are not you he that have today in court
  Professed the disinheriting of your son?
  Perjured yourself? Go home, and die, and stink;
  If you but croak a syllable, all comes out.
  Away, and call your porters! [*Exit* Corbaccio] Go,
      go, stink.
VOLPONE: —Excellent varlet!
VOLTORE: Now, my faithful Mosca,
  I find thy constancy——
MOSCA: Sir!
VOLTORE: Sincere.
MOSCA: 'A table
  Of porphyry'—I mar'l you'll be thus troublesome.
VOLTORE: Nay, leave off now, they are gone.
MOSCA: Why, who are you?
  What! who did send for you? O, cry you mercy,
  Reverend sir! Good faith, I am grieved for you,
  That any chance of mine should thus defeat
  Your—I must needs say—most deserving travails.
  But I protest, sir, it was cast upon me,
  And I could almost wish to be without it,
  But that the will o' th' dead must be observed.
  Marry, my joy is that you need it not;
  You have a gift, sir,—thank your education—
  Will never let you want, while there are men
  And malice to breed causes. Would I had
  But half the like, for all my fortune, sir!
  If I have any suits,—as I do hope,
  Things being so easy and direct, I shall not—
  I will make bold with your obstreperous aid,
  Conceive me, for your fee, sir. In meantime,
  You that have so much law, I know ha' the con-
      science
  Not to be covetous of what is mine.
  Good sir, I thank you for my plate; 'twill help
  To set up a young man. Good faith, you look
  As you were costive; best go home and purge, sir.
                                      [*Exit* Voltore]
VOLPONE: Bid him eat lettuce well! My witty mis-
      chief,
  Let me embrace thee. O that I could now
  Transform thee to a Venus—Mosca, go,
  Straight take my habit of clarissimo,
  And walk the streets; be seen, torment 'em more.
  We must pursue, as well as plot. Who would
  Have lost this feast?
MOSCA: I doubt it will lose them.
VOLPONE: O, my recovery shall recover all.
  That I could now but think on some disguise
  To meet 'em in, and ask 'em questions;
  How I would vex 'em still at every turn!

MOSCA: Sir, I can fit you.
VOLPONE: Canst thou?
MOSCA: Yes, I know
  One o' th' commendatori, sir, so like you,
  Him will I straight make drunk, and bring you his
      habit:
VOLPONE: A rare disguise, and answering thy brain!
  O, I will be a sharp disease unto 'em.
MOSCA: Sir, you must look for curses——
VOLPONE: Till they burst;
  The fox fares ever best when he is curst.   [*Exeunt*]

SCENE 2: *Sir Politic's lodging*

  Enter Peregrine *disguised, and three* Mercatori.
PEREGRINE: Am I enough disguised?
1ST MERCATORE: I warrant you.
PEREGRINE: All my ambition is to fright him only.
2ND MERCATORE: If you could ship him away, 'twere
      excellent.
3RD MERCATORE: To Zant, or to Aleppo!
PEREGRINE: Yes, and ha' his
  Adventures put i' th' book of voyages,
  And his gulled story registered for truth!
  Well, gentlemen, when I am in a while,
  And that you think us warm in our discourse,
  Know your approaches.
1ST MERCATORE: Trust it to our care.
                                [*Exeunt* Mercatori]
  Enter Woman.
PEREGRINE: Save you, fair lady! Is Sir Poll within?
WOMAN: I do not know, sir.
PEREGRINE: Pray you say unto him,
  Here is a merchant, upon urgent business.
  Desires to speak with him.
WOMAN: I will see, sir.   [*Exit*]
PEREGRINE: Pray you.
  I see the family is all female here.

  Re-enter Woman.
WOMAN: He says, sir, he has weighty affairs of state,
  That now require him whole; some other time
  You may possess him.
PEREGRINE: Pray you say again,
  If those require him whole, these will exact him,
  Whereof I bring him tidings. [*Exit* Woman] What
      might be
  His grave affair of state now? how to make
  Bolognian sausages here in Venice, sparing
  One o' th' ingredients.

  Re-enter Woman.
WOMAN: Sir, he says he knows
  By your word 'tidings' that you are no statesman,
  And therefore wills you stay.
PEREGRINE: Sweet, pray you return him,
  I have not read so many proclamations,

And studied them for words, as he has done,
But—Here he deigns to come.

Enter Sir Politic.

SIR POLITIC: Sir, I must crave
Your courteous pardon. There hath chanced today
Unkind disaster 'twixt my lady and me,
And I was penning my apology,
To give her satisfaction, as you came now.

PEREGRINE: Sir, I am grieved I bring you worse disaster:
The gentleman you met at th' port today,
That told you he was newly arrived——

SIR POLITIC: Ay, was
A fugitive punk?

PEREGRINE: No, sir, a spy set on you;
And he has made relation to the Senate,
That you professed to him, to have a plot
To sell the state of Venice to the Turk.

SIR POLITIC: O me!

PEREGRINE: For which warrants are signed by
this time,
To apprehend you, and to search your study
For papers——

SIR POLITIC: Alas, sir, I have none but notes
Drawn out of play-books——

PEREGRINE: All the better, sir.

SIR POLITIC: And some essays. What shall I do?

PEREGRINE: Sir, best
Convey yourself into a sugar-chest,
Or, if you could lie round, a frail were rare;
And I could send you aboard.

SIR POLITIC: Sir, I but talked so,
For discourse sake merely.   [*They knock without*]

PEREGRINE: Hark! they are there.

SIR POLITIC: I am a wretch, a wretch!

PEREGRINE: What will you do, sir?
Ha' you ne'er a currant-butt to leap into?
They'll put you to the rack; you must be sudden.

SIR POLITIC: Sir, I have an engine——

3RD MERCHANT: Sir Politic Wouldbe!

2ND MERCHANT: Where is he?

SIR POLITIC: That I have thought upon beforetime.

PEREGRINE: What is it?

SIR POLITIC: I shall ne'er endure the torture!—
Marry, it is, sir, of a tortoise-shell,
Fitted for these extremities. Pray you, sir, help me.
Here I've a place, sir, to put back my legs;
Please you to lay it on, sir. With this cap,
And my black gloves, I'll lie, sir, like a tortoise,
Till they are gone.

PEREGRINE: And call you this an engine?

SIR POLITIC: Mine own device——Good sir, bid my
wife's women
To burn my papers.

Re-enter three Mercatori.

1ST MERCATORE: Where's he hid?

3RD MERCATORE: We must.
And will sure find him.

2ND MERCATORE: Which is his study?

1ST MERCATORE: What
Are you, sir?

PEREGRINE: I'm a merchant, that came here
To look upon this tortoise.

3RD MERCATORE: How!

1ST MERCATORE: Saint Mark!
What beast is this?

PEREGRINE: It is a fish.

2ND MERCATORE: Come out here!

PEREGRINE: Nay, you may strike him, sir, and tread
upon him.
He'll bear a cart.

1ST MERCATORE: What, to run over him?

PEREGRINE: Yes.

3RD MERCATORE: Let's jump upon him.

2ND MERCATORE: Can he not go?

PEREGRINE: He creeps, sir.

1ST MERCATORE: Let's see him creep.

PEREGRINE: No, good sir, you will hurt him.

2ND MERCATORE: Heart, I'll see him creep, or prick
his guts!

3RD MERCATORE: Come out here!

PEREGRINE: Pray you, sir.—Creep a little.

1ST MERCATORE: Forth.

2ND MERCATORE: Yet further.

PEREGRINE: Good sir!—Creep.

2ND MERCATORE: We'll see his legs.
   [*They pull off the shell and discover* Sir Politic]

3RD MERCATORE: God's so', he has garters!

1ST MERCATORE: Ay, and gloves!

2ND MERCATORE: Is this
Your fearful tortoise?

PEREGRINE: Now, Sir Poll, we are even;
For your next project I shall be prepared.
I am sorry for the funeral of your notes, sir.

1ST MERCATORE: 'Twere a rare motion to be seen in
Fleet Street.

2ND MERCATORE: Ay, i' the term.

1ST MERCATORE: Or Smithfield, in the fair.

3RD MERCATORE: Methinks 'tis but a melancholic
sight.

PEREGRINE: Farewell, most politic tortoise!
              [*Exeunt* Peregrine *and* Mercatori]

SIR POLITIC: Where's my lady?
Knows she of this?

WOMAN: I know not, sir.

SIR POLITIC: Inquire.—
O, I shall be the fable of all feasts,
The freight of the gazetti, ship-boys' tale,
And, which is worst, even talk for ordinaries.

WOMAN: My lady's come most melancholic home,
And says, sir, she will straight to sea, for physic.

SIR POLITIC: And I, to shun this place and clime forever,
Creeping with house on back, and think it well

To shrink my poor head in my politic shell.

[*Exeunt*]

SCENE 3: *Volpone's house*

Enter Volpone *in the habit of a commendatore, and* Mosca *in that of a clarissimo.*

VOLPONE: Am I then like him?

MOSCA: O sir, you are he;
No man can sever you.

VOLPONE: Good.

MOSCA: But what am I?

VOLPONE: 'Fore Heav'n, a brave clarissimo, thou becom'st it!
Pity thou wert not born one.

MOSCA: —If I hold
My made one, 'twill be well.

VOLPONE: I'll go and see
What news first at the court. [*Exit*]

MOSCA: Do so.—My fox
Is out on his hole, and ere he shall re-enter,
I'll make him languish in his borrowed case,
Except he come to composition with me.—
Androgyno, Castrone, Nano!

Enter Androgyno, Castrone, *and* Nano.

ALL: Here.

MOSCA: Go, recreate yourselves abroad; go, sport.

[*Exeunt*]

So, now I have the keys, and am possessed.
Since he will needs be dead afore his time,
I'll bury him or gain by him. I'm his heir,
And so will keep me, till he share at least.
To cozen him of all were but a cheat
Well placed; no man would construe it a sin.
Let his sport pay for 't. This is called the fox-trap.

[*Exit*]

SCENE 4: *A street*

Enter Corbaccio *and* Corvino.

CORBACCIO: They say the court is set.

CORVINO: We must maintain
Our first tale good, for both our reputations.

CORBACCIO: Why, mine's no tale! my son would there have killed me.

CORVINO: That's true, I had forgot.—Mine is, I'm sure.—
But for your will, sir.

CORBACCIO: Ay, I'll come upon him
For that hereafter, now his patron's dead.

Enter Volpone.

VOLPONE: Signior Corvino! and Corbaccio! sir,
Much joy unto you.

CORVINO: Of what?

VOLPONE: The sudden good
Dropped down upon you——

CORBACCIO: Where?

VOLPONE: And none knows how,
From old Volpone, sir.

CORBACCIO: Out, arrant knave!

VOLPONE: Let not your too much wealth, sir, make you furious.

CORBACCIO: Away, thou varlet.

VOLPONE: Why, sir?

CORBACCIO: Dost thou mock me?

VOLPONE: You mock the world, sir; did you not change wills?

CORBACCIO: Out, harlot!

VOLPONE: O! belike you are the man,
Signior Corvino? Faith, you carry it well;
You grow not mad withal. I love your spirit.
You are not over-leavened with your fortune.
You should ha' some would swell now, like a wine-vat,
With such an autumn—Did he gi' you all, sir?

CORVINO: Avoid, you rascal.

VOLPONE: Troth, your wife has shown
Herself a very woman! But you are well,
You need not care; you have a good estate,
To bear it out, sir, better by this chance—
Except Corbaccio have a share.

CORBACCIO: Hence, varlet.

VOLPONE: You will not be a'known, sir? Why, 'tis wise.
Thus do all gamesters, at all games, dissemble.
No man will seem to win. [*Exeunt* Corvino *and* Corbaccio] Here comes my vulture,
Heaving his beak up i' the air, and snuffing.

Enter Voltore.

VOLTORE: Outstripped thus, by a parasite! a slave,
Would run on errands, and make legs for crumbs!
Well, what I'll do——

VOLPONE: The court stays for your worship.
I e'en rejoice, sir, at your worship's happiness,
And that it fell into so learnèd hands,
That understand the fingering——

VOLTORE: What do you mean?

VOLPONE: I mean to be a suitor to your worship,
For the small tenement, out of reparations,
That, at the end of your long row of houses,
By the Pescheria—it was, in Volpone's time,
Your predecessor, ere he grew diseased,
A handsome, pretty, customed bawdy-house
As any was in Venice, none dispraised;
But fell with him. His body and that house
Decayed together.

VOLTORE: Come, sir, leave your prating.

VOLPONE: Why, if your worship give me but your hand,
That I may ha' the refusal, I have done.
'Tis a mere toy to you, sir, candle-rents.
As your learnèd worship knows——

VOLTORE: What do I know?

VOLPONE: Marry, no end o' your wealth, sir, God decrease it!

VOLTORE: Mistaking knave! what, mock'st thou my
    misfortune?   [*Exit*]
VOLPONE: His blessing on your heart, sir; would
    'twere more!
    Now to my first again, at the next corner.

Enter Corbaccio *and* Corvino, Mosca *passing over
    the stage.*
CORBACCIO: See, in our habit! see the impudent var-
    let!
CORVINO: That I could shoot mine eyes at him, like
    gun-stones!
VOLPONE: But is this true, sir, of the parasite?
CORBACCIO: Again, t' afflict us? monster!
VOLPONE: In good faith, sir,
    I'm heartily grieved, a beard of your grave length
    Should be so over-reached. I never brooked
    That parasite's hair; methought his nose should
        cozen.
    There still was somewhat in his look, did promise
    The bane of a clarissimo.
CORBACCIO: Knave——
VOLPONE: Methinks
    Yet you, that are so traded i' the world,
    A witty merchant, the fine bird, Corvino,
    That have such moral emblems on your name,
    Should not have sung your shame; and dropped
        your cheese,
    To let the fox laugh at your emptiness.
CORVINO: Sirrah, you think the privilege of the place,
    And your red saucy cap, that seems to me
    Nailed to your jolt-head with those two sequines,
    Can warrant your abuses. Come you hither.
    You shall perceive, sir, I dare beat you. Approach.
VOLPONE: No haste, sir, I do know your valour well,
    Since you durst publish what you are, sir.
CORVINO: Tarry,
    I'd speak with you.
VOLPONE: Sir, sir, another time——
CORVINO: Nay, now.
VOLPONE: O God, sir! I were a wise man,
    Would stand the fury of a distracted cuckold.
                            [*Mosca walks by them*]
CORBACCIO: What, come again!
VOLPONE: —Upon 'em, Mosca; save me.
CORBACCIO: The air's infected where he breathes.
CORVINO: Let's fly him.
                    [*Exeunt* Corvino *and* Corbaccio]
VOLPONE: Excellent basilisk! turn upon the vulture.

Enter Voltore.
VOLTORE: Well, flesh-fly, it is summer with you now;
    Your winter will come on.
MOSCA: Good advocate,
    Prithee not rail, nor threaten out of place thus;
    Thou'lt make a solecism, as Madam says.
    Get you a biggen more; your brain breaks loose.
                                            [*Exit*]

VOLTORE: Well, sir.
VOLPONE: Would you ha' me beat the in-
    solent slave?
    Throw dirt upon his first good clothes?
VOLTORE: —This same
    Is doubtless some familiar!
VOLPONE: Sir, the court,
    In troth, stays for you. I am mad, a mule
    That never read Justinian, should get up,
    And ride an advocate. Had you no quirk
    To avoid gullage, sir, by such a creature?
    I hope you do but jest; he has not done 't;
    This's but confederacy to blind the rest.
    You are the heir?
VOLTORE: A strange, officious,
    Troublesome knave! thou dost torment me.
VOLPONE: I know——
    It cannot be, sir, that you should be cozened;
    'Tis not within the wit of man to do it.
    You are so wise, so prudent; and 'tis fit
    That wealth and wisdom still should go together.
                                            [*Exeunt*]

SCENE 5: *The Scrutineo*

Enter four Avocatori, Notario, Bonario, Celia,
    Corbaccio, Corvino, Commendatori, &c.
1ST AVOCATORE: Are all the parties here?
NOTARIO: All but the advocate.
2ND AVOCATORE: And here he comes.

Enter Voltore *and* Volpone.
1ST AVOCATORE: Then bring 'em forth to sentence.
VOLTORE: O my most honoured fathers, let your
    mercy
    Once win upon your justice, to forgive——
    I am distracted——
VOLPONE: —What will he do now?
VOLTORE: O,
    I know not which t' address myself to first;
    Whether your fatherhoods, or these innocents——
CORVINO: —Will he betray himself?
VOLTORE: Whom equally
    I have abused, out of most covetous ends——
CORVINO: The man is mad!
CORBACCIO: What's that?
CORVINO: He is possessed.
VOLTORE: For which, now struck in conscience, here
    I prostrate
    Myself at your offended feet, for pardon.
1ST, 2ND AVOCATORI: Arise.
CELIA: O Heaven, how just thou art!
VOLPONE: —I'm caught
    I' mine own noose——
CORVINO: —Be constant, sir; nought now
    Can help but impudence.
1ST AVOCATORE: Speak forward.
COMMENDATORE: Silence!

VOLTORE: It is not passion in me, reverend fathers,
  But only conscience, conscience, my good sires,
  That makes me now tell truth. That parasite,
  That knave, hath been the instrument of all.
1ST AVOCATORE: Where is that knave? fetch him.
VOLPONE: I go. [Exit]
CORVINO: Grave fathers,
  This man's distracted; he confessed it now.
  For, hoping to be old Volpone's heir,
  Who now is dead——
3RD AVOCATORE: How!
2ND AVOCATORE: Is Volpone dead?
CORVINO: Dead since, grave fathers.——
BONARIO: O sure vengeance!
1ST AVOCATORE: Stay,
  Then he was no deceiver.
VOLTORE: O, no, none;
  The parasite, grave fathers.
CORVINO: He does speak
  Out of mere envy, 'cause the servant's made
  The thing he gaped for. Please your fatherhoods,
  This is the truth; though I'll not justify
  The other, but he may be somewhere faulty.
VOLTORE: Ay, to your hopes, as well as mine, Cor-
  vino.
  But I'll use modesty. Pleaseth your wisdoms,
  To view these certain notes, and but confer them;
  As I hope favour, they shall speak clear truth.
CORVINO: The devil has entered him!
BONARIO: Or bides in you.
4TH AVOCATORE: We have done ill, by a public
  officer
  To send for him, if he be heir.
2ND AVOCATORE: For whom?
4TH AVOCATORE: Him that they call the parasite.
3RD AVOCATORE: 'Tis true,
  He is a man of great estate now left.
4TH AVOCATORE: ——Go you, and learn his name, and
  say the court
  Entreats his presence here, but to the clearing
  Of some few doubts.   [Exit Notario]
2ND AVOCATORE: This same's a labyrinth!
1ST AVOCATORE: Stand you unto your first report?
CORVINO: My state,
  My life, my fame——
BONARIO: Where is't?
CORVINO: Are at the stake.
1ST AVOCATORE: Is yours so too?
CORBACCIO: The advocate's a knave,
  And has a forkèd tongue——
2ND AVOCATORE: Speak to the point.
CORBACCIO: So is the parasite too.
1ST AVOCATORE: This is confusion.
VOLTORE: I do beseech your fatherhoods, read but
  those——
CORVINO: And credit nothing the false spirit hath
  writ.
  It cannot be but he's possessed, grave fathers.
                       [The scene closes]

SCENE 6: A street

  Enter Volpone.
VOLPONE: To make a snare for mine own neck! and
  run
  My head into it wilfully, with laughter!
  When I had newly 'scaped, was free and clear!
  Out of mere wantonness! O, the dull devil
  Was in this brain of mine when I devised it,
  And Mosca gave it second; he must now
  Help to sear up this vein, or we bleed dead.

  Enter Nano, Androgyno, and Castrone.
  How now! who let you loose? whither go you now?
  What, to buy gingerbread, or to drown kitlings?
NANO: Sir, Master Mosca called us out of doors,
  And bid us all go play, and took the keys.
ANDROGYNO: Yes.
VOLPONE: Did Master Mosca take the keys? Why, so!
  I'm farther in. These are my fine conceits!
  I must be merry, with a mischief to me!
  What a vile wretch was I, that could not bear
  My fortune soberly. I must ha' my crotchets
  And my conundrums!—Well, go you and seek
  him.—
  His meaning may be truer than my fear.—
  Bid him, he straight come to me to the court;
  Thither will I, and, if't be possible,
  Unscrew my advocate, upon new hopes.
  When I provoked him, then I lost myself.
                       [Exeunt]

SCENE 7: The Scrutineo

  Four Avocatori, Notario, Voltore, Bonario, Celia,
    Corbaccio, Corvino, &c., as before.
1ST AVOCATORE: These things can ne'er be reconciled.
  He here
  Professeth that the gentleman was wronged,
  And that the gentlewoman was brought thither,
  Forced by her husband, and there left.
VOLTORE: Most true.
CELIA: How ready is Heav'n to those that pray!
1ST AVOCATORE: But that
  Volpone would have ravished her, he holds
  Utterly false, knowing his impotence.
CORVINO: Grave fathers, he is possessed; again, I say,
  Possessed. Nay, if there be possession and
  Obsession, he has both.
3RD AVOCATORE: Here comes our officer.

  Enter Volpone.
VOLPONE: The parasite will straight be here, grave
  fathers.
4TH AVOCATORE: You might invent some other name,
  Sir Varlet.
3RD AVOCATORE: Did not the notary meet him?
VOLPONE: Not that I know.
4TH AVOCATORE: His coming will clear all.

2ND AVOCATORE: Yet it is misty.

VOLTORE: May't please your fatherhoods——

VOLPONE: [*Whispers to* Voltore] Sir, the parasite
    Willed me to tell you that his master lives;
    That you are still the man; your hopes the same;
    And this was only a jest——

VOLTORE: How?

VOLPONE: Sir, to try
    If you were firm, and how you stood affected.

VOLTORE: Art sure he lives?

VOLPONE: Do I live, sir?

VOLTORE: O me!
    I was too violent.

VOLPONE: Sir, you may redeem it:
    They said you were possessed; fall down, and seem
    so.
    I'll help to make it good. [Voltore *falls*] God bless
    the man!—
    Stop your wind hard, and swell—See, see, see, see!
    He vomits crooked pins! his eyes are set,
    Like a dead hare's hung in a poulter's shop!
    His mouth's running away! Do you see, signior?
    Now 'tis in his belly.

CORVINO: —Ay, the devil!

VOLPONE: Now in his throat.

CORVINO: —Ay, I perceive it plain.

VOLTORE: 'Twill out, 'twill out! stand clear. See where
    it flies,
    In shape of a blue toad, with a bat's wings!
    Do you not see it, sir?

CORBACCIO: What? I think I do.

CORVINO: —'Tis too manifest.

VOLTORE: Look! he comes t' himself!

VOLTORE: Where am I?

VOLPONE: Take good heart, the worst is past, sir.
    You are dispossessed.

1ST AVOCATORE: What accident is this?

2ND AVOCATORE: Sudden, and full of wonder!

3RD AVOCATORE: If he were
    Possessed, as it appears, all this is nothing.

CORVINO: He has been often subject to these fits.

1ST AVOCATORE: Show him that writing.—Do you
    know it, sir?

VOLPONE: —Deny it, sir, forswear it, know it not.

VOLTORE: Yes, I do know it well, it is my hand;
    But all that it contains is false.

BONARIO: O practice!

2ND AVOCATORE: What maze is this!

1ST AVOCATORE: Is he not guilty then,
    Whom you there name the parasite?

VOLTORE: Grave fathers,
    No more than his good patron, old Volpone.

4TH AVOCATORE: Why, he is dead.

VOLTORE: O, no, my honoured fathers,
    He lives——

1ST AVOCATORE: How! lives?

VOLTORE: Lives.

2ND AVOCATORE: This is subtler yet!

3RD AVOCATORE: You said he was dead.

VOLTORE: Never.

3RD AVOCATORE: You said so!

CORVINO: I heard so.

4TH AVOCATORE: Here comes the gentleman; make
    him way.

3RD AVOCATORE: A stool!   [*Enter* Mosca]

4TH AVOCATORE: —A proper man and, were Volpone
    dead,
    A fit match for my daughter.

3RD AVOCATORE: Give him way.

VOLPONE: —Mosca, I was almost lost; the advocate
    Had betrayed all; but now it is recovered.
    All's o' the hinge again—— Say I am living.

MOSCA: What busy knave is this?—Most reverend
    fathers,
    I sooner had attended your grave pleasures,
    But that my order for the funeral
    Of my dear patron did require me——

VOLPONE: —Mosca!

MOSCA: Whom I intend to bury like a gentleman.

VOLPONE: —Ay, quick, and cozen me of all.

2ND AVOCATORE: Still stranger!
    More intricate!

1ST AVOCATORE: And come about again!

4TH AVOCATORE: —It is a match, my daughter is be-
    stowed.

MOSCA: —Will you gi' me half?

VOLPONE: First I'll be hanged.

MOSCA: I know
    Your voice is good, cry not so loud.

1ST AVOCATORE: Demand.
    The advocate.—Sir, did not you affirm
    Volpone was alive?

VOLPONE: Yes, and he is;
    This gent'man told me so.—Thou shalt have half.

MOSCA: Whose drunkard is this same? speak, some
    that know him.
    I never saw his face.—I cannot now
    Afford it you so cheap.

VOLPONE: No?

1ST AVOCATORE: What say you?

VOLTORE: The officer told me.

VOLPONE: I did, grave fathers,
    And will maintain he lives, with mine own life,
    And that this creature told me.—I was born
    With all good stars my enemies!

MOSCA: Most grave fathers,
    If such an insolence as this must pass
    Upon me, I am silent; 'twas not this
    For which you sent, I hope.

2ND AVOCATORE: Take him away.

VOLPONE: —Mosca!

3RD AVOCATORE: Let him be whipped.

VOLPONE: —Wilt thou betray me?
    Cozen me?

3RD AVOCATORE: And taught to bear himself
    Toward a person of his rank.

4TH AVOCATORE: Away.

MOSCA: I humbly thank your fatherhoods.

VOLPONE: Soft, soft. Whipped!
And lose all that I have! If I confess,
It cannot be much more.
4TH AVOCATORE: Sir, are you married?
VOLPONE: —They'll be allied anon; I must be reso-
lute:
The fox shall here uncase.   [*Puts off his disguise*]
MOSCA: Patron!
VOLPONE: Nay, now
My ruins shall not come alone; your match
I'll hinder sure: my substance shall not glue you
Nor screw you into a family.
MOSCA: Why, patron!
VOLPONE: I am Volpone, and this is my knave;
This, his own knave; this, avarice's fool;
This, a chimera of wittol, fool, and knave.
And, reverend fathers, since we all can hope
Nought but a sentence, let's not now despair it.
You hear me brief.
CORVINO: May it please your fatherhoods——
COMMENDATORE: Silence!
1ST AVOCATORE: The knot is now undone by miracle.
2ND AVOCATORE: Nothing can be more clear.
3RD AVOCATORE: Or can more prove
These innocent.
1ST AVOCATORE: Give 'em their liberty.
BONARIO: Heaven could not long let such gross crimes
be hid.
2ND AVOCATORE: If this be held the highway to get
riches,
May I be poor!
3RD AVOCATORE: This's not the gain, but torment.
1ST AVOCATORE: These possess wealth, as sick men
possess fevers,
Which trulier may be said to possess them.
2ND AVOCATORE: Disrobe that parasite.
CORVINO, MOSCA: Most honoured fathers——
1ST AVOCATORE: Can you plead aught to stay the
course of justice?
If you can, speak.
CORVINO, VOLTORE: We beg favour.
CELIA: And mercy.
1ST AVOCATORE: You hurt your innocence, suing for
the guilty.—
Stand forth; and first the parasite.—You appear
T'have been the chiefest minister, if not plotter,
In all these lewd impostures; and now, lastly,
Have with your impudence abused the court,
And habit of a gentleman of Venice,
Being a fellow of no birth or blood;
For which our sentence is, first thou be whipped;
Then live perpetual prisoner in our galleys.
VOLPONE: I thank you for him.
MOSCA: Bane to thy wolfish nature!
1ST AVOCATORE: Deliver him to the Saffi.—Thou,
Volpone,

By blood and rank a gentleman, canst not fall
Under like censure; but our judgment on thee
Is that thy substance all be straight confiscate
To the hospital of the Incurabili.
And since the most was gotten by imposture,
By feigning lame, gout, palsy, and such diseases,
Thou art to lie in prison, cramped with irons,
Till thou be'st sick and lame indeed.—Remove
him.
VOLPONE: This is called mortifying of a fox.
1ST AVOCATORE: Thou, Voltore, to take away the
scandal,
Thou hast giv'n all worthy men of thy profession,
Art banished from their fellowship, and our
state.—
Corbaccio, bring him near!—We here possess
Thy son of all thy state, and confine thee
To the monastery of San Spirito;
Where, since thou knew'st not how to live well
here,
Thou shalt be learned to die well.
CORBACCIO: Ha! what said he?
COMMENDATORE: You shall know anon, sir.
1ST AVOCATORE: Thou, Corvino, shalt
Be straight embarked from thine own house, and
rowed
Round about Venice, through the Grand Canale,
Wearing a cap, with fair, long ass's ears
Instead of horns; and so to mount, a paper
Pinned on thy breast, to the Berlina—
CORVINO: Yes,
And have mine eyes beat out with stinking fish,
Bruised fruit, and rotten eggs—'Tis well. I'm glad
I shall not see my shame yet.
1ST AVOCATORE: And to expiate
Thy wrongs done to thy wife, thou art to send
her
Home to her father, with her dowry trebled.
And these are all your judgments——
ALL: Honoured fathers!
1ST AVOCATORE: Which may not be revoked. Now
you begin,
When crimes are done, and past, and to be pun-
ished,
To think what your crimes are.—Away with them!
Let all that see these vices thus rewarded,
Take heart, and love to study 'em. Mischiefs feed
Like beasts, till they be fat, and then they bleed.
[*Exeunt*]
Volpone *comes forward.*
The seasoning of a play is the applause.
Now, though the fox be punished by the laws,
He yet doth hope there is no suffering due,
For any fact which he hath done 'gainst you.
If there be, censure him; here he doubtful stands.
If not, fare jovially, and clap your hands.   [*Exit*]

The Man of Mode

by SIR GEORGE ETHEREGE
(1634?–1691?)

The Restoration has as literal a meaning for English comedy as it has for English kings; for it represents—along with the return of Charles II from exile—the reopening of the theaters. They had been shut down during the Civil War and kept shut under Cromwell; and a Puritanism that had put a ban on the stage as part of its condemnation of pleasure would have particularly condemned that most "frivolous" of stage forms, comedy. But with the most "frivolous" of English monarchs on the throne, all puritan and bluenosed restraints were quickly banished; and an England that for years had stifled its lustier impulses now gave unbridled rein to them. An age was opening of hard gay profligacy, when it was quite proper to sin, indeed quite priggish not to; when women were bold and even young girls pert; and when not the errant wife but the cuckold husband was the object of vilification. Or so at least did people ordain things in the theater; but in the theater they ordained, no less, that these things be done with style, and laced with wit, and cleanly starched with artifice.

The men who wrote for the Restoration theater, who created the only large body of English comedy that has homogeneity and lasting merit, were for the most part born with wit, endowed with style, and bred to a life of lustrous artifice—the life of the Court, all smiles and bows and duplicities. These playwrights were gentlemen and even lords; they were often rakes and sometimes fops; and the comedy they created reflects their general experience of life —though it reflects their temperaments, too, and the fashionable taste of the age. That taste is all but unique in rejecting a sentimental portrayal of human nature; in insisting on a worldly, indeed a selfish, basis for human behavior; and in commanding that sex occupy the central stage. In a leisure-class, anti-Puritan, pre-bourgeois society, it would inevitably occupy it.

So far as artificial comedy is concerned, the taste of the times had great value. For artificial comedy thrives on lack of heart, on all avoidance of emotionalism: it must treat social life as in some sense a game—as indeed, since both things rest on established rules and conventions, it is. Restoration playwrights, accustomed to the masks and mazes of Court life, were able to treat it so: and none more than Sir George Etherege. The first of the better known Restoration comedy writers to establish himself in the theater, Etherege brought to his best scenes, and to his one good play, The Man of Mode, a lightness, an airiness, a sense of a game well played, that none of his successors would quite equal. His finest scenes are pure foam; his Man of Mode, the absurd, affected Sir Fopling Flutter, hardly so much dances as floats through the play. And yet for all its froth, The Man of Mode—in the figure of its coldhearted rake, Dorimant, and the women he knows—strikes very close to life. In Dorimant's relations to Mrs. Loveit and Belinda, we have the sense of a real man, able to inspire real sexual love, to rouse real jealousy and cause real unhappiness. Etherege sounds here an inharmonious note, lets us glimpse the lees beneath the froth, feel the chill in the sunlit air: but just so, if he gets outside his proper orbit, he momentarily goes beyond it.

SIR GEORGE ETHEREGE

The Man of Mode

or, Sir Fopling Flutter

THE PERSONS OF THE PLAY

MR. DORIMANT
MR. MEDLEY
OLD BELLAIR
YOUNG BELLAIR
SIR FOPLING FLUTTER
Gentlemen

LADY TOWNLEY
EMILIA
MRS. LOVEIT
BELINDA
LADY WOODVIL
HARRIET, *her daughter*
Gentlewomen

PERT and BUSY, *waiting-women*
A SHOEMAKER
AN ORANGE-WOMAN
THREE SLOVENLY BULLIES
TWO CHAIRMEN
MR. SMIRK, *a parson*
HANDY, *a valet-de-chambre*
PAGES, FOOTMEN, ETC.

THE SCENE: *London*

Act I

SCENE 1: *A Dressing-room. A table covered with a toilet; clothes laid ready*

Enter Dorimant *in his gown and slippers, with a note in his hand made up, repeating verses.*

DORIMANT: Now for some ages had the pride of Spain
Made the sun shine on half the world in vain.

[*Then looking on the note*]

[*For* Mrs. Loveit] What a dull insipid thing is a *billet-doux* written in cold blood, after the heat of the business is over! It is a tax upon good-nature which I have here been labouring to pay, and have done it, but with as much regret as ever fanatic paid the Royal Aid or Church Duties. 'Twill have the same fate, I know, that all my notes to her have

had of late, 'twill not be thought kind enough. Faith, women are i' the right when they jealously examine our letters, for in them we always first discover our decay of passion.—— Hey! Who waits?

Enter Handy.

HANDY: Sir——
DORIMANT: Call a footman.
HANDY: None of 'em are come yet.
DORIMANT: Dogs! Will they ever lie snoring a-bed till noon?
HANDY: 'Tis all one, sir: if they're up, you indulge 'em so they're ever poaching after whores all the morning.
DORIMANT: Take notice henceforward, who's wanting in his duty, the next clap he gets, he shall rot for an example. What vermin are those chattering without?
HANDY: Foggy Nan the orange-woman and swearing Tom the shoemaker.
DORIMANT: Go; call in that overgrown jade with the flasket of guts before her; fruit is refreshing in a morning. [*Exit* Handy]

It is not that I love you less
Than when before your feet I lay.

Enter Orange-Woman *with* Handy.

How now, Double Tripe! what news do you bring?
ORANGE-WOMAN: News! Here's the best fruit has come to town t'year; gad, I was up before four o'clock this morning, and bought all the choice i' the market.
DORIMANT: The nasty refuse of your shop.
ORANGE-WOMAN: You need not make mouths at it; I assure you 'tis all culled ware.
DORIMANT: The citizens buy better on a holiday in their walk to Totnam.
ORANGE-WOMAN: Good or bad, tis all one; I never knew you commend anything. Lord! would the ladies had heard you talk of 'em as I have done. Here, bid your man give me an angel.
[*Sets down the fruit*]
DORIMANT: Give the bawd her fruit again.
ORANGE-WOMAN: Well, on my conscience, there never was the like of you. God's my life, I had almost for-

got to tell you there is a young gentlewoman lately come to town with her mother, that is so taken with you.

DORIMANT: Is she handsome?

ORANGE-WOMAN: Nay, gad, there are few finer women, I tell you but so, and a hugeous fortune, they say. Here, eat this peach, it comes from the stone; 'tis better than any Newington y' have tasted.

DORIMANT: This fine woman, I'll lay my life,
                    [*Taking the peach*]
is some awkward, ill-fashioned, country toad, who, not having above four dozen of black hairs on her head, has adorned her baldness with a large white fruz, that she may look sparkishly in the forefront of the King's box at an old play.

ORANGE-WOMAN: Gad, you'd change your note quickly if you did but see her.

DORIMANT: How came she to know me?

ORANGE-WOMAN: She saw you yesterday at the Change; she told me you came and fooled with the woman at the next shop.

DORIMANT: I remember there was a mask observed me indeed. Fooled, did she say?

ORANGE-WOMAN: Ay, I vow she told me twenty things you said too; and acted with her head and with her body so you——

Enter Medley.

MEDLEY: Dorimant, my life, my joy, my darling sin, how dost thou?

ORANGE-WOMAN: Lord! what a filthy trick these men have got of kissing one another!   [*She spits*]

MEDLEY: Why do you suffer this cartload of scandal to come near you and make your neighbours think you so improvident to need a bawd?

ORANGE-WOMAN: Good, now we shall have it! you did but want him to help you; come, pay me for my fruit.

MEDLEY: Make us thankful for it, huswife; bawds are as much out of fashion as gentlemen-ushers: none but old formal ladies use the one, and none but foppish old strangers employ the other—go, you are an insignificant brandy bottle.

DORIMANT: Nay, there you wrong her, three quarts of canary is her business.

ORANGE-WOMAN: What you please, gentlemen.

DORIMANT: To him! give him as good as he brings.

ORANGE-WOMAN: Hang him, there is not such another heathen in the town again, except it be the shoe-maker without.

MEDLEY: I shall see you hold up your hand at the bar next sessions for murder, huswife; that shoemaker can take his oath you are in fee with the doctors to sell green fruit to the gentry, that the crudities may breed diseases.

ORANGE-WOMAN: Pray give me my money.

DORIMANT: Not a penny; when you bring the gentle-woman hither you spoke of, you shall be paid.

ORANGE-WOMAN: The gentlewoman! the gentle-woman may be as honest as your sister, for aught as I know. Pray pay me, Mr. Dorimant, and do not abuse me so; I have an honester way of living, you know it.

MEDLEY: Was there ever such a restiff bawd?

DORIMANT: Some jade's tricks she has, but she makes amends when she's in good-humour. Come, tell me the lady's name, and Handy shall pay you.

ORANGE-WOMAN: I must not, she forbid me.

DORIMANT: That's a sure sign she would have you.

MEDLEY: Where does she live?

ORANGE-WOMAN: They lodge at my house.

MEDLEY: Nay, then she's in a hopeful way.

ORANGE-WOMAN: Good Mr. Medley, say your pleasure of me, but take heed how you affront my house. God's my life, in a hopeful way!

DORIMANT: Prithee, peace! what kind of woman's the mother?

ORANGE-WOMAN: A goodly grave gentlewoman. Lord! how she talks against the wild young men o' the town! As for your part, she thinks you an arrant devil; should she see you, on my conscience she would look if you had not a cloven foot.

DORIMANT: Does she know me?

ORANGE-WOMAN: Only by hearsay; a thousand horrid stories have been told her of you, and she believes 'em all.

MEDLEY: By the character, this should be the famous Lady Woodvil and her daughter Harriet.

ORANGE-WOMAN: The devil's in him for guessing, I think.

DORIMANT: Do you know 'em?

MEDLEY: Both very well; the mother's a great admirer of the forms and civility of the last age.

DORIMANT: An antiquated beauty may be allowed to be out of humour at the freedoms of the present. This is a good account of the mother; pray, what is the daughter?

MEDLEY: Why, first she's an heiress, vastly rich.

DORIMANT: And handsome?

MEDLEY: What alteration a twelvemonth may have bred in her I know not, but a year ago she was the beautifullest creature I ever saw; a fine, easy, clean shape; light brown hair in abundance; her features regular; her complexion clear and lively; large wanton eyes; but above all, a mouth that has made me kiss it a thousand times in imagination, teeth white and even, and pretty pouting lips, with a little moisture ever hanging on them, that look like the Provence rose fresh on the bush, ere the morning sun has quite drawn up the dew.

DORIMANT: Rapture, mere rapture!

ORANGE-WOMAN: Nay, gad, he tells you true; she's a delicate creature.

DORIMANT: Has she wit?

MEDLEY: More than is usual in her sex, and as much malice. Then she's as wild as you would wish her, and has a demureness in her looks that makes it so surprising.

DORIMANT: Flesh and blood cannot hear this, and not long to know her.

MEDLEY: I wonder what makes her mother bring her up to town; an old doting keeper cannot be more jealous of his mistress.

ORANGE-WOMAN: She made me laugh yesterday; there was a judge came to visit 'em, and the old man, she told me, did so stare upon her, and when he saluted her smacked so heartily; who would think it of 'em?

MEDLEY: God a mercy, a judge!

DORIMANT: Do 'em right, the gentlemen of the long robe have not been wanting by their good examples to countenance the crying sin o' the nation.

MEDLEY: Come, on with your trappings; 'tis later than you imagine.

DORIMANT: Call in the shoemaker, Handy.

ORANGE-WOMAN: Good Mr. Dorimant, pay me; gad, I had rather give you my fruit than stay to be abused by that foul-mouthed rogue; what you gentlemen say, it matters not much, but such a dirty fellow does one more disgrace.

DORIMANT: Give her ten shillings, and be sure you tell the young gentlewoman I must be acquainted with her.

ORANGE-WOMAN: Now do you long to be tempting this pretty creature. Well, heavens mend you!

MEDLEY: Farewell.

[*Exeunt* Orange-Woman *and* Handy]
Dorimant, when did you see your *pis-aller,* as you call her Mrs. Loveit?

DORIMANT: Not these two days.

MEDLEY: And how stand affairs between you?

DORIMANT: There has been great patching of late, much ado; we make a shift to hang together.

MEDLEY: I wonder how her mighty spirit bears it.

DORIMANT: Ill enough, on all conscience; I never knew so violent a creature.

MEDLEY: She's the most passionate in her love, and the most extravagant in her jealousy, of any woman I ever heard of. What note is that?

DORIMANT: An excuse I am going to send her for the neglect I am guilty of.

MEDLEY: Prithee read it.

DORIMANT: No; but if you will take the pains you may.

MEDLEY: [*Reads*] "I never was a lover of business, but now I have a just reason to hate it, since it has kept me these two days from seeing you. I intend to wait upon you in the afternoon, and in the pleasure of your conversation forget all I have suffered during this tedious absence." This business of yours, Dorimant, has been with a vizard at the playhouse; I have had an eye on you. If some malicious body should betray you, this kind note would hardly make your peace with her.

DORIMANT: I desire no better.

MEDLEY: Why, would her knowledge of it oblige you?

DORIMANT: Most infinitely; next to the coming to a good understanding with a new mistress, I love a quarrel with an old one; but the devil's in't, there has been such a calm in my affairs of late, I have not had the pleasure of making a woman so much as break her fan, to be sullen, or forswear herself these three days.

MEDLEY: A very great misfortune. Let me see, I love mischief well enough to forward this business myself; I'll about it presently and though I know the truth of what you've done will set her a-raving, I'll heighten it a little with invention, leave her in a fit o' the mother, and be here again before you're ready.

DORIMANT: Pray stay; you may spare yourself the labour; the business is undertaken already by one who will manage it with as much address, and I think with a little more malice than you can.

MEDLEY: Who i' the devil's name can this be?

DORIMANT: Why the vizard—that very vizard you saw me with.

MEDLEY: Does she love mischief so well as to betray herself to spite another?

DORIMANT: Not so neither, Medley. I will make you comprehend the mystery: this mask, for a farther confirmation of what I have been these two days swearing to her, made me yesterday at the playhouse make her a promise before her face utterly to break off with Loveit; and because she tenders my reputation, and would not have me do a barbarous thing, has contrived a way to give me a handsome occasion.

MEDLEY: Very good.

DORIMANT: She intends, about an hour before me, this afternoon to make Loveit a visit, and (having the privilege, by reason of a professed friendship between 'em) to talk of her concerns.

MEDLEY: Is she a friend?

DORIMANT: Oh, an intimate friend!

MEDLEY: Better and better; pray proceed.

DORIMANT: She means insensibly to insinuate a discourse of me, and artificially raise her jealousy to such a height, that transported with the first motions of her passion, she shall fly upon me with all the fury imaginable as soon as ever I enter; the quarrel being thus happily begun, I am to play my part, confess and justify all my roguery, swear her impertinence and ill-humour makes her intolerable, tax her with the next fop that comes into my head, and in a huff march away; slight her, and leave her to be taken by whosoever thinks it worth his time to lie down before her.

MEDLEY: This vizard is a spark, and has a genius that makes her worthy of yourself, Dorimant.

Enter Handy, Shoemaker, *and* Footman.

DORIMANT: You rogue there, who sneak like a dog that has flung down a dish, if you do not mend your waiting I'll uncase you, and turn you loose to the wheel of fortune. Handy, seal this, and let him run with it presently.

[*Exeunt* Handy[1] *and* Footman]

MEDLEY: Since you're resolved on a quarrel, why do you send her this kind note?

DORIMANT: To keep her at home in order to the business. [*To the* Shoemaker] How now, you drunken sot?

SHOEMAKER: 'Zbud, you have no reason to talk; I have not had a bottle of sack of yours in my belly this fortnight.

MEDLEY: The orange-woman says your neighbours take notice what a heathen you are, and design to inform the bishop and have you burned for an atheist.

SHOEMAKER: Damn her, dunghill! if her husband does not remove her, she stinks so the parish intend to indict him for a nuisance.

MEDLEY: I advise you like a friend, reform your life; you have brought the envy of the world upon you by living above yourself. Whoring and swearing are vices too genteel for a shoemaker.

SHOEMAKER: 'Zbud, I think you men of quality will grow as unreasonable as the women; you would engross the sins o' the nation; poor folks can no sooner be wicked, but they're railed at by their betters.

DORIMANT: Sirrah, I'll have you stand i' the pillory for this libel.

SHOEMAKER: Some of you deserve it, I'm sure; there are so many of 'em, that our journeymen nowadays, instead of harmless ballads, sing nothing but your damned lampoons.

DORIMANT: Our lampoons, you rogue?

SHOEMAKER: Nay, good master, why should not you write your own commentaries as well as Cæsar?

MEDLEY: The rascal's read, I perceive.

SHOEMAKER: You know the old proverb—ale and history.

DORIMANT: Draw on my shoes, sirrah.

SHOEMAKER: Here's a shoe.

DORIMANT: Sits with more wrinkles than there are in an angry bully's forehead.

SHOEMAKER: 'Zbud, as smooth as your mistress's skin does upon her; so strike your foot in home. 'Zbud, if e'er a *monsieur* of 'em all make more fashionable wear, I'll be content to have my ears whipped off with my own paring-knife.

MEDLEY: And served up in a *ragoût* instead of cox-combs to a company of French shoemakers for a collation.

SHOEMAKER: Hold, hold! damn 'em, caterpillars! let 'em feed upon cabbage. Come, master, your health this morning next my heart now.

DORIMANT: Go, get you home, and govern your family better; do not let your wife follow you to the ale-house, beat your whore, and lead you home in triumph.

[1]*Who presently returns, though the entry is not marked.*

SHOEMAKER: 'Zbud, there's never a man i' the town lives more like a gentleman with his wife than I do. I never mind her motions, she never inquires into mine; we speak to one another civilly, hate one another heartily, and because 'tis vulgar to lie and soak together, we have each of us our several settle-bed.

DORIMANT: Give him half-a-crown.

MEDLEY: Not without he will promise to be bloody drunk.

SHOEMAKER: Tope's the word i' the eye of the world, for my master's honour, Robin.

DORIMANT: Do not debauch my servants, sirrah.

SHOEMAKER: I only tip him the wink; he knows an alehouse from a hovel. [*Exit* Shoemaker]

DORIMANT: My clothes, quickly.

MEDLEY: Where shall we dine to-day?

Enter Bellair.

DORIMANT: Where you will; here comes a good third man.

BELLAIR: Your servant, gentlemen.

MEDLEY: Gentle sir, how will you answer this visit to your honourable mistress? 'Tis not her interest you should keep company with men of sense, who will be talking reason.

BELLAIR: I do not fear her pardon, do you but grant me yours for my neglect of late.

MEDLEY: Though you've made us miserable by the want of your good company, to show you I am free from all resentment, may the beautiful cause of our misfortune give you all the joys happy lovers have shared ever since the world began.

BELLAIR: You wish me in heaven, but you believe me on my journey to hell.

MEDLEY: You have a good strong faith, and that may contribute much towards your salvation. I confess I am but of an untoward constitution, apt to have doubts and scruples, and in love they are no less distracting than in religion; were I so near marriage, I should cry out by fits as I ride in my coach, *Cuckold, Cuckold*, with no less fury than the mad fanatic does *Glory* in Bedlam.

BELLAIR: Because religion makes some run mad, must I live an atheist?

MEDLEY: Is it not great indiscretion for a man of credit, who may have money enough on his word, to go and deal with Jews who for little sums make men enter into bonds and give judgments?

BELLAIR: Preach no more on this text, I am determined, and there is no hope of my conversion.

DORIMANT: [*To* Handy, *who is fiddling about him*] Leave your unnecessary fiddling; a wasp that's buzzing about a man's nose at dinner is not more troublesome than thou art.

HANDY: You love to have your clothes hang just, sir.

DORIMANT: I love to be well dressed, sir; and think it no scandal to my understanding.

HANDY: Will you use the essence, or orange-flower water?

DORIMANT: I will smell as I do to-day, no offence to the ladies' noses.

HANDY: Your pleasure, sir.

DORIMANT: That a man's excellency should lie in neatly tying of a ribbon or a cravat! How careful's nature in furnishing the world with necessary cox-combs?

BELLAIR: That's a mighty pretty suit of yours, Dori-mant.

DORIMANT: I am glad't has your approbation.

BELLAIR: No man in town has a better fancy in his clothes than you have.

DORIMANT: You will make me have an opinion of my genius.

MEDLEY: There is a great critic, I hear, in these mat-ters lately arrived piping hot from Paris.

BELLAIR: Sir Fopling Flutter, you mean.

MEDLEY: The same.

BELLAIR: He thinks himself the pattern of modern gallantry.

DORIMANT: He is indeed the pattern of modern fop-pery.

MEDLEY: He was yesterday at the play, with a pair of gloves up to his elbows and a periwig more exactly curled than a lady's head newly dressed for a ball.

BELLAIR: What a pretty lisp he has!

DORIMANT: Ho! that he affects in imitation of the people of quality in France.

MEDLEY: His head stands for the most part on one side, and his looks are more languishing than a lady's when she lolls at stretch in her coach or leans her head carelessly against the side of a box i' the playhouse.

DORIMANT: He is a person indeed of great acquired follies.

MEDLEY: He is like many others, beholding to his education for making him so eminent a coxcomb; many a fool had been lost to the world had their indulgent parents wisely bestowed neither learning nor good breeding on 'em.

BELLAIR: He has been, as the sparkish word is, brisk upon the ladies already; he was yesterday at my Aunt Townley's, and gave Mrs. Loveit a catalogue of his good qualities under the character of a com-plete gentleman, who, according to Sir Fopling, ought to dress well, dance well, fence well, have a genius for love-letters, an agreeable voice for a chamber, be very amorous, something discreet, but not over-constant.

MEDLEY: Pretty ingredients to make an accomplished person.

DORIMANT: I am glad he pitched upon Loveit.

BELLAIR: How so?

DORIMANT: I wanted a fop to lay to her charge, and this is as pat as may be.

BELLAIR: I am confident she loves no man but you.

DORIMANT: The good fortune were enough to make me vain, but that I am in my nature modest.

BELLAIR: Hark you, Dorimant; with your leave, Mr. Medley, 'tis only a secret concerning a fair lady.

MEDLEY: Your good breeding, sir, gives you too much trouble; you might have whispered without all this ceremony.

BELLAIR: [To Dorimant] How stand your affairs with Belinda of late?

DORIMANT: She's a little jilting baggage.

BELLAIR: Nay, I believe her false enough, but she's ne'er the worse for your purpose; she was with you yesterday in a disguise at the play.

DORIMANT: There we fell out, and resolved never to speak to one another more.

BELLAIR: The occasion?

DORIMANT: Want of courage to meet me at the place appointed. These young women apprehend loving as much as the young men do fighting at first; but once entered, like them too, they all turn bullies straight.

Enter Handy.[1]

HANDY: [To Bellair] Sir, your man without desires to speak with you.

BELLAIR: Gentlemen, I'll return immediately.

[*Exit* Bellair]

MEDLEY: A very pretty fellow this.

DORIMANT: He's handsome, well-bred, and by much the most tolerable of all the young men that do not abound in wit.

MEDLEY: Ever well-dressed, always complaisant, and seldom impertinent; you and he are grown very intimate, I see.

DORIMANT: It is our mutual interest to be so: it makes the women think the better of his under-standing and judge more favourably of my reputa-tion; it makes him pass upon some for a man of very good sense and I upon others for a very civil person.

MEDLEY: What was that whisper?

DORIMANT: A thing which he would fain have known, but I did not think it fit to tell him; it might have frighted him from his honourable intentions of marrying.

MEDLEY: Emilia, give her her due, has the best repu-tation of any young woman about the town who has beauty enough to provoke detraction; her car-riage is unaffected, her discourse modest, not at all censorious nor pretending, like the counterfeits of the age.

DORIMANT: She's a discreet maid, and I believe noth-ing can corrupt her but a husband.

MEDLEY: A husband?

DORIMANT: Yes, a husband; I have known many women make a difficulty of losing a maidenhead who have afterwards made none of a cuckold.

MEDLEY: This prudent consideration, I am apt to

[1] *Whose previous exit had not been noticed.*

think, has made you confirm poor Bellair in the desperate resolution he has taken.

DORIMANT: Indeed, the little hope I found there was of her, in the state she was in, has made him by advice contribute something towards the changing of her condition.

Enter Bellair.

Dear Bellair, by heaven I thought we had lost thee; men in love are never to be reckoned on when we would form a company.

BELLAIR: Dorimant I am undone; my man has brought the most surprising news i' the world.

DORIMANT: Some strange misfortune is befallen your love.

BELLAIR: My father came to town last night, and lodges i' the very house where Emilia lies.

MEDLEY: Does he know it is with her you are in love?

BELLAIR: He knows I love, but knows not whom, without some officious sot has betrayed me.

DORIMANT: Your Aunt Townley is your confidante and favours the business.

BELLAIR: I do not apprehend any ill office from her; I have received a letter, in which I am commanded by my father to meet him at my aunt's this afternoon; he tells me farther he has made a match for me, and bids me resolve to be obedient to his will or expect to be disinherited.

MEDLEY: Now's your time, Bellair; never had lover such an opportunity of giving a generous proof of his passion.

BELLAIR: As how, I pray?

MEDLEY: Why, hang an estate, marry Emilia out of hand, and provoke your father to do what he threatens; 'tis but despising a coach, humbling yourself to a pair of goloshes, being out of countenance when you meet your friends, pointed at and pitied wherever you go by all the amorous fops that know you, and your fame will be immortal.

BELLAIR: I could find in my heart to resolve not to marry at all.

DORIMANT: Fie, fie! that would spoil a good jest and disappoint the well-natured town of an occasion of laughing at you.

BELLAIR: The storm I have so long expected hangs o'er my head and begins to pour down upon me; I am on the rack, and can have no rest till I'm satisfied in what I fear; where do you dine?

DORIMANT: At Long's or Locket's.

MEDLEY: At Long's let it be.

BELLAIR: I'll run and see Emilia, and inform myself how matters stand; if my misfortunes are not so great as to make me unfit for company, I'll be with you.   [*Exit* Bellair]

Enter a Footman *with a letter.*

FOOTMAN: [*To* Dorimant] Here's a letter, sir.

DORIMANT: The superscription's right: *For Mr. Dorimant.*

MEDLEY: Let's see: the very scrawl and spelling of a true-bred whore.

DORIMANT: I know the hand; the style is admirable, I assure you.

MEDLEY: Prithee read it.

DORIMANT: [*Reads*] "I told a you you dud not love me, if you dud, you would have seen me again e'er now; I have no mony, and am very mallicolly; pray send me a guynie to see the operies. Your servant to command, Molly."

MEDLEY: Pray let the whore have a favourable answer, that she may spark it in a box and do honour to her profession.

DORIMANT: She shall, and perk up i' the face of quality. Is the coach at door?

HANDY: You did not bid me send for it.

DORIMANT: Eternal blockhead! [Handy *offers to go out*] Hey, sot.

HANDY: Did you call me, sir?

DORIMANT: I hope you have no just exception to the name, sir?

HANDY: I have sense, sir.

DORIMANT: Not so much as a fly in winter.——How did you come, Medley?

MEDLEY: In a chair.

FOOTMAN: You may have a hackney coach if you please, sir.

DORIMANT: I may ride the elephant if I please, sir; call another chair, and let my coach follow to Long's.

[*Exeunt singing,* Be calm, ye great parents, *etc.*]

Act II

SCENE 1

Enter my Lady Townley *and* Emilia.

LADY TOWNLEY: I was afraid, Emilia, all had been discovered.

EMILIA: I tremble with the apprehension still.

LADY TOWNLEY: That my brother should take lodgings i' the very house where you lie!

EMILIA: 'Twas lucky we had timely notice to warn the people to be secret; he seems to be a mighty good-humoured old man.

LADY TOWNLEY: He ever had a notable smirking way with him.

EMILIA: He calls me rogue, tells me he can't abide me, and does so bepat me.

LADY TOWNLEY: On my word you are much in his favour then.

EMILIA: He has been very inquisitive, I am told, about my family, my reputation, and my fortune.

LADY TOWNLEY: I am confident he does not i' the least suspect you are the woman his son's in love with.

EMILIA: What should make him then inform himself so particularly of me?

LADY TOWNLEY: He was always of a very loving temper himself; it may be he has a doting fit upon him; who knows?

EMILIA: It cannot be.

Enter Young Bellair.

LADY TOWNLEY: Here comes my nephew. Where did you leave your father?

YOUNG BELLAIR: Writing a note within. Emilia, this early visit looks as if some kind jealousy would not let you rest at home.

EMILIA: The knowledge I have of my rival gives me a little cause to fear your constancy.

YOUNG BELLAIR: My constancy; I vow——

EMILIA: Do not vow——Our love is frail as is our life, and full as little in our power; and are you sure you shall outlive this day?

YOUNG BELLAIR: I am not; but when we are in perfect health 'twere an idle thing to fright ourselves with the thoughts of sudden death.

LADY TOWNLEY: Pray what has passed between you and your father i' the garden?

YOUNG BELLAIR: He's firm in his resolution, tells me I must marry Mrs. Harriet, or swears he'll marry himself and disinherit me; when I saw I could not prevail with him to be more indulgent, I dissembled an obedience to his will which has composed his passion, and will give us time, and I hope opportunity, to deceive him.

Enter Old Bellair *with a note in his hand.*

LADY TOWNLEY: Peace, here he comes.

OLD BELLAIR: Harry, take this, and let your man carry it for me to Mr. Fourbes's chamber, my lawyer, i' the Temple.　　　[*Exit* Young Bellair] [*To* Emilia] Neighbour, adod, I am glad to see thee here; make much of her, sister, she's one of the best of your acquaintance; I like her countenance and her behaviour well, she has a modesty that is not common i' this age, adod, she has.

LADY TOWNLEY: I know her value, brother, and esteem her accordingly.

OLD BELLAIR: Advise her to wear a little more mirth in her face, adod, she's too serious.

LADY TOWNLEY: The fault is very excusable in a young woman.

OLD BELLAIR: Nay, adod, I like her ne'er the worse, a melancholy beauty has her charms; I love a pretty sadness in a face which varies now and then, like changeable colours, into a smile.

LADY TOWNLEY: Methinks you speak very feelingly, brother.

OLD BELLAIR: I am but five-and-fifty, sister, you know, an age not altogether insensible! [*To* Emilia] Cheer up, sweetheart, I have a secret to tell thee may chance to make thee merry; we three will make collation together anon; i' the meantime mum, I can't abide you; go, I can't abide you.

Enter Young Bellair.

Harry, come, you must along with me to my Lady Woodvil's. I am going to slip the boy at a mistress.

YOUNG BELLAIR: At a wife, sir, you would say.

OLD BELLAIR: You need not look so grum, sir; a wife is no curse when she brings the blessing of a good estate with her; but an idle town flirt, with a painted face, a rotten reputation, and a crazy fortune, adod, is the devil and all; and such a one I hear you are in league with.

YOUNG BELLAIR: I cannot help detraction, sir.

OLD BELLAIR: Out, a pise o' their breeches, there are keeping fools enough for such flaunting baggages, and they are e'en too good for 'em. [*To* Emilia] Remember night, go, you're a rogue, you're a rogue; fare you well, fare you well; come, come, come along, sir.　　　[*Exeunt* Old *and* Young Bellair]

LADY TOWNLEY: On my word the old man comes on apace; I'll lay my life he's smitten.

EMILIA: This is nothing but the pleasantness of his humour.

LADY TOWNLEY: I know him better than you; let it work, it may prove lucky.

Enter a Page.

PAGE: Madam, Mr. Medley has sent to know whether a visit will not be troublesome this afternoon?

LADY TOWNLEY: Send him word his visits never are so.　　　　　　　　　　　　　　　　[*Exit* Page]

EMILIA: He's a very pleasant man.

LADY TOWNLEY: He's a very necessary man among us women; he's not scandalous i' the least, perpetually contriving to bring good company together, and always ready to stop up a gap at ombre; then he knows all the little news o' the town.

EMILIA: I love to hear him talk o' the intrigues; let 'em be never so dull in themselves, he'll make 'em pleasant i' the relation.

LADY TOWNLEY: But he improves things so much one can take no measure of the truth from him. Mr. Dorimant swears a flea or a maggot is not made more monstrous by a magnifying glass than a story is by his telling it.

EMILIA: Hold, here he comes.

Enter Medley.

LADY TOWNLEY: Mr. Medley.

MEDLEY: Your servant, madam.

LADY TOWNLEY: You have made yourself a stranger of late.

EMILIA: I believe you took a surfeit of ombre last time you were here.

MEDLEY: Indeed I had my bellyful of that termagant lady-dealer; there never was so insatiable a carder, an old gleeker never loved to sit to't like her; I have played with her now at least a dozen times till she's worn out all her fine complexion, and her tour[1] would keep in curl no longer.

[1] *Headdress.*

LADY TOWNLEY: Blame her not, poor woman; she loves nothing so well as a black ace.

MEDLEY: The pleasure I have seen her in when she has had hope in drawing for a matadore![1]

EMILIA: 'Tis as pretty sport to her as persuading masks off is to you to make discoveries.

LADY TOWNLEY: Pray, where 's your friend Mr. Dorimant?

MEDLEY: Soliciting his affairs; he's a man of great employment, has more mistresses now depending than the most eminent lawyer in England has causes.

EMILIA: Here has been Mrs. Loveit, so uneasy and out of humour these two days.

LADY TOWNLEY: How strangely love and jealousy rage in that poor woman!

MEDLEY: She could not have picked out a devil upon earth so proper to torment her; he has made her break a dozen or two of fans already, tear half a score points in pieces, and destroy hoods and knots without number.

LADY TOWNLEY: We heard of a pleasant serenade he gave her t'other night.

MEDLEY: A Danish serenade, with kettledrums and trumpets.

EMILIA: Oh, barbarous!

MEDLEY: What, you are of the number of the ladies whose ears are grown so delicate since our operas, you can be charmed with nothing but *flutes douces* and French hautboys.

EMILIA: Leave your raillery, and tell us is there any new wit come forth, songs or novels?

MEDLEY: A very pretty piece of gallantry by an eminent author called *The Diversions of Brussels*; very necessary to be read by all old ladies who are desirous to improve themselves at questions and commands, blindman's buff, and the like fashionable recreations.

EMILIA: Oh, ridiculous!

MEDLEY: Then there is *The Art of Affectation*, written by a late beauty of quality, teaching you how to draw up your breasts, stretch up your neck, to thrust out your breech, to play with your head, to toss up your nose, to bite your lips, to turn up your eyes, to speak in a silly soft tone of a voice, and use all the foolish French words that will infallibly make your person and conversation charming, with a short apology at the latter end, in the behalf of young ladies who notoriously wash and paint, though they have naturally good complexions.

EMILIA: What a deal of stuff you tell us!

MEDLEY: Such as the town affords, madam. The Russians hearing the great respect we have for foreign dancing have lately sent over some of the best balladines, who are now practising a famous ballet, which will be suddenly danced at the Bear Garden.

LADY TOWNLEY: Pray forbear your idle stories, and

[1]*A game at cards.*

give us an account of the state of love as it now stands.

MEDLEY: Truly there has been some revolutions in those affairs, great chopping and changing among the old, and some new lovers, whom malice, indiscretion, and misfortune have luckily brought into play.

LADY TOWNLEY: What think you of walking into the next room, and sitting down before you engage in this business?

MEDLEY: I wait upon you, and I hope (though women are commonly unreasonable) by the plenty of scandal I shall discover to give you very good content, ladies.   [*Exeunt*]

SCENE 2

Enter Mrs. Loveit *and* Pert. Mrs. Loveit *putting up a letter, then pulling out her pocket-glass, and looking in it.*

MRS. LOVEIT: Pert.

PERT: Madam.

MRS. LOVEIT: I hate myself, I look so ill to-day.

PERT: Hate the wicked cause on't, that base man Mr. Dorimant, who makes you torment and vex yourself continually.

MRS. LOVEIT: He is to blame, indeed.

PERT: To blame to be two days without sending, writing, or coming near you, contrary to his oath and covenant! 'twas to much purpose to make him swear: I'll lay my life there's not an article but he has broken——talked to the vizards i' the pit; waited upon the ladies from the boxes to their coaches; gone behind the scenes and fawned upon those little insignificant creatures the players; 'tis impossible for a man of his inconstant temper to forbear, I'm sure.

MRS. LOVEIT: I know he is a devil, but he has something of the angel yet undefaced in him, which makes him so charming and agreeable that I must love him be he never so wicked.

PERT: I little thought, madam, to see your spirit tamed to this degree, who banished poor Mr. Lackwit but for taking up another lady's fan in your presence.

MRS. LOVEIT: My knowing of such odious fools contributes to the making of me love Dorimant the better.

PERT: Your knowing of Mr. Dorimant, in my mind, should rather make you hate all mankind.

MRS. LOVEIT: So it does, besides himself.

PERT: Pray, what excuse does he make in his letter?

MRS. LOVEIT: He has had business.

PERT: Business in general terms would not have been a current excuse for another; a modish man is always very busy when he is in pursuit of a new mistress.

MRS. LOVEIT: Some fop has bribed you to rail at him;

he had business, I will believe it, and will forgive him.

PERT: You may forgive him anything, but I shall never forgive him his turning me into ridicule, as I hear he does.

MRS. LOVEIT: I perceive you are of the number of those fools his wit has made his enemies.

PERT: I am of the number of those he's pleased to rally, madam; and if we may believe Mr. Wagfan and Mr. Caperwell, he sometimes makes merry with yourself too among his laughing companions.

MRS. LOVEIT: Blockheads are as malicious to witty men as ugly women are to the handsome; 'tis their interest, and they make it their business to defame 'em.

PERT: I wish Mr. Dorimant would not make it his business to defame you.

MRS. LOVEIT: Should he, I had rather be made infamous by him than owe my reputation to the dull discretion of those fops you talk of.

Enter Belinda.

Belinda!   [*Running to her*]

BELINDA: My dear.

MRS. LOVEIT: You have been unkind of late.

BELINDA: Do not say unkind, say unhappy!

MRS. LOVEIT: I could chide you; where have you been these two days?

BELINDA: Pity me rather, my dear, where I have been so tired with two or three country gentlewomen, whose conversation has been more insufferable than a country fiddle.

MRS. LOVEIT: Are they relations?

BELINDA: No, Welsh acquaintance I made when I was last year at St. Winifred's; they have asked me a thousand questions of the modes and intrigues of the town, and I have told 'em almost as many things for news that hardly were so when their gowns were in fashion.

MRS. LOVEIT: Provoking creatures, how could you endure 'em?

BELINDA: [*Aside*] Now to carry on my plot; nothing but love could make me capable of so much falsehood; 'tis time to begin, lest Dorimant should come before her jealousy has stung her.

[*Laughs, and then speaks on*]
I was yesterday at a play with 'em, where I was fain to show 'em the living, as the man at Westminster does the dead; that is Mrs. Such-a-one, admired for her beauty; this is Mr. Such-a-one, cried up for a wit; that is sparkish Mr. Such-a-one, who keeps reverend Mrs. Such-a-one, and there sits fine Mrs. Such-a-one, who was lately cast off by my Lord Such-a-one.

MRS. LOVEIT: Did you see Dorimant there?

BELINDA: I did, and imagine you were there with him and have no mind to own it.

MRS. LOVEIT: What should make you think so?

BELINDA: A lady masked in a pretty *déshabillé*, whom

Dorimant entertained with more respect than the gallants do a common vizard.

MRS. LOVEIT: [*Aside*] Dorimant at the play entertaining a mask, oh heavens!

BELINDA: [*Aside*] Good.

MRS. LOVEIT: Did he stay all the while?

BELINDA: Till the play was done, and then led her out, which confirms me it was you.

MRS. LOVEIT: Traitor!

PERT: Now you may believe he had business, and you may forgive him too.

MRS. LOVEIT: Ungrateful, perjured man!

BELINDA: You seem so much concerned, my dear, I fear I have told you unawares what I had better have concealed for your quiet.

MRS. LOVEIT: What manner of shape had she?

BELINDA: Tall and slender, her motions very genteel; certainly she must be some person of condition.

MRS. LOVEIT: Shame and confusion be ever in her face when she shows it!

BELINDA: I should blame your discretion for loving that wild man, my dear; but they say he has a way so bewitching that few can defend their hearts who know him.

MRS. LOVEIT: I will tear him from mine, or die i' the attempt.

BELINDA: Be more moderate.

MRS. LOVEIT: Would I had daggers, darts, or poisoned arrows in my breast, so I could but remove the thoughts of him from thence!

BELINDA: Fie, fie! your transports are too violent, my dear. This may be but an accidental gallantry, and 'tis likely ended at her coach.

PERT: Should it proceed farther, let your comfort be, the conduct Mr. Dorimant affects will quickly make you know your rival, ten to one let you see her ruined, her reputation exposed to the town; a happiness none will envy her but yourself, madam.

MRS. LOVEIT: Whoe'er she be, all the harm I wish her is, may she love him as well as I do, and may he give her as much cause to hate him!

PERT: Never doubt the latter end of your curse, madam.

MRS. LOVEIT: May all the passions that are raised by neglected love, jealousy, indignation, spite, and thirst of revenge, eternally rage in her soul as they do now in mine!

[*Walks up and down with a distracted air*]

Enter a Page.

PAGE: Madam, Mr. Dorimant.

MRS. LOVEIT: I will not see him.

PAGE: I told him you were within, madam.

MRS. LOVEIT: Say you lied, say I'm busy, shut the door; say anything.

PAGE: He's here, madam.

Enter Dorimant.

DORIMANT: They taste of death who do at Heaven arrive,

But we this paradise approach alive.

[*To* Mrs. Loveit] What, dancing the galloping nag without a fiddle?

[*Offers to catch her by the hand; she flings away and walks on*]

I fear this restlessness of the body, madam [*Pursuing her*] proceeds from an unquietness of the mind. What unlucky accident puts you out of humour; a point ill washed, knots spoiled i' the making up, hair shaded awry, or some other little mistake in setting you in order?

PERT: A trifle, in my opinion, sir, more inconsiderable than any you mention.

DORIMANT: Oh, Mrs. Pert, I never knew you sullen enough to be silent; come, let me know the business.

PERT: The business, sir, is the business that has taken you up these two days; how have I seen you laugh at men of business, and now to become a man of business yourself!

DORIMANT: We are not masters of our own affections, our inclinations daily alter; now we love pleasure, and anon we shall dote on business: human frailty will have it so, and who can help it?

MRS. LOVEIT: Faithless, inhuman, barbarous man!——

DORIMANT: Good, now the alarm strikes.——

MRS. LOVEIT: Without sense of love, of honour, or of gratitude, tell me—for I will know—what devil, masked she were you with at the play yesterday?

DORIMANT: Faith, I resolved as much as you, but the devil was obstinate and would not tell me.

MRS. LOVEIT: False in this as in your vows to me! you do know.

DORIMANT: The truth is, I did all I could to know.

MRS. LOVEIT: And dare you own it to my face? Hell and furies!   [*Tears her fan in pieces*]

DORIMANT: Spare your fan, madam; you are growing hot, and will want it to cool you.

MRS. LOVEIT: Horror and distraction seize you, sorrow and remorse gnaw your soul, and punish all your perjuries to me!——   [*Weeps*]

DORIMANT: So thunder breaks the cloud in twain,
And makes a passage for the rain.

[*Turning to* Belinda]

Belinda, you are the devil that have raised this storm; you were at the play yesterday, and have been making discoveries to your dear.

BELINDA: You're the most mistaken man i' the world.

DORIMANT: It must be so, and here I vow revenge; resolve to pursue and persecute you more impertinently than ever any loving fop did his mistress, hunt you i' the Park, trace you i' the Mall, dog you in every visit you make, haunt you at the plays and i' the Drawing-room, hang my nose in your neck, and talk to you whether you will or no, and ever look upon you with such dying eyes, till your friends grow jealous of me, send you out of town,

and make the world suspect your reputation. [*In a lower voice*] At my Lady Townley's when we go from hence.   [*He looks kindly on* Belinda]

BELINDA: I'll meet you there.

DORIMANT: Enough.

MRS. LOVEIT: Stand off, you shall not stare upon her so.   [*Pushing* Dorimant *away*]

DORIMANT: Good! There's one made jealous already.

MRS. LOVEIT: Is this the constancy you vowed?

DORIMANT: Constancy at my years! 'tis not a virtue in season; you might as well expect the fruit the autumn ripens i' the spring.

MRS. LOVEIT: Monstrous principle!

DORIMANT: Youth has a long journey to go, madam: should I have set up my rest at the first inn I lodged at, I should never have arrived at the happiness I now enjoy.

MRS. LOVEIT: Dissembler, damned dissembler!

DORIMANT: I am so, I confess; good nature and good manners corrupt me. I am honest in my inclinations, and would not, were't not to avoid offence, make a lady a little in years believe I think her young, wilfully mistake art for nature, and seem as fond of a thing I am weary of as when I doted on't in earnest.

MRS. LOVEIT: False man!

DORIMANT: True woman!

MRS. LOVEIT: Now you begin to show yourself!

DORIMANT: Love gilds us over and makes us show fine things to one another for a time, but soon the gold wears off, and then again the native brass appears.

MRS. LOVEIT: Think on your oaths, your vows and protestations, perjured man.

DORIMANT: I made 'em when I was in love.

MRS. LOVEIT: And therefore ought they not to bind? Oh, impious!

DORIMANT: What we swear at such a time may be a certain proof of a present passion; but to say truth, in love there is no security to be given for the future.

MRS. LOVEIT: Horrid and ungrateful, begone, and never see me more.

DORIMANT: I am not one of those troublesome coxcombs, who because they were once well received take the privilege to plague a woman with their love ever after; I shall obey you, madam, though I do myself some violence.

[*He offers to go, and* Mrs. Loveit *pulls him back*]

MRS. LOVEIT: Come back, you shall not go. Could you have the ill-nature to offer it?

DORIMANT: When love grows diseased, the best thing we can do is to put it to a violent death; I cannot endure the torture of a lingering and consumptive passion.

MRS. LOVEIT: Can you think mine sickly?

DORIMANT: Oh, 'tis desperately ill! What worse symptoms are there than your being always uneasy when I visit you, your picking quarrels with me on slight occasions, and in my absence kindly listening to the impertinencies of every fashionable fool that talks to you?

MRS. LOVEIT: What fashionable fool can you lay to my charge?

DORIMANT: Why, the very cock-fool of all those fools, Sir Fopling Flutter.

MRS. LOVEIT: I never saw him in my life but once.

DORIMANT: The worse woman you, at first sight to put on all your charms, to entertain him with that softness in your voice and all that wanton kindness in your eyes you so notoriously affect when you design a conquest.

MRS. LOVEIT: So damned a lie did never malice yet invent. Who told you this?

DORIMANT: No matter; that ever I should love a woman that can dote on a senseless caper, a tawdry French ribbon, and a formal cravat.

MRS. LOVEIT: You make me mad.

DORIMANT: A guilty conscience may do much; go on, be the game-mistress o' the town, and enter all our young fops as fast as they come from travel.

MRS LOVEIT: Base and scurrilous!

DORIMANT: A fine mortifying reputation 'twill be for a woman of your pride, wit, and quality!

MRS. LOVEIT: This jealousy's a mere pretence, a cursed trick of your own devising; I know you.

DORIMANT: Believe it, and all the ill of me you can: I would not have a woman have the least good thought of me that can think well of Fopling; farewell; fall to, and much good may [it] do you with your coxcomb.

MRS. LOVEIT: Stay, oh! stay, and I will tell you all.

DORIMANT: I have been told too much already.
                                        [Exit Dorimant]

MRS. LOVEIT: Call him again.

PERT: E'en let him go, a fair riddance.

MRS. LOVEIT: Run, I say; call him again. I will have him called.

PERT: The devil should carry him away first, were it my concern.   [Exit Pert]

BELINDA: He's frightened me from the very thoughts of loving men; for heaven's sake, my dear, do not discover what I told you; I dread his tongue as much as you ought to have done his friendship.

Enter Pert.

PERT: He's gone, madam.

MRS. LOVEIT: Lightning blast him!

PERT: When I told him you desired him to come back, he smiled, made a mouth at me, flung into his coach, and said——

MRS. LOVEIT: What did he say?

PERT: "*Drive away*"; and then repeated verses.

MRS. LOVEIT: Would I had made a contract to be a witch, when first I entertained this great devil, monster, barbarian; I could tear myself in pieces. Revenge, nothing but revenge can ease me: plague, war, famine, fire, all that can bring universal ruin

and misery on mankind; with joy I'd perish to have you in my power but this moment.
                                        [*Exit* Mrs. Loveit]

PERT: Follow, madam; leave her not in this outrageous passion.   [Pert *gathers up the things*]

BELINDA: He's given me the proof which I desired of his love:
  But 'tis a proof of his ill-nature too;
  I wish I had not seen him use her so.
  I sigh to think that Dorimant may be
  One day as faithless and unkind to me.   [*Exeunt*]

Act III

SCENE 1: *Lady Woodvil's Lodgings*

Enter Harriet *and* Busy *her woman.*

BUSY: Dear madam! Let me set that curl in order.

HARRIET: Let me alone, I will shake 'em all out of order.

BUSY: Will you never leave this wildness?

HARRIET: Torment me not.

BUSY: Look! there's a knot falling off.

HARRIET: Let it drop.

BUSY: But one pin, dear madam.

HARRIET: How do I daily suffer under thy officious fingers!

BUSY: Ah, the difference that is between you and my Lady Dapper! How uneasy she is if the least thing be amiss about her!

HARRIET: She is indeed most exact; nothing is ever wanting to make her ugliness remarkable.

BUSY: Jeering people say so.

HARRIET: Her powdering, painting, and her patching never fail in public to draw the tongues and eyes of all the men upon her.

BUSY: She is indeed a little too pretending.

HARRIET: That women should set up for beauty as much in spite of nature as some men have done for wit!

BUSY: I hope, without offence, one may endeavour to make oneself agreeable.

HARRIET: Not when 'tis impossible. Women then ought to be no more fond of dressing than fools should be of talking. Hoods and modesty, masks and silence, things that shadow and conceal: they should think of nothing else.

BUSY: Jesu! madam, what will your mother think is become of you? For heaven's sake, go in again.

HARRIET: I won't.

BUSY: This is the extravagant'st thing that ever you did in your life, to leave her and a gentleman who is to be your husband.

HARRIET: My husband! Hast thou so little wit to think I spoke what I meant when I overjoyed her in the country with a low curtsey and *What you please, madam, I shall ever be obedient?*

BUSY: Nay, I know not, you have so many fetches.

HARRIET: And this was one to get her up to London; nothing else, I assure thee.

BUSY: Well, the man, in my mind, is a fine man.

HARRIET: The man indeed wears his clothes fashionably, and has a pretty negligent way with him, very courtly and much affected; he bows, and talks, and smiles so agreeably as he thinks.

BUSY: I never saw anything so genteel.

HARRIET: Varnished over with good breeding many a blockhead makes a tolerable show.

BUSY: I wonder you do not like him.

HARRIET: I think I might be brought to endure him, and that is all a reasonable woman should expect in a husband; but there is duty i' the case—— and like the haughty Merab,

I find much aversion in my stubborn mind,
Which is bred by being promised and design'd.

BUSY: I wish you do not design your own ruin! I partly guess your inclinations, madam,—— that Mr. Dorimant——

HARRIET: Leave your prating, and sing some foolish song or other.

BUSY: I will; the song you love so well ever since you saw Mr. Dorimant.

SONG

When first Amintas charm'd my heart,
My heedless sheep began to stray;
The wolves soon stole the greatest part,
And all will now be made a prey.

Ah! let not love your thoughts possess,
'Tis fatal to a shepherdess;
The dangerous passion you must shun,
Or else, like me, be quite undone.

HARRIET: Shall I be paid down by a covetous parent for a purchase? I need no land; no, I'll lay myself out all in love. It is decreed——

Enter Young Bellair.

YOUNG BELLAIR: What generous resolution are you making, madam?

HARRIET: Only to be disobedient, sir.

YOUNG BELLAIR: Let me join hands with you in that.

HARRIET: With all my heart; I never thought I should have given you mine so willingly. Here I, Harriet——

YOUNG BELLAIR: And I, Harry——

HARRIET: Do solemnly protest——

YOUNG BELLAIR: And vow——

HARRIET: That I with you——

YOUNG BELLAIR: And I with you——

BOTH: Will never marry.

HARRIET: A match!

YOUNG BELLAIR: And no match! How do you like this indifference now?

HARRIET: You expect I should take it ill, I see.

YOUNG BELLAIR: 'Tis not unnatural for you women to be a little angry [if] you miss a conquest, though you would slight the poor man were he in your power.

HARRIET: There are some, it may be, have an eye like Bartholomew, big enough for the whole fair, but I am not of the number, and you may keep your gingerbread: 'twill be more acceptable to the lady whose dear image it wears, sir.

YOUNG BELLAIR: I must confess, madam, you came a day after the fair.

HARRIET: You own then you are in love.

YOUNG BELLAIR: I do.

HARRIET: The confidence is generous, and in return I could almost find in my heart to let you know my inclinations.

YOUNG BELLAIR: Are you in love?

HARRIET: Yes, with this dear town, to that degree I can scarce endure the country in landscapes and in hangings.

YOUNG BELLAIR: What a dreadful thing 'twould be to be hurried back to Hampshire?

HARRIET: Ah! name it not!

YOUNG BELLAIR: As for us, I find we shall agree well enough! Would we could do something to deceive the grave people!

HARRIET: Could we delay their proceeding, 'twere well; a reprieve is a good step towards the getting of a pardon.

YOUNG BELLAIR: If we give over the game we are undone; what think you of playing it on booty?

HARRIET: What do you mean?

YOUNG BELLAIR: Pretend to be in love with one another; 'twill make some dilatory excuses we may feign pass the better.

HARRIET: Let us do't, if it be but for the dear pleasure of dissembling.

YOUNG BELLAIR: Can you play your part?

HARRIET: I know not what 'tis to love, but I have made pretty remarks by being now and then where lovers meet. Where did you leave their gravities?

YOUNG BELLAIR: I' th' next room; your mother was censuring our modern gallant.

Enter Old Bellair and Lady Woodvil.

HARRIET: Peace! Here they come, I will lean against this wall and look bashfully down upon my fan, while you like an amorous spark modishly entertain me.

LADY WOODVIL: Never go about to excuse 'em; come, come, it was not so when I was a young woman.

OLD BELLAIR: Adod, they're something disrespectful.

LADY WOODVIL: Quality was then considered, and not rallied by every leering fellow.

OLD BELLAIR: Youth will have its jest, adod it will.

LADY WOODVIL: 'Tis good breeding now to be civil to none but players and Exchange women; they are treated by 'em as much above their condition as others are below theirs.

OLD BELLAIR: Out, a pise on 'em! talk no more; the rogues ha' got an ill habit of preferring beauty, no matter where they find it.

LADY WOODVIL: See your son and my daughter, they have improved their acquaintance since they were within.

OLD BELLAIR: Adod, methinks they have; let's keep back and observe.

YOUNG BELLAIR: Now for a look and gestures that may persuade 'em I am saying all the passionate things imaginable.

HARRIET: Your head a little more on one side, ease yourself on your left leg, and play with your right hand.

YOUNG BELLAIR: Thus, is it not?

HARRIET: Now set your right leg firm on the ground, adjust your belt, then look about you.

YOUNG BELLAIR: A little exercising will make me perfect.

HARRIET: Smile, and turn to me again very sparkish.

YOUNG BELLAIR: Will you take your turn and be instructed?

HARRIET: With all my heart.

YOUNG BELLAIR: At one motion play your fan, roll your eyes, and then settle a kind look upon me.

HARRIET: So.

YOUNG BELLAIR: Now spread your fan, look down upon it, and tell the sticks with a finger.

HARRIET: Very modish!

YOUNG BELLAIR: Clap your hand up to your bosom, hold down your gown; shrug a little, draw up your breasts, and let 'em fall again gently, with a sigh or two, etc.

HARRIET: By the good instructions you give, I suspect you for one of those malicious observers who watch people's eyes and from innocent looks make scandalous conclusions.

YOUNG BELLAIR: I know some, indeed, who, out of mere love to mischief, are as vigilant as jealousy itself, and will give you an account of every glance that passes at a play and i' th' circle.[1]

HARRIET: 'Twill not be amiss now to seem a little pleasant.

YOUNG BELLAIR: Clap your fan then in both your hands, snatch it to your mouth, smile, and with a lively motion fling your body a little forwards. So,—— now spread it; fall back on the sudden, cover your face with it, and break out in to a loud laughter—— take up! look grave, and fall a-fanning of yourself—— admirably well acted.

HARRIET: I think I am pretty apt at these matters.

OLD BELLAIR: Adod, I like this well.

LADY WOODVIL: This promises something.

OLD BELLAIR: Come! there is love i' th' case, adod there is, or will be; what say you, young lady?

HARRIET: All in good time, sir; you expect we should

[1]*In Hyde Park.*

fall to and love, as gamecocks fight, as soon as we are set together; adod, you're unreasonable!

OLD BELLAIR: Adod, sirrah, I like thy wit well.

Enter a Servant.

SERVANT: The coach is at the door, madam.

OLD BELLAIR: Go, get you and take the air together.

LADY WOODVIL: Will not you go with us?

OLD BELLAIR: Out a pise. Adod, I ha' business and cannot. We shall meet at night at my sister Townley's.

YOUNG BELLAIR: [*Aside*] He's going to Emilia. I overheard him talk of a collation.   [*Exeunt*]

SCENE 2

Enter Lady Townley, Emilia, *and* Mr. Medley.

LADY TOWNLEY: I pity the young lovers we last talked of; though, to say truth, their conduct has been so indiscreet they deserve to be unfortunate.

MEDLEY: You've had an exact account, from the great lady i' th' box down to the little orange-wench.

EMILIA: You're a living libel, a breathing lampoon; I wonder you are not torn in pieces.

MEDLEY: What think you of setting up an office of intelligence for these matters? The project may get money.

LADY TOWNLEY: You would have great dealings with country ladies.

MEDLEY: More than Muddiman has with their husbands.

Enter Belinda.

LADY TOWNLEY: Belinda, what has been become of you? we have not seen you here of late with your friend Mrs. Loveit.

BELINDA: Dear creature, I left [her] but now so sadly afflicted.

LADY TOWNLEY: With her old distemper, jealousy?

MEDLEY: Dorimant has played her some new prank.

BELINDA: Well, that Dorimant is certainly the worst man breathing.

EMILIA: I once thought so.

BELINDA: And do you not think so still?

EMILIA: No, indeed!

BELINDA: Oh, Jesu!

EMILIA: The town does him a great deal of injury, and I will never believe what it says of a man I do not know again, for his sake.

BELINDA: You make me wonder!

LADY TOWNLEY: He's a very well-bred man.

BELINDA: But strangely ill-natured.

EMILIA: Then he's a very witty man.

BELINDA: But a man of no principles.

MEDLEY: Your man of principles is a very fine thing indeed!

BELINDA: To be preferred to men of parts by women who have regard to their reputation and quiet.

Well, were I minded to play the fool, he should be the last man I'd think of.

MEDLEY: He has been the first in many lady's favours, though you are so severe, madam.

LADY TOWNLEY: What he may be for a lover I know not, but he's a very pleasant acquaintance, I am sure.

BELINDA: Had you seen him use Mrs. Loveit as I have done, you would never endure him more.

EMILIA: What, he has quarrelled with her again?

BELINDA: Upon the slightest occasion; he's jealous of Sir Fopling.

LADY TOWNLEY: She never saw him in her life but yesterday, and that was here.

EMILIA: On my conscience, he's the only man in town that's her aversion; how horribly out of humour she was all the while he talked to her!

BELINDA: And somebody has wickedly told him——

EMILIA: Here he comes.

Enter Dorimant.

MEDLEY: Dorimant! you are luckily come to justify yourself—— here's a lady——

BELINDA: Has a word or two to say to you from a disconsolate person.

DORIMANT: You tender your reputation too much, I know, madam, to whisper with me before this good company.

BELINDA: To serve Mrs. Loveit, I'll make a bold venture.

DORIMANT: Here's Medley, the very spirit of scandal.

BELINDA: No matter!

EMILIA: 'Tis something you are unwilling to hear, Mr. Dorimant.

LADY TOWNLEY: Tell him, Belinda, whether he will or no.

BELINDA: [*Aloud*] Mrs. Loveit——

DORIMANT: Softly, these are laughers, you do not know 'em.

BELINDA: [*To* Dorimant, *apart*] In a word, you've made me hate you, which I thought you never could have done.

DORIMANT: In obeying your commands.

BELINDA: 'Twas a cruel part you played! how could you act it?

DORIMANT: Nothing is cruel to a man who could kill himself to please you; remember, five o'clock tomorrow morning.

BELINDA: I tremble when you name it

DORIMANT: Be sure you come.

BELINDA: I shall not.

DORIMANT: Swear you will.

BELINDA: I dare not.

DORIMANT: Swear, I say.

BELINDA: By my life! by all the happiness I hope for——

DORIMANT: You will.

BELINDA: I will.

DORIMANT: Kind.

BELINDA: I am glad I've sworn, I vow I think I should ha' failed you else!

DORIMANT: Surprisingly kind! In what temper did you leave Loveit?

BELINDA: Her raving was prettily over, and she began to be in a brave way of defying you and all your works. Where have you been since you went from thence?

DORIMANT: I looked in at the play.

BELINDA: I have promised, and must return to her again.

DORIMANT: Persuade her to walk in the Mall this evening.

BELINDA: She hates the place, and will not come.

DORIMANT: Do all you can to prevail with her.

BELINDA: For what purpose?

DORIMANT: Sir Fopling will be here anon; I'll prepare him to set upon her there before me.

BELINDA: You persecute her too much; but I'll do all you'll ha' me.

DORIMANT: [*Aloud*] Tell her plainly, 'tis grown so dull a business I can drudge on no longer.

EMILIA: There are afflictions in love, Mr. Dorimant.

DORIMANT: You women make 'em, who are commonly as unreasonable in that as you are at play; without the advantage be on your side a man can never quietly give over when he's weary.

MEDLEY: If you would play without being obliged to complaisance, Dorimant, you should play in public places.

DORIMANT: Ordinaries were a very good thing for that, but gentlemen do not of late frequent 'em; the deep lay is now in private houses.
                          [Belinda *offering to steal away*]

LADY TOWNLEY: Belinda, are you leaving us so soon?

BELINDA: I am to go to the Park with Mrs. Loveit, madam.   [*Exit* Belinda]

LADY TOWNLEY: This *confidence* will go nigh to spoil this young creature.

MEDLEY: 'Twill do her good, madam. Young men who are brought up under practising lawyers prove the abler counsel when they come to be called to the Bar themselves.

DORIMANT: The town has been very favourable to you this afternoon, my Lady Townley; you use to have an *embarras* of chairs and coaches at your door, an uproar of footmen in your hall, and a noise of fools above here.

LADY TOWNLEY: Indeed my house is the general *rendezvous*, and, next to the playhouse, is the common refuge of all the young idle people.

EMILIA: Company is a very good thing, madam, but I wonder you do not love it a little more chosen.

LADY TOWNLEY: 'Tis good to have an universal taste; we should love wit, but for variety be able to divert ourselves with the extravagancies of those who want it.

MEDLEY: Fools will make you laugh.

EMILIA: For once or twice; but the repetition of their

folly after a visit or two grows tedious and unsufferable.

LADY TOWNLEY: You are a little too delicate, Emilia.

Enter a Page.

PAGE: Sir Fopling Flutter, madam, desires to know if you are to be seen.

LADY TOWNLEY: Here's the freshest fool in town, and one who has not cloyed you yet. Page!

PAGE: Madam!

LADY TOWNLEY: Desire him to walk up.   [*Exit* Page]

DORIMANT: Do not you fall on him, Medley, and snub him. Soothe him up in his extravagance; he will show the better.

MEDLEY: You know I have a natural indulgence for fools, and need not this caution, sir.

Enter Sir Fopling Flutter, *with his* Page *after him.*

SIR FOPLING: Page, wait without. Madam [*To* Lady Townley], I kiss your hands. I see yesterday was nothing of chance; the *belles assemblées* form themselves here every day. Lady [*To* Emilia], your servant. Dorimant, let me embrace thee; without lying, I have not met with any of my acquaintance who retain so much of Paris as thou dost—the very air thou hadst when the marquis mistook thee i' th' Tuileries, and cried, *He! Chevalier!* and then begged thy pardon.

DORIMANT: I would fain wear in fashion as long as I can, sir; 'tis a thing to be valued in men as well as baubles.

SIR FOPLING: Thou art a man of wit, and understandest the town; prithee let thee and I be intimate, there is no living without making some good man the confidant of our pleasures.

DORIMANT: 'Tis true! but there is no man so improper for such a business as I am.

SIR FOPLING: Prithee, why hast thou so modest an opinion of thyself?

DORIMANT: Why, first, I could never keep a secret in my life, and then there is no charm so infallibly makes me fall in love with a woman as my knowing a friend loves her. I deal honestly with you.

SIR FOPLING: Thy humour's very gallant, or let me perish; I knew a French count so like thee.

LADY TOWNLEY: Wit, I perceive, has more power over you than beauty, Sir Fopling, else you would not have let this lady stand so long neglected.

SIR FOPLING: [*To* Emilia] A thousand pardons, madam; some civilities due, of course, upon the meeting a long absent friend. The *éclat* of so much beauty, I confess, ought to have charmed me sooner.

EMILIA: The *brilliant* of so much good language, sir, has much more power than the little beauty I can boast.

SIR FOPLING: I never saw anything prettier than this high work on your *point d' Espagne.*——

EMILIA: 'Tis not so rich as *point de Venise.*——

SIR FOPLING: Not altogether, but looks cooler, and is more proper for the season. Dorimant, is not that Medley?

DORIMANT: The same, sir.

SIR FOPLING: Forgive me, sir; in this *embarras* of civilities I could not come to have you in my arms sooner. You understand an equipage the best of any man in town, I hear.

MEDLEY: By my own you would not guess it.

SIR FOPLING: There are critics who do not write, sir.

MEDLEY: Our peevish poets will scarce allow it.

SIR FOPLING: Damn 'em, they'll allow no man wit who does not play the fool like themselves, and show it! Have you taken notice of the *calèche* I brought over?

MEDLEY: Oh, yes! It has quite another air than the English makes.

SIR FOPLING: 'Tis as easily known from an English tumbril as an Inns of Court man is from one of us.

DORIMANT: Truly, there is a *bel-air* in *calèches* as well as men.

MEDLEY: But there are few so delicate to observe it.

SIR FOPLING: The world is generally very *grossier* here, indeed.

LADY TOWNLEY: He's very fine.

EMILIA: Extreme proper.

SIR FOPLING: A slight suit I made to appear in at my first arrival, not worthy your consideration, ladies.

DORIMANT: The pantaloon is very well mounted.

SIR FOPLING: The tassels are new and pretty.

MEDLEY: I never saw a coat better cut.

SIR FOPLING: It makes me show long-waisted, and, I think slender.

DORIMANT: That's the shape our ladies dote on.

MEDLEY: Your breech, though, is a handful too high in my eye, Sir Fopling.

SIR FOPLING: Peace, Medley; I have wished it lower a thousand times, but a pox on't, 'twill not be.

LADY TOWNLEY: His gloves are well fringed, large and graceful.

SIR FOPLING: I was always eminent for being *biengante.*

EMILIA: He wears nothing but what are originals of the most famous hands in Paris.

SIR FOPLING: You are in the right, madam.

LADY TOWNLEY: The suit?

SIR FOPLING: Barroy.

EMILIA: The garniture?

SIR FOPLING: Le Gras.

MEDLEY: The shoes?

SIR FOPLING: Piccat.

DORIMANT: The periwig?

SIR FOPLING: Chedreux.

LADY TOWNLEY and EMILIA: The gloves?

SIR FOPLING: Orangerie: you know the smell, ladies. Dorimant, I could find in my heart for an amusement to have a gallantry with some of our English ladies.

DORIMANT: 'Tis a thing no less necessary to confirm

the reputation of your wit than a duel will be to satisfy the town of your courage.

SIR FOPLING: Here was a woman yesterday——

DORIMANT: Mistress Loveit.

SIR FOPLING: You have named her.

DORIMANT: You cannot pitch on a better for your purpose.

SIR FOPLING: Prithee, what is she?

DORIMANT: A person of quality, and one who has a rest of reputation enough to make the conquest considerable. Besides, I hear she likes you too.

SIR FOPLING: Methought she seemed, though, very reserved and uneasy all the time I entertained her.

DORIMANT: Grimace and affection. You will see her i' th' Mall to-night.

SIR FOPLING: Prithee let thee and I take the air together.

DORIMANT: I am engaged to Medley, but I'll meet you at St. James's and give you some information upon the which you may regulate your proceedings.

SIR FOPLING: All the world will be in the Park tonight: ladies, 'twere pity to keep so much beauty longer within doors and rob the Ring of all those charms that should adorn it.—— Hey, page!

Enter Page, *and goes out again.*
See that all my people be ready. Dorimant, *au revoir!* [*Exit* Sir Fopling]

MEDLEY: A fine mettled coxcomb.

DORIMANT: Brisk and insipid.

MEDLEY: Pert and dull.

EMILIA: However you despise him, gentlemen, I'll lay my life he passes for a wit with many.

DORIMANT: That may very well be; nature has her cheats, stums a brain, and puts sophisticate dulness often on the tasteless multitude for true wit and good-humour. Medley, come.

MEDLEY: I must go a little way, I will meet you i' the Mall.

DORIMANT: I'll walk through the garden thither. [*To the* Women] We shall meet anon and bow.

LADY TOWNLEY: Not to-night; we are engaged about a business the knowledge of which may make you laugh hereafter.

MEDLEY: Your servant, ladies.

DORIMANT: *Au revoir!* as Sir Fopling says.
[*Exeunt* Medley *and* Dorimant]

LADY TOWNLEY: The old man will be here immediately.

EMILIA: Let's expect him i' th' garden.

LADY TOWNLEY: Go, you are a rogue.

EMILIA: I can't abide you.   [*Exeunt*]

SCENE 3: *The Mall*

Enter Harriet *and* Young Bellair, *she pulling him.*

HARRIET: Come along.

YOUNG BELLAIR: And leave your mother?

HARRIET: Busy will be sent with a hue and cry after us; but that's no matter.

YOUNG BELLAIR: 'Twill look strangely in me.

HARRIET: She'll believe it a freak of mine and never blame your manners.

YOUNG BELLAIR: What reverend acquaintance is that she has met?

HARRIET: A fellow-beauty of the last King's time, though by the ruins you would hardly guess it.
[*Exeunt*]

Enter Dorimant, *who crosses the stage.*

Enter Young Bellair *and* Harriet.

YOUNG BELLAIR: By this time your mother is in a fine taking.

HARRIET: If your friend Mr. Dorimant were but here now, that she might find me talking with him.

YOUNG BELLAIR: She does not know him, but dreads him, I hear, of all mankind.

HARRIET: She concludes if he does but speak to a woman she's undone; is on her knees every day to pray heaven defend me from him.

YOUNG BELLAIR: You do not apprehend him so much as she does.

HARRIET: I never saw anything in him that was frightful.

YOUNG BELLAIR: On the contrary, have you not observed something extreme delightful in his wit and person?

HARRIET: He's agreeable and pleasant I must own, but he does so much affect being so, he displeases me.

YOUNG BELLAIR: Lord, madam, all he does and says is so easy and so natural.

HARRIET: Some men's verses seem so to the unskilful, but labour i' the one and affectation in the other to the judicious plainly appear.

YOUNG BELLAIR: I never heard him accused of affection before.

Enter Dorimant, *who stares upon her.*

HARRIET: It passes on the easy town, who are favourably pleased in him to call it humour.
[*Exeunt* Young Bellair *and* Harriet]

DORIMANT: 'Tis she! it must be she, that lovely hair, that easy shape, those wanton eyes, and all those melting charms about her mouth which Medley spoke of; I'll follow the lottery, and put in for a prize with my friend Bellair.
[*Exit* Dorimant *repeating:*

In love the victors from the vanquish'd fly;
They fly that wound, and they pursue that die.]

Enter Young Bellair *and* Harriet, *and after them* Dorimant, *standing at a distance.*

YOUNG BELLAIR: Most people prefer High Park to this place.

HARRIET: It has the better reputation, I confess; but I abominate the dull diversions there, the formal bows, the affected smiles, the silly by-words, and amorous tweers in passing; here one meets with a little conversation now and then.

YOUNG BELLAIR: These conversations have been fatal to some of your sex, madam.

HARRIET: It may be so; because some who want temper have been undone by gaming, must others who have it wholly deny themselves the pleasure of play?

DORIMANT: Trust me, it were unreasonable, madam.
                    [*Coming up gently, and bowing to her*]

HARRIET: Lord! who's this?
                    [*She starts, and looks grave*]

YOUNG BELLAIR: Dorimant.

DORIMANT: Is this the woman your father would have you marry?

YOUNG BELLAIR: It is.

DORIMANT: Her name?

YOUNG BELLAIR: Harriet.

DORIMANT: I am not mistaken, she's handsome.

YOUNG BELLAIR: Talk to her, her wit is better than her face; we were wishing for you but now.

DORIMANT: [*To Harriet*] Overcast with seriousness o' the sudden! A thousand smiles were shining in that face but now; I never saw so quick a change of weather.

HARRIET: [*Aside*] I feel as great a change within; but he shall never know it.

DORIMANT: You were talking of play, madam; pray what may be your stint?

HARRIET: A little harmless discourse in public walks, or at most an appointment in a box barefaced at the playhouse; you are for masks and private meetings where women engage for all they are worth, I hear.

DORIMANT: I have been used to deep play, but I can make one at small game when I like my gamester well.

HARRIET: And be so unconcerned you'll ha' no pleasure in it.

DORIMANT: Where there is a considerable sum to be won the hope of drawing people in makes every trifle considerable.

HARRIET: The sordidness of men's natures, I know, makes 'em willing to flatter and comply with the rich, though they are sure never to be the better for 'em.

DORIMANT: 'Tis in their power to do us good, and we despair not but at some time or other they may be willing.

HARRIET: To men who have fared on this town like you, 'twould be a great mortification to live on hope; could you keep a Lent for a mistress?

DORIMANT: In expectation of a happy Easter, and though time be very precious, think forty days well lost to gain your favour.

HARRIET: Mr. Bellair! let us walk, 'tis time to leave him; men grow dull when they begin to be particular.

DORIMANT: You're mistaken, flattery will not ensue, though I know you're greedy of the praises of the whole Mall.

HARRIET: You do me wrong.

DORIMANT: I do not; as I followed you I observed how you were pleased when the fops cried: "She's handsome, very handsome, By God she is," and whispered aloud your name, the thousand several forms you put your face into; then, to make yourself more agreeable, how wantonly you played with your head, flung back your locks, and looked smilingly over your shoulder at 'em.

HARRIET: I do not go begging the men's, as you do the ladies' good liking, with a sly softness in your looks and a gentle slowness in your bows as you pass by 'em——as thus, sir;——   [*Acts him*]
Is not this like you?

Enter Lady Woodvil *and* Busy.

YOUNG BELLAIR: Your mother, madam.
                    [*Pulls* Harriet; *she composes herself*]

LADY WOODVIL: Ah, my dear child Harriet!

BUSY: Now is she so pleased with finding her again she cannot chide her.

LADY WOODVIL: Come away!

DORIMANT: 'Tis now but high Mall, madam, the most entertaining time of all the evening.

HARRIET: I would fain see that Dorimant, mother, you so cry out for a monster; he's in the Mall, I hear.

LADY WOODVIL: Come away then! the plague is here, and you should dread the infection.

YOUNG BELLAIR: You may be misinformed of the gentleman.

LADY WOODVIL: Oh, no! I hope you do not know him! He is the prince of all the devils in the town, delights in nothing but in rapes and riots.

DORIMANT: If you did but hear him speak, madam!

LADY WOODVIL: Oh! he has a tongue, they say, would tempt the angels to a second fall.

Enter Sir Fopling *with his Equipage, six* Footmen *and a* Page.

SIR FOPLING: Hey, Champagne, Norman, La Rose, La Fleur, La Tour, La Verdue. Dorimant!——

LADY WOODVIL: Here, here he is among this rout, he names him; come away, Harriet, come away.
                    [*Exeunt* Lady Woodvil, Harriet, Busy, *and* Young Bellair]

DORIMANT: This fool's coming has spoiled all; she's gone, but she has left a pleasing image of herself behind that wanders in my soul——It must not settle there.

SIR FOPLING: What reverie is this? Speak, man.

DORIMANT: Snatch'd from myself, how far behind Already I behold the shore!

Enter Medley.

MEDLEY: Dorimant, a discovery! I met with Bellair.

DORIMANT: You can tell me no news, sir; I know all.

MEDLEY: How do you like the daughter?

DORIMANT: You never came so near truth in your life as you did in her description.

MEDLEY: What think you of the mother?

DORIMANT: Whatever I think of her, she thinks very well of me, I find.

MEDLEY: Did she know you?

DORIMANT: She did not; whether she does now or no, I know not. Here was a pleasant scene towards, when in came Sir Fopling, mustering up his equipage, and at the latter end named me and frighted her away.

MEDLEY: Loveit and Belinda are not far off, I saw 'em alight at St. James's.

DORIMANT: [*Whispers*] Sir Fopling, hark you, a word or two. Look you do not want assurance.

SIR FOPLING: I never do on these occasions.

DORIMANT: Walk on, we must not be seen together; make your advantage of what I have told you; the next turn you will meet the lady.

SIR FOPLING: Hey——Follow me all.

[*Exeunt* Sir Fopling *and his Equipage*]

DORIMANT: Medley, you shall see good sport anon between Loveit and this Fopling.

MEDLEY: I thought there was something toward by that whisper.

DORIMANT: You know a worthy principle of hers?

MEDLEY: Not to be so much as civil to a man who speaks to her in the presence of him she professes to love.

DORIMANT: I have encouraged Fopling to talk to her to-night.

MEDLEY: Now you are here she will go nigh to beat him.

DORIMANT: In the humour she's in, her love will make her do some very extravagant thing, doubtless.

MEDLEY: What was Belinda's business with you at my Lady Townley's?

DORIMANT: To get me to meet Loveit here in order to an *éclaircissement*. I made some difficulty of it, and have prepared this *rencontre* to make good my jealousy.

MEDLEY: Here they come!

Enter Mrs. Loveit, Belinda, *and* Pert.

DORIMANT: I'll meet her and provoke her with a deal of dumb civility in passing by, then turn short and be behind her when Sir Fopling sets upon her.

    See how unregarded now
    That piece of beauty passes.

[*Exeunt* Dorimant *and* Medley]

BELINDA: How wonderful respectfully he bowed!

PERT: He's always over-mannerly when he has done a mischief.

BELINDA: Methought indeed at the same time he had a strange despising countenance.

PERT: The unlucky look, he thinks, becomes him.

BELINDA: I was afraid you would have spoke to him, my dear.

MRS. LOVEIT: I would have died first; he shall no more find me the loving fool he has done.

BELINDA: You love him still!

MRS. LOVEIT: No.

PERT: I wish you did not.

MRS. LOVEIT: I do not, and I will have you think so. What made you hale me to this odious place, Belinda?

BELINDA: I hate to be hulched up in a coach; walking is much better.

MRS. LOVEIT: Would we could meet Sir Fopling now!

BELINDA: Lord! would you not avoid him?

MRS. LOVEIT: I would make him all the advances that may be.

BELINDA: That would confirm Dorimant's suspicion, my dear.

MRS. LOVEIT: He is not jealous, but I will make him so, and be revenged a way he little thinks on.

BELINDA: [*Aside*] If she should make him jealous, that may make him fond of her again: I must dissuade her from it. Lord! my dear, this will certainly make him hate you.

MRS. LOVEIT: 'Twill make him uneasy, though he does not care for me; I know the effects of jealousy on men of his proud temper.

BELINDA: 'Tis a fantastic remedy, its operations are dangerous and uncertain.

MRS. LOVEIT: 'Tis the strongest cordial we can give to dying love, it often brings it back when there's no sign of life remaining. But I design not so much the reviving his, as my revenge.

Enter Sir Fopling *and his Equipage.*

SIR FOPLING: Hey! bid the coachman send home four of his horses, and bring the coach to Whitehall; I'll walk over the Park——Madam, the honour of kissing your fair hands is a happiness I missed this afternoon at my Lady Townley's.

MRS. LOVEIT: You were very obliging, Sir Fopling, the last time I saw you there.

SIR FOPLING: The preference was due to your wit and beauty. Madam, your servant; there never was so sweet an evening.

BELINDA: 'T has drawn all the rabble of the town hither.

SIR FOPLING: 'Tis pity there's not an order made that none but the *beau monde* should walk here.

MRS. LOVEIT: 'Twould add much to the beauty of the place. See what a sort of nasty fellows are coming.

Enter three ill-fashioned Fellows, *singing,*

    'Tis not for kisses alone, etc.

MRS. LOVEIT: Fo! Their periwigs are scented with tobacco so strong——

SIR FOPLING: It overcomes our pulvillio[1]——Methinks I smell the coffee-house they came from.

[1]*A favourite essence.*

1 MAN: Dorimant's convenient, Madam Loveit.

2 MAN: I like the oily buttock with her.

3 MAN: What spruce prig is that?

1 MAN: A caravan lately come from Paris.

2 MAN: Peace, they smoke.

There's something else to be done, etc.

[All of them coughing; exeunt, singing]
Enter Dorimant and Medley.

DORIMANT: They're engaged.

MEDLEY: She entertains him as if she liked him.

DORIMANT: Let us go forward; seem earnest in discourse, and show ourselves. Then you shall see how she'll use him.

BELINDA: Yonder's Dorimant, my dear.

MRS. LOVEIT: [Aside] I see him, he comes insulting; but I will disappoint him in his expectation. [To Sir Fopling] I like this pretty nice humour of yours, Sir Fopling. With what a loathing eye he looked upon those fellows!

SIR FOPLING: I sat near one of 'em at a play to-day, and was almost poisoned with a pair of cordovan gloves he wears.

MRS. LOVEIT: Oh! filthy cordovan, how I hate the smell!   [Laughs in a loud affected way]

SIR FOPLING: Did you observe, madam, how their cravats hung loose an inch from their neck, and what a frightful air it gave 'em?

MRS. LOVEIT: Oh! I took particular notice of one that is always spruced up with a deal of dirty sky-coloured ribbon.

BELINDA: That's one of the walking flageolets who haunt the Mall o' nights.

MRS. LOVEIT: Oh! I remember him; he's a hollow tooth enough to spoil the sweetness of an evening.

SIR FOPLING: I have seen the tallest walk the streets with a dainty pair of boxes neatly buckled on.

MRS. LOVEIT: And a little footboy at his heels pocket-high, with a flat cap——a dirty face.

SIR FOPLING: And a snotty nose.

MRS. LOVEIT: Oh——odious! there's many of my own sex with that Holborn equipage trip to Gray's Inn Walks, and now and then travel hither on a Sunday.

MEDLEY: She takes no notice of you.

DORIMANT: Damn her! I am jealous of a counterplot!

MRS. LOVEIT: Your liveries are the finest, Sir Fopling. ——Oh, that page! that page is the prettily'st dressed——They are all Frenchmen?

SIR FOPLING: There's one damned English blockhead among 'em, you may know him by his mien.

MRS. LOVEIT: Oh! that's he, that's he! what do you call him?

SIR FOPLING: Hey!——I know not what to call him.——

MRS. LOVEIT: What's your name?

FOOTMAN: John Trott, madam!

SIR FOPLING: Oh, unsufferable! Trott, Trott, Trott! there's nothing so barbarous as the names of our English servants. What countryman are you, sirrah?

FOOTMAN: Hampshire, sir.

SIR FOPLING: Then Hampshire be your name. Hey, Hampshire!

MRS. LOVEIT: Oh, that sound! that sound becomes the mouth of a man of quality!

MEDLEY: Dorimant, you look a little bashful on the matter.

DORIMANT: She dissembles better than I thought she could have done.

MEDLEY: You have tempted her with too luscious a bait: she bites at the coxcomb.

DORIMANT: She cannot fall from loving me to that?

MEDLEY: You begin to be jealous in earnest.

DORIMANT: Of one I do not love?

MEDLEY: You did love her.

DORIMANT: The fit has long been over.

MEDLEY: But I have known men fall into dangerous relapses when they have found a woman inclining to another.

DORIMANT: [To himself] He guesses the secret of my heart! I am concerned, but dare not show it lest Belinda should mistrust all I have done to gain her.

BELINDA: [Aside] I have watched his look, and find no alteration there: did he love her, some signs of jealousy would have appeared.

DORIMANT: I hope this happy evening, madam, has reconciled you to the scandalous Mall; we shall have you now hankering here again.

MRS. LOVEIT: Sir Fopling, will you walk?

SIR FOPLING: I am all obedience, madam.

MRS. LOVEIT: Come along then, and let's agree to be malicious on all the ill-fashioned things we meet.

SIR FOPLING: We'll make a critique on the whole Mall, madam.

MRS. LOVEIT: Belinda, you shall engage——

BELINDA: To the reserve of our friends, my dear.

MRS. LOVEIT: No, no exceptions——

SIR FOPLING: We'll sacrifice all to our diversion.

MRS. LOVEIT: All—all——

SIR FOPLING: All.

BELINDA: All? Then let it be.

[Exeunt Sir Fopling, Mrs. Loveit, Belinda, and Pert, laughing]

MEDLEY: Would you had brought some more of your friends, Dorimant, to have been witnesses of Sir Fopling's disgrace and your triumph.

DORIMANT: 'Twere unreasonable to desire you not to laugh at me; but pray do not expose me to the town this day or two.

MEDLEY: By that time you hope to have regained your credit?

DORIMANT: I know she hates Fopling, and only makes use of him in hope to work me on again; had it not been for some powerful considerations which will be removed to-morrow morning, I had made her pluck off this mask and show the passion that lies panting under.

Enter a Footman.

MEDLEY: Here comes a man from Bellair, with news of your last adventure.

DORIMANT: I am glad he sent him. I long to know the consequence of our parting.

FOOTMAN: Sir, my master desires you to come to my Lady Townley's presently, and bring Mr. Medley with you. My Lady Woodvil and her daughter are there.

MEDLEY: Then all's well, Dorimant.

FOOTMAN: They have sent for the fiddles and mean to dance! He bid me tell you, sir, the old lady does not know you, and would have you own yourself to be Mr. Courtage. They are all prepared to receive you by that name.

DORIMANT: That foppish admirer of quality who flatters the very meat at honourable tables, and never offers love to a woman below a lady-grandmother.

MEDLEY: You know the character you are to act, I see.

DORIMANT: This is Harriet's contrivance——wild, witty, lovesome, beautiful and young——come along, Medley.

MEDLEY: This new woman would well supply the loss of Loveit.

DORIMANT: That business must not end so; before to-morrow's sun is set I will revenge and clear it:

> And you and Loveit to her cost shall find,
> I fathom all the depths of womankind. [*Exeunt*]

Act IV

SCENE 1: *The scene opens with the fiddles playing a country dance*

Enter Dorimant, Lady Woodvil, Young Bellair, *and* Mrs. Harriet, Old Bellair, *and* Emilia, Mr. Medley *and* Lady Townley, *as having just ended the dance.*

OLD BELLAIR: So, so, so, a smart bout, a very smart bout, adod!

LADY TOWNLEY: How do you like Emilia's dancing, brother?

OLD BELLAIR: Not at all, not at all.

LADY TOWNLEY: You speak not what you think, I am sure.

OLD BELLAIR: No matter for that; go, bid her dance no more, it don't become her, it don't become her, tell her I say so. [*Aside*] Adod, I love her.

DORIMANT: [*To Lady Woodvil*] All people mingle nowadays, madam, and in public places women of quality have the least respect showed 'em.

LADY WOODVIL: I protest you say the truth, Mr. Courtage.

DORIMANT: Forms and ceremonies, the only things that uphold quality and greatness, are now shamefully laid aside and neglected.

LADY WOODVIL: Well! this is not the women's age, let

'em think what they will; lewdness is the business now, love was the business in my time.

DORIMANT: The women indeed are little beholding to the young men of this age; they're generally only dull admirers of themselves, and make their court to nothing but their periwigs and their cravats, and would be more concerned for the disordering of 'em, though on a good occasion, than a young maid would be for the tumbling of her head or handkerchief.

LADY WOODVIL: I protest you hit 'em.

DORIMANT: They are very assiduous to show themselves at Court well dressed to the women of quality, but their business is with the stale mistresses of the town, who are prepared to receive their lazy addresses by industrious old lovers who have cast 'em off and made 'em easy.

HARRIET: He fits my mother's humour so well, a little more and she'll dance a kissing dance with him anon.

MEDLEY: Dutifully observed, madam.

DORIMANT: They pretend to be great critics in beauty; by their talk you would think they liked no face, and yet can dote on an ill one if it belong to a laundress or a tailor's daughter; they cry a woman's past her prime at twenty, decayed at four-and-twenty, old and unsufferable at thirty.

LADY WOODVIL: Unsufferable at thirty! That they are in the wrong, Mr. Courtage, at five-and-thirty there are living proofs enough to convince 'em.

DORIMANT: Ay, madam, there's Mrs. Setlooks, Mrs. Droplip, and my Lady Lowd; show me among all our opening buds a face that promises so much beauty as the remains of theirs.

LADY WOODVIL: The depraved appetite of this vicious age tastes nothing but green fruit, and loathes it when 'tis kindly ripened.

DORIMANT: Else so many deserving women, madam, would not be so untimely neglected.

LADY WOODVIL: I protest, Mr. Courtage, a dozen such good men as you would be enough to atone for that wicked Dorimant and all the under-debauchees of the town.

> [Harriet, Emilia, Young Bellair, Medley, *and* Lady Townley *break out into laughter*]

What's the matter there?

MEDLEY: A pleasant mistake, madam, that a lady has made, occasions a little laughter.

OLD BELLAIR: Come, come, you keep 'em idle, they are impatient till the fiddles play again.

DORIMANT: You are not weary, madam?

LADY WOODVIL: One dance more; I cannot refuse you, Mr. Courtage.   [*They dance*]

EMILIA: You are very active, sir.

> [*After the dance* Old Bellair *singing and dancing up to* Emilia]

OLD BELLAIR: Adod, sirrah, when I was a young fellow I could ha' capered up to my woman's gorget.

DORIMANT: You are willing to rest yourself, madam?

LADY TOWNLEY: We'll walk into my chamber and sit down.

MEDLEY: Leave us Mr. Courtage, he's a dancer, and the young ladies are not weary yet.

LADY WOODVIL: We'll send him out again.

HARRIET: If you do not quickly, I know where to send for Mr. Dorimant.

LADY WOODVIL: This girl's head, Mr. Courtage, is ever running on that wild fellow.

DORIMANT: 'Tis well you have got her a good husband, madam; that will settle it.

[*Exeunt* Lady Townley, Lady Woodvil, *and* Dorimant]

OLD BELLAIR: [*To* Emilia] Adod, sweetheart, be advised, and do not throw thyself away on a young idle fellow.

EMILIA: I have no such intention, sir.

OLD BELLAIR: Have a little patience, thou shalt have the man I spake of. Adod, he loves thee, and will make a good husband; but no words.

EMILIA: But, sir.——

OLD BELLAIR: No answer——out a pise! peace! and think on't.

Enter Dorimant.

DORIMANT: Your company is desired within, sir.

OLD BELLAIR: I go, I go, good Mr. Courtage—— [*To* Emilia] Fare you well; go, I'll see you no more.

EMILIA: What have I done, sir?

OLD BELLAIR: You are ugly, you are ugly; is she not, Mr. Courtage?

EMILIA: Better words, or I shan't abide you.

OLD BELLAIR: Out a pise——adod, what does she say? Hit her a pat for me there. [*Exit* Old Bellair]

MEDLEY: You have charms for the whole family.

DORIMANT: You'll spoil all with some unseasonable jest, Medley.

MEDLEY: You see I confine my tongue and am content to be a bare spectator, much contrary to my nature.

EMILIA: Methinks, Mr. Dorimant, my Lady Woodvil is a little fond of you.

DORIMANT: Would her daughter were!

MEDLEY: It may be you may find her so; try her, you have an opportunity.

DORIMANT: And I will not lose it. Bellair, here's a lady has something to say to you.

YOUNG BELLAIR: I wait upon her. Mr. Medley, we have both business with you.

DORIMANT: Get you all together then. [*To* Harriet] That demure curtsey is not amiss in jest, but do not think in earnest it becomes you.

HARRIET: Affectation is catching, I find; from your grave bow I got it.

DORIMANT: Where had you all that scorn and coldness in your look?

HARRIET: From nature, sir; pardon my want of art: I have not learnt those softnesses and languishings which now in faces are so much in fashion.

DORIMANT: You need 'em not; you have a sweetness of your own, if you would but calm your frowns and let it settle.

HARRIET: My eyes are wild and wandering like my passions, and cannot yet be tied to rules of charming.

DORIMANT: Women, indeed, have commonly a method of managing those messengers of love; now they will look as if they would kill, and anon they will look as if they were dying. They point and rebate[1] their glances the better to invite us.

HARRIET: I like this variety well enough, but hate the set face that always looks as it would say, Come, love me—a woman who at plays makes the *doux yeux* to a whole audience and at home cannot forbear 'em to her monkey.

DORIMANT: Put on a gentle smile, and let me see how well it will become you.

HARRIET: I am sorry my face does not please you as it is, but I shall not be complaisant and change it.

DORIMANT: Though you are obstinate, I know 'tis capable of improvement, and shall do you justice, madam, if I chance to be at Court when the critics of the circle pass their judgment; for thither you must come.

HARRIET: And expect to be taken in pieces, have all my features examined, every motion censured, and on the whole be condemned to be but pretty, or a beauty of the lowest rate. What think you?

DORIMANT: The women, nay, the very lovers who belong to the drawing-room, will maliciously allow you more than that; they always grant what is apparent that they may the better be believed when they name concealed faults they cannot easily be disproved in.

HARRIET: Beauty runs as great a risk exposed at Court as wit does on the stage, where the ugly and the foolish all are free to censure.

DORIMANT: [*Aside*] I love her, and dare not let her know it; I fear she has an ascendant o'er me, and may revenge the wrongs I have done her sex. [*To her*] Think of making a party, madam, love will engage.

HARRIET: You make me start! I did not think to have heard of love from you.

DORIMANT: I never knew what 'twas to have a settled ague yet, but now and then have had irregular fits.

HARRIET: Take heed! sickness after long health is commonly more violent and dangerous.

DORIMANT: [*Aside*] I have took the infection from her, and feel the disease now spreading in me—— [*To her*] Is the name of love so frightful that you dare not stand it?

HARRIET: 'Twill do little execution out of your mouth on me, I am sure.

DORIMANT: It has been fatal——

[1] *A fencing term.*

HARRIET: To some easy women, but we are not all born to one destiny; I was informed you use to laugh at love, and not make it.

DORIMANT: The time has been, but now I must speak——

HARRIET: If it be on that idle subject, I will put on my serious look, turn my head carelessly from you, drop my lip, let my eyelids fall and hang half o'er my eyes—thus—while you buzz a speech of an hour long in my ear, and I answer never a word; why do you not begin?

DORIMANT: That the company may take notice how passionately I make advances of love, and how disdainfully you receive 'em.

HARRIET: When your love's grown strong enough to make you bear being laughed at, I'll give you leave to trouble me with it: till when, pray forbear, sir.

Enter Sir Fopling *and others in masks.*

DORIMANT: What's here, masquerades?

HARRIET: I thought that foppery had been left off and people might have been in private with a fiddle.

DORIMANT: 'Tis endeavoured to be kept on foot still by some who find themselves the more acceptable the less they are known.

YOUNG BELLAIR: This must be Sir Fopling.

MEDLEY: That extraordinary habit shows it.

YOUNG BELLAIR: What are the rest?

MEDLEY: A company of French rascals whom he picked up in Paris and has brought over to be his dancing equipage on these occasions. Make him own himself; a fool is very troublesome when he presumes he is incognito.

SIR FOPLING: [*To Harriet*] Do you know me?

HARRIET: Ten to one but I guess at you.

SIR FOPLING: Are you women as fond of a vizard as we men are?

HARRIET: I am very fond of a vizard that covers a face I do not like, sir.

YOUNG BELLAIR: Here are no masks, you see, sir, but those which came with you; this was intended a private meeting, but because you look like a gentleman, if you discover yourself, and we know you to be such, you shall be welcome.

SIR FOPLING: [*Pulling off his mask*] Dear Bellair.

MEDLEY: Sir Fopling! how came you hither?

SIR FOPLING: Faith, I was coming late from Whitehall, after the King's *couchée*, one of my people told me he had heard fiddles at my Lady Townley's, and——

DORIMANT: You need not say any more, sir.

SIR FOPLING: Dorimant, let me kiss thee.

DORIMANT: [*Whispers*] Hark you, Sir Fopling.

SIR FOPLING: Enough, enough—Courtage. A pretty kind of young woman that, Medley; I observed her in the Mall; more *éveillée* than our English women commonly are; prithee, what is she?

MEDLEY: The most noted *coquette* in town; beware of her.

SIR FOPLING: Let her be what she will, I know how to take my measures; in Paris the *mode* is to flatter the *prude*, laugh at the *faux-prude*, make serious love to the *demi-prude*, and only rally with the *coquette*. Medley, what think you?

MEDLEY: That for all this smattering of the mathematics, you may be out in your judgment at tennis.

SIR FOPLING: What a *coq-à-l'âne* is this! I talk of women, and thou answer'st tennis.

MEDLEY: Mistakes will be for want of apprehension.

SIR FOPLING: I am very glad of the acquaintance I have with this family.

MEDLEY: My lady truly is a good woman.

SIR FOPLING: Ah! Dorimant—Courtage I would say—would thou hadst spent the last winter in Paris with me. When thou wert there La Corneus and Sallyes were the only habitudes we had; a comedian would have been a *bonne fortune*. No stranger ever passed his time so well as I did some months before I came over. I was well received in a dozen families where all the women of quality used to visit; I have intrigues to tell thee more pleasant than ever thou read'st in a novel.

HARRIET: Write 'em, sir, and oblige us women; our language wants such little stories.

SIR FOPLING: Writing, madam, is a mechanic part of wit; a gentleman should never go beyond a song or a billet.

HARRIET: Bussy was a gentleman.

SIR FOPLING: Who, d'Ambois?

MEDLEY: Was there ever such a brisk blockhead?

HARRIET: Not d'Ambois, sir, but Rabutin—he who writ *The Loves of France.*

SIR FOPLING: That may be madam: many gentlemen do things that are below 'em. Damn your authors, Courtage; women are the prettiest things we can fool away our time with.

HARRIET: I hope ye have wearied yourself to-night at Court sir, and will not think of fooling with anybody here.

SIR FOPLING: I cannot complain of my fortune there, madam——Dorimant——

DORIMANT: Again!

SIR FOPLING: Courtage, a pox on't! I have something to tell thee. When I had made my court within, I came out and flung myself upon the mat under the State i' th' outward room i' th' midst of half a dozen beauties who were withdrawn to jeer among themselves, as they called it.

DORIMANT: Did you know 'em?

SIR FOPLING: Not one of 'em by heavens! not I. But they were all your friends.

DORIMANT: How are you sure of that?

SIR FOPLING: Why we laughed at all the town; spared nobody but yourself; they found me a man for their purpose.

DORIMANT: I know you are malicious to your power.

SIR FOPLING: And faith I had occasion to show it for I never saw more gaping fools at a ball or on a Birthday.

DORIMANT: You learned who the women were?

SIR FOPLING: No matter; they frequent the drawing-room.

DORIMANT: And entertain themselves pleasantly at the expense of all the fops who come there.

SIR FOPLING: That's their business; faith, I sifted 'em, and find they have a sort of wit among them—— Ah! filthy.   [Pinches a tallow candle]

DORIMANT: Look, he has been pinching the tallow candle.

SIR FOPLING: How can you breathe in a room where there's grease frying? Dorimant, thou art intimate with my lady, advise her for her own sake, and the good company that comes hither, to burn wax lights.

HARRIET: What are these masquerades who stand so obsequiously at a distance?

SIR FOPLING: A set of balladins whom I picked out of the best in France, and brought over with a flutes douces or two, my servants; they shall entertain you.

HARRIET: I had rather see you dance yourself, Sir Fopling.

SIR FOPLING: And I had rather do it—all the company knows it—but, madam——

MEDLEY: Come, come, no excuses, Sir Fopling.

SIR FOPLING: By heavens, Medley!

MEDLEY: Like a woman, I find you must be struggled with before one brings you to what you desire.

HARRIET: [Aside] Can he dance?

EMILIA: And fence and sing too, if you'll believe him.

DORIMANT: He has no more excellence in his heels than in his head. He went to Paris a plain bashful English blockhead, and is returned a fine under-taking French fop.

MEDLEY: I cannot prevail.

SIR FOPLING: Do not think it want of complaisance, madam.

HARRIET: You are too well bred to want that, Sir Fopling. I believe it want of power.

SIR FOPLING: By heavens! and so it is. I have sat up so damned late and drunk so cursed hard since I came to this lewd town, that I am fit for nothing but low dancing now, a corant, bourée, or a menuet; but St. André tells me, if I will but be regular, in one month I shall rise again. Pox on this debauchery!   [Endeavours at a caper]

EMILIA: I have heard your dancing much commended.

SIR FOPLING: It had the good fortune to please in Paris. I was judged to rise within an inch as high as the basque, in an entry I danced there.

HARRIET: I am mightily taken with this fool; let us sit. Here's a seat, Sir Fopling.

SIR FOPLING: At your feet, madam; I can be nowhere so much at ease: by your leave, gown.

HARRIET and EMILIA: Ah! you'll spoil it.

SIR FOPLING: No matter, my clothes are my creatures; I make 'em to make my court to you ladies, hey——   [Dances]
Qu'on commence—to an English dancer English motions. I was forced to entertain this fellow, one of my set miscarrying—— Oh, horrid! leave your damned manner of dancing, and put on the French air; have you not a pattern before you——pretty well! Imitation in time may bring him to something.

After the dance enter Old Bellair, Lady Woodvil, *and* Lady Townley.

OLD BELLAIR: Hey, adod! what have we here, a mumming?

LADY WOODVIL: Where's my daughter——Harriet?

DORIMANT: Here, here, madam. I know not but under these disguises there may be dangerous sparks; I gave the young lady warning.

LADY WOODVIL: Lord! I am so obliged to you, Mr. Courtage.

HARRIET: Lord! how you admire this man.

LADY WOODVIL: What have you to except against him?

HARRIET: He's a fop.

LADY WOODVIL: He's not a Dorimant, a wild extravagant fellow of the times.

HARRIET: He's a man made up of forms and commonplaces sucked out of the remaining lees of the last age.

LADY WOODVIL: He's so good a man, that were you not engaged——

LADY TOWNLEY: You'll have but little night to sleep in.

LADY WOODVIL: Lord! 'tis perfect day——

DORIMANT: [Aside] The hour is almost come I appointed Belinda, and I am not so foppishly in love here to forget: I am flesh and blood yet.

LADY TOWNLEY: I am very sensible, madam.

LADY WOODVIL: Lord, madam!

HARRIET: Look, in what struggle is my poor mother yonder?

YOUNG BELLAIR: She has much ado to bring out the compliment.

DORIMANT: She strains hard for it.

HARRIET: See, see! her head tottering, her eyes staring, and her under lip trembling.

DORIMANT: [Aside] Now, now she's in the very convulsions of her civility. 'Sdeath, I shall lose Belinda. I must fright her hence; she'll be an hour in this fit of good manners else. [To Lady Woodvil] Do you not know Sir Fopling, madam?

LADY WOODVIL: I have seen that face. Oh, heaven! 'tis the same we met in the Mall; how came he here?

DORIMANT: A fiddle in this town is a kind of fop-call; no sooner it strikes up but the house is besieged with an army of masquerades straight.

LADY WOODVIL: Lord! I tremble, Mr. Courtage; for certain Dorimant is in the company.

DORIMANT: I cannot confidently say he is not; you had best begone. I will wait upon you; your daughter is in the hands of Mr. Bellair.

LADY WOODVIL: I'll see her before me. Harriet, come away.

YOUNG BELLAIR: Lights! lights!

LADY TOWNLEY: Light down there.

OLD BELLAIR: Adod, it needs not.

DORIMANT: Call my Lady Woodvil's coach to the door quickly.

[Exeunt Dorimant and Young Bellair, with the Ladies]

OLD BELLAIR: Stay, Mr. Medley, let the young fellows do that duty; we will drink a glass of wine together. 'Tis good after dancing; what mumming spark is that?

MEDLEY: He is not to be comprehended in few words.

SIR FOPLING: Hey! La Tour.

MEDLEY: Whither away, Sir Fopling?

SIR FOPLING: I have business with Courtage——

MEDLEY: He'll but put the ladies into their coach, and come up again.

OLD BELLAIR: In the meantime I'll call for a bottle.

[Exit Old Bellair]

Enter Young Bellair.

MEDLEY: Where's Dorimant?

YOUNG BELLAIR: Stolen home; he has had business waiting for him there all this night, I believe, by an impatience I observed in him.

MEDLEY: Very likely; 'tis but dissembling drunkenness, railing at his friends, and the kind soul will embrace the blessing and forget the tedious expectation.

SIR FOPLING: I must speak with him before I sleep.

YOUNG BELLAIR: Emilia and I are resolved on that business.

MEDLEY: Peace, here's your father.

Enter Old Bellair and Butler, with a bottle of wine.

OLD BELLAIR: The women are all gone to bed. Fill, boy; Mr. Medley, begin a health.

MEDLEY: [Whispers] To Emilia.

OLD BELLAIR: Out, a pise! she's a rogue, and I'll not pledge you.

MEDLEY: I know you will.

OLD BELLAIR: Adod, drink it then.

SIR FOPLING: Let us have the new bachique.

OLD BELLAIR: Adod, that is a hard word; what does it mean, sir?

MEDLEY: A catch or drinking song.

OLD BELLAIR: Let us have it then.

SIR FOPLING: Fill the glasses round, and draw up in a body. Hey! music!   [They sing]

The pleasures of love and the joys of good wine
To perfect our happiness wisely we join.
We to beauty all day

Give the sovereign sway,
And her favourite nymphs devoutely obey.
At the plays we are constantly making our court,
And when they are ended we follow the sport,
To the Mall and the Park,
Where we love till 'tis dark;
Then sparkling champagne
Puts an end to their reign;
It quickly recovers
Poor languishing lovers,
Makes us frolic and gay, and drowns all our sorrow;
But, alas! we relapse again on the morrow.
Let ev'ry man stand
With his glass in his hand,
And briskly discharge at the word of command.
Here's a health to all those
Whom to-night we depose:
Wine and beauty by turns great souls should inspire.
Present altogether, and now, boys, give fire!

OLD BELLAIR: Adod, a pretty business, and very merry.

SIR FOPLING: Hark you, Medley, let you and I take the fiddles, and go waken Dorimant.

MEDLEY: We shall do him a courtesy, if it be as I guess. For after the fatigue of this night, he'll quickly have his bellyful, and be glad of an occasion to cry: Take away, Handy.

YOUNG BELLAIR: I'll go with you, and there we'll consult about affairs, Medley.

OLD BELLAIR: [Looks at his watch] Adod, 'tis six o'clock.

SIR FOPLING: Let's away then.

OLD BELLAIR: Mr. Medley, my sister tells me you are an honest man, and, adod, I love you. Few words and hearty—that's the way with old Harry, old Harry.

SIR FOPLING: Light your flambeaux. Hey!

OLD BELLAIR: What does the man mean?

MEDLEY: 'Tis day, Sir Fopling.

SIR FOPLING: No matter. Our serenade will look the greater.   [Exeunt omnes]

SCENE 2: Dorimant's Lodging. A table, a candle, a toilet, etc. Handy tying up linen

Enter Dorimant in his gown, and Belinda.

DORIMANT: Why will you be gone so soon?

BELINDA: Why did you stay out so late?

DORIMANT: Call a chair, Handy.   [Exit Handy] What makes you tremble so?

BELINDA: I have a thousand fears about me. Have I not been seen, think you?

DORIMANT: By nobody but myself and trusty Handy.

BELINDA: Where are all your people?

DORIMANT: I have dispersed 'em on sleeveless errands. What does that sigh mean?

BELINDA: Can you be so unkind to ask me?—Well—
[*Sighs*] were it to do again——

DORIMANT: We should do it, should we not?

BELINDA: I think we should; the wickeder man you
to make me love so well. Will you be discreet
now?

DORIMANT: I will.

BELINDA: You cannot.

DORIMANT: Never doubt it.

BELINDA: I will not expect it.

DORIMANT: You do me wrong.

BELINDA: You have no more power to keep the secret
than I had not to trust you with it.

DORIMANT: By all the joys I have had, and those you
keep in store——

BELINDA: You'll do for my sake what you never did
before——

DORIMANT: By that truth thou hast spoken, a wife
shall sooner betray herself to her husband——

BELINDA: Yet I had rather you should be false in this,
than in any other thing you promised me.

DORIMANT: What's that?

BELINDA: That you would never see Loveit more
but in public places, in the Park, at Court, and
plays.

DORIMANT: 'Tis not likely a man should be fond of
seeing a damned old play when there is a new one
acted.

BELINDA: I dare not trust your promise.

DORIMANT: You may.

BELINDA: This does not satisfy me. You shall swear
you never will see her more.

DORIMANT: I will! A thousand oaths—— By all——

BELINDA: Hold—— You shall not, now I think on't
better.

DORIMANT: I will swear.

BELINDA: I shall grow jealous of the oath, and think
I owe your truth to that, not to your love.

DORIMANT: Then, by my love, no other oath I'll
swear.

Enter Handy.

HANDY: Here's a chair.

BELINDA: Let me go.

DORIMANT: I cannot

BELINDA: Too willingly, I fear.

DORIMANT: Too unkindly feared. When will you
promise me again?

BELINDA: Not this fortnight.

DORIMANT: You will be better than your word.

BELINDA: I think I shall. Will it not make you love
me less? [*Starting*] Hark! what fiddles are these?
[*Fiddles without*]

DORIMANT: Look out Handy.
[*Exit* Handy *and returns*]

HANDY: Mr. Medley, Mr. Bellair, and Sir Fopling;
they are coming up.

DORIMANT: How got they in?

HANDY: The door was open for the chair.

BELINDA: Lord! let me fly——

DORIMANT: Here, here, down the back stairs. I'll see
you into your chair.

BELINDA: No, no, stay and receive 'em, and be sure
you keep your word and never see Loveit more: let
it be a proof of your kindness.

DORIMANT: It shall—— Handy, direct her. Everlast-
ing love go along with thee. [*Kissing her hand*]
[*Exeunt* Belinda *and* Handy]
Enter Young Bellair, Medley, *and* Sir Fopling.

YOUNG BELLAIR: Not a-bed yet!

MEDLEY: You have had an irregular fit, Dorimant?

DORIMANT: I have.

YOUNG BELLAIR: And is it off already?

DORIMANT: Nature has done her part, gentlemen;
when she falls kindly to work, great cures are effected in little time, you know.

SIR FOPLING: We thought there was a wench in the
case by the chair that waited. Prithee make us a
confidence.

DORIMANT: Excuse me.

SIR FOPLING: *Le sage* Dorimant! was she pretty?

DORIMANT: So pretty she may come to keep her coach
and pay parish duties if the good humour of the
age continue.

MEDLEY: And be of the number of the ladies kept by
public-spirited men for the good of the whole
town.

SIR FOPLING: Well said, Medley.
[Sir Fopling *dancing by himself*]

YOUNG BELLAIR: See, Sir Fopling dancing.

DORIMANT: You are practising and have a mind to recover, I see.

SIR FOPLING: Prithee, Dorimant, why hast not thou a
glass hung up here? A room is the dullest thing
without one.

YOUNG BELLAIR: Here is company to entertain you.

SIR FOPLING: But I mean in case of being alone. In a
glass a man may entertain himself.

DORIMANT: The shadow of himself indeed.

SIR FOPLING: Correct the errors of his motions and his
dress.

MEDLEY: I find, Sir Fopling, in your solitude you remember the saying of the wise man, and study
yourself.

SIR FOPLING: 'Tis the best diversion in our retire-
ments. Dorimant, thou art a pretty fellow, and
wear'st thy clothes well, but I never saw thee have
a handsome cravat. Were they made up like mine,
they'd give another air to thy face. Prithee let me
send my man to dress thee but one day. By
heavens! an Englishman cannot tie a ribbon.

DORIMANT: They are something clumsy-fisted.

SIR FOPLING: I have brought over the prettiest fellow
that ever spread a toilet; he served some time under
Merille, the greatest *genie* in the world for a *valet-
de-chambre*.

DORIMANT: What, he who formerly belonged to the
Duke of Candale?

SIR FOPLING: The same, and got him his immortal reputation.

DORIMANT: You've a very fine *brandenburgh* on, Sir Fopling.

SIR FOPLING: It serves to wrap me up after the fatigue of a ball.

MEDLEY: I see you often in it, with your periwig tied up.

SIR FOPLING: We should not always be in a set dress; 'tis more *en cavalier* to appear now and then in a *déshabillé*.

MEDLEY: Pray how goes your business with Loveit?

SIR FOPLING: You might have answered yourself in the Mall last night. Dorimant! did you not see the advances she made me? I have been endeavouring at a song.

DORIMANT: Already!

SIR FOPLING: 'Tis my *coup d'essai* in English; I would fain have thy opinion of it.

DORIMANT: Let's see it.

SIR FOPLING: Hey, Page! give me my song—— Bellair, here, thou hast a pretty voice, sing it.

YOUNG BELLAIR: Sing it yourself, Sir Fopling.

SIR FOPLING: Excuse me.

YOUNG BELLAIR: You learnt to sing in Paris.

SIR FOPLING: I did, of Lambert, the greatest master in the world; but I have his own fault, a weak voice, and care not to sing out of a *ruelle*.[1]

DORIMANT: A *ruelle* is a pretty cage for a singing fop, indeed.

[*Young Bellair reads the song*]

How charming Phyllis is! how fair!
Ah, that she were as willing
To ease my wounded heart of care,
And make her eyes less killing!
I sigh! I sigh! I languish now,
And love will not let me rest;
I drive about the Park, and bow
Still as I meet my dearest.

SIR FOPLING: Sing it, sing it, man; it goes to a pretty new tune, which I am confident was made by Baptiste.

MEDLEY: Sing it yourself, Sir Fopling; he does not know the tune.

SIR FOPLING: I'll venture.   [*Sir Fopling sings*]

DORIMANT: Ay, marry, now 'tis something. I shall not flatter you, Sir Fopling; there is not much thought in't, but 'tis passionate, and well turned.

MEDLEY: After the French way.

SIR FOPLING: That I aimed at. Does it not give you a lively image of the thing? Slap down goes the glass, and thus we are at it.

DORIMANT: It does indeed. I perceive, Sir Fopling, you'll be the very head of the sparks who are lucky in compositions of this nature.

[1]*Properly the ruelle was the space in a bedroom between the bed and the wall.*

Enter Sir Fopling's Footman.

SIR FOPLING: La Tour, is the bath ready?

FOOTMAN: Yes, sir.

SIR FOPLING: *Adieu donc, mes chers.*

[*Exit Sir Fopling*]

MEDLEY: When have you your revenge on Loveit, Dorimant?

DORIMANT: I will but change my linen, and about it.

MEDLEY: The powerful considerations which hindered have been removed then?

DORIMANT: Most luckily this morning; you must along with me, my reputation lies at stake there.

MEDLEY: I am engaged to Bellair.

DORIMANT: What's your business?

MEDLEY: Ma-tri-mony, an't like you.

DORIMANT: It does not, sir.

YOUNG BELLAIR: It may in time, Dorimant; what think you of Mrs. Harriet?

DORIMANT: What does she think of me?

YOUNG BELLAIR: I am confident she loves you.

DORIMANT: How does it appear?

YOUNG BELLAIR: Why, she's never well but when she's talking of you; but then she finds all the faults in you she can. She laughs at all who commend you; but then she speaks ill of all who do not.

DORIMANT: Women of her temper betray themselves by their over-cunning. I had once a growing love with a lady who would always quarrel with me when I came to see her, and yet was never quiet if I stayed a day from her.

YOUNG BELLAIR: My father is in love with Emilia.

DORIMANT: That is a good warrant for your proceedings: go on and prosper; I must to Loveit. Medley, I am sorry you cannot be a witness.

MEDLEY: Make her meet Sir Fopling again in the same place, and use him ill before me.

DORIMANT: That may be brought about, I think. I'll be at your aunt's anon, and give you joy, Mr. Bellair.

YOUNG BELLAIR: You had not best think of Mrs. Harriet too much; without church security there's no taking up there.

DORIMANT: I may fall into the snare too. But

The wise will find a difference in our fate:
You wed a woman, I a good estate.   [*Exeunt*]

SCENE 3

Enter the Chair with Belinda; *the* Men *set it down and open it.* Belinda *starting.*

BELINDA: [*Surprised*] Lord; where am I? in the Mall? Whither have you brought me?

1 CHAIRMAN: You gave us no directions, madam.

BELINDA: [*Aside*] The fright I was in made me forget it.

1 CHAIRMAN: We use to carry a lady from the squire's hither.

BELINDA: [Aside] This is Loveit; I am undone if she sees me. Quickly carry me away.

1 CHAIRMAN: Whither, an't like your honour?

BELINDA: Ask no questions.

Enter Mrs. Loveit's Footman.

FOOTMAN: Have you seen my lady, madam?

BELINDA: I am just come to wait upon her.

FOOTMAN: She will be glad to see you, madam. She sent me to you this morning to desire your company, and I was told you went out by five o'clock.

BELINDA: [Aside] More and more unlucky!

FOOTMAN: Will you walk in, madam?

BELINDA: I'll discharge my chair and follow. Tell your mistress I am here.   [Exit Footman]
                                          [Gives the Chairmen money]
Take this, and if ever you should be examined, be sure you say you took me up in the Strand, over against the Exchange, as you will answer it to Mr. Dorimant.

CHAIRMEN: We will, an't like your honour.
                                          [Exeunt Chairmen]

BELINDA: Now to come off, I must on——
    In confidence and lies some hope is left;
    'Twere hard to be found out in the first theft.
                                                      [Exit]

Act V

SCENE 1

Enter Mistress Loveit *and* Pert, *her woman.*

PERT: Well, in my eyes Sir Fopling is no such despicable person.

MRS. LOVEIT: You are an excellent judge!

PERT: He's as handsome a man as Mr. Dorimant, and as great a gallant.

MRS. LOVEIT: Intolerable! is't not enough I submit to his impertinences, but I must be plagued with yours too?

PERT: Indeed, madam——

MRS. LOVEIT: 'Tis false, mercenary malice——

Enter her Footman.

FOOTMAN: Mrs. Belinda, madam.

MRS. LOVEIT: What of her?

FOOTMAN: She's below.

MRS. LOVEIT: How came she?

FOOTMAN: In a chair; ambling Harry brought her.

MRS. LOVEIT: He bring her! His chair stands near Dorimant's door, and always brings me from thence—— Run and ask him where he took her up; go, there is no truth in friendship neither. Women as well as men—all are false, or all are so to me at least.

PERT: You are jealous of her too.

MRS. LOVEIT: You had best tell her I am. 'Twill become the liberty you take of late. This fellow's

bringing of her, her going out by five o'clock——I know not what to think.

Enter Belinda.

Belinda, you are grown an early riser, I hear.

BELINDA: Do you not wonder, my dear, what made me abroad so soon?

MRS. LOVEIT: You do not use to be so.

BELINDA: The country gentlewomen I told you of (Lord! they have the oddest diversions!) would never let me rest till I promised to go with them to the markets this morning to eat fruit and buy nosegays.

MRS. LOVEIT: Are they so fond of a filthy nosegay?

BELINDA: They complain of the stinks of the town, and are never well but when they have their noses in one.

MRS. LOVEIT: There are essences and sweet waters.

BELINDA: Oh! they cry out upon perfumes they are unwholesome, one of 'em was falling into a fit with the smell of these *narolii*.

MRS. LOVEIT: Methinks, in complaisance you should have had a nosegay too.

BELINDA: Do you think, my dear, I could be so loathsome to trick myself up with carnations and stock gillyflowers? I begged their pardon, and told them I never wore anything but orange flowers and tuberose. That which made me willing to go was a strange desire I had to eat some fresh nectarines.

MRS. LOVEIT: And had you any?

BELINDA: The best I ever tasted.

MRS. LOVEIT: Whence came you now?

BELINDA: From their lodgings, where I crowded out of a coach, and took a chair to come and see you, my dear.

MRS. LOVEIT: Whither did you send for that chair?

BELINDA: 'Twas going by empty.

MRS. LOVEIT: Where do these country gentlewomen lodge, I pray?

BELINDA: In the Strand, over against the Exchange.

PERT: That place is never without a nest of 'em; they are always as one goes by fleering in balconies or staring out of windows.

Enter Footman.

MRS. LOVEIT: [Whispers to the Footman] Come hither.

BELINDA: [Aside] This fellow by her order has been questioning the chairmen—I threatened 'em with the name of Dorimant; if they should have told truth I am lost for ever.

MRS. LOVEIT: In the Strand, said you?

FOOTMAN: Yes, madam, over against the Exchange.
                                          [Exit Footman]

MRS. LOVEIT: She's innocent, and I am much to blame.

BELINDA: [Aside] I am so frighted my countenance will betray me.

MRS. LOVEIT: Belinda! what makes you look so pale?

BELINDA: Want of my usual rest, and jolting up and down so long in an odious hackney.

Enter Footman.

FOOTMAN: Madam, Mr. Dorimant!

MRS. LOVEIT: What makes him here?

BELINDA: [*Aside*] Then I am betrayed indeed; he's broke his word, and I love a man that does not care for me.

MRS. LOVEIT: Lord! you faint, Belinda.

BELINDA: I think I shall; such an oppression here on the sudden.

PERT: She has eaten too much fruit, I warrant you.

MRS. LOVEIT: Not unlikely!

PERT: 'Tis that lies heavy on her stomach.

MRS. LOVEIT: Have her into my chamber, give her some surfeit water, and let her lie down a little.

PERT: Come, madam, I was a strange devourer of fruit when I was young, so ravenous——

[*Exit* Belinda, Pert *leading her off*]

MRS. LOVEIT: Oh, that my love would be but calm awhile! that I might receive this man with all the scorn and indignation he deserves.

Enter Dorimant.

DORIMANT: Now for a touch of Sir Fopling to begin with. Hey—— page—— give positive order that none of my people stir—— let the *canaille* wait as they should do: since noise and nonsense have such powerful charms,

I, that I may successful prove,
Transform myself to what you love.

MRS. LOVEIT: If that would do, you need not change from what you are; you can be vain and loud enough.

DORIMANT: But not with so good a grace as Sir Fopling. Hey, Hampshire!—— Oh! that sound! that sound becomes the mouth of a man of quality.

MRS. LOVEIT: Is there a thing so hateful as a senseless mimic?

DORIMANT: He's a great grievance indeed to all who like yourself, madam, love to play the fool in quiet.

MRS. LOVEIT: A ridiculous animal who has more of the ape than the ape has of the man in him.

DORIMANT: I have as mean an opinion of a sheer mimic as yourself; yet were he all ape I should prefer him to the gay, the giddy, brisk, insipid, noisy fool you dote on.

MRS. LOVEIT: Those noisy fools, however you despise 'em, have good qualities, which weigh more (or ought at least) with us women than all the pernicious wit you have to boast of.

DORIMANT: That I may hereafter have a just value for their merit, pray do me the favour to name 'em.

MRS. LOVEIT: You'll despise 'em as the dull effects of ignorance and vanity, yet I care not if I mention some. First, they really admire us, while you at best but flatter us well.

DORIMANT: Take heed! fools can dissemble too——

MRS. LOVEIT: They may, but not so artificially as you: there is no fear they should deceive us. Then they are assiduous, sir; they are ever offering us their service, and always waiting on our will.

DORIMANT: You owe that to their excessive idleness; they know not how to entertain themselves at home, and find so little welcome abroad, they are fain to fly to you who countenance 'em as a refuge against the solitude they would be otherwise condemned to.

MRS. LOVEIT: Their conversation too diverts us better.

DORIMANT: Playing with your fan, smelling to your gloves, commending your hair, and taking notice how 'tis cut and shaded after the new way.

MRS. LOVEIT: Were it sillier than you can make it, you must allow 'tis pleasanter to laugh at others than to be laughed at ourselves, though never so wittily. Then though they want skill to flatter us, they flatter themselves so well they save us the labour; we need not take that care and pains to satisfy 'em of our love, which we so often lose on you.

DORIMANT: They commonly indeed believe too well of themselves, and always better of you than you deserve.

MRS. LOVEIT: You are in the right; they have an implicit faith in us which keeps 'em from prying narrowly into our secrets, and saves us the vexatious trouble of clearing doubts which your subtle and causeless jealousies every moment raise.

DORIMANT: There is an inbred falsehood in women which inclines 'em still to them whom they may most easily deceive.

MRS. LOVEIT: The man who loves above his quality does not suffer more from the insolent impertinence of his mistress than the woman who loves above her understanding does from the arrogant presumptions of her friend.

DORIMANT: You mistake the use of fools: they are designed for properties, and not for friends. You have an indifferent stock of reputation left yet. Lose it all like a frank gamester on the square; 'twill then be time enough to turn rook and cheat it up again on a good substantial bubble.

MRS. LOVEIT: The old and the ill-favoured are only fit for properties indeed, but young and handsome fools have met with kinder fortunes.

DORIMANT: They have, to the shame of your sex be it spoken; 'twas this, the thought of this, made me, by a timely jealousy, endeavour to prevent the good fortune you are providing for Sir Fopling—— but against a woman's frailty all our care is vain.

MRS. LOVEIT: Had I not with a dear experience bought the knowledge of your falsehood, you might have fooled me yet. This is not the first jealousy you have feigned to make a quarrel with me and get a week to throw away on some such unknown inconsiderable slut as you have been lately lurking with at plays.

DORIMANT: Women, when they would break off with a man, never want th' address to turn the fault on him.

MRS. LOVEIT: You take a pride of late in using of me ill, that the town may know the power you have over me, which now (as unreasonably as yourself) expects that I (do me all the injuries you can) must love you still.

DORIMANT: I am so far from expecting that you should, I begin to think you never did love me.

MRS. LOVEIT: Would the memory of it were so wholly worn out in me that I did doubt it too! What made you come to disturb my growing quiet?

DORIMANT: To give you joy of your growing infamy.

MRS. LOVEIT: Insupportable! insulting devil! this from you, the only author of my shame! This from another had been but justice, but from you 'tis a hellish and inhuman outrage. What have I done?

DORIMANT: A thing that puts you below my scorn and makes my anger as ridiculous as you have made my love.

MRS. LOVEIT: I walked last night with Sir Fopling.

DORIMANT: You did, madam, and you talked and laughed aloud, ha, ha, ha!—— Oh! that laugh! that laugh becomes the confidence of a woman of quality.

MRS. LOVEIT: You, who have more pleasure in the ruin of a woman's reputation than in the endearments of her love, reproach me not with yourself, and I defy you to name the man can lay a blemish on my fame.

DORIMANT: To be seen publicly so transported with the vain follies of that notorious fop, to me is an infamy below the sin of prostitution with another man.

MRS. LOVEIT: Rail on, I am satisfied in the justice of what I did; you had provoked me to't.

DORIMANT: What I did was the effect of a passion whose extravagances you have been willing to forgive.

MRS. LOVEIT: And what I did was the effect of a passion you may forgive if you think fit.

DORIMANT: Are you so indifferent grown?

MRS. LOVEIT: I am.

DORIMANT: Nay! then 'tis time to part. I'll send you back your letters you have so often asked for. I have two or three of 'em about me.

MRS. LOVEIT: Give 'em me.

DORIMANT: You snatch as if you thought I would not—— there—— and may the perjuries in 'em be mine if e'er I see you more.

[Offers to go, she catches him]

MRS. LOVEIT: Stay!

DORIMANT: I will not.

MRS. LOVEIT: You shall.

DORIMANT: What have you to say?

MRS. LOVEIT: I cannot speak it yet.

DORIMANT: Something more in commendation of the fool. Death! I want patience, let me go.

MRS. LOVEIT: [Aside] I cannot. I can sooner part with the limbs that hold him. I hate that nauseous fool, you know I do.

DORIMANT: Was it the scandal you were fond of then?

MRS. LOVEIT: You'd raised my anger equal to my love, a thing you ne'er could do before, and in revenge I did—— I know not what I did.—— Would you would not think on't any more!

DORIMANT: Should I be willing to forget it, I shall be daily minded of it, 'twill be a commonplace for all the town to laugh at me; and Medley, when he is rhetorically drunk, will ever be declaiming on it in my ears.

MRS. LOVEIT: 'Twill be believed a jealous spite! Come, forget it.

DORIMANT: Let me consult my reputation; you are too careless of it. [Pauses] You shall meet Sir Fopling in the Mall again tonight.

MRS. LOVEIT: What mean you?

DORIMANT: I have thought on't, and you must: 'tis necessary to justify my love to the world; you can handle a coxcomb as he deserves when you are not out of humour, madam.

MRS. LOVEIT: Public satisfaction for the wrong I have done you! This is some new device to make me more ridiculous.

DORIMANT: Hear me.

MRS. LOVEIT: I will not.

DORIMANT: You will be persuaded.

MRS. LOVEIT: Never.

DORIMANT: Are you so obstinate?

MRS. LOVEIT: Are you so base?

DORIMANT: You will not satisfy my love?

MRS. LOVEIT: I would die to satisfy that, but I will not to save you from a thousand racks do a shameless thing to please your vanity.

DORIMANT: Farewell, false woman!

MRS. LOVEIT: Do! go!

DORIMANT: You will call me back again.

MRS. LOVEIT: Exquisite fiend! I knew you came but to torment me.

Enter Belinda *and* Pert.

DORIMANT: [Surprised] Belinda here!

BELINDA: [Aside] He starts and looks pale; the sight of me has touched his guilty soul.

PERT: 'Twas but a qualm, as I said, a little indigestion; the surfeit water did it, madam, mixed with a little *mirabilis*.

DORIMANT: I am confounded, and cannot guess how she came hither!

MRS. LOVEIT: 'Tis your fortune, Belinda, ever to be here when I am abused by this prodigy of ill-nature.

BELINDA: I am amazed to find him here! How has he the face to come near you?

DORIMANT: [Aside] Here is fine work towards! I never was at such a loss before.

BELINDA: One who makes a public profession of

breach of faith and ingratitude; I loathe the sight of him.

DORIMANT: [*Aside*] There is no remedy; I must submit to their tongues now, and some other time bring myself off as well as I can.

BELINDA: Other men are wicked, but then they have some sense of shame: he is never well but when he triumphs, nay, glories to a woman's face in his villainies.

MRS. LOVEIT: You are in the right, Belinda; but methinks your kindness for me makes you concern yourself too much with him.

BELINDA: It does indeed, my dear; his barbarous carriage to you yesterday made me hope you ne'er would see him more, and the very next day to find him here again provokes me strangely; but, because I know you love him, I have done.

DORIMANT: You have reproached me handsomely, and I deserve it for coming hither; but——

PERT: You must expect it, sir; all women will hate you for my lady's sake.

DORIMANT: [*Aside to* Belinda] Nay, if she begins too, 'tis time to fly; I shall be scolded to death else. I am to blame in some circumstances, I confess; but as to the main, I am not so guilty as you imagine. I shall seek a more convenient time to clear myself.

MRS. LOVEIT: Do it now! what impediments are here?

DORIMANT: I want time, and you want temper.

MRS. LOVEIT: These are weak pretences!

DORIMANT: You were never more mistaken in your life, and so farewell.   [Dorimant *flings off*]

MRS. LOVEIT: Call a footman, Pert, quickly; I will have him dogged.

PERT: I wish you would not for my quiet and your own.

MRS. LOVEIT: I'll find out the infamous cause of all our quarrels, pluck her mask off, and expose her barefaced to the world.

BELINDA: [*Aside*] Let me but escape this time I'll never venture more.

MRS. LOVEIT: Belinda! you shall go with me.

BELINDA: I have such a heaviness hangs on me with what I did this morning, I would fain go home and sleep, my dear.

MRS. LOVEIT: Death and eternal darkness! I shall never sleep again. Raging fevers seize the world, and make mankind as restless all as I am!
                                [*Exit* Mrs. Loveit]

BELINDA: I knew him false, and helped to make him so. Was not her ruin enough to fright me from the danger? It should have been, but love can take no warning.   [*Exit* Belinda]

SCENE 2: *Lady Townley's house*

Enter Medley, Young Bellair, Lady Townley, Emilia, *and* Chaplain.

MEDLEY: Bear up, Bellair, and do not let us see

that repentance in thine we daily do in married faces.

LADY TOWNLEY: This wedding will strangely surprise my brother when he knows it.

MEDLEY: Your nephew ought to conceal it for a time, madam, since marriage has lost its good name; prudent men seldom expose their own reputations till 'tis convenient to justify their wives.

OLD BELLAIR: [*Without*] Where are you all there? Out, adod, will nobody hear?

LADY TOWNLEY: My brother! quickly, Mr. Smirk, into this closet; you must not be seen yet.
                                [*He goes into the closet*]

Enter Old Bellair *and* Lady Townley's Page.

OLD BELLAIR: Desire Mr. Fourbes to walk into the lower parlour, I will be with him presently. [*To* Young Bellair] Where have you been, sir, you could not wait on me to-day?

YOUNG BELLAIR: About a business.

OLD BELLAIR: Are you so good at business? Adod, I have a business too you shall despatch out of hand, sir. Send for a parson, sister; my Lady Woodvil and her daughter are coming.

LADY TOWNLEY: What need you huddle up things thus!

OLD BELLAIR: Out a pise! youth is apt to play the fool, and 'tis not good it should be in their power.

LADY TOWNLEY: You need not fear your son.

OLD BELLAIR: He's been idling this morning, and, adod, I do not like him. [*To* Emilia] How dost thou do, sweetheart?

EMILIA: You are very severe, sir; married in such haste.

OLD BELLAIR: Go to, thou'rt a rogue, and I will talk with thee anon. Here's my Lady Woodvil come.

Enter Lady Woodvil, Harriet, *and* Busy.
Welcome, madam; Mr. Fourbes is below with the writings.

LADY WOODVIL: Let us down, and make an end then.

OLD BELLAIR: Sister, show the way. [*To* Young Bellair, *who is talking to* Harriet] Harry, your business lies not there yet; excuse him till we have done, lady, and then, adod, he shall be for you. Mr. Medley, we must trouble you to be a witness.

MEDLEY: I luckily came for that purpose, sir.
                [*Exeunt* Old Bellair, Medley, Young Bellair, Lady Townley, *and* Lady Woodvil]

BUSY: What will you do, madam?

HARRIET: Be carried back and mewed up in the country again, run away here, anything rather than be married to a man I do not care for——Dear Emilia, do thou advise me.

EMILIA: Mr. Bellair is engaged you know.

HARRIET: I do, but know not what the fear of losing an estate may fright him to.

EMILIA: In the desperate condition you are in you

should consult with some judicious man; what think you of Mr. Dorimant?

HARRIET: I do not think of him at all.

BUSY: She thinks of nothing else, I am sure.

EMILIA: How fond your mother was of Mr. Courtage!

HARRIET: Because I contrived the mistake to make a little mirth you believe I like the man.

EMILIA: Mr. Bellair believes you love him.

HARRIET: Men are seldom in the right when they guess at a woman's mind; would she whom he loves loved him no better!

BUSY: [Aside] That's e'en well enough, on all conscience.

EMILIA: Mr. Dorimant has a great deal of wit.

HARRIET: And takes a great deal of pains to show it.

EMILIA: He's extremely well-fashioned.

HARRIET: Affectedly grave or ridiculously wild and apish.

BUSY: You defend him still against your mother.

HARRIET: I would not were he justly rallied, but I cannot hear any one undeservedly railed at.

EMILIA: Has your woman learnt the song you were so taken with?

HARRIET: I was fond of a new thing; 'tis dull at second hearing.

EMILIA: Mr. Dorimant made it.

BUSY: She knows it, madam, and has made me sing it at least a dozen times this morning.

HARRIET: Thy tongue is as impertinent as thy fingers.

EMILIA: You have provoked her.

BUSY: 'Tis but singing the song, and I shall appease her.

EMILIA: Prithee do.

HARRIET: She has a voice will grate your ears worse than a cat-call, and dresses so ill she's scarce fit to trick up a yeoman's daughter on a holiday.

BUSY: [Sings]

As Amoret with Phyllis sat
One evening on the plain,
And saw the charming Strephon wait
To tell the nymph his pain,

The threatening danger to remove
She whisper'd in her ear,
Ah, Phyllis! if you would not love,
This shepherd do not hear.

None ever had so strange an art
His passion to convey
Into a listening virgin's heart,
And steal her soul away.

Fly, fly betimes, for fear you give
Occasion for your fate.
In vain, said she, in vain I strive,
Alas! 'tis now too late.

Enter Dorimant.

DORIMANT: Music so softens and disarms the mind——

HARRIET: That not one arrow does resistance find.

DORIMANT: Let us make use of the lucky minute then.

HARRIET: [Aside, turning from Dorimant] My love springs with my blood into my face, I dare not look upon him yet.

DORIMANT: What have we here, the picture of celebrated beauty giving audience in public to a declared lover?

HARRIET: Play the dying fop and make the piece complete, sir.

DORIMANT: What think you if the hint were well improved—the whole mystery of making love pleasantly designed and wrought in a suit of hangings?

HARRIET: 'Twere needless to execute fools in effigy who suffer daily in their own persons.

DORIMANT: [Aside to Emilia] Mrs. Bride, for such I know this happy day has made you.

EMILIA: Defer the formal joy you are to give me and mind your business with her. [Aloud] Here are dreadful preparations, Mr. Dorimant, writings sealing, and a parson sent for.

DORIMANT: To marry this lady?

BUSY: Condemned she is, and what will become of her I know not, without you generously engage in a rescue.

DORIMANT: In this sad condition, madam, I can do no less than offer you my service.

HARRIET: The obligation is not great; you are the common sanctuary for all young women who run from their relations.

DORIMANT: I have always my arms open to receive the distressed. But I will open my heart, and receive you where none yet did ever enter: you have filled it with a secret, might I but let you know it——

HARRIET: Do not speak it if you would have me believe it; your tongue is so famed for falsehood 'twill do the truth an injury.   [Turns away her head]

DORIMANT: Turn not away then; but look on me and guess it.

HARRIET: Did you not tell me there was no credit to be given to faces? that women nowadays have their passions as much at will as they have their complexions, and put on joy and sadness, scorn and kindness, with the same ease they do their paint and patches—— Are they the only counterfeits?

DORIMANT: You wrong your own while you suspect my eyes; by all the hope I have in you, the inimitable colour in your cheeks is not more free from art than are the sighs I offer.

HARRIET: In men who have been long hardened in sin we have reason to mistrust the first signs of repentance.

DORIMANT: The prospect of such a heaven will make me persevere and give you marks that are infallible.

HARRIET: What are those?

DORIMANT: I will renounce all the joys I have in friendship and in wine, sacrifice to you all the interest I have in other women——

HARRIET: Hold!—though I wish you devout I would

not have you turn fanatic—Could you neglect these awhile and make a journey into the country?

DORIMANT: To be with you I could live there and never send one thought to London.

HARRIET: Whate'er you say, I know all beyond High Park's a desert to you, and that no gallantry can draw you farther.

DORIMANT: That has been the utmost limit of my love, but now my passion knows no bounds, and there's no measure to be taken of what I'll do for you from anything I ever did before.

HARRIET: When I hear you talk thus in Hampshire I shall begin to think there may be some truth enlarged upon.

DORIMANT: Is this all?——will you not promise me?——

HARRIET: I hate to promise! What we do then is expected from us, and wants much of the welcome it finds when it surprises.

DORIMANT: May I not hope?

HARRIET: That depends on you and not on me; and 'tis to no purpose to forbid it.   [Turns to Busy]

BUSY: Faith, madam, now I perceive the gentleman loves you too; e'en let him know your mind, and torment yourselves no longer.

HARRIET: Dost think I have no sense of modesty?

BUSY: Think, if you lose this you may never have another opportunity.

HARRIET: May he hate me—a curse that frights me when I speak it—if ever I do a thing against the rules of decency and honour!

DORIMANT: [To Emilia] I am beholding to you for your good intentions, madam.

EMILIA: I thought the concealing of our marriage from her might have done you better service.

DORIMANT: Try her again.

EMILIA: What have you resolved, madam? The time draws near.

HARRIET: To be obstinate, and protest against this marriage.

Enter Lady Townley in haste.

LADY TOWNLEY: [To Emilia] Quickly, quickly, let Mr. Smirk out of the closet.

[Smirk comes out of the closet]

HARRIET: A parson! had you laid him in here?

DORIMANT: I knew nothing of him.

HARRIET: Should it appear you did, your opinion of my easiness may cost you dear.

Enter Old Bellair, Young Bellair, Medley, and Lady Woodvil.

OLD BELLAIR: Out a pise! the canonical hour is almost past. Sister, is the man of God come?

LADY TOWNLEY: He waits your leisure.

OLD BELLAIR: By your favour, sir. Adod, a pretty spruce fellow! what may we call him?

LADY TOWNLEY: Mr. Smirk, my Lady Biggot's chaplain.

OLD BELLAR: A wise woman! adod, she is. The man will serve for the flesh as well as the spirit. Please you, sir, to commission a young couple to go to bed together i' God's name? Harry.

YOUNG BELLAIR: Here, sir.

OLD BELLAIR: Out a pise! without your mistress in your hand!

SMIRK: Is this the gentleman?

OLD BELLAIR: Yes, sir.

SMIRK: Are you not mistaken, sir?

OLD BELLAIR: Adod, I think not, sir.

SMIRK: Sure you are, sir.

OLD BELLAIR: You look as if you would forbid the banns; Mr. Smirk, I hope you have no pretension to the lady?

SMIRK: Wish him joy, sir! I have done him the good office to-day already.

OLD BELLAIR: Out a pise! what do I hear?

LADY TOWNLEY: Never storm, brother, the truth is out.

OLD BELLAIR: How say you, sir? is this your wedding-day?

YOUNG BELLAIR: It is, sir.

OLD BELLAIR: And, adod, it shall be mine too; give me thy hand, sweetheart. [To Emilia] What dost thou mean? give me thy hand, I say.

[Emilia kneels, and Young Bellair]

LADY TOWNLEY: Come, come, give her your blessing; this is the woman your son loved and is married to.

OLD BELLAIR: Ha! cheated! cozened! and by your contrivance, sister!

LADY TOWNLEY: What would you do with her? She's a rogue, and you can't abide her.

MEDLEY: Shall I hit her a pat for you, sir?

OLD BELLAIR: Adod, you are all rogues, and I never will forgive you.

LADY TOWNLEY: Whither! whither away?

MEDLEY: Let him go and cool awhile.

LADY WOODVIL: [To Dorimant] Here's a business broke out now; Mr. Courtage, I am made a fine fool of.

DORIMANT: You see the old gentleman knows nothing of it.

LADY WOODVIL: I find he did not. I shall have some trick put upon me if I stay in this wicked town any longer. Harriet! dear child! where art thou? I'll into the country straight.

OLD BELLAIR: Adod, madam, you shall hear me first.

Enter Mrs. Loveit and Belinda.

MRS. LOVEIT: Hither my man dogged him.

BELINDA: Yonder he stands, my dear.

MRS. LOVEIT: I see him. [Aside] And with the face that has undone me! Oh, that I were but where I might throw out the anguish of my heart! here it must rage within and break it.

LADY TOWNLEY: Mrs. Loveit, are you afraid to come forward?

MRS. LOVEIT: I was amazed to see so much company

here in a morning, the occasion sure is extraordinary.

DORIMANT: [*Aside*] Loveit and Belinda! the devil owes me a shame to-day, and I think never will have done paying it.

MRS. LOVEIT: Married! dear Emilia! how am I transported with the news?

HARRIET: [*To* Dorimant] I little thought Emilia was the woman Mr. Bellair was in love with; I'll chide her for not trusting me with the secret.

DORIMANT: How do you like Mrs. Loveit?

HARRIET: She's a famed mistress of yours, I hear.

DORIMANT: She has been on occasion.

OLD BELLAIR: [*To* Lady Woodvil] Adod, madam, I cannot help it.

LADY WOODVIL: You need make no more apologies, sir.

EMILIA: [*To* Mrs. Loveit] The old gentleman's excusing himself to my Lady Woodvil.

MRS. LOVEIT: Ha, ha, ha! I never heard of anything so pleasant.

HARRIET: [*To* Dorimant] She's extremely overjoyed at something.

DORIMANT: At nothing; she is one of those hoiting ladies who gaily fling themselves about and force a laugh when their aching hearts are full of discontent and malice.

MRS. LOVEIT: Oh, heaven! I was never so near killing myself with laughing. Mr. Dorimant, are you a brideman?

LADY WOODVIL: Mr. Dorimant! Is this Mr. Dorimant, madam?

MRS. LOVEIT: If you doubt it, your daughter can resolve you, I suppose.

LADY WOODVIL: I am cheated too, basely cheated.

OLD BELLAIR: Out a pise! what's here? more knavery yet?

LADY WOODVIL: Harriet! on my blessing, come away, I charge you.

HARRIET: Dear mother, do but stay and hear me.

LADY WOODVIL: I am betrayed, and thou art undone, I fear.

HARRIET: Do not fear it. I have not, nor never will do anything against my duty; believe me, dear mother, do.

DORIMANT: [*To* Mrs. Loveit] I had trusted you with this secret, but that I knew the violence of your nature would ruin my fortune, as now unluckily it has. I thank you, madam.

MRS. LOVEIT: She's an heiress, I know, and very rich.

DORIMANT: To satisfy you I must give up my interest wholly to my love; had you been a reasonable woman, I might have secured 'em both and been happy.

MRS. LOVEIT: You might have trusted me with anything of this kind, you know you might. Why did you go under a wrong name?

DORIMANT: The story is too long to tell you now—be satisfied, this is the business, this is the mask has kept me from you.

BELINDA: [*Aside*] He's tender of my honour, though he's cruel to my love.

MRS. LOVEIT: Was it no idle mistress then?

DORIMANT: Believe me, a wife, to repair the ruins of my estate that needs it.

MRS. LOVEIT: The knowledge of this makes my grief hang lighter on my soul; but I shall never more be happy.

DORIMANT: Belinda!

BELINDA: Do not think of clearing yourself with me, it is impossible. Do all men break their words thus?

DORIMANT: Th' extravagant words they speak in love; 'tis as unreasonable to expect we should perform all we promise then, as do all we threaten when we are angry. When I see you next——

BELINDA: Take no notice of me, and I shall not hate you.

DORIMANT: How came you to Mrs. Loveit?

BELINDA: By a mistake the chairmen made for want of my giving them directions.

DORIMANT: 'Twas a pleasant one. We must meet again.

BELINDA: Never.

DORIMANT: Never?

BELINDA: When we do, may I be as infamous as you are false.

LADY TOWNLEY: Men of Mr. Dorimant's character always suffer in the general opinion of the world.

MEDLEY: You can make no judgment of a witty man from common fame, considering the prevailing faction, madam.

OLD BELLAIR: Adod, he's in the right.

MEDLEY: Besides, 'tis a common error among women to believe too well of them they know and too ill of them they don't.

OLD BELLAIR: Adod, he observes well.

LADY TOWNLEY: Believe me, madam, you will find Mr. Dorimant as civil a gentleman as you thought Mr. Courtage.

HARRIET: If you would but know him better——

LADY WOODVIL: You have a mind to know him better; come away! You shall never see him more.

HARRIET: Dear mother, stay!

LADY WOODVIL: I won't be consenting to your ruin.

HARRIET: Were my fortune in your power.

LADY WOODVIL: Your person is.

HARRIET: Could I be disobedient I might take it out of yours, and put it into his.

LADY WOODVIL: 'Tis that you would be at; you would marry this Dorimant?

HARRIET: I cannot deny it; I would, and never will marry any other man.

LADY WOODVIL: Is this the duty that you promised?

HARRIET: But I will never marry him against your will——

LADY WOODVIL: [*Aside*] She knows the way to melt my heart. [*To* Harriet] Upon yourself light your undoing.

MEDLEY: [*To* Old Bellair] Come, sir, you have not the heart any longer to refuse your blessing.

OLD BELLAIR: Adod, I ha' not——Rise, and God bless you both! Make much of her, Harry, she deserves thy kindness. [*To* Emilia] Adod, sirrah, I did not think it had been in thee.

Enter Sir Fopling *and his* Page.

SIR FOPLING: 'Tis a damned windy day; hey, page? Is my periwig right?

PAGE: A little out of order, sir.

SIR FOPLING: Pox o' this apartment! it wants an antechamber to adjust oneself in. [*To* Mrs. Loveit] Madam, I came from your house, and your servants directed me hither.

MRS. LOVEIT: I will give order hereafter they shall direct you better.

SIR FOPLING: The great satisfaction I had in the Mall last night has given me much disquiet since.

MRS. LOVEIT: 'Tis likely to give me more than I desire.

SIR FOPLING: What the devil makes her so reserved? Am I guilty of an indiscretion, madam?

MRS. LOVEIT: You will be of a great one if you continue your mistake sir.

SIR FOPLING: Something puts you out of humour.

MRS. LOVEIT: The most foolish inconsiderable thing that ever did.

SIR FOPLING: Is it in my power?

MRS. LOVEIT: To hang or drown it; do one of 'em, and trouble me no more.

SIR FOPLING: So *fière? Serviteur, madame.* Medley, where's Dorimant?

MEDLEY: Methinks the lady has not made you those advances to-day she did last night, Sir Fopling.

SIR FOPLING: Prithee do not talk of her.

MEDLEY: She would be a *bonne fortune.*

SIR FOPLING: Not to me, at present.

MEDLEY: How so?

SIR FOPLING: An intrigue now would be but a temptation to me to throw away that vigour on one which I mean shall shortly make my court to the whole sex in a *ballet.*

MEDLEY: Wisely considered, Sir Fopling.

SIR FOPLING: No one woman is worth the loss of a cut in a caper.

MEDLEY: Not when 'tis so universally designed.

LADY WOODVIL: Mr. Dorimant, every one has spoke so much in your behalf that I can no longer doubt but I was in the wrong.

MRS. LOVEIT: There's nothing but falsehood and impertinence in this world; all men are villains or fools. Take example from my misfortunes, Belinda; if thou wouldst be happy, give thyself wholly up to goodness.

HARRIET: [*To* Mrs. Loveit] Mr. Dorimant has been your God Almighty long enough; 'tis time to think of another.

MRS. LOVEIT: Jeered by her! I will lock myself up in my house, and never see the world again.

HARRIET: A nunnery is the more fashionable place for such a retreat, and has been the fatal consequence of many a *belle passion.*

MRS. LOVEIT: Hold, heart! till I get home; should I answer 'twould make her triumph greater.

[*Is going out*]

DORIMANT: Your hand, Sir Fopling.

SIR FOPLING: Shall I wait upon you, madam?

MRS. LOVEIT: Legions of fools, as many devils take thee!   [*Exit* Mrs. Loveit]

MEDLEY: Dorimant! I pronounce thy reputation clear and henceforward when I would know anything of woman, I will consult no other oracle.

SIR FOPLING: Stark mad, by all that's handsome! Dorimant, thou hast engaged me in a pretty business.

DORIMANT: I have not leisure now to talk about it.

OLD BELLAIR: Out a pise! what does this Man of Mode do here again?

LADY TOWNLEY: He'll be an excellent entertainment within, brother, and is luckily come to raise the mirth of the company.

LADY WOODVIL: Madam, I take my leave of you.

LADY TOWNLEY: What do you mean, madam?

LADY WOODVIL: To go this afternoon part of my way to Hartley.

OLD BELLAIR: Adod, you shall stay and dine first; come, we will all be good friends, and you shall give Mr. Dorimant leave to wait upon you and your daughter in the country.

LADY WOODVIL: If his occasions bring him that way, I have now so good an opinion of him he shall be welcome.

HARRIET: To a great rambling lone house that looks as it were not inhabited, the family's so small; there you'll find my mother, an old lame aunt, and myself, sir, perched up on chairs at a distance in a large parlour, sitting moping like three or four melancholy birds in a spacious volery. Does not this stagger your resolution?

DORIMANT: Not at all, madam. The first time I saw you you left me with the pangs of love upon me, and this day my soul has quite given up her liberty.

HARRIET: This is more dismal than the country, Emilia; pity me who am going to that sad place. Methinks I hear the hateful noise of rooks already —knaw, knaw, knaw. There's music in the worst cry in London, *My dill and cucumbers to pickle.*

OLD BELLAIR: Sister, knowing of this matter, I hope you have provided us some good cheer.

LADY TOWNLEY: I have, brother, and the fiddles too.

OLD BELLAIR: Let 'em strike up then; the young lady shall have a dance before she departs.   [*Dance*] [*After the dance*] So, now we'll in and make this an arrant wedding-day.

[*To the pit*] And if these honest gentlemen rejoice, Adod, the boy has made a happy choice.

[*Exeunt omnes*]

The Country Wife

by WILLIAM WYCHERLEY
(1640–1716)

In the popular imagination, Wycherley, more than any other playwright, symbolizes Restoration comedy; suggests what is full-blooded and lusty about it, evokes what is lewd. Although Wycherley himself married a countess and sufficiently led the life of a rake and man of pleasure, there was very little of the foppish courtier about him. Indeed, the feminine side of Restoration comedy—the frilled lace, the feline wit, the dainty prose—is absent from his work; in general, he has neither much of what makes Restoration comedy seem graceful nor much of what makes it seem trifling. For better or worse, he struck at society with a broadsword, not an embroidery needle; he made sex, not a mere elegant accomplishment like tennis, but the fulcrum, the mainspring, the very center of Restoration society life. He was a man of strong feelings, with a strain of coarseness that gives body to his work, whatever it may take off from it in breeding; and his masculinity tends to ally him less with his fellow playwrights than with the English novelists of the following century.

His strong feelings equally affect the sensualist and the moralist in him; violent desire leads, afterwards, to violent disgust. Too often, having drunk to the lees, he was left, first to gaze at them, then angrily to shatter his glass. Having seen all the hypocrisies and betrayals of men and women about him, he could only rail and sputter in a twin revulsion against society and self. His last play, The Plain Dealer—which is sometimes called his masterpiece—pictures this savage mood; but the savagery, the utter intemperateness, mars where it does not half nullify the indictment, so that on grounds of art and objectivity, it is Wycherley who must be indicted himself.

But in The Country Wife, with a gusty humor to fill his sails, and a firm directing hand to hold the rudder, Wycherley produced probably the most robust, and conceivably the most representative, of all Restoration comedies. Sex here takes on a kind of heroic role, dominates men's lives—their talk, their thoughts, their scheming; and in laying bare not just their desires but equally their deceits, it holds them up to laughter. Horner's monstrous ruse of pretending to be a eunuch that he may all the better triumph as a rake is the first of Wycherley's incisions into not only animal but human nature; and not only human nature but leisure-class society. Sex colors Wycherley's whole scene, and with a sharpness that does much to illuminate it. It also, in places, overtaxes Wycherley's story; it is not, indeed, at all a "convincing" story. Such matters as Sparkish's almost wilful refusal to suspect Harcourt or distrust Alithea, or—worse still—Pinchwife's leading Margery, dressed up as Alithea, to Horner's, are wildly improbable. But robustness, not realism, is the true virtue of the play; if it is often excessive as well as implausible, it is from having such tremendous energy, from gathering such huge momentum. The vigor of its protest cannot, and should not, be divorced from the wild romping of its farce.

117

WILLIAM WYCHERLEY

The Country Wife

THE PERSONS OF THE PLAY

MR. HORNER
MR. HARCOURT
MR. DORILANT
MR. PINCHWIFE
MR. SPARKISH
SIR JASPER FIDGET
A BOY
A QUACK
WAITERS, SERVANTS, AND ATTENDANTS
MRS. MARGERY PINCHWIFE
ALITHEA, *Sister of* Pinchwife
LADY FIDGET
MRS. DAINTY FIDGET, *Sister of* Sir Jasper
MRS. SQUEAMISH
OLD LADY SQUEAMISH
LUCY, Alithea's *Maid*

THE SCENE: *London*

Prologue

Poets, like cudgelled bullies, never do
At first or second blow submit to you;
But will provoke you still, and ne'er have done,
Till you are weary first with laying on.
The late so baffled scribbler of this day,
Though he stands trembling, bids me boldly say,
What we before most plays are used to do,
For poets out of fear first draw on you;
In a fierce prologue the still pit defy,
And, ere you speak, like Castril give the lie.
But though our Bayes's battles oft I've fought,
And with bruised knuckles their dear conquests
    bought;
Nay, never yet feared odds upon the stage,
In prologue dare not hector with the age;
But would take quarter from your saving hands,
Though Bayes within all yielding countermands,
Says, you confederate wits no quarter give,
Therefore his play shan't ask your leave to live.
Well, let the vain rash fop, by huffing so,
Think to obtain the better terms of you.

118

But we, the actors, humbly will submit,
Now, and at any time, to a full pit;
Nay, often we anticipate your rage,
And murder poets for you on our stage:
We set no guards upon our tiring-room,
But when with flying colours there you come,
We patiently, you see, give up to you
Our poets, virgins, nay, our matrons too.

Act I

SCENE 1: *Horner's Lodging*

Enter Horner, *and* Quack *following him at a distance.*

HORNER: [*Aside*] A quack is as fit for a pimp, as a midwife for a bawd; they are still but in their way, both helpers of nature.—[*Aloud*] Well, my dear doctor, hast thou done what I desired?

QUACK: I have undone you for ever with the women, and reported you throughout the whole town as bad as an eunuch, with as much trouble as if I had made you one in earnest.

HORNER: But have you told all the midwives you know, the orange wenches at the playhouses, the city husbands, and old fumbling keepers of this end of the town? for they'll be the readiest to report it.

QUACK: I have told all the chambermaids, waiting-women, tire-women, and old women of my acquaintance; nay, and whispered it as a secret to 'em, and to the whisperers of Whitehall; so that you need not doubt 'twill spread, and you will be as odious to the handsome young women, as—

HORNER: As the small-pox. Well—

QUACK: And to the married women of this end of the town, as—

HORNER: As the great one; nay, as their own husbands.

QUACK: And to the city dames, as aniseed Robin, of filthy and contemptible memory; and they will frighten their children with your name, especially their females.

HORNER: And cry, Horner's coming to carry you away. I am only afraid 'twill not be believed. You told 'em it was by an English-French disaster, and an

English-French chirurgeon, who has given me at once not only a cure, but an antidote for the future against that damned malady, and that worse distemper, love, and all other women's evils?

QUACK: Your late journey into France has made it the more credible, and your being here a fortnight before you appeared in public, looks as if you apprehended the shame, which I wonder you do not. Well, I have been hired by young gallants to belie 'em t'other way; but you are the first would be thought a man unfit for women.

HORNER: Dear Mr. Doctor, let vain rogues be contented only to be thought abler men than they are, generally 'tis all the pleasure they have; but mine lies another way.

QUACK: You take, methinks, a very preposterous way to it, and as ridiculous as if we operators in physic should put forth bills to disparage our medicaments, with hopes to gain customers.

HORNER: Doctor, there are quacks in love as well as physic, who get but the fewer and worse patients for their boasting; a good name is seldom got by giving it one's self; and women, no more than honour, are compassed by bragging. Come, come, Doctor, the wisest lawyer never discovers the merits of his cause till the trial; the wealthiest man conceals his riches, and the cunning gamester his play. Shy husbands and keepers, like old rooks, are not to be cheated but by a new unpractised trick: false friendship will pass now no more than false dice upon 'em; no, not in the city.

Enter Boy.

BOY: There are two ladies and a gentleman coming up.　　　　　　　　　　　　　　　　[*Exit*]

HORNER: A pox! some unbelieving sisters of my former acquaintance, who, I am afraid, expect their sense should be satisfied of the falsity of the report. No —this formal fool and women!

Enter Sir Jasper Fidget, Lady Fidget, *and* Mrs. Dainty Fidget.

QUACK: His wife and sister.

SIR JASPER: My coach breaking just now before your door, sir, I look upon as an occasional reprimand to me, sir, for not kissing your hands, sir, since your coming out of France, sir; and so my disaster, sir, has been my good fortune, sir; and this is my wife and sister, sir.

HORNER: What then, sir?

SIR JASPER: My lady, and sister, sir.—Wife, this is Master Horner.

LADY FIDGET: Master Horner, husband!

SIR JASPER: My lady, my Lady Fidget, sir.

HORNER: So, sir.

SIR JASPER: Won't you be acquainted with her, sir?— [*Aside*] So, the report is true, I find, by his coldness or aversion to the sex; but I'll play the wag with him.—[*Aloud*] Pray salute my wife, my lady, sir.

HORNER: I will kiss no man's wife, sir, for him, sir; I have taken my eternal leave, sir, of the sex already, sir.

SIR JASPER: [*Aside*] Ha! ha! ha! I'll plague him yet.— [*Aloud*] Not know my wife, sir?

HORNER: I do know your wife, sir; she's a woman, sir, and consequently a monster, sir, a greater monster than a husband, sir.

SIR JASPER: A husband! how, sir?

HORNER: So, sir; but I make no more cuckolds, sir.
　　　　　　　　　　　　　　　　　　[*Makes horns*]

SIR JASPER: Ha! ha! ha! Mercury! Mercury!

LADY FIDGET: Pray, Sir Jasper, let us be gone from this rude fellow.

MRS. DAINTY: Who, by his breeding, would think he had ever been in France?

LADY FIDGET: Foh! he's but too much a French fellow, such as hate women of quality and virtue for their love to their husbands. Sir Jasper, a woman is hated by 'em as much for loving her husband as for loving their money. But pray let's be gone.

HORNER: You do well, madam; for I have nothing that you came for. I have brought over not so much as a bawdy picture, no new postures, nor the second part of the *Ecole des Filles*; nor—

QUACK: Hold, for shame, sir! what d'ye mean? you'll ruin yourself for ever with the sex—
　　　　　　　　　　　　　　　　[*Apart to* Horner]

SIR JASPER: Ha! ha! ha! he hates women perfectly, I find.

MRS. DAINTY: What pity 'tis he should!

LADY FIDGET: Ay, he's a base fellow for't. But affectation makes not a woman more odious to them than virtue.

HORNER: Because your virtue is your greatest affectation, madam.

LADY FIDGET: How, you saucy fellow! would you wrong my honour?

HORNER: If I could.

LADY FIDGET: How d'ye mean, sir?

SIR JASPER: Ha! ha! ha! no, he can't wrong your ladyship's honour, upon my honour. He, poor man— hark you in your ear—a mere eunuch. [*Whispers*]

LADY FIDGET: O filthy French beast! foh! foh! why do we stay? let's be gone: I can't endure the sight of him.

SIR JASPER: Stay but till the chairs come; they'll be here presently.

LADY FIDGET: No.

SIR JASPER: Nor can I stay longer. 'Tis, let me see, a quarter and a half quarter of a minute past eleven. The council will be sat; I must away. Business must be preferred always before love and ceremony with the wise, Mr. Horner.

HORNER: And the impotent, Sir Jasper.

SIR JASPER: Ay, ay, the impotent, Master Horner; hah! hah! hah!

LADY FIDGET: What, leave us with a filthy man alone in his lodgings?

SIR JASPER: He's an innocent man now, you know. Pray stay, I'll hasten the chairs to you.—Mr. Horner, your servant; I should be glad to see you at my house. Pray come and dine with me, and play at cards with my wife after dinner; you are fit for women at that game yet, ha! ha!—[*Aside*] 'Tis as much a husband's prudence to provide innocent diversion for a wife as to hinder her unlawful pleasures; and he had better employ her than let her employ herself.—[*Aloud*] Farewell.

HORNER: Your servant, Sir Jasper.   [*Exit Sir Jasper*]

LADY FIDGET: I will not stay with him, foh!—

HORNER: Nay, madam, I beseech you stay, if it be but to see I can be as civil to ladies yet as they would desire.

LADY FIDGET: No, no, foh! you cannot be civil to ladies.

MRS. DAINTY: You as civil as ladies would desire?

LADY FIDGET: No, no, no, foh! foh! foh!

[*Exeunt* Lady Fidget *and* Mrs. Dainty Fidget]

QUACK: Now, I think, I, or you yourself, rather, have done your business with the women.

HORNER: Thou art an ass. Don't you see already, upon the report, and my carriage, this grave man of business leaves his wife in my lodgings, invites me to his house and wife, who before would not be acquainted with me out of jealousy?

QUACK: Nay, by this means you may be the more acquainted with the husbands, but the less with the wives.

HORNER: Let me alone; if I can but abuse the husbands, I'll soon disabuse the wives. Stay—I'll reckon you up the advantages I am like to have by my stratagem. First, I shall be rid of all my old acquaintances, the most insatiable sort of duns, that invade our lodgings in a morning; and next to the pleasure of making a new mistress is that of being rid of an old one, and of all old debts. Love, when it comes to be so, is paid the most unwillingly.

QUACK: Well, you may be so rid of your old acquaintances; but how will you get any new ones?

HORNER: Doctor, thou wilt never make a good chemist, thou art so incredulous and impatient. Ask but all the young fellows of the town if they do not lose more time, like huntsmen, in starting the game, than in running it down. One knows not where to find 'em; who will or will not. Women of quality are so civil, you can hardly distinguish love from good breeding, and a man is often mistaken: but now I can be sure she that shows an aversion to me loves the sport, as those women that are gone, whom I warrant to be right. And then the next thing is, your women of honour, as you call 'em, are only chary of their reputations, not their persons; and 'tis scandal they would avoid, not men. Now may I have, by the reputation of an eunuch, the privileges of one, and be seen in a lady's chamber in a morning as early as her hus-

band; kiss virgins before their parents or lovers; and may be, in short, the *passe-partout* of the town. Now, doctor.

QUACK: Nay, now you shall be the doctor; and your process is so new that we do not know but it may succeed.

HORNER: Not so new neither; *probatum est*, doctor.

QUACK: Well, I wish you luck, and many patients, whilst I go to mine.   [*Exit*]

Enter Harcourt *and* Dorilant.

HARCOURT: Come, your appearance at the play yesterday, has, I hope, hardened you for the future against the women's contempt, and the men's raillery; and now you'll abroad as you were wont.

HORNER: Did I not bear it bravely?

DORILANT: With a most theatrical impudence, nay, more than the orange-wenches show there, or a drunken vizard-mask, or a great-bellied actress; nay, or the most impudent of creatures, an ill poet; or what is yet more impudent, a second-hand critic.

HORNER: But what say the ladies? have they no pity?

HARCOURT: What ladies? The vizard-masks, you know, never pity a man when all's gone, though in their service.

DORILANT: And for the women in the boxes, you'd never pity them when 'twas in your power.

HARCOURT: They say 'tis pity but all that deal with common women should be served so.

DORILANT: Nay, I dare swear they won't admit you to play at cards with them, go to plays with 'em, or do the little duties which other shadows of men are wont to do for 'em.

HORNER: What do you call shadows of men?

DORILANT: Half-men.

HORNER: What, boys?

DORILANT: Ay, your old boys, old *beaux garçons*, who, like superannuated stallions, are suffered to run, feed, and whinny with the mares as long as they live, though they can do nothing else.

HORNER: Well, a pox on love and wenching! Women serve but to keep a man from better company. Though I can't enjoy them, I shall you the more. Good fellowship and friendship are lasting, rational, and manly pleasures.

HARCOURT: For all that, give me some of those pleasures you call effeminate too; they help to relish one another.

HORNER: They disturb one another.

HARCOURT: No, mistresses are like books. If you pore upon them too much, they doze you, and make you unfit for company; but if used discreetly, you are the fitter for conversation by 'em.

DORILANT: A mistress should be like a little country retreat near the town; not to dwell in constantly, but only for a night and away, to taste the town the better when a man returns.

HORNER: I tell you, 'tis as hard to be a good fellow, a good friend, and a lover of women, as 'tis to be a good fellow, a good friend, and a lover of money. You cannot follow both, then choose your side. Wine gives you liberty, love takes it away.

DORILANT: Gad, he's in the right on't.

HORNER: Wine gives you joy; love, grief and tortures, besides surgeons. Wine makes us witty; love, only sots. Wine makes us sleep; love breaks it.

DORILANT: By the world he has reason, Harcourt.

HORNER: Wine makes—

DORILANT: Ay, wine makes us—makes us princes; love makes us beggars, poor rogues, egad—and wine—

HORNER: So, there's one converted.—No, no, love and wine, oil and vinegar.

HARCOURT: I grant it; love will still be uppermost.

HORNER: Come, for my part, I will have only those glorious manly pleasures of being very drunk and very slovenly.

Enter Boy.

BOY: Mr. Sparkish is below, sir.   [*Exit*]

HARCOURT: What, my dear friend! a rogue that is fond of me only, I think, for abusing him.

DORILANT: No, he can no more think the men laugh at him than that women jilt him; his opinion of himself is so good.

HORNER: Well, there's another pleasure by drinking I thought not of,—I shall lose his acquaintance, because he cannot drink: and you know 'tis a very hard thing to be rid of him; for he's one of those nauseous offerers at wit, who, like the worst fiddlers, run themselves into all companies.

HARCOURT: One that, by being in the company of men of sense, would pass for one.

HORNER: And may so to the short-sighted world; as a false jewel amongst true ones is not discerned at a distance. His company is as troublesome to us as a cuckold's when you have a mind to his wife's.

HARCOURT: No, the rogue will not let us enjoy one another, but ravishes our conversation; though he signifies no more to't than Sir Martin Mar-all's[1] gaping, and awkward thrumming upon the lute, does to his man's voice and music.

DORILANT: And to pass for a wit in town shows himself a fool every night to us, that are guilty of the plot.

HORNER: Such wits as he are, to a company of reasonable men, like rooks to the gamesters; who only fill a room at the table, but are so far from contributing to the play, that they only serve to spoil the fancy of those that do.

DORILANT: Nay, they are used like rooks too, snubbed, checked, and abused; yet the rogues will hang on.

HORNER: A pox on 'em, and all that force nature, and would be still what she forbids 'em! Affectation is her greatest monster.

HARCOURT: Most men are the contraries to that they would seem. Your bully, you see, is a coward with

[1]Sir Martin Mar-all *is the title of a comedy by Dryden, first produced in* 1667.

a long sword; the little humbly-fawning physician, with his ebony cane, is he that destroys men.

DORILANT: The usurer, a poor rogue, possessed of mouldy bonds and mortgages; and we they call spendthrifts, are only wealthy, who lay out his money upon daily new purchases of pleasure.

HORNER: Ay, your arrantest cheat is your trustee or executor; your jealous man, the greatest cuckold; your churchman the greatest atheist; and your noisy pert rogue of a wit, the greatest fop, dullest ass, and worst company, as you shall see; for here he comes.

Enter Sparkish.

SPARKISH: How is't, sparks? how is't? Well, faith, Harry, I must rally thee a little, ha! ha! ha! upon the report in town of thee, ha! ha! ha! I can't hold i'faith; shall I speak?

HORNER: Yes; but you'll be so bitter then.

SPARKISH: Honest Dick and Frank here shall answer for me; I will not be extreme bitter, by the universe.

HARCOURT: We will be bound in a ten thousand pound bond, he shall not be bitter at all.

DORILANT: Nor sharp, nor sweet.

HORNER: What, not downright insipid?

SPARKISH: Nay then, since you are so brisk, and provoke me, take what follows. You must know, I was discoursing and rallying with some ladies yesterday, and they happened to talk of the fine new signs in town—

HORNER: Very fine ladies, I believe.

SPARKISH: Said I, I know where the best new sign is.—Where? says one of the ladies.—In Covent-Garden, I replied.—Said another, In what street? —In Russel-street, answered I.—Lord, says another, I'm sure there was never a fine new sign there yesterday.—Yes, but there was, said I again; and it came out of France, and has been there a fortnight.

DORILANT: A pox! I can hear no more, prithee.

HORNER: No, hear him out; let him tune his crowd a while.

HARCOURT: The worst music, the greatest preparation.

SPARKISH: Nay, faith, I'll make you laugh.—It cannot be, says a third lady.—Yes, yes, quoth I again.— Says a fourth lady—

HORNER: Look to't, we'll have no more ladies.

SPARKISH: No— then mark, mark, now. Said I to the fourth, Did you never see Mr. Horner? he lodges in Russel-street, and he's a sign of a man, you know, since he came out of France; ha! ha! ha!

HORNER: But the devil take me if thine be the sign of a jest.

SPARKISH: With that they all fell a-laughing, till they bepissed themselves. What, but it does not move you, methinks? Well, I see one had as good go to law without a witness, as break a jest without a laugher on one's side.—Come, come, sparks, but where do we dine? I have left at Whitehall an earl, to dine with you.

DORILANT: Why, I thought thou hadst loved a man with a title, better than a suit with a French trimming to't.

HARCOURT: Go to him again.

SPARKISH: No, sir, a wit to me is the greatest title in the world.

HORNER: But go dine with your earl, sir; he may be exceptious. We are your friends, and will not take it ill to be left, I do assure you.

HARCOURT: Nay, faith, he shall go to him.

SPARKISH: Nay, pray, gentlemen.

DORILANT: We'll thrust you out, if you won't; what, disappoint anybody for us?

SPARKISH: Nay, dear gentlemen, hear me.

HORNER: No, no, sir, by no means; pray go, sir.

SPARKISH: Why, dear rogues—

DORILANT: No, no.

[*They all thrust him out of the room*]

ALL: Ha! ha! ha!

Re-enter Sparkish.

SPARKISH: But, sparks, pray hear me. What, d'ye think I'll eat then with gay shallow fops and silent coxcombs? I think wit as necessary at dinner, as a glass of good wine; and that's the reason I never have any stomach when I eat alone.—Come, but where do we dine?

HORNER: Even where you will.

SPARKISH: At Chateline's?

DORILANT: Yes, if you will.

SPARKISH: Or at the Cock?

DORILANT: Yes, if you please.

SPARKISH: Or at the Dog and Partridge?

HORNER: Ay, if you have a mind to't; for we shall dine at neither.

SPARKISH: Pshaw! with your fooling we shall lose the new play; and I would no more miss seeing a new play the first day, than I would miss sitting in the wit's row. Therefore I'll go fetch my mistress, and away.   [*Exit*]

Enter Pinchwife.

HORNER: Who have we here? Pinchwife?

PINCHWIFE: Gentlemen, your humble servant.

HORNER: Well, Jack, by thy long absence from the town, the grumness of thy countenance, and the slovenliness of thy habit, I should give thee joy, should I not, of marriage?

PINCHWIFE: [*Aside*] Death! does he know I'm married too? I thought to have concealed it from him at least.—[*Aloud*] My long stay in the country will excuse my dress; and I have a suit of law that brings me up to town, that puts me out of humour. Besides, I must give Sparkish to-morrow five thousand pounds to lie with my sister.

HORNER: Nay, you country gentlemen, rather than not purchase, will buy anything; and he is a cracked

title, if we may quibble. Well, but am I to give thee joy? I heard thou wert married.

PINCHWIFE: What then?

HORNER: Why, the next thing that is to be heard, is, thou'rt a cuckold.

PINCHWIFE: Insupportable name!   [*Aside*]

HORNER: But I did not expect marriage from such a whoremaster as you; one that knew the town so much, and women so well.

PINCHWIFE: Why, I have married no London wife.

HORNER: Pshaw! that's all one. That grave circumspection in marrying a country wife, is like refusing a deceitful pampered Smithfield jade, to go and be cheated by a friend in the country.

PINCHWIFE: [*Aside*] A pox on him and his simile!— [*Aloud*] At least we are a little surer of the breed there, know what her keeping has been, whether foiled or unsound.

HORNER: Come, come, I have known a clap gotten in Wales; and there are cousins, justices' clerks, and chaplains in the country, I won't say coachmen. But she's handsome and young?

PINCHWIFE: [*Aside*] I'll answer as I should do.— [*Aloud*] No, no; she has no beauty but her youth, no attraction but her modesty: wholesome, homely, and huswifely; that's all.

DORILANT: He talks as like a grazier as he looks.

PINCHWIFE: She's too awkward, ill-favoured, and silly to bring to town.

HARCOURT: Then methinks you should bring her to be taught breeding.

PINCHWIFE: To be taught! no, sir, I thank you. Good wives and private soldiers should be ignorant—I'll keep her from your instructions, I warrant you.

HARCOURT: The rogue is as jealous as if his wife were not ignorant.   [*Aside*]

HORNER: Why, if she be ill-favoured, there will be less danger here for you than by leaving her in the country. We have such variety of dainties that we are seldom hungry.

DORILANT: But they have always coarse, constant, swingeing stomachs in the country.

HARCOURT: Foul feeders indeed!

DORILANT: And your hospitality is great there.

HARCOURT: Open house; every man's welcome.

PINCHWIFE: So, so, gentlemen.

HORNER: But prithee, why shouldst thou marry her? If she be ugly, ill-bred, and silly, she must be rich then.

PINCHWIFE: As rich as if she brought me twenty thousand pound out of this town; for she'll be as sure not to spend her moderate portion, as a London baggage would be to spend hers, let it be what it would: so 'tis all one. Then, because she's ugly, she's the likelier to be my own; and being ill-bred, she'll hate conversation; and since silly and innocent, will not know the difference betwixt a man of one-and-twenty and one of forty.

HORNER: Nine—to my knowledge. But if she be silly,

she'll expect as much from a man of forty-nine, as from him of one-and-twenty. But methinks wit is more necessary than beauty; and I think no young woman ugly that has it, and no handsome woman agreeable without it.

PINCHWIFE: 'Tis my maxim, he's a fool that marries; but he's a greater that does not marry a fool. What is wit in a wife good for, but to make a man a cuckold?

HORNER: Yes, to keep it from his knowledge.

PINCHWIFE: A fool cannot contrive to make her husband a cuckold.

HORNER: No; but she'll club with a man that can: and what is worse, if she cannot make her husband a cuckold, she'll make him jealous, and pass for one: and then 'tis all one.

PINCHWIFE: Well, well, I'll take care for one. My wife shall make me no cuckold, though she had your help, Mr. Horner. I understand the town, sir.

DORILANT: His help!   [Aside]

HARCOURT: He's come newly to town, it seems, and has not heard how things are with him.   [Aside]

HORNER: But tell me, has marriage cured thee of whoring, which it seldom does?

HARCOURT: 'Tis more than age can do.

HORNER: No, the word is, I'll marry and live honest: but a marriage vow is like a penitent gamester's oath, and entering into bonds and penalties to stint himself to such a particular small sum at play for the future, which makes him but the more eager; and not being able to hold out, loses his money again, and his forfeit to boot.

DORILANT: Ay, ay, a gamester will be a gamester whilst his money lasts, and a whoremaster whilst his vigour.

HARCOURT: Nay, I have known 'em, when they are broke, and can lose no more, keep a fumbling with the box in their hands to fool with only, and hinder other gamesters.

DORILANT: That had wherewithal to make lusty stakes.

PINCHWIFE: Well, gentlemen, you may laugh at me; but you shall never lie with my wife: I know the town.

HORNER: But prithee, was not the way you were in better? is not keeping better than marriage?

PINCHWIFE: A pox on't! the jades would jilt me, I could never keep a whore to myself.

HORNER: So, then you only married to keep a whore to yourself. Well, but let me tell you, women, as you say, are like soldiers, made constant and loyal by good pay, rather than by oaths and covenants. Therefore I'd advise my friends to keep rather than marry, since too I find, by your example, it does not serve one's turn; for I saw you yesterday in the eighteenpenny place with a pretty country-wench.

PINCHWIFE: How the devil! did he see my wife then? I sat there that she might not be seen. But she shall never go to a play again.   [Aside]

HORNER: What! dost thou blush, at nine-and-forty, for having been seen with a wench?

DORILANT: No, faith, I warrant 'twas his wife, which he seated there out of sight; for he's a cunning rogue, and understands the town.

HARCOURT: He blushes. Then 'twas his wife; for men are now more ashamed to be seen with them in public than with a wench.

PINCHWIFE: Hell and damnation! I'm undone, since Horner has seen her, and they know 'twas she.
                                                                [Aside]

HORNER: But prithee, was it thy wife? She was exceeding pretty: I was in love with her at that distance.

PINCHWIFE: You are like never to be nearer to her. Your servant, gentlemen.   [Offers to go]

HORNER: Nay, prithee stay.

PINCHWIFE: I cannot; I will not.

HORNER: Come, you shall dine with us.

PINCHWIFE: I have dined already.

HORNER: Come, I know thou hast not: I'll treat thee, dear rogue; thou sha't spend none of thy Hampshire money to-day.

PINCHWIFE: Treat me! So, he uses me already like his cuckold.   [Aside]

HORNER: Nay, you shall not go.

PINCHWIFE: I must; I have business at home.   [Exit]

HARCOURT: To beat his wife. He's as jealous of her, as a Cheapside husband of a Covent-garden wife.

HORNER: Why, 'tis as hard to find an old whoremaster without jealousy and the gout, as a young one without fear, or the pox:—
As gout in age from pox in youth proceeds,
So wenching past, then jealousy succeeds;
The worst disease that love and wenching breeds.
                                                              [Exeunt]

Act II

SCENE 1:   *A Room in Pinchwife's House*

Mrs. Margery Pinchwife *and* Alithea. Pinchwife *peeping behind at the door.*

MRS. PINCHWIFE: Pray, sister, where are the best fields and woods to walk in, in London?

ALITHEA: [Aside] A pretty question!—[Aloud] Why, sister, Mulberry-garden and St. James's-park; and, for close walks, the New Exchange.

MRS. PINCHWIFE: Pray, sister, tell me why my husband looks so grum here in town, and keeps me up so close, and will not let me go a-walking, nor let me wear my best gown yesterday.

ALITHEA: O, he's jealous, sister.

MRS. PINCHWIFE: Jealous! what's that?

ALITHEA: He's afraid you should love another man.

MRS. PINCHWIFE: How should he be afraid of my loving another man, when he will not let me see any but himself?

ALITHEA: Did he not carry you yesterday to a play?

MRS. PINCHWIFE: Ay; but we sat amongst ugly people. He would not let me come near the gentry, who sat under us, so that I could not see 'em. He told me, none but naughty women sat there, whom they toused and moused. But I would have ventured, for all that.

ALITHEA: But how did you like the play?

MRS. PINCHWIFE: Indeed I was weary of the play; but I liked hugeously the actors. They are the goodliest, properest men, sister!

ALITHEA: O, but you must not like the actors, sister.

MRS. PINCHWIFE: Ay, how should I help it, sister? Pray, sister, when my husband comes in, will you ask leave for me to go a-walking?

ALITHEA: A-walking! ha! ha! Lord, a country-gentle-woman's pleasure is the drudgery of a footpost; and she requires as much airing as her husband's horses. —[Aside] But here comes your husband: I'll ask, though I'm sure he'll not grant it.

MRS. PINCHWIFE: He says he won't let me go abroad for fear of catching the pox.

ALITHEA: Fy! the small-pox you should say.

Enter Pinchwife.

MRS. PINCHWIFE: O my dear, dear bud, welcome home! Why dost thou look so fropish? who has nangered thee?

PINCHWIFE: You're a fool.

               [Mrs. Pinchwife *goes aside, and cries*]

ALITHEA: Faith, so she is, for crying for no fault, poor tender creature!

PINCHWIFE: What, you would have her as impudent as yourself, as arrant a jilflirt, a gadder, a magpie; and to say all, a mere notorious town-woman?

ALITHEA: Brother, you are my only censurer; and the honour of your family will sooner suffer in your wife there than in me, though I take the innocent liberty of the town.

PINCHWIFE: Hark you, mistress, do not talk so before my wife.—The innocent liberty of the town!

ALITHEA: Why, pray, who boasts of any intrigue with me? what lampoon has made my name notorious? what ill women frequent my lodgings? I keep no company with any women of scandalous reputations.

PINCHWIFE: No, you keep the men of scandalous reputations company.

ALITHEA: Where? would you not have me civil? answer 'em in a box at the plays, in the drawing-room at Whitehall, in St. James'-park, Mulberry-garden, or—

PINCHWIFE: Hold, hold! Do not teach my wife where the men are to be found: I believe she's the worse for your town-documents already. I bid you keep her in ignorance, as I do.

MRS. PINCHWIFE: Indeed, be not angry with her, bud, she will tell me nothing of the town, though I ask her a thousand times a day.

PINCHWIFE: Then you are very inquisitive to know, I find?

MRS. PINCHWIFE: Not I indeed, dear; I hate London. Our place-house in the country is worth a thousand of't: would I were there again!

PINCHWIFE: So you shall, I warrant. But were you not talking of plays and players when I came in?—[To Alithea] You are her encourager in such discourses.

MRS. PINCHWIFE: No, indeed, dear; she chid me just now for liking the playermen.

PINCHWIFE: [Aside] Nay, if she be so innocent as to own to me her liking them, there is no hurt in't.— [Aloud] Come, my poor rogue, but thou likest none better than me?

MRS. PINCHWIFE: Yes, indeed, but I do. The player-men are finer folks.

PINCHWIFE: But you love none better than me?

MRS. PINCHWIFE: You are my own dear bud, and I know you. I hate a stranger.

PINCHWIFE: Ay, my dear, you must love me only; and not be like the naughty town-women, who only hate their husbands, and love every man else; love plays, visits, fine coaches, fine clothes, fiddles, balls, treats, and so lead a wicked town-life.

MRS. PINCHWIFE: Nay, if to enjoy all these things be a town-life, London is not so bad a place, dear.

PINCHWIFE: How! if you love me, you must hate London.

ALITHEA: The fool has forbid me discovering to her the pleasures of the town, and he is now setting her agog upon them himself.   [Aside]

MRS. PINCHWIFE: But, husband, do the town-women love the playermen too?

PINCHWIFE: Yes, I warrant you.

MRS. PINCHWIFE: Ay, I warrant you.

PINCHWIFE: Why, you do not, I hope?

MRS. PINCHWIFE: No, no, bud. But why have we no playermen in the country?

PINCHWIFE: Ha!—Mrs. Minx, ask me no more to go to a play.

MRS. PINCHWIFE: Nay, why, love? I did not care for going: but when you forbid me, you make me, as 'twere, desire it.

ALITHEA: So 'twill be in other things, I warrant.
                                                  [Aside]

MRS. PINCHWIFE: Pray let me go to a play, dear.

PINCHWIFE: Hold your peace, I wo' not.

MRS. PINCHWIFE: Why, love?

PINCHWIFE: Why, I'll tell you.

ALITHEA: Nay, if he tell her, she'll give him more cause to forbid her that place.   [Aside]

MRS. PINCHWIFE: Pray why, dear?

PINCHWIFE: First, you like the actors; and the gallants may like you.

MRS. PINCHWIFE: What, a homely country girl! No, bud, nobody will like me.

PINCHWIFE: I tell you yes, they may.

MRS. PINCHWIFE: No, no, you jest—I won't believe you: I will go.

PINCHWIFE: I tell you then, that one of the lewdest fellows in town, who saw you there, told me he was in love with you.

MRS. PINCHWIFE: Indeed! who, who, pray who was't?

PINCHWIFE: I've gone too far, and slipped before I was aware; how overjoyed she is!   [Aside]

MRS. PINCHWIFE: Was it any Hampshire gallant, any of our neighbours? I promise you, I am beholden to him.

PINCHWIFE: I promise you, you lie; for he would but ruin you, as he has done hundreds. He has no other love for women but that; such as he look upon women, like basilisks, but to destroy 'em.

MRS. PINCHWIFE: Ay, but if he loves me, why should he ruin me? answer me to that. Methinks he should not, I would do him no harm.

ALITHEA: Ha! ha! ha!

PINCHWIFE: 'Tis very well; but I'll keep him from doing you any harm, or me either. But here comes company; get you in, get you in.

MRS. PINCHWIFE: But, pray, husband, is he a pretty gentleman that loves me?

PINCHWIFE: In, baggage, in.
                [Thrusts her in, and shuts the door]

Enter Sparkish and Harcourt.
What, all the lewd libertines of the town brought to my lodging by this easy coxcomb! 'sdeath, I'll not suffer it.

SPARKISH: Here, Harcourt, do you approve my choice? —[To Alithea] Dear little rogue, I told you I'd bring you acquainted with all my friends, the wits and—   [Harcourt salutes her]

PINCHWIFE: Ay, they shall know her, as well as you yourself will, I warrant you.

SPARKISH: This is one of those, my pretty rogue, that are to dance at your wedding to-morrow; and him you must bid welcome ever, to what you and I have.

PINCHWIFE: Monstrous!   [Aside]

SPARKISH: Harcourt, how dost thou like her, faith? Nay, dear, do not look down; I should hate to have a wife of mine out of countenance at anything.

PINCHWIFE: Wonderful!   [Aside]

SPARKISH: Tell me, I say, Harcourt, how dost thou like her? Thou hast stared upon her enough, to resolve me.

HARCOURT: So infinitely well, that I could wish I had a mistress too, that might differ from her in nothing but her love and engagement to you.

ALITHEA: Sir, Master Sparkish has often told me that his acquaintance were all wits and raillieurs, and now I find it.

SPARKISH: No, by the universe, madam, he does not rally now; you may believe him. I do assure you, he is the honestest, worthiest, true-hearted gentleman —a man of such perfect honour, he would say nothing to a lady he does not mean.

PINCHWIFE: Praising another man to his mistress!
                [Aside]

HARCOURT: Sir, you are so beyond expectation obliging, that—

SPARKISH: Nay, egad, I am sure you do admire her extremely; I see't in your eyes.—He does admire you, madam.—By the world, don't you?

HARCOURT: Yes, above the world, or the most glorious part of it, her whole sex: and till now I never thought I should have envied you, or any man about to marry, but you have the best excuse for marriage I ever knew.

ALITHEA: Nay, now, sir, I'm satisfied you are of the society of the wits and raillieurs, since you cannot spare your friend, even when he is but too civil to you; but the surest sign is, since you are an enemy to marriage,—for that I hear you hate as much as business or bad wine.

HARCOURT: Truly, madam, I was never an enemy to marriage till now, because marriage was never an enemy to me before.

ALITHEA: But why, sir, is marriage an enemy to you now? because it robs you of your friend here? for you look upon a friend married, as one gone into a monastery, that is, dead to the world.

HARCOURT: 'Tis indeed, because you marry him; I see, madam, you can guess my meaning. I do confess heartily and openly, I wish it were in my power to break the match; by Heavens I would.

SPARKISH: Poor Frank!

ALITHEA: Would you be so unkind to me?

HARCOURT: No, no, 'tis not because I would be unkind to you.

SPARKISH: Poor Frank! no gad, 'tis only his kindness to me.

PINCHWIFE: Great kindness to you indeed! Insensible fop, let a man make love to his wife to his face!
                [Aside]

SPARKISH: Come, dear Frank, for all my wife there, that shall be, thou shalt enjoy me sometimes, dear rogue. By my honour, we men of wit condole for our deceased brother in marriage, as much as for one dead in earnest: I think that was prettily said of me, ha, Harcourt?—But come, Frank, be not melancholy for me.

HARCOURT: No, I assure you, I am not melancholy for you.

SPARKISH: Prithee, Frank, dost think my wife that shall be there, a fine person?

HARCOURT: I could gaze upon her till I became as blind as you are.

SPARKISH: How as I am? how?

HARCOURT: Because you are a lover, and true lovers are blind, stock blind.

SPARKISH: True, true; but by the world she has wit too, as well as beauty: go, go with her into a corner, and try if she has wit; talk to her anything, she's bashful before me.

HARCOURT: Indeed if a woman wants wit in a corner, she has it nowhere.

ALITHEA: Sir, you dispose of me a little before your time—   [*Aside to* Sparkish]

SPARKISH: Nay, nay, madam, let me have an earnest of your obedience, or—go, go, madam—

[Harcourt *courts* Alithea *aside*]

PINCHWIFE: How, sir! if you are not concerned for the honour of a wife, I am for that of a sister; he shall not debauch her. Be a pander to your own wife! bring men to her! let 'em make love before your face! thrust 'em into a corner together, then leave 'em in private! is this your town wit and conduct?

SPARKISH: Ha! ha! ha! a silly wise rogue would make one laugh more than a stark fool, ha! ha! I shall burst. Nay, you shall not disturb 'em; I'll vex thee, by the world.

[*Struggles with* Pinchwife *to keep him from* Harcourt *and* Alithea]

ALITHEA: The writings are drawn, sir, settlements made; 'tis too late, sir, and past all revocation.

HARCOURT: Then so is my death.

ALITHEA: I would not be unjust to him.

HARCOURT: Then why to me so?

ALITHEA: I have no obligation to you.

HARCOURT: My love.

ALITHEA: I had his before.

HARCOURT: You never had it; he wants, you see, jealousy, the only infallible sign of it.

ALITHEA: Love proceeds from esteem; he cannot distrust my virtue: besides, he loves me, or he would not marry me.

HARCOURT: Marrying you is no more sign of his love than bribing your woman, that he may marry you, is a sign of his generosity. Marriage is rather a sign of interest than love; and he that marries a fortune covets a mistress, not loves her. But if you take marriage for a sign of love, take it from me immediately.

ALITHEA: No, now you have put a scruple in my head; but in short, sir, to end our dispute, I must marry him, my reputation would suffer in the world else.

HARCOURT: No; if you do marry him, with your pardon, madam, your reputation suffers in the world, and you would be thought in necessity for a cloak.

ALITHEA: Nay, now you are rude, sir.—Mr. Sparkish, pray come hither, your friend here is very troublesome, and very loving.

HARCOURT: Hold! hold!—   [*Aside to* Alithea]

PINCHWIFE: D'ye hear that?

SPARKISH: Why, d'ye think I'll seem to be jealous, like a country bumpkin?

PINCHWIFE: No, rather be a cuckold, like a credulous cit.

HARCOURT: Madam, you would not have been so little generous as to have told him.

ALITHEA: Yes, since you could be so little generous as to wrong him.

HARCOURT: Wrong him! no man can do't, he's beneath an injury: a bubble, a coward, a senseless idiot, a wretch so contemptible to all the world but you, that—

ALITHEA: Hold, do not rail at him, for since he is like to be my husband, I am resolved to like him: nay, I think I am obliged to tell him you are not his friend.—Master Sparkish, Master Sparkish!

SPARKISH: What, what?—[*To* Harcourt] Now, dear rogue, has not she wit?

HARCOURT: Not so much as I thought, and hoped she had.   [*Speaks surlily*]

ALITHEA: Mr. Sparkish, do you bring people to rail at you?

HARCOURT: Madam—

SPARKISH: How! no; but if he does rail at me, 'tis but in jest, I warrant: what we wits do for one another, and never take any notice of it.

ALITHEA: He spoke so scurrilously of you, I had no patience to hear him; besides, he has been making love to me.

HARCOURT: True, damned tell-tale woman!   [*Aside*]

SPARKISH: Pshaw! to show his parts—we wits rail and make love often, but to show our parts: as we have no affections, so we have no malice, we—

ALITHEA: He said you were a wretch below an injury—

SPARKISH: Pshaw!

HARCOURT: Damned, senseless, impudent, virtuous jade! Well, since she won't let me have her, she'll do as good, she'll make me hate her.   [*Aside*]

ALITHEA: A common bubble—

SPARKISH: Pshaw!

ALITHEA: A coward—

SPARKISH: Pshaw, pshaw!

ALITHEA: A senseless, drivelling idiot—

SPARKISH: How! did he disparage my parts? Nay, then, my honour's concerned, I can't put up that, sir, by the world—brother, help me to kill him—[*Aside*] I may draw now, since we have the odds of him:—'tis a good occasion, too, before my mistress—   [*Offers to draw*]

ALITHEA: Hold, hold!

SPARKISH: What, what?

ALITHEA: [*Aside*] I must not let 'em kill the gentleman neither, for his kindness to me: I am so far from hating him, that I wish my gallant had his person and understanding. Nay, if my honour—

SPARKISH: I'll be thy death.

ALITHEA: Hold, hold! Indeed, to tell the truth, the gentleman said after all, that what he spoke was but out of friendship to you.

SPARKISH: How! say, I am, I am a fool, that is, no wit, out of friendship to me?

ALITHEA: Yes, to try whether I was concerned enough for you; and made love to me only to be satisfied of my virtue, for your sake.

HARCOURT: Kind, however.   [*Aside*]

SPARKISH: Nay, if it were so, my dear rogue, I ask thee pardon; but why would not you tell me so, faith?

HARCOURT: Because I did not think on't, faith.

SPARKISH: Come, Horner does not come; Harcourt, let's be gone to the new play.—Come, madam.

ALITHEA: I will not go, if you intend to leave me alone in the box, and run into the pit, as you use to do.

SPARKISH: Pshaw! I'll leave Harcourt with you in the box to entertain you, and that's as good; if I sat in the box, I should be thought no judge but of trimmings.—Come away, Harcourt, lead her down.

     [*Exeunt* Sparkish, Harcourt, *and* Alithea]

PINCHWIFE: Well, go thy ways, for the flower of the true town fops, such as spend their estates before they come to 'em, and are cuckolds before they're married. But let me go look to my own freehold.— How!

Enter Lady Fidget, Mrs. Dainty Fidget, *and* Mrs. Squeamish.

LADY FIDGET: Your servant, sir: where is your lady? We are come to wait upon her to the new play.

PINCHWIFE: New play!

LADY FIDGET: And my husband will wait upon you presently.

PINCHWIFE: [*Aside*] Damn your civility.—[*Aloud*] Madam, by no means; I will not see Sir Jasper here, till I have waited upon him at home; nor shall my wife see you till she has waited upon your ladyship at your lodgings.

LADY FIDGET: Now we are here, sir?

PINCHWIFE: No, Madam.

MRS. DAINTY: Pray, let us see her.

MRS. SQUEAMISH: We will not stir till we see her.

PINCHWIFE: [*Aside*] A pox on you all!—[*Goes to the door, and returns*] She has locked the door, and is gone abroad.

LADY FIDGET: No, you have locked the door, and she's within.

MRS. DAINTY: They told us below she was here.

PINCHWIFE: [*Aside*] Will nothing do?—[*Aloud*] Well, it must out then. To tell you the truth, ladies, which I was afraid to let you know before, lest it might endanger your lives, my wife has just now the small-pox come out upon her; do not be frightened; but pray be gone, ladies; you shall not stay here in danger of your lives; pray get you gone, ladies.

LADY FIDGET: No, no, we have all had 'em.

MRS. SQUEAMISH: Alack, alack!

MRS. DAINTY: Come, come, we must see how it goes with her; I understand the disease.

LADY FIDGET: Come!

PINCHWIFE: [*Aside*] Well, there is no being too hard for women at their own weapon, lying, therefore I'll quit the field.   [*Exit*]

MRS. SQUEAMISH: Here's an example of jealousy!

LADY FIDGET: Indeed, as the world goes, I wonder there are no more jealous, since wives are so neglected.

MRS. DAINTY: Pshaw! as the world goes, to what end should they be jealous?

LADY FIDGET: Foh! 'tis a nasty world.

MRS. SQUEAMISH: That men of parts, great acquaintance, and quality, should take up with and spend themselves and fortunes in keeping little playhouse creatures, foh!

LADY FIDGET: Nay, that women of understanding, great acquaintance, and good quality, should fall a-keeping too of little creatures, foh!

MRS. SQUEAMISH: Why, 'tis the men of quality's fault; they never visit women of honour and reputation as they used to do; and have not so much as common civility for ladies of our rank, but use us with the same indifference and ill-breeding as if we were all married to 'em.

LADY FIDGET: She says true; 'tis an arrant shame women of quality should be so slighted; methinks birth—birth should go for something; I have known men admired, courted, and followed for their titles only.

MRS. SQUEAMISH: Ay, one would think men of honour should not love, no more than marry, out of their own rank.

MRS. DAINTY: Fy, fy, upon 'em! they are come to think cross breeding for themselves best, as well as for their dogs and horses.

LADY FIDGET: They are dogs and horses for't.

MRS. SQUEAMISH: One would think, if not for love, for vanity a little.

MRS. DAINTY: Nay, they do satisfy their vanity upon us sometimes; and are kind to us in their report, tell all the world they lie with us.

LADY FIDGET: Damned rascals, that we should be only wronged by 'em! To report a man has had a person, when he has not had a person, is the greatest wrong in the whole world that can be done to a person.

MRS. SQUEAMISH: Well, 'tis an arrant shame noble persons should be so wronged and neglected.

LADY FIDGET: But still 'tis an arranter shame for a noble person to neglect her own honour, and defame her own noble person with little inconsiderable fellows, foh!

MRS. DAINTY: I suppose the crime against our honour is the same with a man of quality as with another.

LADY FIDGET: How! no sure, the man of quality is likest one's husband, and therefore the fault should be the less.

MRS. DAINTY: But then the pleasure should be the less.

LADY FIDGET: Fy, fy, fy, for shame, sister! whither shall we ramble? Be continent in your discourse, or I shall hate you.

MRS. DAINTY: Besides, an intrigue is so much the more notorious for the man's quality.

MRS. SQUEAMISH: 'Tis true that nobody takes notice of a private man, and therefore with him 'tis more secret; and the crime's the less when 'tis not known.

LADY FIDGET: You say true; i'faith, I think you are in the right on't: 'tis not an injury to a husband, till it be an injury to our honours; so that a woman of honour loses no honour with a private person; and to say truth—

MRS. DAINTY: So, the little fellow is grown a private person—with her—   [Apart to Mrs. Squeamish]

LADY FIDGET: But still my dear, dear honour—

Enter Sir Jasper Fidget, Horner, and Dorilant.

SIR JASPER: Ay, my dear, dear of honour, thou hast still so much honour in thy mouth—

HORNER: That she has none elsewhere.   [Aside]

LADY FIDGET: Oh, what d'ye mean to bring in these upon us?

MRS. DAINTY: Foh! these are as bad as wits.

MRS. SQUEAMISH: Foh!

LADY FIDGET: Let us leave the room.

SIR JASPER: Stay, stay; faith, to tell you the naked truth—

LADY FIDGET: Fy, Sir Jasper! do not use that word naked.

SIR JASPER: Well, well, in short I have business at Whitehall, and cannot go to the play with you, therefore would have you go—

LADY FIDGET: With those two to a play?

SIR JASPER: No, not with t'other, but with Mr. Horner; there can be no more scandal to go with him than with Mr. Tattle, or Master Limberham.

LADY FIDGET: With that nasty fellow! no—no.

SIR JASPER: Nay, prithee, dear, hear me.
                        [Whispers to Lady Fidget]

HORNER: Ladies—
[Horner and Dorilant draw near Mrs. Squeamish and Mrs. Dainty Fidget]

MRS. DAINTY: Stand off.

MRS. SQUEAMISH: Do not approach us.

MRS. DAINTY: You herd with the wits, you are obscenity all over.

MRS. SQUEAMISH: And I would as soon look upon a picture of Adam and Eve, without fig-leaves, as any of you, if I could help it; therefore keep off, and do not make us sick.

DORILANT: What a devil are these?

HORNER: Why, these are pretenders to honour, as critics to wit, only by censuring others; and as every raw, peevish, out-of-humoured, affected, dull, tea-drinking, arithmetical fop, sets up for a wit by railing at men of sense, so these for honour, by railing at the court, and ladies of as great honour as quality.

SIR JASPER: Come, Mr. Horner, I must desire you to go with these ladies to the play, sir.

HORNER: I, sir?

SIR JASPER: Ay, ay, come, sir.

HORNER: I must beg your pardon, sir, and theirs; I will not be seen in women's company in public again for the world.

SIR JASPER: Ha, ha, strange aversion!

MRS. SQUEAMISH: No, he's for women's company in private.

SIR JASPER: He—poor man—he—ha! ha! ha!

MRS. DAINTY: 'Tis a greater shame amongst lewd fellows to be seen in virtuous women's company, than for the women to be seen with them.

HORNER: Indeed, madam, the time was I only hated virtuous women, but now I hate the other too! I beg your pardon, ladies.

LADY FIDGET: You are very obliging, sir, because we would not be troubled with you.

SIR JASPER: In sober sadness, he shall go.

DORILANT: Nay, if he wo' not, I am ready to wait upon the ladies, and I think I am the fitter man.

SIR JASPER: You sir! no, I thank you for that. Master Horner is a privileged man amongst the virtuous ladies, 'twill be a great while before you are so; he! he! he! he's my wife's gallant; he! he! he! No, pray withdraw, sir, for as I take it, the virtuous ladies have no business with you.

DORILANT: And I am sure he can have none with them. 'Tis strange a man can't come amongst virtuous women now, but upon the same terms as men are admitted into the Great Turk's seraglio. But heavens keep me from being an ombre player with 'em!—But where is Pinchwife?   [Exit]

SIR JASPER: Come, come, man; what, avoid the sweet society of womankind? that sweet, soft, gentle, tame, noble creature, woman, made for man's companion—

HORNER: So is that soft, gentle, tame, and more noble creature a spaniel, and has all their tricks; can fawn, lie down, suffer beating, and fawn the more; barks at your friends when they come to see you, makes your bed hard, gives you fleas, and the mange sometimes. And all the difference is, the spaniel's the more faithful animal, and fawns but upon one master.

SIR JASPER: He! he! he!

MRS. SQUEAMISH: O the rude beast!

MRS. DAINTY: Insolent brute!

LADY FIDGET: Brute! stinking, mortified, rotten French wether, to dare—

SIR JASPER: Hold, an't please your ladyship.—For shame, Master Horner! your mother was a woman—[Aside] Now shall I never reconcile 'em.—[Aside to Lady Fidget] Hark you, madam, take my advice in your anger. You know you often want one to make up your drolling pack of ombre players, and you may cheat him easily; for he's an ill gamester, and consequently loves play. Besides, you know you have but two old civil gentlemen (with stinking breaths too) to wait upon you abroad; take in the third into your service. The other are but crazy; and a lady should have a supernumerary gentleman-usher as a supernumerary coach-horse, lest sometimes you should be forced to stay at home.

LADY FIDGET: But are you sure he loves play, and has money?

SIR JASPER: He loves play as much as you, and has money as much as I.

LADY FIDGET: Then I am contented to make him pay for his scurrility. Money makes up in a measure all other wants in men.—Those whom we cannot make hold for gallants, we make fine.   [Aside]

SIR JASPER: [Aside] So, so; now to mollify, wheedle him.—[Aside to Horner] Master Horner, will you never keep civil company? methinks 'tis time now, since you are only fit for them. Come, come, man, you must e'en fall to visiting our wives, eating at our tables, drinking tea with our virtuous relations after dinner, dealing cards to 'em, reading plays and gazettes to 'em, picking fleas out of their smocks for 'em, collecting receipts, new songs, women, pages, and footmen for 'em.

HORNER: I hope they'll afford me better employment, sir.

SIR JASPER: He! he! he! 'tis fit you know your work before you come into your place. And since you are unprovided of a lady to flatter, and a good house to eat at, pray frequent mine, and call my wife mistress, and she shall call you gallant, according to the custom.

HORNER: Who, I?

SIR JASPER: Faith, thou sha't for my sake; come, for my sake only.

HORNER: For your sake—

SIR JASPER: Come, come, here's a gamester for you; let him be a little familiar sometimes; nay, what if a little rude? Gamesters may be rude with ladies, you know.

LADY FIDGET: Yes; losing gamesters have a privilege with women.

HORNER: I always thought the contrary, that the winning gamester had most privilege with women; for when you have lost your money to a man, you'll lose anything you have, all you have, they say, and he may use you as he pleases.

SIR JASPER: He! he! he! well, win or lose, you shall have your liberty with her.

LADY FIDGET: As he behaves himself; and for your sake I'll give him admittance and freedom.

HORNER: All sorts of freedom, madam?

SIR JASPER: Ay, ay, ay, all sorts of freedom thou canst take. And so go to her, begin thy new employment; wheedle her, jest with her, and be better acquainted one with another.

HORNER: [Aside] I think I know her already; therefore may venture with her my secret for hers.

[Horner and Lady Fidget whisper]

SIR JASPER: Sister cuz, I have provided an innocent playfellow for you there.

MRS. DAINTY: Who, he?

MRS. SQUEAMISH: There's a playfellow, indeed!

SIR JASPER: Yes sure.—What, he is good enough to play at cards, blindman's-buff, or the fool with, sometimes!

MRS. SQUEAMISH: Foh! we'll have no such playfellows.

MRS. DAINTY: No, sir; you shan't choose playfellows for us, we thank you.

SIR JASPER: Nay, pray hear me. [Whispering to them]

LADY FIDGET: But, poor gentleman, could you be so generous, so truly a man of honour, as for the sakes of us women of honour, to cause yourself to be reported no man? No man! and to suffer yourself the greatest shame that could fall upon a man, that none might fall upon us women by your conversation? but, indeed, sir, as perfectly, perfectly the same man as before your going into France, sir? as perfectly, perfectly, sir?

HORNER: As perfectly, perfectly, madam. Nay, I scorn you should take my word; I desire to be tried only, madam.

LADY FIDGET: Well, that's spoken again like a man of honour: all men of honour desire to come to the test. But, indeed, generally you men report such things of yourselves, one does not know how or whom to believe; and it is come to that pass, we dare not take your words no more than your tailor's, without some staid servant of yours be bound with you. But I have so strong a faith in your honour, dear, dear, noble sir, that I'd forfeit mine for yours, at any time, dear sir.

HORNER: No, madam, you should not need to forfeit it for me; I have given you security already to save you harmless, my late reputation being so well known in the world, madam.

LADY FIDGET: But if upon any future falling-out, or upon a suspicion of my taking the trust out of your hands, to employ some other, you yourself should betray your trust, dear sir? I mean, if you'll give me leave to speak obscenely, you might tell, dear sir.

HORNER: If I did, nobody would believe me. The reputation of impotency is as hardly recovered again in the world as that of cowardice, dear madam.

LADY FIDGET: Nay, then, as one may say, you may do your worst, dear, dear sir.

SIR JASPER: Come, is your ladyship reconciled to him yet? have you agreed on matters? for I must be gone to Whitehall.

LADY FIDGET: Why, indeed, Sir Jasper, Master Horner is a thousand, thousand times a better man than I thought him. Cousin Squeamish, sister Dainty, I can name him now. Truly, not long ago, you know, I thought his very name obscenity; and I would as soon have lain with him as have named him.

SIR JASPER: Very likely, poor madam.

MRS. DAINTY: I believe it.

MRS. SQUEAMISH: No doubt on't.

SIR JASPER: Well, well—that your ladyship is as virtuous as any she, I know, and him all the town knows—he! he! he! therefore now you like him, get you gone to your business together, go, go to your business, I say, pleasure, whilst I go to my pleasure, business.

LADY FIDGET: Come, then, dear gallant.

HORNER: Come away, my dearest mistress.

SIR JASPER: So, so; why, 'tis as I'd have it.   [*Exit*]

HORNER: And as I'd have it.

LADY FIDGET: Who for his business from his wife will run,

Takes the best care to have her business done.

[*Exeunt*]

Act III

SCENE 1:   *A Room in Pinchwife's House*

Enter Alithea *and* Mrs. Pinchwife.

ALITHEA: Sister, what ails you? you are grown melancholy.

MRS. PINCHWIFE: Would it not make any one melancholy to see you go every day fluttering about abroad, whilst I must stay at home like a poor lonely sullen bird in a cage?

ALITHEA: Ay, sister; but you came young, and just from the nest to your cage: so that I thought you liked it, and could be as cheerful in't as others that took their flight themselves early, and are hopping abroad in the open air.

MRS. PINCHWIFE: Nay, I confess I was quiet enough till my husband told me what pure lives the London ladies live abroad, with their dancing, meetings, and junketings, and dressed every day in their best gowns; and I warrant you, play at nine-pins every day of the week, so they do.

Enter Pinchwife.

PINCHWIFE: Come, what's here to do? you are putting the town-pleasures in her head, and setting her a-longing.

ALITHEA: Yes, after nine-pins. You suffer none to give her those longings you mean but yourself.

PINCHWIFE: I tell her of the vanities of the town like a confessor.

ALITHEA: A confessor! just such a confessor as he that, by forbidding a silly ostler to grease the horse's teeth, taught him to do't.

PINCHWIFE: Come, Mrs. Flippant, good precepts are lost when bad examples are still before us: the liberty you take abroad makes her hanker after it, and out of humour at home. Poor wretch! she desired not to come to London; I would bring her.

ALITHEA: Very well.

PINCHWIFE: She has been this week in town, and never desired till this afternoon to go abroad.

ALITHEA: Was she not at a play yesterday?

PINCHWIFE: Yes; but she ne'er asked me; I was myself the cause of her going.

ALITHEA: Then if you ask you again, you are the cause of her asking, and not my example.

PINCHWIFE: Well, to-morrow night I shall be rid of you; and the next day, before 'tis light, she and I'll be rid of the town, and my dreadful apprehensions.—Come, be not melancholy; for thou sha't go into the country after to-morrow, dearest.

ALITHEA: Great comfort!

MRS. PINCHWIFE: Pish! what d'ye tell me of the country for?

PINCHWIFE: How's this! what, pish at the country?

MRS. PINCHWIFE: Let me alone; I am not well.

PINCHWIFE: O, if that be all—what ails my dearest?

MRS. PINCHWIFE: Truly, I don't know: but I have not been well since you told me there was a gallant at the play in love with me.

PINCHWIFE: Ha!—

ALITHEA: That's by my example too!

PINCHWIFE: Nay, if you are not well, but are so concerned, because a lewd fellow chanced to lie, and say he liked you, you'll make me sick too.

MRS. PINCHWIFE: Of what sickness?

PINCH: O, of that which is worse than the plague, jealousy.

MRS. PINCHWIFE: Pish, you jeer! I'm sure there's no such disease in our receipt-book at home.

PINCHWIFE: No, thou never met'st with it, poor innocent.—Well, if thou cuckold me, 'twill be my own fault—for cuckolds and bastards are generally makers of their own fortune.   [*Aside*]

MRS. PINCHWIFE: Well, but pray, bud, let's go to a play to-night.

PINCHWIFE: 'Tis just done, she comes from it. But why are you so eager to see a play?

MRS. PINCHWIFE: Faith, dear, not that I care one pin for their talk there; but I like to look upon the player-men, and would see, if I could, the gallant you say loves me: that's all, dear bud.

PINCHWIFE: Is that all, dear bud?

ALITHEA: This proceeds from my example!

MRS. PINCHWIFE: But if the play be done, let's go abroad, however, dear bud.

PINCHWIFE: Come have a little patience and thou shalt go into the country on Friday.

MRS. PINCHWIFE: Therefore I would see first some sights to tell my neighbours of. Nay, I will go abroad, that's once.

ALITHEA: I'm the cause of this desire too!

PINCHWIFE: But now I think on't, who, who was the cause of Horner's coming to my lodgings to-day? That was you.

ALITHEA: No, you, because you would not let him see your handsome wife out of your lodging.

MRS. PINCHWIFE: Why, O Lord! did the gentleman come hither to see me indeed?

PINCHWIFE: No, no.—You are not the cause of that damned question too, Mistress Alithea?—[*Aside*] Well, she's in the right of it. He is in love with my wife—and comes after her—'tis so—but I'll nip his love in the bud; lest he should follow us into the country, and break his chariot-wheel near our house, on purpose for an excuse to come to't. But I think I know the town.

MRS. PINCHWIFE: Come, pray, bud, let's go abroad before 'tis late; for I will go, that's flat and plain.

PINCHWIFE: [Aside] So! the obstinacy already of the townwife; and I must, whilst she's here, humour her like one.—[Aloud] Sister, how shall we do, that she may not be seen, or known?

ALITHEA: Let her put on her mask.

PINCHWIFE: Pshaw! a mask makes people but the more inquisitive, and is as ridiculous a disguise as a stage-beard: her shape, stature, habit will be known. And if we should meet with Horner, he would be sure to take acquaintance with us, must wish her joy, kiss her, talk to her, leer upon her, and the devil and all. No, I'll not use her to a mask, 'tis dangerous; for masks have made more cuckolds than the best faces that ever were known.

ALITHEA: How will you do then?

MRS. PINCHWIFE: Nay, shall we go? The Exchange will be shut, and I have a mind to see that.

PINCHWIFE: So—I have it—I'll dress her up in the suit we are to carry down to her brother, little Sir James; nay, I understand the town-tricks. Come, let's go dress her. A mask! no—a woman masked, like a covered dish, gives a man curiosity and appetite; when, it may be, uncovered, 'twould turn his stomach: no, no.

ALITHEA: Indeed your comparison is something a greasy one: but I had a gentle gallant used to say, A beauty masked, like the sun in eclipse, gathers together more gazers than if it shined out. [Exeunt]

SCENE 2:   *The New Exchange*

Enter Horner, Harcourt, *and* Dorilant.

DORILANT: Engaged to women, and not sup with us!

HORNER: Ay, a pox on 'em all!

HARCOURT: You were much a more reasonable man in the morning, and had as noble resolutions against 'em, as a widower of a week's liberty.

DORILANT: Did I ever think to see you keep company with women in vain?

HORNER: In vain: no—'tis since I can't love 'em, to be revenged on 'em.

HARCOURT: Now your sting is gone, you looked in the box amongst all those women like a drone in the hive; all upon you, shoved and ill-used by 'em all, and thrust from one side to t'other.

DORILANT: Yet he must be buzzing amongst 'em still, like other beetle-headed liquorish drones. Avoid 'em, and hate 'em, as they hate you.

HORNER: Because I do hate 'em, and would hate 'em yet more, I'll frequent 'em. You may see by marriage, nothing makes a man hate a woman more than her constant conversation. In short, I converse with 'em, as you do with rich fools, to laugh at 'em and use 'em ill.

DORILANT: But I would no more sup with women, unless I could lie with 'em, than sup with a rich coxcomb, unless I could cheat him.

HORNER: Yes, I have known thee sup with a fool for his drinking; if he could set out your hand that way only, you were satisfied, and if he were a wine-swallowing mouth, 'twas enough.

HARCOURT: Yes, a man drinks often with a fool, as he tosses with a marker, only to keep his hand in use. But do the ladies drink?

HORNER: Yes, sir; and I shall have the pleasure at least of laying 'em flat with a bottle, and bring as much scandal that way upon 'em as formerly t'other.

HARCOURT: Perhaps you may prove as weak a brother among 'em that way as t'other.

DORILANT: Foh! drinking with women is as unnatural as scolding with 'em. But 'tis a pleasure of decayed fornicators, and the basest way of quenching love.

HARCOURT: Nay, 'tis drowning love, instead of quenching it. But leave us for civil women too!

DORILANT: Ay, when he can't be the better for 'em. We hardly pardon a man that leaves his friend for a wench, and that's a pretty lawful call.

HORNER: Faith, I would not leave you for 'em, if they would not drink.

DORILANT: Who would disappoint his company at Lewis's for a gossiping?

HARCOURT: Foh! Wine and women, good apart, together are as nauseous as sack and sugar. But hark you, sir, before you go, a little of your advice; an old maimed general, when unfit for action, is fittest for counsel. I have other designs upon women than eating and drinking with them; I am in love with Sparkish's mistress, whom he is to marry to-morrow: now how shall I get her?

Enter Sparkish, *looking about.*

HORNER: Why, here comes one will help you to her.

HARCOURT: He! he, I tell you, is my rival, and will hinder my love.

HORNER: No; a foolish rival and a jealous husband assist their rival's designs; for they are sure to make their women hate them, which is the first step to their love for another man.

HARCOURT: But I cannot come near his mistress but in his company.

HORNER: Still the better for you; for fools are most easily cheated when they themselves are accessaries: and he is to be bubbled of his mistress as of his money, the common mistress, by keeping him company.

SPARKISH: Who is that that is to be bubbled? Faith, let me snack; I han't met with a bubble since Christmas. 'Gad, I think bubbles are like their brother woodcocks, go out with the cold weather.

HARCOURT: A pox! he did not hear all, I hope.

[Apart to Horner]

SPARKISH: Come, you bubbling rogues you, where do we sup?—Oh, Harcourt, my mistress tells me you have been making fierce love to her all the play long: ha! ha!—But I—

HARCOURT: I make love to her!

SPARKISH: Nay, I forgive thee, for I think I know thee, and I know her; but I am sure I know myself.

HARCOURT: Did she tell you so? I see all women are like these of the Exchange; who, to enhance the prize of their commodities, report to their fond customers offers which were never made 'em.

HORNER: Ay, women are apt to tell before the intrigue, as men after it, and so show themselves the vainer sex. But hast thou a mistress, Sparkish? 'Tis as hard for me to believe it, as that thou ever hadst a bubble, as you bragged just now.

SPARKISH: O, your servant, sir: are you at your raillery, sir? But we are some of us beforehand with you to-day at the play. The wits were something bold with you, sir; did you not hear us laugh?

HORNER: Yes; but I thought you had gone to plays, to laugh at the poet's wit, not at your own.

SPARKISH: Your servant, sir: no, I thank you. 'Gad I go to a play as to a country treat; I carry my own wine to one, and my own wit to t'other, or else I'm sure I should not be merry at either. And the reason why we are so often louder than the players, is, because we think we speak more wit, and so become the poet's rivals in his audience: for to tell you the truth, we hate the silly rogues; nay, so much, that we find fault even with their bawdy upon the stage, whilst we talk nothing else in the pit as loud.

HORNER: But why shouldst thou hate the silly poets? Thou hast too much wit to be one; and they, like whores, are only hated by each other: and thou dost scorn writing, I'm sure.

SPARKISH: Yes; I'd have you to know I scorn writing: but women, women, that make men do all foolish things, make 'em write songs too. Everybody does it. 'Tis even as common with lovers, as playing with fans; and you can no more help rhyming to your Phillis, than drinking to your Phillis.

HARCOURT: Nay, poetry in love is no more to be avoided than jealousy.

DORILANT: But the poets damned your songs, did they?

SPARKISH: Damn the poets! they have turned 'em into burlesque, as they call it. That burlesque is a hocus-pocus trick they have got, which, by the virtue of *Hictius doctius topsy turvy*, they make a wise and witty man in the world, a fool upon the stage you know not how: and 'tis therefore I hate 'em too, for I know not but it may be my own case; for they'll put a man into a play for looking asquint. Their predecessors were contented to make serving-men only their stage-fools: but these rogues must have gentlemen, with a pox to 'em, nay, knights; and, indeed, you shall hardly see a fool upon the stage but he's a knight. And to tell you the truth, they have kept me these six years from

being a knight in earnest, for fear of being knighted in a play, and dubbed a fool.

DORILANT: Blame 'em not, they must follow their copy, the age.

HARCOURT: But why shouldst thou be afraid of being in a play, who expose yourself every day in the playhouses, and at public places?

HORNER: 'Tis but being on the stage, instead of standing on a bench in the pit.

DORILANT: Don't you give money to painters to draw you like? and are you afraid of your pictures at length in a playhouse, where all your mistresses may see you?

SPARKISH: A pox! painters don't draw the small-pox or pimples in one's face. Come, damn all your silly authors whatever, all books and booksellers, by the world; and all readers, courteous or uncourteous!

HARCOURT: But who comes here, Sparkish?

Enter Pinchwife *and* Mrs. Pinchwife *in man's clothes,* Alithea *and* Lucy.

SPARKISH: Oh, hide me! There's my mistress too.

[Sparkish *hides himself behind* Harcourt]

HARCOURT: She sees you.

SPARKISH: But I will not see her. 'Tis time to go to Whitehall, and I must not fail the drawing-room.

HARCOURT: Pray, first carry me, and reconcile me to her.

SPARKISH: Another time. Faith, the king will have supped.

HARCOURT: Not with the worse stomach for thy absence. Thou art one of those fools that think their attendance at the king's meals as necessary as his physicians, when you are more troublesome to him than his doctors or his dogs.

SPARKISH: Pshaw! I know my interest, sir. Prithee hide me.

HORNER: Your servant, Pinchwife.—What, he knows us not!

PINCHWIFE: Come along.   [*To his* Wife *aside*]

MRS. PINCHWIFE: Pray, have you any ballads? give me six-penny worth.

BOOKSELLER: We have no ballads.

MRS. PINCHWIFE: Then give me "Covent Garden Drollery," and a play or two—Oh, here's "Tarugo's Wiles," and "The Slighted Maiden"; I'll have them.

PINCHWIFE: No; plays are not for your reading. Come along; will you discover yourself?   [*Apart to her*]

HORNER: Who is that pretty youth with him, Sparkish?

SPARKISH: I believe his wife's brother, because he's something like her: but I never saw her but once.

HORNER: Extremely handsome; I have seen a face like it too. Let us follow 'em.

[*Exeunt* Pinchwife, Mrs. Pinchwife, Alithea, *and* Lucy; Horner *and* Dorilant *following them*]

HARCOURT: Come, Sparkish, your mistress saw you,

and will be angry you go not to her. Besides, I would fain be reconciled to her, which none but you can do, dear friend.

SPARKISH: Well, that's a better reason, dear friend. I would not go near her now for hers or my own sake; but I can deny you nothing: for though I have known thee a great while, never go, if I do not love thee as well as a new acquaintance.

HARCOURT: I am obliged to you indeed, dear friend. I would be well with her, only to be well with thee still; for these ties to wives usually dissolve all ties to friends. I would be contented she should enjoy you a-nights, but I would have you to myself a-days as I have had, dear friend.

SPARKISH: And thou shalt enjoy me a-days, dear, dear friend, never stir: and I'll be divorced from her, sooner than from thee. Come along.

HARCOURT: [Aside] So, we are hard put to't, when we make our rival our procurer; but neither she nor her brother would let me come near her now. When all's done, a rival is the best cloak to steal to a mistress under, without suspicion; and when we have once got to her as we desire, we throw him off like other cloaks.

[Exit Sparkish, Harcourt following him]

Re-enter Pinchwife and Mrs. Pinchwife.

PINCHWIFE: [To Alithea] Sister, if you will not go, we must leave you.—[Aside] The fool her gallant and she will muster up all the young saunterers of this place, and they will leave their dear sempstresses to follow us. What a swarm of cuckolds and cuckold-makers are here!—Come, let's be gone, Mistress Margery.

MRS. PINCHWIFE: Don't you believe that; I han't half my bellyfull of sights yet.

PINCHWIFE: Then walk this way.

MRS. PINCHWIFE: Lord, what a power of brave signs are here! stay—the Bull's-Head, the Ram's-Head, and the Stag's-Head, dear—

PINCHWIFE: Nay, if every husband's proper sign here were visible, they would be all alike.

MRS. PINCHWIFE: What d'ye mean by that, bud?

PINCHWIFE: 'Tis no matter—no matter, bud.

MRS. PINCHWIFE: Pray tell me: nay, I will know.

PINCHWIFE: They would be all Bulls, Stags, and Rams-heads.

[Exeunt Pinchwife and Mrs. Pinchwife]

Re-enter Sparkish, Harcourt, Alithea, and Lucy, at the other side.

SPARKISH: Come, dear madam, for my sake you shall be reconciled to him.

ALITHEA: For your sake I hate him.

HARCOURT: That's something too cruel, madam, to hate me for his sake.

SPARKISH: Ay indeed, madam, too, too cruel to me, to hate my friend for my sake.

ALITHEA: I hate him because he is your enemy; and you ought to hate him too, for making love to me, if you love me.

SPARKISH: That's a good one! I hate a man for loving you! If he did love you, 'tis but what he can't help; and 'tis your fault, not his, if he admires you. I hate a man for being of my opinion! I'll n'er do't, by the world.

ALITHEA: Is it for your honour, or mine, to suffer a man to make love to me, who am to marry you to-morrow?

SPARKISH: Is it for your honour, or mine, to have me jealous? That he makes love to you, is a sign you are handsome; and that I am not jealous, is a sign you are virtuous. That I think is for your honour.

ALITHEA: But 'tis your honour too I am concerned for.

HARCOURT: But why, dearest madam, will you be more concerned for his honour than he is himself? Let his honour alone, for my sake and his. He! he has no honour—

SPARKISH: How's that?

HARCOURT: But what my dear friend can guard himself.

SPARKISH: O ho—that's right again.

HARCOURT: Your care of his honour argues his neglect of it, which is no honour to my dear friend here. Therefore once more, let his honour go which way it will, dear madam.

SPARKISH: Ay, ay; were it for my honour to marry a woman whose virtue I suspected, and could not trust her in a friend's hands?

ALITHEA: Are you not afraid to lose me?

HARCOURT: He afraid to lose you, madam! No, no— you may see how the most estimable and most glorious creature in the world is valued by him. Will you not see it?

SPARKISH: Right, honest Frank, I have that noble value for her that I cannot be jealous of her.

ALITHEA: You mistake him. He means, you care not for me, nor who has me.

SPARKISH: Lord, madam, I see you are jealous! Will you wrest a poor man's meaning from his words?

ALITHEA: You astonish me, sir, with your want of jealousy.

SPARKISH: And you make me giddy, madam, with your jealousy and fears, and virtue and honour. 'Gad, I see virtue makes a woman as troublesome as a little reading or learning.

ALITHEA: Monstrous!

LUCY: Well, to see what easy husbands these women of quality can meet with! a poor chambermaid can never have such ladylike luck. Besides, he's thrown away upon her. She'll make no use of her fortune, her blessing, none to a gentleman, for a pure cuckold; for it requires good breeding to be a cuckold.   [Aside]

ALITHEA: I tell you then plainly, he pursues me to marry me.

SPARKISH: Pshaw!

HARCOURT: Come, madam, you see you strive in vain to make him jealous of me. My dear friend is the kindest creature in the world to me.

SPARKISH: Poor fellow!

HARCOURT: But his kindness only is not enough for me, without your favour, your good opinion, dear madam: 'tis that must perfect my happiness. Good gentleman, he believes all I say: would you would do so! Jealous of me! I would not wrong him nor you for the world.

SPARKISH: Look you there. Hear him, hear him, and do not walk away so.

              [Alithea *walks carelessly to and fro*]

HARCOURT: I love you, madam, so—

SPARKISH: How's that? Nay, now you begin to go too far indeed.

HARCOURT: So much, I confess, I say, I love you, that I would not have you miserable, and cast yourself away upon so unworthy and inconsiderable a thing as what you see here.

[*Clapping his hand on his breast, points at* Sparkish]

SPARKISH: No, faith, I believe thou wouldst not: now his meaning is plain; but I knew before thou wouldst not wrong me, nor her.

HARCOURT: No, no, Heavens forbid the glory of her sex should fall so low, as into the embraces of such a contemptible wretch, the least of mankind—my friend here—I injure him!   [*Embracing* Sparkish]

ALITHEA: Very well.

SPARKISH: No, no, dear friend, I knew it.—Madam, you see he will rather wrong himself than me, in giving himself such names.

ALITHEA: Do not you understand him yet?

SPARKISH: Yes: how modestly he speaks of himself, poor fellow!

ALITHEA: Methinks he speaks impudently of yourself, since—before yourself too; insomuch that I can no longer suffer his scurrilous abusiveness to you, no more than his love to me.   [*Offers to go*]

SPARKISH: Nay, nay, madam, pray stay—his love to you! Lord, madam, has he not spoke yet plain enough?

ALITHEA: Yes, indeed, I should think so.

SPARKISH: Well then, by the world, a man can't speak civilly to a woman now, but presently she says, he makes love to her. Nay, madam, you shall stay, with your pardon, since you have not yet understood him, till he has made an eclaircissement of his love to you, that is, what kind of love it is. Answer to thy catechism, friend; do you love my mistress here?

HARCOURT: Yes, I wish she would not doubt it.

SPARKISH: But how do you love her?

HARCOURT: With all my soul.

ALITHEA: I thank him, methinks he speaks plain enough now.

SPARKISH: [*To Alithea*] You are out still.—But with what kind of love, Harcourt?

HARCOURT: With the best and the truest love in the world.

SPARKISH: Look you there then, that is with no matrimonial love, I'm sure.

ALITHEA: How's that? do you say matrimonial love is not best?

SPARKISH: 'Gad, I went too far ere I was aware. But speak for thyself, Harcourt, you said you would not wrong me nor her.

HARCOURT: No, no, madam, e'en take him for Heaven's sake.

SPARKISH: Look you there, madam.

HARCOURT: Who should in all justice be yours, he that loves you most. [*Claps his hand on his breast*]

ALITHEA: Look you there, Mr. Sparkish, who's that?

SPARKISH: Who should it be?—Go on, Harcourt.

HARCOURT: Who loves you more than women titles, or fortune fools.   [*Points at* Sparkish]

SPARKISH: Look you there, he means me still, for he points at me.

ALITHEA: Ridiculous!

HARCOURT: Who can only match your faith and constancy in love.

SPARKISH: Ay.

HARCOURT: Who knows, if it be possible, how to value so much beauty and virtue.

SPARKISH: Ay.

HARCOURT: Whose love can no more be equalled in the world, than that heavenly form of yours.

SPARKISH: No.

HARCOURT: Who could no more suffer a rival, than your absence, and yet could no more suspect your virtue, than his own constancy in his love to you.

SPARKISH: No.

HARCOURT: Who, in fine, loves you better than his eyes, that first made him love you.

SPARKISH: Ay—Nay, madam, faith, you shan't go till—

ALITHEA: Have a care, lest you make me stay too long.

SPARKISH: But till he has saluted you; that I may be assured you are friends, after his honest advice and declaration. Come, pray, madam, be friends with him.

Re-enter Pinchwife *and* Mrs. Pinchwife.

ALITHEA: You must pardon me, sir, that I am not yet so obedient to you.

PINCHWIFE: What, invite your wife to kiss men? Monstrous! are you not ashamed? I will never forgive you.

SPARKISH: Are you not ashamed, that I should have more confidence in the chastity of your family than you have? You must not teach me, I am a man of honour, sir, though I am frank and free; I am frank, sir—

PINCHWIFE: Very frank, sir, to share your wife with your friends.

SPARKISH: He is an humble, menial friend, such as reconciles the differences of the marriage bed; you know man and wife do not always agree; I design him for that use, therefore would have him well with my wife.

PINCHWIFE: A menial friend!—you will get a great many menial friends, by showing your wife as you do.

SPARKISH: What then? It may be I have a pleasure in't, as I have to show fine cloths at a playhouse, the first day, and count money before poor rogues.

PINCHWIFE: He that shows his wife or money, will be in danger of having them borrowed sometimes.

SPARKISH: I love to be envied, and would not marry a wife that I alone could love; loving alone is as dull as eating alone. Is it not a frank age? and I am a frank person; and to tell you the truth, it may be, I love to have rivals in a wife, they make her seem to a man still but as a kept mistress; and so good night, for I must to Whitehall.—Madam, I hope you are now reconciled to my friend; and so I wish you a good night, madam, and sleep if you can: for to-morrow you know I must visit you early with a canonical gentleman. Good night, dear Harcourt.

[Exit]

HARCOURT: Madam, I hope you will not refuse my visit to-morrow, if it should be earlier with a canonical gentleman than Mr. Sparkish's.

PINCHWIFE: This gentlewoman is yet under my care, therefore you must yet forbear your freedom with her, sir.   [Coming between Alithea and Harcourt]

HARCOURT: Must, sir?

PINCHWIFE: Yes, sir, she is my sister.

HARCOURT: 'Tis well she is, sir—for I must be her servant, sir.—Madam—

PINCHWIFE: Come away, sister, we had been gone, if it had not been for you, and so avoided these lewd rake-hells, who seem to haunt us.

Re-enter Horner *and* Dorilant.

HORNER: How now, Pinchwife!

PINCHWIFE: Your servant.

HORNER: What! I see a little time in the country makes a man turn wild and unsociable, and only fit to converse with his horses, dogs, and his herds.

PINCHWIFE: I have business, sir, and must mind it; your business is pleasure, therefore you and I must go different ways.

HORNER: Well, you may go on, but this pretty young gentleman—   [Takes hold of Mrs. Pinchwife]

HARCOURT: The lady—

DORILANT: And the maid—

HORNER: Shall stay with us; for I suppose their business is the same with ours, pleasure.

PINCHWIFE: 'Sdeath, he knows her, she carries it so sillily! yet if he does not, I should be more silly to discover it first.   [Aside]

ALITHEA: Pray, let us go, sir.

PINCHWIFE: Come, come—

HORNER: [To Mrs. Pinchwife] Had you not rather stay with us?—Prithee, Pinchwife, who is this pretty young gentleman?

PINCHWIFE: One to whom I'm a guardian.—[Aside] I wish I could keep her out of your hands.

HORNER: Who is he? I never saw anything so pretty in all my life.

PINCHWIFE: Pshaw! do not look upon him so much, he's a poor bashful youth, you'll put him out of countenance.—Come away, brother.

[Offers to take her away]

HORNER: O, your brother!

PINCHWIFE: Yes, my wife's brother.—Come, come, she'll stay supper for us.

HORNER: I thought so, for he is very like her I saw you at the play with, whom I told you I was in love with.

MRS. PINCHWIFE: [Aside] O jeminy! is that he that was in love with me? I am glad on't, I vow, for he's a curious fine gentleman, and I love him already, too.—[To Pinchwife] Is this he, bud?

PINCHWIFE: Come away, come away.   [To his Wife]

HORNER: Why, what haste are you in? why won't you let me talk with him?

PINCHWIFE: Because you'll debauch him; he's yet young and innocent, and I would not have him debauched for anything in the world.—[Aside] How she gazes on him! the devil!

HORNER: Harcourt, Dorilant, look you here, this is the likeness of that dowdy he told us of, his wife; did you ever see a lovelier creature? The rogue has reason to be jealous of his wife, since she is like him, for she would make all that see her in love with her.

HARCOURT: And, as I remember now, she is as like him here as can be.

DORILANT: She is indeed very pretty, if she be like him.

HORNER: Very pretty? a very pretty commendation!—she is a glorious creature, beautiful beyond all things I ever beheld.

PINCHWIFE: So, so.

HARCOURT: More beautiful than a poet's first mistress of imagination.

HORNER: Or another man's last mistress of flesh and blood.

MRS. PINCHWIFE: Nay, now you jeer, sir; pray don't jeer me.

PINCHWIFE: Come, come.—[Aside] By Heavens, she'll discover herself!

HORNER: I speak of your sister, sir.

PINCHWIFE: Ay, but saying she was handsome, if like him, made him blush.—[Aside] I am upon a rack!

HORNER: Methinks he is so handsome he should not be a man.

PINCHWIFE: [Aside] O, there 'tis out! he has discovered her! I am not able to suffer any longer.—[To his Wife] Come, come away, I say.

HORNER: Nay, by your leave, sir, he shall not go yet.—

[*Aside to them*] Harcourt, Dorilant, let us torment this jealous rogue a little.

HARCOURT, DORILANT: How?

HORNER: I'll show you.

PINCHWIFE: Come, pray let him go, I cannot stay fooling any longer; I tell you his sister stays supper for us.

HORNER: Does she? Come then, we'll all go to sup with he and thee.

PINCHWIFE: No, now I think on't, having stayed so long for us, I warrant she's gone to bed.—[*Aside*] I wish she and I were well out of their hands.—[*To his* Wife] Come, I must rise early to-morrow, come.

HORNER: Well then, if she be gone to bed, I wish her and you a good night. But pray, young gentleman, present my humble service to her.

MRS. PINCHWIFE: Thank you heartily, sir.

PINCHWIFE: [*Aside*] 'Sdeath, she will discover herself yet in spite of me.—[*Aloud*] He is something more civil to you, for your kindness to his sister, than I am, it seems.

HORNER: Tell her, dear sweet little gentleman, for all your brother there, that you have revived the love I had for her at first sight in the playhouse.

MRS. PINCHWIFE: But did you love her indeed, and indeed?

PINCHWIFE: [*Aside*] So, so.—[*Aloud*] Away, I say.

HORNER: Nay, stay.—Yes, indeed, and indeed, pray do you tell her so, and give her this kiss from me.
[*Kisses her*]

PINCHWIFE: [*Aside*] O Heavens! what do I suffer? Now 'tis too plain he knows her, and yet—

HORNER: And this, and this—   [*Kisses her again*]

MRS. PINCHWIFE: What do you kiss me for? I am no woman.

PINCHWIFE: [*Aside*] So, there, 'tis out.—[*Aloud*] Come, I cannot, nor will stay any longer.

HORNER: Nay, they shall send your lady a kiss too. Here, Harcourt, Dorilant, will you not?
[*They kiss her*]

PINCHWIFE: [*Aside*] How! do I suffer this? Was I not accusing another just now for this rascally patience, in permitting his wife to be kissed before his face? Ten thousand ulcers gnaw away their lips.— [*Aloud*] Come, come.

HORNER: Good night, dear little gentleman; madam, good night; farewell, Pinchwife.—[*Apart to* Harcourt *and* Dorilant.] Did not I tell you I would raise his jealous gall?
[*Exeunt* Horner, Harcourt *and* Dorilant]

PINCHWIFE: So, they are gone at last; stay, let me see first if the coach be at this door.   [*Exit*]

Re-enter Horner, Harcourt, *and* Dorilant.

HORNER: What, not gone yet? Will you be sure to do as I desired you, sweet sir?

MRS. PINCHWIFE: Sweet sir, but what will you give me then?

HORNER: Anything. Come away into the next walk.
[*Exit, haling away* Mrs. Pinchwife]

ALITHEA: Hold! hold! what d'ye do?

LUCY: Stay, stay, hold—

HARCOURT: Hold, madam, hold, let him present him —he'll come presently; nay, I will never let you go till you answer my question.

LUCY: For God's sake, sir, I must follow 'em.
[Alithea *and* Lucy, *struggling with* Harcourt *and* Dorilant]

DORILANT: No, I have something to present you with too, you shan't follow them.

Re-enter Pinchwife.

PINCHWIFE: Where?—how—what's become of?— gone!—whither?

LUCY: He's only gone with the gentleman, who will give him something, an't please your worship.

PINCHWIFE: Something!—give him something, with a pox!—where are they?

ALITHEA: In the next walk only, brother.

PINCHWIFE: Only, only! where, where?
[*Exit and returns presently, then goes out again*]

HARCOURT: What's the matter with him? why so much concerned? But, dearest madam—

ALITHEA: Pray let me go, sir; I have said and suffered enough already.

HARCOURT: Then you will not look upon, nor pity, my sufferings?

ALITHEA: To look upon 'em, when I cannot help 'em, were cruelty, not pity; therefore, I will never see you more.

HARCOURT: Let me then, madam, have my privilege of a banished lover, complaining or railing, and giving you but a farewell reason why, if you cannot condescend to marry me, you should not take that wretch, my rival.

ALITHEA: He only, not you, since my honour is engaged so far to him, can give me a reason why I should not marry him; but if he be true, and what I think him to be, I must be so to him. Your servant, sir.

HARCOURT: Have women only constancy when 'tis a vice, and are, like Fortune, only true to fools?

DORILANT: Thou sha't not stir, thou robust creature; you see I can deal with you, therefore you should stay the rather, and be kind.
[*To* Lucy, *who struggles to get from him*]

Re-enter Pinchwife.

PINCHWIFE: Gone, gone, not to be found! quite gone! ten thousand plagues go with 'em! Which way went they?

ALITHEA: But into t'other walk, brother.

LUCY: Their business will be done presently sure, an't please your worship; it can't be long in doing, I'm sure on't.

ALITHEA: Are they not there?

PINCHWIFE: No, you know where they are, you infamous wretch, eternal shame of your family, which you do not dishonour enough yourself you think, but you must help her to do it too, thou legion of bawds!

ALITHEA: Good brother—

PINCHWIFE: Damned, damned sister!

ALITHEA: Look you here, she's coming.

Re-enter Mrs. Pinchwife *running, with her hat full of oranges and dried fruit under her arm,* Horner *following.*

MRS. PINCHWIFE: O dear bud, look you here what I have got, see!

PINCHWIFE: And what I have got here too, which you can't see.　　　　　　[*Aside, rubbing his forehead*]

MRS. PINCHWIFE: The fine gentleman has given me better things yet.

PINCHWIFE: Has he so?—[*Aside*] Out of breath and coloured!—I must hold yet.

HORNER: I have only given your little brother an orange, sir.

PINCHWIFE: [*To* Horner] Thank you, sir.—[*Aside*] You have only squeezed my orange, I suppose, and given it me again; yet I must have a city patience. —[*To his* Wife] Come, come away.

MRS. PINCHWIFE: Stay, till I have put up my fine things, bud.

Enter Sir Jasper Fidget.

SIR JASPER: O, Master Horner, come, come, the ladies stay for you; your mistress, my wife, wonders you make not more haste to her.

HORNER: I have stayed this half hour for you here, and 'tis your fault I am not now with your wife.

SIR JASPER: But, pray, don't let her know so much; the truth on't is, I was advancing a certain project to his majesty about—I'll tell you.

HORNER: No, let's go, and hear it at your house. Good night, sweet little gentleman; one kiss more, you'll remember me now, I hope.　　　　　　[*Kisses her*]

DORILANT: What, Sir Jasper, will you separate friends? He promised to sup with us, and if you take him to your house, you'll be in danger of our company too.

SIR JASPER: Alas! gentlemen, my house is not fit for you; there are none but civil women there, which are not for your turn. He, you know, can bear with the society of civil women now, ha! ha! ha! besides, he's one of my family—he's—he! he! he!

DORILANT: What is he?

SIR JASPER: Faith, my eunuch, since you'll have it; he! he! he!　　[*Exeunt* Sir Jasper Fidget *and* Horner]

DORILANT: I rather wish thou wert his or my cuckold. Harcourt, what a good cuckold is lost there for want of a man to make him one? Thee and I cannot have Horner's privilege, who can make use of it.

HARCOURT: Ay, to poor Horner 'tis like coming to an estate at threescore, when a man can't be the better for't.

PINCHWIFE: Come.

MRS. PINCHWIFE: Presently, bud.

DORILANT: Come, let us go too.—[*To* Alithea] Madam, your servant.—[*To* Lucy] Good night, strapper.

HARCOURT: Madam, though you will not let me have a good day or night, I wish you one; but dare not name the other half of my wish.

ALITHEA: Good night, sir, for ever.

MRS. PINCHWIFE: I don't know where to put this here, dear bud, you shall eat it; nay, you shall have part of the fine gentleman's good things, or treat, as you call it, when we come home.

PINCHWIFE: Indeed, I deserve it, since I furnished the best part of it.　　　　[*Strikes away the orange*]
　The gallant treats presents, and gives the ball;
　But 'tis the absent cuckold pays for all.　[*Exeunt*]

Act IV

SCENE 1:　*Pinchwife's House in the morning*

Enter Alithea *dressed in new clothes, and* Lucy.

LUCY: Well—madam, now have I dressed you, and set you out with so many ornaments, and spent upon you ounces of essence and pulvillio;[1] and all this for no other purpose but as people adorn and perfume a corpse for a stinking second-hand grave: such, or as bad, I think Master Sparkish's bed.

ALITHEA: Hold your peace.

LUCY: Nay, madam, I will ask you the reason why you would banish poor Master Harcourt for ever from your sight; how could you be so hard-hearted?

ALITHEA: 'Twas because I was not hard-hearted.

LUCY: No, no; 'twas stark love and kindness, I warrant.

ALITHEA: It was so; I would see him no more because I love him.

LUCY: Hey day, a very pretty reason!

ALITHEA: You do not understand me.

LUCY: I wish you may yourself.

ALITHEA: I was engaged to marry, you see, another man, whom my justice will not suffer me to deceive or injure.

LUCY: Can there be a greater cheat or wrong done to a man than to give him your person without your heart? I should make a conscience of it.

ALITHEA: I'll retrieve it for him after I am married a while.

LUCY: The woman that marries to love better, will be as much mistaken as the wencher that marries to live better. No, madam, marrying to increase love is like gaming to become rich; alas! you only lose what little stock you had before.

ALITHEA: I find by your rhetoric you have been bribed to betray me.

[1] *A sweet-scented powder.*

LUCY: Only by his merit, that has bribed your heart, you see, against your word and rigid honour. But what a devil is this honour! 'tis sure a disease in the head, like the megrim or falling-sickness, that always hurries people away to do themselves mischief. Men lose their lives by it; women, what's dearer to 'em, their love, the life of life.

ALITHEA: Come, pray talk you no more of honour, nor Master Harcourt; I wish the other would come to secure my fidelity to him and his right in me.

LUCY: You will marry him then?

ALITHEA: Certainly, I have given him already my word, and will my hand too, to make it good, when he comes.

LUCY: Well, I wish I may never stick pin more, if he be not an arrant natural, to t'other fine gentleman.

ALITHEA: I own he wants the wit of Harcourt, which I will dispense withal for another want he has, which is want of jealousy, which men of wit seldom want.

LUCY: Lord, madam, what should you do with a fool to your husband? You intend to be honest, don't you? then that husbandly virtue, credulity, is thrown away upon you.

ALITHEA: He only that could suspect my virtue should have cause to do it; 'tis Sparkish's confidence in my truth that obliges me to be so faithful to him.

LUCY: You are not sure his opinion may last.

ALITHEA: I am satisfied, 'tis impossible for him to be jealous after the proofs I have had of him. Jealousy in a husband—Heaven defend me from it! it begets a thousand plagues to a poor woman, the loss of her honour, her quiet, and her—

LUCY: And her pleasure.

ALITHEA: What d'ye mean, impertinent?

LUCY: Liberty is a great pleasure, madam.

ALITHEA: I say, loss of her honour, her quiet, nay, her life sometimes; and what's as bad almost, the loss of this town; that is, she is sent into the country, which is the last ill-usage of a husband to a wife, I think.

LUCY: [Aside] O, does the wind lie there?—[Aloud] Then of necessity, madam, you think a man must carry his wife into the country, if he be wise. The country is as terrible, I find, to our young English ladies, as a monastery to those abroad; and on my virginity, I think they would rather marry a London jailer, than a high sheriff of a county, since neither can stir from his employment. Formerly women of wit married fools for a great estate, a fine seat, or the like; but now 'tis for a pretty seat only in Lincoln's-Inn-Fields, St. James's-Fields, or the Pall-Mall.

Enter Sparkish, *and* Harcourt, *dressed like a* Parson.

SPARKISH: Madam, your humble servant, a happy day to you, and to us all.

HARCOURT: Amen.

ALITHEA: Who have we here?

SPARKISH: My chaplain, faith—O madam, poor Harcourt remembers his humble service to you; and, in obedience to your last commands, refrains coming into your sight.

ALITHEA: Is not that he?

SPARKISH: No, fy, no; but to show that he ne'er intended to hinder our match, has sent his brother here to join our hands. When I get me a wife, I must get her a chaplain, according to the custom; that is his brother, and my chaplain.

ALITHEA: His brother!

LUCY: And your chaplain, to preach in your pulpit then——   [Aside]

ALITHEA: His brother!

SPARKISH: Nay, I knew you would not believe it.—I told you, sir, she would take you for your brother Frank.

ALITHEA: Believe it!

LUCY: His brother! ha! ha! he! he has a trick left still, it seems.   [Aside]

SPARKISH: Come, my dearest, pray let us go to church before the canonical hour is past.

ALITHEA: For shame, you are abused still.

SPARKISH: By the world, 'tis strange now you are so incredulous.

ALITHEA: 'Tis strange you are so credulous.

SPARKISH: Dearest of my life, hear me. I tell you this is Ned Harcourt of Cambridge, by the world; you see he has a sneaking college look. 'Tis true he's something like his brother Frank; and they differ from each other no more than in their age, for they were twins.

LUCY: Ha! ha! ha!

ALITHEA: Your servant, sir; I cannot be so deceived, though you are. But come, let's hear, how do you know what you affirm so confidently?

SPARKISH: Why, I'll tell you all. Frank Harcourt coming to me this morning to wish me joy, and present his service to you, I asked him if he could help me to a parson. Whereupon he told me, he had a brother in town who was in orders; and he went straight away, and sent him, you see there, to me.

ALITHEA: Yes, Frank goes and puts on a black coat, then tells you he is Ned; that's all you have for't.

SPARKISH: Pshaw! pshaw! I tell you, by the same token, the midwife put her garter about Frank's neck, to know 'em asunder, they were so like.

ALITHEA: Frank tells you this too?

SPARKISH: Ay, and Ned there too: nay, they are both in a story.

ALITHEA: So, so; very foolish.

SPARKISH: Lord, if you won't believe one, you had best try him by your chambermaid there; for chambermaids must needs know chaplains from other men, they are so used to 'em.

LUCY: Let's see: nay, I'll be sworn he has the canonical smirk, and the filthy clammy palm of a chaplain.

ALITHEA: Well, most reverend doctor, pray let us make an end of this fooling.

HARCOURT: With all my soul, divine heavenly creature, when you please.

ALITHEA: He speaks like a chaplain indeed.

SPARKISH: Why, was there not soul, divine, heavenly, in what he said?

ALITHEA: Once more, most impertinent black coat, cease your persecution, and let us have a conclusion of this ridiculous love.

HARCOURT: I had forgot, I must suit my style to my coat, or I wear it in vain.   [Aside]

ALITHEA: I have no more patience left; let us make once an end of this troublesome love, I say.

HARCOURT: So be it, seraphic lady, when your honour shall think it meet and convenient so to do.

SPARKISH: 'Gad I'm sure none but a chaplain could speak so, I think.

ALITHEA: Let me tell you, sir, this dull trick will not serve your turn; though you delay our marriage, you shall not hinder it.

HARCOURT: Far be it from me, munificent patroness, to delay your marriage; I desire nothing more than to marry you presently, which I might do, if you yourself would; for my noble, good-natured, and thrice generous patron here would not hinder it.

SPARKISH: No, poor man, not I, faith.

HARCOURT: And now, madam, let me tell you plainly nobody else shall marry you; by Heavens! I'll die first, for I'm sure I should die after it.

LUCY: How his love has made him forget his function, as I have seen it in real parsons!

ALITHEA: That was spoken like a chaplain too? now you understand him, I hope.

SPARKISH: Poor man, he takes it heinously to be refused; I can't blame him, 'tis putting an indignity upon him, not to be suffered; but you'll pardon me, madam, it shan't be; he shall marry us; come away, pray madam.

LUCY: Ha! ha! he! more ado! 'tis late.

ALITHEA: Invincible stupidity! I tell you, he would marry me as your rival, not as your chaplain.

SPARKISH: Come, come, madam.   [Pulling her away]

LUCY: I pray, madam, do not refuse this reverend divine the honour and satisfaction of marrying you; for I dare say, he has set his heart upon't, good doctor.

ALITHEA: What can you hope or design by this?

HARCOURT: I could answer her, a reprieve for a day only, often revokes a hasty doom. At worst, if she will not take mercy on me, and let me marry her, I have at least the lover's second pleasure, hindering my rival's enjoyment, though but for a time.   [Aside]

SPARKISH: Come, madam, 'tis e'en twelve o'clock, and my mother charged me never to be married out of the canonical hours. Come, come; Lord, here's such a deal of modesty, I warrant, the first day.

LUCY: Yes, an't please your worship, married women show all their modesty the first day, because married men show all their love the first day.

                 [Exeunt]

SCENE 2: *A Bedchamber in Pinchwife's House*

Pinchwife *and* Mrs. Pinchwife *discovered.*

PINCHWIFE: Come, tell me, I say.

MRS. PINCHWIFE: Lord! han't I told it a hundred times over?

PINCHWIFE: [Aside] I would try, if in the repetition of the ungrateful tale, I could find her altering it in the least circumstance; for if her story be false, she is so too.—[Aloud] Come, how was't, baggage?

MRS. PINCHWIFE: Lord, what pleasure you take to hear it sure!

PINCHWIFE: No, you take more in telling it I find; but speak, how was't?

MRS. PINCHWIFE: He carried me up into the house next to the Exchange.

PINCHWIFE: So, and you two were only in the room!

MRS. PINCHWIFE: Yes, for he sent away a youth that was there, for some dried fruit, and China oranges.

PINCHWIFE: Did he so? Damn him for it—and for—

MRS. PINCHWIFE: But presently came up the gentlewoman of the house.

PINCHWIFE: O, 'twas well she did; but what did he do whilst the fruit came?

MRS. PINCHWIFE: He kissed me a hundred times, and told me he fancied he kissed my fine sister, meaning me, you know, whom he said he loved with all his soul, and bid me be sure to tell her so, and to desire her to be at her window, by eleven of the clock this morning, and he would walk under it at that time.

PINCHWIFE: And he was as good as his word, very punctual; a pox reward him for't.   [Aside]

MRS. PINCHWIFE: Well, and he said if you were not within, he would come up to her, meaning me, you know, bud, still.

PINCHWIFE: [Aside] So—he knew her certainly; but for this confession, I am obliged to her simplicity. —[Aloud] But what, you stood very still when he kissed you?

MRS. PINCHWIFE: Yes, I warrant you; would you have had me discovered myself?

PINCHWIFE: But you told me he did some beastliness to you, as you call it; what was't?

MRS. PINCHWIFE: Why, he put—

PINCHWIFE: What?

MRS. PINCHWIFE: Why, he put the tip of his tongue between my lips, and so mousled me—and I said, I'd bite it.

PINCHWIFE: An eternal canker seize it, for a dog!

MRS. PINCHWIFE: Nay, you need not be so angry with him neither, for to say truth, he has the sweetest breath I ever knew.

PINCHWIFE: The devil! you were satisfied with it then, and would do it again?

MRS. PINCHWIFE: Not unless he should force me.

PINCHWIFE: Force you, changeling! I tell you, no woman can be forced.

MRS. PINCHWIFE: Yes, but she may sure, by such a one as he, for he's a proper, goodly, strong man; 'tis hard, let me tell you, to resist him.

PINCHWIFE: [Aside] So, 'tis plain she loves him, yet she has not love enough to make her conceal it from me; but the sight of him will increase her aversion for me and love for him; and that love instruct her how to deceive me and satisfy him, all idiot as she is. Love! 'twas he gave women first their craft, their art of deluding. Out of Nature's hands they came plain, open, silly, and fit for slaves, as she and Heaven intended 'em; but damned Love—well—I must strangle that little monster whilst I can deal with him.—[Aloud] Go fetch pen, ink, and paper out of the next room.

MRS. PINCHWIFE: Yes, bud.   [Exit]

PINCHWIFE: Why should women have more invention in love than men? It can only be, because they have more desires, more soliciting passions, more lust, and more of the devil.

Re-enter Mrs. Pinchwife.
Come, minx, sit down and write.

MRS. PINCHWIFE: Ay, dear bud, but I can't do't very well.

PINCHWIFE: I wish you could not at all.

MRS. PINCHWIFE: But what should I write for?

PINCHWIFE: I'll have you write a letter to your lover.

MRS. PINCHWIFE: O Lord, to the fine gentleman a letter!

PINCHWIFE: Yes, to the fine gentleman.

MRS. PINCHWIFE: Lord, you do but jeer: sure you jest.

PINCHWIFE: I am not so merry: come, write as I bid you.

MRS. PINCHWIFE: What, do you think I am a fool?

PINCHWIFE: [Aside] She's afraid I would not dictate any love to him, therefore she's unwilling.—[Aloud] But you had best begin.

MRS. PINCHWIFE: Indeed, and indeed, but I won't, so I won't.

PINCHWIFE: Why?

MRS. PINCHWIFE: Because he's in town; you may send for him if you will.

PINCHWIFE: Very well, you would have him brought to you; is it come to this? I say, take the pen and write, or you'll provoke me.

MRS. PINCHWIFE: Lord, what d'ye make a fool of me for? Don't I know that letters are never writ but from the country to London, and from London into the country? Now he's in town, and I am in town too; therefore I can't write to him, you know.

PINCHWIFE: [Aside] So, I am glad it is no worse; she is innocent enough yet.—[Aloud] Yes, you may, when your husband bids you, write letters to people that are in town.

MRS. PINCHWIFE: O, may I so? then I'm satisfied.

PINCHWIFE: Come, begin:—"Sir"—   [Dictates]

MRS. PINCHWIFE: Shan't I say, "Dear Sir?"—You know one says always something more than bare "sir."

PINCHWIFE: Write as I bid you, or I will write whore with this penknife in your face.

MRS. PINCHWIFE: Nay, good bud—"Sir"—   [Writes]

PINCHWIFE: "Though I suffered last night your nauseous, loathed kisses and embraces"—Write!

MRS. PINCHWIFE: Nay, why should I say so? You know I told you he had a sweet breath.

PINCHWIFE: Write!

MRS. PINCHWIFE: Let me but put out "loathed."

PINCHWIFE: Write, I say!

MRS. PINCHWIFE: Well then.   [Writes]

PINCHWIFE: Let's see, what have you writ?—[Takes the paper and reads] "Though I suffered last night your kisses and embraces"—Thou impudent creature! where is "nauseous" and "loathed?"

MRS. PINCHWIFE: I can't abide to write such filthy words.

PINCHWIFE: Once more write as I'd have you, and question it not, or I will spoil thy writing with this. I will stab out those eyes that cause my mischief.
                          [Holds up the penknife]

MRS. PINCHWIFE: O Lord! I will.

PINCHWIFE: So—so—let's see now.—[Reads] "Though I suffered last night your nauseous, loathed kisses and embraces"—go on—"yet I would not have you presume that you shall ever repeat them"—so—   [She writes]

MRS. PINCHWIFE: I have writ it.

PINCHWIFE: On, then—"I then concealed myself from your knowledge, to avoid your insolencies."—
                          [She writes]

MRS. PINCHWIFE: So—

PINCHWIFE: "The same reason, now I am out of your hands—"   [She writes]

MRS. PINCHWIFE: So—

PINCHWIFE: "Makes me own to you my unfortunate, though innocent frolic, of being in man's clothes"—   [She writes]

MRS. PINCHWIFE: So—

PINCHWIFE: "That you may for evermore cease to pursue her, who hates and detests you"—
                          [She writes on]

MRS. PINCHWIFE: So—heigh!   [Sighs]

PINCHWIFE: What, do you sigh?—"detests you—as much as she loves her husband and her honour"—

MRS. PINCHWIFE: I vow, husband, he'll ne'er believe I should write such a letter.

PINCHWIFE: What, he'd expect a kinder from you? Come, now your name only.

MRS. PINCHWIFE: What, shan't I say "Your most faithful humble servant till death?"

PINCHWIFE: No, tormenting fiend!—[Aside] Her style, I find, would be very soft.—[Aloud] Come, wrap it up now, whilst I go fetch wax and a candle; and write on the backside, "For Mr. Horner."

[Exit]

MRS. PINCHWIFE: "For Mr. Horner."—So, I am glad he has told me his name. Dear Mr. Horner! but why should I send thee such a letter that will vex thee, and make thee angry with me?—Well, I will not send it.—Ay, but then my husband will kill me—for I see plainly he won't let me love Mr. Horner—but what care I for my husband?—I won't, so I won't, send poor Mr. Horner such a letter—But then my husband—but oh, what if I writ at bottom my husband made me write it?—Ay, but then my husband would see't—Can one have no shift? ah, a London woman would have had a hundred presently. Stay—what if I should write a letter, and wrap it up like this, and write upon't too? Ay, but then my husband would see't —I don't know what to do.—But yet evads I'll try, so I will—for I will not send this letter to poor Mr. Horner, come what will on't.

"Dear, sweet Mr. Horner"—[Writes and repeats what she writes]—so—"my husband would have me send you a base, rude, unmannerly letter; but I won't"—so—"and would have me forbid you loving me; but I won't"—so—"and would have me say to you, I hate you, poor Mr. Horner; but I won't tell a lie for him"—there—"for I'm sure if you and I were in the country at cards together" —so—"I could not help treading on your toe under the table"—so—"or rubbing knees with you, and staring in your face, till you saw me"—very well—"and then looking down, and blushing for an hour together"—so—"but I must make haste before my husband comes: and now he has taught me to write letters, you shall have longer ones from me, who am, dear, dear, poor, dear Mr. Horner, your most humble friend, and servant to command till death,—Margery Pinchwife."

Stay, I must give him a hint at bottom—so— now wrap it up just like t'other—so—now write "For Mr. Horner"—But oh now, what shall I do with it? for here comes my husband.

Re-enter Pinchwife.

PINCHWIFE: [Aside] I have been detained by a spark-ish coxcomb, who pretended a visit to me; but I fear 'twas to my wife—[Aloud] What, have you done?

MRS. PINCHWIFE: Ay, ay, bud, just now.

PINCHWIFE: Let's see't: what d'ye tremble for? what, you would not have it go?

MRS. PINCHWIFE: Here—[Aside] No, I must not give him that: so I had been served if I had given him this.   [He opens and reads the first letter]

PINCHWIFE: Come, where's the wax and seal?

MRS. PINCHWIFE: [Aside] Lord, what shall I do now? Nay, then I have it—[Aloud] Pray let me see't.

Lord, you think me so arrant a fool, I cannot seal a letter; I will do't, so I will.

[Snatches the letter from him, changes it for the other, seals it, and delivers it to him]

PINCHWIFE: Nay, I believe you will learn that, and other things too, which I would not have you.

MRS. PINCHWIFE: So, han't I done it curiously?— [Aside] I think I have; there's my letter going to Mr. Horner, since he'll needs have me send letters to folks.

PINCHWIFE: 'Tis very well; but I warrant, you would not have it go now?

MRS. PINCHWIFE: Yes, indeed, but I would, bud, now.

PINCHWIFE: Well, you are a good girl then. Come, let me lock you up in your chamber, till I come back; and be sure you come not within three strides of the window when I am gone, for I have a spy in the street.—[Exit Mrs. Pinchwife, Pinchwife locks the door] At least, 'tis fit she think so. If we do not cheat women, they'll cheat us, and fraud may be justly used with secret enemies, of which a wife is the most dangerous; and he that has a handsome one to keep, and a frontier town, must provide against treachery, rather than open force. Now I have secured all within, I'll deal with the foe without, with false intelligence.

[Holds up the letter.   Exit]

SCENE 3:   Horner's Lodging

Enter Horner and Quack.

QUACK: Well, sir, how fadges[1] the new design? have you not the luck of all your brother projectors, to deceive only yourself at last?

HORNER: No, good domine doctor, I deceive you, it seems, and others too; for the grave matrons, and old, rigid husbands think me as unfit for love, as they are; but their wives, sisters, and daughters know, some of 'em, better things already.

QUACK: Already!

HORNER: Already, I say. Last night I was drunk with half-a-dozen of your civil persons, as you call 'em, and people of honour, and so was made free of their society and dressing-rooms for ever hereafter; and am already come to the privileges of sleeping upon their pallets, warming smocks, tying shoes and garters, and the like, doctor, already, already, doctor.

QUACK: You have made good use of your time, sir.

HORNER: I tell thee, I am now no more interruption to 'em, when they sing, or talk bawdy, than a little squab French page who speaks no English.

QUACK: But do civil persons and women of honour drink, and sing bawdy songs?

HORNER: O, amongst friends, amongst friends. For your bigots in honour are just like those in religion; they fear the eye of the world more than the eye

[1] Succeeds.

of Heaven; and think there is no virtue, but railing at vice, and no sin, but giving scandal. They rail at a poor, little, kept player, and keep themselves some young, modest pulpit comedian to be privy to their sins in their closets, not to tell 'em of them in their chapels.

QUACK: Nay, the truth on't is, priests, amongst the women now, have quite got the better of us lay-confessors, physicians.

HORNER: And they are rather their patients; but—

Enter Lady Fidget, *looking about her.*

Now we talk of women of honour, here comes one. Step behind the screen there, and but observe, if I have not particular privileges with the women of reputation already, doctor, already. [Quack *retires*]

LADY FIDGET: Well, Horner, am not I a woman of honour? you see, I'm as good as my word.

HORNER: And you shall see, madam, I'll not be be-hindhand with you in honour; and I'll be as good as my word too, if you please but to withdraw into the next room.

LADY FIDGET: But first, my dear sir, you must promise to have a care of my dear honour.

HORNER: If you talk a word more of your honour, you'll make me incapable to wrong it. To talk of honour in the mysteries of love, is like talking of Heaven or the Deity, in an operation of witchcraft, just when you are employing the devil: it makes the charm impotent.

LADY FIDGET: Nay, fy! let us not be smutty. But you talk of mysteries and bewitching to me; I don't understand you.

HORNER: I tell you, madam, the word money in a mistress's mouth, at such a nick of time, is not a more disheartening sound to a younger brother, than that of honour to an eager lover like myself.

LADY FIDGET: But you can't blame a lady of my reputation to be chary.

HORNER: Chary! I have been chary of it already, by the report I have caused of myself.

LADY FIDGET: Ay, but if you should ever let other women know that dear secret, it would come out. Nay, you must have a great care of your conduct; for my acquaintance are so censorious, (oh, 'tis a wicked, censorious world, Mr. Horner!) I say, are so censorious, and detracting, that perhaps they'll talk to the prejudice of my honour, though you should not let them know the dear secret.

HORNER: Nay, madam, rather than they shall preju-dice your honour, I'll prejudice theirs; and, to serve you, I'll lie with 'em all, make the secret their own, and then they'll keep it. I am a Machiavel in love, madam.

LADY FIDGET: O, no sir, not that way.

HORNER: Nay, the devil take me, if censorious women are to be silenced any other way.

LADY FIDGET: A secret is better kept, I hope, by a single person than a multitude; therefore pray do

not trust anybody else with it, dear, dear Mr. Horner.   [*Embracing him*]

Enter Sir Jasper Fidget.

SIR JASPER: How now!

LADY FIDGET: [*Aside*] O my husband!—prevented—and what's almost as bad, found with my arms about another man—that will appear too much—what shall I say?—[*Aloud*] Sir Jasper, come hither: I am trying if Mr. Horner were ticklish, and he's as ticklish as can be. I love to torment the con-founded toad; let you and I tickle him.

SIR JASPER: No, your ladyship will tickle him better without me, I suppose. But is this your buying china? I thought you had been at the china-house.

HORNER: [*Aside*] China-house! that's my cue, I must take it.—[*Aloud*] A pox! can't you keep your im-pertinent wives at home? Some men are troubled with the husbands, but I with the wives; but I'd have you to know, since I cannot be your journey-man by night, I will not be your drudge by day, to squire your wife about, and be your man of straw, or scarecrow only to pies and jays, that would be nibbling at your forbidden fruit; I shall be shortly the hackney gentleman-usher of the town.

SIR JASPER: [*Aside*] He! he! he! poor fellow, he's in the right on't, faith. To squire women about for other folks is as ungrateful an employment, as to tell money for other folks.—[*Aloud*] He! he! he! be'n't angry, Horner.

LADY FIDGET: No, 'tis I have more reason to be angry, who am left by you, to go abroad indecently alone; or, what is more indecent, to pin myself upon such ill-bred people of your acquaintance as this is.

SIR JASPER: Nay, prithee, what has he done?

LADY FIDGET: Nay, he has done nothing.

SIR JASPER: But what d'ye take ill, if he has done nothing?

LADY FIDGET: Ha! ha! ha! faith, I can't but laugh however; why, d'ye think the unmannerly toad would come down to me to the coach? I was fain to come up to fetch him, or go without him, which I was resolved not to do; for he knows china very well, and has himself very good, but will not let me see it, lest I should beg some; but I will find it out, and have what I came for yet.

HORNER: [*Apart to* Lady Fidget, *as he follows her to the door*] Lock the door, madam.—[*Exit* Lady Fidget, *and locks the door*]—[*Aloud*] So, she has got into my chamber and locked me out. Oh the impertinency of woman-kind! Well, Sir Jasper, plain-dealing is a jewel; if ever you suffer your wife to trouble me again here, she shall carry you home a pair of horns; by my lord mayor she shall; though I cannot furnish you myself, you are sure, yet I'll find a way.

SIR JASPER: Ha! ha! he!—[*Aside*] At my first coming in, and finding her arms about him, tickling him it seems, I was half jealous, but now I see my folly. —[*Aloud*] He! he! he! poor Horner.

HORNER: Nay, though you laugh now, 'twill be my turn ere long. Oh women, more impertinent, more cunning, and more mischievous than their monkeys, and to me almost as ugly!—Now is she throwing my things about and rifling all I have; but I'll get into her the back way, and so rifle her for it.

SIR JASPER: Ha! ha! ha! poor angry Horner.

HORNER: Stay here a little, I'll ferret her out to you presently, I warrant.   [*Exit at the other door*]

[*Sir Jasper talks through the door to his* Wife, *she answers from within*]

SIR JASPER: Wife! my Lady Fidget! wife! he is coming in to you the back way.

LADY FIDGET: Let him come, and welcome, which way he will.

SIR JASPER: He'll catch you, and use you roughly, and be too strong for you.

LADY FIDGET: Don't you trouble yourself, let him if he can.

QUACK: [*Aside*] This indeed I could not have believed from him, nor any but my own eyes.

Enter Mrs. Squeamish.

MRS. SQUEAMISH: Where's this woman-hater, this toad, this ugly, greasy, dirty sloven?

SIR JASPER: [*Aside*] So, the women all will have him ugly: methinks he is a comely person, but his wants make his form contemptible to 'em; and 'tis e'en as my wife said yesterday, talking of him, that a proper handsome eunuch was as ridiculous a thing as a gigantic coward.

MRS. SQUEAMISH: Sir Jasper, your servant: where is the odious beast?

SIR JASPER: He's within in his chamber, with my wife; she's playing the wag with him.

MRS. SQUEAMISH: Is she so? and he's a clownish beast, he'll give her no quarter, he'll play the wag with her again, let me tell you: come, let's go help her —What, the door's locked?

SIR JASPER: Ay, my wife locked it.

MRS. SQUEAMISH: Did she so? let's break it open then.

SIR JASPER: No, no, he'll do her no hurt.

MRS. SQUEAMISH: [*Aside*] But is there no other way to get in to 'em? whither goes this? I will disturb 'em.   [*Exit at another door*]

Enter Old Lady Squeamish.

LADY SQUEAMISH: Where is this harlotry, this impudent baggage, this rambling tomrigg? O Sir Jasper, I'm glad to see you here; did you not see my vile grandchild come in hither just now?

SIR JASPER: Yes.

LADY SQUEAMISH: Ay, but where is she then? where is she? Lord, Sir Jasper, I have e'en rattled myself to pieces in pursuit of her: but can you tell what she makes here? they say below, no woman lodges here.

SIR JASPER: No.

LADY SQUEAMISH: No! what does she here then? say, if it be not a woman's lodging, what makes she here? But are you sure no woman lodges here?

SIR JASPER: No, nor no man neither, this is Mr. Horner's lodging.

LADY SQUEAMISH: Is it so, are you sure?

SIR JASPER: Yes, yes.

LADY SQUEAMISH: So; then there's no hurt in't, I hope. But where is he?"

SIR JASPER: He's in the next room with my wife.

LADY SQUEAMISH: Nay, if you trust him with your wife, I may with my Biddy. They say, he's a merry harmless man now, e'en as harmless a man as ever came out of Italy with a good voice, and as pretty, harmless company for a lady, as a snake without his teeth.

SIR JASPER: Ay, ay, poor man.

Re-enter Mrs. Squeamish.

MRS. SQUEAMISH: I can't find 'em—Oh, are you here, grandmother? I followed, you must know, my Lady Fidget hither; 'tis the prettiest lodging, and I have been staring on the prettiest pictures—

Re-enter Lady Fidget *with a piece of china in her hand, and* Horner *following.*

LADY FIDGET: And I have been toiling and moiling for the prettiest piece of china, my dear.

HORNER: Nay, she has been too hard for me, do what I could.

MRS. SQUEAMISH: Oh, lord, I'll have some china too. Good Mr. Horner, don't think to give other people china and me none; come in with me too.

HORNER: Upon my honour, I have none left now.

MRS. SQUEAMISH: Nay, nay, I have known you deny your china before now, but you shan't put me off so. Come.

HORNER: This lady had the last there.

LADY FIDGET: Yes indeed, madam, to my certain knowledge, he has no more left.

MRS. SQUEAMISH: O, but it may be he may have some you could not find.

LADY FIDGET: What, d'ye think if he had had any left, I would not have had it too? for we women of quality never think we have china enough.

HORNER: Do not take it ill, I cannot make china for you all, but I will have a roll-waggon for you too, another time.

MRS. SQUEAMISH: Thank you, dear toad.

LADY FIDGET: What do you mean by that promise?
[*Aside to* Horner]

HORNER: Alas, she has an innocent, literal understanding.   [*Aside to Lady Fidget*]

LADY SQUEAMISH: Poor Mr. Horner! he has enough to do to please you all, I see.

HORNER: Ay, madam, you see how they use me.

LADY SQUEAMISH: Poor gentleman, I pity you.

HORNER: I thank you, madam: I could never find

pity, but from such reverend ladies as you are; the young ones will never spare a man.

MRS. SQUEAMISH: Come, come, beast, and go dine with us; for we shall want a man at ombre after dinner.

HORNER: That's all their use of me, madam, you see.

MRS. SQUEAMISH: Come, sloven, I'll lead you, to be sure of you.   [*Pulls him by the cravat*]

LADY SQUEAMISH: Alas, poor man, how she tugs him! Kiss, kiss her; that's the way to make such nice women quiet.

HORNER: No, madam, that remedy is worse than the torment; they know I dare suffer anything rather than do it.

LADY SQUEAMISH: Prithee kiss her, and I'll give you her picture in little, that you admired so last night; prithee do.

HORNER: Well, nothing but that could bribe me: I love a woman only in effigy, and good painting as much as I hate them.—I'll do't, for I could adore the devil well painted.   [*Kisses* Mrs. Squeamish]

MRS. SQUEAMISH: Foh, you filthy toad! nay, now I've done jesting.

LADY SQUEAMISH: Ha! ha! ha! I told you so.

MRS. SQUEAMISH: Foh! a kiss of his—

SIR JASPER: Has no more hurt in't than one of my spaniel's.

MRS. SQUEAMISH: Nor no more good neither.

QUACK: I will now believe anything he tells me.
                                                    [*Aside*]

Enter Pinchwife.

LADY FIDGET: O lord, here's a man! Sir Jasper, my mask, my mask! I would not be seen here for the world.

SIR JASPER: What, not when I am with you?

LADY FIDGET: No, no, my honour—let's be gone.

MRS. SQUEAMISH: Oh grandmother, let's be gone; make haste, make haste, I know not how he may censure us.

LADY FIDGET: Be found in the lodging of anything like a man!—Away.
            [*Exeunt* Sir Jasper Fidget, Lady Fidget,
            Old Lady Squeamish, *and* Mrs. Squeamish]

QUACK: What's here? another cuckold? he looks like one, and none else sure have any business with him.
                                                    [*Aside*]

HORNER: Well, what brings my dear friend hither?

PINCHWIFE: Your impertinency.

HORNER: My impertinency!—why, you gentlemen that have got handsome wives, think you have a privilege of saying anything to your friends, and are as brutish as if you were our creditors.

PINCHWIFE: No, sir, I'll ne'er trust you any way.

HORNER: But why not, dear Jack? why diffide in me thou know'st so well?

PINCHWIFE: Because I do know you so well.

HORNER: Han't I been always thy friend, honest Jack, always ready to serve thee, in love or battle, before thou wert married, and am so still?

PINCHWIFE: I believe so, you would be my second now, indeed.

HORNER: Well then, dear Jack, why so unkind, so grum, so strange to me? Come, prithee kiss me, dear rogue: gad I was always, I say, and am still as much thy servant as—

PINCHWIFE: As I am yours, sir. What, you would send a kiss to my wife, is that it?

HORNER: So, there 'tis—a man can't show his friendship to a married man, but presently he talks of his wife to you. Prithee, let thy wife alone, and let thee and I be all one, as we were wont. What, thou art as shy of my kindness, as a Lombard-street alderman of a courtier's civility at Locket's!

PINCHWIFE: But you are over-kind to me, as kind as if I were your cuckold already; yet I must confess you ought to be kind and civil to me, since I am so kind, so civil to you, as to bring you this: look you there, sir.   [*Delivers him a letter*]

HORNER: What is't?

PINCHWIFE: Only a love-letter, sir.

HORNER: From whom?—how! this is from your wife —hum—and hum—   [*Reads*]

PINCHWIFE: Even from my wife, sir: am I not wondrous kind and civil to you now too?—[*Aside*] But you'll not think her so.

HORNER: Ha! is this a trick of his or hers?   [*Aside*]

PINCHWIFE: The gentleman's surprised I find.— What, you expected a kinder letter?

HORNER: No faith, not I, how could I?

PINCHWIFE: Yes, yes, I'm sure you did. A man so well made as you are, must needs be disappointed, if the women declare not their passion at first sight or opportunity.

HORNER: [*Aside*] But what should this mean? Stay, the postscript.—[*Reads aside*] "Be sure you love me, whatsoever my husband says to the contrary, and let him not see this, lest he should come home and pinch me, or kill my squirrel."—It seems he knows not what the letter contains.

PINCHWIFE: Come, ne'er wonder at it so much.

HORNER: Faith, I can't help it.

PINCHWIFE: Now, I think I have deserved your infinite friendship and kindness, and have showed myself sufficiently an obliging kind friend and husband; am I not so, to bring a letter from my wife to her gallant?

HORNER: Ay, the devil take me, art thou, the most obliging, kind friend and husband in the world, ha! ha!

PINCHWIFE: Well, you may be merry, sir; but in short I must tell you, sir, my honour will suffer no jesting.

HORNER: What dost thou mean?

PINCHWIFE: Does the letter want a comment? Then, know, sir, though I have been so civil a husband, as to bring you a letter from my wife, to let you kiss and court her to my face, I will not be a cuckold, sir, I will not.

HORNER: Thou art mad with jealousy. I never saw

thy wife in my life but at the play yesterday, and I know not if it were she or no. I court her, kiss her!

PINCHWIFE: I will not be a cuckold, I say; there will be danger in making me a cuckold.

HORNER: Why, wert thou not well cured of thy last clap?

PINCHWIFE: I wear a sword.

HORNER: It should be taken from thee, lest thou shouldst do thyself a mischief with it; thou art mad, man.

PINCHWIFE: As mad as I am, and as merry as you are, I must have more reason from you ere we part. I say again, though you kissed and courted last night my wife in man's clothes, as she confesses in her letter—

HORNER: Ha!   [Aside]

PINCHWIFE: Both she and I say, you must not design it again, for you have mistaken your woman, as you have done your man.

HORNER: [Aside] O—I understand something now— [Aloud] Was that thy wife! Why wouldst thou not tell me 'twas she? Faith, my freedom with her was your fault, not mine.

PINCHWIFE: Faith, so 'twas.   [Aside]

HORNER: Fy! I'd never do't to a woman before her husband's face, sure.

PINCHWIFE: But I had rather you should do't to my wife before my face, than behind my back; and that you shall never do.

HORNER: No—you will hinder me.

PINCHWIFE: If I would not hinder you, you see by her letter she would.

HORNER: Well, I must e'en acquiesce then, and be contented with what she writes.

PINCHWIFE: I'll assure you 'twas voluntarily writ; I had no hand in't you may believe me.

HORNER: I do believe thee, faith.

PINCHWIFE: And believe her too, for she's an innocent creature has no dissembling in her: and so fare you well, sir.

HORNER: Pray, however, present my humble service to her, and tell her, I will obey her letter to a tittle, and fulfil her desires, be what they will, or with what difficulty soever I do't; and you shall be no more jealous of me, I warrant her, and you.

PINCHWIFE: Well then, fare you well; and play with any man's honour but mine, kiss any man's wife but mine, and welcome.   [Exit]

HORNER: Ha! ha! ha! doctor.

QUACK: It seems, he has not heard the report of you, or does not believe it.

HORNER: Ha! ha!—now, doctor, what think you?

QUACK: Pray let's see the letter—hum—"for—dear —love you—"   [Reads the letter]

HORNER: I wonder how she could contrive it! What say'st thou to't? 'tis an original.

QUACK: So are your cuckolds too originals: for they are like no other common cuckolds, and I will

henceforth believe it not impossible for you to cuckold the Grand Signior amidst his guards of eunuchs, that I say.

HORNER: And I say for the letter, 'tis the first love-letter that ever was without flames, darts, fates, destinies, lying and dissembling in't.

Enter Sparkish *pulling in* Pinchwife.

SPARKISH: Come back, you are a pretty brother-in-law, neither go to church nor to dinner with your sister bride!

PINCHWIFE: My sister denies her marriage, and you see is gone away from you dissatisfied.

SPARKISH: Pshaw! upon a foolish scruple, that our parson was not in lawful orders, and did not say all the common-prayer; but 'tis her modesty only I believe. But let all women be never so modest the first day, they'll be sure to come to themselves by night, and I shall have enough of her then. In the meantime, Harry Horner, you must dine with me: I keep my wedding at my aunt's in the Piazza.

HORNER: Thy wedding! what stale maid has lived to despair of a husband, or what young one of a gallant?

SPARKISH: O, your servant, sir—this gentleman's sister then,—no stale maid.

HORNER: I'm sorry for't.

PINCHWIFE: How comes he so concerned for her?
                                              [Aside]

SPARKISH: You sorry for't? why, do you know any ill by her?

HORNER: No, I know none but by thee; 'tis for her sake, not yours, and another man's sake that might have hoped, I thought.

SPARKISH: Another man! another man! what is his name?

HORNER: Nay, since 'tis past, he shall be nameless.— [Aside] Poor Harcourt! I am sorry thou hast missed her.

PINCHWIFE: He seems to be much troubled at the match.   [Aside]

SPARKISH: Prithee, tell me—Nay, you shan't go, brother.

PINCHWIFE: I must of necessity, but I'll come to you to dinner.   [Exit]

SPARKISH: But, Harry, what, have I a rival in my wife already? But with all my heart, for he may be of use to me hereafter; for though my hunger is now my sauce, and I can fall on heartily without, the time will come, when a rival will be as good sauce for a married man to a wife, as an orange to veal.

HORNER: O thou damned rogue! thou hast set my teeth on edge with thy orange.

SPARKISH: Then let's to dinner—there I was with you again. Come.

HORNER: But who dines with thee?

SPARKISH: My friends and relations, my brother Pinchwife, you see, of your acquaintance.

HORNER: And his wife?

SPARKISH: No, 'gad, he'll ne'er let her come amongst us good fellows; your stingy country coxcomb keeps his wife from his friends, as he does his little firkin of ale, for his own drinking, and a gentleman can't get a smack on't; but his servants, when his back is turned, broach it at their pleasures, and dust it away, ha! ha! ha!—'Gad, I am witty, I think, considering I was married to-day, by the world; but come—

HORNER: No, I will not dine with you, unless you can fetch her too.

SPARKISH: Pshaw! what pleasure canst thou have with women now, Harry?

HORNER: My eyes are not gone; I love a good prospect yet, and will not dine with you unless she does too; go fetch her, therefore, but do not tell her husband 'tis for my sake.

SPARKISH: Well, I'll go try what I can do; in the meantime, come away to my aunt's lodging, 'tis in the way to Pinchwife's.

HORNER: The poor woman has called for aid, and stretched forth her hand, doctor; I cannot but help her over the pale out of the briars.   [*Exeunt*]

SCENE 4:   *A Room in Pinchwife's House*

Mrs. Pinchwife *alone, leaning on her elbow.*—A table, pen, ink and paper.

MRS. PINCHWIFE: Well, 'tis e'en so, I have got the London disease they call love; I am sick of my husband, and for my gallant. I have heard this distemper called a fever, but methinks 'tis like an ague; for when I think of my husband, I tremble, and am in a cold sweat, and have inclinations to vomit; but when I think of my gallant, dear Mr. Horner, my hot fit comes, and I am all in a fever indeed; and, as in other fevers, my own chamber is tedious to me, and I would fain be removed to his, and then methinks I should be well. Ah, poor Mr. Horner! Well, I cannot, will not stay here; therefore I'll make an end of my letter to him, which shall be a finer letter than my last, because I have studied it like anything. Oh sick, sick!

[*Takes the pen and writes*]

Enter Pinchwife, *who seeing her writing, steals softly behind her and looking over her shoulder, snatches the paper from her.*

PINCHWIFE: What, writing more letters?

MRS. PINCHWIFE: O Lord, bud, why d'ye fright me so?
[*She offers to run out; he stops her, and reads*]

PINCHWIFE: How's this? nay, you shall not stir, madam:—"Dear, dear, dear Mr. Horner"—very well—I have taught you to write letters to good purpose—but let us see't. "First, I am to beg your pardon for my boldness in writing to you, which I'd have you to know I would not have done, had not you said first you loved me so extremely, which

if you do, you will never suffer me to lie in the arms of another man whom I loathe, nauseate, and detest."—Now you can write these filthy words. But what follows?—"Therefore, I hope you will speedily find some way to free me from this unfortunate match, which was never, I assure you, of my choice, but I'm afraid 'tis already too far gone; however, if you love me, as I do you, you will try what you can do; but you must help me away before to-morrow, or else, alas! I shall be for ever out of your reach, for I can defer no longer our—our—" what is to follow "our"?—speak, what —our journey into the country I suppose—Oh woman, damned woman! and Love, damned Love, their old tempter! for this is one of his miracles; in a moment he can make those blind that could see, and those see that were blind, those dumb that could speak, and those prattle who were dumb before; nay, what is more than all, make these dough-baked, senseless, indocile animals, women, too hard for us their politic lords and rulers, in a moment. But make an end of your letter, and then I'll make an end of you thus, and all my plagues together.   [*Draws his sword*]

MRS. PINCHWIFE: O Lord, O Lord, you are such a passionate man, bud!

Enter Sparkish.

SPARKISH: How now, what's here to do?

PINCHWIFE: This fool here now!

SPARKISH: What! drawn upon your wife? You should never do that, but at night in the dark, when you can't hurt her. This is my sister-in-law, is it not? ay, faith, e'en our country Margery; [*Pulls aside her handkerchief*] one may know her. Come, she and you must go dine with me; dinner's ready, come. But where's my wife? is she not come home yet? where is she?

PINCHWIFE: Making you a cuckold; 'tis that they all do, as soon as they can.

SPARKISH: What, the wedding-day? no, a wife that designs to make a cully of her husband will be sure to let him win the first stake of love, by the world. But come, they stay dinner for us: come, I'll lead down our Margery.

PINCHWIFE: No—sir, go, we'll follow you.

SPARKISH: I will not wag without you.

PINCHWIFE: This coxcomb is a sensible torment to me amidst the greatest in the world.   [*Aside*]

SPARKISH: Come, come, Madam Margery.

PINCHWIFE: No; I'll lead her my way: what, would you treat your friends with mine, for want of your own wife?—[*Leads her to the other door, and locks her in and returns*] I am contented my rage should take breath—   [*Aside*]

SPARKISH: I told Horner this.

PINCHWIFE: Come now.

SPARKISH: Lord, how shy you are of your wife! but let me tell you, brother, we men of wit have amongst us a saying, that cuckolding, like the small-pox, comes with a fear; and you may keep your wife as much as you will out of danger of infection, but if her constitution incline her to't, she'll have it sooner or later, by the world, say they.

PINCHWIFE: [*Aside*] What a thing is a cuckold, that every fool can make him ridiculous!—[*Aloud*] Well, sir—but let me advise you, now you are come to be concerned, because you suspect the danger, not to neglect the means to prevent it, especially when the greatest share of the malady will light upon your own head, for

Hows'e'er the kind wife's belly comes to swell,
The husband breeds for her, and first is ill.

[*Exeunt*]

Act V

SCENE 1: *Pinchwife's House*

Enter Pinchwife *and* Mrs. Pinchwife. *A* table *and* candle.

PINCHWIFE: Come, take the pen and make an end of the letter, just as you intended; if you are false in a tittle, I shall soon perceive it, and punish you as you deserve.—[*Lays his hand on his sword*] Write what was to follow—let's see—"You must make haste, and help me away before to-morrow, or else I shall be for ever out of your reach, for I can defer no longer our"—What follows "our"?

MRS. PINCHWIFE: Must all out, then, bud?—Look you there, then.

[*Mrs. Pinchwife* takes the pen and writes]

PINCHWIFE: Let's see—"For I can defer no longer our—wedding—Your slighted Alithea."—What's the meaning of this? my sister's name to't? speak, unriddle.

MRS. PINCHWIFE: Yes, indeed, bud.

PINCHWIFE: But why her name to't? speak—speak, I say.

MRS. PINCHWIFE: Ay, but you'll tell her then again. If you would not tell her again—

PINCHWIFE: I will not:—I am stunned, my head turns round.—Speak.

MRS. PINCHWIFE: Won't you tell her, indeed, and indeed?

PINCHWIFE: No; speak, I say.

MRS. PINCHWIFE: She'll be angry with me; but I had rather she should be angry with me than you, bud; And, to tell you the truth, 'twas she made me write the letter, and taught me what I should write.

PINCHWIFE: [*Aside*] Ha!—I thought the style was somewhat better than her own.—[*Aloud*] Could she come to you to teach you, since I had locked you up alone?

MRS. PINCHWIFE: O, through the keyhole, bud.

PINCHWIFE: But why should she make you write a letter for her to him, since she can write herself?

MRS. PINCHWIFE: Why, she said because—for I was unwilling to do it—

PINCHWIFE: Because what—because?

MRS. PINCHWIFE: Because, lest Mr. Horner should be cruel, and refuse her; or be vain afterwards, and show the letter, she might disown it, the hand not being hers.

PINCHWIFE: [*Aside*] How's this? Ha!—then I think I shall come to myself again.—This changeling could not invent this lie: but if she could, why should she? she might think I should soon discover it.—Stay—now I think on't too, Horner said he was sorry she had married Sparkish; and her disowning her marriage to me makes me think she has evaded it for Horner's sake: yet why should she take this course? But men in love are fools; women may well be so—[*Aloud*] But hark you, madam, your sister went out in the morning, and I have not seen her within since.

MRS. PINCHWIFE: Alack-a-day, she has been crying all day above, it seems, in a corner.

PINCHWIFE: Where is she? let me speak with her.

MRS. PINCHWIFE: [*Aside*] O Lord, then she'll discover all!—[*Aloud*] Pray hold, bud; what, d'ye mean to discover me? she'll know I have told you then. Pray, bud, let me talk with her first.

PINCHWIFE: I must speak with her, to know whether Horner ever made her any promise, and whether she be married to Sparkish or no.

MRS. PINCHWIFE: Pray, dear bud, don't, till I have spoken with her, and told her that I have told you all; for she'll kill me else.

PINCHWIFE: Go then, and bid her come out to me.

MRS. PINCHWIFE: Yes, yes, bud.

PINCHWIFE: Let me see—   [*Pausing*]

MRS. PINCHWIFE: [*Aside*] I'll go, but she is not within to come to him: I have just got time to know of Lucy her maid, who first set me on work, what lie I shall tell next; for I am e'en at my wit's end.

[*Exit*]

PINCHWIFE: Well, I resolve it, Horner shall have her: I'd rather give him my sister than lend him my wife; and such an alliance will prevent his pretensions to my wife, sure. I'll make him of kin to her, and then he won't care for her.

Re-enter Mrs. Pinchwife.

MRS. PINCHWIFE: O Lord, bud! I told you what anger you would make me with my sister.

PINCHWIFE: Won't she come hither?

MRS. PINCHWIFE: No, no. Lack-a-day, she's ashamed to look you in the face: and she says, if you go in to her, she'll run away down stairs, and shamefully go herself to Mr. Horner, who has promised her marriage, she says; and she will have no other, so she won't.

PINCHWIFE: Did he so?—promise her marriage!—then she shall have no other. Go tell her so; and if she will come and discourse with me a little concerning the means, I will about it immediately. Go.—[Exit Mrs. Pinchwife] His estate is equal to Sparkish's, and his extraction as much better than his, as his parts are; but my chief reason is, I'd rather be akin to him by the name of brother-in-law than that of cuckold.

Re-enter Mrs. Pinchwife.

Well, what says she now?

MRS. PINCHWIFE: Why, she says, she would only have you lead her to Horner's lodging; with whom she first will discourse the matter before she talks with you, which yet she cannot do; for alack, poor creature, she says she can't so much as look you in the face, therefore she'll come to you in a mask. And you must excuse her, if she make you no answer to any question of yours, till you have brought her to Mr. Horner; and if you will not chide her, nor question her, she'll come out to you immediately.

PINCHWIFE: Let her come: I will not speak a word to her, nor require a word from her.

MRS. PINCHWIFE: Oh, I forgot: besides she says, she cannot look you in the face, though through a mask; therefore would desire you to put out the candle.

PINCHWIFE: I agree to all. Let her make haste.—There, 'tis out—[*Puts out the candle. Exit* Mrs. Pinchwife] My case is something better: I'd rather fight with Horner for not lying with my sister, than for lying with my wife; and of the two, I had rather find my sister too forward than my wife. I expected no other from her free education, as she calls it, and her passion for the town. Well, wife and sister are names which make us expect love and duty, pleasure and comfort; but we find 'em plagues and torments, and are equally, though differently, troublesome to their keeper; for we have as much ado to get people to lie with our sisters as to keep 'em from lying with our wives.

Re-enter Mrs. Pinchwife *masked, and in hoods and scarfs, night-gown and petticoat of* Alithea's.

What, are you come, sister? let us go then.—But first, let me lock up my wife. Mrs. Margery, where are you?

MRS. PINCHWIFE: Here, bud.

PINCHWIFE: Come hither, that I may lock you up: get you in.—[*Locks the door*] Come, sister, where are you now?

[Mrs. Pinchwife *gives him her hand; but when he lets her go, she steals softly on to the other side of him, and is led away by him for his sister,* Alithea]

SCENE 2: *Horner's Lodging*

Horner *and* Quack.

QUACK: What, all alone? not so much as one of your cuckolds here, nor one of their wives! They use to take their turns with you, as if they were to watch you.

HORNER: Yes, it often happens that a cuckold is but his wife's spy, and is more upon family duty when he is with her gallant abroad, hindering his pleasure, than when he is at home with her playing the gallant. But the hardest duty a married woman imposes upon a lover is keeping her husband company always.

QUACK: And his fondness wearies you almost as soon as hers.

HORNER: A pox! keeping a cuckold company, after you have had his wife, is as tiresome as the company of a country squire to a witty fellow of the town, when he has got all his money.

QUACK: And as at first a man makes a friend of the husband to get the wife, so at last you are fain to fall out with the wife to be rid of the husband.

HORNER: Ay, most cuckold-makers are true courtiers; when once a poor man has cracked his credit for 'em, they can't abide to come near him.

QUACK: But at first, to draw him in, are so sweet, so kind, so dear! just as you are to Pinchwife. But what becomes of that intrigue with his wife?

HORNER: A pox! he's as surly as an alderman that has been bit; and since he's so coy, his wife's kindness is in vain, for she's a silly innocent.

QUACK: Did she not send you a letter by him?

HORNER: Yes; but that's a riddle I have not yet solved. Allow the poor creature to be willing, she is silly too, and he keeps her up so close—

QUACK: Yes, so close, that he makes her but the more willing, and adds but revenge to her love; which two, when met, seldom fail of satisfying each other one way or other.

HORNER: What! here's the man we are talking of, I think.

Enter Pinchwife, *leading in his* Wife *masked, muffled, and in her* Sister's *gown.*

Pshaw!

QUACK: Bringing his wife to you is the next thing to bringing a love-letter from her.

HORNER: What means this?

PINCHWIFE: The last time, you know, sir, I brought you a love-letter; now, you see, a mistress; I think you'll say I am a civil man to you.

HORNER: Ay, the devil take me, will I say thou art the civilest man I ever met with; and I have known some. I fancy I understand thee now better than I did the letter. But, hark thee, in thy ear—

PINCHWIFE: What?

HORNER: Nothing but the usual question, man: is she sound, on thy word?

PINCHWIFE: What, you take her for a wench, and me for a pimp?

HORNER: Pshaw! wench and pimp, paw[1] words; I know thou art an honest fellow, and hast a great acquaintance among the ladies, and perhaps hast made love for me, rather than let me make love to thy wife.

PINCHWIFE: Come, sir, in short, I am for no fooling.

HORNER: Nor I neither: therefore prithee, let's see her face presently. Make her show, man: art thou sure I don't know her?

PINCHWIFE: I am sure you do know her.

HORNER: A pox! why dost thou bring her to me then?

PINCHWIFE: Because she's a relation of mine—

HORNER: Is she, faith, man? then thou art still more civil and obliging, dear rogue.

PINCHWIFE: Who desired me to bring her to you.

HORNER: Then she is obliging, dear rogue.

PINCHWIFE: You'll make her welcome for my sake, I hope.

HORNER: I hope she is handsome enough to make herself welcome. Prithee let her unmask.

PINCHWIFE: Do you speak to her; she would never be ruled by me.

HORNER: Madam—[Mrs. Pinchwife whispers to Horner] She says she must speak with me in private. Withdraw, prithee.

PINCHWIFE: [Aside] She's unwilling, it seems, I should know all her indecent conduct in this business—[Aloud] Well then, I'll leave you together, and hope when I am gone, you'll agree; if not, you and I shan't agree, sir.

HORNER: What means the fool? if she and I agree 'tis no matter what you and I do.

[Whispers to Mrs. Pinchwife, who makes signs with her hand for him to be gone]

PINCHWIFE: In the mean time I'll fetch a parson, and find out Sparkish, and disabuse him. You would have me fetch a parson, would you not? Well then—now I think I am rid of her, and shall have no more trouble with her—our sisters and daughters, like usurers' money, are safest when put out; but our wives, like their writings, never safe, but in our closets under lock and key. [Exit]

Enter Boy.

BOY: Sir Jasper Fidget, sir, is coming up. [Exit]

HORNER: Here's the trouble of a cuckold now we are talking of. A pox on him! has he not enough to do to hinder his wife's sport, but he must other women's too?—Step in here, madam.

[Exit Mrs. Pinchwife]

Enter Sir Jasper Fidget.

SIR JASPER: My best and dearest friend.

HORNER: [Aside to Quack] The old style, doctor.—[Aloud] Well, be short, for I am busy. What would your impertinent wife have now?

[1]Paw, adj. naughty. An affected word fashionable in the latter half of the seventeenth century.—Wright.

SIR JASPER: Well guessed, i'faith; for I do come from her.

HORNER: To invite me to supper! Tell her, I can't come: go.

SIR JASPER: Nay, now you are out, faith; for my lady, and the whole knot of the virtuous gang, as they call themselves, are resolved upon a frolic of coming to you to-night in masquerade, and are all dressed already.

HORNER: I shan't be at home.

SIR JASPER: [Aside] Lord, how churlish he is to women!—[Aloud] Nay, prithee don't disappoint 'em; they'll think 'tis my fault: prithee don't. I'll send in the banquet and the fiddles. But make no noise on't; for the poor virtuous rogues would not have it known, for the world, that they go a-masquerading; and they would come to no man's ball but yours.

HORNER: Well, well—get you gone; and tell 'em, if they come, 'will be at the peril of their honour and yours.

SIR JASPER: He! he! he!—we'll trust you for that: farewell. [Exit]

HORNER: Doctor, anon you too shall be my guest, But now I'm going to a private feast. [Exeunt]

SCENE 3: The Piazza of Covent Garden

Enter Sparkish with a letter in his hand, Pinchwife following.

SPARKISH: But who would have thought a woman could have been false to me? By the world, I could not have thought it.

PINCHWIFE: You were for giving and taking liberty: she has taken it only, sir, now you find in that letter. You are a frank person, and so is she, you see there.

SPARKISH: Nay, if this be her hand—for I never saw it.

PINCHWIFE: 'Tis no matter whether that be her hand or no; I am sure this hand, at her desire, led her to Mr. Horner, with whom I left her just now, to go fetch a parson to 'em at their desire too, to deprive you of her for ever; for it seems yours was but a mock marriage.

SPARKISH: Indeed, she would needs have it that 'twas Harcourt himself, in a parson's habit, that married us; but I'm sure he told me 'twas his brother Ned.

PINCHWIFE: O, there 'tis out; and you were deceived, not she: for you are such a frank person. But I must be gone.—You'll find her at Mr. Horner's. Go, and believe your eyes. [Exit]

SPARKISH: Nay, I'll to her, and call her as many crocodiles, sirens, harpies, and other heathenish names, as a poet would do a mistress who had refused to hear his suit, nay more, his verses on her.—But stay, is not that she following a torch at t'other end of the Piazza? and from Horner's certainly—'tis so.

Enter Alithea *following a torch, and* Lucy *behind.* You are well met, madam, though you don't think so. What, you have made a short visit to Mr. Horner? but I suppose you'll return to him presently, by that time the parson can be with him.

ALITHEA: Mr. Horner and the parson, sir!

SPARKISH: Come, madam, no more dissembling, no more jilting; for I am no more a frank person.

ALITHEA: How's this?

LUCY: So, 'twill work, I see.   [Aside]

SPARKISH: Could you find out no easy country fool to abuse? none but me, a gentleman of wit and pleasure about the town? But it was your pride to be too hard for a man of parts, unworthy false woman! false as a friend that lends a man money to lose; false as dice, who undo those that trust all they have to 'em.

LUCY: He has been a great bubble, by his similes, as they say.   [Aside]

ALITHEA: You have been too merry, sir, at your wedding-dinner, sure.

SPARKISH: What, d'ye mock me too?

ALITHEA: Or you have been deluded.

SPARKISH: By you.

ALITHEA: Let me understand you.

SPARKISH: Have you the confidence, (I should call it something else, since you know your guilt,) to stand my just reproaches? you did not write an impudent letter to Mr. Horner? who I find now has clubbed with you in deluding me with his aversion for women, that I might not, forsooth, suspect him for my rival.

LUCY: D'ye think the gentleman can be jealous now, madam?   [Aside]

ALITHEA: I write a letter to Mr. Horner!

SPARKISH: Nay, madam, do not deny it. Your brother showed it me just now; and told me likewise, he left you at Horner's lodging to fetch a parson to marry you to him: and I wish you joy, madam, joy, joy; and to him too, much joy; and to myself more joy, for not marrying you.

ALITHEA: [Aside] So, I find my brother would break off the match; and I can consent to't, since I see this gentleman can be made jealous.—[Aloud] O Lucy, by his rude usage and jealousy, he makes me almost afraid I am married to him. Art thou sure 'twas Harcourt himself, and no parson, that married us?

SPARKISH: No, madam, I thank you. I suppose, that was a contrivance too of Mr. Horner's and yours, to make Harcourt play the parson; but I would as little as you have him one now, no, not for the world. For, shall I tell you another truth? I never had any passion for you till now, for now I hate you. 'Tis true, I might have married your portion, as other men of parts of the town do sometimes: and so, your servant. And to show my unconcernedness, I'll come to your wedding, and resign you with as much joy, as I would a stale wench to

a new cully; nay, with as much joy as I would after the first night, if I had been married to you. There's for you; and so your servant, servant.
                                          [Exit]

ALITHEA: How was I deceived in a man!

LUCY: You'll believe then a fool may be made jealous now? for that easiness in him that suffers him to be led by a wife, will likewise permit him to be persuaded against her by others.

ALITHEA: But marry Mr. Horner! my brother does not intend it, sure: if I thought he did, I would take thy advice, and Mr. Harcourt for my husband. And now I wish, that if there be any over-wise woman of the town, who, like me, would marry a fool for fortune, liberty, or title, first, that her husband may love play, and be a cully to all the town but her, and suffer none but Fortune to be mistress of his purse; then, if for liberty, that he may send her into the country, under the conduct of some huswifely mother-in-law; and if for title, may the world give 'em none but that of cuckold.

LUCY: And for her greater curse, madam, may he not deserve it.

ALITHEA: Away, impertinent! Is not this my old Lady Lanterlu's?[1]

LUCY: Yes, madam.—[Aside] And here I hope we shall find Mr. Harcourt.   [Exeunt]

SCENE 4: *Horner's Lodging. A* table, banquet, *and bottles*

Enter Horner, Lady Fidget, Mrs. Dainty Fidget, *and* Mrs. Squeamish.

HORNER: A pox! they are come too soon—before I have sent back my new mistress. All that I have now to do is to lock her in, that they may not see her.   [Aside]

LADY FIDGET: That we may be sure of our welcome, we have brought our entertainment with us, and are resolved to treat thee, dear toad.

MRS. DAINTY: And that we may be merry to purpose, have left Sir Jasper and my old Lady Squeamish, quarrelling at home at backgammon.

MRS. SQUEAMISH: Therefore let us make use of our time, lest they should chance to interrupt us.

LADY FIDGET: Let us sit then.

HORNER: First, that you may be private, let me lock this door and that, and I'll wait upon you presently.

LADY FIDGET: No, sir, shut 'em only, and your lips for ever; for we must trust you as much as our women.

HORNER: You know all vanity's killed in me; I have no occasion for talking.

LADY FIDGET: Now, ladies, supposing we had drank each of us our two bottles, let us speak the truth of our hearts.

MRS. DAINTY and MRS. SQUEAMISH: Agreed.

[1]*"Lanterloo" was the name of a game at cards.*

LADY FIDGET: By this brimmer, for truth is nowhere else to be found—[*Aside to* Horner] not in thy heart, false man!

HORNER: You have found me a true man, I'm sure.
[*Aside to* Lady Fidget]

LADY FIDGET: [*Aside to* Horner] Not every way.—But let us sit and be merry. [*Sings*]

Why should our damned tyrants oblige us to live
On the pittance of pleasure which they only give?
We must not rejoice
With wine and with noise:
In vain we must wake in a dull bed alone,
Whilst to our warm rival the bottle they're gone.
Then lay aside charms,
And take up these arms.
'Tis wine only gives 'em their courage and wit:
Because we live sober, to men we submit.
If for beauties you'd pass,
Take a lick of the glass,
'Twill mend your complexions, and when they are gone,
The best red we have is the red of the grape:
Then, sisters, lay't on,
And damn a good shape.

MRS. DAINTY: Dear brimmer! Well, in token of our openness and plain-dealing, let us throw our masks over our heads.

HORNER: So, 'twill come to the glasses anon. [*Aside*]

MRS. SQUEAMISH: Lovely brimmer! let me enjoy him first.

LADY FIDGET: No, I never part with a gallant till I've tried him. Dear brimmer! that makest our husbands shortsighted.

MRS. DAINTY: And our bashful gallants bold.

MRS. SQUEAMISH: And, for want of a gallant, the butler lovely in our eyes.—Drink, eunuch.

LADY FIDGET: Drink, thou representative of a husband.—Damn a husband!

MRS. DAINTY: And, as it were a husband, an old keeper.

MRS. SQUEAMISH: And an old grandmother.

HORNER: And an English bawd, and a French surgeon.

LADY FIDGET: Ay, we have all reason to curse 'em.

HORNER: For my sake, ladies?

LADY FIDGET: No, for our own; for the first spoils all young gallants' industry.

MRS. DAINTY: And the other's art makes 'em bold only with common women.

MRS. SQUEAMISH: And rather run the hazard of the vile distemper amongst them, than of a denial amongst us.

MRS. DAINTY: The filthy toads choose mistresses now as they do stuffs, for having been fancied and worn by others.

MRS. SQUEAMISH: For being common and cheap.

LADY FIDGET: Whilst women of quality, like the richest stuffs, lie untumbled, and unasked for.

HORNER: Ay, neat, and cheap, and new, often they think best.

MRS. DAINTY: No, sir, the beasts will be known by a mistress longer than by a suit.

MRS. SQUEAMISH: And 'tis not for cheapness neither.

LADY FIDGET: No; for the vain fops will take up druggets, and embroider 'em. But I wonder at the depraved appetites of witty men; they use to be out of the common road, and hate imitation. Pray tell me, beast, when you were a man, why you rather chose to club with a multitude in a common house for an entertainment, than to be the only guest at a good table.

HORNER: Why, faith, ceremony and expectation are unsufferable to those that are sharp bent. People always eat with the best stomach at an ordinary, where every man is snatching for the best bit.

LADY FIDGET: Though he get a cut over the fingers.—But I have heard, that people eat most heartily of another man's meat, that is, what they do not pay for.

HORNER: When they are sure of their welcome and freedom; for ceremony in love and eating is as ridiculous as in fighting: falling on briskly is all should be done on those occasions.

LADY FIDGET: Well then, let me tell you, sir, there is no where more freedom than in our houses; and we take freedom from a young person as a sign of good breeding; and a person may be as free as he pleases with us, as frolic, as gamesome, as wild as he will.

HORNER: Han't I heard you all declaim against wild men?

LADY FIDGET: Yes; but for all that, we think wildness in a man as desirable a quality as in a duck or rabbit: a tame man! foh!

HORNER: I know not, but your reputations frightened me as much as your faces invited me.

LADY FIDGET: Our reputation! Lord, why should you not think that we women make use of our reputation, as you men of yours, only to deceive the world with less suspicion? Our virtue is like the statesman's religion, the quaker's word, the gamester's oath, and the great man's honour; but to cheat those that trust us.

MRS. SQUEAMISH: And that demureness, coyness, and modesty, that you see in our faces in the boxes at plays, is as much a sign of a kind woman, as a vizard-mask in the pit.

MRS. DAINTY: For, I assure you, women are least masked when they have the velvet vizard on.

LADY FIDGET: You would have found us modest women in our denials only.

MRS. SQUEAMISH: Our bashfulness is only the reflection of the men's.

MRS. DAINTY: We blush when they are shamefaced.

HORNER: I beg your pardon, ladies, I was deceived in you devilishly. But why that mighty pretence to honour?

LADY FIDGET: We have told you; but sometimes 'twas for the same reason you men pretend business often, to avoid ill company, to enjoy the better and more privately those you love.

HORNER: But why would you ne'er give a friend a wink then?

LADY FIDGET: Faith, your reputation frightened us, as much as ours did you, you were so notoriously lewd.

HORNER: And you so seemingly honest.

LADY FIDGET: Was that all that deterred you?

HORNER: And so expensive—you allow freedom, you say.

LADY FIDGET: Ay, ay.

HORNER: That I was afraid of losing my little money, as well as my little time, both which my other pleasures required.

LADY FIDGET: Money! foh! you talk like a little fellow now: do such as we expect money?

HORNER: I beg your pardon, madam, I must confess, I have heard that great ladies, like great merchants, set but the higher prices upon what they have, because they are not in necessity of taking the first offer.

MRS. DAINTY: Such as we make sale of our hearts?

MRS. SQUEAMISH: We bribed for our love? foh!

HORNER: With your pardon ladies, I know, like great men in offices, you seem to exact flattery and attendance only from your followers; but you have receivers about you, and such fees to pay, a man is afraid to pass your grants. Besides, we must let you win at cards, or we lose your hearts; and if you make an assignation, 'tis at a goldsmith's, jeweller's, or china-house; where for your honour you deposit to him, he must pawn his to the punctual cit, and so paying for what you take up, pays for what he takes up.

MRS. DAINTY: Would you not have us assured of our gallants' love?

MRS. SQUEAMISH: For love is better known by liberality than by jealousy.

LADY FIDGET: For one may be dissembled, the other not.—[Aside] But my jealousy can be no longer dissembled, and they are telling ripe.—[Aloud]—Come, here's to our gallants in waiting, whom we must name, and I'll begin. This is my false rogue.
[Claps him on the back]

MRS. SQUEAMISH: How!

HORNER: So, all will out now.   [Aside]

MRS. SQUEAMISH: Did you not tell me, 'twas for my sake only you reported yourself no man?
[Aside to Horner]

MRS. DAINTY: Oh, wretch! did you not swear to me, 'twas for my love and honour you passed for that thing you do?   [Aside to Horner]

HORNER: So, so.

LADY FIDGET: Come, speak, ladies: this is my false villain.

MRS. SQUEAMISH: And mine too.

MRS. DAINTY: And mine.

HORNER: Well then, you are all three my false rogues too, and there's an end on't.

LADY FIDGET: Well then, there's no remedy; sister sharers, let us not fall out, but have a care of our honour. Though we get no presents, no jewels of him, we are savers of our honour, the jewel of most value and use, which shines yet to the world unsuspected, though it be counterfeit.

HORNER: Nay, and is e'en as good as if it were true, provided the world think so; for honour, like beauty now, only depends on the opinion of others.

LADY FIDGET: Well, Harry Common, I hope you can be true to three. Swear; but 'tis to no purpose to require your oath, for you are as often forsworn as you swear to new women.

HORNER: Come, faith, madam, let us e'en pardon one another; for all the difference I find betwixt we men and you women, we forswear ourselves at the beginning of an amour, you as long as it lasts.

Enter Sir Jasper Fidget, and Old Lady Squeamish.

SIR JASPER: Oh, my Lady Fidget, was this your cunning, to come to Mr. Horner without me? but you have been nowhere else, I hope.

LADY FIDGET: No, Sir Jasper.

LADY SQUEAMISH: And you came straight hither, Biddy?

MRS. SQUEAMISH: Yes, indeed, lady grandmother.

SIR JASPER: 'Tis well, 'tis well; I knew when once they were thoroughly acquainted with poor Horner, they'd ne'er be from him: you may let her masquerade it with my wife and Horner, and I warrant her reputation safe.

Enter Boy.

BOY: O, sir, here's the gentleman come, whom you bid me not suffer to come up, without giving you notice, with a lady too, and other gentlemen.

HORNER: Do you all go in there, whilst I send 'em away; and, boy, do you desire 'em to stay below till I come, which shall be immediately.
[Exeunt Sir Jasper, Lady Fidget, Lady Squeamish, Mrs. Squeamish, and Mrs. Dainty Fidget]

BOY: Yes, sir.   [Exit]
[Exit Horner at the other door, and returns with Mrs. Pinchwife]

HORNER: You would not take my advice, to be gone home before your husband came back, he'll now discover all; yet pray, my dearest, be persuaded to go home, and leave the rest to my management; I'll let you down the back way.

MRS. PINCHWIFE: I don't know the way home, so I don't.

HORNER: My man shall wait upon you.

MRS. PINCHWIFE: No, don't you believe that I'll go at all; what, are you weary of me already?

HORNER: No, my life, 'tis that I may love you long,

'tis to secure my love, and your reputation with your husband; he'll never receive you again else.

MRS. PINCHWIFE: What care I? d'ye think to frighten me with that? I don't intend to go to him again; you shall be my husband now.

HORNER: I cannot be your husband, dearest, since you are married to him.

MRS. PINCHWIFE: O, would you make me believe that? Don't I see every day at London here, women leave their first husbands, and go and live with other men as their wives? pish, pshaw! you'd make me angry, but that I love you so mainly.

HORNER: So, they are coming up—In again, in, I hear 'em.—[*Exit Mrs. Pinchwife*] Well, a silly mistress is like a weak place, soon got, soon lost, a man has scarce time for plunder; she betrays her husband first to her gallant, and then her gallant to her husband.

Enter Pinchwife, Alithea, Harcourt, Sparkish, Lucy, *and a* Parson.

PINCHWIFE: Come, madam, 'tis not the sudden change of your dress, the confidence of your as-severations, and your false witness there, shall per-suade me I did not bring you hither just now; here's my witness, who cannot deny it, since you must be confronted.—Mr. Horner, did not I bring this lady to you just now?

HORNER: Now must I wrong one woman for another's sake,—but that's no new thing with me, for in these cases I am still on the criminal's side against the innocent.   [*Aside*]

ALITHEA: Pray speak, sir.

HORNER: It must be so. I must be impudent, and try my luck; impudence uses to be too hard for truth.
                                                      [*Aside*]

PINCHWIFE: What, you are studying an evasion or excuse for her! Speak, sir.

HORNER: No, faith, I am something backward only to speak in women's affairs or disputes.

PINCHWIFE: She bids you speak.

ALITHEA: Ay, pray, sir, do, pray satisfy him.

HORNER: Then truly, you did bring that lady to me just now.

PINCHWIFE: O ho!

ALITHEA: How, sir?

HARCOURT: How, Horner?

ALITHEA: What mean you, sir? I always took you for a man of honour.

HORNER: Ay, so much a man of honour, that I must save my mistress, I thank you, come what will on't.
                                                      [*Aside*]

SPARKISH: So, if I had had her, she'd have made me believe the moon had been made of a Christmas pie.

LUCY: Now could I speak, if I durst, and solve the riddle, who am the author of it.   [*Aside*]

ALITHEA: O unfortunate woman! A combination against my honour! which most concerns me now,

because you share in my disgrace, sir, and it is your censure, which I must now suffer, that troubles me, not theirs.

HARCOURT: Madam, then have no trouble, you shall now see 'tis possible for me to love too, without being jealous; I will not only believe your innocence myself, but make all the world believe it.—[*Aside to* Horner] Horner, I must now be concerned for this lady's honour.

HORNER: And I must be concerned for a lady's honour too.

HARCOURT: This lady has her honour, and I will pro-tect it.

HORNER: My lady has not her honour, but has given it me to keep, and I will preserve it.

HARCOURT: I understand you not.

HORNER: I would not have you.

MRS. PINCHWIFE: What's the matter with 'em all?
                                        [*Peeping in behind*]

PINCHWIFE: Come, come, Mr. Horner, no more dis-puting; here's the parson, I brought him not in vain.

HARCOURT: No, sir, I'll employ him, if this lady please.

PINCHWIFE: How! what d'ye mean?

SPARKISH: Ay, what does he mean?

HORNER: Why, I have resigned your sister to him, he has my consent.

PINCHWIFE: But he has not mine, sir; a woman's in-jured honour, no more than a man's, can not be re-paired or satisfied by any but him that first wronged it; and you shall marry her presently, or—
                                  [*Lays his hand on his sword*]

Re-enter Mrs. Pinchwife.

MRS. PINCHWIFE: O Lord, they'll kill poor Mr. Hor-ner! besides, he shan't marry her whilst I stand by, and look on; I'll not lose my second husband so.

PINCHWIFE: What do I see?

ALITHEA: My sister in my clothes!

SPARKISH: Ha!

MRS. PINCHWIFE: Nay, pray now don't quarrel about finding work for the parson, he shall marry me to Mr. Horner; or now, I believe, you have enough of me.   [*To Pinchwife*]

HORNER: Damned, damned loving changeling! [*Aside*]

MRS. PINCHWIFE: Pray, sister, pardon me for telling so many lies of you.

HORNER: I suppose the riddle is plain now.

LUCY: No, that must be my work.—Good sir, hear me.
[*Kneels to* Pinchwife, *who stands doggedly with his hat over his eyes*]

PINCHWIFE: I will never hear woman again, but make 'em all silent thus—
                              [*Offers to draw upon his* Wife]

HORNER: No, that must not be.

PINCHWIFE: You then shall go first, 'tis all one to me.

[*Offers to draw on* Horner, *but is stopped by* Harcourt]

HARCOURT: Hold!

Re-enter Sir Jasper Fidget, Lady Fidget, Lady Squeamish, Mrs. Dainty Fidget, *and* Mrs. Squeamish.

SIR JASPER: What's the matter? what's the matter? pray, what's the matter, sir? I beseech you communicate, sir.

PINCHWIFE: Why, my wife has communicated, sir, as your wife may have done too, sir, if she knows him, sir.

SIR JASPER: Pshaw, with him! ha! ha! he!

PINCHWIFE: D'ye mock me, sir? a cuckold is a kind of a wild beast; have a care, sir.

SIR JASPER: No, sure, you mock me, sir. He cuckold you! it can't be, ha! ha! he! why, I'll tell you, sir—
[*Offers to whisper*]

PINCHWIFE: I tell you again, he has whored my wife, and yours too, if he knows her, and all the women he comes near; 'tis not his dissembling, his hypocrisy, can wheedle me.

SIR JASPER: How! does he dissemble? is he a hypocrite? Nay, then—how—wife—sister, is he a hypocrite?

LADY SQUEAMISH: A hypocrite! a dissembler! Speak, young harlotry, speak, how?

SIR JASPER: Nay, then—O my head too!—O thou libidinous lady!

LADY SQUEAMISH: O thou harloting harlotry! has thou done't then?

SIR JASPER: Speak, good Horner, art thou a dissembler, a rogue? hast thou—

HORNER: So!

LUCY: I'll fetch you off, and her too, if she will but hold her tongue.   [*Apart to* Horner]

HORNER: Canst thou? I'll give thee— [*Apart to* Lucy]

LUCY: [*To Pinchwife*] Pray have but patience to hear me, sir, who am the unfortunate cause of all this confusion. Your wife is innocent, I only culpable; for I put her upon telling you all these lies concerning my mistress, in order to the breaking off the match between Mr. Sparkish and her, to make way for Mr. Harcourt.

SPARKISH: Did you so, eternal rotten tooth? Then, it seems, my mistress was not false to me, I was only deceived by you. Brother, that should have been, now man of conduct, who is a frank person now, to bring your wife to her lover, ha?

LUCY: I assure you, sir, she came not to Mr. Horner out of love, for she loves him no more—

MRS. PINCHWIFE: Hold, I told lies for you, but you shall tell none for me, for I do love Mr. Horner with all my soul, and nobody shall say me nay; pray, don't you go to make poor Mr. Horner believe to the contrary; 'tis spitefully done of you, I'm sure.

HORNER: Peace, dear idiot. [*Aside to* Mrs. Pinchwife]

MRS. PINCHWIFE: Nay, I will not peace.

PINCHWIFE: Not till I make you.

Enter Dorilant *and* Quack.

DORILANT: Horner, your servant; I am the doctor's guest, he must excuse our intrusion.

QUACK: But what's the matter, gentlemen? for Heaven's sake, what's the matter?

HORNER: Oh, 'tis well you are come. 'Tis a censorious world we live in; you may have brought me a reprieve, or else I had died for a crime I never committed, and these innocent ladies had suffered with me; therefore, pray satisfy these worthy, honourable, jealous gentlemen—that—   [*Whispers*]

QUACK: O, I understand you, is that all?—Sir Jasper, by Heavens, and upon the word of a physician, sir—   [*Whispers to* Sir Jasper]

SIR JASPER: Nay, I do believe you truly.—Pardon me, my virtuous lady, and dear of honour.

LADY SQUEAMISH: What, then all's right again?

SIR JASPER: Ay, ay, and now let us satisfy him too.
[*They whisper with* Pinchwife]

PINCHWIFE: An eunuch! Pray, no fooling with me.

QUACK: I'll bring half the chirurgeons in town to swear it.

PINCHWIFE: They!—they'll swear a man that bled to death through his wounds, died of an apoplexy.

QUACK: Pray, hear me, sir—why, all the town has heard the report of him.

PINCHWIFE: But does all the town believe it?

QUACK: Pray, inquire a little, and first of all these.

PINCHWIFE: I'm sure when I left the town, he was the lewdest fellow in't.

QUACK: I tell you, sir, he has been in France since; pray, ask but these ladies and gentlemen, your friend Mr. Dorilant. Gentlemen and ladies, han't you all heard the late sad report of poor Mr. Horner?

ALL THE LADIES: Ay, ay, ay.

DORILANT: Why, thou jealous fool, dost thou doubt it? he's an arrant French capon.

MRS. PINCHWIFE: 'Tis false, sir, you shall not disparage poor Mr. Horner, for to my certain knowledge—

LUCY: O, hold!

MRS. SQUEAMISH: Stop her mouth!   [*Aside to* Lucy]

LADY FIDGET: Upon my honour, sir, 'tis as true—
[*To* Pinchwife]

MRS. DAINTY: D'ye think we would have been seen in his company?

MRS. SQUEAMISH: Trust our unspotted reputations with him?

LADY FIDGET: This you get, and we too, by trusting your secret to a fool.   [*Aside to* Horner]

HORNER: Peace, madam.—[*Aside to* Quack] Well, doctor, is not this a good design, that carries a man on unsuspected, and brings him off safe?

PINCHWIFE: Well, if this were true—but my wife—
[*Aside*]
[Dorilant *whispers with* Mrs. Pinchwife]

ALITHEA: Come, brother, your wife is yet innocent, you see; but have a care of too strong an imagination, lest, like an over-concerned timorous gamester, by fancying an unlucky cast, it should come. Women and fortune are truest still to those that trust 'em.

LUCY: And any wild thing grows but the more fierce and hungry for being kept up, and more dangerous to the keeper.

ALITHEA: There's doctrine for all husbands, Mr. Harcourt.

HARCOURT: I edify, madam, so much, that I am impatient till I am one.

DORILANT: And I edify so much by example, I will never be one.

SPARKISH: And because I will not disparage my parts, I'll ne'er be one.

HORNER: And I, alas! can't be one.

PINCHWIFE: But I must be one—against my will to a country wife, with a country murrain to me!

MRS. PINCHWIFE: And I must be a country wife still too, I find; for I can't, like a city one, be rid of my musty husband, and do what I list.   [Aside]

HORNER: Now, sir, I must pronounce your wife innocent, though I blush whilst I do it; and I am the only man by her now exposed to shame, which I will straight drown in wine, as you shall your suspicion; and the ladies' troubles we'll divert with a ballad.—Doctor, where are your maskers?

LUCY: Indeed, she's innocent, sir, I am her witness; and her end of coming out was but to see her sister's wedding; and what she has said to your face of her love to Mr. Horner, was but the usual innocent revenge on a husband's jealousy;—was it not, madam, speak?

MRS. PINCHWIFE: [Aside to Lucy and Horner] Since you'll have me tell more lies—[Aloud] Yes, indeed, bud.

PINCHWIFE: For my own sake fain I would all believe; Cuckolds, like lovers, should themselves deceive. But—   [Sighs] His honour is least safe (too late I find) Who trusts it with a foolish wife or friend.

A Dance of Cuckolds.

HORNER: Vain fops but court and dress, and keep a pother, To pass for women's men with one another; But he who aims by women to be prized, First by the men, you see, must be despised.
                                        [Exeunt]

Epilogue

Now you the vigorous who daily here
O'er vizard-mask in public domineer,
And what you'd do to her, if in place where;
Nay, have the confidence to cry, "Come out!"
Yet when she says, "Lead on!" you are not stout;
But to your well-dressed brother straight turn round,
    And cry "Pox on her, Ned, she can't be sound!"
Then slink away, a fresh one to engage,
With so much seeming heat and loving rage,
You'd frighten listening actress on the stage;
Till she at last has seen you huffing come,
And talk of keeping in the tiring-room,
Yet cannot be provoked to lead her home.
Next, you Falstaffs of fifty, who beset
Your buckram maidenheads, which your friends get
And whilst to them you of achievements boast,
They share the booty, and laugh at your cost.
In fine, you essenced boys, both old and young,
Who would be thought so eager, brisk, and strong,
Yet do the ladies, not their husbands wrong;
Whose purses for your manhood make excuse,
And keep your Flanders mares for show not use;
Encouraged by our woman's man to-day,
A Horner's part may vainly think to play;
And may intrigues so bashfully disown,
That they may doubted be by few or none;
May kiss the cards at picquet, ombre, loo,
And so be taught to kiss the lady too;
But, gallants, have a care, faith, what you do.
The world, which to no man his due will give,
You by experience know you can deceive,
And men may still believe you vigorous,
But then we women—there's no cozening us.

Love for Love

by WILLIAM CONGREVE
(1670–1729)

Restoration comedy reaches its summit in Congreve, who, without destroying its spirit, greatly refined it. Burke said that, with Marie Antoinette, vice lost half its evil by losing all its grossness; just so Congreve mitigated the Restoration's coldhearted salacity by embossing it with notable wit and style. Congreve is decidedly the child of his time: he can accept, he can even embody, its faults; he can often enough exhibit its cynicism; he does not protest much against vice, or put much credence in virtue. But he is also the child of a tradition, and much less a case-hardened worldling than an unillusioned, civilized homme du monde. He looks, if a little coldly, then a little sadly, too, at the world about him and the way of the world. He is not warmhearted but neither is he callous: there are things about life he regrets; but he will never remonstrate. We may fairly call him detached.

Endowed with such a temperament, Congreve was granted one supreme and, for him, completely harmonious talent: a wit that was more than decorative, better than glittering; one that could pervade his plays and give them not just their brilliance, but their very character, almost their very substance. Wit, we might say, determined how he judged things no less than how he phrased them: it was much more than a form of cleverness, it was a point of view, almost a criticism of life, and it made Congreve enormously aware of the ironies, the anomalies, the incongruities in life—of what was rueful as well as comic.

But Congreve, however detached, could enter very fully into the kind of fun, could deal brightly with the kind of foibles, that his age delighted in. He could relish its stage jokes, and go it one better at cracking them. Indeed Congreve's first play, The Old Bachelor, is a pastiche of every stock figure and routine situation in Restoration comedy; but though everything he wears is a loan or a hand-me-down, he already cuts something of a figure by the way he wears it and the way he moves, by his inborn elegance. And by the time he wrote Love for Love he had become master of his materials, so that they suggest the whole Restoration theater at its liveliest rather than bits and pieces from other Restoration plays; and he was master of his medium as well, of all that is vital to artificial comedy, and essential to the stage.

Love for Love perhaps ranks with The Country Wife as the most stageworthy Restoration comedy for the twentieth-century theater. This is to attest, in the end, its soundness as a play over and above its effectiveness as a picture: this is Congreve's best theater piece, but not his best piece of writing. Love for Love is the finest type of what we might call acquiescent art: the ingredients and methods are above criticism, but the recipe is not quite Congreve's own. Some of the characters—Foresight and Sir Sampson—are as old as Ben Jonson; some, like Ben and Miss Prue, are of the very broadest kind. But Valentine, and his servant Jeremy, and his young lady Angelica, are in the best traditional style; while Mrs. Frail and Mrs. Foresight are much more Congreve's own. As acquiescent art, Love for Love stands halfway between the public's taste and the author's talent, which means that it makes a certain conscious effort to please; and such are its blandishments that it still manages, with a very large public, to please today. In his next and final comedy, Congreve would make no such effort, and have no such success: in The Way of the World he so failed with the public as to quit the theater. But the play, as art, is the supreme comedy of the Restoration.

WILLIAM CONGREVE

Love for Love

THE PERSONS OF THE PLAY

SIR SAMPSON LEGEND, *Father of* Valentine *and* Ben

VALENTINE, *fallen under his Father's displeasure by his expensive way of living, in love with* Angelica

SCANDAL, *his Friend, a free speaker*

TATTLE, *a half-witted Beau, vain of his amours, yet valuing himself for secrecy*

BEN, Sir Sampson's *younger Son, half home-bred, and half sea-bred, designed to marry* Miss Prue

FORESIGHT, *an illiterate old fellow, peevish and positive, superstitious, and pretending to understand* Astrology, Palmistry, Physiognomy, Omens, Dreams, &c., *Uncle to* Angelica

JEREMY, *Servant to* Valentine

TRAPLAND, *a Scrivener*

BUCKRAM, *a Lawyer*

SNAP, *a Bailiff*

ANGELICA, *Niece to* Foresight, *of a considerable Fortune in her own hands*

MRS. FORESIGHT, *second Wife of* Foresight

MRS. FRAIL, *Sister to* Mrs. Foresight, *a Woman of the Town*

MISS PRUE, *Daughter of* Foresight *by a former Wife, a silly awkward country Girl*

NURSE *to* Miss Prue

JENNY, *Maid to* Angelica

STEWARDS, SAILORS, AND SERVANTS

THE SCENE: *London*

Prologue

The husbandman in vain renews his toil,
To cultivate each year a hungry soil;
And fondly hopes for rich and generous fruit,
When what should feed the tree devours the root;
The unladen boughs, he sees, bode certain dearth,
Unless transplanted to more kindly earth.
So, the poor husbands of the stage, who found
Their labours lost upon ungrateful ground
This last and only remedy have proved,
And hope new fruit from ancient stocks removed.
Well may they hope, when you so kindly aid,
Well plant a soil which you so rich have made.
As Nature gave the world to man's first age,
So from your bounty we receive this stage;
The freedom man was born to you've restored.
And to our world such plenty you afford,
It seems like Eden, fruitful of its own accord.
But since in Paradise frail flesh gave way,
And when but two were made, both went astray;
Forbear your wonder and the fault forgive,
If in our larger family we grieve
One falling Adam, and one tempted Eve.
We who remain would gratefully repay
What our endeavours can, and bring, this day,
The first-fruit offering of a virgin play.
We hope there's something that may please each taste,
And though of homely fare we make the feast,
Yet you will find variety at least.
There's humour, which for cheerful friends we got,
And for the thinking party there's a plot.
We've something, too, to gratify ill-nature,
(If there be any here) and that is satire;
Though satire scarce dares grin, 'tis grown so mild,
Or only shows its teeth as if it smiled.
As asses thistles, poets mumble wit,
And dare not bite, for fear of being bit.
They hold their pens, as swords are held by fools,
And are afraid to use their own edge-tools.
Since *The Plain Dealer's* scenes of manly rage,
Not one has dared to lash this crying age.
This time the poet owns the bold essay,
Yet hopes there's no ill-manners in his play:
And he declares by me, he has designed
Affront to none, but frankly speaks his mind.
And should the ensuing scenes not chance to hit,
He offers but this one excuse, 'twas writ
Before your late encouragement of wit.

Act I

SCENE 1: *Valentine's Lodging*

Valentine *discovered reading*, Jeremy *waiting: several books upon the table.*

VALENTINE: Jeremy!

JEREMY: Sir?

VALENTINE: Here, take away; I'll walk a turn, and digest what I have read.

JEREMY: [*Aside*] You'll grow devilish fat upon this paper diet.   [*Takes away the books*]

VALENTINE: And d'ye hear, you go to breakfast.— There's a page doubled down in Epictetus that is a feast for an emperor.

JEREMY: Was Epictetus a real cook, or did he only write receipts?

VALENTINE: Read, read, sirrah! and refine your appetite; learn to live upon instruction; feast your mind, and mortify your flesh; read, and take your nourishment in at your eyes; shut up your mouth, and chew the cud of understanding; so Epictetus advises.

JEREMY: O Lord! I have heard much of him, when I waited upon a gentleman at Cambridge. Pray what was that Epictetus?

VALENTINE: A very rich man—not worth a groat.

JEREMY: Humph, and so he has made a very fine feast where there is nothing to be eaten?

VALENTINE: Yes.

JEREMY: Sir, you're a gentleman, and probably understand this fine feeding; but if you please, I had rather be at board-wages. Does your Epictetus, or your Seneca here, or any of these poor rich rogues, teach you how to pay your debts without money? Will they shut up the mouths of your creditors? Will Plato be bail for you? or Diogenes, because he understands confinement, and lived in a tub, go to prison for you? 'Slife, sir, what do you mean? to mew yourself up here with three or four musty books, in commendation of starving and poverty?

VALENTINE: Why, sirrah, I have no money, you know it; and therefore resolve to rail at all that have; and in that I but follow the examples of the wisest and wittiest men in all ages; these poets and philosophers whom you naturally hate, for just such another reason, because they abound in sense, and you are a fool.

JEREMY: Ay, sir, I am a fool, I know it; and yet, Heaven help me, I'm poor enough to be a wit;— but I was always a fool when I told you what your expenses would bring you to; your coaches and your liveries, your treats and your balls; your being in love with a lady that did not care a farthing for you in your prosperity; and keeping company with wits that cared for nothing but your prosperity, and now, when you are poor, hate you as much as they do one another.

VALENTINE: Well, and now I am poor I have an opportunity to be revenged on 'em all; I'll pursue Angelica with more love than ever, and appear more notoriously her admirer in this restraint, than when I openly rivalled the rich fops that made court to her; so shall my poverty be a mortification to her pride, and perhaps make her compassionate of the love, which has principally reduced me to this lowness of fortune. And for the wits, I'm sure I am in a condition to be even with them.

JEREMY: Nay, your position is pretty even with theirs, that's the truth on't.

VALENTINE: I'll take some of their trade out of their hands.

JEREMY: Now Heaven, of mercy, continue the tax upon paper! you don't mean to write?

VALENTINE: Yes, I do; I'll write a play.

JEREMY: Hem!—Sir, if you please to give me a small certificate of three lines;—only to certify those whom it may concern, that the bearer hereof, Jeremy Fetch by name, has for the space of seven years, truly and faithfully served Valentine Legend, Esq.; and that he is not now turned away for any misdemeanor, but does voluntarily dismiss his master from any future authority over him.

VALENTINE: No, sirrah, you shall live with me still.

JEREMY: Sir, it's impossible:—I may die with you, starve with you, or be damned with your works; but to live, even three days, the life of a play, I no more expect it, than to be canonised for a Muse after my decease.

VALENTINE: You are witty, you rogue! I shall want your help; I'll have you learn to make couplets, to tag the ends of acts; d'ye hear, get the maids to crambo in an evening, and learn the knack of rhyming: you may arrive at the height of a song sent by an unknown hand or a chocolate-house lampoon.

JEREMY: But, sir, is this the way to recover your father's favour? why, Sir Sampson will be irreconcilable. If your younger brother should come from sea, he'd never look upon you again. You're undone, sir, you're ruined, you won't have a friend left in the world if you turn poet.—Ah, pox confound that Will's Coffee-house! it has ruined more young men than the Royal Oak lottery;—nothing thrives that belongs to't. The man of the house would have been an alderman by this time with half the trade, if he had set up in the city. For my part, I never sit at the door that I don't get double the stomach that I do at a horse-race:—the air upon Banstead downs is nothing to it for a whetter. Yet I never see it, but the spirit of famine appears to me, sometimes like a decayed porter, worn out with pimping, and carrying billets-doux and songs; not like other porters for hire, but for the jest's sake:—now like a thin chairman, melted down to half his proportion with carrying a poet upon tick, to visit some great fortune, and his fare to be paid him, like the wages of sin, either at the day of marriage, or the day of death.

VALENTINE: Very well, sir; can you proceed?

JEREMY: Sometimes like a bilked bookseller, with a meagre terrified countenance, that looks as if he had written for himself, or were resolved to turn author, and bring the rest of his brethren into the same condition:—and lastly, in the form of a worn-out punk, with verses in her hand, which her vanity had preferred to settlements, without a whole tatter to her tail, but as ragged as one of the Muses; or as if she were carrying her linen to the paper-mill, to be converted into folio books of warning to all young maids, not to prefer poetry to good sense, or lying in the arms of a needy wit, before the embraces of a wealthy fool.

Enter Scandal.

SCANDAL: What, Jeremy holding forth?

VALENTINE: The rogue has (with all the wit he could muster up) been declaiming against wit.

SCANDAL: Ay? why then I'm afraid Jeremy has wit: for wherever it is, it's always contriving its own ruin.

JEREMY: Why, so I have been telling my master, sir; Mr. Scandal, for Heaven's sake, sir, try if you can dissuade him from turning poet.

SCANDAL: Poet! he shall turn soldier first, and rather depend upon the outside of his head, than the lining. Why, what the devil! has not your poverty made you enemies enough? must you needs show your wit to get more?

JEREMY: Ay, more indeed; for who cares for anybody that has more wit than himself?

SCANDAL: Jeremy speaks like an oracle. Don't you see how worthless great men, and dull rich rogues, avoid a witty man of small fortune? Why, he looks like a writ of inquiry into their titles and estates; and seems commissioned by Heaven to seize the better half.

VALENTINE: Therefore I would rail in my writings, and be revenged.

SCANDAL: Rail? at whom? the whole world? Impotent and vain! who would die a martyr to sense in a country where the religion is folly? you may stand at bay for a while; but when the full cry is against you, you shan't have fair play for your life. If you can't be fairly run down by the hounds, you will be treacherously shot by the huntsmen. No, turn pimp, flatterer, quack, lawyer, parson, be chaplain to an atheist, or stallion to an old woman, anything but poet; a modern poet is worse, more servile, timorous and fawning, than any I have named: without you could retrieve the ancient honours of the name, recall the stage of Athens, and be allowed the force of open, honest satire.

VALENTINE: You are as inveterate against our poets

as if your character had been lately exposed upon the stage.—Nay, I am not violently bent upon the trade.—[*Knocking at the door*] Jeremy, see who's there.—[*Exit* Jeremy] But tell me what you would have me do? What does the world say of me, and my forced confinement?

SCANDAL: The world behaves itself as it uses to do on such occasions; some pity you and condemn your father; others excuse him and blame you; only the ladies are merciful, and wish you well; since love and pleasurable expense have been your greatest faults.

Re-enter Jeremy.

VALENTINE: How now?

JEREMY: Nothing new, sir; I have despatched some half-a-dozen duns with as much dexterity as a hungry judge does causes at dinner time.

VALENTINE: What answer have you given 'em?

SCANDAL: Patience, I suppose? the old receipt.

JEREMY: No, faith, sir; I have put 'em off so long with patience and forbearance, and other fair words, that I was forced now to tell 'em in plain downright English—

VALENTINE: What?

JEREMY: That they should be paid.

VALENTINE: When?

JEREMY: To-morrow.

VALENTINE: And how the devil do you mean to keep your word?

JEREMY: Keep it! not at all; it has been so very much stretched that I reckon it will break of course by to-morrow, and nobody be surprised at the matter. —[*Knocking*] Again!—Sir, if you don't like my negotiation, will you be pleased to answer these yourself?

VALENTINE: See who they are.   [*Exit* Jeremy]

VALENTINE: By this, Scandal, you may see what it is to be great; secretaries of state, presidents of the council, and generals of an army, lead just such a life as I do; have just such crowds of visitants in a morning, all soliciting of past promises; which are but a civiler sort of duns, that lay claim to voluntary debts.

SCANDAL: And you, like a true great man, having engaged their attendance, and promised more than ever you intend to perform, are more perplexed to find evasions than you would be to invent the honest means of keeping your word, and gratifying your creditors.

VALENTINE: Scandal, learn to spare your friends, and do not provoke your enemies: this liberty of your tongue will one day bring a confinement on your body, my friend.

Re-enter Jeremy.

JEREMY: O sir, there's Trapland the scrivener, with two suspicious fellows like lawful pads, that would knock a man down with pocket-tipstaves;—and there's your father's steward, and the nurse with one of your children from Twitnam.

VALENTINE: Pox on her! could she find no other time to fling my sins in my face? Here, give her this [*Gives money*], and bid her trouble me no more;—a thoughtless, two-handed whore! she knows my condition well enough, and might have overlaid the child a fortnight ago, if she had had any forecast in her.

SCANDAL: What, is it bouncing Margery with my godson?

JEREMY: Yes, sir.

SCANDAL: My blessing to the boy, with this token of my love.—[*Gives money*] And, d'ye hear, bid Margery put more flocks in her bed, shift twice a-week, and not work so hard, that she may not smell so vigorously. I shall take the air shortly.

VALENTINE: Scandal, don't spoil my boy's milk.—[*To Jeremy*] Bid Trapland come in. [*Exit Jeremy*] If I can give that Cerberus a sop, I shall be at rest for one day.

Re-enter Jeremy *with* Trapland.

VALENTINE: O Mr. Trapland, my old friend, welcome!—Jeremy, a chair quickly; a bottle of sack and a toast;—fly—a chair first.

TRAPLAND: A good morning to you, Mr. Valentine, and to you, Mr. Scandal.

SCANDAL: The morning's a very good morning, if you don't spoil it.

VALENTINE: Come sit you down, you know his way.

TRAPLAND: [*Sits*] There is a debt, Mr. Valentine, of fifteen hundred pounds of pretty long standing—

VALENTINE: I cannot talk about business with a thirsty palate.—[*To Jeremy*] Sirrah, the sack.

TRAPLAND: And I desire to know what course you have taken for the payment?

VALENTINE: Faith and troth, I am heartily glad to see you:—my service to you. [*Drinks*] Fill, fill, to honest Mr. Trapland, fuller.

TRAPLAND: Hold, sweetheart;—this is not to our business. My service to you, Mr. Scandal. [*Drinks*] I have forborne as long—

VALENTINE: T'other glass, and then we'll talk.—Fill, Jeremy.

TRAPLAND: No more, in truth.—I have forborne, I say—

VALENTINE: [*To Jeremy*] Sirrah, fill when I bid you.—[*To Trapland*] And how does your handsome daughter? Come, a good husband to her. [*Drinks*]

TRAPLAND: Thank you.—I have been out of this money—

VALENTINE: Drink first.—Scandal, why do you not drink?   [*They drink*]

TRAPLAND: And in short, I can be put off no longer.

VALENTINE: I was much obliged to you for your supply: it did me signal service in my necessity. But you delight in doing good.—Scandal, drink to me my friend Trapland's health. An honester man

lives not, nor one more ready to serve his friend in distress, though I say it to his face. Come, fill each man his glass.

SCANDAL: What, I know Trapland has been a whoremaster, and loves a wench still. You never knew a whoremaster that was not an honest fellow.

TRAPLAND: Fy, Mr. Scandal! you never knew—

SCANDAL: What, don't I know?—I know the buxom black widow in the Poultry—eight hundred pounds a-year, jointure, and twenty thousand pounds in money. Aha, old Trap!

VALENTINE: Say you so, i'faith? come, we'll remember the widow: I know whereabouts you are; come, to the widow—

TRAPLAND: No more, indeed.

VALENTINE: What, the widow's health.—[*To Jeremy*] Give it him.—Off with it. [*They drink*] A lovely girl, i'faith, black sparkling eyes, soft pouting ruby lips; better sealing there than a bond for a million, ha!

TRAPLAND: No, no, there's no such thing, we'd better mind our business;—you're a wag.

VALENTINE: No, faith, we'll mind the widow's business, fill again.—Pretty round heaving breasts, a Barbary shape, and a jut with her bum would stir an anchorite, and the prettiest foot! Oh, if a man could but fasten his eyes to her feet, as they steal in and out, and play at bo-peep under her petticoats! ah, Mr. Trapland?

TRAPLAND: Verily, give me a glass—you're a wag—and here's to the widow.   [*Drinks*]

SCANDAL: [*Aside to* Valentine] He begins to chuckle; ply him close, or he'll relapse into a dun.
                                                    [*Exit* Jeremy]

Enter Snap.

SNAP: By your leave, gentlemen.—Mr. Trapland, if we must do our office, tell us: we have half-a-dozen gentlemen to arrest in Pall Mall and Covent Garden; and if we don't make haste, the chairmen will be abroad, and block up the chocolate-houses, and then our labour's lost.

TRAPLAND: Udso, that's true.—Mr. Valentine, I love mirth, but business must be done; are you ready to—

Re-enter Jeremy.

JEREMY: Sir, your father's steward says he comes to make proposals concerning your debts.

VALENTINE: Bid him come in.—Mr. Trapland, send away your officer; you shall have an answer presently.

TRAPLAND: Mr. Snap, stay within call.   [*Exit* Snap]

Enter Steward, *who whispers* Valentine.

SCANDAL: Here's a dog now, a traitor in his wine; [*To* Trapland]—sirrah, refund the sack.—Jeremy, fetch him some warm water, or I'll rip up his stomach, and go the shortest way to his conscience.

TRAPLAND: Mr. Scandal, you are uncivil; I did not

value your sack; but you cannot expect it again, when I have drunk it.

SCANDAL: And how do you expect to have your money again, when a gentleman has spent it?

VALENTINE: [*To* Steward] You need say no more, I understand the conditions, they are very hard, but my necessity is very pressing; I agree to 'em. Take Mr. Trapland with you, and let him draw the writing.—Mr. Trapland, you know this man, he shall satisfy you.

TRAPLAND: I am loth to be thus pressing, but my necessity—

VALENTINE: No apology, good Mr. Scrivener, you shall be paid.

TRAPLAND: I hope you forgive me, my business requires— [*Exeunt* Trapland, Steward, *and* Jeremy]

SCENE 2:   *The Same.*

Valentine *and* Scandal *seated.*

SCANDAL: He begs pardon like a hangman at an execution.

VALENTINE: But I have got a reprieve.

SCANDAL: I am surprised; what, does your father relent?

VALENTINE: No; he has sent me the hardest conditions in the world. You have heard of a booby brother of mine that was sent to sea three years ago? this brother my father hears is landed; whereupon he very affectionately sends me word, if I will make a deed of conveyance of my right to his estate after his death to my younger brother, he will immediately furnish me with four thousand pounds to pay my debts, and make my fortune. This was once proposed before, and I refused it; but the present impatience of my creditors for their money, and my own impatience of confinement, and absence from Angelica, force me to consent.

SCANDAL: A very desperate demonstration of your love to Angelica; and I think she has never given you any assurance of hers.

VALENTINE: You know her temper; she never gave me any great reason either for hope or despair.

SCANDAL: Women of her airy temper, as they seldom think before they act, so they rarely give us any light to guess at what they mean; but you have little reason to believe that a woman of this age, who has had an indifference for you in your prosperity, will fall in love with your ill-fortune; besides, Angelica has a great fortune of her own; and great fortunes either expect another great fortune, or a fool.

Enter Jeremy.

JEREMY: More misfortunes, sir.

VALENTINE: What, another dun?

JEREMY: No, sir, but Mr. Tattle is come to wait upon you.

VALENTINE: Well, I can't help it;—you must bring him up; he knows I don't go abroad. [*Exit* Jeremy]

SCANDAL: Pox on him! I'll be gone.

VALENTINE: No, prithee stay: Tattle and you should never be asunder; you are light and shadow, and show one another; he is perfectly thy reverse both in humour and understanding; and, as you set up for defamation, he is a mender of reputations.

SCANDAL: A mender of reputations! ay, just as he is a keeper of secrets, another virtue that he sets up for in the same manner. For the rogue will speak aloud in the posture of a whisper; and deny a woman's name, while he gives you the marks of her person: he will forswear receiving a letter from her, and at the same time show you her hand in the superscription; and yet perhaps he has counterfeited the hand too, and sworn to a truth; but he hopes not to be believed; and refuses the reputation of a lady's favour, as a doctor says *No* to a bishopric, only that it may be granted him.—In short, he is a public professor of secrecy, and makes proclamation that he holds private intelligence.—He's here.

Enter Tattle.

TATTLE: Valentine, good morrow; Scandal, I am yours,—that is, when you speak well of me.

SCANDAL: That is, when I am yours; for while I am my own, or anybody's else, that will never happen.

TATTLE: How inhuman!

VALENTINE: Why, Tattle, you need not be much concerned at anything that he says: for to converse with Scandal, is to play at Losing Loadum: you must lose a good name to him, before you can win it for yourself.

TATTLE: But how barbarous that is, and how unfortunate for him, that the world should think the better of any person for his calumniation!—I thank heaven, it has always been a part of my character to handle the reputation of others very tenderly indeed.

SCANDAL: Ay, such rotten reputations as you have to deal with, are to be handled tenderly indeed.

TATTLE: Nay, but why rotten; why should you say rotten, when you know not the persons of whom you speak? how cruel that is!

SCANDAL: Not know 'em? why, thou never hadst to do with anybody that did not stink to all the town.

TATTLE: Ha! ha! ha! nay, now you make a jest of it indeed; for there is nothing more known, than that nobody knows anything of that nature of me.—As I hope to be saved, Valentine, I never exposed a woman since I knew what woman was.

VALENTINE: And yet you have conversed with several.

TATTLE: To be free with you, I have;—I don't care if I own that;—nay more (I'm going to say a bold word now), I never could meddle with a woman that had to do with anybody else.

SCANDAL: How!

VALENTINE: Nay, faith, I'm apt to believe him.—Except her husband, Tattle.

TATTLE: Oh, that—

SCANDAL: What think you of that noble commoner Mrs. Drab?

TATTLE: Pooh, I know Madam Drab has made her brags in three or four places, that I said this and that, and writ to her, and did I know not what;—but upon my reputation she did me wrong.—Well, well, that was malice:—but I know the bottom of it. She was bribed to that by one we all know;—a man too—only to bring me into disgrace with a certain woman of quality—

SCANDAL: Whom we all know.

TATTLE: No matter for that.—Yes, yes, everybody knows—no doubt on't, everybody knows my secret.—But I soon satisfied the lady of my innocence; for I told her—Madam, says I, there are some persons who make it their business to tell stories, and say this and that of one and t'other, and everything in the world; and, say I, if your grace—

SCANDAL: Grace!

TATTLE: O Lord! what have I said? my unlucky tongue!

VALENTINE: Ha! ha! ha!

SCANDAL: Why, Tattle, thou hast more impudence than one can in reason expect: I shall have an esteem for thee. Well, and, ha! ha! ha! well, go on: and what did you say to her grace?

VALENTINE: I confess this is something extraordinary.

TATTLE: Not a word, as I hope to be saved; an arrant *lapsus linguæ*.—Come, let's talk of something else.

VALENTINE: Well, but how did you acquit yourself?

TATTLE: Pooh! pooh! nothing at all, I only rallied with you—a woman of ordinary rank was a little jealous of me, and I told her something or other, faith—I know not what.—Come, let's talk of something else.   [*Hums a song*]

SCANDAL: Hang him, let him alone, he has a mind we should inquire.

TATTLE: Valentine, I supped last night with your mistress, and her uncle old Foresight; I think your father lies at Foresight's.

VALENTINE: Yes.

TATTLE: Upon my soul, Angelica's a fine woman.—And so is Mrs. Foresight, and her sister Mrs. Frail.

SCANDAL: Yes, Mrs. Frail is a very fine woman; we all know her.

TATTLE: Oh, that is not fair!

SCANDAL: What?

TATTLE: To tell.

SCANDAL: To tell what? why, what do you know of Mrs. Frail?

TATTLE: Who, I? upon honour I don't know whether she be man or woman; but, by the smoothness of her chin, and roundness of her hips.

SCANDAL: No!

TATTLE: No.

SCANDAL: She says otherwise.

TATTLE: Impossible!

SCANDAL: Yes, faith. Ask Valentine else.

TATTLE: Why then, as I hope to be saved, I believe a woman only obliges a man to secrecy, that she may have the pleasure of telling herself.

SCANDAL: No doubt on't. Well, but has she done you wrong, or no? you have had her? ha?

TATTLE: Though I have more honour than to tell first, I have more manners than to contradict what a lady has declared.

SCANDAL: Well, you own it?

TATTLE: I am strangely surprised!—Yes, yes, I can't deny't, if she taxes me with it.

SCANDAL: She'll be here by-and-by, she sees Valentine every morning.

TATTLE: How?

VALENTINE: She does me the favour, I mean, of a visit sometimes. I did not think she had granted more to anybody.

SCANDAL: Nor I, faith; but Tattle does not use to belie a lady; it is contrary to his character.—How one may be deceived in a woman, Valentine!

TATTLE: Nay, what do you mean, gentlemen?

SCANDAL: I'm resolved I'll ask her.

TATTLE: O barbarous! why, did you not tell me—

SCANDAL: No, you told us.

TATTLE: And bid me ask Valentine?

VALENTINE: What did I say? I hope you won't bring me to confess an answer, when you never asked me the question?

TATTLE: But, gentlemen, this is the most inhuman proceeding—

VALENTINE: Nay, if you have known Scandal thus long, and cannot avoid such a palpable decoy as this was, the ladies have a fine time whose reputations are in your keeping.

Re-enter Jeremy.

JEREMY: Sir, Mrs. Frail has sent to know if you are stirring.

VALENTINE: Show her up when she comes.
                                          [*Exit* Jeremy]

TATTLE: I'll be gone.

VALENTINE: You'll meet her.

TATTLE: Is there not a back way?

VALENTINE: If there were, you have more discretion than to give Scandal such an advantage; why, your running away will prove all that he can tell her.

TATTLE: Scandal, you will not be so ungenerous?—Oh, I shall lose my reputation of secrecy for ever!—I shall never be received but upon public days; and my visits will never be admitted beyond a drawing-room: I shall never see a bedchamber again, never be locked in a closet, nor run behind a screen, or under a table; never be distinguished among the waiting-women by the name of trusty Mr. Tattle more.—You will not be so cruel.

VALENTINE: Scandal, have pity on him; he'll yield to any conditions.

TATTLE: Any, any terms.

SCANDAL: Come, then, sacrifice half-a-dozen women of good reputation to me presently.—Come, where are you familiar?—and see that they are women of quality too, the first quality.

TATTLE: 'Tis very hard.—Won't a baronet's lady pass?

SCANDAL: No, nothing under a right honourable.

TATTLE: O inhuman! you don't expect their names?

SCANDAL: No, their titles shall serve.

TATTLE: Alas! that's the same thing: pray spare me their titles; I'll describe their persons.

SCANDAL: Well, begin then: but take notice, if you are so ill a painter, that I cannot know the person by your picture of her, you must be condemned, like other bad painters, to write the name at the bottom.

TATTLE: Well, first then—

Enter Mrs. Frail.

TATTLE: O unfortunate! she's come already; will you have patience till another time;—I'll double the number.

SCANDAL: Well, on that condition.—Take heed you don't fail me.

MRS. FRAIL: I shall get a fine reputation by coming to see fellows in a morning.—Scandal, you devil, are you here too?—Oh, Mr. Tattle, everything is safe with you, we know.

SCANDAL: Tattle!

TATTLE: Mum.—O madam, you do me too much honour.

VALENTINE: Well, lady galloper, how does Angelica?

MRS. FRAIL: Angelica? manners!

VALENTINE: What, you will allow an absent lover—

MRS. FRAIL: No, I'll allow a lover present with his mistress to be particular;—but otherwise I think his passion ought to give place to his manners.

VALENTINE: But what if he has more passion than manners?

MRS. FRAIL: Then let him marry and reform.

VALENTINE: Marriage indeed may qualify the fury of his passion, but it very rarely mends a man's manners.

MRS. FRAIL: You are the most mistaken in the world; there is no creature perfectly civil but a husband. For in a little time he grows only rude to his wife, and that is the highest good breeding, for it begets his civility to other people.—Well, I'll tell you news; but I suppose you hear your brother Benjamin is landed. And my brother Foresight's daughter is come out of the country—I assure you there's a match talked of by the old people.—Well, if he be but as great a sea-beast as she is a land monster, we shall have a most amphibious breed. —The progeny will be all otters; he has been bred at sea, and she has never been out of the country.

VALENTINE: Pox take 'em! their conjunction bodes me no good, I'm sure.

MRS. FRAIL: Now you talk of conjunction, my brother Foresight has cast both their nativities, and prognosticates an admiral and an eminent justice of the peace to be the issue male of their two bodies. —'Tis the most superstitious old fool! he would have persuaded me, that this was an unlucky day, and would not let me come abroad; but I invented a dream, and sent him to Artemidorus for interpretation, and so stole out to see you. Well, and what will you give me now? come, I must have something.

VALENTINE: Step into the next room—and I'll give you something.

SCANDAL: Ay, we'll all give you something.

MRS. FRAIL: Well, what will you all give me?

VALENTINE: Mine's a secret.

MRS. FRAIL: I thought you would give me something that would be a trouble to you to keep.

VALENTINE: And Scandal shall give you a good name.

MRS. FRAIL: That's more than he has for himself.— And what will you give me, Mr. Tattle?

TATTLE: I? my soul, madam.

MRS. FRAIL: Pooh, no, I thank you, I have enough to do to take care of my own. Well; but I'll come and see you one of these mornings: I hear you have a great many pictures.

TATTLE: I have a pretty good collection at your service, some originals.

SCANDAL: Hang him, he has nothing but the Seasons and the Twelve Cæsars, paltry copies; and the Five Senses, as ill represented as they are in himself; and he himself is the only original you will see there.

MRS. FRAIL: Ay, but I hear he has a closet of beauties.

SCANDAL: Yes, all that have done him favours, if you will believe him.

MRS. FRAIL: Ay, let me see those, Mr. Tattle.

TATTLE: Oh, madam, those are sacred to love and contemplation. No man but the painter and myself was ever blest with the sight.

MRS. FRAIL: Well, but a woman—

TATTLE: Nor woman, 'till she consented to have her picture there too;—for then she's obliged to keep the secret.

SCANDAL: No, no; come to me if you'd see pictures.

MRS. FRAIL: You?

SCANDAL: Yes, faith, I can show you your own picture, and most of your acquaintance to the life, and as like as at Kneller's.

MRS. FRAIL: O lying creature!—Valentine, does not he lie?—I can't believe a word he says.

VALENTINE: No, indeed, he speaks truth now; for as Tattle has pictures of all that have granted him favours, he has the pictures of all that have refused him; if satires, descriptions, characters, and lampoons are pictures.

SCANDAL: Yes, mine are most in black and white;—

and yet there are some set out in their true colours, both men and women. I can show you pride, folly, affectation, wantonness, inconstancy, covetousness, dissimulation, malice, and ignorance, all in one piece. Then I can show you lying, foppery, vanity, cowardice, bragging, lechery, impotence, and ugliness in another piece; and yet one of these is a celebrated beauty, and t'other a professed beau. I have paintings too, some pleasant enough.

MRS. FRAIL: Come, let's hear 'em.

SCANDAL: Why, I have a beau in a bagnio, cupping for a complexion, and sweating for a shape.

MRS. FRAIL: So.

SCANDAL: Then I have a lady burning brandy in a cellar with a hackney coachman.

MRS. FRAIL: O devil! Well, but that story is not true.

SCANDAL: I have some hieroglyphics too; I have a lawyer with a hundred hands, two heads, and but one face; a divine with two faces, and one head; and I have a soldier with his brains in his belly, and his heart where his head should be.

MRS. FRAIL: And no head?

SCANDAL: No head.

MRS. FRAIL: Pooh, this is all invention. Have you ne'er a poet?

SCANDAL: Yes, I have a poet weighing words, and selling praise for praise, and a critic picking his pocket. I have another large piece too, representing a school; where there are huge-proportioned critics, with long wigs, laced coats, Steenkirk cravats, and terrible faces; with catcalls in their hands, and horn-books about their necks. I have many more of this kind, very well painted as you shall see.

MRS. FRAIL: Well, I'll come, if it be but to disprove you.

Re-enter Jeremy.

JEREMY: Sir, here's the steward again from your father.

VALENTINE: I'll come to him.—Will you give me leave? I'll wait on you again presently.

MRS. FRAIL: No, I'll be gone. Come, who squires me to the Exchange? I must call my sister Foresight there.

SCANDAL: I will: I have a mind to your sister.

MRS. FRAIL: Civil!

TATTLE: I will, because I have a *tendre* for your ladyship.

MRS. FRAIL: That's somewhat the better reason, to my opinion.

SCANDAL: Well, if Tattle entertains you, I have the better opportunity to engage your sister.

VALENTINE: Tell Angelica, I am about making hard conditions to come abroad, and be at liberty to see her.

SCANDAL: I'll give an account of you and your proceedings. If indiscretion be a sign of love, you are the most a lover of anybody that I know: you fancy that parting with your estate will help you to your

mistress.—In my mind he is a thoughtless adventurer,

Who hopes to purchase wealth by selling land,
Or win a mistress with a losing hand. [*Exeunt*]

Act II

SCENE 1:   *A Room in Foresight's House*

Foresight *and* Servant.

FORESIGHT: Heyday! what are all the women of my family abroad? Is not my wife come home, nor my sister, nor my daughter?

SERVANT: No, sir.

FORESIGHT: Mercy on us, what can be the meaning of it? Sure the moon is in all her fortitudes. Is my niece Angelica at home?

SERVANT: Yes, sir.

FORESIGHT: I believe you lie, sir.

SERVANT: Sir?

FORESIGHT: I say you lie, sir. It is impossible that anything should be as I would have it; for I was born, sir, when the Crab was ascending, and all my affairs go backward.

SERVANT: I can't tell, indeed, sir.

FORESIGHT: No, I know you can't, sir; but I can tell, sir, and foretell, sir.

Enter Nurse.

FORESIGHT: Nurse, where's your young mistress?

NURSE: Wee'st heart, I know not, they're none of 'em come home yet. Poor child! I warrant she's fond o' seeing the town;—marry, pray heaven, they ha' given her any dinner.—Good lack-a-day, ha! ha! ha! Oh strange! I'll vow and swear now, ha! ha! ha! marry, and did you ever see the like?

FORESIGHT: Why, how now, what's the matter?

NURSE: Pray Heaven send your worship good luck! marry and amen with all my heart; for you have put on one stocking with the wrong side outward.

FORESIGHT: Ha, how? faith and troth I'm glad of it! —And so I have; that may be good luck in troth, in troth it may, very good luck; nay, I have had some omens: I got out of bed backwards too this morning, without premeditation; pretty good that too; but then I stumbled coming down stairs, and met a weasel; bad omens those: some bad, some good, our lives are chequered: mirth and sorrow, want and plenty, night and day, make up our time. —But in troth I am pleased at my stocking; very well pleased at my stocking.—Oh, here's my niece! —Sirrah, go tell Sir Sampson Legend I'll wait on him if he's at leisure; 'tis now three o'clock, a very good hour for business. Mercury governs this hour.
[*Exit* Servant]

Enter Angelica.

ANGELICA: Is it not a good hour for pleasure too,

uncle? pray lend me your coach, mine's out of order.

FORESIGHT: What, would you be gadding too? sure all females are mad to-day. It is of evil portent, and bodes mischief to the master of a family.—I remember an old prophecy written by Messahalah the Arabian, and thus translated by a reverend Buckinghamshire bard.

"When housewives all the house forsake,
And leave goodman to brew and bake,
Withouten guile then be it said,
That house doth stond upon its head;
And when the head is set in ground,
Ne mar'l if it be fruitful found."

Fruitful, the head fruitful;—that bodes horns; the fruit of the head is horns.—Dear niece, stay at home; for by the head of the house is meant the husband; the prophecy needs no explanation.

ANGELICA: Well, but I can neither make you a cuckold, uncle, by going abroad; nor secure you from being one, by staying at home.

FORESIGHT: Yes, yes; while there's one woman left, the prophecy is not in full force.

ANGELICA: But my inclinations are in force; I have a mind to go abroad; and if you won't lend me your coach, I'll take a hackney, or a chair, and leave you to erect a scheme, and find who's in conjunction with your wife. Why don't you keep her at home, if you're jealous of her when she's abroad? You know my aunt is a little retrograde (as you call it) in her nature. Uncle, I'm afraid you are not lord of the ascendant, ha! ha! ha!

FORESIGHT: Well, jill-flirt, you are very pert—and always ridiculing that celestial science.

ANGELICA: Nay, uncle, don't be angry;—if you are, I'll rip up all your false prophecies, ridiculous dreams, and idle divinations: I'll swear you are a nuisance to the neighbourhood.—What a bustle did you keep against the last invisible eclipse, laying in provision, as 'twere for a siege! What a world of fire and candle, matches and tinderboxes did you purchase! One would have thought we were ever after to live underground, or at least making a voyage to Greenland, to inhabit there all the dark season.

FORESIGHT: Why, you malapert slut!

ANGELICA: Will you lend me your coach, or I'll go on?—Nay, I'll declare how you prophesied popery was coming, only because the butler had mislaid some of the apostle spoons, and thought they were lost. Away went religion and spoonmeat together.—Indeed, uncle, I'll indict you for a wizard.

FORESIGHT: How, hussy! was there ever such a provoking minx!

NURSE: O merciful Father, how she talks!

ANGELICA: Yes, I can make oath of your unlawful midnight practices; you and the old nurse there—

NURSE: Marry, Heaven defend!—I at midnight practices!—O Lord, what's here to do!—I in unlawful doings with my master's worship!—Why, did you ever hear the like now?—Sir, did ever I do anything of your midnight concerns—but warm your bed, and tuck you up, and set the candle and your tobacco-box and your urinal by you, and now and then rub the soles of your feet?—O Lord, I?—

ANGELICA: Yes, I saw you together, through the keyhole of the closet, one night, like Saul and the witch of Endor, turning the sieve and shears, and pricking your thumbs to write poor innocent servants' names in blood, about a little nutmeg-grater, which she had forgot in the caudle-cup.—Nay, I know something worse, if I would speak of it.

FORESIGHT: I defy you, hussy! but I'll remember this, I'll be revenged on you, cockatrice; I'll hamper you.—You have your fortune in your own hands,—but I'll find a way to make your lover, your prodigal spendthrift gallant, Valentine, pay for all, I will.

ANGELICA: Will you? I care not but all shall out then.—Look to't, nurse; I can bring witness that you have a great unnatural teat under your left arm, and he another; and that you suckle a young devil in the shape of a tabby-cat, by turns, I can.

NURSE: A teat! a teat! I an unnatural teat! O the false, slanderous thing; feel, feel here, if I have anything but like another Christian.   [Crying]

FORESIGHT: I will have patience, since it is the will of the stars I should be thus tormented.—This is the effect of the malicious conjunctions and oppositions in the third house of my nativity; there the curse of kindred was foretold.—But I will have my doors locked up—I'll punish you, not a man shall enter my house.

ANGELICA: Do, uncle, lock 'em up quickly before my aunt comes home;—you'll have a letter for alimony to-morrow morning,—but let me begone first, and then let no mankind come near the house, but converse with spirits and the celestial signs, the Bull, and the Ram, and the Goat. Bless me! there are a great many horned beasts among the Twelve Signs, uncle;—but cuckolds go to Heaven.

FORESIGHT: But there's but one virgin among the twelve signs, spitfire, but one virgin. ·

ANGELICA: Nor there had not been that one, if she had had to do with anything but astrologers, uncle. That makes my aunt go abroad.

FORESIGHT: How? how? is that the reason? Come, you know something: tell me and I'll forgive you; do, good niece.—Come, you shall have my coach and horses;—faith and troth you shall.—Does my wife complain? come, I know women tell one another.—She is young and sanguine, has a wanton hazel eye, and was born under Gemini, which may incline her to society; she has a mole upon her lip, with a moist palm, and an open liberality on the mount of Venus.

ANGELICA: Ha! ha! ha!

FORESIGHT: Do you laugh?—Well, gentlewoman, I'll —but come, be a good girl, don't perplex your poor uncle, tell me; won't you speak?—Odd, I'll—

Re-enter Servant.

SERVANT: Sir Sampson is coming down to wait upon you.

ANGELICA: Good b'w'ye, uncle.—Call me a chair.— [*Exit* Servant] I'll find out my aunt, and tell her she must not come home.   [*Exit*]

FORESIGHT: I'm so perplexed and vexed, I am not fit to receive him; I shall scarce recover myself before the hour be past.—Go, nurse, tell Sir Sampson I'm ready to wait on him.

NURSE: Yes, sir.   [*Exit*]

FORESIGHT: Well—why, if I was born to be a cuckold there's no more to be said—he's here already.

Enter Sir Sampson *with a paper.*

SIR SAMPSON: Nor no more to be done, old boy; that's plain.—Here 'tis, I have it in my hand, old Ptolomee; I'll make the ungracious prodigal know who begat him; I will, old Nostrodamus. What, I warrant my son thought nothing belonged to a father but forgiveness and affection; no authority, no correction, no arbitrary power; nothing to be done, but for him to offend, and me to pardon. I warrant you, if he danced till doomsday, he thought I was to pay the piper. Well, but here it is under black and white, *signatum, sigillatum,* and *deliberatum;* that as soon as my son Benjamin is arrived, he is to make over to him his right of inheritance. Where's my daughter that is to be—ha! old Merlin! body o' me, I'm so glad I'm revenged on this undutiful rogue.

FORESIGHT: Odso, let me see; let me see the paper. —Ay, faith and troth, here 'tis, if it will but hold. I wish things were done, and the conveyance made. When was this signed, what hour? Odso, you should have consulted me for the time. Well, but we'll make haste.

SIR SAMPSON: Haste, ay, ay; haste enough, my son Ben will be in town to-night.—I have ordered my lawyer to draw up writings of settlement and jointure:—all shall be done to-night. No matter for the time: prithee, Brother Foresight, leave superstition. Pox o' th' time! there's no time but the time present, there's no more to be said of what's past, and all that is to come will happen. If the sun shine by day, and the stars by night, why, we shall know one another's faces without the help of a candle, and that's all the stars are good for.

FORESIGHT: How, how, Sir Sampson? that all? Give me leave to contradict you, and tell you, you are ignorant.

SIR SAMPSON: I tell you I am wise; and *sapiens dominabitur astris;* there's Latin for you to prove it, and an argument to confound your ephemeris.—Ignorant!—I tell you, I have travelled, old Fircu, and know the globe. I have seen the antipodes, where the sun rises at midnight, and sets at noonday.

FORESIGHT: But I tell you, I have travelled, and travelled in the celestial spheres, know the signs and the planets, and their houses. Can judge of motions direct and retrograde, of sextiles, quadrates, trines and oppositions, fiery trigons and aquatical trigons. Know whether life shall be long or short, happy or unhappy, whether diseases are curable or incurable. If journeys shall be prosperous, undertakings successful; or goods stolen recovered, I know—

SIR SAMPSON: I know the length of the Emperor of China's foot; have kissed the Great Mogul's slipper, and rid a hunting upon an elephant with the Cham of Tartary.—Body o' me, I have made a cuckold of a king, and the present majesty of Bantam is the issue of these loins.

FORESIGHT: I know when travellers lie or speak truth, when they don't know it themselves.

SIR SAMPSON: I have known an astrologer made a cuckold in the twinkling of a star; and seen a conjurer that could not keep the devil out of his wife's circle.

FORESIGHT: [*Aside*] What, does he twit me with my wife too? I must be better informed of this.— [*Aloud*] Do you mean my wife, Sir Sampson? Though you made a cuckold of the King of Bantam, yet by the body of the sun—

SIR SAMPSON: By the horns of the moon, you would say, brother Capricorn.

FORESIGHT: Capricorn in your teeth, thou modern Mandeville! Ferdinand Mendez Pinto was but a type of thee, thou liar of the first magnitude! Take back your paper of inheritance; send your son to sea again. I'll wed my daughter to an Egyptian mummy, ere she shall incorporate with a contemner of sciences, and a defamer of virtue.

SIR SAMPSON: [*Aside*] Body o'me, I have gone too far;—I must not provoke honest Albumazar.[1]— [*Aloud*] An Egyptian mummy is an illustrious creature, my trusty hieroglyphic; and may have significations of futurity about him; odsbud, I would my son were an Egyptian mummy for thy sake. What, thou art not angry for a jest, my good Haly?—I reverence the sun, moon, and stars with all my heart. What, I'll make thee a present of a mummy: now I think on't, body o'me, I have a shoulder of an Egyptian king, that I purloined from one of the pyramids, powdered with hieroglyphics; thou shalt have it brought home to thy house, and make an entertainment for all the philomaths, and students in physic and astrology, in and about London.

FORESIGHT: But what do you know of my wife, Sir Sampson?

[1] *A Persian astrologer who has given his name to a play.*

SIR SAMPSON: Thy wife is a constellation of virtues; she's the moon, and thou art the man in the moon: nay, she is more illustrious than the moon; for she has her chastity without her inconstancy; 'sbud, I was but in jest.

Enter Jeremy.

SIR SAMPSON: How now, who sent for you? ha! what would you have? [Jeremy *whispers to* Sir Sampson]

FORESIGHT: Nay, if you were but in jest—Who's that fellow? I don't like his physiognomy.

SIR SAMPSON: [*To* Jeremy] My son, sir; what son, sir? my son Benjamin, hoh?

JEREMY: No, sir; Mr. Valentine, my master.—'Tis the first time he has been abroad since his confinement, and he comes to pay his duty to you.

SIR SAMPSON: Well, sir.

Enter Valentine.

JEREMY: He is here, sir.

VALENTINE: Your blessing, sir.

SIR SAMPSON: You've had it already, sir. I think I sent it you to-day in a bill of four thousand pounds.—A great deal of money, Brother Foresight.

FORESIGHT: Ay, indeed, Sir Sampson, a great deal of money for a young man; I wonder what he can do with it.

SIR SAMPSON: Body o'me, so do I.—Hark ye, Valentine, if there be too much, refund the superfluity, dost hear, boy?

VALENTINE: Superfluity, sir! it will scarce pay my debts. I hope you will have more indulgence, than to oblige me to those hard conditions which my necessity signed to.

SIR SAMPSON: Sir, how, I beseech you, what were you pleased to intimate concerning indulgence?

VALENTINE: Why, sir, that you would not go to the extremity of the conditions, but release me at least from some part.

SIR SAMPSON: Oh, sir, I understand you—that's all, ha?

VALENTINE: Yes, sir, all that I presume to ask;—but what you, out of fatherly fondness, will be pleased to add shall be doubly welcome.

SIR SAMPSON: No doubt of it, sweet sir, but your filial piety and my fatherly fondness would fit like two tallies.—Here's a rogue, Brother Foresight, makes a bargain under hand and seal in the morning, and would be released from it in the afternoon; here's a rogue, dog, here's conscience and honesty; this is your wit now, this is the morality of your wits! You are a wit, and have been a beau, and may be a—why, sirrah, is it not here under hand and seal? —can you deny it?

VALENTINE: Sir, I don't deny it.

SIR SAMPSON: Sirrah, you'll be hanged; I shall live to see you go up Holborn Hill.—Has he not a rogue's face?—Speak, brother, you understand physiognomy, a hanging look to me;—of all my boys the most unlike me; he has a damned Tyburn-face, without the benefit o' the clergy.

FORESIGHT: Hum—truly I don't care to discourage a young man. He has a violent death in his face; but I hope no danger of hanging.

VALENTINE: Sir, is this usage for your son?—for that old weather-headed fool, I know how to laugh at him; but you, sir—

SIR SAMPSON: You, sir; and you, sir;—why, who are you, sir?

VALENTINE: Your son, sir.

SIR SAMPSON: That's more than I know, sir, and I believe not.

VALENTINE: Faith, I hope not.

SIR SAMPSON: What, would you have your mother a whore!—Did you ever hear the like! did you ever hear the like! Body o'me—

VALENTINE: I would have an excuse for your barbarity and unnatural usage.

SIR SAMPSON: Excuse! impudence! Why, sirrah, mayn't I do what I please? are not you my slave? did not I beget you? and might not I have chosen whether I would have begot you or no? 'Oons! who are you? whence came you? what brought you into the world? how came you here, sir? here, to stand here, upon those two legs, and look erect with that audacious face, hah? answer me that? Did you come a volunteer into the world? or did I, with the lawful authority of a parent, press you to the service?

VALENTINE: I know no more why I came than you do why you called me. But here I am, and if you don't mean to provide for me, I desire you would leave me as you found me.

SIR SAMPSON: With all my heart: come, uncase, strip, and go naked out of the world as you came into't.

VALENTINE: My clothes are soon put off;—but you must also divest me of reason, thought, passions, inclinations, affections, appetites, senses, and the huge train of attendants that you begot along with me.

SIR SAMPSON: Body o'me, what a many-headed monster have I propagated!

VALENTINE: I am of myself a plain, easy, simple creature, and to be kept at small expense; but the retinue that you gave me are craving and invincible; they are so many devils that you have raised, and will have employment.

SIR SAMPSON: 'Oons, what had I to do to get children! ——can't a private man be born without all these followers?—Why, nothing under an emperor should be born with appetites.—Why, at this rate, a fellow that has but a groat in his pocket, may have a stomach capable of a ten-shilling ordinary.

JEREMY: Nay, that's as clear as the sun; I'll make oath of it before any justice in Middlesex.

SIR SAMPSON: Here's a cormorant too.—'S'heart, this fellow was not born with you?—I did not beget him, did I?

JEREMY: By the provision that's made for me, you might have begot me too:—nay, and to tell your worship another truth, I believe you did, for I find I was born with those same whoreson appetites too that my master speaks of.

SIR SAMPSON: Why, look you there now—I'll maintain it, that by the rule of right reason, this fellow ought to have been born without a palate.— 'S'heart, what should he do with a distinguishing taste?—I warrant now he'd rather eat a pheasant than a piece of poor John: and smell now—why, I warrant he can smell, and loves perfumes above a stink.—Why, there's it; and music—don't you love music, scoundrel?

JEREMY: Yes, I have a reasonable good ear, sir, as to jigs and country dances, and the like; I don't much matter your solos or sonatas; they give me the spleen.

SIR SAMPSON: The spleen, ha! ha! ha! a pox confound you!—solos or sonatas? 'Oons, whose son are you? how were you engendered, muckworm?

JEREMY: I am by my father the son of a chairman; my mother sold oysters in winter and cucumbers in summer; and I came up-stairs into the world; for I was born in a cellar.

FORESIGHT: By your looks, you should go up-stairs out of the world too, friend.

SIR SAMPSON: And if this rogue were anatomised now, and dissected, he has his vessels of digestion and concoction, and so forth, large enough for the inside of a cardinal, this son of a cucumber!— These things are unaccountable and unreasonable. —Body o'me, why was not I a bear? that my cubs might have lived upon sucking their paws. Nature has been provident only to bears and spiders; the one has its nutriment in his own hands, and t'other spins his habitation out of his own entrails.

VALENTINE: Fortune was provident enough to supply all the necessities of my nature, if I had my right of inheritance.

SIR SAMPSON: Again! 'Oons, han't you four thousand pounds—if I had it again, I would not give thee a groat.—What, wouldst thou have me turn pelican, and feed thee out of my own vitals?—'S'heart, live by your wits,—you were always fond of the wits:—now let's see if you have wit enough to keep yourself.—Your brother will be in town to-night or to-morrow morning, and then look you, perform covenants, and so your friend and servant. —Come, Brother Foresight.

[Exeunt Sir Sampson and Foresight]

JEREMY: I told you what your visit would come to.

VALENTINE: 'Tis as much as I expected.—I did not come to see him: I came to Angelica; but since she was gone abroad it was easily turned another way; and at least looked well on my side.—What's here? Mrs. Foresight and Mrs. Frail; they are earnest.— I'll avoid 'em.—Come this way, and go and inquire when Angelica will return.   [Exeunt]

SCENE 2:   A Room in Foresight's house

Mrs. Foresight and Mrs. Frail.

MRS. FRAIL: What have you to do to watch me! 'slife, I'll do what I please.

MRS. FORESIGHT: You will?

MRS. FRAIL: Yes, marry will I.—A great piece of business to go to Covent-Garden square in a hackney-coach, and take a turn with one's friend!

MRS. FORESIGHT: Nay, two or three turns, I'll take my oath.

MRS. FRAIL: Well, what if I took twenty?—I warrant if you had been there, it had been only innocent recreation.—Lord, where's the comfort of this life, if we can't have the happiness of conversing where we like?

MRS. FORESIGHT: But can't you converse at home?— I own it, I think there is no happiness like conversing with an agreeable man; I don't quarrel at that, nor I don't think but your conversation was very innocent; but the place is public, and to be seen with a man in a hackney-coach is scandalous: what if anybody else should have seen you alight, as I did?—How can anybody be happy, while they're in perpetual fear of being seen and censured?—Besides, it would not only reflect upon you, sister, but me.

MRS. FRAIL: Pooh, here's a clutter!—Why should it reflect upon you?—I don't doubt but you have thought yourself happy in a hackney-coach before now.—If I had gone to Knightsbridge, or to Chelsea, or to Spring Gardens, or Barn Elms, with a man alone—something might have been said.

MRS. FORESIGHT: Why, was I ever in any of those places? what do you mean, sister?

MRS. FRAIL: Was I? what do you mean?

MRS. FORESIGHT: You have been at a worse place.

MRS. FRAIL: I at a worse place, and with a man!

MRS. FORESIGHT: I suppose you would not go alone to the World's-End.

MRS. FRAIL: The world's-end! what, do you mean to banter me?

MRS. FORESIGHT: Poor innocent! you don't know that there's a place called the World's-End? I'll swear you can keep your countenance purely, you'd make an admirable player.

MRS. FRAIL: I'll swear you have a great deal of confidence, and in my mind too much for the stage.

MRS. FORESIGHT: Very well, that will appear who has most; you never were at the World's-End?

MRS. FRAIL: No.

MRS. FORESIGHT: You deny it positively to my face?

MRS. FRAIL: Your face! what's your face?

MRS. FORESIGHT: No matter for that, it's as good a face as yours.

MRS. FRAIL: Not by a dozen years' wearing.—But I do deny it positively to your face then.

MRS. FORESIGHT: I'll allow you now to find fault with my face;—for I'll swear your impudence has put me out of countenance:—but look you here now—where did you lose this gold bodkin?—O sister, sister!

MRS. FRAIL: My bodkin?

MRS. FORESIGHT: Nay, 'tis yours, look at it.

MRS. FRAIL: Well, if you go to that, where did you find this bodkin?—O sister, sister!—sister every way.

MRS. FORESIGHT: [Aside] O devil on't, that I could not discover her without betraying myself!

MRS. FRAIL: I have heard gentlemen say, sister, that one should take great care, when one makes a thrust in fencing, not to lie open one's self.

MRS. FORESIGHT: It's very true, sister; well, since all's out, and as you say, since we are both wounded, let us do what is often done in duels, take care of one another, and grow better friends than before.

MRS. FRAIL: With all my heart: ours are but slight flesh wounds, and if we keep 'em from air, not at all dangerous: well, give me your hand in token of sisterly secrecy and affection.

MRS. FORESIGHT: Here 'tis with all my heart.

MRS. FRAIL: Well, as an earnest of friendship and confidence, I'll acquaint you with a design that I have. To tell truth, and speak openly one to another, I'm afraid the world have observed us more than we have observed one another. You have a rich husband, and are provided for; I am at a loss, and have no great stock either of fortune or reputation; and therefore must look sharply about me. Sir Sampson has a son that is expected to-night; and by the account I have heard of his education, can be no conjuror; the estate you know is to be made over to him:—now if I could wheedle him, sister, ha? you understand me?

MRS. FORESIGHT: I do; and will help you to the utmost of my power.—And I can tell you one thing that falls out luckily enough; my awkward daughter-in-law, who you know is designed to be his wife, is grown fond of Mr. Tattle; now if we can improve that, and make her have an aversion for the booby, it may go a great way towards his liking you. Here they come together; and let us contrive some way or other to leave 'em together.

Enter Tattle *and* Miss Prue.

PRUE: Mother, mother, mother, look you here!

MRS. FORESIGHT: Fy, fy, miss! how you bawl.—Besides, I have told you, you must not call me mother.

PRUE: What must I call you then? are you not my father's wife?

MRS. FORESIGHT: Madam; you must say madam.—By my soul, I shall fancy myself old indeed, to have this great girl call me mother!—Well, but, miss, what are you so overjoyed at?

PRUE: Look you here, madam, then, what Mr. Tattle has given me.—Look you here, cousin, here's a snuff-box; nay, there's snuff in't;—here, will you

have any?—Oh good! how sweet it is.—Mr. Tattle is all over sweet, his peruke is sweet, and his gloves are sweet, and his handkerchief is sweet, pure sweet, sweeter than roses.—Smell him, mother, madam, I mean.—He gave me this ring for a kiss.

TATTLE: O fy, miss! you must not kiss and tell.

PRUE: Yes; I may tell my mother.—And he says he'll give me something to make me smell so.—[To Tattle] Oh pray lend me your handkerchief.—Smell, cousin; he says, he'll give me something that will make my smocks smell this way.—Is not it pure?—It's better than lavender, mun—I'm resolved I won't let nurse put any more lavender among my smocks—ha, cousin?

MRS. FRAIL: Fy, miss! amongst your linen, you must say;—you must never say smock.

PRUE: Why, it is not bawdy, is it, cousin?

TATTLE: Oh, madam, you are too severe upon miss; you must not find fault with her pretty simplicity, it becomes her strangely.—Pretty miss, don't let 'em persuade you out of your innocency.

MRS. FORESIGHT: Oh, demn you, toad!—I wish you don't persuade her out of her innocency.

TATTLE: Who I, madam?—Oh Lord, how can your ladyship have such a thought—sure you don't know me?

MRS. FRAIL: Ah, devil! sly devil!—He's as close, sister, as a confessor.—He thinks we don't observe him.

MRS. FORESIGHT: A cunning cur! how soon he could find out a fresh harmless creature! and left us, sister, presently.

TATTLE: Upon reputation—

MRS. FORESIGHT: They're all so, sister, these men:—they love to have the spoiling of a young thing, they are as fond of it, as of being first in the fashion, or of seeing a new play the first day.—I warrant it would break Mr. Tattle's heart, to think that anybody else should be beforehand with him.

TATTLE: Oh Lord, I swear I would not for the world—

MRS. FRAIL: O hang you! who'll believe you?—You'd be hanged before you'd confess—we know you—she's very pretty!—Lord, what pure red and white!—she looks so wholesome;—ne'er stir, I don't know, but I fancy, if I were a man—

PRUE: How you love to jeer one, cousin!

MRS. FORESIGHT: Hark ye, sister.—By my soul the girl is spoiled already—d'ye think she'll ever endure a great lubberly tarpaulin!—gad, I warrant you, she won't let him come near her, after Mr. Tattle.

MRS. FRAIL: O' my soul, I'm afraid not—eh!—filthy creature, that smells of all pitch and tar.—[To Tattle] Devil take you, you confounded toad!—why did you see her before she was married?

MRS. FORESIGHT: Nay, why did we let him?—My husband will hang us;—he'll think we brought 'em acquainted.

MRS. FRAIL: Come, faith, let us begone.—If my

brother Foresight should find us with them, he'd think so, sure enough.

MRS. FORESIGHT: So he would—but then leaving 'em together is as bad.—And he's such a sly devil, he'll never miss an opportunity.

MRS. FRAIL: I don't care; I won't be seen in't.

MRS. FORESIGHT: Well, if you should, Mr. Tattle, you'll have a world to answer for;—remember I wash my hands of it.—I'm thoroughly innocent.

[Exeunt Mrs. Foresight and Mrs. Frail]

PRUE: What makes 'em go away, Mr. Tattle? what do they mean, do you know?

TATTLE: Yes, my dear,—I think I can guess;—but hang me if I know the reason of it.

PRUE: Come, must not we go too?

TATTLE: No, no, they don't mean that.

PRUE: No! what then? what shall you and I do together?

TATTLE: I must make love to you, pretty miss; will you let me make love to you?

PRUE: Yes, if you please.

TATTLE: [Aside] Frank, egad, at least. What a pox does Mrs. Foresight mean by this civility? Is it to make a fool of me? or does she leave us together out of good morality, and do as she would be done by?—Gad, I'll understand it so.

PRUE: Well; and how will you make love to me? come, I long to have you begin. Must I make love too? you must tell me how.

TATTLE: You must let me speak, miss, you must not speak first; I must ask you questions, and you must answer.

PRUE: What, is it like the catechism?—come then, ask me.

TATTLE: D'ye think you can love me?

PRUE: Yes.

TATTLE: Pooh! pox! you must not say yes already; I shan't care a farthing for you then in a twinkling.

PRUE: What must I say then?

TATTLE: Why, you must say no, or you believe not, or you can't tell.

PRUE: Why, must I tell a lie then?

TATTLE: Yes, if you'd be well-bred;—all well-bred persons lie.—Besides, you are a woman, you must never speak what you think: your words must contradict your thoughts; but your actions may contradict your words. So, when I ask you, if you can love me, you must say no, but you must love me too. If I tell you you are handsome, you must deny it, and say I flatter you. But you must think yourself more charming than I speak you: and like me, for the beauty which I say you have, as much as if I had it myself. If I ask you to kiss me, you must be angry, but you must not refuse me. If I ask you for more, you must be more angry,—but more complying; and as soon as ever I make you say you'll cry out, you must be sure to hold your tongue.

PRUE: O Lord, I swear this is pure!—I like it better

than our old-fashioned country way of speaking one's mind;—and must not you lie too?

TATTLE: Hum!—Yes; but you must believe I speak truth.

PRUE: O Gemini! well, I always had a great mind to tell lies: but they frighted me, and said it was a sin.

TATTLE: Well, my pretty creature; will you make me happy by giving me a kiss?

PRUE: No, indeed; I'm angry at you.

[Runs and kisses him]

TATTLE: Hold, hold, that's pretty well;—but you should not have given it me, but have suffered me to have taken it.

PRUE: Well, we'll do't again.

TATTLE: With all my heart.—Now then, my little angel!   [Kisses her]

PRUE: Pish!

TATTLE: That's right—again, my charmer!

[Kisses her again]

PRUE: O fy! nay, now I can't abide you.

TATTLE: Admirable! that was as well as if you had been born and bred in Covent Garden. And won't you show me, pretty miss, where your bedchamber is?

PRUE: No, indeed, won't I; but I'll run there and hide myself from you behind the curtains.

TATTLE: I'll follow you.

PRUE: Ah, but I'll hold the door with both hands, and be angry;—and you shall push me down before you come in.

TATTLE: No, I'll come in first, and push you down afterwards.

PRUE: Will you? then I'll be more angry, and more complying.

TATTLE: Then I'll make you cry out.

PRUE: Oh, but you shan't; for I'll hold my tongue.

TATTLE: Oh, my dear apt scholar!

PRUE: Well, now I'll run, and make more haste than you.

TATTLE: You shall not fly so fast as I'll pursue.

[Exeunt]

Act III

SCENE 1: *The Gallery adjoining Prue's Bed-chamber*

Enter Nurse.

NURSE: Miss! miss! Miss Prue!—mercy on me, marry and amen!—Why, what's become of the child? why miss? Miss Foresight!—Sure, she has locked herself up in her chamber, and gone to sleep, or to prayers.—Miss! miss! I hear her;—come to your father, child; open the door—open the door, miss! —I hear you cry "Hush!"—O Lord who's there? —[Peeps through the keyhole]—What's here to do? O the father! a man with her!—Why, miss, I say! God's my life, here's fine doings towards!—O

Lord, we're all undone!—O you young harlotry!
—[*Knocks*] Od's my life! won't you open the
door?—I'll come in the back way.   [*Exit*]

SCENE 2: *Prue's Bedchamber*

Tattle *and* Miss Prue.

PRUE: O Lord, she's coming!—and she'll tell my
father; what shall I do now!

TATTLE: Pox take her!—if she had stayed two minutes longer, I should have wished for her coming.

PRUE: Oh dear, what shall I say? tell me Mr. Tattle,
tell me a lie.

TATTLE: There's no occasion for a lie; I could never
tell a lie to no purpose;—but since we have done
nothing, we must say nothing, I think. I hear her;
I'll leave you together, and come off as you can.
[*Thrusts her back, and shuts the door*]

SCENE 3: *A Room in Foresight's House*

Tattle, Valentine, Scandal, *and* Angelica.

ANGELICA: You can't accuse me of inconstancy; I
never told you that I loved you.

VALENTINE: But I can accuse you of uncertainty, for
not telling me whether you did or not.

ANGELICA: You mistake indifference for uncertainty;
I never had concern enough to ask myself the
question.

SCANDAL: Nor good-nature enough to answer him that
did ask you; I'll say that for you, madam.

ANGELICA: What, are you setting up for good-nature?

SCANDAL: Only the affectation of it, as the women
do for ill-nature.

ANGELICA: Persuade your friend that it is all affectation.

SCANDAL: I shall receive no benefit from the opinion;
for I know no effectual difference between continued affectation and reality.

TATTLE: [*Coming up*] Scandal, are you in private
discourse? anything of secrecy?   [*Aside to Scandal*]

SCANDAL: Yes, but I dare trust you! we were talking
of Angelica's love for Valentine; you won't speak
of it?

TATTLE: No, no, not a syllable;—I know that's a
secret, for it's whispered everywhere.

SCANDAL: Ha! ha! ha!

ANGELICA: What is, Mr. Tattle? I heard you say
something was whispered everywhere.

SCANDAL: Your love of Valentine.

ANGELICA: How!

TATTLE: No, madam, his love for your ladyship.—
Gad take me, I beg your pardon;—for I never
heard a word of your ladyship's passion till this
instant.

ANGELICA: My passion! and who told you of my
passion, pray, sir?

SCANDAL: [*Aside to* Tattle] Why, is the devil in you?
did not I tell it you for a secret?

TATTLE: [*Aside to* Scandal] Gad so, but I thought
she might have been trusted with her own affairs.

SCANDAL: Is that your discretion? trust a woman with
her self?

TATTLE: You say true, I beg your pardon;—I'll bring
all off.—[*Aloud*] It was impossible, madam, for me
to imagine, that a person of your ladyship's wit
and gallantry could have so long received the passionate addresses of the accomplished Valentine,
and yet remain insensible; therefore you will pardon me, if, from a just weight of his merit, with
your ladyship's good judgment, I formed the balance of a reciprocal affection.

VALENTINE: O the devil! what damned costive poet
has given thee this lesson of fustian to get by
rote?

ANGELICA: I dare swear you wrong him, it is his own;
and Mr. Tattle only judges of the success of others
from the effects of his own merit. For certainly
Mr. Tattle was never denied anything in his life.

TATTLE: O Lord! yes, indeed, madam, several times.

ANGELICA: I swear I don't think 'tis possible.

TATTLE: Yes, I vow and swear I have: Lord, madam,
I'm the most unfortunate man in the world, and
the most cruelly used by the ladies.

ANGELICA: Nay, now you are ungrateful.

TATTLE: No, I hope not:—'tis as much ingratitude
to own some favours as to conceal others.

VALENTINE: There, now it's out.

ANGELICA: I don't understand you now: I thought
you had never asked anything but what a lady
might modestly grant, and you confess.

SCANDAL: So, faith, your business is done here; now
you may go brag somewhere else.

TATTLE: Brag! O heavens! why, did I name anybody?

ANGELICA: No, I suppose that is not in your power:
but you would if you could, no doubt on't.

TATTLE: Not in my power, madam! what, does your
ladyship mean that I have no woman's reputation
in my power?

SCANDAL: [*Aside to* Tattle] 'Oons, why, you won't
own it, will you?

TATTLE: Faith, madam, you're in the right: no more
I have, as I hope to be saved; I never had it in my
power to say anything to a lady's prejudice in my
life. For, as I was telling you, madam, I have been
the most unsuccessful creature living, in things
of that nature; and never had the good fortune to
be trusted once with a lady's secret, not once.

ANGELICA: No!

VALENTINE: Not once, I dare answer for him.

SCANDAL: And I'll answer for him; for I'm sure if he
had, he would have told me.—I find, madam, you
don't know Mr. Tattle.

TATTLE: No, indeed, madam, you don't know me at
all, I find. For sure my intimate friends would have
known—

ANGELICA: Then it seems you would have told, if you had been trusted.

TATTLE: O pox, Scandal! that was too far put.—Never have told particulars, madam. Perhaps I might have talked as of a third person, or have introduced an amour of my own, in conversation, by way of novel; but never have explained particulars.

ANGELICA: But whence comes the reputation of Mr. Tattle's secrecy, if he was never trusted?

SCANDAL: Why thence it arises: the thing is proverbially spoken; but may be applied to him.—As if we should say in general terms, "He only is secret who never was trusted"; a satirical proverb upon our sex.—There's another upon yours, as "She is chaste who was never asked the question." That's all.

VALENTINE: A couple of very civil proverbs truly: 'tis hard to tell whether the lady or Mr. Tattle be the more obliged to you. For you found her virtue upon the backwardness of the men, and his secrecy upon the mistrust of the women.

TATTLE: Gad, it's very true, madam, I think we are obliged to acquit ourselves; and for my part—but your ladyship is to speak first.

ANGELICA: Am I? well, I freely confess I have resisted a great deal of temptation.

TATTLE: And, egad, I have given some temptation that has not been resisted.

VALENTINE: Good!

ANGELICA: I cite Valentine here, to declare to the court how fruitless he has found his endeavours, and to confess all his solicitations and my denials.

VALENTINE: I am ready to plead not guilty for you, and guilty for myself.

SCANDAL: So, why this is fair, here's demonstration with a witness!

TATTLE: Well, my witnesses are not present. But I confess I have had favours from persons—but as the favours are numberless, so the persons are nameless.

SCANDAL: Pooh, this proves nothing.

TATTLE: No? I can show letters, lockets, pictures, and rings; and if there be occasion for witnesses, I can summon the maids at the chocolate-houses, all the porters at Pall-Mall and Covent-Garden, the door-keepers at the playhouse, the drawers at Locket's, Pontac's, the Rummer, Spring-Garden; my own landlady, and valet-de-chambre; all who shall make oath, that I receive more letters than the Secretary's Office; and that I have more vizor-masks to inquire for me than ever went to see the Hermaphrodite, or the Naked Prince. And it is notorious, that in a country church, once, an inquiry being made who I was, it was answered, I was the famous Tattle, who had ruined so many women.

VALENTINE: It was there, I suppose, you got the nickname of the Great Turk.

TATTLE: True, I was called Turk-Tattle all over the parish.—The next Sunday all the old women kept their daughters at home, and the parson had not half his congregation. He would have brought me into the spiritual court, but I was revenged upon him, for he had a handsome daughter, whom I initiated into the science. But I repented it afterwards, for it was talked of in town; and a lady of quality, that shall be nameless, in a raging fit of jealousy, came down in her coach and six horses, and exposed herself upon my account; gad, I was sorry for it with all my heart.—You know whom I mean—you know where we raffled—

SCANDAL: Mum, Tattle.

VALENTINE: 'Sdeath, are not you ashamed?

ANGELICA: O barbarous! I never heard so insolent a piece of vanity.—Fy, Mr. Tattle!—I'll swear I could not have believed it.—Is this your secrecy?

TATTLE: Gad so, the heat of my story carried me beyond my discretion, as the heat of the lady's passion hurried her beyond her reputation.—But I hope you don't know whom I mean; for there were a great many ladies raffled.—Pox on't! now could I bite off my tongue.

SCANDAL: No, don't; for then you'll tell us no more.—Come, I'll recommend a song to you upon the hint of my two proverbs, and I see one in the next room that will sing it.   [Exit]

TATTLE: For Heaven's sake if you do guess, say nothing; gad, I'm very unfortunate.

Re-enter Scandal *with one to sing.*

SCANDAL: Pray sing the first song in the last new play.

SONG

A nymph and a swain to Apollo once prayed,
The swain had been jilted, the nymph been betrayed:
Their intent was to try if his oracle knew
E'er a nymph that was chaste, or a swain that was true.

Apollo was mute, and had like t'have been posed,
But sagely at length he this secret disclosed:
"He alone won't betray in whom none will confide:
And the nymph may be chaste that has never been tried."   [Exit Singer]

Enter Sir Sampson, Mrs. Frail, Miss Prue, *and* Servant.

SIR SAMPSON: Is Ben come? odso, my son Ben come? odd I'm glad on't: where is he? I long to see him.—Now, Mrs. Frail, you shall see my son Ben.—Body o'me, he's the hopes of my family.—I han't seen him these three years.—I warrant he's grown.—Call him in, bid him make haste.—[*Exit* Servant] I'm ready to cry for joy.

MRS. FRAIL: Now, Miss, you shall see your husband.

PRUE: [*Aside to* Mrs. Frail] Pish, he shall be none of my husband.

MRS. FRAIL: [*Aside to* Prue] Hush: well he shan't, leave that to me.—I'll beckon Mr. Tattle to us.

ANGELICA: Won't you stay and see your brother?

VALENTINE: We are the twin-stars, and cannot shine in one sphere; when he rises I must set.—Besides, if I should stay, I don't know but my father in good-nature may press me to the immediate signing the deed of conveyance of my estate; and I'll defer it as long as I can.—Well, you'll come to a resolution?

ANGELICA: I can't. Resolution must come to me, or I shall never have one.

SCANDAL: Come, Valentine, I'll go with you; I've something in my head to communicate to you.

[*Exeunt* Valentine *and* Scandal]

SIR SAMPSON: What, is my son Valentine gone? what, is he sneaked off, and would not see his brother? There's an unnatural whelp! there's an ill-natured dog!—What, were you here too, madam, and could not keep him? could neither love, nor duty, nor natural affection, oblige him? Odsbud, madam, have no more to say to him; he is not worth your consideration. The rogue has not a drachm of generous love about him: all interest, all interest; he's an undone scoundrel, and courts your estate: body o' me, he does not care a doit for your person.

ANGELICA: I'm pretty even with him, Sir Sampson; for if ever I could have liked anything in him, it should have been his estate, too: but since that's gone, the bait's off, and the naked hook appears.

SIR SAMPSON: Odsbud, well spoken; and you are a wiser woman than I thought you were: for most young women now-a-days are to be tempted with a naked hook.

ANGELICA: If I marry, Sir Sampson, I'm for a good estate with any man, and for any man with a good estate: therefore if I were obliged to make a choice, I declare I'd rather have you than your son.

SIR SAMPSON: Faith and troth, you're a wise woman, and I'm glad to hear you say so; I was afraid you were in love with the reprobate; odd, I was sorry for you with all my heart: hang him, mongrel; cast him off; you shall see the rogue show himself, and make love to some desponding Cadua of fourscore for sustenance. Odd, I love to see a young spendthrift forced to cling to an old woman for support, like ivy round a dead oak: faith I do; I love to see 'em hug and cotton together, like down upon a thistle.

Enter Ben *and* Servant.

BEN: Where's father?

SERVANT: There, sir, his back's toward you.

SIR SAMPSON: My son Ben! bless thee, my dear boy; body o' me, thou art heartily welcome.

BEN: Thank you, father, and I'm glad to see you.

SIR SAMPSON: Odsbud, and I am glad to see thee; kiss me, boy, kiss me again and again, dear Ben. [*Kisses him*]

BEN: So, so, enough, father.—Mess,[1] I'd rather kiss these gentlewomen.

SIR SAMPSON: And so thou shalt.—Mrs. Angelica, my son Ben.

BEN: Forsooth, if you please.—[*Salutes her*] Nay, mistress, I'm not for dropping anchor here; about ship i'faith.—[*Kisses* Mrs. Frail] Nay, and you, too, my little cock-boat—so. [*Kisses* Miss Prue]

TATTLE: Sir, you're welcome ashore.

BEN: Thank you, thank you, friend.

SIR SAMPSON: Thou hast been many a weary league, Ben, since I saw thee.

BEN: Ey, ey, been! been far enough, an that be all.
—Well, father, and how do all at home? how does brother Dick, and brother Val?

SIR SAMPSON: Dick! body o' me, Dick has been dead these two years! I writ you word when you were at Leghorn.

BEN: Mess, that's true; marry, I had forgot. Dick's dead, as you say.—Well, and how? I have many questions to ask you. Well, you ben't married again, father, be you?

SIR SAMPSON: No, I intend you shall marry, Ben; I would not marry for thy sake.

BEN: Nay, what does that signify?—An you marry again—why, then, I'll go to sea again, so there's one for t'other, an that be all.—Pray don't let me be your hindrance; e'en marry a' God's name, an the wind sit that way. As for my part, mayhap I have no mind to marry.

MRS. FRAIL: That would be a pity, such a handsome young gentleman.

BEN: Handsome! he! he! he! nay, forsooth, an you be for joking, I'll joke with you; for I love my jest, an the ship were sinking, as we say'n at sea. But I'll tell you why I don't much stand toward matrimony. I love to roam about from port to port, and from land to land: I could never abide to be portbound, as we call it; now, a man that is married has, as it were, d'ye see, his feet in the bilboes, and mayhap mayn't get 'em out again when he would.

SIR SAMPSON: Ben's a wag.

BEN: A man that is married, d'ye see, is no more like another man than a galley-slave is like one of us free sailors; he is chained to an oar all his life; and mayhap forced to tug a leaky vessel into the bargain.

SIR SAMPSON: A very wag! Ben's a very wag! only a little rough, he wants a little polishing.

MRS. FRAIL: Not at all; I like his humour mightily, it's plain and honest; I should like such a humour in a husband extremely.

BEN: Say'n you so, forsooth? Marry, and I should like such a handsome gentlewoman for a bedfellow

A survival of the old oath, By the mass!

hugely; how say you, mistress, would you like going to sea? Mess, you're a tight vessel! and well rigged, an you were but as well manned.

MRS. FRAIL: I should not doubt that, if you were master of me.

BEN: But I'll tell you one thing, an you come to sea in a high wind, or that lady—you mayn't carry so much sail o' your head.—Top and top-gallant, by the mess.

MRS. FRAIL: No, why so?

BEN: Why, an you do, you may run the risk to be overset, and then you'll carry your keels above water, he! he! he!

ANGELICA: I swear, Mr. Benjamin is the veriest wag in nature; an absolute sea-wit.

SIR SAMPSON: Nay, Ben has parts, but, as I told you before, they want a little polishing: you must not take anything ill, madam.

BEN: No, I hope the gentlewoman is not angry; I mean all in good part; for if I give a jest I'll take a jest: and so, forsooth, you may be as free with me.

ANGELICA: I thank you, sir, I am not at all offended. —But methinks, Sir Sampson, you should leave him alone with his mistress.—Mr. Tattle, we must not hinder lovers.

TATTLE: [Aside to Miss Prue] Well, miss, I have your promise.

SIR SAMPSON: Body o' me, madam, you say true.— Look you, Ben, this is your mistress.—Come, miss, you must not be shamefaced; we'll leave you together.

PRUE: I can't abide to be left alone, mayn't my cousin stay with me?

SIR SAMPSON: No, no.—Come, let's away.

BEN: Look you, father, mayhap the young woman mayn't take a liking to me.

SIR SAMPSON: I warrant thee, boy; come, come, we'll be gone; I'll venture that.

[Exeunt Sir Sampson, Angelica, Tattle, and Mrs. Frail]

BEN: Come, mistress, will you please to sit down? for an you stand astern a that'n, we shall never grapple together.—Come, I'll haul a chair; there, an you please to sit I'll sit by you.

PRUE: You need not sit so near one; if you have anything to say I can hear you farther off, I an't deaf.

BEN: Why, that's true, as you say; nor I an't dumb; I can be heard as far as another;—I'll heave off to please you.—[Sits farther off] An we were a league asunder, I'd undertake to hold discourse with you, an 'twere not a main high wind indeed, and full in my teeth. Look you, forsooth, I am, as it were, bound for the land of matrimony; 'tis a voyage, d'ye see, that was none of my seeking, I was commanded by father, and if you like of it mayhap I may steer into your harbour. How say you, mistress? The short of the thing is, that if you like

me, and I like you, we may chance to swing in a hammock together.

PRUE: I don't know what to say to you, nor I don't care to speak with you at all.

BEN: No? I'm sorry for that.—But pray, why are you so scornful?

PRUE: As long as one must not speak one's mind, one had better not speak at all, I think, and truly I won't tell a lie for the matter.

BEN: Nay, you say true in that, 'tis but a folly to lie: for to speak one thing, and to think just the contrary way, is, as it were, to look one way and row another. Now, for my part, d'ye see, I'm for carrying things above board, I'm not for keeping anything under hatches,—so that if you ben't as willing as I, say so a' God's name, there's no harm done. Mayhap you may be shamefaced? some maidens, tho'f they love a man well enough, yet they don't care to tell'n so to's face: if that's the case, why silence gives consent.

PRUE: But I'm sure it is not so, for I'll speak sooner than you should believe that; and I'll speak truth, though one should always tell a lie to a man; and I don't care, let my father do what he will; I'm too big to be whipped so I'll tell you plainly I don't like you, nor love you at all, nor never will, that's more: so, there's your answer for you; and don't trouble me no more, you ugly thing!

BEN: Look you, young woman, you may learn to give good words however. I spoke you fair, d'ye see, and civil.—As for your love or your liking, I don't value it of a rope's end;—and mayhap I like you as little as you do me.—What I said was in obedience to father; gad, I fear a whipping no more than you do. But I tell you one thing, if you should give such language at sea you'd have a cat o' nine-tails laid across your shoulders. Flesh! who are you? You heard t'other handsome young woman speak civilly to me, of her own accord: whatever you think of yourself, gad, I don't think you are any more to compare to her than a can of small beer to a bowl of punch.

PRUE: Well, and there's a handsome gentleman, and a fine gentleman, and a sweet gentleman, that was here, that loves me, and I love him; and if he sees you speak to me any more he'll thrash your jacket for you, he will, you great sea-calf!

BEN: What, do you mean that fair-weather spark that was here just now? will he thrash my jacket?— let'n—let'n. But an he comes near me, mayhap I may giv'n a salt eel for's supper, for all that. What does father mean to leave me alone as soon as I come home, with such a dirty dowdy? Sea-calf! I an't calf enough to lick your chalked face, you cheese-curd you!—Marry thee! 'oons, I'll marry a Lapland witch as soon, and live upon selling contrary winds and wrecked vessels.

PRUE: I won't be called names, nor I won't be abused thus, so I won't.—If I were a man [Cries], you durst not talk at this rate;—no, you durst not, you stinking tar-barrel!

Enter Mrs. Foresight *and* Mrs. Frail

MRS. FORESIGHT: [*Aside to* Mrs. Frail] They have quarrelled just as we could wish.

BEN: Tar-barrel? let your sweetheart there call me so if he'll take your part, your Tom Essence, and I'll say something to him; gad, I'll lace his musk doublet for him! I'll make him stink! he shall smell more like a weasel than a civet cat afore I ha' done with 'en.

MRS. FORESIGHT: Bless me, what's the matter, miss? What, does she cry?—Mr. Benjamin, what have you done to her?

BEN: Let her cry: the more she cries, the less she'll —she has been gathering foul weather in her mouth, and now it rains out at her eyes.

MRS. FORESIGHT: Come, miss, come along with me, and tell me, poor child.

MRS. FRAIL: Lord, what shall we do? there's my brother Foresight and Sir Sampson coming.— Sister, do you take miss down into the parlour, and I'll carry Mr. Benjamin into my chamber, for they must not know that they are fallen out.— Come, sir, will you venture yourself with me?
[*Looking kindly on him*]

BEN: Venture, mess, and that I will, though 'twere to sea in a storm.   [*Exeunt*]

SCENE 4: *The same*

Enter Sir Sampson *and* Foresight.

SIR SAMPSON: I left 'em together here; what, are they gone? Ben's a brisk boy; he has got her into a corner; father's own son, faith, he'll touzle her, and mouzle her; the rogue's sharp set, coming from sea; if he should not stay for saying grace, old Foresight, but fall to without the help of a parson, ha? Odd, if he should, I could not be angry with him; 'twould be but like me, *a chip of the old block*. Ha! thou'rt melancholic, old prognostication; as melancholic as if thou hadst spilt the salt, or pared thy nails on a Sunday.—Come, cheer up, look about thee: look up, old star-gazer.—[*Aside*] Now is he poring upon the ground for a crooked pin, or an old horse-nail, with the head towards him.

FORESIGHT: Sir Sampson, we'll have the wedding to-morrow morning.

SIR SAMPSON: With all my heart.

FORESIGHT: At ten o'clock, punctually at ten.

SIR SAMPSON: To a minute, to a second; thou shalt set thy watch, and the bridegroom shall observe its motions; they shall be married to a minute; go to bed to a minute; and when the alarm strikes, they shall keep time like the figures of St. Dunstan's

clock, and *consummatum est* shall ring all over the parish.

Enter Scandal.

SCANDAL: Sir Sampson, sad news!

FORESIGHT: Bless us!

SIR SAMPSON: Why, what's the matter?

SCANDAL: Can't you guess at what ought to afflict you and him, and all of us more than anything else?

SIR SAMPSON: Body o' me, I don't know any universal grievance but a new tax, or the loss of the Canary fleet. Unless popery should be landed in the west, or the French fleet were at anchor at Black-wall.

SCANDAL: No! undoubtedly Mr. Foresight knew all this, and might have prevented it.

FORESIGHT: 'Tis no earthquake!

SCANDAL: No, not yet; nor whirlwind. But we don't know what it may come to.—But it has had a consequence already that touches us all.

SIR SAMPSON: Why, body o' me, out with't.

SCANDAL: Something has appeared to your son Valentine.—He's gone to bed upon't, and very ill.— He speaks little, yet says he has a world to say. Asks for his father and the wise Foresight; talks of Raymond Lully, and the ghost of Lilly. He has secrets to impart I suppose to you two. I can get nothing out of him but sighs. He desires he may see you in the morning, but would not be disturbed to-night, because he has some business to do in a dream.

SIR SAMPSON: Hoity, toity, what have I to do with his dreams or his divinations?—Body o' me, this is a trick to defer signing the conveyance. I warrant the devil will tell him in a dream, that he must not part with his estate; but I'll bring him a parson, to tell him that the devil's a liar; or, if that won't do, I'll bring a lawyer that shall outlie the devil. And so I'll try whether my blackguard or his shall get the better of the day.   [*Exit*]

SCANDAL: Alas, Mr. Foresight! I'm afraid all is not right.—You are a wise man, and a conscientious man; a searcher into obscurity and futurity; and if you commit an error, it is with a great deal of consideration and discretion and caution.

FORESIGHT: Ah, good Mr. Scandal—

SCANDAL: Nay, nay, 'tis manifest; I do not flatter you. —But Sir Sampson is hasty, very hasty;—I'm afraid he is not scrupulous enough, Mr. Foresight. —He has been wicked, and Heaven grant he may mean well in his affair with you.—But my mind gives me, these things cannot be wholly insignificant. You are wise, and should not be over-reached, methinks you should not.

FORESIGHT: Alas, Mr. Scandal!—*Humanum est errare.*

SCANDAL: You say true, man will err; mere man will err—but you are something more.—There have been wise men; but they were such as you;—men who consulted the stars, and were observers of omens.—Solomon was wise, but how?—by his judgment in astrology:—so says Pineda in his third book and eighth chapter.

FORESIGHT: You are learned, Mr. Scandal!

SCANDAL: A trifler—but a lover of art.—And the wise men of the East owed their instruction to a star, which is rightly observed by Gregory the Great in favour of astrology! And Albertus Magnus makes it the most valuable science: because (says he) it teaches us to consider the causation of causes, in the causes of things.

FORESIGHT: I protest I honour you, Mr. Scandal:—I did not think you had been read in these matters. —Few young men are inclined—

SCANDAL: I thank my stars that have inclined me.— But I fear this marriage, and making over this estate, this transferring of a rightful inheritance, will bring judgments upon us. I prophesy it, and I would not have the fate of Cassandra, not to be believed. Valentine is disturbed, what can be the cause of that? and Sir Sampson is hurried on by an unusual violence.—I fear he does not act wholly from himself; methinks he does not look as he used to do.

FORESIGHT: He was always of an impetuous nature. —But as to this marriage, I have consulted the stars, and all appearances are prosperous.

SCANDAL: Come, come, Mr. Foresight, let not the prospect of worldly lucre carry you beyond your judgment, nor against your conscience:—you are not satisfied that you act justly.

FORESIGHT: How?

SCANDAL: You are not satisfied, I say.—I am loath to discourage you—but it is palpable that you are not satisfied.

FORESIGHT: How does it appear, Mr. Scandal? I think I am very well satisfied.

SCANDAL: Either you suffer yourself to deceive yourself; or you do not know yourself.

FORESIGHT: Pray explain yourself.

SCANDAL: Do you sleep well o' nights?

FORESIGHT: Very well.

SCANDAL: Are you certain? you do not look so.

FORESIGHT: I am in health, I think.

SCANDAL: So was Valentine this morning; and looked just so.

FORESIGHT: How! am I altered any way? I don't perceive it.

SCANDAL: That may be, but your beard is longer than it was two hours ago.

FORESIGHT: Indeed! bless me!

Enter Mrs. Foresight.

MRS. FORESIGHT: Husband, will you go to bed? it's ten o'clock.—Mr. Scandal, your servant.

SCANDAL: [*Aside*] Pox on her! she has interrupted my design:—but I must work her into the project.— [*Aloud*] You keep early hours, madam.

MRS. FORESIGHT: Mr. Foresight is punctual, we sit up after him.

FORESIGHT: My dear, pray lend me your glass, your little looking-glass.

SCANDAL: Pray, lend it him, madam—I'll tell you the reason.—[*She gives him the glass:* Scandal *and she talk aside*] My passion for you is grown so violent, that I am no longer master of myself.— I was interrupted in the morning, when you had charity enough to give me your attention, and I had hopes of finding another opportunity of explaining myself to you;—but was disappointed all this day; and the uneasiness that has attended me ever since, brings me now hither at this unseasonable hour.

MRS. FORESIGHT: Was there ever such impudence! to make love to me before my husband's face! I'll swear I'll tell him.

SCANDAL: Do; I'll die a martyr, rather than disclaim my passion. But come a little farther this way, and I'll tell you what project I had to get him out of the way, that I might have an opportunity of waiting upon you.

FORESIGHT: [*Looking in the glass*] I do not see any revolution here;—methinks I look with a serene and benign aspect—pale, a little pale—but the roses of these cheeks have been gathered many years.—Ha! I do not like that sudden flushing;— gone already!—hem, hem, hem! faintish. My heart is pretty good; yet it beats; and my pulses, ha!—I have none—mercy on me!—hum—yes, here they are—gallop, gallop, gallop, gallop, gallop, gallop, hey! whither will they hurry me?—Now they're gone again—and now I'm faint again; and pale again, and, hem; and my, hem!—breath, hem!— grows short; hem! hem! he, he, hem!

SCANDAL: [*Aside to* Mrs. Foresight] It takes; pursue it, in the name of love and pleasure!

MRS. FORESIGHT: How do you do, Mr. Foresight?

FORESIGHT: Hum, not so well as I thought I was. Lend me your hand.

SCANDAL: Look you there now—your lady says your sleep has been unquiet of late.

FORESIGHT: Very likely.

MRS. FORESIGHT: O mighty restless; but I was afraid to tell him so.—He has been subject to talking and starting.

SCANDAL: And did not use to be so?

MRS. FORESIGHT: Never, never, till within these three nights; I cannot say that he has once broken my rest since we have been married.

FORESIGHT: I will go to bed.

SCANDAL: Do so, Mr. Foresight, and say your prayers. —He looks better than he did.

MRS. FORESIGHT: Nurse, nurse!   [*Calls*]

FORESIGHT: Do you think so, Mr. Scandal?

SCANDAL: Yes, yes; I hope this will be gone by morning, taking it in time.

FORESIGHT: I hope so.

Enter Nurse.

MRS. FORESIGHT: Nurse, your master is not well; put him to bed.

SCANDAL: I hope you will be able to see Valentine in the morning. You had best take a little diacodian and cowslip water, and lie upon your back, may be you may dream.

FORESIGHT: I thank you, Mr. Scandal, I will.—Nurse, let me have a watch-light, and lay *The Crumbs of Comfort* by me.

NURSE: Yes, sir.

FORESIGHT: And—hem, hem! I am very faint.

SCANDAL: No, no; you look much better.

FORESIGHT: Do I?—[*To Nurse*] And, d'ye hear, bring me, let me see—within a quarter of twelve—hem —he, hem!—just upon the turning of the tide, bring me the urinal. And I hope neither the lord of my ascendant, nor the moon, will be combust; and then I may do well.

SCANDAL: I hope so. Leave that to me; I will erect a scheme; and I hope I shall find both Sol and Venus in the sixth house.

FORESIGHT: I thank you, Mr. Scandal; indeed that would be a great comfort to me. Hem, hem; good night.   [*Exit with* Nurse]

SCANDAL: Good night, good Mr. Foresight; and I hope Mars and Venus will be in conjunction, while your wife and I are together.

MRS. FORESIGHT: Well, and what use do you hope to make of this project? you don't think that you are ever like to succeed in your design upon me?

SCANDAL: Yes, faith, I do; I have a better opinion both of you and myself than to despair.

MRS. FORESIGHT: Did you ever hear such a toad? Hark ye, devil! do you think any woman honest?

SCANDAL: Yes, several very honest; they'll cheat little at cards, sometimes; but that's nothing.

MRS. FORESIGHT: Pshaw! but virtuous, I mean.

SCANDAL: Yes, faith; I believe some women are virtuous too; but 'tis as I believe some men are valiant, through fear. For why should a man court danger, or a woman shun pleasure?

MRS. FORESIGHT: O monstrous! what are conscience and honour?

SCANDAL: Why, honour is a public enemy; and conscience a domestic thief; and he that would secure his pleasure, must pay a tribute to one, and go halves with t'other. As for honour, that you have secured; for you have purchased a perpetual opportunity for pleasure.

MRS. FORESIGHT: An opportunity for pleasure?

SCANDAL: Ay, your husband; a husband is an opportunity for pleasure; so you have taken care of honour, and 'tis the least I can do to take care of conscience.

MRS. FORESIGHT: And so you think we are free for one another.

SCANDAL: Yes, faith, I think so; I love to speak my mind.

MRS. FORESIGHT: Why, then I'll speak my mind. Now, as to this affair between you and me. Here you make love to me; why, I'll confess, it does not displease me. Your person is well enough, and your understanding is not amiss.

SCANDAL: I have no great opinion of myself; but I think I'm neither deformed nor a fool.

MRS. FORESIGHT: But you have a villainous character; you are a libertine in speech as well as practice.

SCANDAL: Come, I know what you would say; you think it more dangerous to be seen in conversation with me, than to allow some other men the last favour. You mistake; the liberty I take in talking is purely affected, for the service of your sex. He that first cries out, *Stop thief!* is often he that has stolen the treasure. I am a juggler, that act by confederacy; and, if you please, we'll put a trick upon the world.

MRS. FORESIGHT: Ay; but you are such a universal juggler, that I'm afraid you have a great many confederates.

SCANDAL: Faith, I'm sound.

MRS. FORESIGHT: O, fy!—I'll swear you're impudent.

SCANDAL: I'll swear you're handsome.

MRS. FORESIGHT: Pish! you'd tell me so, though you did not think so.

SCANDAL: And you'd think so, though I should not tell you so. And now I think we know one another pretty well.

MRS. FORESIGHT: O Lord, who's here?

Enter Mrs. Frail *and* Ben.

BEN: Mess, I love to speak my mind; father has nothing to do with me. Nay, I can't say that neither; he has something to do with me. But what does that signify? if so be, that I be'n't minded to be steered by him, 'tis as tho'f he should strive against wind and tide.

MRS. FRAIL: Ay, but, my dear, we must keep it secret till the estate be settled; for you know marrying without an estate is like sailing in a ship without ballast.

BEN: He! he! he! why, that's true; just so for all the world it is indeed, as like as two cable-ropes.

MRS. FRAIL: And though I have a good portion, you know one would not venture all in one bottom.

BEN: Why, that's true again; for mayhap one bottom may spring a leak. You have hit it indeed, mess, you've nicked the channel.

MRS. FRAIL: Well, but if you should forsake me after all, you'd break my heart.

BEN: Break your heart! I'd rather the Marygold should break her cable in a storm, as well as I love her. Flesh, you don't think I'm false-hearted like a landman! A sailor will be honest, tho'f mayhap he has never a penny of money in his pocket.— Mayhap I may not have so fair a face as a good citizen or a courtier; but for all that, I've as good blood in my veins, and a heart as sound as a biscuit.

MRS. FRAIL: And will you love me always?

BEN: Nay, an I love once, I'll stick like pitch; I'll tell you that. Come, I'll sing you a song for a sailor.

MRS. FRAIL: Hold, there's my sister; I'll call her to hear it.

MRS. FORESIGHT: Well, I won't go to bed to my husband to-night; because I'll retire to my own chamber, and think of what you have said.

SCANDAL: Well; you'll give me leave to wait upon you to your chamber door, and leave you my last instructions?

MRS. FORESIGHT: Hold, here's my sister coming towards us.

MRS. FRAIL: If it won't interrupt you, I'll entertain you with a song.

BEN: The song was made upon one of our ship's crew's wife; our boatswain made the song; mayhap you may know her, sir. Before she was married, she was called buxom Joan of Deptford.

SCANDAL: I have heard of her.   [Ben sings]

A soldier and a sailor,
A tinker and a tailor,
Had once a doubtful strife, sir,
To make a maid a wife, sir,
    Whose name was buxom Joan.
For now the time was ended,
When she no more intended
To lick her lips at men, sir,
And gnaw the sheets in vain, sir,
    And lie o' nights alone.

The soldier swore like thunder,
He loved her more than plunder;
And showed her many a scar, sir,
That he had brought from far, sir,
    With fighting for her sake.
The tailor thought to please her,
With offering her his measure.
The tinker too with mettle,
Said he could mend her kettle,
    And stop up every leak.

But while these three were prating,
The sailor slily waiting,
Thought if it came about, sir,
That they should all fall out, sir,
    He then might play his part.
And just e'en as he meant, sir,
To loggerheads they went, sir,
And then he let fly at her
A shot 'twixt wind and water,
    That won this fair maid's heart.

If some of our crew that came to see me are not gone, you shall see that we sailors can dance some-times as well as other folks.—[Whistles] I warrant that brings 'em, an they be within hearing.

Enter Sailors.

Oh, here they be!—and fiddles along with 'em. Come, my lads, let's have a round, and I'll make one.   [They dance]

BEN: We're merry folks, we sailors, we han't much to care for. Thus we live at sea; eat biscuit, and drink flip; put on a clean shirt once a quarter—come home and lie with our landladies once a year, get rid of a little money; and then put off with the next fair wind. How d'ye like us?

MRS. FRAIL: O you are the happiest, merriest men alive!

MRS. FORESIGHT: We're beholden to Mr. Benjamin for this entertainment.—I believe it's late.

BEN: Why, forsooth, an you think so, you had best go to bed. For my part, I mean to toss a can, and remember my sweetheart, afore I turn in; mayhap I may dream of her.

MRS. FORESIGHT: Mr. Scandal, you had best go to bed and dream too.

SCANDAL: Why faith, I have a good lively imagina-tion; and can dream as much to the purpose as another, if I set about it; but dreaming is the poor retreat of a lazy, hopeless, and imperfect lover; 'tis the last glimpse of love to worn-out sinners, and the faint dawning of a bliss to wishing girls and growing boys.
There's nought but willing, waking love that can
Make blest the ripened maid and finished man.
                                          [Exeunt]

Act IV

SCENE 1: An Ante-room at Valentine's Lodging

Scandal and Jeremy.

SCANDAL: Well, is your master ready? does he look madly, and talk madly?

JEREMY: Yes, sir; you need make no great doubt of that; he that was so near turning poet yesterday morning, can't be much to seek in playing the madman to-day.

SCANDAL: Would he have Angelica acquainted with the reason of his design?

JEREMY: No, sir, not yet;—he has a mind to try, whether his playing the madman won't make her play the fool, and fall in love with him; or at least own that she has loved him all this while and concealed it.

SCANDAL: I saw her take coach just now with her maid; and think I heard her bid the coachman drive hither.

JEREMY: Like enough, sir, for I told her maid this morning my master was run stark mad only for love of her mistress. I hear a coach stop; if it should be she, sir, I believe he would not see her, till he hears how she takes it.

SCANDAL: Well, I'll try her:—'tis she, here she comes.

Enter Angelica *and* Jenny.

ANGELICA: Mr. Scandal, I suppose you don't think it a novelty to see a woman visit a man at his own lodgings in a morning?

SCANDAL: Not upon a kind occasion, madam. But when a lady comes tyrannically to insult a ruined lover, and make manifest the cruel triumphs of her beauty, the barbarity of it something surprises me.

ANGELICA: I don't like raillery from a serious face.— Pray tell me what is the matter?

JEREMY: No strange matter, madam; my master's mad, that's all: I suppose your ladyship has thought him so a great while.

ANGELICA: How d'ye mean, mad?

JEREMY: Why, faith, madam, he's mad for want of his wits, just as he was poor for want of money; his head is e'en as light as his pockets; and anybody that has a mind to a bad bargain, can't do better than to beg him for his estate.

ANGELICA: If you speak truth, your endeavouring at wit is very unseasonable.

SCANDAL: [*Aside*] She's concerned, and loves him.

ANGELICA: Mr. Scandal, you cannot think me guilty of so much inhumanity, as not to be concerned for a man I must own myself obliged to; pray tell me the truth.

SCANDAL: Faith, madam, I wish telling a lie would mend the matter. But this is no new effect of an unsuccessful passion.

ANGELICA: [*Aside*] I know not what to think.—Yet I should be vexed to have a trick put upon me.— [*Aloud*] May I not see him?

SCANDAL: I'm afraid the physician is not willing you should see him yet.—Jeremy, go in and inquire.

[*Exit* Jeremy]

ANGELICA: [*Aside*] Ha! I saw him wink and smile—I fancy 'tis a trick—I'll try.—[*Aloud*] I would disguise to all the world a failing which I must own to you.—I fear my happiness depends upon the recovery of Valentine. Therefore I conjure you, as you are his friend, and as you have compassion upon one fearful of affliction, to tell me what I am to hope for.—I cannot speak—but you may tell me, for you know what I would ask.

SCANDAL: [*Aside*] So, this is pretty plain.—[*Aloud*] Be not too much concerned, madam, I hope his condition is not desperate: an acknowledgment of love from you, perhaps, may work a cure; as the fear of your aversion occasioned his distemper.

ANGELICA: [*Aside*] Say you so? nay, then I'm convinced; and if I don't play trick for trick, may I never taste the pleasure of revenge!—[*Aloud*] Acknowledgment of love! I find you have mistaken my compassion, and think me guilty of a weakness I'm a stranger to. But I have too much sincerity to deceive you, and too much charity to suffer him to be deluded with vain hopes. Good-nature and humanity oblige me to be concerned for him; but

to love is neither in my power nor inclination; and if he can't be cured without I suck the poison from his wounds, I'm afraid he won't recover his senses till I lose mine.

SCANDAL: [*Aside*] Hey, brave woman, i'faith!— [*Aloud*] Won't you see him then, if he desire it?

ANGELICA: What signify a madman's desires? besides, 'twould make me uneasy. If I don't see him, perhaps my concern for him may lessen. If I forget him, 'tis no more than he has done by himself; and now the surprise is over, methinks I am not half so sorry as I was.

SCANDAL: So, faith, good nature works apace; you were confessing just now an obligation to his love.

ANGELICA: But I have considered that passions are unreasonable and involuntary; if he loves, he can't help it; and if I don't love, I can't help it; no more than he can help his being a man, or I my being a woman; or no more than I can help my want of inclination to stay longer here.—Come, Jenny. [*Exeunt* Angelica *and* Jenny]

SCANDAL: Humph!—An admirable composition, faith, this same womankind!

Re-enter Jeremy.

JEREMY: What, is she gone, sir?

SCANDAL: Gone? why she was never here; nor anywhere else; nor I don't know her if I see her; nor you neither.

JEREMY: Good lack! what's the matter now? are any more of us to be mad? Why, sir, my master longs to see her; and is almost mad in good earnest with the joyful news of her being here.

SCANDAL: We are all under a mistake. Ask no questions, for I can't resolve you; but I'll inform your master. In the mean time, if our project succeed no better with his father than it does with his mistress, he may descend from his exaltation of madness into the road of common sense, and be content only to be made a fool with other reasonable people.—I hear Sir Sampson. You know your cue; I'll to your master. [*Exit*]

Enter Sir Sampson *and* Buckram.

SIR SAMPSON: D'ye see, Mr. Buckram, here's the paper signed with his own hand.

BUCKRAM: Good, sir. And the conveyance is ready drawn in this box, if he be ready to sign and seal.

SIR SAMPSON: Ready, body o' me, he must be ready! his sham-sickness shan't excuse him.—O, here's his scoundrel.—Sirrah, where's your master?

JEREMY: Ah, sir, he's quite gone.

SIR SAMPSON: Gone! what, he is not dead?

JEREMY: No, sir, not dead.

SIR SAMPSON: What, is he gone out of town? run away, ha! he has tricked me? speak, varlet.

JEREMY: No, no, sir, he's safe enough, sir, an he were but as sound, poor gentleman. He is, indeed, here, sir, and not here, sir.

SIR SAMPSON: Heyday, rascal, do you banter me? sirrah, d'ye banter me?—Speak, sirrah, where is he? for I will find him.

JEREMY: Would you could, sir! for he has lost himself. Indeed, sir, I have almost broke my heart about him—I can't refrain tears when I think of him, sir: I'm as melancholy for him as a passing-bell, sir; or a horse in a pound.

SIR SAMPSON: A pox confound your similitudes, sir!—Speak to be understood, and tell me in plain terms what the matter is with him, or I'll crack your fool's skull.

JEREMY: Ah, you've hit it, sir! that's the matter with him, sir; his skull's cracked, poor gentleman! he's stark mad, sir.

SIR SAMPSON: Mad!

BUCKRAM: What, is he *non compos*?

JEREMY: Quite *non compos*, sir.

BUCKRAM: Why, then all's obliterated, Sir Sampson; if he be *non compos mentis*, his act and deed will be of no effect, it is not good in law.

SIR SAMPSON: 'Oons, I won't believe it! let me see him, sir.—Mad! I'll make him find his senses.

JEREMY: Mr. Scandal is with him, sir; I'll knock at the door.   [*Goes to the Scene, which opens*]

SCENE 2:   *Another Room at Valentine's Lodgings*

Sir Sampson, Valentine, Scandal, Jeremy, *and* Buckram. Valentine *upon a couch, disorderly dressed.*

SIR SAMPSON: How now! what's here to do?

VALENTINE: [*Starting*] Ha! who's that?

SCANDAL: For Heaven's sake softly, sir, and gently! don't provoke him.

VALENTINE: Answer me, who is that, and that?

SIR SAMPSON: Gadsobs, does he not know me? Is he mischievous? I'll speak gently.—Val, Val, dost thou not know me, boy? not know thy own father, Val? I am thy own father, and this is honest Brief Buckram the lawyer.

VALENTINE: It may be so—I did not know you—the world is full.—There are people that we do know and people that we do not know; and yet the sun shines upon all alike.—There are fathers that have many children; and there are children that have many fathers.—'Tis strange! but I am Truth, and come to give the world the lie.

SIR SAMPSON: Body o' me, I know not what to say to him!

VALENTINE: Why does that lawyer wear black?—does he carry his conscience withoutside?—Lawyer, what art thou? dost thou know me?

BUCKRAM: O Lord! what must I say?—Yes, sir.

VALENTINE: Thou liest, for I am Truth. 'Tis hard I cannot get a livelihood amongst you. I have been sworn out of Westminster-Hall the first day of every term—let me see—no matter how long—but I'll tell you one thing; it's a question that would puzzle an arithmetician, if you should ask him, whether the Bible saves more souls in Westminster-Abbey or damns more in Westminster-Hall; for my part, I am Truth; and can't tell; I have very few acquaintance.

SIR SAMPSON: Body o' me, he talks sensibly in his madness! has he no intervals?

JEREMY: Very short, sir.

BUCKRAM: Sir, I can do you no service while he's in this condition; here's your paper, sir—he may do me a mischief if I stay—the conveyance is ready, sir, if he recover his senses.   [*Exit Buckram*]

SIR SAMPSON: Hold, hold, hold, don't you go yet.

SCANDAL: You'd better let him go, sir; and send for him if there be occasion; for I fancy his presence provokes him more.

VALENTINE: Is the lawyer gone? 'tis well; then we may drink about without going together by the ears—heigh-ho! What o'clock is 't?—My father here! your blessing, sir.

SIR SAMPSON: He recovers.—Bless thee, Val,—how dost thou do, boy?

VALENTINE: Thank you, sir, pretty well—I have been a little out of order—won't you please to sit, sir?

SIR SAMPSON: Ay, boy.—Come, thou shalt sit down by me.

VALENTINE: Sir, 'tis my duty to wait.

SIR SAMPSON: No, no, come, come, sit thee down, honest Val; how dost thou do? let me feel thy pulse.—Oh, pretty well now, Val; body o' me, I was sorry to see thee indisposed! but I'm glad thou art better, honest Val.

VALENTINE: I thank you, sir.

SCANDAL: Miracle! the monster grows loving, [*Aside*]

SIR SAMPSON: Let me feel thy hand again, Val; it does not shake—I believe thou canst write, Val; ha, boy, thou canst write thy name, Val?—Jeremy, step and overtake Mr. Buckram, bid him make haste back with the conveyance! quick! quick!
            [*Whispers to Jeremy, who goes out*]

SCANDAL: [*Aside*] That ever I should suspect such a heathen of any remorse!

SIR SAMPSON: Dost thou know this paper, Val? I know thou'rt honest, and wilt perform articles. [*Shows him the paper, but holds it out of his reach*]

VALENTINE: Pray, let me see it, sir. You hold it so far off, that I can't tell whether I know it or no.

SIR SAMPSON: See it, boy? ay, ay, why thou dost see it—'tis thy own hand, Vally. Why, let me see, I can read it as plain as can be; look you here— [*Reads*] "The conditions of this obligation"—look you, as plain as can be, so it begins—and then at the bottom—"As witness my hand, Valentine Legend," in great letters; why, 'tis as plain as the nose in one's face; what, are my eyes better than thine? I believe I can read it farther off yet—let me see.   [*Stretches out his arm as far as he can*]

VALENTINE: Will you please to let me hold it, sir?

SIR SAMPSON: Let thee hold it, sayest thou?—ay, with all my heart.—What matter is it who holds it? what need anybody hold it?—I'll put it in my pocket, Val, and then nobody need hold it.— [*Puts the paper in his pocket*] There, Val, it's safe enough, boy—but thou shalt have it as soon as thou hast set thy hand to another paper, little Val.

Re-enter Jeremy *and* Buckram.

VALENTINE: What, is my bad genius here again! Oh, no, it is the lawyer with his itching palm; and he's come to be scratched—my nails are not long enough—let me have a pair of red-hot tongs, quickly! quickly! and you shall see me act St. Dunstan, and lead the devil by the nose.

BUCKRAM: O Lord, let me be gone! I'll not venture myself with a madman.   [*Exit*]

VALENTINE: Ha! ha! ha! you need not run so fast, honesty will not overtake you.—Ha! ha! ha! the rogue found me out to be *in formâ pauperis* presently.

SIR SAMPSON: 'Oons! what a vexation is here! I know not to do or say, or which way to go.

VALENTINE: Who's that, that's out of his way! I am Truth, and can set him right.—Hark ye, friend, the straight road is the worst way you can go:—he that follows his nose always, will very often be led into a stink.—*Probatum est.*—But what are you for, religion or politics? There's a couple of topics for you, no more like one another than oil and vinegar; and yet those two beaten together by a state-cook, make sauce for the whole nation.

SIR SAMPSON: What the devil had I to do, ever to beget sons? why did I ever marry?

VALENTINE: Because thou wert a monster, old boy; the two greatest monsters in the world are a man and a woman; what's thy opinion?

SIR SAMPSON: Why, my opinion is that those two monsters joined together, make a yet greater, that's a man and his wife.

VALENTINE: Aha, old truepenny! sayest thou so? thou hast nicked it.—But, it's wonderful strange, Jeremy.

JEREMY: What is, sir?

VALENTINE: That grey hairs should cover a green head, and I make a fool of my father.—What's here! *Erra Pater*, or a bearded Sibyl? If Prophecy comes, Truth must give place.   [*Exeunt*]

SCENE 3:   *An Ante-room at Valentine's Lodgings*

Enter Sir Sampson, Scandal, Foresight, Mrs. Foresight, *and* Mrs. Frail.

FORESIGHT: What says he? what, did he prophesy?— Ha, Sir Sampson, bless us! how are we?

SIR SAMPSON: Are we! a pox o' your prognostication —why, we are fools as we used to be.—'Oons, that you could not foresee that the moon would predominate, and my son be mad!—Where's your oppositions, your trines, and your quadrates?— What did your Cardan and your Ptolemy tell you? your Messahalah and your Longomontanus, your harmony of chiromancy with astrology? Ah! pox on't, that I that know the world, and men and manners, that don't believe a syllable in the sky and stars, and suns, and almanacs, and trash, should be directed by a dreamer, an omen-hunter, and defer business in expectation of a lucky hour! when, body o' me, there never was a lucky hour after the first opportunity.   [*Exit Sir Sampson*]

FORESIGHT: Ah, Sir Sampson, Heaven help your head! This is none of your lucky hour! *Nemo omnibus horis sapit.* What, is he gone, and in contempt of science? Ill stars and unconvertible ignorance attend him!

SCANDAL: You must excuse his passion, Mr. Foresight, for he has been heartily vexed.—His son is *non compos mentis*, and thereby incapable of making any conveyance in law; so that all his measures are disappointed.

FORESIGHT: Ha! say you so?

MRS. FRAIL: [*Aside to* Mrs. Foresight] What, has my sea-lover lost his anchor of hope then?

MRS. FORESIGHT: Oh, sister, what will you do with him?

MRS. FRAIL: Do with him! send him to sea again in the next foul weather.—He's used to an inconstant element, and won't be surprised to see the tide turned.

FORESIGHT: Wherein was I mistaken, not to foresee this?   [*Considers*]

SCANDAL: [*Aside to* Mrs. Foresight] Madam, you and I can tell him something else that he did not foresee, and more particularly relating to his own fortune.

MRS. FORESIGHT: [*Aside to* Scandal] What do you mean? I don't understand you.

SCANDAL: Hush, softly—the pleasures of last night, my dear! too considerable to be forgot so soon.

MRS. FORESIGHT: Last night! and what would your impudence infer from last night! last night was like the night before, I think.

SCANDAL: 'Sdeath, do you make no difference between me and your husband?

MRS. FORESIGHT: Not much;—he's superstitious, and you are mad, in my opinion.

SCANDAL: You make me mad.—You are not serious; —pray, recollect yourself.

MRS. FORESIGHT: O yes, now I remember, you were very impertinent and impudent,—and would have come to bed to me.

SCANDAL: And did not?

MRS. FORESIGHT: Did not! with what face can you ask the question?

SCANDAL: [*Aside*] This I have heard of before, but never believed. I have been told she had that admirable quality of forgetting to a man's face in the morning that she had lain with him all night, and denying that she had done favours with more impudence than she could grant 'em.—Madam, I'm your humble servant, and honour you.—[*Aloud*] You look pretty well, Mr. Foresight.—How did you rest last night?

FORESIGHT: Truly, Mr. Scandal, I was so taken up with broken dreams and distracted visions, that I remember little.

SCANDAL: 'Twas a very forgetting night.—But would you not talk with Valentine, perhaps you may understand him? I'm apt to believe there is something mysterious in his discourses, and sometimes rather think him inspired than mad.

FORESIGHT: You speak with singular good judgment, Mr. Scandal, truly.—I am inclining to your Turkish opinion in this matter, and do reverence a man whom the vulgar think mad. Let us go to him.

[*Exeunt* Foresight *and* Scandal]

MRS. FRAIL: Sister, do you stay with them; I'll find out my lover, and give him his discharge, and come to you.—O' my conscience here he comes.

[*Exit* Mrs. Foresight]

Enter Ben.

BEN: All mad, I think.—Flesh, I believe all the calentures of the sea are come ashore, for my part!

MRS. FRAIL: Mr. Benjamin in choler!

BEN: No, I'm pleased well enough now I have found you.—Mess, I have had such a hurricane upon your account yonder!

MRS. FRAIL: My account! pray what's the matter?

BEN: Why, father came and found me squabbling with yon chitty-faced thing as he would have me marry,—so he asked what was the matter.—He asked in a surly sort of a way.—It seems brother Val is gone mad, and so that put'n into a passion: but what did I know that, what's that to me?—So he asked in a surly sort of manner,—and gad I answered 'en as surlily; what tho'f he be my father? I an't bound prentice to 'en:—so faith I told'n in plain terms, if I were minded to marry I'd marry to please myself, not him: and for the young woman that he provided for me, I thought it more fitting for her to learn her sampler and make dirt-pies, than to look after a husband; for my part I was none of her man.—I had another voyage to make, let him take it as he will.

MRS. FRAIL: So then, you intend to go to sea again?

BEN: Nay, nay, my mind run upon you,—but I would not tell him so much.—So he said he'd make my heart ache; and if so be that he could get a woman to his mind, he'd marry himself. Gad, says I, an you play the fool and marry at these years, there's more danger of your head's aching than my heart.—He was woundy angry when I gav'n that wipe.—He hadn't a word to say, and so I left'n and the green girl together; mayhap the bee may bite, and he'll marry her himself; with all my heart.

MRS. FRAIL: And were you this undutiful and graceless wretch to your father?

BEN: Then why was he graceless first?—If I am undutiful and graceless, why did he beget me so? I did not get myself.

MRS. FRAIL: O impiety! how have I been mistaken! what an inhuman merciless creature have I set my heart upon! O, I am happy to have discovered the shelves and quicksands that lurk beneath that faithless smiling face!

BEN: Hey toss? what's the matter now? why, you ben't angry, be you?

MRS. FRAIL: O see me no more! for thou wert born amongst rocks, suckled by whales, cradled in a tempest, and whistled to by winds; and thou art come forth with fins and scales, and three rows of teeth, a most outrageous fish of prey.

BEN: O Lord, O Lord, she's mad! poor young woman; love has turned her senses, her brain is quite overset! Well-a-day, how shall I do to set her to rights?

MRS. FRAIL: No, no, I am not mad, monster, I am wise enough to find you out. Hadst thou the impudence to aspire at being a husband with that stubborn and disobedient temper?—You that know not how to submit to a father, presume to have a sufficient stock of duty to undergo a wife? I should have been finely fobbed indeed, very finely fobbed.

BEN: Hark ye, forsooth; if so be that you are in your right senses, d'ye see; for aught as I perceive I'm like to be finely fobbed,—if I have got anger here upon your account, and you are tacked about already.—What d'ye mean, after all your fair speeches and stroking my cheeks, and kissing, and hugging, what, would you sheer off so? would you, and leave me aground?

MRS. FRAIL: No, I'll leave you adrift, and go which way you will.

BEN: What, are you false-hearted, then?

MRS. FRAIL: Only the wind's changed.

BEN: More shame for you:—the wind's changed! It's an ill wind blows nobody good,—mayhap I have a good riddance on you, if these be your tricks. What did you mean all this while, to make a fool of me?

MRS. FRAIL: Any fool but a husband.

BEN: Husband! gad, I would not be your husband, if you would have me, now I know your mind, tho'f you had your weight in gold and jewels, and tho'f I loved you never so well.

MRS. FRAIL: Why, canst thou love, porpoise?

BEN: No matter what I can do; don't call names,—I don't love you so well as to bear that, whatever I did. I'm glad you show yourself, mistress.—Let them marry you, as don't know you:—gad, I know you too well, by sad experience; I believe he that marries you will go to sea in a hen-pecked frigate—I believe that, young woman—and mayhap may come to an anchor at Cuckold's-point; so there's a dash for you, take it as you will, mayhap you may holla after me when I can't come to. [*Exit*]

MRS. FRAIL: Ha! ha! ha! no doubt on't;—

[*Sings*] My true love is gone to sea—

Re-enter MRS. FORESIGHT.

MRS. FRAIL: O sister, had you come a minute sooner, you would have seen the resolution of a lover.—Honest Tar and I are parted,—and with the same indifference that we met.—O' my life I am half vexed at the insensibility of a brute that I despised.

MRS. FORESIGHT: What, then, he bore it most heroically?

MRS. FRAIL: Most tyrannically,—for you see he has got the start of me; and I the poor forsaken maid am left complaining on the shore. But I'll tell you a hint that he has given me; Sir Sampson is enraged, and talks desperately of committing matrimony himself;—if he has a mind to throw himself away, he can't do it more effectually than upon me, if we could bring it about.

MRS. FORESIGHT: Oh, hang him, old fox! he's too cunning; besides he hates both you and me. But I have a project in my head for you, and I have gone a good way towards it. I have almost made a bargain with Jeremy, Valentine's man, to sell his master to us.

MRS. FRAIL: Sell him! how?

MRS. FORESIGHT: Valentine raves upon Angelica, and took me for her, and Jeremy says will take anybody for her that he imposes on him. Now I have promised him mountains, if in one of his mad fits he will bring you to him in her stead, and get you married together, and put to bed together; and after consummation, girl, there's no revoking. And if he should recover his senses, he'll be glad at least to make you a good settlement.—Here they come: stand aside a little, and tell me how you like the design.

Enter Valentine, Scandal, Foresight, *and* Jeremy.

SCANDAL: [*To* Jeremy] And have you given your master a hint of their plot upon him?

JEREMY: Yes, sir; he says he'll favour it, and mistake her for Angelica.

SCANDAL: It may make us sport.

FORESIGHT: Mercy on us!

VALENTINE: Hush!—interrupt me not: I'll whisper prediction to thee, and thou shalt prophesy. I am Truth, and can teach thy tongue a new trick:—I have told thee what's past—now I'll tell what's to come. Dost thou know what will happen to-morrow?—answer me not—for I will tell thee. To-morrow, knaves will thrive through craft, and fools through fortune, and honesty will go as it did, frost-nipped in a summer suit. Ask me questions concerning to-morrow.

SCANDAL: Ask him, Mr. Foresight.

FORESIGHT: Pray, what will be done at court?

VALENTINE: Scandal will tell you:—I am Truth, I never come there.

FORESIGHT: In the city?

VALENTINE: Oh, prayers will be said in empty churches, at the usual hours. Yet you will see such zealous faces behind the counters, as if religion were to be sold in every shop. Oh, things will go methodically, in the city; the clocks will strike twelve at noon, and the horned herd buzz in the Exchange at two. Husbands and wives will drive distinct trades, and care and pleasure separately occupy the family. Coffee-houses will be full of smoke and stratagem. And the cropt prentice, that sweeps his master's shop in the morning, may, ten to one, dirty his sheets before night. But there are two things that you will see very strange; which are wanton wives with their legs at liberty, and tame cuckolds with chains about their necks.—But hold, I must examine you before I go further; you look suspiciously. Are you a husband?

FORESIGHT: I am married.

VALENTINE: Poor creature! is your wife of Covent-garden parish?

FORESIGHT: No; St. Martin's-in-the-fields.

VALENTINE: Alas, poor man! his eyes are sunk, and his hands shrivelled; his legs dwindled, and his back bowed; pray, pray, for a metamorphosis. Change thy shape, and shake off age; get thee Medea's kettle, and be boiled anew; come forth with labouring callous hands, a chine of steel, and Atlas shoulders. Let Taliacotius trim the calves of twenty chairmen, and make thee pedestals to stand erect upon, and look matrimony in the face. Ha! ha! ha! that a man should have a stomach to a wedding supper, when the pigeons ought rather to be laid to his feet, ha! ha! ha!

FORESIGHT: His frenzy is very high now, Mr. Scandal.

SCANDAL: I believe it is a spring-tide.

FORESIGHT: Very likely, truly; you understand these matters;—Mr. Scandal, I shall be very glad to confer with you about these things which he has uttered—his sayings are very mysterious and hieroglyphical.

VALENTINE: Oh, why would Angelica be absent from my eyes so long?

JEREMY: She's here, sir.

MRS. FORESIGHT: Now, sister.

MRS. FRAIL: O Lord, what must I say?

SCANDAL: Humour him, madam, by all means.

VALENTINE: Where is she? oh, I see her;—she comes like riches, health, and liberty at once, to a despairing, starving, and abandoned wretch. Oh welcome, welcome.

MRS. FRAIL: How d'ye, sir? can I serve you?

VALENTINE: Hark ye—I have a secret to tell you—Endymion and the moon shall meet us upon Mount Latmos, and we'll be married in the dead of night—but say not a word. Hymen shall put his torch into a dark lantern, that it may be secret; and Juno shall give her peacock poppy-water, that he may fold his ogling tail, and Argus's hundred eyes be shut, ha! Nobody shall know but Jeremy.

MRS. FRAIL: No, no, we'll keep it secret, it shall be done presently.

VALENTINE: The sooner the better.—Jeremy, come hither—closer—that none may overhear us—Jeremy, I can tell you news; Angelica is turned nun, and I am turning friar, and yet we'll marry one another in spite of the pope. Get me a cowl and beads, that I may play my part; for she'll meet me two hours hence in black and white, and a long veil to cover the project, and we won't see one another's faces, till we have done something to be ashamed of, and then we'll blush once for all.

Enter Tattle *and* Angelica.

JEREMY: I'll take care, and—

VALENTINE: Whisper.

ANGELICA: Nay, Mr. Tattle, if you make love to me, you spoil my design, for I intend to make you my confidant.

TATTLE: But, madam, to throw away your person, such a person, and such a fortune, on a madman?

ANGELICA: I never loved him till he was mad; but don't tell anybody so.

SCANDAL: [*Aside*] How's this! Tattle making love to Angelica?

TATTLE: Tell, madam! alas, you don't know me—I have much ado to tell your ladyship how long I have been in love with you; but encouraged by the impossibility of Valentine's making any more addresses to you, I have ventured to declare the very inmost passion of my heart. Oh, madam, look upon us both; there you see the ruins of a poor decayed creature,—here a complete and lively figure, with youth and health, and all his five senses in perfection, madam; and to all this, the most passionate lover—

ANGELICA: O fy, for shame! hold your tongue; a passionate lover and five senses in perfection! when you are as mad as Valentine, I'll believe you love me, and the maddest shall take me.

VALENTINE: It is enough.—Ha, who's here?

MRS. FRAIL: [*Aside to* Jeremy] O Lord, her coming will spoil all!

JEREMY: [*Aside to* Mrs. Frail] No, no, madam, he won't know her; if he should, I can persuade him.

VALENTINE: Scandal, who are these? foreigners? If they are, I'll tell you what I think.—[*Whispers*] Get away all the company but Angelica, that I may discover my design to her.

SCANDAL: [*Whispers*] I will; I have discovered something of Tattle that is of a piece with Mrs. Frail. He courts Angelica; if we could contrive to couple 'em together; hark ye.

MRS. FORESIGHT: He won't know you, cousin, he knows nobody.

FORESIGHT: But he knows more than anybody. Oh, niece, he knows things past and to come, and all the profound secrets of time.

TATTLE: Look you, Mr. Foresight, it is not my way to make many words of matters, and so I shan't say much; but, in short, d'ye see, I will hold you a hundred pounds now, that I know more secrets than he.

FORESIGHT: How! I cannot read that knowledge in your face, Mr. Tattle. Pray, what do you know?

TATTLE: Why, d'ye think I'll tell you, sir? Read it in my face! no, sir, 'tis written in my heart; and safer there, sir, than letters writ in juice of lemon; for no fire can fetch it out. I am no blab, sir.

VALENTINE: [*Aside to* Scandal] Acquaint Jeremy with it, he may easily bring it about.—[*Aloud*] They are welcome, and I'll tell 'em so myself. What, do you look strange upon me? then I must be plain.—[*Coming up to them*] I am Truth, and hate an old acquaintance with a new face.

[Scandal *goes aside with* Jeremy]

TATTLE: Do you know me, Valentine?

VALENTINE: You? who are you? no, I hope not.

TATTLE: I am Jack Tattle, your friend.

VALENTINE: My friend? what to do? I am no married man, and thou canst not lie with my wife; I am very poor, and thou canst not borrow money of me; then what employment have I for a friend?

TATTLE: Ha! a good open speaker, and not to be trusted with a secret.

ANGELICA: Do you know me Valentine?

VALENTINE: Oh, very well.

ANGELICA: Who am I?

VALENTINE: You're a woman,—one to whom Heaven gave beauty, when it grafted roses on a briar. You are the reflection of Heaven in a pond, and he that leaps at you is sunk. You are all white, a sheet of lovely, spotless paper, when you first are born; but you are to be scrawled and blotted by every goose's quill. I know you; for I loved a woman, and loved her so long, that I found out a strange thing; I found out what a woman was good for.

TATTLE: Ay, prithee, what's that?

VALENTINE: Why, to keep a secret.

TATTLE: O Lord!

VALENTINE: O, exceeding good to keep a secret: for though she should tell, yet she is not to be believed.

TATTLE: Ha! good again, faith.

VALENTINE: I would have music.—Sing me the song that I like.

SONG

I tell thee, Charmion, could I time retrieve,
And could again begin to love and live,
To you I should my earliest offering give;

I know, my eyes would lead my heart to you,
And I should all my vows and oaths renew;
But, to be plain, I never would be true.

For by our weak and weary truth I find,
Love hates to centre in a point assigned;
But runs with joy the circle of the mind:

Then never let us chain what should be free,
But for relief of either sex agree:
Since women love to change, and so do we.

VALENTINE: No more, for I am melancholy.
                                        [*Walks musing*]
JEREMY: [*Aside to* Scandal] I'll do't, sir.
SCANDAL: Mr. Foresight, we had best leave him. He
may grow outrageous, and do mischief.
FORESIGHT: I will be directed by you.
JEREMY: [*Aside to* Mrs. Frail] You'll meet, madam?
I'll take care everything shall be ready.
MRS. FRAIL: Thou shalt do what thou wilt; in short,
I will deny thee nothing.
TATTLE: [*To* Angelica] Madam, shall I wait upon
you?
ANGELICA: No, I'll stay with him; Mr. Scandal will
protect me.—Aunt, Mr. Tattle desires you would
give him leave to wait on you.
TATTLE: [*Aside*] Pox on't! there's no coming off, now
she has said that.—[*Aloud*] Madam, will you do
me the honour?
MRS. FORESIGHT: Mr. Tattle might have used less
ceremony.
                      [*Exeunt* Foresight, Mrs. Frail, Mrs. Fore-
                      sight, *and* Tattle]
SCANDAL: Jeremy, follow Tattle.   [*Exit* Jeremy]
ANGELICA: Mr. Scandal, I only stay till my maid
comes, and because I had a mind to be rid of Mr.
Tattle.
SCANDAL: Madam, I am very glad that I overheard a
better reason, which you gave to Mr. Tattle; for
his impertinence forced you to acknowledge a
kindness for Valentine which you denied to all his
sufferings and my solicitations. So I'll leave him to
make use of the discovery, and your ladyship to
the free confession of your inclinations.
ANGELICA: Oh Heavens! you won't leave me alone
with a madman?
SCANDAL: No, madam, I only leave a madman to his
remedy.   [*Exit* Scandal]
VALENTINE: Madam, you need not be very much
afraid, for I fancy I begin to come to myself.
ANGELICA: [*Aside*] Ay, but if I don't fit you, I'll be
hanged.
VALENTINE: You see what disguises love makes us put
on: gods have been in counterfeited shapes for the
same reason; and the divine part of me, my mind,
has worn this mask of madness, and this motley
livery, only as the slave of love, and menial creature
of your beauty.
ANGELICA: Mercy on me, how he talks! poor Valentine!
VALENTINE: Nay, faith, now let us understand one
another, hypocrisy apart.—The comedy draws
toward an end, and let us think of leaving acting,
and be ourselves; and since you have loved me,
you must own, I have at length deserved you
should confess it.

ANGELICA: [*Sighs*] I would I had loved you!—for
Heaven knows I pity you; and could I have foreseen the bad effects, I would have striven; but
that's too late.   [*Sighs*]
VALENTINE: What bad effects?—what's too late? My
seeming madness has deceived my father, and procured me time to think of means to reconcile me to
him, and preserve the right of my inheritance to
his estate; which otherwise by articles I must this
morning have resigned: and this I had informed
you of to-day, but you were gone, before I knew
you had been here.
ANGELICA: How! I thought your love of me had
caused this transport in your soul; which it seems
you only counterfeited, for mercenary ends and
sordid interest!
VALENTINE: Nay, now you do me wrong; for if any
interest was considered it was yours; since I
thought I wanted more than love to make me
worthy of you.
ANGELICA: Then you thought me mercenary.—But
how am I deluded by this interval of sense, to
reason with a madman!
VALENTINE: Oh, 'tis barbarous to misunderstand me
longer.

Enter Jeremy.
ANGELICA: Oh, here's a reasonable creature—sure he
will not have the impudence to persevere.—Come,
Jeremy, acknowledge your trick, and confess your
master's madness counterfeit.
JEREMY: Counterfeit, madam! I'll maintain him to
be as absolutely and substantially mad as any free-
holder in Bethlehem; nay, he's as mad as any pro-
jector, fanatic, chemist, lover, or poet in Europe.
VALENTINE: Sirrah, you lie! I am not mad.
ANGELICA: Ha! ha! ha! you see he denies it.
JEREMY: O Lord, madam, did you ever know any
madman mad enough to own it?
VALENTINE: Sot, can't you comprehend?
ANGELICA: Why, he talked very sensible just now.
JEREMY: Yes, madam, he has intervals; but you see
he begins to look wild again now.
VALENTINE: Why, you thick-skulled rascal, I tell you
the farce is done, and I will be mad no longer.
                                              [*Beats him*]
ANGELICA: Ha! ha! ha! is he mad or no, Jeremy?
JEREMY: Partly I think—for he does not know his
own mind two hours.—I'm sure I left him just now
in the humour to be mad; and I think I have not
found him very quiet at this present!—[*Knocking
at the door*] Who's there?
VALENTINE: Go see, you sot.—[*Exit* Jeremy] I'm very
glad that I can move your mirth, though not your
compassion.
ANGELICA: I did not think you had apprehension
enough to be exceptious: but madmen show themselves most, by over-pretending to a sound understanding; as drunken men do by over-acting

sobriety. I was half-inclining to believe you, till I accidentally touched upon your tender part; but now you have restored me to my former opinion and compassion.

Re-enter Jeremy.

JEREMY: Sir, your father has sent to know if you are any better yet.—Will you please to be mad, sir, or how?

VALENTINE: Stupidity! you know the penalty of all I'm worth must pay for the confession of my senses; I'm mad, and will be mad to everybody but this lady.

JEREMY: So;—Just the very backside of truth.—But lying is a figure in speech, that interlards the greatest part of my conversation.—Madam, your ladyship's woman.   [*Exit*]

Enter Jenny.

ANGELICA: Well, have you been there?—Come hither.

JENNY: [*Aside to* Angelica] Yes, madam, Sir Sampson will wait upon you presently.

VALENTINE: You are not leaving me in this uncertainty?

ANGELICA: Would anything but a madman complain of uncertainty? Uncertainty and expectation are the joys of life. Security is an insipid thing, and the overtaking and possessing of a wish, discovers the folly of the chase. Never let us know one another better: for the pleasure of a masquerade is done, when we come to show our faces; but I'll tell you two things before I leave you; I am not the fool you take me for; and you are mad, and don't know it.   [*Exeunt* Angelica *and* Jenny]

VALENTINE: From a riddle you can expect nothing but a riddle. There's my instruction, and the moral of my lesson.

Re-enter Jeremy.

JEREMY: What, is the lady gone again, sir? I hope you understood one another before she went?

VALENTINE: Understood! she is harder to be understood than a piece of Egyptian antiquity, or an Irish manuscript; you may pore till you spoil your eyes, and not improve your knowledge.

JEREMY: I have heard 'em say, sir, they read hard Hebrew books backwards; may be you begin to read at the wrong end.

VALENTINE: They say so of a witch's prayer: and dreams and Dutch almanacs are to be understood by contraries. But there's regularity and method in that; she is a medal without a reverse or inscription, for indifference has both sides alike. Yet while she does not seem to hate me, I will pursue her, and know her if it be possible, in spite of the opinion of my satirical friend, Scandal, who says,

That women are like tricks by sleight of hand,
Which, to admire, we should not understand.
                                                    [*Exeunt*]

Act V

SCENE 1: *A Room in* Foresight's *House*

Enter Angelica *and* Jenny.

ANGELICA: Where is Sir Sampson? did you not tell me he would be here before me?

JENNY: He's at the great glass in the dining-room, madam, setting his cravat and wig.

ANGELICA: How! I'm glad on't.—If he has a mind I should like him, it's a sign he likes me; and that's more than half my design.

JENNY: I hear him, madam.

ANGELICA: Leave me; and d'ye hear, if Valentine should come or send, I am not to be spoken with.
                                                [*Exit* Jenny]

Enter Sir Sampson.

SIR SAMPSON: I have not been honoured with the commands of a fair lady, a great while:—odd, madam, you have revived me!—not since I was five-and-thirty.

ANGELICA: Why, you have no great reason to complain, Sir Sampson, that is not long ago.

SIR SAMPSON: Zooks, but it is, madam, a very great while to a man that admires a fine woman as much as I do.

ANGELICA: You're an absolute courtier, Sir Sampson.

SIR SAMPSON: Not at all, madam; odsbud you wrong me; I am not so old neither to be a bare courtier, only a man of words: odd, I have warm blood about me yet, and can serve a lady any way.— Come, come, let me tell you, you women think a man old too soon, faith and troth, you do!—Come, don't despise fifty; odd, fifty, in a hale constitution, is no such contemptible age.

ANGELICA: Fifty a contemptible age! not at all, a very fashionable age, I think.—I assure you, I know very considerable beaux that set a good face upon fifty:—fifty! I have seen fifty in a side-box, by candle-light, out-blossom five-and-twenty.

SIR SAMPSON: Outsides, outsides; a pize take 'em, mere outsides! hang your side-box beaux! no, I'm none of those, none of your forced trees, that pretend to blossom in the fall, and bud when they should bring forth fruit; I am of a long-lived race, and inherit vigour: none of my ancestors married till fifty; yet they begot sons and daughters till fourscore; I am of your patriarchs, I, a branch of one of your antediluvian families, fellows that the flood could not wash away. Well, madam, what are your commands? has any young rogue affronted you, and shall I cut his throat? or—

ANGELICA: No, Sir Sampson, I have no quarrel upon my hands—I have more occasion for your conduct than your courage at this time. To tell you the truth, I'm weary of living single, and want a husband.

SIR SAMPSON: Odsbud, and 'tis pity you should!—[Aside] Odd, would she would like me, then I should hamper my young rogues: odd, would she would; faith and troth she's devilish handsome!—[Aloud] Madam, you deserve a good husband, and 'twere pity you should be thrown away upon any of these young idle rogues about the town. Odd, there's ne'er a young fellow worth hanging!—that is a very young fellow.—Pize on 'em! they never think beforehand of anything;—and if they commit matrimony, 'tis as they commit murder; out of a frolic, and are ready to hang themselves, or to be hanged by the law, the next morning:—odso, have a care, madam.

ANGELICA: Therefore I ask your advice, Sir Sampson: I have fortune enough to make any man easy that I can like; if there were such a thing as a young agreeable man with a reasonable stock of good-nature and sense.—For I would neither have an absolute wit nor a fool.

SIR SAMPSON: Odd, you are hard to please, madam; to find a young fellow that is neither a wit in his own eye, nor a fool in the eye of the world, is a very hard task. But, faith and troth, you speak very discreetly; for I hate both a wit and a fool.

ANGELICA: She that marries a fool, Sir Sampson, forfeits the reputation of her honesty or understanding: and she that marries a very witty man is a slave to the severity and insolent conduct of her husband. I should like a man of wit for a lover, because I would have such a one in my power; but I would no more be his wife than his enemy. For his malice is not a more terrible consequence of his aversion than his jealousy is of his love.

SIR SAMPSON: None of old Foresight's Sibyls ever uttered such a truth. Odsbud, you have won my heart! I hate a wit; I had a son that was spoiled among 'em; a good hopeful lad, till he learned to be a wit—and might have risen in the state.—But a pox on't! his wit run him out of his money, and now his poverty has run him out of his wits.

ANGELICA: Sir Sampson, as your friend, I must tell you, you are very much abused in that matter: he's no more mad than you are.

SIR SAMPSON: How, madam! would I could prove it!

ANGELICA: I can tell you how that may be done.—But it is a thing that would make me appear to be too much concerned in your affairs.

SIR SAMPSON: [Aside] Odsbud, I believe she likes me! [Aloud] Ah, madam, all my affairs are scarce worthy to be laid at your feet; and I wish, madam, they were in a better posture, that I might make a more becoming offer to a lady of your incomparable beauty and merit.—If I had Peru in one hand, and Mexico in t'other, and the eastern empire under my feet, it would make me only a more glorious victim to be offered at the shrine of your beauty.

ANGELICA: Bless me, Sir Sampson, what's the matter?

SIR SAMPSON: Odd, madam, I love you!—and if you would take my advice in a husband—

ANGELICA: Hold, hold, Sir Sampson. I asked your advice for a husband, and you are giving me your consent.—I was indeed thinking to propose something like it in jest, to satisfy you about Valentine: for if a match were seemingly carried on between you and me, it would oblige him to throw off his disguise of madness, in apprehension of losing me: for you know he has long pretended a passion for me.

SIR SAMPSON: Gadzooks, a most ingenious contrivance!—if we were to go through with it. But why must the match only be seemingly carried on?—Odd, let it be a real contract.

ANGELICA: O fy, Sir Sampson! what would the world say?

SIR SAMPSON: Say! they would say you were a wise woman and I a happy man. Odd, madam, I'll love you as long as I live, and leave you a good jointure when I die.

ANGELICA: Ay; but that is not in your power, Sir Sampson; for when Valentine confesses himself in his senses, he must make over his inheritance to his younger brother.

SIR SAMPSON: Odd, you're cunning, a wary baggage! faith and troth, I like you the better.—But, I warrant you, I have a proviso in the obligation in favour of myself.—Body o' me, I have a trick to turn the settlement upon issue male of our two bodies begotten. Odsbud, let us find children, and I'll find an estate.

ANGELICA: Will you? well do you find the estate, and leave the other to me.

SIR SAMPSON: O rogue! but I'll trust you. And will you consent! is it a match then?

ANGELICA: Let me consult my lawyer concerning this obligation; and if I find what you propose practicable, I'll give you my answer.

SIR SAMPSON: With all my heart: come in with me, and I'll lend you the bond.—You shall consult your lawyer, and I'll consult a parson. Odzooks I'm a young man: odzooks, I'm a young man, and I'll make it appear. Odd, you're devilish handsome: faith and troth, you're very handsome; and I'm very young, and very lusty. Odsbud, hussy, you know how to choose, and so do I;—odd, I think we are very well met. Give me your hand, odd, let me kiss it; 'tis as warm and as soft—as what?—Odd, as t'other hand; give me t'other hand, and I'll mumble 'em and kiss 'em till they melt in my mouth.

ANGELICA: Hold, Sir Sampson: you're profuse of your vigour before your time: you'll spend your estate before you come to it.

SIR SAMPSON: No, no, only give you a rent-roll of my possessions,—ha! baggage!—I warrant you for little Sampson: odd, Sampson's a very good name for an able fellow: your Sampsons were strong dogs from the beginning.

ANGELICA: Have a care, and don't overact your part. If you remember, Sampson, the strongest of the name, pulled an old house over his head at last.

SIR SAMPSON: Say you so, hussy? Come, let's go then; odd, I long to be pulling too, come away.—Odso, here's somebody coming.   [*Exeunt*]

SCENE 2: *The same*

Enter Tattle *and* Jeremy.

TATTLE: Is not that she, gone out just now?

JEREMY: Ay, sir, she's just going to the place of appointment. Ah, sir, if you are not very faithful and close in this business, you'll certainly be the death of a person that has a most extraordinary passion for your honour's service.

TATTLE: Ay, who's that?

JEREMY: Even my unworthy self, sir. Sir, I have had an appetite to be fed with your commands a great while; and now, sir, my former master having much troubled the fountain of his understanding, it is a very plausible occasion for me to quench my thirst at the spring of your bounty. I thought I could not recommend myself better to you, sir, than by the delivery of a great beauty and fortune into your arms, whom I have heard you sigh for.

TATTLE: I'll make thy fortune; say no more. Thou art a pretty fellow, and canst carry a message to a lady, in a pretty soft kind of phrase, and with a good persuading accent.

JEREMY: Sir, I have the seeds of rhetoric and oratory in my head; I have been at Cambridge.

TATTLE: Ay! 'tis well enough for a servant to be bred at a university: but the education is a little too pedantic for a gentleman. I hope you are secret in your nature, private, close, ha?

JEREMY: O sir, for that, sir, 'tis my chief talent: I'm as secret as the head of Nilus.

TATTLE: Ay! who is he, though? a privy counsellor?

JEREMY: [*Aside*] O ignorance!—[*Aloud*] A cunning Egyptian, sir, that with his arms would overrun the country: yet nobody could ever find out his head-quarters.

TATTLE: Close dog! a good whoremaster, I warrant him. The time draws nigh, Jeremy. Angelica will be veiled like a nun; and I must be hooded like a friar; ha, Jeremy?

JEREMY: Ay, sir, hooded like a hawk, to seize at first sight upon the quarry. It is the whim of my master's madness to be so dressed; and she is so in love with him, she'll comply with anything to please him. Poor lady, I'm sure she'll have reason to pray for me, when she finds what a happy exchange she has made, between a madman and so accomplished a gentleman.

TATTLE: Ay, faith, so she will, Jeremy; you're a good friend to her, poor creature. I swear I do it hardly so much in consideration of myself as compassion to her.

JEREMY: 'Tis an act of charity, sir, to save a fine woman with thirty thousand pounds, from throwing herself away.

TATTLE: So 'tis, faith. I might have saved several others in my time; but egad, I could never find in my heart to marry anybody before.

JEREMY: Well, sir, I'll go and tell her my master is coming; and meet you in half a quarter of an hour, with your disguise, at your own lodgings. You must talk a little madly, she won't distinguish the tone of your voice.

TATTLE: No, no, let me alone for a counterfeit; I'll be ready for you.   [*Exit* Jeremy]

Enter Miss Prue.

PRUE: O Mr. Tattle, are you here! I'm glad I have found you; I have been looking up and down for you like anything, 'till I am as tired as anything in the world.

TATTLE: [*Aside*] A pox, how shall I get rid of this foolish girl!

PRUE: O I have pure news, I can tell you, pure news. I must not marry the seaman now—my father says so. Why won't you be my husband? you say you love me, and you won't be my husband. And I know you may be my husband now if you please.

TATTLE: O fy, miss! who told you so, child?

PRUE: Why, my father. I told him that you loved me.

TATTLE: O fy, miss! why did you do so? and who told you so, child?

PRUE: Who! why you did; did not you?

TATTLE: O pox! that was yesterday, miss, that was a great while ago, child. I have been asleep since; slept a whole night, and did not so much as dream of the matter.

PRUE: Pshaw! O but I dreamt that it was so though.

TATTLE: Ay, but your father will tell you that dreams come by contraries, child. O fy! what, we must not love one another now—pshaw, that would be a foolish thing indeed! Fy! fy! you're a woman now, and must think of a new man every morning, and forget him every night.—No, no, to marry is to be a child again, and play with the same rattle always; O fy! marrying is a paw thing.

PRUE: Well, but don't you love me as well as you did last night then?

TATTLE: No, no, child, you would not have me.

PRUE: No! yes, but I would though.

TATTLE: Pshaw! but I tell you, you would not—You forget you're a woman, and don't know your own mind.

PRUE: But here's my father, and he knows my mind.

Enter Foresight.

FORESIGHT: O, Mr. Tattle, your servant, you are a close man; but methinks your love to my daughter was a secret I might have been trusted with; or had you a mind to try if I could discover it by my art?

Hum, ha! I think there is something in your physiognomy that has a resemblance of her; and the girl is like me.

TATTLE: And so you would infer, that you and I are alike?—[*Aside*] What does the old prig mean? I'll banter him, and laugh at him, and leave him.—[*Aloud*] I fancy you have a wrong notion of faces.

FORESIGHT: How? what? a wrong notion! how so?

TATTLE: In the way of art: I have some taking features, not obvious to vulgar eyes; that are indications of a sudden turn of good fortune in the lottery of wives; and promise a great beauty and great fortune reserved alone for me, by a private intrigue of destiny, kept secret from the piercing eye of perspicuity; from all astrologers and the stars themselves.

FORESIGHT: How? I will make it appear that what you say is impossible.

TATTLE: Sir, I beg your pardon, I'm in haste—

FORESIGHT: For what?

TATTLE: To be married, sir, married.

FORESIGHT: Ay, but pray take me along with you,[1] sir—

TATTLE: No, sir: 'tis to be done privately. I never make confidants.

FORESIGHT: Well, but my consent, I mean.—You won't marry my daughter without my consent.

TATTLE: Who, I, sir? I'm an absolute stranger to you and your daughter, sir.

FORESIGHT: Heyday! what time of the moon is this?

TATTLE: Very true, sir, and desire to continue so. I have no more love for your daughter than I have likeness of you; and I have a secret in my heart, which you would be glad to know, and shan't know; and yet you shall know it too, and be sorry for it afterwards. I'd have you to know, sir, that I am as knowing as the stars, and as secret as the night. And I'm going to be married just now, yet did not know of it half an hour ago; and the lady stays for me, and does not know of it yet. There's a mystery for you!—I know you love to untie difficulties—or if you can't solve this, stay here a quarter of an hour, and I'll come and explain it to you.
[*Exit*]

PRUE: O father, why will you let him go? won't you make him to be my husband?

FORESIGHT: Mercy on us! what do these lunacies portend?—Alas! he's mad, child, stark wild.

PRUE: What, and must not I have e'er a husband then? What, must I go to bed to nurse again, and be a child as long as she's an old woman? Indeed but I won't; for now my mind is set upon a man, I will have a man some way or other. Oh! methinks I'm sick when I think of a man; and if I can't have one I would go to sleep all my life: for when I'm awake it makes me wish and long, and I don't know for what:—and I'd rather be always asleep, than sick with thinking.

[1]i.e. *Let me understand you.*

FORESIGHT: O fearful! I think the girl's influenced too. —Hussy, you shall have a rod.

PRUE: A fiddle of a rod! I'll have a husband: and if you won't get me one I'll get one for myself. I'll marry our Robin the butler; he says he loves me, and he's a handsome man, and shall be my husband: I warrant he'll be my husband, and thank me too, for he told me so.

Enter Scandal, Mrs. Foresight, *and* Nurse.

FORESIGHT: Did he so? I'll dispatch him for it presently; rogue!—Oh, nurse, come hither.

NURSE: What is your worship's pleasure?

FORESIGHT: Here take your young mistress, and lock her up presently, till farther orders from me.—Not a word, hussy. Do what I bid you; no reply; away! And bid Robin make ready to give an account of his plate and linen, d'ye hear: begone when I bid you.

MRS. FORESIGHT: What is the matter, husband?

FORESIGHT: 'Tis not convenient to tell you now.— Mr. Scandal, heaven keep us all in our senses!—I fear there is a contagious frenzy abroad. How does Valentine?

SCANDAL: O, I hope he will do well again:—I have a message from him to your niece Angelica.

FORESIGHT: I think she has not returned since she went abroad with Sir Sampson.—Nurse, why are you not gone?   [*Exit* Nurse]

Enter Ben.

MRS. FORESIGHT: Here's Mr. Benjamin; he can tell us if his father be come home.

BEN: Who father? ay, he's come home with a vengeance.

MRS. FORESIGHT: Why, what's the matter?

BEN: Matter! why, he's mad.

FORESIGHT: Mercy on us! I was afraid of this.

BEN: And there's the handsome young woman, she, as they say, brother Val went mad for, she's mad too, I think.

FORESIGHT: O my poor niece, my poor niece, is she gone too? Well, I shall run mad next.

MRS. FORESIGHT: Well, but how mad? how d'ye mean?

BEN: Nay, I'll give you leave to guess:—I'll undertake to make a voyage to Antegoa—no, hold, I mayn't say so neither—but I'll sail as far as Leghorn, and back again, before you shall guess at the matter, and do nothing else; mess, you may take in all the points of the compass and not hit right.

MRS. FORESIGHT: Your experiment will take up a little too much time.

BEN: Why then I'll tell you: there's a new wedding upon the stocks, and they two are a-going to be married to-night.

SCANDAL: Who?

BEN: My father, and—the young woman. I can't hit on her name.

SCANDAL: Angelica?

BEN: Ay, the same.

MRS. FORESIGHT: Sir Sampson and Angelica: impossible!

BEN: That may be—but I'm sure it is as I tell you.

SCANDAL: 'Sdeath, it's a jest! I can't believe it.

BEN: Look you, friend, it's nothing to me whether you believe it or no. What I say is true, d'ye see; they are married, or just going to be married, I know not which.

FORESIGHT: Well, but they are not mad, that is not lunatic?

BEN: I don't know what you may call madness; but she's mad for a husband, and he's horn mad, I think, or they'd ne'er make a match together.— Here they come.

Enter Sir Sampson, Angelica, *and* Buckram.

SIR SAMPSON: Where is this old soothsayer? this uncle of mine elect?—Aha! old Foresight, Uncle Foresight, wish me joy, Uncle Foresight, double joy, both as uncle and astrologer; here's a conjunction that was not foretold in all your Ephemeris. The brightest star in the blue firmament—is *shot from above in a jelly of love*, and so forth; and I'm lord of the ascendant. Odd, you're an old fellow, Foresight, uncle I mean; a very old fellow, Uncle Foresight; and yet you shall live to dance at my wedding, faith and troth you shall. Odd, we'll have the music of the spheres for thee, old Lilly, that we will, and thou shalt lead up a dance *in via lactea!*

FORESIGHT: I'm thunderstruck!—You are not married to my niece?

SIR SAMPSON: Not absolutely married, uncle; but very near it, within a kiss of the matter, as you see.
                                                    [*Kisses* Angelica]

ANGELICA: 'Tis very true, indeed, uncle; I hope you'll be my father, and give me.

SIR SAMPSON: That he shall, or I'll burn his globes. Body o' me, he shall be thy father, I'll make him thy father, and thou shalt make me a father, and I'll make thee a mother, and we'll beget sons and daughters enough to put the weekly bills out of countenance.

SCANDAL: Death and hell! where's Valentine? [*Exit*]

MRS. FORESIGHT: This is so surprising—

SIR SAMPSON: How! what does my aunt say? Surprising, aunt! not at all, for a young couple to make a match in winter: not at all.—It's a plot to undermine cold weather, and destroy that usurper of a bed called a warming-pan.

MRS. FORESIGHT: I'm glad to hear you have so much fire in you, Sir Sampson.

BEN: Mess, I fear his fire's little better than tinder; mayhap it will only serve to light up a match for somebody else. The young woman's a handsome young woman, I can't deny it; but, father, if I might be your pilot in this case, you should not

marry her. It's just the same thing, as if so be you should sail so far as the Straits without provision.

SIR SAMPSON: Who gave you authority to speak, sirrah? To your element, fish! be mute, fish, and to sea! rule your helm, sirrah, don't direct me.

BEN: Well, well, take you care of your own helm, or you mayn't keep your new vessel steady.

SIR SAMPSON: Why, you impudent tarpaulin! sirrah, do you bring your forecastle jests upon your father? but I shall be even with you, I won't give you a groat.—Mr. Buckram, is the conveyance so worded that nothing can possibly descend to this scoundrel? I would not so much as have him have the prospect of an estate; though there were no way to come to it but by the north-east passage.

BUCKRAM: Sir, it is drawn according to your directions, there is not the least cranny of the law unstopped.

BEN: Lawyer, I believe there's many a cranny and leak unstopped in your conscience.—If so be that one had a pump to your bosom, I believe we should discover a foul hold. They say a witch will sail in a sieve,—but I believe the devil would not venture aboard o' your conscience. And that's for you.

SIR SAMPSON: Hold your tongue, sirrah!—How now? who's here?

Enter Tattle *and* Mrs. Frail.

MRS. FRAIL: O sister, the most unlucky accident!

MRS. FORESIGHT: What's the matter?

TATTLE: Oh, the two most unfortunate poor creatures in the world we are!

FORESIGHT: Bless us! how so?

MRS. FRAIL: Ah, Mr. Tattle and I, poor Mr. Tattle and I are—I can't speak it out.

TATTLE: Nor I—but poor Mrs. Frail and I are—

MRS. FRAIL: Married.

MRS. FORESIGHT: Married! How?

TATTLE: Suddenly—before we knew where we were —that villain Jeremy, by the help of disguises, tricked us into one another.

FORESIGHT: Why, you told me just now, you went hence in haste to be married.

ANGELICA: But I believe Mr. Tattle meant the favour to me: I thank him.

TATTLE: I did, as I hope to be saved, madam; my intentions were good.—But this is the most cruel thing, to marry one does not know how, nor why, nor wherefore.—The devil take me if ever I was so much concerned at anything in my life!

ANGELICA: 'Tis very unhappy, if you don't care for one another.

TATTLE: The least in the world;—that is, for my part; I speak for myself. Gad, I never had the least thought of serious kindness: I never liked anybody less in my life. Poor woman! gad, I'm sorry for her, too; for I have no reason to hate her neither; but I believe I shall lead her a damned sort of life.

MRS. FORESIGHT: [*Aside to* Mrs. Frail] He's better than no husband at all—though he's a coxcomb.

MRS. FRAIL: [*Aside to* Mrs. Foresight] Ay, ay, it's well it's no worse.—[*Aloud*] Nay, for my part I always despised Mr. Tattle of all things; nothing but his being my husband could have made me like him less.

TATTLE: Look you there, I thought as much!—Pox on't, I wish we could keep it secret! why, I don't believe any of this company would speak of it.

MRS. FRAIL: But, my dear, that's impossible; the parson and that rogue Jeremy will publish it.

TATTLE: Ay, my dear, so they will, as you say.

ANGELICA: O you'll agree very well in a little time; custom will make it easy to you.

TATTLE: Easy! pox on't! I don't believe I shall sleep to-night.

SIR SAMPSON: Sleep, quotha! no; why you would not sleep o' your wedding night! I'm an older fellow than you, and don't mean to sleep.

BEN: Why, there's another match now, as tho'f a couple of privateers were looking for a prize, and should fall foul of one another. I'm sorry for the young man with all my heart. Look you, friend, if I may advise you, when she's going, for that you must expect, I have experience of her, when she's going, let her go. For no matrimony is tough enough to hold her, and if she can't drag her anchor along with her, she'll break her cable, I can tell you that.—Who's here? the madman?

Enter Valentine, Scandal, *and* Jeremy.

VALENTINE: No; here's the fool; and, if occasion be, I'll give it under my hand.

SIR SAMPSON: How now!

VALENTINE: Sir, I'm come to acknowledge my errors, and ask your pardon.

SIR SAMPSON: What, have you found your senses at last then? in good time, sir.

VALENTINE: You were abused, sir, I never was distracted.

FORESIGHT: How, not mad! Mr. Scandal?

SCANDAL: No, really, sir; I'm his witness, it was all counterfeit.

VALENTINE: I thought I had reasons.—But it was a poor contrivance; the effect has shown it such.

SIR SAMPSON: Contrivance! what, to cheat me? to cheat your father? sirrah, could you hope to prosper?

VALENTINE: Indeed, I thought, sir, when the father endeavoured to undo the son, it was a reasonable return of nature.

SIR SAMPSON: Very good, sir!—Mr. Buckram, are you ready?—[*To* Valentine] Come, sir, will you sign and seal?

VALENTINE: If you please, sir; but first I would ask this lady one question.

SIR SAMPSON: Sir, you must ask me leave first.—That lady! no, sir; you shall ask that lady no questions,

till you have asked her blessing, sir; that lady is to be my wife.

VALENTINE: I have heard as much, sir; but I would have it from her own mouth.

SIR SAMPSON: That's as much as to say, I lie, sir, and you don't believe what I say.

VALENTINE: Pardon me, sir. But I reflect that I very lately counterfeited madness; I don't know but the frolic may go round.

SIR SAMPSON: Come, chuck, satisfy him, answer him.—Come, come, Mr. Buckram, the pen and ink.

BUCKRAM: Here it is, sir, with the deed; all is ready.

[*Valentine goes to* Angelica]

ANGELICA: 'Tis true, you have a great while pretended love to me; nay, what if you were sincere; still you must pardon me, if I think my own inclinations have a better right to dispose of my person, than yours.

SIR SAMPSON: Are you answered now, sir?

VALENTINE: Yes, sir.

SIR SAMPSON: Where's your plot, sir; and your contrivance now, sir? Will you sign, sir? come, will you sign and seal?

VALENTINE: With all my heart, sir.

SCANDAL: 'Sdeath, you are not mad indeed, to ruin yourself?

VALENTINE: I have been disappointed of my only hope; and he that loses hope may part with anything. I never valued fortune, but as it was subservient to my pleasure; and my only pleasure was to please this lady; I have made many vain attempts, and find at last that nothing but my ruin can effect it; which, for that reason I will sign to.—Give me the paper.

ANGELICA: [*Aside*] Generous Valentine!

BUCKRAM: Here is the deed, sir.

VALENTINE: But where is the bond, by which I am obliged to sign this?

BUCKRAM: Sir Sampson, you have it.

ANGELICA: No, I have it; and I'll use it, as I would everything that is an enemy to Valentine.

[*Tears the paper*]

SIR SAMPSON: How now!

VALENTINE: Ha!

ANGELICA: [*To* Valentine] Had I the world to give you, it could not make me worthy of so generous and faithful a passion; here's my hand, my heart was always yours, and struggled very hard to make this utmost trial of your virtue.

VALENTINE: Between pleasure and amazement, I am lost.—But on my knees I take the blessing.

SIR SAMPSON: Oons, what is the meaning of this?

BEN: Mess, here's the wind changed again! Father, you and I may make a voyage together now.

ANGELICA: Well, Sir Sampson, since I have played you a trick, I'll advise you how you may avoid such another. Learn to be a good father, or you'll never get a second wife. I always loved your son, and hated your unforgiving nature. I was resolved to try him to the utmost; I have tried you too, and know you both. You have not more faults than he has virtues; and 'tis hardly more pleasure to me, that I can make him and myself happy, than that I can punish you.

VALENTINE: If my happiness could receive addition, this kind surprise would make it double.

SIR SAMPSON: Oons, you're a crocodile!

FORESIGHT: Really, Sir Sampson, this is a sudden eclipse.

SIR SAMPSON: You're an illiterate old fool, and I'm another!   [Exit]

TATTLE: If the gentleman is in disorder for want of a wife, I can spare him mine.—[To Jeremy] Oh, are you there, sir? I'm indebted to you for my happiness.

JEREMY: Sir, I ask you ten thousand pardons; 'twas an arrant mistake.—You see, sir, my master was never mad, or anything like it:—then how could it be otherwise?

VALENTINE: Tattle, I thank you, you would have interposed between me and Heaven; but Providence laid purgatory in your way:—you have but justice.

SCANDAL: I hear the fiddles that Sir Sampson provided for his own wedding; methinks 'tis pity they should not be employed when the match is so much mended.—Valentine, though it be morning, we may have a dance.

VALENTINE: Anything, my friend, everything that looks like joy and transport.

SCANDAL: Call 'em, Jeremy.   [Exit Jeremy]

ANGELICA: I have done dissembling now, Valentine; and if that coldness which I have always worn before you, should turn to an extreme fondness, you must not suspect it.

VALENTINE: I'll prevent that suspicion:—for I intend to dote to that immoderate degree, that your fondness shall never distinguish itself enough to be taken notice of. If ever you seem to love too much, it must be only when I can't love enough.

ANGELICA: Have a care of promises; you know you are apt to run more in debt than you are able to pay.

VALENTINE: Therefore I yield my body as your prisoner, and make your best on't.

Re-enter Jeremy.

JEREMY: The music stays for you.   [A dance]

SCANDAL: Well, madam, you have done exemplary justice, in punishing an inhuman father, and rewarding a faithful lover: but there is a third good work, which I, in particular, must thank you for; I was an infidel to your sex, and you have converted me.—For now I am convinced that all women are not like Fortune, blind in bestowing favours, either on those who do not merit, or who do not want 'em.

ANGELICA: 'Tis an unreasonable accusation, that you lay upon our sex: you tax us with injustice, only to cover your own want of merit. You would all have the reward of love; but few have the constancy to stay till it becomes your due. Men are generally hypocrites and infidels, they pretend to worship, but have neither zeal nor faith: how few, like Valentine, would persevere even to martyrdom, and sacrifice their interest to their constancy! In admiring me you misplace the novelty:—

The miracle to-day is, that we find
A lover true: not that a woman's kind.
                                        [*Exeunt omnes*]

Epilogue

Sure Providence at first designed this place
To be the player's refuge in distress;
For still in every storm they all run hither,
As to a shed that shields 'em from the weather.
But thinking of this change which last befell us,
It's like what I have heard our poets tell us:
For when behind our scenes their suits are pleading,
To help their love sometimes they show their reading;
And wanting ready cash to pay for hearts,
They top their learning on us and their parts.
Once of philosophers they told us stories,
Whom, as I think, they called—Py—Pythagories;—
I'm sure 'tis some such *Latin* name they give 'em,
And we, who know no better, must believe 'em.
Now to these men (say they) such souls were given,
That after death ne'er went to hell nor heaven,
But lived, I know not how, in beasts; and then,
When many years were passed, in men again.
Methinks, we players resemble such a soul;
That does from bodies, we from houses stroll.
Thus Aristotle's soul, of old that was,
May now be damned to animate an ass;
Or in this very house, for aught we know,
Is doing painful penance in some beau:
And thus, our audience, which did once resort
To shining theatres to see our sport,
Now, find us tossed into a tennis-court.
These walls but t'other day were filled with noise
Of roaring gamesters, and your *damn-me* boys;
Then bounding balls and rackets they encompast,
And now they're filled with jests, and flights, and bombast!
I vow, I don't much like this transmigration,
Strolling from place to place by circulation;
Grant, Heaven, we don't return to our first station
I know not what these think, but, for my part,
I can't reflect without an aching heart,
How we should end in our original, a cart.
But we can't fear, since you're so good to save us
That you have only set us up,—to leave us.
Thus from the past, we hope for future grace
I beg it———
And some here know I have a begging face.
Then pray continue this your kind behaviour,
For a clear stage won't do, without your favour.

The Way of the World

by WILLIAM CONGREVE

In The Way of the World Congreve, with no thought of consequences, gave his temperament free rein; and it thus expresses his way of regarding the world no less than the way of the world itself. Here, while impaling a callous, self-seeking society, Congreve himself maintained the note of civilization and culture, so that while he mirrors, he also refines. This is by no means—as Charles Lamb chose to call it—fairyland. The motives here are all too harsh, the moments of enchantment all too fleeting. In what fairyland, moreover, should we find age-blotched, sex-ravenous Lady Wishforts, or even Fainalls and Mrs. Marwoods so unscrupulously, so unhappily allied? But neither is this reality; though there is no sense of rose-colored glasses about it, it is lifted high above life by style, and crisped and waxed—beyond human wear and tear—by wit.

Indeed, The Way of the World is not only too witty for real life; it is very probably too witty for the stage. Hearing it spoken, we have to pant to keep up with it: we can barely absorb it and can never, where we might like to, linger over it. For beyond the wit itself, there is the whole matter of texture and tone; this is high comedy, the distillation of what Congreve felt about life. And this is as delicately complex as the surface action of the play is tediously complicated. There is something elegiac—a kind of reserved and aristocratic pathos—about it all; a touch of melancholy when it is most mocking, of chill where it seems most bright. We begin to understand a little better why Congreve never remonstrates: there would never, in his view of things, be any use.

Thanks to Millamant, The Way of the World boasts something radiant as well as glittering: from her glorious first entrance, she is at once a captivating stage figure and an entrancing heroine. And if only one scene—in prose—of love or courtship were to be chosen from all the comedies in the language, it is unthinkable that any but that between Millamant and Mirabell should even be considered.

WILLIAM CONGREVE

The Way of the World

THE PERSONS OF THE PLAY

FAINALL, *in love with* Mrs. Marwood

MIRABELL, *in love with* Mrs. Millamant

WITWOUD, } *Followers of* Mrs. Millamant
PETULANT, }

SIR WILFULL WITWOUD, *Half brother to* Witwoud, *and Nephew to* Lady Wishfort

WAITWELL, *Servant to* Mirabell

LADY WISHFORT, *Enemy to* Mirabell, *for having falsely pretended love to her*

MRS. MILLAMANT, *a fine Lady, Niece to* Lady Wishfort, *and loves* Mirabell

MRS. MARWOOD, *Friend to* Mr. Fainall, *and likes* Mirabell

MRS. FAINALL, *Daughter to* Lady Wishfort, *and Wife to* Fainall, *formerly Friend to* Mirabell

FOIBLE, *Woman to* Lady Wishfort

MINCING, *Woman to* Mrs. Millamant

BETTY, *Waiting-maid at a Chocolate-house*

PEG, *Maid to* Lady Wishfort

COACHMEN, DANCERS, FOOTMEN, AND ATTENDANTS

THE SCENE: *London*

This author heretofore has found your favour;
But pleads no merit from his past behaviour.
To build on that might prove a vain presumption,
Should grants, to poets made, admit resumption:
And in Parnassus he must lose his seat,
If that be found a forfeited estate.

He owns with toil he wrought the following scenes;
But, if they're naught, ne'er spare him for his pains:
Damn him the more; have no commiseration
For dulness on mature deliberation,
He swears he'll not resent one hissed-off scene,
Nor, like those peevish wits, his play maintain,
Who, to assert their sense, your taste arraign.
Some plot we think he has, and some new thought;
Some humour too, no farce; but that's a fault.
Satire, he thinks, you ought not to expect;
For so reformed a town who dares correct?
To please, this time, has been his sole pretence,
He'll not instruct, lest it should give offence.
Should he by chance a knave or fool expose,
That hurts none here, sure here are none of those:
In short, our play shall (with your leave to show it)
Give you one instance of a passive poet,
Who to your judgments yields all resignation;
So save or damn, after your own discretion.

Prologue

Of those few fools who with ill stars are curst,
Sure scribbling fools, called poets, fare the worst:
For they're a sort of fools which Fortune makes,
And after she has made 'em fools, forsakes.
With Nature's oafs 'tis quite a different case,
For Fortune favours all her idiot-race.
In her own nest the cuckoo-eggs we find,
O'er which she broods to hatch the changeling-kind.
No portion for her own she has to spare,
So much she dotes on her adopted care.

Poets are bubbles, by the town drawn in,
Suffered at first some trifling stakes to win;
But what unequal hazards do they run!
Each time they write they venture all they've won:
The squire that's buttered still, is sure to be undone.

Act I

SCENE 1: *A Chocolate House*

Mirabell *and* Fainall, *rising from cards*, Betty *waiting*.

MIRABELL: You are a fortunate man, Mr. Fainall!

FAINALL: Have we done?

MIRABELL: What you please: I'll play on to entertain you.

FAINALL: No, I'll give you your revenge another time, when you are not so indifferent; you are thinking of something else now, and play too negligently; the coldness of a losing gamester lessens the pleasure of the winner. I'd no more play with a man that slighted his ill fortune than I'd make love to a woman who undervalued the loss of her reputation.

MIRABELL: You have a taste extremely delicate, and are for refining on your pleasures.

FAINALL: Prithee, why so reserved? Something has put you out of humour.

MIRABELL: Not at all: I happen to be grave to day, and you are gay; that's all.

FAINALL: Confess, Millamant and you quarrelled last night after I left you; my fair cousin has some humours that would tempt the patience of a Stoic. What, some coxcomb came in, and was well received by her, while you were by?

MIRABELL: Witwoud and Petulant; and what was worse, her aunt, your wife's mother, my evil genius: or to sum up all in her own name, my old Lady Wishfort came in.

FAINALL: O there it is then! She has a lasting passion for you, and with reason.—What, then my wife was there?

MIRABELL: Yes, and Mrs. Marwood, and three or four more, whom I never saw before. Seeing me, they all put on their grave faces, whispered one another; then complained aloud of the vapours, and after fell into a profound silence.

FAINALL: They had a mind to be rid of you.

MIRABELL: For which reason I resolved not to stir. At last the good old lady broke through her painful taciturnity with an invective against long visits. I would not have understood her, but Millamant joining in the argument, I rose, and, with a constrained smile, told her, I thought nothing was so easy as to know when a visit began to be troublesome. She reddened, and I withdrew, without expecting her reply.

FAINALL: You were to blame to resent what she spoke only in compliance with her aunt.

MIRABELL: She is more mistress of herself than to be under the necessity of such a resignation.

FAINALL: What! though half her fortune depends upon her marrying with my lady's approbation?

MIRABELL: I was then in such a humour, that I should have been better pleased if she had been less discreet.

FAINALL: Now, I remember, I wonder not they were weary of you; last night was one of their cabal nights; they have 'em three times a-week, and meet by turns at one another's apartments, where they come together like the coroner's inquest, to sit upon the murdered reputations of the week. You and I are excluded; and it was once proposed that all the male sex should be excepted; but somebody moved that, to avoid scandal, there might be one man of the community; upon which motion Witwoud and Petulant were enrolled members.

MIRABELL: And who may have been the foundress of this sect? My Lady Wishfort, I warrant, who publishes her detestation of mankind; and full of the vigour of fifty-five, declares for a friend and ratafia; and let posterity shift for itself, she'll breed no more.

FAINALL: The discovery of your sham addresses to her, to conceal your love to her niece, has provoked this separation; had you dissembled better, things might have continued in the state of nature.

MIRABELL: I did as much as man could, with any reasonable conscience; I proceeded to the very last act of flattery with her, and was guilty of a song in her commendation. Nay, I got a friend to put her into a lampoon, and compliment her with the imputation of an affair with a young fellow, which I carried so far, that I told her the malicious town took notice that she was grown fat of a sudden; and when she lay in of a dropsy, persuaded her she was reported to be in labour. The devil's in't, if an old woman is to be flattered further, unless a man should endeavour downright personally to debauch her; and that my virtue forbade me. But for the discovery of this amour I am indebted to your friend, or your wife's friend, Mrs. Marwood.

FAINALL: What should provoke her to be your enemy, unless she has made you advances which you have slighted? Women do not easily forgive omissions of that nature.

MIRABELL: She was always civil to me till of late.—I confess I am not one of those coxcombs who are apt to interpret a woman's good manners to her prejudice, and think that she who does not refuse 'em everything, can refuse 'em nothing.

FAINALL: You are a gallant man, Mirabell; and though you may have cruelty enough not to satisfy a lady's longing, you have too much generosity not to be tender of her honour. Yet you speak with an indifference which seems to be affected, and confesses you are conscious of a negligence.

MIRABELL: You pursue the argument with a distrust that seems to be unaffected, and confesses you are conscious of a concern for which the lady is more indebted to you than is your wife.

FAINALL: Fy, fy, friend! if you grow censorious I must leave you.—I'll look upon the gamesters in the next room.

MIRABELL: Who are they?

FAINALL: Petulant and Witwoud.—[To Betty] Bring me some chocolate.   [Exit]

MIRABELL: Betty, what says your clock?

BETTY: Turned of the last canonical hour, sir.   [Exit]

MIRABELL: How pertinently the jade answers me!— [Looking on his watch]—Ha! almost one o'clock! —O, y'are come!

Enter Footman.
Well, is the grand affair over? You have been something tedious.

FOOTMAN: Sir, there's such coupling at Pancras, that they stand behind one another, as 'twere in a country dance. Ours was the last couple to lead up; and no hopes appearing of despatch: besides, the parson growing hoarse, we were afraid his lungs would have failed before it came to our turn; so we drove round to Duke's-place; and there they were rivetted in a trice.

MIRABELL: So, so, you are sure they are married.

FOOTMAN: Married and bedded, sir; I am witness.

MIRABELL: Have you the certificate?

FOOTMAN: Here it is, sir.

MIRABELL: Has the tailor brought Waitwell's clothes home, and the new liveries?

FOOTMAN: Yes, sir.

MIRABELL: That's well. Do you go home again, d'ye hear, and adjourn the consummation till further orders. Bid Waitwell shake his ears, and Dame Partlet rustle up her feathers, and meet me at one o'clock by Rosamond's Pond, that I may see her before she returns to her lady; and as you tender your ears be secret.   [*Exeunt*]

SCENE 2: *The same*

Mirabell, Fainall, *and* Betty.

FAINALL: Joy of your success, Mirabell; you look pleased.

MIRABELL: Ay; I have been engaged in a matter of some sort of mirth, which is not yet ripe for discovery. I am glad this is not a cabal night. I wonder, Fainall, that you who are married, and of consequence should be discreet, will suffer your wife to be of such a party.

FAINALL: Faith, I am not jealous. Besides, most who are engaged are women and relations; and for the men, they are of a kind too contemptible to give scandal.

MIRABELL: I am of another opinion. The greater the coxcomb, always the more the scandal: for a woman, who is not a fool, can have but one reason for associating with a man who is one.

FAINALL: Are you jealous as often as you see Witwoud entertained by Millamant?

MIRABELL: Of her understanding I am, if not of her person.

FAINALL: You do her wrong; for, to give her her due, she has wit.

MIRABELL: She has beauty enough to make any man think so; and complaisance enough not to contradict him who shall tell her so.

FAINALL: For a passionate lover, methinks you are a man somewhat too discerning in the failings of your mistress.

MIRABELL: And for a discerning man, somewhat too passionate a lover; for I like her with all her faults; nay, like her for her faults. Her follies are so natural, or so artful, that they become her; and those affectations which in another woman would be odious, serve but to make her more agreeable. I'll tell thee, Fainall, she once used me with that insolence, that in revenge I took her to pieces; sifted her, and separated her failings; I studied 'em, and got 'em by rote. The catalogue was so large, that I was not without hopes one day or other to hate her heartily: to which end I so used myself to think of 'em, that at length, contrary to my design and expectation, they gave me every hour less and less disturbance; till in a few days it became habitual to me to remember 'em without being displeased. They are now grown as familiar to me as my own frailties; and in all probability, in a little time longer, I shall like 'em as well.

FAINALL: Marry her, marry her! be half as well acquainted with her charms, as you are with her defects, and my life on't, you are your own man again.

MIRABELL: Say you so?

FAINALL: Ay, ay, I have experience: I have a wife, and so forth.

Enter Messenger.

MESSENGER: Is one Squire Witwoud here?

BETTY: Yes, what's your business?

MESSENGER: I have a letter for him, from his brother Sir Wilfull, which I am charged to deliver into his own hands.

BETTY: He's in the next room, friend—that way.
                                    [*Exit* Messenger]

MIRABELL: What, is the chief of that noble family in town, Sir Wilfull Witwoud?

FAINALL: He is expected to-day. Do you know him?

MIRABELL: I have seen him. He promises to be an extraordinary person; I think you have the honour to be related to him.

FAINALL: Yes; he is half brother to this Witwoud by a former wife, who was sister to my Lady Wishfort, my wife's mother. If you marry Millamant, you must call cousins too.

MIRABELL: I had rather be his relation than his acquaintance.

FAINALL: He comes to town in order to equip himself for travel.

MIRABELL: For travel! why, the man that I mean is above forty.

FAINALL: No matter for that; 'tis for the honour of England, that all Europe should know we have blockheads of all ages.

MIRABELL: I wonder there is not an act of parliament to save the credit of the nation, and prohibit the exportation of fools.

FAINALL: By no means; 'tis better as 'tis. 'Tis better to trade with a little loss, than to be quite eaten up with being overstocked.

MIRABELL: Pray, are the follies of this knight-errant, and those of the squire his brother, anything related?

FAINALL: Not at all; Witwoud grows by the knight, like a medlar grafted on a crab. One will melt in your mouth, and t'other set your teeth on edge; one is all pulp, and the other all core.

MIRABELL: So one will be rotten before he be ripe, and the other will be rotten without ever being ripe at all.

FAINALL: Sir Wilfull is an odd mixture of bashfulness and obstinacy.—But when he's drunk he's as loving as the monster in the Tempest, and much after the same manner. To give t'other his due, he has something of good-nature, and does not always want wit.

MIRABELL: Not always: but as often as his memory fails him, and his common-place of comparisons. He is a fool with a good memory, and some few scraps of other folks' wit. He is one whose conversation can never be approved, yet it is now and then to be endured. He has indeed one good quality, he is not exceptious; for he so passionately affects the reputation of understanding raillery, that he will construe an affront into a jest; and call downright rudeness and ill language, satire and fire.

FAINALL: If you have a mind to finish his picture, you have an opportunity to do it at full length. Behold the original!

Enter Witwoud.

WITWOUD: Afford me your compassion, my dears! pity me, Fainall! Mirabell, pity me!

MIRABELL: I do from my soul.

FAINALL: Why, what's the matter?

WITWOUD: No letters for me, Betty?

BETTY: Did not a messenger bring you one but now, sir?

WITWOUD: Ay, but no other?

BETTY: No, sir.

WITWOUD: That's hard, that's very hard.—A messenger! a mule, a beast of burden! he has brought me a letter from the fool my brother, as heavy as a panegyric in a funeral sermon, or a copy of commendatory verses from one poet to another: and what's worse, 'tis as sure a forerunner of the author, as an epistle dedicatory.

MIRABELL: A fool, and your brother, Witwoud!

WITWOUD: Ay, ay, my half brother. My half brother he is, no nearer upon honour.

MIRABELL: Then 'tis possible he may be but half a fool.

WITWOUD: Good, good, Mirabell, *le drôle!* good, good; hang him, don't let's talk of him.—Fainall, how does your lady? Gad, I say anything in the world to get this fellow out of my head. I beg pardon that I should ask a man of pleasure, and the town, a question at once so foreign and domestic. But I talk like an old maid at a marriage; I don't know what I say: but she's the best woman in the world.

FAINALL: 'Tis well you don't know what you say, or else your commendation would go near to make me either vain or jealous.

WITWOUD: No man in town lives well with a wife but Fainall.—Your judgment, Mirabell.

MIRABELL: You had better step and ask his wife, if you would be credibly informed.

WITWOUD: Mirabell?

MIRABELL: Ay.

WITWOUD: My dear, I ask ten thousand pardons;—gad, I have forgot what I was going to say to you!

MIRABELL: I thank you heartily, heartily.

WITWOUD: No, but prithee excuse me:—my memory is such a memory.

MIRABELL: Have a care of such apologies, Witwoud; for I never knew a fool but he affected to complain, either of the spleen or his memory.

FAINALL: What have you done with Petulant?

WITWOUD: He's reckoning his money—my money it was.—I have no luck to-day.

FAINALL: You may allow him to win of you at play: for you are sure to be too hard for him at repartee; since you monopolise the wit that is between you, the fortune must be his of course.

MIRABELL: I don't find that Petulant confesses the superiority of wit to be your talent, Witwoud.

WITWOUD: Come, come, you are malicious now, and would breed debates.—Petulant's my friend, and a very honest fellow, and a very pretty fellow, and has a smattering—faith and troth, a pretty deal of an odd sort of a small wit: nay, I'll do him justice. I'm his friend, I won't wrong him neither.—And if he had any judgment in the world, he would not be altogether contemptible. Come, come, don't detract from the merits of my friend.

FAINALL: You don't take your friend to be over-nicely bred?

WITWOUD: No, no, hang him, the rogue has no manners at all, that I must own:—no more breeding than a bum-bailiff, that I grant you:—'tis pity, faith; the fellow has fire and life.

MIRABELL: What, courage?

WITWOUD: Hum, faith I don't know as to that, I can't say as to that—Yes, faith, in a controversy, he'll contradict anybody.

MIRABELL: Though 'twere a man whom he feared, or a woman whom he loved.

WITWOUD: Well, well, he does not always think before he speaks;—we have all our failings: you are too hard upon him, you are, faith. Let me excuse him—I can defend most of his faults, except one or two: one he has, that's the truth on't; if he were my brother, I could not acquit him:—that, indeed, I could wish were otherwise.

MIRABELL: Ay, marry, what's that, Witwoud?

WITWOUD: O pardon me!—expose the infirmities of my friend!—No, my dear, excuse me there.

FAINALL: What, I warrant he's unsincere, or 'tis some such trifle.

WITWOUD: No, no; what if he be? 'tis no matter for that, his wit will excuse that: a wit should no more be sincere, than a woman constant; one argues a decay of parts, as t'other of beauty.

MIRABELL: Maybe you think him too positive?

WITWOUD: No, no, his being positive is an incentive to argument, and keeps up conversation.

FAINALL: Too illiterate?

WITWOUD: That! that's his happiness:—his want of

learning gives him the more opportunities to show his natural parts.

MIRABELL: He wants words?

WITWOUD: Ay: but I like him for that now; for his want of words gives me the pleasure very often to explain his meaning.

FAINALL: He's impudent?

WITWOUD: No, that's not it.

MIRABELL: Vain?

WITWOUD: No.

MIRABELL: What! he speaks unseasonable truths sometimes, because he has not wit enough to invent an evasion?

WITWOUD: Truths! ha! ha! ha! no, no; since you will have it,—I mean, he never speaks truth at all,—that's all. He will lie like a chambermaid, or a woman of quality's porter. Now that is a fault.

Enter Coachman.

COACHMAN: Is Master Petulant here, mistress?

BETTY: Yes.

COACHMAN: Three gentlewomen in a coach would speak with him.

FAINALL: O brave Petulant! three!

BETTY: I'll tell him.

COACHMAN: You must bring two dishes of chocolate and a glass of cinnamon-water.

[*Exeunt* Betty *and* Coachman]

WITWOUD: That should be for two fasting strumpets, and a bawd troubled with the wind. Now you may know what the three are.

MIRABELL: You are very free with your friend's acquaintance.

WITWOUD: Ay, ay, friendship without freedom is as dull as love without enjoyment, or wine without toasting. But to tell you a secret, these are trulls whom he allows coach-hire, and something more, by the week, to call on him once a-day at public places.

MIRABELL: How!

WITWOUD: You shall see he won't go to 'em, because there's no more company here to take notice of him.—Why this is nothing to what he used to do:—before he found out this way, I have known him call for himself.

FAINALL: Call for himself! what dost thou mean?

WITWOUD: Mean! why he would slip you out of this chocolate-house, just when you had been talking to him—as soon as your back was turned—whip he was gone!—then trip to his lodging, clap on a hood and scarf, and a mask, slap into a hackney-coach, and drive hither to the door again in a trice, where he would send in for himself; that I mean, call for himself, wait for himself; nay, and what's more, not finding himself, sometimes leave a letter for himself.

MIRABELL: I confess this is something extraordinary. —I believe he waits for himself now, he is so long a-coming: Oh! I ask his pardon.

Enter Petulant *and* Betty.

BETTY: Sir, the coach stays.

PETULANT: Well, well;—I come.—'Sbud, a man had as good be a professed midwife, as a professed whoremaster, at this rate! to be knocked up and raised at all hours, and in all places. Pox on 'em, I won't come!—D'ye hear, tell 'em I won't come:— let 'em snivel and cry their hearts out.

FAINALL: You are very cruel, Petulant.

PETULANT: All's one, let it pass:—I have a humour to be cruel.

MIRABELL: I hope they are not persons of condition that you use at this rate.

PETULANT: Condition! condition's a dried fig, if I am not in humour!—By this hand, if they were your—a—a—your what d'ye-call-'ems themselves, they must wait or rub off, if I want appetite.

MIRABELL: What d'ye-call-'ems! what are they, Witwoud?

WITWOUD: Empresses, my dear:—by your what-d'ye-call-'ems he means sultana queens.

PETULANT: Ay, Roxolanas.

MIRABELL: Cry you mercy!

FAINALL: Witwoud says they are—

PETULANT: What does he say th'are?

WITWOUD: I? fine ladies, I say.

PETULANT: Pass on, Witwoud.—Hark'ee, by this light his relations:—two co-heiresses his cousins, and an old aunt, who loves caterwauling better than a conventicle.

WITWOUD: Ha! ha! ha! I had a mind to see how the rogue would come off.—Ha! ha! ha! gad, I can't be angry with him, if he had said they were my mother and my sisters.

MIRABELL: No!

WITWOUD: No; the rogue's wit and readiness of invention charm me. Dear Petulant.

BETTY: They are gone, sir, in great anger.

PETULANT: Enough, let 'em trundle. Anger helps complexion, saves paint.

FAINALL: This continence is all dissembled; this is in order to have something to brag of the next time he makes court to Millamant, and swear he has abandoned the whole sex for her sake.

MIRABELL: Have you not left off your impudent pretensions there yet? I shall cut your throat some time or other, Petulant, about that business.

PETULANT: Ay, ay, let that pass—there are other throats to be cut.

MIRABELL: Meaning mine, sir?

PETULANT: Not I—I mean nobody—I know nothing:—but there are uncles and nephews in the world—and they may be rivals—what then! all's one for that.

MIRABELL: How! hark'ee, Petulant, come hither:— explain, or I shall call your interpreter.

PETULANT: Explain! I know nothing.—Why, you have an uncle, have you not, lately come to town, and lodges by my Lady Wishfort's?

MIRABELL: True.

PETULANT: Why, that's enough—you and he are not friends; and if he should marry and have a child, you may be disinherited, ha?

MIRABELL: Where hast thou stumbled upon all this truth?

PETULANT: All's one for that; why then say I know something.

MIRABELL: Come, thou art an honest fellow, Petulant, and shalt make love to my mistress, thou sha't, faith. What hast thou heard of my uncle?

PETULANT: I? nothing I. If throats are to be cut, let swords clash! snug's the word, I shrug and am silent.

MIRABELL: Oh, raillery, raillery! Come, I know thou art in the women's secrets.—What, you're a cabalist; I know you stayed at Millamant's last night, after I went. Was there any mention made of my uncle or me? tell me. If thou hadst but good-nature equal to thy wit, Petulant, Tony Witwoud, who is now thy competitor in fame, would show as dim by thee as a dead whiting's eye by a pearl of orient; he would no more be seen by thee, than Mercury is by the sun. Come, I'm sure thou wo't tell me.

PETULANT: If I do, will you grant me common sense then for the future?

MIRABELL: Faith, I'll do what I can for thee, and I'll pray that Heaven may grant it thee in the meantime.

PETULANT: Well, hark'ee.

[Mirabell *and* Petulant *talk apart*]

FAINALL: Petulant and you both will find Mirabell as warm a rival as a lover.

WITWOUD: Pshaw! pshaw! that she laughs at Petulant is plain. And for my part, but that it is almost a fashion to admire her, I should—hark'ee—to tell you a secret, but let it go no further—between friends, I shall never break my heart for her.

FAINALL: How!

WITWOUD: She's handsome; but she's a sort of an uncertain woman.

FAINALL: I thought you had died for her.

WITWOUD: Umh—no—

FAINALL: She has wit.

WITWOUD: 'Tis what she will hardly allow anybody else:—now, demme, I should hate that, if she were as handsome as Cleopatra. Mirabell is not so sure of her as he thinks for.

FAINALL: Why do you think so?

WITWOUD: We stayed pretty late there last night, and heard something of an uncle to Mirabell, who is lately come to town—and is between him and the best part of his estate. Mirabell and he are at some distance, as my Lady Wishfort has been told; and you know she hates Mirabell worse than a quaker hates a parrot, or than a fishmonger hates a hard frost. Whether this uncle has seen Mrs. Millamant or not, I cannot say, but there were items of such a treaty being in embryo; and if it should come to

life, poor Mirabell would be in some sort unfortunately fobbed, i'faith.

FAINALL: 'Tis impossible Millamant should hearken to it.

WITWOUD: Faith, my dear, I can't tell; she's a woman, and a kind of humourist.

MIRABELL: And this is the sum of what you could collect last night?

PETULANT: The quintessence. Maybe Witwoud knows more, he staid longer:—besides, they never mind him; they say anything before him.

MIRABELL: I thought you had been the greatest favourite.

PETULANT: Ay, *tête-à-tête*, but not in public, because I make remarks.

MIRABELL: You do?

PETULANT: Ay, ay; pox, I'm malicious, man! Now he's soft you know; they are not in awe of him—the fellow's well-bred; he's what you call a—what-d'ye-call-'em, a fine gentleman; but he's silly withal.

MIRABELL: I thank you, I know as much as my curiosity requires.—Fainall, are you for the Mall?

FAINALL: Ay, I'll take a turn before dinner.

WITWOUD: Ay, we'll all walk in the Park; the ladies talked of being there.

MIRABELL: I thought you were obliged to watch for your brother Sir Wilfull's arrival.

WITWOUD: No, no; he comes to his aunt's, my lady Wishfort. Pox on him! I shall be troubled with him too; what shall I do with the fool?

PETULANT: Beg him for his estate, that I may beg you afterwards: and so have but one trouble with you both.

WITWOUD: O rare Petulant! thou art as quick as fire in a frosty morning; thou shalt to the Mall with us, and we'll be very severe.

PETULANT: Enough, I'm in a humour to be severe.

MIRABELL: Are you? pray then walk by yourselves: let not us be accessory to your putting the ladies out of countenance with your senseless ribaldry, which you roar out aloud as often as they pass by you; and when you have made a handsome woman blush, then you think you have been severe.

PETULANT: What, what! then let 'em either show their innocence by not understanding what they hear, or else show their discretion by not hearing what they would not be thought to understand.

MIRABELL: But hast not thou then sense enough to know that thou oughtest to be most ashamed thyself, when thou hast put another out of countenance?

PETULANT: Not I, by this hand!—I always take blushing either for a sign of guilt, or ill-breeding.

MIRABELL: I confess you ought to think so. You are in the right, that you may plead the error of your judgment in defence of your practice.

    Where modesty's ill-manners, 'tis but fit
    That impudence and malice pass for wit.

[*Exeunt*]

Act II

SCENE 1: *St. James's Park.*

Mrs. Fainall *and* Mrs. Marwood.

MRS. FAINALL: Ay, ay, dear Marwood, if we will be happy, we must find the means in ourselves, and among ourselves. Men are ever in extremes; either doating or averse. While they are lovers, if they have fire and sense, their jealousies are insupportable; and when they cease to love (we ought to think at least) they loathe; they look upon us with horror and distaste; they meet us like the ghosts of what we were, and as such, fly from us.

MRS. MARWOOD: True, 'tis an unhappy circumstance of life, that love should ever die before us; and that the man so often should outlive the lover. But say what you will, 'tis better to be left, than never to have been loved. To pass our youth in dull indifference, to refuse the sweets of life because they once must leave us, is as preposterous as to wish to have been born old, because we one day must be old. For my part, my youth may wear and waste, but it shall never rust in my possession.

MRS. FAINALL: Then it seems you dissemble an aversion to mankind, only in compliance to my mother's humour?

MRS. MARWOOD: Certainly. To be free; I have no taste of those insipid dry discourses, with which our sex of force must entertain themselves, apart from men. We may affect endearments to each other, profess eternal friendships, and seem to doat like lovers; but 'tis not in our natures long to persevere. Love will resume his empire in our breasts; and every heart, or soon or late, receive and readmit him as its lawful tyrant.

MRS. FAINALL: Bless me, how have I been deceived! why you profess a libertine.

MRS. MARWOOD: You see my friendship by my freedom. Come, be as sincere, acknowledge that your sentiments agree with mine.

MRS. FAINALL: Never!

MRS. MARWOOD: You hate mankind?

MRS. FAINALL: Heartily, inveterately.

MRS. MARWOOD: Your husband?

MRS. FAINALL: Most transcendently; ay, though I say it, meritoriously.

MRS. MARWOOD: Give me your hand upon it.

MRS. FAINALL: There.

MRS. MARWOOD: I join with you; what I have said has been to try you.

MRS. FAINALL: Is it possible? dost thou hate those vipers, men?

MRS. MARWOOD: I have done hating 'em, and am now come to despise 'em; the next thing I have to do, is eternally to forget 'em.

MRS. FAINALL: There spoke the spirit of an Amazon, a Penthesilea!

MRS. MARWOOD: And yet I am thinking sometimes to carry my aversion further.

MRS. FAINALL: How?

MRS. MARWOOD: Faith, by marrying; if I could but find one that loved me very well, and would be thoroughly sensible of ill usage, I think I should do myself the violence of undergoing the ceremony.

MRS. FAINALL: You would not make him a cuckold?

MRS. MARWOOD: No; but I'd make him believe I did, and that's as bad.

MRS. FAINALL: Why, had not you as good do it?

MRS. MARWOOD: Oh! if he should ever discover it, he would then know the worst, and be out of his pain; but I would have him ever to continue upon the rack of fear and jealousy.

MRS. FAINALL: Ingenious mischief! would thou wert married to Mirabell.

MRS. MARWOOD: Would I were!

MRS. FAINALL: You change colour.

MRS. MARWOOD: Because I hate him.

MRS. FAINALL: So do I; but I can hear him named. But what reason have you to hate him in particular?

MRS. MARWOOD: I never loved him; he is, and always was, insufferably proud.

MRS. FAINALL: By the reason you give for your aversion, one would think it dissembled; for you have laid a fault to his charge, of which his enemies must acquit him.

MRS. MARWOOD: Oh then, it seems, you are one of his favourable enemies! Methinks you look a little pale, and now you flush again.

MRS. FAINALL: Do I? I think I am a little sick o' the sudden.

MRS. MARWOOD: What ails you?

MRS. FAINALL: My husband. Don't you see him? He turned short upon me unawares, and has almost overcome me.

Enter Fainall *and* Mirabell.

MRS. MARWOOD: Ha! ha! ha! he comes opportunely for you.

MRS. FAINALL: For you, for he has brought Mirabell with him.

FAINALL: My dear!

MRS. FAINALL: My soul!

FAINALL: You don't look well to-day, child.

MRS. FAINALL: D'ye think so?

MIRABELL: He is the only man that does, madam.

MRS. FAINALL: The only man that would tell me so at least; and the only man from whom I could hear it without mortification.

FAINALL: O my dear, I am satisfied of your tenderness; I know you cannot resent anything from me; especially what is an effect of my concern.

MRS. FAINALL: Mr. Mirabell, my mother interrupted

you in a pleasant relation last night; I would fain hear it out.

MIRABELL: The persons concerned in that affair have yet a tolerable reputation.—I am afraid Mr. Fainall will be censorious.

MRS. FAINALL: He has a humour more prevailing than his curiosity, and will willingly dispense with the hearing of one scandalous story, to avoid giving an occasion to make another by being seen to walk with his wife. This way, Mr. Mirabell, and I dare promise you will oblige us both.

[*Exeunt* Mrs. Fainall *and* Mirabell]

FAINALL: Excellent creature! Well, sure if I should live to be rid of my wife, I should be a miserable man.

MRS. MARWOOD: Ay!

FAINALL: For having only that one hope, the accomplishment of it, of consequence, must put an end to all my hopes; and what a wretch is he who must survive his hopes! Nothing remains when that day comes, but to sit down and weep like Alexander, when he wanted other worlds to conquer.

MRS. MARWOOD: Will you not follow 'em?

FAINALL: Faith, I think not.

MRS. MARWOOD: Pray let us; I have a reason.

FAINALL: You are not jealous?

MRS. MARWOOD: Of whom?

FAINALL: Of Mirabell.

MRS. MARWOOD: If I am, is it inconsistent with my love to you that I am tender of your honour?

FAINALL: You would intimate, then, as if there were a fellow-feeling between my wife and him.

MRS. MARWOOD: I think she does not hate him to that degree she would be thought.

FAINALL: But he, I fear, is too insensible.

MRS. MARWOOD: It may be you are deceived.

FAINALL: It may be so. I do now begin to apprehend it.

MRS. MARWOOD: What?

FAINALL: That I have been deceived, madam, and you are false.

MRS. MARWOOD: That I am false! what mean you?

FAINALL: To let you know I see through all your little arts.—Come, you both love him; and both have equally dissembled your aversion. Your mutual jealousies of one another have made you clash till you have both struck fire. I have seen the warm confession reddening on your cheeks, and sparkling from your eyes.

MRS. MARWOOD: You do me wrong.

FAINALL: I do not. 'Twas for my ease to oversee and wilfully neglect the gross advances made him by my wife; that by permitting her to be engaged, I might continue unsuspected in my pleasures; and take you oftener to my arms in full security. But could you think, because the nodding husband would not wake, that e'er the watchful lover slept?

MRS. MARWOOD: And wherewithal can you reproach me?

FAINALL: With infidelity, with loving another, with love of Mirabell.

MRS. MARWOOD: 'Tis false! I challenge you to show an instance that can confirm your groundless accusation. I hate him.

FAINALL: And wherefore do you hate him? he is insensible, and your resentment follows his neglect. An instance! the injuries you have done him are a proof: your interposing in his love. What cause had you to make discoveries of his pretended passion? to undeceive the credulous aunt, and be the officious obstacle of his match with Millamant?

MRS. MARWOOD: My obligations to my lady urged me; I had professed a friendship to her; and could not see her easy nature so abused by that dissembler.

FAINALL: What, was it conscience then? Professed a friendship! O the pious friendships of the female sex!

MRS. MARWOOD: More tender, more sincere, and more enduring, than all the vain and empty vows of men, whether professing love to us, or mutual faith to one another.

FAINALL: Ha! ha! ha! you are my wife's friend too.

MRS. MARWOOD: Shame and ingratitude! do you reproach me? you, you upbraid me? Have I been false to her, through strict fidelity to you, and sacrificed my friendship to keep my love inviolate? And have you the baseness to charge me with the guilt, unmindul of the merit? To you it should be meritorious, that I have been vicious: and do you reflect that guilt upon me, which should lie buried in your bosom?

FAINALL: You misinterpret my reproof. I meant but to remind you of the slight account you once could make of strictest ties, when set in competition with your love to me.

MRS. MARWOOD: 'Tis false, you urged it with deliberate malice! 'twas spoken in scorn, and I never will forgive it.

FAINALL: Your guilt, not your resentment, begets your rage. If yet you loved, you could forgive a jealousy: but you are stung to find you are discovered.

MRS. MARWOOD: It shall be all discovered. You too shall be discovered; be sure you shall. I can but be exposed.—If I do it myself I shall prevent your baseness.

FAINALL: Why, what will you do?

MRS. MARWOOD: Disclose it to your wife; own what has passed between us.

FAINALL: Frenzy!

MRS. MARWOOD: By all my wrongs I'll do't!—I'll publish to the world the injuries you have done me, both in my fame and fortune! With both I trusted you, you bankrupt in honour, as indigent of wealth.

FAINALL: Your fame I have preserved: your fortune has been bestowed as the prodigality of your love would have it, in pleasures which we both have shared. Yet, had not you been false, I had ere this repaid it—'tis true—had you permitted Mirabell with Millamant to have stolen their marriage, my lady had been incensed beyond all means of reconcilement: Millamant had forfeited the moiety of her fortune; which then would have descended to my wife;—and wherefore did I marry, but to make lawful prize of a rich widow's wealth, and squander it on love and you?

MRS. MARWOOD: Deceit and frivolous pretence!

FAINALL: Death, am I not married? What's pretence? Am I not imprisoned, fettered? Have I not a wife? nay a wife that was a widow, a young widow, a handsome widow, and would be again a widow, but that I have a heart of proof, and something of a constitution to bustle through the ways of wedlock and this world! Will you yet be reconciled to truth and me?

MRS. MARWOOD: Impossible. Truth and you are inconsistent: I hate you, and shall for ever.

FAINALL: For loving you?

MRS. MARWOOD: I loathe the name of love after such usage; and next to the guilt with which you would asperse me, I scorn you most. Farewell!

FAINALL: Nay, we must not part thus.

MRS. MARWOOD: Let me go.

FAINALL: Come, I'm sorry.

MRS. MARWOOD: I care not—let me go—break my hands, do—I'd leave 'em to get loose.

FAINALL: I would not hurt you for the world. Have I no other hold to keep you here?

MRS. MARWOOD: Well, I have deserved it all.

FAINALL: You know I love you.

MRS. MARWOOD: Poor dissembling!—O that—well, it is not yet—

FAINALL: What? what is it not? what is it not yet? It is not yet too late—

MRS. MARWOOD: No, it is not yet too late;—I have that comfort.

FAINALL: It is, to love another.

MRS. MARWOOD: But not to loathe, detest, abhor mankind, myself, and the whole treacherous world.

FAINALL: Nay, this is extravagance.—Come, I ask your pardon—no tears—I was to blame, I could not love you and be easy in my doubts. Pray forbear—I believe you; I'm convinced I've done you wrong; and any way, every way will make amends. I'll hate my wife yet more, damn her! I'll part with her, rob her of all she's worth, and we'll retire somewhere, anywhere, to another world. I'll marry thee—be pacified.—'Sdeath, they come, hide your face, your tears;—you have a mask, wear it a moment. This way, this way—be persuaded. [Exeunt]

SCENE 2: The same

Mirabell and Mrs. Fainall.

MRS. FAINALL: They are here yet.

MIRABELL: They are turning into the other walk.

MRS. FAINALL: While I only hated my husband, I could bear to see him; but since I have despised him, he's too offensive.

MIRABELL: O you should hate with prudence.

MRS. FAINALL: Yes, for I have loved with indiscretion.

MIRABELL: You should have just so much disgust for your husband, as may be sufficient to make you relish your lover.

MRS. FAINALL: You have been the cause that I have loved without bounds, and would you set limits to that aversion of which you have been the occasion? why did you make me marry this man?

MIRABELL: Why do we daily commit disagreeable and dangerous actions? to save that idol, reputation. If the familiarities of our loves had produced that consequence of which you were apprehensive, where could you have fixed a father's name with credit, but on a husband? I knew Fainall to be a man lavish of his morals, an interested and professing friend, a false and a designing lover; yet one whose wit and outward fair behaviour have gained a reputation with the town enough to make that woman stand excused who has suffered herself to be won by his addresses. A better man ought not to have been sacrificed to the occasion; a worse had not answered to the purpose. When you are weary of him you know your remedy.

MRS. FAINALL: I ought to stand in some degree of credit with you, Mirabell.

MIRABELL: In justice to you, I have made you privy to my whole design, and put it in your power to ruin or advance my fortune.

MRS. FAINALL: Whom have you instructed to represent your pretended uncle?

MIRABELL: Waitwell, my servant.

MRS. FAINALL: He is an humble servant to Foible my mother's woman, and may win her to your interest.

MIRABELL: Care is taken for that—she is won and worn by this time. They were married this morning.

MRS. FAINALL: Who?

MIRABELL: Waitwell and Foible. I would not tempt my servant to betray me by trusting him too far. If your mother, in hopes to ruin me, should consent to marry my pretended uncle, he might, like Mosca in the Fox,[1] stand upon terms; so I made him sure beforehand.

MRS. FAINALL: So if my poor mother is caught in a contract, you will discover the imposture betimes; and release her by producing a certificate of her gallant's former marriage?

MIRABELL: Yes, upon condition that she consent to my marriage with her niece, and surrender the moiety of her fortune in her possession.

MRS. FAINALL: She talked last night of endeavouring at a match between Millamant and your uncle.

[1] i.e. Ben Jonson's comedy, Volpone.

MIRABELL: That was by Foible's direction, and my instruction, that she might seem to carry it more privately.

MRS. FAINALL: Well, I have an opinion of your success; for I believe my lady will do anything to get a husband; and when she has this, which you have provided for her, I suppose she will submit to anything to get rid of him.

MIRABELL: Yes, I think the good lady would marry anything that resembled a man, though 'twere no more than what a butler could pinch out of a napkin.

MRS. FAINALL: Female frailty! we must all come to it, if we live to be old, and feel the craving of a false appetite when the true is decayed.

MIRABELL: An old woman's appetite is depraved like that of a girl—'tis the green sickness of a second childhood; and, like the faint offer of a latter spring, serves but to usher in the fall, and withers in an affected bloom.

MRS. FAINALL: Here's your mistress.

Enter Mrs. Millamant, Witwoud, *and* Mincing.

MIRABELL: Here she comes, i'faith, full sail, with her fan spread and her streamers out, and a shoal of fools for tenders; ha, no, I cry her mercy!

MRS. FAINALL: I see but one poor empty sculler; and he tows her woman after him.

MIRABELL: [*To* Mrs. Millamant] You seem to be unattended, madam—you used to have the *beau monde* throng after you; and a flock of gay fine perukes hovering round you.

WITWOUD: Like moths about a candle.—I had like to have lost my comparison for want of breath.

MRS. MILLAMANT: O I have denied myself airs today, I have walked as fast through the crowd.

WITWOUD: As a favourite just disgraced; and with as few followers.

MRS. MILLAMANT: Dear Mr. Witwoud, truce with your similitudes; for I'm as sick of 'em—

WITWOUD: As a physician of a good air.—I cannot help it, madam, though 'tis against myself.

MRS. MILLAMANT: Yet, again! Mincing, stand between me and his wit.

WITWOUD: Do, Mrs. Mincing, like a screen before a great fire.—I confess I do blaze to-day, I am too bright.

MRS. FAINALL: But, dear Millamant, why were you so long?

MRS. MILLAMANT: Long! Lord, have I not made violent haste; I have asked every living thing I met for you; I have inquired after you, as after a new fashion.

WITWOUD: Madam, truce with your similitudes.—No, you met her husband, and did not ask him for her.

MRS. MILLAMANT: By your leave, Witwoud, that were like inquiring after an old fashion, to ask a husband for his wife.

WITWOUD: Hum, a hit! a hit! a palpable hit! I confess it.

MRS. FAINALL: You were dressed before I came abroad.

MRS. MILLAMANT: Ay, that's true.—O but then I had—Mincing, what had I? why was I so long?

MINCING: O mem, your la'ship stayed to peruse a packet of letters.

MRS. MILLAMANT: O ay, letters—I had letters—I am persecuted with letters—I hate letters—Nobody knows how to write letters, and yet one has 'em, one does not know why. They serve one to pin up one's hair.

WITWOUD: Is that the way? Pray, madam, do you pin up your hair with all your letters? I find I must keep copies.

MRS. MILLAMANT: Only with those in verse, Mr. Witwoud, I never pin up my hair with prose.—I think I tried once, Mincing.

MINCING: O mem, I shall never forget it.

MRS. MILLAMANT: Ay, poor Mincing tift and tift all the morning.

MINCING: Till I had the cramp in my fingers, I'll vow, mem: and all to no purpose. But when your la'ship pins it up with poetry, it sits so pleasant the next day as anything, and is so pure and so crips.

WITWOUD: Indeed, so crips?

MINCING: You're such a critic, Mr. Witwoud.

MRS. MILLAMANT: Mirabell, did you take exceptions last night? O ay, and went away.—Now I think on't I'm angry—no, now I think on't I'm pleased —for I believe I gave you some pain.

MIRABELL: Does that please you?

MRS. MILLAMANT: Infinitely; I love to give pain.

MIRABELL: You would affect a cruelty which is not in your nature; your true vanity is in the power of pleasing.

MRS. MILLAMANT: Oh I ask you pardon for that—one's cruelty is one's power; and when one parts with one's cruelty, one parts with one's power; and when one has parted with that, I fancy one's old and ugly.

MIRABELL: Ay, ay, suffer your cruelty to ruin the object of your power, to destroy your lover—and then how vain, how lost a thing you'll be! Nay, 'tis true: you are no longer handsome when you've lost your lover; your beauty dies upon the instant; for beauty is the lover's gift; 'tis he bestows your charms—your glass is all a cheat. The ugly and the old, whom the looking-glass mortifies, yet after commendation can be flattered by it, and discover beauties in it; for that reflects our praises, rather than your face.

MRS. MILLAMANT: O the vanity of these men!—Fainall, d'ye hear him? If they did not commend us, we were not handsome! Now you must know they could not commend one, if one was not handsome. Beauty the lover's gift!—Lord, what is a lover, that it can give? Why, one makes lovers as fast as one pleases, and they live as long as one pleases, and they die as soon as one pleases; and then, if one pleases, one makes more.

WITWOUD: Very pretty. Why, you make no more of making of lovers, madam, than of making so many card-matches.

MRS. MILLAMANT: One no more owes one's beauty to a lover, than one's wit to an echo. They can but reflect what we look and say; vain empty things if we are silent or unseen, and want a being.

MIRABELL: Yet to those two vain empty things you owe the two greatest pleasures of your life.

MRS. MILLAMANT: How so?

MIRABELL: To your lover you owe the pleasure of hearing yourselves praised; and to an echo the pleasure of hearing yourselves talk.

WITWOUD: But I know a lady that loves talking so incessantly, she won't give an echo fair play; she has that everlasting rotation of tongue, that an echo must wait till she dies, before it can catch her last words.

MRS. MILLAMANT: O fiction!—Fainall, let us leave these men.

MIRABELL: Draw off Witwoud.
                                    [Aside to Mrs. Fainall]

MRS. FAINALL: Immediately.—I have a word or two for Mr. Witwoud.
                        [Exeunt Mrs. Fainall and Witwoud]

MIRABELL: I would beg a little private audience too. —You had the tyranny to deny me last night; though you knew I came to impart a secret to you that concerned my love.

MRS. MILLAMANT: You saw I was engaged.

MIRABELL: Unkind! You had the leisure to entertain a herd of fools; things who visit you from their excessive idleness; bestowing on your easiness that time which is the incumbrance of their lives. How can you find delight in such society? It is impossible they should admire you, they are not capable: or if they were, it should be to you as a mortification; for sure to please a fool is some degree of folly.

MRS. MILLAMANT: I please myself:—besides, sometimes to converse with fools is for my health.

MIRABELL: Your health! is there a worse disease than the conversation of fools?

MRS. MILLAMANT: Yes, the vapours; fools are physic for it, next to asafœtida.

MIRABELL: You are not in a course of fools?

MRS. MILLAMANT: Mirabell, if you persist in this offensive freedom, you'll displease me.—I think I must resolve, after all, not to have you:—we shan't agree.

MIRABELL: Not in our physic, it may be.

MRS. MILLAMANT: And yet our distemper, in all likelihood, will be the same; for we shall be sick of one another. I shan't endure to be reprimanded nor instructed: 'tis so dull to act always by advice,

and so tedious to be told of one's faults—I can't bear it. Well, I won't have you, Mirabell—I'm resolved—I think—you may go.—Ha! ha! ha! what would you give, that you could help loving me?

MIRABELL: I would give something that you did not know I could not help it.

MRS. MILLAMANT: Come, don't look grave then. Well, what do you say to me?

MIRABELL: I say that a man may as soon make a friend by his wit, or a fortune by his honesty, as win a woman by plain-dealing and sincerity.

MRS. MILLAMANT: Sententious Mirabell!—Prithee, don't look with that violent and inflexible wise face, like Solomon at the dividing of the child in an old tapestry hanging.

MIRABELL: You are merry, madam, but I would persuade you for a moment to be serious.

MRS. MILLAMANT: What, with that face? no, if you keep your countenance, 'tis impossible I should hold mine. Well, after all, there is something very moving in a love-sick face. Ha! ha! ha!—well, I won't laugh, don't be peevish—Heigho! now I'll be melancholy, as melancholy as a watch-light. Well, Mirabell, if ever you will win me woo me now.— Nay, if you are so tedious, fare you well;—I see they are walking away.

MIRABELL: Can you not find in the variety of your disposition one moment—

MRS. MILLAMANT: To hear you tell me Foible's married, and your plot like to speed;—no.

MIRABELL: But how come you to know it?

MRS. MILLAMANT: Without the help of the devil, you can't imagine; unless she should tell me herself. Which of the two it may have been I will leave you to consider; and when you have done thinking of that, think of me.   [Exit]

MIRABELL: I have something more.—Gone!—Think of you? to think of a whirlwind, though't were in a whirlwind, were a case of more steady contemplation; a very tranquillity of mind and mansion. A fellow that lives in a windmill, has not a more whimsical dwelling than the heart of a man that is lodged in a woman. There is no point of the compass to which they cannot turn, and by which they are not turned; and by one as well as another; for motion, not method, is their occupation. To know this, and yet continue to be in love, is to be made wise from the dictates of reason, and yet persevere to play the fool by the force of instinct.—Oh, here come my pair of turtles!—What, billing so sweetly! is not Valentine's day over with you yet?

Enter Waitwell and Foible.
Sirrah, Waitwell, why sure you think you were married for your own recreation, and not for my conveniency.

WAITWELL: Your pardon, sir. With submission, we have indeed been solacing in lawful delights; but still with an eye to business, sir. I have instructed her as well as I could. If she can take your directions as readily as my instructions, sir, your affairs are in a prosperous way.

MIRABELL: Give you joy, Mrs. Foible.

FOIBLE: O las, sir, I'm so ashamed!—I'm afraid my lady has been in a thousand inquietudes for me. But I protest, sir, I made as much haste as I could.

WAITWELL: That she did indeed, sir. It was my fault that she did not make more.

MIRABELL: That I believe.

FOIBLE: But I told my lady as you instructed me, sir, that I had a prospect of seeing Sir Rowland your uncle; and that I would put her ladyship's picture in my pocket to show him; which I'll be sure to say has made him so enamoured of her beauty, that he burns with impatience to lie at her ladyship's feet, and worship the original.

MIRABELL: Excellent Foible! matrimony has made you eloquent in love.

WAITWELL: I think she has profited, sir, I think so.

FOIBLE: You have seen Madam Millamant, sir?

MIRABELL: Yes.

FOIBLE: I told her, sir, because I did not know that you might find an opportunity; she had so much company last night.

MIRABELL: Your diligence will merit more—in the mean time—   [Gives money]

FOIBLE: O dear sir, your humble servant!

WAITWELL: Spouse.

MIRABELL: Stand off, sir, not a penny!—Go on and prosper, Foible:—the lease shall be made good, and the farm stocked, if we succeed.

FOIBLE: I don't question your generosity, sir: and you need not doubt of success. If you have no more commands, sir, I'll be gone; I'm sure my lady is at her toilet, and can't dress till I come.—O dear, I'm sure that [Looking out] was Mrs. Marwood that went by in a mask! If she has seen me with you I'm sure she'll tell my lady. I'll make haste home and prevent her. Your servant, sir.—B'w'y, Waitwell.
                                              [Exit]

WAITWELL: Sir Rowland, if you please.—The jade's so pert upon her preferment she forgets herself.

MIRABELL: Come, sir, will you endeavour to forget yourself, and transform into Sir Rowland?

WAITWELL: Why, sir, it will be impossible I should remember myself.—Married, knighted, and attended all in one day! 'tis enough to make any man forget himself. The difficulty will be how to recover my acquaintance and familiarity with my former self, and fall from my transformation to a reformation into Waitwell. Nay, I shan't be quite the same Waitwell neither; for now, I remember me, I'm married, and can't be my own man again.

    Ay there's my grief; that's the sad change of life,
To lose my title, and yet keep my wife. [Exeunt]

Act III

SCENE 1: A Room in Lady Wishfort's House

Lady Wishfort at her toilet, Peg waiting.

LADY WISHFORT: Merciful! no news of Foible yet?

PEG: No, madam.

LADY WISHFORT: I have no more patience.—If I have not fretted myself till I am pale again, there's no veracity in me! Fetch me the red—the red, do you hear, sweetheart?—An arrant ash-colour, as I am a person! Look you how this wench stirs! Why dost thou not fetch me a little red? didst thou not hear me, Mopus?

PEG: The red ratafia does your ladyship mean, or the cherry-brandy?

LADY WISHFORT: Ratafia, fool! no, fool. Not the ratafia, fool—grant me patience!—I mean the Spanish paper, idiot—complexion, darling. Paint, paint, paint, dost thou understand that, changeling, dangling thy hands like bobbins before thee? Why dost thou not stir, puppet? thou wooden thing upon wires!

PEG: Lord, madam, your ladyship is so impatient!—I cannot come at the paint, madam; Mrs. Foible has locked it up, and carried the key with her.

LADY WISHFORT: A pox take you both!—fetch me the cherry-brandy then. [Exit Peg] I'm as pale and as faint, I look like Mrs. Qualmsick, the curate's wife, that's always breeding.—Wench, come, come, wench, what art thou doing? sipping, tasting?—Save thee, dost thou not know the bottle?

Re-enter Peg with a bottle and china cup.

PEG: Madam, I was looking for a cup.

LADY WISHFORT: A cup, save thee! and what a cup hast thou brought!—Dost thou take me for a fairy, to drink out of an acorn? Why didst thou not bring thy thimble? Hast thou ne'er a brass thimble clinking in thy pocket with a bit of nutmeg?—I warrant thee. Come, fill, fill!—So—again.— [Knocking at the door]—See who that is.—Set down the bottle first—here, here, under the table. —What, wouldst thou go with the bottle in thy hand, like a tapster? As I am a person, this wench has lived in an inn upon the road, before she came to me, like Maritornes the Asturian in Don Quixote!—No Foible yet?

PEG: No, madam; Mrs. Marwood.

LADY WISHFORT: Oh, Marwood; let her come in.— Come in, good Marwood.

Enter Mrs. Marwood.

MRS. MARWOOD: I'm surprised to find your ladyship in dishabille at this time of day.

LADY WISHFORT: Foible's a lost thing; has been abroad since morning, and never heard of since.

MRS. MARWOOD: I saw her but now, as I came masked through the park, in conference with Mirabell.

LADY WISHFORT: With Mirabell!—You call my blood into my face, with mentioning that traitor. She durst not have the confidence! I sent her to negotiate an affair, in which, if I'm detected, I'm undone. If that wheedling villain has wrought upon Foible to detect me, I'm ruined. O my dear friend, I'm a wretch of wretches if I'm detected.

MRS. MARWOOD: O madam, you cannot suspect Mrs. Foible's integrity!

LADY WISHFORT: Oh, he carries poison in his tongue that would corrupt integrity itself! If she has given him an opportunity, she has as good as put her integrity into his hands. Ah, dear Marwood, what's integrity to an opportunity?—Hark! I hear her!—dear friend, retire into my closet, that I may examine her with more freedom.—You'll pardon me, dear friend; I can make bold with you.—There are books over the chimney.—Quarles and Prynne, and "The Short View of the Stage," with Bunyan's works, to entertain you.—[To Peg]—Go, you thing, and send her in.

[Exeunt Mrs. Marwood and Peg]

Enter Foible.

LADY WISHFORT: O Foible, where hast thou been? what hast thou been doing?

FOIBLE: Madam, I have seen the party.

LADY WISHFORT: But what hast thou done?

FOIBLE: Nay, 'tis your ladyship has done, and are to do; I have only promised. But a man so enamoured —so transported!—Well, here it is, all that is left; all that is not kissed away.—Well, if worshipping of pictures be a sin——poor Sir Rowland, I say.

LADY WISHFORT: The miniature has been counted like;—but hast thou not betrayed me, Foible? hast thou not detected me to that faithless Mirabell? —What hadst thou to do with him in the Park? Answer me, has he got nothing out of thee?

FOIBLE: [Aside] So the devil has been beforehand with me. What shall I say?—[Aloud]—Alas, madam, could I help it, if I met that confident thing? was I in fault? If you had heard how he used me, and all upon your ladyship's account, I'm sure you would not suspect my fidelity. Nay, if that had been the worst, I could have borne; but he had a fling at your ladyship too; and then I could not hold; but i'faith I gave him his own.

LADY WISHFORT: Me? what did the filthy fellow say?

FOIBLE: O madam! 'tis a shame to say what he said— with his taunts and his fleers, tossing up his nose. Humph! (says he) what, you are a hatching some plot (says he), you are so early abroad, or catering (says he), ferreting for some disbanded officer, I warrant.—Half-pay is but thin subsistence (says he);—well, what pension does your lady propose? Let me see (says he), what, she must come down

pretty deep now, she's superannuated (says he) and—

LADY WISHFORT: Odds my life, I'll have him, I'll have him murdered! I'll have him poisoned! Where does he eat?—I'll marry a drawer to have him poisoned in his wine. I'll send for Robin from Locket's immediately.

FOIBLE: Poison him! poisoning's too good for him. Starve him, madam, starve him; marry Sir Rowland, and get him disinherited. Oh you would bless yourself to hear what he said!

LADY WISHFORT: A villain! superannuated!

FOIBLE: Humph (says he), I hear you are laying designs against me too (says he), and Mrs. Millamant is to marry my uncle (he does not suspect a word of your ladyship); but (says he) I'll fit you for that. I warrant you (says he) I'll hamper you for that (says he); you and your old frippery too (says he); I'll handle you—

LADY WISHFORT: Audacious villain! handle me; would he durst!—Frippery! old frippery! was there ever such a foul-mouthed fellow? I'll be married to-morrow, I'll be contracted to-night.

FOIBLE: The sooner the better, madam.

LADY WISHFORT: Will Sir Rowland be here, sayest thou? when, Foible?

FOIBLE: Incontinently, madam. No new sheriff's wife expects the return of her husband after knighthood with that impatience in which Sir Rowland burns for the dear hour of kissing your ladyship's hand after dinner.

LADY WISHFORT: Frippery! superannuated frippery! I'll frippery the villain; I'll reduce him to frippery and rags! a tatterdemalion! I hope to see him hung with tatters, like a Long-lane pent-house or a gibbet thief. A slander-mouthed railer! I warrant the spendthrift prodigal's in debt as much as the million lottery, or the whole court upon a birthday. I'll spoil his credit with his tailor. Yes, he shall have my niece with her fortune, he shall.

FOIBLE: He! I hope to see him lodge in Ludgate first, and angle into Blackfriars for brass farthings with an old mitten.

LADY WISHFORT: Ay, dear Foible; thank thee for that, dear Foible. He has put me out of all patience. I shall never recompose my features to receive Sir Rowland with any economy of face. This wretch has fretted me that I am absolutely decayed. Look, Foible.

FOIBLE: Your ladyship has frowned a little too rashly, indeed, madam. There are some cracks discernible in the white varnish.

LADY WISHFORT: Let me see the glass.—Cracks, sayest thou?—why, I am errantly flayed—I look like an old peeled wall. Thou must repair me, Foible, before Sir Rowland comes, or I shall never keep up to my picture.

FOIBLE: I warrant you, madam, a little art once made your picture like you; and now a little of the same art must make you like your picture. Your picture must sit for you, madam.

LADY WISHFORT: But art thou sure Sir Rowland will not fail to come? or will he not fail when he does come? Will he be importunate, Foible, and push? For if he should not be importunate, I shall never break decorums:—I shall die with confusion, if I am forced to advance.—Oh no, I can never advance!—I shall swoon if he should expect advances. No, I hope Sir Rowland is better bred than to put a lady to the necessity of breaking her forms. I won't be too coy, neither.—I won't give him despair—but a little disdain is not amiss; a little scorn is alluring.

FOIBLE: A little scorn becomes your ladyship.

LADY WISHFORT: Yes, but tenderness becomes me best—a sort of dyingness—you see that picture has a sort of a—ha, Foible! a swimmingness in the eye —yes, I'll look so—my niece affects it; but she wants features. Is Sir Rowland handsome? Let my toilet be removed—I'll dress above. I'll receive Sir Rowland here. Is he handsome? Don't answer me. I won't know: I'll be surprised, I'll be taken by surprise.

FOIBLE: By storm, madam, Sir Rowland's a brisk man.

LADY WISHFORT: Is he! O then he'll importune, if he's a brisk man. I shall save decorums if Sir Rowland importunes. I have a mortal terror at the apprehension of offending against decorums. O, I'm glad he's a brisk man. Let my things be removed, good Foible.   [Exit]

Enter Mrs. Fainall.

MRS. FAINALL: O Foible, I have been in a fright, lest I should come too late! That devil Marwood saw you in the Park with Mirabell, and I'm afraid will discover it to my lady.

FOIBLE: Discover what, madam!

MRS. FAINALL: Nay, nay, put not on that strange face, I am privy to the whole design, and know that Waitwell, to whom thou wert this morning married, is to personate Mirabell's uncle, and as such, winning my lady, to involve her in those difficulties from which Mirabell only must release her, by his making his conditions to have my cousin and her fortune left to her own disposal.

FOIBLE: O dear madam, I beg your pardon. It was not my confidence in your ladyship that was deficient; but I thought the former good correspondence between your ladyship and Mr. Mirabell might have hindered his communicating this secret.

MRS. FAINALL: Dear Foible, forget that.

FOIBLE: O dear madam, Mr. Mirabell is such a sweet, winning gentleman—but your ladyship is the pattern of generosity.—Sweet lady, to be so good! Mr. Mirabell cannot choose but be grateful. I find your ladyship has his heart still. Now, madam, I can safely tell your ladyship our success; Mrs. Marwood had told my lady; but I warrant I managed myself; I turned it all for the better. I told my lady that Mr. Mirabell railed at her; I laid horrid things to his charge, I'll vow; and my lady is so incensed that she'll be contracted to Sir Rowland to-night, she says; I warrant I worked her up, that he may have her for asking for, as they say of a Welsh maidenhead.

MRS. FAINALL: O rare Foible!

FOIBLE: Madam, I beg your ladyship to acquaint Mr. Mirabell of his success. I would be seen as little as possible to speak to him:—besides, I believe Madam Marwood watches me.—She has a month's mind; but I know Mr. Mirabell can't abide her.— John!—[Calls] remove my lady's toilet.—Madam, your servant: my lady is so impatient, I fear she'll come for me if I stay.

MRS. FAINALL: I'll go with you up the back-stairs, lest I should meet her.   [Exeunt]

SCENE 2: Lady Wishfort's Closet

Mrs. Marwood.

MRS. MARWOOD: Indeed, Mrs. Engine, is it thus with you? are you become a go-between of this importance? yes, I shall watch you. Why this wench is the passe-partout, a very master-key to everybody's strong-box. My friend Fainall, have you carried it so swimmingly? I thought there was something in it; but it seems 'tis over with you. Your loathing is not from a want of appetite, then, but from a surfeit. Else you could never be so cool to fall from a principal to be an assistant; to procure for him! a pattern of generosity that, I confess. Well, Mr. Fainall, you have met with your match.—O man, man! woman, woman! the devil's an ass: if I were a painter, I would draw him like an idiot, a driveller with a bib and bells: man should have his head and horns, and woman the rest of him. Poor simple fiend!—"Madam Marwood has a month's mind, but he can't abide her."—'Twere better for him you had not been his confessor in that affair, without you could have kept his counsel closer. I shall not prove another pattern of generosity: he has not obliged me to that with those excesses of himself! and now I'll have none of him. Here comes the good lady, panting ripe; with a heart full of hope, and a head full of care, like any chemist upon the day of projection.

Enter Lady Wishfort.

LADY WISHFORT: O dear, Marwood, what shall I say for this rude forgetfulness?—but my dear friend is all goodness.

MRS. MARWOOD: No apologies, dear madam, I have been very well entertained.

LADY WISHFORT: As I'm a person, I am in a very chaos to think I should so forget myself:—but I have such an olio of affairs, really I know not what to do.—Foible!—[*Calls*] I expect my nephew, Sir Wilfull, every moment too.—Why, Foible!—He means to travel for improvement.

MRS. MARWOOD: Methinks Sir Wilfull should rather think of marrying than travelling at his years. I hear he is turned of forty.

LADY WISHFORT: O he's in less danger of being spoiled by his travels—I am against my nephew's marrying too young. It will be time enough when he comes back, and has acquired discretion to choose for himself.

MRS. MARWOOD: Methinks Mrs. Millamant and he would make a very fit match. He may travel afterwards. 'Tis a thing very usual with young gentlemen.

LADY WISHFORT: I promise you I have thought on't—and since 'tis your judgment, I'll think on't again. I assure you I will; I value your judgment extremely. On my word, I'll propose it.

Enter Foible.

LADY WISHFORT: Come, come, Foible—I had forgot my nephew will be here before dinner:—I must make haste.

FOIBLE: Mr. Witwoud and Mr. Petulant are come to dine with your ladyship.

LADY WISHFORT: O dear, I can't appear till I'm dressed.—Dear Marwood, shall I be free with you again, and beg you to entertain 'em? I'll make all imaginable haste. Dear friend, excuse me.

[*Exeunt*]

SCENE 3:   *A Room in Lady Wishfort's House*

Mrs. Marwood, Mrs. Millamant *and* Mincing.

MRS. MILLAMANT: Sure never anything was so unbred as that odious man!—Marwood, your servant.

MRS. MARWOOD: You have a colour; what's the matter?

MRS. MILLAMANT: That horrid fellow, Petulant, has provoked me into a flame:—I have broken my fan. —Mincing, lend me yours; is not all the powder out of my hair?

MRS. MARWOOD: No. What has he done?

MRS. MILLAMANT: Nay, he has done nothing; he has only talked—nay, he has said nothing neither; but he has contradicted everything that has been said. For my part, I thought Witwoud and he would have quarrelled.

MINCING: I vow, mem, I thought once they would have fit.

MRS. MILLAMANT: Well, 'tis a lamentable thing, I swear, that one has not the liberty of choosing one's acquaintance as one does one's clothes.

MRS. MARWOOD: If we had that liberty, we should be as weary of one set of acquaintance, though never

so good, as we are of one suit though never so fine. A fool and a doily stuff would now and then find days of grace, and be worn for variety.

MRS. MILLAMANT: I could consent to wear 'em, if they would wear alike; but fools never wear out—they are such *drap de Berri* things! without one could give 'em to one's chambermaid after a day or two.

MRS. MARWOOD: 'Twere better so indeed. Or what think you of the playhouse? A fine gay glossy fool should be given there, like a new masking habit, after the masquerade is over, and we have done with the disguise. For a fool's visit is always a disguise; and never admitted by a woman of wit, but to blind her affair with a lover of sense. If you would but appear barefaced now, and own Mirabell, you might as easily put off Petulant and Witwoud as your hood and scarf. And indeed, 'tis time, for the town has found it; the secret is grown too big for the pretence. 'Tis like Mrs. Primly's great belly; she may lace it down before, but it burnishes on her hips. Indeed, Millamant, you can no more conceal it, than my Lady Strammel can her face; that goodly face, which in defiance of her Rhenish wine tea, will not be comprehended in a mask.

MRS. MILLAMANT: I'll take my death, Marwood, you are more censorious than a decayed beauty, or a discarded toast.—Mincing, tell the men they may come up.—My aunt is not dressing here; their folly is less provoking than your malice. [*Exit Mincing*] The town has found it! what has it found? That Mirabell loves me is no more a secret, than it is a secret that you discovered it to my aunt, or than the reason why you discovered it is a secret.

MRS. MARWOOD: You are nettled.

MRS. MILLAMANT: You're mistaken. Ridiculous!

MRS. MARWOOD: Indeed, my dear, you'll tear another fan, if you don't mitigate those violent airs.

MRS. MILLAMANT: O silly! ha! ha! ha! I could laugh immoderately. Poor Mirabell! his constancy to me has quite destroyed his complaisance for all the world beside. I swear, I never enjoined it him to be so coy—If I had the vanity to think he would obey me, I would command him to show more gallantry—'tis hardly well-bred to be so particular on one hand, and so insensible on the other. But I despair to prevail, and so let him follow his own way. Ha! ha! ha! pardon me, dear creature, I must laugh, ha! ha! ha! though I grant you 'tis a little barbarous, ha! ha! ha!

MRS. MARWOOD: What pity 'tis so much fine raillery, and delivered with so significant gesture, should be so unhappily directed to miscarry!

MRS. MILLAMANT: Ha! dear creature, I ask your pardon—I swear I did not mind you.

MRS. MARWOOD: Mr. Mirabell and you both may think it a thing impossible, when I shall tell him by telling you—

MRS. MILLAMANT: O dear, what? for it is the same thing if I hear it—ha! ha! ha!

MRS. MARWOOD: That I detest him, hate him, madam.

MRS. MILLAMANT: O madam, why so do I—and yet the creature loves me, ha! ha! ha! how can one forbear laughing to think of it.—I am a sibyl if I am not amazed to think what he can see in me. I'll take my death, I think you are handsomer—and within a year or two as young—if you could but stay for me, I should overtake you—but that cannot be.—Well, that thought makes me melancholic.—Now, I'll be sad.

MRS. MARWOOD: Your merry note may be changed sooner than you think.

MRS. MILLAMANT: D'ye say so? Then I'm resolved I'll have a song to keep up my spirits.

Re-enter Mincing.

MINCING: The gentlemen stay but to comb, madam, and will wait on you.

MRS. MILLAMANT: Desire Mrs. — that is in the next room to sing the song I would have learned yesterday.—You shall hear it, madam—not that there's any great matter in it—but 'tis agreeable to my humour.

SONG

Love's but the frailty of the mind,
    When 'tis not with ambition joined;
A sickly flame, which, if not fed, expires,
And feeding, wastes in self-consuming fires.

'Tis not to wound a wanton boy
    Or amorous youth, that gives the joy;
But 'tis the glory to have pierced a swain,
For whom inferior beauties sighed in vain.

Then I alone the conquest prize,
    When I insult a rival's eyes:
If there's delight in love, 'tis when I see
That heart, which others bleed for, bleed for me.

Enter Petulant *and* Witwoud.

MRS. MILLAMANT: Is your animosity composed, gentlemen?

WITWOUD: Raillery, raillery, madam; we have no animosity—we hit off a little wit now and then, but no animosity.—The falling-out of wits is like the falling-out of lovers:—we agree in the main, like treble and bass.—Ha, Petulant?

PETULANT: Ay, in the main—but when I have a humour to contradict—

WITWOUD: Ay, when he has a humour to contradict, then I contradict too. What, I know my cue. Then we contradict one another like two battledores; for contradictions beget one another like Jews.

PETULANT: If he says black's black—if I have a humour to say 'tis blue—let that pass—all's one

for that. If I have a humour to prove it, it must be granted.

WITWOUD: Not positively must—but it may—it may.

PETULANT: Yes, it positively must, upon proof positive.

WITWOUD: Ay, upon proof positive it must; but upon proof presumptive it only may.—That's a logical distinction now, madam.

MRS. MARWOOD: I perceive your debates are of importance, and very learnedly handled.

PETULANT: Importance is one thing, and learning's another, but a debate's a debate, that I assert.

WITWOUD: Petulant's an enemy to learning; he relies altogether on his parts.

PETULANT: No, I'm no enemy to learning; it hurts not me.

MRS. MARWOOD: That's a sign indeed it's no enemy to you.

PETULANT: No, no, it's no enemy to anybody but them that have it.

MRS. MILLAMANT: Well, an illiterate man's my aversion: I wonder at the impudence of any illiterate man to offer to make love.

WITWOUD: That I confess I wonder at too.

MRS. MILLAMANT: Ah! to marry an ignorant that can hardly read or write!

PETULANT: Why should a man be any further from being married, though he can't read, than he is from being hanged? The ordinary's paid for setting the psalm, and the parish-priest for reading the ceremony. And for the rest which is to follow in both cases, a man may do it without book— so all's one for that.

MRS. MILLAMANT: D'ye hear the creature?—Lord, here's company, I'll be gone.   [*Exit*]

Enter Sir Wilfull Witwoud *in a riding dress, followed by* Footman.

WITWOUD: In the name of Bartlemew and his fair, what have we here?

MRS. MARWOOD: 'Tis your brother, I fancy. Don't you know him?

WITWOUD: Not I.—Yes, I think it is he—I've almost forgot him; I have not seen him since the Revolution.

FOOTMAN: [*To Sir Wilfull*] Sir, my lady's dressing. Here's company; if you please to walk in, in the mean time.

SIR WILFULL: Dressing! what, it's but morning here, I warrant, with you in London; we should count it towards afternoon in our parts, down in Shropshire.—Why then, belike, my aunt han't dined yet, ha, friend?

FOOTMAN: Your aunt, sir?

SIR WILFULL: My aunt, sir! yes, my aunt, sir, and your lady, sir; your lady is my aunt, sir.—Why, what dost thou not know me, friend? why then send somebody hither that does. How long hast thou lived with thy lady, fellow, ha?

FOOTMAN: A week, sir; longer than anybody in the house, except my lady's woman.

SIR WILFULL: Why then belike thou dost not know thy lady, if thou seest her, ha, friend?

FOOTMAN: Why, truly, sir, I cannot safely swear to her face in a morning, before she is dressed. 'Tis like I may give a shrewd guess at her by this time.

SIR WILFULL: Well, prithee try what thou canst do; if thou canst not guess, inquire her out, dost hear, fellow? and tell her, her nephew, Sir Wilfull Witwoud, is in the house.

FOOTMAN: I shall, sir.

SIR WILFULL: Hold ye, hear me, friend; a word with you in your ear; prithee who are these gallants?

FOOTMAN: Really, sir, I can't tell; here come so many here, 'tis hard to know 'em all.　　　　[Exit]

SIR WILFULL: Oons, this fellow knows less than a starling; I don't think a' knows his own name.

MRS. MARWOOD: Mr. Witwoud, your brother is not behindhand in forgetfulness—I fancy he has forgot you too.

WITWOUD: I hope so—the devil take him that remembers first, I say.

SIR WILFULL: Save you, gentlemen and lady!

MRS. MARWOOD: For shame, Mr. Witwoud; why don't you speak to him?—And you, sir.

WITWOUD: Petulant, speak.

PETULANT: And you, sir.

SIR WILFULL: No offence, I hope.
　　　　　　　[Salutes Mrs. Marwood]

MRS. MARWOOD: No sure, sir.

WITWOUD: This is a vile dog, I see that already. No offence! ha! ha! ha! To him; to him, Petulant, smoke him.

PETULANT: It seems as if you had come a journey, sir; hem, hem.　　　[Surveying him round]

SIR WILFULL: Very likely, sir, that it may seem so.

PETULANT: No offence, I hope, sir.

WITWOUD: Smoke the boots, the boots; Petulant, the boots: ha! ha! ha!

SIR WILFULL: May be not, sir; thereafter, as 'tis meant, sir.

PETULANT: Sir, I presume upon the information of your boots.

SIR WILFULL: Why, 'tis like you may, sir: if you are not satisfied with the information of my boots, sir, if you will step to the stable, you may inquire further of my horse, sir.

PETULANT: Your horse, sir! your horse is an ass, sir!

SIR WILFULL: Do you speak by way of offence, sir?

MRS. MARWOOD: The gentleman's merry, that's all sir. —[Aside] S'life, we shall have a quarrel betwixt an horse and an ass before they find one another out.—[Aloud] You must not take anything amiss from your friends, sir. You are among your friends here, though it may be you don't know it.—If I am not mistaken, you are Sir Wilfull Witwoud.

SIR WILFULL: Right, lady; I am Sir Wilfull Witwoud, so I write myself; no offence to anybody, I hope;

and nephew to the Lady Wishfort of this mansion.

MRS. MARWOOD: Don't you know this gentleman, sir?

SIR WILFULL: Hum! what, sure 'tis not—yea by'r Lady, but 'tis—s'heart, I know not whether 'tis or no—yea, but 'tis, by the Wrekin. Brother Anthony! what Tony, i'faith! what, dost thou not know me? By'r Lady, nor I thee, thou art so becravated, and so beperiwigged.—S'heart, why dost not speak? art thou overjoyed?

WITWOUD: Odso, brother, is it you? your servant, brother.

SIR WILFULL: Your servant! why yours, sir. Your servant again—s'heart, and your friend and servant to that—and a—and a—flap-dragon for your service, sir! and a hare's foot and a hare's scut for your service, sir! an you be so cold and so courtly.

WITWOUD: No offence, I hope, brother.

SIR WILFULL: S'heart, sir, but there is, and much offence!—A pox, is this your inns o' court breeding, not to know your friends and your relations, your elders and your betters?

WITWOUD: Why, brother Wilfull of Salop, you may be as short as a Shrewsbury-cake, if you please. But I tell you 'tis not modish to know relations in town: you think you're in the country, where great lubberly brothers slabber and kiss one another when they meet, like a call of serjeants— 'tis not the fashion here; 'tis not indeed, dear brother.

SIR WILFULL: The fashion's a fool; and you're a fop, dear brother. S'heart, I've suspected this—by'r Lady, I conjectured you were a fop, since you began to change the style of your letters, and write on a scrap of paper gilt round the edges, no bigger than a subpœna. I might expect this when you left off, "Honoured brother;" and "hoping you are in good health," and so forth—to begin with a "Rat me, knight, I'm so sick of a last night's debauch" —'ods heart, and then tell a familiar tale of a cock and a bull, and a whore and a bottle, and so conclude.—You could write news before you were out of your time, when you lived with honest Pimple Nose the attorney of Furnival's Inn—you could entreat to be remembered then to your friends round the Wrekin. We could have gazettes, then, and Dawks's Letter, and the Weekly Bill, till of late days.

PETULANT: S'life, Witwoud, were you ever an attorney's clerk? of the family of the Furnival? Ha! ha! ha!

WITWOUD: Ay, ay, but that was but for a while: not long, not long. Pshaw! I was not in my own power then;—an orphan, and this fellow was my guardian; ay, ay, I was glad to consent to that, man, to come to London: he had the disposal of me then. If I had not agreed to that, I might have been bound 'prentice to a felt-maker in Shrewsbury;

this fellow would have bound me to a maker of fells.

SIR WILFULL: S'heart, and better than to be bound to a maker of fops; where, I suppose, you have served your time; and now you may set up for yourself.

MRS. MARWOOD: You intend to travel, sir, as I'm informed.

SIR WILFULL: Belike I may, madam. I may chance to sail upon the salt seas, if my mind hold.

PETULANT: And the wind serve.

SIR WILFULL: Serve or not serve, I shan't ask licence of you, sir; nor the weathercock your companion: I direct my discourse to the lady, sir.—'Tis like my aunt may have told you, madam—yes, I have settled my concerns, I may say now, and am minded to see foreign parts. If an how that the peace holds, whereby that is, taxes abate.

MRS. MARWOOD: I thought you had designed for France at all adventures.

SIR WILFULL: I can't tell that; 'tis like I may, and 'tis like I may not. I am somewhat dainty in making a resolution—because when I make it I keep it. I don't stand shill I, shall I, then; if I say't, I'll do't; but I have thoughts to tarry a small matter in town, to learn somewhat of your lingo first, before I cross the seas. I'd gladly have a spice of your French as they say, whereby to hold discourse in foreign countries.

MRS. MARWOOD: Here's an academy in town for that use.

SIR WILFULL: There is? 'Tis like there may.

MRS. MARWOOD: No doubt you will return very much improved.

WITWOUD: Yes, refined, like a Dutch skipper from a whale fishing.

Enter Lady Wishfort *and* Fainall.

LADY WISHFORT: Nephew, you are welcome.

SIR WILFULL: Aunt, your servant.

FAINALL: Sir Wilfull, your most faithful servant.

SIR WILFULL: Cousin Fainall, give me your hand.

LADY WISHFORT: Cousin Witwoud, your servant; Mr. Petulant, your servant—nephew, you are welcome again. Will you drink anything after your journey, nephew; before you eat? dinner's almost ready.

SIR WILFULL: I'm very well, I thank you, aunt—however, I thank you for your courteous offer. S'heart I was afraid you would have been in the fashion too, and have remembered to have forgot your relations. Here's your cousin Tony, belike, I mayn't call him brother for fear of offence.

LADY WISHFORT: O, he's a railleur, nephew—my cousin's a wit: and your great wits always rally their best friends to choose. When you have been abroad, nephew, you'll understand raillery better.

[Fainall *and* Mrs. Marwood *talk apart*]

SIR WILFULL: Why then let him hold his tongue in the mean time; and rail when that day comes.

Enter Mincing.

MINCING: Mem, I am come to acquaint your la'ship that dinner is impatient.

SIR WILFULL: Impatient! why then belike it won't stay till I pull off my boots.—Sweetheart, can you help me to a pair of slippers?—My man's with his horses, I warrant.

LADY WISHFORT: Fy, fy, nephew! you would not pull off your boots here?—Go down into the hall—dinner shall stay for you.—My nephew's a little unbred, you'll pardon him, madam.—Gentlemen, will you walk?—Marwood—

MRS. MARWOOD: I'll follow you, madam—before Sir Wilfull is ready.

[*Exeunt all but* Mrs. Marwood *and* Fainall]

FAINALL: Why then, Foible's a bawd, an arrant, rank, match-making bawd: and I, it seems, am a husband, a rank husband; and my wife a very arrant, rank wife—all in the way of the world. 'Sdeath, to be a cuckold by anticipation, a cuckold in embryo! sure I was born with budding antlers, like a young satyr, or a citizen's child. 'Sdeath! to be out-witted—to be out-jilted—out-matrimony'd!—If I had kept my speed like a stag, 'twere somewhat,—but to crawl after, with my horns, like a snail, and be outstripped by my wife—'tis scurvy wedlock.

MRS. MARWOOD: Then shake it off; you have often wished for an opportunity to part—and now you have it. But first prevent their plot—the half of Millamant's fortune is too considerable to be parted with, to a foe, to Mirabell.

FAINALL: Damn him! that had been mine—had you not made that fond discovery—that had been forfeited, had they been married. My wife had added lustre to my horns by that increase of fortune; I could have worn 'em tipped with gold, though my forehead had been furnished like a deputy-lieutenant's hall.

MRS. MARWOOD: They may prove a cap of maintenance to you still, if you can away with your wife. And she's no worse than when you had her—I dare swear she had given up her game before she was married.

FAINALL: Hum! that may be.

MRS. MARWOOD: You married her to keep you; and if you can contrive to have her keep you better than you expected, why should you not keep her longer than you intended?

FAINALL: The means, the means.

MRS. MARWOOD: Discover to my lady your wife's conduct; threaten to part with her!—my lady loves her, and will come to any composition to save her reputation. Take the opportunity of breaking it, just upon the discovery of this imposture. My lady will be enraged beyond bounds, and sacrifice niece, and fortune, and all, at that conjuncture. And let me alone to keep her warm; if she should flag in her part, I will not fail to prompt her.

FAINALL: Faith, this has an appearance.

MRS. MARWOOD: I'm sorry I hinted to my lady to endeavour a match between Millamant and Sir Wilfull: that may be an obstacle.

FAINALL: Oh, for that matter, leave me to manage him: I'll disable him for that; he will drink like a Dane; after dinner, I'll set his hand in.

MRS. MARWOOD: Well, how do you stand affected towards your lady?

FAINALL: Why, faith, I'm thinking of it.—Let me see—I am married already, so that's over:—my wife has played the jade with me—well, that's over too:—I never loved her, or if I had, why that would have been over too by this time:—jealous of her I cannot be, for I am certain; so there's an end of jealousy:—weary of her I am, and shall be—no, there's no end of that—no, no, that were too much to hope. Thus far concerning my repose; now for my reputation. As to my own, I married not for it, so that's out of the question;—and as to my part in my wife's—why, she had parted with hers before; so bringing none to me, she can take none from me; 'tis against all rule of play, that I should lose to one who has not wherewithal to stake.

MRS. MARWOOD: Besides, you forget, marriage is honourable.

FAINALL: Hum, faith, and that's well thought on; marriage is honourable as you say; and if so, wherefore should cuckoldom be a discredit, being derived from so honourable a root?

MRS. MARWOOD: Nay, I know not; if the root be honourable, why not the branches?

FAINALL: So, so, why this point's clear—well, how do we proceed?

MRS. MARWOOD: I will contrive a letter which shall be delivered to my lady at the time when that rascal who is to act Sir Rowland is with her. It shall come as from an unknown hand—for the less I appear to know of the truth, the better I can play the incendiary. Besides, I would not have Foible provoked if I could help it—because you know she knows some passages—nay, I expect all will come out—but let the mine be sprung first, and then I care not if I am discovered.

FAINALL: If the worst come to the worst—I'll turn my wife to grass—I have already a deed of settlement of the best part of her estate; which I wheedled out of her; and that you shall partake at least.

MRS. MARWOOD: I hope you are convinced that I hate Mirabell now; you'll be no more jealous?

FAINALL: Jealous! no—by this kiss—let husbands be jealous; but let the lover still believe; or if he doubt, let it be only to endear his pleasure, and prepare the joy that follows, when he proves his mistress true. But let husbands' doubts convert to endless jealousy; or if they have belief, let it corrupt to superstition and blind credulity. I am single, and will herd no more with 'em. True, I

wear the badge, but I'll disown the order. And since I take my leave of 'em, I care not if I leave 'em a common motto to their common crest:—

All husbands must or pain or shame endure;
The wise too jealous are, fools too secure.

[Exeunt]

Act IV

SCENE 1: *A Room in Lady* Wishfort's *House*

Lady Wishfort *and* Foible.

LADY WISHFORT: Is Sir Rowland coming, sayest thou, Foible? and are things in order?

FOIBLE: Yes, madam, I have put wax lights in the sconces, and placed the footmen in a row in the hall, in their best liveries, with the coachman and postillion to fill up the equipage.

LADY WISHFORT: Have you pulvilled the coachman and postillion, that they may not stink of the stable when Sir Rowland comes by.

FOIBLE: Yes, madam.

LADY WISHFORT: And are the dancers and the music ready, that he may be entertained in all points with correspondence to his passion?

FOIBLE: All is ready, madam.

LADY WISHFORT: And—well—and how do I look, Foible?

FOIBLE: Most killing well, madam.

LADY WISHFORT: Well, and how shall I receive him? in what figure shall I give his heart the first impression? there is a great deal in the first impression. Shall I sit?—no, I won't sit—I'll walk—ay, I'll walk from the door upon his entrance; and then turn full upon him—no, that will be too sudden. I'll lie—ay, I'll lie down—I'll receive him in my little dressing-room, there's a couch—yes, yes, I'll give the first impression on a couch.—I won't lie neither, but loll and lean upon one elbow: with one foot a little dangling off, jogging in a thoughtful way—yes—and then as soon as he appears, start, ay, start and be surprised, and rise to meet him in a pretty disorder—yes—O, nothing is more alluring than a levee from a couch, in some confusion:—it shows the foot to advantage, and furnishes with blushes, and recomposing airs beyond comparison. Hark! there's a coach.

FOIBLE: 'Tis he, madam.

LADY WISHFORT: O dear!—Has my nephew made his addresses to Millamant? I ordered him.

FOIBLE: Sir Wilfull is set in to drinking, madam, in the parlour.

LADY WISHFORT: Odds my life, I'll send him to her. Call her down, Foible; bring her hither. I'll send him as I go—when they are together, then come to me, Foible, that I may not be too long alone with Sir Rowland.   [Exit]

Enter Mrs. Millamant *and* Mrs. Fainall.

FOIBLE: Madam, I stayed here, to tell your ladyship that Mr. Mirabell has waited this half hour for an opportunity to talk with you: though my lady's orders were to leave you and Sir Wilfull together. Shall I tell Mr. Mirabell that you are at leisure?

MRS. MILLAMANT: No,—what would the dear man have? I am thoughtful, and would amuse myself—bid him come another time.

"There never yet was woman made
        Nor shall but to be cursed."

        [*Repeating, and walking about*]
That's hard.

MRS. FAINALL: You are very fond of Sir John Suckling to-day, Millamant, and the poets.

MRS. MILLAMANT: He? Ay, and filthy verses—so I am.

FOIBLE: Sir Wilfull is coming, madam. Shall I send Mr. Mirabell away.

MRS. MILLAMANT: Ay, if you please, Foible, send him away—or send him hither—just as you will, dear Foible.—I think I'll see him—shall I? ay, let the wretch come.   [*Exit* Foible]
"Thyrsis, a youth of the inspirèd train."
                                          [*Repeating*]
Dear Fainall, entertain Sir Wilfull—thou hast philosophy to undergo a fool, thou art married and hast patience—I would confer with my own thoughts.

MRS. FAINALL: I am obliged to you, that you would make me your proxy in this affair; but I have business of my own.

Enter Sir Wilfull.

MRS. FAINALL: O Sir Wilfull, you are come at the critical instant. There's your mistress up to the ears in love and contemplation; pursue your point now or never.

SIR WILFULL: Yes; my aunt will have it so—I would gladly have been encouraged with a bottle or two, because I'm somewhat wary at first before I am acquainted.—[*This while* Millamant *walks about repeating to herself*]—But I hope, after a time, I shall break my mind—that is, upon further acquaintance—so for the present, cousin, I'll take my leave—if so be you'll be so kind to make my excuse, I'll return to my company—

MRS FAINALL: O fy, Sir Wilfull! what, you must not be daunted.

SIR WILFULL: Daunted! no, that's not it, it is not so much for that—for if so be that I set on't, I'll do't. But only for the present, 'tis sufficient till further acquaintance, that's all—your servant.

MRS. FAINALL: Nay, I'll swear you shall never lose so favourable an opportunity, if I can help it. I'll leave you together, and lock the door.   [*Exit*]

SIR WILFULL: Nay, nay, cousin—I have forgot my gloves—what d'ye do?—S'heart, a'has locked the door indeed, I think—nay, Cousin Fainall, open the door—pshaw, what a vixen trick is this?—Nay,

now a'has seen me too.—Cousin, I made bold to pass through as it were—I think this door's enchanted!

MRS. MILLAMANT: [*Repeating*]
    "I prithee spare me, gentle boy,
    Press me no more for that slight toy."

SIR WILFULL: Anan? Cousin, your servant.

MRS. MILLAMANT: [*Repeating*]
    "That foolish trifle of a heart."
Sir Wilfull!

SIR WILFULL: Yes—your servant. No offence, I hope, cousin.

MRS. MILLAMANT: [*Repeating*]
    "I swear it will not do its part,
    Though thou dost thine, employest thy power and art."
Natural, easy Suckling!

SIR WILFULL: Anan? Suckling! no such suckling neither, cousin, nor stripling: I thank Heaven, I'm no minor.

MRS. MILLAMANT: Ah, rustic, ruder than Gothic!

SIR WILFULL: Well, well, I shall understand your lingo one of these days, cousin; in the meanwhile I must answer in plain English.

MRS. MILLAMANT: Have you any business with me, Sir Wilfull?

SIR WILFULL: Not at present, cousin—yes I make bold to see, to come and know if that how you were disposed to fetch a walk this evening, if so be that I might not be troublesome, I would have sought a walk with you.

MRS. MILLAMANT: A walk! what then?

SIR WILFULL: Nay, nothing—only for the walk's sake, that's all.

MRS. MILLAMANT: I nauseate walking; 'tis a country diversion; I loathe the country, and everything that relates to it.

SIR WILFULL: Indeed! ha! look ye, look ye, you do? Nay, 'tis like you may—here are choice of pastimes here in town, as plays and the like; that must be confessed indeed.

MRS. MILLAMANT: *Ah l'étour di!* I hate the town too.

SIR WILFULL: Dear heart, that's much—ha! that you should hate 'em both! ha! 'tis like you may; there are some can't relish the town, and others can't away with the country—'tis like you may be one of those, cousin.

MRS. MILLAMANT: Ha! ha! ha! yes, 'tis like I may.—You have nothing further to say to me?

SIR WILFULL: Not at present, cousin.—'Tis like when I have an opportunity to be more private—I may break my mind in some measure—I conjecture you partly guess—however, that's as time shall try—but spare to speak and spare to speed, as they say.

MRS. MILLAMANT: If it is of no great importance, Sir Wilfull, you will oblige me to leave me; I have just now a little business—

SIR WILFULL: Enough, enough, cousin: yes, yes, all a case—when you're disposed: now's as well as another time; and another time as well as now. All's one for that—yes, yes, if your concerns call you, there's no haste; it will keep cold, as they say.— Cousin, your servant—I think this door's locked.

MRS. MILLAMANT: You may go this way, sir.

SIR WILFULL: Your servant; then with your leave I'll return to my company.   [*Exit*]

MRS. MILLAMANT: Ay, ay; ha! ha! ha!

"Like Phœbus sung the no less amorous boy."

Enter Mirabell.

MIRABELL: "Like Daphne she, as lovely and as coy." Do you lock yourself up from me, to make my search more curious? or is this pretty artifice contrived to signify that here the chase must end, and my pursuits be crowned? For you can fly no further.

MRS. MILLAMANT: Vanity! no—I'll fly, and be followed to the last moment. Though I am upon the very verge of matrimony, I expect you should solicit me as much as if I were wavering at the grate of a monastery, with one foot over the threshold. I'll be solicited to the very last, nay, and afterwards.

MIRABELL: What, after the last?

MRS. MILLAMANT: Oh, I should think I was poor and had nothing to bestow, if I were reduced to an inglorious ease, and freed from the agreeable fatigues of solicitation.

MIRABELL: But do not you know, that when favours are conferred upon instant and tedious solicitation, that they diminish in their value, and that both the giver loses the grace, and the receiver lessens his pleasure?

MRS. MILLAMANT: It may be in things of common application; but never sure in love. Oh, I hate a lover that can dare to think he draws a moment's air, independent of the bounty of his mistress. There is not so impudent a thing in nature, as the saucy look of an assured man, confident of success. The pedantic arrogance of a very husband has not so pragmatical an air. Ah! I'll never marry, unless I am first made sure of my will and pleasure.

MIRABELL: Would you have 'em both before marriage? or will you be contented with the first now, and stay for the other till after grace?

MRS. MILLAMANT: Ah! don't be impertinent.—My dear liberty, shall I leave thee? my faithful solitude, my darling contemplation, must I bid you then adieu? Ay-h adieu—my morning thoughts, agreeable wakings, indolent slumbers, all ye *douceurs*, ye *sommeils du matin*, adieu?—I can't do't, 'tis more than impossible—positively, Mirabell, I'll lie abed in a morning as long as I please.

MIRABELL: Then I'll get up in a morning as early as I please.

MRS. MILLAMANT: Ah! idle creature, get up when you will—and d'ye hear, I won't be called names after I'm married; positively I won't be called names.

MIRABELL: Names!

MRS. MILLAMANT: Ay, as wife, spouse, my dear, joy, jewel, love, sweetheart, and the rest of that nauseous cant, in which men and their wives are so fulsomely familiar—I shall never bear that—good Mirabell, don't let us be familiar or fond, nor kiss before folks, like my Lady Fadler and Sir Francis: nor go to Hyde-park together the first Sunday in a new chariot, to provoke eyes and whispers, and then never to be seen there together again; as if we were proud of one another the first week, and ashamed of one another ever after. Let us never visit together, nor go to a play together; but let us be very strange and well-bred: let us be as strange as if we had been married a great while; and as well bred as if we were not married at all.

MIRABELL: Have you any more conditions to offer? Hitherto your demands are pretty reasonable.

MRS. MILLAMANT: Trifles!—As liberty to pay and receive visits to and from whom I please; to write and receive letters, without interrogatories or wry faces on your part; to wear what I please; and choose conversation with regard only to my own taste; to have no obligation upon me to converse with wits that I don't like, because they are your acquaintance: or to be intimate with fools, because they may be your relations. Come to dinner when I please; dine in my dressing-room when I'm out of humour, without giving a reason. To have my closet inviolate; to be sole empress of my tea-table, which you must never presume to approach without first asking leave. And lastly, wherever I am, you shall always knock at the door before you come in. These articles subscribed, if I continue to endure you a little longer, I may by degrees dwindle into a wife.

MIRABELL: Your bill of fare is something advanced in this latter account.—Well, have I liberty to offer conditions—that when you are dwindled into a wife, I may not be beyond measure enlarged into a husband?

MRS. MILLAMANT: You have free leave; propose your utmost, speak and spare not.

MIRABELL: I thank you.—*Imprimis* then, I covenant, that your acquaintance be general; that you admit no sworn confidant, or intimate of your own sex; no she friend to screen her affairs under your countenance, and tempt you to make trial of a mutual secrecy. No decoy duck to wheedle you a fop-scrambling to the play in a mask—then bring you home in a pretended fright, when you think you shall be found out—and rail at me for missing the play, and disappointing the frolic which you had to pick me up, and prove my constancy.

MRS. MILLAMANT: Detestable *imprimis*! I go to the play in a mask!

MIRABELL: *Item*, I article, that you continue to like your own face, as long as I shall: and while it passes current with me, that you endeavour not to new-coin it. To which end, together with all vizards for the day, I prohibit all masks for the night, made of oiled-skins, and I know not what—hogs' bones, hares' gall, pig-water, and the marrow of a roasted cat. In short, I forbid all commerce with the gentlewoman in what d'ye call it court. *Item*, I shut my doors against all bawds with baskets, and pennyworths of muslin, china, fans, atlasses, etc. —*Item*, when you shall be breeding—

MRS. MILLAMANT: Ah! name it not.

MIRABELL: Which may be presumed with a blessing on our endeavours.

MRS. MILLAMANT: Odious endeavours!

MIRABELL: I denounce against all strait lacing, squeezing for a shape, till you mould my boy's head like a sugar-loaf, and instead of a man child, make me father to a crooked billet. Lastly, to the dominion of the tea-table I submit—but with proviso, that you exceed not in your province; but restrain yourself to native and simple tea-table drinks, as tea, chocolate, and coffee: as likewise to genuine and authorised tea-table talk—such as mending of fashions, spoiling reputations, railing at absent friends, and so forth—but that on no account you encroach upon the men's prerogative, and presume to drink healths, or toast fellows; for prevention of which I banish all foreign forces, all auxiliaries to the tea-table, as orange-brandy, all aniseed, cinnamon, citron, and Barbadoes waters, together with ratafia, and the most noble spirit of clary—but for cowslip wine, poppy water, and all dormitives, those I allow.—These provisos admitted, in other things I may prove a tractable and complying husband.

MRS. MILLAMANT: O horrid provisos! filthy strong-waters! I toast fellows! odious men! I hate your odious provisos.

MIRABEL: Then we are agreed! shall I kiss your hand upon the contract? And here comes one to be a witness to the sealing of the deed.

Enter Mrs. Fainall.

MRS. MILLAMANT: Fainall, what shall I do? shall I have him? I think I must have him.

MRS. FAINALL: Ay, ay, take him, take him, what should you do?

MRS. MILLAMANT: Well then—I'll take my death I'm in a horrid fright—Fainall, I shall never say it—well—I think—I'll endure you.

MRS. FAINALL: Fy! fy! have him, have him, and tell him so in plain terms: for I am sure you have a mind to him.

MRS. MILLAMANT: Are you? I think I have—and the horrid man looks as if he thought so too—well, you ridiculous thing you, I'll have you—I won't be kissed, nor I won't be thanked—here kiss my hand though.—So, hold your tongue now, don't say a word.

MRS. FAINALL: Mirabell, there's a necessity for your

obedience;—you have neither time to talk nor stay. My mother is coming; and in my conscience if she should see you, would fall into fits, and maybe not recover time enough to return to Sir Rowland, who, as Foible tells me, is in a fair way to succeed. Therefore spare your ecstacies for another occasion, and slip down the backstairs, where Foible waits to consult you.

MRS. MILLAMANT: Ay, go, go. In the mean time I suppose you have said something to please me.

MIRABELL: I am all obedience.　　　　[*Exit*]

MRS. FAINALL: Yonder Sir Wilfull's drunk, and so noisy that my mother has been forced to leave Sir Rowland to appease him; but he answers her only with singing and drinking—what they may have done by this time I know not; but Petulant and he were upon quarrelling as I came by.

MRS. MILLAMANT: Well, if Mirabell should not make a good husband, I am a lost thing,—for I find I love him violently.

MRS. FAINALL: So it seems; for you mind not what's said to you.—If you doubt him, you had best take up with Sir Wilfull.

MRS. MILLAMANT: How can you name that super-annuated lubber? foh!

Enter Witwoud.

MRS. FAINALL: So, is the fray made up, that you have left 'em?

WITWOUD: Left 'em? I could stay no longer—I have laughed like ten christnings—I am tipsy with laughing—if I had stayed any longer I should have burst,—I must have been let out and pieced in the sides like an unsized camlet.—Yes, yes, the fray is composed; my lady came in like a *noli prosequi*, and stopped the proceedings.

MRS. MILLAMANT: What was the dispute?

WITWOUD: That's the jest; there was no dispute. They could neither of 'em speak for rage, and so fell a sputtering at one another like two roasting apples.

Enter Petulant, *drunk*.

WITWOUD: Now, Petulant, all's over, all's well. Gad, my head begins to whim it about—why dost thou not speak? thou art both as drunk and as mute as a fish.

PETULANT: Look you, Mrs. Millamant—if you can love me, dear nymph—say it—and that's the conclusion—pass on, or pass off—that's all.

WITWOUD: Thou hast uttered volumes, folios, in less than *decimo sexto*, my dear Lacedemonian. Sirrah, Petulant, thou art an epitomiser of words.

PETULANT: Witwoud—you are an annihilator of sense.

WITWOUD: Thou art a retailer of phrases; and dost deal in remnants of remnants, like a maker of pin-cushions—thou art in truth (metaphorically speaking) a speaker of shorthand.

PETULANT: Thou art (without a figure) just one half

of an ass, and Baldwin yonder, thy half-brother, is the rest.—A Gemini of asses split would make just four of you.

WITWOUD: Thou dost bite, my dear mustard-seed; kiss me for that.

PETULANT: Stand off!—I'll kiss no more males—I have kissed your twin yonder in a humour of reconciliation, till he [Hiccups] rises upon my stomach like a radish.

MRS. MILLAMANT: Eh! filthy creature! what was the quarrel?

PETULANT: There was no quarrel—there might have been a quarrel.

WITWOUD: If there had been words enow between 'em to have expressed provocation, they had gone together by the ears like a pair of castanets.

PETULANT: You were the quarrel.

MRS. MILLAMANT: Me!

PETULANT: If I have a humour to quarrel, I can make less matters conclude premises.—If you are not handsome, what then, if I have a humour to prove it? If I shall have my reward, say so; if not, fight for your face the next time yourself—I'll go sleep.

WITWOUD: Do, wrap thyself up like a wood-louse, and dream revenge—and hear me, if thou canst learn to write by to-morrow morning, pen me a challenge.—I'll carry it for thee.

PETULANT: Carry your mistress's monkey a spider!— Go flea dogs, and read romances!—I'll go to bed to my maid.   [Exit]

MRS. FAINALL: He's horridly drunk.—How came you all in this pickle?

WITWOUD: A plot! a plot! to get rid of the night— your husband's advice; but he sneaked off.

SCENE 2: *The Dining-room in Lady Wishfort's House*

Sir Wilfull *drunk*, Lady Wishfort, Witwoud, Mrs. Millamant, *and* Mrs. Fainall.

LADY WISHFORT: Out upon't, out upon't! At years of discretion, and comport yourself at this rantipole rate!

SIR WILFULL: No offence, aunt.

LADY WISHFORT: Offence! as I'm a person, I'm ashamed of you—foh! how you stink of wine! D'ye think my niece will ever endure such a Borachio! you're an absolute Borachio.

SIR WILFULL: Borachio?

LADY WISHFORT: At a time when you should commence an amour, and put your best foot foremost—

SIR WILFULL: S'heart, an you grutch me your liquor, make a bill—give me more drink, and take my purse—   [Sings]

"Prithee fill me the glass,
    Till it laugh in my face,

With ale that is potent and mellow;
    He that whines for a lass,
    Is an ignorant ass,
For a bumper has not its fellow."

But if you would have me marry my cousin—say the word, and I'll do't—Wilfull will do't, that's the word—Wilfull will do't, that's my crest—my motto I have forgot.

LADY WISHFORT: My nephew's a little overtaken, cousin—but 'tis with drinking your health.—O' my word you are obliged to him.

SIR WILFULL: *In vino veritas*, aunt.—If I drunk your health to-day, cousin—I am a Borachio. But if you have a mind to be married, say the word, and send for the piper; Wilfull will do't. If not, dust it away, and let's have t'other round.—Tony!—Odds heart, where's Tony!—Tony's an honest fellow; but he spits after a bumper, and that's a fault.—   [Sings]

"We'll drink, and we'll never ha' done, boys,
    Put the glass then around with the sun, boys,
Let Apollo's example invite us;
    For he's drunk every night,
    And that makes him so bright,
That he's able next morning to light us."

The sun's a good pimple, an honest soaker; he has a cellar at your Antipodes. If I travel, aunt, I touch at your Antipodes.—Your Antipodes are a good, rascally sort of topsy-turvy fellows: if I had a bumper, I'd stand upon my head and drink a health to 'em.—A match or no match, cousin with the hard name?—Aunt, Wilfull will do't. If she has her maidenhead, let her look to't; if she has not, let her keep her own counsel in the meantime, and cry out at the nine months' end.

MRS. MILLAMANT: Your pardon, madam, I can stay no longer—Sir Wilfull grows very powerful. Eh! how he smells! I shall be overcome, if I stay.— Come, cousin.

            [Exeunt Mrs. Millamant *and* Mrs. Fainall]

LADY WISHFORT: Smells! he would poison a tallow-chandler and his family! Beastly creature, I know not what to do with him!—Travel, quotha! ay, travel, travel, get thee gone, get thee gone, get thee but far enough, to the Saracens, or the Tartars, or the Turks!—for thou art not fit to live in a Christian commonwealth, thou beastly Pagan!

SIR WILFULL: Turks, no; no Turks, aunt: your Turks are infidels, and believe not in the grape. Your Mahometan, your Mussulman, is a dry stinkard— no offence, aunt. My map says that your Turk is not so honest a man as your Christian. I cannot find by the map that your Mufti is orthodox— whereby it is a plain case, that orthodox is a hard word, aunt, and [Hiccups] Greek for claret.—

                                    [Sings]

"To drink is a Christian diversion,
　　Unknown to the Turk or the Persian:
　　　　Let Mahometan fools
　　　　Live by heathenish rules,
　　And be damned over tea-cups and coffee.
　　　　But let British lads sing,
　　　　Crown a health to the king,
　　And a fig for your sultan and sophy!"

Ah Tony!

Enter Foible, *who whispers to* Lady Wishfort.

LADY WISHFORT: [*Aside to* Foible]—Sir Rowland impatient? Good lack! what shall I do with this beastly tumbril?—[*Aloud*] Go lie down and sleep, you sot!—or, as I'm a person, I'll have you bastinadoed with broomsticks.—Call up the wenches.

SIR WILFULL: Ahey! wenches, where are the wenches?

LADY WISHFORT: Dear Cousin Witwoud, get him away, and you will bind me to you inviolably. I have an affair of moment that invades me with some precipitation—you will oblige me to all futurity.

WITWOUD: Come, knight.—Pox on him, I don't know what to say to him.—Will you go to a cock-match?

SIR WILFULL: With a wench, Tony! Is she a shake-bag, sirrah? Let me bite your cheek for that.

WITWOUD: Horrible! he has a breath like a bag-pipe! —Ay, ay; come, will you march, my Salopian?

SIR WILFULL: Lead on, little Tony—I'll follow thee, my Anthony, my Tantony, sirrah, thou shalt be my Tantony, and I'll be thy pig. [*Sings*]

"And a fig for your sultan and sophy."
　　　　　　[*Exeunt* Sir Wilfull *and* Witwoud]

LADY WISHFORT: This will never do. It will never make a match—at least before he has been abroad.

Enter Waitwell, *disguised as* Sir Rowland.

LADY WISHFORT: Dear Sir Rowland, I am confounded with confusion at the retrospection of my own rudeness!—I have more pardons to ask than the pope distributes in the year of jubilee. But I hope, where there is likely to be so near an alliance, we may unbend the severity of decorums, and dispense with a little ceremony.

WAITWELL: My impatience, madam, is the effect of my transport; and till I have the possession of your adorable person, I am tantalised on the rack; and do but hang, madam, on the tenter of expectation.

LADY WISHFORT: You have excess of gallantry, Sir Rowland, and press things to a conclusion with a most prevailing vehemence.—But a day or two for decency of marriage—

WAITWELL: For decency of funeral, madam! The delay will break my heart—or, if that should fail, I shall be poisoned. My nephew will get an inkling of my designs, and poison me—and I would willingly starve him before I die—I would gladly go out of the world with that satisfaction.—That would be some comfort to me, if I could but live so long as to be revenged on that unnatural viper!

LADY WISHFORT: Is he so unnatural, say you? Truly I would contribute much both to the saving of your life, and the accomplishment of your revenge.— Not that I respect myself, though he has been a perfidious wretch to me.

WAITWELL: Perfidious to you!

LADY WISHFORT: O Sir Rowland, the hours that he has died away at my feet, the tears that he has shed, the oaths that he has sworn, the palpitations that he has felt, the trances and the tremblings, the ardours and the ecstacies, the kneelings and the risings, the heart-heavings and the hand-gripings, the pangs and the pathetic regards of his protesting eyes!—Oh, no memory can register!

WAITWELL: What, my rival! is the rebel my rival?— a' dies.

LADY WISHFORT: No, don't kill him at once, Sir Rowland, starve him gradually, inch by inch.

WAITWELL: I'll do't. In three weeks he shall be barefoot; in a month out at knees with begging an alms.—He shall starve upward and upward, till he has nothing living but his head, and then go out in a stink like a candle's end upon a save-all.

LADY WISHFORT: Well, Sir Rowland, you have the way—you are no novice in the labyrinth of love— you have the clue.—But as I am a person, Sir Rowland, you must not attribute my yielding to any sinister appetite, or indigestion of widowhood; nor impute my complacency to any lethargy of continence—I hope you do not think me prone to any iteration of nuptials—

WAITWELL: Far be it from me—

LADY WISHFORT: If you do, I protest I must recede— or think that I have made a prostitution of decorums; but in the vehemence of compassion, and to save the life of a person of so much importance—

WAITWELL: I esteem it so.

LADY WISHFORT: Or else you wrong my condescension.

WAITWELL: I do not, I do not!

LADY WISHFORT: Indeed you do.

WAITWELL: I do not, fair shrine of virtue!

LADY WISHFORT: If you think the least scruple of carnality was an ingredient—

WAITWELL: Dear madam, no. You are all camphor and frankincense, all chastity and odour.

LADY WISHFORT: Or that—

Enter Foible.

FOIBLE: Madam, the dancers are ready; and there's one with a letter, who must deliver it into your own hands.

LADY WISHFORT: Sir Rowland, will you give me leave? Think favourably, judge candidly, and conclude you have found a person who would suffer racks in honour's cause, dear Sir Rowland, and will wait on you incessantly.   [*Exit*]

WAITWELL: Fy, fy!—What a slavery have I undergone! Spouse, hast thou any cordial; I want spirits.

FOIBLE: What a washy rogue art thou, to pant thus for a quarter of an hour's lying and swearing to a fine lady!

WAITWELL: Oh, she is the antidote to desire! Spouse, thou wilt fare the worse for't—I shall have no appetite to iteration of nuptials this eight-and-forty hours.—By this hand I'd rather be a chairman in the dog-days—than act Sir Rowland till this time to-morrow!

Re-enter Lady Wishfort, *with a letter.*

LADY WISHFORT: Call in the dancers.—Sir Rowland, we'll sit, if you please, and see the entertainment. [*A Dance*] Now, with your permission, Sir Rowland, I will peruse my letter.—I would open it in your presence, because I would not make you uneasy. If it should make you uneasy, I would burn it.—Speak, if it does—but you may see the superscription is like a woman's hand.

FOIBLE: [*Aside to* Waitwell] By Heaven! Mrs. Marwood's, I know it.—My heart aches—get it from her.

WAITWELL: A woman's hand! no, madam, that's no woman's hand, I see that already. That's somebody whose throat must be cut.

LADY WISHFORT: Nay, Sir Rowland, since you give me a proof of your passion by your jealousy, I promise you I'll make a return, by a frank communication.—You shall see it—we'll open it together—look you here.—[*Reads*]—"Madam, though unknown to you"—Look you there, 'tis from nobody that I know—"I have that honour for your character, that I think myself obliged to let you know you are abused. He who pretends to be Sir Rowland, is a cheat and a rascal."—Oh Heavens! what's this?

FOIBLE: [*Aside*] Unfortunate! all's ruined!

WAITWELL: How, how, let me see, let me see!—[*Reads*] "A rascal, and disguised and suborned for that imposture,"—O villainy! O villainy!—"by the contrivance of—"

LADY WISHFORT: I shall faint, I shall die, oh!

FOIBLE: [*Aside to* Waitwell] Say 'tis your nephew's hand—quickly, his plot, swear it, swear it!

WAITWELL: Here's a villain! madam, don't you perceive it, don't you see it?

LADY WISHFORT: Too well, too well! I have seen too much.

WAITWELL: I told you at first I knew the hand.—A woman's hand! The rascal writes a sort of a large hand; your Roman hand—I saw there was a throat to be cut presently. If he were my son, as he is my nephew, I'd pistol him!

FOIBLE: O treachery!—But are you sure, Sir Rowland, it is his writing?

WAITWELL: Sure! am I here? do I live? do I love this

pearl of India? I have twenty letters in my pocket from him in the same character.

LADY WISHFORT: How!

FOIBLE: O what luck it is, Sir Rowland, that you were present at this juncture!—This was the business that brought Mr. Mirabell disguised to Madam Millamant this afternoon. I thought something was contriving, when he stole by me and would have hid his face.

LADY WISHFORT: How, how!—I heard the villain was in the house indeed; and now I remember, my niece went away abruptly, when Sir Wilfull was to have made his addresses.

FOIBLE: Then, then, madam, Mr. Mirabell waited for her in her chamber! but I would not tell your ladyship to discompose you when you were to receive Sir Rowland.

WAITWELL: Enough, his date is short.

FOIBLE: No, good Sir Rowland, don't incur the law.

WAITWELL: Law! I care not for law. I can but die, and 'tis in a good cause.—My lady shall be satisfied of my truth and innocence, though it cost me my life.

LADY WISHFORT: No, dear Sir Rowland, don't fight; if you should be killed I must never show my face; or hanged—O, consider my reputation, Sir Rowland!—No, you shan't fight—I'll go in and examine my niece; I'll make her confess. I conjure you, Sir Rowland, by all your love, not to fight.

WAITWELL: I am charmed, madam, I obey. But some proof you must let me give you; I'll go for a black box, which contains the writings of my whole estate, and deliver them into your hands.

LADY WISHFORT: Ay, dear Sir Rowland, that will be some comfort, bring the black box.

WAITWELL: And may I presume to bring a contract to be signed this night? may I hope so far?

LADY WISHFORT: Bring what you will; but come alive, pray come alive. Oh, this is a happy discovery!

WAITWELL: Dead or alive I'll come—and married we will be in spite of treachery; ay, and get an heir that shall defeat the last remaining glimpse of hope in my abandoned nephew. Come, my buxom widow:—

Ere long you shall substantial proofs receive,
That I'm an errant knight—

FOIBLE [*Aside*]   Or errant knave.
                                        [*Exeunt*]

Act V

SCENE 1: *A Room in Lady Wishfort's House*

Lady Wishfort *and* Foible.

LADY WISHFORT: Out of my house, out of my house, thou viper! thou serpent, that I have fostered! thou bosom traitress, that I raised from nothing!—Begone! begone! begone!—go! go!—That I took from washing of old gauze and weaving of dead hair, with a bleak blue nose over a chafing-dish of starved embers, and dining behind a traverse rag, in a shop no bigger than a birdcage!—Go, go! starve again, do, do!

FOIBLE: Dear madam, I'll beg pardon on my knees.

LADY WISHFORT: Away! out! out!—Go, set up for yourself again!—Do, drive a trade, do, with your threepennyworth of small ware, flaunting upon a packthread, under a brandy-seller's bulk, or against a dead wall by a ballad-monger! Go, hang out an old Frisoneer gorget,[1] with a yard of yellow colberteen[2] again. Do; an old gnawed mask, two rows of pins, and a child's fiddle; a glass necklace with the beads broken, and a quilted nightcap with one ear. Go, go, drive a trade!—These were your commodities, you treacherous trull! this was the merchandise you dealt in when I took you into my house, placed you next myself, and made you governante of my whole family! You have forgot this, have you, now you have feathered your nest?

FOIBLE: No, no, dear madam. Do but hear me, have but a moment's patience, I'll confess all. Mr. Mirabell seduced me; I am not the first that he has wheedled with his dissembling tongue; your ladyship's own wisdom has been deluded by him; then how should I, a poor ignorant, defend myself? O madam, if you knew but what he promised me, and how he assured me your ladyship should come to no damage!—Or else the wealth of the Indies should not have bribed me to conspire against so good, so sweet, so kind a lady as you have been to me.

LADY WISHFORT: No damage! What, to betray me, and marry me to a cast-servingman! to make me a receptacle, an hospital for a decayed pimp! No damage! O thou frontless impudence, more than a big-bellied actress!

FOIBLE: Pray, do but hear me, madam; he could not marry your ladyship, madam.—No, indeed, his marriage was to have been void in law, for he was married to me first, to secure your ladyship. He could not have bedded your ladyship; for if he had consummated with your ladyship, he must have run the risk of the law, and been put upon his clergy.—Yes, indeed, I inquired of the law in that case before I would meddle or make.

LADY WISHFORT: What then, I have been your property, have I? I have been convenient to you, it seems!—While you were catering for Mirabell, I have been broker for you! What, have you made a passive bawd of me?—This exceeds all precedent; I am brought to fine uses, to become a botcher of second-hand marriages between Abigails and Andrews!—I'll couple you!—Yes, I'll baste you together, you and your Philander! I'll Duke's-place you, as I am a person! Your turtle is in custody

[1] A kerchief worn by women over their bosoms.
[2] A kind of lace.

already: you shall coo in the same cage, if there be a constable or warrant in the parish.   [Exit]

FOIBLE: Oh that ever I was born! Oh that I was ever married!—A bride!—ay, I shall be a Bridewell-bride[3]—Oh!

Enter Mrs. Fainall.

MRS. FAINALL: Poor Foible, what's the matter?

FOIBLE: O madam, my lady's gone for a constable. I shall be had to a justice, and put to Bridewell to beat hemp. Poor Waitwell's gone to prison already.

MRS. FAINALL: Have a good heart, Foible; Mirabell's gone to give security for him. This is all Marwood's and my husband's doing.

FOIBLE: Yes, yes; I know it, madam: she was in my lady's closet, and overheard all that you said to me before dinner. She sent the letter to my lady; and that missing effect, Mr. Fainall laid this plot to arrest Waitwell, when he pretended to go for the papers; and in the meantime Mrs. Marwood declared all to my lady.

MRS. FAINALL: Was there no mention made of me in the letter? My mother does not suspect my being in the confederacy? I fancy Marwood has not told her, though she has told my husband.

FOIBLE: Yes, madam; but my lady did not see that part; we stifled the letter before she read so far,—Has that mischievous devil told Mr. Fainall of your ladyship then?

MRS. FAINALL: Ay, all's out—my affair with Mirabell—everything discovered. This is the last day of our living together, that's my comfort.

FOIBLE: Indeed, madam; and so 'tis a comfort if you knew all;—he has been even with your ladyship, which I could have told you long enough since, but I love to keep peace and quietness by my goodwill. I had rather bring friends together, than set 'em at distance: but Mrs. Marwood and he are nearer related than ever their parents thought for.

MRS. FAINALL: Sayest thou so, Foible? canst thou prove this?

FOIBLE: I can take my oath of it, madam; so can Mrs. Mincing. We have had many a fair word from Madam Marwood, to conceal something that passed in our chamber one evening when you were at Hyde-park; and we were thought to have gone a-walking, but we went up unawares;—though we were sworn to secrecy too. Madam Marwood took a book and swore us upon it, but it was but a book of poems. So long as it was not a bible-oath, we may break it with a safe conscience.

MRS. FAINALL: This discovery is the most opportune thing I could wish.—Now, Mincing!

Enter Mincing.

MINCING: My lady would speak with Mrs. Foible, mem. Mr. Mirabell is with her; he has set your spouse at liberty, Mrs. Foible, and would have you

[3] Bridewell, situated between Fleet Ditch and Bride Lane, was a House of Correction for the loose and disorderly.

hide yourself in my lady's closet till my old lady's anger is abated. Oh, my old lady is in a perilous passion at something Mr. Fainall has said; he swears, and my old lady cries. There's a fearful hurricane, I vow. He says, mem, how that he'll have my lady's fortune made over to him, or he'll be divorced.

MRS. FAINALL: Does your lady or Mirabell know that?

MINCING: Yes, mem; they have sent me to see if Sir Wilfull be sober, and to bring him to them. My lady is resolved to have him, I think, rather than lose such a vast sum as six thousand pounds.—O come, Mrs. Foible, I hear my old lady.

MRS. FAINALL: Foible, you must tell Mincing that she must prepare to vouch when I call her.

FOIBLE: Yes, yes, madam.

MINCING: O yes, mem, I'll vouch anything for your ladyship's service, be what it will.

SCENE 2: *Another Room in Lady Wishfort's House*

Mrs. Fainall, Lady Wishfort, *and* Mrs. Marwood.

LADY WISHFORT: O my dear friend, how can I enumerate the benefits that I have received from your goodness! To you I owe the timely discovery of the false vows of Mirabell; to you I owe the detection of the impostor Sir Rowland. And now you are become an intercessor with my son-in-law, to save the honour of my house, and compound for the frailties of my daughter. Well, friend, you are enough to reconcile me to the bad world, or else I would retire to deserts and solitudes, and feed harmless sheep by groves and purling streams. Dear Marwood, let us leave the world, and retire by ourselves and be shepherdesses.

MRS. MARWOOD: Let us first despatch the affair in hand, madam. We shall have leisure to think of retirement afterwards. Here is one who is concerned in the treaty.

LADY WISHFORT: Oh daughter, daughter! is it possible thou shouldst be my child, bone of my bone, and flesh of my flesh, and, as I may say, another me, and yet transgress the most minute particle of severe virtue? Is it possible you should lean aside to iniquity, who have been cast in the direct mould of virtue? I have not only been a mould but a pattern for you, and a model for you, after you were brought into the world.

MRS. FAINALL: I don't understand your ladyship.

LADY WISHFUL: Not understand! Why, have you not been naught? have you not been sophisticated? Not understand! here I am ruined to compound for your caprices and your cuckoldoms. I must pawn my plate and my jewels, and ruin my niece, and all little enough——

MRS. FAINALL: I am wronged and abused, and so are you. 'Tis a false accusation, as false as hell, as false as your friend there, ay, or your friend's friend, my false husband.

MRS. MARWOOD: My friend, Mrs. Fainall! your husband my friend! what do you mean?

MRS. FAINALL: I know what I mean, madam, and so do you; and so shall the world at a time convenient.

MRS. MARWOOD: I am sorry to see you so passionate, madam. More temper would look more like innocence. But I have done. I am sorry my zeal to serve your ladyship and family should admit of misconstruction, or make me liable to affronts. You will pardon me, madam, if I meddle no more with an affair in which I am not personally concerned.

LADY WISHFORT: O dear friend, I am so ashamed that you should meet with such returns!—[*To Mrs. Fainall*] You ought to ask pardon on your knees, ungrateful creature! she deserves more from you than all your life can accomplish.—[*To Mrs. Marwood*] Oh, don't leave me destitute in this perplexity!—no, stick to me, my good genius.

MRS. FAINALL: I tell you, madam, you are abused.— Stick to you! ay, like a leech, to suck your best blood—she'll drop off when she's full. Madam, you shan't pawn a bodkin, nor part with a brass counter, in composition for me. I defy 'em all. Let 'em prove their aspersions; I know my own innocence, and dare stand a trial.   [*Exit*]

LADY WISHFORT: Why, if she should be innocent, if she should be wronged after all, ha?—I don't know what to think;—and I promise you her education has been unexceptionable—I may say it; for I chiefly made it my own care to initiate her very infancy in the rudiments of virtue, and to impress upon her tender years a young odium and aversion to the very sight of men:—ay, friend, she would ha' shrieked if she had but seen a man, till she was in her teens. As I am a person 'tis true;—she was never suffered to play with a male child, though but in coats; nay, her very babies were of the feminine gender. Oh, she never looked a man in the face but her own father, or the chaplain, and him we made a shift to put upon her for a woman, by the help of his long garments, and his sleek face, till she was going in her fifteeen.

MRS. MARWOOD: 'Twas much she should be deceived so long.

LADY WISHFORT: I warrant you, or she would never have borne to have been catechised by him; and have heard his long lectures against singing and dancing, and such debaucheries; and going to filthy plays, and profane music-meetings, where the lewd trebles squeak nothing but bawdy, and the basses roar blasphemy. Oh, she would have swooned at the sight or name of an obscene playbook!—and can I think, after all this, that my daughter can be naught? What, a whore? and thought it excommunication to set her foot within the door of a playhouse! O dear friend, I can't believe it, no, no! as she says, let him prove it, let him prove it.

MRS. MARWOOD: Prove it, madam! What, and have

your name prostituted in a public court! yours and your daughter's reputation worried at the bar by a pack of bawling lawyers! To be ushered in with an O yes of scandal; and have your case opened by an old fumbling lecher in a quoif like a man-midwife; to bring your daughter's infamy to light; to be a theme for legal punsters and quibblers by the statute; and become a jest against a rule of court, where there is no precedent for a jest in any record —not even in doomsday-book; to discompose the gravity of the bench, and provoke naughty interrogatories in more naughty law Latin; while the good judge, tickled with the proceeding, simpers under a grey beard, and fidgets off and on his cushion as if he had swallowed cantharides, or sat upon cow-itch!——

LADY WISHFORT: Oh, 'tis very hard!

MRS. MARWOOD: And then to have my young revellers of the Temple take notes, like 'prentices at a conventicle; and after talk it over again in commons, or before drawers in an eating-house.

LADY WISHFORT: Worse and worse!

MRS. MARWOOD: Nay, this is nothing; if it would end here 'twere well. But it must, after this, be consigned by the short-hand writers to the public press; and from thence be transferred to the hands, nay into the throats and lungs of hawkers, with voices more licentious than the loud flounderman's: and this you must hear till you are stunned; nay, you must hear nothing else for some days.

LADY WISHFORT: Oh, 'tis insupportable! No, no, dear friend, make it up, make it up; ay, ay, I'll compound. I'll give up all, myself and my all, my niece and her all—anything, everything for composition.

MRS. MARWOOD: Nay, madam, I advise nothing, I only lay before you, as a friend, the inconveniences which perhaps you have overseen. Here comes Mr. Fainall; if he will be satisfied to huddle up all in silence, I shall be glad. You must think I would rather congratulate than condole with you.

Enter Fainall.

LADY WISHFORT: Ay, ay, I do not doubt it, dear Marwood; no, no, I do not doubt it.

FAINALL: Well, madam; I have suffered myself to be overcome by the importunity of this lady your friend; and am content you shall enjoy your own proper estate during life, on condition you oblige yourself never to marry, under such penalty as I think convenient.

LADY WISHFUL: Never to marry!

FAINALL: No more Sir Rowlands;—the next imposture may not be so timely detected.

MRS. MARWOOD: That condition, I dare answer, my lady will consent to without difficulty; she has already but too much experienced the perfidiousness of men.—Besides, madam, when we retire to our pastoral solitude we shall bid adieu to all other thoughts.

LADY WISHFORT: Ay, that's true; but in case of necessity, as of health, or some such emergency——

FAINALL: Oh, if you are prescribed marriage, you shall be considered; I will only reserve to myself the power to choose for you. If your physic be wholesome, it matters not who is your apothecary. Next, my wife shall settle on me the remainder of her fortune, not made over already; and for her maintenance depend entirely on my discretion.

LADY WISHFORT: This is most inhumanly savage; exceeding the barbarity of a Muscovite husband.

FAINALL: I learned it from his Czarish majesty's retinue, in a winter evening's conference over brandy and pepper, amongst other secrets of matrimony and policy, as they are at present practised in the northern hemisphere. But this must be agreed unto, and that positively. Lastly, I will be endowed, in right of my wife, with that six thousand pounds, which is the moiety of Mrs. Millamant's fortune in your possession; and which she has forfeited (as will appear by the last will and testament of your deceased husband, Sir Jonathan Wishfort) by her disobedience in contracting herself against your consent or knowledge; and by refusing the offered match with Sir Wilfull Witwoud, which you, like a careful aunt, had provided for her.

LADY WISHFORT: My nephew was *non compos*, and could not make his addresses.

FAINALL: I come to make demands—I'll hear no objections.

LADY WISHFORT: You will grant me time to consider?

FAINALL: Yes, while the instrument is drawing, to which you must set your hand till more sufficient deeds can be perfected: which I will take care shall be done with all possible speed. In the meantime I'll go for the said instrument, and till my return you may balance this matter in your own discretion.   [*Exit*]

LADY WISHFORT: This insolence is beyond all precedent, all parallel; must I be subject to this merciless villain?

MRS. MARWOOD: 'Tis severe indeed, madam, that you should smart for your daughter's wantonness.

LADY WISHFORT: 'Twas against my consent that she married this barbarian, but she would have him, though her year was not out.—Ah! her first husband, my son Languish, would not have carried it thus. Well, that was my choice, this is hers: she is matched now with a witness.—I shall be mad!— Dear friend, is there no comfort for me? must I live to be confiscated at this rebel-rate?—Here come two more of my Egyptian plagues too.

Enter Mrs. Millamant, *and* Sir Wilfull Witwoud.

SIR WILFULL: Aunt, your servant.

LADY WISHFORT: Out, caterpillar, call not me aunt! I know thee not!

SIR WILFULL: I confess I have been a little in disguise, as they say.—S'heart! and I'm sorry for't.

What would you have? I hope I have committed no offence, aunt—and if I did I am willing to make satisfaction; and what can a man say fairer? If I have broke anything I'll pay for't, an it cost a pound. And so let that content for what's past, and make no more words. For what's to come, to pleasure you I'm willing to marry my cousin. So pray let's all be friends, she and I are agreed upon the matter before a witness.

LADY WISHFORT: How's this, dear niece? have I any comfort? can this be true?

MRS. MILLAMANT: I am content to be a sacrifice to your repose, madam; and to convince you that I had no hand in the plot, as you were misinformed, I have laid my commands on Mirabell to come in person, and be a witness that I give my hand to this flower of knighthood: and for the contract that passed between Mirabell and me, I have obliged him to make a resignation of it in your ladyship's presence;—he is without, and waits your leave for admittance.

LADY WISHFORT: Well, I'll swear I am something revived at this testimony of your obedience; but I cannot admit that traitor.—I fear I cannot fortify myself to support his appearance. He is as terrible to me as a gorgon; if I see him I fear I shall turn to stone, and petrify incessantly.

MRS. MILLAMANT: If you disoblige him, he may resent your refusal, and insist upon the contract still. Then 'tis the last time he will be offensive to you.

LADY WISHFORT: Are you sure it will be the last time?—If I were sure of that—shall I never see him again?

MRS. MILLAMANT: Sir Wilfull, you and he are to travel together, are you not?

SIR WILFULL: S'heart, the gentleman's a civil gentleman, aunt, let him come in; why, we are sworn brothers and fellow-travellers.—We are to be Pylades and Orestes, he and I.—He is to be my interpreter in foreign parts. He has been over-seas once already; and with proviso that I marry my cousin, will cross 'em once again, only to bear me company.—S'heart, I'll call him in,—an I set on't once, he shall come in; and see who'll hinder him.

[Goes to the door and hems]

MRS. MARWOOD: This is precious fooling, if it would pass; but I'll know the bottom of it.

LADY WISHFORT: O dear Marwood, you are not going.

MRS. MARWOOD: Not far, madam; I'll return immediately.   [Exit]

Enter Mirabell.

SIR WILFULL: Look up, man, I'll stand by you; 'sbud an she do frown, she can't kill you;—besides—harkee, she dare not frown desperately, because her face is none of her own. S'heart, an she should, her forehead would wrinkle like the coat of a cream-cheese; but mum for that, fellow-traveller.

MIRABELL: If a deep sense of the many injuries I have offered to so good a lady, with a sincere remorse, and a hearty contrition, can but obtain the least glance of compassion, I am too happy.—Ah, madam, there was a time!—but let it be forgotten—I confess I have deservedly forfeited the high place I once held of sighing at your feet. Nay, kill me not, by turning from me in disdain.—I come not to plead for favour;—nay, not for pardon; I am a suppliant only for pity—I am going where I never shall behold you more—

SIR WILFULL: How, fellow-traveller! you shall go by yourself then.

MIRABELL: Let me be pitied first, and afterwards forgotten.—I ask no more.

SIR WILFULL: By'r lady, a very reasonable request, and will cost you nothing, aunt! Come, come, forgive and forget, aunt; why you must, an you are a Christian.

MIRABELL: Consider, madam, in reality, you could not receive much prejudice; it was an innocent device; though I confess it had a face of guiltiness,—it was at most an artifice which love contrived;—and errors which love produces have ever been accounted venial. At least think it is punishment enough, that I have lost what in my heart I hold most dear, that to your cruel indignation I have offered up this beauty, and with her my peace and quiet; nay, all my hopes of future comfort.

SIR WILFULL: An he does not move me, would I may never be o' the quorum!—an it were not as good a deed as to drink, to give her to him again, I would I might never take shipping!—Aunt, if you don't forgive quickly, I shall melt, I can tell you that. My contract went no farther than a little mouth-glue, and that's hardly dry;—one doleful sigh more from my fellow-traveller, and 'tis dissolved.

LADY WISHFORT: Well, nephew, upon your account—Ah, he has a false insinuating tongue!—Well, sir, I will stifle my just resentment at my nephew's request.—I will endeavour what I can to forget,—but on proviso that you resign the contract with my niece immediately.

MIRABELL: It is in writing, and with papers of concern; but I have sent my servant for it, and will deliver it to you, with all acknowledgments for your transcendent goodness.

LADY WISHFORT: [Aside] Oh, he has witchcraft in his eyes and tongue!—When I did not see him, I could have bribed a villain to his assassination; but his appearance rakes the embers which have so long lain smothered in my breast.

SCENE 3: *The same*

Lady Wishfort, Mrs. Millamant, Sir Wilfull, Mirabell, Fainall, *and* Mrs. Marwood.

FAINALL: Your date of deliberation, madam, is expired. Here is the instrument; are you prepared to sign?

LADY WISHFORT: If I were prepared, I am not impowered. My niece exerts a lawful claim, having matched herself by my direction to Sir Wilfull.

FAINALL: That sham is too gross to pass on me—though 'tis imposed on you, madam.

MRS. MILLAMANT: Sir, I have given my consent.

MIRABELL: And, sir, I have resigned my pretensions.

SIR WILFULL: And, sir, I assert my right; and will maintain it in defiance of you, sir, and of your instrument. S'heart, an you talk of an instrument, sir, I have an old fox by my thigh that shall hack your instrument of ram vellum to shreds, sir!—it shall not be sufficient for a mittimus or a tailor's measure. Therefore withdraw your instrument, sir, or by'r lady, I shall draw mine.

LADY WISHFORT: Hold, nephew, hold!

MRS. MILLAMANT: Good Sir Wilfull, respite your valour.

FAINALL: Indeed! Are you provided of your guard, with your single beef-eater there? but I'm prepared for you, and insist upon my first proposal. You shall submit your own estate to my management, and absolutely make over my wife's to my sole use, as pursuant to the purport and tenor of this other covenant.—I suppose, madam, your consent is not requisite in this case; nor, Mr. Mirabell, your resignation; nor, Sir Wilfull, your right.—You may draw your fox if you please, sir, and make a bear-garden flourish somewhere else; for here it will not avail. This, my Lady Wishfort, must be subscribed, or your darling daughter's turned adrift, like a leaky hulk, to sink or swim, as she and the current of this lewd town can agree.

LADY WISHFORT: Is there no means, no remedy to stop my ruin? Ungrateful wretch! dost thou not owe thy being, thy subsistence, to my daughter's fortune?

FAINALL: I'll answer you when I have the rest of it in my possession.

MIRABELL: But that you would not accept of a remedy from my hands—I own I have not deserved you should owe any obligation to me; or else perhaps I could advise—

LADY WISHFORT: O what? what? to save me and my child from ruin, from want, I'll forgive all that's past; nay, I'll consent to anything to come, to be delivered from this tyranny.

MIRABELL: Ay, madam; but that is too late, my reward is intercepted. You have disposed of her who only could have made me a compensation for all my services; but be it as it may, I am resolved I'll serve you! you shall not be wronged in this savage manner.

LADY WISHFORT: How! dear Mr. Mirabell, can you be so generous at last! But it is not possible. Harkee, I'll break my nephew's match; you shall have my niece yet, and all her fortune, if you can but save me from this imminent danger.

MIRABELL: Will you? I'll take you at your word. I ask no more. I must have leave for two criminals to appear.

LADY WISHFORT: Ay, ay, anybody, anybody!

MIRABELL: Foible is one, and a penitent.

Enter Mrs. Fainall, Foible, and Mincing.

MRS. MARWOOD: O my shame! [Mirabell *and* Lady Wishfort *go to* Mrs. Fainall *and* Foible] These corrupt things are brought hither to expose me. [*To* Fainall]

FAINALL: If it must all come out, why let 'em know it; 'tis but the way of the world. That shall not urge me to relinquish or abate one tittle of my terms; no, I will insist the more.

FOIBLE: Yes, indeed, madam, I'll take my Bible oath of it.

MINCING: And so will I, mem.

LADY WISHFORT: O Marwood, Marwood, art thou false? my friend deceive me! hast thou been a wicked accomplice with that profligate man?

MRS. MARWOOD: Have you so much ingratitude and injustice to give credit against your friend, to the aspersions of two such mercenary trulls.

MINCING: Mercenary, mem? I scorn your words. 'Tis true we found you and Mr. Fainall in the blue garret; by the same token, you swore us to secrecy upon Messalina's poems. Mercenary! No, if we would have been mercenary, we should have held our tongues; you would have bribed us sufficiently.

FAINALL: Go, you are an insignificant thing!—Well, what are you the better for this; is this Mr. Mirabell's expedient? I'll be put off no longer.—You thing, that was a wife, shall smart for this! I will not leave thee wherewithall to hide thy shame; your body shall be naked as your reputation.

MRS. FAINALL: I despise you, and defy your malice!—you have aspersed me wrongfully—I have proved your falsehood—go you and your treacherous—I will not name it, but starve together—perish!

FAINALL: Not while you are worth a groat, indeed, my dear.—Madam, I'll be fooled no longer.

LADY WISHFORT: Ah, Mr. Mirabell, this is small comfort, the detection of this affair.

MIRABELL: Oh, in good time—your leave for the other offender and penitent to appear, madam.

Enter Waitwell with a box of writings.

LADY WISHFORT: O Sir Rowland!—Well, rascal!

WAITWELL: What your ladyship pleases. I have brought the black box at last, madam.

MIRABELL: Give it me.—Madam, you remember your promise.

LADY WISHFORT: Ay, dear sir.

MIRABELL: Where are the gentlemen?

WAITWELL: At hand, sir, rubbing their eyes—just risen from sleep.

FAINALL: 'Sdeath, what's this to me? I'll not wait your private concerns.

Enter Petulant *and* Witwoud.

PETULANT: How now? What's the matter? whose hand's out?

WITWOUD: Heyday! what, are you all got together, like players at the end of the last act?

MIRABELL: You may remember, gentlemen, I once requested your hands as witnesses to a certain parchment.

WITWOUD: Ay, I do, my hand I remember—Petulant set his mark.

MIRABELL: You wrong him, his name is fairly written, as shall appear.—You do not remember, gentlemen, anything of what that parchment contains?— [*Undoing the box*]

WITWOUD: No.

PETULANT: Not I; I writ, I read nothing.

MIRABELL: Very well, now you shall know.—Madam, your promise.

LADY WISHFORT: Ay, ay, sir, upon my honour.

MIRABELL: Mr. Fainall, it is now time that you should know, that your lady, while she was at her own disposal, and before you had by your insinuations wheedled her out of a pretended settlement of the greatest part of her fortune—

FAINALL: Sir! pretended!

MIRABELL: Yes, sir. I say that this lady while a widow, having it seems received some cautions respecting your inconstancy and tyranny of temper, which from her own partial opinion and fondness of you she could never have suspected—she did, I say, by the wholesome advice of friends, and of sages learned in the laws of this land, deliver this same as her act and deed to me in trust, and to the uses within mentioned. You may read if you please—[*Holding out the parchment*] though perhaps what is written on the back may serve your occasions.

FAINALL: Very likely, sir. What's here?—Damnation! [*Reads*] "A deed of conveyance of the whole estate real of Arabella Languish, widow, in trust to Edward Mirabell."—Confusion!

MIRABELL: Even so, sir; 'tis the Way of the World, sir, of the widows of the world. I suppose this deed may bear an elder date than what you have obtained from your lady.

FAINALL: Perfidious fiend! then thus I'll be revenged. [*Offers to run at* Mrs. Fainall]

SIR WILFULL: Hold, sir! now you may make your bear-garden flourish somewhere else, sir.

FAINALL: Mirabell, you shall hear of this, sir, be sure you shall.—Let me pass, oaf! [*Exit*]

MRS. FAINALL: Madam, you seem to stifle your resentment; you had better give it vent.

MRS. MARWOOD: Yes, it shall have vent—and to your confusion; or I'll perish in the attempt. [*Exit*]

LADY WISHFORT: O daughter, daughter! 'tis plain thou hast inherited thy mother's prudence.

MRS. FAINALL: Thank Mr. Mirabell, a cautious friend, to whose advice all is owing.

LADY WISHFORT: Well, Mr. Mirabell, you have kept your promise—and I must perform mine.—First, I pardon, for your sake, Sir Rowland there, and Foible; the next thing is to break the matter to my nephew—and how to do that—

MIRABELL: For that, madam, give yourself no trouble; let me have your consent. Sir Wilfull is my friend; he has had compassion upon lovers, and generously engaged a volunteer in this action, for our service; and now designs to prosecute his travels.

SIR WILFULL: S'heart, aunt, I have no mind to marry. My cousin's a fine lady, and the gentleman loves her, and she loves him, and they deserve one another; my resolution is to see foreign parts—I have set on't—and when I'm set on't I must do't. And if these two gentlemen would travel too, I think they may be spared.

PETULANT: For my part, I say little—I think things are best off or on.

WITWOUD: I'gad, I understand nothing of the matter; I'm in a maze yet, like a dog in a dancing-school.

LADY WISHFORT: Well, sir, take her, and with her all the joy I can give you.

MRS. MILLAMANT: Why does not the man take me? would you have me give myself to you over again?

MIRABELL: Ay, and over and over again; [*Kisses her hand*] I would have you as often as possibly I can. Well, Heaven grant I love you not too well, that's all my fear.

SIR WILFULL: S'heart, you'll have time enough to toy after you're married; or if you will toy now, let us have a dance in the mean time, that we who are not lovers may have some other employment besides looking on.

MIRABELL: With all my heart, dear Sir Wilfull. What shall we do for music?

FOIBLE: O sir, some that were provided for Sir Rowland's entertainment are yet within call. [*A Dance*]

LADY WISHFORT: As I am a person, I can hold out no longer;—I have wasted my spirits so to-day already, that I am ready to sink under the fatigue; and I cannot but have some fears upon me yet, that my son Fainall will pursue some desperate course.

MIRABELL: Madam, disquiet not yourself on that account; to my knowledge his circumstances are such he must of force comply. For my part, I will contribute all that in me lies to a reunion; in the mean time, madam,—[*To* Mrs. Fainall] let me before these witnesses restore to you this deed of trust; it may be a means, well-managed, to make you live easily together.

> From hence let those be warned who mean to wed;
> Lest mutual falsehood stain the bridal bed;
> For each deceiver to his cost may find,
> That marriage-frauds too oft are paid in kind.
> [*Exeunt omnes*]

Epilogue

After our Epilogue this crowd dismisses,
I'm thinking how this play'll be pulled to pieces.
But pray consider, ere you doom its fall,
How hard a thing 'twould be to please you all.
There are some critics so with spleen diseased,
They scarcely come inclining to be pleased:
And sure he must have more than mortal skill,
Who pleases any one against his will.
Then all bad poets we are sure are foes,
And how their number's swelled, the town well
   knows:
In shoals I've marked 'em judging in the pit;
Though they're, on no pretence, for judgment fit,
But that they have been damned for want of
   wit.
Since when, they by their own offences taught,
Set up for spies on plays, and finding fault.

Others there are whose malice we'd prevent;
Such who watch plays with scurrilous intent
To mark out who by characters are meant.
And though no perfect likeness they can trace,
Yet each pretends to know the copied face.
These with false glosses feed their own ill nature,
And turn to libel what was meant a satire.
May such malicious fops this fortune find,
To think themselves alone the fools designed:
If any are so arrogantly vain,
To think they singly can support a scene,
And furnish fool enough to entertain.
For well the learned and the judicious know
That satire scorns to stoop so meanly low,
As any one abstracted fop to show.
For, as when painters form a matchless face,
They from each fair one catch some different grace;
And shining features in one portrait blend,
To which no single beauty must pretend;
So poets oft do in one piece expose
Whole belles-assemblées of coquettes and beaux.

The Confederacy

by SIR JOHN VANBRUGH
(1664–1726)

With The Confederacy, the last and I think the best of Vanbrugh's plays, the curtain may be said to come down on true Restoration comedy. Already in Vanbrugh, there is a note that we do not find in Etherege or Wycherley, in the Restoration proper; and after Vanbrugh there is distinctly a new note— more romantic, more respectable—that, gradually swelling, drowns out the old Restoration tune. Even in Vanbrugh, we have the sense of someone who is falling in with a tradition rather than helping to create it; for whom the tradition is congenial enough, but not compulsive—no part of his blood or temperament. Vanbrugh, it might be said, displays absence of feeling rather than want of heart; offers what audiences are used to, rather than what playwrights are driven to say. Everyone, of course, is influenced by his age; but Vanbrugh seems less the child of his times than the child of the theater of his times—though, even as he writes, the times are changing, are growing seemlier; and the theater is all poised for change.

Hence Vanbrugh's comedies have less critical, satirical, in a sense moral, value than (artificial though they are) the best of Etherege's or Congreve's: Vanbrugh's are more in the nature of outright theater pieces. They have a playwright's professional liveliness rather than the sharpness of an individual man or mind. In The Confederacy we get the sense of a mere game, of the stratagems of a theater intrigue rather than the duplicities of human beings; we feel that the plot—borrowed from the French—has all the sprightliness but none of the seriousness of the Restoration-comedy tradition.

And yet The Confederacy seems to me, stagewise, at once the best of Vanbrugh's comedies and among the best of the whole rich period it brings to an end. It turns on a very nice point—the fact that husbands will spend money on other men's wives that they refuse to spend on their own. This is no basis for any criticism of life, but it is an excellent and valid one for a comedy of manners. The Confederacy treats, too, of a class of people—what today we should call the up-and-coming middle class—who, in comedy-of-manners terms, have an interest, both social and historical, of their own; there is, among other things, their keen consciousness of not being well born. Much less ironic- and philosophic-minded than a Congreve, more a man of the theater than a man of the world, Vanbrugh had yet a good eye and a good ear for detail; and though not a first-rate wit or a first-rate humorist, had a liveliness with something in it of wit and humor both. And though, by comparison with the comedies that precede it, The Confederacy deals very little in sex, happily, by comparison with the comedies that come after, it traffics very little in sentiment. It has rather to do with the old, Jonsonian, Jacobean world of fraud, and is thus part of a set framework of comedy. The Restoration writers were most decidedly, in tone and impulse, of an age. Vanbrugh is less individual than they; hence, in a not altogether laudable sense, is theatrically more of all time.

SIR JOHN VANBRUGH

The Confederacy

THE PERSONS OF THE PLAY

GRIPE,
MONEY-TRAP } *Two rich Money-scriveners*

DICK, *a Gamester, son to* Mrs. Amlet

BRASS, *his Companion, passes for his Valet de Chambre*

CLIP, *a Goldsmith*

JESSAMIN, *Foot-boy to* Clarissa

CLARISSA, *Wife to* Gripe, *an expensive luxurious woman, a great admirer of quality*

ARAMINTA, *Wife to* Moneytrap, *very intimate with* Clarissa, *of the same humour*

CORINNA, *Daughter to* Gripe *by a former wife, a good fortune, young, and kept very close by her father*

FLIPPANTA, Clarissa's *Maid*

MRS. AMLET, *a seller of all sorts of private affairs to the ladies*

MRS. CLOGGIT, *her Neighbour*

THE SCENE: *London*

Prologue

SPOKEN BY A SHABBY POET

Ye Gods! what crime had my poor father done,
That you should make a poet of his son?
Or is't for some great services of his,
Y'are pleas'd to compliment his boy——with this?
            [*Shewing his crown of laurel*]
    The honour, I must needs confess, is great,
If, with his crown, you'd tell him where to eat.
'Tis well——But I have more complaints—look here!
            [*Shewing his ragged coat*]
Hark ye:—D'ye think this suit good winter wear?
In a cold morning; whu——at a lord's gate,
How you have let the porter let me wait!
You'll say, perhaps, you knew I'd get no harm,
You'd given me fire enough to keep me warm.
Ah——
A world of blessings to that fire we owe;

Without it I'd ne'er made this princely show.
I have a brother too, now in my sight,
            [*Looking behind the scenes*]
A busy man amongst us here to-night:
Your fire has made him play a thousand pranks,
For which, no doubt, you've had his daily thanks;
He'as thank'd you, first, for all his decent plays,
Where he so nick'd it, when he writ for praise.
Next for his meddling with some folks in black,
And bringing——Souse——a priest upon his back;
For building houses here t'oblige the peers,
And fetching all their house about his ears;
For a new play, he'as now thought fit to write,
To sooth the town——which they——will damn to-night.
    These benefits are such, no man can doubt
But he'll go on, and set your fancy out,
Till for reward of all his noble deeds,
At last like other sprightly folks he speeds:
Has this great recompence fix'd on his brow
At fam'd *Parnassus*; has your leave to bow
And walk about the streets——equip'd——as I am now.

Act I

SCENE 1: *Covent Garden*

Enter Mrs. Amlet *and* Mrs. Cloggit, *meeting.*

AMLET: Good-morrow, neighbour; good-morrow, neighbour Cloggit! How does all at your house this morning?

CLOGGIT: Thank you kindly, Mrs. Amlet, thank you kindly; how do you do, I pray?

AMLET: At the old rate, neighbour, poor and honest; these are hard times good lack.

CLOGGIT: If they are hard with you, what are they with us? You have a good trade going, all the great folks in town help you off with your merchandise.

AMLET: Yes, they do help us off with 'em indeed; they buy all.

CLOGGIT: And pay——

AMLET: For some.

CLOGGIT: Well, 'tis a thousand pities, Mrs. Amlet, they are not as ready at one, as they are at t'other: For, not to wrong 'em, they give very good rates.

227

AMLET: O for that, let's do 'em justice, neighbour; they never make two words upon the price, all they haggle about is the day of payment.

CLOGGIT: There's all the dispute, as you say.

AMLET: But that's a wicked one: For my part, neighbour, I'm just tir'd off my legs with trotting after 'em; besides, it eats out all our profit. Would you believe it, Mrs. Cloggit, I have worn out four pair of pattins, with following my old Lady Youthful, for one set of false teeth, and but three pots of paint.

CLOGGIT: Look you there now.

AMLET: If they wou'd but once let me get enough by 'em, to keep a coach to carry me a dunning after 'em, there would be some conscience in it.

CLOGGIT: Ay, that were something. But now you talk of conscience, Mrs. Amlet, how do you speed amongst your city customers?

AMLET: My city customers! Now by my truth, neighbour, between the city and the court (with reverence be it spoken) there's not a——to choose. My ladies in the city, in times past, were as full of gold as they were of religion, and as punctual in their payments as they were in their prayers; but since they have set their minds upon quality, adieu one, adieu t'other, their money and their consciences are gone, heav'n knows where. There is not a goldsmith's wife to be found in town, but's as hard-hearted as an antient judge, and as poor as a towering dutchess.

CLOGGIT: But what the murrain have they to do with quality, why don't their husbands make 'em mind their shops?

AMLET: Their husbands! their husbands, say'st thou, woman? Alack, alack, they mind their husbands, neighbour, no more than they do a sermon.

CLOGGIT: Good lack a day, that women born of sober parents, should be prone to follow ill examples! But now we talk of quality, when did you hear of your son, Richard, Mrs. Amlet? My daughter Flipp says she met him t'other day in a lac'd coat, with three fine ladies, his footman at his heels, and as gay as a bridegroom.

AMLET: Is it possible! Ah the rogue! Well neighbour, all's well that end's well; but Dick will be hang'd.

CLOGGIT: That were pity.

AMLET: Pity indeed; for he's a hopeful young man to look on; but he leads a life—Well—Where he has it, heav'n knows; but they say, he pays his club with the best of 'em. I have seen him but once these three months, neighbour, and then the varlet wanted money; but I bid him march, and march he did to some purpose; for in less than an hour back comes my gentleman into the house, walks to and fro in the room, with his wig over his shoulder, his hat on one side, whistling a minuet, and tossing a purse of gold from one hand to t'other, with no more respect (heaven bless us!) than if it had been an orange. "Sirrah," says I,

"where have you got that?" He answers me never a word, but sets his arms akimbo, cocks his saucy hat in my face, turns about upon his ungracious heel, as much as say kiss—and I've never set eye on him since.

CLOGGIT: Look you there now; to see what the youth of this age are come to!

AMLET: See what they will come to, neighbour. Heaven shield, I say; but Dick's upon the gallop. Well, I must bid you good-morrow; I'm going where I doubt I shall meet but a sorry welcome.

CLOGGIT: To get in some old debt, I'll warrant you?

AMLET: Neither better nor worse.

CLOGGIT: From a lady of quality?

AMLET: No, she's but a scrivener's wife; but she lives as well, and pays as ill, as the stateliest countess of 'em all.   [*Exeunt several ways*]

SCENE 2

Enter Brass, *Solus.*

BRASS: Well surely thro' the world's wide extent, there never appear'd so impudent a fellow as my school-fellow Dick, pass himself upon the town for a gentleman, drop into all the best company with an easy air, as if his natural element were in the sphere of quality; when the rogue had a kettle-drum to his father, who was hang'd for robbing a church, and has a pedlar to his mother, who carries her shop under her arm. But here he comes.

Enter Dick.

DICK: Well, Brass, what news? Hast thou given my letter to Flippanta?

BRASS: I'm but just come; I han't knock'd at the door yet. But I have a damn'd piece of news for you.

DICK: As how?

BRASS: We must quit this country.

DICK: We'll be hang'd first.

BRASS: So you will if you stay.

DICK: Why, what's the matter?

BRASS: There's a storm a coming.

DICK: From whence?

BRASS: From the worst point in the compass, the law.

DICK: The law! Why what have I to do with the law?

BRASS: Nothing; and therefore it has something to do with you.

DICK: Explain.

BRASS: You know you cheated a young fellow at picquet t'other day, of the money he had to raise his company.

DICK: Well, what then?

BRASS: Why, he's sorry he lost it.

DICK: Who doubts that?

BRASS: Ay, but that is not all, he's such a fool to think of complaining on't.

DICK: Then I must be so wise to stop his mouth.

BRASS: How?

DICK: Give him a little back; if that won't do, strangle him.

BRASS: You are very quick in your methods.

DICK: Men must be so that will dispatch business.

BRASS: Hark you, colonel, your father dy'd in's bed?

DICK: He might have done, if he had not been a fool.

BRASS: Why, he robb'd a church.

DICK: Ay, but he forgot to make sure of the sexton.

BRASS: Are not you a great rogue?

DICK: Or I should wear worse clothes.

BRASS: Hark you, I would advise you to change your life.

DICK: And turn ballad-singer.

BRASS: Not so neither.

DICK: What then?

BRASS: Why, if you can get this young wench, reform, and live honest.

DICK: That's the way to be starv'd.

BRASS: No, she has money enough to buy you a good place, and pay me into the bargain for helping her to so good a match. You have but this throw left to save you, for you are not ignorant, youngster, that your morals begin to be pretty well known about town; have a care your noble birth and your honourable relations are not discover'd too: there needs but that to have you toss'd in a blanket, for the entertainment of the first company of ladies you intrude into; and then like a dutiful son, you may daggle about with your mother, and sell paint: She's old and weak, and wants somebody to carry her goods after her. How like a dog will you look, with a pair of plod shoes, your hair crop'd up to your ears, and a band-box under your arm!

DICK: Why faith, Brass, I think thou art in the right on't; I must fix my affairs quickly, or Madam Fortune will be playing some of her bitch-tricks with me: Therefore I'll tell thee what we'll do; we'll pursue this old rogue's daughter heartily; we'll cheat his family to purpose, and they shall atone for the rest of mankind.

BRASS: Have at her then; I'll about your business presently.

DICK: One kiss—and success attend thee. [Exit Dick]

BRASS: A great rogue—Well, I say nothing. But when I have got the thing into a good posture, he shall sign and seal, or I'll have him tumbled out of the house, like a cheese. Now for Flippanta.

[He knocks]

Enter Flippanta.

FLIPPANTA: Who's that? Brass!

BRASS: Flippanta!

FLIPPANTA: What want you, rogue's-face?

BRASS: Is your mistress dress'd?

FLIPPANTA: What, already? Is the fellow drunk?

BRASS: Why, with respect to her looking-glass, it's almost two.

FLIPPANTA: What then, fool?

BRASS: Why then it's time for the mistress of the house to come down, and look after her family.

FLIPPANTA: Pr'ythee don't be an owl. Those that go to bed at night may rise in the morning; we that go to bed in the morning rise in the afternoon.

BRASS: When does she make her visits then?

FLIPPANTA: By candle-light; it helps off a muddy complexion; we women hate inquisitive sunshine: But do you know that my lady is going to turn good housewife?

BRASS: What, is she going to die?

FLIPPANTA: Die!

BRASS: Why, that's the only way to save money for her family.

FLIPPANTA: No; but she has thought of a project to save chair-hire.

BRASS: As how?

FLIPPANTA: Why all the company she us'd to keep abroad she now intends shall meet at her own house. Your master has advis'd her to set up a basset-table.[1]

BRASS: Nay, if he advis'd her to it, it's right; but has she acquainted her husband with it yet?

FLIPPANTA: What to do? When the company meet, he'll see them.

BRASS: Nay, that's true, as you say, he'll know it soon enough.

FLIPPANTA: Well, I must be gone; have you any business with my lady?

BRASS: Yes; as ambassador from Araminta, I have a letter for her.

FLIPPANTA: Give it me.

BRASS: Hold—and as first minister of state to the colonel, I have an affair to communicate to thee.

FLIPPANTA: What is't? quick.

BRASS: Why—he's in love.

FLIPPANTA: With what?

BRASS: A woman—and her money together.

FLIPPANTA: Who is she?

BRASS: Corinna.

FLIPPANTA: What wou'd he be at?

BRASS: At her——if she's at leisure.

FLIPPANTA: Which way?

BRASS: Honourably——He has ordered me to demand her of thee in marriage.

FLIPPANTA: Of me?

BRASS: Why, when a man of quality has a mind to a City-fortune, would'st have him apply to her father and mother?

FLIPPANTA: No.

BRASS: No, so I think: Men of our end of the town are better bred than to use ceremony. With a long periwig we strike the lady, with a you-know-what we soften the maid; and when the parson has done his job, we open the affair to the family. Will you slip this letter into her prayer-book, my little queen? It's a very passionate one—It's seal'd with

[1] Basset is an obsolete game of cards, resembling Faro.

a heart and a dagger; you may see by that what he
intends to do with himself.

FLIPPANTA: Are there any verses in it? If not, I won't
touch it.

BRASS: Not one word in prose, it's dated in rhyme.

FLIPPANTA: Well, but have you brought nothing
else?   [*She takes it*]

BRASS: Gad forgive me; I'm the forgetfullest dog—I
have a letter for you too—here—'tis in a purse,
but it's in prose; you won't touch it.

FLIPPANTA: Yes, hang it, it is not good to be too
dainty.

BRASS: How useful a virtue is humility! Well, child,
we shall have an answer to-morrow, shan't we?

FLIPPANTA: I can't promise you that; for our young
gentlewoman is not so often in my way as she
would be. Her father (who is a citizen from the
foot to the forehead of him) lets her seldom converse with her mother-in-law[1] and me, for fear she
should learn the airs of a woman of quality. But I'll
take the first occasion: See there's my lady, go in
and deliver your letter to her.   [*Exeunt*]

SCENE 3:   *A Parlour*

Enter Clarissa, *follow'd by* Flippanta *and* Brass.

CLARISSA: No messages this morning from any body,
Flippanta? Lard, how dull that is! O, there's Brass!
I did not see thee, Brass. What news dost thou
bring?

BRASS: Only a letter from Araminta, madam.

CLARISSA: Give it me—open it for me, Flippanta, I
am so lazy to-day.

BRASS: [*To Flippanta*] Be sure now you deliver my
master's as carefully as I do this.

FLIPPANTA: Don't trouble thy self, I'm no novice.

CLARISSA: [*To Brass*] 'Tis well, there needs no answer,
since she'll be here so soon.

BRASS: Your ladyship has no farther commands,
then?

CLARISSA: Not at this time, honest Brass!—Flippanta!   [*Exit Brass*]

FLIPPANTA: Madam.

CLARISSA: My husband's in love.

FLIPPANTA: In love?

CLARISSA: With Araminta.

FLIPPANTA: Impossible!

CLARISSA: This letter from her, is to give me an account of it.

FLIPPANTA: Methinks you are not very much alarm'd.

CLARISSA: No; thou know'st I'm not much tortur'd
with jealousy.

FLIPPANTA: Nay, you are much in the right on't,
madam, for jealousy's a City-passion, 'tis a thing
unknown amongst people of quality.

CLARISSA: Fy! A woman must indeed be of a mechanick mould, who is either troubled or pleas'd

[1] *i.e. Stepmother.*

with any thing her husband can do to her. Pr'ythee
mention him no more; 'tis the dullest theme.

FLIPPANTA: 'Tis splenetick, indeed. But when once
you open your basset-table, I hope that will put
him out of your head.

CLARISSA: Alas, Flippanta, I begin to grow weary
even of the thoughts of that too.

FLIPPANTA: How so?

CLARISSA: Why, I have thought on't a day and a
night already; and four and twenty hours, thou
know'st, is enough to make one weary of any thing.

FLIPPANTA: Now, by my conscience, you have more
woman in you than all your sex together: You
never know what you would have.

CLARISSA: Thou mistakest the thing quite. I always
know what I lack, but I am never pleas'd with
what I have. The want of a thing is perplexing
enough, but the possession of it is intolerable.

FLIPPANTA: Well, I don't know what you are made
of, but other women would think themselves blest
in your case; handsome, witty, lov'd by every body,
and of so happy a composure, to care a fig for no
body. You have no one passion, but that of your
pleasures, and you have in me a servant devoted to
all your desires, let them be as extravagant as they
will: Yet all this is nothing; you can still be out of
humour.

CLARISSA: Alas, I have but too much cause.

FLIPPANTA: Why, what have you to complain of?

CLARISSA: Alas, I have more subjects for spleen than
one: Is it not a most horrible thing that I should
be but a scrivener's wife?—Come,—don't flatter
me, don't you think nature design'd me for something *plus élevée*?

FLIPPANTA: Nay, that's certain; but on th' other side,
methinks, you ought to be in some measure content, since you live like a woman of quality, tho'
you are none.

CLARISSA: O fy! the very quintessence of it is wanting.

FLIPPANTA: What's that!

CLARISSA: Why, I dare abuse no body: I'm afraid to
affront people, tho' I don't like their faces; or to
ruin their reputations, tho' they pique me to it, by
taking ever so much pains to preserve 'em: I dare
not raise a lye of a man, tho' he neglects to make
love to me; nor report a woman to be a fool, tho'
she's handsomer than I am. In short, I dare not so
much as bid my footman kick the people out of
doors, tho' they come to ask me for what I owe
them.

FLIPPANTA: All this is very hard indeed.

CLARISSA: Ah, Flippanta, the perquisites of quality
are of an unspeakable value.

FLIPPANTA: They are of some use, I must confess;
but we must not expect to have every thing. You
have wit and beauty, and a fool to your husband:
Come, come, madam, that's a good portion for
one.

CLARISSA: Alas, what signifies beauty and wit, when

one dares neither jilt the men, nor abuse the women? 'Tis a sad thing, Flippanta, when wit's confin'd, 'tis worse than the rising of the lights; I have been sometimes almost chok'd with scandal, and durst not cough it up for want of being a countess.

FLIPPANTA: Poor lady!

CLARISSA: O! liberty is a fine thing, Flippanta; it's a great help in conversation to have leave to say what one will. I have seen a woman of quality, who has not had one grain of wit, entertain a whole company the most agreeably in the world, only with her malice. But 'tis in vain to repine, I can't mend my condition till my husband dies; so I'll say no more on't, but think of making the most of the state I am in.

FLIPPANTA: That's your best way, madam; and in order to it, pray consider how you'll get some ready money to set your basset-table a going; for that's necessary.

CLARISSA: Thou say'st true; but what trick I shall play my husband to get some, I don't know: For my pretence of losing my diamond necklace has put the man into such a passion, I'm afraid he won't hear reason.

FLIPPANTA: No matter; he begins to think 'tis lost in earnest: So I fancy you may venture to sell it, and raise money that way.

CLARISSA: That can't be, for he has left odious notes with all the goldsmiths in town.

FLIPPANTA: Well, we must pawn it then.

CLARISSA: I'm quite tir'd with dealing with those pawnbrokers.

FLIPPANTA: I'm afraid you'll continue the trade a great while, for all that.   [Aside]

Enter Jessamin.

JESSAMIN: Madam, there's the woman below that sells paint and patches, iron-bodice, false teeth, and all sorts of things to the ladies; I can't think of her name.   [Exit]

FLIPPANTA: 'Tis Mrs. Amlet, she wants money.

CLARISSA: Well, I han't enough for my self, it's an unreasonable thing she should think I have any for her.

FLIPPANTA: She's a troublesome jade!

CLARISSA: So are all people that come a dunning.

FLIPPANTA: What will you do with her?

CLARISSA: I have just now thought on't. She's very rich, that woman is, Flippanta, I'll borrow some money of her.

FLIPPANTA: Borrow! Sure, you jest, madam.

CLARISSA: No, I'm in earnest; I give thee commission to do it for me.

FLIPPANTA: Me!

CLARISSA: Why dost thou stare, and look so ungainly? Don't I speak to be understood?

FLIPPANTA: Yes, I understand you well enough; but Mrs. Amlet——

CLARISSA: But Mrs. Amlet must lend me some money, where shall I have any to pay her else?

FLIPPANTA: That's true; I never thought of that truly. But here she is.

Enter Mrs. Amlet.

CLARISSA: How d'you do? How d'you do, Mrs. Amlet? I han't seen you these thousand years, and yet I believe I'm down in your books.

AMLET: O, madam, I don't come for that, alack.

FLIPPANTA: Good-morrow, Mrs. Amlet.

AMLET: Good-morrow, Mrs. Flippanta.

CLARISSA: How much am I indebted to you, Mrs. Amlet?

AMLET: Nay, if your ladyship desires to see your bill, I believe I may have it about me.—There, madam, if it ben't too much fatigue to you to look it over.

CLARISSA: Let me see it, for I hate to be in debt, where I am obliged to pay. [*Aside. Reads*] "Imprimis, *For bolstering out the Countess of* Crump's *left hip*"—O fy, this does not belong to me.

AMLET: I beg your ladyship's pardon. I mistook indeed; 'tis a countess's bill I have writ out to little purpose. I furnish'd her two years ago with three pair of hips, and am not paid for them yet: But some are better customers than some. There's your ladyship's bill, Madam.   [*Giving the bill*]

CLARISSA: "*For the idea of a new-invented commode!*"—Ay, this may be mine, but 'tis of a preposterous length. Do you think I can waste time to read every article, Mrs. Amlet? I'd as lief read a sermon.

AMLET: Alack-a-day, there's no need of fatiguing yourself at that rate; cast an eye only, if your honour pleases, upon the sum total.

CLARISSA: Total; fifty six pound—and odd things.

FLIPPANTA: But six and fifty pound!

AMLET: Nay, another body would have made it twice as much, but there's a blessing goes along with a moderate profit.

CLARISSA: Flippanta, go to my cashier, let him give you six and fifty pound. Make haste: Don't you hear me? six and fifty pound. Is it so difficult to be comprehended?

FLIPPANTA: No, madam, I, I comprehend, six and fifty pound, but——

CLARISSA: But go and fetch it then.

FLIPPANTA: What she means, I don't know; [*Aside*] but I shall, I suppose, before I bring her the money.   [*Exit* Flippanta]

CLARISSA: [*Setting her hair in a pocket-glass*] The trade you follow gives you a great deal of trouble, Mrs. Amlet?

AMLET: Alack-a-day, a world of pain, madam, and yet there's small profit, as your honour sees by your bill.

CLARISSA: Poor woman! Sometimes you have great losses, Mrs. Amlet?

AMLET: I have two thousand pounds owing me, of which I shall never get ten shillings.

CLARISSA: Poor woman! you have a great charge of children, Mrs. Amlet?

AMLET: Only one wicked rogue, madam, who, I think, will break my heart.

CLARISSA: Poor woman!

AMLET: He'll be hang'd, madam—that will be the end of him. Where he gets it, heav'n knows; but he's always shaking his heels with the ladies, and his elbows with the lords. He's as fine as a prince, and as gim as the best of them; but the ungracious rogue tells all he comes near that his mother is dead, and I am but his nurse.

CLARISSA: Poor woman!

AMLET: Alas, madam, he's like the rest of the world; every body's for appearing to be more than they are, and that ruins all.

CLARISSA: Well, Mrs. Amlet, you'll excuse me, I have a little business, Flippanta will bring you your money presently. Adieu, Mrs. Amlet.

[Exit Clarissa]

AMLET: I return your honour many thanks. [Sola] Ah, there's my good lady, not so much as read her bill; if the rest were like her, I should soon have money enough to go as fine as Dick himself.

Enter Dick.

DICK: Sure Flippanta must have given my letter by this time; [Aside] I long to know how it has been received.

AMLET: Misericord! what do I see!

DICK: Fiends and hags——the witch my mother!

AMLET: Nay, 'tis he; ah, my poor Dick, what art thou doing here?

DICK: What a misfortune——   [Aside]

AMLET: Good lard! how thou art bravely deck'd. But it's all one, I am thy mother still; and tho' thou art a wicked child, nature will speak, I love thee still, ah, Dick, my poor Dick.   [Embracing him]

DICK: Blood and thunder! will you ruin me?

[Breaking from her]

AMLET: Ah, the blasphemous rogue, how he swears!

DICK: You destroy all my hopes.

AMLET: Will your mother's kiss destroy you, varlet? Thou art an ungracious bird; kneel down, and ask me blessing, sirrah.

DICK: Death and furies!

AMLET: Ah, he's a proper young man, see what a shape he has: ah, poor child.

[Running to embrace him, he still avoiding her]

DICK: Oons, keep off, the woman's mad. If any body comes my fortune's lost.

AMLET: What fortune, ha? Speak graceless. Ah Dick, thou'lt be hang'd, Dick.

DICK: Good dear mother now, don't call me Dick here.

AMLET: Not call thee Dick? Is it not thy name? What shall I call thee? Mr. Amlet? ha! Art not

thou a presumptuous rascal? Hark you, sirrah, I hear of your tricks; you disown me for your mother, and say I am but your nurse. Is not this true?

DICK: No, I love you; I respect you [Taking her hand]; I am all duty. But if you discover me here, you ruin the fairest prospect that man ever had.

AMLET: What prospect? ha! Come, this is a lye now.

DICK: No, my honour'd parent, what I say is true, I'm about a great fortune. I'll bring you home a daughter-in-law, in a coach and six horses, if you'll but be quiet: I can't tell you more now.

AMLET: Is it possible?

DICK: 'Tis true, by Jupiter.

AMLET: My dear lad——

DICK: For heaven's sake——

AMLET: But tell me, Dick——

DICK: I'll follow you home in a moment, and tell you all.

AMLET: What a shape is there——

DICK: Pray mother go.

AMLET: I must receive some money here first, which shall go for thy wedding-dinner.

DICK: Here's somebody coming; 'Sdeath, she'll betray me.   [He makes signs to his mother]

Enter Flippanta.

Good-morrow, dear Flippanta; how do all the ladies within?

FLIPPANTA: At your service, colonel; as far at least as my interest goes.

AMLET: Colonel!—Law you now, how Dick's respected!   [Aside]

DICK: Waiting for thee, Flippanta; I was making acquaintance with this old gentlewoman here.

AMLET: The pretty lad, he's as impudent as a page.   [Aside]

DICK: Who is this good woman, Flippanta?

FLIPPANTA: A gin of all trades; an old daggling cheat, that hobbles about from house to house to bubble the ladies of their money. I have a small business of yours in my pocket, colonel.

DICK: An answer to my letter?

FLIPPANTA: So quick indeed! No, it's your letter it self.

DICK: Hast thou not given it then yet?

FLIPPANTA: I han't had an opportunity; but 'twon't be long first. Won't you go in and see my lady?

DICK: Yes, I'll go make her a short visit. But, dear Flippanta, don't forget: My life and fortune are in your hands.

FLIPPANTA: Ne'er fear, I'll take care of 'em.

AMLET: How he traps 'em; let Dick alone.   [Aside]

DICK: Your servant, good madam [To his mother]

[Exit Dick]

AMLET: Your honour's most devoted.—A pretty, civil, well-bred gentleman this, Mrs. Flippanta. Pray whom may he be?

FLIPPANTA: A man of great note; Colonel Shapely.

AMLET: Is it possible! I have heard much of him indeed, but never saw him before: One may see quality in every limb of him: He's a fine man truly.

FLIPPANTA: I think you are in love with him, Mrs. Amlet.

AMLET: Alas, those days are done with me; but if I were as fair as I was once, and had as much money as some folks, Colonel Shapely should not catch cold for want of a bedfellow. I love your men of rank, they have something in their air does so distinguish 'em from the rascality.

FLIPPANTA: People of quality are fine things indeed, Mrs. Amlet, if they had but a little more money; but for want of that, they are forc'd to do things their great souls are asham'd of. For example— here's my lady—she owes you but six and fifty pounds—

AMLET: Well!

FLIPPANTA: Well, and she has it not by her to pay you.

AMLET: How can that be?

FLIPPANTA: I don't know; her cash-keeper's out of humour, he says he has no money.

AMLET: What a presumptuous piece of vermin is a cash-keeper! Tell his lady he has no money!—Now, Mrs. Flippanta, you may see his bags are full, by his being so saucy.

FLIPPANTA: If they are, there's no help for't; he'll do what he pleases, till he comes to make up his yearly accounts.

AMLET: But madam plays sometimes, so when she has good fortune, she may pay me out of her winnings.

FLIPPANTA: O ne'er think of that, Mrs. Amlet; if she had won a thousand pounds, she'd rather die in a gaol than pay off a farthing with it: Play-money, Mrs. Amlet, amongst people of quality, is a sacred thing, and not to be profan'd. The deux—'tis consecrated to their pleasures, 'twould be sacrilege to pay their debts with it.

AMLET: Why what shall we do then? For I han't one penny to buy bread.

FLIPPANTA:—I'll tell you—it just now comes in my head: I know my lady has a little occasion for money at this time; so—if you lend her—a hundred pound—do you see, then she may pay you your six and fifty out of it.

AMLET: Sure, Mrs. Flippanta, you think to make a fool of me?

FLIPPANTA: No, the devil fetch me if I do—— You shall have a diamond necklace in pawn.

AMLET: O ho, a pawn! That's another case. And when must she have this money?

FLIPPANTA: In a quarter of an hour.

AMLET: Say no more. Bring the necklace to my house, it shall be ready for you.

FLIPPANTA: I'll be with you in a moment.

AMLET: Adieu, Mrs. Flippanta.

FLIPPANTA: Adieu, Mrs. Amlet. [*Exit* Amlet, Flippanta *sola*] So—this ready money will make us all

happy. This spring will set our basset going, and that's a wheel that will turn twenty others. My lady's young and handsome; she'll have a dozen intrigues upon her hands, before she has been twice at her prayers. So much the better; the more the grist, the richer the miller. Sure never wench got into so hopeful a place: Here's a fortune to be sold, a mistress to be debauch'd, and a master to be ruin'd. If I don't feather my nest, and get a good husband, I deserve to die, both a maid and a beggar.

Act II

SCENE 1: *Mr. Gripe's House*

Enter Clarissa *and* Dick.

CLARISSA: What in the name of dulness is the matter with you, colonel? You are as studious as a crack'd chymist.

DICK: My head, madam, is full of your husband.

CLARISSA: The worst furniture for a head in the universe.

DICK: I am thinking of his passion for your friend Araminta.

CLARISSA: Passion!—Dear colonel, give it a less violent name.

Enter Brass.

DICK: Well, sir, what want you?

BRASS: The affair I told you of goes ill. [*To Dick aside*] There's an action out.

DICK: The devil there is!

CLARISSA: What news brings Brass?

DICK: Before Gad I can't tell, madam; the dog will never speak out. My Lord what-d'ye-call-him waits for me at my lodging: Is not that it?

BRASS: Yes, sir.

DICK: Madam, I ask your pardon.

CLARISSA: Your servant, sir. [*Exeunt* Dick *and* Brass] Jessamin!   [*She sits down*]

Enter Jessamin.

JESSAMIN: Madam.

CLARISSA: Where's Corinna? Call her to me, if her father han't lock'd her up: I want her company.

JESSAMIN: Madam, her guitar-master is with her.

CLARISSA: Pshaw! she's taken up with her impertinent guitar-man. Flippanta stays an age with that old fool, Mrs. Amlet. And Araminta, before she can come abroad, is so long a placing her coquet-patch, that I must be a year without company. How insupportable is a moment's uneasiness to a woman of spirit and pleasure.

Enter Flippanta.

O, art thou come at last? Pr'ythee, Flippanta, learn to move a little quicker, thou know'st how impatient I am.

FLIPPANTA: Yes, when you expect money: If you had sent me to buy a prayer-book, you'd have thought I had flown.

CLARISSA: Well, hast thou brought me any, after all?

FLIPPANTA: Yes, I have brought some. There [*Giving her a purse*], the old hag has struck off her bill, the rest is in that purse.

CLARISSA: 'Tis well; but take care, Flippanta, my husband don't suspect any thing of this, 'twould vex him, and I don't love to make him uneasy: So I would spare him these little sort of troubles, by keeping 'em from his knowledge.

FLIPPANTA: See the tenderness she has for him, and yet he's always a complaining of you.

CLARISSA: 'Tis the nature of 'em, Flippanta; a husband is a growling animal.

FLIPPANTA: How exactly you define 'em!

CLARISSA: O! I know 'em, Flippanta: though I confess my poor wretch diverts me sometimes with his ill-humours. I wish he wou'd quarrel with me to-day a little, to pass away the time, for I find my self in a violent spleen.

FLIPPANTA: Why, if you please to drop your self in his way, six to four but he scolds one rubbers with you.

CLARISSA: Ay, but thou know'st he's as uncertain as the wind, and if instead of quarrelling with me, he shou'd chance to be fond, he'd make me as sick as a dog.

FLIPPANTA: If he's kind, you must provoke him, if he kisses you, spit in his face.

CLARISSA: Alas! when men are in the kissing fit, (like lap-dogs) they take that for a favour.

FLIPPANTA: Nay, then I don't know what you'll do with him.

CLARISSA: I'll e'en do nothing at all with him.—Flippanta! [*Yawning*]

FLIPPANTA: Madam.

CLARISSA: My hoods and scarf, and a coach to the door.

FLIPPANTA: Why, whither are you going?

CLARISSA: I can't tell yet, but I wou'd go spend some money, since I have it.

FLIPPANTA: Why, you want nothing that I know of.

CLARISSA: How awkward an objection now is that, as if a woman of education bought things because she wanted 'em. Quality always distinguishes itself; and therefore, as the mechanick people buy things, because they have occasion for 'em, you see women of rank always buy things, because they have not occasion for 'em. Now there, Flippanta, you see the difference between a woman that has breeding, and one that has none. O ho, here's Araminta come at last.

Enter Araminta.

Lard, what a tedious while you have let me expect you! I was afraid you were not well; how d'ye do to-day?

ARAMINTA: As well as a woman can do, that has not slept all night.

FLIPPANTA: Methinks, madam, you are pretty well awake, however.

ARAMINTA: O, 'tis not a little thing will make a woman of my vigour look drowsy.

CLARISSA: But pr'ythee what was't disturb'd you?

ARAMINTA: Not your husband, don't trouble yourself; at least, I am not in love with him yet.

CLARISSA: Well remember'd, I had quite forgot that matter. I wish you much joy, you have made a noble conquest indeed.

ARAMINTA: But now I have subdu'd the country, pray is it worth my keeping? You know the ground, you have try'd it.

CLARISSA: A barren soil, Heaven can tell.

ARAMINTA: Yet if it were well cultivated, it would produce something to my knowledge. Do you know 'tis in my power to ruin this poor thing of yours? His whole estate is at my service.

FLIPPANTA: Cods-fish, strike him, madam, and let my lady go your halves. There's no sin in plundering a husband, so his wife has share of the booty.

ARAMINTA: Whenever she gives me her orders, I shall be very ready to obey 'em.

CLARISSA: Why, as odd a thing as such a project may seem, Araminta, I believe I shall have a little serious discourse with you about it. But pr'ythee tell me how you have pass'd the night? For I am sure your mind has been roving upon some pretty thing or other.

ARAMINTA: Why, I have been studying all the ways my brain could produce to plague my husband.

CLARISSA: No wonder indeed you look so fresh this morning, after the satisfaction of such pleasing ideas all night.

ARAMINTA: Why, can a woman do less than study mischief, when she has tumbled and toss'd herself into a burning-fever, for want of sleep, and sees a fellow lie snoring by her, stock-still, in a fine breathing sweat?

CLARISSA: Now see the difference of women's tempers: If my dear wou'd make but one nap of his whole life, and only waken to make his will, I shou'd be the happiest wife in the universe. But we'll discourse more of these matters as we go, for I must make a tour among the shops.

ARAMINTA: I have a coach waits at the door, we'll talk of 'em as we rattle along.

CLARISSA: The best place in nature, for you know a hackney-coach is a natural enemy to a husband.

[*Exeunt* Clarissa *and* Araminta]

Flippanta *sola*.

FLIPPANTA: What a pretty little pair of amiable persons are there gone to hold a council of war together! Poor birds! what wou'd they do with their time, if the plaguing their husbands did not help 'em to employment! Well, if idleness be the root of all evil, then matrimony's good for something, for it sets many a poor woman to work. But here comes miss. I hope I shall help her into the holy state too ere long. And when she's once there, if she don't play her part as well as the best of 'em, I'm mistaken. Han't I lost the letter I'm to give her?—No, here 'tis; so, now we shall see how pure nature will work with her, for art she knows none yet.

Enter Corinna.

CORINNA: What does my mother-in-law want with me, Flippanta? They tell me, she was asking for me.

FLIPPANTA: She's just gone out, so I suppose 'twas no great business.

CORINNA: Then I'll go into my chamber again.

FLIPPANTA: Nay, hold a little if you please. I have some business with you my self, of more concern than what she had to say to you.

CORINNA: Make haste then, for you know my father won't let me keep you company; he says, you'll spoil me.

FLIPPANTA: I spoil you! He's an unworthy man to give you such ill impressions of a woman of my honour.

CORINNA: Nay, never take it to heart, Flippanta, for I don't believe a word he says. But he does so plague me with his continual scolding, I'm almost weary of my life.

FLIPPANTA: Why, what is't he finds fault with?

CORINNA: Nay, I don't know, for I never mind him; when he has babbled for two hours together, me-thinks I have heard a mill going, that's all. It does not at all change my opinion, Flippanta, it only makes my head ache.

FLIPPANTA: Nay, if you can bear it so, you are not to be pity'd so much as I thought.

CORINNA: Not pity'd! Why is it not a miserable thing, such a young creature as I am shou'd be kept in perpetual solitude, with no other company but a parcel of old fumbling masters, to teach me geography, arithmetick, philosophy, and a thousand useless things? Fine entertainment, indeed, for a young maid at sixteen! methinks one's time might be better employ'd.

FLIPPANTA: Those things will improve your wit.

CORINNA: Fiddle, faddle; han't I wit enough already? My mother-in-law has learn'd none of this trump-ery, and is not she as happy as the day is long?

FLIPPANTA: Then you envy her, I find?

CORINNA: And well I may. Does she not do what she has a mind to, in spite of her husband's teeth?

FLIPPANTA: Look you there now [*Aside*], if she has not already conceived that, as the supreme blessing of life.

CORINNA: I'll tell you what, Flippanta; if my mother-in-law would but stand by me a little, and en-courage me, and let me keep her company, I'd rebel against my father to-morrow, and throw all my books in the fire. Why, he can't touch a groat of my portion; do you know that, Flippanta?

FLIPPANTA: So—I shall spoil her! [*Aside*] Pray heaven the girl don't debauch me.

CORINNA: Look you: In short, he may think what he pleases, he may think himself wise; but thoughts are free, and I may think in my turn. I'm but a girl 'tis true, and a fool too, if you believe him; but let him know, a foolish girl may make a wise man's heart ache; so he had as good be quiet—Now it's out—

FLIPPANTA: Very well. I love to see a young woman have spirit, it's a sign she'll come to something.

CORINNA: Ah, Flippanta, if you wou'd but encourage me, you'll find me quite another thing. I'm a devilish girl in the bottom; I wish you'd but let me make one amongst you.

FLIPPANTA: That never can be, 'till you are marry'd. Come, examine your strength a little. Do you think, you durst venture upon a husband?

CORINNA: A husband! Why a—if you wou'd but en-courage me. Come, Flippanta, be a true friend now. I'll give you advice, when I have got a little more experience. Do you in your very conscience and soul think I am old enough to be marry'd?

FLIPPANTA: Old enough! Why you are sixteen, are you not?

CORINNA: Sixteen! I am sixteen, two months, and odd days, woman. I keep an exact account.

FLIPPANTA: The duce you are!

CORINNA: Why, do you then truly and sincerely think I am old enough?

FLIPPANTA: I do upon my faith, child.

CORINNA: Why then, to deal as fairly with you, Flip-panta, as you do with me, I have thought so any time these three years.

FLIPPANTA: Now I find you have more wit than ever I thought you had; and to shew you what an opinion I have of your discretion, I'll shew you a thing I thought to have thrown in the fire.

CORINNA: What is it, for Jupiter's sake?

FLIPPANTA: Something will make your heart chuck within you.

CORINNA: My dear Flippanta!

FLIPPANTA: What do you think it is?

CORINNA: I don't know, nor I don't care; but I'm mad to have it.

FLIPPANTA: It's a four-corner'd thing.

CORINNA: What, like a cardinal's cap?

FLIPPANTA: No, 'tis worth a whole conclave of 'em. How do you like it? [*Shewing the letter*]

CORINNA: O lard, a letter!—Is there ever a token in it?

FLIPPANTA: Yes, and a precious one too. There's a handsome young gentleman's heart.

CORINNA: A handsome young gentleman's heart! Nay, then it's time to look grave. [*Aside*]

FLIPPANTA: There.

CORINNA: I shan't touch it.

FLIPPANTA: What's the matter now?

CORINNA: I shan't receive it.

FLIPPANTA: Sure you jest.

CORINNA: You'll find I don't. I understand my self better, than to take letters, when I don't know who they are from.

FLIPPANTA: I'm afraid I commended your wit too soon.

CORINNA: 'Tis all one, I shan't touch it, unless I know who it comes from.

FLIPPANTA: Hey-day! Open it, and you'll see.

CORINNA: Indeed I shall not.

FLIPPANTA: Well—then I must return it where I had it.

CORINNA: That won't serve your turn, madam. My father must have an account of this.

FLIPPANTA: Sure you are not in earnest?

CORINNA: You'll find I am.

FLIPPANTA: So, here's fine work! This 'tis to deal with girls before they come to know the distinction of sexes.

CORINNA: Confess who you had it from, and perhaps, for this once, I mayn't tell my father.

FLIPPANTA: Why then, since it must out, 'twas the Colonel: But why are you so scrupulous, madam?

CORINNA: Because if it had come from any body else —I would not have given a farthing for it. [Twitching it eagerly out of her hand]

FLIPPANTA: Ah, my dear little rogue! [Kissing her] You frighten'd me out of my wits.

CORINNA: Let me read it, let me read it, let me read it, let me read it, I say. Um, um, um, Cupid's, um, um, um, darts, um, um, um, beauty, um, charms, um, um, um, angel, um, goddess, um—[Kissing the letter], um, um, um, truest lover, hum, um, eternal constancy, um, um, um, cruel, um, um, um, racks, um, um, tortures, um, um, fifty daggers, um, um, bleeding heart, um, um, dead man. Very well, a mighty civil letter, I promise you; not one smutty word in it: I'll go lock it up in my comb-box.

FLIPPANTA: Well—but what does he say to you?

CORINNA: Not a word of news, Flippanta; 'tis all about business.

FLIPPANTA: Does he not tell you he's in love with you?

CORINNA: Ay, but he told me that before.

FLIPPANTA: How so? He never spoke to you.

CORINNA: He sent me word by his eyes.

FLIPPANTA: Did he so? mighty well. I thought you had been to learn that language.

CORINNA: O, but you thought wrong, Flippanta. What, because I don't go a visiting, and see the world, you think I know nothing. But you shou'd consider, Flippanta, that the more one's alone, the more one thinks; and 'tis thinking that improves a girl. I'll have you to know, when I was younger than I am now, by more than I'll boast of, I thought of things would have made you stare again.

FLIPPANTA: Well, since you are so well vers'd in your business, I suppose I need not inform you, that if you don't write your gallant an answer—he'll die.

CORINNA: Nay, now, Flippanta, I confess you tell me something I did not know before. Do you speak in serious sadness? Are men given to die, if their mistresses are sour to 'em?

FLIPPANTA: Um——I can't say they all die——No, I can't say they do; but truly, I believe it wou'd go very hard with the Colonel.

CORINNA: Lard, I would not have my hands in blood for thousands; and therefore Flippanta——if ou'll encourage me——

FLIPPANTA: O, by all means an answer.

CORINNA: Well, since you say it then, I'll e'en in and do it, tho' I protest to you (lest you should think me too forward now) he's the only man that wears a beard, I'd ink my fingers for. May be, if I marry him, in a year or two's time I mayn't be so nice. [Aside]
[Exit Corinna]

Flippanta sola.

Now heaven give him joy; he's like to have a rare wife o'thee. But where there's money, a man has a plaister to his sore. They have a blessed time on't, who marry for love. See!—here comes an example ——Araminta's dread lord.

Enter Money-trap.

MONEY-TRAP: Ah, Flippanta! How do you do, good Flippanta? How do you do?

FLIPPANTA: Thank you, sir, well, at your service.

MONEY-TRAP: And how does the good family, your master, and your fair mistress? Are they at home?

FLIPPANTA: Neither of them; my master has been gone out these two hours, and my lady is just gone with your wife.

MONEY-TRAP: Well, I won't say I have lost my labour however, as long as I have met with you, Flippanta. For I have wish'd a great while for an opportunity to talk with you a little. You won't take it amiss, if I should ask you a few questions?

FLIPPANTA: Provided you leave me to my liberty in my answers. What's this Cot-quean going to pry into now! [Aside]

MONEY-TRAP: Pr'ythee, good Flippanta, how do your master and mistress live together?

FLIPPANTA: Live! Why—like man and wife, generally out of humour, quarrel often, seldom agree, complain of one another; and perhaps have both reason. In short, 'tis much as 'tis at your house.

MONEY-TRAP: Good-lack! but whose side are you generally of?

FLIPPANTA: O' the right side always, my lady's. And if you'll have me give you my opinion of these matters, sir, I do not think a husband can ever be in the right.

MONEY-TRAP: Ha!

FLIPPANTA: Little, peeking, creeping, sneaking, stingy, covetous, cowardly, dirty, cuckoldy things.

MONEY-TRAP: Ha!

FLIPPANTA: Fit for nothing but taylors and dry-nurses.

MONEY-TRAP: Ha!

FLIPPANTA: A dog in a manger, snarling and biting, to starve gentlemen with good stomachs.

MONEY-TRAP: Ha!

FLIPPANTA: A centry upon pleasure, set to be a plague on lovers, and damn poor women before their time.

MONEY-TRAP: A husband is indeed——

FLIPPANTA: Sir, I say, he is nothing——A beetle without wings, a windmill without sails, a ship in a calm.

MONEY-TRAP: Ha!

FLIPPANTA: A bag without money——an empty bottle——dead small-beer.

MONEY-TRAP: Ha!

FLIPPANTA: A quack without drugs.

MONEY-TRAP: Ha!

FLIPPANTA: A lawyer without knavery.

MONEY-TRAP: Ha!

FLIPPANTA: A courtier without flattery.

MONEY-TRAP: Ha!

FLIPPANTA: A king without an army——or a people with one. Have I drawn him, sir?

MONEY-TRAP: Why truly, Flippanta, I can't deny but there are some general lines of resemblance. But you know there may be exceptions.

FLIPPANTA: Hark you, sir, shall I deal plainly with you? Had I got a husband, I wou'd put him in mind, that he was marry'd as well as I.　[*Sings*]

For were I the thing call'd a wife,
And my fool grew too fond of his power
He shou'd look like an ass all his life,
For a prank that I'd play him in an hour.

Tol lol la ra tol lol, &c.—Do you observe that, sir?

MONEY-TRAP: I do: and think you wou'd be in the right on't. But, pr'ythee, why dost not give this advice to thy mistress?

FLIPPANTA: For fear it should go round to your wife, sir, for you know they are play-fellows.

MONEY-TRAP: O, there's no danger of my wife; she knows I'm none of those husbands.

FLIPPANTA: Are you sure she knows that, sir?

MONEY-TRAP: I'm sure she ought to know it, Flippanta, for really I have but four faults in the world.

FLIPPANTA: And, pray what may they be?

MONEY-TRAP: Why, I'm a little slovenly, I shift but once a week.

FLIPPANTA: Fough!

MONEY-TRAP: I am sometimes out of humour.

FLIPPANTA: Provoking!

MONEY-TRAP: I don't give her so much money as she'd have.

FLIPPANTA: Insolent!

MONEY-TRAP: And a——perhaps I mayn't be quite so young as I was.

FLIPPANTA: The devil!

MONEY-TRAP: O, but then consider how 'tis on her side, Flippanta. She ruins me with washing, is always out of humour, ever wanting money, and will never be older.

FLIPPANTA: That last article, I must confess, is a little hard upon you.

MONEY-TRAP: Ah, Flippanta, didst thou but know the daily provocations I have, thou'dst be the first to excuse my faults. But now I think on't——Thou art none of my friend, thou dost not love me at all; no, not at all.

FLIPPANTA: And whither is this little reproach going to lead us now?

MONEY-TRAP: You have power over your fair mistress, Flippanta.

FLIPPANTA: Sir!

MONEY-TRAP: But what then? You hate me.

FLIPPANTA: I understand you not.

MONEY-TRAP: There's not a moment's trouble her naughty husband gives her, but I feel it too.

FLIPPANTA: I don't know what you mean.

MONEY-TRAP: If she did but know what part I take in her sufferings——

FLIPPANTA: Mighty obscure.

MONEY-TRAP: Well, I'll say no more; but——

FLIPPANTA: All Hebrew.

MONEY-TRAP: If thou wou'dst but tell her on't.

FLIPPANTA: Still darker and darker.

MONEY-TRAP: I shou'd not be ungrateful.

FLIPPANTA: Ah, now I begin to understand you.

MONEY-TRAP: Flippanta—there's my purse.

FLIPPANTA: Say no more; now you explain, indeed——You are in love?

MONEY-TRAP: Bitterly—and I do swear by all the Gods——

FLIPPANTA: Hold—Spare 'em for another time, you stand in no need of 'em now. An usurer that parts with his purse, gives sufficient proof of his sincerity.

MONEY-TRAP: I hate my wife, Flippanta.

FLIPPANTA: That we'll take upon your bare word.

MONEY-TRAP: She's the devil, Flippanta.

FLIPPANTA: You like your neighbour's better.

MONEY-TRAP: Oh!——an angel!

FLIPPANTA: What pity it is the law don't allow trucking!

MONEY-TRAP: If it did, Flippanta!

FLIPPANTA: But since it don't, sir——keep the reins upon your passion: Don't let your flame rage too high, lest my lady shou'd be cruel, and it should dry you up to a mummy.

MONEY-TRAP: 'Tis impossible she can be so barbarous, to let me die. Alas, Flippanta, a very small matter wou'd save my life.

FLIPPANTA: Then y'are dead—for we women never grant any thing to a man who will be satisfied with a little.

MONEY-TRAP: Dear Flippanta, that was only my modesty; but since you'll have it out——I am a very dragon: And so your lady'll find——if ever she thinks fit to be——Now I hope you'll stand my friend.

FLIPPANTA: Well, sir, as far as my credit goes, it shall be employ'd in your service.

MONEY-TRAP: My best Flippanta—tell her—I'm all hers—tell her—my body's hers—tell her—my soul's hers—and tell her—my estate's hers. Lard have mercy upon me, how I'm in love!

FLIPPANTA: Poor man! what a sweat he's in! But hark—I hear my master; for heaven's sake compose your self a little, you are in such a fit, o' my conscience he'll smell you out.

MONEY-TRAP: Ah dear, I'm in such an emotion, I dare not be seen; put me in this closet for a moment.

FLIPPANTA: Closet, man! it's too little, your love wou'd stifle you. Go air your self in the garden a little, you have need on't, i'faith.

[She puts him out]

Flippanta sola.

A rare adventure, by my troth. This will be curious news to the wives. Fortune has now put their husbands into their hands, and I think they are too sharp to neglect its favours.

Enter Gripe.

GRIPE: O, here's the right-hand; the rest of the body can't be far off. Where's my wife, huswife?

FLIPPANTA: An admirable question!——Why, she's gone abroad, sir.

GRIPE: Abroad, abroad, abroad already? Why, she uses to be stewing in her bed three hours after this time, as late as 'tis: What makes her gadding so soon?

FLIPPANTA: Business, I suppose.

GRIPE: Business! she has a pretty head for business truly: O ho, let her change her way of living, or I'll make her change a light heart for a heavy one.

FLIPPANTA: And why would you have her change her way of living, sir? You see it agrees with her. She never look'd better in her life.

GRIPE: Don't tell me of her looks, I have done with her looks long since. But I'll make her change her life, or——

FLIPPANTA: Indeed, sir, you won't.

GRIPE: Why, what shall hinder me, insolence?

FLIPPANTA: That which hinders most husbands; contradiction.

GRIPE: Suppose I resolve I won't be contradicted?

FLIPPANTA: Suppose she resolves you shall?

GRIPE: A wife's resolution is not good by law.

FLIPPANTA: Nor a husband's by custom.

GRIPE: I tell thee I will not bear it.

FLIPPANTA: I tell you, sir, you will bear it.

GRIPE: Oons, I have borne it three years already.

FLIPPANTA: By that you see 'tis but giving your mind to it.

GRIPE: My mind to it! Death and the devil! My mind to it!

FLIPPANTA: Look ye, sir, you may swear and damn, and call the furies to assist you; but 'till you apply the remedy to the right place, you'll never cure the disease. You fancy you have got an extravagant wife, is't not so?

GRIPE: Pr'ythee change me that word fancy, and it is so.

FLIPPANTA: Why there's it. Men are strangely troubled with the vapours of late. You'll wonder now, if I tell you, you have the most reasonable wife in town: And that all the disorders you think you see in her, are only here, here, here, in your own head.   [Thumping his forehead]

GRIPE: She is then, in thy opinion, a reasonable woman?

FLIPPANTA: By my faith I think so.

GRIPE: I shall run mad——Name me an extravagance in the world she is not guilty of.

FLIPPANTA: Name me an extravagance in the world she is guilty of.

GRIPE: Come then: Does not she put the whole house in disorder?

FLIPPANTA: Not that I know of, for she never comes into it but to sleep.

GRIPE: 'Tis very well: Does she employ any one moment of her life in the government of her family?

FLIPPANTA: She is so submissive a wife, she leaves it entirely to you.

GRIPE: Admirable! Does not she spend more money in coach-hire, and chair-hire than would maintain six children?

FLIPPANTA: She's too nice of your credit to be seen daggling in the streets.

GRIPE: Good! Do I set eye on her sometimes in a week together?

FLIPPANTA: That, sir, is because you are never stirring at the same time; you keep odd hours; you are always going to bed when she's rising, and rising just when she's coming to bed.

GRIPE: Yes truly, night into day, and day into night, bawdy-house play, that's her trade; but these are trifles: Has she not lost her diamond necklace? Answer me to that, Trapes.

FLIPPANTA: Yes, and has sent as many tears after it, as if it had been her husband.

GRIPE: Ah!——the pox take her; but enough. 'Tis resolv'd, and I will put a stop to the course of her life, or I will put a stop to the course of her blood, and so she shall know, the first time I meet with her; [Aside] which tho' we are man and wife, and lie under one roof, 'tis very possible may not be this fortnight.   [Exit Gripe]

Flippanta sola.

Nay, thou hast a blessed time on't, that must be confessed. What a miserable devil is a husband!

Insupportable to himself, and a plague to every thing about them. Their wives do by them, as children do by dogs, teaze and provoke 'em, 'till they make them so curs'd, they snarl and bite at every thing that comes in their reach. This wretch here is grown perverse to that degree, he's for his wife's keeping home, and making hell of his house, so he may be the devil in it, to torment her. How niggardly soever he is, of all things he possesses, he is willing to purchase her misery, at the expence of his own peace. But he'd as good be still, for he'll miss of his aim. If I know her (which I think I do) she'll set his blood in such a ferment, it shall bubble out at every pore of him; whilst hers is so quiet in her veins, her pulse shall go like a pendulum. [Exit]

Act III

SCENE 1: *Mrs. Amlet's House*

Enter Dick.
Where's this old woman?——A hey. What the devil, no body at home? Ha! her strong box!—— And the key in't! 'tis so. Now fortune be my friend. What the duce——Not a penny of money in cash!—Nor a chequer note!—Nor a Bank bill —[*Searches the strong box*]—Nor a crooked stick![1] Nor a—Mum—here's something—A diamond necklace, by all the Gods! Oons the old woman ——Zest.   [*Claps the necklace in his pocket, then runs and asks her blessing*]

Enter Mrs. Amlet.
——Pray mother, pray to, &c.
AMLET: Is it possible!—Dick upon his humble knee! Ah my dear child!—May heaven be good unto thee.
DICK: I'm come, my dear mother, to pay my duty to you, and to ask your consent to——
AMLET: What a shape is there!
DICK: To ask your consent, I say, to marry a great fortune; for what is riches in this world without a blessing? And how can there be a blessing without respect and duty to parents?
AMLET: What a nose he has!
DICK: And therefore it being the duty of every good child not to dispose of himself in marriage, without the——
AMLET: Now the Lord love thee [*Kissing him*]—— for thou art a goodly young man: Well, Dick,—— And how goes it with the lady? Are her eyes open to thy charms? Does she see what's for her own good? Is she sensible of the blessings thou hast in store for her? Ha! is all sure? Hast thou broke a piece of money with her? Speak, bird, do: Don't

[1]i.e., an *Exchequer tally.*

be modest and hide thy love from thy mother, for I'm an indulgent parent.
DICK: Nothing under heaven can prevent my good fortune, but its being discover'd I am your son——
AMLET: Then thou art still asham'd of thy natural mother—Graceless! Why, I'm no whore, sirrah.
DICK: I know you are not—A whore! Bless us all——
AMLET: No; my reputation's as good as the best of 'em; and tho' I'm old, I'm chaste, you rascal you.
DICK: Lord, that is not the thing we talk of, mother; but——
AMLET: I think, as the world goes, they may be proud of marrying their daughter into a vartuous family.
DICK: Oons, vartue is not the case——
AMLET: Where she may have a good example before her eyes.
DICK: O Lord! O Lord! O Lord!
AMLET: I'm a woman that don't so much as encourage an incontinent look towards me.
DICK: I tell you, 'sdeath, I tell you——
AMLET: If a man shou'd make an uncivil motion to me, I'd spit in his lascivious face: And all this you may tell them, sirrah.
DICK: Death and furies! the woman's out of her——
AMLET: Don't you swear, you rascal you, don't you swear; we shall have thee damn'd at last, and then I shall be disgrac'd.
DICK: Why then in cold blood hear me speak to you: I tell you it's a City-fortune I'm about, she cares not a fig for your virtue; she'll hear of nothing but quality: She has quarrell'd with one of her friends for having a better complexion, and is resolv'd she'll marry, to take place of her.
AMLET: What a cherry lip is there!
DICK: Therefore, good dear mother, now have a care and don't discover me; for if you do, all's lost.
AMLET: Dear, dear, how thy fair bride will be delighted: Go, get thee gone, go: Go fetch her home, go fetch her home; I'll give her a sack-posset, and a pillow of down she shall lay her head upon. Go, fetch her home, I say.
DICK: Take care then of the main chance, my dear mother; remember, if you discover me——
AMLET: Go, fetch her home, I say.
DICK: You promise me then——
AMLET: March.
DICK: But swear to me——
AMLET: Be gone, sirrah.
DICK: Well, I'll rely upon you—But one kiss before I go.   [*Kisses her heartily, and runs off*]
AMLET: Now the Lord love thee! for thou art a comfortable young man.   [*Exit* Mrs. Amlet]

SCENE 2: *Gripe's House*

Enter Corinna *and* Flippanta.
CORINNA: But hark you, Flippanta, if you don't think

he loves me dearly, don't give him my letter, after all.

FLIPPANTA: Let me alone.

CORINNA: When he has read it, let him give it you again.

FLIPPANTA: Don't trouble your self.

CORINNA: And not a word of the pudding to my mother-in-law.

FLIPPANTA: Enough.

CORINNA: When we come to love one another to the purpose, she shall know all.

FLIPPANTA: Ay, then 'twill be time.

CORINNA: But remember 'tis you make me do all this now, so if any mischief comes on't, 'tis you must answer for't.

FLIPPANTA: I'll be your security.

CORINNA: I'm young, and know nothing of the matter; but you have experience, so it's your business to conduct me safe.

FLIPPANTA: Poor innocence!

CORINNA: But tell me in serious sadness, Flippanta, does he love me with the very soul of him?

FLIPPANTA: I have told you so an hundred times, and yet you are not satisfied.

CORINNA: But, methinks, I'd fain have him tell me so himself.

FLIPPANTA: Have patience, and it shall be done.

CORINNA: Why, patience is a virtue; that we must all confess——But I fancy, the sooner it's done the better, Flippanta.

Enter Jessamin.

JESSAMIN: Madam, yonder's your geography-master waiting for you.   [*Exit*]

CORINNA: Ah! how I am tir'd with these old fumbling fellows, Flippanta.

FLIPPANTA: Well, don't let them break your heart, you shall be rid of them all ere long.

CORINNA: Nay, 'tis not the study I'm so weary of, Flippanta, 'tis the odious thing that teaches me. Were the Colonel my master, I fancy I could take pleasure in learning every thing he could shew me.

FLIPPANTA: And he can shew you a great deal, I can tell you that. But get you gone in, here's somebody coming, we must not be seen together.

CORINNA: I will, I will, I will——O the dear Colonel.
                                                [*Running off*]

Enter Mrs. Amlet.

FLIPPANTA: O ho, it's Mrs. Amlet——What brings you so soon to us again, Mrs. Amlet?

AMLET: Ah! my dear Mrs. Flippanta, I'm in a furious fright.

FLIPPANTA: Why, what's come to you?

AMLET: Ah! Mercy on us all——Madam's diamond necklace——

FLIPPANTA: What of that?

AMLET: Are you sure you left it at my house?

FLIPPANTA: Sure I left it! a very pretty question truly!

AMLET: Nay, don't be angry; say nothing to madam

of it, I beseech you: It will be found again, if it be heav'n's good will. At least 'tis I must bear the loss on't. 'Tis my rogue of a son has laid his birdlime fingers on't.

FLIPPANTA: Your son, Mrs. Amlet! Do you breed your children up to such tricks as these then?

AMLET: What shall I say to you, Mrs. Flippanta? Can I help it? He has been a rogue from his cradle, Dick has. But he has his deserts too. And now it comes in my head, mayhap he may have no ill design in this neither.

FLIPPANTA: No ill design, woman! He's a pretty fellow if he can steal a diamond necklace with a good one.

AMLET: You don't know him, Mrs. Flippanta, so well as I that bore him. Dick's a rogue, 'tis true, but ——Mum——

FLIPPANTA: What does the woman mean?

AMLET: Hark you, Mrs. Flippanta, is not here a young gentlewoman in your house that wants a husband?

FLIPPANTA: Why do you ask?

AMLET: By way of conversation only, it does not concern me; but when she marries, I may chance to dance at the wedding. Remember I tell you so; I who am but Mrs. Amlet.

FLIPPANTA: You dance at her wedding! you!

AMLET: Yes, I, I; but don't trouble madam about her necklace, perhaps it mayn't go out of the family. Adieu, Mrs. Flippanta.   [*Exit* Mrs. Amlet]

FLIPPANTA: What—what—what does the woman mean? Mad! What a capilotade[1] of a story's here! The necklace lost; and her son Dick; and a fortune to marry; and she shall dance at the wedding; and ——She does not intend, I hope, to propose a match between her son Dick and Corinna? By my conscience I believe she does. An old beldam!

Enter Brass.

BRASS: Well, hussy, how stand our affairs? Has miss writ us an answer yet? My master's very impatient yonder.

FLIPPANTA: And why the duce does not he come himself? What does he send such idle fellows as thee of his errands? Here I had her alone just now: He won't have such an opportunity again this month, I can tell him that.

BRASS: So much the worse for him; 'tis his business ——But now, my dear, let thee and I talk a little of our own: I grow most damnably in love with thee; dost hear that?

FLIPPANTA: Phu! thou art always timing things wrong; my head is full, at present, of more important things than love.

BRASS: Then it's full of important things indeed: Dost want a privy-counsellor?

FLIPPANTA: I want an assistant.

BRASS: To do what?

[1] *A cooked-up story, hash, medley.*

FLIPPANTA: Mischief.

BRASS: I'm thy man——touch.

FLIPPANTA: But before I venture to let thee into my project, pr'ythee tell me, whether thou find'st a natural disposition to ruin a husband to oblige his wife?

BRASS: Is she handsome?

FLIPPANTA: Yes.

BRASS: Why then my disposition's at her service.

FLIPPANTA: She's beholden to thee.

BRASS: Not she alone neither, therefore don't let her grow vain upon't; for I have three or four affairs of that kind going at this time.

FLIPPANTA: Well, go carry this epistle from miss to thy master; and when thou com'st back, I'll tell thee thy business.

BRASS: I'll know it before I go, if you please.

FLIPPANTA: Thy master waits for an answer.

BRASS: I'd rather he shou'd wait than I.

FLIPPANTA: Why then, in short, Araminta's husband is in love with my lady.

BRASS: Very well, child, we have a Rowland for her Oliver: Thy lady's husband is in love with Araminta.

FLIPPANTA: Who told you that, sirrah?

BRASS: 'Tis a negotiation I am charged with, Pert. Did not I tell thee I did business for half the town? I have manag'd Master Gripe's little affairs for him these ten years, you slut you.

FLIPPANTA: Hark thee, Brass, the game's in our hands, if we can but play the cards.

BRASS: Pique and repique, you jade you, if the wives will fall into a good intelligence.

FLIPPANTA: Let them alone; I'll answer for them they don't slip the occasion.——See here they come. They little think what a piece of good news we have for 'em.

Enter Clarissa *and* Araminta.

CLARISSA: Jessamin! here, boy, carry up these things into my dressing-room, and break as many of them by the way as you can, be sure.——O! art thou there, Brass! What news?

BRASS: Madam, I only call'd in as I was going by ——But some little propositions Mrs. Flippanta has been starting, have kept me here to offer your ladyship my humble service.

CLARISSA: What propositions?

BRASS: She'll acquaint you, madam.

ARAMINTA: Is there any thing new, Flippanta?

FLIPPANTA: Yes, and pretty too.

CLARISSA: That follows of course, but let's have it quick.

FLIPPANTA: Why, Madam, you have made a conquest.

CLARISSA: Hussy——But of who? quick.

FLIPPANTA: Of Mr. Money-trap, that's all.

ARAMINTA: My husband?

FLIPPANTA: Yes, your husband, Madam: You thought fit to corrupt ours, so now we are even with you.

ARAMINTA: Sure thou art in jest, Flippanta.

FLIPPANTA: Serious as my devotions.

BRASS: And the cross intrigue, ladies, is what our brains have been at work about.

ARAMINTA: My dear!   [*To Clarissa*]

CLARISSA: My life!

ARAMINTA: My angel!

CLARISSA: My soul!   [*Hugging one another*]

ARAMINTA: The stars have done this.

CLARISSA: The pretty little twinklers.

FLIPPANTA: And what will you do for them now?

CLARISSA: What grateful creatures ought; shew 'em we don't despise their favours.

ARAMINTA: But is not this a wager between these two blockheads?

CLARISSA: I would not give a shilling to go the winner's halves.

ARAMINTA: Then 'tis the most fortunate thing that ever cou'd have happen'd.

CLARISSA: All your last night's ideas, Araminta, were trifles to it.

ARAMINTA: Brass (my dear) will be useful to us.

BRASS: At your service, Madam.

CLARISSA: Flippanta will be necessary, my life!

FLIPPANTA: She waits your commands, Madam.

ARAMINTA: For my part then, I recommend my husband to thee, Flippanta, and make it my earnest request thou won't leave him one half-crown.

FLIPPANTA: I'll do all I can to obey you, Madam.

BRASS: [*To Clarissa*] If your ladyship wou'd give me the same kind orders for yours.

CLARISSA: O——if thou spar'st him, Brass, I'm thy enemy till I die.

BRASS: 'Tis enough, Madam, I'll be sure to give you a reasonable account of him. But how do you intend we shall proceed, ladies? Must we storm the purse at once, or break ground in form, and carry it by little and little?

CLARISSA: Storm, dear Brass, storm: ever whilst you live, storm.

ARAMINTA: O by all means; must it not be so, Flippanta?

FLIPPANTA: In four and twenty hours, two hundred pounds a-piece, that's my sentence.

BRASS: Very well. But, ladies, you'll give me leave to put you in mind of some little expence in favours, 'twill be necessary you are at, to these honest gentlemen.

ARAMINTA: Favours, Brass!

BRASS: Um——a——some small matters, Madam, I doubt must be.

CLARISSA: Now that's a vile article, Araminta; for that thing your husband is so like mine——

FLIPPANTA: Phu, there's a scruple indeed. Pray, Madam, don't be so squeamish; tho' the meat be a little flat, we'll find you savoury sauce to it.

CLARISSA: This wench is so mad.

FLIPPANTA: Why, what in the name of Lucifer, is it you have to do, that's so terrible?

BRASS: A civil look only.

ARAMINTA: There's no great harm in that.

FLIPPANTA: An obliging word.

CLARISSA: That one may afford 'em.

BRASS: A little smile, à propos.

ARAMINTA: That's but giving one's self an air.

FLIPPANTA: Receive a little letter, perhaps.

CLARISSA: Women of quality do that from fifty odious fellows.

BRASS: Suffer (may be) a squeeze by the hand.

ARAMINTA: One's so us'd to that, one does not feel it.

FLIPPANTA: Or if a kiss wou'd do't?

CLARISSA: I'd die first.

BRASS: Indeed, ladies, I doubt 'twill be necessary to——

CLARISSA: Get their wretched money without paying so dear for it.

FLIPPANTA: Well, just as you please for that, my ladies: But I suppose you'll play upon the square with your favours, and not pique your selves upon being one more grateful than another.

BRASS: And state a fair account of receipts and disbursements.

ARAMINTA: That I think shou'd be, indeed.

CLARISSA: With all my heart, and Brass shall be our book-keeper. So get thee to work, man, as fast as thou canst; but not a word of all this to thy master.

BRASS: I'll observe my order, Madam.   [Exit Brass]

CLARISSA: I'll have the pleasure of telling him my self; he'll be violently delighted with it: 'Tis the best man in the world, Araminta; he'll bring us rare company to-morrow, all sorts of gamesters; and thou shalt see my husband will be such a beast to be out of humour at it.

ARAMINTA: The monster——But hush, here's my dear approaching; pr'ythee let's leave him to Flippanta.

FLIPPANTA: Ah, pray do, I'll bring you a good account of him, I'll warrant you.

CLARISSA: Dispatch then, for the basset-table's in haste.   [Exit Clarissa and Araminta]

Flippanta sola.

So, now have at him; here he comes: We'll try if we can pillage the usurer, as he does other folks.

Enter Money-trap.

MONEY-TRAP: Well, my pretty Flippanta, is thy mistress come home?

FLIPPANTA: Yes, Sir.

MONEY-TRAP: And where is she, pr'ythee?

FLIPPANTA: Gone abroad, Sir.

MONEY-TRAP: How dost mean?

FLIPPANTA: I mean right, Sir; my lady'll come home and go abroad ten times in an hour, when she's either in very good humour, or very bad.

MONEY-TRAP: Good-lack! But I'll warrant, in general,

'tis her naughty husband that makes her house uneasy to her. But hast thou said a little something to her, chicken, for an expiring lover? ha!

FLIPPANTA: Said——yes, I have said, much good may it do me.

MONEY-TRAP: Well! and how?

FLIPPANTA: And how!——And how do you think you wou'd have me do't? And you have such a way with you, one can refuse you nothing. But I have brought my self into a fine business by it.

MONEY-TRAP: Good lack:——But, I hope, Flippanta——

FLIPPANTA: Yes your hopes will do much, when I am turn'd out of doors.

MONEY-TRAP: Was she then terrible angry?

FLIPPANTA: Oh! had you seen how she flew, when she saw where I was pointing; for you must know I went round the bush, and round the bush, before I came to the matter.

MONEY-TRAP: Nay, 'tis a ticklish point, that must be own'd.

FLIPPANTA: On my word is it——I mean where a lady's truly virtuous; for that's our case, you must know.

MONEY-TRAP: A very dangerous case indeed.

FLIPPANTA: But I can tell you one thing——she has an inclination to you.

MONEY-TRAP: Is it possible?

FLIPPANTA: Yes, and I told her so at last.

MONEY-TRAP: Well, and what did she answer thee?

FLIPPANTA: Slap——and bid me bring it you for a token.   [Giving him a slap on the face]

MONEY-TRAP: And you have lost none on't by the way, with a pox t'ye.   [Aside]

FLIPPANTA: Now this, I think, looks the best in the world.

MONEY-TRAP: Yea, but really it feels a little oddly.

FLIPPANTA: Why, you must know, ladies have different ways of expressing their kindness, according to the humour they are in: If she had been in a good one, it had been a kiss; but as long as she sent you something, your affairs go well.

MONEY-TRAP: Why, truly, I am a little ignorant in the mysterious paths of love, so I must be guided by thee. But, pr'ythee, take her in a good humour next token she sends me.

FLIPPANTA: Ah——good humour?

MONEY-TRAP: What's the matter?

FLIPPANTA: Poor lady!

MONEY-TRAP: Ha!

FLIPPANTA: If I durst tell you all——

MONEY-TRAP: What then?

FLIPPANTA: You wou'd not expect to see her in one a good while.

MONEY-TRAP: Why, I pray?

FLIPPANTA: I must own I did take an unseasonable time to talk of love-matters to her.

MONEY-TRAP: Why, what's the matter?

FLIPPANTA: Nothing.

MONEY-TRAP: Nay, pr'ythee tell me.

FLIPPANTA: I dare not.

MONEY-TRAP: You must indeed.

FLIPPANTA: Why, when women are in difficulties, how can they think of pleasure?

MONEY-TRAP: Why, what difficulties can she be in?

FLIPPANTA: Nay, I do but guess after all: for she has that grandeur of soul, she'd die before she'd tell.

MONEY-TRAP: But what dost thou suspect?

FLIPPANTA: Why, what should one suspect, where a husband loves nothing but getting of money, and a wife nothing but spending on't?

MONEY-TRAP: So she wants that same then?

FLIPPANTA: I say no such thing, I know nothing of the matter; pray make no wrong interpretation of what I say, my lady wants nothing that I know of. 'Tis true——she has had ill luck at cards of late, I believe she has not won once this month: But what of that?

MONEY-TRAP: Ha!

FLIPPANTA: 'Tis true, I know her spirit's that, she'd see her husband hang'd, before she'd ask him for a farthing.

MONEY-TRAP: Ha!

FLIPPANTA: And then I know him again, he'd see her drown'd before he'd give her a farthing; but that's a help to your affair, you know.

MONEY-TRAP: 'Tis so indeed.

FLIPPANTA: Ah——well, I'll say nothing; but if she had none of these things to fret her——

MONEY-TRAP: Why really, Flippanta——

FLIPPANTA: I know what you are going to say now; you are going to offer your service, but 'twon't do; you have a mind to play the gallant now, but it must not be; you want to be shewing your liberality, but 'twon't be allow'd; you'll be pressing me to offer it, and she'll be in a rage. We shall have the Devil to do.

MONEY-TRAP: You mistake me, Flippanta; I was only going to say——

FLIPPANTA: Ay, I know what you were going to say well enough; but I tell you it will never do so. If one cou'd find out some way now——ay——let me see——

MONEY-TRAP: Indeed I hope——

FLIPPANTA: Pray be quiet——no——but I'm thinking——hum——she'll smoke that tho'——let us consider——If one cou'd find a way to——'Tis the nicest point in the world to bring about, she'll never touch it, if she knows from whence it comes.

MONEY-TRAP: Shall I try if I can reason her husband out of twenty pounds, to make her easy the rest of her life?

FLIPPANTA: Twenty pounds, man?——why you shall see her set that upon a card. O——she has a great soul.——Besides, if her husband should oblige her, it might, in time, take off her aversion to him, and by consequence, her inclination to you. No, no, it must never come that way.

MONEY-TRAP: What shall we do then?

FLIPPANTA: Hold still——I have it. I'll tell you what you shall do.

MONEY-TRAP: Ay.

FLIPPANTA: You shall make her—a restitution—of two hundred pounds.

MONEY-TRAP: Ha!—Restitution!

FLIPPANTA: Yes, yes, 'tis the luckiest thought in the world; madam often plays, you know, and folks who do so, meet now and then with sharpers. Now you shall be a sharper.

MONEY-TRAP: A sharper!

FLIPPANTA: Ay, ay, a sharper; and having cheated her of two hundred pounds, shall be troubled in mind, and send it her back again. You comprehend me?

MONEY-TRAP: Yes, I, I comprehend, but a——won't she suspect if it be so much?

FLIPPANTA: No, no, the more the better.

MONEY-TRAP: Two hundred pound!

FLIPPANTA: Yes, two hundred pound——Or let me see——so even a sum may look a little suspicious, ——ay——let it be two hundred and thirty; that odd thirty will make it look so natural, the devil won't find it out.

MONEY-TRAP: Ha!

FLIPPANTA: Pounds, too, look I don't know how; guineas I fancy were better——ay, guineas, it shall be guineas. You are of that mind, are you not?

MONEY-TRAP: Um—a guinea you know, Flippanta, is——

FLIPPANTA: A thousand times genteeler, you are certainly in the right on't; it shall be as you say, two hundred and thirty guineas.

MONEY-TRAP: Ho——well, if it must be guineas, let's see, two hundred guineas.

FLIPPANTA: And thirty; two hundred and thirty: If you mistake the sum, you spoil all. So go put them in a purse, while it's fresh in your head, and send 'em to me with a penitential letter, desiring I'll do you the favour to restore them to her.

MONEY-TRAP: Two hundred and thirty pounds in a bag!

FLIPPANTA: Guineas, I say, guineas.

MONEY-TRAP: Ay, guineas, that's true. But, Flippanta, if she don't know they come from me, then I give my money for nothing, you know.

FLIPPANTA: Phu, leave that to me, I'll manage the stock for you; I'll make it produce something, I'll warrant you.

MONEY-TRAP: Well, Flippanta, 'tis a great sum indeed; but I'll go try what I can do for her. You say, two hundred guineas in a purse?

FLIPPANTA: And thirty; if the man's in his senses.

MONEY-TRAP: And thirty, 'tis true, I always forget that thirty.   [Exit Money-trap]

FLIPPANTA: So, get thee gone, thou art a rare fellow, i'faith. Brass!——it's thee, is't not?

Enter Brass.

BRASS: It is, huswife. How go matters? I staid till thy gentleman was gone. Hast done any thing towards our common purse?

FLIPPANTA: I think I have; he's going to make us a restitution of two or three hundred pounds.

BRASS: A restitution!——good.

FLIPPANTA: A new way, sirrah, to make a lady take a present without putting her to the blush.

BRASS: 'Tis very well, mighty well indeed. Pr'ythee where's thy master? let me try if I can persuade him to be troubled in mind too.

FLIPPANTA: Not so hasty; he's gone into his closet to prepare himself for a quarrel, I have advis'd him to——with his wife.

BRASS: What to do?

FLIPPANTA: Why, to make her stay at home, now she has resolv'd to do it beforehand. You must know, sirrah, we intend to make a merit of our basset-table, and get a good pretence for the merry companions we intend to fill his house with.

BRASS: Very nicely spun, truly, thy husband will be a happy man.

FLIPPANTA: Hold your tongue, you fool you. See here comes your master.

BRASS: He's welcome.

Enter Dick.

DICK: My dear Flippanta! how many thanks have I to pay thee?

FLIPPANTA: Do you like her style?

DICK: The kindest little rogue! there's nothing but she gives me leave to hope. I am the happiest man the world has in its care.

FLIPPANTA: Not so happy as you think for neither, perhaps; you have a rival, Sir, I can tell you that.

DICK: A rival!

FLIPPANTA: Yes, and a dangerous one too.

DICK: Who, in the name of terror?

FLIPPANTA: A devilish fellow, one Mr. Amlet.

DICK: Amlet! I know no such man.

FLIPPANTA: You know the man's mother tho'; you met her here, and are in her favour, I can tell you. If he worst you in your mistress, you shall e'en marry her, and disinherit him.

DICK: If I have no other rival but Mr. Amlet, I believe I shan't be much disturb'd in my amour. But can't I see Corinna?

FLIPPANTA: I don't know, she has always some of her masters with her: But I'll go see if she can spare you a moment, and bring you word.

[*Exit* Flippanta]

DICK: I wish my old hobbling mother han't been blabbing something here she should not do.

BRASS: Fear nothing, all's safe on that side yet. But, how speaks young mistress's epistle? soft and tender?

DICK: As pen can write.

BRASS: So you think all goes well there?

DICK: As my heart can wish.

BRASS: You are sure on't?

DICK: Sure on't!

BRASS: Why then ceremony aside. [*Putting on his hat*] You and I must have a little talk, Mr. Amlet.

DICK: Ah, Brass, what art thou going to do? Wou't ruin me?

BRASS: Look you, Dick, few words; you are in a smooth way of making your fortune. I hope all will roll on. But how do you intend matters shall pass 'twixt you and me in this business?

DICK: Death and Furies! What a time dost take to talk on't?

BRASS: Good words, or I betray you; they have already heard of one Mr. Amlet in the house.

DICK: Here's a son of a whore!   [*Aside*]

BRASS: In short, look smooth, and be a good prince: I am your valet, 'tis true; your footman sometimes, which I'm enrag'd at; but you have always had the ascendant, I confess: when we were school-fellows, you made me carry your books, make your exercise, own your rogueries, and sometimes take a whipping for you. When we were fellow-prentices, tho' I was your senior, you made me open the shop, clean my master's shoes, cut last at dinner, and eat all the crust. In our sins too, I must own you still kept me under; you soar'd up to adultery with our mistress, while I was at humble fornication with the maid. Nay, in our punishments you still made good your post; for when once upon a time I was sentenc'd but to be whipp'd, I cannot deny but you were condemn'd to be hang'd. So that in all times, I must confess, your inclinations have been greater and nobler than mine; however, I cannot consent that you shou'd at once fix fortune for life, and I dwell in my humilities for the rest of my days.

DICK: Hark thee, Brass, if I do not most nobly by thee, I'm a dog.

BRASS: And when?

DICK: As soon as ever I am married.

BRASS: Ah, the pox take thee.

DICK: Then you mistrust me?

BRASS: I do, by my faith. Look you, Sir, some folks we mistrust, because we don't know them; others we mistrust, because we do know them: And for one of these reasons I desire there may be a bargain beforehand: If not [*Raising his voice*] look ye, Dick Amlet——

DICK: Soft, my dear friend and companion. The dog will ruin me. [*Aside*] Say, what is't will content thee?

BRASS: O ho!

DICK: But how canst thou be such a barbarian?

BRASS: I learnt it at Algiers.

DICK: Come, make thy Turkish demand then.

BRASS: You know you gave me a bank-bill this morning to receive for you.

DICK: I did so, of fifty pounds, 'tis thine. So, now thou art satisfy'd, all's fix'd.

BRASS: It is not indeed. There's a diamond necklace you robb'd your mother of ev'n now.

DICK: Ah, you Jew.

BRASS: No words.

DICK: My dear Brass!

BRASS: I insist.

DICK: My old friend.

BRASS: Dick Amlet [*Raising his voice*] I insist.

DICK: Ah the cormorant——Well, 'tis thine: But thou'lt never thrive with it.

BRASS: When I find it begins to do me mischief, I'll give it you again. But I must have a wedding-suit.

DICK: Well.

BRASS: Some good lace

DICK: Thou sha't.

BRASS: A stock of linen

DICK: Enough.

BRASS: Not yet——a silver sword.

DICK: Well, thou sha't have that too. Now thou hast every thing.

BRASS: Gad forgive me, I forgot a ring of remembrance; I wou'd not forget all these favours for the world: A sparkling diamond will be always playing in my eye, and put me in mind of them.

DICK: This unconscionable rogue! [*Aside*] Well I'll bespeak one for thee.

BRASS: Brilliant.

DICK: It shall. But if the thing don't succeed after all?——

BRASS: I'm a man of honour, and restore: And so the treaty being finish'd, I strike my flag of defiance, and fall into my respects again. [*Taking off his hat*]

Enter Flippanta.

FLIPPANTA: I have made you wait a little, but I cou'd not help it, her master is but just gone. He has been shewing her Prince Eugene's march into Italy.

DICK: Pr'ythee let me come to her, I'll shew her a part of the world he has never shewn her yet.

FLIPPANTA: So I told her, you must know; and she said, she cou'd like to travel in good company: so if you'll slip up those back-stairs, you shall try if you can agree upon the journey.

DICK: My dear Flippanta!

FLIPPANTA: None of your dear acknowledgments, I beseech you, but up stairs as hard as you can drive.

DICK: I'm gone.   [*Exit Dick*]

FLIPPANTA: And do you follow him, Jack-a-dandy, and see he is not surpriz'd.

BRASS: I thought that was your post, Mrs. Useful: But if you'll come and keep me in humour, I don't care if I share the duty with you.

FLIPPANTA: No words, sirrah, but follow him, I have somewhat else to do.

BRASS: The jade's so absolute there's no contesting with her. One kiss tho', to keep the centinel warm. [*Gives her a long kiss*]——So.   [*Exit Brass*]

Flippanta *sola*.

——A nasty rogue [*Wiping her mouth*]. But, let me see what have I to do now? This *restitution* will be here quickly, I suppose; in the mean time I'll go know if my lady's ready for the quarrel yet. Master, yonder, is so full on't, he's ready to burst; but we'll give him vent by and by with a witness.

[*Exit Flippanta*]

Act IV

SCENE 1: *Gripe's House*

Enter Corinna, Dick, *and* Brass.

BRASS: Don't fear, I'll give you timely notice.

[*Goes to the door*]

DICK: Come, you must consent, you shall consent. How can you leave me thus upon the rack? A man who loves you to that excess that I do.

CORINNA: Nay, that you love me, Sir, that I'm satisfy'd in, for you have sworn you do: And I'm so pleas'd with it, I'd fain have you do so as long as you live, so we must never marry.

DICK: Not marry, my dear! why, what's our love good for if we don't marry?

CORINNA: Ah——I'm afraid 'twill be good for little if we do.

DICK: Why do you think so?

CORINNA: Because I hear my father and mother, and my uncle and aunt, and Araminta and her husband, and twenty other marry'd folks, say so from morning to night.

DICK: Oh, that's because they are bad husbands and bad wives; but in our case there will be a good husband and a good wife, and so we shall love for ever.

CORINNA: Why there may be something in that truly; and I'm always willing to hear reason, as a reasonable young woman ought to do. But are you sure, Sir, tho' we are very good now, we shall be so when we come to be better acquainted?

DICK: I can answer for my self, at least.

CORINNA: I wish you cou'd answer for me too. You see I am a plain-dealer, Sir, I hope you don't like me the worse for it.

DICK: O, by no means, 'tis a sign of admirable morals; and I hope, since you practise it your self, you'll approve of it in your lover. In one word, therefore (for 'tis in vain to mince the matter), my resolution's fix'd, and the world can't stagger me, I marry ——or I die.

CORINNA: Indeed, Sir, I have much ado to believe you; the disease of love is seldom so violent.

DICK: Madam, I have two diseases to end my miseries; if the first don't do't, the latter shall; [*Drawing his sword*] one's in my heart, t'other's in my scabbard.

CORINNA: Not for a diadem. [*Catching hold of him.*] Ah, put it up, put it up.

DICK: How absolute is your command! [*Dropping his sword*] A word, you see, disarms me.

CORINNA: What a power I have over him! [*Aside*] The wondrous deeds of love!——Pray, Sir, let me have no more of these rash doings tho'; perhaps I mayn't be always in the saving humour——I'm sure if I had let him stick himself, I shou'd have been envy'd by all the great ladies in the town.
[*Aside*]

DICK: Well, madam, have I then your promise? You'll make me the happiest of mankind.

CORINNA: I don't know what to say to you; but I believe I had as good promise, for I find I shall certainly do't.

DICK: Then let us seal the contract thus. [*Kisses her*]

CORINNA: Um——he has almost taken away my breath: He kisses purely. [*Aside*]

DICK: Hark——some body comes. [Brass *peeping in*]

BRASS: Gar there, the enemy——no, hold y'are safe, 'tis Flippanta.

Enter Flippanta.

FLIPPANTA: Come, have you agreed the matter? If not, you must end it another time, for your father's in motion, so pray kiss and part.

CORINNA: That's sweet and sour. [*They kiss*] Adieu t'ye, Sir. [*Exit* Dick *and* Corinna]

Enter Clarissa.

CLARISSA: Have you told him I'm at home, Flippanta?

FLIPPANTA: Yes, madam.

CLARISSA: And that I'll see him?

FLIPPANTA: Yes, that too: But here's news for you; I have just now receiv'd the restitution.

CLARISSA: That's killing pleasure; and how much has he restor'd me?

FLIPPANTA: Two hundred and thirty.

CLARISSA: Wretched rogue! but retreat, your master's coming to quarrel.

FLIPPANTA: I'll be within call, if things run high.
[*Exit Flippanta*]

Enter Gripe.

GRIPE: O ho!——are you there, i'faith? Madam, your humble servant, I'm very glad to see you at home. I thought I shou'd never have had that honour again.

CLARISSA: Good-morrow, my dear, how d'ye do? Flippanta says you are out of humour, and that you have a mind to quarrel with me: Is it true? ha!—— I have a terrible pain in my head, I give you notice on't beforehand.

GRIPE: And how the pox shou'd it be otherwise? It's a wonder you are not dead [as a'wou'd you were, *aside*] with the life you lead. Are you not asham'd? and do you not blush to——

CLARISSA: My dear child, you crack my brain; soften the harshness of your voice: Say what thou wou't, but let it be in an agreeable tone——

GRIPE: Tone, Madam, don't tell me of a tone——

CLARISSA: O——if you will quarrel, do it with temperance; let it be all in cool blood, even and smooth, as if you were not mov'd with what you said; and then I'll hear you, as if I were not mov'd with it neither.

GRIPE: Had ever man such need of patience? Madam, Madam, I must tell you, Madam——

CLARISSA: Another key, or I'll walk off.

GRIPE: Don't provoke me.

CLARISSA: Shall you be long, my dear, in your remonstrances?

GRIPE: Yes, madam, and very long.

CLARISSA: If you wou'd quarrel *en abrégé*, I shou'd have a world of obligation to you.

GRIPE: What I have to say, forsooth, is not to be express'd *en abrégé*, my complaints are too numerous.

CLARISSA: Complaints! of what, my dear? Have I ever given you subject of complaint, my life?

GRIPE: O pox! my dear and my life! I desire none of your *tendres*.

CLARISSA: How! find fault with my kindness, and my expressions of affection and respect? the world will guess by this what the rest of your complaints may be. I must tell you, I am scandaliz'd at your procedure.

GRIPE: I must tell you, I am running mad with yours.

CLARISSA: Ah! how insupportable are the humours of some husbands, so full of fancies, and so ungovernable: What have you in the world to disturb you?

GRIPE: What have I to disturb me! I have you, Death and the Devil!

CLARISSA: Ay, merciful heaven! how he swears! You should never accustom your self to such words as these; indeed, my dear, you shou'd not; your mouth's always full of them.

GRIPE: Blood and thunder! Madam——

CLARISSA: Ah, he'll fetch the house down: Do you know you make me tremble for you? Flippanta! who's there? Flippanta!

GRIPE: Here's a provoking devil for you!

Enter Flippanta.

FLIPPANTA: What, in the name of Jove's the matter? you raise the neighbourhood.

CLARISSA: Why here's your master in a most violent fuss, and no mortal soul can tell for what.

GRIPE: Not tell for what!

CLARISSA: No, my life. I have begg'd him to tell me his griefs, Flippanta; and then he swears, good Lord! how he does swear.

GRIPE: Ah you wicked jade! Ah you wicked jade!

CLARISSA: Do you hear him, Flippanta! do you hear him!

FLIPPANTA: Pray, Sir, let's know a little what puts you in all this fury?

CLARISSA: Pr'ythee stand near me, Flippanta, there's an odd froth about his mouth, looks as if his poor head were going wrong, I'm afraid he'll bite.

GRIPE: The wicked woman, Flippanta, the wicked woman.

CLARISSA: Can any body wonder I shun my own house, when he treats me at this rate in it?

GRIPE: At this rate! why in the devil's name——

CLARISSA: Do you hear him again?

FLIPPANTA: Come, a little moderation, Sir, and try what that will produce.

GRIPE: Hang her, 'tis all a pretence to justify her going abroad.

CLARISSA: A pretence! a pretence! Do you hear how black a charge he loads me with? Charges me with a pretence? Is this the return for all my down-right open actions? You know, my dear, I scorn pretences: Whene'er I go abroad, it is without pretence.

GRIPE: Give me patience.

FLIPPANTA: You have a great deal, Sir.

CLARISSA: And yet he's never content, Flippanta.

GRIPE: What shall I do?

CLARISSA: What a reasonable man wou'd do; own your self in the wrong, and be quiet. Here's Flippanta has understanding, and I have moderation; I'm willing to make her judge of our differences.

FLIPPANTA: You do me a great deal of honour, Madam: But I tell you beforehand, I shall be a little on Master's side.

GRIPE: Right, Flippanta has sense. Come let her decide. Have I not reason to be in a passion? tell me that.

CLARISSA: You must tell her for what, my life.

GRIPE: Why, for the trade you drive, my soul.

FLIPPANTA: Look you, Sir, pray take things right. I know madam does fret you a little now and then, that's true; but in the fund she is the softest, sweetest, gentlest lady breathing: Let her but live entirely to her own fancy, and she'll never say a word to you from morning to night.

GRIPE: Oons; let her but stay at home, and she shall do what she will: In reason, that is.

FLIPPANTA: D'ye hear that, Madam? Nay, now I must be on master's side; you see how he loves you, he desires only your company: Pray give him that satisfaction, or I must pronounce against you.

CLARISSA: Well I agree. Thou know'st I don't love to grieve him: Let him be always in good humour, and I'll be always at home.

FLIPPANTA: Look you there, Sir, what wou'd you have more?

GRIPE: Well, let her keep her word, and I'll have done quarrelling.

CLARISSA: I must not, however, so far lose the merit of my consent, as to let you think I'm weary of going abroad, my dear: what I do, is purely to oblige you; which, that I may be able to perform, without a relapse, I'll invent what ways I can to make my prison supportable to me.

FLIPPANTA: Her prison! pretty bird! her prison! don't that word melt you, Sir?

GRIPE: I must confess I did not expect to find her so reasonable.

FLIPPANTA: O, Sir, soon or late wives come into good humour: Husbands must only have a little patience to wait for it.

CLARISSA: The innocent little diversions, dear, that I shall content my self with, will be chiefly play and company.

GRIPE: O, I'll find you employment, your time shan't lie upon your hands, tho' if you have a mind now for such a companion as a——let me see——Araminta for example, why I shan't be against her being with you from morning 'till night.

CLARISSA: You can't oblige me more, 'tis the best woman in the world.

GRIPE: Is not she?

FLIPPANTA: Ah, the old satyr!   [Aside]

GRIPE: Then we'll have, besides her, may be sometimes——her husband; and we shall see my niece that writes verses, and my sister Fidget: With her husband's brother that's always merry; and his little cousin, that's to marry the fat curate; and my uncle the apothecary, with his wife and all his children. O we shall divert ourselves rarely.

FLIPPANTA: Good.   [Aside]

CLARISSA: O, for that, my dear child, I must be plain with you, I'll see none of 'em but Araminta, who has the manners of the court; for I'll converse with none but women of quality.

GRIPE: Ay, ay, they shall all have one quality or other.

CLARISSA: Then, my dear, to make our home pleasant, we'll have consorts of musick sometimes.

GRIPE: Musick in my house!

CLARISSA: Yes my child, we must have musick, or the house will be so dull I shall get the spleen, and be going abroad again.

FLIPPANTA: Nay, she has so much complaisance for you, Sir, you can't dispute such things with her.

GRIPE: Ay, but if I have musick——

CLARISSA: Ay, but Sir, I must have musick——

FLIPPANTA: Not every day, Madam don't mean.

CLARISSA: No bless me, no; but three consorts a week: three days more we'll play after dinner at ombre, picquet, basset, and so forth, and close the evening with a handsome supper and a ball.

GRIPE: A ball!

CLARISSA: Then, my love, you know there is but one day more upon our hands, and that shall be the day of conversation, we'll read verses, talk of books, invent modes, tell lyes, scandalize our friends, be pert upon religion; and in short, employ every moment of it, in some pretty witty exercise or other.

FLIPPANTA: What order you see 'tis she proposes to live in! A most wonderful regularity!

GRIPE: Regularity with a pox——   [Aside]

CLARISSA: And as this kind of life, so soft, so smooth, so agreeable, must needs invite a vast deal of company to partake of it, 'twill be necessary to have the decency of a porter at our door, you know.

GRIPE: A porter——a scrivener have a porter, madam!

CLARISSA: Positively, a porter.

GRIPE: Why, no scrivener since Adam ever had a porter, woman!

CLARISSA: You will therefore be renown'd· in story, for having the first, my life.

GRIPE: Flippanta.

FLIPPANTA: Hang it, Sir, never dispute a trifle; if you vex her, perhaps she'll insist upon a Swiss.   [Aside to Gripe]

GRIPE: But, Madam——

CLARISSA: But, Sir, a porter, positively a porter; without that the treaty's null, and I go abroad this moment.

FLIPPANTA: Come, Sir, never lose so advantageous a peace for a pitiful porter.

GRIPE: Why, I shall be hooted at, the boys will throw stones at my porter. Besides, where shall I have money for all this expence?

CLARISSA: My dear, who asks you for any? Don't be in a fright, chicken.

GRIPE: Don't be in a fright, Madam! But where, I say——

FLIPPANTA: Madam plays, Sir, think on that; women that play have inexhaustible mines, and wives who receive least money from their husbands, are many times those who spend the most.

CLARISSA: So, my dear, let what Flippanta says content you. Go, my life, trouble your self with nothing, but let me do just as I please, and all will be well. I'm going into my closet, to consider of some more things to enable me to give you the pleasure of my company at home, without making it too great a misery to a yielding wife.   [Exit Clarissa]

FLIPPANTA: Mirror of goodness! Pattern to all wives! well sure, Sir, you are the happiest of all husbands.

GRIPE: Yes——and a miserable dog for all that too, perhaps.

FLIPPANTA: Why what can you ask more, than this matchless complaisance?

GRIPE: I don't know what I can ask, and yet I'm not satisfy'd with what I have neither, the devil mixes in it all, I think; complaisant or perverse, it feels just as't did.

FLIPPANTA: Why then your uneasiness is only a disease, Sir, perhaps a little bleeding and purging wou'd relieve you.

CLARISSA: Flippanta!   [Clarissa calls within]

FLIPPANTA: Madam calls. I come, Madam. Come, be merry, be merry, sir, you have cause, take my word for't.—Poor devil. [Aside]   [Exit Flippanta]

GRIPE: I don't know that, I don't know that: But this I do know, that an honest man, who has marry'd a jade, whether she's pleas'd to spend her time at home or abroad, had better have liv'd a bachelor.

Enter Brass.

BRASS: O, Sir, I'm mighty glad I have found you.

GRIPE: Why, what's the matter, pr'ythee?

BRASS: Can no body hear us?

GRIPE: No, no, speak quickly.

BRASS: You han't seen Araminta, since the last letter I carry'd her from you?

GRIPE: Not I, I go prudently; I don't press things like your young firebrand lovers.

BRASS: But seriously, Sir, are you very much in love with her?

GRIPE: As mortal man has been.

BRASS: I'm sorry for't.

GRIPE: Why so, dear Brass?

BRASS: If you were never to see her more now? Suppose such a thing, d'you think 'twould break your heart?

GRIPE: Oh!

BRASS: Nay, now I see you love her; wou'd you did not.

GRIPE: My dear friend.

BRASS: I'm in your interest deep; you see it.

GRIPE: I do: but speak, what miserable story hast thou for me?

BRASS: I had rather the devil had, phu—flown away with you quick, than to see you so much in love, as I perceive you are, since——

GRIPE: Since what?—ho.

BRASS: Araminta, Sir.

GRIPE: Dead?

BRASS: No.

GRIPE: How then?

BRASS: Worse.

GRIPE: Out with't.

BRASS: Broke.

GRIPE: Broke!

BRASS: She is, poor lady, in the most unfortunate situation of affairs. But I have said too much.

GRIPE: No, no, 'tis very sad, but let's hear it.

BRASS: Sir, she charg'd me, on my life, never to mention it to you, of all men living.

GRIPE: Why, who should'st thou tell it to, but to the best of her friends?

BRASS: Ay, why there's it now, it's going just as I fancy'd. Now will I be hang'd if you are not enough in love to be engaging in this matter. But I must tell you, Sir, that as much concern as I have for that most excellent, beautiful, agreeable, distress'd, unfortunate lady, I'm too much your friend and servant, ever to let it be said I was the means of your being ruin'd for a woman——by letting you know, she esteem'd you more than any other man upon earth.

GRIPE: Ruin'd! what dost thou mean?

BRASS: Mean! Why I mean that women always ruin those that love 'em, that's the rule.

GRIPE: The rule!

BRASS: Yes the rule; why, wou'd you have 'em ruin those that don't? How shall they bring that about?

GRIPE: But is there a necessity then, they shou'd ruin somebody?

BRASS: Yes, marry is there; how wou'd you have 'em

support their expence else? Why, Sir, you can't conceive now——you can't conceive what Araminta's privy-purse requires. Only her privy-purse, Sir! Why, what do you imagine now she gave me for the last letter I carry'd her from you? 'Tis true, 'twas from a man she lik'd, else, perhaps, I had had my bones broke. But what do you think she gave me?

GRIPE: Why, mayhap——a shilling.

BRASS: A guinea, Sir, a guinea. You see by that how fond she was on't, by the by. But then, Sir, her coach-hire, her chair-hire, her pin-money, her play-money, her china, and her charity——wou'd consume peers: A great soul, a very great soul! but what's the end of all this?

GRIPE: Ha!

BRASS: Why, I'll tell you what the end is——a nunnery.

GRIPE: A nunnery!

BRASS: A nunnery.——In short, she is at last reduc'd to that extremity, and attack'd with such a battalion of duns, that rather than tell her husband (who you know is such a dog, he'd let her go if she did) she has e'en determin'd to turn papist, and bid the world adieu for life.

GRIPE: O terrible! a papist!

BRASS: Yes, when a handsome woman has brought her self into difficulties, the devil can't help her out of——To a nunnery, that's another rule, Sir.

GRIPE: But, but, but, pr'ythee Brass, but——

BRASS: But all the buts in the world, Sir, won't stop her; she's a woman of a noble resolution. So, Sir, your humble servant; I pity her, I pity you. Turtle and mate; but the Fates will have it so, all's packt up, and I am now going to call her a coach, for she resolves to slip off without saying a word: and the next visit she receives from her friends, will be through a melancholy grate, with a veil instead of a top-knot.   [Going]

GRIPE: It must not be, by the Powers it must not; she was made for the world, and the world was made for her.

BRASS: And yet you see, Sir, how small a share she has on't.

GRIPE: Poor woman! Is there no way to save her?

BRASS: Save her! No, how can she be sav'd? why she owes above five hundred pound.

GRIPE: Oh!

BRASS: Five hundred pound, Sir; she's like to be sav'd indeed.——Not but that I know them in this town wou'd give me one of the five, if I wou'd persuade her to accept of th' other four: But she had forbid me mentioning it to any soul living; and I have disobey'd her only to you; and so—I'll go and call a coach.

GRIPE: Hold!——dost think, my poor Brass, one might not order it so, as to compound those debts for——for——twelve pence in the pound?

BRASS: Sir, d'ye hear? I have already try'd 'em with

ten shillings, and not a rogue will prick up his ear at it. Tho' after all, for three hundred pounds all in glittering gold, I could set their chaps a watering. But where's that to be had with honour? there's the thing, Sir——I'll go and call a coach.

GRIPE: Hold, once more: I have a note in my closet of two hundred, ay——and fifty, I'll go and give it her my self.

BRASS: You will; very genteel truly. Go, slap-dash, and offer a woman of her scruples, money! bolt in her face: Why, you might as well offer her a scorpion, and she'd as soon touch it.

GRIPE: Shall I carry it to her creditors then, and treat with them?

BRASS: Ay, that's a rare thought.

GRIPE: Is not it, Brass?

BRASS: Only one little inconvenience by the way.

GRIPE: As how?

BRASS: That they are your wife's creditors as well as hers; and perhaps it might not be altogether so well to see you clearing the debts of your neighbour's wife, and leaving those of your own unpaid.

GRIPE: Why that's true now.

BRASS: I'm wise you see, Sir.

GRIPE: Thou art; and I'm but a young lover: But what shall we do then?

BRASS: Why, I'm thinking, that if you give me the note, do you see; and that I promise to give you an account of it——

GRIPE: Ay, but look you, Brass——

BRASS: But look you!——Why what, d'ye think I'm a pick-pocket? D'ye think I intend to run away with your note? your paltry note.

GRIPE: I don't say so——I say only that in case——

BRASS: Case, Sir! there is no case but the case I have put you; and since you heap cases upon cases, where there is but three hundred rascally pounds in the case——I'll go and call a coach.

GRIPE: Pr'ythee don't be so testy; come, no more words, follow me to my closet, and I'll give thee the money.

BRASS: A terrible effort you make indeed; you are so much in love, your wits are all upon the wing, just a going; and for three hundred pounds you put a stop to their flight: Sir, your wits are worth that, or your wits are worth nothing. Come away.

GRIPE: Well, say no more, thou shalt be satisfy'd.
                                                    [Exeunt]

Enter Dick.

DICK: S't——Brass! S't——

Re-enter Brass.

BRASS: Well, Sir!

DICK: 'Tis not well, Sir, 'tis very ill, Sir; we shall be all blown up.

BRASS: What, with pride and plenty?

DICK: No, Sir, with an officious slut that will spoil

all. In short, Flippanta has been telling her mistress and Araminta, of my passion for the young gentlewoman; and truly to oblige me (suppos'd no ill match by the by) they are resolv'd to propose it immediately to her father.

BRASS: That's the devil! we shall come to papers and parchments, jointures and settlements, relations meet on both sides; that's the devil.

DICK: I intended this very day to propose to Flippanta, the carrying her off: And I'm sure the young housewife wou'd have tuck'd up her coats, and have march'd.

BRASS: Ay, with the body and the soul of her.

DICK: Why then, what damn'd luck is this?

BRASS: 'Tis your damn'd luck, not mine: I have always seen it in your ugly phiz, in spite of your powder'd periwig——pox take ye——he'll be hang'd at last. Why don't you try to get her off yet?

DICK: I have no money, you dog; you know you have stript me of every penny.

BRASS: Come, damn it, I'll venture one cargo more upon your rotten bottom: But if ever I see one glance of your hempen fortune again, I'm off your partnership for ever——I shall never thrive with him.

DICK: An impudent rogue, but he's in possession of my estate, so I must bear with him.   [Aside]

BRASS: Well, come, I'll raise a hundred pounds for your use, upon my wife's jewels here; [Pulling out the necklace] her necklace shall pawn for't.

DICK: Remember tho', that if things fail, I'm to have the necklace again; you know you agreed to that.

BRASS: Yes, and if I make it good, you'll be the better for't; if not, I shall: so you see where the cause will pinch.

DICK: Why, you barbarous dog, you won't offer to——

BRASS: No words now; about your business, march. Go stay for me at the next tavern: I'll go to Flippanta, and try what I can do for you.

DICK: Well, I'll go, but don't think to——O pox, Sir——   [Exit Dick]

Brass solus.

BRASS: Will you be gone? A pretty title you'd have to sue me upon truly, if I shou'd have a mind to stand upon the defensive, as perhaps I may; I have done the rascal service enough to lull my conscience upon't I'm sure: But 'tis time enough for that. Let me see——First I'll go to Flippanta, and put a stop to this family way of match-making, then sell our necklace for what ready money 'twill produce; and by this time to-morrow I hope we shall be in possession of——t'other jewel here; a precious jewel, as she's set in gold: I believe for the stone it self we may part with't again to a friend——for a tester.   [Exit]

Act V

SCENE 1: *Gripe's House*

Enter Brass *and* Flippanta.

BRASS: Well, you agree I'm in the right, don't you?

FLIPPANTA: I don't know; if your master has the estate he talks of, why not do't all above-board? Well, tho' I am not much of his mind, I'm much in his interest, and will therefore endeavour to serve him in his own way.

BRASS: That's kindly said, my child, and I believe I shall reward thee one of these days, with as pretty a fellow to thy husband for't, as——

FLIPPANTA: Hold your prating, Jackadandy, and leave me to my business.

BRASS: I obey—adieu. [Kisses her]   [Exit Brass]

FLIPPANTA: Rascal!

Enter Corinna.

CORINNA: Ah, Flippanta, I'm ready to sink down, my legs tremble under me, my dear Flippy.

FLIPPANTA: And what's the affair?

CORINNA: My father's there within, with my mother and Araminta; I never saw him in so good a humour in my life.

FLIPPANTA: And is that it that frightens you so?

CORINNA: Ah, Flippanta, they are just going to speak to him, about my marrying the Colonel.

FLIPPANTA: Are they so? so much the worse; they're too hasty.

CORINNA: O no, not a bit: I slipt out on purpose, you must know, to give 'em an opportunity; wou'd 'twere done already.

FLIPPANTA: I tell you no; get you in again immediately, and prevent it.

CORINNA: My dear, dear, I am not able; I never was in such a way before.

FLIPPANTA: Never in a way to be marry'd before, ha? is not that it?

CORINNA: Ah, Lord, if I'm thus before I come to't, Flippanta, what shall I be upon the very spot? Do but feel with what a thumpaty thump it goes.
                            [Putting her hand to her heart]

FLIPPANTA: Nay, it does make a filthy bustle, that's the truth on't, child. But I believe I shall make it leap another way, when I tell you, I'm cruelly afraid your father won't consent, after all.

CORINNA: Why, he won't be the death o'me, will he?

FLIPPANTA: I don't know, old folks are cruel; but we'll have a trick for him. Brass and I have been consulting upon the matter, and agreed upon a surer way of doing it in spite of his teeth.

CORINNA: Ay, marry, sir, that were something.

FLIPPANTA: But then he must not know a word of any thing towards it.

CORINNA: No, no.

FLIPPANTA: So, get you in immediately.

CORINNA: One, two, three and away. [Running off]

FLIPPANTA: And prevent your mother's speaking on't.

CORINNA: But is t'other way sure, Flippanta?

FLIPPANTA: Fear nothing, 'twill only depend upon you.

CORINNA: Nay then——O ho, ho, ho, how pure that is? [Exit Corinna]

Flippanta sola.

Poor child! we may do what we will with her, as far as marrying her goes: when that's over, 'tis possible she mayn't prove altogether so tractable. But who's here? my sharper, I think: Yes.

Enter Money-trap.

MONEY-TRAP: Well, my best friend, how go matters? Has the restitution been receiv'd, ha? Was she pleas'd with it?

FLIPPANTA: Yes, truly; that is, she was pleas'd to see there was so honest a man in this immoral age.

MONEY-TRAP: Well, but a——does she know that 'twas I that——

FLIPPANTA: Why, you must know I begun to give her a little sort of a hint, and——and so——why, and so she begun to put on a sort of a severe, haughty, reserv'd, angry, forgiving air. But soft; here she comes: You'll see how you stand with her presently: But don't be afraid. Courage.

MONEY-TRAP: He, hem.

Enter Clarissa.

'Tis no small piece of good fortune, Madam, to find you at home: I have often endeavour'd it in vain.

CLARISSA: 'Twas then unknown to me, for if I cou'd often receive the visits of so good a friend at home, I shou'd be more reasonably blam'd for being so much abroad.

MONEY-TRAP: Madam, you make me——

CLARISSA: You are the man of the world whose company I think is most to be desir'd. I don't compliment you when I tell you so, I assure you.

MONEY-TRAP: Alas, Madam, your poor humble servant——

CLARISSA: My poor humble servant however (with all the esteem I have for him) stands suspected with me for a vile trick, I doubt he has play'd me, which if I could prove upon him, I'm afraid I shou'd punish him very severely.

MONEY-TRAP: I hope, Madam, you'll believe I am not capable of——

CLARISSA: Look you, look you, you are capable of whatever you please, you have a great deal of wit, and know how to give a nice and gallant turn to every thing; but if you will have me continue your friend, you must leave me in some uncertainty in this matter.

MONEY-TRAP: Madam, I do then protest to you——

CLARISSA: Come protest nothing about it, I am but too penetrating, as you may perceive; but we sometimes shut our eyes, rather than break with our friends; for a thorough knowledge of the truth of this business, wou'd make me very seriously angry.

MONEY-TRAP: 'Tis very certain, Madam, that——

CLARISSA: Come, say no more on't, I beseech you, for I'm in a good deal of heat while I but think on't; if you'll walk in, I'll follow you presently.

MONEY-TRAP: Your goodness, Madam, is——

FLIPPANTA: War, horse.   [Aside to Money-trap] No fine speeches, you'll spoil all.

MONEY-TRAP: Thou art a most incomparable person.

FLIPPANTA: Nay, it goes rarely; but get you in, and I'll say a little something to my lady for you, while she's warm.

MONEY-TRAP: But S't, Flippanta, how long do'st think she may hold out?

FLIPPANTA: Phu, not a twelvemonth.

MONEY-TRAP: Boo.

FLIPPANTA: Away, I say.   [Pushing him out]

CLARISSA: Is he gone? What a wretch it is! he never was quite such a beast before.

FLIPPANTA: Poor mortal, his money's finely laid out truly.

CLARISSA: I suppose there may have been much such another scene within between Araminta and my dear: But I left him so insupportably brisk, 'tis impossible he can have parted with any money: I'm afraid Brass has not succeeded as thou hast done, Flippanta.

FLIPPANTA: By my faith but he has, and better too; he presents his humble duty to Araminta, and has sent her——this.   [Shewing the note]

CLARISSA: A bill from my love for two hundred and fifty pounds. The monster! he wou'd not part with ten to save his lawful wife from everlasting torment.

FLIPPANTA: Never complain of his avarice, Madam, as long as you have his money.

CLARISSA: But is not he a beast, Flippanta? methinks the restitution look'd better by half.

FLIPPANTA: Madam, the man's beast enough, that's certain; but which way will you go to receive his beastly money, for I must not appear with his note?

CLARISSA: That's true; why send for Mrs. Amlet; that's a mighty useful woman, that Mrs. Amlet.

FLIPPANTA: Marry is she; we shou'd have been basely puzzled how to dispose of the necklace without her, 'twou'd have been dangerous offering it to sale.

CLARISSA: It wou'd so, for I know your master has been laying out for't among the goldsmiths. But I stay here too long, I must in and coquet it a little more to my lover, Araminta will get ground on me else.   [Exit Clarissa]

FLIPPANTA: And I'll go send for Mrs. Amlet.

[*Exit* Flippanta]

SCENE 2: *The same*

Araminta, Corinna, Gripe, *and* Money-trap *at a tea-table, very gay and laughing.* Clarissa *comes in to 'em.*

OMNES: Ha! ha! ha! ha!

MONEY-TRAP: Mighty well, O mighty well indeed!

CLARISSA: Save you, save you good folks, you are all in rare humour methinks.

GRIPE: Why, what shou'd we be otherwise for, Madam?

CLARISSA: Nay, I don't know, not I, my dear; but I han't had the happiness of seeing you so since our honey-moon was over, I think.

GRIPE: Why to tell you the truth, my dear, 'tis the joy of seeing you at home. [*Kisses her.*] You see what charms you have, when you are pleased to make use of 'em.

ARAMINTA: Very gallant truly.

CLARISSA: Nay, and what's more, you must know, he's never to be otherwise henceforwards; we have come to an agreement about it.

MONEY-TRAP: Why, here's my love and I have been upon just such another treaty too.

ARAMINTA: Well, sure there's some very peaceful star rules at present. Pray heaven continue its reign.

MONEY-TRAP: Pray do you continue its reign, you ladies; for 'tis all in your power.

[*Leering at* Clarissa]

GRIPE: My neighbour Money-trap says true, at least I'll confess frankly [*Ogling* Araminta] 'tis in one lady's power to make me the best-humour'd man on earth.

MONEY-TRAP: And I'll answer for another, that has the same over me.   [*Ogling* Clarissa]

CLARISSA: 'Tis mighty fine, gentlemen, mighty civil husbands indeed.

GRIPE: Nay, what I say's true, and so true, that all quarrels being now at an end, I am willing, if you please, to dispense with all that fine company we talk'd of to-day, be content with the friendly conversation of our two good neighbours here, and spend all my toying hours alone with my sweet wife.

MONEY-TRAP: Why, truly, I think now, if these good women pleas'd, we might make up the prettiest little neighbourly company between our two families, and set a defiance to all the impertinent people in the world.   [*Aside*]

CLARISSA: The rascals!

ARAMINTA: Indeed I doubt you'd soon grow weary, if we grew fond.

GRIPE: Never, never, for our wives have wit, neighbour, and that never palls.

CLARISSA: And our husbands have generosity, Araminta, and that seldom palls.

GRIPE: So that's a wipe for me now, because I did give her a new-year's gift last time; but be good, and I'll think of some tea-cups for you, next year.

MONEY-TRAP: And perhaps I mayn't forget a fan, or as good a thing——hum, hussy.

CLARISSA: Well, upon these encouragements, Araminta, we'll try how good we can be.

GRIPE: Well, this goes most rarely: Poor Money-trap, he little thinks what makes his wife so easy in his company.   [*Aside*]

MONEY-TRAP: I can but pity poor neighbour Gripe. Lard, Lard, what a fool does his wife and I make of him!   [*Aside*]

CLARISSA: Are not these two wretched rogues, Araminta?   [*Aside to* Araminta]

ARAMINTA: They are indeed.   [*Aside to* Clarissa]

Enter Jessamin.

JESSAMIN: Sir, here's Mr. Clip, the goldsmith, desires to speak with you.

GRIPE: Cods so, perhaps some news of your necklace, my dear.

CLARISSA: That would be news indeed.

GRIPE: Let him come in.

Enter Mr. Clip.

GRIPE: Mr. Clip, your servant, I'm glad to see you: How do you do?

CLIP: At your service, Sir, very well. Your servant, Madam Gripe.

CLARISSA: Horrid fellow!   [*Aside*]

GRIPE: Well, Mr. Clip, no news yet of my wife's necklace?

CLIP: If you please to let me speak with you in the next room, I have something to say to you.

GRIPE: Ay, with all my heart. Shut the door after us. [*They come forward, and the scene shuts behind them*] Well, any news?

CLIP: Look you, Sir, here's a necklace brought me to sell, at least very like that you describ'd to me.

GRIPE: Let's see't——Victoria! the very same. Ah, my dear Mr. Clip.——[*Kisses him*] But who brought it you? you should have seiz'd him.

CLIP: 'Twas a young fellow that I know: I can't tell whether he may be guilty, tho' it's like enough. But he has only left it me now, to shew a brother of our trade, and will call upon me again presently.

GRIPE: Wheedle him hither, dear Mr. Clip. Here's my neighbour Money-trap in the house; he's a justice, and will commit him presently.

CLIP: 'Tis enough.

Enter Brass.

GRIPE: O, my friend Brass!

BRASS: Hold, sir, I think that's a gentleman I'm looking for. Mr. Clip, O your servant; what, are you acquainted here? I have just been at your shop.

CLIP: I only stept here to shew Mr. Gripe the necklace you left.

BRASS: Why, Sir, do you understand jewels? [*To Gripe*] I thought you only dealt in gold. But I smoak the matter, hark you——a word in your ear——you are going to play the gallant again, and make a purchase on't for Araminta; ha, ha?

GRIPE: Where had you the necklace?

BRASS: Look you, don't trouble your self about that; it's in commission with me, and I can help you to a pennyworth on't.

GRIPE: A pennyworth on't villain? [*Strikes at him*]

BRASS: Villain! a hey, a hey. Is't you or me, Mr. Clip, he's pleas'd to compliment?

CLIP: What do you think on't, Sir?

BRASS: Think on't, now the devil fetch me if I know what to think on't.

GRIPE: You'll sell a pennyworth, rogue! of a thing you have stoln from me.

BRASS: Stoln! pray, Sir——what wine have you drank to-day? It has a very merry effect upon you.

GRIPE: You villain; either give me an account how you stole it, or——

BRASS: O ho, Sir, if you please, don't carry your jest too far, I don't understand hard words, I give you warning on't: If you han't a mind to buy the necklace, you may let it alone, I know how to dispose on't. What a pox!——

GRIPE: O, you shan't have that trouble, Sir. Dear Mr. Clip, you may leave the necklace here. I'll call at your shop, and thank you for your care.

CLIP: Sir, your humble servant.   [*Going*]

BRASS: O ho, Mr. Clip, if you please, Sir, this won't do. [*Stopping him*] I don't understand raillery in such matters.

CLIP: I leave it with Mr. Gripe, do you and he dispute it.   [*Exit Clip*]

BRASS: Ay, but 'tis from you, by your leave, Sir, that I expect it.   [*Going after him*]

GRIPE: You expect, you rogue, to make your escape, do you? But I have other accounts besides this, to make up with you. To be sure the dog has cheated me of two hundred and fifty pound. Come, villain, give me an account of——

BRASS: Account of!——Sir, give me an account of my necklace, or I'll make such a noise in your house, I'll raise the devil in't.

GRIPE: Well said, courage.

BRASS: Blood and thunder, give it me, or——

GRIPE: Come, hush, be wise, and I'll make no noise of this affair.

BRASS: You'll make no noise! But I'll make a noise, and a damn'd noise too. O, don't think to——

GRIPE: I tell thee I will not hang thee.

BRASS: But I tell you I will hang you, if you don't give me my necklace, I will, rot me.

GRIPE: Speak softly, be wise; how came it thine? who gave it thee?

BRASS: A gentleman, a friend of mine.

GRIPE: What's his name?

BRASS: His name!——I'm in such a passion I have forgot it.

GRIPE: Ah, brazen rogue——thou hast stole it from my wife: 'tis the same she lost six weeks ago.

BRASS: This has not been in England a month.

GRIPE: You are a son of a whore.

BRASS: Give me my necklace.

GRIPE: Give me my two hundred and fifty pound note.

BRASS: Yet I offer peace: one word without passion. The case stands thus, either I'm out of my wits, or you are out of yours: Now 'tis plain I am not out of my wits, *Ergo*——

GRIPE: My bill, hang-dog, or I'll strangle thee.

BRASS: Murder, murder!   [*They struggle*]

Enter Clarissa, Araminta, Corinna, Flippanta, *and* Money-trap.

FLIPPANTA: What's the matter? What's the matter here?

GRIPE: I'll matter him.

CLARISSA: Who makes thee cry out thus, poor Brass?

BRASS: Why, your husband, madam, he's in his altitudes here.

GRIPE: Robber.

BRASS: Here, he has cheated me of a diamond necklace.

CORINNA: Who, Papa? Ah dear me!

CLARISSA: Pr'ythee what's the meaning of this great emotion, my dear?

GRIPE: The meaning is that——I'm quite out of breath——this son of a whore has got our necklace, that's all.

CLARISSA: My necklace!

GRIPE: That birdlime there—stole it.

CLARISSA: Impossible!

BRASS: Madam, you see master's a little——touch'd, that's all. Twenty ounces of blood let loose, wou'd set all right again.

GRIPE: Here, call a constable presently. Neighbour Money-trap, you'll commit him.

BRASS: D'ye hear? d'ye hear? See how wild he looks: how his eyes roll in his head: tye him down, or he'll do some mischief or other.

GRIPE: Let me come at him.

CLARISSA: Hold—pr'ythee, my dear, reduce things to a little temperance, and let us coolly into the secret of this disagreeable rupture.

GRIPE: Well then, without passion: Why, you must know (but I'll have him hang'd), you must know that he came to Mr. Clip, to Mr. Clip the dog did——with a necklace to sell; so Mr. Clip having notice before that (can you deny this, sirrah?) that you had lost yours, brings it to me. Look at it here, do you know it again? Ah, you traitor.

[*To Brass*]

BRASS: He makes me mad. Here's an appearance of something now to the company, and yet nothing in't in the bottom.

Enter Constable.

CLARISSA: Flippanta! [*Aside to* Flippanta, *shewing the necklace*]

FLIPPANTA: 'Tis it, 'faith; here's some mystery in this, we must look about us.

CLARISSA: The safest way is point blank to disown the necklace.

FLIPPANTA: Right, stick to that.

GRIPE: Well, madam, do you know your old acquaintance, ha?

CLARISSA: Why, truly, my dear, tho' (as you may all imagine) I shou'd be very glad to recover so valuable a thing as my necklace, yet I must be just to all the world, this necklace is not mine.

BRASS: Huzza——here constable, do your duty; Mr. Justice, I demand my necklace, and satisfaction of him.

GRIPE: I'll die before I part with it, I'll keep it, and have him hang'd.

CLARISSA: But be a little calm, my dear, do my bird, and then thou'lt be able to judge rightly of things.

GRIPE: O good lack, O good lack.

CLARISSA: No, but don't give way to fury and interest both, either of 'em are passions strong enough to lead a wise man out of the way. The necklace not being really mine, give it the man again, and come drink a dish of tea.

BRASS: Ay, Madam says right.

GRIPE: Oons, if you with your addle head don't know your own jewels, I with my solid one do. And if I part with it, may famine be my portion.

CLARISSA: But don't swear and curse thy self at this fearful rate; don't my dove: Be temperate in your words, and just in all your actions, 'twill bring a blessing upon you and your family.

GRIPE: Bring thunder and lightning upon me and my family, if I part with my necklace.

CLARISSA: Why, you'll have the lightning burn your house about your ears, my dear, if you go on in these practices.

MONEY-TRAP: A most excellent woman this! [*Aside*]

Enter Mrs. Amlet.

GRIPE: I'll keep my necklace.

BRASS: Will you so? Then here comes one has a title to it, if I han't; let Dick bring himself off with her as he can. Mrs. Amlet, you are come in a very good time, you lost a necklace t'other day, and who do you think has got it?

AMLET: Marry that I know not, I wish I did.

BRASS: Why then here's Mr. Gripe has it, and swears 'tis his wife's.

GRIPE: And so I do, sirrah——look here, Mistress, do you pretend this is yours?

AMLET: Not for the round world I wou'd not say it; I only kept it to do Madam a small courtesy, that's all.

CLARISSA: Ah, Flippanta, all will out now.
                                        [*Aside to* Flippanta]

GRIPE: Courtesy! what courtesy?

AMLET: A little money only that madam had present need of, please to pay me that, and I demand no more.

BRASS: So here's fresh game, I have started a new hare, I find.   [*Aside*]

GRIPE: How forsooth, is this true?   [*To* Clarissa]

CLARISSA: You are in a humour at present, love, to believe any thing, so I won't take the pains to contradict it.

BRASS: This damn'd necklace will spoil all our affairs, this is Dick's luck again.   [*Aside*]

GRIPE: Are you not asham'd of these ways? Do you see how you are expos'd before your best friends here? don't you blush at it?

CLARISSA: I do blush, my dear, but 'tis for you, that here it shou'd appear to the world, you keep me so bare of money, I'm forc'd to pawn my jewels.

GRIPE: Impudent houswife!
                          [*Raising his hand to strike her*]

CLARISSA: Softly, chicken: you might have prevented all this by giving me the two hundred and fifty pounds, you sent to Araminta e'en now.

BRASS: You see, Sir, I deliver'd your note: How I have been abus'd to-day!

GRIPE: I'm betray'd——jades on both sides, I see that.   [*Aside*]

MONEY-TRAP: But Madam, Madam, is this true I hear? Have you taken a present of two hundred and fifty pound? Pray what were you to return for these pounds, Madam, ha?

ARAMINTA: Nothing, my dear, I only took 'em to reimburse you of about the same sum you sent to Clarissa.

MONEY-TRAP: Hum, hum, hum.

GRIPE: How gentlewoman, did you receive money from him?

CLARISSA: O, my dear, 'twas only in jest, I knew you'd give it again to his wife.

AMLET: But amongst all this tintamar, I don't hear a word of my hundred pounds. Is it Madam will pay me, or Master?

GRIPE: I pay? the Devil shall pay.

CLARISSA: Look you, my dear, malice apart, pay Mrs. Amlet her money, and I'll forgive you the wrong you intended my bed with Araminta: Am not I a good wife now?

GRIPE: I burst with rage, and will get rid of this noose, tho' I tuck my self up in another.

MONEY-TRAP: Nay, pray, e'en tuck me up with you.
[*Exit* Money-trap *and* Gripe]
CLARISSA & ARAMINTA: B'y, dearies.

Enter Dick.

CORINNA: Look, look, Flippanta, here's the Colonel come at last.
DICK: Ladies, I ask your pardon, I have stay'd so long, but——
AMLET: Ah rogue's face, have I got thee, old Good-for-nought? Sirrah, sirrah, do you think to amuse me with your marriages, and your great fortunes? Thou hast play'd me a rare prank, by my conscience. Why you ungracious rascal, what do you think will be the end of all this? Now Heaven forgive me, but I have a great mind to hang thee for't.
CORINNA: She talks to him very familiarly, Flippanta.
FLIPPANTA: So methinks, by my faith.
BRASS: Now the rogue's star is making an end of him. [*Aside*]
DICK: What shall I do with her? [*Aside*]
AMLET: Do but look at him, my dames, he has the countenance of a cherubim, but he's a rogue in his heart.
CLARISSA: What is the meaning of all this, Mrs. Amlet?
AMLET: The meaning, good lack! Why this all-to-bepowder'd rascal here, is my son, an't please you; ha, graceless? Now I'll make you own your mother, vermine.
CLARISSA: What, the Colonel your son?
AMLET: 'Tis Dick, Madam, that rogue Dick, I have so often told you of, with tears trickling down my old cheeks.
ARAMINTA: The woman's mad, it can never be.
AMLET: Speak, rogue, am I not thy mother, ha? Did I not bring thee forth? say then.
DICK: What will you have me say? you had a mind to ruin me, and you have don't; wou'd you do any more?
CLARISSA: Then, Sir, you are son to good Mrs. Amlet?
ARAMINTA: And have had the assurance to put upon us all this while?
FLIPPANTA: And the confidence to think of marrying Corinna.
BRASS: And the impudence to hire me for your servant, who am as well born as your self.
CLARISSA: Indeed I think he shou'd be corrected.
ARAMINTA: Indeed I think he deserves to be cudgell'd.
FLIPPANTA: Indeed I think he might be pumpt.
BRASS: Indeed I think he will be hang'd.
AMLET: Good lack-a-day, good lack-a-day! there's no need to be so smart upon him neither: If he is not a gentleman, he's a gentleman's fellow. Come hither, Dick, they shan't run thee down neither: Cock up thy hat, Dick, and tell them tho' Mrs. Amlet is thy mother, she can make thee amends, with ten thousand good pounds to buy thee some lands, and build thee a house in the midst on't.
OMNES: How!
CLARISSA: Ten thousand pounds, Mrs. Amlet?
AMLET: Yes forsooth; tho' I shou'd lose the hundred, you pawn'd your necklace for. Tell 'em of that, Dick.
CORINNA: Look you, Flippanta, I can hold no longer, and I hate to see the young man abus'd. And so, Sir, if you please, I'm your friend and servant, and what's mine is yours; and when our estates are put together, I don't doubt but we shall do as well as the best of 'em.
DICK: Say'st thou so, my little queen? Why then if dear mother will give us her blessing, the parson shall give us a tack. We'll get her a score of grandchildren, and a merry house we'll make her.
[*They kneel to* Mrs. Amlet]
AMLET: Ah——ha, ha, ha, ha, the pretty pair, the pretty pair! rise my chickens, rise, rise and face the proudest of them. And if Madam does not deign to give her consent, a fig for her, Dick—— Why how now?
CLARISSA: Pray, Mrs. Amlet, don't be in a passion, the girl is my husband's girl, and if you can have his consent, upon my word you shall have mine, for any thing belongs to him.
FLIPPANTA: Then all's peace again, but we have been more lucky than wise.
ARAMINTA: And I suppose, for us, Clarissa, we are to go on with our dears, as we us'd to do.
CLARISSA: Just in the same track, for this late treaty of agreement with 'em, was so unnatural, you see it cou'd not hold. But 'tis just as well with us, as if it had. Well, 'tis a strange fate, good folks. But while you live, every thing gets well out of a broil, but a husband.

Epilogue

I've heard wise men in politicks lay down
What feats by little England might be done,
Were all agreed, and all would act as one.
Ye wives a useful hint from this might take,
The heavy, old, despotick kingdom shake,
And make your matrimonial *Monsieurs* quake.
Our heads are feeble, and we're cramp'd by laws;
Our hands are weak, and not too strong our cause:
Yet would those heads and hands, such as they are,
In firm confed'racy resolve on war,
You'd find your tyrants——what I've found my dear.
What only two united can produce
You've seen to-night, a sample for your use;
Single, we found we nothing could obtain;
We join our force—and we subdu'd our men.
Believe me (my dear sex) they are not brave;
Try each your man, you'll quickly find your slave.

I know they'll make campaigns, risk blood and life;
But this is a more terrifying strife;
They'll stand a shot, who'll tremble at a wife.
Beat then your drums, and your shrill trumpets sound,
Let all your visits of your feats resound,
And deeds of war in cups of tea go round:
The stars are with you, fate is in your hand,
In twelve months time you've vanquish'd half the land;
Be wise, and keep 'em under good command.
This year will to your glory long be known,
And deathless ballads hand your triumphs down;
Your late achievements ever will remain,
For tho' you cannot boast of many slain,
Your pris'ners shew, you've made a brave campaign.

She Stoops to Conquer

by OLIVER GOLDSMITH
(1728–1774)

As a playwright, Oliver Goldsmith occupies a position of considerable historical importance. As a rule, such an opening sentence is to be received with foreboding; for nine times out of ten, people who occupy positions of considerable historical importance are interesting for very little else. They were the first to develop one thing or dispense with another, to fish in strange waters or explore new terrain. They were the first to use a particular verse form—and are quite unpoetical; the first to introduce a new style of humor —and seem monumentally unfunny. Oliver Goldsmith, however, is an exception: he is historically significant for having opened fire on the genteel sentimental comedy that had dominated the English stage from Farquhar's time on; but he is artistically significant for writing reasonably ungenteel—and thoroughly unsentimental—comedy that is still, after almost two centuries, bright and entertaining. As a playwright, he was not only a weed-killer; he grew a flower that still has fragrance. Indeed, Goldsmith, a man whose life was lived in disorder and even in some distress, enjoys a delightful and unusual form of immortality. He wrote one play, She Stoops to Conquer, that is an unquestionable classic; one poem, The Deserted Village; and one novel, The Vicar of Wakefield.

Dust has gathered on the English comic drama of the sixty years following The Beaux' Stratagem because, paradoxically, it was in its own days soaked with tears. There are comedies that escaped the tears, but they for the most part yet deserve the dust. What humor, what gaiety, what amusement brightened the stage during those sixty years came in the form of the pantomime, of the burlesques of Fielding and others, and of the ballad operas, one of which— The Beggars' Opera—is securely immortal. But for the most part the stage had become as grimly respectable as during Restoration times it was unseemly and lewd. It had become the property of that sanctimonious institution, the middle-class family; and it soon lost, as a result, every property of Art. The burden was on any aspiring playwright of comedy to concoct something that, in the most chilling sense, would be good clean fun. And such is man's incurable waywardness—which even hypocrisy cannot down— that this is very difficult to do.

Yet just this, precisely this, is what in She Stoops to Conquer Goldsmith did. It achieved the rare feat that while making no woman blush, it made no man yawn. To be sure, had Goldsmith written in an age not so given to blushes, he might have raised She Stoops to Conquer to a higher pitch of gaiety; and might have given the subtitle, The Mistakes of a Night, a more convivial and less merely temporal meaning. But in view of the age he wrote for, his play is impressively successful; truly comic; consistently animated—and, best of all, a sound farce-comedy of situation, that by holding up through all five acts holds up today after 180 years. It rests, of course, on that idea of misunderstanding, of people at cross-purposes, that is almost the pedestal on which Comedy itself rests. And the kind of misunderstanding, which involves a whole code of social behavior, makes it a sort of inverted comedy of manners: everyone, that is, behaves as he should behave were only the circumstances what he thought them. To misdirect two young gentlemen to a private house with the information that it is an inn, and for that very private house to be their real reason for coming into the neighborhood: this still diverts us because in the proper hands such a situation always will; diverts us because it proves but the first of many mistakes of a night; because it is all humor and not wit; all farce and not satire; robustly old-fashioned, not—even for its own time—skimpily up-to-date. Few plays can have seemed less chic when first produced, or have grown less dowdy afterward.

OLIVER GOLDSMITH

She Stoops to Conquer
or, The Mistakes of a Night

THE PERSONS OF THE PLAY

SIR CHARLES MARLOW
YOUNG MARLOW, *his Son*
HARDCASTLE
HASTINGS
TONY LUMPKIN
DIGGORY
MRS. HARDCASTLE
MISS HARDCASTLE
MISS NEVILLE
MAID

LANDLORDS, SERVANTS, &c., &c.

Act I

SCENE: *A Chamber in an old-fashioned House*

Enter Mrs. Hardcastle *and* Mr. Hardcastle.

MRS. HARDCASTLE: I vow, Mr. Hardcastle, you're very particular. Is there a creature in the whole country, but ourselves, that does not take a trip to town now and then, to rub off the rust a little? There's the two Miss Hoggs, and our neighbour, Mrs. Grigsby, go to take a month's polishing every winter.

HARDCASTLE: Ay, and bring back vanity and affectation to last them the whole year. I wonder why London cannot keep its own fools at home. In my time, the follies of the town crept slowly among us, but now they travel faster than a stage-coach. Its fopperies come down, not only as inside passengers, but in the very basket.

MRS. HARDCASTLE: Ay, *your* times were fine times, indeed; you have been telling us of *them* for many a long year. Here we live in an old rumbling mansion, that looks for all the world like an inn, but that we never see company. Our best visitors are old Mrs. Oddfish, the curate's wife, and little Cripplegate, the lame dancing-master: And all our

entertainment your old stories of Prince Eugene and the Duke of Marlborough. I hate such old-fashioned trumpery.

HARDCASTLE: And I love it. I love everything that's old: old friends, old times, old manners, old books, old wine; and, I believe, Dorothy [*Taking her hand*], you'll own I have been pretty fond of an old wife.

MRS. HARDCASTLE: Lord, Mr. Hardcastle, you're for ever at your Dorothys and your old wifes. You may be a Darby, but I'll be no Joan, I promise you. I'm not so old as you'd make me, by more than one good year. Add twenty to twenty, and make money of that.

HARDCASTLE: Let me see; twenty added to twenty, makes just fifty and seven!

MRS. HARDCASTLE: It's false, Mr. Hardcastle: I was but twenty when I was brought to bed of Tony, that I had by Mr. Lumpkin, my first husband; and he's not come to years of discretion yet.

HARDCASTLE: Nor ever will, I dare answer for him. Ay, you have taught *him* finely!

MRS. HARDCASTLE: No matter, Tony Lumpkin has a good fortune. My son is not to live by his learning. I don't think a boy wants much learning to spend fifteen hundred a year.

HARDCASTLE: Learning, quotha! A mere composition of tricks and mischief!

MRS. HARDCASTLE: Humour, my dear: nothing but humour. Come, Mr. Hardcastle, you must allow the boy a little humour.

HARDCASTLE: I'd sooner allow him a horse-pond! If burning the footmen's shoes, frightening the maids, and worrying the kittens, be humour, he has it. It was but yesterday he fastened my wig to the back of my chair, and when I went to make a bow, I popped my bald head in Mrs. Frizzle's face!

MRS. HARDCASTLE: And am I to blame? The poor boy was always too sickly to do any good. A school would be his death. When he comes to be a little stronger, who knows what a year or two's Latin may do for him?

HARDCASTLE: Latin for him! A cat and fiddle! No, no, the ale-house and the stable are the only schools he'll ever go to!

MRS. HARDCASTLE: Well, we must not snub the poor boy now, for I believe we shan't have him long among us. Anybody that looks in his face may see he's consumptive.

HARDCASTLE: Ay, if growing too fat be one of the symptoms.

MRS. HARDCASTLE: He coughs sometimes.

HARDCASTLE: Yes, when his liquor goes the wrong way.

MRS. HARDCASTLE: I'm actually afraid of his lungs.

HARDCASTLE: And truly, so am I; for he sometimes whoops like a speaking-trumpet—[Tony *hallooing behind the Scenes*]—O, there he goes.—A very consumptive figure, truly!

Enter Tony, *crossing the stage.*

MRS. HARDCASTLE: Tony, where are you going, my charmer? Won't you give papa and I a little of your company, lovey?

TONY: I'm in haste, mother, I cannot stay.

MRS. HARDCASTLE: You shan't venture out this raw evening, my dear: You look most shockingly.

TONY: I can't stay, I tell you. The Three Pigeons expects me down every moment. There's some fun going forward.

HARDCASTLE: Ay; the ale-house, the old place: I thought so.

MRS. HARDCASTLE: A low, paltry set of fellows.

TONY: Not so low, neither. There's Dick Muggins the exciseman, Jack Slang the horse doctor, Little Aminadab that grinds the music-box, and Tom Twist that spins the pewter platter.

MRS. HARDCASTLE: Pray, my dear, disappoint them for one night, at least.

TONY: As for disappointing *them*, I should not much mind; but I can't abide to disappoint *myself!*

MRS. HARDCASTLE: [*Detaining him*] You shan't go.

TONY: I will, I tell you.

MRS. HARDCASTLE: I say you shan't.

TONY: We'll see which is strongest, you or I.
                              [*Exit hauling her out*]

Hardcastle *solus.*

HARDCASTLE: Ay, there goes a pair that only spoil each other. But is not the whole age in a combination to drive sense and discretion out of doors? There's my pretty darling Kate; the fashions of the times have almost infected her too. By living a year or two in town, she is as fond of gauze, and French frippery, as the best of them.

Enter Miss Hardcastle.

HARDCASTLE: Blessings on my pretty innocence! Dressed out as my usual, my Kate! Goodness! What a quantity of superfluous silk hast thou got about thee, girl! I could never teach the fools of this age, that the indigent world could be clothed out of the trimmings of the vain.

MISS HARDCASTLE: You know our agreement, sir. You allow me the morning to receive and pay visits, and to dress in my own manner; and in the evening, I put on my housewife's dress, to please you.

HARDCASTLE: Well, remember, I insist on the terms of our agreement; and, by-the-bye, I believe I shall have occasion to try your obedience this very evening.

MISS HARDCASTLE: I protest, sir, I don't comprehend your meaning.

HARDCASTLE: Then to be plain with you, Kate, I expect the young gentleman I have chosen to be your husband from town this very day. I have his father's letter, in which he informs me his son is set out, and that he intends to follow himself shortly after.

MISS HARDCASTLE: Indeed! I wish I had known something of this before. Bless me, how shall I behave? It's a thousand to one I shan't like him; our meeting will be so formal, and so like a thing of business, that I shall find no room for friendship or esteem.

HARDCASTLE: Depend upon it, child, I'll never control your choice; but Mr. Marlow, whom I have pitched upon, is the son of my old friend, Sir Charles Marlow, of whom you have heard me talk so often. The young gentleman has been bred a scholar, and is designed for an employment in the service of his country. I am told he's a man of an excellent understanding.

MISS HARDCASTLE: Is he?

HARDCASTLE: Very generous.

MISS HARDCASTLE: I believe I shall like him.

HARDCASTLE: Young and brave.

MISS HARDCASTLE: I'm sure I shall like him.

HARDCASTLE: And very handsome.

MISS HARDCASTLE: My dear papa, say no more [*Kissing his hand*], he's mine, I'll have him!

HARDCASTLE: And, to crown all, Kate, he's one of the most bashful and reserved young fellows in all the world.

MISS HARDCASTLE: Eh! you have frozen me to death again. That word reserved has undone all the rest of his accomplishments. A reserved lover, it is said, always makes a suspicious husband.

HARDCASTLE: On the contrary, modesty seldom resides in a breast that is not enriched with nobler virtues. It was the very feature in his character that first struck me.

MISS HARDCASTLE: He must have more striking features to catch me, I promise you. However, if he be so young, so handsome, and so everything, as you mention, I believe he'll do still. I think I'll have him.

HARDCASTLE: Ay, Kate, but there is still an obstacle. It is more than an even wager, he may not have *you.*

MISS HARDCASTLE: My dear papa, why will you mortify one so?—Well, if he refuses, instead of breaking my heart at his indifference, I'll only break my glass for its flattery. Set my cap to some newer fashion, and look out for some less difficult admirer.

HARDCASTLE: Bravely resolved! In the meantime I'll go prepare the servants for his reception; as we seldom see company, they want as much training as a company of recruits the first day's muster.   [Exit]

Miss Hardcastle *sola.*

MISS HARDCASTLE: Lud, this news of papa's puts me all in a flutter. Young, handsome; these he put last; but I put them foremost. Sensible, good-natur'd; I like all that. But then reserved, and sheepish, that's much against him. Yet can't he be cured of his timidity, by being taught to be proud of his wife. Yes, and can't I— But I vow I'm disposing of the husband before I have secured the lover!

Enter Miss Neville.

MISS HARDCASTLE: I'm glad you're come, Neville, my dear. Tell me, Constance, how do I look this evening? Is there anything whimsical about me? Is it one of my well-looking days, child? Am I in face to-day?

MISS NEVILLE: Perfectly, my dear. Yet, now I look again—bless me!—sure no accident has happened among the canary birds or the goldfishes? Has your brother or the cat been meddling? Or has the last novel been too moving?

MISS HARDCASTLE: No; nothing of all this. I have been threatened—I can scarce get it out—I have been threatened with a lover!

MISS NEVILLE: And his name——

MISS HARDCASTLE: Is Marlow.

MISS NEVILLE: Indeed!

MISS HARDCASTLE: The son of Sir Charles Marlow.

MISS NEVILLE: As I live, the most intimate friend of Mr. Hastings, *my* admirer. They are never asunder. I believe you must have seen him when we lived in town.

MISS HARDCASTLE: Never.

MISS NEVILLE: He's a very singular character, I assure you. Among women of reputation and virtue, he is the modestest man alive: but his acquaintance give him a very different character among creatures of another stamp: you understand me?

MISS HARDCASTLE: An odd character, indeed! I shall never be able to manage him. What shall I do? Pshaw, think no more of him, but trust to occurrences for success. But how goes on your own affair, my dear? Has my mother been courting you for my brother Tony, as usual?

MISS NEVILLE: I have just come from one of our agreeable *tête-à-têtes.* She has been saying a hundred tender things, and setting off her pretty monster as the very pink of perfection.

MISS HARDCASTLE: And her partiality is such, that she actually thinks him so. A fortune like yours is no small temptation. Besides, as she has the sole management of it, I'm not surprised to see her unwilling to let it go out of the family.

MISS NEVILLE: A fortune like mine, which chiefly consists in jewels, is no such mighty temptation. But, at any rate, if my dear Hastings be but constant, I make no doubt to be too hard for her at last. However, I let her suppose that I am in love with her son, and she never once dreams that my affections are fixed upon another.

MISS HARDCASTLE: My good brother holds out stoutly. I could almost love him for hating you so.

MISS NEVILLE: It is a good-natur'd creature at bottom, and I'm sure would wish to see me married to anybody but himself. But my aunt's bell rings for our afternoon's walk through the improvements. *Allons.* Courage is necessary, as our affairs are critical.

MISS HARDCASTLE: Would it were bed-time and all were well.   [Exeunt]

SCENE: *An Alehouse Room. Several shabby fellows, with punch and tobacco.* Tony *at the head of the table, a little higher than the rest: a mallet in his hand.*

OMNES: Hurrea, hurrea, hurrea, bravo!

FIRST FELLOW: Now, gentlemen, silence for a song. The 'Squire is going to knock himself down for a song.

OMNES: Ay, a song, a song.

TONY: Then I'll sing you, gentlemen, a song I made upon this ale-house, the Three Pigeons.

SONG

Let school-masters puzzle their brain,
    With grammar, and nonsense, and learning;
Good liquor, I stoutly maintain,
    Gives *genus* a better discerning,
Let them brag of their Heathenish Gods,
    Their Lethes, their Styxes, and Stygians;
Their Quis, and their Quæs, and their Quods,
    They're all but a parcel of Pigeons.
            Toroddle, toroddle, toroll!

When Methodist preachers come down,
    A-preaching that drinking is sinful,
I'll wager the rascals a crown,
    They always preach best with a skinful.
But when you come down with your pence,
    For a slice of their scurvy religion,
I'll leave it to all men of sense,
    But you, my good friend, are the pigeon.
            Toroddle, toroddle, toroll!

Then come, put the jorum about,
    And let us be merry and clever,
Our hearts and our liquors are stout,
    Here's the Three Jolly Pigeons for ever.

Let some cry up woodcock or hare,
  Your bustards, your ducks, and your widgeons:
But of all the birds in the air,
  Here's a health to the Three Jolly Pigeons.
                    Toroddle, toroddle, toroll!

OMNES: Bravo, bravo!

FIRST FELLOW: The 'Squire has got spunk in him.

SECOND FELLOW: I loves to hear him sing, bekeays he
never gives us nothing that's *low*.

THIRD FELLOW: O damn anything that's *low*, I cannot bear it!

FOURTH FELLOW: The genteel thing is the genteel
thing at any time. If so be that a gentleman bees
in a concatenation accordingly.

THIRD FELLOW: I like the maxum of it, Master Muggins. What, though I am obligated to dance a
bear, a man may be a gentleman for all that. May
this be my poison if my bear ever dances but to the
very genteelest of tunes. Water Parted, or the
minuet in Ariadne.

SECOND FELLOW: What a pity it is the 'Squire is not
come to his own. It would be well for all the pub-
licans within ten miles round of him.

TONY: Ecod, and so it would, Master Slang. I'd then
show what it was to keep choice of company.

SECOND FELLOW: O, he takes after his own father for
that. To be sure, old 'Squire Lumpkin was the
finest gentleman I ever set my eyes on. For winding
the straight horn, or beating a thicket for a hare,
or a wench, he never had his fellow. It was a saying
in the place, that he kept the best horses, dogs,
and girls in the whole county.

TONY: Ecod, and when I'm of age I'll be no bastard,
I promise you. I have been thinking of Bet
Bouncer and the miller's grey mare to begin with.
But come, my boys, drink about and be merry, for
you pay no reckoning. Well, Stingo, what's the
matter?

Enter Landlord.

LANDLORD: There be two gentlemen in a post-chaise
at the door. They have lost their way upo' the
forest; and they are talking something about Mr.
Hardcastle.

TONY: As sure as can be, one of them must be the
gentleman that's coming down to court my sister.
Do they seem to be Londoners?

LANDLORD: I believe they may. They look woundily
like Frenchmen.

TONY: Then desire them to step this way, and I'll set
them right in a twinkling. [*Exit* Landlord] Gentlemen, as they mayn't be good enough company for
you, step down for a moment, and I'll be with you
in the squeezing of a lemon.   [*Exeunt Mob*]

Tony *solus.*

TONY: Father-in-law has been calling me whelp, and
hound, this half year. Now, if I pleased, I could be

so revenged upon the old grumbletonian. But then
I'm afraid—afraid of what? I shall soon be worth
fifteen hundred a year, and let him frighten me
out of *that* if he can!

Enter Landlord, *conducting* Marlow *and* Hastings.

MARLOW: What a tedious uncomfortable day have
we had of it! We were told it was but forty miles
across the country, and we have come above three-
score!

HASTINGS: And all, Marlow, from that unaccountable
reserve of yours, that would not let us enquire
more frequently on the way.

MARLOW: I own, Hastings, I am unwilling to lay
myself under an obligation to every one I meet;
and often stand the chance of an unmannerly answer.

HASTINGS: At present, however, we are not likely to
receive any answer.

TONY: No offence, gentlemen. But I'm told you have
been enquiring for one Mr. Hardcastle, in these
parts. Do you know what part of the country you
are in?

HASTINGS: Not in the least, sir, but should thank you
for information.

TONY: Nor the way you came?

HASTINGS: No, sir, but if you can inform us——

TONY: Why, gentlemen, if you know neither the
road you are going, nor where you are, nor the
road you came, the first thing I have to inform is,
that—you have lost your way.

MARLOW: We wanted no ghost to tell us that.

TONY: Pray, gentlemen, may I be so bold as to ask
the place from whence you came?

MARLOW: That's not necessary towards directing us
where we are to go.

TONY: No offence; but question for question is all
fair, you know. Pray, gentlemen, is not this same
Hardcastle a cross-grained, old-fashioned, whimsical fellow with an ugly face; a daughter, and a
pretty son?

HASTINGS: We have not seen the gentleman, but he
has the family you mention.

TONY: The daughter, a tall, trapesing, trolloping, talkative maypole—— The son, a pretty, well-bred,
agreeable youth, that everybody is fond of!

MARLOW: Our information differs in this. The daughter is said to be well-bred and beautiful; the son,
an awkward booby, reared up and spoiled at his
mother's apron-string.

TONY: He-he-hem—then, gentlemen, all I have to
tell you is, that you won't reach Mr. Hardcastle's
house this night, I believe.

HASTINGS: Unfortunate!

TONY: It's a damned long, dark, boggy, dirty, dangerous way. Stingo, tell the gentlemen the way to Mr.
Hardcastle's. [*Winking upon the* Landlord] Mr.
Hardcastle's of Quagmire Marsh, you understand
me.

LANDLORD: Master Hardcastle's! Lack-a-daisy, my masters, you're come a deadly deal wrong! When you came to the bottom of the hill, you should have crossed down Squash Lane.

MARLOW: Cross down Squash Lane!

LANDLORD: Then you were to keep straight forward, until you came to four roads.

MARLOW: Come to where four roads meet!

TONY: Ay, but you must be sure to take only one of them.

MARLOW: O, sir, you're facetious!

TONY: Then, keeping to the right, you are to go sideways till you come upon Crack-skull common: there you must look sharp for the track of the wheel, and go forward, till you come to farmer Murrain's barn. Coming to the farmer's barn, you are to turn to the right, and then to the left, and then to the right about again, till you find out the old mill——

MARLOW: Zounds, man! we could as soon find out the longitude!

HASTINGS: What's to be done, Marlow?

MARLOW: This house promises but a poor reception, though, perhaps, the landlord can accommodate us.

LANDLORD: Alack, master, we have but one spare bed in the whole house.

TONY: And to my knowledge, that's taken up by three lodgers already. [*After a pause, in which the rest seem disconcerted*] I have hit it. Don't you think, Stingo, our landlady could accommodate the gentlemen by the fire-side, with——three chairs and a bolster?

HASTINGS: I hate sleeping by the fire-side.

MARLOW: And I detest your three chairs and a bolster.

TONY: You do, do you?—then let me see—what—if you go on a mile further, to the Buck's Head; the old Buck's Head on the hill, one of the best inns in the whole country?

HASTINGS: Oh, oh! so we have escaped an adventure for this night, however.

LANDLORD: [*Apart to Tony*] Sure, you ben't sending them to your father's as an inn, be you?

TONY: Mum, you fool, you. Let *them* find that out. [*To them*] You have only to keep on straight forward, till you come to a large old house by the roadside. You'll see a pair of large horns over the door. That's the sign. Drive up the yard, and call stoutly about you.

HASTINGS: Sir, we are obliged to you. The servants can't miss the way?

TONY: No, no: But I tell you though, the landlord is rich, and going to leave off business; so he wants to be thought a gentleman, saving your presence, he! he! he! He'll be for giving you his company, and, ecod, if you mind him, he'll persuade you that his mother was an alderman, and his aunt a justice of the peace!

LANDLORD: A troublesome old blade, to be sure; but 'a keeps as good wines and beds as any in the whole country.

MARLOW: Well, if he supplies us with these, we shall want no further connection. We are to turn to the right, did you say?

TONY: No, no; straight forward. I'll just step myself, and show you a piece of the way. [*To the* Landlord] Mum.

LANDLORD: Ah, bless your heart, for a sweet, pleasant ——damned mischievous son of a whore. [*Exeunt*]

Act II

SCENE: *An old-fashioned House*

Enter Hardcastle *followed by three or four awkward* Servants.

HARDCASTLE: Well, I hope you're perfect in the table exercise I have been teaching you these three days. You all know your posts and your places, and can show that you have been used to good company, without ever stirring from home.

OMNES: Ay, ay.

HARDCASTLE: When company comes, you are not to pop out and stare, and then run in again, like frightened rabbits in a warren.

OMNES: No, no.

HARDCASTLE: You, Diggory, whom I have taken from the barn are to make a show at the side-table; and you, Roger, whom I have advanced from the plough, are to place yourself behind *my* chair. But you're not to stand so, with your hands in your pockets. Take your hands from your pockets, Roger; and from your head, you blockhead, you. See how Diggory carries his hands. They're a little too stiff, indeed, but that's no great matter.

DIGGORY: Ay, mind how I hold them. I learned to hold my hands this way, when I was upon drill for the militia. And so being upon drill——

HARDCASTLE: You must not be so talkative, Diggory. You must be all attention to the guests. You must hear us talk, and not think of talking; you must see us drink and not think of drinking; you must see us eat and not think of eating.

DIGGORY: By the laws, your worship, that's perfectly unpossible. Whenever Diggory sees yeating going forward, ecod, he's always wishing for a mouthful himself.

HARDCASTLE: Blockhead! Is not a bellyful in the kitchen as good as a bellyful in the parlour? Stay your stomach with that reflection.

DIGGORY: Ecod, I thank your worship, I'll make a shift to stay my stomach with a slice of cold beef in the pantry.

HARDCASTLE: Diggory, you are too talkative. Then, if I happen to say a good thing, or tell a good story at table, you must not all burst out a-laughing, as if you made part of the company.

DIGGORY: Then, ecod, your worship must not tell the story of Ould Grouse in the gun-room: I can't help laughing at that—he! he! he!—for the soul of me! We have laughed at that these twenty years—ha! ha! ha!

HARDCASTLE: Ha! ha! ha! The story is a good one. Well, honest Diggory, you may laugh at that—but still remember to be attentive. Suppose one of the company should call for a glass of wine, how will you behave? A glass of wine, sir, if you please [*To* Diggory]—Eh, why don't you move?

DIGGORY: Ecod, your worship, I never have courage till I see the eatables and drinkables brought upo' the table, and then I'm as bauld as a lion.

HARDCASTLE: What, will nobody move?

FIRST SERVANT: I'm not to leave this pleace.

SECOND SERVANT: I'm sure it's no pleace of mine.

THIRD SERVANT: Nor mine for sartain.

DIGGORY: Wauns, and I'm sure it canna be mine.

HARDCASTLE: You numskulls! and so while, like your betters, you are quarrelling for places, the guests must be starved. O, you dunces! I find I must begin all over again.—But don't I hear a coach drive into the yard? To your posts, you blockheads! I'll go in the meantime and give my old friend's son a hearty reception at the gate.   [*Exit* Hardcastle]

DIGGORY: By the elevens, my pleace is gone quite out of my head!

ROGER: I know that my pleace is to be everywhere!

FIRST SERVANT: Where the devil is mine?

SECOND SERVANT: My pleace is to be nowhere at all; and so I ze go about my business!

[*Exeunt* Servants, *running about as if frighted, different ways*]

Enter Servants *with Candles, showing in* Marlow *and* Hastings.

SERVANT: Welcome, gentlemen, very welcome. This way.

HASTINGS: After the disappointments of the day, welcome once more, Charles, to the comforts of a clean room and a good fire. Upon my word, a very well-looking house; antique but creditable.

MARLOW: The usual fate of a large mansion. Having first ruined the master by good housekeeping, it at last comes to levy contributions as an inn.

HASTINGS: As you say, we passengers are to be taxed to pay all these fineries. I have often seen a good sideboard, or a marble chimney-piece, though not actually put in the bill, inflame a reckoning confoundedly.

MARLOW: Travellers, George, must pay in all places. The only difference is, that in good inns, you pay dearly for luxuries; in bad inns, you are fleeced and starved.

HASTINGS: You have lived pretty much among them. In truth, I have been often surprised, that you who have seen so much of the world, with your natural good sense, and your many opportunities, could never yet acquire a requisite share of assurance.

MARLOW: The Englishman's malady. But tell me, George, where could I have learned that assurance you talk of? My life has been chiefly spent in a college, or an inn, in seclusion from that lovely part of the creation that chiefly teach men confidence. I don't know that I was ever familiarly acquainted with a single modest woman—except my mother—but among females of another class, you know—

HASTINGS: Ay, among them you are impudent enough of all conscience!

MARLOW: They are of *us*, you know.

HASTINGS: But in the company of women of reputation I never saw such an idiot, such a trembler; you look for all the world as if you wanted an opportunity of stealing out of the room.

MARLOW: Why, man, that's because I *do* want to steal out of the room. Faith, I have often formed a resolution to break the ice, and rattle away at any rate. But I don't know how, a single glance from a pair of fine eyes has totally overset my resolution. An impudent fellow may counterfeit modesty, but I'll be hanged if a modest man can ever counterfeit impudence.

HASTINGS: If you could but say half the fine things to them that I have heard you lavish upon the barmaid of an inn, or even a college bedmaker—

MARLOW: Why, George, I can't say fine things to them. They freeze, they petrify me. They may talk of a comet, or a burning mountain, or some such bagatelle. But to me, a modest woman, dressed out in all her finery, is the most tremendous object of the whole creation.

HASTINGS: Ha! ha! ha! At this rate, man, how can you ever expect to marry!

MARLOW: Never, unless, as among kings and princes, my bride were to be courted by proxy. If, indeed, like an Eastern bridegroom, one were to be introduced to a wife he never saw before, it might be endured. But to go through all the terrors of a formal courtship, together with the episode of aunts, grandmothers and cousins, and at last to blurt out the broad staring question of, *madam, will you marry me?* No, no, that's a strain much above me, I assure you!

HASTINGS: I pity you. But how do you intend behaving to the lady you are come down to visit at the request of your father?

MARLOW: As I behave to all other ladies. Bow very low. Answer yes, or no, to all her demands—But for the rest, I don't think I shall venture to look in her face, till I see my father's again.

HASTINGS: I'm surprised that one who is so warm a friend can be so cool a lover.

MARLOW: To be explicit, my dear Hastings, my chief inducement down was to be instrumental in forwarding your happiness, not my own. Miss Neville loves you, the family don't know you, as my friend you are sure of a reception, and let honour do the rest.

HASTINGS: My dear Marlow! But I'll suppress the emotion. Were I a wretch, meanly seeking to carry off a fortune, you should be the last man in the world I would apply to for assistance. But Miss Neville's person is all I ask, and that is mine, both from her deceased father's consent and her own inclination.

MARLOW: Happy man! You have talents and art to captivate any woman. I'm doomed to adore the sex, and yet to converse with the only part of it I despise. This stammer in my address, and this awkward prepossessing visage of mine, can never permit me to soar above the reach of a milliner's apprentice, or one of the duchesses of Drury Lane. Pshaw! this fellow here to interrupt us.

Enter Hardcastle.

HARDCASTLE: Gentlemen, once more you are heartily welcome. Which is Mr. Marlow? Sir, you're heartily welcome. It's not my way, you see, to receive my friends with my back to the fire. I like to give them a hearty reception in the old style at my gate. I like to see their horses and trunks taken care of.

MARLOW: [*Aside*] He has got our names from the servants already. [*To him*] We approve your caution and hospitality, sir. [*To Hastings*] I have been thinking, George, of changing our travelling dresses in the morning. I am grown confoundedly ashamed of mine.

HARDCASTLE: I beg, Mr. Marlow, you'll use no ceremony in this house.

HASTINGS: I fancy, George, you're right: the first blow is half the battle. I intend opening the campaign with the white and gold.

HARDCASTLE: Mr. Marlow—Mr. Hastings—gentlemen—pray be under no constraint in this house. This is Liberty Hall, gentlemen. You may do just as you please here.

MARLOW: Yet, George if we open the campaign too fiercely at first, we may want ammunition before it is over. I think to reserve the embroidery to secure a retreat.

HARDCASTLE: Your talking of a retreat, Mr. Marlow, puts me in mind of the Duke of Marlborough, when we went to besiege Denain. He first summoned the garrison——

MARLOW: Don't you think the *ventre d'or* waistcoat will do with the plain brown.

HARDCASTLE: He first summoned the garrison, which might consist of about five thousand men——

HASTINGS: I think not: brown and yellow mix but very poorly.

HARDCASTLE: I say, gentlemen, as I was telling you, he summoned the garrison, which might consist of about five thousand men——

MARLOW: The girls like finery.

HARDCASTLE: Which might consist of about five thousand men, well appointed with stores, ammunition, and other implements of war. "Now," says the Duke of Marlborough to George Brooks, that stood next to him—you must have heard of George Brooks; "I'll pawn my Dukedom," says he, "but I take that garrison without spilling a drop of blood!" So——

MARLOW: What, my good friend, if you gave us a glass of punch in the meantime, it would help us to carry on the siege with vigour.

HARDCASTLE: Punch, sir!——[*Aside*] This is the most unaccountable kind of modesty I ever met with!

MARLOW: Yes, sir, punch! A glass of warm punch, after our journey, will be comfortable. This is Liberty Hall, you know.

HARDCASTLE: Here's punch, sir.

MARLOW: [*Aside*] So this fellow, in his Liberty Hall, will only let us have just what he pleases.

HARDCASTLE: [*Taking the cup*] I hope you'll find it to your mind. I have prepared it with my own hands, and I believe you'll own the ingredients are tolerable. Will you be so good as to pledge me, sir? Here, Mr. Marlow, here is our better acquaintance!
[*Drinks*]

MARLOW: [*Aside*] A very impudent fellow this! but he's a character, and I'll humour him a little. Sir, my service to you.   [*Drinks*]

HASTINGS: [*Aside*] I see this fellow wants to give us his company, and forgets that he's an innkeeper, before he has learned to be a gentleman.

MARLOW: From the excellence of your cup, my old friend, I suppose you have a good deal of business in this part of the country. Warm work, now and then, at elections, I suppose?

HARDCASTLE: No, sir, I have long given that work over. Since our betters have hit upon the expedient of electing each other, there's no business *for us that sell ale.*

HASTINGS: So, then you have no turn for politics, I find.

HARDCASTLE: Not in the least. There was a time, indeed, I fretted myself about the mistakes of government, like other people; but finding myself every day grow more angry, and the government growing no better, I left it to mend itself. Since that, I no more trouble my head about *Heyder Ally, Ally Cawn,* than about *Ally Croker.* Sir, my service to you.

HASTINGS: So that, with eating above stairs, and drinking below, with receiving your friends within, and amusing them without, you lead a good pleasant bustling life of it.

HARDCASTLE: I do stir about a great deal, that's certain. Half the differences of the parish are adjusted in this very parlour.

MARLOW: [*After drinking*] And you have an argument in your cup, old gentleman, better than any in Westminster Hall.

HARDCASTLE: Ay, young gentleman, that, and a little philosophy.

MARLOW: [*Aside*] Well, this is the first time I ever heard of an innkeeper's philosophy.

HASTINGS: So then, like an experienced general, you attack them on every quarter. If you find their reason manageable, you attack it with your philosophy; if you find they have no reason, you attack them with this. Here's your health, my philosopher.   [*Drinks*]

HARDCASTLE: Good, very good, thank you; ha! ha! Your generalship puts me in mind of Prince Eugene, when he fought the Turks at the battle of Belgrade. You shall hear.

MARLOW: Instead of the battle of Belgrade, I believe it's almost time to talk about supper. What has your philosophy got in the house for supper?

HARDCASTLE: For supper, sir!——[*Aside*] Was ever such a request to a man in his own house!

MARLOW: Yes, sir, supper, sir; I begin to feel an appetite. I shall make devilish work to-night in the larder, I promise you.

HARDCASTLE: [*Aside*] Such a brazen dog sure never my eyes beheld. [*To him*] Why, really, sir, as for supper I can't well tell. My Dorothy, and the cook maid, settle these things between them. I leave these kind of things entirely to them.

MARLOW: You do, do you?

HARDCASTLE: Entirely. By-the-bye, I believe they are in actual consultation upon what's for supper this moment in the kitchen.

MARLOW: Then I beg they'll admit *me* as one of their privy council. It's a way I have got. When I travel, I always choose to regulate my own supper. Let the cook be called. No offence, I hope, sir.

HARDCASTLE: O, no, sir, none in the least; yet, I don't know how: our Bridget, the cook maid, is not very communicative upon these occasions. Should we send for her, she might scold us all out of the house.

HASTINGS: Let's see your list of the larder, then. I ask it as a favour. I always match my appetite to my bill of fare.

MARLOW: [*To Hardcastle, who looks at them with surprise*] Sir, he's very right, and it's my way, too.

HARDCASTLE: Sir, you have a right to command here. Here, Roger, bring us the bill of fare for to-night's supper. I believe it's drawn out. Your manner, Mr. Hastings, puts me in mind of my uncle, Colonel Wallop. It was a saying of his, that no man was sure of his supper till he had eaten it.

HASTING: [*Aside*] All upon the high ropes! His uncle a colonel! We shall soon hear of his mother being a justice of peace. But let's hear the bill of fare.

MARLOW: [*Perusing*] What's here? For the first course; for the second course; for the dessert. The devil, sir, do you think we have brought down the whole Joiners' Company, or the Corporation of Bedford, to eat up such a supper? Two or three little things, clean and comfortable, will do.

HASTINGS: But let's hear it.

MARLOW: [*Reading*] For the first course at the top, a pig, and prune sauce.

HASTINGS: Damn your pig, I say!

MARLOW: And damn your prune sauce, say I!

HARDCASTLE: And yet, gentlemen, to men that are hungry, pig, with prune sauce, is very good eating.

MARLOW: At the bottom, a calf's tongue and brains.

HASTINGS: Let your brains be knocked out, my good sir; I don't like them.

MARLOW: Or you may clap them on a plate by themselves; I do.

HARDCASTLE: [*Aside*] Their impudence confounds me. [*To them*] Gentlemen, you are my guests, make what alterations you please. Is there anything else you wish to retrench or alter, gentlemen?

MARLOW: Item. A pork pie, a boiled rabbit and sausages, a florentine, a shaking pudding, and a dish of tiff—taff—taffety cream!

HASTINGS: Confound your made dishes, I shall be as much at a loss in this house as at a green and yellow dinner at the French ambassador's table. I'm for plain eating.

HARDCASTLE: I'm sorry, gentlemen, that I have nothing you like, but if there be anything you have a particular fancy to——

MARLOW: Why, really, sir, your bill of fare is so exquisite, that any one part of it is full as good as another. Send us what you please. So much for supper. And now to see that our beds are aired, and properly taken care of.

HARDCASTLE: I entreat you'll leave all that to me. You shall not stir a step.

MARLOW: Leave that to you! I protest, sir, you must excuse me, I always look to these things myself.

HARDCASTLE: I must insist, sir, you'll make yourself easy on that head.

MARLOW: You see I'm resolved on it.—[*Aside*] A very troublesome fellow this, as ever I met with.

HARDCASTLE: Well, sir, I'm resolved at least to attend you.—[*Aside*] This may be modern modesty, but I never saw anything look so like old-fashioned impudence.   [*Exeunt* Marlow *and* Hardcastle]

Hastings solus.

HASTINGS: So I find this fellow's civilities begin to grow troublesome. But who can be angry at those assiduities which are meant to please him! Miss Neville, by all that's happy!

Enter Miss Neville.

MISS NEVILLE: My dear Hastings! To what unexpected good fortune? to what accident am I to ascribe this happy meeting?

HASTINGS: Rather let me ask the same question, as I could never have hoped to meet my dearest Constance at an inn.

MISS NEVILLE: An inn! sure you mistake! my aunt, my guardian, lives here. What could induce you to think this house an inn?

HASTINGS: My friend, Mr. Marlow, with whom I came down, and I, have been sent here as to an inn, I assure you. A young fellow whom we accidentally met at a house hard by directed us hither.

MISS NEVILLE: Certainly it must be one of my hopeful cousin's tricks, of whom you have heard me talk so often, ha! ha! ha! ha!

HASTINGS: He whom your aunt intends for you? He of whom I have such just apprehensions?

MISS NEVILLE: You have nothing to fear from him, I assure you. You'd adore him if you knew how heartily he despises me. My aunt knows it too, and has undertaken to court me for him, and actually begins to think she has made a conquest.

HASTINGS: Thou dear dissembler! You must know, my Constance, I have just seized this happy opportunity of my friend's visit here to get admittance into the family. The horses that carried us down are now fatigued with their journey, but they'll soon be refreshed; and then if my dearest girl will trust in her faithful Hastings, we shall soon be landed in France, where even among slaves the laws of marriage are respected.

MISS NEVILLE: I have often told you, that though ready to obey you, I yet should leave my little fortune behind with reluctance. The greatest part of it was left me by my uncle, the India Director, and chiefly consists in jewels. I have been for some time persuading my aunt to let me wear them. I fancy I'm very near succeeding. The instant they are put into my possession you shall find me ready to make them and myself yours.

HASTINGS: Perish the baubles! Your person is all I desire. In the meantime, my friend Marlow must not be let into his mistake. I know the strange reserve of his temper is such, that if abruptly informed of it, he would instantly quit the house before our plan was ripe for execution.

MISS NEVILLE: But how shall we keep him in the deception? Miss Hardcastle is just returned from walking; what if we still continue to deceive him? —This, this way——   [They confer]

Enter Marlow.

MARLOW: The assiduities of these good people tease me beyond bearing. My host seems to think it ill manners to leave me alone, and so he claps not only himself, but his old-fashioned wife on my back. They talk of coming to sup with us, too; and then, I suppose, we are to run the gauntlet through all the rest of the family.—What have we got here?

HASTINGS: My dear Charles! Let me congratulate you!—The most fortunate accident!—Who do you think is just alighted?

MARLOW: Cannot guess.

HASTINGS: Our mistresses, boy, Miss Hardcastle and Miss Neville. Give me leave to introduce Miss Constance Neville to your acquaintance. Happening to dine in the neighbourhood, they called, on their return to take fresh horses, here. Miss Hardcastle has just stept into the next room, and will be back in an instant. Wasn't it lucky? eh!

MARLOW: [*Aside*] I have just been mortified enough of all conscience, and here comes something to complete my embarrassment.

HASTINGS: Well! but wasn't it the most fortunate thing in the world?

MARLOW: Oh! yes. Very fortunate—a most joyful encounter——But our dresses, George, you know, are in disorder——What if we should postpone the happiness till to-morrow?——To-morrow at her own house——It will be every bit as convenient——And rather more respectful——To-morrow let it be.   [*Offering to go*]

MISS NEVILLE: By no means, sir. Your ceremony will displease her. The disorder of your dress will shew the ardour of your impatience. Besides, she knows you are in the house, and will permit you to see her.

MARLOW: O! the devil! how shall I support it? Hem! hem! Hastings, you must not go. You are to assist me, you know. I shall be confoundedly ridiculous. Yet, hang it! I'll take courage. Hem!

HASTINGS: Pshaw, man! it's but the first plunge, and all's over. She's but a woman, you know.

MARLOW: And of all women, she that I dread most to encounter!

Enter Miss Hardcastle, *as returned from walking, a Bonnet, &c.*

HASTINGS: [*Introducing them*] Miss Hardcastle, Mr. Marlow, I'm proud of bringing two persons of such merit together, that only want to know, to esteem each other.

MISS HARDCASTLE: [*Aside*] Now, for meeting my modest gentleman with a demure face, and quite in his own manner. [*After a pause, in which he appears very uneasy and disconcerted*] I'm glad of your safe arrival, sir——I'm told you had some accidents by the way.

MARLOW: Only a few, madam. Yes, we had some. Yes, madam, a good many accidents, but should be sorry—madam—or rather glad of any accidents —that are so agreeably concluded. Hem!

HASTING: [*To him*] You never spoke better in your whole life. Keep it up, and I'll insure you the victory.

MISS HARDCASTLE: I'm afraid you flatter, sir. You that have seen so much of the finest company can find little entertainment in an obscure corner of the country.

MARLOW: [*Gathering courage*] I have lived, indeed, in the world, madam; but I have kept very little company. I have been but an observer upon life, madam, while others were enjoying it.

MISS NEVILLE: But that, I am told, is the way to enjoy it at last.

HASTINGS: [*To him*] Cicero never spoke better. Once more, and you are confirmed in assurance for ever.

MARLOW: [*To him*] Hem! Stand by me, then, and when I'm down, throw in a word or two to set me up again.

MISS HARDCASTLE: An observer, like you, upon life, were, I fear, disagreeably employed, since you must have had much more to censure than to approve.

MARLOW: Pardon me, madam. I was always willing to be amused. The folly of most people is rather an object of mirth than uneasiness.

HASTINGS: [*To him*] Bravo, bravo. Never spoke so well in your whole life. Well, Miss Hardcastle, I see that you and Mr. Marlow are going to be very good company. I believe our being here will but embarrass the interview.

MARLOW: Not in the least, Mr. Hastings. We like your company of all things. [*To him*] Zounds! George, sure you won't go? How can you leave us?

HASTINGS: Our presence will but spoil conversation, so we'll retire to the next room. [*To him*] You don't consider, man, that we are to manage a little *tête-à-tête* of our own.   [*Exeunt*]

MISS HARDCASTLE: [*After a pause*] But you have not been wholly an observer, I presume, sir. The ladies, I should hope, have employed some part of your addresses.

MARLOW: [*Relapsing into timidity*] Pardon me, madam, I—I—I—as yet have studied—only—to—deserve them.

MISS HARDCASTLE: And that some say is the very worst way to obtain them.

MARLOW: Perhaps so, madam. But I love to converse only with the more grave and sensible part of the sex.——But I'm afraid I grow tiresome.

MISS HARDCASTLE: Not at all sir; there is nothing I like so much as grave conversation myself: I could hear it for ever. Indeed, I have often been surprised how a man of *sentiment* could ever admire those light airy pleasures, where nothing reaches the heart.

MARLOW: It's—a disease—of the mind, madam.`In the variety of tastes there must be some who, wanting a relish for—um-a-um.

MISS HARDCASTLE: I understand you, sir. There must be some, who, wanting a relish for refined pleasures, pretend to despise what they are incapable of tasting.

MARLOW: My meaning, madam, but infinitely better expressed. And I can't help observing—a——

MISS HARDCASTLE: [*Aside*] Who could ever suppose this fellow impudent upon some occasions. [*To him*] You were going to observe, sir——

MARLOW: I was observing, madam——I protest, madam, I forget what I was going to observe.

MISS HARDCASTLE: [*Aside*] I vow and so do I. [*To him*] You were observing, sir, that in this age of hypocrisy—something about hypocrisy, sir.

MARLOW: Yes, madam. In this age of hypocrisy, there are few who upon strict enquiry do not—a—a—a——

MISS HARDCASTLE: I understand you perfectly, sir.

MARLOW: [*Aside*] Egad! and that's more than I do myself!

MISS HARDCASTLE: You mean that in this hypocritical age there are few that do not condemn in public what they practise in private, and think they pay every debt to virtue when they praise it.

MARLOW: True, madam; those who have most virtue in their mouths, have least of it in their bosoms. But I'm sure I tire you, madam.

MISS HARDCASTLE: Not in the least, sir; there's something so agreeable and spirited in your manner, such life and force——pray, sir, go on.

MARLOW: Yes, madam. I was saying——that there are some occasions——when a total want of courage, madam, destroys all the——and puts us——upon a——a——a——

MISS HARDCASTLE: I agree with you entirely, a want of courage upon some occasions assumes the appearance of ignorance, and betrays us when we most want to excel. I beg you'll proceed.

MARLOW: Yes, Madam. Morally speaking, madam——but I see Miss Neville expecting us in the next room. I would not intrude for the world.

MISS HARDCASTLE: I protest, sir, I never was more agreeably entertained in all my life. Pray go on.

MARLOW: Yes, Madam. I was——But she beckons us to join her. Madam, shall I do myself the honour to attend you?

MISS HARDCASTLE: Well then, I'll follow.

MARLOW: [*Aside*] This pretty smooth dialogue has done for me.   [*Exit*]

Miss Hardcastle *sola*.

MISS HARDCASTLE: Ha! ha! ha! Was there ever such a sober sentimental interview? I'm certain he scarce looked in my face the whole time. Yet the fellow, but for his unaccountable bashfulness, is pretty well, too. He has good sense, but then so buried in his fears, that it fatigues one more than ignorance. If I could teach him a little confidence, it would be doing somebody that I know of a piece of service. But who is that somebody?—that, faith, is a question I can scarce answer.   [*Exit*]

Enter Tony *and* Miss Neville, *followed by* Mrs. Hardcastle *and* Hastings.

TONY: What do you follow me for, cousin Con? I wonder you're not ashamed to be so very engaging.

MISS NEVILLE: I hope, cousin, one may speak to one's own relations, and not be to blame.

TONY: Ay, but I know what sort of a relation you want to make me, though; but it won't do. I tell you, cousin Con, it won't do, so I beg you'll keep your distance, I want no nearer relationship.

[*She follows coquetting him to the back scene*]

MRS. HARDCASTLE: Well! I vow, Mr. Hastings, you are

very entertaining. There's nothing in the world I love to talk of so much as London, and the fashions, though I was never there myself.

HASTINGS: Never there! You amaze me! From your air and manner, I concluded you had been bred all your life either at Ranelagh, St. James's, or Tower Wharf.

MRS. HARDCASTLE: O! sir, you're only pleased to say so. We country persons can have no manner at all. I'm in love with the town, and that serves to raise me above some of our neighbouring rustics; but who can have a manner, that has never seen the Pantheon, the Grotto Gardens, the Borough, and such places where the nobility chiefly resort? All I can do is to enjoy London at second-hand. I take care to know every *tête-à-tête* from the Scandalous Magazine, and have all the fashions as they come out, in a letter from the two Miss Rickets of Crooked Lane. Pray how do you like this head, Mr. Hastings?

HASTINGS: Extremely elegant and *degagée*, upon my word, madam. Your friseur is a Frenchman, I suppose?

MRS. HARDCASTLE: I protest, I dressed it myself from a print in the Ladies' Memorandum-book for the last year.

HASTINGS: Indeed. Such a head in a side-box, at the Play-house, would draw as many gazers as my Lady Mayoress at a City Ball.

MRS. HARDCASTLE: I vow, since inoculation began, there is no such thing to be seen as a plain woman; so one must dress a little particular or one may escape in the crowd.

HASTINGS: But that can never be your case, madam, in any dress! [*Bowing*]

MRS. HARDCASTLE: Yet, what signifies *my* dressing when I have such a piece of antiquity by my side as Mr. Hardcastle: all I can say will never argue down a single button from his clothes. I have often wanted him to throw off his great flaxen wig, and where he was bald, to plaster it over like my Lord Pately, with powder.

HASTINGS: You are right, madam; for, as among the ladies there are none ugly, so among the men there are none old.

MRS. HARDCASTLE: But what do you think his answer was? Why, with his usual Gothic vivacity, he said I only wanted him to throw off his wig to convert it into a *tête* for my own wearing!

HASTINGS: Intolerable! At your age you may wear what you please, and it must become you.

MRS. HARDCASTLE: Pray, Mr. Hastings, what do you take to be the most fashionable age about town?

HASTINGS: Some time ago forty was all the mode; but I'm told the ladies intend to bring up fifty for the ensuing winter.

MRS. HARDCASTLE: Seriously. Then I shall be too young for the fashion!

HASTINGS: No lady begins now to put on jewels till she's past forty. For instance, miss there, in a polite circle, would be considered as a child, as a mere maker of samplers.

MRS. HARDCASTLE: And yet Mrs. Niece thinks herself as much a woman, and is as fond of jewels as the oldest of us all.

HASTINGS: Your niece, is she? And that young gentleman, a brother of yours, I should presume?

MRS. HARDCASTLE: My son, sir. They are contracted to each other. Observe their little sports. They fall in and out ten times a day, as if they were man and wife already. [*To them*] Well, Tony, child, what soft things are you saying to your cousin Constance, this evening?

TONY: I have been saying no soft things; but that it's very hard to be followed about so. Ecod! I've not a place in the house now that's left to myself but the stable.

MRS. HARDCASTLE: Never mind him, Con, my dear. He's in another story behind your back.

MISS NEVILLE: There's something generous in my cousin's manner. He falls out before faces to be forgiven in private.

TONY: That's a damned confounded——crack.

MRS. HARDCASTLE: Ah! he's a sly one. Don't you think they're like each other about the mouth, Mr. Hastings? The Blenkinsop mouth to a T. They're of a size, too. Back to back, my pretties, that Mr. Hastings may see you. Come, Tony.

TONY: You had as good not make me, I tell you.
                                                    [*Measuring*]

MISS NEVILLE: O lud! he has almost cracked my head.

MRS. HARDCASTLE: O, the monster! For shame, Tony. You a man, and behave so!

TONY: If I'm a man, let me have my fortin. Ecod! I'll not be made a fool of no longer.

MRS. HARDCASTLE: Is this, ungrateful boy, all that I'm to get for the pains I have taken in your education? I that have rocked you in your cradle, and fed that pretty mouth with a spoon! Did not I work that waistcoat to make you genteel? Did not I prescribe for you every day, and weep while the receipt was operating?

TONY: Ecod! you had reason to weep, for you have been dosing me ever since I was born. I have gone through every receipt in the complete housewife ten times over; and you have thoughts of coursing me through *Quincy* next spring. But, ecod! I tell you, I'll not be made a fool of no longer.

MRS. HARDCASTLE: Wasn't it all for your good, viper? Wasn't it all for your good?

TONY: I wish you'd let me and my good alone, then. Snubbing this way when I'm in spirits. If I'm to have any good, let it come of itself; not to keep dinging it, dinging it into one so.

MRS. HARDCASTLE: That's false; I never see you when you're in spirits. No, Tony, you then go to the ale-house or kennel. I'm never to be delighted with your agreeable, wild notes, unfeeling monster!

TONY: Ecod! Mamma, your own notes are the wildest of the two.

MRS. HARDCASTLE: Was ever the like? But I see he wants to break my heart, I see he does.

HASTINGS: Dear Madam, permit me to lecture the young gentleman a little. I'm certain I can persuade him to his duty.

MRS. HARDCASTLE: Well! I must retire. Come, Constance, my love. You see, Mr. Hastings, the wretchedness of my situation. Was ever poor woman so plagued with a dear, sweet, pretty, provoking, undutiful boy.

[*Exeunt* Mrs. Hardcastle *and* Miss Neville]

TONY: [*Singing*] *There was a young man riding by, and fain would have his will. Rang do didlo dee.* Don't mind her. Let her cry. It's the comfort of her heart. I have seen her and sister cry over a book for an hour together, and they said, they liked the book the better the more it made them cry.

HASTINGS: Then you're no friend to the ladies, I find, my pretty young gentleman?

TONY: That's as I find 'um.

HASTINGS: Not to her of your mother's choosing, I dare answer! And yet she appears to me a pretty, well-tempered girl.

TONY: That's because you don't know her as well as I. Ecod! I know every inch about her; and there's not a more bitter cantankerous toad in all Christendom!

HASTINGS: [*Aside*] Pretty encouragement, this, for a lover.

TONY: I have seen her since the height of that. She has as many tricks as a hare in a thicket, or a colt the first day's breaking.

HASTINGS: To me she appears sensible and silent!

TONY: Ay, before company. But when she's with her playmates she's as loud as a hog in a gate.

HASTINGS: But there is a meek modesty about her that charms me.

TONY: Yes, but curb her never so little, she kicks up, and you're flung in a ditch.

HASTINGS: Well, but you must allow her a little beauty.—Yes, you must allow her some beauty.

TONY: Bandbox! She's all a made up thing, mun. Ah! could you but see Bet Bouncer of these parts, you might then talk of beauty. Ecod, she has two eyes as black as sloes, and cheeks as broad and red as a pulpit cushion. She'd make two of she.

HASTINGS: Well, what say you to a friend that would take this bitter bargain off your hands?

TONY: Anon.

HASTINGS: Would you thank him that would take Miss Neville, and leave you to happiness and your dear Betsy?

TONY: Ay; but where is there such a friend, for who would take *her*?

HASTINGS: I am he. If you but assist me, I'll engage to whip her off to France, and you shall never hear more of her.

TONY: Assist you! Ecod, I will, to the last drop of my blood. I'll clap a pair of horses to your chaise that shall trundle you off in a twinkling, and may be get you a part of her fortin besides, in jewels, that you little dream of.

HASTINGS: My dear 'Squire, this looks like a lad of spirit.

TONY: Come along then, and you shall see more of my spirit before you have done with me. [*Singing*]

> We are the boys
> That fears no noise
> Where the thundering cannons roar.
>
> [*Exeunt*]

Act III

Enter Hardcastle *solus.*

HARDCASTLE: What could my old friend Sir Charles mean by recommending his son as the modestest young man in town? To me he appears the most impudent piece of brass that ever spoke with a tongue. He has taken possession of the easy chair by the fireside already. He took off his boots in the parlour, and desired me to see them taken care of. I'm desirous to know how his impudence affects my daughter.—She will certainly be shocked at it.

Enter Miss Hardcastle *plainly dressed.*

HARDCASTLE: Well, my Kate, I see you have changed your dress as I bid you; and yet, I believe, there was no great occasion.

MISS HARDCASTLE: I find such a pleasure, sir, in obeying your commands, that I take care to observe them without ever debating their propriety.

HARDCASTLE: And yet, Kate, I sometimes give you some cause, particularly when I recommended my *modest* gentleman to you as a lover to-day.

MISS HARDCASTLE: You taught me to expect something extraordinary, and I find the original exceeds the description!

HARDCASTLE: I was never so surprised in my life! He has quite confounded all my faculties!

MISS HARDCASTLE: I never saw anything like it: And a man of the world, too!

HARDCASTLE: Ay, he learned it all abroad,—what a fool was I, to think a young man could learn modesty by travelling. He might as soon learn wit at a masquerade.

MISS HARDCASTLE: It seems all natural to him.

HARDCASTLE: A good deal assisted by bad company and a French dancing-master.

MISS HARDCASTLE: Sure, you mistake, papa! a French dancing-master could never have taught him that timid look,—that awkward address,—that bashful manner——

HARDCASTLE: Whose look? whose manner? child!

MISS HARDCASTLE: Mr. Marlow's: his *mauvaise honte*, his timidity struck me at the first sight.

HARDCASTLE: Then your first sight deceived you; for I think him one of the most brazen first sights that ever astonished my senses!

MISS HARDCASTLE: Sure, sir, you rally! I never saw anyone so modest.

HARDCASTLE: And can you be serious! I never saw such a bouncing swaggering puppy since I was born. Bully Dawson was but a fool to him.

MISS HARDCASTLE: Surprising! He met me with a respectful bow, a stammering voice, and a look fixed on the ground.

HARDCASTLE: He met me with a loud voice, a lordly air, and a familiarity that made my blood freeze again.

MISS HARDCASTLE: He treated me with diffidence and respect; censured the manners of the age; admired the prudence of girls that never laughed; tired me with apologies for being tiresome; then left the room with a bow, and, madam, I would not for the world detain you.

HARDCASTLE: He spoke to me as if he knew me all his life before. Asked twenty questions, and never waited for an answer. Interrupted my best remarks with some silly pun, and when I was in my best story of the Duke of Marlborough and Prince Eugene, he asked if I had not a good hand at making punch. Yes, Kate, he asked your father if he was a maker of punch!

MISS HARDCASTLE: One of us must certainly be mistaken.

HARDCASTLE: If he be what he has shown himself, I'm determined he shall never have my consent.

MISS HARDCASTLE: And if he be the sullen thing I take him, he shall never have mine.

HARDCASTLE: In one thing then we are agreed—to reject him.

MISS HARDCASTLE: Yes. But upon conditions. For if you should find him less impudent, and I more presuming; if you find him more respectful, and I more importunate—I don't know—the fellow is well enough for a man—Certainly we don't meet many such at a horse race in the country.

HARDCASTLE: If we should find him so——— But that's impossible. The first appearance has done my business. I'm seldom deceived in that.

MISS HARDCASTLE: And yet there may be many good qualities under that first appearance.

HARDCASTLE: Ay, when a girl finds a fellow's outside to her taste, she then sets about guessing the rest of his furniture. With her, a smooth face stands for good sense, and a genteel figure for every virtue.

MISS HARDCASTLE: I hope, sir, a conversation begun with a compliment to my good sense won't end with a sneer at my understanding?

HARDCASTLE: Pardon me, Kate. But if young Mr. Brazen can find the art of reconciling contradictions, he may please us both, perhaps.

MISS HARDCASTLE: And as one of us must be mistaken, what if we go to make further discoveries?

HARDCASTLE: Agreed. But depend on't I'm in the right.

MISS HARDCASTLE: And depend on't I'm not much in the wrong.   [Exeunt]

Enter Tony running in with a casket.

TONY: Ecod! I have got them. Here they are. My Cousin Con's necklaces, bobs and all. My mother shan't cheat the poor souls out of their fortin neither. O! my genus, is that you?

Enter Hastings.

HASTINGS: My dear friend, how have you managed with your mother? I hope you have amused her with pretending love for your cousin, and that you are willing to be reconciled at last? Our horses will be refreshed in a short time, and we shall soon be ready to set off.

TONY: And here's something to bear your charges by the way. [Giving the casket] Your sweetheart's jewels. Keep them, and hang those, I say, that would rob you of one of them!

HASTINGS: But how have you procured them from your mother?

TONY: Ask me no questions, and I'll tell you no fibs. I procured them by the rule of thumb. If I had not a key to every drawer in mother's bureau, how could I go to the alehouse so often as I do? An honest man may rob himself of his own at any time.

HASTINGS: Thousands do it every day. But to be plain with you; Miss Neville is endeavouring to procure them from her aunt this very instant. If she succeeds, it will be the most delicate way at least of obtaining them.

TONY: Well, keep them, till you know how it will be. But I know how it will be well enough, she'd as soon part with the only sound tooth in her head!

HASTINGS: But I dread the effects of her resentment, when she finds she has lost them.

TONY: Never you mind her resentment, leave me to manage that. I don't value her resentment the bounce of a cracker. Zounds! here they are! Morrice, Prance!   [Exit Hastings]

Tony, Mrs. Hardcastle, Miss Neville.

MRS. HARDCASTLE: Indeed, Constance, you amaze me. Such a girl as you want jewels? It will be time enough for jewels, my dear, twenty years hence, when your beauty begins to want repairs.

MISS NEVILLE: But what will repair beauty at forty, will certainly improve it at twenty, madam.

MRS. HARDCASTLE: Yours, my dear, can admit of none. That natural blush is beyond a thousand ornaments. Besides, child, jewels are quite out at present. Don't you see half the ladies of our acquaintance, my lady Killdaylight, and Mrs. Crump, and the rest of them, carry their jewels to town, and bring nothing but paste and marcasites back?

MISS NEVILLE: But who knows, madam, but somebody that shall be nameless would like me best with all my little finery about me?

MRS. HARDCASTLE: Consult your glass, my dear, and then see, if with such a pair of eyes, you want any better sparklers. What do you think, Tony, my dear, does your cousin Con want any jewels, in your eyes, to set off her beauty?

TONY: That's as thereafter may be.

MISS NEVILLE: My dear aunt, if you knew how it would oblige me.

MRS. HARDCASTLE: A parcel of old-fashioned rose and tablecut things. They would make you look like the court of King Solomon at a puppet-show. Besides, I believe I can't readily come at them. They may be missing, for aught I know to the contrary.

TONY: [Apart to Mrs. Hardcastle] Then why don't you tell her so at once, as she's so longing for them? Tell her they're lost. It's the only way to quiet her. Say they're lost, and call me to bear witness.

MRS. HARDCASTLE: [Apart to Tony] You know, my dear, I'm only keeping them for you. So if I say they're gone, you'll bear me witness, will you? He! he! he!

TONY: Never fear me. Ecod! I'll say I saw them taken out with my own eyes.

MISS NEVILLE: I desire them but for a day, madam. Just to be permitted to show them as relics, and then they may be locked up again.

MRS. HARDCASTLE: To be plain with you, my dear Constance, if I could find them, you should have them. They're missing, I assure you. Lost, for aught I know; but we must have patience wherever they are.

MISS NEVILLE: I'll not believe it; this is but a shallow pretence to deny me. I know they're too valuable to be so slightly kept, and as you are to answer for the loss.

MRS. HARDCASTLE: Don't be alarmed, Constance. If they be lost, I must restore an equivalent. But my son knows they are missing, and not to be found.

TONY: That I can bear witness to. They are missing, and not to be found, I'll take my oath on't!

MRS. HARDCASTLE: You must learn resignation, my dear; for though we lose our fortune, yet we should not lose our patience. See me, how calm I am!

MISS NEVILLE: Ay, people are generally calm at the misfortunes of others.

MRS. HARDCASTLE: Now, I wonder a girl of your good sense should waste a thought upon such trumpery. We shall soon find them; and, in the meantime, you shall make use of my garnets till your jewels be found.

MISS NEVILLE: I detest garnets!

MRS. HARDCASTLE: The most becoming things in the world to set off a clear complexion. You have often seen how well they look upon me. You *shall* have them.   [Exit]

MISS NEVILLE: I dislike them of all things. You shan't stir.—Was ever anything so provoking to mislay my own jewels, and force me to wear her trumpery?

TONY: Don't be a fool. If she gives you the garnets, take what you can get. The jewels are your own already. I have stolen them out of her bureau, and she does not know it. Fly to your spark, he'll tell you more of the matter. Leave me to manage *her*.

MISS NEVILLE: My dear cousin!

TONY: Vanish. She's here, and has missed them already. Zounds! how she fidgets and spits about like a Catharine wheel.

Enter Mrs. Hardcastle.

MRS. HARDCASTLE: Confusion! thieves! robbers! We are cheated, plundered, broke open, undone!

TONY: What's the matter, what's the matter, mamma? I hope nothing has happened to any of the good family!

MRS. HARDCASTLE: We are robbed. My bureau has been broke open, the jewels taken out, and I'm undone!

TONY: Oh! is that all? Ha! ha! ha! By the laws, I never saw it better acted in my life. Ecod, I thought you was ruined in earnest, ha, ha, ha!

MRS. HARDCASTLE: Why, boy, I *am* ruined in earnest. My bureau has been broke open, and all taken away.

TONY: Stick to that; ha, ha, ha! stick to that. I'll bear witness, you know, call me to bear witness.

MRS. HARDCASTLE: I tell you, Tony, by all that's precious, the jewels are gone, and I shall be ruined for ever.

TONY: Sure I know they're gone, and I am to say so.

MRS. HARDCASTLE: My dearest Tony, but hear me. They're gone, I say.

TONY: By the laws, mamma, you make me for to laugh, ha! ha! I know who took them well enough, ha! ha! ha!

MRS. HARDCASTLE: Was there ever such a blockhead, that can't tell the difference between jest and earnest. I tell you I'm not in jest, booby!

TONY: That's right, that's right: You must be in a bitter passion, and then nobody will suspect either of us. I'll bear witness that they are gone.

MRS. HARDCASTLE: Was there ever such a cross-grained brute, that won't hear me! Can you bear witness that you're no better than a fool? Was ever poor woman so beset with fools on one hand, and thieves on the other?

TONY: I can bear witness to that.

MRS. HARDCASTLE: Bear witness again, you blockhead, you, and I'll turn you out of the room directly. My poor niece, what will become of *her*? Do you laugh, you unfeeling brute, as if you enjoyed my distress?

TONY: I can bear witness to that.

MRS. HARDCASTLE: Do you insult me, monster? I'll teach you to vex your mother, I will!

TONY: I can bear witness to that.

[He runs off, she follows him]

Enter Miss Hardcastle *and* Maid.

MISS HARDCASTLE: What an unaccountable creature is that brother of mine, to send them to the house as an inn, ha! ha! I don't wonder at his impudence.

MAID: But what is more, madam, the young gentleman as you passed by in your present dress, asked me if you were the barmaid? He mistook you for the barmaid, madam!

MISS HARDCASTLE: Did he? Then as I live I'm resolved to keep up the delusion. Tell me, Pimple, how do you like my present dress? Don't you think I look something like Cherry in the Beaux' Stratagem?

MAID: It's the dress, madam, that every lady wears in the country, but when she visits or receives company.

MISS HARDCASTLE: And are you sure he does not remember my face or person?

MAID: Certain of it!

MISS HARDCASTLE: I vow, I thought so; for though we spoke for some time together, yet his fears were such, that he never once looked up during the interview. Indeed, if he had, my bonnet would have kept him from seeing me.

MAID: But what do you hope from keeping him in his mistake?

MISS HARDCASTLE: In the first place, I shall be *seen*, and that is no small advantage to a girl who brings her face to market. Then I shall perhaps make an acquaintance, and that's no small victory gained over one who never addresses any but the wildest of her sex. But my chief aim is to take my gentleman off his guard, and like an invisible champion of romance examine the giant's force before I offer to combat.

MAID: But you are sure you can act your part, and disguise your voice, so that he may mistake that, as he has already mistaken your person?

MISS HARDCASTLE: Never fear me. I think I have got the true bar cant:—Did your honour call?——Attend the Lion there.——Pipes and tobacco for the Angel.——The Lamb has been outrageous this half hour!

MAID: It will do, madam. But he's here. [*Exit* Maid]

Enter Marlow.

MARLOW: What a bawling in every part of the house; I have scarce a moment's repose. If I go to the best room, there I find my host and his story. If I fly to the gallery, there we have my hostess with her curtsey down to the ground. I have at last got a moment to myself, and now for recollection. [*Walks and muses*]

MISS HARDCASTLE: Did you call, sir? did your honour call?

MARLOW: [*Musing*] As for Miss Hardcastle, she's too grave and sentimental for me.

MISS HARDCASTLE: Did your honour call?

[*She still places herself before him, he turning away*]

MARLOW: No, child! [*Musing*] Besides from the glimpse I had of her, I think she squints.

MISS HARDCASTLE: I'm sure, sir, I heard the bell ring.

MARLOW: No! no! [*Musing*] I have pleased my father, however, by coming down, and I'll to-morrow please myself by returning.

[*Taking out his tablets, and perusing*]

MISS HARDCASTLE: Perhaps the other gentleman called, sir?

MARLOW: I tell you, no.

MISS HARDCASTLE: I should be glad to know, sir. We have such a parcel of servants.

MARLOW: No, no, I tell you. [*Looks full in her face*] Yes, child, I think I did call. I wanted——I wanted——I vow, child, you are vastly handsome!

MISS HARDCASTLE: O la, sir, you'll make one ashamed.

MARLOW: Never saw a more sprightly malicious eye. Yes, yes, my dear, I did call. Have you got any of your——a——what d'ye call it in the house?

MISS HARDCASTLE: No, sir, we have been out of that these ten days.

MARLOW: One may call in this house, I find, to very little purpose. Suppose I should call for a taste, just by way of trial, of the nectar of your lips; perhaps I might be disappointed in that, too!

MISS HARDCASTLE: Nectar! nectar! that's a liquor there's no call for in these parts. French, I suppose. We keep no French wines here, sir.

MARLOW: Of true English growth, I assure you.

MISS HARDCASTLE: Then it's odd I should not know it. We brew all sorts of wines in this house, and I have lived here these eighteen years.

MARLOW: Eighteen years! Why one would think, child, you kept the bar before you were born. How old are you?

MISS HARDCASTLE: O! sir, I must not tell my age. They say women and music should never be dated.

MARLOW: To guess at this distance, you can't be much above forty. [*Approaching*] Yet nearer I don't think so much. [*Approaching*] By coming close to some women they look younger still; but when we come very close indeed.

[*Attempting to kiss her*]

MISS HARDCASTLE: Pray, sir, keep your distance. One would think you wanted to know one's age as they do horses, by mark of mouth.

MARLOW: I protest, child, you use me extremely ill. If you keep me at this distance, how is it possible you and I can be ever acquainted?

MISS HARDCASTLE: And who wants to be acquainted with you? I want no such acquaintance, not I. I'm sure you did not treat Miss Hardcastle that was here awhile ago in this obstropalous manner. I'll warrant me, before her you looked dashed, and kept bowing to the ground, and talked, for all the world, as if you was before a justice of peace.

MARLOW: [*Aside*] Egad! she has hit it, sure enough. [*To her*] In awe of her, child? Ha! ha! ha! A mere awkward, squinting thing, no, no! I find you don't know me. I laughed, and rallied her a little; but I was unwilling to be too severe. No, I could not be too severe, curse me!

MISS HARDCASTLE: O! then, sir, you are a favourite, I find, among the ladies?

MARLOW: Yes, my dear, a great favourite. And yet, hang me, I don't see what they find in me to follow. At the Ladies' Club in town I'm called their agreeable Rattle. Rattle, child, is not my real name, but one I'm known by. My name is Solomons. Mr. Solomons, my dear, at your service.

[Offering to salute her]

MISS HARDCASTLE: Hold, sir; you were introducing me to your club, not to yourself. And you're so great a favourite there you say?

MARLOW: Yes, my dear. There's Mrs. Mantrap, Lady Betty Blackleg, the Countess of Sligo, Mrs. Longhorns, old Miss Biddy Buckskin, and your humble servant, keep up the spirit of the place.

MISS HARDCASTLE: Then it's a very merry place, I suppose.

MARLOW: Yes, as merry as cards, suppers, wine, and old women can make us.

MISS HARDCASTLE: And their agreeable Rattle, ha! ha! ha!

MARLOW: [Aside] Egad! I don't quite like this chit. She looks knowing, methinks. You laugh, child!

MISS HARDCASTLE: I can't but laugh to think what time they all have for minding their work or their family.

MARLOW: [Aside] All's well, she don't laugh at me. [To her] Do you ever work, child?

MISS HARDCASTLE: Ay, sure. There's not a screen or a quilt in the whole house but what can bear witness to that.

MARLOW: Odso! Then you must show me your embroidery. I embroider and draw patterns myself a little. If you want a judge of your work you must apply to me.   [Seizing her hand]

MISS HARDCASTLE: Ay, but the colours don't look well by candle light. You shall see all in the morning.   [Struggling]

MARLOW: And why not now, my angel? Such beauty fires beyond the power of resistance.——Pshaw! the father here! My old luck: I never nicked seven that I did not throw ames-ace[1] three times following.   [Exit Marlow]

Enter Hardcastle, who stands in surprise.

HARDCASTLE: So, madam! So I find this is your modest lover. This is your humble admirer that kept his eyes fixed on the ground, and only adored at humble distance. Kate, Kate, art thou not ashamed to deceive your father so?

MISS HARDCASTLE: Never trust me, dear papa, but he's still the modest man I first took him for, you'll be convinced of it as well as I.

[1]Ambs-ace, i.e. a cast of double ace.

HARDCASTLE: By the hand of my body, I believe his impudence is infectious! Didn't I see him seize your hand? Didn't I see him haul you about like a milkmaid? and now you talk of his respect and his modesty, forsooth!

MISS HARDCASTLE: But if I shortly convince you of his modesty, that he has only the faults that will pass off with time, and the virtues that will improve with age, I hope you'll forgive him.

HARDCASTLE: The girl would actually make one run mad! I tell you I'll not be convinced. I am convinced. He has scarcely been three hours in the house, and he has already encroached on all my prerogatives. You may like his impudence, and call it modesty. But my son-in-law, madam, must have very different qualifications.

MISS HARDCASTLE: Sir, I ask but this night to convince you.

HARDCASTLE: You shall not have half the time, for I have thoughts of turning him out this very hour.

MISS HARDCASTLE: Give me that hour then, and I hope to satisfy you.

HARDCASTLE: Well, an hour let it be then. But I'll have no trifling with your father. All fair and open, do you mind me?

MISS HARDCASTLE: I hope, sir, you have ever found that I considered your commands as my pride; for your kindness is such, that my duty as yet has been inclination.   [Exeunt]

Act IV

Enter Hastings and Miss Neville.

HASTINGS: You surprise me! Sir Charles Marlow expected here this night? Where have you had your information?

MISS NEVILLE: You may depend upon it. I just saw his letter to Mr. Hardcastle, in which he tells him he intends setting out a few hours after his son.

HASTINGS: Then, my Constance, all must be completed before he arrives. He knows me; and should he find me here, would discover my name, and perhaps my designs, to the rest of the family.

MISS NEVILLE: The jewels, I hope, are safe.

HASTINGS: Yes, yes. I have sent them to Marlow, who keeps the keys of our baggage. In the meantime, I'll go to prepare matters for our elopement. I have had the Squire's promise of a fresh pair of horses; and, if I should not see him again, will write him further directions.   [Exit]

MISS NEVILLE: Well! success attend you. In the meantime, I'll go amuse my aunt with the old pretence of a violent passion for my cousin. [Exit]

Enter Marlow, followed by a Servant.

MARLOW: I wonder what Hastings could mean by sending me so valuable a thing as a casket to keep for him, when he knows the only place I have is the seat of a post-coach at an Inn-door. Have you deposited the casket with the landlady, as I ordered you? Have you put it into her own hands?

SERVANT: Yes, your honour.

MARLOW: She said she'd keep it safe, did she?

SERVANT: Yes, she said she'd keep it safe enough; she asked me how I came by it? and she said she had a great mind to make me give an account of myself.   [Exit Servant]

MARLOW: Ha! ha! ha! They're safe, however. What an unaccountable set of beings have we got amongst! This little barmaid though runs in my head most strangely, and drives out the absurdities of all the rest of the family. She's mine, she must be mine, or I'm greatly mistaken!

Enter Hastings.

HASTINGS: Bless me! I quite forgot to tell her that I intended to prepare at the bottom of the garden. Marlow here, and in spirits too!

MARLOW: Give me joy, George! Crown me, shadow me with laurels! Well, George, after all, we modest fellows don't want for success among the women.

HASTINGS: Some women, you mean. But what success has your honour's modesty been crowned with now, that it grows so insolent upon us?

MARLOW: Didn't you see the tempting, brisk, lovely little thing that runs about the house with a bunch of keys to its girdle?

HASTINGS: Well! and what then?

MARLOW: She's mine, you rogue, you. Such fire, such motion, such eyes, such lips——but egad! she would not let me kiss them though.

HASTINGS: But are you sure, so very sure of her?

MARLOW: Why, man, she talked of showing me her work above-stairs, and I am to improve the pattern.

HASTINGS: But how can you, Charles, go about to rob a woman of her honour?

MARLOW: Pshaw! pshaw! we all know the honour of the barmaid of an inn. I don't intend to rob her, take my word for it, there's nothing in this house, I shan't honestly pay for!

HASTINGS: I believe the girl has virtue.

MARLOW: And if she has, I should be the last man in the world that would attempt to corrupt it.

HASTINGS: You have taken care, I hope, of the casket I sent you to lock up? It's in safety?

MARLOW: Yes, yes. It's safe enough. I have taken care of it. But how could you think the seat of a post-coach at an Inn-door a place of safety? Ah! numskull! I have taken better precautions for you than you did for yourself.——I have——

HASTINGS: What!

MARLOW: I have sent it to the landlady to keep for you.

HASTINGS: To the landlady!

MARLOW: The landlady.

HASTINGS: You did!

MARLOW: I did. She's to be answerable for its forthcoming, you know.

HASTINGS: Yes, she'll bring it forth with a witness.

MARLOW: Wasn't I right? I believe you'll allow that I acted prudently upon this occasion?

HASTINGS: [Aside] He must not see my uneasiness.

MARLOW: You seem a little disconcerted, though, methinks. Sure nothing has happened?

HASTINGS: No, nothing. Never was I in better spirits in all my life. And so you left it with the landlady, who, no doubt, very readily undertook the charge?

MARLOW: Rather too readily. For she not only kept the casket, but, through her great precaution, was going to keep the messenger too. Ha! ha! ha!

HASTINGS: He! he! he! They're safe, however.

MARLOW: As a guinea in a miser's purse.

HASTINGS: [Aside] So now all hopes of fortune are at an end, and we must set off without it. [To him] Well, Charles, I'll leave you to your meditations on the pretty barmaid, and, he! he! he! may you be as successful for yourself as you have been for me.   [Exit]

MARLOW: Thank ye, George! I ask no more. Ha! ha! ha!

Enter Hardcastle.

HARDCASTLE: I no longer know my own house. It's turned all topsy-turvy. His servants have got drunk already. I'll bear it no longer, and yet, from my respect for his father, I'll be calm. [To him] Mr. Marlow, your servant. I'm your very humble servant.   [Bowing low]

MARLOW: Sir, your humble servant. [Aside] What's to be the wonder now?

HARDCASTLE: I believe, sir, you must be sensible, sir, that no man alive ought to be more welcome than your father's son, sir. I hope you think so?

MARLOW: I do, from my soul, sir. I don't want much entreaty. I generally make my father's son welcome wherever he goes.

HARDCASTLE: I believe you do, from my soul, sir. But though I say nothing to your own conduct, that of your servants is insufferable. Their manner of drinking is setting a very bad example in this house, I assure you.

MARLOW: I protest, my very good sir, that's no fault of mine. If they don't drink as they ought they are to blame. I ordered them not to spare the cellar, I did, I assure you. [To the side scene] Here, let one of my servants come up. [To him] My positive directions were, that as I did not drink myself, they should make up for my deficiencies below.

HARDCASTLE: Then they had your orders for what they do! I'm satisfied!

MARLOW: They had, I assure you. You shall hear from one of themselves.

Enter Servant, drunk.

MARLOW: You, Jeremy! Come forward, sirrah! What were my orders? Were you not told to drink freely, and call for what you thought fit, for the good of the house?

HARDCASTLE: [*Aside*] I begin to lose my patience.

JEREMY: Please your honour, liberty and Fleet Street for ever! Though I'm but a servant, I'm as good as another man. I'll drink for no man before supper, sir, dammy! Good liquor will sit upon a good supper, but a good supper will not sit upon—— hiccup——upon my conscience, sir.

MARLOW: You see, my old friend, the fellow is as drunk as he can possibly be. I don't know what you'd have more, unless you'd have the poor devil soused in a beer-barrel.

HARDCASTLE: Zounds! He'll drive me distracted if I contain myself any longer. Mr. Marlow. Sir; I have submitted to your insolence for more than four hours, and I see no likelihood of its coming to an end. I'm now resolved to be master here, sir, and I desire that you and your drunken pack may leave my house directly.

MARLOW: Leave your house!—Sure, you jest, my good friend! What, when I'm doing what I can to please you!

HARDCASTLE: I tell you, sir, you don't please me; so I desire you'll leave my house.

MARLOW: Sure, you cannot be serious! At this time of night, and such a night! You only mean to banter me!

HARDCASTLE: I tell you, sir, I'm serious; and, now that my passions are roused, I say this house is mine, sir; this house is mine, and I command you to leave it directly.

MARLOW: Ha! ha! ha! A puddle in a storm. I shan't stir a step, I assure you. [*In a serious tone*] This your house, fellow! It's my house. This is my house. Mine, while I choose to stay. What right have you to bid me leave this house, sir? I never met with such impudence, curse me, never in my whole life before!

HARDCASTLE: Nor I, confound me if ever I did! To come to my house, to call for what he likes, to turn me out of my own chair, to insult the family, to order his servants to get drunk, and then to tell me *This house is mine, sir*. By all that's impudent, it makes me laugh. Ha! ha! ha! Pray, sir, [*Bantering*] as you take the house, what think you of taking the rest of the furniture? There's a pair of silver candlesticks, and there's a fire-screen, and here's a pair of brazen-nosed bellows, perhaps you may take a fancy to them?

MARLOW: Bring me your bill, sir, bring me your bill, and let's make no more words about it.

HARDCASTLE: There are a set of prints, too. What think you of the Rake's Progress for your own apartment?

MARLOW: Bring me your bill, I say; and I'll leave you and your infernal house directly.

HARDCASTLE: Then there's a mahogany table, that you may see your own face in.

MARLOW: My bill, I say.

HARDCASTLE: I had forgot the great chair, for your own particular slumbers, after a hearty meal.

MARLOW: Zounds! bring me my bill, I say, and let's hear no more on't.

HARDCASTLE: Young man, young man, from your father's letter to me, I was taught to expect a well-bred modest man, as a visitor here, but now I find him no better than a coxcomb and a bully; but he will be down here presently, and shall hear more of it.   [*Exit*]

MARLOW: How's this! Sure, I have not mistaken the house? Everything looks like an inn. The servants cry "coming." The attendance is awkward; the barmaid, too, to attend us. But she's here, and will further inform me. Whither so fast, child? A word with you.

Enter Miss Hardcastle.

MISS HARDCASTLE: Let it be short, then. I'm in a hurry.—[*Aside*] I believe he begins to find out his mistake, but it's too soon quite to undeceive him.

MARLOW: Pray, child, answer me one question. What are you, and what may your business in this house be?

MISS HARDCASTLE: A relation of the family, sir.

MARLOW: What? A poor relation?

MISS HARDCASTLE: Yes, sir. A poor relation appointed to keep the keys, and to see that the guests want nothing in my power to give them.

MARLOW: That is, you act as the barmaid of this inn.

MISS HARDCASTLE: Inn! O law!—What brought that in your head? One of the best families in the county keep an inn! Ha, ha, ha, old Mr. Hardcastle's house an inn!

MARLOW: Mr. Hardcastle's house! Is this house Mr. Hardcastle's house, child?

MISS HARDCASTLE: Ay, sure. Whose else should it be?

MARLOW: So then all's out, and I have been damnably imposed on. O, confound my stupid head, I shall be laughed at over the whole town. I shall be stuck up in caricature in all the print-shops. The Dullissimo Macaroni. To mistake this house of all others for an inn, and my father's old friend for an innkeeper! What a swaggering puppy must he take me for. What a silly puppy do I find myself. There again, may I be hanged, my dear, but I mistook you for the barmaid!

MISS HARDCASTLE: Dear me! dear me! I'm sure there's nothing in my *behaviour* to put me upon a level with one of that stamp.

MARLOW: Nothing, my dear, nothing. But I was in for a list of blunders, and could not help making you a subscriber. My stupidity saw everything the wrong way. I mistook your assiduity for assurance, and your simplicity for allurement. But it's over— this house I no more show *my* face in!

MISS HARDCASTLE: I hope, sir, I have done nothing

to disoblige you. I'm sure I should be sorry to affront any gentleman who has been so polite, and said so many civil things to me. I'm sure I should be sorry [*Pretending to cry*] if he left the family upon my account. I'm sure I should be sorry people said anything amiss, since I have no fortune but my character.

MARLOW: [*Aside*] By heaven, she weeps. This is the first mark of tenderness I ever had from a modest woman, and it touches me. [*To her*] Excuse me, my lovely girl, you are the only part of the family I leave with reluctance. But to be plain with you, the difference of our birth, fortune and education, make an honourable connexion impossible; and I can never harbour a thought of seducing simplicity that trusted in my honour, or bringing ruin upon one whose only fault was being too lovely.

MISS HARDCASTLE: [*Aside*] Generous man! I now begin to admire him. [*To him*] But I'm sure my family is as good as Miss Hardcastle's, and though I'm poor, that's no great misfortune to a contented mind, and, until this moment, I never thought that it was bad to want fortune.

MARLOW: And why now, my pretty simplicity?

MISS HARDCASTLE: Because it puts me at a distance from one, that if I had a thousand pound I would give it all to.

MARLOW: [*Aside*] This simplicity bewitches me, so that if I stay I'm undone. I must make one bold effort, and leave her. [*To her*] Your partiality in my favour, my dear, touches me most sensibly, and were I to live for myself alone, I could easily fix my choice. But I owe too much to the opinion of the world, too much to the authority of a father, so that—I can scarcely speak it—it affects me! Farewell! [*Exit*]

MISS HARDCASTLE: I never knew half his merit till now. He shall not go, if I have power or art to detain him. I'll still preserve the character in which I stooped to conquer, but will undeceive my papa, who, perhaps, may laugh him out of his resolution. [*Exit*]

Enter Tony, Miss Neville.

TONY: Ay, you may steal for yourselves the next time. I have done my duty. She has got the jewels again, that's a sure thing; but she believes it was all a mistake of the servants.

MISS NEVILLE: But, my dear cousin, sure, you won't forsake us in this distress. If she in the least suspects that I am going off, I shall certainly be locked up, or sent to my aunt Pedigree's, which is ten times worse.

TONY: To be sure, aunts of all kinds are damned bad things. But what can I do? I have got you a pair of horses that will fly like Whistlejacket,[1] and I'm sure you can't say but I have courted you nicely

[1] *A famous racer, painted by Stubbs.*

before her face. Here she comes, we must court a bit or two more, for fear she should suspect us. [*They retire, and seem to fondle*]

Enter Mrs. Hardcastle.

MRS. HARDCASTLE: Well, I was greatly fluttered, to be sure. But my son tells me it was all a mistake of the servants. I shan't be easy, however, till they are fairly married, and then let her keep her own fortune. But what do I see! Fondling together, as I'm alive! I never saw Tony so sprightly before. Ah! have I caught you, my pretty doves! What, billing, exchanging stolen glances, and broken murmurs! Ah!

TONY: As for murmurs, mother, we grumble a little now and then, to be sure. But there's no love lost between us.

MRS. HARDCASTLE: A mere sprinkling, Tony, upon the flame, only to make it burn brighter.

MISS NEVILLE: Cousin Tony promises to give us more of his company at home. Indeed, he shan't leave us any more. It won't leave us, cousin Tony, will it?

TONY: O! it's a pretty creature. No, I'd sooner leave my horse in a pound, than leave you when you smile upon one so. Your laugh makes you so becoming.

MISS NEVILLE: Agreeable cousin! Who can help admiring that natural humour, that pleasant, broad, red, thoughtless, [*Patting his cheek*] ah! it's a bold face.

MRS. HARDCASTLE: Pretty innocence!

TONY: I'm sure I always loved cousin Con's hazel eyes, and her pretty long fingers, that she twists this way and that, over the haspicholls, like a parcel of bobbins.

MRS. HARDCASTLE: Ah, he would charm the bird from the tree. I was never so happy before. My boy takes after his father, poor Mr. Lumpkin, exactly. The jewels, my dear Con, shall be yours incontinently. You shall have them. Isn't he a sweet boy, my dear? You shall be married to-morrow, and we'll put off the rest of his education, like Dr. Drowsy's sermons, to a fitter opportunity.

Enter Diggory.

DIGGORY: Where's the 'Squire? I have got a letter for your worship.

TONY: Give it to my mamma. She reads all my letters first.

DIGGORY: I had orders to deliver it into your own hands.

TONY: Who does it come from?

DIGGORY: Your worship mun ask that of the letter itself.

TONY: I could wish to know, though. [*Turning the letter, and gazing on it*]

MISS NEVILLE: [*Aside*] Undone, undone! A letter to him from Hastings. I know the hand. If my aunt

sees it we are ruined for ever. I'll keep her employed a little if I can. [*To* Mrs. Hardcastle] But
I have not told you, madam, of my cousin's smart
answer just now to Mr. Marlow. We so laughed—
you must know, madam—this way a little, for he
must not hear us.   [*They confer*]

TONY: [*Still gazing*] A damned cramp piece of pen-
manship, as ever I saw in my life. I can read the
print-hand very well. But here there are such
handles, and shanks, and dashes, that one can
scarce tell the head from the tail. *To Anthony
Lumpkin, Esquire.* It's very odd, I can read the
outside of my letters, where my own name is, well
enough. But when I come to open it, it's all—
buzz. That's hard, very hard; for the inside of the
letter is always the cream of the correspondence.

MRS. HARDCASTLE: Ha! ha! ha! Very well, very well.
And so my son was too hard for the philosopher!

MISS NEVILLE: Yes, madam; but you must hear the
rest, madam. A little more this way, or he may
hear us. You'll hear how he puzzled him again.

MRS. HARDCASTLE: He seems strangely puzzled now
himself, methinks.

TONY: [*Still gazing*] A damned up and down hand,
as if it was disguised in liquor. [*Reading*] *Dear
Sir.* Ay, that's that. Then there's an *M*, and a *T*,
and an *S*, but whether the next be an *izzard* or an
R, confound me, I cannot tell!

MRS. HARDCASTLE: What's that, my dear? Can I
give you any assistance?

MISS NEVILLE: Pray, aunt, let me read it. Nobody
reads a cramp hand better than I. [*Twitching the
letter from her*] Do you know who it is from?

TONY: Can't tell, except from Dick Ginger the
feeder.

MISS NEVILLE: Ay, so it is. [*Pretending to read*] Dear
'Squire, Hoping that you're in health, as I am
at this present. The gentlemen of the Shakebag
club has cut the gentlemen of Goose-green quite
out of feather. The odds—um—odd battle—um
—long fighting—um, here, here, it's all about
cocks, and fighting; it's of no consequence, here,
put it up, put it up.

[*Thrusting the crumpled letter upon him*]

TONY: But I tell you, miss, it's of all the consequence in the world! I would not lose the rest of
it for a guinea! Here, mother, do you make it out?
Of no consequence!

[*Giving* Mrs. Hardcastle *the letter*]

MRS. HARDCASTLE: How's this! [*Reads*] Dear 'Squire,
I'm now waiting for Miss Neville, with a post-
chaise and pair, at the bottom of the garden, but
I find my horses yet unable to perform the journey. I expect you'll assist us with a pair of fresh
horses, as you promised. Dispatch is necessary,
as the *hag* (ay, the hag) your mother, will otherwise suspect us. Yours, Hastings. Grant me patience. I shall run distracted! My rage chokes
me.

MISS NEVILLE: I hope, madam, you'll suspend your
resentment for a few moments, and not impute
to me any impertinence, or sinister design that
belongs to another.

MRS. HARDCASTLE: [*Curtseying very low*] Fine spoken,
madam, you are most miraculously polite and
engaging, and quite the very pink of courtesy
and circumspection, madam. [*Changing her
tone*] And you, you great ill-fashioned oaf, with
scarce sense enough to keep your mouth shut.
Were you too joined against me? But I'll defeat
all your plots in a moment. As for you, madam,
since you have got a pair of fresh horses ready,
it would be cruel to disappoint them. So, if you
please, instead of running away with your spark,
prepare, this very moment, to run off with *me*.
Your old aunt Pedigree will keep you secure, I'll
warrant me. You too, sir, may mount your horse,
and guard us upon the way. Here, Thomas, Roger,
Diggory, I'll show you that I wish you better than
you do yourselves.   [*Exit*]

MISS NEVILLE: So now I'm completely ruined.

TONY: Ay, that's a sure thing.

MISS NEVILLE: What better could be expected from
being connected with such a stupid fool, and after
all the nods and signs I made him.

TONY: By the laws, miss, it was your own cleverness,
and not my stupidity, that did your business. You
were so nice and so busy with your Shakebags and
Goosegreens, that I thought you could never be
making believe.

Enter Hastings.

HASTINGS: So, sir, I find by my servant, that you
have shown my letter, and betrayed us. Was this
well done, young gentleman?

TONY: Here's another. Ask miss there who betrayed
you. Ecod, it was her doing, not mine.

Enter Marlow.

MARLOW: So I have been finely used here among
you. Rendered contemptible, driven into ill manners, despised, insulted, laughed at.

TONY: Here's another. We shall have old Bedlam
broke loose presently.

MISS NEVILLE: And there, sir, is the gentleman to
whom we all owe every obligation.

MARLOW: What can I say to him, a mere boy, an
idiot, whose ignorance and age are a protection?

HASTINGS: A poor contemptible booby, that would
but disgrace correction.

MISS NEVILLE: Yet with cunning and malice enough
to make himself merry with all our embarrass-
ments.

HASTINGS: An insensible cub.

MARLOW: Replete with tricks and mischief.

TONY: Baw! damme, but I'll fight you both one after
the other,——with baskets.

MARLOW: As for him, he's below resentment. But
your conduct, Mr. Hastings, requires an explana-

tion. You knew of my mistakes, yet would not undeceive me.

HASTINGS: Tortured as I am with my own disappointments, is this a time for explanation? It is not
friendly, Mr. Marlow.

MARLOW: But, sir——

MISS NEVILLE: Mr. Marlow, we never kept on your
mistake, till it was too late to undeceive you. Be
pacified.

Enter Servant.

SERVANT: My mistress desires you'll get ready immediately, madam. The horses are putting to. Your
hat and things are in the next room. We are to
go thirty miles before morning.   [*Exit* Servant]

MISS NEVILLE: Well, well; I'll come presently.

MARLOW: [*To* Hastings] Was it well done, sir, to
assist in rendering me ridiculous? To hang me
out for the scorn of all my acquaintance? Depend
upon it, sir, I shall expect an explanation.

HASTINGS: Was it well done, sir, if you're upon that
subject, to deliver what I entrusted to yourself, to
the care of another, sir?

MISS NEVILLE: Mr. Hastings. Mr. Marlow. Why
will you increase my distress by this groundless
dispute? I implore, I entreat you——

Enter Servant.

SERVANT: Your cloak, madam. My mistress is impatient.

MISS NEVILLE: I come. Pray be pacified. If I leave
you thus, I shall die with apprehension!

Enter Servant.

SERVANT: Your fan, muff, and gloves, madam. The
horses are waiting.

MISS NEVILLE: O, Mr. Marlow! if you knew what a
scene of constraint and ill-nature lies before me,
I'm sure it would convert your resentment into
pity.

MARLOW: I'm so distracted with a variety of passions, that I don't know what I do. Forgive me,
madam. George, forgive me. You know my hasty
temper, and should not exasperate it.

HASTINGS: The torture of my situation is my only
excuse.

MISS NEVILLE: Well, my dear Hastings, if you have
that esteem for me that I think, that I am sure
you have, your constancy for three years will but
increase the happiness of our future connection.
If——

MRS. HARDCASTLE: [*Within*] Miss Neville. Constance, why, Constance, I say.

MISS NEVILLE: I'm coming. Well, constancy. Remember, constancy is the word.   [*Exit*]

HASTINGS: My heart! How can I support this! To
be so near happiness, and such happiness!

MARLOW: [*To* Tony] You see now, young gentleman, the effects of your folly. What might be

amusement to you, is here disappointment, and
even distress.

TONY: [*From a reverie*] Ecod, I have hit it. It's here.
Your hands. Yours and yours, my poor Sulky.
My boots there, ho! Meet me two hours hence
at the bottom of the garden; and if you don't
find Tony Lumpkin a more good-natur'd fellow
than you thought for, I'll give you leave to take
my best horse, and Bet Bouncer into the bargain!
Come along. My boots, ho!   [*Exeunt*]

Act V

SCENE: *Continues*

Enter Hastings *and* Servant.

HASTINGS: You saw the old lady and Miss Neville
drive off, you say?

SERVANT: Yes, your honour. They went off in a post-
coach, and the young 'Squire went on horseback.
They're thirty miles off by this time.

HASTINGS: Then all my hopes are over.

SERVANT: Yes, sir. Old Sir Charles is arrived. He
and the old gentleman of the house have been
laughing at Mr. Marlow's mistake this half hour.
They are coming this way.

HASTINGS: Then I must not be seen. So now to my
fruitless appointment at the bottom of the garden.
This is about the time.   [*Exit*]

Enter Sir Charles *and* Hardcastle.

HARDCASTLE: Ha! ha! ha! The peremptory tone in
which he sent forth his sublime commands.

SIR CHARLES: And the reserve with which I suppose
he treated all your advances.

HARDCASTLE: And yet he might have seen something
in me above a common innkeeper, too.

SIR CHARLES: Yes, Dick, but he mistook you for an
uncommon innkeeper, ha! ha! ha!

HARDCASTLE: Well, I'm in too good spirits to think
of anything but joy. Yes, my dear friend, this
union of our families will make our personal
friendships hereditary: and though my daughter's
fortune is but small——

SIR CHARLES: Why, Dick, will you talk of fortune
to *me*? My son is possessed of more than a competence already, and can want nothing but a good
and virtuous girl to share his happiness and increase it. If they like each other, as you say they
do——

HARDCASTLE: *If*, man! I tell you they *do* like each
other. My daughter as good as told me so.

SIR CHARLES: But girls are apt to flatter themselves,
you know.

HARDCASTLE: I saw him grasp her hand in the warmest manner myself; and here he comes to put you
out of your *ifs*, I warrant him.

Enter Marlow.

MARLOW: I come, sir, once more, to ask pardon for my strange conduct. I can scarce reflect on my insolence without confusion.

HARDCASTLE: Tut, boy, a trifle. You take it too gravely. An hour or two's laughing with my daughter will set all to rights again. She'll never like you the worse for it.

MARLOW: Sir, I shall be always proud of her approbation.

HARDCASTLE: Approbation is but a cold word, Mr. Marlow; if I am not deceived, you have something more than approbation thereabouts. You take me.

MARLOW: Really, sir, I have not that happiness.

HARDCASTLE: Come, boy, I'm an old fellow, and know what's what, as well as you that are younger. I know what has passed between you; but mum.

MARLOW: Sure, sir, nothing has passed between us but the most profound respect on my side, and the most distant reserve on hers. You don't think, sir, that my impudence has been passed upon all the rest of the family.

HARDCASTLE: Impudence! No, I don't say that— Not quite impudence—Though girls like to be played with, and rumpled a little too, sometimes. But she has told no tales, I assure you.

MARLOW: I never gave her the slightest cause.

HARDCASTLE: Well, well, I like modesty in its place well enough. But this is over-acting, young gentleman. You *may* be open. Your father and I will like you the better for it.

MARLOW: May I die, sir, if I ever——

HARDCASTLE: I tell you, she don't dislike you; and as I'm sure you like her——

MARLOW: Dear sir—I protest, sir——

HARDCASTLE: I see no reason why you should not be joined as fast as the parson can tie you.

MARLOW: But hear me, sir——

HARDCASTLE: Your father approves the match, I admire it, every moment's delay will be doing mischief, so——

MARLOW: But why won't you hear me? By all that's just and true, I never gave Miss Hardcastle the slightest mark of my attachment, or even the most distant hint to suspect me of affection. We had but one interview, and that was formal, modest and uninteresting.

HARDCASTLE: [*Aside*] This fellow's formal modest impudence is beyond bearing.

SIR CHARLES: And you never grasped her hand, or made any protestations?

MARLOW: As heaven is my witness, I came down in obedience to your commands. I saw the lady without emotion, and parted without reluctance. I hope you'll exact no further proofs of my duty, nor prevent me from leaving a house in which I suffer so many mortifications.   [*Exit*]

SIR CHARLES: I'm astonished at the air of sincerity with which he parted.

HARDCASTLE: And I'm astonished at the deliberate intrepidity of his assurance.

SIR CHARLES: I dare pledge my life and honour upon his truth.

HARDCASTLE: Here comes my daughter, and I would stake my happiness upon her veracity.

Enter Miss Hardcastle.

HARDCASTLE: Kate, come hither, child. Answer us sincerely, and without reserve; has Mr. Marlow made you any professions of love and affection?

MISS HARDCASTLE: The question is very abrupt, sir! But since you require unreserved sincerity, I think he has.

HARDCASTLE: [*To Sir Charles*] You see.

SIR CHARLES: And pray, madam, have you and my son had more than one interview?

MISS HARDCASTLE: Yes, sir, several.

HARDCASTLE: [*To Sir Charles*] You see.

SIR CHARLES: But did he profess any attachment?

MISS HARDCASTLE: A lasting one.

SIR CHARLES: Did he talk of love?

MISS HARDCASTLE: Much, sir.

SIR CHARLES: Amazing! And all this formally?

MISS HARDCASTLE: Formally.

HARDCASTLE: Now, my friend, I hope you are satisfied.

SIR CHARLES: And how did he behave, madam?

MISS HARDCASTLE: As most professed admirers do. Said some civil things of my face, talked much of his want of merit, and the greatness of mine; mentioned his heart, gave a short tragedy speech, and ended with pretended rapture.

SIR CHARLES: Now I'm perfectly convinced, indeed I know his conversation among women to be modest and submissive. This forward, canting, ranting manner by no means describes him, and I am confident he never sat for the picture.

MISS HARDCASTLE: Then what, sir, if I should convince you to your face of my sincerity? If you and my papa, in about half-an-hour, will place yourselves behind that screen, you shall hear him declare his passion to me in person.

SIR CHARLES: Agreed. And if I find him what you describe, all my happiness in him must have an end.   [*Exit*]

MISS HARDCASTLE: And if you don't find him what I describe—I fear my happiness must never have a beginning.   [*Exeunt*]

SCENE: *Changes to the back of the Garden*

Enter Hastings.

HASTINGS: What an idiot am I, to wait here for a fellow, who probably takes a delight in mortifying me. He never intended to be punctual, and I'll wait no longer. What do I see? It is he, and perhaps with news of my Constance.

Enter Tony, *booted and spattered.*

HASTINGS: My honest 'Squire! I now find you a man of your word. This looks like friendship.

TONY: Ay, I'm your friend, and the best friend you have in the world, if you knew but all. This riding by night, by-the-bye, is cursedly tiresome. It has shook me worse than the basket of a stage-coach.

HASTINGS: But how? Where did you leave your fellow-travellers? Are they in safety? Are they housed?

TONY: Five and twenty miles in two hours and a half is no such bad driving. The poor beasts have smoked for it: Rabbit me, but I'd rather ride forty miles after a fox, than ten with such *varmint*.

HASTINGS: Well, but where have you left the ladies? I die with impatience.

TONY: Left them? Why, where should I leave them, but where I found them?

HASTINGS: This is a riddle.

TONY: Riddle me this, then. What's that goes round the house, and round the house, and never touches the house?

HASTINGS: I'm still astray.

TONY: Why, that's it, mon. I have led them astray. By jingo, there's not a pond or slough within five miles of the place but they can tell the taste of.

HASTINGS: Ha, ha, ha, I understand; you took them in a round, while they supposed themselves going forward. And so you have at last brought them home again.

TONY: You shall hear. I first took them down Featherbed-lane, where we stuck fast in the mud. I then rattled them crack over the stones of Up-and-down Hill—I then introduced them to the gibbet on Heavytree Heath, and from that, with a circumbendibus, I fairly lodged them in the horsepond at the bottom of the garden.

HASTINGS: But no accident, I hope.

TONY: No, no. Only mother is confoundedly frightened. She thinks herself forty miles off. She's sick of the journey, and the cattle can scarce crawl. So, if your own horses be ready, you may whip off with cousin, and I'll be bound that no soul here can budge a foot to follow you.

HASTINGS: My dear friend, how can I be grateful?

TONY: Ay, now it's dear friend, noble 'Squire. Just now, it was all idiot, cub, and run me through the guts. Damn *your* way of fighting, I say. After we take a knock in this part of the country, we kiss and be friends. But if you had run me through the guts, then I should be dead, and you might go kiss the hangman.

HASTINGS: The rebuke is just. But I must hasten to relieve Miss Neville; if you keep the old lady employed, I promise to take care of the young one.

[*Exit* Hastings]

TONY: Never fear me. Here she comes. Vanish. She's got from the pond, and draggled up to the waist like a mermaid.

Enter Mrs. Hardcastle.

MRS. HARDCASTLE: Oh, Tony, I'm killed. Shook. Battered to death. I shall never survive it. That last jolt that laid us against the quickset hedge has done my business.

TONY: Alack, mamma, it was all your own fault. You would be for running away by night, without knowing one inch of the way.

MRS. HARDCASTLE: I wish we were at home again. I never met so many accidents in so short a journey. Drenched in the mud, overturned in a ditch, stuck fast in a slough, jolted to a jelly, and at last to lose our way! Whereabouts do you think we are, Tony?

TONY: By my guess we should be upon Crackskull Common, about forty miles from home.

MRS. HARDCASTLE: O lud! O lud! the most notorious spot in all the country. We only want a robbery to make a complete night on't.

TONY: Don't be afraid, mamma, don't be afraid. Two of the five that kept here are hanged, and the other three may not find us. Don't be afraid. Is that a man that's galloping behind us? No; its only a tree. Don't be afraid.

MRS. HARDCASTLE: The fright will certainly kill me.

TONY: Do you see anything like a black hat moving behind the thicket?

MRS. HARDCASTLE: O death!

TONY: No, it's only a cow. Don't be afraid, mamma, don't be afraid.

MRS. HARDCASTLE: As I'm alive, Tony, I see a man coming towards us. Ah! I'm sure on't. If he perceives us, we are undone.

TONY: [*Aside*] Father-in-law, by all that's unlucky, come to take one of his night walks. [*To her*] Ah, it's a highwayman, with pistols as long as my arm. A damned ill-looking fellow.

MRS. HARDCASTLE: Good heaven defend us! He approaches.

TONY: Do you hide yourself in that thicket, and leave me to manage him. If there be any danger I'll cough and cry hem. When I cough be sure to keep close. [Mrs. Hardcastle *hides behind a tree in the back scene*]

Enter Hardcastle.

HARDCASTLE: I'm mistaken, or I heard voices of people in want of help. Oh, Tony, is that you? I did not expect you so soon back. Are your mother and her charge in safety?

TONY: Very safe, sir, at my aunt Pedigree's. Hem.

MRS. HARDCASTLE: [*From behind*] Ah! I find there's danger.

HARDCASTLE: Forty miles in three hours; sure, that's too much, my youngster.

TONY: Stout horses and willing minds make short journeys, as they say. Hem.

MRS. HARDCASTLE: [*From behind*] Sure he'll do the dear boy no harm.

HARDCASTLE: But I heard a voice here; I should be glad to know from whence it came.

TONY: It was I, sir, talking to myself, sir. I was saying that forty miles in four hours was very good going. Hem. As to be sure it was. Hem. I have got a sort of cold by being out in the air. We'll go in if you please. Hem.

HARDCASTLE: But if you talked to yourself, you did not answer yourself. I am certain I heard two voices, and am resolved [*Raising his voice*] to find the other out.

MRS. HARDCASTLE: [*From behind*] Oh! he's coming to find me out. Oh!

TONY: What need you go, sir, if I tell you? Hem. I'll lay down my life for the truth—hem—I'll tell you all, sir.   [*Detaining him*]

HARDCASTLE: I tell you I will not be detained. I insist on seeing. It's in vain to expect I'll believe you.

MRS. HARDCASTLE: [*Running forward from behind*] O lud, he'll murder my poor boy, my darling. Here, good gentleman, whet your rage upon me. Take my money, my life, but spare that young gentleman, spare my child, if you have any mercy.

HARDCASTLE: My wife! as I'm a Christian. From whence can she come, or what does she mean?

MRS. HARDCASTLE: [*Kneeling*] Take compassion on us, good Mr. Highwayman. Take our money, our watches, all we have, but spare our lives. We will never bring you to justice, indeed we won't, good Mr. Highwayman.

HARDCASTLE: I believe the woman's out of her senses. What, Dorothy, don't you know *me*?

MRS. HARDCASTLE: Mr. Hardcastle, as I'm alive! My fears blinded me. But who, my dear, could have expected to meet you here, in this frightful place, so far from home. What has brought you to follow us?

HARDCASTLE: Sure, Dorothy, you have not lost your wits! So far from home, when you are within forty yards of your own door! [*To him*] This is one of your old tricks, you graceless rogue, you! [*To her*] Don't you know the gate, and the mulberry-tree; and don't you remember the horsepond, my dear?

MRS. HARDCASTLE: Yes, I shall remember the horsepond as long as I live; I have caught my death in it. [*To Tony*] And is it to you, you graceless varlet, I owe all this? I'll teach you to abuse your mother, I will.

TONY: Ecod, mother, all the parish says you have spoiled me, and so you may take the fruits on't.

MRS. HARDCASTLE: I'll spoil you, I will.
                    [*Follows him off the stage. Exit*]

HARDCASTLE: There's morality, however in his reply.
                                          [*Exit*]

Enter Hastings *and* Miss Neville.

HASTINGS: My dear Constance, why will you deliberate thus? If we delay a moment, all is lost for ever.

Pluck up a little resolution, and we shall soon be out of the reach of her malignity.

MISS NEVILLE: I find it impossible. My spirits are so sunk with the agitations I have suffered, that I am unable to face any new danger. Two or three years' patience will at last crown us with happiness.

HASTINGS: Such a tedious delay is worse than inconstancy. Let us fly, my charmer. Let us date our happiness from this very moment. Perish fortune. Love and content will increase what we possess beyond a monarch's revenue. Let me prevail.

MISS NEVILLE: No, Mr. Hastings, no. Prudence once more comes to my relief, and I will obey its dictates. In the moment of passion, fortune may be despised, but it ever produces a lasting repentance. I'm resolved to apply to Mr. Hardcastle's compassion and justice for redress.

HASTINGS: But though he had the will, he has not the power to relieve you.

MISS NEVILLE: But he has influence, and upon that I am resolved to rely.

HASTINGS: I have no hopes. But since you persist, I must reluctantly obey you.   [*Exeunt*]

SCENE: *Changes*

Enter Sir Charles *and* Miss Hardcastle.

SIR CHARLES: What a situation am I in! If what you say appears, I shall then find a guilty son. If what he says be true, I shall then lose one that, of all others, I most wished for a daughter.

MISS HARDCASTLE: I am proud of your approbation; and, to show I merit it, if you place yourselves as I directed, you shall hear his explicit declaration. But he comes.

SIR CHARLES: I'll to your father, and keep him to the appointment.   [*Exit Sir Charles*]

Enter Marlow.

MARLOW: Though prepared for setting out, I come once more to take leave, nor did I, till this moment, know the pain I feel in the separation.

MISS HARDCASTLE: [*In her own natural manner*] I believe these sufferings cannot be very great, sir, which you can so easily remove. A day or two longer, perhaps, might lessen your uneasiness, by showing the little value of what you think proper to regret.

MARLOW: [*Aside*] This girl every moment improves upon me. [*To her*] It must not be, madam. I have already trifled too long with my heart. My very pride begins to submit to my passion. The disparity of education and fortune, the anger of a parent, and the contempt of my equals, begin to lose their weight; and nothing can restore me to myself but this painful effort of resolution.

MISS HARDCASTLE: Then go, sir. I'll urge nothing more to detain you. Though my family be as good as hers you came down to visit, and my education, I hope, not inferior, what are these advantages without equal affluence? I must remain contented with the slight approbation of imputed merit; I must have only the mockery of your addresses, while all your serious aims are fixed on fortune.

Enter Hardcastle *and* Sir Charles *from behind.*

SIR CHARLES: Here, behind this screen.

HARDCASTLE: Ay, ay, make no noise. I'll engage my Kate covers him with confusion at last.

MARLOW: By heavens, madam, fortune was ever my smallest consideration. Your beauty at first caught my eye; for who could see that without emotion? But every moment that I converse with you, steals in some new grace, heightens the picture, and gives it stronger expression. What at first seemed rustic plainness, now appears refined simplicity. What seemed forward assurance, now strikes me as the result of courageous innocence, and conscious virtue.

SIR CHARLES: What can it mean? He amazes me!

HARDCASTLE: I told you how it would be. Hush!

MARLOW: I am now determined to stay, madam, and I have too good an opinion of my father's discernment, when he sees you, to doubt his approbation.

MISS HARDCASTLE: No, Mr. Marlow, I will not, cannot detain you. Do you think I could suffer a connection, in which there is the smallest room for repentance? Do you think I would take the mean advantage of a transient passion, to load you with confusion? Do you think I could ever relish that happiness, which was acquired by lessening yours?

MARLOW: By all that's good, I can have no happiness but what's in your power to grant me. Nor shall I ever feel repentance, but in not having seen your merits before. I will stay, even contrary to your wishes; and though you should persist to shun me, I will make my respectful assiduities atone for the levity of my past conduct.

MISS HARDCASTLE: Sir, I must entreat you'll desist. As our acquaintance began, so let it end, in indifference. I might have given an hour or two to levity; but, seriously, Mr. Marlow, do you think I could ever submit to a connection, where I must appear mercenary, and *you* imprudent? Do you think I could ever catch at the confident addresses of a secure admirer?

MARLOW: [*Kneeling*] Does this look like security? Does this look like confidence? No, madam, every moment that shows me your merit, only serves to increase my diffidence and confusion. Here let me continue——

SIR CHARLES: I can hold it no longer. Charles, Charles, how hast thou deceived me! Is this your indifference, your uninteresting conversation!

HARDCASTLE: Your cold contempt! your formal interview! What have you to say now?

MARLOW: That I'm all amazement! What can it mean?

HARDCASTLE: It means that you can say and unsay things at pleasure. That you can address a lady in private, and deny it in public; that you have one story for us, and another for my daughter!

MARLOW: Daughter!—this lady your daughter!

HARDCASTLE: Yes, sir, my only daughter. My Kate, whose else should she be?

MARLOW: Oh, the devil.

MISS HARDCASTLE: Yes, sir, that very identical tall squinting lady you were pleased to take me for. [*Curtseying*] She that you addressed as the mild, modest, sentimental man of gravity, and the bold, forward, agreeable Rattle of the ladies' club: ha, ha, ha!

MARLOW: Zounds, there's no bearing this; it's worse than death!

MISS HARDCASTLE: In which of your characters, sir, will you give us leave to address you? As the faltering gentleman, with looks on the ground, that speaks just to be heard, and hates hypocrisy: or the loud confident creature, that keeps it up with Mrs. Mantrap, and old Miss Biddy Buckskin, till three in the morning; ha, ha, ha!

MARLOW: Oh, curse on my noisy head. I never attempted to be impudent yet, that I was not taken down. I must be gone.

HARDCASTLE: By the hand of my body, but you shall not. I see it was all a mistake, and I am rejoiced to find it. You shall not, sir, I tell you. I know she'll forgive you. Won't you forgive him, Kate? We'll all forgive you. Take courage, man. [*They retire, she tormenting him to the back scene*]

Enter Mrs. Hardcastle, Tony.

MRS. HARDCASTLE: So, so, they're gone off. Let them go, I care not.

HARDCASTLE: Who gone?

MRS. HARDCASTLE: My dutiful niece and her gentleman, Mr. Hastings, from town. He who came down with our modest visitor, here.

SIR CHARLES: Who, my honest George Hastings? As worthy a fellow as lives, and the girl could not have made a more prudent choice.

HARDCASTLE: Then, by the hand of my body, I'm proud of the connection.

MRS. HARDCASTLE: Well, if he has taken away the lady, he has not taken her fortune, that remains in this family to console us for her loss.

HARDCASTLE: Sure, Dorothy, you would not be so mercenary?

MRS. HARDCASTLE: Ay, that's my affair, not yours. But you know, if your son when of age, refuses to marry his cousin, her whole fortune is then at her own disposal.

HARDCASTLE: Ay, but he's not of age, and she has not thought proper to wait for his refusal.

Enter Hastings *and* Miss Neville.

MRS. HARDCASTLE: [*Aside*] What! returned so soon? I begin not to like it.

HASTINGS: [*To Hardcastle*] For my late attempt to fly off with your niece, let my present confusion be my punishment. We are now come back, to appeal from your justice to your humanity. By her father's consent, I first paid her my addresses, and our passions were first founded in duty.

MISS NEVILLE: Since his death, I have been obliged to stoop to dissimulation to avoid oppression. In an hour of levity, I was ready even to give up my fortune to secure my choice. But I'm now recovered from the delusion, and hope from your tenderness what is denied me from a nearer connection.

MRS. HARDCASTLE: Pshaw, pshaw! this is all but the whining end of a modern novel.

HARDCASTLE: Be it what it will, I'm glad they're come back to reclaim their due. Come hither, Tony, boy. Do you refuse this lady's hand whom I now offer you?

TONY: What signifies my refusing? You know I can't refuse her till I'm of age, father.

HARDCASTLE: While I thought concealing your age, boy, was likely to conduce to your improvement, I concurred with your mother's desire to keep it secret. But since I find she turns it to a wrong use, I must now declare, you have been of age these three months.

TONY: Of age! Am I of age, father?

HARDCASTLE: Above three months.

TONY: Then you'll see the first use I'll make of my liberty. [*Taking* Miss Neville's *hand*] Witness all men by these presents, that I, Anthony Lumpkin, Esquire, of BLANK place, refuse you, Constantia Neville, spinster, of no place at all, for my true and lawful wife. So Constance Neville may marry whom she pleases, and Tony Lumpkin is his own man again!

SIR CHARLES: O brave 'Squire!

HASTINGS: My worthy friend!

MRS. HARDCASTLE: My undutiful offspring!

MARLOW: Joy, my dear George, I give you joy sincerely. And could I prevail upon my little tyrant here to be less arbitrary, I should be the happiest man alive, if you would return me the favour.

HASTINGS: [*To Miss Hardcastle*] Come, madam, you are now driven to the very last scene of all your contrivances. I know you like him, I'm sure he loves you, and you must and shall have him.

HARDCASTLE: [*Joining their hands*] And I say so, too. And Mr. Marlow, if she makes as good a wife as she has a daughter, I don't believe you'll ever repent your bargain. So now to supper, to-morrow we shall gather all the poor of the parish about us, and the Mistakes of the Night shall be crowned with a merry morning; so boy, take her; as you have been mistaken in the mistress, my wish is, that you may never be mistaken in the wife.

Epilogue

Well, having stooped to conquer with success,
And gained a husband without aid from dress,
Still as a Barmaid, I could wish it too,
As I have conquered him to conquer you:
And let me say, for all your resolution,
That pretty Barmaids have done execution.
Our life is all a play, composed to please,
"We have our exits and our entrances."
The first act shows the simple country maid,
Harmless and young, of everything afraid;
Blushes when hired, and with unmeaning action,
I hopes as how to give you satisfaction.
Her second act displays a livelier scene,—
Th' unblushing Barmaid of a country inn.
Who whisks about the house, at market caters,
Talks loud, coquets the guests, and scolds the waiters.
Next the scene shifts to town, and there she soars,
The chop-house toast of ogling connoisseurs.
On 'Squires and Cits she there displays her arts,
And on the gridiron broils her lovers' hearts—
And as she smiles, her triumphs to complete,
Even Common Councilmen forget to eat.
The fourth act shows her wedded to the 'Squire,
And madam now begins to hold it higher;
Pretends to taste, at Operas cries *caro*,
And quits her *Nancy Dawson*, for *Che Faro*.
Doats upon dancing, and in all her pride,
Swims round the room, the *Heinel* of Cheapside:
Ogles and leers with artificial skill,
Till having lost in age the power to kill,
She sits all night at cards, and ogles at spadille.
Such, through our lives, the eventful history—
The fifth and last act still remains for me.
The Barmaid now for your protection prays,
Turns female Barrister, and pleads for Bayes.

The School for Scandal

by RICHARD BRINSLEY SHERIDAN
(1751–1816)

Goldsmith, with his humor, had restored Comedy to dry land; and now, with wit and a sharp satiric point of view, Sheridan was to raise it to an eminence. In theatrical history the two playwrights, from having flourished during the same years and having alone survived their period, are always bracketed together; but in temperament and concrete talent, they stood very far apart. Goldsmith was a social stutterer, a man who "talked like Poor Poll"; Sheridan was an accomplished worldling who delivered the most brilliant parliamentary oration of his age; and we are fully aware of how much the two men differ when, after the rustic shenanigans of She Stoops to Conquer, we turn to the polished backbiting and intrigue of The School for Scandal.

We have turned, as a matter of fact, off an old-fashioned country lane back onto the broad highroad, the great avenue, the principal artery of the English comic drama—the comedy of manners. We have only to open The School for Scandal, to hear Mr. Snake in conference with Lady Sneerwell, to know where we stand; a Tony Lumpkin, here, is as inconceivable as a Macbeth, and far more out of place than an Iago. Reading on, moreover, we become quickly conscious of how deft, how knowledgeable is Sheridan at his trade: as deft and knowledgeable as Mr. Snake and Lady Sneerwell at theirs. Surely these two are among the very greatest of scandalmongers, compounding their little pellets of slander and abuse like master pharmacists making up their pills and powders. To say that they turn scandal into an art is not enough; they make it as fascinating, as rich in shop talk and trade secrets, as any business or profession. And with their vivacious, venomous tattle, we are launched on what —in theater annals and textbook opinion and the general public's knowledge—is surely the most famous comedy of manners in the language.

It is not hard to understand its fame; nor too hard to justify it. Sheridan had genuine wit and polish; he had, too, an eye for social detail, a born instinct for satire. He, like Congreve, understood the way of the world; he, even more than Congreve, understood the ways and wiles of the theater. With a plot not a third as complicated as several of Congreve's, Sheridan provided something that seems just as conspiratorial and sinful, and ten times more effective. Master of stage devices, he is equally master of the Big Scene—indeed, so much so as to cap the Big Scene with a Bigger One. First, in the picture scene, Charles is prettily redeemed; then, in the screen scene, his brother is damningly exposed. It is this gift for something more than comedy, this sharp sense of theater, that has gone far toward making The School for Scandal the most famous comedy of manners in the language.

Once we are conscious of how, even more than he was a stylist or a satirist, Sheridan was a knowing playwright, we can grasp how much his play deserves its fame. If there is any catch to it all, it is that these virtues, in combination, less enhance than diminish one another; that the artificial begins to smack of the contrived; that the characters seem more puppets than points of view; that the polish, in consequence, suggests only the very best veneer; that the very pretenses Sheridan is satirizing have sneaked into his own act. Thus, for all the fine talk (and furtive whispers), there is only a pretense, here, of sinning: at any rate, the villain no more sins than the hero, the men than the women. Though Sheridan has vividly, and up to a point quite accurately, mirrored worldly society, he has, if not misrepresented, then at least sidestepped, the question of human nature. His is almost as good a school to learn stage tricks in as scandal. For all its brilliance, his play is a conventional and even cautious one. But, however debatable the uses to which it has been put, the brilliance is the thing that must ultimately be stressed.

RICHARD B. SHERIDAN

The School for Scandal

THE PERSONS OF THE PLAY

SIR PETER TEAZLE
SIR OLIVER SURFACE
SIR HARRY BUMPER
SIR BENJAMIN BACKBITE
JOSEPH SURFACE
CHARLES SURFACE
CARELESS
SNAKE
CRABTREE
ROWLEY
MOSES
TRIP
LADY TEAZLE
LADY SNEERWELL
MRS. CANDOUR
MARIA
GENTLEMEN, MAID, AND SERVANTS

THE SCENE: *London*

Prologue

A School for Scandal! tell me, I beseech you,
Needs there a school this modish art to teach you
No need of lessons now, the knowing think;
We might as well be taught to eat and drink.
Caused by a dearth of scandal, should the vapours
Distress our fair ones—let them read the papers;
Their powerful mixtures such disorders hit;
Crave what you will—there's *quantum suffict.*
"Lord!" cries my Lady Wormwood (who loves tattle,
And puts much salt and pepper in her prattle),
Just risen at noon, all night at cards when threshing
Strong tea and scandal—"Bless me, how refreshing!
Give me the papers, Lisp—how bold and free! [*Sips*]
Last night Lord L. [*Sips*] *was caught with Lady D.*
For aching heads what charming sal volatile! [*Sips*]
If Mrs. B will still continue flirting,
We hope she'll DRAW, *or we'll* UNDRAW *the curtain.*
Fine satire, poz—in public all abuse it,
But, by ourselves [*Sips*], our praise we can't refuse it.
Now, Lisp, read you—there, at that dash and star."

"Yes, ma'am—*A certain Lord had best beware,*
Who lives not twenty miles from Grosvenor Square;
For should he Lady W. find willing,
Wormwood is bitter"——"Oh! that's me! the villain!
Throw it behind the fire, and never more
Let that vile paper come within my door."
Thus at our friends we laugh, who feel the dart;
To reach our feelings, we ourselves must smart.
Is our young bard so young, to think that he
Can stop the full spring-tide of calumny?
Knows he the world so little, and its trade?
Alas! the devil's sooner raised than laid.
So strong, so swift, the monster there's no gagging:
Cut Scandal's head off, still the tongue is wagging.
Proud of your smiles once lavishly bestow'd,
Again our young Don Quixote takes the road;
To show his gratitude he draws his pen,
And seeks his hydra, Scandal, in his den.
For your applause all perils he would through—
He'll fight—that's write—a cavalliero true,
Till every drop of blood—that's ink—is spilt for you.

Act I

SCENE 1: *Lady Sneerwell's Dressing-room*

Lady Sneerwell *discovered at her toilet;* Snake *drinking cholocate.*

LADY SNEERWELL: The paragraphs, you say, Mr. Snake, were all inserted?

SNAKE: They were, madam; and, as I copied them myself in a feigned hand, there can be no suspicion whence they came.

LADY SNEERWELL: Did you circulate the report of Lady Brittle's intrigue with Captain Boastall?

SNAKE: That's in as fine a train as your ladyship could wish. In the common course of things, I think it must reach Mrs. Clackitt's ears within four-and-twenty hours; and then, you know, the business is as good as done.

LADY SNEERWELL: Why, truly, Mrs. Clackitt has a very pretty talent, and a great deal of industry.

SNAKE: True, madam, and has been tolerably successful in her day. To my knowledge, she has been the cause of six matches being broken off, and three sons being disinherited; of four forced elopements, and as many close confinements; nine separate maintenances, and two divorces. Nay, I have more than once traced her causing a *tête-à-tête* in the "Town and Country Magazine," when the parties, perhaps, had never seen each other's face before in the course of their lives.

LADY SNEERWELL: She certainly has talents, but her manner is gross.

SNAKE: 'Tis very true. She generally designs well, has a free tongue and a bold invention; but her colouring is too dark, and her outlines often extravagant. She wants that delicacy of tint, and mellowness of sneer, which distinguish your ladyship's scandal.

LADY SNEERWELL: You are partial, Snake.

SNAKE: Not in the least; everybody allows that Lady Sneerwell can do more with a word or look than many can with the most laboured detail, even when they happen to have a little truth on their side to support it.

LADY SNEERWELL: Yes, my dear Snake; and I am no hypocrite to deny the satisfaction I reap from the success of my efforts. Wounded myself, in the early part of my life, by the envenomed tongue of slander, I confess I have since known no pleasure equal to the reducing others to the level of my own injured reputation.

SNAKE: Nothing can be more natural. But, Lady Sneerwell, there is one affair in which you have lately employed me, wherein, I confess, I am at a loss to guess your motives.

LADY SNEERWELL: I conceive you mean with respect to my neighbour, Sir Peter Teazle, and his family?

SNAKE: I do. Here are two young men, to whom Sir Peter has acted as a kind of guardian since their father's death; the eldest possessing the most amiable character, and universally well spoken of—the youngest, the most dissipated and extravagant young fellow in the kingdom, without friends or character: the former an avowed admirer of your ladyship, and apparently your favourite; the latter attached to Maria, Sir Peter's ward, and confessedly beloved by her. Now, on the face of these circumstances, it is utterly unaccountable to me, why you, the widow of a city knight, with a good jointure, should not close with the passion of a man of such character and expectations as Mr. Surface; and more so why you should be so uncommonly earnest to destroy the mutual attachment subsisting between his brother Charles and Maria.

LADY SNEERWELL: Then, at once to unravel this mystery, I must inform you that love has no share whatever in the intercourse between Mr. Surface and me.

SNAKE: No!

LADY SNEERWELL: His real attachment is to Maria or her fortune; but, finding in his brother a favoured rival, he has been obliged to mask his pretensions, and profit by my assistance.

SNAKE: Yet still I am more puzzled why you should interest yourself in his success.

LADY SNEERWELL: Heavens! how dull you are! Cannot you surmise the weakness which I hitherto, through shame, have concealed even from you? Must I confess that Charles—that libertine, that extravagant, that bankrupt in fortune and reputation—that he it is for whom I am thus anxious and malicious, and to gain whom I would sacrifice everything?

SNAKE: Now, indeed, your conduct appears consistent; but how came you and Mr. Surface so confidential?

LADY SNEERWELL: For our mutual interest. I have found him out a long time since. I know him to be artful, selfish, and malicious—in short, a sentimental knave; while with Sir Peter, and indeed with all his acquaintance, he passes for a youthful miracle of prudence, good sense, and benevolence.

SNAKE: Yes; yet Sir Peter vows he has not his equal in England; and, above all, he praises him as a man of sentiment.

LADY SNEERWELL: True; and with the assistance of his sentiment and hypocrisy he has brought Sir Peter entirely into his interest with regard to Maria; while poor Charles has no friend in the house—though, I fear, he has a powerful one in Maria's heart, against whom we must direct our schemes.

Enter Servant.

SERVANT: Mr. Surface.

LADY SNEERWELL: Show him up.—[*Exit* Servant] He generally calls about this time. I don't wonder at people giving him to me for a lover.

Enter Joseph Surface.

JOSEPH SURFACE: My dear Lady Sneerwell, how do you do to-day? Mr. Snake, your most obedient.

LADY SNEERWELL: Snake has just been rallying me on our mutual attachment; but I have informed him of our real views. You know how useful he has been to us; and, believe me, the confidence is not ill-placed.

JOSEPH SURFACE: Madam, it is impossible for me to suspect a man of Mr. Snake's sensibility and discernment.

LADY SNEERWELL: Well, well, no compliments now; but tell me when you saw your mistress, Maria—or, what is more material to me, your brother.

JOSEPH SURFACE: I have not seen either since I left you; but I can inform you that they never meet. Some of your stories have taken a good effect on Maria.

LADY SNEERWELL: Ah, my dear Snake! the merit of this belongs to you. But do your brother's distresses increase?

JOSEPH SURFACE: Every hour. I am told he has had another execution in the house yesterday. In short, his dissipation and extravagance exceed anything I have ever heard of.

LADY SNEERWELL: Poor Charles!

JOSEPH SURFACE: True, madam; notwithstanding his vices, one can't help feeling for him. Poor Charles! I'm sure I wish it were in my power to be of any essential service to him; for the man who does not share in the distresses of a brother, even though merited by his own misconduct, deserves——

LADY SNEERWELL: O Lud! you are going to be moral, and forget that you are among friends.

JOSEPH SURFACE: Egad, that's true! I'll keep that sentiment till I see Sir Peter. However, it is certainly a charity to rescue Maria from such a libertine, who, if he is to be reclaimed, can be so only by a person of your ladyship's superior accomplishments and understanding.

SNAKE: I believe, Lady Sneerwell, here's company coming: I'll go and copy the letter I mentioned to you. Mr. Surface, your most obedient.

JOSEPH SURFACE: Sir, your very devoted.—[Exit Snake] Lady Sneerwell, I am very sorry you have put any farther confidence in that fellow.

LADY SNEERWELL: Why so?

JOSEPH SURFACE: I have lately detected him in frequent conference with old Rowley, who was formerly my father's steward, and has never, you know, been a friend of mine.

LADY SNEERWELL: And do you think he would betray us?

JOSEPH SURFACE: Nothing more likely: take my word for't, Lady Sneerwell, that fellow hasn't virtue enough to be faithful even to his own villainy. Ah, Maria!

Enter Maria.

LADY SNEERWELL: Maria, my dear, how do you do? What's the matter?

MARIA: Oh! there's that disagreeable lover of mine, Sir Benjamin Backbite, has just called at my guardian's, with his odious uncle, Crabtree; so I slipped out, and ran hither to avoid them.

LADY SNEERWELL: Is that all?

JOSEPH SURFACE: If my brother Charles had been of the party, madam, perhaps you would not have been so much alarmed.

LADY SNEERWELL: Nay, now you are severe; for I dare swear the truth of the matter is, Maria heard you were here. But, my dear, what has Sir Benjamin done, that you should avoid him so?

MARIA: Oh, he has done nothing—but 'tis for what he has said: his conversation is a perpetual libel on all his acquaintance.

JOSEPH SURFACE: Ay, and the worst of it is, there is no advantage in not knowing him; for he'll abuse a stranger just as soon as his best friend: and his uncle's as bad.

LADY SNEERWELL: Nay, but we should make allowance; Sir Benjamin is a wit and a poet.

MARIA: For my part, I own, madam, wit loses its respect with me, when I see it in company with malice. What do you think, Mr. Surface?

JOSEPH SURFACE: Certainly, madam; to smile at the jest which plants a thorn in another's breast is to become a principal in the mischief.

LADY SNEERWELL: Psha! there's no possibility of being witty without a little ill-nature: the malice of a good thing is the barb that makes it stick. What's your opinion, Mr. Surface?

JOSEPH SURFACE: To be sure, madam; that conversation, where the spirit of raillery is suppressed, will ever appear tedious and insipid.

MARIA: Well, I'll not debate how far scandal may be allowable; but in a man, I am sure, it is always contemptible. We have pride, envy, rivalship, and a thousand motives to depreciate each other; but the male slanderer must have the cowardice of a woman before he can traduce one.

Re-enter Servant.

SERVANT: Madam, Mrs. Candour is below, and, if your ladyship's at leisure, will leave her carriage.

LADY SNEERWELL: Beg her to walk in.—[Exit Servant] Now, Maria, here is a character to your taste; for, though Mrs. Candour is a little talkative, everybody knows her to be the best-natured and best sort of woman.

MARIA: Yes, with a very gross affectation of good nature and benevolence, she does more mischief than the direct malice of old Crabtree.

JOSEPH SURFACE: I'faith that's true, Lady Sneerwell: whenever I hear the current running against the characters of my friends, I never think them in such danger as when Candour undertakes their defence.

LADY SNEERWELL: Hush!—here she is!

Enter Mrs. Candour.

MRS. CANDOUR: My dear Lady Sneerwell, how have you been this century?—Mr. Surface, what news do you hear?—though indeed it is no matter, for I think one hears nothing else but scandal.

JOSEPH SURFACE: Just so, indeed, ma'am.

MRS. CANDOUR: Oh, Maria! child,—what, is the whole affair off between you and Charles? His extravagance, I presume—the town talks of nothing else.

MARIA: I am very sorry, ma'am, the town has so little to do.

MRS. CANDOUR: True, true, child: but there's no stopping people's tongues. I own I was hurt to hear it, as I indeed was to learn, from the same quarter, that your guardian, Sir Peter, and Lady Teazle have not agreed lately as well as could be wished.

MARIA: 'Tis strangely impertinent for people to busy themselves so.

MRS. CANDOUR: Very true, child; but what's to be done? People will talk—there's no preventing it.

Why, it was but yesterday I was told that Miss Gadabout had eloped with Sir Filagree Flirt. But, Lord! there's no minding what one hears; though, to be sure, I had this from very good authority.

MARIA: Such reports are highly scandalous.

MRS. CANDOUR: So they are, child—shameful, shameful! But the world is so censorious, no character escapes. Lord, now who would have suspected your friend, Miss Prim, of an indiscretion? Yet such is the ill-nature of people, that they say her uncle stopped her last week, just as she was stepping into the York mail with her dancing-master.

MARIA: I'll answer for't there are no grounds for that report.

MRS. CANDOUR: Ah, no foundation in the world, I dare swear: no more, probably, than for the story circulated last month, of Mrs. Festino's affair with Colonel Cassino—though, to be sure, that matter was never rightly cleared up.

JOSEPH SURFACE: The license of invention some people take is monstrous indeed.

MARIA: 'Tis so; but, in my opinion, those who report such things are equally culpable.

MRS. CANDOUR: To be sure they are; tale-bearers are as bad as the tale-makers—'tis an old observation, and a very true one: but what's to be done, as I said before? how will you prevent people from talking? To-day, Mrs. Clackitt assured me, Mr. and Mrs. Honeymoon were at last become mere man and wife, like the rest of their acquaintance. She likewise hinted that a certain widow, in the next street, had got rid of her dropsy and recovered her shape in a most surprising manner. And at the same time Miss Tattle, who was by, affirmed, that Lord Buffalo had discovered his lady at a house of no extraordinary fame; and that Sir Harry Bouquet and Tom Saunter were to measure swords on a similar provocation. But, Lord, do you think I would report these things! No, no! tale-bearers, as I said before, are just as bad as the tale-makers.

JOSEPH SURFACE: Ah! Mrs. Candour, if everybody had your forbearance and good nature!

MRS. CANDOUR: I confess, Mr. Surface, I cannot bear to hear people attacked behind their backs; and when ugly circumstances come out against our acquaintance I own I always love to think the best. By-the-by, I hope 'tis not true that your brother is absolutely ruined?

JOSEPH SURFACE: I am afraid his circumstances are very bad indeed, ma'am.

MRS. CANDOUR: Ah!—I heard so—but you must tell him to keep up his spirits; everybody almost is in the same way: Lord Spindle, Sir Thomas Splint, Captain Quinze, and Mr. Nickit—all up, I hear, within this week; so, if Charles is undone, he'll find half his acquaintance ruined too, and that, you know, is a consolation.

JOSEPH SURFACE: Doubtless, ma'am—a very great one.

Re-enter Servant.

SERVANT: Mr. Crabtree and Sir Benjamin Backbite.

[*Exit*]

LADY SNEERWELL: So, Maria, you see your lover pursues you; positively you shan't escape.

Enter Crabtree *and* Sir Benjamin Backbite.

CRABTREE: Lady Sneerwell, I kiss your hand. Mrs. Candour, I don't believe you are acquainted with my nephew, Sir Benjamin Backbite? Egad, ma'am, he has a pretty wit, and is a pretty poet too. Isn't he, Lady Sneerwell?

SIR BENJAMIN: Oh, fie, uncle!

CRABTREE: Nay, egad it's true: I back him at a rebus or a charade against the best rhymer in the kingdom. Has your ladyship heard the epigram he wrote last week on Lady Frizzle's feather catching fire?—Do, Benjamin, repeat it, or the charade you made last night extempore at Mrs. Drowzie's conversazione. Come now; your first is the name of a fish, your second a great naval commander, and——

SIR BENJAMIN: Uncle, now—pr'ythee——

CRABTREE: I'faith, ma'am, 'twould surprise you to hear how ready he is at all these sort of things.

LADY SNEERWELL: I wonder, Sir Benjamin, you never publish anything.

SIR BENJAMIN: To say truth, ma'am, 'tis very vulgar to print; and, as my little productions are mostly satires and lampoons on particular people, I find they circulate more by giving copies in confidence to the friends of the parties. However, I have some love elegies, which, when favoured with this lady's smiles, I mean to give the public.

[*Pointing to* Maria]

CRABTREE: [*To Maria*] 'Fore heaven, ma'am, they'll immortalize you!—you will be handed down to posterity, like Petrarch's Laura, or Waller's Sacharissa.

SIR BENJAMIN: [*To Maria*] Yes, madam, I think you will like them, when you shall see them on a beautiful quarto page, where a neat rivulet of text shall meander through a meadow of margin. 'Fore Gad, they will be the most elegant things of their kind!

CRABTREE: But, ladies, that's true—have you heard the news?

MRS. CANDOUR: What, sir, do you mean the report of—

CRABTREE: No, ma'am, that's not it.—Miss Nicely is going to be married to her own footman.

MRS. CANDOUR: Impossible!

CRABTREE: Ask Sir Benjamin.

SIR BENJAMIN: 'Tis very true, ma'am: everything is fixed, and the wedding liveries bespoke.

CRABTREE: Yes—and they do say there were pressing reasons for it.

LADY SNEERWELL: Why, I have heard something of this before.

MRS. CANDOUR: It can't be—and I wonder any one

should believe such a story of so prudent a lady as Miss Nicely.

SIR BENJAMIN: O Lud! ma'am, that's the very reason 'twas believed at once. She has always been so cautious and so reserved, that everybody was sure there was some reason for it at bottom.

MRS. CANDOUR: Why, to be sure, a tale of scandal is as fatal to the credit of a prudent lady of her stamp as a fever is generally to those of the strongest constitutions. But there is a sort of puny sickly reputation, that is always ailing, yet will outlive the robuster characters of a hundred prudes.

SIR BENJAMIN: True, madam, there are valetudinarians in reputation as well as constitution, who, being conscious of their weak part, avoid the least breath of air, and supply their want of stamina by care and circumspection.

MRS. CANDOUR: Well, but this may be all a mistake. You know, Sir Benjamin, very trifling circumstances often give rise to the most injurious tales.

CRABTREE: That they do, I'll be sworn, ma'am. Did you ever hear how Miss Piper came to lose her lover and her character last summer at Tunbridge? —Sir Benjamin, you remember it?

SIR BENJAMIN: Oh, to be sure!—the most whimsical circumstance.

LADY SNEERWELL: How was it, pray?

CRABTREE: Why, one evening, at Mrs. Ponto's assembly, the conversation happened to turn on the breeding of Nova Scotia sheep in this country. Says a young lady in company, I have known instances of it; for Miss Letitia Piper, a first cousin of mine, had a Nova Scotia sheep that produced her twins. "What!" cries the Lady Dowager Dundizzy (who you know is as deaf as a post), "has Miss Piper had twins?" This mistake, as you may imagine, threw the whole company into a fit of laughter. However, 'twas the next morning everywhere reported, and in a few days believed by the whole town, that Miss Letitia Piper had actually been brought to bed of a fine boy and girl: and in less than a week there were some people who could name the father, and the farm-house where the babies were put to nurse.

LADY SNEERWELL: Strange, indeed!

CRABTREE: Matter of fact, I assure you. O Lud! Mr. Surface, pray is it true that your uncle, Sir Oliver, is coming home?

JOSEPH SURFACE: Not that I know of, indeed, sir.

CRABTREE: He has been in the East Indies a long time. You can scarcely remember him, I believe? Sad comfort, whenever he returns, to hear how your brother has gone on!

JOSEPH SURFACE: Charles has been imprudent, sir, to be sure; but I hope no busy people have already prejudiced Sir Oliver against him. He may reform.

SIR BENJAMIN: To be sure he may; for my part I never believed him to be so utterly void of principle as people say; and though he has lost all his

friends, I am told nobody is better spoken of by the Jews.

CRABTREE: That's true, egad, nephew. If the old Jewry was a ward, I believe Charles would be an alderman: no man more popular there, 'fore Gad! I hear he pays as many annuities as the Irish tontine; and that, whenever he is sick, they have prayers for the recovery of his health in all the synagogues.

SIR BENJAMIN: Yet no man lives in greater splendour. They tell me, when he entertains his friends he will sit down to dinner with a dozen of his own securities; have a score of tradesmen in the antechamber, and an officer behind every guest's chair.

JOSEPH SURFACE: This may be entertainment to you, gentlemen, but you pay very little regard to the feelings of a brother.

MARIA: [Aside] Their malice is intolerable!—[Aloud] Lady Sneerwell, I must wish you a good morning: I'm not very well.   [Exit]

MRS. CANDOUR: O dear! she changes colour very much.

LADY SNEERWELL: Do, Mrs. Candour, follow her; she may want your assistance.

MRS. CANDOUR: That I will, with all my soul, ma'am. —Poor dear girl, who knows what her situation may be!   [Exit]

LADY SNEERWELL: 'Twas nothing but that she could not bear to hear Charles reflected on, notwithstanding their difference.

SIR BENJAMIN: The young lady's *penchant* is obvious.

CRABTREE: But, Benjamin, you must not give up the pursuit for that: follow her, and put her into good humour. Repeat her some of your own verses. Come, I'll assist you.

SIR BENJAMIN: Mr. Surface, I did not mean to hurt you; but depend on't your brother is utterly undone.

CRABTREE: O Lud, ay! undone as ever man was— can't raise a guinea.

SIR BENJAMIN: And everything sold, I'm told, that was movable.

CRABTREE: I have seen one that was at his house. Not a thing left but some empty bottles that were overlooked, and the family pictures, which I believe are framed in the wainscots.

SIR BENJAMIN: And I'm very sorry also to hear some bad stories against him.   [Going]

CRABTREE: Oh, he has done many mean things, that's certain.

SIR BENJAMIN: But, however, as he's your brother——
                                              [Going]

CRABTREE: We'll tell you all another opportunity.
                        [Exeunt Crabtree and Sir Benjamin]

LADY SNEERWELL: Ha, ha! 'tis very hard for them to leave a subject they have not quite run down.

JOSEPH SURFACE: And I believe the abuse was no more acceptable to your ladyship than to Maria.

LADY SNEERWELL: I doubt her affections are further

engaged than we imagine. But the family are to be here this evening, so you may as well dine where you are, and we shall have an opportunity of observing further; in the meantime, I'll go and plot mischief, and you shall study sentiment. [*Exeunt*]

SCENE 2:   *A Room in Sir Peter Teazle's House*

Enter Sir Peter Teazle.

SIR PETER: When an old bachelor marries a young wife, what is he to expect? 'Tis now six months since Lady Teazle made me the happiest of men —and I have been the most miserable dog ever since! We tift a little going to church, and fairly quarrelled before the bells had done ringing. I was more than once nearly choked with gall during the honeymoon, and had lost all comfort in life before my friends had done wishing me joy. Yet I chose with caution—a girl bred wholly in the country, who never knew luxury beyond one silk gown, nor dissipation above the annual gala of a race ball. Yet she now plays her part in all the extravagant fopperies of fashion and the town, with as ready a grace as if she never had seen a bush or a grass-plot out of Grosvenor Square! I am sneered at by all my acquaintance, and paragraphed in the newspapers. She dissipates my fortune, and contradicts all my humours; yet the worst of it is, I doubt I love her, or I should never bear all this. However, I'll never be weak enough to own it.

Enter Rowley.

ROWLEY: Oh! Sir Peter, your servant: how is it with you, sir?

SIR PETER: Very bad, Master Rowley, very bad. I meet with nothing but crosses and vexations.

ROWLEY: What can have happened since yesterday?

SIR PETER: A good question to a married man!

ROWLEY: Nay, I'm sure, Sir Peter, your lady can't be the cause of your uneasiness.

SIR PETER: Why, has anybody told you she was dead?

ROWLEY: Come, come, Sir Peter, you love her, notwithstanding your tempers don't exactly agree.

SIR PETER: But the fault is entirely hers, Master Rowley. I am, myself, the sweetest-tempered man alive, and hate a teasing temper; and so I tell her a hundred times a day.

ROWLEY: Indeed!

SIR PETER: Ay; and what is very extraordinary, in all our disputes she is always in the wrong! But Lady Sneerwell, and the set she meets at her house, encourage the perverseness of her disposition. Then, to complete my vexation, Maria, my ward, whom I ought to have the power of a father over, is determined to turn rebel too, and absolutely refuses the man whom I have long resolved on for her husband; meaning, I suppose, to bestow herself on his profligate brother.

ROWLEY: You know, Sir Peter, I have always taken the liberty to differ with you on the subject of these two young gentlemen. I only wish you may not be deceived in your opinion of the elder. For Charles, my life on't! he will retrieve his errors yet. Their worthy father, once my honoured master, was, at his years, nearly as wild a spark; yet, when he died, he did not leave a more benevolent heart to lament his loss.

SIR PETER: You are wrong, Master Rowley. On their father's death, you know, I acted as a kind of guardian to them both, till their uncle Sir Oliver's liberality gave them an early independence: of course, no person could have more opportunities of judging of their hearts, and I was never mistaken in my life. Joseph is indeed a model for the young men of the age. He is a man of sentiment, and acts up to the sentiments he professes; but, for the other, take my word for't, if he had any grain of virtue by descent, he has dissipated it with the rest of his inheritance. Ah! my old friend, Sir Oliver, will be deeply mortified when he finds how part of his bounty has been misapplied.

ROWLEY: I am sorry to find you so violent against the young man, because this may be the most critical period of his fortune. I came hither with news that will surprise you.

SIR PETER: What! let me hear.

ROWLEY: Sir Oliver is arrived, and at this moment in town.

SIR PETER: How! you astonish me! I thought you did not expect him this month.

ROWLEY: I did not: but his passage has been remarkably quick.

SIR PETER: Egad, I shall rejoice to see my old friend. 'Tis sixteen years since we met. We have had many a day together: but does he still enjoin us not to inform his nephews of his arrival?

ROWLEY: Most strictly. He means, before it is known, to make some trial of their dispositions.

SIR PETER: Ah! There needs no art to discover their merits—however, he shall have his way; but, pray, does he know I am married?

ROWLEY: Yes, and will soon wish you joy.

SIR PETER: What, as we drink health to a friend in consumption! Ah, Oliver will laugh at me. We used to rail at matrimony together, but he has been steady to his text. Well, he must be soon at my house, though—I'll instantly give orders for his reception. But, Master Rowley, don't drop a word that Lady Teazle and I ever disagree.

ROWLEY: By no means.

SIR PETER: For I should never be able to stand Noll's jokes; so I'll have him think, Lord forgive me! that we are a very happy couple.

ROWLEY: I understand you:—but then you must be very careful not to differ while he is in the house with you.

SIR PETER: Egad, and so we must—and that's impossible. Ah! Master Rowley, when an old bachelor marries a young wife, he deserves—no—the crime carries its punishment along with it.　[*Exeunt*]

Act II

SCENE 1:　*A Room in Sir Peter Teazle's House*

Enter Sir Peter *and* Lady Teazle.

SIR PETER: Lady Teazle, Lady Teazle, I'll not bear it!

LADY TEAZLE: Sir Peter, Sir Peter, you may bear it or not, as you please; but I ought to have my own way in everything, and what's more, I will too. What though I was educated in the country, I know very well that women of fashion in London are accountable to nobody after they are married.

SIR PETER: Very well, ma'am, very well; so a husband is to have no influence, no authority?

LADY TEAZLE: Authority! No, to be sure:—if you wanted authority over me, you should have adopted me, and not married me: I am sure you were old enough.

SIR PETER: Old enough!—ay, there it is! Well, well, Lady Teazle, though my life may be made unhappy by your temper, I'll not be ruined by your extravagance!

LADY TEAZLE: My extravagance! I'm sure I'm not more extravagant than a woman of fashion ought to be.

SIR PETER: No, no, madam, you shall throw away no more sums on such unmeaning luxury. 'Slife! to spend as much to furnish your dressing-room with flowers in winter as would suffice to turn the Pantheon into a greenhouse, and give a *fête champêtre* at Christmas.

LADY TEAZLE: And am I to blame, Sir Peter, because flowers are dear in cold weather? You should find fault with the climate, and not with me. For my part, I'm sure I wish it was spring all the year round, and that roses grew under our feet!

SIR PETER: Oons! madam—if you had been born to this, I shouldn't wonder at your talking thus; but you forget what your situation was when I married you.

LADY TEAZLE: No, no, I don't; 'twas a very disagreeable one, or I should never have married you.

SIR PETER: Yes, yes, madam, you were then in somewhat a humbler style—the daughter of a plain country squire. Recollect, Lady Teazle, when I saw you first sitting at your tambour, in a pretty figured linen gown, with a bunch of keys at your side, your hair combed smooth over a roll, and your apartment hung round with fruits in worsted, of your own working.

LADY TEAZLE: Oh, yes! I remember it very well, and a curious life I led. My daily occupation to inspect the dairy, superintend the poultry, make extracts from the family receipt-book, and comb my aunt Deborah's lapdog.

SIR PETER: Yes, yes, ma'am, 'twas so indeed.

LADY TEAZLE: And then, you know, my evening amusements! To draw patterns for ruffles, which I had not the materials to make up; to play Pope Joan with the Curate; to read a sermon to my aunt; or to be stuck down to an old spinet to strum my father to sleep after a fox-chase.

SIR PETER: I am glad you have so good a memory. Yes, madam, these were the recreations I took you from; but now you must have your coach—*vis-à-vis* —and three powdered footmen before your chair; and, in the summer, a pair of white cats to draw you to Kensington Gardens. No recollection, I suppose, when you were content to ride double, behind the butler, on a docked coach-horse?

LADY TEAZLE: No—I swear I never did that; I deny the butler and the coach-horse.

SIR PETER: This, madam, was your situation; and what have I done for you? I have made you a woman of fashion, of fortune, of rank—in short, I have made you my wife.

LADY TEAZLE: Well, then, and there is but one thing more you can make me to add to that obligation, that is——

SIR PETER: My widow, I suppose?

LADY TEAZLE: Hem! hem!

SIR PETER: I thank you, madam—but don't flatter yourself; for, though your ill-conduct may disturb my peace of mind, it shall never break my heart, I promise you: however, I am equally obliged to you for the hint.

LADY TEAZLE: Then why will you endeavour to make yourself so disagreeable to me, and thwart me in every little elegant expense?

SIR PETER: 'Slife, madam, I say, had you any of these little elegant expenses when you married me?

LADY TEAZLE: Lud, Sir Peter! would you have me be out of the fashion?

SIR PETER: The fashion, indeed! what had you to do with the fashion before you married me?

LADY TEAZLE: For my part, I should think you would like to have your wife thought a woman of taste.

SIR PETER: Ay—there again—taste! Zounds! madam, you had no taste when you married me!

LADY TEAZLE: That's very true, indeed, Sir Peter! and, after having married you, I should never pretend to taste again, I allow. But now, Sir Peter, since we have finished our daily jangle, I presume I may go to my engagement at Lady Sneerwell's?

SIR PETER: Ay, there's another precious circumstance —a charming set of acquaintance you have made there!

LADY TEAZLE: Nay, Sir Peter, they are all people of rank and fortune, and remarkably tenacious of reputation.

SIR PETER: Yes, egad, they are tenacious of reputation with a vengeance; for they don't choose anybody should have a character but themselves! Such a crew! Ah! many a wretch has rid on a hurdle who has done less mischief than these utterers of forged tales, coiners of scandal, and clippers of reputation.

LADY TEAZLE: What, would you restrain the freedom of speech?

SIR PETER: Ah! they have made you just as bad as any one of the society.

LADY TEAZLE: Why, I believe I do bear a part with a tolerable grace. But I vow I bear no malice against the people I abuse: when I say an ill-natured thing, 'tis out of pure good humour; and I take it for granted they deal exactly in the same manner with me. But, Sir Peter, you know you promised to come to Lady Sneerwell's too.

SIR PETER: Well, well, I'll call in just to look after my own character.

LADY TEAZLE: Then, indeed, you must make haste after me or you'll be too late. So good-bye to ye. [Exit]

SIR PETER: So—I have gained much by my intended expostulation! Yet with what a charming air she contradicts everything I say, and how pleasantly she shows her contempt for my authority! Well, though I can't make her love me, there is great satisfaction in quarrelling with her; and I think she never appears to such advantage as when she is doing everything in her power to plague me. [Exit]

SCENE 2: A Room in Lady Sneerwell's House

Lady Sneerwell, Mrs. Candour, Crabtree, Sir Benjamin Backbite, and Joseph Surface, discovered.

LADY SNEERWELL: Nay, positively, we will hear it.

JOSEPH SURFACE: Yes, yes, the epigram, by all means.

SIR BENJAMIN: O plague on't, uncle! 'tis mere nonsense.

CRABTREE: No, no; 'fore Gad, very clever for an extempore!

SIR BENJAMIN: But, ladies, you should be acquainted with the circumstance. You must know, that one day last week, as Lady Betty Curricle was taking the dust in Hyde Park, in a sort of duodecimo phaeton, she desired me to write some verses on her ponies; upon which, I took out my pocketbook, and in one moment produced the following:—

Sure never were seen two such beautiful ponies;
Other horses are clowns, but these macaronies:
To give them this title I am sure can't be wrong.
Their legs are so slim, and their tails are so long.

CRABTREE: There, ladies, done in the smack of a whip, and on horseback too.

JOSEPH SURFACE: A very Phœbus, mounted—indeed, Sir Benjamin!

SIR BENJAMIN: Oh dear, sir!—trifles—trifles.—

Enter Lady Teazle and Maria.

MRS. CANDOUR: I must have a copy.

LADY SNEERWELL: Lady Teazle, I hope we shall see Sir Peter?

LADY TEAZLE: I believe he'll wait on your ladyship presently.

LADY SNEERWELL: Maria, my love, you look grave. Come, you shall sit down to piquet with Mr. Surface.

MARIA: I take very little pleasure in cards—however, I'll do as your ladyship pleases.

LADY TEAZLE: I am surprised Mr. Surface should sit down with her; I thought he would have embraced this opportunity of speaking to me before Sir Peter came. [Aside]

MRS. CANDOUR: Now, I'll die; but you are so scandalous, I'll forswear your society.

LADY TEAZLE: What's the matter, Mrs. Candour?

MRS. CANDOUR: They'll not allow our friend Miss Vermillion to be handsome.

LADY SNEERWELL: Oh, surely she is a pretty woman.

CRABTREE: I am very glad you think so, ma'am.

MRS. CANDOUR: She has a charming fresh colour.

LADY TEAZLE: Yes, when it is fresh put on.

MRS. CANDOUR: Oh, fie! I'll swear her colour is natural: I have seen it come and go!

LADY TEAZLE: I dare swear you have, ma'am: it goes off at night, and comes again in the morning.

SIR BENJAMIN: True, ma'am, it not only comes and goes; but, what's more, egad, her maid can fetch and carry it!

MRS. CANDOUR: Ha! ha! ha! how I hate to hear you talk so! But surely, now, her sister is, or was, very handsome.

CRABTREE: Who? Mrs. Evergreen? O Lord! she's six-and-fifty if she's an hour!

MRS. CANDOUR: Now positively you wrong her; fifty-two or fifty-three is the utmost—and I don't think she looks more.

SIR BENJAMIN: Ah! there's no judging by her looks, unless one could see her face.

LADY SNEERWELL: Well, well, if Mrs. Evergreen does take some pains to repair the ravages of time, you must allow she effects it with great ingenuity; and surely that's better than the careless manner in which the widow Ochre caulks her wrinkles.

SIR BENJAMIN: Nay, now, Lady Sneerwell, you are severe upon the widow. Come, come, 'tis not that she paints so ill—but, when she has finished her face, she joins it on so badly to her neck, that she looks like a mended statue, in which the connoisseur may see at once that the head's modern, though the trunk's antique!

CRABTREE: Ha! ha! ha! Well said, nephew!

MRS. CANDOUR: Ha! ha! ha! Well, you make me laugh; but I vow I hate you for it. What do you think of Miss Simper?

SIR BENJAMIN: Why, she has very pretty teeth.

LADY TEAZLE: Yes; and on that account, when she is

neither speaking nor laughing (which very seldom happens), she never absolutely shuts her mouth, but leaves it always on ajar, as it were—thus.

[Shows her teeth]

MRS. CANDOUR: How can you be so ill-natured?

LADY TEAZLE: Nay, I allow even that's better than the pains Mrs. Prim takes to conceal her losses in front. She draws her mouth till it positively resembles the aperture of a poor's-box, and all her words appear to slide out edgewise, as it were—thus: *How do you do, madam? Yes, madam.*

LADY SNEERWELL: Very well, Lady Teazle; I see you can be a little severe.

LADY TEAZLE: In defence of a friend it is but justice. But here comes Sir Peter to spoil our pleasantry.

Enter Sir Peter Teazle.

SIR PETER: Ladies, your most obedient—[Aside] Mercy on me, here is the whole set! a character dead at every word, I suppose.

MRS. CANDOUR: I am rejoiced you are come, Sir Peter. They have been so censorious—and Lady Teazle as bad as any one.

SIR PETER: That must be very distressing to you, Mrs. Candour, I dare swear.

MRS. CANDOUR: Oh, they will allow good qualities to nobody; not even good nature to our friend Mrs. Pursy.

LADY TEAZLE: What, the fat dowager who was at Mrs. Quadrille's last night?

MRS. CANDOUR: Nay, her bulk is her misfortune; and, when she takes so much pains to get rid of it, you ought not to reflect on her.

LADY SNEERWELL: That's very true, indeed.

LADY TEAZLE: Yes, I know she almost lives on acids and small whey; laces herself by pulleys; and often, in the hottest noon in summer, you may see her on a little squat pony, with her hair plaited up behind like a drummer's and puffing round the Ring on a full trot.

MRS. CANDOUR: I thank you, Lady Teazle, for defending her.

SIR PETER: Yes, a good defence, truly.

MRS. CANDOUR: Truly, Lady Teazle is as censorious as Miss Sallow.

CRABTREE: Yes, and she is a curious being to pretend to be censorious—an awkward gawky, without any one good point under heaven.

MRS. CANDOUR: Positively you shall not be so very severe. Miss Sallow is a near relation of mine by marriage, and, as for her person, great allowance is to be made; for, let me tell you, a woman labours under many disadvantages who tries to pass for a girl of six-and-thirty.

LADY SNEERWELL: Though, surely, she is handsome still—and for the weakness in her eyes, considering how much she reads by candle-light, it is not to be wondered at.

MRS. CANDOUR: True; and then as to her manner, upon my word I think it is particularly graceful, considering she never had the least education; for you know her mother was a Welsh milliner, and her father a sugar-baker at Bristol.

SIR BENJAMIN: Ah! you are both of you too good-natured!

SIR PETER: Yes, damned good-natured! This their own relation! mercy on me!   [Aside]

MRS. CANDOUR: For my part, I own I cannot bear to hear a friend ill-spoken of.

SIR PETER: No, to be sure!

SIR BENJAMIN: Oh! you are of a moral turn. Mrs. Candour and I can sit for an hour and hear Lady Stucco talk sentiment.

LADY TEAZLE: Nay, I vow Lady Stucco is very well with the dessert after dinner; for she's just like the French fruit one cracks for mottoes—made up of paint and proverb.

MRS. CANDOUR: Well, I will never join in ridiculing a friend; and so I constantly tell my cousin Ogle, and you all know what pretensions she has to be critical on beauty.

CRABTREE: Oh, to be sure! she has herself the oddest countenance that ever was seen; 'tis a collection of features from all the different countries of the globe.

SIR BENJAMIN: So she has, indeed—an Irish front——

CRABTREE: Caledonian locks——

SIR BENJAMIN: Dutch nose——

CRABTREE: Austrian lips——

SIR BENJAMIN: Complexion of a Spaniard——

CRABTREE: And teeth *à la Chinoise*——

SIR BENJAMIN: In short, her face resembles a *table d'hôte* at Spa—where no two guests are of a nation——

CRABTREE: Or a congress at the close of a general war—wherein all the members, even to her eyes, appear to have a different interest, and her nose and chin are the only parties likely to join issue.

MRS. CANDOUR: Ha! ha! ha!

SIR PETER: Mercy on my life!—a person they dine with twice a week!   [Aside]

LADY SNEERWELL: Go—go—you are a couple of provoking Toads.

MRS. CANDOUR: Nay, but I vow you shall not carry the laugh off so—for give me leave to say, that Mrs. Ogle——

SIR PETER: Madam, madam, I beg your pardon—there's no stopping these good gentlemen's tongues. But when I tell you, Mrs. Candour, that the lady they are abusing is a particular friend of mine, I hope you'll not take her part.

LADY SNEERWELL: Ha! ha! ha! well said, Sir Peter! but you are a cruel creature—too phlegmatic yourself for a jest, and too peevish to allow wit in others.

SIR PETER: Ah, madam, true wit is more nearly allied to good nature than your ladyship is aware of.

LADY TEAZLE: True, Sir Peter: I believe they are so near akin that they can never be united.

SIR BENJAMIN: Or rather, madam, suppose them man and wife, because one seldom sees them together.

LADY TEAZLE: But Sir Peter is such an enemy to scandal, I believe he would have it put down by parliament.

SIR PETER: 'Fore heaven, madam, if they were to consider the sporting with reputation of as much importance as poaching on manors, and pass an act for the preservation of fame, I believe many would thank them for the bill.

LADY SNEERWELL: O Lud! Sir Peter, would you deprive us of our privileges?

SIR PETER: Ay, madam; and then no person should be permitted to kill characters and run down reputations, but qualified old maids and disappointed widows.

LADY SNEERWELL: Go, you monster!

MRS. CANDOUR: But, surely, you would not be quite so severe on those who only report what they hear?

SIR PETER: Yes, madam, I would have law merchant for them too; and in all cases of slander currency, whenever the drawer of the lie was not to be found, the injured parties should have a right to come on any of the indorsers.

CRABTREE: Well, for my part, I believe there never was a scandalous tale without some foundation.

LADY SNEERWELL: Come, ladies, shall we sit down to cards in the next room?

Enter Servant, *who whispers* Sir Peter.

SIR PETER: I'll be with them directly.—[*Exit* Servant] I'll get away unperceived.   [*Aside*]

LADY SNEERWELL: Sir Peter, you are not going to leave us?

SIR PETER: Your ladyship must excuse me; I'm called away by particular business. But I leave my character behind me.   [*Exit*]

SIR BENJAMIN: Well—certainly, Lady Teazle, that lord of yours is a strange being: I could tell you some stories of him would make you laugh heartily if he were not your husband.

LADY TEAZLE: Oh, pray don't mind that; come, do let's hear them.

[*Exeunt all but* Joseph Surface *and* Maria]

JOSEPH SURFACE: Maria, I see you have no satisfaction in this society.

MARIA: How is it possible I should? If to raise malicious smiles at the infirmities or misfortunes of those who have never injured us be the province of wit or humour, Heaven grant me a double portion of dulness!

JOSEPH SURFACE: Yet they appear more ill-natured than they are; they have no malice at heart.

MARIA: Then is their conduct still more contemptible; for, in my opinion, nothing could excuse the intemperance of their tongues but a natural and uncontrollable bitterness of mind.

JOSEPH SURFACE: Undoubtedly, madam; and it has always been a sentiment of mine, that to propagate a malicious truth wantonly is more despicable than to falsify from revenge. But can you, Maria, feel thus for others, and be unkind to me alone? Is hope to be denied the tenderest passion?

MARIA: Why will you distress me by renewing this subject?

JOSEPH SURFACE: Ah, Maria! you would not treat me thus, and oppose your guardian, Sir Peter's will, but that I see that profligate Charles is still a favoured rival.

MARIA: Ungenerously urged! But, whatever my sentiments are for that unfortunate young man, be assured I shall not feel more bound to give him up, because his distresses have lost him the regard even of a brother.

JOSEPH SURFACE: Nay, but, Maria, do not leave me with a frown: by all that's honest, I swear——

[*Kneels*]

Re-enter Lady Teazle *behind.*

[*Aside*] Gad's life, here's Lady Teazle.—[*Aloud to* Maria] You must not—no, you shall not—for, though I have the greatest regard for Lady Teazle——

MARIA: Lady Teazle!

JOSEPH SURFACE: Yet were Sir Peter to suspect——

LADY TEAZLE: [*Coming forward*] What is this, pray? Do you take her for me?—Child, you are wanted in the next room.—[*Exit* Maria] What is all this, pray?

JOSEPH SURFACE: Oh, the most unlucky circumstance in nature! Maria has somehow suspected the tender concern I have for your happiness, and threatened to acquaint Sir Peter with her suspicions, and I was just endeavouring to reason with her when you came in.

LADY TEAZLE: Indeed! but you seemed to adopt a very tender mode of reasoning—do you usually argue on your knees?

JOSEPH SURFACE: Oh, she's a child, and I thought a little bombast——but, Lady Teazle, when are you to give me your judgment on my library, as you promised?

LADY TEAZLE: No, no; I begin to think it would be imprudent, and you know I admit you as a lover no farther than fashion requires.

JOSEPH SURFACE: True—a mere Platonic cicisbeo, what every wife is entitled to.

LADY TEAZLE: Certainly, one must not be out of the fashion. However, I have so many of my country prejudices left, that, though Sir Peter's ill humour may vex me ever so, it never shall provoke me to——

JOSEPH SURFACE: The only revenge in your power. Well, I applaud your moderation.

LADY TEAZLE: Go—you are an insinuating wretch! But we shall be missed—let us join the company.

JOSEPH SURFACE: But we had best not return together.

LADY TEAZLE: Well, don't stay; for Maria shan't come to hear any more of your reasoning, I promise you.   [Exit]

JOSEPH SURFACE: A curious dilemma, truly, my politics have run me into! I wanted, at first, only to ingratiate myself with Lady Teazle, that she might not be my enemy with Maria; and I have, I don't know how, become her serious lover. Sincerely I begin to wish I had never made such a point of gaining so very good a character, for it has led me into so many cursed rogueries that I doubt I shall be exposed at last.   [Exit]

SCENE 3: *A Room in Sir Peter Teazle's House*

Enter Sir Oliver Surface *and* Rowley.

SIR OLIVER: Ha! ha! ha! so my old friend is married, hey?—a young wife out of the country. Ha! ha! ha! that he should have stood bluff to old bachelor so long, and sink into a husband at last!

ROWLEY: But you must not rally him on the subject, Sir Oliver; 'tis a tender point, I assure you, though he has been married only seven months.

SIR OLIVER: Then he has been just half a year on the stool of repentance!—Poor Peter! But you say he has entirely given up Charles—never sees him, hey?

ROWLEY: His prejudice against him is astonishing, and I am sure greatly increased by a jealousy of him with Lady Teazle, which he has industriously been led into by a scandalous society in the neighbourhood, who have contributed not a little to Charles's ill name. Whereas the truth is, I believe, if the lady is partial to either of them, his brother is the favourite.

SIR OLIVER: Ay, I know there are a set of malicious, prating, prudent gossips, both male and female, who murder characters to kill time, and will rob a young fellow of his good name before he has years to know the value of it. But I am not to be prejudiced against my nephew by such, I promise you! No, no: if Charles has done nothing false or mean, I shall compound for his extravagance.

ROWLEY: Then, my life on't, you will reclaim him. Ah, sir, it gives me new life to find that your heart is not turned against him, and that the son of my good old master has one friend, however, left.

SIR OLIVER: What! shall I forget, Master Rowley, when I was at his years myself? Egad, my brother and I were neither of us very prudent youths; and yet, I believe, you have not seen many better men than your old master was?

ROWLEY: Sir, 'tis this reflection gives me assurance that Charles may yet be a credit to his family. But here comes Sir Peter.

SIR OLIVER: Egad, so he does! Mercy on me, he's greatly altered, and seems to have a settled married look! One may read husband in his face at this distance!

Enter Sir Peter Teazle.

SIR PETER: Ha! Sir Oliver—my old friend! Welcome to England a thousand times!

SIR OLIVER: Thank you, thank you, Sir Peter! and i'faith I am glad to find you well, believe me!

SIR PETER: Oh! 'tis a long time since we met—fifteen years, I doubt, Sir Oliver, and many a cross accident in the time.

SIR OLIVER: Ay, I have had my share. But, what! I find you are married, hey, my old boy? Well, well, it can't be helped; and so—I wish you joy with all my heart!

SIR PETER: Thank you, thank you, Sir Oliver.—Yes, I have entered into—the happy state; but we'll not talk of that now.

SIR OLIVER: True, true, Sir Peter; old friends should not begin on grievances at first meeting. No, no, no.

ROWLEY: [*Aside to* Sir Oliver] Take care, pray, sir.

SIR OLIVER: Well, so one of my nephews is a wild rogue, hey?

SIR PETER: Wild! Ah! my old friend, I grieve for your disappointment there; he's a lost young man, indeed. However, his brother will make you amends; Joseph is, indeed, what a youth should be—everybody in the world speaks well of him.

SIR OLIVER: I am sorry to hear it; he has too good a character to be an honest fellow. Everybody speaks well of him! Psha! then he has bowed as low to knaves and fools as to the honest dignity of genius and virtue.

SIR PETER: What, Sir Oliver! do you blame him for not making enemies?

SIR OLIVER: Yes, if he has merit enough to deserve them.

SIR PETER: Well, well—you'll be convinced when you know him. 'Tis edification to hear him converse; he professes the noblest sentiments.

SIR OLIVER: Oh, plague of his sentiments! If he salutes me with a scrap of morality in his mouth, I shall be sick directly. But, however, don't mistake me, Sir Peter; I don't mean to defend Charles's errors: but, before I form my judgment of either of them, I intend to make a trial of their hearts; and my friend Rowley and I have planned something for the purpose.

ROWLEY: And Sir Peter shall own for once he has been mistaken.

SIR PETER: Oh, my life on Joseph's honour!

SIR OLIVER: Well—come, give us a bottle of good wine, and we'll drink the lads' health, and tell you our scheme.

SIR PETER: *Allons*, then!

SIR OLIVER: And don't, Sir Peter, be so severe against your old friend's son. Odds my life! I am not sorry that he has run out of the course a little: for my part, I hate to see prudence clinging to the green suckers of youth; 'tis like ivy round a sapling, and spoils the growth of the tree.   [*Exeunt*]

Act III

SCENE 1: A *Room in Sir Peter Teazle's House*

Enter Sir Peter Teazle, Sir Oliver Surface, *and* Rowley.

SIR PETER: Well, then, we will see this fellow first, and have our wine afterwards. But how is this, Master Rowley? I don't see the jet of your scheme.

ROWLEY: Why, sir, this Mr. Stanley, whom I was speaking of, is nearly related to them by their mother. He was once a merchant in Dublin, but has been ruined by a series of undeserved misfortunes. He has applied, by letter, since his confinement, both to Mr. Surface and Charles: from the former he has received nothing but evasive promises of future service, while Charles has done all that his extravagance has left him power to do; and he is, at this time, endeavouring to raise a sum of money, part of which, in the midst of his own distresses, I know he intends for the service of poor Stanley.

SIR OLIVER: Ah! he is my brother's son.

SIR PETER: Well, but how is Sir Oliver personally to——

ROWLEY: Why, sir, I will inform Charles and his brother that Stanley has obtained permission to apply personally to his friends; and, as they have neither of them ever seen him, let Sir Oliver assume his character, and he will have a fair opportunity of judging, at least, of the benevolence of their dispositions: and believe me, sir, you will find in the youngest brother one who, in the midst of folly and dissipation, has still, as our immortal bard expresses it,—

"a heart to pity, and a hand
Open as day, for melting charity."

SIR PETER: Psha! What signifies his having an open hand or purse either, when he has nothing left to give? Well, well, make the trial, if you please. But where is the fellow whom you brought for Sir Oliver to examine, relative to Charles's affairs?

ROWLEY: Below, waiting his commands, and no one can give him better intelligence.—This, Sir Oliver, is a friendly Jew, who, to do him justice, has done everything in his power to bring your nephew to a proper sense of his extravagance.

SIR PETER: Pray let us have him in.

ROWLEY: Desire Mr. Moses to walk upstairs.
[*Calls to* Servant]

SIR PETER: But, pray, why should you suppose he will speak the truth?

ROWLEY: Oh, I have convinced him that he has no chance of recovering certain sums advanced to Charles but through the bounty of Sir Oliver, who

he knows is arrived; so that you may depend on his fidelity to his own interests. I have also another evidence in my power, one Snake, whom I have detected in a matter little short of forgery, and shall shortly produce to remove some of your prejudices, Sir Peter, relative to Charles and Lady Teazle.

SIR PETER: I have heard too much on that subject.

ROWLEY: Here comes the honest Israelite.

Enter Moses.
—This is Sir Oliver.

SIR OLIVER: Sir, I understand you have lately had great dealings with my nephew Charles.

MOSES: Yes, Sir Oliver, I have done all I could for him; but he was ruined before he came to me for assistance.

SIR OLIVER: That was unlucky, truly; for you have had no opportunity of showing your talents.

MOSES: None at all; I hadn't the pleasure of knowing his distresses till he was some thousands worse than nothing.

SIR OLIVER: Unfortunate, indeed! But I suppose you have done all in your power for him, honest Moses?

MOSES: Yes, he knows that. This very evening I was to have brought him a gentleman from the city, who does not know him, and will, I believe, advance him some money.

SIR PETER: What, one Charles has never had money from before?

MOSES: Yes, Mr. Premium, of Crutched Friars, formerly a broker.

SIR PETER: Egad, Sir Oliver, a thought strikes me!—Charles, you say, does not know Mr. Premium?

MOSES: Not at all.

SIR PETER: Now then, Sir Oliver, you may have a better opportunity of satisfying yourself than by an old romancing tale of a poor relation: go with my friend Moses, and represent Premium, and then, I'll answer for it, you'll see your nephew in all his glory.

SIR OLIVER: Egad, I like this idea better than the other, and I may visit Joseph afterwards as old Stanley.

SIR PETER: True—so you may.

ROWLEY: Well, this is taking Charles rather at a disadvantage, to be sure. However, Moses, you understand Sir Peter, and will be faithful?

MOSES: You may depend upon me.—[*Looks at his watch*] This is near the time I was to have gone.

SIR OLIVER: I'll accompany you as soon as you please, Moses—— But hold! I have forgot one thing—how the plague shall I be able to pass for a Jew?

MOSES: There's no need—the principal is Christian.

SIR OLIVER: Is he? I'm very sorry to hear it. But, then again, an't I rather too smartly dressed to look like a money-lender?

SIR PETER: Not at all; 'twould not be out of character, if you went in your carriage—would it, Moses?

MOSES: Not in the least.

SIR OLIVER: Well, but how must I talk? there's certainly some cant of usury and mode of treating that I ought to know.

SIR PETER: Oh, there's not much to learn. The great point, as I take it, is to be exorbitant enough in your demands. Hey, Moses?

MOSES: Yes, that's a very great point.

SIR OLIVER: I'll answer for't I'll not be wanting in that. I'll ask him eight or ten per cent. on the loan, at least.

MOSES: If you ask him no more than that, you'll be discovered immediately.

SIR OLIVER: Hey! what, the plague! how much then?

MOSES: That depends upon the circumstances. If he appears not very anxious for the supply, you should require only forty or fifty per cent.; but if you find him in great distress, and want the moneys very bad, you may ask double.

SIR PETER: A good honest trade you're learning, Sir Oliver!

SIR OLIVER: Truly I think so—and not unprofitable.

MOSES: Then, you know, you haven't the moneys yourself, but are forced to borrow them for him of a friend.

SIR OLIVER: Oh! I borrow it of a friend, do I?

MOSES: And your friend is an unconscionable dog: but you can't help that.

SIR OLIVER: My friend an unconscionable dog, is he?

MOSES: Yes, and he himself has not the moneys by him, but is forced to sell stock at a great loss.

SIR OLIVER: He is forced to sell stock at a great loss, is he? Well, that's very kind of him.

SIR PETER: I'faith, Sir Oliver—Mr. Premuim, I mean—you'll soon be master of the trade. But, Moses! would not you have him run out a little against the annuity bill? That would be in character, I should think.

MOSES: Very much.

ROWLEY: And lament that a young man now must be at years of discretion before he is suffered to ruin himself?

MOSES: Ay, great pity!

SIR PETER: And abuse the public for allowing merit to an act whose only object is to snatch misfortune and imprudence from the rapacious grip of usury, and give the minor a chance of inheriting his estate without being undone by coming into possession.

SIR OLIVER: So, so—Moses shall give me further instructions as we go together.

SIR PETER: You will not have much time, for your nephew lives hard by.

SIR OLIVER: Oh, never fear! my tutor appears so able, that though Charles lived in the next street, it must be my own fault if I am not a complete rogue before I turn the corner.   [Exit with Moses]

SIR PETER: So, now, I think Sir Oliver will be convinced: you are partial, Rowley, and would have prepared Charles for the other plot.

ROWLEY: No, upon my word, Sir Peter.

SIR PETER: Well, go bring me this Snake, and I'll hear what he has to say presently. I see Maria, and want to speak with her.—[Exit Rowley] I should be glad to be convinced my suspicions of Lady Teazle and Charles were unjust. I have never yet opened my mind on this subject to my friend Joseph—I am determined I will do it—he will give me his opinion sincerely.

Enter Maria.

So, child, has Mr. Surface returned with you?

MARIA: No, sir; he was engaged.

SIR PETER: Well, Maria, do you not reflect, the more you converse with that amiable young man, what return his partiality for you deserves?

MARIA: Indeed, Sir Peter, your frequent importunity on this subject distresses me extremely—you compel me to declare, that I know no man who has ever paid me a particular attention whom I would not prefer to Mr. Surface.

SIR PETER: So—here's perverseness! No, no, Maria, 'tis Charles only whom you would prefer. 'Tis evident his vices and follies have won your heart.

MARIA: This is unkind, sir. You know I have obeyed you in neither seeing nor corresponding with him: I have heard enough to convince me that he is unworthy my regard. Yet I cannot think it culpable, if, while my understanding severely condemns his vices, my heart suggests pity for his distresses.

SIR PETER: Well, well, pity him as much as you please; but give your heart and hand to a worthier object.

MARIA: Never to his brother!

SIR PETER: Go, perverse and obstinate! But take care, madam; you have never yet known what the authority of a guardian is: don't compel me to inform you of it.

MARIA: I can only say, you shall not have just reason. 'Tis true, by my father's will, I am for a short period bound to regard you as his substitute; but must cease to think you so, when you would compel me to be miserable.   [Exit]

SIR PETER: Was ever man so crossed as I am, everything conspiring to fret me! I had not been involved in matrimony a fortnight, before her father, a hale and hearty man, died, on purpose, I believe, for the pleasure of plaguing me with the care of his daughter.—[Lady Teazle sings without] But here comes my helpmate! She appears in great good humour. How happy I should be if I could tease her into loving me, though but a little!

Enter Lady Teazle.

LADY TEAZLE: Lud! Sir Peter, I hope you haven't been quarrelling with Maria? It is not using me well to be ill humoured when I am not by.

SIR PETER: Ah, Lady Teazle, you might have the power to make me good humoured at all times.

LADY TEAZLE: I am sure I wish I had; for I want you to be in a charming sweet temper at this moment. Do be good humoured now, and let me have two hundred pounds, will you?

SIR PETER: Two hundred pounds; what, an't I to be in a good humour without paying for it! But speak to me thus, and i'faith there's nothing I could refuse you. You shall have it; but seal me a bond for the repayment.

LADY TEAZLE: Oh, no—there—my note of hand will do as well.   [Offering her hand]

SIR PETER: And you shall no longer reproach me with not giving you an independent settlement. I mean shortly to surprise you; but shall we always live thus, hey?

LADY TEAZLE: If you please. I'm sure I don't care how soon we leave off quarrelling, provided you'll own you were tired first.

SIR PETER: Well—then let our future contest be, who shall be most obliging.

LADY TEAZLE: I assure you, Sir Peter, good nature becomes you. You look now as you did before we were married, when you used to walk with me under the elms, and tell me stories of what a gallant you were in your youth, and chuck me under the chin, you would; and ask me if I thought I could love an old fellow, who would deny me nothing—didn't you?

SIR PETER: Yes, yes, and you were as kind and attentive——

LADY TEAZLE: Ay, so I was, and would always take your part, when my acquaintance used to abuse you, and turn you into ridicule.

SIR PETER: Indeed!

LADY TEAZLE: Ay, and when my cousin Sophy has called you a stiff, peevish old bachelor, and laughed at me for thinking of marrying one who might be my father, I have always defended you, and said, I didn't think you so ugly by any means, and that you'd make a very good sort of a husband.

SIR PETER: And you prophesied right; and we shall now be the happiest couple——

LADY TEAZLE: And never differ again?

SIR PETER: No, never—though at the same time, indeed, my dear Lady Teazle, you must watch your temper very seriously; for in all our little quarrels, my dear, if you recollect, my love, you always began first.

LADY TEAZLE: I beg your pardon, my dear Sir Peter: indeed, you always gave the provocation.

SIR PETER: Now, see, my angel! take care—contradicting isn't the way to keep friends.

LADY TEAZLE: Then, don't you begin it, my love!

SIR PETER: There, now! you—you are going on. You don't perceive, my life, that you are just doing the very thing which you know always makes me angry.

LADY TEAZLE: Nay, you know if you will be angry without any reason, my dear——

SIR PETER: There! now you want to quarrel again.

LADY TEAZLE: No, I'm sure I don't: but, if you will be so peevish——

SIR PETER: There now! who begins first?

LADY TEAZLE: Why, you, to be sure. I said nothing—but there's no bearing your temper.

SIR PETER: No, no, madam: the fault's in your own temper.

LADY TEAZLE: Ay, you are just what my cousin Sophy said you would be.

SIR PETER: Your cousin Sophy is a forward, impertinent gipsy.

LADY TEAZLE: You are a great bear, I am sure, to abuse my relations.

SIR PETER: Now may all the plagues of marriage be doubled on me, if ever I try to be friends with you any more!

LADY TEAZLE: So much the better.

SIR PETER: No, no, madam: 'tis evident you never cared a pin for me, and I was a madman to marry you—a pert, rural coquette, that had refused half the honest 'squires in the neighbourhood!

LADY TEAZLE: And I am sure I was a fool to marry you—an old dangling bachelor, who was single at fifty, only because he never could meet with any one who would have him.

SIR PETER: Ay, ay, madam; but you were pleased enough to listen to me: you never had such an offer before.

LADY TEAZLE: No! didn't I refuse Sir Tivy Terrier, who everybody said would have been a better match? for his estate is just as good as yours, and he has broke his neck since we have been married.

SIR PETER: I have done with you, madam! You are an unfeeling, ungrateful—but there's an end of everything. I believe you capable of everything that is bad. Yes, madam, I now believe the reports relative to you and Charles, madam. Yes, madam, you and Charles are, not without grounds——

LADY TEAZLE: Take care, Sir Peter! you had better not insinuate any such thing! I'll not be suspected without cause, I promise you.

SIR PETER: Very well, madam! very well! a separate maintenance as soon as you please. Yes, madam, or a divorce! I'll make an example of myself for the benefit of all old bachelors. Let us separate, madam.

LADY TEAZLE: Agreed! agreed! And now, my dear Sir Peter, we are of a mind once more, we may be the happiest couple, and never differ again, you know: ha! ha! ha! Well, you are going to be in a passion, I see, and I shall only interrupt you—so, bye! bye!   [Exit]

SIR PETER: Plagues and tortures! can't I make her angry either! Oh, I am the most miserable fellow! But I'll not bear her presuming to keep her temper: no! she may break my heart, but she shan't keep her temper.   [Exit]

SCENE 2:   *A Room in Charles Surface's House*

Enter Trip, Moses, *and* Sir Oliver Surface.

TRIP: Here, Master Moses; if you'll stay a moment, I'll try whether—what's the gentleman's name?

SIR OLIVER: Mr. Moses, what is my name?
                                    [*Aside to* Moses]

MOSES: Mr. Premium.

TRIP: Premium—very well.   [*Exit, taking snuff*]

SIR OLIVER: To judge by the servants, one wouldn't believe the master was ruined. But what!—sure, this was my brother's house?

MOSES: Yes, sir; Mr. Charles bought it of Mr. Joseph, with the furniture, pictures, &c., just as the old gentleman left it. Sir Peter thought it a piece of extravagance in him.

SIR OLIVER: In my mind, the other's economy in selling it to him was more reprehensible by half.

Re-enter Trip.

TRIP: My master says you must wait, gentlemen: he has company, and can't speak with you yet.

SIR OLIVER: If he knew who it was wanted to see him, perhaps he would not send such a message?

TRIP: Yes, yes, sir; he knows you are here—I did not forget little Premium: no, no, no.

SIR OLIVER: Very well; and I pray, sir, what may be your name?

TRIP: Trip, sir; my name is Trip, at your service.

SIR OLIVER: Well, then, Mr. Trip, you have a pleasant sort of place here, I guess?

TRIP: Why, yes—here are three or four of us pass our time agreeably enough; but then our wages are sometimes a little in arrear—and not very great either—but fifty pounds a year, and find our own bags and bouquets.

SIR OLIVER: Bags and bouquets! halters and bastinadoes!   [*Aside*]

TRIP: And *à propos*, Moses, have you been able to get me that little bill discounted?

SIR OLIVER: Wants to raise money, too!—mercy on me! Has his distresses too, I warrant, like a lord, and affects creditors and duns.   [*Aside*]

MOSES: 'Twas not to be done, indeed, Mr. Trip.

TRIP: Good lack, you surprise me! My friend Brush has indorsed it, and I thought when he put his name at the back of a bill 'twas the same as cash.

MOSES: No, 'twouldn't do.

TRIP: A small sum—but twenty pounds. Hark'ee, Moses, do you think you couldn't get it me by way of annuity?

SIR OLIVER: An annuity! ha! ha! a footman raise money by way of annuity! Well done, luxury, egad!
                                    [*Aside*]

MOSES: Well, but you must insure your place.

TRIP: Oh, with all my heart! I'll insure my place, and my life too, if you please.

SIR OLIVER: It's more than I would your neck.
                                    [*Aside*]

MOSES: But is there nothing you could deposit?

TRIP: Why, nothing capital of my master's wardrobe has dropped lately; but I could give you a mortgage on some of his winter clothes, with equity of redemption before November—or you shall have the reversion of the French velvet, or a post-obit on the blue and silver;—these, I should think, Moses, with a few pair of point ruffles, as a collateral security—hey, my little fellow?

MOSES: Well, well.   [*Bell rings*]

TRIP: Egad, I heard the bell! I believe, gentlemen, I can now introduce you. Don't forget the annuity, little Moses! This way, gentlemen, I'll insure my place, you know.

SIR OLIVER: [*Aside*] If the man be a shadow of the master, this is the temple of dissipation indeed!   [*Exeunt*]

SCENE 3:   *Another Room in the same*

Charles Surface, Sir Harry Bumper, Careless, *and* Gentlemen, *discovered drinking.*

CHARLES SURFACE: 'Fore heaven, 'tis true!—there's the great degeneracy of the age. Many of our acquaintance have taste, spirit, and politeness; but plague on't they won't drink.

CARELESS: It is so, indeed, Charles! they give in to all the substantial luxuries of the table, and abstain from nothing but wine and wit. Oh, certainly society suffers by it intolerably! for now, instead of the social spirit of raillery that used to mantle over a glass of bright Burgundy, their conversation is become just like the Spa-water they drink, which has all the pertness and flatulency of champagne, without its spirit or flavour.

1 GENTLEMAN: But what are they to do who love play better than wine?

CARELESS: True! there's Sir Harry diets himself for gaming, and is now under a hazard regimen.

CHARLES SURFACE: Then he'll have the worst of it. What! you wouldn't train a horse for the course by keeping him from corn? For my part, egad, I'm never so successful as when I am a little merry: let me throw on a bottle of champagne, and I never lose—at least I never feel my losses, which is exactly the same thing.

2 GENTLEMAN: Ay, that I believe.

CHARLES SURFACE: And, then, what man can pretend to be a believer in love, who is an abjurer of wine? 'Tis the test by which the lover knows his own heart. Fill a dozen bumpers to a dozen beauties, and she that floats at the top is the maid that has bewitched you.

CARELESS: Now then, Charles, be honest, and give us your real favourite.

CHARLES SURFACE: Why, I have withheld her only in compassion to you. If I toast her, you must give a round of her peers, which is impossible—on earth.

CARELESS: Oh, then we'll find some canonised vestals or heathen goddesses that will do, I warrant!

CHARLES SURFACE: Here then, bumpers, you rogues! bumpers! Maria! Maria—

SIR HARRY: Maria who?

CHARLES SURFACE: Oh, damn the surname!—'tis too formal to be registered in Love's calendar—but now, Sir Harry, beware, we must have beauty superlative.

CARELESS: Nay, never study, Sir Harry: we'll stand to the toast, though your mistress should want an eye, and you know you have a song will excuse you.

SIR HARRY: Egad, so I have! and I'll give him the song instead of the lady.   [Sings]

Here's to the maiden of bashful fifteen;
    Here's to the widow of fifty;
Here's to the flaunting extravagant quean,
    And here's to the housewife that's thrifty.

Chorus: Let the toast pass,—
    Drink to the lass,
I'll warrant she'll prove an excuse for a glass.

Here's to the charmer whose dimples we prize;
    Now to the maid who has none, sir;
Here's to the girl with a pair of blue eyes,
    And here's to the nymph with but one, sir.

Chorus: Let the toast pass,—
    Drink to the lass,
I'll warrant she'll prove an excuse for a glass.

Here's to the maid with a bosom of snow:
    Now to her that's as brown as a berry:
Here's to the wife with a face full of woe,
    And now to the damsel that's merry.

Chorus: Let the toast pass,—
    Drink to the lass,
I'll warrant she'll prove an excuse for a glass.

For let 'em be clumsy, or let 'em be slim,
    Young or ancient, I care not a feather;
So fill a pint bumper quite up to the brim,
So fill up your glasses, nay, fill to the brim,
    And let us e'en toast them together.

Chorus: Let the toast pass,—
    Drink to the lass,
I'll warrant she'll prove an excuse for a glass.

ALL: Bravo! Bravo!

Enter Trip, and whispers Charles Surface.

CHARLES SURFACE: Gentlemen, you must excuse me a little.—Careless, take the chair, will you?

CARELESS: Nay, pr'ythee, Charles, what now? This is one of your peerless beauties, I suppose, dropped in by chance?

CHARLES SURFACE: No, faith! To tell you the truth, 'tis a Jew and a broker, who are come by appointment.

CARELESS: Oh, damn it! let's have the Jew in.

1 GENTLEMAN: Ay, and the broker too, by all means.

2 GENTLEMAN: Yes, yes, the Jew and the broker.

CHARLES SURFACE: Egad, with all my heart!—Trip, bid the gentlemen walk in.—[Exit Trip] Though there's one of them a stranger, I can tell you.

CARELESS: Charles, let us give them some generous Burgundy, and perhaps they'll grow conscientious.

CHARLES SURFACE: Oh, hang 'em, no! wine does but draw forth a man's natural qualities; and to make them drink would only be to whet their knavery.

Re-enter Trip, with Sir Oliver Surface and Moses.

CHARLES SURFACE: So, honest Moses; walk in, pray, Mr. Premium—that's the gentleman's name, isn't it, Moses?

MOSES: Yes, sir.

CHARLES SURFACE: Set chairs, Trip.—Sit down, Mr. Premium.—Glasses, Trip.—[Trip gives chairs and glasses, and exits] Sit down, Moses.—Come, Mr. Premium, I'll give you a sentiment; here's Success to usury!—Moses, fill the gentleman a bumper.

MOSES: Success to usury!   [Drinks]

CARELESS: Right, Moses—usury is prudence and industry, and deserves to succeed.

SIR OLIVER: Then here's—All the success it deserves!   [Drinks]

CARELESS: No, no, that won't do! Mr. Premium, you have demurred at the toast, and must drink it in a pint bumper.

1 GENTLEMAN: A pint bumper, at least.

MOSES: Oh, pray, sir, consider—Mr. Premium's a gentleman.

CARELESS: And therefore loves good wine.

2 GENTLEMAN: Give Moses a quart glass—this is mutiny, and a high contempt for the chair.

CARELESS: Here, now for't! I'll see justice done, to the last drop of my bottle.

SIR OLIVER: Nay, pray, gentlemen—I did not expect this usage.

CHARLES SURFACE: No, hang it, you shan't; Mr. Premium's a stranger.

SIR OLIVER: Odd! I wish I was well out of their company.   [Aside]

CARELESS: Plague on 'em then! if they won't drink, we'll not sit down with them. Come, Harry, the dice are in the next room.—Charles, you'll join us when you have finished your business with the gentlemen?

CHARLES SURFACE: I will! I will!—[Exeunt Sir Harry Bumper and Gentlemen; Careless following] Careless.

CARELESS: [Returning] Well!

CHARLES SURFACE: Perhaps I may want you.

CARELESS: Oh, you know I am always ready: word, note, or bond, 'tis all the same to me.   [Exit]

MOSES: Sir, this is Mr. Premium, a gentleman of the strictest honour and secrecy; and always performs what he undertakes. Mr. Premium, this is——

CHARLES SURFACE: Psha! have done. Sir, my friend Moses is a very honest fellow, but a little slow at expression: he'll be an hour giving us our titles. Mr. Premium, the plain state of the matter is this: I am an extravagant young fellow who wants to borrow money; you I take to be a prudent old fellow, who has got money to lend. I am blockhead enough to give fifty per cent. sooner than not have it! and you, I presume, are rogue enough to take a hundred if you can get it. Now, sir, you see we are acquainted at once, and may proceed to business without further ceremony.

SIR OLIVER: Exceeding frank, upon my word. I see, sir, you are not a man of many compliments.

CHARLES SURFACE: Oh, no, sir! plain dealing in business I always think best.

SIR OLIVER: Sir, I like you the better for it. However, you are mistaken in one thing; I have no money to lend, but I believe I could procure some of a friend; but then he's an unconscionable dog. Isn't he, Moses? And must sell stock to accommodate you. Mustn't he, Moses?

MOSES: Yes, indeed! You know I always speak the truth, and scorn to tell a lie!

CHARLES SURFACE: Right. People that speak truth generally do. But these are trifles, Mr. Premium. What! I know money isn't to be bought without paying for't!

SIR OLIVER: Well, but what security could you give? You have no land, I suppose?

CHARLES SURFACE: Not a mole-hill, nor a twig, but what's in the bough-pots out of the window!

SIR OLIVER: Nor any stock, I presume?

CHARLES SURFACE: Nothing but live stock—and that's only a few pointers and ponies. But pray, Mr. Premium, are you acquainted at all with any of my connections?

SIR OLIVER: Why, to say the truth, I am.

CHARLES SURFACE: Then you must know that I have a devilish rich uncle in the East Indies, Sir Oliver Surface, from whom I have the greatest expectations?

SIR OLIVER: That you have a wealthy uncle, I have heard; but how your expectations will turn out is more, I believe, than you can tell.

CHARLES SURFACE: Oh, no!—there can be no doubt. They tell me I'm a prodigious favourite, and that he talks of leaving me everything.

SIR OLIVER: Indeed! this is the first I've heard of it.

CHARLES SURFACE: Yes, yes, 'tis just so. Moses knows 'tis true; don't you, Moses?

MOSES: Oh, yes! I'll swear to't.

SIR OLIVER: Egad, they'll persuade me presently I'm at Bengal.   [Aside]

CHARLES SURFACE: Now I propose, Mr. Premium, if it's agreeable to you, a post-obit on Sir Oliver's life:

though at the same time the old fellow has been so liberal to me, that I give you my word, I should be very sorry to hear that anything had happened to him.

SIR OLIVER: Not more than I should, I assure you. But the bond you mention happens to be just the worst security you could offer me—for I might live to a hundred and never see the principal.

CHARLES SURFACE: Oh, yes, you would! the moment Sir Oliver dies, you know, you would come on me for the money.

SIR OLIVER: Then I believe I should be the most unwelcome dun you ever had in your life.

CHARLES SURFACE: What! I suppose you're afraid that Sir Oliver is too good a life?

SIR OLIVER: No, indeed I am not; though I have heard he is as hale and healthy as any man of his years in Christendom.

CHARLES SURFACE: There again, now, you are misinformed. No, no, the climate has hurt him considerably, poor uncle Oliver. Yes, yes, he breaks apace, I'm told—and is so much altered lately that his nearest relations would not know him.

SIR OLIVER: No! Ha! ha! ha! so much altered lately that his nearest relations would not know him! Ha! ha! ha! egad—ha! ha! ha!

CHARLES SURFACE: Ha! ha!—you're glad to hear that, little Premium?

SIR OLIVER: No, no, I'm not.

CHARLES SURFACE: Yes, yes, you are—ha! ha! ha!—you know that mends your chance.

SIR OLIVER: But I'm told Sir Oliver is coming over; nay, some say he has actually arrived.

CHARLES SURFACE: Psha! sure I must know better than you whether he's come or not. No, no, rely on't he's at this moment at Calcutta. Isn't he, Moses?

MOSES: Oh, yes, certainly.

SIR OLIVER: Very true, as you say, you must know better than I, though I have it from pretty good authority. Haven't I, Moses?

MOSES: Yes, most undoubted!

SIR OLIVER: But, sir, as I understand you want a few hundreds immediately, is there nothing you could dispose of?

CHARLES SURFACE: How do you mean?

SIR OLIVER: For instance, now, I have heard that your father left behind him a great quantity of massy old plate.

CHARLES SURFACE: O Lud! that's gone long ago. Moses can tell you how better than I can.

SIR OLIVER: [Aside] Good lack! all the family race-cups and corporation-bowls!—[Aloud] Then it was also supposed that his library was one of the most valuable and compact.

CHARLES SURFACE: Yes, yes, so it was—vastly too much so for a private gentleman. For my part, I was always of a communicative disposition, so I thought it a shame to keep so much knowledge to myself.

SIR OLIVER: [Aside] Mercy upon me! learning that had run in the family like an heir-loom!—[Aloud] Pray, what has become of the books?

CHARLES SURFACE: You must inquire of the auctioneer, Master Premium, for I don't believe even Moses can direct you.

MOSES: I know nothing of books.

SIR OLIVER: So, so, nothing of the family property left, I suppose?

CHARLES SURFACE: Not much, indeed; unless you have a mind to the family pictures. I have got a room full of ancestors above: and if you have a taste for old paintings, egad, you shall have 'em a bargain!

SIR OLIVER: Hey! what the devil! sure, you wouldn't sell your forefathers, would you?

CHARLES SURFACE: Every man of them, to the best bidder.

SIR OLIVER: What! your great-uncles and aunts?

CHARLES SURFACE: Ay, and my great-grandfathers and grandmothers too.

SIR OLIVER: [Aside] Now I give him up!—[Aloud] What the plague, have you no bowels for your own kindred? Odd's life! do you take me for Shylock in the play, that you would raise money of me on your own flesh and blood?

CHARLES SURFACE: Nay, my little broker, don't be angry: what need you care, if you have your money's worth?

SIR OLIVER: Well, I'll be the purchaser: I think I can dispose of the family canvas.—[Aside] Oh, I'll never forgive him this! never!

Re-enter Careless.

CARELESS: Come, Charles, what keeps you?

CHARLES SURFACE: I can't come yet. I'faith, we are going to have a sale above stairs, here's little Premium will buy all my ancestors!

CARELESS: Oh, burn your ancestors!

CHARLES SURFACE: No, he may do that afterwards, if he pleases. Stay, Careless, we want you: egad, you shall be auctioneer—so come along with us.

CARELESS: Oh, have with you, if that's the case. I can handle a hammer as well as a dice box! Going! going!

SIR OLIVER: Oh, the profligates!   [Aside]

CHARLES SURFACE: Come, Moses, you shall be appraiser, if we want one. Gad's life, little Premium, you don't seem to like the business?

SIR OLIVER: Oh, yes, I do, vastly! Ha! ha! ha! yes, yes, I think it a rare joke to sell one's family by auction —ha! ha!—[Aside] Oh, the prodigal!

CHARLES SURFACE: To be sure! when a man wants money, where the plague should he get assistance, if he can't make free with his own relations?

[Exeunt]

SIR OLIVER: I'll never forgive him; never! never!

Act IV

SCENE 1: A *Picture Room in Charles Surface's House*

Enter Charles Surface, Sir Oliver Surface, Moses, *and* Careless.

CHARLES SURFACE: Walk in, gentlemen, pray walk in; —here they are, the family of the Surfaces, up to the Conquest.

SIR OLIVER: And, in my opinion, a goodly collection.

CHARLES SURFACE: Ay, ay, these are done in the true spirit of portrait-painting; no *volontière grace* or expression. Not like the works of your modern Raphaels, who give you the strongest resemblance, yet contrive to make your portrait independent of you; so that you may sink the original and not hurt the picture. No, no; the merit of these is the inveterate likeness—all stiff and awkward as the originals, and like nothing in human nature besides.

SIR OLIVER: Ah! we shall never see such figures of men again.

CHARLES SURFACE: I hope not. Well, you see, Master Premium, what a domestic character I am; here I sit of an evening surrounded by my family. But come, get to your pulpit, Mr. Auctioneer; here's an old gouty chair of my grandfather's will answer the purpose.

CARELESS: Ay, ay, this will do. But, Charles, I haven't a hammer; and what's an auctioneer without his hammer?

CHARLES SURFACE: Egad, that's true. What parchment have we here? Oh, our genealogy in full. [*Taking pedigree down*] Here, Careless, you shall have no common bit of mahogany, here's the family tree for you, you rogue! This shall be your hammer, and now you may knock down my ancestors with their own pedigree.

SIR OLIVER: What an unnatural rogue!—*an ex post facto* parricide!   [Aside]

CARELESS: Yes, yes, here's a list of your generation indeed;—faith, Charles, this is the most convenient thing you could have found for the business, for 'twill not only serve as a hammer, but a catalogue into the bargain. Come, begin—A-going, a-going, a-going!

CHARLES SURFACE: Bravo, Careless! Well, here's my great uncle, Sir Richard Ravelin, a marvellous good general in his day, I assure you. He served in all the Duke of Marlborough's wars, and got that cut over his eye at the battle of Malplaquet. What say you, Mr. Premium? look at him—there's a hero! not cut out of his feathers, as your modern clipped captains are, but enveloped in wig and regimentals, as a general should be. What do you bid?

SIR OLIVER: [Aside to Moses] Bid him speak.

MOSES: Mr. Premium would have you speak.

CHARLES SURFACE: Why, then, he shall have him for ten pounds, and I'm sure that's not dear for a staff-officer.

SIR OLIVER: [Aside] Heaven deliver me! his famous uncle Richard for ten pounds!—[Aloud] Very well, sir, I take him at that.

CHARLES SURFACE: Careless, knock down my uncle Richard.—Here, now, is a maiden sister of his, my great-aunt Deborah, done by Kneller, in his best manner, and esteemed a very formidable likeness. There she is, you see, a shepherdess feeding her flock. You shall have her for five pounds ten—the sheep are worth the money.

SIR OLIVER: [Aside] Ah! poor Deborah! a woman who set such a value on herself!—[Aloud] Five pounds ten—she's mine.

CHARLES SURFACE: Knock down my aunt Deborah! Here, now, are two that were a sort of cousins of theirs.—You see, Moses, these pictures were done some time ago, when beaux wore wigs, and the ladies their own hair.

SIR OLIVER: Yes, truly, head-dresses appear to have been a little lower in those days.

CHARLES SURFACE: Well, take that couple for the same.

MOSES: 'Tis a good bargain.

CHARLES SURFACE: Careless!—This, now, is a grandfather of my mother's, a learned judge, well known on the western circuit.—What do you rate him at, Moses?

MOSES: Four guineas.

CHARLES SURFACE: Four guineas! Gad's life, you don't bid me the price of his wig.—Mr. Premium, you have more respect for the woolsack; do let us knock his lordship down at fifteen.

SIR OLIVER: By all means.

CARELESS: Gone!

CHARLES SURFACE: And there are two brothers of his, William and Walter Blunt, Esquires, both members of Parliament, and noted speakers; and, what's very extraordinary, I believe, this is the first time they were ever bought or sold.

SIR OLIVER: That is very extraordinary, indeed! I'll take them at your own price, for the honour of Parliament.

CARELESS: Well said, little Premium! I'll knock them down at forty.

CHARLES SURFACE: Here's a jolly fellow—I don't know what relation, but he was mayor of Norwich: take him at eight pounds.

SIR OLIVER: No, no; six will do for the mayor.

CHARLES SURFACE: Come, make it guineas, and I'll throw you the two aldermen there into the bargain.

SIR OLIVER: They're mine.

CHARLES SURFACE: Careless, knock down the mayor and aldermen. But, plague on't! we shall be all day retailing in this manner; do let us deal wholesale: what say you, little Premium? Give me three hundred pounds for the rest of the family in the lump.

CARELESS: Ay, ay, that will be the best way.

SIR OLIVER: Well, well, anything to accommodate you; they are mine. But there is one portrait which you have always passed over.

CARELESS: What, that ill-looking little fellow over the settee?

SIR OLIVER: Yes, sir, I mean that; though I don't think him so ill-looking a little fellow, by any means.

CHARLES SURFACE: What, that? Oh; that's my uncle Oliver! 'Twas done before he went to India.

CARELESS: Your uncle Oliver! Gad, then you'll never be friends, Charles. That, now, to me, is as stern a looking rogue as ever I saw; an unforgiving eye, and a damned disinheriting countenance! an inveterate knave, depend on't. Don't you think so, little Premium?

SIR OLIVER: Upon my soul, sir, I do not; I think it is as honest a looking face as any in the room, dead or alive. But I suppose uncle Oliver goes with the rest of the lumber?

CHARLES SURFACE: No, hang it! I'll not part with poor Noll. The old fellow has been very good to me, and, egad, I'll keep his picture while I've a room to put it in.

SIR OLIVER: [Aside] The rogue's my nephew after all!—[Aloud] But, sir, I have somehow taken a fancy to that picture.

CHARLES SURFACE: I'm sorry for't, for you certainly will not have it. Oons, haven't you got enough of them?

SIR OLIVER: [Aside] I forgive him everything!—[Aloud] But, sir, when I take a whim in my head, I don't value money. I'll give you as much for that as for all the rest.

CHARLES SURFACE: Don't tease me, master broker; I tell you I'll not part with it, and there's an end of it.

SIR OLIVER: [Aside] How like his father the dog is.—[Aloud] Well, well, I have done.—[Aside] I did not perceive it before, but I think I never saw such a striking resemblance.—[Aloud] Here is a draught for your sum.

CHARLES SURFACE: Why, 'tis for eight hundred pounds!

SIR OLIVER: You will not let Sir Oliver go?

CHARLES SURFACE: Zounds! no! I tell you, once more.

SIR OLIVER: Then never mind the difference, we'll balance that another time. But give me your hand on the bargain; you are an honest fellow, Charles—I beg pardon, sir, for being so free.—Come, Moses.

CHARLES SURFACE: Egad, this is a whimsical old fellow!—But hark'ee, Premium, you'll prepare lodgings for these gentlemen.

SIR OLIVER: Yes, yes, I'll send for them in a day or two.

CHARLES SURFACE: But hold; do now send a genteel

conveyance for them, for, I assure you, they were most of them used to ride in their own carriages.

SIR OLIVER: I will, I will—for all but Oliver.

CHARLES SURFACE: Ay, all but the little nabob.

SIR OLIVER: You're fixed on that?

CHARLES SURFACE: Peremptorily.

SIR OLIVER: [Aside] A dear extravagant rogue!— [Aloud] Good day!—Come, Moses,—[Aside] Let me hear now who dares call him profligate!

[Exit with Moses]

CARELESS: Why, this is the oddest genius of the sort I ever met with!

CHARLES SURFACE: Egad, he's the prince of brokers, I think. I wonder how the devil Moses got acquainted with so honest a fellow.—Ha! here's Rowley.—Do, Careless, say I'll join the company in a few moments.

CARELESS: I will—but don't let that old blockhead persuade you to squander any of that money on old musty debts, or any such nonsense; for tradesmen, Charles, are the most exorbitant fellows.

CHARLES SURFACE: Very true, and paying them is only encouraging them.

CARELESS: Nothing else.

CHARLES SURFACE: Ay, ay, never fear.—[Exit Careless] So! this was an odd old fellow, indeed. Let me see, two-thirds of these five hundred and thirty odd pounds are mine by right. 'Fore Heaven! I find one's ancestors are more valuable relations than I took them for!—Ladies and gentlemen, your most obedient and very grateful servant.

[Bows ceremoniously to the pictures]

Enter Rowley.

Ha! old Rowley! egad, you are just come in time to take leave of your old acquaintance.

ROWLEY: Yes, I heard they were a-going. But I wonder you can have such spirits under so many distresses.

CHARLES SURFACE: Why, there's the point! my distresses are so many, that I can't afford to part with my spirits; but I shall be rich and splenetic, all in good time. However, I suppose you are surprised that I am not more sorrowful at parting with so many near relations; to be sure, 'tis very affecting; but you see they never move a muscle, so why should I?

ROWLEY: There's no making you serious a moment.

CHARLES SURFACE: Yes, faith, I am so now. Here, my honest Rowley, here, get me this changed directly, and take a hundred pounds of it immediately to old Stanley.

ROWLEY: A hundred pounds! Consider only——

CHARLES SURFACE: Gad's life, don't talk about it! poor Stanley's wants are pressing, and, if you don't make haste, we shall have some one call that has a better right to the money.

ROWLEY: Ah! there's the point! I never will cease dunning you with the old proverb——

CHARLES SURFACE: Be just before you're generous.— Why, so I would if I could; but Justice is an old hobbling beldame, and I can't get her to keep pace with Generosity, for the soul of me.

ROWLEY: Yet, Charles, believe me, one hour's reflection——

CHARLES SURFACE: Ay, ay, it's very true; but, hark'ee, Rowley, while I have, by Heaven I'll give; so, damn your economy! and now for hazard.   [Exeunt]

SCENE 2:   Another room in the same

Enter Sir Oliver Surface and Moses.

MOSES: Well, sir, I think, as Sir Peter said, you have seen Mr. Charles in high glory; 'tis great pity he's so extravagant.

SIR OLIVER: True, but he would not sell my picture.

MOSES: And loves wine and women so much.

SIR OLIVER: But he would not sell my picture.

MOSES: And games so deep.

SIR OLIVER: But he would not sell my picture. Oh, here's Rowley.

Enter Rowley.

ROWLEY: So, Sir Oliver, I find you have made a purchase——

SIR OLIVER: Yes, yes, our young rake has parted with his ancestors like old tapestry.

ROWLEY: And here has he commissioned me to re-deliver you part of the purchase-money—I mean, though, in your necessitous character of old Stanley.

MOSES: Ah! there is the pity of all: he is so damned charitable.

ROWLEY: And I left a hosier and two tailors in the hall, who, I'm sure, won't be paid, and this hundred would satisfy them.

SIR OLIVER: Well, well, I'll pay his debts, and his benevolence too. But now I am no more a broker, and you shall introduce me to the elder brother as old Stanley.

ROWLEY: Not yet awhile; Sir Peter, I know, means to call there about this time.

Enter Trip.

TRIP: Oh, gentlemen, I beg pardon for not showing you out; this way—Moses, a word.

[Exit with Moses]

SIR OLIVER: There's a fellow for you! Would you believe it, that puppy intercepted the Jew on our coming, and wanted to raise money before he got to his master!

ROWLEY: Indeed.

SIR OLIVER: Yes, they are now planning an annuity business. Ah, Master Rowley, in my days servants were content with the follies of their masters, when they were worn a little threadbare; but now they have their vices, like their birthday clothes, with the gloss on.   [Exeunt]

SCENE 3: A *Library in Joseph Surface's House*

Enter Joseph Surface *and* Servant.

JOSEPH SURFACE: No letter from Lady Teazle?

SERVANT: No, sir.

JOSEPH SURFACE: [*Aside*] I am surprised she has not sent, if she is prevented from coming. Sir Peter certainly does not suspect me. Yet I wish I may not lose the heiress, through the scrape I have drawn myself into with the wife; however, Charles's imprudence and bad character are great points in my favour.   [*Knocking without*]

SERVANT: Sir, I believe that must be Lady Teazle.

JOSEPH SURFACE: Hold! See whether it is or not, before you go to the door: I have a particular message for you if it should be my brother.

SERVANT: 'Tis her ladyship, sir; she always leaves the chair at the milliner's in the next street.

JOSEPH SURFACE: Stay, stay: draw that screen before the window—that will do;—my opposite neighbour is a maiden lady of so curious a temper.— [*Servant draws the screen, and exits*] I have a difficult hand to play in this affair. Lady Teazle has lately suspected my views on Maria; but she must by no means be let into that secret,—at least, till I have her more in my power.

Enter Lady Teazle.

LADY TEAZLE: What sentiment in soliloquy now? Have you been very impatient? O Lud! don't pretend to look grave. I vow I couldn't come before.

JOSEPH SURFACE: O madam, punctuality is a species of constancy very unfashionable in a lady of quality.   [*Places chairs, and sits after* Lady Teazle *is seated*]

LADY TEAZLE: Upon my word, you ought to pity me. Do you know Sir Peter is grown so ill-natured to me of late, and so jealous of Charles too—that's the best of the story, isn't it?

JOSEPH SURFACE: I am glad my scandalous friends keep that up.   [*Aside*]

LADY TEAZLE: I am sure I wish he would let Maria marry him, and then perhaps he would be convinced; don't you, Mr. Surface?

JOSEPH SURFACE: [*Aside*] Indeed I do not.—[*Aloud*] Oh, certainly I do! for then my dear Lady Teazle would also be convinced how wrong her suspicions were of my having any design on the silly girl.

LADY TEAZLE: Well, well, I'm inclined to believe you. But isn't it provoking, to have the most ill-natured things said of one? And there's my friend Lady Sneerwell has circulated I don't know how many scandalous tales of me, and all without any foundation, too; that's what vexes me.

JOSEPH SURFACE: Ay, madam, to be sure, that is the provoking circumstance—without foundation; yes, yes, there's the mortification, indeed; for, when a scandalous story is believed against one, there certainly is no comfort like the consciousness of having deserved it.

LADY TEAZLE: No, to be sure, then I'd forgive their malice; but to attack me, who am really so innocent, and who never say an ill-natured thing of anybody—that is, of any friend; and then Sir Peter, too, to have him so peevish, and so suspicious, when I know the integrity of my own heart—indeed 'tis monstrous!

JOSEPH SURFACE: But, my dear Lady Teazle, 'tis your own fault if you suffer it. When a husband entertains a groundless suspicion of his wife, and withdraws his confidence from her, the original compact is broken, and she owes it to the honour of her sex to endeavour to outwit him.

LADY TEAZLE: Indeed! So that, if he suspects me without cause, it follows, that the best way of curing his jealousy is to give him reason for't?

JOSEPH SURFACE: Undoubtedly—for your husband should never be deceived in you: and in that case it becomes you to be frail in compliment to his discernment.

LADY TEAZLE: To be sure, what you say is very reasonable, and when the consciousness of my innocence——

JOSEPH SURFACE: Ah, my dear madam, there is the great mistake; 'tis this very conscious innocence that is of the greatest prejudice to you. What is it makes you negligent of forms, and careless of the world's opinion? why, the consciousness of your own innocence. What makes you thoughtless in your conduct, and apt to run into a thousand little imprudences? why, the consciousness of your own innocence. What makes you impatient of Sir Peter's temper, and outrageous at his suspicions? why, the consciousness of your innocence.

LADY TEAZLE: 'Tis very true!

JOSEPH SURFACE: Now, my dear Lady Teazle, if you would but once make a trifling *faux pas*, you can't conceive how cautious you would grow, and how ready to humour and agree with your husband.

LADY TEAZLE: Do you think so?

JOSEPH SURFACE: Oh, I'm sure on't; and then you would find all scandal would cease at once, for—in short, your character at present is like a person in a plethora, absolutely dying from too much health.

LADY TEAZLE: So, so; then I perceive your prescription is, that I must sin in my own defence, and part with my virtue to preserve my reputation?

JOSEPH SURFACE: Exactly so, upon my credit, ma'am.

LADY TEAZLE: Well, certainly this is the oddest doctrine, and the newest receipt for avoiding calumny?

JOSEPH SURFACE: An infallible one, believe me. Prudence, like experience, must be paid for.

LADY TEAZLE: Why, if my understanding were once convinced——

JOSEPH SURFACE: Oh, certainly, madam, your understanding should be convinced. Yes, yes—Heaven forbid I should persuade you to do anything you thought wrong. No, no, I have too much honour to desire it.

LADY TEAZLE: Don't you think we may as well leave honour out of the argument?   [Rises]

JOSEPH SURFACE: Ah, the ill effects of your country education, I see, still remain with you.

LADY TEAZLE: I doubt they do, indeed; and I will fairly own to you, that if I could be persuaded to do wrong, it would be by Sir Peter's ill-usage sooner than your honourable logic, after all.

JOSEPH SURFACE: Then, by this hand, which he is unworthy of——   [Taking her hand]

Re-enter Servant.
'Sdeath, you blockhead—what do you want?

SERVANT: I beg your pardon, sir, but I thought you would not choose Sir Peter to come up without announcing him.

JOSEPH SURFACE: Sir Peter!—Oons—the devil!

LADY TEAZLE: Sir Peter! O Lud! I'm ruined! I'm ruined!

SERVANT: Sir, 'twasn't I let him in.

LADY TEAZLE: Oh! I'm quite undone! What will become of me? Now, Mr. Logic—Oh! mercy, sir, he's on the stairs—I'll get behind here—and if ever I'm so imprudent again——
          [Goes behind the screen]

JOSEPH SURFACE: Give me that book.
          [Sits down. Servant pretends to adjust his chair]

Enter Sir Peter Teazle.

SIR PETER: Ay, ever improving himself. Mr. Surface, Mr. Surface——   [Pats Joseph on the shoulder]

JOSEPH SURFACE: Oh, my dear Sir Peter, I beg your pardon. [Gaping, throws away the book] I have been dozing over a stupid book. Well, I am much obliged to you for this call. You haven't been here, I believe, since I fitted up this room. Books, you know, are the only things I am a coxcomb in.

SIR PETER: 'Tis very neat indeed. Well, well, that's proper; and you can make even your screen a source of knowledge—hung, I perceive, with maps.

JOSEPH SURFACE: Oh, yes, I find great use in that screen.

SIR PETER: I dare say you must, certainly, when you want to find anything in a hurry.

JOSEPH SURFACE: Ay, or to hide anything in a hurry either.   [Aside]

SIR PETER: Well, I have a little private business——

JOSEPH SURFACE: You need not stay.   [To Servant]

SERVANT: No, sir.   [Exit]

JOSEPH SURFACE: Here's a chair, Sir Peter—I beg——

SIR PETER: Well, now we are alone, there is a subject, my dear friend, on which I wish to unburden my mind to you—a point of the greatest moment to my peace; in short, my good friend, Lady Teazle's conduct of late has made me very unhappy.

JOSEPH SURFACE: Indeed! I am very sorry to hear it.

SIR PETER: Yes, 'tis but too plain she has not the least regard for me; but, what's worse, I have pretty good authority to suppose she has formed an attachment to another.

JOSEPH SURFACE: Indeed! you astonish me!

SIR PETER: Yes! and, between ourselves, I think I've discovered the person.

JOSEPH SURFACE: How! you alarm me exceedingly.

SIR PETER: Ay, my dear friend, I knew you would sympathize with me!

JOSEPH SURFACE: Yes, believe me, Sir Peter, such a discovery would hurt me just as much as it would you.

SIR PETER: I am convinced of it. Ah! it is a happiness to have a friend whom we can trust even with one's family secrets. But have you no guess who I mean?

JOSEPH SURFACE: I haven't the most distant idea. It can't be Sir Benjamin Backbite!

SIR PETER: Oh, no! What say you to Charles?

JOSEPH SURFACE: My brother! impossible!

SIR PETER: Oh, my dear friend, the goodness of your own heart misleads you. You judge of others by yourself.

JOSEPH SURFACE: Certainly, Sir Peter, the heart that is conscious of its own integrity is ever slow to credit another's treachery.

SIR PETER: True; but your brother has no sentiment —you never hear him talk so.

JOSEPH SURFACE: Yet I can't but think Lady Teazle herself has too much principle.

SIR PETER: Ay; but what is principle against the flattery of a handsome, lively young fellow?

JOSEPH SURFACE: That's very true.

SIR PETER: And then, you know, the difference of our ages makes it very improbable that she should have any great affection for me; and if she were to be frail, and I were to make it public, why the town would only laugh at me, the foolish old bachelor, who had married a girl.

JOSEPH SURFACE: That's true, to be sure—they would laugh.

SIR PETER: Laugh! ay, and make ballads, and paragraphs, and the devil knows what of me.

JOSEPH SURFACE: No, you must never make it public.

SIR PETER: But then again—that the nephew of my old friend, Sir Oliver, should be the person to attempt such a wrong, hurts me more nearly.

JOSEPH SURFACE: Ay, there's the point. When ingratitude barbs the dart of injury, the wound has double danger in it.

SIR PETER: Ay—I, that was, in a manner, left his guardian: in whose house he had been so often entertained; who never in my life denied him—my advice!

JOSEPH SURFACE: Oh, 'tis not to be credited! There may be a man capable of such baseness, to be sure; but, for my part, till you can give me positive proofs, I cannot but doubt it. However, if it should be proved on him, he is no longer a brother of mine—I disclaim kindred with him: for the man who can break the laws of hospitality, and tempt the wife of his friend, deserves to be branded as the pest of society.

SIR PETER: What a difference there is between you! What noble sentiments!

JOSEPH SURFACE: Yet I cannot suspect Lady Teazle's honour.

SIR PETER: I am sure I wish to think well of her, and to remove all ground of quarrel between us. She has lately reproached me more than once with having made no settlement on her; and, in our last quarrel, she almost hinted that she should not break her heart if I was dead. Now, as we seem to differ in our ideas of expense, I have resolved she shall have her own way, and be her own mistress in that respect for the future; and, if I were to die, she will find I have not been inattentive to her interest while living. Here, my friend, are the drafts of two deeds, which I wish to have your opinion on. By one, she will enjoy eight hundred a year independent while I live; and, by the other, the bulk of my fortune at my death.

JOSEPH SURFACE: This conduct, Sir Peter, is indeed truly generous.—[Aside] I wish it may not corrupt my pupil.

SIR PETER: Yes, I am determined she shall have no cause to complain, though I would not have her acquainted with the latter instance of my affection yet awhile.

JOSEPH SURFACE: Nor I, if I could help it.   [Aside]

SIR PETER: And now, my dear friend, if you please, we will talk over the situation of your hopes with Maria.

JOSEPH SURFACE: [Softly] Oh, no, Sir Peter; another time, if you please.

SIR PETER: I am sensibly chagrined at the little progress you seem to make in her affections.

JOSEPH SURFACE: [Softly] I beg you will not mention it. What are my disappointments when your happiness is in debate!—[Aside] 'Sdeath, I shall be ruined every way!

SIR PETER: And though you are averse to my acquainting Lady Teazle with your passion, I'm sure she's not your enemy in the affair.

JOSEPH SURFACE: Pray, Sir Peter, now oblige me. I am really too much affected by the subject we have been speaking of to bestow a thought on my own concerns. The man who is entrusted with his friend's distresses can never——

Re-enter Servant.
Well, sir?

SERVANT: Your brother, sir, is speaking to a gentleman in the street, and says he knows you are within.

JOSEPH SURFACE: 'Sdeath, blockhead, I'm not within —I'm out for the day.

SIR PETER: Stay—hold—a thought has struck me: you shall be at home.

JOSEPH SURFACE: Well, well, let him up.—[Exit Servant] He'll interrupt Sir Peter, however. [Aside]

SIR PETER: Now, my good friend, oblige me, I entreat you. Before Charles comes, let me conceal myself somewhere, then do you tax him on the point we have been talking, and his answer may satisfy me at once.

JOSEPH SURFACE: Oh, fie, Sir Peter! would you have me join in so mean a trick?—to trepan my brother too?

SIR PETER: Nay, you tell me you are sure he is innocent; if so, you do him the greatest service by giving him an opportunity to clear himself, and you will set my heart at rest. Come, you shall not refuse me: [Going up] here, behind the screen will be—Hey! what the devil! there seems to be one listener here already—I'll swear I saw a petticoat!

JOSEPH SURFACE: Ha! ha! ha! Well, this is ridiculous enough. I'll tell you, Sir Peter, though I hold a man of intrigue to be a most despicable character, yet you know, it does not follow that one is to be an absolute Joseph either! Hark'ee, 'tis a little French milliner, a silly rogue that plagues me; and having some character to lose, on your coming, sir, she ran behind the screen.

SIR PETER: Ah, a rogue—— But, egad, she has overheard all I have been saying of my wife.

JOSEPH SURFACE: Oh, 'twill never go any farther, you may depend upon it!

SIR PETER: No! then, faith, let her hear it out.— Here's a closet will do as well.

JOSEPH SURFACE: Well, go in there.

SIR PETER: Sly rogue! sly rogue! [Goes into the closet]

JOSEPH SURFACE: A narrow escape, indeed! and a curious situation I'm in, to part man and wife in this manner.

LADY TEAZLE: [Peeping] Couldn't I steal off?

JOSEPH SURFACE: Keep close, my angel!

SIR PETER: [Peeping] Joseph, tax him home.

JOSEPH SURFACE: Back, my dear friend!

LADY TEAZLE: [Peeping] Couldn't you lock Sir Peter in?

JOSEPH SURFACE: Be still, my life!

SIR PETER: [Peeping] You're sure the little milliner won't blab?

JOSEPH SURFACE: In, in, my dear Sir Peter!—'Fore Gad, I wish I had a key to the door.

Enter Charles Surface.

CHARLES SURFACE: Holla! brother, what has been the matter? Your fellow would not let me up at first. What! have you had a Jew or a wench with you?

JOSEPH SURFACE: Neither, brother, I assure you.

CHARLES SURFACE: But what has made Sir Peter steal off? I thought he had been with you.

JOSEPH SURFACE: He was, brother; but, hearing you were coming, he did not choose to stay.

CHARLES SURFACE: What! was the old gentleman afraid I wanted to borrow money of him!

JOSEPH SURFACE: No, sir: but I am sorry to find, Charles, you have lately given that worthy man grounds for great uneasiness.

CHARLES SURFACE: Yes, they tell me I do that to a great many worthy men. But how so, pray?

JOSEPH SURFACE: To be plain with you, brother, he thinks you are endeavouring to gain Lady Teazle's affections from him.

CHARLES SURFACE: Who, I? O Lud! not I, upon my word.—Ha! ha! ha! ha! so the old fellow has found out that he has got a young wife, has he?—or, what is worse, Lady Teazle has found out she has an old husband?

JOSEPH SURFACE: This is no subject to jest on, brother. He who can laugh——

CHARLES SURFACE: True, true, as you were going to say—then, seriously, I never had the least idea of what you charge me with, upon my honour.

JOSEPH SURFACE: Well, it will give Sir Peter great satisfaction to hear this.   [Raising his voice]

CHARLES SURFACE: To be sure, I once thought the lady seemed to have taken a fancy to me; but, upon my soul, I never gave her the least encouragement. Besides, you know my attachment to Maria.

JOSEPH SURFACE: But sure, brother, even if Lady Teazle had betrayed the fondest partiality for you——

CHARLES SURFACE: Why, look'ee, Joseph, I hope I shall never deliberately do a dishonourable action; but if a pretty woman was purposely to throw herself in my way—and that pretty woman married to a man old enough to be her father——

JOSEPH SURFACE: Well!

CHARLES SURFACE: Why, I believe I should be obliged to borrow a little of your morality, that's all. But, brother, do you know now that you surprise me exceedingly, by naming me with Lady Teazle; for i'faith, I always understood you were her favourite.

JOSEPH SURFACE: Oh, for shame, Charles! This retort is foolish.

CHARLES SURFACE: Nay, I swear I have seen you exchange such significant glances——

JOSEPH SURFACE: Nay, nay, sir, this is no jest.

CHARLES SURFACE: Egad, I'm serious! Don't you remember one day, when I called here——

JOSEPH SURFACE: Nay, pr'ythee, Charles——

CHARLES SURFACE: And found you together——

JOSEPH SURFACE: Zounds, sir, I insist——

CHARLES SURFACE: And another time, when your servant——

JOSEPH SURFACE: Brother, brother, a word with you! —[Aside] Gad, I must stop him.

CHARLES SURFACE: Informed, I say, that——

JOSEPH SURFACE: Hush! I beg your pardon, but Sir Peter has overheard all we have been saying. I knew you would clear yourself, or I should not have consented.

CHARLES SURFACE: How, Sir Peter! Where is he?

JOSEPH SURFACE: Softly, there! [Points to the closet]

CHARLES SURFACE: Oh, 'fore Heaven, I'll have him out. Sir Peter, come forth!

JOSEPH SURFACE: No, no——

CHARLES SURFACE: I say, Sir Peter, come into court. —[Pulls in Sir Peter] What! my old guardian!— What!—turn inquisitor, and take evidence, incog.? Oh, fie! Oh, fie!

SIR PETER: Give me your hand, Charles—I believe I have suspected you wrongfully; but you mustn't be angry with Joseph—'twas my plan!

CHARLES SURFACE: Indeed!

SIR PETER: But I acquit you. I promise you I don't think near so ill of you as I did. What I have heard has given me great satisfaction.

CHARLES SURFACE: Egad, then, 'twas lucky you didn't hear any more. Wasn't it, Joseph?

SIR PETER: Ah! you would have retorted on him.

CHARLES SURFACE: Ah, ay, that was a joke.

SIR PETER: Yes, yes, I know his honour too well.

CHARLES SURFACE: But you might as well have suspected him as me in this matter, for all that. Mightn't he, Joseph?

SIR PETER: Well, well, I believe you.

JOSEPH SURFACE: Would they were both out of the room!   [Aside]

SIR PETER: And in future, perhaps, we may not be such strangers.

Re-enter Servant and whispers Joseph Surface.

SERVANT: Lady Sneerwell is below, and says she will come up.

JOSEPH SURFACE: Gentlemen, I beg pardon—I must wait on you downstairs; here's a person come on particular business.

CHARLES SURFACE: Well, you can see him in another room. Sir Peter and I have not met a long time, and I have something to say to him.

JOSEPH SURFACE: [Aside] They must not be left together.—[Aloud] I'll send Lady Sneerwell away, and return directly.—[Aside to Sir Peter] Sir Peter, not a word of the French milliner.

SIR PETER: [Aside to Joseph Surface] I! not for the world!—[Exit Joseph Surface] Ah, Charles, if you associated more with your brother, one might indeed hope for your reformation. He is a man of sentiment. Well, there is nothing in the world so noble as a man of sentiment.

CHARLES SURFACE: Psha! he is too moral by half; and so apprehensive of his good name, as he calls it, that I suppose he would as soon let a priest into his house as a wench.

SIR PETER: No, no,—come, come—you wrong him. No, no, Joseph is no rake, but he is no such saint either, in that respect.—[Aside] I have a great mind to tell him—we should have such a laugh at Joseph.

CHARLES SURFACE: Oh, hang him! he's a very anchorite, a young hermit!

SIR PETER: Hark'ee—you must not abuse him: he

may chance to hear of it again, I promise you.

CHARLES SURFACE: Why, you won't tell him?

SIR PETER: No—but—this way.—[*Aside*] Egad, I'll tell him. [*Aloud*] Hark'ee, have you a mind to have a good laugh at Joseph?

CHARLES SURFACE: I should like it of all things.

SIR PETER: Then, i'faith, we will! I'll be quit with him for discovering me. He had a girl with him when I called.   [*Whispers*]

CHARLES SURFACE: What! Joseph? you jest.

SIR PETER: Hush!—a little French milliner—and the best of the jest is—she's in the room now.

CHARLES SURFACE: The devil she is!

SIR PETER: Hush! I tell you.

                    [*Points to the screen*]

CHARLES SURFACE: Behind the screen! Odds life, let's unveil her!

SIR PETER: No, no, he's coming:—you shan't, indeed!

CHARLES SURFACE: Oh, egad, we'll have a peep at the little milliner!

SIR PETER: Not for the world!—Joseph will never forgive me.

CHARLES SURFACE: I'll stand by you——

SIR PETER: Odds, here he is!

          [*Charles Surface* throws down the screen]

Re-enter Joseph Surface.

CHARLES SURFACE: Lady Teazle, by all that's wonderful!

SIR PETER: Lady Teazle, by all that's damnable!

CHARLES SURFACE: Sir Peter, this is one of the smartest French milliners I ever saw. Egad, you seem all to have been diverting yourselves here at hide and seek, and I don't see who is out of the secret. Shall I beg your ladyship to inform me? Not a word!— Brother, will you be pleased to explain this matter? What! is Morality dumb too?—Sir Peter, though I found you in the dark, perhaps you are not so now! All mute! Well—though I can make nothing of the affair, I suppose you perfectly understand one another; so I'll leave you to yourselves.— [*Going*] Brother, I'm sorry to find you have given that worthy man grounds for so much uneasiness. —Sir Peter! there's nothing in the world so noble as a man of sentiment!   [*Exit*]

JOSEPH SURFACE: Sir Peter—notwithstanding—I confess—that appearances are against me—if you will afford me your patience—I make no doubt—but I shall explain everything to your satisfaction.

SIR PETER: If you please, sir.

JOSEPH SURFACE: The fact is, sir, that Lady Teazle, knowing my pretensions to your ward Maria—I say, sir, Lady Teazle, being apprehensive of the jealousy of your temper—and knowing my friendship to the family—she, sir, I say—called here— in order that—I might explain these pretensions— but on your coming—being apprehensive—as I said—of your jealousy—she withdrew—and this,

you may depend on it, is the whole truth of the matter.

SIR PETER: A very clear account, upon my word; and I dare swear the lady will vouch for every article of it.

LADY TEAZLE: For not one word of it, Sir Peter.

SIR PETER: How! don't you think it worth while to agree in the lie?

LADY TEAZLE: There is not one syllable of truth in what that gentleman has told you.

SIR PETER: I believe you, upon my soul, ma'am!

JOSEPH SURFACE: [*Aside to* Lady Teazle] 'Sdeath, madam, will you betray me?

LADY TEAZLE: Good Mr. Hypocrite, by your leave, I'll speak for myself.

SIR PETER: Ay, let her alone, sir; you'll find she'll make out a better story than you, without prompting.

LADY TEAZLE: Hear me, Sir Peter!—I came here on no matter relating to your ward, and even ignorant of this gentleman's pretensions to her. But I came, seduced by his insidious arguments, at least to listen to his pretended passion, if not to sacrifice your honour to his baseness.

SIR PETER: Now, I believe, the truth is coming, indeed!

JOSEPH SURFACE: The woman's mad!

LADY TEAZLE: No, sir; she has recovered her senses, and your own arts have furnished her with the means.—Sir Peter, I do not expect you to credit me—but the tenderness you expressed for me, when I am sure you could not think I was a witness to it, has penetrated so to my heart, that had I left the place without the shame of this discovery, my future life should have spoken the sincerity of my gratitude. As for that smooth-tongued hypocrite, who would have seduced the wife of his too credulous friend, while he affected honourable addresses to his ward—I behold him now in a light so truly despicable, that I shall never again respect myself for having listened to him.   [*Exit*]

JOSEPH SURFACE: Notwithstanding all this, Sir Peter, Heaven knows——

SIR PETER: That you are a villain! and so I leave you to your conscience.

JOSEPH SURFACE: You are too rash, Sir Peter; you shall hear me. The man who shuts out conviction by refusing to——

          [*Exeunt* Sir Peter *and* Joseph Surface, *talking*]

Act V

SCENE 1: *The Library in Joseph Surface's House*

Enter Joseph Surface *and* Servant.

JOSEPH SURFACE: Mr. Stanley! and why should you think I would see him? you must know he comes to ask something.

SERVANT: Sir, I should not have let him in, but that Mr. Rowley came to the door with him.

JOSEPH SURFACE: Psha! blockhead! to suppose that I should now be in a temper to receive visits from poor relations!—Well, why don't you show the fellow up?

SERVANT: I will, sir.—Why, sir, it was not my fault that Sir Peter discovered my lady——

JOSEPH SURFACE: Go, fool!—[*Exit* Servant] Sure Fortune never played a man of my policy such a trick before! My character with Sir Peter, my hopes with Maria, destroyed in a moment! I'm in a rare humour to listen to other people's distresses! I shan't be able to bestow even a benevolent sentiment on Stanley.—So! here he comes, and Rowley with him. I must try to recover myself, and put a little charity into my face, however.   [*Exit*]

Enter Sir Oliver Surface *and* Rowley.

SIR OLIVER: What! does he avoid us? That was he, was it not?

ROWLEY: It was, sir. But I doubt you are come a little too abruptly. His nerves are so weak, that the sight of a poor relation may be too much for him. I should have gone first to break it to him.

SIR OLIVER: Oh, plague of his nerves! Yet this is he whom Sir Peter extols as a man of the most benevolent way of thinking!

ROWLEY: As to his way of thinking, I cannot pretend to decide; for, to do him justice, he appears to have as much speculative benevolence as any private gentleman in the kingdom, though he is seldom so sensual as to indulge himself in the exercise of it.

SIR OLIVER: Yet he has a string of charitable sentiments at his fingers' ends.

ROWLEY: Or, rather, at his tongue's end, Sir Oliver; for I believe there is no sentiment he has such faith in as that *Charity begins at home*.

SIR OLIVER: And his, I presume, is of that domestic sort which never stirs abroad at all.

ROWLEY: I doubt you'll find it so;—but he's coming. I mustn't seem to interrupt you; and you know, immediately as you leave him, I come in to announce your arrival in your real character.

SIR OLIVER: True; and afterwards you'll meet me at Sir Peter's.

ROWLEY: Without losing a moment.   [*Exit*]

SIR OLIVER: I don't like the complaisance of his features.

Re-enter Joseph Surface.

JOSEPH SURFACE: Sir, I beg you ten thousand pardons for keeping you a moment waiting.—Mr. Stanley, I presume.

SIR OLIVER: At your service.

JOSEPH SURFACE: Sir, I beg you will do me the honour to sit down—I entreat you, sir.

SIR OLIVER: Dear sir—there's no occasion.—[*Aside*] Too civil by half!

JOSEPH SURFACE: I have not the pleasure of knowing you, Mr. Stanley; but I am extremely happy to see you look so well. You were nearly related to my mother, I think, Mr. Stanley?

SIR OLIVER: I was, sir; so nearly that my present poverty, I fear, may do discredit to her wealthy children, else I should not have presumed to trouble you.

JOSEPH SURFACE: Dear sir, there needs no apology: he that is in distress, though a stranger, has a right to claim kindred with the wealthy. I am sure I wish I was one of that class, and had it in my power to offer you even a small relief.

SIR OLIVER: If your uncle, Sir Oliver, were here, I should have a friend.

JOSEPH SURFACE: I wish he was, sir, with all my heart: you should not want an advocate with him, believe me, sir.

SIR OLIVER: I should not need one—my distresses would recommend me. But I imagined his bounty would enable you to become the agent of his charity.

JOSEPH SURFACE: My dear sir, you were strangely misinformed. Sir Oliver is a worthy man, a very worthy man; but avarice, Mr. Stanley, is the vice of age. I will tell you, my good sir, in confidence, what he has done for me has been a mere nothing; though people, I know, have thought otherwise, and, for my part, I never chose to contradict the report.

SIR OLIVER: What! has he never transmitted you bullion—rupees—pagodas?

JOSEPH SURFACE: Oh, dear sir, nothing of the kind! No, no; a few presents now and then—china, shawls, congou tea, avadavats, and Indian crackers—little more, believe me.

SIR OLIVER: Here's gratitude for twelve thousand pounds!—Avadavats and Indian crackers! [*Aside*]

JOSEPH SURFACE: Then, my dear sir, you have heard, I doubt not, of the extravagance of my brother; there are very few would credit what I have done for that unfortunate young man.

SIR OLIVER: Not I, for one!   [*Aside*]

JOSEPH SURFACE: The sums I have lent him! Indeed I have been exceedingly to blame; it was an amiable weakness; however, I don't pretend to defend it—and now I feel it doubly culpable, since it has deprived me of the pleasure of serving you, Mr. Stanley, as my heart dictates.

SIR OLIVER: [*Aside*] Dissembler!—[*Aloud*] Then, sir, you can't assist me?

JOSEPH SURFACE: At present, it grieves me to say, I cannot; but, whenever I have the ability, you may depend upon hearing from me.

SIR OLIVER: I am extremely sorry——

JOSEPH SURFACE: Not more than I, believe me; to pity, without the power to relieve, is still more painful than to ask and be denied.

SIR OLIVER: Kind sir, your most obedient humble servant.

JOSEPH SURFACE: You leave me deeply affected, Mr. Stanley.—William, be ready to open the door.
                                    [*Calls to* Servant]

SIR OLIVER: O, dear sir, no ceremony.

JOSEPH SURFACE: Your very obedient.

SIR OLIVER: Your most obsequious.

JOSEPH SURFACE: You may depend upon hearing from me, whenever I can be of service.

SIR OLIVER: Sweet sir, you are too good.

JOSEPH SURFACE: In the meantime I wish you health and spirits.

SIR OLIVER: Your ever grateful and perpetual humble servant.

JOSEPH SURFACE: Sir, yours as sincerely.

SIR OLIVER: Charles!—you are my heir.   [*Exit*]

JOSEPH SURFACE: This is one bad effect of a good character; it invites application from the unfortunate, and there needs no small degree of address to gain the reputation of benevolence without incurring the expense. The silver ore of pure charity is an expensive article in the catalogue of a man's good qualities; whereas the sentimental French plate I use instead of it makes just as good a show, and pays no tax.

Re-enter Rowley.

ROWLEY: Mr. Surface, your servant: I was apprehensive of interrupting you, though my business demands immediate attention, as this note will inform you.

JOSEPH SURFACE: Always happy to see Mr. Rowley.—[*Aside. Reads the letter*] Sir Oliver Surface!—My uncle arrived!

ROWLEY: He is, indeed: we have just parted—quite well, after a speedy voyage, and impatient to embrace his worthy nephew.

JOSEPH SURFACE: I am astonished!—William! stop Mr. Stanley, if he's not gone.   [*Calls to* Servant]

ROWLEY: Oh! he's out of reach, I believe.

JOSEPH SURFACE: Why did you not let me know this when you came in together?

ROWLEY: I thought you had particular business. But I must be gone to inform your brother, and appoint him here to meet your uncle. He will be with you in a quarter of an hour.

JOSEPH SURFACE: So he says. Well, I am strangely overjoyed at his coming.—[*Aside*] Never, to be sure, was anything so damned unlucky!

ROWLEY: You will be delighted to see how well he looks.

JOSEPH SURFACE: Oh! I'm overjoyed to hear it.—[*Aside*]—Just at this time!

ROWLEY: I'll tell him how impatiently you expect him.

JOSEPH SURFACE: Do, do; pray give my best duty and affection. Indeed, I cannot express the sensations I feel at the thought of seeing him.—[*Exit* Rowley] Certainly his coming just at this time is the cruellest piece of ill fortune.   [*Exit*]

SCENE 2: A *Room in Sir Peter Teazle's House*

Enter Mrs. Candour *and* Maid.

MAID: Indeed, ma'am, my lady will see nobody at present.

MRS. CANDOUR: Did you tell her it was her friend Mrs. Candour?

MAID: Yes, ma'am; but she begs you will excuse her.

MRS. CANDOUR: Do go again; I shall be glad to see her, if it be only for a moment, for I am sure she must be in great distress.—[*Exit* Maid] Dear heart, how provoking! I'm not mistress of half the circumstances! We shall have the whole affair in the newspapers, with the names of the parties at length, before I have dropped the story at a dozen houses.

Enter Sir Benjamin Backbite.

Oh, dear Sir Benjamin! you have heard, I suppose——

SIR BENJAMIN: Of Lady Teazle and Mr. Surface——

MRS. CANDOUR: And Sir Peter's discovery——

SIR BENJAMIN: Oh, the strangest piece of business, to be sure!

MRS. CANDOUR: Well, I never was so surprised in my life. I am so sorry for all parties, indeed.

SIR BENJAMIN: Now, I don't pity Sir Peter at all: he was so extravagantly partial to Mr. Surface.

MRS. CANDOUR: Mr. Surface! Why, 'twas with Charles Lady Teazle was detected.

SIR BENJAMIN: No, no, I tell you: Mr. Surface is the gallant.

MRS. CANDOUR: No such thing! Charles is the man. 'Twas Mr. Surface brought Sir Peter on purpose to discover them.

SIR BENJAMIN: I tell you I had it from one——

MRS. CANDOUR: And I have it from one——

SIR BENJAMIN: Who had it from one, who had it——

MRS. CANDOUR: From one immediately——But here comes Lady Sneerwell; perhaps she knows the whole affair.

Enter Lady Sneerwell.

LADY SNEERWELL: So, my dear Mrs. Candour, here's a sad affair of our friend Lady Teazle!

MRS. CANDOUR: Ay, my dear friend, who would have thought——

LADY SNEERWELL: Well, there is no trusting to appearances; though indeed, she was always too lively for me.

MRS. CANDOUR: To be sure, her manners were a little too free; but then she was so young!

LADY SNEERWELL: And had, indeed, some good qualities.

MRS. CANDOUR: So she had, indeed. But have you heard the particulars?

LADY SNEERWELL: No; but everybody says that Mr. Surface——

SIR BENJAMIN: Ay, there; I told you Mr. Surface was the man.

MRS. CANDOUR: No, no: indeed the assignation was with Charles.

LADY SNEERWELL: With Charles! You alarm me, Mrs. Candour.

MRS. CANDOUR: Yes, yes: he was the lover. Mr. Surface, to do him justice, was only the informer.

SIR BENJAMIN: Well, I'll not dispute with you, Mrs. Candour; but, be it which it may, I hope that Sir Peter's wound will not——

MRS. CANDOUR: Sir Peter's wound! Oh, mercy! I didn't hear a word of their fighting.

LADY SNEERWELL: Nor I, a syllable.

SIR BENJAMIN: No! what, no mention of the duel?

MRS. CANDOUR: Not a word.

SIR BENJAMIN: Oh, yes: they fought before they left the room.

LADY SNEERWELL: Pray let us hear.

MRS. CANDOUR: Ay, do oblige us with the duel.

SIR BENJAMIN: "Sir," says Sir Peter, immediately after the discovery, "you are a most ungrateful fellow."

MRS. CANDOUR: Ay, to Charles——

SIR BENJAMIN: No, no—to Mr. Surface—"a most ungrateful fellow; and old as I am, sir," says he, "I insist on immediate satisfaction."

MRS. CANDOUR: Ay, that must have been to Charles; for 'tis very unlikely Mr. Surface should fight in his own house.

SIR BENJAMIN: 'Gad's life, ma'am, not at all—"giving me immediate satisfaction."—On this, ma'am, Lady Teazle, seeing Sir Peter in such danger, ran out of the room in strong hysterics, and Charles after her, calling out for hartshorn and water; then, madam, they began to fight with swords——

Enter Crabtree.

CRABTREE: With pistols, nephew—pistols! I have it from undoubted authority.

MRS. CANDOUR: Oh, Mr. Crabtree, then it is all true!

CRABTREE: Too true, indeed, madam, and Sir Peter is dangerously wounded——

SIR BENJAMIN: By a thrust in second quite through his left side——

CRABTREE: By a bullet lodged in the thorax.

MRS. CANDOUR: Mercy on me! Poor Sir Peter!

CRABTREE: Yes, madam; though Charles would have avoided the matter, if he could.

MRS. CANDOUR: I knew Charles was the person.

SIR BENJAMIN: My uncle, I see, knows nothing of the matter.

CRABTREE: But Sir Peter taxed him with the basest ingratitude——

SIR BENJAMIN: That I told you, you know——

CRABTREE: Do, nephew, let me speak!—and insisted on immediate——

SIR BENJAMIN: Just as I said——

CRABTREE: Odds life, nephew, allow others to know something too! A pair of pistols lay on the bureau (for Mr. Surface, it seems, had come home the night before late from Salthill, where he had been to see the Montem with a friend, who has a son at Eton), so, unluckily, the pistols were left charged.

SIR BENJAMIN: I heard nothing of this.

CRABTREE: Sir Peter forced Charles to take one, and they fired, it seems, pretty nearly together. Charles's shot took effect, as I tell you, and Sir Peter's missed; but, what is very extraordinary, the ball struck against a little bronze Shakespeare that stood over the fireplace, grazed out of the window at a right angle, and wounded the postman, who was just coming to the door with a double letter from Northamptonshire.

SIR BENJAMIN: My uncle's account is more circumstantial, I confess; but I believe mine is the true one, for all that.

LADY SNEERWELL: [*Aside*] I am more interested in this affair than they imagine, and must have better information.   [*Exit*]

SIR BENJAMIN: Ah! Lady Sneerwell's alarm is very easily accounted for.

CRABTREE: Yes, yes, they certainly do say—but that's neither here nor there.

MRS. CANDOUR: But, pray, where is Sir Peter at present?

CRABTREE: Oh! they brought him home, and he is now in the house, though the servants are ordered to deny him.

MRS. CANDOUR: I believe so, and Lady Teazle, I suppose, attending him.

CRABTREE: Yes, yes; and I saw one of the faculty enter just before me.

SIR BENJAMIN: Hey! who comes here?

CRABTREE: Oh, this is he: the physician, depend on't.

MRS. CANDOUR: Oh, certainly! it must be the physician; and now we shall know.

Enter Sir Oliver Surface.

CRABTREE: Well, doctor, what hopes?

MRS. CANDOUR: Ay, doctor, how's your patient?

SIR BENJAMIN: Now, doctor, isn't it a wound with a small-sword?

CRABTREE: A bullet lodged in the thorax, for a hundred!

SIR OLIVER: Doctor! a wound with a small-sword! and a bullet in the thorax?—Oons! are you mad, good people?

SIR BENJAMIN: Perhaps, sir, you are not a doctor?

SIR OLIVER: Truly, I am to thank you for my degree, if I am.

CRABTREE: Only a friend of Sir Peter's, then, I presume. But, sir, you must have heard of his accident?

SIR OLIVER: Not a word!

CRABTREE: Not of his being dangerously wounded?

SIR OLIVER: The devil he is!

SIR BENJAMIN: Run through the body——

CRABTREE: Shot in the breast——

SIR BENJAMIN: By one Mr. Surface——

CRABTREE: Ay, the younger.

SIR OLIVER: Hey! what the plague! you seem to differ strangely in your accounts: however, you agree that Sir Peter is dangerously wounded.

SIR BENJAMIN: Oh, yes, we agree in that.

CRABTREE: Yes, yes, I believe there can be no doubt in that.

SIR OLIVER: Then, upon my word, for a person in that situation, he is the most imprudent man alive; for here he comes, walking as if nothing at all was the matter.

Enter Sir Peter Teazle.

Odds heart, Sir Peter! you are come in good time, I promise you; for we had just given you over!

SIR BENJAMIN: [*Aside to* Crabtree] Egad, uncle, this is the most sudden recovery!

SIR OLIVER: Why, man! what do you do out of bed with a small-sword through your body, and a bullet lodged in your thorax?

SIR PETER: A small-sword and a bullet?

SIR OLIVER: Ay; these gentlemen would have killed you without law or physic, and wanted to dub me a doctor, to make me an accomplice.

SIR PETER: Why, what is all this?

SIR BENJAMIN: We rejoice, Sir Peter, that the story of the duel is not true, and are sincerely sorry for your other misfortune.

SIR PETER: So, so; all over the town already. [*Aside*]

CRABTREE: Though, Sir Peter, you were certainly vastly to blame to marry at your years.

SIR PETER: Sir, what business is that of yours?

MRS. CANDOUR: Though, indeed, as Sir Peter made so good a husband, he's very much to be pitied.

SIR PETER: Plague on your pity, ma'am! I desire none of it.

SIR BENJAMIN: However, Sir Peter, you must not mind the laughing and jests you will meet with on the occasion.

SIR PETER: Sir, sir! I desire to be master in my own house.

CRABTREE: 'Tis no uncommon case, that's one comfort.

SIR PETER: I insist on being left to myself: without ceremony, I insist on your leaving my house directly!

MRS. CANDOUR: Well, well, we are going; and depend on't, we'll make the best report of it we can. [*Exit*]

SIR PETER: Leave my house!

CRABTREE: And tell how hardly you've been treated. [*Exit*]

SIR PETER: Leave my house!

SIR BENJAMIN: And how patiently you bear it. [*Exit*]

SIR PETER: Fiends! vipers! furies! Oh! that their own venom would choke them!

SIR OLIVER: They are very provoking indeed, Sir Peter.

Enter Rowley.

ROWLEY: I heard high words: what has ruffled you, sir?

SIR PETER: Psha! what signifies asking? Do I ever pass a day without my vexations?

ROWLEY: Well, I'm not inquisitive.

SIR OLIVER: Well, Sir Peter, I have seen both my nephews in the manner we proposed.

SIR PETER: A precious couple they are!

ROWLEY: Yes, and Sir Oliver is convinced that your judgment was right, Sir Peter.

SIR OLIVER: Yes, I find Joseph is indeed the man, after all.

ROWLEY: Ay, as Sir Peter says, he is a man of sentiment.

SIR OLIVER: And acts up to the sentiments he professes.

ROWLEY: It certainly is edification to hear him talk.

SIR OLIVER: Oh, he's a model for the young men of the age! But how's this, Sir Peter? you don't join us in your friend Joseph's praise, as I expected.

SIR PETER: Sir Oliver, we live in a damned wicked world, and the fewer we praise the better.

ROWLEY: What! do you say so, Sir Peter, who were never mistaken in your life?

SIR PETER: Psha! plague on you both! I see by your sneering you have heard the whole affair. I shall go mad among you!

ROWLEY: Then, to fret you no longer, Sir Peter, we are indeed acquainted with it all. I met Lady Teazle coming from Mr. Surface's so humbled, that she deigned to request me to be her advocate with you.

SIR PETER: And does Sir Oliver know all this?

SIR OLIVER: Every circumstance.

SIR PETER: What, of the closet and the screen, hey?

SIR OLIVER: Yes, yes, and the little French milliner. Oh, I have been vastly diverted with the story! ha! ha! ha!

SIR PETER: 'Twas very pleasant.

SIR OLIVER: I never laughed more in my life, I assure you: ha! ha! ha!

SIR PETER: Oh, vastly diverting! ha! ha! ha!

ROWLEY: To be sure, Joseph with his sentiments! ha! ha! ha!

SIR PETER: Yes, his sentiments! ha! ha! ha! Hypocritical villain!

SIR OLIVER: Ay, and that rogue Charles to pull Sir Peter out of the closet: ha! ha! ha!

SIR PETER: Ha! ha! 'twas devilish entertaining, to be sure!

SIR OLIVER: Ha! ha! ha! Egad, Sir Peter, I should like to have seen your face when the screen was thrown down: ha! ha!

SIR PETER: Yes, my face when the screen was thrown down: ha! ha! ha! Oh, I must never show my head again!

SIR OLIVER: But come, come, it isn't fair to laugh at you neither, my old friend; though, upon my soul, I can't help it.

SIR PETER: Oh, pray don't restrain your mirth on my account: it does not hurt me at all! I laugh at the whole affair myself. Yes, yes, I think being a standing jest for all one's acquaintance a very happy situation. Oh, yes, and then of a morning to read the paragraphs about Mr. S——, Lady T——, and Sir P——, will be so entertaining!

ROWLEY: Without affectation, Sir Peter, you may despise the ridicule of fools. But I see Lady Teazle going towards the next room; I am sure you must desire a reconciliation as earnestly as she does.

SIR OLIVER: Perhaps my being here prevents her coming to you. Well, I'll leave honest Rowley to mediate between you; but he must bring you all presently to Mr. Surface's, where I am now returning, if not to reclaim a libertine, at least to expose hypocrisy.

SIR PETER: Ah, I'll be present at your discovering yourself there with all my heart; though 'tis a vile unlucky place for discoveries.

ROWLEY: We'll follow.   [Exit Sir Oliver Surface]

SIR PETER: She is not coming here, you see, Rowley.

ROWLEY: No, but she has left the door of that room open, you perceive. See, she is in tears.

SIR PETER: Certainly a little mortification appears very becoming in a wife. Don't you think it will do her good to let her pine a little?

ROWLEY: Oh, this is ungenerous in you!

SIR PETER: Well, I know not what to think. You remember the letter I found of hers evidently intended for Charles!

ROWLEY: A mere forgery, Sir Peter! laid in your way on purpose. This is one of the points which I intend Snake shall give you conviction of.

SIR PETER: I wish I were once satisfied of that. She looks this way. What a remarkably elegant turn of the head she has. Rowley, I'll go to her.

ROWLEY: Certainly.

SIR PETER: Though, when it is known that we are reconciled, people will laugh at me ten times more.

ROWLEY: Let them laugh, and retort their malice only by showing them you are happy in spite of it.

SIR PETER: I'faith, so I will! and, if I'm not mistaken, we may yet be the happiest couple in the country.

ROWLEY: Nay, Sir Peter, he who once lays aside suspicion——

SIR PETER: Hold, Master Rowley! if you have any regard for me, never let me hear you utter anything like a sentiment: I have had enough of them to serve me the rest of my life.   [Exeunt]

SCENE 3:   *The Library in Joseph Surface's House*

Enter Joseph Surface *and* Lady Sneerwell.

LADY SNEERWELL: Impossible! Will not Sir Peter immediately be reconciled to Charles, and of course no longer oppose his union with Maria? The thought is distraction to me.

JOSEPH SURFACE: Can passion furnish a remedy?

LADY SNEERWELL: No, nor cunning either. Oh, I was a fool, an idiot, to league with such a blunderer!

JOSEPH SURFACE: Surely, Lady Sneerwell, I am the greatest sufferer; yet you see I bear the accident with calmness.

LADY SNEERWELL: Because the disappointment doesn't reach your heart; your interest only attached you to Maria. Had you felt for her what I have for that ungrateful libertine, neither your temper nor hypocrisy could prevent your showing the sharpness of your vexation.

JOSEPH SURFACE: But why should your reproaches fall on me for this disappointment?

LADY SNEERWELL: Are you not the cause of it? Had you not a sufficient field for your roguery in imposing upon Sir Peter, and supplanting your brother, but you must endeavour to seduce his wife? I hate such an avarice of crimes; 'tis an unfair monopoly, and never prospers.

JOSEPH SURFACE: Well, I admit I have been to blame. I confess I deviated from the direct road of wrong, but I don't think we're so totally defeated either.

LADY SNEERWELL: No!

JOSEPH SURFACE: You tell me you have made a trial of Snake since we met, and that you still believe him faithful to us?

LADY SNEERWELL: I do believe so.

JOSEPH SURFACE: And that he has undertaken, should it be necessary, to swear and prove, that Charles is at this time contracted by vows and honour to your ladyship, which some of his former letters to you will serve to support?

LADY SNEERWELL: This, indeed, might have assisted.

JOSEPH SURFACE: Come, come; it is not too late yet. —[Knocking at the door] But hark! this is probably my uncle, Sir Oliver: retire to that room; we'll consult further when he's gone.

LADY SNEERWELL: Well, but if he should find you out too.

JOSEPH SURFACE: Oh, I have no fear of that. Sir Peter will hold his tongue for his own credit's sake—and you may depend on it I shall soon discover Sir Oliver's weak side!

LADY SNEERWELL: I have no diffidence of your abilities! only be constant to one roguery at a time.

JOSEPH SURFACE: I will, I will!—[Exit Lady Sneerwell] So! 'tis confounded hard, after such bad fortune, to be baited by one's confederate in evil. Well, at all events, my character is so much better than Charles's, that I certainly—hey!—what—this is not Sir Oliver, but old Stanley again. Plague on't that he should return to tease me just now! I shall have Sir Oliver come and find him here—and——

Enter Sir Oliver Surface.
Gad's life, Mr. Stanley, why have you come back to plague me at this time? You must not stay now, upon my word.

SIR OLIVER: Sir, I hear your uncle Oliver is expected

here, and though he has been so penurious to you, I'll try what he'll do for me.

JOSEPH SURFACE: Sir, 'tis impossible for you to stay now, so I must beg——Come any other time, and I promise you, you shall be assisted.

SIR OLIVER: No: Sir Oliver and I must be acquainted.

JOSEPH SURFACE: Zounds, sir! then I insist on your quitting the room directly.

SIR OLIVER: Nay, sir——

JOSEPH SURFACE: Sir, I insist on't!—Here, William! show this gentleman out. Since you compel me, sir, not one moment—this is such insolence.

[*Going to push him out*]

Enter Charles Surface.

CHARLES SURFACE: Heyday! what's the matter now? What the devil have you got hold of my little broker here? Zounds, brother, don't hurt little Premium. What's the matter, my little fellow?

JOSEPH SURFACE: So! he has been with you, too, has he?

CHARLES SURFACE: To be sure he has. Why, he's as honest a little—— But sure, Joseph, you have not been borrowing money too, have you?

JOSEPH SURFACE: Borrowing! no! But, brother, you know we expect Sir Oliver here every——

CHARLES SURFACE: O Gad, that's true! Noll mustn't find the little broker here, to be sure.

JOSEPH SURFACE: Yet, Mr. Stanley insists

CHARLES SURFACE: Stanley! why his name's Premium.

JOSEPH SURFACE: No, sir, Stanley.

CHARLES SURFACE: No, no, Premium.

JOSEPH SURFACE: Well, no matter which—but——

CHARLES SURFACE: Ay, ay, Stanley or Premium, 'tis the same thing, as you say; for I suppose he goes by half a hundred names, besides A. B. at the coffee-house.   [*Knocking*]

JOSEPH SURFACE: 'Sdeath! here's Sir Oliver at the door. Now I beg, Mr. Stanley——

CHARLES SURFACE: Ay, ay, and I beg, Mr. Premium——

SIR OLIVER: Gentlemen——

JOSEPH SURFACE: Sir, by heaven you shall go!

CHARLES SURFACE: Ay, out with him, certainly.

SIR OLIVER: This violence——

JOSEPH SURFACE: Sir, 'tis your own fault.

CHARLES SURFACE: Out with him, to be sure.

[*Both forcing* Sir Oliver *out*]

Enter Sir Peter *and* Lady Teazle, Maria, *and* Rowley.

SIR PETER: My old friend, Sir Oliver—hey! What in the name of wonder!—here are dutiful nephews—assault their uncle at his first visit!

LADY TEAZLE: Indeed, Sir Oliver, 'twas well we came in to rescue you.

ROWLEY: Truly it was; for I perceive, Sir Oliver, the character of old Stanley was no protection to you.

SIR OLIVER: Nor of Premium either: the necessities of the former could not extort a shilling from that benevolent gentleman; and with the other I stood a chance of faring worse than my ancestors, and being knocked down without being bid for.

JOSEPH SURFACE: Charles!

CHARLES SURFACE: Joseph!

JOSEPH SURFACE: 'Tis now complete!

CHARLES SURFACE: Very.

SIR OLIVER: Sir Peter, my friend, and Rowley too—look on that elder nephew of mine. You know what he has already received from my bounty; and you also know how gladly I would have regarded half my fortune as held in trust for him? judge, then, my disappointment in discovering him to be destitute of truth, charity, and gratitude!

SIR PETER: Sir Oliver, I should be more surprised at this declaration, if I had not myself found him to be mean, treacherous, and hypocritical.

LADY TEAZLE: And if the gentleman pleads not guilty to these, pray let him call me to his character.

SIR PETER: Then, I believe, we need add no more: if he knows himself, he will consider it as the most perfect punishment that he is known to the world.

CHARLES SURFACE: If they talk this way to Honesty, what will they say to me, by-and-by?   [*Aside*]

[*Sir Peter, Lady Teazle, and* Maria *retire*]

SIR OLIVER: As for that prodigal, his brother, there——

CHARLES SURFACE: Ay, now comes my turn: the damned family pictures will ruin me!   [*Aside*]

JOSEPH SURFACE: Sir Oliver—uncle, will you honour me with a hearing?

CHARLES SURFACE: Now, if Joseph would make one of his long speeches, I might recollect myself a little.

[*Aside*]

SIR OLIVER: I suppose you would undertake to justify yourself?   [*To* Joseph Surface]

JOSEPH SURFACE: I trust I could.

SIR OLIVER: [*To* Charles Surface] Well, sir!—and you could justify yourself too, I suppose?

CHARLES SURFACE: Not that I know of, Sir Oliver.

SIR OLIVER: What!—Little Premium has been let too much into the secret, I suppose?

CHARLES SURFACE: True, sir; but they were family secrets, and should not be mentioned again, you know.

ROWLEY: Come, Sir Oliver, I know you cannot speak of Charles's follies with anger.

SIR OLIVER: Odd's heart, no more I can; nor with gravity either. Sir Peter, do you know the rogue bargained with me for all his ancestors; sold me judges and generals by the foot, and maiden aunts as cheap as broken china.

CHARLES SURFACE: To be sure, Sir Oliver, I did make a little free with the family canvas, that's the truth on't. My ancestors may rise in judgment against me, there's no denying it; but believe me sincere when I tell you—and upon my soul I would not say so if I was not—that if I do not appear mortified at the exposure of my follies, it is because I feel at this moment the warmest satisfaction at seeing you, my liberal benefactor.

SIR OLIVER: Charles, I believe you. Give me your hand again: the ill-looking little fellow over the settee has made your peace.

CHARLES SURFACE: Then, sir, my gratitude to the original is still increased.

LADY TEAZLE: [*Advancing*] Yet, I believe, Sir Oliver, here is one whom Charles is still more anxious to be reconciled to.   [*Pointing to* Maria]

SIR OLIVER: Oh, I have heard of his attachment there; and, with the young lady's pardon, if I construe right—that blush——

SIR PETER: Well, child, speak your sentiments.

MARIA: Sir, I have little to say, but that I shall rejoice to hear that he is happy; for me, whatever claim I had to his attention, I willingly resign to one who has a better title.

CHARLES SURFACE: How, Maria!

SIR PETER: Heyday! what's the mystery now? While he appeared an incorrigible rake, you would give your hand to no one else; and now that he is likely to reform I'll warrant you won't have him.

MARIA: His own heart and Lady Sneerwell know the cause.

CHARLES SURFACE: Lady Sneerwell!

JOSEPH SURFACE: Brother, it is with great concern I am obliged to speak on this point, but my regard to justice compels me, and Lady Sneerwell's injuries can no longer be concealed. [*Opens the door*]

Enter Lady Sneerwell.

SIR PETER: So! another French milliner! Egad, he has one in every room in the house, I suppose!

LADY SNEERWELL: Ungrateful Charles! Well may you be surprised, and feel for the indelicate situation your perfidy has forced me into.

CHARLES SURFACE: Pray, uncle, is this another plot of yours? For, as I have life, I don't understand it.

JOSEPH SURFACE: I believe, sir, there is but the evidence of one person more necessary to make it extremely clear.

SIR PETER: And that person, I imagine, is Mr. Snake. —Rowley, you were perfectly right to bring him with us, and pray let him appear.

ROWLEY: Walk in, Mr. Snake.

Enter Snake.
I thought his testimony might be wanted; however, it happens unluckily, that he comes to confront Lady Sneerwell, not to support her.

LADY SNEERWELL: A villain! Treacherous to me at last! Speak, fellow, have you too conspired against me?

SNAKE: I beg your ladyship ten thousand pardons: you paid me extremely liberally for the lie in question; but I unfortunately have been offered double to speak the truth.

LADY SNEERWELL: The torments of shame and disappointment on you all!   [*Going*]

LADY TEAZLE: Hold, Lady Sneerwell—before you go, let me thank you for the trouble you and that gentleman have taken, in writing letters from me to Charles, and answering them yourself; and let me also request you to make my respects to the scandalous college, of which you are president, and inform them, that Lady Teazle, licentiate, begs leave to return the diploma they granted her, as she leaves off practice, and kills characters no longer.

LADY SNEERWELL: You too, madam!—provoking—insolent! May your husband live these fifty years!
                                                  [*Exit*]

SIR PETER: Oons! what a fury!

LADY TEAZLE: A malicious creature, indeed!

SIR PETER: What! not for her last wish?

LADY TEAZLE: Oh, no!

SIR OLIVER: Well, sir, and what have you to say now?

JOSEPH SURFACE: Sir, I am so confounded, to find that Lady Sneerwell could be guilty of suborning Mr. Snake in this manner, to impose on us all, that I know not what to say: however, lest her revengeful spirit should prompt her to injure my brother, I had certainly better follow her directly.   [*Exit*]

SIR PETER: Moral to the last drop!

SIR OLIVER: Ay, and marry her, Joseph, if you can. Oil and vinegar!—egad you'll do very well together.

ROWLEY: I believe we have no more occasion for Mr. Snake at present?

SNAKE: Before I go, I beg pardon once for all, for whatever uneasiness I have been the humble instrument of causing to the parties present.

SIR PETER: Well, well, you have made atonement by a good deed at last.

SNAKE: But I must request of the company, that it shall never be known.

SIR PETER: Hey! what the plague! are you ashamed of having done a right thing once in your life?

SNAKE: Ah, sir, consider—I live by the badness of my character; and, if it were once known that I had been betrayed into an honest action, I should lose every friend I have in the world.

SIR OLIVER: Well, well—we'll not traduce you by saying anything in your praise, never fear. [*Exit* Snake]

SIR PETER: There's a precious rogue!

LADY TEAZLE: See, Sir Oliver, there needs no persuasion now to reconcile your nephew and Maria.

SIR OLIVER: Ay, ay, that's as it should be, and, egad, we'll have the wedding to-morrow morning.

CHARLES SURFACE: Thank you, dear uncle.

SIR PETER: What, you rogue! don't you ask the girl's consent first?

CHARLES SURFACE: Oh, I have done that a long time —a minute ago—and she has looked yes.

MARIA: For shame, Charles!—I protest, Sir Peter, there has not been a word——

SIR OLIVER: Well, then, the fewer the better: may your love for each other never know abatement.

SIR PETER: And may you live as happily together as Lady Teazle and I intend to do!

CHARLES SURFACE: Rowley, my old friend, I am sure you congratulate me; and I suspect that I owe you much.

SIR OLIVER: You do, indeed, Charles.

ROWLEY: If my efforts to serve you had not succeeded you would have been in my debt for the attempt—but deserve to be happy—and you over-repay me.

SIR PETER: Ay, honest Rowley always said you would reform.

CHARLES SURFACE: Why as to reforming, Sir Peter, I'll make no promises, and that I take to be a proof that I intend to set about it. But here shall be my monitor—my gentle guide.—Ah! can I leave the virtuous path those eyes illumine?

> Though thou, dear maid, shouldst wave thy beauty's sway,
> Thou still must rule, because I will obey:
> An humble fugitive from Folly view,
> No sanctuary near but Love and you:

[*To the audience*]

> You can, indeed, each anxious fear remove,
> For even Scandal dies, if you approve.

[*Exeunt omnes*]

The Importance of Being Earnest

by OSCAR WILDE

(1856–1900)

Between Sheridan and Oscar Wilde, England produced many masters of comedy—only none of them happened to write for the stage. For stage comedy, the hundred years after Sheridan have come to be an arctic night. To be sure, just before Wilde emerged as a playwright, wit and satire re-emerged in the man who spoofed Wilde as a poet. But W. S. Gilbert's real success in the theater was not as playwright but librettist, one might really say lyric writer. And though he has not survived by the plays he wrote without Sullivan, Gilbert—with his consistent mockery—was in the truest sense far more a comedy writer than, in three comedies out of four, Wilde was. For, reading Lady Windermere's Fan, An Ideal Husband, and A Woman of No Importance today, we are as often appalled by the plots with their guilty secrets as we are delighted by the prattle with its gay nonsensical charm; we are as often staggered by the highbusted language in which characters avow their penitence and shame as we are dazzled by the epigrams with which Wilde polished off, and now and then pulverized, human pretension. There is beyond that the trashy high-society world, crammed with peers and snob-appeal, in which all this melodrama goes on. Yet if these three of Wilde's plays are, for all their wit, not real comedies, they are at any rate real plays; for Wilde was a master of complication and suspense, and used his bag of stage tricks with a kind of shameless skill.

It is only in The Importance of Being Earnest that Wilde truly achieved comedy; and, paradoxical ever, he there achieved it by exchanging it for farce. But the play is not only a comedic high-water mark for its century, it remains a comedic milestone within its medium. Instead of using the drawing room for old-fashioned society melodrama, Wilde here used it for something quite new. He wedded the utmost propriety to the utmost preposterousness; in the most elegant of settings, he reeled off the topsy-turviest of plots. He blended Gilbert with Sheridan, he interleaved Alice in Wonderland with Debrett. The plot here, too, might seem melodramatic were it not so blandly mad. For Miss Prism here, like Mrs. Erlynne or Mrs. Arbuthnot before her, is a Woman with a Past; Jack Worthing, like Gerald Arbuthnot, is a young man of clouded parentage; here, too, characters not only tell lies but live them; and the plot has the same need of a handbag as it earlier did of a fan. Only here, it is not rankly incredible but delightfully impossible; here the most distinguished cold-bloodedness replaces the most detestable emotionalism; and a joke is executed with so highborn an air as to attain to a kind of grandeur.

Beyond the story that grows out of one young man inventing a wicked brother as a way of coming to London, and another young man inventing an invalid friend as a way of leaving it, there are delightful characters, like Lady Bracknell; and notable interludes, like the interview scene; and witty lines; and brilliant touches, like Jack's sudden appearance in deep mourning for the brother who at that moment is not ten feet away. The Importance of Being Earnest is wonderful fun on condition it be treated, throughout, as an exercise in manner. It is uproarious, that is to say, if—and only if—nothing about it and no one in it ever cracks a smile.

OSCAR WILDE

The Importance of Being Earnest

CHARACTERS

JOHN WORTHING, J.P.

ALGERNON MONCRIEFF

REV. CANON CHASUBLE, D.D.

MERRIMAN, *Butler*

LANE, *Manservant*

LADY BRACKNELL

HON. GWENDOLEN FAIRFAX

CECILY CARDEW

MISS PRISM, *Governess*

THE SCENES IN THE PLAY

ACT I: *Algernon Moncrieff's Flat in Half-Moon Street, W.*

ACT II: *The Garden at the Manor House, Woolton*

ACT III: *Drawing-Room of the Manor House, Woolton*

TIME: *The Present*

PLACE: *London*

Act I

SCENE: *Morning-room in Algernon's flat in Half-Moon Street. The room is luxuriously and artistically furnished. The sound of a piano is heard in the adjoining room.*

[Lane *is arranging afternoon tea on the table, and after the music has ceased,* Algernon *enters*]

ALGERNON: Did you hear what I was playing, Lane?

LANE: I didn't think it polite to listen, sir.

ALGERNON: I'm sorry for that, for your sake. I don't play accurately—anyone can play accurately—but I play with wonderful expression. As far as the piano is concerned, sentiment is my forte. I keep science for Life.

LANE: Yes, sir.

ALGERNON: And, speaking of the science of Life, have you got the cucumber sandwiches cut for Lady Bracknell?

LANE: Yes, sir. [*Hands them on a salver*]

ALGERNON: [*Inspects them, takes two, and sits down on the sofa*] Oh! . . . by the way, Lane, I see from your book that on Thursday night, when Lord Shoreman and Mr. Worthing were dining with me, eight bottles of champagne are entered as having been consumed.

LANE: Yes, sir; eight bottles and a pint.

ALGERNON: Why is it that in a bachelor's establishment the servants invariably drink the champagne? I ask merely for information.

LANE: I attribute it to the superior quality of the wine, sir. I have often observed that in married households the champagne is rarely of a first-rate brand.

ALGERNON: Good Heavens! Is marriage so demoralizing as that?

LANE: I believe it *is* a very pleasant state, sir. I have had very little experience of it myself up to the present. I have only been married once. That was in consequence of a misunderstanding between myself and a young woman.

ALGERNON: [*Languidly*] I don't know that I am much interested in your family life, Lane.

LANE: No, sir; it is not a very interesting subject. I never think of it myself.

ALGERNON: Very natural, I am sure. That will do, Lane, thank you.

LANE: Thank you, sir. [*Lane goes out*]

ALGERNON: Lane's views on marriage seem somewhat lax. Really, if the lower orders don't set us a good example, what on earth is the use of them? They seem, as a class, to have absolutely no sense of moral responsibility.

[*Enter Lane*]

LANE: Mr. Ernest Worthing.

[*Enter Jack. Lane goes out*]

ALGERNON: How are you, my dear Ernest? What brings you up to town?

JACK: Oh, pleasure, pleasure! What else should bring one anywhere? Eating as usual, I see, Algy!

ALGERNON: [*Stiffly*] I believe it is customary in good society to take some slight refreshment at five o'clock. Where have you been since last Thursday?

JACK: [*Sitting down on the sofa*] In the country.

ALGERNON: What on earth do you do there?

319

JACK: [*Pulling off his gloves*] When one is in town one amuses oneself. When one is in the country one amuses other people. It is excessively boring.

ALGERNON: And who are the people you amuse?

JACK: [*Airily*] Oh, neighbors, neighbors.

ALGERNON: Got nice neighbors in your part of Shropshire?

JACK: Perfectly horrid! Never speak to one of them.

ALGERNON: How immensely you must amuse them! [*Goes over and takes sandwich*] By the way, Shropshire is your county, is it not?

JACK: Eh? Shropshire? Yes, of course. Hallo! Why all these cups? Why cucumber sandwiches? Why such reckless extravagance in one so young? Who is coming to tea?

ALGERNON: Oh! merely Aunt Augusta and Gwendolen.

JACK: How perfectly delightful!

ALGERNON: Yes, that is all very well; but I am afraid Aunt Augusta won't quite approve of your being here.

JACK: May I ask why?

ALGERNON: My dear fellow, the way you flirt with Gwendolen is perfectly disgraceful. It is almost as bad as the way Gwendolen flirts with you.

JACK: I am in love with Gwendolen. I have come up to town expressly to propose to her.

ALGERNON: I thought you had come for pleasure? . . . I call that business.

JACK: How utterly unromantic you are!

ALGERNON: I really don't see anything romantic in proposing. It is very romantic to be in love. But there is nothing romantic about a definite proposal. Why, one may be accepted. One usually is, I believe. Then the excitement is all over. The very essence of romance is uncertainty. If ever I get married, I'll certainly try to forget the fact.

JACK: I have no doubt about that, dear Algy. The Divorce Court was specially invented for people whose memories are so curiously constituted.

ALGERNON: Oh! there is no use speculating on that subject. Divorces are made in Heaven—[*Jack puts out his hand to take a sandwich. Algernon at once interferes*] Please don't touch the cucumber sandwiches. They are ordered specially for Aunt Augusta. [*Takes one and eats it*]

JACK: Well, you have been eating them all the time.

ALGERNON: That is quite a different matter. She is my aunt. [*Takes plate from below*] Have some bread and butter. The bread and butter is for Gwendolen. Gwendolen is devoted to bread and butter.

JACK: [*Advancing to table and helping himself*] And very good bread and butter it is, too.

ALGERNON: Well, my dear fellow, you need not eat as if you were going to eat it all. You behave as if you were married to her already. You are not married to her already, and I don't think you will ever be.

JACK: Why on earth do you say that?

ALGERNON: Well, in the first place girls never marry the men they flirt with. Girls don't think it right.

JACK: Oh, that is nonsense!

ALGERNON: It isn't. It is a great truth. It accounts for the extraordinary number of bachelors that one sees all over the place. In the second place, I don't give my consent.

JACK: Your consent!

ALGERNON: My dear fellow, Gwendolen is my first cousin. And before I allow you to marry her, you will have to clear up the whole question of Cecily.
                                              [*Rings bell*]

JACK: Cecily! What on earth do you mean? What do you mean, Algy, by Cecily! I don't know anyone of the name Cecily.

[*Enter* Lane]

ALGERNON: Bring me that cigarette case Mr. Worthing left in the smoking-room the last time he dined here.

LANE: Yes, sir.   [*Lane goes out*]

JACK: Do you mean to say you have had my cigarette case all this time? I wish to goodness you had let me know. I have been writing frantic letters to Scotland Yard about it. I was very nearly offering a large reward.

ALGERNON: Well, I wish you would offer one. I happen to be more than usually hard up.

JACK: There is no good offering a large reward now that the thing is found.

[*Enter* Lane *with the cigarette case on a salver. Algernon takes it at once. Lane goes out*]

ALGERNON: I think that is rather mean of you, Ernest, I must say. [*Opens case and examines it*] However, it makes no matter, for, now that I look at the inscription, I find that the thing isn't yours after all.

JACK: Of course it's mine. [*Moving to him*] You have seen me with it a hundred times, and you have no right whatsoever to read what is written inside. It is a very ungentlemanly thing to read a private cigarette case.

ALGERNON: Oh! it is absurd to have a hard-and-fast rule about what one should read and what one shouldn't. More than half of modern culture depends on what one shouldn't read.

JACK: I am quite aware of the fact, and I don't propose to discuss modern culture. It isn't the sort of thing one should talk of in private. I simply want my cigarette case back.

ALGERNON: Yes; but this isn't your cigarette case. This cigarette case is a present from someone of the name of Cecily, and you said you didn't know anyone of that name.

JACK: Well, if you want to know, Cecily happens to be my aunt.

ALGERNON: Your aunt!

JACK: Yes. Charming old lady she is, too. Lives at Tunbridge Wells. Just give it back to me, Algy.

ALGERNON: [*Retreating to back of sofa*] But why does she call herself little Cecily if she is your aunt and lives at Tunbridge Wells? [*Reading*] "From little Cecily with her fondest love."

JACK: [*Moving to sofa and kneeling upon it*] My dear fellow, what on earth is there in that? Some aunts are tall, some aunts are not tall. That is a matter that surely an aunt may be allowed to decide for herself. You seem to think that every aunt should be exactly like your aunt! That is absurd! For Heaven's sake give me back my cigarette case.

[*Follows* Algernon *round the room*]

ALGERNON: Yes. But why does your aunt call you her uncle? "From little Cecily, with her fondest love to her dear Uncle Jack." There is no objection, I admit, to an aunt being a small aunt, but why an aunt, no matter what her size may be, should call her own nephew her uncle, I can't quite make out. Besides, your name isn't Jack at all; it's Ernest.

JACK: It isn't Ernest; it's Jack.

ALGERNON: You have always told me it was Ernest. I have introduced you to everyone as Ernest. You answer to the name of Ernest. You look as if your name was Ernest. You are the most earnest-looking person I ever saw in my life. It is perfectly absurd your saying that your name isn't Ernest. It's on your cards. Here is one of them. [*Taking it from case*] "Mr. Ernest Worthing, B 4, The Albany." I'll keep this as a proof your name is Ernest if ever you attempt to deny it to me, or to Gwendolen, or to anyone else. [*Puts the card in his pocket*]

JACK: Well, my name is Ernest in town and Jack in the country, and the cigarette case was given to me in the country.

ALGERNON: Yes, but that does not account for the fact that your small Aunt Cecily, who lives at Tunbridge Wells, calls you her dear uncle. Come, old boy, you had much better have the thing out at once.

JACK: My dear Algy, you talk exactly as if you were a dentist. It is very vulgar to talk like a dentist when one isn't a dentist. It produces a false impression.

ALGERNON: Well, that is exactly what dentists always do. Now, go on! Tell me the whole thing. I may mention that I have always suspected you of being a confirmed and secret Bunburyist; and I am quite sure of it now.

JACK: Bunburyist? What on earth do you mean by a Bunburyist?

ALGERNON: I'll reveal to you the meaning of that incomparable expression as soon as you are kind enough to inform me why you are Ernest in town and Jack in the country.

JACK: Well, produce my cigarette case first.

ALGERNON: Here it is. [*Hands cigarette case*] Now produce your explanation, and pray make it improbable.   [*Sits on sofa*]

JACK: My dear fellow, there is nothing improbable about my explanation at all. In fact it's perfectly ordinary. Old Mr. Thomas Cardew, who adopted me when I was a little boy, made me in his will guardian to his grand-daughter, Miss Cecily Cardew. Cecily, who addresses me as her uncle from motives of respect that you could not possibly appreciate, lives at my place in the country under the charge of her admirable governess, Miss Prism.

ALGERNON: Where is that place in the country, by the way?

JACK: That is nothing to you, dear boy. You are not going to be invited. . . . I may tell you candidly that the place is not in Shropshire.

ALGERNON: I suspected that, my dear fellow! I have Bunburyed all over Shropshire on two separate occasions. Now, go on. Why are you Ernest in town and Jack in the country?

JACK: My dear Algy, I don't know whether you will be able to understand my real motives. You are hardly serious enough. When one is placed in the position of guardian, one has to adopt a very high moral tone on all subjects. It's one's duty to do so. And as a high moral tone can hardly be said to conduce very much to either one's health or one's happiness, in order to get up to town I have always pretended to have a younger brother of the name of Ernest, who lives in the Albany, and gets into the most dreadful scrapes. That, my dear Algy, is the whole truth pure and simple.

ALGERNON: The truth is rarely pure and never simple. Modern life would be very tedious if it were either, and modern literature a complete impossibility!

JACK: That wouldn't be at all a bad thing.

ALGERNON: Literary criticism is not your forte, my dear fellow. Don't try it. You should leave that to people who haven't been at a University. They do it so well in the daily papers. What you really are is a Bunburyist. I was quite right in saying you were a Bunburyist. You are one of the most advanced Bunburyists I know.

JACK: What on earth do you mean?

ALGERNON: You have invented a very useful younger brother called Ernest, in order that you may be able to come up to town as often as you like. I have invented an invaluable permanent invalid called Bunbury, in order that I may be able to go down into the country whenever I choose. Bunbury is perfectly invaluable. If it wasn't for Bunbury's extraordinary bad health, for instance, I wouldn't be able to dine with you at Willis' to-night, for I have been really engaged to Aunt Augusta for more than a week.

JACK: I haven't asked you to dine with me anywhere to-night.

ALGERNON: I know. You are absolutely careless about sending out invitations. It is very foolish of you. Nothing annoys people so much as not receiving invitations.

JACK: You had much better dine with your Aunt Augusta.

ALGERNON: I haven't the smallest intention of doing anything of the kind. To begin with, I dined there on Monday, and once a week is quite enough to dine with one's own relatives. In the second place, whenever I do dine there I am always treated as a member of the family, and sent down with either no woman at all, or two. In the third place, I know perfectly well whom she will place me next, to-night. She will place me next Mary Farquhar, who always flirts with her own husband across the dinner-table. That is not very pleasant. Indeed, it is not even decent . . . and that sort of thing is enormously on the increase. The amount of women in London who flirt with their own husbands is perfectly scandalous. It looks so bad. It is simply washing one's clean linen in public. Besides, now that I know you to be a confirmed Bunburyist I naturally want to talk to you about Bunburying. I want to tell you the rules.

JACK: I'm not a Bunburyist at all. If Gwendolen accepts me, I am going to kill my brother, indeed I think I'll kill him in any case. Cecily is a little too much interested in him. It is rather a bore. So I am going to get rid of Ernest. And I strongly advise you to do the same with Mr. . . . with your invalid friend who has the absurd name.

ALGERNON: Nothing will induce me to part with Bunbury, and if you ever get married, which seems to me extremely problematic, you will be very glad to know Bunbury. A man who marries without knowing Bunbury has a very tedious time of it.

JACK: That is nonsense. If I marry a charming girl like Gwendolen, and she is the only girl I ever saw in my life that I would marry, I certainly won't want to know Bunbury.

ALGERNON: Then your wife will. You don't seem to realize, that in married life three is company and two is none.

JACK: [Sententiously] That, my dear young friend, is the theory that the corrupt French Drama has been propounding for the last fifty years.

ALGERNON: Yes; and that the happy English home has proved in half the time.

JACK: For heaven's sake, don't try to be cynical. It's perfectly easy to be cynical.

ALGERNON: My dear fellow, it isn't easy to be anything now-a-days. There's such a lot of beastly competition about. [The sound of an electric bell is heard] Ah! that must be Aunt Augusta. Only relatives, or creditors, ever ring in that Wagnerian manner. Now, if I get her out of the way for ten minutes, so that you can have an opportunity for proposing to Gwendolen, may I dine with you to-night at Willis'?

JACK: I suppose so, if you want to.

ALGERNON: Yes, but you must be serious about it. I hate people who are not serious about meals. It is so shallow of them.

[Enter Lane]

LANE: Lady Bracknell and Miss Fairfax.

[Algernon goes forward to meet them. Enter Lady Bracknell and Gwendolen]

LADY BRACKNELL: Good afternoon, dear Algernon, I hope you are behaving very well.

ALGERNON: I'm feeling very well, Aunt Augusta.

LADY BRACKNELL: That's not quite the same thing. In fact the two things rarely go together. [Sees Jack and bows to him with icy coldness]

ALGERNON: [To Gwendolen] Dear me, you are smart!

GWENDOLEN: I am always smart! Aren't I, Mr. Worthing?

JACK: You're quite perfect, Miss Fairfax.

GWENDOLEN: Oh! I hope I am not that. It would leave no room for developments, and I intend to develop in many directions.

[Gwendolen and Jack sit down together in the corner]

LADY BRACKNELL: I'm sorry if we are a little late, Algernon, but I was obliged to call on dear Lady Harbury. I hadn't been there since her poor husband's death. I never saw a woman so altered; she looks quite twenty years younger. And now I'll have a cup of tea, and one of those nice cucumber sandwiches you promised me.

ALGERNON: Certainly, Aunt Augusta.

[Goes over to tea-table]

LADY BRACKNELL: Won't you come and sit here, Gwendolen?

GWENDOLEN: Thanks, mamma, I'm quite comfortable where I am.

ALGERNON: [Picking up empty plate in horror] Good heavens! Lane! Why are there no cucumber sandwiches? I ordered them specially.

LANE: [Gravely] There were no cucumbers in the market this morning, sir. I went down twice.

ALGERNON: No cucumbers!

LANE: No, sir. Not even for ready money.

ALGERNON: That will do, Lane, thank you.

LANE: Thank you, sir.   [Goes out]

ALGERNON: I am greatly distressed, Aunt Augusta, about there being no cucumbers, not even for ready money.

LADY BRACKNELL: It really makes no matter, Algernon. I had some crumpets with Lady Harbury, who seems to me to be living entirely for pleasure now.

ALGERNON: I hear her hair has turned quite gold from grief.

LADY BRACKNELL: It certainly has changed its color. From what cause I, of course, cannot say. [Algernon crosses and hands tea] Thank you. I've quite a treat for you to-night, Algernon. I am going to send you down with Mary Farquhar. She is such a nice woman, and so attentive to her husband. It's delightful to watch them.

ALGERNON: I am afraid, Aunt Augusta, I shall have

to give up the pleasure of dining with you to-night after all.

LADY BRACKNELL: [Frowning] I hope not, Algernon. It would put my table completely out. Your uncle would have to dine upstairs. Fortunately he is accustomed to that.

ALGERNON: It is a great bore, and, I need hardly say, a terrible disappointment to me, but the fact is I have just had a telegram to say that my poor friend Bunbury is very ill again. [Exchanges glances with Jack] They seem to think I should be with him.

LADY BRACKNELL: It is very strange. This Mr. Bunbury seems to suffer from curiously bad health.

ALGERNON: Yes; poor Bunbury is a dreadful invalid.

LADY BRACKNELL: Well, I must say, Algernon, that I think it is high time that Mr. Bunbury made up his mind whether he was going to live or to die. This shilly-shallying with the question is absurd. Nor do I in any way approve of the modern sympathy with invalids. I consider it morbid. Illness of any kind is hardly a thing to be encouraged in others. Health is the primary duty of life. I am always telling that to your poor uncle, but he never seems to take much notice . . . as far as any improvement in his ailments goes. I should be much obliged if you would ask Mr. Bunbury, from me, to be kind enough not to have a relapse on Saturday, for I rely on you to arrange my music for me. It is my last reception and one wants something that will encourage conversation, particularly at the end of the season when everyone has practically said whatever they had to say, which, in most cases, was probably not much.

ALGERNON: I'll speak to Bunbury, Aunt Augusta, if he is still conscious, and I think I can promise you he'll be all right by Saturday. You see, if one plays good music, people don't listen, and if one plays bad music people don't talk. But I'll run over the program I've drawn out, if you will kindly come into the next room for a moment.

LADY BRACKNELL: Thank you, Algernon. It is very thoughtful of you. [Rising, and following Algernon] I'm sure the program will be delightful, after a few expurgations. French songs I cannot possibly allow. People always seem to think that they are improper, and either look shocked, which is vulgar, or laugh, which is worse. But German sounds a thoroughly respectable language, and indeed, I believe is so. Gwendolen, you will accompany me.

GWENDOLEN: Certainly, mamma.

[Lady Bracknell and Algernon go into the music-room, Gwendolen remains behind]

JACK: Charming day it has been, Miss Fairfax.

GWENDOLEN: Pray don't talk to me about the weather, Mr. Worthing. Whenever people talk to me about the weather, I always feel quite certain that they mean something else. And that makes me so nervous.

JACK: I do mean something else.

GWENDOLEN: I thought so. In fact, I am never wrong.

JACK: And I would like to be allowed to take advantage of Lady Bracknell's temporary absence . . .

GWENDOLEN: I would certainly advise you to do so. Mamma has a way of coming back suddenly into a room that I have often had to speak to her about.

JACK: [Nervously] Miss Fairfax, ever since I met you I have admired you more than any girl . . . I have ever met since . . . I met you.

GWENDOLEN: Yes, I am quite aware of the fact. And I often wish that in public, at any rate, you had been more demonstrative. For me you have always had an irresistible fascination. Even before I met you I was far from indifferent to you. [Jack looks at her in amazement] We live, as I hope you know, Mr. Worthing, in an age of ideals. The fact is constantly mentioned in the more expensive monthly magazines, and has reached the provincial pulpits I am told: and my ideal has always been to love some one of the name of Ernest. There is something in that name that inspires absolute confidence. The moment Algernon first mentioned to me that he had a friend called Ernest, I knew I was destined to love you.

JACK: You really love me, Gwendolen?

GWENDOLEN: Passionately!

JACK: Darling! You don't know how happy you've made me.

GWENDOLEN: My own Ernest!

JACK: But you don't really mean to say that you couldn't love me if my name wasn't Ernest?

GWENDOLEN: But your name is Ernest.

JACK: Yes, I know it is. But supposing it was something else? Do you mean to say you couldn't love me then?

GWENDOLEN: [Glibly] Ah! that is clearly a metaphysical speculation, and like most metaphysical speculations has very little reference at all to the actual facts of real life, as we know them.

JACK: Personally, darling, to speak quite candidly, I don't much care about the name of Ernest . . . I don't think that name suits me at all.

GWENDOLEN: It suits you perfectly. It is a divine name. It has a music of its own. It produces vibrations.

JACK: Well, really, Gwendolen, I must say that I think there are lots of other much nicer names. I think, Jack, for instance, a charming name.

GWENDOLEN: Jack? . . . No, there is very little music in the name Jack, if any at all, indeed. It does not thrill. It produces absolutely no vibrations. . . . I have known several Jacks, and they all, without exception, were more than usually plain. Besides, Jack is a notorious domesticity for John! And I pity any woman who is married to a man called John. She would probably never be allowed to know the entrancing pleasure of a single moment's solitude. The only really safe name is Ernest.

JACK: Gwendolen, I must get christened at once—I mean we must get married at once. There is no time to be lost.

GWENDOLEN: Married, Mr. Worthing?

JACK: [Astounded] Well . . . surely. You know that I love you, and you led me to believe, Miss Fairfax, that you were not absolutely indifferent to me.

GWENDOLEN: I adore you. But you haven't proposed to me yet. Nothing has been said at all about marriage. The subject has not even been touched on.

JACK: Well . . . may I propose to you now?

GWENDOLEN: I think it would be an admirable opportunity. And to spare you any possible disappointment, Mr. Worthing, I think it only fair to tell you quite frankly beforehand that I am fully determined to accept you.

JACK: Gwendolen!

GWENDOLEN: Yes, Mr. Worthing, what have you got to say to me?

JACK: You know what I have got to say to you.

GWENDOLEN: Yes, but you don't say it.

JACK: Gwendolen, will you marry me?
[Goes on his knees]

GWENDOLEN: Of course I will, darling. How long you have been about it! I am afraid you have had very little experience in how to propose.

JACK: My own one, I have never loved anyone in the world but you.

GWENDOLEN: Yes, but men often propose for practice. I know my brother Gerald does. All my girl-friends tell me so. What wonderfully blue eyes you have, Ernest! They are quite, quite blue. I hope you will always look at me just like that, especially when there are other people present.

[Enter Lady Bracknell]

LADY BRACKNELL: Mr. Worthing! Rise, sir, from this semi-recumbent posture. It is most indecorous.

GWENDOLEN: Mamma! [He tries to rise; she restrains him] I must beg you to retire. This is no place for you. Besides, Mr. Worthing has not quite finished yet.

LADY BRACKNELL: Finished what, may I ask?

GWENDOLEN: I am engaged to Mr. Worthing, mamma.   [They rise together]

LADY BRACKNELL: Pardon me, you are not engaged to anyone. When you do become engaged to some one, I, or your father, should his health permit him, will inform you of the fact. An engagement should come on a young girl as a surprise, pleasant or unpleasant, as the case may be. It is hardly a matter that she could be allowed to arrange for herself. . . . And now I have a few questions to put to you, Mr. Worthing. While I am making these inquiries, you, Gwendolen, will wait for me below in the carriage.

GWENDOLEN: [Reproachfully] Mamma!

LADY BRACKNELL: In the carriage, Gwendolen!
[Gwendolen goes to the door. She and

Jack blow kisses to each other behind Lady Bracknell's back. Lady Bracknell looks vaguely about as if she could not understand what the noise was. Finally turns round]
Gwendolen, the carriage!

GWENDOLEN: Yes, mamma.
[Goes out, looking back at Jack]

LADY BRACKNELL: [Sitting down] You can take a seat, Mr. Worthing. [Looks in her pocket for note-book and pencil]

JACK: Thank you, Lady Bracknell, I prefer standing.

LADY BRACKNELL: [Pencil and note-book in hand] I feel bound to tell you that you are not down on my list of eligible young men, although I have the same list as the dear Duchess of Bolton has. We work together, in fact. However, I am quite ready to enter your name, should your answers be what a really affectionate mother requires. Do you smoke?

JACK: Well, yes, I must admit I smoke.

LADY BRACKNELL: I am glad to hear it. A man should always have an occupation of some kind. There are far too many idle men in London as it is. How old are you?

JACK: Twenty-nine.

LADY BRACKNELL: A very good age to be married at. I have always been of opinion that a man who desires to get married should know either everything or nothing. Which do you know?

JACK: [After some hesitation] I know nothing, Lady Bracknell.

LADY BRACKNELL: I am pleased to hear it. I do not approve of anything that tampers with natural ignorance. Ignorance is like a delicate exotic fruit; touch it and the bloom is gone. The whole theory of modern education is radically unsound. Fortunately in England, at any rate, education produces no effect whatsoever. If it did, it would prove a serious danger to the upper classes, and probably lead to acts of violence in Grosvenor Square. What is your income?

JACK: Between seven and eight thousand a year.

LADY BRACKNELL: [Makes a note in her book] In land, or in investments?

JACK: In investments, chiefly.

LADY BRACKNELL: That is satisfactory. What between the duties expected of one during one's lifetime, and the duties exacted from one after one's death, land has ceased to be either a profit or a pleasure. It gives one position, and prevents one from keeping it up. That's all that can be said about land.

JACK: I have a country house with some land, of course, attached to it, about fifteen hundred acres, I believe; but I don't depend on that for my real income. In fact, as far as I can make out, the poachers are the only people who make anything out of it.

LADY BRACKNELL: A country house! How many bedrooms? Well, that point can be cleared up afterwards. You have a town house, I hope? A girl with a simple, unspoiled nature, like Gwendolen, could hardly be expected to reside in the country.

JACK: Well, I own a house in Belgrave Square, but it is let by the year to Lady Bloxham. Of course, I can get it back whenever I like, at six months' notice.

LADY BRACKNELL: Lady Bloxham? I don't know her.

JACK: Oh, she goes about very little. She is a lady considerably advanced in years.

LADY BRACKNELL: Ah, now-a-days that is no guarantee of respectability of character. What number in Belgrave Square?

JACK: 149.

LADY BRACKNELL: [Shaking her head] The unfashionable side. I thought there was something. However, that could easily be altered.

JACK: Do you mean the fashion, or the side?

LADY BRACKNELL: [Sternly] Both, if necessary, I presume. What are your politics?

JACK: Well, I am afraid I really have none. I am a Liberal Unionist.

LADY BRACKNELL: Oh, they count as Tories. They dine with us. Or come in the evening, at any rate. Now to minor matters. Are your parents living?

JACK: I have lost both my parents.

LADY BRACKNELL: Both? . . . That seems like carelessness. Who was your father? He was evidently a man of some wealth. Was he born in what the Radical papers call the purple of commerce, or did he rise from the ranks of the aristocracy?

JACK: I am afraid I really don't know. The fact is, Lady Bracknell, I said I had lost my parents. It would be nearer the truth to say that my parents seem to have lost me . . . I don't actually know who I am by birth. I was . . . well, I was found.

LADY BRACKNELL: Found!

JACK: The late Mr. Thomas Cardew, an old gentleman of a very charitable and kindly disposition, found me, and gave me the name of Worthing, because he happened to have a first-class ticket for Worthing in his pocket at the time. Worthing is a place in Sussex. It is a seaside resort.

LADY BRACKNELL: Where did the charitable gentleman who had a first-class ticket for this seaside find you?

JACK: [Gravely] In a hand-bag.

LADY BRACKNELL: A hand-bag?

JACK: [Very seriously] Yes, Lady Bracknell. I was in a hand-bag—a somewhat large, black leather hand-bag, with handles to it—an ordinary hand-bag in fact.

LADY BRACKNELL: In what locality did this Mr. James, or Thomas, Cardew come across this ordinary hand-bag?

JACK: In the cloak-room at Victoria Station. It was given to him in mistake for his own.

LADY BRACKNELL: The cloak-room at Victoria Station?

JACK: Yes. The Brighton line.

LADY BRACKNELL: The line is immaterial. Mr. Worthing, I confess I feel somewhat bewildered by what you have just told me. To be born, or at any rate bred, in a hand-bag, whether it had handles or not, seems to me to display a contempt for the ordinary decencies of family life that remind one of the worst excesses of the French Revolution. And I presume you know what that unfortunate movement led to? As for the particular locality in which the hand-bag was found, a cloak-room at a railway station might serve to conceal a social indiscretion—has probably, indeed, been used for that purpose before now—but it could hardly be regarded as an assured basis for a recognized position in good society.

JACK: May I ask you then what you would advise me to do? I need hardly say I would do anything in the world to ensure Gwendolen's happiness.

LADY BRACKNELL: I would strongly advise you, Mr. Worthing, to try and acquire some relations as soon as possible, and to make a definite effort to produce at any rate one parent, of either sex, before the season is quite over.

JACK: Well, I don't see how I could possibly manage to do that. I can produce the hand-bag at any moment. It is in my dressing-room at home. I really think that should satisfy you, Lady Bracknell.

LADY BRACKNELL: Me, sir! What has it to do with me? You can hardly imagine that I and Lord Bracknell would dream of allowing our only daughter—a girl brought up with the utmost care—to marry into a cloak-room, and form an alliance with a parcel? Good morning, Mr. Worthing!

[Lady Bracknell *sweeps out in majestic indignation*]

JACK: Good morning!

[Algernon *from the other room, strikes up the Wedding March. Jack looks perfectly furious, and goes to the door*]
For goodness' sake don't play that ghastly tune, Algy! How idiotic you are!

[*The music stops, and* Algernon *enters cheerily*]

ALGERNON: Didn't it go off all right, old boy? You don't mean to say Gwendolen refused you? I know it is a way she has. She is always refusing people. I think it is most ill-natured of her.

JACK: Oh, Gwendolen is as right as a trivet. As far as she is concerned, we are engaged. Her mother is perfectly unbearable. Never met such a Gorgon . . . I don't really know what a Gorgon is like, but I am quite sure that Lady Bracknell is one. In any case, she is a monster, without being a myth, which is rather unfair. . . . I beg your pardon, Algy, I suppose I shouldn't talk about your own aunt in that way before you.

ALGERNON: My dear boy, I love hearing my relations abused. It is the only thing that makes me put up with them at all. Relations are simply a tedious pack of people, who haven't got the remotest knowledge of how to live, nor the smallest instinct about when to die.

JACK: Oh, that is nonsense!

ALGERNON: It isn't!

JACK: Well, I won't argue about the matter. You always want to argue about things.

ALGERNON: That is exactly what things were originally made for.

JACK: Upon my word, if I thought that, I'd shoot myself. . . . [A pause] You don't think there is any chance of Gwendolen becoming like her mother in about a hundred and fifty years, do you, Algy?

ALGERNON: All women become like their mothers. That is their tragedy. No man does. That's his.

JACK: Is that clever?

ALGERNON: It is perfectly phrased! and quite as true as any observation in civilized life should be.

JACK: I am sick to death of cleverness. Everybody is clever now-a-days. You can't go anywhere without meeting clever people. The thing has become an absolute public nuisance. I wish to goodness we had a few fools left.

ALGERNON: We have.

JACK: I should extremely like to meet them. What do they talk about?

ALGERNON: The fools! Oh! about the clever people, of course.

JACK: What fools!

ALGERNON: By the way, did you tell Gwendolen the truth about your being Ernest in town, and Jack in the country?

JACK: [In a very patronizing manner] My dear fellow, the truth isn't quite the sort of thing one tells to a nice, sweet, refined girl. What extraordinary ideas you have about the way to behave to a woman!

ALGERNON: The only way to behave to a woman is to make love to her, if she is pretty, and to someone else if she is plain.

JACK: Oh, that is nonsense.

ALGERNON: What about your brother? What about the profligate Ernest?

JACK: Oh, before the end of the week I shall have got rid of him. I'll say he died in Paris of apoplexy. Lots of people die of apoplexy, quite suddenly, don't they?

ALGERNON: Yes, but it's hereditary, my dear fellow. It's a sort of thing that runs in families. You had much better say a severe chill.

JACK: You are sure a severe chill isn't hereditary, or anything of that kind?

ALGERNON: Of course it isn't!

JACK: Very well, then. My poor brother Ernest is carried off suddenly in Paris, by a severe chill. That gets rid of him.

ALGERNON: But I thought you said that . . . Miss Cardew was a little too much interested in your poor brother Ernest? Won't she feel his loss a good deal?

JACK: Oh, that is all right. Cecily is not a silly, romantic girl, I am glad to say. She has got a capital appetite, goes for long walks, and pays no attention at all to her lessons.

ALGERNON: I would rather like to see Cecily.

JACK: I will take very good care you never do. She is excessively pretty, and she is only just eighteen.

ALGERNON: Have you told Gwendolen yet that you have an excessively pretty ward who is only just eighteen?

JACK: Oh! one doesn't blurt these things out to people. Cecily and Gwendolen are perfectly certain to be extremely great friends. I'll bet you anything you like that half an hour after they have met, they will be calling each other sister.

ALGERNON: Women only do that when they have called each other a lot of other things first. Now, my dear boy, if we want to get a good table at Willis', we really must go and dress. Do you know it is nearly seven?

JACK: [Irritably] Oh! it always is nearly seven.

ALGERNON: Well, I'm hungry.

JACK: I never knew you when you weren't. . . .

ALGERNON: What shall we do after dinner? Go to a theater?

JACK: Oh, no! I loathe listening.

ALGERNON: Well, let us go to the Club?

JACK: Oh, no! I hate talking.

ALGERNON: Well, we might trot round to the Empire at ten?

JACK: Oh, no! I can't bear looking at things. It is so silly.

ALGERNON: Well, what shall we do?

JACK: Nothing!

ALGERNON: It is awfully hard work doing nothing. However, I don't mind hard work where there is no definite object of any kind.

[Enter Lane]

LANE: Miss Fairfax.

[Enter Gwendolen. Lane goes out.]

ALGERNON: Gwendolen, upon my word!

GWENDOLEN: Algy, kindly turn your back. I have something very particular to say to Mr. Worthing.

ALGERNON: Really, Gwendolen, I don't think I can allow this at all.

GWENDOLEN: Algy, you always adopt a strictly immoral attitude towards life. You are not quite old enough to do that.

[Algernon retires to the fireplace]

JACK: My own darling!

GWENDOLEN: Ernest, we may never be married. From the expression on mamma's face I fear we never shall. Few parents now-a-days pay any regard to what their children say to them. The old-fashioned respect for the young is fast dying out. Whatever influence I ever had over mamma, I lost at the age of three. But although she may prevent us from becoming man and wife, and I may marry someone else, and marry often, nothing that she can possibly do can alter my eternal devotion to you.

JACK: Dear Gwendolen.

GWENDOLEN: The story of your romantic origin, as related to me by mamma, with unpleasing comments, has naturally stirred the deeper fibers of my nature. Your Christian name has an irresistible fascination. The simplicity of your character makes you exquisitely incomprehensible to me. Your town address at the Albany I have. What is your address in the country?

JACK: The Manor House, Woolton, Hertfordshire. [Algernon, *who has been carefully listening, smiles to himself, and writes the address on his shirt-cuff. Then picks up the Railway Guide*]

GWENDOLEN: There is a good postal service, I suppose? It may be necessary to do something desperate. That, of course, will require serious consideration. I will communicate with you daily.

JACK: My own one!

GWENDOLEN: How long do you remain in town?

JACK: Till Monday.

GWENDOLEN: Good! Algy, you may turn round now.

ALGERNON: Thanks, I've turned round already.

GWENDOLEN: You may also ring the bell.

JACK: You will let me see you to your carriage, my own darling?

GWENDOLEN: Certainly.

JACK: [*To Lane, who now enters*] I will see Miss Fairfax out.

LANE: Yes, sir.

[Jack *and* Gwendolen *go off.* Lane *presents several letters on a salver to* Algernon. *It is to be surmised that they are bills, as* Algernon, *after looking at the envelopes, tears them up*]

ALGERNON: A glass of sherry, Lane.

LANE: Yes, sir.

ALGERNON: To-morrow, Lane, I'm going Bunburying.

LANE: Yes, sir.

ALGERNON: I shall probably not be back till Monday. You can put up my dress clothes, my smoking jacket, and all the Bunbury suits . . .

LANE: Yes, sir. [*Handing sherry*]

ALGERNON: I hope to-morrow will be a fine day, Lane.

LANE: It never is, sir.

ALGERNON: Lane, you're a perfect pessimist.

LANE: I do my best to give satisfaction, sir.

[*Enter* Jack. Lane *goes off*]

JACK: There's a sensible, intellectual girl! the only girl I ever cared for in my life. [Algernon *is laughing immoderately*] What on earth are you so amused at?

ALGERNON: Oh, I'm a little anxious about poor Bunbury, that's all.

JACK: If you don't take care, your friend Bunbury will get you into a serious scrape some day.

ALGERNON: I love scrapes. They are the only things that are never serious.

JACK: Oh, that's nonsense, Algy. You never talk anything but nonsense.

ALGERNON: Nobody ever does. [Jack *looks indignantly at him, and leaves the room.* Algernon *lights a cigarette, reads his shirt-cuff and smiles*]

Act II

SCENE: *Garden at the Manor House. A flight of gray stone steps leads up to the house. The garden, an old-fashioned one, full of roses. Time of year, July. Basket chairs, and a table covered with books, are set under a large yew tree.*

[Miss Prism *discovered seated at the table.* Cecily *is at the back watering flowers*]

MISS PRISM: [*Calling*] Cecily, Cecily! Surely such a utilitarian occupation as the watering of flowers is rather Moulton's duty than yours? Especially at a moment when intellectual pleasures await you. Your German grammar is on the table. Pray open it at page fifteen. We will repeat yesterday's lesson.

CECILY: [*Coming over very slowly*] But I don't like German. It isn't at all a becoming language. I know perfectly well that I look quite plain after my German lesson.

MISS PRISM: Child, you know how anxious your guardian is that you should improve yourself in every way. He laid particular stress on your German, as he was leaving for town yesterday. Indeed, he always lays stress on your German when he is leaving for town.

CECILY: Dear Uncle Jack is so very serious! Sometimes he is so serious that I think he cannot be quite well.

MISS PRISM: [*Drawing herself up*] Your guardian enjoys the best of health, and his gravity of demeanor is especially to be commended in one so comparatively young as he is. I know no one who has a higher sense of duty and responsibility.

CECILY: I suppose that is why he often looks a little bored when we three are together.

MISS PRISM: Cecily! I am surprised at you. Mr. Worthing has many troubles in his life. Idle merriment and triviality would be out of place in his conversation. You must remember his constant anxiety about that unfortunate young man, his brother.

CECILY: I wish Uncle Jack would allow that unfortunate young man, his brother, to come down here sometimes. We might have a good influence over him, Miss Prism. I am sure you certainly would. You know German, and geology, and things of that kind influence a man very much. [Cecily *begins to write in her diary*]

MISS PRISM: [*Shaking her head*] I do not think that even I could produce any effect on a character that, according to his own brother's admission, is irretrievably weak and vacillating. Indeed, I am not sure that I would desire to reclaim him. I am not in favor of this modern mania for turning bad people into good people at a moment's notice. As a man sows so let him reap. You must put away your diary, Cecily. I really don't see why you should keep a diary at all.

CECILY: I keep a diary in order to enter the wonderful secrets of my life. If I didn't write them down I should probably forget all about them.

MISS PRISM: Memory, my dear Cecily, is the diary that we all carry about with us.

CECILY: Yes, but it usually chronicles the things that have never happened, and couldn't possibly have happened. I believe that Memory is responsible for nearly all the three-volume novels that Mudie sends us.

MISS PRISM: Do not speak slightingly of the three-volume novel, Cecily. I wrote one myself in earlier days.

CECILY: Did you really, Miss Prism? How wonderfully clever you are! I hope it did not end happily? I don't like novels that end happily. They depress me so much.

MISS PRISM: The good ended happily, and the bad unhappily. That is what Fiction means.

CECILY: I suppose so. But it seems very unfair. And was your novel ever published?

MISS PRISM: Alas! no. The manuscript unfortunately was abandoned. I use the word in the sense of lost or mislaid. To your work, child, these speculations are profitless.

CECILY: [*Smiling*] But I see dear Dr. Chasuble coming up through the garden.

MISS PRISM: [*Rising and advancing*] Dr. Chasuble! This is indeed a pleasure.

[*Enter* Canon Chasuble]

CHASUBLE: And how are we this morning? Miss Prism, you are, I trust, well?

CECILY: Miss Prism has just been complaining of a slight headache. I think it would do her so much good to have a short stroll with you in the park, Dr. Chasuble.

MISS PRISM: Cecily, I have not mentioned anything about a headache.

CECILY: No, dear Miss Prism, I know that, but I felt instinctively that you had a headache. Indeed I was thinking about that, and not about my German lesson when the Rector came in.

CHASUBLE: I hope, Cecily, you are not inattentive.

CECILY: Oh, I am afraid I am.

CHASUBLE: That is strange. Were I fortunate enough to be Miss Prism's pupil, I would hang upon her lips. [Miss Prism *glares*] I spoke metaphorically.—My metaphor was drawn from bees. Ahem! Mr. Worthing, I suppose, has not returned from town yet?

MISS PRISM: We do not expect him till Monday afternoon.

CHASUBLE: Ah yes, he usually likes to spend his Sunday in London. He is not one of those whose sole aim is enjoyment, as, by all accounts, that unfortunate young man, his brother, seems to be. But I must not disturb Egeria and her pupil any longer.

MISS PRISM: Egeria? My name is Lætitia, Doctor.

CHASUBLE: [*Bowing*] A classical allusion merely, drawn from the Pagan authors. I shall see you both no doubt at Evensong.

MISS PRISM: I think, dear Doctor, I will have a stroll with you. I find I have a headache after all, and a walk might do it good.

CHASUBLE: With pleasure, Miss Prism, with pleasure. We might go as far as the schools and back.

MISS PRISM: That would be delightful. Cecily, you will read your Political Economy in my absence. The chapter on the Fall of the Rupee you may omit. It is somewhat too sensational. Even these metallic problems have their melodramatic side. [*Goes down the garden with* Dr. Chasuble]

CECILY: [*Picks up books and throws them back on table*] Horrid Political Economy! Horrid Geography! Horrid, horrid German!

[*Enter* Merriman *with a card on a salver*]

MERRIMAN: Mr. Ernest Worthing has just driven over from the station. He has brought his luggage with him.

CECILY: [*Takes the card and reads it*] "Mr. Ernest Worthing, B 4 The Albany, W." Uncle Jack's brother! Did you tell him Mr. Worthing was in town?

MERRIMAN: Yes, Miss. He seemed very much disappointed. I mentioned that you and Miss Prism were in the garden. He said he was anxious to speak to you privately for a moment.

CECILY: Ask Mr. Ernest Worthing to come here. I suppose you had better talk to the housekeeper about a room for him.

MERRIMAN: Yes, Miss.   [Merriman *goes off*]

CECILY: I have never met any really wicked person before. I feel rather frightened. I am so afraid he will look just like everyone else.

[*Enter* Algernon, *very gay and debonair*] He does!

ALGERNON: [*Raising his hat*] You are my little Cousin Cecily, I'm sure.

CECILY: You are under some strange mistake. I am not little. In fact, I am more than usually tall for my age. [Algernon *is rather taken aback*] But I am your Cousin Cecily. You, I see from your card, are Uncle Jack's brother, my Cousin Ernest, my wicked Cousin Ernest.

ALGERNON: Oh! I am not really wicked at all, Cousin Cecily. You mustn't think that I am wicked.

CECILY: If you are not, then you have certainly been deceiving us all in a very inexcusable manner. I hope you have not been leading a double life, pretending to be wicked and being really good all the time. That would be hypocrisy.

ALGERNON: [Looks at her in amazement] Oh! Of course I have been rather reckless.

CECILY: I am glad to hear it.

ALGERNON: In fact, now you mention the subject, I have been very bad in my own small way.

CECILY: I don't think you should be so proud of that, though I am sure it must have been very pleasant.

ALGERNON: It is much pleasanter being here with you.

CECILY: I can't understand how you are here at all. Uncle Jack won't be back till Monday afternoon.

ALGERNON: That is a great disappointment. I am obliged to go up by the first train on Monday morning. I have a business appointment that I am anxious . . . to miss.

CECILY: Couldn't you miss it anywhere but in London?

ALGERNON: No; the appointment is in London.

CECILY: Well, I know, of course, how important it is not to keep a business engagement, if one wants to retain any sense of the beauty of life, but still I think you had better wait till Uncle Jack arrives. I know he wants to speak to you about your emigrating.

ALGERNON: About my what?

CECILY: Your emigrating. He has gone up to buy your outfit.

ALGERNON: I certainly wouldn't let Jack buy my outfit. He has no taste in neckties at all.

CECILY: I don't think you will require neckties. Uncle Jack is sending you to Australia.

ALGERNON: Australia! I'd sooner die.

CECILY: Well, he said at dinner on Wednesday night, that you would have to choose between this world, the next world, and Australia.

ALGERNON: Oh, well! The accounts I have received of Australia and the next world, are not particularly encouraging. This world is good enough for me, Cousin Cecily.

CECILY: Yes, but are you good enough for it?

ALGERNON: I'm afraid I'm not that. That is why I want you to reform me. You might make that your mission, if you don't mind, Cousin Cecily.

CECILY: I'm afraid I've not time, this afternoon.

ALGERNON: Well, would you mind my reforming myself this afternoon?

CECILY: That is rather Quixotic of you. But I think you should try.

ALGERNON: I will. I feel better already

CECILY: You are looking a little worse.

ALGERNON: That is because I am hungry.

CECILY: How thoughtless of me. I should have remembered that when one is going to lead an entirely new life, one requires regular and wholesome meals. Won't you come in?

ALGERNON: Thank you. Might I have a button-hole first? I never have any appetite unless I have a button-hole first.

CECILY: A Maréchal Niel? [Picks up scissors]

ALGERNON: No, I'd sooner have a pink rose.

CECILY: Why? [Cuts a flower]

ALGERNON: Because you are like a pink rose, Cousin Cecily.

CECILY: I don't think it can be right for you to talk to me like that. Miss Prism never says such things to me.

ALGERNON: Then Miss Prism is a short-sighted old lady. [Cecily puts the rose in his button-hole] You are the prettiest girl I ever saw.

CECILY: Miss Prism says that all good looks are a snare.

ALGERNON: They are a snare that every sensible man would like to be caught in.

CECILY: Oh! I don't think I would care to catch a sensible man. I shouldn't know what to talk to him about.

[They pass into the house. Miss Prism and Dr. Chasuble return]

MISS PRISM: You are too much alone, dear Dr. Chasuble. You should get married. A misanthrope I can understand—a womanthrope, never!

CHASUBLE: [With a scholar's shudder] Believe me, I do not deserve so neologistic a phrase. The precept as well as the practice of the Primitive Church was distinctly against matrimony.

MISS PRISM: [Sententiously] That is obviously the reason why the Primitive Church has not lasted up to the present day. And you do not seem to realize, dear Doctor, that by persistently remaining single, a man converts himself into a permanent public temptation. Men should be careful; this very celibacy leads weaker vessels astray.

CHASUBLE: But is a man not equally attractive when married?

MISS PRISM: No married man is ever attractive except to his wife.

CHASUBLE: And often, I've been told, not even to her.

MISS PRISM: That depends on the intellectual sympathies of the woman. Maturity can always be depended on. Ripeness can be trusted. Young women are green. [Dr. Chasuble starts] I spoke horticulturally. My metaphor was drawn from fruits. But where is Cecily?

CHASUBLE: Perhaps she followed us to the schools.

[Enter Jack slowly from the back of the garden. He is dressed in the deepest mourning, with crape hat-band and black gloves]

MISS PRISM: Mr. Worthing!

CHASUBLE: Mr. Worthing?

MISS PRISM: This is indeed a surprise. We did not look for you till Monday afternoon.

JACK: [Shakes Miss Prism's *hand in a tragic manner*] I have returned sooner than I expected. Dr. Chasuble, I hope you are well?

CHASUBLE: Dear Mr. Worthing, I trust this garb of woe does not betoken some terrible calamity?

JACK: My brother.

MISS PRISM: More shameful debts and extravagance?

CHASUBLE: Still leading his life of pleasure?

JACK: [*Shaking his head*] Dead.

CHASUBLE: Your brother Ernest dead?

JACK: Quite dead.

MISS PRISM: What a lesson for him! I trust he will profit by it.

CHASUBLE: Mr. Worthing, I offer you my sincere condolence. You have at least the consolation of knowing that you were always the most generous and forgiving of brothers.

JACK: Poor Ernest! He had many faults, but it is a sad, sad blow.

CHASUBLE: Very sad indeed. Were you with him at the end?

JACK: No. He died abroad; in Paris, in fact. I had a telegram last night from the manager of the Grand Hotel.

CHASUBLE: Was the cause of death mentioned?

JACK: A severe chill, it seems.

MISS PRISM: As a man sows, so shall he reap.

CHASUBLE: [*Raising his hand*] Charity, dear Miss Prism, charity! None of us are perfect. I myself am peculiarly susceptible to draughts. Will the interment take place here?

JACK: No. He seems to have expressed a desire to be buried in Paris.

CHASUBLE: In Paris! [*Shakes his head*] I fear that hardly points to any very serious state of mind at the last. You would no doubt wish me to make some slight allusion to this tragic domestic affliction next Sunday. [Jack *presses his hand convulsively*] My sermon on the meaning of the manna in the wilderness can be adapted to almost any occasion, joyful, or, as in the present case, distressing. [*All sigh*] I have preached it at harvest celebrations, christenings, confirmations, on days of humiliation and festal days. The last time I delivered it was in the Cathedral, as a charity sermon on behalf of the Society for the Prevention of Discontentment among the Upper Orders. The Bishop, who was present, was much struck by some of the analogies I drew.

JACK: Ah, that reminds me, you mentioned christenings I think, Dr. Chasuble? I suppose you know how to christen all right? [Dr. Chasuble *looks astounded*] I mean, of course, you are continually christening, aren't you?

MISS PRISM: It is, I regret to say, one of the Rector's most constant duties in this parish. I have often spoken to the poorer classes on the subject. But they don't seem to know what thrift is.

CHASUBLE: But is there any particular infant in whom you are interested, Mr. Worthing? Your brother was, I believe, unmarried, was he not?

JACK: Oh, yes.

MISS PRISM: [*Bitterly*] People who live entirely for pleasure usually are.

JACK: But it is not for any child, dear Doctor. I am very fond of children. No! the fact is, I would like to be christened myself, this afternoon, if you have nothing better to do.

CHASUBLE: But surely, Mr. Worthing, you have been christened already?

JACK: I don't remember anything about it.

CHASUBLE: But have you any grave doubts on the subject?

JACK: I certainly intend to have. Of course, I don't know if the thing would bother you in any way, or if you think I am a little too old now.

CHASUBLE: Not at all. The sprinkling, and, indeed, the immersion of adults is a perfectly canonical practice.

JACK: Immersion!

CHASUBLE: You need have no apprehensions. Sprinkling is all that is necessary, or indeed I think advisable. Our weather is so changeable. At what hour would you wish the ceremony performed?

JACK: Oh, I might trot around about five if that would suit you.

CHASUBLE: Perfectly, perfectly! In fact I have two similar ceremonies to perform at that time. A case of twins that occurred recently in one of the outlying cottages on your own estate. Poor Jenkins the carter, a most hard-working man.

JACK: Oh! I don't see much fun in being christened along with other babies. It would be childish. Would half-past five do?

CHASUBLE: Admirably! Admirably! [*Takes out watch*] And now, dear Mr. Worthing, I will not intrude any longer into a house of sorrow. I would merely beg you not to be too much bowed down by grief. What seem to us bitter trials at the moment are often blessings in disguise.

MISS PRISM: This seems to me a blessing of an extremely obvious kind.

[*Enter* Cecily *from the house*]

CECILY: Uncle Jack! Oh, I am pleased to see you back. But what horrid clothes you have on! Do go and change them.

MISS PRISM: Cecily!

CHASUBLE: My child! my child!

[Cecily *goes towards* Jack; *he kisses her brow in a melancholy manner*]

CECILY: What is the matter, Uncle Jack? Do look happy! You look as if you had a toothache and I have such a surprise for you. Who do you think is in the dining-room? Your brother!

JACK: Who?

CECILY: Your brother Ernest. He arrived about half an hour ago.

JACK: What nonsense! I haven't got a brother.

CECILY: Oh, don't say that. However badly he may have behaved to you in the past he is still your brother. You couldn't be so heartless as to disown him. I'll tell him to come out. And you will shake hands with him, won't you, Uncle Jack? [*Runs back into the house*]

CHASUBLE: These are very joyful tidings.

MISS PRISM: After we had all been resigned to his loss, his sudden return seems to me peculiarly distressing.

JACK: My brother is in the dining-room? I don't know what it all means. I think it is perfectly absurd.

[*Enter Algernon and Cecily hand in hand. They come slowly up to* Jack]

JACK: Good heavens! [*Motions Algernon away*]

ALGERNON: Brother John, I have come down from town to tell you that I am very sorry for all the trouble I have given you, and that I intend to lead a better life in the future. [*Jack glares at him and does not take his hand*]

CECILY: Uncle Jack, you are not going to refuse your own brother's hand?

JACK: Nothing will induce me to take his hand. I think his coming down here disgraceful. He knows perfectly well why.

CECILY: Uncle, do be nice. There is some good in everyone. Ernest has just been telling me about his poor invalid friend, Mr. Bunbury, whom he goes to visit so often. And surely there must be much good in one who is kind to an invalid, and leaves the pleasures of London to sit by a bed of pain.

JACK: Oh, he has been talking about Bunbury, has he?

CECILY: Yes, he has told me all about poor Mr. Bunbury, and his terrible state of health.

JACK: Bunbury! Well, I won't have him talk to you about Bunbury or about anything else. It is enough to drive one perfectly frantic.

ALGERNON: Of course I admit that the faults were all on my side. But I must say that I think that Brother John's coldness to me is peculiarly painful. I expected a more enthusiastic welcome, especially considering it is the first time I have come here.

CECILY: Uncle Jack, if you don't shake hands with Ernest I will never forgive you.

JACK: Never forgive me?

CECILY: Never, never, never!

JACK: Well, this is the last time I shall ever do it. [*Shakes hands with* Algernon *and glares*]

CHASUBLE: It's pleasant, is it not, to see so perfect a reconciliation? I think we might leave the two brothers together.

MISS PRISM: Cecily, you will come with us.

CECILY: Certainly, Miss Prism. My little task of reconciliation is over.

CHASUBLE: You have done a beautiful action today, dear child.

MISS PRISM: We must not be premature in our judgments.

CECILY: I feel very happy.   [*They all go off*]

JACK: You young scoundrel, Algy, you must get out of this place as soon as possible. I don't allow any Bunburying here.

[*Enter Merriman*]

MERRIMAN: I have put Mr. Ernest's things in the room next to yours, sir. I suppose that is all right?

JACK: What?

MERRIMAN: Mr. Ernest's luggage, sir. I have unpacked it and put it in the room next to your own.

JACK: His luggage?

MERRIMAN: Yes, sir. Three portmanteaus, a dressing-case, two hat-boxes, and a large luncheon-basket.

ALGERNON: I am afraid I can't stay more than a week this time.

JACK: Merriman, order the dog-cart at once. Mr. Ernest has been suddenly called back to town.

MERRIMAN: Yes, sir.   [*Goes back into the house*]

ALGERNON: What a fearful liar you are, Jack. I have not been called back to town at all.

JACK: Yes, you have.

ALGERNON: I haven't heard anyone call me.

JACK: Your duty as a gentleman calls you back.

ALGERNON: My duty as a gentleman has never interfered with my pleasures in the smallest degree.

JACK: I can quite understand that.

ALGERNON: Well, Cecily is a darling.

JACK: You are not to talk of Miss Cardew like that. I don't like it.

ALGERNON: Well, I don't like your clothes. You look perfectly ridiculous in them. Why on earth don't you go up and change? It is perfectly childish to be in deep mourning for a man who is actually staying for a whole week with you in your house as a guest. I call it grotesque.

JACK: You are certainly not staying with me for a whole week as a guest or anything else. You have got to leave . . . by the four-five train.

ALGERNON: I certainly won't leave you so long as you are in mourning. It would be most unfriendly. If I were in mourning you would stay with me, I suppose. I should think it very unkind if you didn't.

JACK: Well, will you go if I change my clothes?

ALGERNON: Yes, if you are not too long. I never saw anybody take so long to dress, and with such little result.

JACK: Well, at any rate, that is better than being always over-dressed as you are.

ALGERNON: If I am occasionally a little over-dressed, I make up for it by being always immensely over-educated.

JACK: Your vanity is ridiculous, your conduct an outrage, and your presence in my garden utterly absurd. However you have got to catch the four-five, and I hope you will have a pleasant journey back to town. This Bunburying, as you call it, has not been a great success for you. [*Goes into the house*]

ALGERNON: I think it has been a great success. I'm in love with Cecily, and that is everything.

[*Enter* Cecily *at the back of the garden. She picks up the can and begins to water the flowers*]

But I must see her before I go, and make arrangements for another Bunbury. Ah, there she is.

CECILY: Oh, I merely came back to water the roses. I thought you were with Uncle Jack.

ALGERNON: He's gone to order the dog-cart for me.

CECILY: Oh, is he going to take you for a nice drive?

ALGERNON: He's going to send me away.

CECILY: Then have we got to part?

ALGERNON: I am afraid so. It's a very painful parting.

CECILY: It is always painful to part from people whom one has known for a very brief space of time. The absence of old friends one can endure with equanimity. But even a momentary separation from anyone to whom one has just been introduced is almost unbearable.

ALGERNON: Thank you.

[*Enter* Merriman]

MERRIMAN: The dog-cart is at the door, sir. [*Algernon looks appealingly at* Cecily]

CECILY: It can wait, Merriman . . . for . . . five minutes.

MERRIMAN: Yes, miss.   [*Exit* Merriman]

ALGERNON: I hope, Cecily, I shall not offend you if I state quite frankly and openly that you seem to me to be in every way the visible personification of absolute perfection.

CECILY: I think your frankness does you great credit, Ernest. If you will allow me I will copy your remarks into my diary. [*Goes over to table and begins writing in diary*]

ALGERNON: Do you really keep a diary? I'd give anything to look at it. May I?

CECILY: Oh, no. [*Puts her hand over it*] You see, it is simply a very young girl's record of her own thoughts and impressions, and consequently meant for publication. When it appears in volume form I hope you will order a copy. But pray, Ernest, don't stop. I delight in taking down from dictation. I have reached "absolute perfection." You can go on. I am quite ready for more.

ALGERNON: [*Somewhat taken aback*] Ahem! Ahem!

CECILY: Oh, don't cough, Ernest. When one is dictating one should speak fluently and not cough. Besides, I don't know how to spell a cough. [*Writes as* Algernon *speaks*]

ALGERNON: [*Speaking very rapidly*] Cecily, ever since I first looked upon your wonderful and incomparable beauty, I have dared to love you wildly, passionately, devotedly, hopelessly.

CECILY: I don't think that you should tell me that you love me wildly, passionately, devotedly, hope-lessly. Hopelessly doesn't seem to make much sense, does it?

ALGERNON: Cecily!

[*Enter* Merriman]

MERRIMAN: The dog-cart is waiting, sir.

ALGERNON: Tell it to come round next week, at the same hour.

MERRIMAN: [*Looks at* Cecily, *who makes no sign*] Yes, sir.   [Merriman *retires*]

CECILY: Uncle Jack would be very much annoyed if he knew you were staying on till next week, at the same hour.

ALGERNON: Oh, I don't care about Jack. I don't care for anybody in the whole world but you. I love you, Cecily. You will marry me, won't you?

CECILY: You silly you! Of course. Why, we have been engaged for the last three months.

ALGERNON: For the last three months?

CECILY: Yes, it will be exactly three months on Thursday.

ALGERNON: But how did we become engaged?

CECILY: Well, ever since dear Uncle Jack first confessed to us that he had a younger brother who was very wicked and bad, you of course have formed the chief topic of conversation between myself and Miss Prism. And of course a man who is much talked about is always very attractive. One feels there must be something in him after all. I daresay it was foolish of me, but I fell in love with you, Ernest.

ALGERNON: Darling! And when was the engagement actually settled?

CECILY: On the 14th of February last. Worn out by your entire ignorance of my existence, I determined to end the matter one way or the other, and after a long struggle with myself I accepted you under this dear old tree here. The next day I bought this little ring in your name, and this is the little bangle with the true lovers' knot I promised you always to wear.

ALGERNON: Did I give you this? It's very pretty, isn't it?

CECILY: Yes, you've wonderfully good taste, Ernest. It's the excuse I've always given for your leading such a bad life. And this is the box in which I keep all your dear letters. [*Kneels at table, opens box, and produces letters tied up with blue ribbon*]

ALGERNON: My letters! But my own sweet Cecily, I have never written you any letters.

CECILY: You need hardly remind me of that, Ernest. I remember only too well that I was forced to write your letters for you. I wrote always three times a week, and sometimes oftener.

ALGERNON: Oh, do let me read them, Cecily?

CECILY: Oh, I couldn't possibly. They would make you far too conceited. [*Replaces box*] The three you wrote me after I had broken off the engagement are so beautiful, and so badly spelled, that even now I can hardly read them without crying a little.

ALGERNON: But was our engagement ever broken off?

CECILY: Of course it was. On the 22nd of last March. You can see the entry if you like. [*Shows diary*] "To-day I broke off my engagement with Ernest. I feel it is better to do so. The weather still continues charming."

ALGERNON: But why on earth did you break it off? What had I done? I had done nothing at all. Cecily, I am very much hurt indeed to hear you broke it off. Particularly when the weather was so charming.

CECILY: It would hardly have been a really serious engagement if it hadn't been broken off at least once. But I forgave you before the week was out.

ALGERNON: [*Crossing to her, and kneeling*] What a perfect angel you are, Cecily.

CECILY: You dear romantic boy. [*He kisses her, she puts her fingers through his hair*] I hope your hair curls naturally, does it?

ALGERNON: Yes, darling, with a little help from others.

CECILY: I am so glad.

ALGERNON: You'll never break off our engagement again, Cecily?

CECILY: I don't think I could break it off now that I have actually met you. Besides, of course, there is the question of your name.

ALGERNON: Yes, of course. [*Nervously*]

CECILY: You must not laugh at me, darling, but it had always been a girlish dream of mine to love some one whose name was Ernest. [Algernon *rises*, Cecily *also*] There is something in that name that seems to inspire absolute confidence. I pity any poor married woman whose husband is not called Ernest.

ALGERNON: But, my dear child, do you mean to say you could not love me if I had some other name?

CECILY: But what name?

ALGERNON: Oh, any name you like—Algernon, for instance. . . .

CECILY: But I don't like the name of Algernon.

ALGERNON: Well, my dear, sweet, loving little darling, I really can't see why you should object to the name of Algernon. It is not at all a bad name. In fact, it is rather an aristocratic name. Half of the chaps who get into the Bankruptcy Court are called Algernon. But seriously, Cecily . . . [*Moving to her*] . . . if my name was Algy, couldn't you love me?

CECILY: [*Rising*] I might respect you, Ernest, I might admire your character, but I fear that I should not be able to give you my undivided attention.

ALGERNON: Ahem! Cecily! [*Picking up hat*] Your Rector here is, I suppose, thoroughly experienced in the practice of all the rites and ceremonials of the church?

CECILY: Oh, yes. Dr. Chasuble is a most learned man.

He has never written a single book, so you can imagine how much he knows.

ALGERNON: I must see him at once on a most important christening—I mean on most important business.

CECILY: Oh!

ALGERNON: I sha'n't be away more than half an hour.

CECILY: Considering that we have been engaged since February the 14th, and that I only met you to-day for the first time, I think it is rather hard that you should leave me for so long a period as half an hour. Couldn't you make it twenty minutes?

ALGERNON: I'll be back in no time. [*Kisses her and rushes down the garden*]

CECILY: What an impetuous boy he is. I like his hair so much. I must enter his proposal in my diary.

[*Enter* Merriman]

MERRIMAN: A Miss Fairfax has just called to see Mr. Worthing. On very important business, Miss Fairfax states.

CECILY: Isn't Mr. Worthing in his library?

MERRIMAN: Mr. Worthing went over in the direction of the Rectory some time ago.

CECILY: Pray ask the lady to come out here; Mr. Worthing is sure to be back soon. And you can bring tea.

MERRIMAN: Yes, miss.   [*Goes out*]

CECILY: Miss Fairfax! I suppose one of the many good elderly women who are associated with Uncle Jack in some of his philanthropic work in London. I don't quite like women who are interested in philanthropic work. I think it is so forward of them.

[*Enter* Merriman]

MERRIMAN: Miss Fairfax.

[*Enter* Gwendolen]

[*Exit* Merriman]

CECILY: [*Advancing to meet her*] Pray let me introduce myself to you. My name is Cecily Cardew.

GWENDOLEN: Cecily Cardew? [*Moving to her and shaking hands*] What a very sweet name! Something tells me that we are going to be great friends. I like you already more than I can say. My first impressions of people are never wrong.

CECILY: How nice of you to like me so much after we have known each other such a comparatively short time. Pray sit down.

GWENDOLEN: [*Still standing up*] I may call you Cecily, may I not?

CECILY: With pleasure!

GWENDOLEN: And you will always call me Gwendolen, won't you?

CECILY: If you wish.

GWENDOLEN: Then that is all quite settled, is it not?

CECILY: I hope so. [*A pause. They both sit down together*]

GWENDOLEN: Perhaps this might be a favorable opportunity for my mentioning who I am. My father is Lord Bracknell. You have never heard of papa, I suppose?

CECILY: I don't think so.

GWENDOLEN: Outside the family circle, papa, I am glad to say, is entirely unknown. I think that is quite as it should be. The home seems to me to be the proper sphere for the man. And certainly once a man begins to neglect his domestic duties he becomes painfully effeminate, does he not? And I don't like that. It makes men so very attractive. Cecily, mamma, whose views on education are remarkably strict, has brought me up to be extremely short-sighted; it is part of her system; so do you mind my looking at you through my glasses?

CECILY: Oh, not at all, Gwendolen. I am very fond of being looked at.

GWENDOLEN: [After examining Cecily carefully through a lorgnette] You are here on a short visit, I suppose.

CECILY: Oh, no, I live here.

GWENDOLEN: [Severely] Really? Your mother, no doubt, or some female relative of advanced years, resides here also?

CECILY: Oh, no. I have no mother, nor, in fact, any relations.

GWENDOLEN: Indeed?

CECILY: My dear guardian, with the assistance of Miss Prism, has the arduous task of looking after me.

GWENDOLEN: Your guardian?

CECILY: Yes, I am Mr. Worthing's ward.

GWENDOLEN: Oh! It is strange he never mentioned to me that he had a ward. How secretive of him! He grows more interesting hourly. I am not sure, however, that the news inspires me with feelings of unmixed delight. [Rising and going to her] I am very fond of you, Cecily; I have liked you ever since I met you. But I am bound to state that now that I know that you are Mr. Worthing's ward, I cannot help expressing a wish you were—well, just a little older than you seem to be—and not quite so very alluring in appearance. In fact, if I may speak candidly——

CECILY: Pray do! I think that whenever one has anything unpleasant to say, one should always be quite candid.

GWENDOLEN: Well, to speak with perfect candor, Cecily, I wish that you were fully forty-two, and more than usually plain for your age. Ernest has a strong upright nature. He is the very soul of truth and honor. Disloyalty would be as impossible to him as deception. But even men of the noblest possible moral character are extremely susceptible to the influence of the physical charms of others. Modern, no less than Ancient History, supplies us with most painful examples of what I refer to. If it were not so, indeed, History would be quite unreadable.

CECILY: I beg your pardon, Gwendolen, did you say Ernest?

GWENDOLEN: Yes.

CECILY: Oh, but it is not Mr. Ernest Worthing who is my guardian. It is his brother—his elder brother.

GWENDOLEN: [Sitting down again] Ernest never mentioned to me that he had a brother.

CECILY: I am sorry to say they have not been on good terms for a long time.

GWENDOLEN: Ah! that accounts for it. And now that I think of it I have never heard any man mention his brother. The subject seems distasteful to most men. Cecily, you have lifted a load from my mind. I was growing almost anxious. It would have been terrible if any cloud had come across a friendship like ours, would it not? Of course you are quite, quite sure that it is not Mr. Ernest Worthing who is your guardian?

CECILY: Quite sure. [A pause] In fact, I am going to be his.

GWENDOLEN: [Enquiringly] I beg your pardon?

CECILY: [Rather shy and confidingly] Dearest Gwendolen, there is no reason why I should make a secret of it to you. Our little county newspaper is sure to chronicle the fact next week. Mr. Ernest Worthing and I are engaged to be married.

GWENDOLEN: [Quite politely, rising] My darling Cecily, I think there must be some slight error. Mr. Ernest Worthing is engaged to me. The announcement will appear in the Morning Post on Saturday at the latest.

CECILY: [Very politely, rising] I am afraid you must be under some misconception. Ernest proposed to me exactly ten minutes ago. [Shows diary]

GWENDOLEN: [Examines diary through her lorgnette carefully] It is certainly very curious, for he asked me to be his wife yesterday afternoon at 5.30. If you would care to verify the incident, pray do so. [Produces diary of her own] I never travel without my diary. One should always have something sensational to read in the train. I am so sorry, dear Cecily, if it is any disappointment to you, but I am afraid I have the prior claim.

CECILY: It would distress me more than I can tell you, dear Gwendolen, if it caused you any mental or physical anguish, but I feel bound to point out that since Ernest proposed to you he clearly has changed his mind.

GWENDOLEN: [Meditatively] If the poor fellow has been entrapped into any foolish promise I shall consider it my duty to rescue him at once, and with a firm hand.

CECILY: [Thoughtfully and sadly] Whatever unfortunate entanglement my dear boy may have got into, I will never reproach him with it after we are married.

GWENDOLEN: Do you allude to me, Miss Cardew, as an entanglement? You are presumptuous. On an occasion of this kind it becomes more than a moral duty to speak one's mind. It becomes a pleasure.

CECILY: Do you suggest, Miss Fairfax, that I entrapped Ernest into an engagement? How dare you? This is no time for wearing the shallow mask of manners. When I see a spade I call it a spade.

GWENDOLEN: [*Satirically*] I am glad to say that I have never seen a spade. It is obvious that our social spheres have been widely different.

[*Enter Merriman, followed by the footman. He carries a salver, tablecloth, and plate-stand. Cecily is about to retort. The presence of the servants exercises a restraining influence, under which both girls chafe*]

MERRIMAN: Shall I lay tea here as usual, miss?

CECILY: [*Sternly, in a calm voice*] Yes, as usual. [*Merriman begins to clear and lay cloth. A long pause. Cecily and Gwendolen glare at each other*]

GWENDOLEN: Are there many interesting walks in the vicinity, Miss Cardew?

CECILY: Oh, yes, a great many. From the top of one of the hills quite close one can see five counties.

GWENDOLEN: Five counties! I don't think I should like that. I hate crowds.

CECILY: [*Sweetly*] I suppose that is why you live in town? [*Gwendolen bites her lip, and beats her foot nervously with her parasol*]

GWENDOLEN: [*Looking round*] Quite a well-kept garden this is, Miss Cardew.

CECILY: So glad you like it, Miss Fairfax.

GWENDOLEN: I had no idea there were any flowers in the country.

CECILY: Oh, flowers are as common here, Miss Fairfax, as people are in London.

GWENDOLEN: Personally I cannot understand how anybody manages to exist in the country, if anybody who is anybody does. The country always bores me to death.

CECILY: Ah! This is what the newspapers call agricultural depression, is it not? I believe the aristocracy are suffering very much from it just at present. It is almost an epidemic amongst them, I have been told. May I offer you some tea, Miss Fairfax?

GWENDOLEN: [*With elaborate politeness*] Thank you. [*Aside*] Detestable girl! But I require tea!

CECILY: [*Sweetly*] Sugar?

GWENDOLEN: [*Superciliously*] No, thank you. Sugar is not fashionable any more. [*Cecily looks angrily at her, takes up the tongs and puts four lumps of sugar into the cup*]

CECILY: [*Severely*] Cake or bread and butter?

GWENDOLEN: [*In a bored manner*] Bread and butter, please. Cake is rarely seen at the best houses nowadays.

CECILY: [*Cuts a very large slice of cake, and puts it on the tray*] Hand that to Miss Fairfax. [*Merriman does so, and goes out with footman. Gwendolen drinks the tea and makes a grimace. Puts down cup at once, reaches out her hand to the bread and butter, looks at it, and finds it is cake. Rises in indignation*]

GWENDOLEN: You have filled my tea with lumps of sugar, and though I asked most distinctly for bread and butter, you have given me cake. I am known for the gentleness of my disposition, and the extraordinary sweetness of my nature, but I warn you, Miss Cardew, you may go too far.

CECILY: [*Rising*] To save my poor, innocent, trusting boy from the machinations of any other girl there are no lengths to which I would not go.

GWENDOLEN: From the moment I saw you I distrusted you. I felt that you were false and deceitful. I am never deceived in such matters. My first impressions of people are invariably right.

CECILY: It seems to me, Miss Fairfax, that I am trespassing on your valuable time. No doubt you have many other calls of a similar character to make in the neighborhood.

[*Enter* Jack]

GWENDOLEN: [*Catching sight of him*] Ernest! My own Ernest!

JACK: Gwendolen! Darling! [*Offers to kiss her*]

GWENDOLEN: [*Drawing back*] A moment! May I ask if you are engaged to be married to this young lady? [*Points to* Cecily]

JACK: [*Laughing*] To dear little Cecily! Of course not! What could have put such an idea into your pretty little head?

GWENDOLEN: Thank you. You may. [*Offers her cheek*]

CECILY: [*Very sweetly*] I knew there must be some misunderstanding, Miss Fairfax. The gentleman whose arm is at present around your waist is my dear guardian, Mr. John Worthing.

GWENDOLEN: I beg your pardon?

CECILY: This is Uncle Jack.

GWENDOLEN: [*Receding*] Jack! Oh!

[*Enter* Algernon]

CECILY: Here is Ernest.

ALGERNON: [*Goes straight over to Cecily without noticing anyone else*] My own love! [*Offers to kiss her*]

CECILY: [*Drawing back*] A moment, Ernest! May I ask you—are you engaged to be married to this young lady?

ALGERNON: [*Looking round*] To what young lady? Good heavens! Gwendolen!

CECILY: Yes, to good heavens, Gwendolen, I mean to Gwendolen.

ALGERNON: [*Laughing*] Of course not! What could have put such an idea into your pretty little head?

CECILY: Thank you. [*Presenting her cheek to be kissed*] You may. [*Algernon kisses her*]

GWENDOLEN: I felt there was some slight error, Miss Cardew. The gentleman who is now embracing you is my cousin, Mr. Algernon Moncrieff.

CECILY: [*Breaking away from* Algernon] Algernon Moncrieff! Oh! [*The two girls move towards each other and put their arms round each other's waists as if for protection*]

CECILY: Are you called Algernon?

ALGERNON: I cannot deny it.

CECILY: Oh!

GWENDOLEN: Is your name really John?

JACK: [*Standing rather proudly*] I could deny it if I liked. I could deny anything if I liked. But my name certainly is John. It has been John for years.

CECILY: [*To Gwendolen*] A gross deception has been practised on both of us.

GWENDOLEN: My poor wounded Cecily!

CECILY: My sweet, wronged Gwendolen!

GWENDOLEN: [*Slowly and seriously*] You will call me sister, will you not? [*They embrace.* Jack *and* Algernon *groan and walk up and down*]

CECILY: [*Rather brightly*] There is just one question I would like to be allowed to ask my guardian.

GWENDOLEN: An admirable idea! Mr. Worthing, there is just one question I would like to be permitted to put to you. Where is your brother Ernest? We are both engaged to be married to your brother Ernest, so it is a matter of some importance to us to know where your brother Ernest is at present.

JACK: [*Slowly and hesitatingly*] Gwendolen—Cecily —it is very painful for me to be forced to speak the truth. It is the first time in my life that I have ever been reduced to such a painful position, and I am really quite inexperienced in doing anything of the kind. However I will tell you quite frankly that I have no brother Ernest. I have no brother at all. I never had a brother in my life, and I certainly have not the smallest intention of ever having one in the future.

CECILY: [*Surprised*] No brother at all?

JACK: [*Cheerily*] None!

GWENDOLEN: [*Severely*] Had you never a brother of any kind?

JACK: [*Pleasantly*] Never. Not even of any kind.

GWENDOLEN: I am afraid it is quite clear, Cecily, that neither of us is engaged to be married to anyone.

CECILY: It is not a very pleasant position for a young girl suddenly to find herself in. Is it?

GWENDOLEN: Let us go into the house. They will hardly venture to come after us there.

CECILY: No, men are so cowardly, aren't they? [*They retire into the house with scornful looks*]

JACK: This ghastly state of things is what you call Bunburying, I suppose?

ALGERNON: Yes, and a perfectly wonderful Bunbury it is. The most wonderful Bunbury I have ever had in my life.

JACK: Well, you've no right whatsoever to Bunbury here.

ALGERNON: That is absurd. One has a right to Bunbury anywhere one chooses. Every serious Bunburyist knows that.

JACK: Serious Bunburyist! Good heavens!

ALGERNON: Well, one must be serious about something, if one wants to have any amusement in life. I happen to be serious about Bunburying. What on earth you are serious about I haven't got the remotest idea. About everything, I should fancy. You have such an absolutely trivial nature.

JACK: Well, the only small satisfaction I have in the whole of this wretched business is that your friend Bunbury is quite exploded. You won't be able to run down to the country quite so often as you used to do, dear Algy. And a very good thing, too.

ALGERNON: Your brother is a little off color, isn't he, dear Jack? You won't be able to disappear to London quite so frequently as your wicked custom was. And not a bad thing, either.

JACK: As for your conduct towards Miss Cardew, I must say that your taking in a sweet, simple, innocent girl like that is quite inexcusable. To say nothing of the fact that she is my ward.

ALGERNON: I can see no possible defence at all for your deceiving a brilliant, clever, thoroughly experienced young lady like Miss Fairfax. To say nothing of the fact that she is my cousin.

JACK: I wanted to be engaged to Gwendolen, that is all. I love her.

ALGERNON: Well, I simply wanted to be engaged to Cecily. I adore her.

JACK: There is certainly no chance of your marrying Miss Cardew.

ALGERNON: I don't think there is much likelihood, Jack, of you and Miss Fairfax being united.

JACK: Well, that is no business of yours.

ALGERNON: If it was my business, I wouldn't talk about it. [*Begins to eat muffins*] It is very vulgar to talk about one's business. Only people like stockbrokers do that, and then merely at dinner parties.

JACK: How you can sit there, calmly eating muffins, when we are in this horrible trouble, I can't make out. You seem to me to be perfectly heartless.

ALGERNON: Well, I can't eat muffins in an agitated manner. The butter would probably get on my cuffs. One should always eat muffins quite calmly. It is the only way to eat them.

JACK: I say it's perfectly heartless your eating muffins at all, under the circumstances.

ALGERNON: When I am in trouble, eating is the only thing that consoles me. Indeed, when I am in really great trouble, as anyone who knows me intimately will tell you, I refuse everything except food and drink. At the present moment I am eating muffins because I am unhappy. Besides, I am particularly fond of muffins. [*Rising*]

JACK: [*Rising*] Well, that is no reason why you should eat them all in that greedy way. [*Takes muffins from* Algernon]

ALGERNON: [*Offering tea-cake*] I wish you would have tea-cake instead. I don't like tea-cake.

JACK: Good heavens! I suppose a man may eat his own muffins in his own garden.

ALGERNON: But you have just said it was perfectly heartless to eat muffins.

JACK: I said it was perfectly heartless of you, under the circumstances. That is a very different thing.

ALGERNON: That may be. But the muffins are the same. [*He seizes the muffin-dish from* Jack]

JACK: Algy, I wish to goodness you would go.

ALGERNON: You can't possibly ask me to go without having some dinner. It's absurd. I never go without my dinner. No one ever does, except vegetarians and people like that. Besides I have just made arrangements with Dr. Chasuble to be christened at a quarter to six under the name of Ernest.

JACK: My dear fellow, the sooner you give up that nonsense the better. I made arrangements this morning with Dr. Chasuble to be christened myself at 5.30, and I naturally will take the name of Ernest. Gwendolen would wish it. We can't both be christened Ernest. It's absurd. Besides, I have a perfect right to be christened if I like. There is no evidence at all that I ever have been christened by anybody. I should think it extremely probable I never was, and so does Dr. Chasuble. It is entirely different in your case. You have been christened already.

ALGERNON: Yes, but I have not been christened for years.

JACK: Yes, but you have been christened. That is the important thing.

ALGERNON: Quite so. So I know my constitution can stand it. If you are not quite sure about your ever having been christened, I must say I think it rather dangerous your venturing on it now. It might make you very unwell. You can hardly have forgotten that someone very closely connected with you was very nearly carried off this week in Paris by a severe chill.

JACK: Yes, but you said yourself that a severe chill was not hereditary.

ALGERNON: It usedn't to be, I know—but I daresay it is now. Science is always making wonderful improvements in things.

JACK: [*Picking up the muffin-dish*] Oh, that is nonsense; you are always talking nonsense.

ALGERNON: Jack, you are at the muffins again! I wish you wouldn't. There are only two left. [*Takes them*] I told you I was particularly fond of muffins.

JACK: But I hate tea-cake.

ALGERNON: Why on earth then do you allow tea-cake to be served up for your guests? What ideas you have of hospitality!

JACK: Algernon! I have already told you to go. I don't want you here. Why don't you go?

ALGERNON: I haven't quite finished my tea yet, and there is still one muffin left. [Jack *groans, and sinks into a chair.* Algernon *still continues eating*]

Act III

SCENE: *Morning-room at the Manor House.* Gwendolen *and* Cecily *are at the window, looking out into the garden.*

GWENDOLEN: The fact that they did not follow us at once into the house, as anyone else would have done, seems to me to show that they have some sense of shame left.

CECILY: They have been eating muffins. That looks like repentance.

GWENDOLEN: [*After a pause*] They don't seem to notice us at all. Couldn't you cough?

GWENDOLEN: They're looking at us. What effrontery!

CECILY: They're approaching. That's very forward of them.

GWENDOLEN: Let us preserve a dignified silence.

CECILY: Certainly. It's the only thing to do now.

[*Enter* Jack, *followed by* Algernon. *They whistle some dreadful popular air from a British opera*]

GWENDOLEN: This dignified silence seems to produce an unpleasant effect.

CECILY: A most distasteful one.

GWENDOLEN: But we will not be the first to speak.

CECILY: Certainly not.

GWENDOLEN: Mr. Worthing, I have something very particular to ask you. Much depends on your reply.

CECILY: Gwendolen, your common sense is invaluable. Mr. Moncrieff, kindly answer me the following question. Why did you pretend to be my guardian's brother?

ALGERNON: In order that I might have an opportunity of meeting you.

CECILY: [*To* Gwendolen] That certainly seems a satisfactory explanation, does it not?

GWENDOLEN: Yes, dear, if you can believe him.

CECILY: I don't. But that does not affect the wonderful beauty of his answer.

GWENDOLEN: True. In matters of grave importance, style, not sincerity, is the vital thing. Mr. Worthing, what explanation can you offer to me for pretending to have a brother? Was it in order that you might have an opportunity of coming up to town to see me as often as possible?

JACK: Can you doubt it, Miss Fairfax?

GWENDOLEN: I have the gravest doubts upon the subject. But I intend to crush them. This is not the moment for German scepticism. [*Moving to* Cecily] Their explanations appear to be quite satisfactory, especially Mr. Worthing's. That seems to me to have the stamp of truth upon it.

CECILY: I am more than content with what Mr.

Moncrieff said. His voice alone inspires one with absolute credulity.

GWENDOLEN: Then you think we should forgive them?

CECILY: Yes. I mean no.

GWENDOLEN: True! I had forgotten. There are principles at stake that one cannot surrender. Which of us should tell them? The task is not a pleasant one.

CECILY: Could we not both speak at the same time?

GWENDOLEN: An excellent idea! I nearly always speak at the same time as other people. Will you take the time from me?

CECILY: Certainly. [Gwendolen *beats time with uplifted finger*]

GWENDOLEN AND CECILY: [*Speaking together*] Your Christian names are still an insuperable barrier. That is all!

JACK AND ALGERNON: [*Speaking together*] Our Christian names! Is that all? But we are going to be christened this afternoon.

GWENDOLEN: [*To* Jack] For my sake you are prepared to do this terrible thing?

JACK: I am.

CECILY: [*To* Algernon] To please me you are ready to face this fearful ordeal?

ALGERNON: I am.

GWENDOLEN: How absurd to talk of the equality of the sexes! Where questions of self-sacrifice are concerned, men are infinitely beyond us.

JACK: We are. [*Clasps hands with* Algernon]

CECILY: They have moments of physical courage of which we women know absolutely nothing.

GWENDOLEN: [*To* Jack] Darling!

ALGERNON: [*To* Cecily] Darling!

[*They fall into each other's arms*]

[*Enter* Merriman. *When he enters he coughs loudly, seeing the situation*]

MERRIMAN: Ahem! Ahem! Lady Bracknell!

JACK: Good heavens!

[*Enter* Lady Bracknell. *The couples separate in alarm. Exit* Merriman]

LADY BRACKNELL: Gwendolen! What does this mean?

GWENDOLEN: Merely that I am engaged to be married to Mr. Worthing, Mamma.

LADY BRACKNELL: Come here. Sit down. Sit down immediately. Hesitation of any kind is a sign of mental decay in the young, of physical weakness in the old. [*Turns to* Jack] Apprised, sir, of my daughter's sudden flight by her trusty maid, whose confidence I purchased by means of a small coin, I followed her at once by a luggage train. Her unhappy father is, I am glad to say, under the impression that she is attending a more than usually lengthy lecture by the University Extension Scheme on the Influence of a Permanent Income on Thought. I do not propose to undeceive him. Indeed I have never undeceived him on any ques-

tion. I would consider it wrong. But of course, you will clearly understand that all communication between yourself and my daughter must cease immediately from this moment. On this point, as indeed on all points, I am firm.

JACK: I am engaged to be married to Gwendolen, Lady Bracknell!

LADY BRACKNELL: You are nothing of the kind, sir. And now, as regards Algernon! . . . Algernon!

ALGERNON: Yes, Aunt Augusta.

LADY BRACKNELL: May I ask if it is in this house that your invalid friend Mr. Bunbury resides?

ALGERNON: [*Stammering*] Oh, no! Bunbury doesn't live here. Bunbury is somewhere else at present. In fact, Bunbury is dead.

LADY BRACKNELL: Dead! When did Mr. Bunbury die? His death must have been extremely sudden.

ALGERNON: [*Airily*] Oh, I killed Bunbury this afternoon. I mean poor Bunbury died this afternoon.

LADY BRACKNELL: What did he die of?

ALGERNON: Bunbury? Oh, he was quite exploded.

LADY BRACKNELL: Exploded! Was he the victim of a revolutionary outrage? I was not aware that Mr. Bunbury was interested in social legislation. If so, he is well punished for his morbidity.

ALGERNON: My dear Aunt Augusta, I mean he was found out! The doctors found out that Bunbury could not live, that is what I mean—so Bunbury died.

LADY BRACKNELL: He seems to have had great confidence in the opinion of his physicians. I am glad, however, that he made up his mind at the last to some definite course of action, and acted under proper medical advice. And now that we have finally got rid of this Mr. Bunbury, may I ask, Mr. Worthing, who is that young person whose hand my nephew Algernon is now holding in what seems to me a peculiarly unnecessary manner?

JACK: That lady is Miss Cecily Cardew, my ward.
                [Lady Bracknell *bows coldly to* Cecily]

ALGERNON: I am engaged to be married to Cecily, Aunt Augusta.

LADY BRACKNELL: I beg your pardon?

CECILY: Mr. Moncrieff and I are engaged to be married, Lady Bracknell.

LADY BRACKNELL: [*With a shiver, crossing to the sofa and sitting down*] I do not know whether there is anything peculiarly exciting in the air in this particular part of Hertfordshire, but the number of engagements that go on seems to me considerably above the proper average that statistics have laid down for our guidance. I think some preliminary enquiry on my part would not be out of place. Mr. Worthing, is Miss Cardew at all connected with any of the larger railway stations in London? I merely desire information. Until yesterday I had no idea that there were any families or persons whose origin was a Terminus. [Jack *looks perfectly furious, but restrains himself*]

JACK: [*In a clear, cold voice*] Miss Cardew is the granddaughter of the late Mr. Thomas Cardew of 149, Belgrave Square, S.W.; Gervase Park, Dorking, Surrey; and the Sporran, Fifeshire, N.B.

LADY BRACKNELL: That sounds not unsatisfactory. Three addresses always inspire confidence, even in tradesmen. But what proof have I of their authenticity?

JACK: I have carefully preserved the Court Guide of the period. They are open to your inspection, Lady Bracknell.

LADY BRACKNELL: [*Grimly*] I have known strange errors in that publication.

JACK: Miss Cardew's family solicitors are Messrs. Markby, Markby, and Markby.

LADY BRACKNELL: Markby, Markby, and Markby? A firm of the very highest position in their profession. Indeed I am told that one of the Mr. Markbys is occasionally to be seen at dinner parties. So far I am satisfied.

JACK: [*Very irritably*] How extremely kind of you, Lady Bracknell! I have also in my possession, you will be pleased to hear, certificates of Miss Cardew's birth, baptism, whooping cough, registration, vaccination, confirmation, and the measles; both the German and the English variety.

LADY BRACKNELL: Ah! A life crowded with incident, I see; though perhaps somewhat too exciting for a young girl. I am not myself in favor of premature experiences. [*Rises, looks at her watch*] Gwendolen! the time approaches for our departure. We have not a moment to lose. As a matter of form, Mr. Worthing, I had better ask you if Miss Cardew has any little fortune?

JACK: Oh, about a hundred and thirty thousand pounds in the Funds. That is all. Good-bye, Lady Bracknell. So pleased to have seen you.

LADY BRACKNELL: [*Sitting down again*] A moment, Mr. Worthing. A hundred and thirty thousand pounds! And in the Funds! Miss Cardew seems to me a most attractive young lady, now that I look at her. Few girls of the present day have any really solid qualities, any of the qualities that last, and improve with time. We live, I regret to say, in an age of surfaces. [*To Cecily*] Come over here, dear. [*Cecily goes across*] Pretty child! your dress is sadly simple, and your hair seems almost as Nature might have left it. But we can soon alter all that. A thoroughly experienced French maid produces a really marvelous result in a very brief space of time. I remember recommending one to young Lady Lancing, and after three months her own husband did not know her.

JACK: [*Aside*] And after six months nobody knew her.

LADY BRACKNELL: [*Glares at Jack for a few moments. Then bends, with a practised smile, to Cecily*] Kindly turn round, sweet child. [*Cecily turns completely round*] No, the side view is what I want. [*Cecily presents her profile*] Yes, quite as I expected. There are distinct social possibilities in your profile. The two weak points in our age are its want of principle and its want of profile. The chin a little higher, dear. Style largely depends on the way the chin is worn. They are worn very high, just at present. Algernon!

ALGERNON: Yes, Aunt Augusta!

LADY BRACKNELL: There are distinct social possibilities in Miss Cardew's profile.

ALGERNON: Cecily is the sweetest, dearest, prettiest girl in the whole world. And I don't care twopence about social possibilities.

LADY BRACKNELL: Never speak disrespectfully of society, Algernon. Only people who can't get into it do that. [*To Cecily*] Dear child, of course you know that Algernon has nothing but his debts to depend upon. But I do not approve of mercenary marriages. When I married Lord Bracknell I had no fortune of any kind. But I never dreamed for a moment of allowing that to stand in my way. Well, I suppose I must give my consent.

ALGERNON: Thank you, Aunt Augusta.

LADY BRACKNELL: Cecily, you may kiss me!

CECILY: [*Kisses her*] Thank you, Lady Bracknell.

LADY BRACKNELL: You may also address me as Aunt Augusta for the future.

CECILY: Thank you, Aunt Augusta.

LADY BRACKNELL: The marriage, I think, had better take place quite soon.

ALGERNON: Thank you, Aunt Augusta.

CECILY: Thank you, Aunt Augusta.

LADY BRACKNELL: To speak frankly, I am not in favor of long engagements. They give people the opportunity of finding out each other's character before marriage, which I think is never advisable.

JACK: I beg your pardon for interrupting you, Lady Bracknell, but this engagement is quite out of the question. I am Miss Cardew's guardian, and she cannot marry without my consent until she comes of age. That consent I absolutely decline to give.

LADY BRACKNELL: Upon what grounds, may I ask? Algernon is an extremely, I may almost say an ostentatiously, eligible young man. He has nothing, but he looks everything. What more can one desire?

JACK: It pains me very much to have to speak frankly to you, Lady Bracknell, about your nephew, but the fact is that I do not approve at all of his moral character. I suspect him of being untruthful. [*Algernon and Cecily look at him in indignant amazement*]

LADY BRACKNELL: Untruthful! My nephew Algernon? Impossible! He is an Oxonian.

JACK: I fear there can be no possible doubt about the matter. This afternoon, during my temporary absence in London on an important question of romance, he obtained admission to my house by means of the false pretense of being my brother. Under an assumed name he drank, I've just been informed by my butler, an entire pint bottle of my Perrier-Jouet, Brut, '89; a wine I was specially reserving for myself. Continuing his disgraceful deception, he succeeded in the course of the afternoon in alienating the affections of my only ward. He subsequently stayed to tea, and devoured every single muffin. And what makes his conduct all the more heartless is, that he was perfectly well aware from the first that I have no brother, that I never had a brother, and that I don't intend to have a brother, not even of any kind. I distinctly told him so myself yesterday afternoon.

LADY BRACKNELL: Ahem! Mr. Worthing, after careful consideration I have decided entirely to overlook my nephew's conduct to you.

JACK: That is very generous of you, Lady Bracknell. My own decision, however, is unalterable. I decline to give my consent.

LADY BRACKNELL: [To Cecily] Come here, sweet child. [Cecily goes over] How old are you, dear?

CECILY: Well, I am really only eighteen, but I always admit to twenty when I go to evening parties.

LADY BRACKNELL: You are perfectly right in making some slight alteration. Indeed, no woman should ever be quite accurate about her age. It looks so calculating. . . . [In meditative manner] Eighteen, but admitting to twenty at evening parties. Well, it will not be very long before you are of age and free from the restraints of tutelage. So I don't think your guardian's consent is, after all, a matter of any importance.

JACK: Pray excuse me, Lady Bracknell, for interrupting you again, but it is only fair to tell you that according to the terms of her grandfather's will Miss Cardew does not come legally of age till she is thirty-five.

LADY BRACKNELL: That does not seem to me to be a grave objection. Thirty-five is a very attractive age. London society is full of women of the very highest birth who have, of their own free choice, remained thirty-five for years. Lady Dumbleton is an instance in point. To my own knowledge she has been thirty-five ever since she arrived at the age of forty, which was many years ago now. I see no reason why our dear Cecily should not be even still more attractive at the age you mention than she is at present. There will be a large accumulation of property.

CECILY: Algy, could you wait for me till I was thirty-five?

ALGERNON: Of course I could, Cecily. You know I could.

CECILY: Yes, I felt it instinctively, but I couldn't wait all that time. I hate waiting even five minutes for anybody. It always makes me rather cross. I am not punctual myself, I know, but I do like punctuality in others, and waiting, even to be married, is quite out of the question.

ALGERNON: Then what is to be done, Cecily?

CECILY: I don't know, Mr. Moncrieff.

LADY BRACKNELL: My dear Mr. Worthing, as Miss Cardew states positively that she cannot wait till she is thirty-five—a remark which I am bound to say seems to me to show a somewhat impatient nature—I would beg of you to reconsider your decision.

JACK: But my dear Lady Bracknell, the matter is entirely in your own hands. The moment you consent to my marriage with Gwendolen, I will most gladly allow your nephew to form an alliance with my ward.

LADY BRACKNELL: [Rising and drawing herself up] You must be quite aware that what you propose is out of the question.

JACK: Then a passionate celibacy is all that any of us can look forward to.

LADY BRACKNELL: That is not the destiny I propose for Gwendolen. Algernon, of course, can choose for himself. [Pulls out her watch] Come, dear, [Gwendolen rises] we have already missed five, if not six, trains. To miss any more might expose us to comment on the platform.

[Enter Dr. Chasuble]

CHASUBLE: Everything is quite ready for the christenings.

LADY BRACKNELL: The christenings, sir! Is not that somewhat premature?

CHASUBLE: [Looking rather puzzled, and pointing to Jack and Algernon] Both these gentlemen have expressed a desire for immediate baptism.

LADY BRACKNELL: At their age? The idea is grotesque and irreligious! Algernon, I forbid you to be baptized. I will not hear of such excesses. Lord Bracknell would be highly displeased if he learned that that was the way in which you wasted your time and money.

CHASUBLE: Am I to understand then that there are to be no christenings at all this afternoon?

JACK: I don't think that, as things are now, it would be of much practical value to either of us, Dr. Chasuble.

CHASUBLE: I am grieved to hear such sentiments from you, Mr. Worthing. They savor of the heretical views of the Anabaptists, views that I have completely refuted in four of my unpublished sermons. However, as your present mood seems to be one peculiarly secular, I will return to the church at once. Indeed, I have just been informed by the pew-opener that for the last hour and a half Miss Prism has been waiting for me in the vestry.

LADY BRACKNELL: [Starting] Miss Prism! Did I hear you mention a Miss Prism?

CHASUBLE: Yes, Lady Bracknell. I am on my way to join her.

LADY BRACKNELL: Pray allow me to detain you for a moment. This matter may prove to be one of vital importance to Lord Bracknell and myself. Is this

Miss Prism a female of repellent aspect, remotely connected with education?

CHASUBLE: [*Somewhat indignantly*] She is the most cultivated of ladies, and the very picture of respectability.

LADY BRACKNELL: It is obviously the same person. May I ask what position she holds in your household?

CHASUBLE: [*Severely*] I am a celibate, madam.

JACK: [*Interposing*] Miss Prism, Lady Bracknell, has been for the last three years Miss Cardew's esteemed governess and valued companion.

LADY BRACKNELL: In spite of what I hear of her, I must see her at once. Let her be sent for.

CHASUBLE: [*Looking off*] She approaches; she is nigh.

[*Enter* Miss Prism *hurriedly*]

MISS PRISM: I was told you expected me in the vestry, dear Canon. I have been waiting for you there for an hour and three-quarters. [*Catches sight of* Lady Bracknell, *who has fixed her with a stony glare.* Miss Prism *grows pale and quails. She looks anxiously round as if desirous to escape*]

LADY BRACKNELL: [*In a severe, judicial voice*] Prism! [Miss Prism *bows her head in shame*] Come here, Prism! [Miss Prism *approaches in a humble manner*] Prism! Where is that baby? [*General consternation. The* Canon *starts back in horror.* Algernon *and* Jack *pretend to be anxious to shield* Cecily *and* Gwendolen *from hearing the details of a terrible public scandal*] Twenty-eight years ago, Prism, you left Lord Bracknell's house, Number 104, Upper Grosvenor Street, in charge of a perambulator that contained a baby, of the male sex. You never returned. A few weeks later, through the elaborate investigations of the Metropolitan police, the perambulator was discovered at midnight, standing by itself in a remote corner of Bayswater. It contained the manuscript of a three-volume novel of more than usually revolting sentimentality. [Miss Prism *starts in involuntary indignation*] But the baby was not there! [*Everyone looks at* Miss Prism] Prism, where is that baby?   [*A pause*]

MISS PRISM: Lady Bracknell, I admit with shame that I do not know. I only wish I did. The plain facts of the case are these. On the morning of the day you mention, a day that is forever branded on my memory, I prepared as usual to take the baby out in its perambulator. I had also with me a somewhat old but capacious handbag in which I had intended to place the manuscript of a work of fiction that I had written during my few unoccupied hours. In a moment of mental abstraction, for which I never can forgive myself, I deposited the manuscript in the bassinette, and placed the baby in the handbag.

JACK: [*Who has been listening attentively*] But where did you deposit the handbag?

MISS PRISM: Do not ask me, Mr. Worthing.

JACK: Miss Prism, this is a matter of no small importance to me. I insist on knowing where you deposited the handbag that contained that infant.

MISS PRISM: I left it in the cloak-room of one of the larger railway stations in London.

JACK: What railway station?

MISS PRISM: [*Quite crushed*] Victoria. The Brighton line. [*Sinks into a chair*]

JACK: I must retire to my room for a moment. Gwendolen, wait here for me.

GWENDOLEN: If you are not too long, I will wait here for you all my life.

[*Exit* Jack *in great excitement*]

CHASUBLE: What do you think this means, Lady Bracknell?

LADY BRACKNELL: I dare not even suspect, Dr. Chasuble. I need hardly tell you that in families of high position strange coincidences are not supposed to occur. They are hardly considered the thing.

[*Noises heard overhead as if someone was throwing trunks about. Everybody looks up*]

CECILY: Uncle Jack seems strangely agitated.

CHASUBLE: Your guardian has a very emotional nature.

LADY BRACKNELL: This noise is extremely unpleasant. It sounds as if he was having an argument. I dislike arguments of any kind. They are always vulgar, and often convincing.

CHASUBLE: [*Looking up*] It has stopped now.

[*The noise is redoubled*]

LADY BRACKNELL: I wish he would arrive at some conclusion.

GWENDOLEN: This suspense is terrible. I hope it will last.

[*Enter* Jack *with a handbag of black leather in his hand*]

JACK: [*Rushing over to* Miss Prism] Is this the handbag, Miss Prism? Examine it carefully before you speak. The happiness of more than one life depends on your answer.

MISS PRISM: [*Calmly*] It seems to be mine. Yes, here is the injury it received through the upsetting of a Gower Street omnibus in younger and happier days. Here is the stain on the lining caused by the explosion of a temperance beverage, an incident that occurred at Leamington. And here, on the lock, are my initials. I had forgotten that in an extravagant mood I had had them placed there. The bag is undoubtedly mine. I am delighted to have it so unexpectedly restored to me. It has been a great inconvenience being without it all these years.

JACK: [*In a pathetic voice*] Miss Prism, more is restored to you than this handbag. I was the baby you placed in it.

MISS PRISM: [*Amazed*] You?

JACK: [*Embracing her*] Yes . . . mother!

MISS PRISM: [*Recoiling in indignant astonishment*] Mr. Worthing! I am unmarried!

JACK: Unmarried! I do not deny that is a serious blow. But after all, who has the right to cast a stone against one who has suffered? Cannot repentance wipe out an act of folly? Why should there be one law for men and another for women? Mother, I forgive you.   [*Tries to embrace her again*]

MISS PRISM: [*Still more indignant*] Mr. Worthing, there is some error. [*Pointing to* Lady Bracknell] There is the lady who can tell you who you really are.

JACK: [*After a pause*] Lady Bracknell, I hate to seem inquisitive, but would you kindly inform me who I am?

LADY BRACKNELL: I am afraid that the news I have to give you will not altogether please you. You are the son of my poor sister, Mrs. Moncrieff, and consequently Algernon's elder brother.

JACK: Algy's elder brother! Then I have a brother after all. I knew I had a brother! I always said I had a brother! Cecily—how could you have ever doubted that I had a brother? [*Seizes hold of Algernon*] Dr. Chasuble, my unfortunate brother. Miss Prism, my unfortunate brother. Gwendolen, my unfortunate brother. Algy, you young scoundrel, you will have to treat me with more respect in the future. You have never behaved to me like a brother in all your life.

ALGERNON: Well, not till to-day, old boy, I admit. I did my best, however, though I was out of practice.   [*Shakes hands*]

GWENDOLEN: [*To Jack*] My own! But what own are you? What is your Christian name, now that you have become someone else?

JACK: Good heavens! . . . I had quite forgotten that point. Your decision on the subject of my name is irrevocable, I suppose?

GWENDOLEN: I never change, except in my affections.

CECILY: What a noble nature you have, Gwendolen!

JACK: Then the question had better be cleared up at once. Aunt Augusta, a moment. At the time when Miss Prism left me in the handbag, had I been christened already?

LADY BRACKNELL: Every luxury that money could buy, including christening, had been lavished on you by your fond and doting parents.

JACK: Then I was christened! That is settled. Now, what name was I given? Let me know the worst.

LADY BRACKNELL: Being the eldest son you were naturally christened after your father.

JACK: [*Irritably*] Yes, but what was my father's Christian name?

LADY BRACKNELL: [*Meditatively*] I cannot at the present moment recall what the General's Christian name was. But I have no doubt he had one. He was eccentric, I admit. But only in later years. And that was the result of the Indian climate, and marriage, and indigestion, and other things of that kind.

JACK: Algy! Can't you recollect what our father's Christian name was?

ALGERNON: My dear boy, we were never even on speaking terms. He died before I was a year old.

JACK: His name would appear in the Army Lists of the period, I suppose, Aunt Augusta?

LADY BRACKNELL: The General was essentially a man of peace, except in his domestic life. But I have no doubt his name would appear in any military directory.

JACK: The Army Lists of the last forty years are here. These delightful records should have been my constant study. [*Rushes to bookcase and tears the books out*] M. Generals . . . Mallam, Maxbohm, Magley, what ghastly names they have—Markby, Migsby, Mobbs, Moncrieff! Lieutenant 1840, Captain, Lieutenant-Colonel, Colonel, General 1869, Christian names, Ernest John. [*Puts book very quietly down and speaks quite calmly*] I always told you, Gwendolen, my name was Ernest, didn't I? Well, it is Ernest after all. I mean it naturally is Ernest.

LADY BRACKNELL: Yes, I remember that the General was called Ernest. I knew I had some particular reason for disliking the name.

GWENDOLEN: Ernest! My own Ernest! I felt from the first that you could have no other name!

JACK: Gwendolen, it is a terrible thing for a man to find out suddenly that all his life he has been speaking nothing but the truth. Can you forgive me?

GWENDOLEN: I can. For I feel that you are sure to change.

JACK: My own one!

CHASUBLE: [*To Miss Prism*] Lætitia! [*Embraces her*]

MISS PRISM: [*Enthusiastically*] Frederick! At last!

ALGERNON: Cecily! [*Embraces her*] At last!

JACK: Gwendolen! [*Embraces her*] At last!

LADY BRACKNELL: My nephew, you seem to be displaying signs of triviality.

JACK: On the contrary, Aunt Augusta, I've now realized for the first time in my life the vital Importance of Being Earnest.

                                        TABLEAU

Androcles and the Lion

by GEORGE BERNARD SHAW

(1856–1950)

Though Shaw wrote no single comic masterpiece like The Alchemist, he perhaps wrote more comedy classics than any other one playwright, Shakespeare included, has written in English. The word classic can surely be applied without argument to Candida, Caesar and Cleopatra, Man and Superman, Major Barbara, Androcles and the Lion, Pygmalion, and Heartbreak House; and the term can very nearly be applied, and doubtless is very frequently applied, to half a dozen other Shaw plays as well. Of course, Shaw wrote more plays than virtually any other modern playwright of standing; and this fact is an important fact, for it is Shaw's oeuvre that most matters; it is not by the best of his work but by the body of it that he chiefly stands forth as great. His characters approximate the population of a thriving community, and indeed he gives us, as do Dickens and Trollope, Balzac and Henry James, the sense not of a few houses to live in or families to know, but of whole streets to investigate, and squares to traverse, and passageways to explore. And as with these other creators of large personal worlds, there is a particular architecture about it all, a special, characterizing light that hangs over it. And as with Dickens—it is at once his huge merit and the key to his faults—there is a sense of careless, limitless energy about Shaw. We feel that he could have written twice again as much as he did, while simultaneously suspecting that he wrote twice as much as he should have.

What is additionally remarkable, beyond the several dozen plays, is that he treated in them—or in retrospect seems to have treated—several dozen subjects. He canvassed modern life, from slums to throne rooms, from brothels to country houses, from medicine to munitions, from phonetics to peace conferences; he dove backward in time all the way to ancient heroes and fabled beasts; he plunged forward into the wild far future; he redecorated Hell and toned down Heaven. He went everywhere, in fact, including a number of places that do not—nor ever did—exist. But Shaw the traveler dwindles beside Shaw the teacher: he has been guide, philosopher, and enemy to almost every ism: and next only to the many things he attacked are those he espoused; and next come the things he attacked and espoused by turn. Exalting the Life Force in Man and Superman, he championed the Death Force in Major Barbara; in Major Barbara,

again, a daughter is reconciled to a parent for pretty much what alienates her in Mrs. Warren's Profession. Shaw exalts dictators, he assails dictators; he hails poets, he hoots at poets; he is the arch-priest of reason and then, suddenly, of mysticism. No one ever had so many ideas—or rather, so many ideas about ideas.

No one, indeed—no playwright or novelist—has at once so continuously mocked and so incessantly moralized; and hence acquired, among other things, two such large and dissimilar audiences: those who reveled in Shaw's manner and those who took very seriously his beliefs. Now and then, so great was his personal force and showmanship, a few who came to scoff with him may have remained to pray; but the important thing is that almost all who came remained, if only to marvel. Again and again he puts on an extraordinary, an unpredictable show: exhibits verbal battlegrounds whose missiles reverse their direction, so that bombs become boomerangs and combatants fire into their own ranks. But there are mockery and morality of a different kind, where the joke is very much a lesson—a lesson in the folly of all absolute positions; a demonstration of the virtue residing in vice, or of the ill effects of overrighteousness. Like most such demonstrations, Shaw's are about equally illuminating and confusing, about equally inspire faith and foster doubt; but however much Shaw messes up men's thoughts, at least he goads them into thinking for themselves.

Being so superb an entertainer, Shaw has made almost everyone listen: though were this he speaking of someone else, he might inquire whether he had made anyone learn. We come away from the Hell scene murmuring "A plague o' both your afterworlds"; from John Bull's Other Island with misdoubts of England and Ireland alike; from Man and Superman shown that man proposes—after woman has done the courting. The moral can be too ambiguous to have any moral value; and we have often the sense that Shaw has simply been a gay, slightly mischievous host; has poured words, epigrams, paradoxes, insults, riddles, jests from a kind of intellectual cocktail shaker—so that everyone, departing, is sure that he had a good time and that many of the guests were brilliant and fascinating, but is a little hazy about what was said—or, worse yet, meant. Man (perhaps quite rightly, since he takes his own salvation seriously) is not going to pin his faith on an evangelist who is so good an entertainer. Besides, we are so constituted as to desire, in our leaders, a certain gravity, even solemnity, of manner: if not the frock coat, then the clerical gown—but at any rate not motley; if not the pious sigh, then the thundering voice—but at any rate, not buffoonery. And so, despite the many things Shaw really cared about and militantly fought for, or loathed and fiercely inveighed against, he has—by virtue of seeing both sides of every argument and what is funny in every situation or struggle—triumphed, not as a philosopher but as a comedian.

Yet, reading Androcles and the Lion, an opéra bouffe if there ever was one, a wild extravaganza even for Shaw, we are not just wonderfully exhilarated and amused, but are somehow touched, somehow moved to admire these early Christians, to feel their nobility and courage. And we are touched as we very well might not be were the tone more serious or the treatment more straightforward. About Androcles and Lavinia there is a kind of beauty from their being so gaily high-hearted, so almost casually heroic: and at least at moments, the comic approach can penetrate more deeply, can touch more sensitive and special chords, than the dramatic. And as this was not to be tragedy—as Shaw's martyrs were to be deprived, in the end, of martyrdom—it is as well that it should have been the sunny, small-scaled comedy he made it. It is a perfect little thing of its kind; and the kind of thing that Shaw not only brought to perfection, but well-nigh invented into the bargain.

GEORGE BERNARD SHAW

Androcles and the Lion

Preface on the Prospects of Christianity

Why Not Give Christianity a Trial?

The question seems a hopeless one after 2000 years of resolute adherence to the old cry of "Not this man, but Barabbas." Yet it is beginning to look as if Barabbas was a failure, in spite of his strong right hand, his victories, his empires, his millions of money, and his moralities and churches and political constitutions. "This man" has not been a failure yet; for nobody has ever been sane enough to try his way. But he has had one quaint triumph. Barabbas has stolen his name and taken his cross as a standard. There is a sort of compliment in that. There is even a sort of loyalty in it, like that of the brigand who breaks every law and yet claims to be a patriotic subject of the king who makes them. We have always had a curious feeling that though we crucified Christ on a stick, he somehow managed to get hold of the right end of it, and that if we were better men we might try his plan. There have been one or two grotesque attempts at it by inadequate people, such as the Kingdom of God in Munster, which was ended by a crucifixion so much more atrocious that the one on Calvary that the bishop who took the part of Annas went home and died of horror. But responsible people have never made such attempts. The moneyed, respectable, capable world has been steadily anti-Christian and Barabbasque since the crucifixion; and the specific doctrine of Jesus has not in all that time been put into political or general social practice. I am no more a Christian than Pilate was, or you, gentle reader; and yet, like Pilate, I greatly prefer Jesus to Annas and Caiaphas; and I am ready to admit that after contemplating the world and human nature for nearly sixty years, I see no way out of the world's misery but the way which would have been found by Christ's will if he had undertaken the work of a modern practical statesman.

Pray do not at this early point lose patience with me and shut the book. I assure you I am as sceptical and scientific and modern a thinker as you will find anywhere. I grant you I know a great deal more about economics and politics than Jesus did, and can do things he could not do. I am by all Barabbasque standards a person of much better character and standing, and greater practical sense. I have no sympathy with vagabonds and talkers who try to reform society by taking men away from their regular productive work and making vagabonds and talkers of them too; and if I had been Pilate I should have recognized as plainly as he the necessity for suppressing attacks on the existing social order, however corrupt that order might be, by people with no knowledge of government and no power to construct political machinery to carry out their views, acting on the very dangerous delusion that the end of the world was at hand. I make no defence of such Christians as Savonarola and John of Leyden: they were scuttling the ship before they had learned how to build a raft; and it became necessary to throw them overboard to save the crew. I say this to set myself right with respectable society; but I must still insist that if Jesus could have worked out the practical problems of a Communist constitution, an admitted obligation to deal with crime without revenge or punishment, and a full assumption by humanity of divine responsibilities, he would have conferred an incalculable benefit on mankind, because these distinctive demands of his are now turning out to be good sense and sound economics.

I say distinctive, because his common humanity and his subjection to time and space (that is, to the Syrian life of his period) involved his belief in many things, true and false, that in no way distinguish him from other Syrians of that time. But such common beliefs do not constitute specific Christianity any more than wearing a beard, working in a carpenter's shop, or believing that the earth is flat and that the stars could drop on it from heaven like hailstones. Christianity interests practical statesmen now because of the doctrines that distinguished Christ from the Jews and the Barabbasques generally, including ourselves.

Why Jesus More Than Another?

I do not imply, however, that these doctrines were peculiar to Christ. A doctrine peculiar to one man would be only a craze, unless its comprehension depended on a development of human faculty so rare that only one exceptionally gifted man possessed it.

But even in this case it would be useless, because incapable of spreading. Christianity is a step in moral evolution which is independent of any individual preacher. If Jesus had never existed (and that he ever existed in any other sense than that in which Shakespear's Hamlet existed has been vigorously questioned) Tolstoy would have thought and taught and quarrelled with the Greek Church all the same. Their creed has been fragmentarily practised to a considerable extent in spite of the fact that the laws of all countries treat it, in effect, as criminal. Many of its advocates have been militant atheists. But for some reason the imagination of white mankind has picked out Jesus of Nazareth as *the* Christ, and attributed all the Christian doctrines to him; and as it is the doctrine and not the man that matters, and, as, besides, one symbol is as good as another provided everyone attaches the same meaning to it, I raise, for the moment, no question as to how far the gospels are original, and how far they consist of Greek and Chinese interpolations. The record that Jesus said certain things is not invalidated by a demonstration that Confucius said them before him. Those who claim a literal divine paternity for him cannot be silenced by the discovery that the same claim was made for Alexander and Augustus. And I am not just now concerned with the credibility of the gospels as records of fact; for I am not acting as a detective, but turning our modern lights on to certain ideas and doctrines in them which disentangle themselves from the rest because they are flatly contrary to common practice, common sense, and common belief, and yet have, in the teeth of dogged incredulity and recalcitrance, produced an irresistible impression that Christ, though rejected by his posterity as an unpractical dreamer, and executed by his contemporaries as a dangerous anarchist and blasphemous madman, was greater than his judges.

Was Jesus a Coward?

I know quite well that this impression of superiority is not produced on everyone, even of those who profess extreme susceptibility to it. Setting aside the huge mass of inculcated Christ-worship which has no real significance because it has no intelligence, there is, among people who are really free to think for themselves on the subject, a great deal of hearty dislike of Jesus and of contempt for his failure to save himself and overcome his enemies by personal bravery and cunning as Mahomet did. I have heard this feeling expressed far more impatiently by persons brought up in England as Christians than by Mahometans, who are, like their prophet, very civil to Jesus, and allow him a place in their esteem and veneration at least as high as we accord to John the Baptist. But this British bulldog contempt is founded on a complete misconception of his reasons for submitting voluntarily to an ordeal of torment and death. The modern Sec-

ularist is often so determined to regard Jesus as a man like himself and nothing more, that he slips unconsciously into the error of assuming that Jesus shared that view. But it is quite clear from the New Testament writers (the chief authorities for believing that Jesus ever existed) that Jesus at the time of his death believed himself to be the Christ, a divine personage. It is therefore absurd to criticize his conduct before Pilate as if he were Colonel Roosevelt or Admiral von Tirpitz or even Mahomet. Whether you accept his belief in his divinity as fully as Simon Peter did, or reject it as a delusion which led him to submit to torture and sacrifice his life without resistance in the conviction that he would presently rise again in glory, you are equally bound to admit that, far from behaving like a coward or a sheep, he shewed considerable physical fortitude in going through a cruel ordeal against which he could have defended himself as effectually as he cleared the money-changers out of the temple. "Gentle Jesus, meek and mild" is a snivelling modern invention, with no warrant in the gospels. St Matthew would as soon have thought of applying such adjectives to Judas Maccabeus as to Jesus; and even St Luke, who makes Jesus polite and gracious, does not make him meek. The picture of him as an English curate of the farcical comedy type, too meek to fight a policeman, and everybody's butt, may be useful in the nursery to soften children; but that such a figure could ever have become a centre of the world's attention is too absurd for discussion: grown men and women may speak kindly of a harmless creature who utters amiable sentiments and is a helpless nincompoop when he is called on to defend them; but they will not follow him, nor do what he tells them, because they do not wish to share his defeat and disgrace.

Was Jesus a Martyr?

It is important therefore that we should clear our minds of the notion that Jesus died, as some of us are in the habit of declaring, for his social and political opinions. There have been many martyrs to those opinions; but he was not one of them, nor, as his words shew, did he see any more sense in martyrdom than Galileo did. He was executed by the Jews for the blasphemy of claiming to be a God; and Pilate, to whom this was a mere piece of superstitious nonsense, let them execute him as the cheapest way of keeping them quiet, on the formal plea that he had committed treason against Rome by saying that he was the King of the Jews. He was not falsely accused, nor denied full opportunities of defending himself. The proceedings were quite straightforward and regular; and Pilate, to whom the appeal lay, favored him and despised his judges, and was evidently willing enough to be conciliated. But instead of denying the charge, Jesus repeated the offence. He knew what he was doing: he had alienated numbers of his own disciples and been stoned in the streets for doing it before. He was not lying: he believed literally what he said. The horror of the High Priest was perfectly natural: he was a Primate confronted with a heterodox street preacher uttering what seemed to him an appalling and impudent blasphemy. The fact that the blasphemy was to Jesus a simple statement of fact, and that it has since been accepted as such by all western nations, does not invalidate the proceedings, nor give us the right to regard Annas and Caiaphas as worse men than the Archbishop of Canterbury and the Head Master of Eton. If Jesus had been indicted in a modern court, he would have been examined by two doctors; found to be obsessed by a delusion; declared incapable of pleading; and sent to an asylum: that is the whole difference. But please note that when a man is charged before a modern tribunal (to take a case that happened the other day) of having asserted and maintained that he was an officer returned from the front to receive the Victoria Cross at the hands of the King, although he was in fact a mechanic, nobody thinks of treating him as afflicted with a delusion. He is punished for false pretences, because his assertion is credible and therefore misleading. Just so, the claim to divinity made by Jesus was to the High Priest, who looked forward to the coming of a Messiah, one that might conceivably have been true, and might therefore have misled the people in a very dangerous way. That was why he treated Jesus as an impostor and a blasphemer where we should have treated him as a madman.

The Gospels Without Prejudice

All this will become clear if we read the gospels without prejudice. When I was young it was impossible to read them without fantastic confusion of thought. The confusion was so utterly confounded that it was called the proper spirit to read the Bible in. Jesus was a baby; and he was older than creation. He was a man who could be persecuted, stoned, scourged, and killed; and he was a god, immortal and all-powerful, able to raise the dead and call millions of angels to his aid. It was a sin to doubt either view of him: that is, it was a sin to reason about him; and the end was that you did not reason about him, and read about him only when you were compelled. When you heard the gospel stories read in church, or learnt them from painters and poets, you came out with an impression of their contents that would have astonished a Chinaman who had read the story without prepossession. Even sceptics who were specially on their guard, put the Bible in the dock, and read the gospels with the object of detecting discrepancies in the four narratives to shew that the writers were as subject to error as the writers of yesterday's newspaper.

All this has changed greatly within two generations. Today the Bible is so little read that the language of the Authorized Version is rapidly becoming obsolete; so that even in the United States, where the old tradition of the verbal infallibility of "the book of books" lingers more strongly than anywhere else except perhaps in Ulster, retranslations into modern English have been introduced perforce to save its bare intelligibility. It is quite easy today to find cultivated persons who have never read the New Testament, and on whom therefore it is possible to try the experiment of asking them to read the gospels and state what they have gathered as to the history and views and character of Christ.

The Gospels Now Unintelligible to Novices

But it will not do to read the gospels with a mind furnished only for the reception of, say, a biography of Goethe. You will not make sense of them, nor even be able without impatient weariness to persevere in the task of going steadily through them, unless you know something of the history of the human imagination as applied to religion. Not long ago I asked a writer of distinguished intellectual competence whether he had made a study of the gospels since his childhood. His reply was that he had lately tried, but "found it all such nonsense that I could not stick it." As I do not want to send anyone to the gospels with this result, I had better here give a brief exposition of how much of the history of religion is needed to make the gospels and the conduct and ultimate fate of Jesus intelligible and interesting.

Worldliness of the Majority

The first common mistake to get rid of is that mankind consists of a great mass of religious people and a few eccentric atheists. It consists of a huge mass of worldly people, and a small percentage of persons deeply interested in religion and concerned about their own souls and other people's; and this section consists mostly of those who are passionately affirming the established religion and those who are passionately attacking it, the genuine philosophers being very few. Thus you never have a nation of millions of Wesleys and one Tom Paine. You have a million Mr Worldly Wisemans, one Wesley, with his small congregation, and one Tom Paine, with *his* smaller congregation. The passionately religious are a people apart; and if they were not hopelessly outnumbered by the worldly, they would turn the world upside down, as St Paul was reproached, quite justly, for wanting to do. Few people can number among their personal acquaintances a single atheist or a single Plymouth Brother. Unless a religious turn in ourselves has led us to seek the little Societies to which these rare birds belong, we pass our lives among people who, whatever creeds they may repeat, and in whatever temples they may avouch their respectability and wear their Sunday clothes, have robust consciences, and hunger and thirst, not for righteousness, but for rich feeding and comfort and social position and attractive mates and ease and pleasure and respect and consideration: in short, for love and money. To these people one morality is as good as another provided they are used to it and can put up with its restrictions without unhappiness; and in the maintenance of this morality they will fight and punish and coerce without scruple. They may not be the salt of the earth, these Philistines; but they are the substance of civilization; and they save society from ruin by criminals and conquerors as well as by Savonarolas and Knipperdollings. And as they know, very sensibly, that a little religion is good for children and serves morality, keeping the poor in goodhumor or in awe by promising rewards in heaven or threatening torments in hell, they encourage the religious people up to a certain point: for instance, if Savonarola only tells the ladies of Florence that they ought to tear off their jewels and finery and sacrifice them to God, they offer him a cardinal's hat, and praise him as a saint; but if he induces them to actually do it, they burn him as a public nuisance.

Religion of the Minority. Salvationism

The religion of the tolerated religious minority has always been essentially the same religion: that is why its changes of name and form have made so little difference. That is why, also, a nation so civilized as the English can convert negroes to their faith with great ease, but cannot convert Mahometans or Jews. The negro finds in civilized Salvationism an unspeakably more comforting version of his crude creed; but neither Saracen nor Jew sees any advantage in it over his own version. The Crusader was surprised to find the Saracen quite as religious and moral as himself, and rather more than less civilized. The Latin Christian has nothing to offer the Greek Christian that Greek Christianity has not already provided. They are all, at root, Salvationists.

Let us trace this religion of Salvation from its beginnings. So many things that man does not himself contrive or desire are always happening: death, plagues, tempests, blights, floods, sunrise and sunset, growths and harvests and decay, and Kant's two wonders of the starry heavens above us and the moral law within us, that we conclude that somebody must be doing it all, or that somebody is doing the good and somebody else doing the evil, or that armies of invisible persons, beneficent and malevolent, are doing it; hence you postulate gods and devils, angels and demons. You propitiate these powers with presents, called sacrifices, and flatteries, called praises. Then the Kantian moral law within you makes you conceive your god as a judge; and straightway you try to corrupt him, also with presents and flatteries. This seems shocking to us; but our objection to it is quite a recent development: no longer ago than Shakespear's time it was thought quite natural that litigants should give presents to human judges; and the buying off of divine wrath by actual money payments to priests, or, in the reformed churches which discountenance this, by subscriptions to charities and church building and the like, is still in full swing. Its practical disadvantage is that though it makes matters very easy for the rich, it cuts off the poor from all hope of divine favor. And this quickens the moral criticism of the poor to such an extent, that they soon find the moral law within them revolting against the idea of buying off the deity with gold and gifts, though they are still quite ready to buy him off with the paper money of praise and professions of repentance. Accordingly, you will find that though a religion may last unchanged for many centuries in primitive communities where the conditions of life leave no room for poverty and riches, and the process of propitiating the supernatural powers is as well within the means of the least of the members as within those of the headman, yet when commercial civilization arrives, and capitalism divides the people into a few rich and a great many so poor that they can barely live, a movement for religious reform will arise among the poor, and will be essentially a movement for cheap or entirely gratuitous salvation.

To understand what the poor mean by propitiation, we must examine for a moment what they mean by justice.

The Difference Between Atonement and Punishment

The primitive idea of justice is partly legalized revenge and partly expiation by sacrifice. It works out from both sides in the notion that two blacks make a white, and that when a wrong has been done, it should be paid for by an equivalent suffering. It seems to the Philistine majority a matter of course that this compensating suffering should be inflicted on the wrongdoer for the sake of its deterrent effect on other would-be wrongdoers; but a moment's reflection will shew that this utilitarian application corrupts the whole transaction. For example, the shedding of innocent blood cannot be balanced by the shedding of guilty blood. Sacrificing a criminal to propitiate God for the murder of one of his righteous servants is like sacrificing a mangy sheep or an ox with the rinderpest: it calls down divine wrath instead of appeasing it. In doing it we offer God as a sacrifice the gratification of our own revenge and the protection of our own lives without cost to ourselves; and cost to ourselves is the essence of sacrifice and expiation. However much the Philistines have succeeded in confusing these things in practice, they are to the Salvationist sense distinct and even contrary. The Baronet's cousin in Dickens's novel, who, perplexed by the failure of the police to discover the murderer of the baronet's solicitor, said "Far better hang wrong fellow than no fellow," was not only expressing a very common sentiment, but trembling on the brink of the rarer Salvationist opinion that it is much better to hang the wrong fellow: that, in fact, the wrong fellow is the right fellow to hang.

The point is a cardinal one, because until we grasp it not only does historical Christianity remain unintelligible to us, but those who do not care a rap about historical Christianity may be led into the mistake of supposing that if we discard revenge, and treat murderers exactly as God treated Cain: that is, exempt them from punishment by putting a brand on them as unworthy to be sacrificed, and let them face the world as best they can with that brand on them, we should get rid both of punishment and sacrifice. It would not at all follow: on the contrary, the feeling that there must be an expiation of the murder might quite possibly lead to our putting some innocent person—the more innocent the better—to a cruel death to balance the account with divine justice.

Salvation at First a Class Privilege; and the Remedy

Thus, even when the poor decide that the method of purchasing salvation by offering rams and goats or bringing gold to the altar must be wrong because they cannot afford it, we still do not feel "saved" without a sacrifice and a victim. In vain do we try to substitute mystical rites that cost nothing, such as circumcision, or, as a substitute for that, baptism. Our sense of justice still demands an expiation, a sacrifice, a sufferer for our sins. And this leaves the poor man still in his old difficulty; for if it was impossible for him to procure rams and goats and shekels, how much more impossible is it for him to find a neighbor who will voluntarily suffer for his sins: one who will say cheerfully "You have committed a murder. Well, never mind: I am willing to be hanged for it in your stead"?

Our imagination must come to our rescue. Why not, instead of driving ourselves to despair by insisting on a separate atonement by a separate redeemer for every sin, have one great atonement and one great redeemer to compound for the sins of the world once for all? Nothing easier, nothing cheaper. The yoke is easy, the burden light. All you have to do when the redeemer is once found (or invented by the imagination) is to believe in the efficacy of the transaction, and you are saved. The rams and goats cease to bleed; the altars which ask for expensive gifts and continually renewed sacrifices are torn down; and the Church of the single redeemer and the single atonement rises on the ruins of the old temples, and becomes a single Church of the Christ.

Retrospective Atonement; and the Expectation of the Redeemer

But this does not happen at once. Between the old costly religion of the rich and the new gratuitous religion of the poor there comes an interregnum in which the redeemer, though conceived by the human imagination, is not yet found. He is awaited and expected under the names of the Christ, the Messiah, Baldur the Beautiful, or what not; but he has not yet come. Yet the sinners are not therefore in despair. It is true that they cannot say, as we say, "The Christ has come, and has redeemed us"; but they can say "The Christ will come, and will redeem us," which, as the atonement is conceived as retrospective, is equally consoling. There are periods when nations are seething with this expectation and crying aloud with prophecy of the Redeemer through their poets. To feel that atmosphere we have only to take up the Bible and read Isaiah at one end of such a period and Luke and John at the other.

Completion of the Scheme by Luther and Calvin

We now see our religion as a quaint but quite intelligible evolution from crude attempts to propitiate the destructive forces of Nature among savages to a subtle theology with a costly ritual of sacrifice possible only to the rich as a luxury, and finally to the religion of Luther and Calvin. And it must be said for the earlier forms that they involved very real sacrifices. The sacrifice was not always vicarious, and is not yet universally so. In India men pay with their own skins, torturing themselves hideously to attain holiness. In the west, saints amazed the world with their austerities and self-scourgings and confessions and vigils. But Luther delivered us from all that. His reformation was a triumph of imagination and a triumph of cheapness. It brought you complete salvation and asked you for nothing but faith. Luther did not know what he was doing in the scientific sociological way in which we know it; but his instinct served him better than knowledge could have done; for it was instinct rather than theological casuistry that made him hold so resolutely to Justification by Faith as the trump card by which he should beat the Pope, or, as he would have put it, the sign in which he should conquer. He may be said to have abolished the charge for admission to heaven. Paul had advocated this; but Luther and Calvin did it.

John Barleycorn

There is yet another page in the history of religion which must be conned and digested before the career of Jesus can be fully understood. People who can read long books will find it in Frazer's Golden Bough. Simpler folk will find it in the peasant's song of John Barleycorn, now made accessible to our drawing room amateurs in the admirable collections of Somersetshire Folk Songs by Mr. Cecil Sharp. From Frazer's *magnum opus* you will learn how the same primitive logic which makes the Englishman believe today that by eating a beefsteak he can acquire the strength and courage of the bull, and to hold that belief in the face of the most ignominious defeats by vegetarian wrestlers and racers and bicyclists, led the first men who conceived God as capable of incarnation to believe that they could acquire a spark of his divinity by eating his flesh and drinking his blood. And from the song of John Barleycorn you may learn how the miracle of the seed, the growth, and the harvest, still the most wonderful of all the miracles and as inexplicable as ever, taught the primitive husbandman, and, as we must now affirm, taught him quite rightly, that God is in the seed, and that God is immortal. And thus it became the test of Godhead that nothing that you could do to it could kill it, and that when you buried it, it would rise again in renewed life and beauty and give mankind eternal life on condition that it was eaten and drunk, and again slain and buried, to rise again for ever and ever. You may, and indeed must, use John Barleycorn "right barbarouslee," cutting him "off at knee" with your scythes, scourging him with your flails, burying him in the earth; and he will not resist you nor reproach you, but will rise again in golden beauty amidst a great burst of sunshine and bird music, and save you and renew your life. And from the interweaving of these two traditions with the craving for the Redeemer, you at last get the conviction that when the Redeemer comes he will be immortal; he will give us his body to eat and his blood to drink; and he will prove his divinity by suffering a barbarous death without resistance or reproach, and rise from the dead and return to the earth in glory as the giver of life eternal.

Looking for the End of the World

Yet another persistent belief has beset the imagination of the religious ever since religion spread among the poor, or, rather, ever since commercial civilization produced a hopelessly poor class cut off from enjoyment in this world. That belief is that the end of this world is at hand, and that it will presently pass away and be replaced by a kingdom of happiness, justice, and bliss in which the rich and the oppressors and the unjust shall have no share. We are all familiar with this expectation: many of us cherish some pious relative who sees in every great calamity a sign of the approaching end. Warning pamphlets are in constant circulation: advertisements are put in the papers and paid for by those who are convinced, and who are horrified at the indifference of the irreligious to the approaching doom. And revivalist preachers, now as in the days of John the Baptist, seldom fail to warn their flocks to watch and pray, as the great day will steal upon them like a thief in the night, and cannot be long deferred in a world so wicked. This belief also associates itself with Barleycorn's second coming; so that the two events become identified at last.

There is the other and more artificial side of this belief, on which it is an inculcated dread. The ruler who appeals to the prospect of heaven to console the poor and keep them from insurrection also curbs the vicious by threatening them with hell. In the Koran we find Mahomet driven more and more to this expedient of government; and experience confirms his evident belief that it is impossible to govern without it in certain phases of civilization. We shall see later on that it gives a powerful attraction to the belief in a Redeemer, since it adds to remorse of conscience, which hardened men bear very lightly, a definite dread of hideous and eternal torture.

The Honor of Divine Parentage

One more tradition must be noted. The consummation of praise for a king is to declare that he is the son of no earthly father, but of a god. His mother goes into the temple of Apollo, and Apollo comes to her in the shape of a serpent, or the like. The Roman emperors, following the example of Augustus, claimed the title of God. Illogically, such divine kings insist a good deal on their royal human ancestors. Alexander, claiming to be the son of Apollo, is equally determined to be the son of Philip. As the gospels stand, St Matthew and St Luke give genealogies (the two are different) establishing the descent of Jesus through Joseph from the royal house of David, and yet declare that not Joseph but the Holy Ghost was the father of Jesus. It is therefore now held that the story of the Holy Ghost is a later interpolation borrowed from the Greek and Roman imperial tradition. But experience shews that simultaneous faith in the descent from David and the conception by the Holy Ghost is possible. Such double beliefs are entertained by the human mind without uneasiness or consciousness of the contradiction involved. Many instances might be given: a familiar one to my generation being that of the Tichborne claimant, whose attempt to pass himself off as a baronet was supported by an association of laborers on the ground that the Tichborne family, in resisting it, were trying to do a laborer out of his rights. It is quite possible that Matthew and Luke may have been unconscious of the contradiction: indeed the interpolation theory does not remove the difficulty, as the interpolators themselves must have been unconscious of it. A better ground for suspecting interpolation is that St Paul knew nothing of the divine birth, and taught that Jesus came into the world at his birth as the son of Joseph, but rose from the dead after three days as the son of God. Here again, few notice the discrepancy: the three views are accepted simultaneously without intellectual discomfort. We can provisionally entertain half a dozen contradictory versions of an event if we feel either that it does not greatly matter, or that there is a category attainable in which the contradictions are reconciled.

But that is not the present point. All that need be noted here is that the legend of divine birth was sure to be attached sooner or later to very eminent persons in Roman imperial times, and that modern theologians, far from discrediting it, have very logically affirmed the miraculous conception not only of Jesus but of his mother.

With no more scholarly equipment than a knowledge of these habits of the human imagination, anyone may now read the four gospels without bewilderment, and without the contemptuous incredulity which spoils the temper of many modern atheists, or the senseless credulity which sometimes makes pious people force us to shove them aside in emergencies as impracticable lunatics when they ask us to meet violence and injustice with dumb submission in the belief that the strange demeanor of Jesus before Pilate was meant as an example of normal human conduct. Let us admit that without the proper clues the gospels are, to a modern educated person, nonsensical and incredible, whilst the apostles are unreadable. But with the clues, they are fairly plain sailing. Jesus becomes an intelligible and consistent person. His reasons for going "like a lamb to the slaughter" instead of saving himself as Mahomet did, become quite clear. The narrative becomes as credible as any other historical narrative of its period.

Matthew

THE ANNUNCIATION:
THE MASSACRE: THE FLIGHT

Let us begin with the gospel of Matthew, bearing in mind that it does not profess to be the evidence of an eyewitness. It is a chronicle, founded, like other chronicles, on such evidence and records as the chronicler could get hold of. The only one of the evangelists who professes to give first-hand evidence as an eyewitness naturally takes care to say so; and the fact that Matthew makes no such pretension, and writes throughout as a chronicler, makes it clear that he is telling the story of Jesus as Holinshed told the story of Macbeth, except that, for a reason to be given later on, he must have collected his material and completed his book within the lifetime of persons contemporary with Jesus. Allowance must also be made for the fact that the gospel is written in the Greek language, whilst the first-hand traditions and the actual utterances of Jesus must have been in Aramaic, the dialect of Palestine. These distinctions are important, as you will find if you read Holinshed or Froissart and then read Benvenuto Cellini. You do not blame Holinshed or Froissart for believing and repeating the things they had read or been told, though you cannot always believe these things yourself. But when Cellini tells you that he saw this or did that, and you find it impossible to believe him,

you lose patience with him, and are disposed to doubt everything in his autobiography. Do not forget, then, that Matthew is Holinshed and not Benvenuto. The very first pages of his narrative will put your attitude to the test.

Matthew tells us that the mother of Jesus was betrothed to a man of royal pedigree named Joseph, who was rich enough to live in a house in Bethlehem to which kings could bring gifts of gold without provoking any comment. An angel announces to Joseph that Jesus is the son of the Holy Ghost, and that he must not accuse her of infidelity because of her bearing a son of which he is not the father; but this episode disappears from the subsequent narrative: there is no record of its having been told to Jesus, nor any indication of his having any knowledge of it. The narrative, in fact, proceeds in all respects as if the annunciation formed no part of it.

Herod the Tetrarch, believing that a child has been born who will destroy him, orders all the male children to be slaughtered; and Jesus escapes by the flight of his parents into Egypt, whence they return to Nazareth when the danger is over. Here it is necessary to anticipate a little by saying that none of the other evangelists accepts this story, as none of them except John, who throws over Matthew altogether, shares his craze for treating history and biography as mere records of the fulfilment of ancient Jewish prophecies. This craze no doubt led him to seek for some legend bearing out Hosea's "Out of Egypt have I called my son," and Jeremiah's Rachel weeping for her children: in fact, he says so. Nothing that interests us nowadays turns on the credibility of the massacre of the innocents and the flight into Egypt. We may forget them, and proceed to the important part of the narrative, which skips at once to the manhood of Jesus.

John the Baptist

At this moment, a Salvationist prophet named John is stirring the people very strongly. John has declared that the rite of circumcision is insufficient as a dedication of the individual to God, and has substituted the rite of baptism. To us, who are accustomed to baptism as a matter of course, and to whom circumcision is a rather ridiculous foreign practice of no consequence, the sensational effect of such a heresy as this on the Jews is not apparent: it seems to us as natural that John should have baptized people as that the rector of our village should do so. But, as St Paul found to his cost later on, the discarding of circumcision for baptism was to the Jews as startling a heresy as the discarding of transubstantiation in the Mass was to the Catholics of the XVI century.

Jesus Joins the Baptists

Jesus entered as a man of thirty (Luke says) into the religious life of his time by going to John the Baptist and demanding baptism from him, much as certain well-to-do young gentlemen forty years ago "joined the Socialists." As far as established Jewry was concerned, he burnt his boats by this action, and cut himself off from the routine of wealth, respectability, and orthodoxy. He then began preaching John's gospel, which, apart from the heresy of baptism, the value of which lay in its bringing the Gentiles (that is, the uncircumcized) within the pale of salvation, was a call to the people to repent of their sins, as the kingdom of heaven was at hand. Luke adds that he also preached the communism of charity; told the surveyors of taxes not to over-assess the taxpayers; and advised soldiers to be content with their wages and not to be violent or lay false accusations. There is no record of John going beyond this.

The Savage John and the Civilized Jesus

Jesus went beyond it very rapidly, according to Matthew. Though, like John, he became an itinerant preacher, he departed widely from John's manner of life. John went into the wilderness, not into the synagogues; and his baptismal font was the river Jordan. He was an ascetic, clothed in skins and living on locusts and wild honey, practising a savage austerity. He courted martyrdom, and met it at the hands of Herod. Jesus saw no merit either in asceticism or martyrdom. In contrast to John he was essentially a highly-civilized, cultivated person. According to Luke, he pointed out the contrast himself, chaffing the Jews for complaining that John must be possessed by the devil because he was a teetotaller and vegetarian, whilst, because Jesus was neither one nor the other, they reviled him as a gluttonous man and a wine-bibber, the friend of the officials and their mistresses. He told straitlaced disciples that they would have trouble enough from other people without making any for themselves, and that they should avoid martyrdom and enjoy themselves whilst they had the chance. "When they persecute you in this city," he says, "flee into the next." He preaches in the synagogues and in the open air indifferently, just as they come. He repeatedly says, "I desire mercy and not sacrifice," meaning evidently to clear himself of the inveterate superstition that suffering is gratifying to God. "Be not, as the Pharisees, of a sad countenance," he says. He is convivial, feasting with Roman officials and sinners. He is careless of his person, and is remonstrated with for not washing his hands before sitting down to table. The followers of John the Baptist, who fast, and who expect to find the Christians greater ascetics than themselves, are disappointed at finding that Jesus and his twelve friends do not fast; and Jesus tells them that they should rejoice in him instead of being melancholy. He is jocular, and tells them they will all have as much

fasting as they want soon enough, whether they like it or not. He is not afraid of disease, and dines with a leper. A woman, apparently to protect him against infection, pours a costly unguent on his head, and is rebuked because what it cost might have been given to the poor. He poohpoohs that lowspirited view, and says, as he said when he was reproached for not fasting, that the poor are always there to be helped, but that he is not there to be anointed always, implying that you should never lose a chance of being happy when there is so much misery in the world. He breaks the Sabbath; is impatient of conventionality when it is uncomfortable or obstructive; and outrages the feelings of the Jews by breaches of it. He is apt to accuse people who feel that way of hypocrisy. Like the late Samuel Butler, he regards disease as a department of sin, and on curing a lame man, says "Thy sins are forgiven" instead of "Arise and walk," subsequently maintaining, when the Scribes reproach him for assuming power to forgive sin as well as to cure disease, that the two come to the same thing. He has no modest affectations, and claims to be greater than Solomon or Jonah. When reproached, as Bunyan was, for resorting to the art of fiction when teaching in parables, he justifies himself on the ground that art is the only way in which the people can be taught. He is, in short, what we should call an artist and a Bohemian in his manner of life.

Jesus Not a Proselytist

A point of considerable practical importance today is that he expressly repudiates the idea that forms of religion, once rooted, can be weeded out and replanted with the flowers of a foreign faith. "If you try to root up the tares you will root up the wheat as well." Our proselytizing missionary enterprises are thus flatly contrary to his advice; and their results appear to bear him out in his view that if you convert a man brought up in another creed, you inevitably demoralize him. He acts on this view himself, and does not convert his disciples from Judaism to Christianity. To this day a Christian would be in religion a Jew initiated by baptism instead of circumcision, and accepting Jesus as the Messiah, and his teachings as of higher authority than those of Moses, but for the action of the Jewish priests, who, to save Jewry from being submerged in the rising flood of Christianity after the capture of Jerusalem and the destruction of the Temple, set up what was practically a new religious order, with new Scriptures and elaborate new observances, and to their list of the accursed added one Jeschu, a bastard magician, whose comic rogueries brought him to a bad end like Punch or Til Eulenspiegel: an invention which cost them dear when the Christians got the upper hand of them politically. The Jew as Jesus, himself a Jew, knew him, never dreamt of such things, and could follow Jesus without ceasing to be a Jew.

The Teachings of Jesus

So much for his personal life and temperament. His public career as a popular preacher carries him equally far beyond John the Baptist. He lays no stress on baptism or vows, and preaches conduct incessantly. He advocates communism, the widening of the private family with its cramping ties into the great family of mankind under the fatherhood of God, the abandonment of revenge and punishment, the counteracting of evil by good instead of by a hostile evil, and an organic conception of society in which you are not an independent individual but a member of society, your neighbor being another member, and each of you members one of another, as two fingers on a hand, the obvious conclusion being that unless you love your neighbor as yourself and he reciprocates you will both be the worse for it. He conveys all this with extraordinary charm, and entertains his hearers with fables (parables) to illustrate them. He has no synagogue or regular congregation, but travels from place to place with twelve men whom he has called from their work as he passed, and who have abandoned it to follow him.

The Miracles

He has certain abnormal powers by which he can perform miracles. He is ashamed of these powers, but, being extremely compassionate, cannot refuse to exercise them when afflicted people beg him to cure them, when multitudes of people are hungry, and when his disciples are terrified by storms on the lakes. He asks for no reward, but begs the people not to mention these powers of his. There are two obvious reasons for his dislike of being known as a worker of miracles. One is the natural objection of all men who possess such powers, but have far more important business in the world than to exhibit them, to be regarded primarily as charlatans, besides being pestered to give exhibitions to satisfy curiosity. The other is that his view of the effect of miracles upon his mission is exactly that taken later on by Rousseau. He perceives that they will discredit him and divert attention from his doctrine by raising an entirely irrelevant issue between his disciples and his opponents.

Possibly my readers may not have studied Rousseau's Letters Written From The Mountain, which may be regarded as the classic work on miracles as credentials of divine mission. Rousseau shews, as Jesus foresaw, that the miracles are the main obstacle to the acceptance of Christianity, because their incredibility (if they were not incredible they would not be miracles) makes people sceptical as to the whole narrative, credible enough in the main, in which they occur, and suspicious of the doctrine with which they are thus associated. "Get rid of the miracles," said Rousseau, "and the whole world will fall at the feet of Jesus Christ." He points out that miracles offered as evidence of divinity, and failing to convince, make divinity ridiculous. He says, in effect, there is nothing in making a lame man walk: thousands of lame men have been cured and have walked without any miracle. Bring me a man with only one leg and make another grow instantaneously on him before my eyes, and I will be really impressed; but mere cures of ailments that have often been cured before are quite useless as evidence of anything else than desire to help and power to cure.

Jesus, according to Matthew, agreed so entirely with Rousseau, and felt the danger so strongly, that when people who were not ill or in trouble came to him and asked him to exercise his powers as a sign of his mission, he was irritated beyond measure, and refused with an indignation which they, not seeing Rousseau's point, must have thought very unreasonable. To be called "an evil and adulterous generation" merely for asking a miracle worker to give an exhibition of his powers, is rather a startling experience. Mahomet, by the way, also lost his temper when people asked him to perform miracles. But Mahomet expressly disclaimed any unusual powers; whereas it is clear from Matthew's story that Jesus (unfortunately for himself, as he thought) had some powers of healing. It is also obvious that the exercise of such powers would give rise to wild tales of magical feats which would expose their hero to condemnation as an impostor among people whose good opinion was of great consequence to the movement started by his mission.

But the deepest annoyance arising from the miracles would be the irrelevance of the issue raised by them. Jesus's teaching has nothing to do with miracles. If his mission had been simply to demonstrate a new method of restoring lost eyesight, the miracle of curing the blind would have been entirely relevant. But to say "You should love your enemies; and to convince you of this I will now proceed to cure this gentleman of cataract" would have been, to a man of Jesus's intelligence, the proposition of an idiot. If it could be proved today that not one of the miracles of Jesus actually occurred, that proof would not invalidate a single one of his didactic utterances; and conversely, if it could be proved that not only did the miracles actually occur, but that he had wrought a thousand other miracles a thousand times more wonderful, not a jot of weight would be added to his doctrine. And yet the intellectual energy of sceptics and divines has been wasted for generations in arguing about the miracles on the assumption that Christianity is at stake in the controversy as to whether the stories of Matthew are false or true. According to Matthew himself, Jesus must have known this only too well; for wherever he went he was assailed with a clamor for miracles, though his doctrine created bewilderment.

So much for the miracles! Matthew tells us further,

that Jesus declared that his doctrines would be attacked by Church and State, and that the common multitude were the salt of the earth and the light of the world. His disciples, in their relations with the political and ecclesiastical organizations, would be as sheep among wolves.

Matthew Imputes Bigotry to Jesus

Matthew, like most biographers, strives to identify the opinions and prejudices of his hero with his own. Although he describes Jesus as tolerant even to carelessness, he draws the line at the Gentile, and represents Jesus as a bigoted Jew who regards his mission as addressed exclusively to "the lost sheep of the house of Israel." When a woman of Canaan begged Jesus to cure her daughter, he first refused to speak to her, and then told her brutally that "It is not meet to take the children's bread and cast it to the dogs." But when the woman said, "Truth, Lord; yet the dogs eat of the crumbs which fall from their master's table," she melted the Jew out of him and made Christ a Christian. To the woman whom he had just called a dog he said, "O woman, great is thy faith: be it unto thee even as thou wilt." This is somehow one of the most touching stories in the gospel; perhaps because the woman rebukes the prophet by a touch of his own finest quality. It is certainly out of character; but as the sins of good men are always out of character, it is not safe to reject the story as invented in the interest of Matthew's determination that Jesus shall have nothing to do with the Gentiles. At all events, there the story is; and it is by no means the only instance in which Matthew reports Jesus, in spite of the charm of his preaching, as extremely uncivil in private intercourse.

The Great Change

So far the history is that of a man sane and interesting apart from his special gifts as orator, healer, and prophet. But a startling change occurs. One day, after the disciples have discouraged him for a long time by their misunderstandings of his mission, and their speculations as to whether he is one of the old prophets come again, and if so, which, his disciple Peter suddenly solves the problem by exclaiming, "Thou art the Christ, the son of the living God." At this Jesus is extraordinarily pleased and excited. He declares that Peter has had a revelation straight from God. He makes a pun on Peter's name, and declares him the founder of his Church. And he accepts his destiny as a god by announcing that he will be killed when he goes to Jerusalem; for if he is really the Christ, it is a necessary part of his legendary destiny that he shall be slain. Peter, not understanding this, rebukes him for what seems mere craven melancholy; and Jesus turns fiercely on him and cries, "Get thee behind me, Satan."

Jesus now becomes obsessed with a conviction of his divinity, and talks about it continually to his disciples, though he forbids them to mention it to others. They begin to dispute among themselves as to the position they shall occupy in heaven when his kingdom is established. He rebukes them strenuously for this, and repeats his teaching that greatness means service and not domination; but he himself, always instinctively somewhat haughty, now becomes arrogant, dictatorial, and even abusive, never replying to his critics without an insulting epithet, and even cursing a fig-tree which disappoints him when he goes to it for fruit. He assumes all the traditions of the folk-lore gods, and announces that, like John Barleycorn, he will be barbarously slain and buried, but will rise from the earth and return to life. He attaches to himself the immemorial tribal ceremony of eating the god, by blessing bread and wine and handing them to his disciples with the words "This is my body: this is my blood." He forgets his own teaching and threatens eternal fire and eternal punishment. He announces, in addition to his Barleycorn resurrection, that he will come to the world a second time in glory and establish his kingdom on earth. He fears that this may lead to the appearance of impostors claiming to be himself, and declares explicitly and repeatedly that no matter what wonders these impostors may perform, his own coming will be unmistakable, as the stars will fall from heaven, and trumpets be blown by angels. Further he declares that this will take place during the lifetime of persons then present.

Jerusalem and the Mystical Sacrifice

In this new frame of mind he at last enters Jerusalem amid great popular curiosity; drives the money-changers and sacrifice sellers out of the temple in a riot; refuses to interest himself in the beauties and wonders of the temple building on the ground that presently not a stone of it shall be left on another; reviles the high priests and elders in intolerable terms; and is arrested by night in a garden to avoid a popular disturbance. He makes no resistance, being persuaded that it is part of his destiny as a god to be murdered and to rise again. One of his followers shews fight, and cuts off the ear of one of his captors. Jesus rebukes him, but does not attempt to heal the wound, though he declares that if he wished to resist he could easily summon twelve million angels to his aid. He is taken before the high priest and by him handed over to the Roman governor, who is puzzled by his silent refusal to defend himself in any way, or to contradict his accusers or their witnesses, Pilate having naturally no idea that the prisoner conceives himself as going through an inevitable process of torment, death, and burial as a prelude to resurrection. Before the high priest he has also been silent except that when the priest asks him is he the Christ, the Son of God, he replies that they shall all see the Son of Man sitting at the right hand of power, and coming on the clouds of heaven. He maintains this attitude with frightful fortitude whilst they scourge him, mock him, torment him, and finally crucify him between two thieves. His prolonged agony of thirst and pain on the cross at last breaks his spirit, and he dies with a cry of "My God: why hast Thou forsaken me?"

Not This Man but Barabbas

Meanwhile he has been definitely rejected by the people as well as by the priests. Pilate, pitying him, and unable to make out exactly what he has done (the blasphemy that has horrified the high priest does not move the Roman), tries to get him off by reminding the people that they have, by custom, the right to have a prisoner released at that time, and suggests that he should release Jesus. But they insist on his releasing a prisoner named Barabbas instead, and on having Jesus crucified. Matthew gives no clue to the popularity of Barabbas, describing him simply as "a notable prisoner." The later gospels make it clear, very significantly, that his offence was sedition and insurrection; that he was an advocate of physical force; and that he had killed his man. The choice of Barabbas thus appears as a popular choice of the militant advocate of physical force as against the unresisting advocate of mercy.

The Resurrection

Matthew then tells how after three days an angel opened the family vault of one Joseph, a rich man of Arimathea, who had buried Jesus in it, whereupon Jesus rose and returned from Jerusalem to Galilee and resumed his preaching with his disciples, assuring them that he would now be with them to the end of the world.

At that point the narrative abruptly stops. The story has no ending.

Date of Matthew's Narrative

One effect of the promise of Jesus to come again in glory during the lifetime of some of his hearers is to date the gospel without the aid of any scholarship. It must have been written during the lifetime of Jesus's contemporaries: that is, whilst it was still possible for the promise of his Second Coming to be fulfilled. The death of the last person who had been alive when Jesus said "There be some of them that stand here that shall in no wise taste death til they see the Son of Man coming in his kingdom" destroyed the last possibility of the promised Second Coming, and bore out the incredulity of Pilate and the Jews. And

as Matthew writes as one believing in that Second Coming, and in fact left his story unfinished to be ended by it, he must have produced his gospel within a lifetime of the crucifixion. Also, he must have believed that reading books would be one of the pleasures of the kingdom of heaven on earth.

Class Type of Matthew's Jesus

One more circumstance must be noted as gathered from Matthew. Though he begins his story in such a way as to suggest that Jesus belonged to the privileged classes, he mentions later on that when Jesus attempted to preach in his own country, and had no success there, the people said, "Is not this the carpenter's son?" But Jesus's manner throughout is that of an aristocrat, or at the very least the son of a rich bourgeois, and by no means a lowly-minded one at that. We must be careful therefore to conceive Joseph, not as a modern proletarian carpenter working for weekly wages, but as a master craftsman of royal descent. John the Baptist may have been a Keir Hardie; but the Jesus of Matthew is of the Ruskin-Morris class.

This haughty characterization is so marked that if we had no other documents concerning Jesus than the gospel of Matthew, we should not feel as we do about him. We should have been much less loth to say, "There is a man here who was sane until Peter hailed him as the Christ, and who then became a monomaniac." We should have pointed out that his delusion is a very common delusion among the insane, and that such insanity is quite consistent with the retention of the argumentative cunning and penetration which Jesus displayed in Jerusalem after his delusion had taken complete hold of him. We should feel horrified at the scourging and mocking and crucifixion just as we should if Ruskin had been treated in that way when he also went mad, instead of being cared for as an invalid. And we should have had no clear perception of any special significance in his way of calling the Son of God the Son of Man. We should have noticed that he was a Communist; that he regarded much of what we call law and order as machinery for robbing the poor under legal forms; that he thought domestic ties a snare for the soul; that he agreed with the proverb "The nearer the Church, the farther from God"; that he saw very plainly that the masters of the community should be its servants and not its oppressors and parasites; and that though he did not tell us not to fight our enemies, he did tell us to love them, and warned us that they who draw the sword shall perish by the sword. All this shews a great power of seeing through vulgar illusions, and a capacity for a higher morality than has yet been established in any civilized community; but it does not place Jesus above Confucius or Plato, not to mention more modern philosophers and moralists.

Mark

THE WOMEN DISCIPLES AND THE ASCENSION

Let us see whether we can get anything more out of Mark, whose gospel, by the way, is supposed to be older than Matthew's. Mark is brief; and it does not take long to discover that he adds nothing to Matthew except the ending of the story by Christ's ascension into heaven, and the news that many women had come with Jesus to Jerusalem, including Mary Magdalene, out of whom he had cast seven devils. On the other hand Mark says nothing about the birth of Jesus, and does not touch his career until his adult baptism by John. He apparently regards Jesus as a native of Nazareth, as John does, and not of Bethlehem, as Matthew and Luke do, Bethlehem being the city of David, from whom Jesus is said by Matthew and Luke to be descended. He describes John's doctrine as "Baptism of repentance unto remission of sins": that is, a form of Salvationism. He tells us that Jesus went into the synagogues and taught, not as the Scribes but as one having authority: that is, we infer, he preaches his own doctrine as an original moralist instead of repeating what the books say. He describes the miracle of Jesus reaching the boat by walking across the sea, but says nothing about Peter trying to do the same. Mark sees what he relates more vividly than Matthew, and gives touches of detail that bring the event more clearly before the reader. He says, for instance, that when Jesus walked on the waves to the boat, he was passing it by when the disciples called out to him. He seems to feel that Jesus's treatment of the woman of Canaan requires some apology, and therefore says that she was a Greek of Syrophenician race, which probably excused any incivility to her in Mark's eyes. He represents the father of the boy whom Jesus cured of epilepsy after the transfiguration as a sceptic who says "Lord, I believe: help thou mine unbelief." He tells the story of the widow's mite, omitted by Matthew. He explains that Barabbas was "lying bound with them that made insurrection, men who in the insurrection had committed murder." Joseph of Arimathea, who buried Jesus in his own tomb, and who is described by Matthew as a disciple, is described by Mark as "one who also himself was looking for the kingdom of God," which suggests that he was an independent seeker. Mark earns our gratitude by making no mention of the old prophecies, and thereby not only saves time, but avoids the absurd implication that Christ was merely going through a predetermined ritual, like the works of a clock, instead of living. Finally Mark reports Christ as saying, after his resurrection, that those who believe in him will be saved and those who do not, damned; but it is impossible to discover whether he means anything by a state of damnation beyond a state of error. The paleographers regard this passage as tacked on by a later scribe.

On the whole Mark leaves the modern reader where Matthew left him.

Luke

LUKE THE LITERARY ARTIST

When we come to Luke, we come to a later story-teller, and one with a stronger natural gift for his art. Before you have read twenty lines of Luke's gospel you are aware that you have passed from the chronicler writing for the sake of recording important facts, to the artist, telling the story for the sake of telling it. At the very outset he achieves the most charming idyll in the Bible: the story of Mary crowded out of the inn into the stable and laying her newly-born son in the manger, and of the shepherds abiding in the field keeping watch over their flocks by night, and how the angel of the Lord came upon them, and the glory of the Lord shone around them, and suddenly there was with the angel a multitude of the heavenly host. These shepherds go to the stable and take the place of the kings in Matthew's chronicle. So completely has this story conquered and fascinated our imagination that most of us suppose all the gospels to contain it; but it is Luke's story and his alone: none of the others have the smallest hint of it.

The Charm of Luke's Narrative

Luke gives the charm of sentimental romance to every incident. The Annunciation, as described by Matthew, is made to Joseph, and is simply a warning to him not to divorce his wife for misconduct. In Luke's gospel it is made to Mary herself, at much greater length, with a sense of the ecstasy of the bride of the Holy Ghost. Jesus is refined and softened almost out of recognition: the stern peremptory disciple of John the Baptist, who never addresses a Pharisee or a Scribe without an insulting epithet, becomes a considerate, gentle, sociable, almost urbane person; and the Chauvinist Jew becomes a pro-Gentile who is thrown out of the synagogue in his own town for reminding the congregation that the prophets had sometimes preferred Gentiles to Jews. In fact they try to throw him down from a sort of Tarpeian rock which they use for executions; but he makes his way through them and escapes: the only suggestion of a feat of arms on his part in the gospels. There is not a word of the Syrophenician woman. At the end he is calmly superior to his sufferings; delivers an address on his way to execution with unruffled composure; does not despair on the cross; and dies with perfect dignity, commending his spirit to God, after praying for the forgiveness of his persecutors on the ground that "They know not what they do." According to Matthew, it is part of the bitterness of his death that even the thieves who are crucified with him revile him. According to Luke, only one of them does this; and he is rebuked by the other, who begs

Jesus to remember him when he comes into his kingdom. To which Jesus replies, "This day shalt thou be with me in Paradise," implying that he will spend the three days of his death there. In short, every device is used to get rid of the ruthless horror of the Matthew chronicle, and to relieve the strain of the Passion by touching episodes, and by representing Christ as superior to human suffering. It is Luke's Jesus who has won our hearts.

The Touch of Parisian Romance

Luke's romantic shrinking from unpleasantness, and his sentimentality, are illustrated by his version of the woman with the ointment. Matthew and Mark describe it as taking place in the house of Simon the Leper, where it is objected to as a waste of money. In Luke's version the leper becomes a rich Pharisee; the woman becomes a Dame aux Camellias; and nothing is said about money and the poor. The woman washes the feet of Jesus with her tears and dries them with her hair; and he is reproached for suffering a sinful woman to touch him. It is almost an adaptation of the unromantic Matthew to the Parisian stage. There is a distinct attempt to increase the feminine interest all through. The slight lead given by Mark is taken up and developed. More is said about Jesus's mother and her feelings. Christ's following of women, just mentioned by Mark to account for their presence at his tomb, is introduced earlier; and some of the women are named; so that we are introduced to Joanna the wife of Chuza, Herod's steward, and Susanna. There is the quaint little domestic episode between Mary and Martha. There is the parable of the Prodigal Son, appealing to the indulgence romance has always shewn to Charles Surface and Des Grieux. Women follow Jesus to the cross; and he makes them a speech beginning "Daughters of Jerusalem." Slight as these changes may seem, they make a great change in the atmosphere. The Christ of Matthew could never have become what is vulgarly called a woman's hero (though the truth is that the popular demand for sentiment, as far as it is not simply human, is more manly than womanly); but the Christ of Luke has made possible those pictures which now hang in many ladies' chambers, in which Jesus is represented exactly as he is represented in the Lourdes cinematograph, by a handsome actor. The only touch of realism which Luke does not instinctively suppress for the sake of producing this kind of amenity is the reproach addressed to Jesus for sitting down to table without washing his hands; and that is retained because an interesting discourse hangs on it.

Waiting for the Messiah

Another new feature in Luke's story is that it begins in a world in which everyone is expecting the advent of the Christ. In Matthew and Mark, Jesus comes into a normal Philistine world like our own of today. Not until the Baptist foretells that one greater than himself shall come after him does the old Jewish hope of a Messiah begin to stir again; and as Jesus begins as a disciple of John, and is baptized by him, nobody connects him with that hope until Peter has the sudden inspiration which produces so startling an effect on Jesus. But in Luke's gospel men's minds, and especially women's minds, are full of eager expectation of a Christ not only before the birth of Jesus, but before the birth of John the Baptist, the events with which Luke begins his story. Whilst Jesus and John are still in their mothers' wombs, John leaps at the approach of Jesus when the two mothers visit one another. At the circumcision of Jesus pious men and women hail the infant as the Christ.

The Baptist himself is not convinced; for at quite a late period in his former disciple's career he sends two young men to ask Jesus is he really the Christ. This is noteworthy because Jesus immediately gives them a deliberate exhibition of miracles, and bids them tell John what they have seen, and ask him what he thinks *now*. This is in complete contradiction to what I have called the Rousseau view of miracles as inferred from Matthew. Luke shews all a romancer's thoughtlessness about miracles: he regards them as "signs": that is, as proofs of the divinity of the person performing them, and not merely of thaumaturgic powers. He revels in miracles just as he revels in parables: they make such capital stories. He cannot allow the calling of Peter, James, and John from their boats to pass without a comic miraculous overdraft of fishes, with the net sinking the boats and provoking Peter to exclaim, "Depart from me; for I am a sinful man, O Lord," which should probably be translated, "I want no more of your miracles: natural fishing is good enough for my boats."

There are some other novelties in Luke's version. Pilate sends Jesus to Herod, who happens to be in Jerusalem just then, because Herod had expressed some curiosity about him; but nothing comes of it: the prisoner will not speak to him. When Jesus is ill received in a Samaritan village James and John propose to call down fire from heaven and destroy it; and Jesus replies that he is come not to destroy lives but to save them. The bias of Jesus against lawyers is emphasized, and also his resolution not to admit that he is more bound to his relatives than to strangers. He snubs a woman who blesses his mother. As this is contrary to the traditions of sentimental romance, Luke would presumably have avoided it had he not become persuaded that the brotherhood of Man and the Fatherhood of God are superior even to sentimental considerations. The story of the lawyer asking what are the two chief commandments is changed by making Jesus put the question to the lawyer instead of answering it.

As to doctrine, Luke is only clear when his feelings are touched. His logic is weak; for some of the sayings of Jesus are pieced together wrongly, as anyone who has read them in the right order and context in Matthew will discover at once. He does not make anything new out of Christ's mission, and, like the other evangelists, thinks that the whole point of it is that Jesus was the long expected Christ, and that he will presently come back to earth and establish his kingdom, having duly died and risen again after three days. Yet Luke not only records the teachings as to communism and the discarding of hate, which have, of course, nothing to do with the Second Coming, but quotes one very remarkable saying which is not compatible with it, which is, that people must not go about asking where the kingdom of heaven is, and saying "Lo, here!" and "Lo, there!" because the kingdom of heaven is within them. But Luke has no sense that this belongs to a quite different order of thought to his Christianity, and retains undisturbed his view of the kingdom as a locality as definite as Jerusalem or Madagascar.

John

A NEW STORY AND A NEW CHARACTER

The gospel of John is a surprise after the others. Matthew, Mark and Luke describe the same events in the same order (the variations in Luke are negligible), and their gospels are therefore called the synoptic gospels. They tell substantially the same story of a wandering preacher who at the end of his life came to Jerusalem. John describes a preacher who spent practically his whole adult life in the capital, with occasional visits to the provinces. His circumstantial account of the calling of Peter and the sons of Zebedee is quite different from the others; and he says nothing about their being fishermen. He says expressly that Jesus, though baptized by John, did not himself practice baptism, and that his disciples did. Christ's agonized appeal against his doom in the garden of Gethsemane becomes a cold-blooded suggestion made in the temple at a much earlier period. Jesus argues much more; complains a good deal of the unreasonableness and dislike with which he is met; is by no means silent before Caiaphas and Pilate; lays much greater stress on his resurrection and on the eating of his body (losing all his disciples except the twelve in consequence); says many apparently contradictory and nonsensical things to which no ordinary reader can now find any clue; and gives the impression of an educated, not to say sophisticated mystic, different both in character and schooling from the simple and downright preacher of Matthew and Mark, and the urbane easy-minded charmer of Luke. Indeed, the Jews say of him "How knoweth this man letters, having never learnt?"

John the Immortal Eye-Witness

John, moreover, claims to be not only a chronicler but a witness. He declares that he is "the disciple whom Jesus loved," and that he actually leaned on the bosom of Jesus at the last supper and asked in a whisper which of them it was that should betray him. Jesus whispered that he would give a sop to the traitor, and thereupon handed one to Judas, who ate it and immediately became possessed by the devil. This is more natural than the other accounts, in which Jesus openly indicates Judas without eliciting any protest or exciting any comment. It also implies that Jesus deliberately bewitched Judas in order to bring about his own betrayal. Later on John claims that Jesus said to Peter "If I will that John tarry til I come, what is that to thee?" and John, with a rather obvious mock modesty, adds that he must not claim to be immortal, as the disciples concluded; for Christ did not use that expression, but merely remarked "If I will that he tarry til I come." No other evangelist claims personal intimacy with Christ, or even pretends to be his contemporary (there is no ground for identifying Matthew the publican with Matthew the Evangelist); and John is the only evangelist whose account of Christ's career and character is hopelessly irreconcilable with Matthew's. He is almost as bad as Matthew, by the way, in his repeated explanations of Christ's actions as having no other purpose than to fulfill the old prophecies. The impression is more unpleasant, because, as John, unlike Matthew, is educated, subtle, and obsessed with artificial intellectual mystifications, the discovery that he is stupid or superficial in so simple a matter strikes one with distrust and dislike, in spite of his great literary charm, a good example of which is his transfiguration of the harsh episode of the Syrophenician woman into the pleasant story of the woman of Samaria. This perhaps is why his claim to be John the disciple, or to be a contemporary of Christ or even of any survivor of Christ's generation, has been disputed, and finally, it seems, disallowed. But I repeat, I take no note here of the disputes of experts as to the date of the gospels, not because I am not acquainted with them, but because, as the earliest codices are Greek manuscripts of the fourth century A. D., and the Syrian ones are translations from the Greek, the paleographic expert has no difficulty in arriving at whatever conclusion happens to suit his beliefs or disbeliefs; and he never succeeds in convincing the other experts except when they believe or disbelieve exactly as he does. Hence I conclude that the dates of the original narratives cannot be ascertained, and that we must make the best of the evangelists' own accounts of themselves. There is, as we have seen, a very marked difference between them, leaving no doubt that we are dealing with four authors of well-marked diversity; but they all end in an attitude of expectancy of the Second Coming which they agree in declaring Jesus to have positively and unequivocally promised within the lifetime of his contemporaries. Any believer compiling a gospel after the last of these contemporaries had passed away, would either reject and omit the tradition of that promise on the ground that since it was not fulfilled, and could never now be fulfilled, it could not have been made, or else have had to confess to the Jews, who were the keenest critics of the Christians, that Jesus was either an impostor or the victim of a delusion. Now all the evangelists except Matthew expressly declare themselves to be believers; and Matthew's narrative is obviously not that of a sceptic. I therefore assume as a matter of common sense that, interpolations apart, the gospels are derived from narratives written in the first century A. D. I include John, because though it may be claimed that he hedged his position by claiming that Christ, who specially loved him, endowed him with a miraculous life until the Second Coming, the conclusion being that John is alive at this moment, I cannot believe that a literary forger could hope to save the situation by so outrageous a pretension. Also, John's narrative is in many passages nearer to the realities of public life than the simple chronicle of Matthew or the sentimental romance of Luke. This may be because John was obviously more a man of the world than the others, and knew, as mere chroniclers and romancers never know, what actually happens away from books and desks. But it may also be because he saw and heard what happened instead of collecting traditions about it. The paleographers and daters of first quotations may say what they please: John's claim to give evidence as an eye-witness whilst the others are only compiling history is supported by a certain verisimilitude which appeals to me as one who has preached a new doctrine and argued about it, as well as written stories. This verisimilitude may be dramatic art backed by knowledge of public life; but even at that we must not forget that the best dramatic art is the operation of a divinatory instinct for truth. Be that as it may, John was certainly not the man to believe in the Second Coming and yet give a date for it after that date had passed. There is really no escape from the conclusion that the originals of all the gospels date from the period within which there was still a possibility of the Second Coming occurring at the promised time.

The Peculiar Theology of Jesus

In spite of the suspicions roused by John's idiosyncrasies, his narrative is of enormous importance to those who go to the gospels for a credible modern religion. For it is John who adds to the other records such sayings as that "I and my father are one"; that "God is a spirit"; that the aim of Jesus is not only that the people should have life, but that they should have it "more abundantly" (a distinction much needed by people who think a man is either alive or

dead, and never consider the important question how much alive he is); and that men should bear in mind what they were told in the 82nd Psalm: that they are gods, and are responsible for the doing of the mercy and justice of God. The Jews stoned him for saying these things, and, when he remonstrated with them for stupidly stoning one who had done nothing to them but good works, replied "For a good work we stone thee not; but for blasphemy, because that thou, being a man, makest thyself God." He insists (referring to the 82nd Psalm) that if it is part of their own religion that they are gods on the assurance of God himself, it cannot be blasphemy for him, whom the Father sanctified and sent into the world, to say "I am the son of God." But they will not have this at any price; and he has to escape from their fury. Here the point is obscured by the distinction made by Jesus between himself and other men. He says, in effect, "If you are gods, then, à fortiori, I am a god." John makes him say this, just as he makes him say "I am the light of the world." But Matthew makes him say to the people "Ye are the light of the world." John has no grip of the significance of these scraps which he has picked up: he is far more interested in a notion of his own that men can escape death and do even more extraordinary things than Christ himself: in fact, he actually represents Jesus as promising this explicitly, and is finally led into the audacious hint that he, John, is himself immortal in the flesh. Still, he does not miss the significant sayings altogether. However inconsistent they may be with the doctrine he is consciously driving at, they appeal to some sub-intellectual instinct in him that makes him stick them in, like a child sticking tinsel stars on the robe of a toy angel.

John does not mention the ascension; and the end of his narrative leaves Christ restored to life, and appearing from time to time among his disciples. It is on one of these occasions that John describes the miraculous draught of fishes which Luke places at the other end of Christ's career, at the call of the sons of Zebedee.

John Agreed as to the Trial and Crucifixion

Although John, following his practice of shewing Jesus's skill as a debater, makes him play a less passive part at his trial, he still gives substantially the same account of it as all the rest. And the question that would occur to any modern reader never occurs to him, any more than it occurred to Matthew, Mark, or Luke. That question is, Why on earth did not Jesus defend himself, and make the people rescue him from the High Priest? He was so popular that they were unable to prevent him driving the money-changers out of the temple, or to arrest him for it. When they did arrest him afterwards, they had to do it at night in a garden. He could have argued with them as he had often done in the temple, and justified himself both to the Jewish law and to Caesar. And he had physical force at his command to back up his arguments: all that was needed was a speech to rally his followers; and he was not gagged. The reply of the evangelists would have been that all these inquiries are idle, because if Jesus had wished to escape, he could have saved himself all that trouble by doing what John describes him as doing: that is, casting his captors to the earth by an exertion of his miraculous power. If you asked John why he let them get up again and torment and execute him, John would have replied that it was part of the destiny of God to be slain and buried and to rise again, and that to have avoided this destiny would have been to repudiate his Godhead. And that is the only apparent explanation. Whether you believe with the evangelists that Christ could have rescued himself by a miracle, or, as a modern Secularist, point out that he could have defended himself effectually, the fact remains that according to all the narratives he did not do so. He had to die like a god, not to save himself "like one of the princes."[1] The consensus on this point is important, because it proves the absolute sincerity of Jesus's declaration that he was a god. No impostor would have accepted such dreadful consequences without an effort to save himself. No impostor would have been nerved to endure them by the conviction that he would rise from the grave and live again after three days. If we accept the story at all, we must believe this, and believe also that his promise to return in glory and establish his kingdom on earth within the lifetime of men then living, was one which he believed that he could, and indeed must fulfil. Two evangelists declare that in his last agony he despaired, and reproached God for forsaking him. The other two represent him as dying in unshaken conviction and charity with the simple remark that the ordeal was finished. But all four testify that his faith was not deceived, and that he actually rose again after three days. And I think it unreasonable to doubt that all four wrote their narratives in full faith that the other promise would be fulfilled too, and that they themselves might live to witness the Second Coming.

Credibility of the Gospels

It will be noted by the older among my readers, who are sure to be obsessed more or less by elderly wrangles as to whether the gospels are credible as matter-of-fact narratives, that I have hardly raised

[1] *Jesus himself had referred to that psalm (LXXXII) in which men who have judged unjustly and accepted the persons of the wicked (including by anticipation practically all the white inhabitants of the British Isles and the North American continent, to mention no other places) are condemned in the words, "I have said, ye are gods; and all of ye are children of the Most High; but ye shall die like men, and fall like one of the princes."*

this question, and have accepted the credible and incredible with equal complacency. I have done this because credibility is a subjective condition, as the evolution of religious belief clearly shews. Belief is not dependent on evidence and reason. There is as much evidence that the miracles occurred as that the battle of Waterloo occurred, or that a large body of Russian troops passed through England in 1914 to take part in the war on the western front. The reasons for believing in the murder of Pompey are the same as the reasons for believing in the raising of Lazarus. Both have been believed and doubted by men of equal intelligence. Miracles, in the sense of phenomena we cannot explain, surround us on every hand: life itself is the miracle of miracles. Miracles in the sense of events that violate the normal course of our experience are vouched for every day: the flourishing Church of Christ Scientist is founded on a multitude of such miracles. Nobody believes all the miracles: everybody believes some of them. I cannot tell why men who will not believe that Jesus ever existed yet believe firmly that Shakespear was Bacon. I cannot tell why people who believe that angels appeared and fought on our side at the battle of Mons, and who believe that miracles occur quite frequently at Lourdes, nevertheless boggle at the miracle of the liquefaction of the blood of St Januarius, and reject it as a trick of priestcraft. I cannot tell why people who will not believe Matthew's story of three kings bringing costly gifts to the cradle of Jesus, believe Luke's story of the shepherds and the stable. I cannot tell why people, brought up to believe the Bible in the old literal way as an infallible record and revelation, and rejecting that view later on, begin by rejecting the Old Testament, and give up the belief in a brimstone hell before they give up (if they ever do) the belief in a heaven of harps, crowns, and thrones. I cannot tell why people who will not believe in baptism on any terms believe in vaccination with the cruel fanaticism of inquisitors. I am convinced that if a dozen sceptics were to draw up in parallel columns a list of the events narrated in the gospels which they consider credible and incredible respectively, their lists would be different in several particulars. Belief is literally a matter of taste.

Fashions in Belief

Now matters of taste are mostly also matters of fashion. We are conscious of a difference between medieval fashions in belief and modern fashions. For instance, though we are more credulous than men were in the Middle Ages, and entertain such crowds of fortune-tellers, magicians, miracle workers, agents of communication with the dead, discoverers of the elixir of life, transmuters of metals, and healers of all sorts, as the Middle Ages never dreamed of as possible, yet we will not take our miracles in the form that convinced the Middle Ages. Arithmetical numbers appealed to the Middle Ages just as they do to us, because they are difficult to deal with, and because the greatest masters of numbers, the Newtons and Leibnitzes, rank among the greatest men. But there are fashions in numbers too. The Middle Ages took a fancy to some familiar number like seven; and because it was an odd number, and the world was made in seven days, and there are seven stars in Charles's Wain, and for a dozen other reasons, they were ready to believe anything that had a seven or a seven times seven in it. Seven deadly sins, seven swords of sorrow in the heart of the Virgin, seven champions of Christendom, seemed obvious and reasonable things to believe in simply because they were seven. To us, on the contrary, the number seven is the stamp of superstition. We will believe in nothing less than millions. A medieval doctor gained his patient's confidence by telling him that his vitals were being devoured by seven worms. Such a diagnosis would ruin a modern physician. The modern physician tells his patient that he is ill because every drop of his blood is swarming with a million microbes; and the patient believes him abjectly and instantly. Had a bishop told William the Conqueror that the sun was seventy-seven miles distant from the earth, William would have believed him not only out of respect for the Church, but because he would have felt that seventy-seven miles was the proper distance. The Kaiser, knowing just as little about it as the Conqueror, would send that bishop to an asylum. Yet he (I presume) unhesitatingly accepts the estimate of ninety-two and nine-tenths millions of miles, or whatever the latest big figure may be.

Credibility and Truth

And here I must remind you that our credulity is not to be measured by the truth of the things we believe. When men believed that the earth was flat, they were not credulous: they were using their common sense, and, if asked to prove that the earth was flat, would have said simply, "Look at it." Those who refuse to believe that it is round are exercising a wholesome scepticism. The modern man who believes that the earth is round is grossly credulous. Flat Earth men drive him to fury by confuting him with the greatest ease when he tries to argue about it. Confront him with a theory that the earth is cylindrical, or annular, or hour-glass shaped, and he is lost. The thing he believes may be true, but that is not why he believes it: he believes it because in some mysterious way it appeals to his imagination. If you ask him why he believes that the sun is ninety-odd million miles off, either he will have to confess that he doesn't know, or he will say that Newton proved it. But he has not read the treatise in which Newton proved it, and does not even know that it was written in Latin. If you press an Ulster Protestant as to why he regards Newton as an infallible authority, and

St Thomas Aquinas or the Pope as superstitious liars whom, after his death, he will have the pleasure of watching from his place in heaven whilst they roast in eternal flame, or if you ask me why I take into serious consideration Colonel Sir Almroth Wright's estimates of the number of streptococci contained in a given volume of serum whilst I can only laugh at the earlier estimates of the number of angels that can be accommodated on the point of a needle, no reasonable reply is possible except that somehow sevens and angels are out of fashion, and billions and streptococci are all the rage. I simply cannot tell you why Bacon, Montaigne, and Cervantes had a quite different fashion of credulity and incredulity from the Venerable Bede and Piers Plowman and the divine doctors of the Aquinas-Aristotle school, who were certainly no stupider, and had the same facts before them. Still less can I explain why, if we assume that these leaders of thought had all reasoned out their beliefs, their authority seemed conclusive to one generation and blasphemous to another, neither generation having followed the reasoning or gone into the facts of the matter for itself at all.

It is therefore idle to begin disputing with the reader as to what he should believe in the gospels and what he should disbelieve. He will believe what he can, and disbelieve what he must. If he draws any lines at all, they will be quite arbitrary ones. St John tells us that when Jesus explicitly claimed divine honors by the sacrament of his body and blood, so many of his disciples left him that their number was reduced to twelve. Many modern readers will not hold out so long: they will give in at the first miracle. Others will discriminate. They will accept the healing miracles, and reject the feeding of the multitude. To some the walking on the water will be a legendary exaggeration of a swim, ending in an ordinary rescue of Peter; and the raising of Lazarus will be only a similar glorification of a commonplace feat of artificial respiration, whilst others will scoff at it as a planned imposture in which Lazarus acted as a confederate. Between the rejection of the stories as wholly fabulous and the acceptance of them as the evangelists themselves mean them to be accepted, there will be many shades of belief and disbelief, of sympathy and derision. It is not a question of being a Christian or not. A Mahometan Arab will accept literally and without question parts of the narrative which an English Archbishop has to reject or explain away; and many Theosophists and lovers of the wisdom of India, who never enter a Christian Church except as sightseers, will revel in parts of John's gospel which mean nothing to a pious matter-of-fact Bradford manufacturer. Every reader takes from the Bible what he can get. In submitting a précis of the gospel narratives I have not implied any estimate either of their credibility or of their truth. I have simply informed him or reminded him, as the case may be, of what those narratives tell us about their hero.

Christian Iconolatry and the Peril of the Iconoclast

I must now abandon this attitude, and make a serious draft on the reader's attention by facing the question whether, if and when the medieval and Methodist will-to-believe the Salvationist and miraculous side of the gospel narratives fails us, as it plainly has failed the leaders of modern thought, there will be anything left of the mission of Jesus: whether, in short, we may not throw the gospels into the wastepaper basket, or put them away on the fiction shelf of our libraries. I venture to reply that we shall be, on the contrary, in the position of the man in Bunyan's riddle who found that "the more he threw away, the more he had." We get rid, to begin with, of the idolatrous or iconographic worship of Christ. By this I mean literally that worship which is given to pictures and statues of him, and to finished and unalterable stories about him. The test of the prevalence of this is that if you speak or write of Jesus as a real live person, or even as a still active God, such worshippers are more horrified than Don Juan was when the statue stepped from its pedestal and came to supper with him. You may deny the divinity of Jesus; you may doubt whether he ever existed; you may reject Christianity for Judaism, Mahometanism, Shintoism, or Fire Worship; and the iconolaters, placidly contemptuous, will only classify you as a freethinker or a heathen. But if you venture to wonder how Christ would have looked if he had shaved and had his hair cut, or what size in shoes he took, or whether he swore when he stood on a nail in the carpenter's shop, or could not button his robe when he was in a hurry, or whether he laughed over the repartees by which he baffled the priests when they tried to trap him into sedition and blasphemy, or even if you tell any part of his story in the vivid terms of modern colloquial slang, you will produce an extraordinary dismay and horror among the iconolaters. You will have made the picture come out of its frame, the statue descend from its pedestal, the story become real, with all the incalculable consequences that may flow from this terrifying miracle. It is at such moments that you realize that the iconolaters have never for a moment conceived Christ as a real person who meant what he said, as a fact, as a force like electricity, only needing the invention of suitable political machinery to be applied to the affairs of mankind with revolutionary effect.

Thus it is not disbelief that is dangerous in our society: it is belief. The moment it strikes you (as it may any day) that Christ is not the lifeless harmless image he has hitherto been to you, but a rallying centre for revolutionary influences which all established States and Churches fight, you must look to yourselves; for you have brought the image to life; and the mob may not be able to bear that horror.

The Alternative to Barabbas

But mobs must be faced if civilization is to be saved. It did not need the present war to shew that neither the iconographic Christ nor the Christ of St Paul has succeeded in effecting the salvation of human society. Whilst I write, the Turks are said to be massacring the Armenian Christians on an unprecedented scale; but Europe is not in a position to remonstrate; for her Christians are slaying one another by every device which civilization has put within their reach as busily as they are slaying the Turks. Barabbas is triumphant everywhere; and the final use he makes of his triumph is to lead us all to suicide with heroic gestures and resounding lies. Now those who, like myself, see the Barabbasque social organization as a failure, and are convinced that the Life Force (or whatever you choose to call it) cannot be finally beaten by any failure, and will even supersede humanity by evolving a higher species if we cannot master the problems raised by the multiplication of our own numbers, have always known that Jesus had a real message, and have felt the fascination of his character and doctrine. Not that we should nowadays dream of claiming any supernatural authority for him, much less the technical authority which attaches to an educated modern philosopher and jurist. But when, having entirely got rid of Salvationist Christianity, and even contracted a prejudice against Jesus on the score of his involuntary connection with it, we engage on a purely scientific study of economics, criminology, and biology, and find that our practical conclusions are virtually those of Jesus, we are distinctly pleased and encouraged to find that we were doing him an injustice, and that the nimbus that surrounds his head in the pictures may be interpreted some day as a light of science rather than a declaration of sentiment or a label of idolatry.

The doctrines in which Jesus is thus confirmed are, roughly, the following:

1. The kingdom of heaven is within you. You are the son of God; and God is the son of man. God is a spirit, to be worshipped in spirit and in truth, and not an elderly gentleman to be bribed and begged from. We are members one of another; so that you cannot injure or help your neighbor without injuring or helping yourself. God is your father: you are here to do God's work; and you and your father are one.

2. Get rid of property by throwing it into the common stock. Dissociate your work entirely from money payments. If you let a child starve you are letting God starve. Get rid of all anxiety about tomorrow's dinner and clothes, because you cannot serve two masters: God and Mammon.

3. Get rid of judges and punishment and revenge. Love your neighbor as yourself, he being a part of yourself. And love your enemies: they are your neighbors.

4. Get rid of your family entanglements. Every

mother you meet is as much your mother as the woman who bore you. Every man you meet is as much your brother as the man she bore after you. Don't waste your time at family funerals grieving for your relatives: attend to life, not to death: there are as good fish in the sea as ever came out of it, and better. In the kingdom of heaven, which, as aforesaid, is within you, there is no marriage nor giving in marriage, because you cannot devote your life to two divinities: God and the person you are married to.

Now these are very interesting propositions; and they become more interesting every day, as experience and science drive us more and more to consider them favorably. In considering them, we shall waste our time unless we give them a reasonable construction. We must assume that the man who saw his way through such a mass of popular passion and illusion as stands between us and a sense of the value of such teaching was quite aware of all the objections that occur to an average stockbroker in the first five minutes. It is true that the world is governed to a considerable extent by the considerations that occur to stockbrokers in the first five minutes; but as the result is that the world is so badly governed that those who know the truth can hardly bear to live in it, an objection from an average stockbroker constitutes in itself a *prima facie* case for any social reform.

The Reduction to Modern Practice of Christianity

All the same, we must reduce the ethical counsels and proposals of Jesus to modern practice if they are to be of any use to us. If we ask our stockbroker to act simply as Jesus advised his disciples to act, he will reply, very justly, "You are advising me to become a tramp." If we urge a rich man to sell all that he has and give it to the poor, he will inform us that such an operation is impossible. If he sells his shares and his lands, their purchaser will continue all those activities which oppress the poor. If all the rich men take the advice simultaneously the shares will fall to zero and the lands be unsaleable. If one man sells out and throws the money into the slums, the only result will be to add himself and his dependents to the list of the poor, and to do no good to the poor beyond giving a chance few of them a drunken spree. We must therefore bear in mind that whereas, in the time of Jesus, and in the ages which grew darker and darker after his death until the darkness, after a brief false dawn in the Reformation and the Renascence, culminated in the commercial night of the nineteenth century, it was believed that you could not make men good by Act of Parliament, we now know that you cannot make them good in any other way, and that a man who is better than his fellows is a nuisance. The rich man must sell up not only himself but his whole class; and that can be done only through the Chancellor of the Exchequer. The disciple cannot have his

bread without money until there is bread for everybody without money; and that requires an elaborate municipal organization of the food supply, rate supported. Being members one of another means One Man One Vote, and One Woman One Vote, and universal suffrage and equal incomes and all sorts of modern political measures. Even in Syria in the time of Jesus his teachings could not possibly have been realized by a series of independent explosions of personal righteousness on the part of the separate units of the population. Jerusalem could not have done what even a village community cannot do, and what Robinson Crusoe himself could not have done if his conscience, and the stern compulsion of Nature, had not imposed a common rule on the half dozen Robinson Crusoes who struggled within him for not wholly compatible satisfactions. And what cannot be done in Jerusalem or Juan Fernandez cannot be done in London, New York, Paris, and Berlin.

In short, Christianity, good or bad, right or wrong, must perforce be left out of the question in human affairs until it is made practically applicable to them by complicated political devices; and to pretend that a field preacher under the governorship of Pontius Pilate, or even Pontius Pilate himself in council with all the wisdom of Rome, could have worked out applications of Christianity or any other system of morals for the twentieth century, is to shelve the subject much more effectually than Nero and all its other persecutors ever succeeded in doing. Personal righteousness, and the view that you cannot make people moral by Act of Parliament, is, in fact, the favorite defensive resort of the people who, consciously or subconsciously, are quite determined not to have their property meddled with by Jesus or any other reformer.

Modern Communism

Now let us see what modern experience and sociology have to say to the suggestion of Jesus that you should get rid of your property by throwing it into the common stock. One can hear the Pharisees of Jerusalem and Chorazin and Bethsaida saying, "My good fellow, if you were to divide up the wealth of Judea equally today, before the end of the year you would have rich and poor, poverty and affluence, just as you have today; for there will always be the idle and the industrious, the thrifty and the wasteful, the drunken and the sober; and, as you yourself have very justly observed, the poor we shall have always with us." And we can hear the reply, "Woe unto you, liars and hypocrites; for ye have this very day divided up the wealth of the country yourselves, as must be done every day (for man liveth not otherwise than from hand to mouth, nor can fish and eggs endure for ever); and ye have divided it unjustly; also ye have said that my reproach to you for having the poor always with you was a law unto you that this evil should persist and stink in the nostrils of God to all eternity; wherefore I think that Lazarus will yet see you beside Dives in hell." Modern Capitalism has made short work of the primitive pleas for inequality. The Pharisees themselves have organized communism in capital. Joint stock is the order of the day. An attempt to return to individual properties as the basis of our production would smash civilization more completely than ten revolutions. You cannot get the fields tilled today until the farmer becomes a co-operator. Take the shareholder to his railway, and ask him to point out to you the particular length of rail, the particular seat in the railway carriage, the particular lever in the engine that is his very own and nobody elses; and he will shun you as a madman, very wisely. And if, like Ananias and Sapphira, you try to hold back your little shop or what not from the common stock, represented by the Trust, or Combine, or Kartel, the Trust will presently freeze you out and rope you in and finally strike you dead industrially as thoroughly as St Peter himself. There is no longer any practical question open as to Communism in production: the struggle today is over the distribution of the product: that is, over the daily dividing-up which is the first necessity of organized society.

Redistribution

Now it needs no Christ to convince anybody today that our system of distribution is wildly and monstrously wrong. We have million-dollar babies side by side with paupers worn out by a long life of unremitted drudgery. One person in every five dies in a workhouse, a public hospital, or a madhouse. In cities like London the proportion is very nearly one in two. Naturally so outrageous a distribution has to be effected by violence pure and simple. If you demur, you are sold up. If you resist the selling up you are bludgeoned and imprisoned, the process being euphemistically called the maintenance of law and order. Iniquity can go no further. By this time nobody who knows the figures of the distribution defends them. The most bigoted British Conservative hesitates to say that his king should be much poorer than Mr Rockefeller, or to proclaim the moral superiority of prostitution to needlework on the ground that it pays better. The need for a drastic redistribution of income in all civilized countries is now as obvious and as generally admitted as the need for sanitation.

Shall He Who Makes, Own?

It is when we come to the question of the proportions in which we are to redistribute that controversy begins. We are bewildered by an absurdly unpractical notion that in some way a man's income should be given to him, not to enable him to live, but as a sort of Sunday School Prize for good behavior. And this folly is complicated by a less ridiculous but quite as unpractical belief that it is possible to assign to each person the exact portion of the national income that he or she has produced. To a child it seems that the blacksmith has made a horse-shoe, and that therefore the horse-shoe is his. But the blacksmith knows that the horse-shoe does not belong solely to him, but to his landlord, to the rate collector and taxgatherer, to the men from whom he bought the iron and anvil and the coals, leaving only a scrap of its value for himself; and this scrap he has to exchange with the butcher and baker and the clothier for the things that he really appropriates as living tissue or its wrappings, paying for all of them more than their cost; for these fellow traders of his have also their landlords and moneylenders to satisfy. If, then, such simple and direct village examples of apparent individual production turn out on a moment's examination to be the products of an elaborate social organization, what is to be said of such products as dreadnoughts, factory-made pins and needles, and steel pens? If God takes the dreadnought in one hand and a steel pen in the other, and asks Job who made them, and to whom they should belong by maker's right, Job must scratch his puzzled head with a potsherd and be dumb, unless indeed it strikes him that God is the ultimate maker, and that all we have a right to do with the product is to feed his lambs.

Labor Time

So maker's right as an alternative to taking the advice of Jesus would not work. In practice nothing was possible in that direction but to pay a worker by labor time: so much an hour or day or week or year. But how much? When that question came up, the only answer was "as little as he can be starved into accepting," with the ridiculous results already mentioned, and the additional anomaly that the largest share went to the people who did not work at all, and the least to those who worked hardest. In England nine-tenths of the wealth goes into the pockets of one-tenth of the population.

The Dream of Distribution According to Merit

Against this comes the protest of the Sunday School theorists "Why not distribute according to merit?" Here one imagines Jesus, whose smile has been broadening down the ages as attempt after attempt to escape from his teaching has led to deeper and deeper disaster, laughing outright. Was ever so idiotic a project mooted as the estimation of virtue in money? The London School of Economics is, we must suppose, to set examination papers with such questions as, "Taking the money value of the virtues of Jesus as 100, and of Judas Iscariot as zero, give the correct figures for, respectively, Pontius Pilate, the proprietor of the Gadarene swine, the widow who put her mite in the poor-box, Mr Horatio Bottomley, Shakespear,

Mr Jack Johnson, Sir Isaac Newton, Palestrina, Offenbach, Sir Thomas Lipton, Mr Paul Cinquevalli, your family doctor, Florence Nightingale, Mrs Siddons, your charwoman, the Archbishop of Canterbury, and the common hangman." Or "The late Mr Barney Barnato received as his lawful income three thousand times as much money as an English agricultural laborer of good general character. Name the principal virtues in which Mr Barnato exceeded the laborer three thousandfold; and give in figures the loss sustained by civilization when Mr Barnato was driven to despair and suicide by the reduction of his multiple to one thousand." The Sunday School idea, with its principle "to each the income he deserves," is really too silly for discussion. Hamlet disposed of it three hundred years ago. "Use every man after his deserts, and who shall scape whipping?" Jesus remains unshaken as the practical man; and we stand exposed as the fools, the blunderers, the unpractical visionaries. The moment you try to reduce the Sunday School idea to figures you find that it brings you back to the hopeless plan of paying for a man's time; and your examination paper will read "The time of Jesus was worth nothing (he complained that the foxes had holes and the birds of the air nests whilst he had not a place to lay his head). Dr Crippen's time was worth, say, three hundred and fifty pounds a year. Criticize this arrangement; and, if you dispute its justice, state in pounds, dollars, francs and marks, what their relative time wages ought to have been." Your answer may be that the question is in extremely bad taste and that you decline to answer it. But you cannot object to being asked how many minutes of a bookmaker's time are worth two hours of an astronomer's?

Vital Distribution

In the end you are forced to ask the question you should have asked at the beginning. What do you give a man an income for? Obviously to keep him alive. Since it is evident that the first condition on which he can be kept alive without enslaving somebody else is that he shall produce an equivalent for what it costs to keep him alive, we may quite rationally compel him to abstain from idling by whatever means we employ to compel him to abstain from murder, arson, forgery, or any other crime. The one supremely foolish thing to do with him is to do nothing: that is, to be as idle, lazy, and heartless in dealing with him as he is in dealing with us. Even if we provided work for him instead of basing, as we do, our whole industrial system on successive competitive waves of overwork with their ensuing troughs of unemployment, we should still sternly deny him the alternative of not doing it; for the result must be that he will become poor and make his children poor if he has any; and poor people are cancers in the commonwealth, costing far more than if they were

handsomely pensioned off as incurables. Jesus had more sense than to propose anything of the sort. He said to his disciples, in effect, "Do your work for love; and let the other people lodge and feed and clothe you for love." Or, as we should put it nowadays, "for nothing." All human experience and all natural uncommercialized human aspiration point to this as the right path. The Greeks said, "First secure an independent income; and then practise virtue." We all strive towards an independent income. We all know as well as Jesus did that if we have to take thought for the morrow as to whether there shall be anything to eat or drink it will be impossible for us to think of nobler things, or live a higher life than that of a mole, whose life is from beginning to end a frenzied pursuit of food. Until the community is organized in such a way that the fear of bodily want is forgotten as completely as the fear of wolves already is in civilized capitals, we shall never have a decent social life. Indeed the whole attraction of our present arrangement lies in the fact that it does relieve a handful of us from this fear; but as the relief is effected stupidly and wickedly by making the favored handful parasitic on the rest, they are smitten with the degeneracy which seems to be the inevitable biological penalty of complete parasitism. They corrupt culture and statecraft instead of contributing to them, their excessive leisure being as mischievous as the excessive toil of the laborers. Anyhow, the moral is clear. The two main problems of organized society: how to produce subsistence enough for all its members, and how to prevent the theft of that subsistence by idlers, should be carefully dissociated; for the triumphant solution of the first by our inventors and chemists has been offset by the disastrous failure of our rulers to solve the other. Optimism on this point is only wilful blindness: we all have the hard fact of the failure before us. The only people who cling to the lazy delusion that it is possible to find a just distribution that will work automatically are those who postulate some revolutionary change like land nationalization, which by itself would obviously only force into greater urgency the problem of how to distribute the product of the land among all the individuals in the community.

Equal Distribution

When that problem is at last faced, the question of the proportion in which the national income shall be distributed can have only one answer. All our shares must be equal. It has always been so: it always will be so. It is true that the incomes of robbers vary considerably from individual to individual; and the variation is reflected in the incomes of their parasites. The commercialization of certain exceptional talents has also produced exceptional incomes, direct and derivative. Persons who live on rent of land and capital are economically, though not legally, in the category of robbers, and have grotesquely different incomes. But in the huge mass of mankind variation of income from individual to individual is unknown, because it is ridiculously impracticable. As a device for persuading a carpenter that a judge is a creature of superior nature to himself, to be deferred and submitted to even to the death, we may give a carpenter a hundred pounds a year and a judge five thousand; but the wage for one carpenter is the wage for all the carpenters: the salary for one judge is the salary for all the judges.

The Captain and the Cabin Boy

Nothing, therefore, is really in question, or ever has been, but the differences between class incomes. Already there is economic equality between captains, and economic equality between cabin boys. What is at issue still is whether there shall be economic equality between captains and cabin boys. What would Jesus have said? Presumably he would have said that if your only object is to produce a captain and a cabin boy for the purpose of transferring you from Liverpool to New York, or to manœuvre a fleet and carry powder from the magazine to the gun, then you need give no more than a shilling to the cabin boy for every pound you give to the more expensively trained captain. But if in addition to this you desire to allow the two human souls which are inseparable from the captain and the cabin boy, and which alone differentiate them from the donkey-engine, to develop all their possibilities, then you may find the cabin boy costing rather more than the captain, because cabin boy's work does not do so much for the soul as captain's work. Consequently you will have to give him at least as much as the captain unless you definitely wish him to be a lower creature, in which case the sooner you are hanged as an abortionist the better. That is the fundamental argument.

The Political and Biological Objections to Inequality

But there are other reasons for objecting to class stratification of income which have heaped themselves up since the time of Jesus. In politics it defeats every form of government except that of a necessarily corrupt oligarchy. Democracy in the most democratic modern republics: France and the United States for example, is an imposture and a delusion. It reduces justice and law to a farce: law becomes merely an instrument for keeping the poor in subjection; and accused workmen are tried, not by a jury of their peers, but by conspiracies of their exploiters. The press is the press of the rich and the curse of the poor: it becomes dangerous to teach men to read. The priest becomes the mere complement of the policeman in the machinery by which the countryhouse oppresses the village. Worst of all, marriage becomes a class affair:

the infinite variety of choice which nature offers to the young in search of a mate is narrowed to a handful of persons of similar income; and beauty and health become the dreams of artists and the advertisements of quacks instead of the normal conditions of life. Society is not only divided but actually destroyed in all directions by inequality of income between classes: such stability as it has is due to the huge blocks of people between whom there is equality of income.

Jesus as Economist

It seems therefore that we must begin by holding the right to an income as sacred and equal, just as we now begin by holding the right to life as sacred and equal. Indeed the one right is only a restatement of the other. To hang me for cutting a dock laborer's throat after making much of me for leaving him to starve when I do not happen to have a ship for him to unload is idiotic; for as he does far less mischief with his throat cut than when he is starving, a rational society would esteem the cutthroat more highly than the capitalist. The thing has become so obvious, and the evil so unendurable, that if our attempt at civilization is not to perish like all the previous ones, we shall have to organize our society in such a way as to be able to say to every person in the land, "Take no thought, saying What shall we eat? or What shall we drink? or Wherewithal shall we be clothed?" We shall then no longer have a race of men whose hearts are in their pockets and safes and at their bankers. As Jesus said, where your treasure is, there will your heart be also. That was why he recommended that money should cease to be a treasure, and that we should take steps to make ourselves utterly reckless of it, setting our minds free for higher uses. In other words, that we should all be gentlemen and take care of our country because our country takes care of us, instead of the commercialized cads we are, doing everything and anything for money, and selling our souls and bodies by the pound and the inch after wasting half the day haggling over the price. Decidedly, whether you think Jesus was God or not, you must admit that he was a first-rate political economist.

Jesus as Biologist

He was also, as we now see, a first-rate biologist. It took a century and a half of evolutionary preachers, from Buffon and Goethe to Butler and Bergson, to convince us that we and our father are one; that as the kingdom of heaven is within us we need not go about looking for it and crying Lo here! and Lo there!; that God is not a picture of a pompous person in white robes in the family Bible, but a spirit; that it is through this spirit that we evolve towards greater abundance of life; that we are the lamps in which the light of the world burns: that, in short, we are gods though we die like men. All that is today sound biology and psychology; and the efforts of Natural Selectionists like Weismann to reduce evolution to mere automatism have not touched the doctrine of Jesus, though they have made short work of the theologians who conceived God as a magnate keeping men and angels as Lord Rothschild keeps buffaloes and emus at Tring.

Money the Midwife of Scientific Communism

It may be asked here by some simple-minded reader why we should not resort to crude Communism as the disciples were told to do. This would be quite practicable in a village where production was limited to the supply of the primitive wants which nature imposes on all human beings alike. We know that people need bread and boots without waiting for them to come and ask for these things and offer to pay for them. But when civilization advances to the point at which articles are produced that no man absolutely needs and that only some men fancy or can use, it is necessary that individuals should be able to have things made to their order and at their own cost. It is safe to provide bread for everybody because everybody wants and eats bread; but it would be absurd to provide microscopes and trombones, pet snakes and polo mallets, alembics and test tubes for everybody, as ninetenths of them would be wasted; and the nine-tenths of the population who do not use such things would object to their being provided at all. We have in the invaluable instrument called money a means of enabling every individual to order and pay for the particular things he desires over and above the things he must consume in order to remain alive, plus the things the State insists on his having and using whether he wants to or not: for example, clothes, sanitary arrangements, armies and navies. In large communities, where even the most eccentric demands for manufactured articles average themselves out until they can be foreseen within a negligible margin of error, direct communism (Take what you want without payment, as the people do in Morris's News From Nowhere) will, after a little experience, be found not only practicable but highly economical to an extent that now seems impossible. The sportsmen, the musicians, the physicists, the biologists will get their apparatus for the asking as easily as their bread, or, as at present, their paving, street lighting, and bridges; and the deaf man will not object to contribute to communal flutes when the musician has to contribute to communal ear trumpets. There are cases (for example, radium) in which the demand may be limited to the merest handful of laboratory workers, and in which nevertheless the whole community must pay because the price is beyond the means of any individual worker. But even when the utmost allowance is made for extensions of communism that now seem fabulous, there will still remain for a long time to come regions of supply and demand in which men will need and use money or individual credit, and for which, therefore, they must have individual incomes. Foreign travel is an obvious instance. We are so far from even national communism still, that we shall probably have considerable developments of local communism before it becomes possible for a Manchester man to go up to London for a day without taking any money with him. The modern practical form of the communism of Jesus is therefore, for the present, equal distribution of the surplus of the national income that is not absorbed by simple communism.

Judge Not

In dealing with crime and the family, modern thought and experience have thrown no fresh light on the views of Jesus. When Swift had occasion to illustrate the corruption of our civilization by making a catalogue of the types of scoundrels it produces, he always gave judges a conspicuous place alongside of them they judged. And he seems to have done this not as a restatement of the doctrine of Jesus, but as the outcome of his own observation and judgment. One of Mr Gilbert Chesterton's stories has for its hero a judge who, whilst trying a criminal case, is so overwhelmed by the absurdity of his position and the wickedness of the things it forces him to do, that he throws off the ermine there and then, and goes out into the world to live the life of an honest man instead of that of a cruel idol. There has also been a propaganda of a soulless stupidity called Determinism, representing man as a dead object driven hither and thither by his environment, antecedents, circumstances, and so forth, which nevertheless does remind us that there are limits to the number of cubits an individual can add to his stature morally or physically, and that it is silly as well as cruel to torment a man five feet high for not being able to pluck fruit that is within the reach of men of average height. I have known a case of an unfortunate child being beaten for not being able to tell the time after receiving an elaborate explanation of the figures on a clock dial, the fact being that she was short-sighted and could not see them. This is a typical illustration of the absurdities and cruelties into which we are led by the counter-stupidity to Determinism: the doctrine of Free Will. The notion that people can be good if they like, and that you should give them a powerful additional motive for goodness by tormenting them when they do evil, would soon reduce itself to absurdity if its application were not kept within the limits which nature sets to the self-control of most of us. Nobody supposes that a man with no ear for music or no mathematical faculty could be compelled on pain of death, however cruelly inflicted, to hum all the themes of Beethoven's symphonies or to complete Newton's work on fluxions.

Limits to Free Will

Consequently such of our laws as are not merely the intimidations by which tyrannies are maintained under pretext of law, can be obeyed through the exercise of a quite common degree of reasoning power and self-control. Most men and women can endure the ordinary annoyances and disappointments of life without committing murderous assaults. They conclude therefore that any person can refrain from such assaults if he or she chooses to, and proceed to reinforce self-control by threats of severe punishment. But in this they are mistaken. There are people, some of them possessing considerable powers of mind and body, who can no more restrain the fury into which a trifling mishap throws them than a dog can restrain himself from snapping if he is suddenly and painfully pinched. People fling knives and lighted paraffin lamps at one another in a dispute over a dinner-table. Men who have suffered several long sentences of penal servitude for murderous assaults will, the very day after they are released, seize their wives and cast them under drays at an irritating word. We have not only people who cannot resist an opportunity of stealing for the sake of satisfying their wants, but even people who have a specific mania for stealing, and do it when they are in no need of the things they steal. Burglary fascinates some men as sailoring fascinates some boys. Among respectable people how many are there who can be restrained by the warnings of their doctors and the lessons of experience from eating and drinking more than is good for them? It is true that between self-controlled people and ungovernable people there is a narrow margin of moral malingerers who can be made to behave themselves by the fear of consequences; but it is not worth while maintaining an abominable system of malicious, deliberate, costly and degrading ill-treatment of criminals for the sake of these marginal cases. For practical dealing with crime, Determinism or Predestination is quite a good working rule. People without self-control enough for social purposes may be killed, or may be kept in asylums with a view to studying their condition and ascertaining whether it is curable. To torture them and give ourselves virtuous airs at their expense is ridiculous and barbarous; and the desire to do it is vindictive and cruel. And though vindictiveness and cruelty are at least human qualities when they are frankly proclaimed and indulged, they are loathsome when they assume the robes of Justice. Which, I take it, is why Shakespear's Isabella gave such a dressing-down to Judge Angelo, and why Swift reserved the hottest corner of his hell for judges. Also, of course, why Jesus said "Judge not that ye be not judged" and "If any man hear my words and believe not, I judge

him not" because "he hath one that judgeth him": namely, the Father who is one with him.

When we are robbed we generally appeal to the criminal law, not considering that if the criminal law were effective we should not have been robbed. That convicts us of vengeance.

I need not elaborate the argument further. I have dealt with it sufficiently elsewhere. I have only to point out that we have been judging and punishing ever since Jesus told us not to; and I defy anyone to make out a convincing case for believing that the world has been any better than it would have been if there had never been a judge, a prison, or a gallows in it all that time. We have simply added the misery of punishment to the misery of crime, and the cruelty of the judge to the cruelty of the criminal. We have taken the bad man, and made him worse by torture and degradation, incidentally making ourselves worse in the process. It does not seem very sensible, does it? It would have been far easier to kill him as kindly as possible, or to label him and leave him to his conscience, or to treat him as an invalid or a lunatic is now treated (it is only of late years, by the way, that madmen have been delivered from the whip, the chain, and the cage); and this, I presume, is the form in which the teaching of Jesus could have been put into practice.

Jesus on Marriage and the Family

When we come to marriage and the family, we find Jesus making the same objection to that individual appropriation of human beings which is the essence of matrimony as to the individual appropriation of wealth. A married man, he said, will try to please his wife, and a married woman to please her husband, instead of doing the work of God. This is another version of "Where your treasure is, there will your heart be also." Eighteen hundred years later we find a very different person from Jesus, Talleyrand to wit, saying the same thing. A married man with a family, said Talleyrand, will do anything for money. Now this, though not a scientifically precise statement, is true enough to be a moral objection to marriage. As long as a man has a right to risk his life or his livelihood for his ideas he needs only courage and conviction to make his integrity unassailable. But he forfeits that right when he marries. It took a revolution to rescue Wagner from his Court appointment at Dresden; and his wife never forgave him for being glad and feeling free when he lost it and threw her back into poverty. Millet might have gone on painting potboiling nudes to the end of his life if his wife had not been of a heroic turn herself. Women, for the sake of their children and parents, submit to slaveries and prostitutions that no unattached woman would endure.

This was the beginning and the end of the objection of Jesus to marriage and family ties, and the explanation of his conception of heaven as a place where there should be neither marrying nor giving in marriage. Now there is no reason to suppose that when he said this he did not mean it. He did not, as St Paul did afterwards in his name, propose celibacy as a rule of life; for he was not a fool, nor, when he denounced marriage, had he yet come to believe, as St Paul did, that the end of the world was at hand and there was therefore no more need to replenish the earth. He must have meant that the race should be continued without dividing with women and men the allegiance the individual owes to God within him. This raises the practical problem of how we are to secure the spiritual freedom and integrity of the priest and the nun without their barrenness and uncompleted experience. Luther the priest did not solve the problem by marrying a nun: he only testified in the most convincing and practical way to the fact that celibacy was a worse failure than marriage.

Why Jesus Did Not Marry

To all appearance the problem oppresses only a few exceptional people. Thoroughly conventional women married to thoroughly conventional men should not be conscious of any restriction: the chain not only leaves them free to do whatever they want to do, but greatly facilitates their doing it. To them an attack on marriage is not a blow struck in defence of their freedom but at their rights and privileges. One would expect that they would not only demur vehemently to the teachings of Jesus in this matter, but object strongly to his not having been a married man himself. Even those who regard him as a god descended from his throne in heaven to take on humanity for a time might reasonably declare that the assumption of humanity must have been incomplete at its most vital point if he were a celibate. But the facts are flatly contrary. The mere thought of Jesus as a married man is felt to be blasphemous by the most conventional believers; and even those of us to whom Jesus is no supernatural personage, but a prophet only as Mahomet was a prophet, feel that there was something more dignified in the bachelordom of Jesus than in the spectacle of Mahomet lying distracted on the floor of his harem whilst his wives stormed and squabbled and henpecked round him. We are not surprised that when Jesus called the sons of Zebedee to follow him, he did not call their father, and that the disciples, like Jesus himself, were all men without family entanglements. It is evident from his impatience when people excused themselves from following him because of their family funerals, or when they assumed that his first duty was to his mother, that he had found family ties and domestic affections in his way at every turn, and had become persuaded at last that no man could follow his inner light until he was free from their compulsion. The absence of any protest against this tempts us to declare that on this question of marriage there are no conventional

people; and that everyone of us is at heart a good Christian sexually.

Inconsistency of the Sex Instinct

But the question is not so simple as that. Sex is an exceedingly subtle and complicated instinct; and the mass of mankind neither know nor care much about freedom of conscience, which is what Jesus was thinking about, and are concerned almost to obsession with sex, as to which Jesus said nothing. In our sexual natures we are torn by an irresistible attraction and an overwhelming repugnance and disgust. We have two tyrannous physical passions: concupiscence and chastity. We become mad in pursuit of sex: we become equally mad in the persecution of that pursuit. Unless we gratify our desire the race is lost: unless we restrain it we destroy ourselves. We are thus led to devise marriage institutions which will at the same time secure opportunities for the gratification of sex and raise up innumerable obstacles to it; which will sanctify and brand it as infamous; which will identify it with virtue and with sin simultaneously. Obviously it is useless to look for any consistency in such institutions; and it is only by continual reform and readjustment, and by a considerable elasticity in their enforcement, that a tolerable result can be arrived at. I need not repeat here the long and elaborate examination of them that I prefixed to my play entitled Getting Married. Here I am concerned only with the views of Jesus on the question; and it is necessary, in order to understand the attitude of the world towards them, that we should not attribute the general approval of the decision of Jesus to remain unmarried as an endorsement of his views. We are simply in a state of confusion on the subject; but it is part of the confusion that we should conclude that Jesus was a celibate, and shrink even from the idea that his birth was a natural one, yet cling with ferocity to the sacredness of the institution which provides a refuge from celibacy.

For Better For Worse

Jesus, however, did not express a complicated view of marriage. His objection to it was quite simple, as we have seen. He perceived that nobody could live the higher life unless money and sexual love were obtainable without sacrificing it; and he saw that the effect of marriage as it existed among the Jews (and as it still exists among ourselves) was to make the couples sacrifice every higher consideration until they had fed and pleased one another. The worst of it is that this dangerous preposterousness in marriage, instead of improving as the general conduct of married couples improves, becomes much worse. The selfish man to whom his wife is nothing but a slave, the selfish woman to whom her husband is nothing but a scapegoat and a breadwinner, are not held back from spiritual or any other adventures by fear of their effect on the welfare of their mates. Their wives do not make recreants and cowards of them: their husbands do not chain them to the cradle and the cooking range when their feet should be beautiful on the mountains. It is precisely as people become more kindly, more conscientious, more ready to shoulder the heavier part of the burden (which means that the strong shall give way to the weak and the slow hold back the swift), that marriage becomes an intolerable obstacle to individual evolution. And that is why the revolt against marriage of which Jesus was an exponent always recurs when civilization raises the standard of marital duty and affection, and at the same time produces a greater need for individual freedom in pursuit of a higher evolution.

The Remedy

This, fortunately, is only one side of marriage; and the question arises, can it not be eliminated? The reply is reassuring: of course it can. There is no mortal reason in the nature of things why a married couple should be economically dependent on one another. The Communism advocated by Jesus, which we have seen to be entirely practicable, and indeed inevitable if our civilization is to be saved from collapse, gets rid of that difficulty completely. And with the economic dependence will go the force of the outrageous claims that derive their real sanction from the economic pressure behind them. When a man allows his wife to turn him from the best work he is capable of doing, and to sell his soul at the highest commercial prices obtainable; when he allows her to entangle him in a social routine that is wearisome and debilitating to him, or tie him to her apron strings when he needs that occasional solitude which is one of the most sacred of human rights, he does so because he has no right to impose eccentric standards of expenditure and unsocial habits on her, and because these conditions have produced by their pressure so general a custom of chaining wedded couples to one another that married people are coarsely derided when their partners break the chain. And when a woman is condemned by her parents to wait in genteel idleness and uselessness for a husband when all her healthy social instincts call her to acquire a profession and work, it is again her economic dependence on them that makes their tyranny effective.

The Case for Marriage

Thus, though it would be too much to say that everything that is obnoxious in marriage and family life will be cured by Communism, yet it can be said that it will cure what Jesus objected to in these institutions. He made no comprehensive study of them: he only expressed his own grievance with an overwhelming sense that it is a grievance so deep that all the

considerations on the other side are as dust in the balance. Obviously there are such considerations, and very weighty ones too. When Talleyrand said that a married man with a family is capable of anything, he meant anything evil; but an optimist may declare, with equal half truth, that a married man is capable of anything good; that marriage turns vagabonds into steady citizens; and that men and women will, for love of their mates and children, practise virtues that unattached individuals are incapable of. It is true that too much of this domestic virtue is self-denial, which is not a virtue at all; but then the following of the inner light at all costs is largely self-indulgence, which is just as suicidal, just as weak, just as cowardly as self-denial. Ibsen, who takes us into the matter far more resolutely than Jesus, is unable to find any golden rule: both Brand and Peer Gynt come to a bad end; and though Brand does not do as much mischief as Peer, the mischief he does do is of extraordinary intensity.

Celibacy No Remedy

We must, I think, regard the protest of Jesus against marriage and family ties as the claim of a particular kind of individual to be free from them because they hamper his own work intolerably. When he said that if we are to follow him in the sense of taking up his work we must give up our family ties, he was simply stating a fact; and to this day the Roman Catholic priest, the Buddhist lama, and the fakirs of all the eastern denominations accept the saying. It is also accepted by the physically enterprising, the explorers, the restlessly energetic of all kinds: in short, by the adventurous. The greatest sacrifice in marriage is the sacrifice of the adventurous attitude towards life: the being settled. Those who are born tired may crave for settlement; but to fresher and stronger spirits it is a form of suicide.

Now to say of any institution that it is incompatible with both the contemplative and adventurous life is to disgrace it so vitally that all the moralizings of all the Deans and Chapters cannot reconcile our souls to its slavery. The unmarried Jesus and the unmarried Beethoven, the unmarried Joan of Arc, Clare, Teresa, Florence Nightingale seem as they should be; and the saying that there is always something ridiculous about a married philosopher becomes inevitable. And yet the celibate is still more ridiculous than the married man: the priest, in accepting the alternative of celibacy, disables himself; and the best priests are those who have been men of this world before they became men of the world to come. But as the taking of vows does not annul an existing marriage, and a married man cannot become a priest, we are again confronted with the absurdity that the best priest is a reformed rake. Thus does marriage, itself intolerable, thrust us upon intolerable alternatives. The practical solution is to make the individual economically independent of marriage and the family, and to make marriage as easily dissoluble as any other partnership: in other words, to accept the conclusions to which experience is slowly driving both our sociologists and our legislators. This will not instantly cure all the evils of marriage, nor root up at one stroke its detestable tradition of property in human bodies. But it will leave Nature free to effect a cure; and in free soil the root may wither and perish.

This disposes of all the opinions and teachings of Jesus which are still matters of controversy. They are all in line with the best modern thought. He told us what we have to do; and we have had to find the way to do it. Most of us are still, as most were in his own time, extremely recalcitrant, and are being forced along that way by painful pressure of circumstances, protesting at every step that nothing will induce us to go; that it is a ridiculous way, a disgraceful way, a socialistic way, an atheistic way, an immoral way, and that the vanguard ought to be ashamed of themselves and must be made to turn back at once. But they find that they have to follow the vanguard all the same if their lives are to be worth living.

After the Crucifixion

Let us now return to the New Testament narrative; for what happened after the disappearance of Jesus is instructive. Unfortunately, the crucifixion was a complete political success. I remember that when I described it in these terms once before, I greatly shocked a most respectable newspaper in my native town, the Dublin Daily Express, because my journalistic phrase shewed that I was treating it as an ordinary event like Home Rule or the Insurance Act: that is (though this did not occur to the editor), as a real event which had really happened, instead of a portion of the Church service. I can only repeat, assuming as I am that it *was* a real event and did actually happen, that it was as complete a success as any in history. Christianity as a specific doctrine was slain with Jesus, suddenly and utterly. He was hardly cold in his grave, or high in his heaven (as you please), before the apostles dragged the tradition of him down to the level of the thing it has remained ever since. And that thing the intelligent heathen may study, if they would be instructed in it by modern books, in Samuel Butler's novel, The Way of All Flesh.

The Vindictive Miracles and the Stoning of Stephen

Take, for example, the miracles. Of Jesus alone of all the Christian miracle workers there is no record, except in certain gospels that all men reject, of a malicious or destructive miracle. A barren fig-tree was the only victim of his anger. Every one of his miracles on sentient subjects was an act of kindness. John declares that he healed the wound of the man whose ear was cut off (by Peter, John says) at the arrest in the garden. One of the first things the apostles did with their miraculous power was to strike dead a wretched man and his wife who had defrauded them by holding back some money from the common stock. They struck people blind or dead without remorse, judging because they had been judged. They healed the sick and raised the dead apparently in a spirit of pure display and advertisement. Their doctrine did not contain a ray of that light which reveals Jesus as one of the redeemers of men from folly and error. They cancelled him, and went back straight to John the Baptist and his formula of securing remission of sins by repentance and the rite of baptism (being born again of water and the spirit). Peter's first harangue softens us by the human touch of its exordium, which was a quaint assurance to his hearers that they must believe him to be sober because it was too early in the day to get drunk; but of Jesus he had nothing to say except that he was the Christ foretold by the prophets as coming from the seed of David, and that they must believe this and be baptized. To this the other apostles added incessant denunciations of the Jews for having crucified him, and threats of the destruction that would overtake them if they did not repent: that is, if they did not join the sect which the apostles were now forming. A quite intolerable young speaker named Stephen delivered an oration to the council, in which he first inflicted on them a tedious sketch of the history of Israel, with which they were presumably as well acquainted as he, and then reviled them in the most insulting terms as "stiffnecked and uncircumcised." Finally, after boring and annoying them to the utmost bearable extremity, he looked up and declared that he saw the heavens open, and Christ standing on the right hand of God. This was too much: they threw him out of the city and stoned him to death. It was a severe way of suppressing a tactless and conceited bore; but it was pardonable and human in comparison to the slaughter of poor Ananias and Sapphira.

Paul

Suddenly a man of genius, Paul, violently anti-Christian, enters on the scene, holding the clothes of the men who are stoning Stephen. He persecutes the Christians with great vigor, a sport which he combines with the business of a tentmaker. This temperamental hatred of Jesus, whom he has never seen, is a pathological symptom of that particular sort of conscience and nervous constitution which brings its victims under the tyranny of two delirious terrors: the terror of sin and the terror of death, which may be called also the terror of sex and the terror of life. Now Jesus, with his healthy conscience on his higher plane, was free from these terrors. He consorted freely with sinners, and was never concerned for a moment, as far as we know, about whether his conduct was sinful or not; so that he has forced us to accept him as the man without sin. Even if we reckon his last days as the days of his delusion, he none the less gave a fairly convincing exhibition of superiority to the fear of death. This must have both fascinated and horrified Paul, or Saul, as he was first called. The horror accounts for his fierce persecution of the Christians. The fascination accounts for the strangest of his fancies: the fancy for attaching the name of Jesus Christ to the great idea which flashed upon him on the road to Damascus, the idea that he could not only make a religion of his two terrors, but that the movement started by Jesus offered him the nucleus for his new Church. It was a monstrous idea; and the shock of it, as he afterwards declared, struck him blind for days. He heard Jesus calling to him from the clouds, "Why persecute me?" His natural hatred of the teacher for whom Sin and Death had no terrors turned into a wild personal worship of him which has the ghastliness of a beautiful thing seen in a false light.

The chronicler of the Acts of the Apostles sees nothing of the significance of this. The great danger of conversion in all ages has been that when the religion of the high mind is offered to the lower mind, the lower mind, feeling its fascination without understanding it, and being incapable of rising to it, drags it down to its level by degrading it. Years ago I said that the conversion of a savage to Christianity is the conversion of Christianity to savagery. The conversion of Paul was no conversion at all: it was Paul who converted the religion that had raised one man above sin and death into a religion that delivered millions of men so completely into their dominion that their own common nature became a horror to them, and the religious life became a denial of life. Paul had no intention of surrendering either his Judaism or his Roman citizenship to the new moral world (as Robert Owen called it) of Communism and Jesuism. Just as in our own time Karl Marx, not content to take political economy as he found it, insisted on rebuilding it from the bottom upwards in his own way, and thereby gave a new lease of life to the errors it was just outgrowing, so Paul reconstructed the old Salvationism from which Jesus had vainly tried to redeem him, and produced a fantastic theology which is still the most amazing thing of the kind known to us. Being intellectually an inveterate Roman Rationalist, always discarding the irrational real thing for the unreal but ratiocinable postulate, he began by discarding Man as he is, and substituted a postulate which he called Adam. And when he was asked, as he surely must have been in a world not wholly mad, what had become of the natural man, he replied "Adam *is* the natural man." This was confusing to simpletons, because according to tradition Adam was certainly the name of the natural man as created in the garden of Eden. It was as if a preacher of our own time had described as typically British Frankenstein's monster, and called him Smith, and somebody, on demanding

what about the man in the street, had been told "Smith *is* the man in the street." The thing happens often enough; for indeed the world is full of these Adams and Smiths and men in the street and average sensual men and economic men and womanly women and what not, all of them imaginary Atlases carrying imaginary worlds on their unsubstantial shoulders.

The Eden story provided Adam with a sin: the "original sin" for which we are all damned. Badly stated, this seems ridiculous; nevertheless it corresponds to something actually existent not only in Paul's consciousness but in our own. The original sin was not the eating of the forbidden fruit, but the consciousness of sin which the fruit produced. The moment Adam and Eve tasted the apple they found themselves ashamed of their sexual relation, which until then had seemed quite innocent to them; and there is no getting over the hard fact that this shame, or state of sin, has persisted to this day, and is one of the strongest of our instincts. Thus Paul's postulate of Adam as the natural man was pragmatically true: it worked. But the weakness of Pragmatism is that most theories will work if you put your back into making them work, provided they have some point of contact with human nature. Hedonism will pass the pragmatic test as well as Stoicism. Up to a certain point every social principle that is not absolutely idiotic works: Autocracy works in Russia and Democracy in America; Atheism works in France, Polytheism in India, Monotheism throughout Islam, and Pragmatism, or No-ism, in England. Paul's fantastic conception of the damned Adam, represented by Bunyan as a pilgrim with a great burden of sins on his back, corresponded to the fundamental condition of evolution, which is, that life, including human life, is continually evolving, and must therefore be continually ashamed of itself and its present and past. Bunyan's pilgrim wants to get rid of his bundle of sins; but he also wants to reach "yonder shining light"; and when at last his bundle falls off him into the sepulchre of Christ, his pilgrimage is still unfinished and his hardest trials still ahead of him. His conscience remains uneasy; "original sin" still torments him; and his adventure with Giant Despair, who throws him into the dungeon of Doubting Castle, from which he escapes by the use of a skeleton key, is more terrible than any he met whilst the bundle was still on his back. Thus Bunyan's allegory of human nature breaks through the Pauline theology at a hundred points. His theological allegory, The Holy War, with its troops of Election Doubters, and its cavalry of "those that rode Reformadoes," is, as a whole, absurd, impossible, and, except in passages where the artistic old Adam momentarily got the better of the Salvationist theologian, hardly readable.

Paul's theory of original sin was to some extent idiosyncratic. He tells us definitely that he finds himself quite well able to avoid the sinfulness of sex by practising celibacy; but he recognizes, rather contemptuously, that in this respect he is not as other men are, and says that they had better marry than burn, thus admitting that though marriage may lead to placing the desire to please wife or husband before the desire to please God, yet preoccupation with unsatisfied desire may be even more ungodly than preoccupation with domestic affection. This view of the case inevitably led him to insist that a wife should be rather a slave than a partner, her real function being, not to engage a man's love and loyalty, but on the contrary to release them for God by relieving the man of all preoccupation with sex just as in her capacity of housekeeper and cook she relieves his preoccupation with hunger by the simple expedient of satisfying his appetite. This slavery also justifies itself pragmatically by working effectively; but it has made Paul the eternal enemy of Woman. Incidentally it has led to many foolish surmises about Paul's personal character and circumstances, by people so enslaved by sex that a celibate appears to them a sort of monster. They forget that not only whole priesthoods, official and unofficial, from Paul to Carlyle and Ruskin, have defied the tyranny of sex, but immense numbers of ordinary citizens of both sexes have, either voluntarily or under pressure of circumstances easily surmountable, saved their energies for less primitive activities.

Howbeit, Paul succeeded in stealing the image of Christ crucified for the figure-head of his Salvationist vessel, with its Adam posing as the natural man, its doctrine of original sin, and its damnation avoidable only by faith in the sacrifice of the cross. In fact, no sooner had Jesus knocked over the dragon of superstition than Paul boldly set it on its legs again in the name of Jesus.

The Confusion of Christendom

Now it is evident that two religions having such contrary effects on mankind should not be confused as they are under a common name. There is not one word of Pauline Christianity in the characteristic utterances of Jesus. When Saul watched the clothes of the men who stoned Stephen, he was not acting upon beliefs which Paul renounced. There is no record of Christ's having ever said to any man: "Go and sin as much as you like: you can put it all on me." He said "Sin no more," and insisted that he was putting up the standard of conduct, not debasing it, and that the righteousness of the Christian must exceed that of the Scribe and Pharisee. The notion that he was shedding his blood in order that every petty cheat and adulterator and libertine might wallow in it and come out whiter than snow, cannot be imputed to him on his own authority. "I come as an infallible patent medicine for bad consciences" is not one of the sayings in the gospels. If Jesus could have been consulted on Bunyan's allegory as to that business of the burden of sin dropping from the pilgrim's back when he caught sight of the cross, we must infer from his teaching

that he would have told Bunyan in forcible terms that he had never made a greater mistake in his life, and that the business of a Christ was to make self-satisfied sinners feel the burden of their sins and stop committing them instead of assuring them that they could not help it, as it was all Adam's fault, but that it did not matter as long as they were credulous and friendly about himself. Even when he believed himself to be a god, he did not regard himself as a scapegoat. He was to take away the sins of the world by good government, by justice and mercy, by setting the welfare of little children above the pride of princes, by casting all the quackeries and idolatries which now usurp and malversate the power of God into what our local authorities quaintly call the dust destructor, and by riding on the clouds of heaven in glory instead of in a thousand-guinea motor car. That was delirious, if you like; but it was the delirium of a free soul, not of a shamebound one like Paul's. There has really never been a more monstrous imposition perpetrated than the imposition of the limitations of Paul's soul upon the soul of Jesus.

The Secret of Paul's Success

Paul must soon have found that his followers had gained peace of mind and victory over death and sin at the cost of all moral responsibility; for he did his best to reintroduce it by making good conduct the test of sincere belief, and insisting that sincere belief was necessary to salvation. But as his system was rooted in the plain fact that as what he called sin includes sex and is therefore an ineradicable part of human nature (why else should Christ have had to atone for the sin of all future generations?) it was impossible for him to declare that sin, even in its wickedest extremity, could forfeit the sinner's salvation if he repented and believed. And to this day Pauline Christianity is, and owes its enormous vogue to being, a premium on sin. Its consequences have had to be held in check by the worldlywise majority through a violently anti-Christian system of criminal law and stern morality. But of course the main restraint is human nature, which has good impulses as well as bad ones, and refrains from theft and murder and cruelty, even when it is taught that it can commit them all at the expense of Christ and go happily to heaven afterwards, simply because it does not always want to murder or rob or torture.

It is now easy to understand why the Christianity of Jesus failed completely to establish itself politically and socially, and was easily suppressed by the police and the Church, whilst Paulinism overran the whole western civilized world, which was at that time the Roman Empire, and was adopted by it as its official faith, the old avenging gods falling helplessly before the new Redeemer. It still retains, as we may see in Africa, its power of bringing to simple people a message of hope and consolation that no other religion offers. But this enchantment is produced by its spurious association with the personal charm of Jesus, and exists only for untrained minds. In the hands of a logical Frenchman like Calvin, pushing it to its utmost conclusions, and devising "institutes" for hardheaded adult Scots and literal Swiss, it becomes the most infernal of fatalisms; and the lives of civilized children are blighted by its logic whilst negro piccaninnies are rejoicing in its legends.

Paul's Qualities

Paul, however, did not get his great reputation by mere imposition and reaction. It is only in comparison with Jesus (to whom many prefer him) that he appears common and conceited. Though in The Acts he is only a vulgar revivalist, he comes out in his own epistles as a genuine poet, though by flashes only. He is no more a Christian than Jesus was a Baptist: he is a disciple of Jesus only as Jesus was a disciple of John. He does nothing that Jesus would have done, and says nothing that Jesus would have said, though much, like the famous ode to charity, that he would have admired. He is more Jewish than the Jews, more Roman than the Romans, proud both ways, full of startling confessions and self-revelations that would not surprise us if they were slipped into the pages of Nietzsche, tormented by an intellectual conscience that demanded an argued case even at the cost of sophistry, with all sorts of fine qualities and occasional illuminations, but always hopelessly in the toils of Sin, Death, and Logic, which had no power over Jesus. As we have seen, it was by introducing this bondage and terror of his into the Christian doctrine that he adapted it to the Church and State systems which Jesus transcended, and made it practicable by destroying the specifically Jesuist side of it. He would have been quite in his place in any modern Protestant State; and he, not Jesus, is the true head and founder of our Reformed Church, as Peter is of the Roman Church. The followers of Paul and Peter made Christendom, whilst the Nazarenes were wiped out.

The Acts of the Apostles

Here we may return to the narrative called The Acts of the Apostles, which we left at the point where the stoning of Stephen was followed by the introduction of Paul. The author of The Acts, though a good storyteller, like Luke, was (herein also like Luke) much weaker in power of thought than in imaginative literary art. Hence we find Luke credited with the authorship of The Acts by people who like stories and have no aptitude for theology, whilst the book itself is denounced as spurious by Pauline theologians because Paul, and indeed all the apostles, are represented in it as very commonplace revivalists, interesting us by their adventures more than by any qualities of mind or character. Indeed, but for the epistles, we should have a very poor opinion of the apostles. Paul in particular is described as setting a fashion which has remained in continual use to this day. Whenever he addresses an audience, he dwells with great zest on his misdeeds before his pseudo conversion, with the effect of throwing into stronger relief his present state of blessedness; and he tells the story of that conversion over and over again, ending with exhortations to the hearers to come and be saved, and threats of the wrath that will overtake them if they refuse. At any revival meeting today the same thing may be heard, followed by the same conversions. This is natural enough; but it is totally unlike the preaching of Jesus, who never talked about his personal history, and never "worked up" an audience to hysteria. It aims at a purely nervous effect; it brings no enlightenment; the most ignorant man has only to become intoxicated with his own vanity, and mistake his self-satisfaction for the Holy Ghost, to become qualified as an apostle; and it has absolutely nothing to do with the characteristic doctrines of Jesus. The Holy Ghost may be at work all round producing wonders of art and science, and strengthening men to endure all sorts of martyrdoms for the enlargement of knowledge, and the enrichment and intensification of life ("that ye may have life more abundantly"); but the apostles, as described in The Acts, take no part in the struggle except as persecutors and revilers. To this day, when their successors get the upper hand, as in Geneva (Knox's "perfect city of Christ") and in Scotland and Ulster, every spiritual activity but moneymaking and churchgoing is stamped out; heretics are ruthlessly persecuted; and such pleasures as money can purchase are suppressed so that its possessors are compelled to go on making money because there is nothing else to do. And the compensation for all this privation is partly an insane conceit of being the elect of God, with a reserved seat in heaven, and partly, since even the most infatuated idiot cannot spend his life admiring himself, the less innocent excitement of punishing other people for not admiring him, and the nosing out of the sins of the people who, being intelligent enough to be incapable of mere dull self-righteousness, and highly susceptible to the beauty and interest of the real workings of the Holy Ghost, try to live more rational and abundant lives. The abominable amusement of terrifying children with threats of hell is another of these diversions, and perhaps the vilest and most mischievous of them. The net result is that the imitators of the apostles, whether they are called Holy Willies or Stigginses in derision, or, in admiration, Puritans or saints, are, outside their own congregations, and to a considerable extent inside them, heartily detested. Now nobody detests Jesus, though many who have been tormented in their childhood in his name include him in their general loathing of everything connected with the word religion; whilst others, who know him only by misrepresentation as a sentimental pacifist and an ascetic, include him in their general dislike of that type of character. In the same way a student who has had to "get up" Shakespear as a college subject may hate Shakespear; and people who dislike the theatre may include Molière in that dislike without ever having read a line of his or witnessed one of his plays; but nobody with any knowledge of Shakespear or Molière could possibly detest them, or read without pity and horror a description of their being insulted, tortured, and killed. And the same is true of Jesus. But it requires the most strenuous effort of conscience to refrain from crying "Serve him right" when we read of the stoning of Stephen; and nobody has ever cared twopence about the martyrdom of Peter: many better men have died worse deaths: for example, honest Hugh Latimer, who was burned by us, was worth fifty Stephens and a dozen Peters. One feels at last that when Jesus called Peter from his boat, he spoiled an honest fisherman, and made nothing better out of the wreck than a salvation monger.

The Controversies on Baptism and Transubstantiation

Meanwhile the inevitable effect of dropping the peculiar doctrines of Jesus and going back to John the Baptist, was to make it much easier to convert Gentiles than Jews; and it was by following the line of least resistance that Paul became the apostle to the Gentiles. The Jews had their own rite of initiation: the rite of circumcision; and they were fiercely jealous for it, because it marked them as the chosen people of God, and set them apart from the Gentiles, who were simply the uncircumcised. When Paul, finding that baptism made way faster among the Gentiles than among the Jews, as it enabled them to plead that they too were sanctified by a rite of later and higher authority than the Mosaic rite, he was compelled to admit that circumcision did not matter; and this, to the Jews, was an intolerable blasphemy. To Gentiles like ourselves, a good deal of the Epistle to the Romans is now tedious to unreadableness because it consists of a hopeless attempt by Paul to evade the conclusion that if a man were baptized it did not matter a rap whether he was circumcized or not. Paul claims circumcision as an excellent thing in its way for a Jew; but if it has no efficacy towards salvation, and if salvation is the one thing needful—and Paul was committed to both propositions—his pleas in mitigation only made the Jews more determined to stone him.

Thus from the very beginning of apostolic Christianity, it was hampered by a dispute as to whether salvation was to be attained by a surgical operation or by a sprinkling of water: mere rites on which Jesus would not have wasted twenty words. Later on, when the new sect conquered the Gentile west, where the dispute had no practical application, the other ceremony—that of eating the god—produced a still more disastrous dispute, in which a difference of belief, not as to the obligation to perform the ceremony, but as to whether it was a symbolic or a real ingestion of divine substance, produced persecution, slaughter, hatred, and everything that Jesus loathed, on a monstrous scale.

But long before that, the superstitions which had fastened on the new faith made trouble. The parthenogenetic birth of Christ, simple enough at first as a popular miracle, was not left so simple by the theologians. They began to ask of what substance Christ was made in the womb of the virgin. When the Trinity was added to the faith the question arose, was the virgin the mother of God or only the mother of Jesus? Arian schisms and Nestorian schisms arose on these questions; and the leaders of the resultant agitations rancorously deposed one another and excommunicated one another according to their luck in enlisting the emperors on their side. In the IV century they began to burn one another for differences of opinion in such matters. In the VIII century Charlemagne made Christianity compulsory by killing those who refused to embrace it; and though this made an end of the voluntary character of conversion, Charlemagne may claim to be the first Christian who put men to death for any point of doctrine that really mattered. From his time onward the history of Christian controversy reeks with blood and fire, torture and warfare. The Crusades, the persecutions in Albi and elsewhere, the Inquisition, the "wars of religion" which followed the Reformation, all presented themselves as Christian phenomena; but who can doubt that they would have been repudiated with horror by Jesus? Our own notion that the massacre of St Bartholomew's was an outrage on Christianity, whilst the campaigns of Gustavus Adolphus, and even of Frederick the Great, were a defence of it, is as absurd as the opposite notion that Frederick was Antichrist and Torquemada and Ignatius Loyola men after the very heart of Jesus. Neither they nor their exploits had anything to do with him. It is probable that Archbishop Laud and John Wesley died equally persuaded that he in whose name they had made themselves famous on earth would receive them in Heaven with open arms. George Fox the Quaker would have had ten times their chance; and yet Fox made rather a miserable business of life.

Nevertheless all these perversions of the doctrine of Jesus derived their moral force from his credit, and so had to keep his gospel alive. When the Protestants translated the Bible into the vernacular and let it loose among the people, they did an extremely dangerous thing, as the mischief which followed proves; but they incidentally let loose the sayings of Jesus in open competition with the sayings of Paul and Koheleth and David and Solomon and the authors of Job and the Pentateuch; and, as we have seen, Jesus seems to be the winning name. The glaring contradiction between his teaching and the practice of all the States and all the Churches is no longer hidden. And it may be that though nineteen centuries have passed since Jesus was born (the date of his birth is now quaintly given as 7 B.C., though some contend for 100 B.C.), and though his Church has not yet been founded nor his political system tried, the bankruptcy of all the other systems when audited by our vital statistics, which give us a final test for all political systems, is driving us hard into accepting him, not as a scapegoat, but as one who was much less of a fool in practical matters than we have hitherto all thought him.

The Alternative Christs

Let us now clear up the situation a little. The New Testament tells two stories for two different sorts of readers. One is the old story of the achievement of our salvation by the sacrifice and atonement of a divine personage who was barbarously slain and rose again on the third day: the story as it was accepted by the apostles. And in this story the political, economic, and moral views of the Christ have no importance: the atonement is everything; and we are saved by our faith in it, and not by works or opinions (other than that particular opinion) bearing on practical affairs.

The other is the story of a prophet who, after expressing several very interesting opinions as to practical conduct, both personal and political, which are now of pressing importance, and instructing his disciples to carry them out in their daily life, lost his head; believed himself to be a crude legendary form of god; and under that delusion courted and suffered a cruel execution in the belief that he would rise from the dead and come in glory to reign over a regenerated world. In this form, the political, economic, and moral opinions of Jesus, as guides to conduct, are interesting and important: the rest is mere psychopathy and superstition. The accounts of the resurrection, the parthenogenetic birth, and the more incredible miracles are rejected as inventions; and such episodes as the conversation with the devil are classed with similar conversations recorded of St Dunstan, Luther, Bunyan, Swedenborg, and Blake.

Credulity No Criterion

This arbitrary acceptance and rejection of parts of the gospel is not peculiar to the Secularist view. We have seen Luke and John reject Matthew's story of the massacre of the innocents and the flight into Egypt without ceremony. The notion that Matthew's manuscript is a literal and infallible record of facts, not subject to the errors that beset all earthly chroniclers, would have made John stare, being as it is a comparatively modern fancy of intellectually untrained people who keep the Bible on the same shelf

with Napoleon's Book of Fate, Old Moore's Almanack, and handbooks of therapeutic herbalism. You may be a fanatical Salvationist and reject more miracle stories than Huxley did; and you may utterly repudiate Jesus as the Savior and yet cite him as a historical witness to the possession by men of the most marvellous thaumaturgical powers. "Christ Scientist" and Jesus the Mahatma are preached by people whom Peter would have struck dead as worse infidels than Simon Magus; and the Atonement is preached by Baptist and Congregationalist ministers whose views of the miracles are those of Ingersoll and Bradlaugh. Luther, who made a clean sweep of all the saints with their million miracles, and reduced the Blessed Virgin herself to the status of an idol, concentrated Salvationism to a point at which the most execrable murderer who believes in it when the rope is round his neck, flies straight to the arms of Jesus, whilst Tom Paine and Shelley fall into the bottomless pit to burn there to all eternity. And sceptical physicists like Sir William Crookes demonstrate by laboratory experiments that "mediums" like Dunglas Home can make the pointer of a spring-balance go round without touching the weight suspended from it.

Belief in Personal Immortality No Criterion

Nor is belief in individual immortality any criterion. Theosophists, rejecting vicarious atonement so sternly that they insist that the smallest of our sins brings its Karma, also insist on individual immortality and metempsychosis in order to provide an unlimited field for Karma to be worked out by the unredeemed sinner. The belief in the prolongation of individual life beyond the grave is far more real and vivid among table-rapping Spiritualists than among conventional Christians. The notion that those who reject the Christian (or any other) scheme of salvation by atonement must reject also belief in personal immortality and in miracles is as baseless as the notion that if a man is an atheist he will steal your watch.

I could multiply these instances to weariness. The main difference that set Gladstone and Huxley by the ears is not one between belief in supernatural persons or miraculous events and the sternest view of such belief as a breach of intellectual integrity: it is the difference between belief in the efficacy of the crucifixion as an infallible cure for guilt, and a congenital incapacity for believing this, or (the same thing) desiring to believe it.

The Secular View Natural, Not Rational, Therefore Inevitable

It must therefore be taken as a flat fundamental modern fact, whether we like it or not, that whilst many of us cannot believe that Jesus got his curious grip of our souls by mere sentimentality, neither can we believe that he was John Barleycorn. The more our reason and study lead us to believe that Jesus was talking the most penetrating good sense when he preached Communism; when he declared that the reality behind the popular belief in God was a creative spirit in ourselves called by him the Heavenly Father and by us Evolution, Élan Vital, Life Force and other names; when he protested against the claims of marriage and the family to appropriate that high part of our energy that was meant for the service of his Father, the more impossible it becomes for us to believe that he was talking equally good sense when he so suddenly announced that he was himself a visible concrete God; that his flesh and blood were miraculous food for us; that he must be tortured and slain in the traditional manner and would rise from the dead after three days; and that at his Second Coming the stars would fall from heaven and he become king of an earthly paradise. But it is easy and reasonable to believe that an overwrought preacher at last went mad as Swift and Ruskin and Nietzsche went mad. Every asylum has in it a patient suffering from the delusion that he is a god, yet otherwise sane enough. These patients do not nowadays declare that they will be barbarously slain and will rise from the dead, because they have lost that tradition of the destiny of godhead; but they claim everything appertaining to divinity that is within their knowledge.

Thus the gospels as memoirs and suggestive statements of sociological and biological doctrine, highly relevant to modern civilization, though ending in the history of a psychopathic delusion, are quite credible, intelligible, and interesting to modern thinkers. In any other light they are neither credible, intelligible, nor interesting except to people upon whom the delusion imposes.

"The Higher Criticism"

Historical research and paleographic criticism will no doubt continue their demonstrations that the New Testament, like the Old, seldom tells a single story or expounds a single doctrine, and gives us often an accretion and conglomeration of widely discrete and even unrelated traditions and doctrines. But these disintegrations, though technically interesting to scholars, and gratifying or exasperating, as the case may be, to people who are merely defending or attacking the paper fortifications of the infallibility of the Bible, have hardly anything to do with the purpose of these pages. I have mentioned the fact that most of the authorities are now agreed (for the moment) that the date of the birth of Jesus may be placed at about 7 B.C.; but they do not therefore date their letters 1923, nor, I presume, do they expect me to do so. What I am engaged in is a criticism (in the Kantian sense) of an established body of belief which has become an actual part of the mental

fabric of my readers; and I should be the most exasperating of triflers and pedants if I were to digress into a criticism of some other belief or no-belief which my readers might conceivably profess if they were erudite Scriptural paleographers and historians, in which case, by the way, they would have to change their views so frequently that the gospel they received in their childhood would dominate them after all by its superior persistency. The chaos of mere facts in which the Sermon on the Mount and the Ode to Charity suggest nothing but disputes as to whether they are interpolations or not, in which Jesus becomes nothing but a name suspected of belonging to ten different prophets or executed persons, in which Paul is only the man who could not possibly have written the epistles attributed to him, in which Chinese sages, Greek philosophers, Latin authors, and writers of ancient anonymous inscriptions are thrown at our heads as the sources of this or that scrap of the Bible, is neither a religion nor a criticism of religion: one does not offer the fact that a good deal of the medieval building in Peterborough Cathedral was found to be flagrant jerry-building as a criticism of the Dean's sermons. For good or evil, we have made a synthesis out of the literature we call the Bible; and though the discovery that there is a good deal of jerry-building in the Bible is interesting in its way, because everything about the Bible is interesting, it does not alter the synthesis very materially even for the paleographers, and does not alter it at all for those who know no more about modern paleography than Archbishop Ussher did. I have therefore indicated little more of the discoveries than Archbishop Ussher might have guessed for himself if he had read the Bible without prepossessions.

For the rest, I have taken the synthesis as it really lives and works in men. After all, a synthesis is what you want: it is the case you have to judge brought to an apprehensible issue for you. Even if you have little more respect for synthetic biography than for synthetic rubber, synthetic milk, and the still unachieved synthetic protoplasm which is to enable us to make different sorts of men as a pastrycook makes different sorts of tarts, the practical issue still lies as plainly before you as before the most credulous votaries of what pontificates as the Higher Criticism.

The Perils of Salvationism

The secular view of Jesus is powerfully reinforced by the increase in our day of the number of people who have had the means of educating and training themselves to the point at which they are not afraid to look facts in the face, even such terrifying facts as sin and death. The result is greater sternness in modern thought. The conviction is spreading that to encourage a man to believe that though his sins be as scarlet he can be made whiter than snow by an easy exercise of self-conceit, is to encourage him to be a rascal. It did not work so badly when you could also conscientiously assure him that if he let himself be caught napping in the matter of faith by death, a red-hot hell would roast him alive to all eternity. In those days a sudden death—the most enviable of all deaths—was regarded as the most frightful calamity. It was classed with plague, pestilence, and famine, battle and murder, in our prayers. But belief in that hell is fast vanishing. All the leaders of thought have lost it; and even for the rank and file it has fled to those parts of Ireland and Scotland which are still in the seventeenth century. Even there, it is tacitly reserved for the other fellow.

The Importance of Hell in the Salvation Scheme

The seriousness of throwing over hell whilst still clinging to the Atonement is obvious. If there is no punishment for sin there can be no self-forgiveness for it. If Christ paid our score, and if there is no hell and therefore no chance of our getting into trouble by forgetting the obligation, then we can be as wicked as we like with impunity inside the secular law, even from self-approach, which becomes mere ingratitude to the Savior. On the other hand, if Christ did not pay our score, it still stands against us; and such debts make us extremely uncomfortable. The drive of evolution, which we call conscience and honor, seizes on such slips, and shames us to the dust for being so low in the scale as to be capable of them. The "saved" thief experiences an ecstatic happiness which can never come to the honest atheist: he is tempted to steal again to repeat the glorious sensation. But if the atheist steals he has no such happiness. He is a thief and knows that he is a thief. Nothing can rub that off him. He may try to soothe his shame by some sort of restitution or equivalent act of benevolence; but that does not alter the fact that he did steal; and his conscience will not be easy until he has conquered his will to steal and changed himself into an honest man by developing that divine spark within him which Jesus insisted on as the everyday reality of what the atheist denies.

Now though the state of the believers in the Atonement may thus be the happier, it is most certainly not more desirable from the point of view of the community. The fact that a believer is happier than a sceptic is no more to the point than the fact that a drunken man is happier than a sober one. The happiness of credulity is a cheap and dangerous quality of happiness, and by no means a necessity of life. Whether Socrates got as much happiness out of life as Wesley is an unanswerable question; but a nation of Socrateses would be much safer and happier than a nation of Wesleys; and its individuals would be higher in the evolutionary scale. At all events it is in the Socratic man and not in the Wesleyan that our hope lies now.

The Right to Refuse Atonement

Consequently, even if it were mentally possible for all of us to believe in the Atonement, we should have to cry off it, as we evidently have a right to do. Every man to whom salvation is offered has an inalienable natural right to say "No, thank you: I prefer to retain my full moral responsibility: it is not good for me to be able to load a scapegoat with my sins: I should be less careful how I committed them if I knew they would cost me nothing." Then, too, there is the attitude of Ibsen: that iron moralist to whom the whole scheme of salvation was only an ignoble attempt to cheat God; to get into heaven without paying the price. To be let off, to beg for and accept eternal life as a present instead of earning it, would be mean enough even if we accepted the contempt of the Power on whose pity we were trading; but to bargain for a crown of glory as well! that was too much for Ibsen: it provoked him to exclaim, "Your God is an old man whom you cheat," and to lash the deadened conscience of the nineteenth century back to life with a whip of scorpions.

The Teaching of Christianity

And there I must leave the matter to such choice as your nature allows you. The honest teacher who has to make known to a novice the facts about Christianity cannot in any essential regard, I think, put the facts otherwise than as I have put them. If children are to be delivered from the proselytizing atheist on the one hand, and the proselytizing nun in the convent school on the other, with all the other proselytizers that lie between them, they must not be burdened with idle controversies as to whether there was ever such a person as Jesus or not. When Hume said that Joshua's campaigns were impossible, Whately did not wrangle about it: he proved, on the same lines, that the campaigns of Napoleon were impossible. Only fictitious characters will stand Hume's sort of examination: nothing will ever make Edward the Confessor and St Louis as real to us as Don Quixote and Mr Pickwick. We must cut the controversy short by declaring that there is the same evidence for the existence of Jesus as for that of any other person of his time; and the fact that you may not believe everything Matthew tells you no more disproves the existence of Jesus than the fact that you do not believe everything Macaulay tells you disproves the existence of William III. The gospel narratives in the main give you a biography which is quite credible and accountable on purely secular grounds when you have trimmed off everything that Hume or Grimm or Rousseau or Huxley or any modern bishop could reject as fanciful. Without going further than this, you can become a follower of Jesus just as you can become a follower of Confucius or Lao Tse, and may therefore call yourself a Jesuist, or even a Christian, if you hold, as the strictest Secularist quite legitimately may, that all prophets are inspired, and all men with a mission, Christs.

The teacher of Christianity has then to make known to the child, first the song of John Barleycorn, with the fields and seasons as witness to its eternal truth. Then, as the child's mind matures, it can learn, as historical and psychological phenomena, the tradition of the scapegoat, the Redeemer, the Atonement, the Resurrection, the Second Coming, and how, in a world saturated with this tradition, Jesus has been largely accepted as the long expected and often prophesied Redeemer, the Messiah, *the* Christ. It is open to the child also to accept him. If the child is built like Gladstone, he will accept Jesus as his Savior, and Peter and John the Baptist as the Savior's revealer and forerunner respectively. If he is built like Huxley, he will take the secular view, in spite of all that a pious family can do to prevent him. The important thing now is that the Gladstones and Huxleys should no longer waste their time irrelevantly and ridiculously wrangling about the Gadarene swine, and that they should make up their minds as to the soundness of the secular doctrines of Jesus; for it is about these that they may come to blows in our own time.

Christianity and the Empire

Finally, let us ask why it is that the old superstitions have so suddenly lost countenance that although, to the utter disgrace of the nation's leaders and rulers, the laws by which persecutors can destroy or gag all freedom of thought and speech in these matters are still unrepealed and ready to the hand of our bigots and fanatics (quite recently a respectable shopkeeper was convicted of "blasphemy" for saying that if a modern girl accounted for an illicit pregnancy by saying she had conceived of the Holy Ghost, we should know what to think: a remark which would never have occurred to him had he been properly taught how the story was grafted on the gospel), yet somehow they are used only against poor men, and that only in a half-hearted way. When we consider that from the time when the first scholar ventured to whisper as a professional secret that the Pentateuch could not possibly have been written by Moses to the time within my own recollection when Bishop Colenso, for saying the same thing openly, was inhibited from preaching and actually excommunicated, eight centuries elapsed (the point at issue, though technically interesting to paleographers and historians, having no more bearing on human welfare than the controversy as to whether uncial or cursive is the older form of writing); yet now, within fifty years of Colenso's heresy, there is not a Churchman of any authority living, or an educated layman, who could without ridicule declare that Moses wrote the Pentateuch as Pascal wrote his Thoughts or D'Aubigny his

History of the Reformation, or that St Jerome wrote the passage about the three witnesses in the Vulgate, or that there are less than three different accounts of the creation jumbled together in the book of Genesis. Now the maddest Progressive will hardly contend that our growth in wisdom and liberality has been greater in the last half century than in the sixteen half centuries preceding: indeed it would be easier to sustain the thesis that the last fifty years have witnessed a distinct reaction from Victorian Liberalism to Collectivism which has perceptibly strengthened the State Churches. Yet the fact remains that whereas Byron's Cain, published a century ago, is a leading case on the point that there is no copyright in a blasphemous book, the Salvation Army might now include it among its publications without shocking anyone.

I suggest that the causes which have produced this sudden clearing of the air include the transformation of many modern States, notably the old self-contained French Republic and the tight little Island of Britain, into empires which overflow the frontiers of all the Churches. In India, for example, there are less than four million Christians out of a population of three hundred and sixteen and a half millions. The King of England is the defender of the faith; but what faith is now *the* faith? The inhabitants of this island would, within the memory of persons still living, have claimed that their faith is surely *the* faith of God, and that all others are heathen. But we islanders are only forty-five millions; and if we count ourselves all as Christians, there are still seventy-seven and a quarter million Mahometans in the Empire. Add to these the Hindoos and Buddhists, Sikhs and Jains, whom I was taught in my childhood, by way of religious instruction, to regard as gross idolaters consigned to eternal perdition, but whose faith I can now be punished for disparaging by a provocative word, and you have a total of over three hundred and forty-two and a quarter million heretics to swamp our forty-five million Britons, of whom, by the way, only six thousand call themselves distinctively "disciples of Christ," the rest being members of the Church of England and other denominations whose discipleship is less emphatically affirmed. In short, the Englishman of today, instead of being, like the forefathers whose ideas he clings to, a subject of a State practically wholly Christian, is now crowded, and indeed considerably overcrowded, into a corner of an Empire in which the Christians are a mere eleven per cent of the population; so that the Nonconformist who allows his umbrella stand to be sold up rather than pay rates towards the support of a Church of England school, finds himself paying taxes not only to endow the Church of Rome in Malta, but to send Christians to prison for the blasphemy of offering Bibles for sale in the streets of Khartoum.

Turn to France, a country ten times more insular

in its preoccupation with its own language, its own history, its own character, than we, who have always been explorers and colonizers and grumblers. This once self-centred nation is forty millions strong. The total population of the French Republic is about one hundred and fourteen millions. The French are not in our hopeless Christian minority of eleven per cent; but they are in a minority of thirty-five per cent, which is fairly conclusive. And, being a more logical people than we, they have officially abandoned Christianity and declared that the French State has no specific religion.

Neither has the British State, though it does not say so. No doubt there are many innocent people in England who take Charlemagne's view, and would, as a matter of course, offer our eighty-nine per cent of "pagans, I regret to say" the alternative of death or Christianity but for a vague impression that these lost ones are all being converted gradually by the missionaries. But no statesman can entertain such ludicrously parochial delusions. No English king or French president can possibly govern on the assumption that the theology of Peter and Paul, Luther and Calvin, has any objective validity, or that the Christ is more than the Buddha or Jehovah more than Krishna, or Jesus more or less human than Mahomet or Zoroaster or Confucius. He is actually compelled, in so far as he makes laws against blasphemy at all, to treat all the religions, including Christianity, as blasphemous when paraded before people who are not accustomed to them and do not want them. And even that is a concession to a mischievous intolerance which an empire should use its control of education to eradicate.

On the other hand, Governments cannot really divest themselves of religion, or even of dogma. When Jesus said that people should not only live but live more abundantly, he was dogmatizing; and many Pessimist sages, including Shakespear, whose hero begged his friend to refrain from suicide in the words "Absent thee from felicity awhile," would say dogmatizing very perniciously. Indeed many preachers and saints declare, some of them in the name of Jesus himself, that this world is a vale of tears, and that our lives had better be passed in sorrow and even in torment, as a preparation for a better life to come. Make these sad people comfortable; and they baffle you by putting on hair shirts.

None the less, Governments must proceed on dogmatic assumptions, whether they call them dogmas or not; and they must clearly be assumptions common enough to stamp those who reject them as eccentrics or lunatics. And the greater and more heterogeneous the population the commoner the assumptions must be. A Trappist monastery can be conducted on assumptions which would in twenty-four hours provoke the village at its gates to insurrection. That is because the monastery selects its people; and if a Trappist does not like it he can leave it. But

a subject of the British Empire or the French Republic is not selected; and if he does not like it he must lump it; for emigration is practicable only within narrow limits, and seldom provides an effective remedy, all civilizations being now much alike.

To anyone capable of comprehending government at all it must be evident without argument that the set of fundamental assumptions drawn up in the thirty-nine articles or in the Westminster Confession are wildly impossible as political constitutions for modern empires. A personal profession of them by any person disposed to take such professions seriously would practically disqualify him for high imperial office. A Calvinist Viceroy of India and a Particular Baptist Secretary of State for Foreign Affairs would wreck the empire. The Stuarts wrecked even the tight little island which was the nucleus of the empire by their Scottish logic and theological dogma; and it may be sustained very plausibly that the alleged aptitude of the English for self-government, which is contradicted by every chapter of their history, is really only an incurable inaptitude for theology, and indeed for co-ordinated thought in any direction, which makes them equally impatient of systematic despotism and systematic good government: their history being that of a badly governed and accidentally free people (comparatively). Thus our success in colonizing, as far as it has not been produced by exterminating the natives, has been due to our indifference to the salvation of our subjects. Ireland is the exception which proves the rule; for Ireland, the standing instance of the inability of the English to colonize without extermination of natives, is also the one country under British rule in which the conquerors and colonizers proceeded on the assumption that their business was to establish Protestantism as well as to make money and thereby secure at least the lives of the unfortunate inhabitants out of whose labor it could be made. At this moment Ulster is refusing to accept fellow-citizenship with the other Irish provinces because the south believes in St Peter and Bossuet, and the north in St Paul and Calvin. Imagine the effect of trying to govern India or Egypt from Belfast or from the Vatican!

The position is perhaps graver for France than for England, because the sixty-five per cent of French subjects who are neither French nor Christian nor Modernist includes some thirty millions of negroes who are susceptible, and indeed highly susceptible, of conversion to those salvationist forms of pseudo-Christianity which have produced all the persecutions and religious wars of the last fifteen hundred years. When the late explorer Sir Henry Stanley told me of the emotional grip which Christianity had over the Baganda tribes, and read me their letters, which were exactly like medieval letters in their literal faith and ever-present piety, I said "Can these men handle a rifle?" To which Stanley replied with some scorn "Of course they can, as well as any white man." Now at this moment (1915) a vast European war is being waged, in which the French are using Senegalese soldiers. I ask the French Government, which, like our own Government, is deliberately leaving the religious instruction of these negroes in the hands of missions of Petrine Catholics and Pauline Calvinists, whether they have considered the possibility of a new series of crusades, by ardent African Salvationists, to rescue Paris from the grip of the modern scientific "infidel," and to raise the cry of "Back to the Apostles: back to Charlemagne!"

We are more fortunate in that an overwhelming majority of our subjects are Hindoos, Mahometans, and Buddhists: that is, they have, as a prophylactic against salvationist Christianity, highly civilized religions of their own. Mahometanism, which Napoleon at the end of his career classed as perhaps the best popular religion for modern political use, might in some respects have arisen as a reformed Christianity if Mahomet had had to deal with a population of seventeenth-century Christians instead of Arabs who worshipped stones. As it is, men do not reject Mahomet for Calvin; and to offer a Hindoo so crude a theology as ours in exchange for his own, or our Jewish canonical literature as an improvement on Hindoo scripture, is to offer old lamps for older ones in a market where the oldest lamps, like old furniture in England, are the most highly valued.

Yet, I repeat, government is impossible without a religion: that is, without a body of common assumptions. The open mind never acts: when we have done our utmost to arrive at a reasonable conclusion, we still, when we can reason and investigate no more, must close our minds for the moment with a snap, and act dogmatically on our conclusions. The man who waits to make an entirely reasonable will dies intestate. A man so reasonable as to have an open mind about theft and murder, or about the need for food and reproduction, might just as well be a fool and a scoundrel for any use he could be as a legislator or a State official. The modern pseudo-democratic statesman, who says that he is only in power to carry out the will of the people, and moves only as the cat jumps, is clearly a political and intellectual brigand. The rule of the negative man who has no convictions means in practice the rule of the positive mob. Freedom of conscience as Cromwell used the phrase is an excellent thing; nevertheless if any man had proposed to give effect to freedom of conscience as to cannibalism in England, Cromwell would have laid him by the heels almost as promptly as he would have laid a Roman Catholic, though in Fiji at the same moment

he would have supported heartily the freedom of conscience of a vegetarian who disparaged the sacred diet of Long Pig.

Here then comes in the importance of the repudiation by Jesus of proselytism. His rule "Don't pull up the tares: sow the wheat: if you try to pull up the tares you will pull up the wheat with it" is the only possible rule for a statesman governing a modern empire, or a voter supporting such a statesman. There is nothing in the teaching of Jesus that cannot be assented to by a Brahman, a Mahometan, a Buddhist or a Jew, without any question of their conversion to Christianity. In some ways it is easier to reconcile a Mahometan to Jesus than a British parson, because the idea of a professional priest is unfamiliar and even monstrous to a Mahometan (the tourist who persists in asking who is the dean of St Sophia puzzles beyond words the sacristan who lends him a huge pair of slippers); and Jesus never suggested that his disciples should separate themselves from the laity: he picked them up by the wayside, where any man or woman might follow him. For priests he had not a civil word; and they shewed their sense of his hostility by getting him killed as soon as possible. He was, in short, a thorough-going anti-Clerical. And though, as we have seen, it is only by political means that his doctrine can be put into practice, he not only never suggested a sectarian theocracy as a form of government, and would certainly have prophesied the downfall of the late President Kruger if he had survived to his time, but, when challenged, he refused to teach his disciples not to pay tribute to Caesar, admitting that Caesar, who presumably had the kingdom of heaven within him as much as any disciple, had his place in the scheme of things. Indeed the apostles made this an excuse for carrying subservience to the State to a pitch of idolatry that ended in the theory of the divine right of kings, and provoked men to cut kings' heads off to restore some sense of proportion in the matter. Jesus certainly did not consider the overthrow of the Roman empire or the substitution of a new ecclesiastical organization for the Jewish Church or for the priesthood of the Roman gods as part of his program. He said that God was better than Mammon; but he never said that Tweedledum was better than Tweedledee; and that is why it is now possible for British citizens and statesmen to follow Jesus, though they cannot possibly follow either Tweedledum or Tweedledee without bringing the empire down with a crash on their heads. And at that I must leave it.

LONDON, *December* 1915.

Androcles and the Lion

Prologue

OVERTURE: *forest sounds, roaring of lions, Christian hymn faintly.*

A jungle path. A lion's roar, a melancholy suffering roar, comes from the jungle. It is repeated nearer. The lion limps from the jungle on three legs, holding up his right forepaw, in which a huge thorn sticks. He sits down and contemplates it. He licks it. He shakes it. He tries to extract it by scraping it along the ground, and hurts himself worse. He roars piteously. He licks it again. Tears drop from his eyes. He limps painfully off the path and lies down under the trees, exhausted with pain. Heaving a long sigh, like wind in a trombone, he goes to sleep.

Androcles and his wife Megaera *come along the path. He is a small, thin, ridiculous little man who might be any age from thirty to fifty-five. He has sandy hair, watery compassionate blue eyes, sensitive nostrils, and a very presentable forehead; but his good points go no further: his arms and legs and back, though wiry of their kind, look shrivelled and starved. He carries a big bundle, is very poorly clad, and seems tired and hungry.*

His wife is a rather handsome pampered slattern, well fed and in the prime of life. She has nothing to carry, and has a stout stick to help her along.

MEGAERA: [*Suddenly throwing down her stick*] I wont go another step.

ANDROCLES: [*Pleading wearily*] Oh, not again, dear. Whats the good of stopping every two miles and saying you wont go another step? We must get on to the next village before night. There are wild beasts in this wood: lions, they say.

MEGAERA: I dont believe a word of it. You are always threatening me with wild beasts to make me walk the very soul out of my body when I can hardly drag one foot before another. We havnt seen a single lion yet.

ANDROCLES: Well, dear, do you want to see one?

MEGAERA: [*Tearing the bundle from his back*] You cruel brute, you dont care how tired I am, or what becomes of me [*She throws the bundle on the ground*]: always thinking of yourself. Self! self! self! always yourself! [*She sits down on the bundle*]

ANDROCLES: [*Sitting down sadly on the ground with his elbows on his knees and his head in his hands*] We all have to think of ourselves occasionally, dear.

MEGAERA: A man ought to think of his wife sometimes.

ANDROCLES: He cant always help it, dear. You make me think of you a good deal. Not that I blame you.

MEGAERA: Blame me! I should think not indeed. Is it my fault that I'm married to you?

ANDROCLES: No, dear: that is my fault.

MEGAERA: Thats a nice thing to say to me. Arnt you happy with me?

ANDROCLES: I dont complain, my love.

MEGAERA: You ought to be ashamed of yourself.

ANDROCLES: I am, my dear.

MEGAERA: Youre not: you glory in it.

ANDROCLES: In what, darling?

MEGAERA: In everything. In making me a slave, and making yourself a laughing-stock. It's not fair. You get me the name of being a shrew with your meek ways, always talking as if butter wouldnt melt in your mouth. And just because I look a big strong woman, and because I'm goodhearted and a bit hasty, and because youre always driving me to do things I'm sorry for afterwards, people say "Poor man: what a life his wife leads him!" Oh, if they only knew! And you think I dont know. But I do, I do, [*Screaming*] I do.

ANDROCLES: Yes, my dear: I know you do.

MEGAERA: Then why dont you treat me properly and be a good husband to me?

ANDROCLES: What can I do, my dear?

MEGAERA: What can you do! You can return to your duty, and come back to your home and your friends, and sacrifice to the gods as all respectable people do, instead of having us hunted out of house and home for being dirty disreputable blaspheming atheists.

ANDROCLES: I'm not an atheist, dear: I am a Christian.

MEGAERA: Well, isnt that the same thing, only ten times worse? Everybody knows that the Christians are the very lowest of the low.

ANDROCLES: Just like us, dear.

MEGAERA: Speak for yourself. Dont you dare to compare me to common people. My father owned his own public-house; and sorrowful was the day for me when you first came drinking in our bar.

ANDROCLES: I confess I was addicted to it, dear. But I gave it up when I became a Christian.

MEGAERA: Youd much better have remained a drunkard. I can forgive a man being addicted to drink: it's only natural; and I dont deny I like a drop myself sometimes. What I cant stand is your being addicted to Christianity. And whats worse again, your being addicted to animals. How is any woman to keep her house clean when you bring in every stray cat and lost cur and lame duck in the whole countryside? You took the bread out of my mouth to feed them: you know you did: dont attempt to deny it.

ANDROCLES: Only when they were hungry and you were getting too stout, dearie.

MEGAERA: Yes: insult me, do. [*Rising*] Oh! I wont bear it another moment. You used to sit and talk to those dumb brute beasts for hours, when you hadnt a word for me.

ANDROCLES: They never answered back, darling. [*He rises and again shoulders the bundle*]

MEGAERA: Well, if youre fonder of animals than of your own wife, you can live with them here in the jungle. Ive had enough of them and enough of you. I'm going back. I'm going home.

ANDROCLES: [*Barring the way back*] No, dearie: dont take on like that. We cant go back. Weve sold everything: we should starve; and I should be sent to Rome and thrown to the lions—

MEGAERA: Serve you right! I wish the lions joy of you. [*Screaming*] Are you going to get out of my way and let me go home?

ANDROCLES: No, dear—

MEGAERA: Then I'll make my way through the forest; and when I'm eaten by the wild beasts youll know what a wife youve lost. [*She dashes into the jungle and nearly falls over the sleeping lion*] Oh! Oh! Andy! Andy! [*She totters back and collapses into the arms of* Androcles, *who, crushed by her weight, falls on his bundle*]

ANDROCLES: [*Extracting himself from beneath her and slapping her hands in great anxiety*] What is it, my precious, my pet? Whats the matter? [*He raises her head. Speechless with terror, she points in the direction of the sleeping lion. He steals cautiously towards the spot indicated by* Megaera. *She rises with an effort and totters after him*]

MEGAERA: No, Andy: youll be killed. Come back.

[*The lion utters a long snoring sigh.* Androcles *sees the lion, and recoils fainting into the arms of* Megaera, *who falls back on the bundle. They roll apart and lie staring in terror at one another. The lion is heard groaning heavily in the jungle*]

ANDROCLES: [*Whispering*] Did you see? A lion.

MEGAERA: [*Despairing*] The gods have sent him to punish us because youre a Christian. Take me away, Andy. Save me.

ANDROCLES: [*Rising*] Meggy: theres one chance for you. Itll take him pretty nigh twenty minutes to eat me (I'm rather stringy and tough) and you can escape in less time than that.

MEGAERA: Oh, dont talk about eating. [*The lion rises with a great groan and limps towards them*] Oh! [*She faints*]

ANDROCLES: [*Quaking, but keeping between the lion and* Megaera] Dont you come near my wife, do you hear? [*The lion groans.* Androcles *can hardly stand from trembling*] Meggy: run. Run for your life. If I take my eye off him it's all up. [*The lion holds up his wounded paw and flaps it piteously before* Androcles] Oh, he's lame, poor old chap! He's got a thorn in his paw. A frightfully big thorn. [*Full of sympathy*] Oh, poor old man! Did um get an awful thorn into um's tootsums wootsums? Has it made um too sick to eat a nice little Christian man for um's breakfast? Oh, a nice little Christian man will get um's thorn out for um; and then um shall eat the nice Christian man and the nice Christian man's nice big tender wifey pifey. [*The lion responds by moans of self-pity*] Yes, yes, yes, yes, yes. Now, now [*Taking the paw in his hand*], um is not to bite and not to scratch, not even if it hurts a very very little. Now make velvet paws. Thats right. [*He pulls gingerly at the thorn. The lion, with an angry yell of pain, jerks back his paw so abruptly that* Androcles *is thrown on his back*] Steadeee! Oh, did the nasty cruel little Christian man hurt the sore paw? [*The lion moans assentingly but apologetically*] Well, one more little pull and it will be all over. Just one little, little, leetle pull; and then um will live happily ever after. [*He gives the thorn another pull. The lion roars and snaps his jaws with a terrifying clash*] Oh, mustnt frighten um's good kind doctor, um's affectionate nursey. That didnt hurt at all: not a bit. Just one more. Just to shew how the brave big lion can bear pain, not like the little crybaby Christian man. Oopsh! [*The thorn comes out. The lion yells with pain, and shakes his paw wildly*] Thats it! [*Holding up the thorn*] Now it's out. Now lick um's paw to take away the nasty inflammation. See? [*He licks his own hand. The lion nods intelligently and licks his paw industriously*] Clever little liony-piony! Understands um's dear old friend Andy Wandy. [*The lion licks his face*] Yes, kissums Andy Wandy. [*The lion, wagging his tail violently, rises on his hind legs, and embraces* Androcles, *who makes a wry face and cries*] Velvet paws! Velvet paws! [*The lion draws in his claws*] Thats right. [*He embraces the lion, who finally takes the end of his tail in one paw, places that tight round Androcles' waist, resting it on his hip.* Androcles *takes the other paw in his hand, stretches out his arm, and the two waltz rapturously round and round and finally away through the jungle*]

MEGAERA: [*Who has revived during the waltz*] Oh, you coward, you havnt danced with me for years; and now you go off dancing with a great brute beast that you havnt known for ten minutes and that wants to eat your own wife. Coward! Coward! Coward! [*She rushes off after them into the jungle*]

Act I

EVENING: *The end of three converging roads to Rome. Three triumphal arches span them where they debouch on a square at the gate of the city. Looking north through the arches one can see the campagna threaded by the three long dusty tracks. On the east and west sides of the square are long stone benches. An old beggar sits on the east side, his bowl at his feet.*

Through the eastern arch a squad of Roman soldiers tramps along escorting a batch of Christian prisoners of both sexes and all ages, among them one Lavinia, *a good-looking resolute young woman, apparently of higher social standing than her fellow-prisoners. A* Centurion, *carrying his vinewood cudgel, trudges alongside the squad, on its right, in command of it. All are tired and dusty; but the soldiers are dogged and indifferent, the* Christians *lighthearted and determined to treat their hardships as a joke and encourage one another.*

A bugle is heard far behind on the road, where the rest of the cohort is following.

CENTURION: [*Stopping*] Halt! Orders from the Captain. [*They halt and wait*] Now then, you Christians, none of your larks. The Captain's coming. Mind you behave yourselves. No singing. Look respectful. Look serious, if youre capable of it. See that big building over there! Thats the Coliseum. Thats where youll be thrown to the lions or set to fight the gladiators presently. Think of that; and itll help you to behave properly before the Captain. [*The* Captain *arrives*] Attention! Salute! [*The soldiers salute*]

A CHRISTIAN: [*Cheerfully*] God bless you, Captain!

THE CENTURION: [*Scandalized*] Silence!

[*The* Captain, *a patrician, handsome, about thirty-five, very cold and distinguished, very superior and authoritative, steps up on a stone seat at the west side of the square, behind the centurion, so as to dominate the others more effectually*]

THE CAPTAIN: Centurion.

THE CENTURION: [*Standing at attention and saluting*] Sir?

THE CAPTAIN: [*Speaking stiffly and officially*] You will remind your men, Centurion, that we are now entering Rome. You will instruct them that once inside the gates of Rome they are in the presence of the Emperor. You will make them understand that the lax discipline of the march cannot be permitted here. You will instruct them to shave every day, not every week. You will impress on them particularly that there must be an end to the profanity and blasphemy of singing Christian hymns on the march. I have to reprimand you, Centurion, for not only allowing this, but actually doing it yourself.

THE CENTURION: [*Apologetic*] The men march better, Captain.

THE CAPTAIN: No doubt. For that reason an exception is made in the case of the march called Onward Christian Soldiers. This may be sung, except when marching through the forum or within hearing of the Emperor's palace; but the words must be altered to "Throw them to the Lions."

[*The* Christians *burst into shrieks of uncontrollable laughter, to the great scandal of the* Centurion]

CENTURION: Silence! Silen-n-n-nce! Wheres your behavior? Is that the way to listen to an officer? [*To the* Captain] Thats what we have to put up with from these Christians every day, sir. Theyre always laughing and joking something scandalous. Theyve no religion: thats how it is.

LAVINIA: But I think the Captain meant us to laugh, Centurion. It was so funny.

CENTURION: Youll find out how funny it is when youre thrown to the lions tomorrow. [*To the* Captain, *who looks displeased*] Beg pardon, sir. [*To the* Christians] Silennnnce!

THE CAPTAIN: You are to instruct your men that all intimacy with Christian prisoners must now cease. The men have fallen into habits of dependence upon the prisoners, especially the female prisoners, for cooking, repairs to uniforms, writing letters, and advice in their private affairs. In a Roman soldier such dependence is inadmissible. Let me see no more of it whilst we are in the city. Further, your orders are that in addressing Christian prisoners, the manners and tone of your men must express abhorrence and contempt. Any shortcoming in this respect will be regarded as a breach of discipline. [*He turns to the prisoners*] Prisoners.

CENTURION: [*Fiercely*] Prisonerrrrrs! Tention! Silence!

THE CAPTAIN: I call your attention, prisoners, to the fact that you may be called on to appear in the Imperial Circus at any time from tomorrow onwards according to the requirements of the managers. I may inform you that as there is a shortage of Christians just now, you may expect to be called on very soon.

LAVINIA: What will they do to us, Captain?

CENTURION: Silence!

THE CAPTAIN: The women will be conducted into the arena with the wild beasts of the Imperial Menagerie, and will suffer the consequences. The men, if of an age to bear arms, will be given weapons to defend themselves, if they choose, against the Imperial Gladiators.

LAVINIA: Captain: is there no hope that this cruel persecution—

CENTURION: [*Shocked*] Silence! Hold your tongue, there. Persecution, indeed!

THE CAPTAIN: [*Unmoved and somewhat sardonic*] Persecution is not a term applicable to the acts of the Emperor. The Emperor is the Defender of the Faith. In throwing you to the lions he will be upholding the interests of religion in Rome. If you were to throw him to the lions, that would no doubt be persecution.

[*The* Christians *again laugh heartily*]

CENTURION: [*Horrified*] Silence, I tell you! Keep silence there. Did anyone ever hear the like of this?

LAVINIA: Captain: there will be nobody to appreciate your jokes when we are gone.

THE CAPTAIN: [*Unshaken in his official delivery*] I call the attention of the female prisoner Lavinia to the fact that as the Emperor is a divine personage, her imputation of cruelty is not only treason, but sacrilege. I point out to her further that there is no foundation for the charge, as the Emperor does not desire that any prisoner should suffer; nor can any Christian be harmed save through his or her own obstinacy. All that is necessary is to sacrifice to the gods: a simple and convenient ceremony effected by dropping a pinch of incense on the altar, after which the prisoner is at once set free. Under such circumstances you have only your own perverse folly to blame if you suffer. I suggest to you that if you cannot burn a morsel of incense as a matter of conviction, you might at least do so as a matter of good taste, to avoid shocking the religious convictions of your fellow citizens. I am aware that these considerations do not weigh with Christians; but it is my duty to call your attention to them in order that you may have no ground for complaining of your treatment, or of accusing the Emperor of cruelty when he is shewing you the most signal clemency. Looked at from this point of view, every Christian who has perished in the arena has really committed suicide.

LAVINIA: Captain: your jokes are too grim. Do not think it is easy for us to die. Our faith makes life far stronger and more wonderful in us than when we walked in darkness and had nothing to live for. Death is harder for us than for you: the martyr's agony is as bitter as his triumph is glorious.

THE CAPTAIN: [*Rather troubled, addressing her personally and gravely*] A martyr, Lavinia, is a fool. Your death will prove nothing.

LAVINIA: Then why kill me?

THE CAPTAIN: I mean that truth, if there be any truth, needs no martyrs.

LAVINIA: No; but my faith, like your sword, needs testing. Can you test your sword except by staking your life on it?

THE CAPTAIN: [*Suddenly resuming his official tone*] I call the attention of the female prisoner to the fact that Christians are not allowed to draw the Emperor's officers into arguments and put questions to them for which the military regulations provide no answer.

[*The* Christians *titter*]

LAVINIA: Captain: how can you?

THE CAPTAIN: I call the female prisoner's attention specially to the fact that four comfortable homes

have been offered her by officers of this regiment, of which she can have her choice the moment she chooses to sacrifice as all wellbred Roman ladies do. I have no more to say to the prisoners.

CENTURION: Dismiss! But stay where you are.

THE CAPTAIN: Centurion: you will remain here with your men in charge of the prisoners until the arrival of three Christian prisoners in the custody of a cohort of the tenth legion. Among these prisoners you will particularly identify an armorer named Ferrovius, of dangerous character and great personal strength, and a Greek tailor reputed to be a sorcerer, by name Androcles. You will add the three to your charge here and march them all to the Coliseum, where you will deliver them into the custody of the master of the gladiators and take his receipt, countersigned by the keeper of the beasts and the acting manager. You understand your instructions?

CENTURION: Yes, sir.

THE CAPTAIN: Dismiss. [*He throws off his air of parade, and descends from his perch. The* Centurion *seats himself on it and prepares for a nap, whilst his men stand at ease. The* Christians *sit down on the west side of the square, glad to rest.* Lavinia *alone remains standing to speak to the* Captain]

LAVINIA: Captain: is this man who is to join us the famous Ferrovius, who has made such wonderful conversions in the northern cities?

THE CAPTAIN: Yes. We are warned that he has the strength of an elephant and the temper of a mad bull. Also that he is stark mad. Not a model Christian, it would seem.

LAVINIA: You need not fear him if he is a Christian, Captain.

THE CAPTAIN: [*Coldly*] I shall not fear him in any case, Lavinia.

LAVINIA: [*Her eyes dancing*] How brave of you, Captain!

THE CAPTAIN: You are right: it was a silly thing to say. [*In a lower tone, humane and urgent*] Lavinia: do Christians know how to love?

LAVINIA: [*Composedly*] Yes, Captain: they love even their enemies.

THE CAPTAIN: Is that easy?

LAVINIA: Very easy, Captain, when their enemies are as handsome as you.

THE CAPTAIN: Lavinia: you are laughing at me.

LAVINIA: At you, Captain! Impossible.

THE CAPTAIN: Then you are flirting with me, which is worse. Dont be foolish.

LAVINIA: But such a very handsome captain.

THE CAPTAIN: Incorrigible! [*Urgently*] Listen to me. The men in that audience tomorrow will be the vilest of voluptuaries: men in whom the only passion excited by a beautiful woman is a lust to see her tortured and torn shrieking limb from limb. It is a crime to gratify that passion. It is offering yourself for violation by the whole rabble of the streets and the riff-raff of the court at the same time. Why will you not choose rather a kindly love and an honorable alliance?

LAVINIA: They cannot violate my soul. I alone can do that by sacrificing to false gods.

THE CAPTAIN: Sacrifice then to the true God. What does his name matter? We call him Jupiter. The Greeks call him Zeus. Call him what you will as you drop the incense on the alter flame: He will understand.

LAVINIA: No. I couldnt. That is the strange thing, Captain, that a little pinch of incense should make all that difference. Religion is such a great thing that when I meet really religious people we are friends at once, no matter what name we give to the divine will that made us and moves us. Oh, do you think that I, a woman, would quarrel with you for sacrificing to a woman god like Diana, if Diana meant to you what Christ means to me? No: we should kneel side by side before her altar like two children. But when men who believe neither in my god nor in their own—men who do not know the meaning of the word religion—when these men drag me to the foot of an iron statue that has become the symbol of the terror and darkness through which they walk, of their cruelty and greed, of their hatred of God and their oppression of man—when they ask me to pledge my soul before the people that this hideous idol is God, and that all this wickedness and falsehood is divine truth, I cannot do it, not if they could put a thousand cruel deaths on me. I tell you, it is physically impossible. Listen, Captain: did you ever try to catch a mouse in your hand? Once there was a dear little mouse that used to come out and play on my table as I was reading. I wanted to take him in my hand and caress him; and sometimes he got among my books so that he could not escape me when I stretched out my hand. And I did stretch out my hand; but it always came back in spite of me. I was not afraid of him in my heart; but my hand refused: it is not in the nature of my hand to touch a mouse. Well, Captain, if I took a pinch of incense in my hand and stretched it out over the altar fire, my hand would come back. My body would be true to my faith even if you could corrupt my mind. And all the time I should believe more in Diana than my persecutors have ever believed in anything. Can you understand that?

THE CAPTAIN: [Simply] Yes: I understand that. But my hand would not come back. The hand that holds the sword has been trained not to come back from anything but victory.

LAVINIA: Not even from death?

THE CAPTAIN: Least of all from death.

LAVINIA: Then I must not come back from death either. A woman has to be braver than a soldier.

THE CAPTAIN: Prouder, you mean.

LAVINIA: [Startled] Prouder! You call our courage pride?

THE CAPTAIN: There is no such thing as courage: there is only pride. You Christians are the proudest devils on earth.

LAVINIA: [Hurt] Pray God then my pride may never become a false pride. [She turns away as if she did not wish to continue the conversation, but softens and says to him with a smile] Thank you for trying to save me.

THE CAPTAIN: I knew it was no use; but one tries in spite of one's knowledge.

LAVINIA: Something stirs, even in the iron breast of a Roman soldier?

THE CAPTAIN: It will soon be iron again. I have seen many women die, and forgotten them in a week.

LAVINIA: Remember me for a fortnight, handsome Captain. I shall be watching you, perhaps.

THE CAPTAIN: From the skies? Do not deceive yourself, Lavinia. There is no future for you beyond the grave.

LAVINIA: What does that matter? Do you think I am only running away from the terrors of life into the comfort of heaven? If there were no future, or if the future were one of torment, I should have to go just the same. The hand of God is upon me.

THE CAPTAIN: Yes: when all is said, we are both patricians, Lavinia, and must die for our beliefs. Farewell. [He offers her his hand. She takes it and presses it. He walks away, trim and calm. She looks after him for a moment, and cries a little as he disappears through the eastern arch. A trumpet-call is heard from the road through the western arch]

CENTURION: [Waking up and rising] Cohort of the tenth with prisoners. Two file out with me to receive them. [He goes out through the western arch, followed by four soldiers in two files]

[Lentulus and Metellus come into the square from the west side with a little retinue of servants. Both are young courtiers, dressed in the extremity of fashion. Lentulus is slender, fair-haired, epicene. Metellus is manly, compactly built, olive skinned, not a talker]

LENTULUS: Christians, by Jove! Lets chaff them.

METELLUS: Awful brutes. If you knew as much about them as I do you wouldnt want to chaff them. Leave them to the lions.

LENTULUS: [Indicating Lavinia, who is still looking towards the arches after the Captain] That woman's got a figure. [He walks past her, staring at her invitingly; but she is preoccupied and is not conscious of him] Do you turn the other cheek when they kiss you?

LAVINIA: [Starting] What?

LENTULUS: Do you turn the other cheek when they kiss you, fascinating Christian?

LAVINIA: Dont be foolish. [To Metellus, who has remained on her right, so that she is between them] Please dont let your friend behave like a cad before the soldiers. How are they to respect and obey patricians if they see them behaving like street boys? [Sharply to Lentulus] Pull yourself together, man. Hold your head up. Keep the corners of your mouth firm; and treat me respectfully. What do you take me for?

LENTULUS: [Irresolutely] Look here, you know: I— you—I—

LAVINIA: Stuff! Go about your business. [She turns decisively away and sits down with her comrades, leaving him disconcerted]

METELLUS: You didnt get much out of that. I told you they were brutes.

LENTULUS: Plucky little filly! I suppose she thinks I care. [With an air of indifference he strolls with Metellus to the east side of the square, where they stand watching the return of the Centurion through the western arch with his men, escorting three prisoners: Ferrovius, Androcles, and Spintho. Ferrovius is a powerful, choleric man in the prime of life, with large nostrils, staring eyes, and a thick neck: a man whose sensibilities are keen and violent to the verge of madness. Spintho is a debauchee, the wreck of a good-looking man gone hopelessly to the bad. Androcles is overwhelmed with grief, and is restraining his tears with great difficulty]

THE CENTURION: [To Lavinia] Here are some pals for you. This little bit is Ferrovius that you talk so much about. [Ferrovius turns on him threateningly. The Centurion holds up his left forefinger in admonition] Now remember that youre a Christian, and that youve got to return good for evil. [Ferrovius controls himself convulsively; moves away from temptation to the east side near Lentulus; clasps his hands in silent prayer; and throws himself on his knees] Thats the way to manage them, eh! This fine fellow [Indicating Androcles, who comes to his left, and makes Lavinia a heartbroken salutation] is a sorcerer. A Greek tailor, he is. A real sorcerer, too: no mistake about it. The tenth marches with a leopard at the head of the column. He made a pet of the leopard; and now he's crying at being parted from it. [Androcles sniffs lamentably] Aint you, old chap? Well, cheer up, we march with a Billy goat [Androcles brightens up] thats killed two leopards and ate a turkey-cock. You can have him for a pet if you like. [Androcles, quite consoled, goes past the Centurion to Lavinia, and sits down contentedly on the ground on her left] This dirty dog [Collaring Spintho] is a real Christian. He mobs the temples, he does [At each accusation he gives the neck of Spintho's tunic a twist]; he goes smashing things mad drunk, he does; he steals the gold vessels, he does; he assaults the priestesses, he does—yah! [He flings Spintho into the middle of the group of

prisoners] Youre the sort that makes duty a pleasure, you are.

SPINTHO: [Gasping] Thats it: strangle me. Kick me. Beat me. Revile me. Our Lord was beaten and reviled. Thats my way to heaven. Every martyr goes to heaven, no matter what he's done. That is so, isnt it, brother?

CENTURION: Well, if youre going to heaven, I dont want to go there. I wouldnt be seen with you.

LENTULUS: Haw! Good! [Indicating the kneeling Ferrovius] Is this one of the turn-the-other-cheek gentlemen, Centurion?

CENTURION: Yes, sir. Lucky for you too, sir, if you want to take any liberties with him.

LENTULUS: [To Ferrovius] You turn the other cheek when youre struck, I'm told.

FERROVIUS: [Slowly turning his great eyes on him] Yes, by the grace of God, I do, now.

LENTULUS: Not that youre a coward, of course; but out of pure piety.

FERROVIUS: I fear God more than man; at least I try to.

LENTULUS: Lets see. [He strikes him on the cheek. Androcles makes a wild movement to rise and interfere; but Lavinia holds him down, watching Ferrovius intently. Ferrovius, without flinching, turns the other cheek. Lentulus, rather out of countenance, titters foolishly, and strikes him again feebly] You know, I should feel ashamed if I let myself be struck like that, and took it lying down. But then I'm not a Christian: I'm a man. [Ferrovius rises impressively and towers over him. Lentulus becomes white with terror; and a shade of green flickers in his cheek for a moment]

FERROVIUS: [With the calm of a steam hammer] I have not always been faithful. The first man who struck me as you have just struck me was a stronger man than you: he hit me harder than I expected. I was tempted and fell; and it was then that I first tasted bitter shame. I never had a happy moment after that until I had knelt and asked his forgiveness by his bedside in the hospital. [Putting his hands on Lentulus's shoulders with paternal weight] But now I have learnt to resist with a strength that is not my own. I am not ashamed now, nor angry.

LENTULUS: [Uneasily] Er—good evening. [He tries to move away]

FERROVIUS: [Gripping his shoulders] Oh, do not harden your heart, young man. Come: try for yourself whether our way is not better than yours. I will now strike you on one cheek; and you will turn the other and learn how much better you will feel than if you gave way to the promptings of anger. [He holds him with one hand and clenches the other fist]

LENTULUS: Centurion: I call on you to protect me.

CENTURION: You asked for it, sir. It's no business of

ours. Youve had two whacks at him. Better pay him a trifle and square it that way.

LENTULUS: Yes, of course. [*To Ferrovius*] It was only a bit of fun, I assure you: I meant no harm. Here. [*He proffers a gold coin*]

FERROVIUS: [*Taking it and throwing it to the old beggar, who snatches it up eagerly, and hobbles off to spend it*] Give all thou hast to the poor. Come, friend: courage! I may hurt your body for a moment; but your soul will rejoice in the victory of the spirit over the flesh. [*He prepares to strike*]

ANDROCLES: Easy, Ferrovius, easy: you broke the last man's jaw.

[Lentulus, *with a moan of terror, attempts to fly; but* Ferrovius *holds him ruthlessly*]

FERROVIUS: Yes; but I saved his soul. What matters a broken jaw?

LENTULUS: Dont touch me, do you hear? The law—

FERROVIUS: The law will throw me to the lions tomorrow: what worse could it do were I to slay you? Pray for strength; and it shall be given to you.

LENTULUS: Let me go. Your religion forbids you to strike me.

FERROVIUS: On the contrary, it commands me to strike you. How can you turn the other cheek, if you are not first struck on the one cheek?

LENTULUS: [*Almost in tears*] But I'm convinced already that what you said is quite right. I apologize for striking you.

FERROVIUS: [*Greatly pleased*] My son: have I softened your heart? Has the good seed fallen in a fruitful place? Are your feet turning towards a better path?

LENTULUS: [*Abjectly*] Yes, yes. Theres a great deal in what you say.

FERROVIUS: [*Radiant*] Join us. Come to the lions. Come to suffering and death.

LENTULUS: [*Falling on his knees and bursting into tears*] Oh, help me. Mother! mother!

FERROVIUS: These tears will water your soul and make it bring forth good fruit, my son. God has greatly blessed my efforts at conversion. Shall I tell you a miracle—yes, a miracle—wrought by me in Cappadocia? A young man—just such a one as you, with golden hair like yours—scoffed at and struck me as you scoffed at and struck me. I sat up all night with that youth wrestling for his soul; and in the morning not only was he a Christian, but his hair was as white as snow. [Lentulus *falls in a dead faint*] There, there: take him away. The spirit has overwrought him, poor lad. Carry him gently to his house; and leave the rest to heaven.

CENTURION: Take him home. [*The servants, intimidated, hastily carry him out.* Metellus *is about to follow when* Ferrovius *lays his hand on his shoulder*]

FERROVIUS: You are his friend, young man. You will see that he is taken safely home.

METELLUS: [*With awestruck civility*] Certainly, sir. I shall do whatever you think best. Most happy to have made your acquaintance, I'm sure. You may depend on me. Good evening, sir.

FERROVIUS: [*With unction*] The blessing of heaven upon you and him.

[Metellus *follows* Lentulus. *The* Centurion *returns to his seat to resume his interrupted nap. The deepest awe has settled on the spectators.* Ferrovius, *with a long sigh of happiness, goes to* Lavinia, *and offers her his hand*]

LAVINIA: [*Taking it*] So that is how you convert people, Ferrovius.

FERROVIUS: Yes: there has been a blessing on my work in spite of my unworthiness and my backslidings— all through my wicked, devilish temper. This man—

ANDROCLES: [*Hastily*] Dont slap me on the back, brother. She knows you mean me.

FERROVIUS: How I wish I were weak like our brother here! for then I should perhaps be meek and gentle like him. And yet there seems to be a special providence that makes my trials less than his. I hear tales of the crowd scoffing and casting stones and reviling the brethren; but when I come, all this stops: my influence calms the passions of the mob: they listen to me in silence; and infidels are often converted by a straight heart-to-heart talk with me. Every day I feel happier, more confident. Every day lightens the load of the great terror.

LAVINIA: The great terror? What is that?

[Ferrovius *shakes his head and does not answer. He sits down beside her on her left, and buries his face in his hands in gloomy meditation*]

ANDROCLES: Well, you see, sister, he's never quite sure of himself. Suppose at the last moment in the arena, with the gladiators there to fight him, one of them was to say anything to annoy him, he might forget himself and lay that gladiator out.

LAVINIA: That would be splendid.

FERROVIUS: [*Springing up in horror*] What!

ANDROCLES: Oh, sister!

FERROVIUS: Splendid to betray my master, like Peter! Splendid to act like any common blackguard in the day of my proving! Woman: you are no Christian. [*He moves away from her to the middle of the square, as if her neighborhood contaminated him*]

LAVINIA: [*Laughing*] You know, Ferrovius, I am not always a Christian. I dont think anybody is. There are moments when I forget all about it, and something comes out quite naturally, as it did then.

SPINTHO: What does it matter? If you die in the arena, youll be a martyr; and all martyrs go to heaven, no matter what they have done. Thats so, isnt it, Ferrovius?

FERROVIUS: Yes: that is so, if we are faithful to the end.

LAVINIA: I'm not so sure.

SPINTHO: Dont say that. Thats blasphemy. Dont say

that, I tell you. We shall be saved, no matter WHAT we do.

LAVINIA: Perhaps you men will all go into heaven bravely and in triumph, with your heads erect and golden trumpets sounding for you. But I am sure I shall only be allowed to squeeze myself in through a little crack in the gate after a great deal of begging. I am not good always: I have moments only.

SPINTHO: Youre talking nonsense, woman. I tell you, martyrdom pays all scores.

ANDROCLES: Well, let us hope so, brother, for your sake. Youve had a gay time, havent you? with your raids on the temples. I cant help thinking that heaven will be very dull for a man of your temperament. [Spintho *snarls*] Dont be angry: I say it only to console you in case you should die in your bed tonight in the natural way. Theres a lot of plague about.

SPINTHO: [*Rising and running about in abject terror*] I never thought of that. Oh Lord, spare me to be martyred. Oh, what a thought to put into the mind of a brother! Oh, let me be martyred today, now. I shall die in the night and go to hell. Youre a sorcerer: youve put death into my mind. Oh, curse you, curse you! [*He tries to seize* Androcles *by the throat*]

FERROVIUS: [*Holding him in a grasp of iron*] Whats this, brother? Anger! Violence! Raising your hand to a brother Christian!

SPINTHO: It's easy for you. Youre strong. Your nerves are all right. But I'm full of disease. [Ferrovius *takes his hand from him with instinctive disgust*] Ive drunk all my nerves away. I shall have the horrors all night.

ANDROCLES: [*Sympathetic*] Oh, don't take on so, brother. We're all sinners.

SPINTHO: [*Snivelling, trying to feel consoled*] Yes: I daresay if the truth were known, youre all as bad as I am.

LAVINIA: [*Contemptuously*] Does that comfort you?

FERROVIUS: [*Sternly*] Pray, man, pray.

SPINTHO: Whats the good of praying? If we're martyred we shall go to heaven, shant we, whether we pray or not?

FERROVIUS: Whats that? Not pray! [*Seizing him again*] Pray this instant, you dog, you rotten hound, you slimy snake, you beastly goat, or—

SPINTHO: Yes: beat me: kick me. I forgive you: mind that.

FERROVIUS: [*Spurning him with loathing*] Yah! [Spintho *reels away and falls in front of* Ferrovius]

ANDROCLES: [*Reaching out and catching the skirt of* Ferrovius's *tunic*] Dear brother: if you wouldnt mind—just for my sake—

FERROVIUS: Well?

ANDROCLES: Dont call him by the names of the animals. Weve no right to. Ive had such friends in dogs. A pet snake is the best of company. I was nursed on goat's milk. Is it fair to them to call the like of him a dog or a snake or a goat?

FERROVIUS: I only meant that they have no souls.

ANDROCLES: [*Anxiously protesting*] Oh, believe me, they have. Just the same as you and me. I really dont think I could consent to go to heaven if I thought there were to be no animals there. Think of what they suffer here.

FERROVIUS: Thats true. Yes: that is just. They will have their share in heaven.

SPINTHO: [*Who has picked himself up and is sneaking past* Ferrovius *on his left, sneers derisively*]!!

FERROVIUS: [*Turning on him fiercely*] Whats that you say?

SPINTHO: [*Cowering*] Nothing.

FERROVIUS: [*Clenching his fist*] Do animals go to heaven or not?

SPINTHO: I never said they didnt.

FERROVIUS: [*Implacable*] Do they or do they not?

SPINTHO: They do: they do. [*Scrambling out of* Ferrovius's *reach*] Oh, curse you for frightening me!

[*A bugle call is heard*]

CENTURION: [*Waking up*] Tention! Form as before. Now then, prisoners: up with you and trot along spry.

[*The soldiers fall in. The Christians rise*]

[*A man with an ox goad comes running through the central arch*]

THE OX DRIVER: Here, you soldiers! clear out of the way for the Emperor.

THE CENTURION: Emperor! Wheres the Emperor? You aint the Emperor, are you?

THE OX DRIVER: It's the menagerie service. My team of oxen is drawing the new lion to the Coliseum. You clear the road.

CENTURION: What! Go in after you in your dust, with half the town at the heels of you and your lion! Not likely. We go first.

THE OX DRIVER: The menagerie service is the Emperor's personal retinue. You clear out, I tell you.

CENTURION: You tell me, do you? Well, I'll tell you something. If the lion is menagerie service, the lion's dinner is menagerie service too. This [*Pointing to the* Christians] is the lion's dinner. So back with you to your bullocks double quick; and learn your place. March. [*The soldiers start*] Now then, you Christians: step out there.

LAVINIA: [*Marching*] Come along, the rest of the dinner. I shall be the olives and anchovies.

ANOTHER CHRISTIAN: [*Laughing*] I shall be the soup.

ANOTHER: I shall be the fish.

ANOTHER: Ferrovius shall be the roast boar.

FERROVIUS: [*Heavily*] I see the joke. Yes, yes: I shall be the roast boar. Ha! ha! [*He laughs conscientiously and marches out with them*]

ANDROCLES: [*Following*] I shall be the mince pie. [*Each announcement is received with a louder laugh by all the rest as the joke catches on*]

CENTURION: [*Scandalized*] Silence! Have some sense of your situation. Is this the way for martyrs to behave? [*To* Spintho, *who is quaking and loitering*] I know what youll be at that dinner. Youll be the emetic. [*He shoves him rudely along*]

SPINTHO: It's too dreadful: I'm not fit to die.

CENTURION: Fitter than you are to live, you swine.

[*They pass from the square westward. The oxen, drawing a waggon with a great wooden cage and the lion in it, arrive through the central arch*]

Act II

BEHIND *the Emperor's box at the Coliseum, where the performers assemble before entering the arena. In the middle a wide passage leading to the arena descends from the floor level under the imperial box. On both sides of this passage steps ascend to a landing at the back entrance to the box. The landing forms a bridge across the passage. At the entrance to the passage are two bronze mirrors, one on each side.*

On the west side of this passage, on the right hand of anyone coming from the box and standing on the bridge, the martyrs are sitting on the steps. Lavinia is seated half-way up, thoughtful, trying to look death in the face. On her left Androcles *consoles himself by nursing a cat.* Ferrovius *stands behind them, his eyes blazing, his figure stiff with intense resolution. At the foot of the steps crouches* Spintho, *with his head clutched in his hands, full of horror at the approach of martyrdom.*

On the east side of the passage the gladiators are standing and sitting at ease, waiting, like the Christians, *for their turn in the arena. One (Retiarius) is a nearly naked man with a net and a trident. Another (Secutor) is in armor with a sword. He carries a helmet with a barred visor. The editor of the gladiators sits on a chair a little apart from them.*

The Call Boy *enters from the passage.*

THE CALL BOY: Number six. Retiarius versus Secutor.

[*The gladiator with the net picks it up. The gladiator with the helmet puts it on; and the two go into the arena, the net thrower taking out a little brush and arranging his hair as he goes, the other tightening his straps and shaking his shoulders loose. Both look at themselves in the mirrors before they enter the passage*]

LAVINIA: Will they really kill one another?

SPINTHO: Yes, if the people turn down their thumbs.

THE EDITOR: You know nothing about it. The people indeed! Do you suppose we would kill a man worth perhaps fifty talents to please the riffraff? I should like to catch any of my men at it.

SPINTHO: I thought—

THE EDITOR: [*Contemptuously*] You thought! Who cares what you think? Youll be killed all right enough.

SPINTHO: [*Groans and again hides his face*]!!!

LAVINIA: Then is nobody ever killed except us poor Christians?

THE EDITOR: If the vestal virgins turn down their thumbs, thats another matter. Theyre ladies of rank.

LAVINIA: Does the Emperor ever interfere?

THE EDITOR: Oh, yes: he turns his thumb up fast enough if the vestal virgins want to have one of his pet fighting men killed.

ANDROCLES: But dont they ever just only pretend to kill one another? Why shouldnt you pretend to die, and get dragged out as if you were dead; and then get up and go home, like an actor?

THE EDITOR: See here: you want to know too much. There will be no pretending about the new lion: let that be enough for you. He's hungry.

SPINTHO: [*Groaning with horror*] Oh, Lord! cant you stop talking about it? Isnt it bad enough for us without that?

ANDROCLES: I'm glad he's hungry. Not that I want him to suffer, poor chap! but then he'll enjoy eating me so much more. Theres a cheerful side to everything.

THE EDITOR: [*Rising and striding over to* Androcles] Here: dont you be obstinate. Come with me and drop the pinch of incense on the altar. Thats all you need do to be let off.

ANDROCLES: No: thank you very much indeed; but I really mustnt.

THE EDITOR: What! Not to save your life?

ANDROCLES: I'd rather not. I couldnt sacrifice to Diana: she's a huntress, you know, and kills things.

THE EDITOR: That dont matter. You can choose your own altar. Sacrifice to Jupiter: he likes animals: he turns himself into an animal when he goes off duty.

ANDROCLES: No: it's very kind of you; but I feel I cant save myself that way.

THE EDITOR: But I dont ask you to do it to save yourself: I ask you to do it to oblige me personally.

ANDROCLES: [*Scrambling up in the greatest agitation*] Oh, please dont say that. This is dreadful. You mean so kindly by me that it seems quite horrible to disoblige you. If you could arrange for me to sacrifice when theres nobody looking, I shouldnt mind. But I must go into the arena with the rest. My honor, you know.

THE EDITOR: Honor! The honor of a tailor?

ANDROCLES: [*Apologetically*] Well, perhaps honor is too strong an expression. Still, you know, I couldnt allow the tailors to get a bad name through me.

THE EDITOR: How much will you remember of all that when you smell the beast's breath and see his jaws opening to tear out your throat?

SPINTHO: [*Rising with a yell of terror*] I cant bear it. Wheres the altar? I'll sacrifice.

FERROVIUS: Dog of an apostate. Iscariot!

SPINTHO: I'll repent afterwards. I fully mean to die in the arena: I'll die a martyr and go to heaven; but not this time, not now, not until my nerves are better. Besides, I'm too young: I want to have just one more good time. [*The gladiators laugh at him*] Oh, will no one tell me where the altar is? [*He dashes into the passage and vanishes*]

ANDROCLES: [*To the* Editor, *pointing after* Spintho] Brother: I cant do that, not even to oblige you. Dont ask me.

THE EDITOR: Well, if youre determined to die, I cant help you. But I wouldnt be put off by a swine like that.

FERROVIUS: Peace, peace: tempt him not. Get thee behind him, Satan.

THE EDITOR: [*Flushing with rage*] For two pins I'd take a turn in the arena myself today, and pay you out for daring to talk to me like that.

[*Ferrovius springs forward*]

LAVINIA: [*Rising quickly and interposing*] Brother, brother: you forget.

FERROVIUS: [*Curbing himself by a mighty effort*] Oh, my temper, my wicked temper! [*To the* Editor, *as* Lavinia *sits down again, reassured*]: Forgive me, brother. My heart was full of wrath: I should have been thinking of your dear precious soul.

THE EDITOR: Yah! [*He turns his back on* Ferrovius *contemptuously, and goes back to his seat*]

FERROVIUS: [*Continuing*] And I forgot it all: I thought of nothing but offering to fight you with one hand tied behind me.

THE EDITOR: [*Turning pugnaciously*] What!

FERROVIUS: [*On the border line between zeal and ferocity*] Oh, dont give way to pride and wrath, brother. I could do it so easily. I could—

[*They are separated by the* Menagerie Keeper, *who rushes in from the passage, furious*]

THE KEEPER: Heres a nice business! Who let that Christian out of here down to the dens when we were changing the lion into the cage next the arena?

THE EDITOR: Nobody let him. He let himself.

THE KEEPER: Well, the lion's ate him.

[*Consternation. The* Christians *rise, greatly agitated. The gladiators sit callously, but are highly amused. All speak or cry out or laugh at once. Tumult*]

LAVINIA: Oh, poor wretch! FERROVIUS: The apostate has perished. Praise be to God's justice! ANDROCLES: The poor beast was starving. It couldnt help itself. THE CHRISTIANS: What! Ate him! How frightful! How terrible! Without a moment to repent! God be merciful to him, a sinner! Oh, I cant bear to think of it! In the midst of his sin! Horrible, horrible! THE EDITOR: Serve the rotter right! THE GLADIATORS: Just walked into it, he did. He's martyred all right enough. Good old lion! Old Jock doesnt like that: look at his face. Devil a better!

The Emperor will laugh when he hears of it. I cant help smiling. Ha ha ha!!!!!

THE KEEPER: Now his appetite's taken off, he wont as much as look at another Christian for a week.

ANDROCLES: Couldnt you have saved him, brother?

THE KEEPER: Saved him! Saved him from a lion that I'd just got mad with hunger! a wild one that came out of the forest not four weeks ago! He bolted him before you could say Balbus.

LAVINIA: [*Sitting down again*] Poor Spintho! And it wont even count as martyrdom!

THE KEEPER: Serve him right! What call had he to walk down the throat of one of my lions before he was asked?

ANDROCLES: Perhaps the lion wont eat me now.

THE KEEPER: Yes: thats just like a Christian: think only of yourself! What am I to do? What am I to say to the Emperor when he sees one of my lions coming into the arena half asleep?

THE EDITOR: Say nothing. Give your old lion some bitters and a morsel of fried fish to wake up his appetite. [*Laughter*]

THE KEEPER: Yes: it's easy for you to talk; but—

THE EDITOR: [*Scrambling to his feet*] Sh! Attention there! The Emperor.

[*The* Keeper *bolts precipitately into the passage. The gladiators rise smartly and form into line*]

[*The* Emperor *enters on the* Christians' *side, conversing with* Metellus, *and followed by his suite*]

THE GLADIATORS: Hail, Caesar! those about to die salute thee.

CAESAR: Good morrow, friends.

[*Metellus* shakes hands with the Editor, *who accepts his condescension with bluff respect*]

LAVINIA: Blessing, Caesar, and forgiveness!

CAESAR: [*Turning in some surprise at the salutation*] There is no forgiveness for Christianity.

LAVINIA: I did not mean that, Caesar. I mean that we forgive you.

METELLUS: An inconceivable liberty! Do you not know, woman, that the Emperor can do no wrong and therefore cannot be forgiven?

LAVINIA: I expect the Emperor knows better. Anyhow, we forgive him.

THE CHRISTIANS: Amen!

CAESAR: Metellus: you see now the disadvantage of too much severity. These people have no hope; therefore they have nothing to restrain them from saying what they like to me. They are almost as impertinent as the gladiators. Which is the Greek sorcerer?

ANDROCLES: [*Humbly touching his forelock*] Me, your Worship.

CAESAR: My Worship! Good! A new title. Well: what miracles can you perform?

ANDROCLES: I can cure warts by rubbing them with

my tailor's chalk; and I can live with my wife without beating her.

CAESAR: Is that all?

ANDROCLES: You dont know her, Caesar, or you wouldnt say that.

CAESAR: Ah, well, my friend, we shall no doubt contrive a happy release for you. Which is Ferrovius?

FERROVIUS: I am he.

CAESAR: They tell me you can fight.

FERROVIUS: It is easy to fight. *I* can die, Caesar.

CAESAR: That is still easier, is it not?

FERROVIUS: Not to me, Caesar. Death comes hard to my flesh; and fighting comes very easily to my spirit. [*Beating his breast and lamenting*] Oh, sinner that I am! [*He throws himself down on the steps, deeply discouraged*]

CAESAR: I should like to have this man in the Pretorian Guard.

METELLUS: *I* should not, Caesar. He looks a spoilsport. There are men in whose presence it is impossible to have any fun: men who are a sort of walking conscience. He would make us all uncomfortable.

CAESAR: For that reason, perhaps, it might be well to have him. An Emperor can hardly have too many consciences. [*To Ferrovius*] Listen, Ferrovius. [*Ferrovius shakes his head and will not look up*] You and your friends shall not be outnumbered today in the arena. You shall have arms; and there will be no more than one gladiator to each Christian. If you come out of the arena alive, I will consider favorably any request of yours, and give you a place in the Pretorian Guard. Even if the request be that no questions be asked about your faith I shall perhaps not refuse it.

FERROVIUS: I will not fight. I will die. Better stand with the archangels than with the Pretorian Guard.

CAESAR: I cannot believe that the archangels—whoever they may be—would not prefer to be recruited from the Pretorian Guard. However, as you please. Come: let us see the show.

[*As the Court ascends the steps,* Secutor *and* Retiarius *return from the arena through the passage:* Secutor *covered with dust and very angry:* Retiarius *grinning*]

SECUTOR: Ha, the Emperor. Now we shall see. Caesar: I ask you whether it is fair for the Retiarius, instead of making a fair throw of his net at me, to swish it along the ground and throw the dust in my eyes, and then catch me when I'm blinded. If the vestals had not turned up their thumbs I should have been a dead man.

CAESAR: [*Halting on the stair*] There is nothing in the rules against it.

SECUTOR: [*Indignantly*] Caesar: is it a dirty trick or is it not?

CAESAR: It is a dusty one, my friend. [*Obsequious laughter*] Be on your guard next time.

SECUTOR: Let him be on his guard. Next time I'll throw my sword at his heels and strangle him with his own net before he can hop off. [*To the* Retiarius] You see if I dont. [*He goes out past the gladiators, sulky and furious*]

CAESAR: [*To the chuckling* Retiarius] These tricks are not wise, my friend. The audience likes to see a dead man in all his beauty and splendor. If you smudge his face and spoil his armor they will shew their displeasure by not letting you kill him. And when your turn comes, they will remember it against you and turn their thumbs down.

THE RETIARIUS: Perhaps that is why I did it, Caesar. He bet me ten sesterces that he would vanquish me. If I had had to kill him I should not have had the money.

CAESAR: [*Indulgent, laughing*] You rogues: there is no end to your tricks. I'll dismiss you all and have elephants to fight. They fight fairly. [*He goes up to his box, and knocks at it. It is opened from within by the* Captain, *who stands as on parade to let him pass*]

[*The* Call Boy *comes from the passage, followed by three attendants carrying respectively a bundle of swords, some helmets, and some breastplates and pieces of armor which they throw down in a heap*]

THE CALL BOY: By your leave, Caesar. Number eleven! Gladiators and Christians!

[*Ferrovius springs up, ready for martyrdom. The other* Christians *take the summons as best they can, some joyful and brave, some patient and dignified, some tearful and helpless, some embracing one another with emotion. The* Call Boy *goes back into the passage*]

CAESAR: [*Turning at the door of the box*] The hour has come, Ferrovius. I shall go into my box and see you killed, since you scorn the Pretorian Guard.

[*He goes into the box. The* Captain *shuts the door, remaining inside with the* Emperor. Metellus *and the rest of the suite disperse to their seats. The* Christians, *led by* Ferrovius, *move towards the passage*]

LAVINIA: [*To Ferrovius*] Farewell.

THE EDITOR: Steady there. You Christians have got to fight. Here! arm yourselves.

FERROVIUS: [*Picking up a sword*] I'll die sword in hand to shew people that I could fight if it were my Master's will, and that I could kill the man who kills me if I chose.

THE EDITOR: Put on that armor.

FERROVIUS: No armor.

THE EDITOR: [*Bullying him*] Do what youre told. Put on that armor.

FERROVIUS: [*Gripping the sword and looking dangerous*] I said, No armor.

THE EDITOR: And what am I to say when I am accused of sending a naked man in to fight my men in armor?

FERROVIUS: Say your prayers, brother; and have no fear of the princes of this world.

THE EDITOR: Tsha! You obstinate fool! [*He bites his lips irresolutely, not knowing exactly what to do*]

ANDROCLES: [*To Ferrovius*] Farewell, brother, till we meet in the sweet by-and-by.

THE EDITOR: [*To Androcles*] You are going too. Take a sword there; and put on any armor you can find to fit you.

ANDROCLES: No, really: I cant fight: I never could: I cant bring myself to dislike anyone enough. I'm to be thrown to the lions with the lady.

THE EDITOR: Then get out of the way and hold your noise. [*Androcles steps aside with cheerful docility*] Now then! Are you all ready there?

[*A trumpet is heard from the arena*]

FERROVIUS: [*Starting convulsively*] Heaven give me strength!

THE EDITOR: Aha! That frightens you, does it?

FERROVIUS: Man: there is no terror like the terror of that sound to me. When I hear a trumpet or a drum or the clash of steel or the hum of the cata-pult as the great stone flies, fire runs through my veins: I feel my blood surge up hot behind my eyes: I must charge: I must strike: I must conquer: Caesar himself will not be safe in his imperial seat if once that spirit gets loose in me. Oh, brothers, pray! exhort me! remind me that if I raise my sword my honor falls and my Master is crucified afresh.

ANDROCLES: Just keep thinking how cruelly you might hurt the poor gladiators.

FERROVIUS: It does not hurt a man to kill him.

LAVINIA: Nothing but faith can save you.

FERROVIUS: Faith! Which faith? There are two faiths. There is our faith. And there is the warrior's faith, the faith in fighting, the faith that sees God in the sword. How if that faith should overwhelm me?

LAVINIA: You will find your real faith in the hour of trial.

FERROVIUS: That is what I fear. I know that I am a fighter. How can I feel sure that I am a Christian?

ANDROCLES: Throw away the sword, brother.

FERROVIUS: I cannot. It cleaves to my hand. I could as easily throw a woman I loved from my arms. [*Starting*] Who spoke that blasphemy? Not I.

LAVINIA: I cant help you, friend. I cant tell you not to save your own life. Something wilful in me wants to see you fight your way into heaven.

FERROVIUS: Ha!

ANDROCLES: But if you are going to give up our faith, brother, why not do it without hurting anybody? Dont fight them. Burn the incense.

FERROVIUS: Burn the incense! Never.

LAVINIA: This is only pride, Ferrovius.

FERROVIUS: Only pride! What is nobler than pride?

[*Conscience stricken*] Oh, I'm steeped in sin. I'm proud of my pride.

LAVINIA: They say we Christians are the proudest devils on earth—that only the weak are meek. Oh, I am worse than you. I ought to send you to death; and I am tempting you.

ANDROCLES: Brother, brother: let them rage and kill: let us be brave and suffer. You must go as a lamb to the slaughter.

FERROVIUS: Aye, aye: that is right. Not as a lamb is slain by the butcher; but as a butcher might let himself be slain by a [*Looking at the* Editor] by a silly ram whose head he could fetch off in one twist.

[*Before the* Editor *can retort, the* Call Boy *rushes up through the passage, and the* Captain *comes from the* Emperor's *box and descends the steps*]

THE CALL BOY: In with you: into the arena. The stage is waiting.

THE CAPTAIN: The Emperor is waiting. [*To the* Editor] What are you dreaming of, man? Send your men in at once.

THE EDITOR: Yes, sir: it's these Christians hanging back.

FERROVIUS: [*In a voice of thunder*] Liar!

THE EDITOR: [*Not heeding him*] March. [*The gladi-ators told off to fight with the* Christians *march down the passage*] Follow up there, you.

THE CHRISTIAN MEN AND WOMEN: [*As they part*] Be steadfast, brother. Farewell. Hold up the faith, brother. Farewell. Go to glory, dearest. Farewell. Remember: we are praying for you. Farewell. Be strong, brother. Farewell. Dont forget that the divine love and our love surround you. Farewell. Nothing can hurt you: remember that, brother. Farewell. Eternal glory, dearest. Farewell.

THE EDITOR: [*Out of patience*] Shove them in, there.

[*The remaining gladiators and the* Call Boy *make a movement towards them*]

FERROVIUS: [*Interposing*] Touch them, dogs; and we die here, and cheat the heathen of their spectacle. [*To his fellow* Christians] Brothers: the great mo-ment has come. That passage is your hill to Calvary. Mount it bravely, but meekly; and re-member! not a word of reproach, not a blow nor a struggle. Go. [*They go out through the passage. He turns to* Lavinia] Farewell.

LAVINIA: You forget: I must follow before you are cold.

FERROVIUS: It is true. Do not envy me because I pass before you to glory. [*He goes through the pas-sage*]

THE EDITOR: [*To the* Call Boy] Sickening work, this. Why cant they all be thrown to the lions? It's not a man's job. [*He throws himself moodily into his chair*]

[*The remaining gladiators go back to their former places indifferently. The*

Call Boy *shrugs his shoulders and squats down at the entrance to the passage, near the* Editor] [Lavinia *and the Christian women sit down again, wrung with grief, some weeping silently, some praying, some calm and steadfast.* Androcles *sits down at* Lavinia's *feet. The Captain stands on the stairs, watching her curiously*]

ANDROCLES: I'm glad I havent to fight. That would really be an awful martyrdom. I am lucky.

LAVINIA: [*Looking at him with a pang of remorse*] Androcles: burn the incense: youll be forgiven. Let my death atone for both. I feel as if I were killing you.

ANDROCLES: Dont think of me, sister. Think of yourself. That will keep your heart up.

[*The* Captain *laughs sardonically*]

LAVINIA: [*Startled: she had forgotten his presence*] Are you there, handsome Captain? Have you come to see me die?

THE CAPTAIN: [*Coming to her side*] I am on duty with the Emperor, Lavinia.

LAVINIA: Is it part of your duty to laugh at us?

THE CAPTAIN: No: that is part of my private pleasure. Your friend here is a humorist. I laughed at his telling you to think of yourself to keep up your heart. I say, think of yourself and burn the incense.

LAVINIA: He is not a humorist: he was right. You ought to know that, Captain: you have been face to face with death.

THE CAPTAIN: Not with certain death, Lavinia. Only death in battle, which spares more men than death in bed. What you are facing is certain death. You have nothing left now but your faith in this craze of yours: this Christianity. Are your Christian fairy stories any truer than our stories about Jupiter and Diana, in which, I may tell you, I believe no more than the Emperor does, or any educated man in Rome?

LAVINIA: Captain: all that seems nothing to me now. I'll not say that death is a terrible thing; but I will say that it is so real a thing that when it comes close, all the imaginary things—all the stories, as you call them—fade into mere dreams beside that inexorable reality. I know now that I am not dying for stories or dreams. Did you hear of the dreadful thing that happened here while we were waiting?

THE CAPTAIN: I heard that one of your fellows bolted, and ran right into the jaws of the lion. I laughed. I still laugh.

LAVINIA: Then you dont understand what that meant?

THE CAPTAIN: It meant that the lion had a cur for his breakfast.

LAVINIA: It meant more than that, Captain. It meant that a man cannot die for a story and a dream. None of us believed the stories and the dreams more devoutly than poor Spintho; but he could not face the great reality. What he would have called my faith has been oozing away minute by minute whilst Ive been sitting here, with death coming nearer and nearer, with reality become realler and realler, with stories and dreams fading away into nothing.

THE CAPTAIN: Are you then going to die for nothing?

LAVINIA: Yes: that is the wonderful thing. It is since all the stories and dreams have gone that I have now no doubt at all that I must die for something greater than dreams or stories.

THE CAPTAIN: But for what?

LAVINIA: I dont know. If it were for anything small enough to know, it would be too small to die for. I think I'm going to die for God. Nothing else is real enough to die for.

THE CAPTAIN: What is God?

LAVINIA: When we know that, Captain, we shall be gods ourselves.

THE CAPTAIN: Lavinia: come down to earth. Burn the incense and marry me.

LAVINIA: Handsome Captain: would you marry me if I hauled down the flag in the day of battle and burnt the incense? Sons take after their mothers, you know. Do you want your son to be a coward?

THE CAPTAIN: [*Strongly moved*] By great Diana, I think I would strangle you if you gave in now.

LAVINIA: [*Putting her hand on the head of* Androcles] The hand of God is on us three, Captain.

THE CAPTAIN: What nonsense it all is! And what a monstrous thing that you should die for such nonsense, and that I should look on helplessly when my whole soul cries out against it! Die then if you must; but at least I can cut the Emperor's throat and then my own when I see your blood.

[*The* Emperor *throws open the door of his box angrily, and appears in wrath on the threshold. The* Editor, *the* Call Boy, *and the gladiators spring to their feet*]

THE EMPEROR: The Christians will not fight; and your curs cannot get their blood up to attack them. It's all that fellow with the blazing eyes. Send for the whip. [*The* Call Boy *rushes out on the east side for the whip*] If that will not move them, bring the hot irons. The man is like a mountain. [*He returns angrily into the box and slams the door*]

[*The* Call Boy *returns with a man in a hideous Etruscan mask, carrying a whip. They both rush down the passage into the arena*]

LAVINIA: [*Rising*] Oh, that is unworthy. Can they not kill him without dishonoring him?

ANDROCLES: [*Scrambling to his feet and running into the middle of the space between the staircases*] It's dreadful. Now *I* want to fight. I cant bear the sight of a whip. The only time I ever hit a man was when he lashed an old horse with a whip. It was terrible: I danced on his face when he was on the ground. He mustnt strike Ferrovius: I'll go into the arena and kill him first. [*He makes a wild dash into the passage. As he does so a great clamor is heard from the arena, ending in wild applause. The gladiators listen and look inquiringly at one another*]

THE EDITOR: Whats up now?

LAVINIA: [*To the* Captain] What has happened, do you think?

THE CAPTAIN: What can happen? They are killing them, I suppose.

ANDROCLES: [*Running in through the passage, screaming with horror and hiding his eyes*]!!!

LAVINIA: Androcles, Androcles: whats the matter?

ANDROCLES: Oh don't ask me, don't ask me. Something too dreadful. Oh! [*He crouches by her and hides his face in her robe, sobbing*]

THE CALL BOY: [*Rushing through from the passage as before*] Ropes and hooks there! Ropes and hooks!

THE EDITOR: Well, need you excite yourself about it?
                                      [*Another burst of applause*]

[*Two slaves in Etruscan masks, with ropes and drag hooks, hurry in*]

ONE OF THE SLAVES: How many dead?

THE CALL BOY: Six. [*The slave blows a whistle twice; and four more masked slaves rush through into the arena with the same apparatus*] And the basket. Bring the baskets. [*The slave whistles three times, and runs through the passage with his companion*]

THE CAPTAIN: Who are the baskets for?

THE CALL BOY: For the whip. He's in pieces. Theyre all in pieces, more or less. [*Lavinia hides her face*]

[*Two more masked slaves come in with a basket and follow the others into the arena, as the* Call Boy *turns to the gladiators and exclaims, exhausted*]: Boys: he's killed the lot.

THE EMPEROR: [*Again bursting from his box, this time in an ecstasy of delight*] Where is he? Magnificent! He shall have a laurel crown.

[Ferrovius, *madly waving his bloodstained sword, rushes through the passage in despair, followed by his co-religionists, and by the menagerie keeper, who goes to the gladiators. The gladiators draw their swords nervously*]

FERROVIUS: Lost! lost for ever! I have betrayed my Master. Cut off this right hand: it has offended. Ye have swords, my brethren: strike.

LAVINIA: No, no. What have you done, Ferrovius?

FERROVIUS: I know not; but there was blood behind my eyes; and theres blood on my sword. What does that mean?

THE EMPEROR: [*Enthusiastically, on the landing outside his box*] What does it mean? It means that you are the greatest man in Rome. It means that you shall have a laurel crown of gold. Superb fighter: I could almost yield you my throne. It is a record for my reign: I shall live in history. Once,

in Domitian's time, a Gaul slew three men in the arena and gained his freedom. But when before has one naked man slain six armed men of the bravest and best? The persecution shall cease: if Christians can fight like this, I shall have none but Christians to fight for me. [*To the gladiators*] You are ordered to become Christians, you there: do you hear?

RETIARIUS: It is all one to us, Caesar. Had I been there with my net, the story would have been different.

THE CAPTAIN: [*Suddenly seizing* Lavinia *by the wrist and dragging her up the steps to the* Emperor] Caesar: this woman is the sister of Ferrovius. If she is thrown to the lions he will fret. He will lose weight; get out of condition—

THE EMPEROR: The lions? Nonsense! [*To* Lavinia] Madam: I am proud to have the honor of making your acquaintance. Your brother is the glory of Rome.

LAVINIA: But my friends here. Must they die?

THE EMPEROR: Die! Certainly not. There has never been the slightest idea of harming them. Ladies and gentlemen: you are all free. Pray go into the front of the house and enjoy the spectacle to which your brother has so splendidly contributed. Captain: oblige me by conducting them to the seats reserved for my personal friends.

THE MENAGERIE KEEPER: Caesar: I must have one Christian for the lion. The people have been promised it; and they will tear the decorations to bits if they are disappointed.

THE EMPEROR: True, true: we must have somebody for the new lion.

FERROVIUS: Throw me to him. Let the apostate perish.

THE EMPEROR: No, no: you would tear him in pieces, my friend; and we cannot afford to throw away lions as if they were mere slaves. But we must have somebody. This is really extremely awkward.

THE MENAGERIE KEEPER: Why not that little Greek chap? He's not a Christian: he's a sorcerer.

THE EMPEROR: The very thing: he will do very well.

THE CALL BOY: [*Issuing from the passage*] Number twelve. The Christian for the new lion.

ANDROCLES: [*Rising, and pulling himself sadly together*] Well, it was to be, after all.

LAVINIA: I'll go in his place, Caesar. Ask the captain whether they do not like best to see a woman torn to pieces. He told me so yesterday.

THE EMPEROR: There is something in that: there is certainly something in that—if only I could feel sure that your brother would not fret.

ANDROCLES: No: I should never have another happy hour. No: on the faith of a Christian and the honor of a tailor, I accept the lot that has fallen on me. If my wife turns up, give her my love and say that my wish was that she should be happy with her next, poor fellow! Caesar: go to your box and see how a tailor can die. Make way for number twelve there. [*He marches out along the passage*]

[*The vast audience in the amphitheatre now sees the* Emperor *re-enter his box and take his place as* Androcles, *desperately frightened, but still marching with piteous devotion, emerges from the other end of the passage, and finds himself at the focus of thousands of eager eyes. The lion's cage, with a heavy portcullis grating, is on his left. The* Emperor *gives a signal. A gong sounds.* Androcles *shivers at the sound; then falls on his knees and prays. The grating rises with a clash. The lion bounds into the arena. He rushes round frisking in his freedom. He sees* Androcles. *He stops; rises stiffly by straightening his legs; stretches out his nose forward and his tail in a horizontal line behind, like a pointer, and utters an appalling roar.* Androcles *crouches and hides his face in his hands. The lion gathers himself for a spring, swishing his tail to and fro through the dust in an ecstasy of anticipation.* Androcles *throws up his hands in supplication to heaven. The lion checks at the sight of* Androcles's *face. He then steals towards him; smells him; arches his back; purrs like a motor car; finally rubs himself against* Androcles, *knocking him over.* Androcles, *supporting himself on his wrist, looks affrightedly at the lion. The lion limps on three paws, holding up the other as if it was wounded. A flash of recognition lights up the face of* Androcles. *He flaps his hand as if it had a thorn in it, and pretends to pull the thorn out and to hurt himself. The lion nods repeatedly.* Androcles *holds out his hands to the lion, who gives him both paws, which he shakes with enthusiasm. They embrace rapturously, finally waltz round the arena amid a sudden burst of deafening applause, and out through the passage, the* Emperor *watching them in breathless astonishment until they disappear, when he rushes from his box and descends the steps in frantic excitement*]

THE EMPEROR: My friends, an incredible! an amazing thing! has happened. I can no longer doubt the truth of Christianity. [*The* Christians *press to him joyfully*] This Christian sorcerer—[*With a yell, he breaks off as he sees* Androcles *and the lion emerge from the passage, waltzing. He bolts wildly up the steps into his box, and slams the door. All,* Christians *and gladiators alike, fly for their lives, the gladiators bolting into the arena, the others in all directions. The place is emptied with magical suddenness*]

ANDROCLES: [*Naïvely*] Now I wonder why they all run away from us like that. [*The lion, combining a series of yawns, purrs, and roars, achieves something very like a laugh*]

THE EMPEROR: [*Standing on a chair inside his box and looking over the wall*] Sorcerer: I command

you to put that lion to death instantly. It is guilty of high treason. Your conduct is most disgra—[*The lion charges at him up the stairs*] Help! [*He disappears. The lion rears against the box; looks over the partition at him; and roars. The* Emperor *darts out through the door and down to* Androcles, *pursued by the lion*]

ANDROCLES: Dont run away, sir: he cant help springing if you run. [*He seizes the* Emperor *and gets between him and the lion, who stops at once*] Dont be afraid of him.

THE EMPEROR: I am not afraid of him. [*The lion crouches, growling. The* Emperor *clutches* Androcles] Keep between us.

ANDROCLES: Never be afraid of animals, your worship: thats the great secret. He'll be as gentle as a lamb when he knows that you are his friend. Stand quite still; and smile; and let him smell you all over just to reassure him; for, you see, he's afraid of you; and he must examine you thoroughly before he gives you his confidence. [*To the lion*] Come now, Tommy; and speak nicely to the Emperor, the great good Emperor who has power to have all our heads cut off if we dont behave very very respectfully to him.

[*The lion utters a fearful roar. The* Emperor *dashes madly up the steps, across the landing, and down again on the other side, with the lion in hot pursuit.* Androcles *rushes after the lion; overtakes him as he is descending; and throws himself on his back, trying to use his toes as a brake. Before he can stop him the lion gets hold of the trailing end of the* Emperor's *robe*]

ANDROCLES: Oh bad wicked Tommy, to chase the Emperor like that! Let go the Emperor's robe at once, sir: wheres your manners? [*The lion growls and worries the robe*] Dont pull it away from him, your worship. He's only playing. Now I shall be really angry with you, Tommy, if you dont let go. [*The lion growls again*] I'll tell you what it is, sir: he thinks you and I are not friends.

THE EMPEROR: [*Trying to undo the clasp of his brooch*] Friends! You infernal scoundrel [*The lion growls*]—dont let him go. Curse this brooch! I cant get it loose.

ANDROCLES: We mustnt let him lash himself into a rage. You must shew him that you are my particular friend—if you will have the condescension. [*He seizes the* Emperor's *hands and shakes them cordially*] Look, Tommy: the nice Emperor is the dearest friend Andy Wandy has in the whole world: he loves him like a brother.

THE EMPEROR: You little brute, you damned filthy little dog of a Greek tailor: I'll have you burnt alive for daring to touch the divine person of the Emperor. [*The lion growls*]

ANDROCLES: Oh dont talk like that, sir. He understands every word you say: all animals do: they take it from the tone of your voice. [*The lion growls and lashes his tail*] I think he's going to spring at your worship. If you wouldnt mind saying something affectionate.   [*The lion roars*]

THE EMPEROR: [*Shaking* Androcles's *hands frantically*] My dearest Mr Androcles, my sweetest friend, my long lost brother, come to my arms. [*He embraces* Androcles] Oh, what an abominable smell of garlic!

[*The lion lets go the robe and rolls over on his back, clasping his forepaws over one another coquettishly above his nose*]

ANDROCLES: There! You see, your worship, a child might play with him now. See! [*He tickles the lion's belly. The lion wriggles ecstatically*] Come and pet him.

THE EMPEROR: I must conquer these unkingly terrors. Mind you dont go away from him, though. [*He pats the lion's chest*]

ANDROCLES: Oh, sir, how few men would have the courage to do that!

THE EMPEROR: Yes: it takes a bit of nerve. Let us have the Court in and frighten them. Is he safe, do you think?

ANDROCLES: Quite safe now, sir.

THE EMPEROR: [*Majestically*] What ho, there! All who are within hearing, return without fear. Caesar has tamed the lion. [*All the fugitives steal cautiously in. The* Menagerie Keeper *comes from the passage with other keepers armed with iron bars and tridents*] Take those things away. I have subdued the beast. [*He places his foot on it*]

FERROVIUS: [*Timidly approaching the* Emperor *and looking down with awe on the lion*] It is strange that I, who fear no man, should fear a lion.

THE CAPTAIN: Every man fears something, Ferrovius.

THE EMPEROR: How about the Pretorian Guard now?

FERROVIUS: In my youth I worshipped Mars, the God of War. I turned from him to serve the Christian god; but today the Christian god forsook me; and Mars overcame me and took back his own. The Christian god is not yet. He will come when Mars and I are dust; but meanwhile I must serve the gods that are, not the God that will be. Until then I accept service in the Guard, Caesar.

THE EMPEROR: Very wisely said. All really sensible men agree that the prudent course is to be neither bigoted in our attachment to the old nor rash and unpractical in keeping an open mind for the new, but to make the best of both dispensations.

THE CAPTAIN: What do you say, Lavinia? Will you too be prudent?

LAVINIA: [*On the stairs*] No: I'll strive for the coming of the God who is not yet.

THE CAPTAIN: May I come and argue with you occasionally?

LAVINIA: Yes, handsome Captain: you may.

[*He kisses her hand*]

THE EMPEROR: And now, my friends, though I do not, as you see, fear this lion, yet the strain of his presence is considerable; for none of us can feel quite sure what he will do next.

THE MENAGERIE KEEPER: Caesar: give us this Greek sorcerer to be a slave in the menagerie. He has a way with the beasts.

ANDROCLES: [*Distressed*] Not if they are in cages. They should not be kept in cages. They must be all let out.

THE EMPEROR: I give this sorcerer to be a slave to the first man who lays hands on him. [*The menagerie keepers and the gladiators rush for* Androcles. *The lion starts up and faces them. They surge back*] You see how magnanimous we Romans are, Androcles. We suffer you to go in peace.

ANDROCLES: I thank your worship. I thank you all, ladies and gentlemen. Come, Tommy. Whilst we stand together, no cage for you: no slavery for me. [*He goes out with the lion, everybody crowding away to give him as wide a berth as possible*]

In this play I have presented one of the Roman persecutions of the early Christians, not as the conflict of a false theology with a true, but as what all such persecutions essentially are: an attempt to suppress a propaganda that seemed to threaten the interests involved in the established law and order, organized and maintained in the name of religion and justice by politicians who are pure opportunist Have-and-Holders. People who are shewn by their inner light the possibility of a better world based on the demand of the spirit for a nobler and more abundant life, not for themselves at the expense of others, but for everybody, are naturally dreaded and therefore hated by the Have-and-Holders, who keep always in reserve two sure weapons against them. The first is a persecution effected by the provocation, organization, and arming of that herd instinct which makes men abhor all departures from custom, and, by the most cruel punishments and the wildest calumnies, force eccentric people to behave and profess exactly as other people do. The second is by leading the herd to war, which immediately and infallibly makes them forget everything, even their most cherished and hard won public liberties and private interests, in the irresistible surge of their pugnacity and the tense preoccupation of their terror.

There is no reason to believe that there was anything more in the Roman persecutions than this. The attitude of the Roman Emperor and the officers of his staff towards the opinions at issue were much the same as those of a modern British Home Secretary towards members of the lower middle classes when some pious policeman charges them with Bad Taste, technically called blasphemy: Bad Taste being a violation of Good Taste, which in such matters practically means Hypocrisy. The Home Secretary and the judges who try the case are usually far more sceptical and blasphemous than the poor men whom they persecute; and their professions of horror at the blunt utterance of their own opinions are revolting to those behind the scenes who have any genuine religious sensibility; but the thing is done because the governing classes, provided only the law against blasphemy is not applied to themselves, strongly approve of such persecution because it enables them to represent their own privileges as part of the religion of the country.

Therefore my martyrs are the martyrs of all time, and my persecutors the persecutors of all time. My Emperor, who has no sense of the value of common people's lives, and amuses himself with killing as carelessly as with sparing, is the sort of monster you can make of any silly-clever gentleman by idolizing him. We are still so easily imposed on by such idols that one of the leading pastors of the Free Churches in London denounced my play on the ground that my persecuting Emperor is a very fine fellow, and the persecuted Christians ridiculous. From which I conclude that a popular pulpit may be as perilous to a man's soul as an imperial throne.

All my articulate Christians, the reader will notice, have different enthusiasms, which they accept as the same religion only because it involves them in a common opposition to the official religion and consequently in a common doom. Androcles is a humanitarian naturalist, whose views surprise everybody. Lavinia, a clever and fearless freethinker, shocks the Pauline Ferrovius, who is comparatively stupid and conscience ridden. Spintho, the blackguardly debauchee, is presented as one of the typical Christians of that period on the authority of St Augustine, who seems to have come to the conclusion at one period of his development that most Christians were what we call wrong uns. No doubt he was to some extent right: I have had occasion often to point out that revolutionary movements attract those who are not good enough for established institutions as well as those who are too good for them.

But the most striking aspect of the play at this moment is the terrible topicality given it by the war. We were at peace when I pointed out, by the mouth of Ferrovius, the path of an honest man who finds out, when the trumpet sounds, that he cannot follow Jesus. Many years earlier, in The Devil's Disciple, I touched the same theme even more definitely, and shewed the minister throwing off his black coat for ever when he discovered, amid the thunder of the captains and the shouting, that he was a born fighter. Great numbers of our clergy have found themselves of late in the position of Ferrovius and Anthony Anderson. They have discovered that they hate not only their enemies but everyone who does not share their hatred, and that they want to fight and to force other people to fight. They have turned their churches into recruiting stations and their vestries

into munition workshops. But it has never occurred to them to take off their black coats and say quite simply, "I find in the hour of trial that the Sermon on the Mount is tosh, and that I am not a Christian. I apologize for all the unpatriotic nonsense I have been preaching all these years. Have the goodness to give me a revolver and a commission in a regiment which has for its chaplain a priest of the god Mars: my God." Not a bit of it. They have stuck to their livings and served Mars in the name of Christ, to the scandal of all religious mankind. When the Archbishop of York behaved like a gentleman and the Head Master of Eton preached a Christian sermon, and were reviled by the rabble, the Martian parsons encouraged the rabble. For this they made no apologies or excuses, good or bad. They simply indulged their passions, just as they had always indulged their class prejudices and commercial interests, without troubling themselves for a moment as to whether they were Christians or not. They did not protest even when a body calling itself the Anti-German League (not having noticed, apparently, that it had been anticipated by the British Empire, the French Republic, and the Kingdoms of Italy, Japan, and Serbia) actually succeeded in closing a church at Forest Hill in which God was worshipped in the German language. One would have supposed that this grotesque outrage on the commonest decencies of religion would have provoked a remonstrance from even the worldliest bench of bishops. But no: apparently it seemed to the bishops as natural that the House of God should be looted when He allowed German to be spoken in it as that a baker's shop with a German name over the door should be pillaged. Their verdict was, in effect, "Serve God right, for creating the Germans!" The incident would have been impossible in a country where the Church was as powerful as the Church of England, had it had at the same time a spark of catholic as distinguished from tribal religion in it. As it is, the thing occurred; and as far as I have observed, the only people who gasped were the Freethinkers.

Thus we see that even among men who make a profession of religion the great majority are as Martian as the majority of their congregations. The average clergyman is an official who makes his living by christening babies, marrying adults, conducting a ritual, and making the best he can (when he has any conscience about it) of a certain routine of school superintendence, district visiting, and organization of almsgiving, which does not necessarily touch Christianity at any point except the point of the tongue. The exceptional or religious clergyman may be an ardent Pauline salvationist, in which case his more cultivated parishioners dislike him, and say that he ought to have joined the Methodists. Or he may be an artist expressing religious emotion without intellectual definition by means of poetry, music, vestments, and architecture, also producing religious ecstasy by physical expedients, such as fasts and vigils, in which case he is denounced as a Ritualist. Or he may be either a Unitarian Deist like Voltaire or Tom Paine, or the more modern sort of Anglican Theosophist to whom the Holy Ghost is the Élan Vital of Bergson, and the Father and Son are an expression of the fact that our functions and aspects are manifold, and that we are all sons and all either potential or actual parents, in which case he is strongly suspected by the straiter Salvationists of being little better than an Atheist. All these varieties, you see, excite remark. They may be very popular with their congregations; but they are regarded by the average man as the freaks of the Church. The Church, like the society of which it is an organ, is balanced and steadied by the great central Philistine mass above whom theology looms as a highly spoken of and doubtless most important thing, like Greek Tragedy, or classical music, or the higher mathematics, but who are very glad when church is over and they can go home to lunch or dinner, having in fact, for all practical purposes, no reasoned convictions at all, and being equally ready to persecute a poor Freethinker for saying that St James was not infallible, and to send one of the Peculiar People to prison for being so very peculiar as to take St James seriously.

In short, a Christian martyr was thrown to the lions not because he was a Christian, but because he was a crank: that is, an unusual sort of person. And multitudes of people, quite as civilized and amiable as we, crowded to see the lions eat him just as they now crowd the lion-house in the Zoo at feeding-time, not because they really cared twopence about Diana or Christ, or could have given you any intelligent or correct account of the things Diana and Christ stood against one another for, but simply because they wanted to see a curious and exciting spectacle. You,

dear reader, have probably run to see a fire; and if somebody came in now and told you that a lion was chasing a man down the street you would rush to the window. And if anyone were to say that you were as cruel as the people who let the lion loose on the man, you would be justly indignant. Now that we may no longer see a man hanged, we assemble outside the jail to see the black flag run up. That is our duller method of enjoying ourselves in the old Roman spirit. And if the Government decided to throw persons of unpopular or eccentric views to the lions in the Albert Hall or the Earl's Court stadium tomorrow, can you doubt that all the seats would be crammed, mostly by people who could not give you the most superficial account of the views in question. Much less unlikely things have happened. It is true that if such a revival does take place soon, the martyrs will not be members of heretical religious sects: they will be Peculiars, Anti-Vivisectionists, Flat-Earth men, scoffers at the laboratories, or infidels who refuse to kneel down when a procession of doctors goes by. But the lions will hurt them just as much, and the spectators will enjoy themselves just as much, as the Roman lions and spectators used to do.

It was currently reported in the Berlin newspapers that when Androcles was first performed in Berlin, the Crown Prince rose and left the house, unable to endure the (I hope) very clear and fair exposition of autocratic Imperialism given by the Roman captain to his Christian prisoners. No English Imperialist was intelligent and earnest enough to do the same in London. If the report is correct, I confirm the logic of the Crown Prince, and am glad to find myself so well understood. But I can assure him that the Empire which served for my model when I wrote Androcles was, as he is now finding to his cost, much nearer my home than the German one.

Pygmalion

by GEORGE BERNARD SHAW

Pygmalion is one of the most satisfying of G.B.S.'s comedies, and one of the most pleasantly Shavian. Who else, we might ask, would forge a plot—a fairy-tale plot—out of phonetics? And yet it is only the dry scientific word that is so anomalous. For in England the thing the word represents is of vast social importance, and it is largely through how he pronounces his words whether an Englishman shall be himself pronounced a gentleman. What is Shavian about the play in a far deeper sense is that its Pygmalion turns out to be not the sculptor but the statue. It is he, Higgins, who remains a man of stone when confronted with the woman he has brought to life: indeed, this Galatea must face the fact that she is a mere offshoot of science and not at all a creature of romance.

Yet it is just this unlustrous variation, this drastic violation, of the legend that constitutes the dramatic merit—more even than it does the intellectual meaning—of the play. With Pygmalion, as opposed to its heroine, the scientific rather than romantic approach is a great gain: the play emerges a fresh and novel stage experiment rather than just one more obvious, conventional romance. It is because Higgins doesn't fall in love with Liza that she is really able to come to life. It is his lack of interest in her as a woman that turns her into one; it is his caring only about how she speaks, and not at all about what she says, that provokes her into saying such sharp-tongued things. It is the sexlessness of the professor with a mother fixation that turns Pygmalion, more than most Shaw plays, into genuine sexual comedy.

As social comedy, the play has, of course, all the amusing detail that goes into the creation of a lady. There is in particular Mrs. Higgins' famous At Home scene; and for picturesque contrast, there is the figure of Liza's dustman father, that fine representation of the unworthy poor. But I strongly suspect that it is all the paraphernalia of the Cinderella story that gives Pygmalion a kind of primitive charm: even knowing Shaw, we can't quite believe that the glass coach—or, as actually happens, the Fairy Prince—will turn into a pumpkin. Indeed, Shaw half encourages us not to believe it, and only informs us in an epilogue not meant for the stage that it was Freddie Liza married rather than Higgins or a duke; and a florist shop that became her destiny. Was it sound sense on Shaw's part, or ultimate irony, that Liza should end up spang in the bosom of the bourgeoisie?

GEORGE BERNARD SHAW

Pygmalion

A ROMANCE IN FIVE ACTS

Preface

A Professor of Phonetics

As will be seen later on, Pygmalion needs, not a preface, but a sequel, which I have supplied in its due place.

The English have no respect for their language, and will not teach their children to speak it. They spell it so abominably that no man can teach himself what it sounds like. It is impossible for an Englishman to open his mouth without making some other Englishman hate or despise him. German and Spanish are accessible to foreigners: English is not accessible even to Englishmen. The reformer England needs today is an energetic phonetic enthusiast: that is why I have made such a one the hero of a popular play. There have been heroes of that kind crying in the wilderness for many years past. When I became interested in the subject towards the end of the eighteen-seventies, the illustrious Alexander Melville Bell, the inventor of Visible Speech, had emigrated to Canada, where his son invented the telephone; but Alexander J. Ellis was still a London patriarch, with an impressive head always covered by a velvet skull cap, for which he would apologize to public meetings in a very courtly manner. He and Tito Pagliardini, another phonetic veteran, were men whom it was impossible to dislike. Henry Sweet, then a young man, lacked their sweetness of character: he was about as conciliatory to conventional mortals as Ibsen or Samuel Butler. His great ability as a phonetician (he was, I think, the best of them all at his job) would have entitled him to high official recognition, and perhaps enabled him to popularize his subject, but for his Satanic contempt for all academic dignitaries and persons in general who thought more of Greek than of phonetics. Once, in the days when the Imperial Institute rose in South Kensington, and Joseph Chamberlain was booming the Empire, I induced the editor of a leading monthly review to commission an article from Sweet on the imperial importance of his subject. When it arrived, it contained nothing but a savagely derisive attack on a professor of language and literature whose chair Sweet re-

garded as proper to a phonetic expert only. The article, being libellous, had to be returned as impossible; and I had to renounce my dream of dragging its author into the limelight. When I met him afterwards, for the first time for many years, I found to my astonishment that he, who had been a quite tolerably presentable young man, had actually managed by sheer scorn to alter his personal appearance until he had become a sort of walking repudiation of Oxford and all its traditions. It must have been largely in his own despite that he was squeezed into something called a Readership of phonetics there. The future of phonetics rests probably with his pupils, who all swore by him; but nothing could bring the man himself into any sort of compliance with the university to which he nevertheless clung by divine right in an intensely Oxonian way. I daresay his papers, if he has left any, include some satires that may be published without too destructive results fifty years hence. He was, I believe, not in the least an illnatured man: very much the opposite, I should say; but he would not suffer fools gladly.

Those who knew him will recognize in my third act the allusion to the patent shorthand in which he used to write postcards, and which may be acquired from a four and sixpenny manual published by the Clarendon Press. The postcards which Mrs Higgins describes are such as I have received from Sweet. I would decipher a sound which a cockney would represent by *zerr*, and a Frenchman by *seu*, and then write demanding with some heat what on earth it meant. Sweet, with boundless contempt for my stupidity, would reply that it not only meant but obviously was the word Result, as no other word containing that sound, and capable of making sense with the context, existed in any language spoken on earth. That less expert mortals should require fuller indications was beyond Sweet's patience. Therefore, though the whole point of his Current Shorthand is that it can express every sound in the language perfectly, vowels as well as consonants, and that your hand has to make no stroke except the easy and current ones with which you write m, n, and u, l, p, and q, scribbling them at whatever angle comes easiest to you, his unfortunate determination to make this remarkable and quite legible script serve also as a shorthand reduced it in his own practice to the most inscrutable of cryptograms. His true objective was the provision of a full, accurate, legible script for our noble but ill-dressed language; but he was led past that by his contempt for the popular Pitman system of shorthand, which he called the Pitfall system. The triumph of Pitman was a triumph of business organization: there was a weekly paper to persuade you to learn Pitman: there were cheap textbooks and exercise books and transcripts of speeches for you to copy, and schools where experienced teachers coached you up to the necessary proficiency. Sweet could not organize his market in that fashion. He might as well have been the Sybil who tore up the leaves of prophecy that nobody would attend to. The four and sixpenny manual, mostly in his lithographed handwriting, that was never vulgarly advertized, may perhaps some day be taken up by a syndicate and pushed upon the public as The Times pushed the Encyclopædia Britannica; but until then it will certainly not prevail against Pitman. I have bought three copies of it during my lifetime; and I am informed by the publishers that its cloistered existence is still a steady and healthy one. I actually learned the system two several times; and yet the shorthand in which I am writing these lines is Pitman's. And the reason is, that my secretary cannot transcribe Sweet, having been perforce taught in the schools of Pitman. Therefore, Sweet railed at Pitman as vainly as Thersites railed at Ajax: his raillery, however it may have eased his soul, gave no popular vogue to Current Shorthand.

Pygmalion Higgins is not a portrait of Sweet, to whom the adventure of Eliza Doolittle would have been impossible; still, as will be seen, there are touches of Sweet in the play. With Higgins's physique and temperament Sweet might have set the Thames on fire. As it was, he impressed himself professionally on Europe to an extent that made his comparative personal obscurity, and the failure of Oxford to do justice to his eminence, a puzzle to foreign specialists in his subject. I do not blame Oxford, because I think Oxford is quite right in demanding a certain social amenity from its nurslings

(heaven knows it is not exorbitant in its requirements!); for although I well know how hard it is for a man of genius with a seriously underrated subject to maintain serene and kindly relations with the men who underrate it, and who keep all the best places for less important subjects which they profess without originality and sometimes without much capacity for them, still, if he overwhelms them with wrath and disdain, he cannot expect them to heap honors on him.

Of the later generations of phoneticians I know little. Among them towers the Poet Laureate, to whom perhaps Higgins may owe his Miltonic sympathies, though here again I must disclaim all portraiture. But if the play makes the public aware that there are such people as phoneticians, and that they are among the most important people in England at present, it will serve its turn.

I wish to boast that Pygmalion has been an extremely successful play all over Europe and North America as well as at home. It is so intensely and deliberately didactic, and its subject is esteemed so dry, that I delight in throwing it at the heads of the wiseacres who repeat the parrot cry that art should never be didactic. It goes to prove my contention that art should never be anything else.

Finally, and for the encouragement of people troubled with accents that cut them off from all high employment, I may add that the change wrought by Professor Higgins in the flower-girl is neither impossible nor uncommon. The modern concierge's daughter who fulfils her ambition by playing the Queen of Spain in Ruy Blas at the Théâtre Français is only one of many thousands of men and women who have sloughed off their native dialects and acquired a new tongue. But the thing has to be done scientifically, or the last state of the aspirant may be worse than the first. An honest and natural slum dialect is more tolerable than the attempt of a phonetically untaught person to imitate the vulgar dialect of the golf club; and I am sorry to say that in spite of the efforts of our Royal Academy of Dramatic Art, there is still too much sham golfing English on our stage, and too little of the noble English of Forbes-Robertson.

Pygmalion

Act I

Covent Garden at 11.15 p.m. Torrents of heavy summer rain. Cab whistles blowing frantically in

all directions. Pedestrians running for shelter into the market and under the portico of St Paul's Church, where there are already several people, among them a lady and her daughter in evening dress. They are all peering out gloomily at the rain, except one man with his back turned to the rest, who seems wholly preoccupied with a notebook in which he is writing busily.

The church clock strikes the first quarter.

THE DAUGHTER: [*In the space between the central pillars, close to the one on her left*] I'm getting chilled to the bone. What can Freddy be doing all this time? He's been gone twenty minutes.

THE MOTHER: [*On her daughter's right*] Not so long. But he ought to have got us a cab by this.

A BYSTANDER: [*On the lady's right*] He wont get no cab not until half-past eleven, missus, when they come back after dropping their theatre fares.

THE MOTHER: But we must have a cab. We cant stand here until half-past eleven. It's too bad.

THE BYSTANDER: Well, it aint my fault, missus.

THE DAUGHTER: If Freddy had a bit of gumption, he would have got one at the theatre door.

THE MOTHER: What could he have done, poor boy?

THE DAUGHTER: Other people got cabs. Why couldnt he?

[*Freddy rushes in out of the rain from the Southampton Street side, and comes between them closing a dripping umbrella. He is a young man of twenty, in evening dress, very wet round the ankles*]

THE DAUGHTER: Well, havent you got a cab?

FREDDY: Theres not one to be had for love or money.

THE MOTHER: Oh, Freddy, there must be one. You cant have tried.

THE DAUGHTER: It's too tiresome. Do you expect us to go and get one ourselves?

FREDDY: I tell you theyre all engaged. The rain was so sudden: nobody was prepared; and everybody had to take a cab. Ive been to Charing Cross one way and nearly to Ludgate Circus the other; and they were all engaged.

THE MOTHER: Did you try Trafalgar Square?

THE DAUGHTER: Did you try?

FREDDY: I tried as far as Charing Cross Station. Did you expect me to walk to Hammersmith?

THE DAUGHTER: You havent tried at all.

THE MOTHER: You really are very helpless, Freddy. Go again; and dont come back until you have found a cab.

FREDDY: I shall simply get soaked for nothing.

THE DAUGHTER: And what about us? Are we to stay here all night in this draught, with next to nothing on? You selfish pig—

FREDDY: Oh, very well: I'll go, I'll go. [*He opens his umbrella and dashes off Strandwards, but comes into collision with a flower girl, who is hurrying in for shelter, knocking her basket out of her hands. A blinding flash of lightning, followed instantly by a rattling peal of thunder, orchestrates the incident*]

THE FLOWER GIRL: Nah then, Freddy: look wh'y' gowin, deah.

FREDDY: Sorry. [*He rushes off*]

THE FLOWER GIRL: [*Picking up her scattered flowers and replacing them in the basket*] Theres menners f' yer! Te-oo banches o voylets trod into the mad. [*She sits down on the plinth of the column, sorting her flowers, on the lady's right. She is not at all an attractive person. She is perhaps eighteen, perhaps twenty, hardly older. She wears a little sailor hat of black straw that has long been exposed to the dust and soot of London and has seldom if ever been brushed. Her hair needs washing rather badly: its mousy color can hardly be natural. She wears a shoddy black coat that reaches nearly to her knees and is shaped to her waist. She has a brown skirt with a coarse apron. Her boots are much the worse for wear. She is no doubt as clean as she can afford to be; but compared to the ladies she is very dirty. Her features are no worse than theirs; but their condition leaves something to be desired; and she needs the services of a dentist*]

THE MOTHER: How do you know that my son's name is Freddy, pray?

THE FLOWER GIRL: Ow, eez ye-ooa san, is e? Wal, fewd dan y' de-ooty bawmz a mather should, eed now bettern to spawl a pore gel's flahrzn than ran awy athaht pyin. Will ye-oo py me f'them? [*Here, with apologies, this desperate attempt to represent her dialect without a phonetic alphabet must be abandoned as unintelligible outside London*]

THE DAUGHTER: Do nothing of the sort, mother. The idea!

THE MOTHER: Please allow me, Clara. Have you any pennies?

THE DAUGHTER: No. I've nothing smaller than sixpence.

THE FLOWER GIRL: [*Hopefully*] I can give you change for a tanner, kind lady.

THE MOTHER: [*To Clara*] Give it to me. [*Clara parts reluctantly*] Now [*To the girl*] this is for your flowers.

THE FLOWER GIRL: Thank you kindly, lady.

THE DAUGHTER: Make her give you the change. These things are only a penny a bunch.

THE MOTHER: Do hold your tongue, Clara. [*To the girl*] You can keep the change.

THE FLOWER GIRL: Oh, thank you, lady.

THE MOTHER: Now tell me how you know that young gentleman's name.

THE FLOWER GIRL: I didnt.

THE MOTHER: I heard you call him by it. Dont try to deceive me.

THE FLOWER GIRL: [*Protesting*] Who's trying to deceive you? I called him Freddy or Charlie same as you might yourself if you was talking to a stranger and wished to be pleasant. [*She sits down beside her basket*]

THE DAUGHTER: Sixpence thrown away! Really, mamma, you might have spared Freddy that. [*She retreats in disgust behind the pillar*]

[*An elderly gentleman of the amiable military type rushes into the shelter, and closes a dripping umbrella. He is in the same plight as* Freddy, *very wet about the ankles. He is in evening dress, with a light overcoat. He takes the place left vacant by the daughter's retirement*]

THE GENTLEMAN: Phew!

THE MOTHER: [*To the gentleman*] Oh, sir, is there any sign of its stopping?

THE GENTLEMAN: I'm afraid not. It started worse than ever about two minutes ago. [*He goes to the plinth beside the flower girl; puts up his foot on it; and stoops to turn down his trouser ends*]

THE MOTHER: Oh dear! [*She retires sadly and joins her daughter*]

THE FLOWER GIRL: [*Taking advantage of the military gentleman's proximity to establish friendly relations with him*] If it's worse, it's a sign it's nearly over. So cheer up, Captain; and buy a flower off a poor girl.

THE GENTLEMAN: I'm sorry. I havnt any change.

THE FLOWER GIRL: I can give you change, Captain.

THE GENTLEMAN: For a sovereign? Ive nothing less.

THE FLOWER GIRL: Garn! Oh do buy a flower off me, Captain. I can change half-a-crown. Take this for tuppence.

THE GENTLEMAN: Now dont be troublesome: theres a good girl. [*Trying his pockets*] I really havnt any change—Stop: heres three hapence, if thats any use to you. [*He retreats to the other pillar*]

THE FLOWER GIRL: [*Disappointed, but thinking three halfpence better than nothing*] Thank you, sir.

THE BYSTANDER: [*To the girl*] You be careful: give him a flower for it. Theres a bloke here behind taking down every blessed word youre saying.

[*All turn to the man who is taking notes*]

THE FLOWER GIRL: [*Springing up terrified*] I aint done nothing wrong by speaking to the gentleman. Ive a right to sell flowers if I keep off the kerb. [*Hysterically*] I'm a respectable girl: so help me, I never spoke to him except to ask him to buy a flower off me. [*General hubbub, mostly sympathetic to the flower girl, but deprecating her excessive sensibility. Cries of* Dont start hollerin. Who's hurting you? Nobody's going to touch you. Whats the good of fussing? Steady on. Easy easy, etc., *come from the elderly staid spectators, who pat her comfortingly. Less patient ones bid her shut her head, or ask her roughly what is wrong with her. A remoter group, not knowing what the matter is, crowd in and increase the noise with question and answer:* Whats the row? Whatshe do? Where is he? A tec taking her down. What! him? Yes: him over there: Took money off the gentleman, etc. *The flower girl, distraught and mobbed, breaks through them to the gentleman, crying wildly*] Oh, sir, dont let him charge me. You dunno what it means to me. Theyll take away

my character and drive me on the streets for speaking to gentlemen. They—

THE NOTE TAKER: [*Coming forward on her right, the rest crowding after him*] There, there, there, there! who's hurting you, you silly girl? What do you take me for?

THE BYSTANDER: It's all right: he's a gentleman: look at his boots. [*Explaining to the note taker*] She thought you was a copper's nark, sir.

THE NOTE TAKER: [*With quick interest*] Whats a copper's nark?

THE BYSTANDER: [*Inapt at definition*] It's a—well, it's a copper's nark, as you might say. What else would you call it? A sort of informer.

THE FLOWER GIRL: [*Still hysterical*] I take my Bible oath I never said a word—

THE NOTE TAKER: [*Overbearing but good-humored*] Oh, shut up, shut up. Do I look like a policeman?

THE FLOWER GIRL: [*Far from reassured*] Then what did you take down my words for? How do I know whether you took me down right? You just shew me what youve wrote about me. [*The note taker opens his book and holds it steadily under her nose, though the pressure of the mob trying to read it over his shoulders would upset a weaker man*] Whats that? That aint proper writing. I cant read that.

THE NOTE TAKER: I can. [*Reads, reproducing her pronunciation exactly*] "Cheer ap, Keptin; n' baw ya flahr orf a pore gel."

THE FLOWER GIRL: [*Much distressed*] It's because I called him Captain. I meant no harm. [*To the gentleman*] Oh, sir, dont let him lay a charge agen me for a word like that. You—

THE GENTLEMAN: Charge! I make no charge. [*To the note taker*] Really, sir, if you are a detective, you need not begin protecting me against molestation by young women until I ask you. Anybody could see that the girl meant no harm.

THE BYSTANDERS GENERALLY: [*Demonstrating against police espionage*] Course they could. What business is it of yours? You mind your own affairs. He wants promotion, he does. Taking down people's words! Girl never said a word to him. What harm if she did? Nice thing a girl cant shelter from the rain without being insulted, etc., etc., etc. [*She is conducted by the more sympathetic demonstrators back to her plinth, where she resumes her seat and struggles with her emotion*]

THE BYSTANDER: He aint a tec. He's a blooming busybody: thats what he is. I tell you, look at his boots.

THE NOTE TAKER: [*Turning on him genially*] And how are all your people down at Selsey?

THE BYSTANDER: [*Suspiciously*] Who told you my people come from Selsey?

THE NOTE TAKER: Never you mind. They did. [*To the girl*] How do you come to be up so far east? You were born in Lisson Grove.

THE FLOWER GIRL: [*Appalled*] Oh, what harm is there in my leaving Lisson Grove? It wasnt fit for a pig to live in; and I had to pay four-and-six a week. [*In tears*] Oh, boo—hoo—oo—

THE NOTE TAKER: Live where you like; but stop that noise.

THE GENTLEMAN: [*To the girl*] Come, come! he cant touch you: you have a right to live where you please.

A SARCASTIC BYSTANDER: [*Thrusting himself between the note taker and the gentleman*] Park Lane, for instance. I'd like to go into the Housing Question with you, I would.

THE FLOWER GIRL: [*Subsiding into a brooding melancholy over her basket, and talking very low-spiritedly to herself*] I'm a good girl, I am.

THE SARCASTIC BYSTANDER: [*Not attending to her*] Do you know where I come from?

THE NOTE TAKER: [*Promptly*] Hoxton.

[*Titterings. Popular interest in the note taker's performance increases*]

THE SARCASTIC ONE: [*Amazed*] Well, who said I didnt? Bly me! You know everything, you do.

THE FLOWER GIRL: [*Still nursing her sense of injury*] Aint no call to meddle with me, he aint.

THE BYSTANDER: [*To her*] Of course he aint. Dont you stand it from him. [*To the note taker*] See here: what call have you to know about people what never offered to meddle with you? Wheres your warrant?

SEVERAL BYSTANDERS: [*Encouraged by this seeming point of law*] Yes: wheres your warrant?

THE FLOWER GIRL: Let him say what he likes. I dont want to have no truck with him.

THE BYSTANDER: You take us for dirt under your feet, dont you? Catch you taking liberties with a gentleman!

THE SARCASTIC BYSTANDER: Yes: tell him where he come from if you want to go fortune-telling.

THE NOTE TAKER: Cheltenham, Harrow, Cambridge, and India.

THE GENTLEMAN: Quite right. [*Great laughter. Reaction in the note taker's favor. Exclamations of He knows all about it. Told him proper. Hear him tell the toff where he come from? etc.*] May I ask, sir, do you do this for your living at a music hall?

THE NOTE TAKER: Ive thought of that. Perhaps I shall some day.

[*The rain has stopped; and the persons on the outside of the crowd begin to drop off*]

THE FLOWER GIRL: [*Resenting the reaction*] He's no gentleman, he aint, to interfere with a poor girl.

THE DAUGHTER: [*Out of patience, pushing her way rudely to the front and displacing the gentleman, who politely retires to the other side of the pillar*] What on earth is Freddy doing? I shall get pneumonia if I stay in this draught any longer.

THE NOTE TAKER: [*To himself, hastily making a note of her pronunciation of "monia"*] Earlscourt.

THE DAUGHTER: [*Violently*] Will you please keep your impertinent remarks to yourself.

THE NOTE TAKER: Did I say that out loud? I didnt mean to. I beg your pardon. Your mother's Epsom, unmistakably.

THE MOTHER: [*Advancing between her daughter and the note taker*] How very curious! I was brought up in Largelady Park, near Epsom.

THE NOTE TAKER: [*Uproariously amused*] Ha! ha! What a devil of a name! Excuse me. [*To the daughter*] You want a cab, do you?

THE DAUGHTER: Dont dare speak to me.

THE MOTHER: Oh please, please, Clara. [*Her daughter repudiates her with an angry shrug and retires haughtily*] We should be so grateful to you, sir, if you found us a cab. [*The note taker produces a whistle*] Oh, thank you. [*She joins her daughter*] [*The note taker blows a piercing blast*]

THE SARCASTIC BYSTANDER: There! I knowed he was a plain-clothes copper.

THE BYSTANDER: That aint a police whistle: thats a sporting whistle.

THE FLOWER GIRL: [*Still preoccupied with her wounded feelings*] He's no right to take away my character. My character is the same to me as any lady's.

THE NOTE TAKER: I dont know whether youve noticed it; but the rain stopped about two minutes ago.

THE BYSTANDER: So it has. Why didnt you say so before? and us losing our time listening to your silliness! [*He walks off towards the Strand*]

THE SARCASTIC BYSTANDER: I can tell where y o u come from. You come from Anwell. Go back there.

THE NOTE TAKER: [*Helpfully*] Hanwell.

THE SARCASTIC BYSTANDER: [*Affecting great distinction of speech*] Thenk you, teacher. Haw haw! So long. [*He touches his hat with mock respect and strolls off*]

THE FLOWER GIRL: Frightening people like that! How would he like it himself?

THE MOTHER: It's quite fine now, Clara. We can walk to a motor bus. Come. [*She gathers her skirts above her ankles and hurries off towards the Strand*]

THE DAUGHTER: But the cab—[*Her mother is out of hearing*] Oh, how tiresome! [*She follows angrily*]

[*All the rest have gone except the note taker, the gentleman, and the flower girl, who sits arranging her basket and still pitying herself in murmurs*]

THE FLOWER GIRL: Poor girl! Hard enough for her to live without being worrited and chivied.

THE GENTLEMAN: [*Returning to his former place on the note taker's left*] How do you do it, if I may ask?

THE NOTE TAKER: Simply phonetics. The science of speech. Thats my profession: also my hobby. Happy is the man who can make a living by his hobby! Y o u can spot an Irishman or a Yorkshireman by his brogue. *I* can place any man within six miles. I can place him within two miles in London. Sometimes within two streets.

THE FLOWER GIRL: Ought to be ashamed of himself, unmanly coward!

THE GENTLEMAN: But is there a living in that?

THE NOTE TAKER: Oh yes. Quite a fat one. This is an age of upstarts. Men begin in Kentish Town with £80 a year, and end in Park Lane with a hundred thousand. They want to drop Kentish Town; but they give themselves away every time they open their mouths. Now I can teach them—

THE FLOWER GIRL: Let him mind his own business and leave a poor girl—

THE NOTE TAKER: [*Explosively*] Woman: cease this detestable boohooing instantly; or else seek the shelter of some other place of worship.

THE FLOWER GIRL: [*With feeble defiance*] Ive a right to be here if I like, same as you.

THE NOTE TAKER: A woman who utters such depressing and disgusting sounds has no right to be anywhere—no right to live. Remember that you are a human being with a soul and the divine gift of articulate speech: that your native language is the language of Shakespear and Milton and The Bible: and dont sit there crooning like a bilious pigeon.

THE FLOWER GIRL: [*Quite overwhelmed, looking up at him in mingled wonder and deprecation without daring to raise her head*] Ah-ah-ah-ow-ow-ow-oo!

THE NOTE TAKER: [*Whipping out his book*] Heavens! what a sound! [*He writes; then holds out the book and reads, reproducing her vowels exactly*] Ah-ah-ah-ow-ow-ow-oo!

THE FLOWER GIRL: [*Tickled by the performance, and laughing in spite of herself*] Garn!

THE NOTE TAKER: You see this creature with her kerbstone English: the English that will keep her in the gutter to the end of her days. Well, sir, in three months I could pass that girl off as a duchess at an ambassador's garden party. I could even get her a place as lady's maid or shop assistant, which requires better English. Thats the sort of thing I do for commercial millionaires. And on the profits of it I do genuine scientific work in phonetics, and a little as a poet on Miltonic lines.

THE GENTLEMAN: I am myself a student of Indian dialects; and—

THE NOTE TAKER: [*Eagerly*] Are you? Do you know Colonel Pickering, the author of Spoken Sanscrit?

THE GENTLEMAN: I am Colonel Pickering. Who are you?

THE NOTE TAKER: Henry Higgins, author of Higgins's Universal Alphabet.

PICKERING: [*With enthusiasm*] I came from India to meet you.

HIGGINS: I was going to India to meet you.

PICKERING: Where do you live?

HIGGINS: 27A Wimpole Street. Come and see me tomorrow.

PICKERING: I'm at the Carlton. Come with me now and lets have a jaw over some supper.

HIGGINS: Right you are.

THE FLOWER GIRL: [*To Pickering, as he passes her*] Buy a flower, kind gentleman. I'm short for my lodging.

PICKERING: I really havnt any change. I'm sorry. [*He goes away*]

HIGGINS: [*Shocked at the girl's mendacity*] Liar. You said you could change half-a-crown.

THE FLOWER GIRL: [*Rising in desperation*] You ought to be stuffed with nails, you ought. [*Flinging the basket at his feet*] Take the whole blooming basket for sixpence.

[*The church clock strikes the second quarter*]

HIGGINS: [*Hearing in it the voice of God, rebuking him for his Pharisaic want of charity to the poor girl*] A reminder. [*He raises his hat solemnly; then throws a handful of money into the basket and follows* Pickering]

THE FLOWER GIRL: [*Picking up a half-crown*] Ah-ow-ooh! [*Picking up a couple of florins*] Aaah-ow-ooh! [*Picking up several coins*] Aaaaaah-ow-ooh! [*Picking up a half-sovereign*] Aaaaaaaaaaaah-ow-ooh!!!

FREDDY: [*Springing out of a taxicab*] Got one at last. Hallo! [*To the girl*] Where are the two ladies that were here?

THE FLOWER GIRL: They walked to the bus when the rain stopped.

FREDDY: And left me with a cab on my hands! Damnation!

THE FLOWER GIRL: [*With grandeur*] Never mind, young man. *I'm* going home in a taxi. [*She sails off to the cab. The driver puts his hand behind him and holds the door firmly shut against her. Quite understanding his mistrust, she shews him her handful of money*] Eightpence aint no object to me, Charlie. [*He grins and open the door*] Angel Court, Drury Lane, round the corner of Micklejohn's oil shop. Lets see how fast you can make her hop it. [*She gets in and pulls the door to with a slam as the taxicab starts*]

FREDDY: Well, I'm dashed!

Act II

Next day at 11 a.m. Higgins's laboratory in Wimpole Street. It is a room on the first floor, looking on the street, and was meant for the drawing room. The double doors are in the middle of the back wall; and persons entering find in the corner to their right two tall file cabinets at right angles to one another against the walls. In this corner stands a flat writing-table, on which are a phonograph, a laryngoscope, a row of tiny organ

pipes with bellows, a set of lamp chimneys for singing flames with burners attached to a gas plug in
the wall by an indiarubber tube, several tuning-
forks of different sizes, a life-size image of half a
human head, shewing in section the vocal organs,
and a box containing a supply of wax cylinders for
the phonograph.

Further down the room, on the same side, is a
fireplace, with a comfortable leather-covered easy-
chair at the side of the hearth nearest the door,
and a coal-scuttle. There is a clock on the mantelpiece. Between the fireplace and the phonograph
table is a stand for newspapers.

On the other side of the central door, to the left
of the visitor, is a cabinet of shallow drawers. On it
is a telephone and the telephone directory. The corner beyond, and most of the side wall, is occupied
by a grand piano, with the keyboard at the end
furthest from the door, and a bench for the player
extending the full length of the keyboard. On the
piano is a dessert dish heaped with fruit and
sweets, mostly chocolates.

The middle of the room is clear. Besides the
easy-chair, the piano bench, and two chairs at
the phonograph table, there is one stray chair. It
stands near the fireplace. On the walls, engravings:
mostly Piranesi and mezzotint portraits. No paintings.

Pickering is seated at the table, putting down
some cards and a tuning-fork which he has been
using. Higgins is standing up near him, closing two
or three file drawers which are hanging out. He
appears in the morning light as a robust, vital,
appetizing sort of man of forty or thereabouts,
dressed in a professional-looking black frock-coat
with a white linen collar and black silk tie. He is of
the energetic, scientific type, heartily, even violently interested in everything that can be studied
as a scientific subject, and careless about himself
and other people, including their feelings. He is,
in fact, but for his years and size, rather like a
very impetuous baby "taking notice" eagerly and
loudly, and requiring almost as much watching to
keep him out of unintended mischief. His manner
varies from genial bullying when he is in a good
humor to stormy petulance when anything goes
wrong; but he is so entirely frank and void of
malice that he remains likeable even in his least
reasonable moments.

HIGGINS: [As he shuts the last drawer] Well, I think
thats the whole show.

PICKERING: It's really amazing. I havnt taken half of
it in, you know.

HIGGINS: Would you like to go over any of it again?

PICKERING: [Rising and coming to the fireplace,
where he plants himself with his back to the fire]
No, thank you; not now. I'm quite done up for this
morning.

HIGGINS: [Following him, and standing beside him
on his left] Tired of listening to sounds?

PICKERING: Yes. It's a fearful strain. I rather fancied
myself because I can pronounce twenty-four distinct vowel sounds; but your hundred and thirty
beat me. I cant hear a bit of difference between
most of them.

HIGGINS: [Chuckling, and going over to the piano to
eat sweets] Oh, that comes with practice. You hear
no difference at first; but you keep on listening,
and presently you find theyre all as different as A
from B. [Mrs Pearce looks in: she is Higgins's
housekeeper] Whats the matter?

MRS PEARCE: [Hesitating, evidently perplexed] A
young woman wants to see you, sir.

HIGGINS: A young woman! What does she want?

MRS PEARCE: Well, sir, she says youll be glad to see
her when you know what she's come about. She's
quite a common girl, sir. Very common indeed. I
should have sent her away, only I thought perhaps
you wanted her to talk into your machines. I hope
Ive not done wrong; but really you see such queer
people sometimes—youll excuse me, I'm sure,
sir—

HIGGINS: Oh, thats all right, Mrs Pearce. Has she
an interesting accent?

MRS PEARCE: Oh, something dreadful, sir, really. I
dont know how you can take an interest in it.

HIGGINS: [To Pickering] Lets have her up. Shew her
up, Mrs Pearce. [He rushes across to his working
table and picks out a cylinder to use on the phono-
graph]

MRS PEARCE: [Only half resigned to it] Very well,
sir. It's for you to say.   [She goes downstairs]

HIGGINS: This is rather a bit of luck. I'll shew you
how I make records. We'll set her talking; and I'll
take it down first in Bell's visible Speech; then in
broad Romic; and then we'll get her on the phonograph so that you can turn her on as often as you
like with the written transcript before you.

MRS PEARCE: [Returning] This is the young woman,
sir.

[The flower girl enters in state. She has a hat with
three ostrich feathers, orange, sky-blue, and red.
She has a nearly clean apron, and the shoddy
coat has been tidied a little. The pathos of this
deplorable figure, with its innocent vanity and
consequential air, touches Pickering, who has
already straightened himself in the presence of
Mrs Pearce. But as to Higgins, the only distinction he makes between men and women is that
when he is neither bullying nor exclaiming to
the heavens against some feather-weight cross,
he coaxes women as a child coaxes its nurse
when it wants to get anything out of her]

HIGGINS: [Brusquely, recognizing her with uncon-
cealed disappointment, and at once, babylike, making an intolerable grievance of it] Why, this is the

girl I jotted down last night. She's no use: Ive got all the records I want of the Lisson Grove lingo; and I'm not going to waste another cylinder on it. [To the girl] Be off with you: I dont want you.

THE FLOWER GIRL: Dont you be so saucy. You aint heard what I come for yet. [To Mrs Pearce, who is waiting at the door for further instructions] Did you tell him I come in a taxi?

MRS PEARCE: Nonsense, girl! what do you think a gentleman like Mr Higgins cares what you came in?

THE FLOWER GIRL: Oh, we a r e proud! He aint above giving lessons, not him: I heard him say so. Well, I aint come here to ask for any compliment; and if my money's not good enough I can go elsewhere.

HIGGINS: Good enough for what?

THE FLOWER GIRL: Good enough for ye-oo. Now you know, dont you? I'm come to have lessons, I am. And to pay for em too: make no mistake.

HIGGINS: [Stupent] Well!!! [Recovering his breath with a gasp] What do you expect me to say to you?

THE FLOWER GIRL: Well, if you was a gentleman, you might ask me to sit down, I think. Dont I tell you I'm bringing you business?

HIGGINS: Pickering: shall we ask this baggage to sit down, or shall we throw her out of the window?

THE FLOWER GIRL: [Running away in terror to the piano, where she turns at bay] Ah-ah-oh-ow-ow-ow-oo! [Wounded and whimpering] I wont be called a baggage when Ive offered to pay like any lady.

[Motionless, the two men stare at her from the other side of the room, amazed]

PICKERING: [Gently] What is it you want, my girl?

THE FLOWER GIRL: I want to be a lady in a flower shop stead of selling at the corner of Tottenham Court Road. But they wont take me unless I can talk more genteel. He said he could teach me. Well, here I am ready to pay him—not asking any favor—and he treats me as if I was dirt.

MRS PEARCE: How can you be such a foolish ignorant girl as to think you could afford to pay Mr Higgins?

THE FLOWER GIRL: Why shouldnt I? I know what lessons cost as well as you do; and I'm ready to pay.

HIGGINS: How much?

THE FLOWER GIRL: [Coming back to him, triumphant] Now youre talking! I thought youd come off it when you saw a chance of getting back a bit of what you chucked at me last night. [Confidentially] Youd had a drop in, hadnt you?

HIGGINS: [Peremptorily] Sit down.

THE FLOWER GIRL: Oh, if youre going to make a compliment of it—

HIGGINS: [Thundering at her] Sit down.

MRS PEARCE: [Severely] Sit down, girl. Do as youre told. [She places the stray chair near the hearthrug between Higgins and Pickering, and stands behind it waiting for the girl to sit down]

THE FLOWER GIRL: Ah-ah-ah-ow-ow-oo! [She stands, half rebellious, half bewildered]

PICKERING: [Very courteous] Wont you sit down?

LIZA: [Coyly] Dont mind if I do. [She sits down. Pickering returns to the hearthrug]

HIGGINS: Whats your name?

THE FLOWER GIRL: Liza Doolittle.

HIGGINS: [Declaiming gravely]
    Eliza, Elizabeth, Betsy and Bess,
    They went to the woods to get a bird's nes':

PICKERING: They found a nest with four eggs in it:

HIGGINS: They took one apiece, and left three in it.
    [They laugh heartily at their own wit]

LIZA: Oh, dont be silly.

MRS PEARCE: You mustnt speak to the gentleman like that.

LIZA: Well, why wont he speak sensible to me?

HIGGINS: Come back to business. How much do you propose to pay me for the lessons?

LIZA: Oh, I know whats right. A lady friend of mine gets French lessons for eighteenpence an hour from a real French gentleman. Well, you wouldnt have the face to ask me the same for teaching me my own language as you would for French; so I wont give more than a shilling. Take it or leave it.

HIGGINS: [Walking up and down the room, rattling his keys and his cash in his pockets] You know, Pickering, if you consider a shilling, not as a simple shilling, but as a percentage of this girl's income, it works out as fully equivalent to sixty or seventy guineas from a millionaire.

PICKERING: How so?

HIGGINS: Figure it out. A millionaire has about £150 a day. She earns about half-a-crown.

LIZA: [Haughtily] Who told you I only—

HIGGINS: [Continuing] She offers me two-fifths of her day's income for a lesson. Two-fifths of a millionaire's income for a day would be somewhere about £60. It's handsome. By George, it's enormous! it's the biggest offer I ever had.

LIZA: [Rising, terrified] Sixty pounds! What are you talking about? I never offered you sixty pounds. Where would I get—

HIGGINS: Hold your tongue.

LIZA: [Weeping] But I aint got sixty pounds. Oh—

MRS PEARCE: Dont cry, you silly girl. Sit down. Nobody is going to touch your money.

HIGGINS: Somebody is going to touch you, with a broomstick, if you dont stop snivelling. Sit down.

LIZA: [Obeying slowly] Ah-ah-ah-ow-ee-o! One would think you was my father.

HIGGINS: If I decide to teach you, I'll be worse than two fathers to you. Here! [He offers her his silk handkerchief]

LIZA: Whats this for?

HIGGINS: To wipe your eyes. To wipe any part of your face that feels moist. Remember: thats your handkerchief; and thats your sleeve. Dont mistake the one for the other if you wish to become a lady in a shop.

[Liza, utterly bewildered, stares helplessly at him]

MRS PEARCE: It's no use talking to her like that, Mr Higgins: she doesnt understand you. Besides, youre quite wrong: she doesnt do it that way at all.

[She takes the handkerchief]

LIZA: [Snatching it] Here! You give me that hand-kerchief. He give it to me, not to you.

PICKERING: [Laughing] He did. I think it must be re-garded as her property, Mrs Pearce.

MRS PEARCE: [Resigning herself] Serve you right, Mr Higgins.

PICKERING: Higgins: I'm interested. What about the ambassador's garden party? I'll say youre the greatest teacher alive if you make that good. I'll bet you all the expenses of the experiment you cant do it. And I'll pay for the lessons.

LIZA: Oh, you are real good. Thank you, Captain.

HIGGINS: [Tempted, looking at her] It's almost irre-sistible. She's so deliciously low—so horribly dirty—

LIZA: [Protesting extremely] Ah-ah-ah-ah-ow-ow-oo-oo!!! I aint dirty: I washed my face and hands afore I come, I did.

PICKERING: Youre certainly not going to turn her head with flattery, Higgins.

MRS PEARCE: [Uneasy] Oh, dont say that, sir: theres more ways than one of turning a girl's head; and nobody can do it better than Mr Higgins, though he may not always mean it. I do hope, sir, you wont encourage him to do anything foolish.

HIGGINS: [Becoming excited as the idea grows on him] What is life but a series of inspired follies? The difficulty is to find them to do. Never lose a chance: it doesnt come every day. I shall make a duchess of this draggletailed guttersnipe.

LIZA: [Strongly deprecating this view of her] Ah-ah-ah-ow-ow-oo!

HIGGINS: [Carried away] Yes: in six months—in three if she has a good ear and a quick tongue—I'll take her anywhere and pass her off as anything. We'll start today: now! this moment! Take her away and clean her, Mrs Pearce. Monkey Brand, if it wont come off any other way. Is there a good fire in the kitchen?

MRS PEARCE: [Protesting] Yes; but—

HIGGINS: [Storming on] Take all her clothes off and burn them. Ring up Whiteley or somebody for new ones. Wrap her up in brown paper til they come.

LIZA: Youre no gentleman, youre not, to talk of such things. I'm a good girl, I am; and I know what the like of you are, I do.

HIGGINS: We want none of your Lisson Grove prudery here, young woman. Youve got to learn to behave like a duchess. Take her away, Mrs Pearce. If she gives you any trouble, wallop her.

LIZA: [Springing up and running between Pickering and Mrs Pearce for protection] No! I'll call the police, I will.

MRS PEARCE: But Ive no place to put her.

HIGGINS: Put her in the dustbin.

LIZA: Ah-ah-ah-ow-ow-oo!

PICKERING: Oh come, Higgins! be reasonable.

MRS PEARCE: [Resolutely] You m u s t be reasonable, Mr Higgins: really you must. You cant walk over everybody like this.

[Higgins, thus scolded, subsides. The hur-ricane is succeeded by a zephyr of amiable surprise]

HIGGINS: [With professional exquisiteness of modu-lation] I walk over everybody! My dear Mrs Pearce, my dear Pickering, I never had the slightest intention of walking over anyone. All I propose is that we should be kind to this poor girl. We must help her to prepare and fit herself for her new station in life. If I did not express myself clearly it was because I did not wish to hurt her delicacy, or yours.   [Liza, reassured, steals back to her chair]

MRS PEARCE: [To Pickering] Well, did you ever hear anything like that, sir?

PICKERING: [Laughing heartily] Never, Mrs Pearce: never.

HIGGINS: [Patiently] Whats the matter?

MRS PEARCE: Well, the matter is, sir, that you cant take a girl up like that as if you were picking up a pebble on the beach.

HIGGINS: Why not?

MRS PEARCE: Why not! But you dont know anything about her. What about her parents? She may be married.

LIZA: Garn!

HIGGINS: There! As the girl very properly says, Garn! Married indeed! Dont you know that a woman of that class looks a worn out drudge of fifty a year after she's married?

LIZA: Whood marry me?

HIGGINS: [Suddenly resorting to the most thrillingly beautiful low tones in his best elocutionary style] By George, Eliza, the streets will be strewn with the bodies of men shooting themselves for your sake before Ive done with you.

MRS PEARCE: Nonsense, sir. You mustnt talk like that to her.

LIZA: [Rising and squaring herself determinedly] I'm going away. He's off his chump, he is. I dont want no balmies teaching me.

HIGGINS: [Wounded in his tenderest point by her in-sensibility to his elocution] Oh, indeed! I'm mad, am I? Very well, Mrs Pearce: you neednt order the new clothes for her. Throw her out.

LIZA: [Whimpering] Nah-ow. You got no right to touch me.

MRS PEARCE: You see now what comes of being saucy. [Indicating the door] This way, please.

LIZA: [*Almost in tears*] I didnt want no clothes. I wouldnt have taken them. [*She throws away the handkerchief*] I can buy my own clothes.

HIGGINS: [*Deftly retrieving the handkerchief and intercepting her on her reluctant way to the door*] Youre an ungrateful wicked girl. This is my return for offering to take you out of the gutter and dress you beautifully and make a lady of you.

MRS PEARCE: Stop, Mr Higgins. I wont allow it. It's you that are wicked. Go home to your parents, girl; and tell them to take better care of you.

LIZA: I aint got no parents. They told me I was big enough to earn my own living and turned me out.

MRS PEARCE: Wheres your mother?

LIZA: I aint got no mother. Her that turned me out was my sixth stepmother. But I done without them. And I'm a good girl, I am.

HIGGINS: Very well, then, what on earth is all this fuss about? The girl doesnt belong to anybody—is no use to anybody but me. [*He goes to* Mrs Pearce *and begins coaxing*] You can adopt her, Mrs Pearce: I'm sure a daughter would be a great amusement to you. Now dont make any more fuss. Take her downstairs; and—

MRS PEARCE: But whats to become of her? Is she to be paid anything? Do be sensible, sir.

HIGGINS: Oh, pay her whatever is necessary: put it down in the housekeeping book. [*Impatiently*] What on earth will she want with money? She'll have her food and her clothes. She'll only drink if you give her money.

LIZA: [*Turning on him*] Oh you are a brute. It's a lie: nobody ever saw the sign of liquor on me. [*She goes back to her chair and plants herself there defiantly*]

PICKERING: [*In good-humored remonstrance*] Does it occur to you, Higgins, that the girl has some feelings?

HIGGINS: [*Looking critically at her*] Oh no, I dont think so. Not any feelings that we need bother about. [*Cheerily*] Have you, Eliza?

LIZA: I got my feelings same as anyone else.

HIGGINS: [*To Pickering, reflectively*] You see the difficulty?

PICKERING: Eh? What difficulty?

HIGGINS: To get her to talk grammar. The mere pronunciation is easy enough.

LIZA: I dont want to talk grammar. I want to talk like a lady.

MRS PEARCE: Will you please keep to the point, Mr Higgins? I want to know on what terms the girl is to be here. Is she to have any wages? And what is to become of her when youve finished your teaching? You must look ahead a little.

HIGGINS: [*Impatiently*] Whats to become of her if I leave her in the gutter? Tell me that, Mrs Pearce.

MRS PEARCE: Thats her own business, not yours, Mr Higgins.

HIGGINS: Well, when Ive done with her, we can throw her back into the gutter; and then it will be her own business again; so thats all right.

LIZA: Oh, youve no feeling heart in you: you dont care for nothing but yourself. [*She rises and takes the floor resolutely*] Here! Ive had enough of this. I'm going. [*Making for the door*] You ought to be ashamed of yourself, you ought.

HIGGINS: [*Snatching a chocolate cream from the piano, his eyes suddenly beginning to twinkle with mischief*] Have some chocolates, Eliza.

LIZA: [*Halting, tempted*] How do I know what might be in them? Ive heard of girls being drugged by the like of you.

[Higgins *whips out his penknife; cuts a chocolate in two; puts one half into his mouth and bolts it; and offers her the other half*]

HIGGINS: Pledge of good faith, Eliza. I eat one half: you eat the other. [Liza *opens her mouth to retort: he pops the half chocolate into it*] You shall have boxes of them, barrels of them, every day. You shall live on them. Eh?

LIZA: [*Who has disposed of the chocolate after being nearly choked by it*] I wouldnt have ate it, only I'm too ladylike to take it out of my mouth.

HIGGINS: Listen, Eliza. I think you said you came in a taxi.

LIZA: Well, what if I did? Ive as good a right to take a taxi as anyone else.

HIGGINS: You have, Eliza; and in future you shall have as many taxis as you want. You shall go up and down and round the town in a taxi every day. Think of that, Eliza.

MRS PEARCE: Mr Higgins: youre tempting the girl. It's not right. She should think of the future.

HIGGINS: At her age! Nonsense! Time enough to think of the future when you havnt any future to think of. No, Eliza: do as this lady does: think of other people's futures; but never think of your own. Think of chocolates, and taxis, and gold, and diamonds.

LIZA: No: I dont want no gold and no diamonds. I'm a good girl, I am. [*She sits down again, with an attempt at dignity*]

HIGGINS: You shall remain so, Eliza, under the care of Mrs Pearce. And you shall marry an officer in the Guards, with a beautiful moustache: the son of a marquis, who will disinherit him for marrying you, but will relent when he sees your beauty and goodness—

PICKERING: Excuse me, Higgins; but I really must interfere. Mrs Pearce is quite right. If this girl is to put herself in your hands for six months for an experiment in teaching, she must understand thoroughly what she's doing.

HIGGINS: How can she? She's incapable of understanding anything. Besides, do any of us understand what we are doing? If we did, would we ever do it?

PICKERING: Very clever, Higgins; but not sound sense. [*To Eliza*] Miss Doolittle—

LIZA: [*Overwhelmed*] Ah-ah-ow-oo!

HIGGINS: There! Thats all youll get out of Eliza. Ah-ah-ow-oo! No use explaining. As a military man you ought to know that. Give her her orders: thats what she wants. Eliza: you are to live here for the next six months, learning how to speak beautifully, like a lady in a florist's shop. If youre good and do whatever youre told, you shall sleep in a proper bedroom, and have lots to eat, and money to buy chocolates and take rides in taxis. If youre naughty and idle you will sleep in the back kitchen among the black beetles, and be walloped by Mrs Pearce with a broomstick. At the end of six months you shall go to Buckingham Palace in a carriage, beautifully dressed. If the King finds out youre not a lady, you will be taken by the police to the Tower of London, where your head will be cut off as a warning to other presumptuous flower girls. If you are not found out, you shall have a present of seven-and-sixpence to start life with as a lady in a shop. If you refuse this offer you will be a most ungrateful and wicked girl; and the angels will weep for you. [*To Pickering*] Now are you satisfied, Pickering? [*To Mrs Pearce*] Can I put it more plainly and fairly, Mrs Pearce?

MRS PEARCE: [*Patiently*] I think youd better let me speak to the girl properly in private. I dont know that I can take charge of her or consent to the arrangement at all. Of course I know you dont mean her any harm; but when you get what you call interested in people's accents, you never think or care what may happen to them or you. Come with me, Eliza.

HIGGINS: Thats all right. Thank you, Mrs Pearce. Bundle her off to the bath-room.

LIZA: [*Rising reluctantly and suspiciously*] Youre a great bully, you are. I wont stay here if I dont like. I wont let nobody wallop me. I never asked to go to Bucknam Palace, I didnt. I was never in trouble with the police, not me. I'm a good girl—

MRS PEARCE: Dont answer back, girl. You dont understand the gentleman. Come with me. [*She leads the way to the door, and holds it open for Eliza*]

LIZA: [*As she goes out*] Well, what I say is right. I wont go near the King, not if I'm going to have my head cut off. If I'd known what I was letting myself in for, I wouldnt have come here. I always been a good girl; and I never offered to say a word to him; and I dont owe him nothing; and I dont care; and I wont be put upon; and I have my feelings the same as anyone else—

[*Mrs Pearce shuts the door; and Eliza's plaints are no longer audible. Pickering comes from the hearth to the chair and sits astride it with his arms on the back*]

PICKERING: Excuse the straight question, Higgins. Are you a man of good character where women are concerned?

HIGGINS: [*Moodily*] Have you ever met a man of good character where women are concerned?

PICKERING: Yes: very frequently.

HIGGINS: [*Dogmatically, lifting himself on his hands to the level of the piano, and sitting on it with a bounce*] Well, I havnt. I find that the moment I let a woman make friends with me, she becomes jealous, exacting, suspicious, and a damned nuisance. I find that the moment I let myself make friends with a woman, I become selfish and tyrannical. Women upset everything. When you let them into your life, you find that the woman is driving at one thing and youre driving at another.

PICKERING: At what, for example?

HIGGINS: [*Coming off the piano restlessly*] Oh, Lord knows! I suppose the woman wants to live her own life; and the man wants to live his; and each tries to drag the other on to the wrong track. One wants to go north and the other south; and the result is that both have to go east, though they both hate the east wind. [*He sits down on the bench at the keyboard*] So here I am, a confirmed old bachelor, and likely to remain so.

PICKERING: [*Rising and standing over him gravely*] Come, Higgins! You know what I mean. If I'm to be in this business I shall feel responsible for that girl. I hope it's understood that no advantage is to be taken of her position.

HIGGINS: What! That thing! Sacred, I assure you. [*Rising to explain*] You see, she'll be a pupil; and teaching would be impossible unless pupils were sacred. Ive taught scores of American millionairesses how to speak English: the best looking women in the world. I'm seasoned. They might as well be blocks of wood. *I* might as well be a block of wood. It's—

[*Mrs Pearce opens the door. She has Eliza's hat in her hand. Pickering retires to the easy-chair at the hearth and sits down*]

HIGGINS: [*Eagerly*] Well, Mrs Pearce: is it all right?

MRS PEARCE: [*At the door*] I just wish to trouble you with a word, if I may, Mr Higgins.

HIGGINS: Yes, certainly. Come in. [*She comes forward*] Dont burn that, Mrs Pearce. I'll keep it as a curiosity. [*He takes the hat*]

MRS PEARCE: Handle it carefully, sir, please. I had to promise her not to burn it; but I had better put it in the oven for a while.

HIGGINS: [*Putting it down hastily on the piano*] Oh! thank you. Well, what have you to say to me?

PICKERING: Am I in the way?

MRS PEARCE: Not at all, sir. Mr Higgins: will you please be very particular what you say before the girl?

HIGGINS: [*Sternly*] Of course. I'm always particular about what I say. Why do you say this to me?

MRS PEARCE: [*Unmoved*] No, sir: youre not at all particular when youve mislaid anything or when you get a little impatient. Now it doesnt matter before me: I'm used to it. But you really must not swear before the girl.

HIGGINS: [*Indignantly*] I swear! [*Most emphatically*] I never swear. I detest the habit. What the devil do you mean?

MRS PEARCE: [*Stolidly*] Thats what I mean, sir. You swear a great deal too much. I dont mind your damning and blasting, and what the devil and where the devil and who the devil—

HIGGINS: Mrs Pearce: this language from your lips! Really!

MRS PEARCE: [*Not to be put off*]—but there is a certain word I must ask you not to use. The girl has just used it herself because the bath was too hot. It begins with the same letter as bath. She knows no better: she learnt it at her mother's knee. But she must not hear it from your lips.

HIGGINS: [*Loftily*] I cannot charge myself with having ever uttered it, Mrs Pearce. [*She looks at him steadfastly. He adds, hiding an uneasy conscience with a judicial air*] Except perhaps in a moment of extreme and justifiable excitement.

MRS PEARCE: Only this morning, sir, you applied it to your boots, to the butter, and to the brown bread.

HIGGINS: Oh, that! Mere alliteration, Mrs Pearce, natural to a poet.

MRS PEARCE: Well, sir, whatever you choose to call it, I beg you not to let the girl hear you repeat it.

HIGGINS: Oh, very well, very well. Is that all?

MRS PEARCE: No, sir. We shall have to be very particular with this girl as to personal cleanliness.

HIGGINS: Certainly. Quite right. Most important.

MRS PEARCE: I mean not to be slovenly about her dress or untidy in leaving things about.

HIGGINS: [*Going to her solemnly*] Just so. I intended to call your attention to that. [*He passes on to Pickering, who is enjoying the conversation immensely*] It is these little things that matter, Pickering. Take care of the pence and the pounds will take care of themselves is as true of personal habits as of money. [*He comes to anchor on the hearthrug, with the air of a man in an unassailable position*]

MRS PEARCE: Yes, sir. Then might I ask you not to come down to breakfast in your dressing-gown, or at any rate not to use it as a napkin to the extent you do, sir. And if you would be so good as not to eat everything off the same plate, and to remember not to put the porridge saucepan out of your hand on the clean tablecloth, it would be a better example to the girl. You know you nearly choked yourself with a fishbone in the jam only last week.

HIGGINS: [*Routed from the hearthrug and drifting back to the piano*] I may do these things sometimes in absence of mind; but surely I dont do them habitually. [*Angrily*] By the way: my dressing-gown smells most damnably of benzine.

MRS PEARCE: No doubt it does, Mr Higgins. But if you will wipe your fingers—

HIGGINS: [*Yelling*] Oh very well, very well: I'll wipe them in my hair in future.

MRS PEARCE: I hope youre not offended, Mr Higgins.

HIGGINS: [*Shocked at finding himself thought capable of an unamiable sentiment*] Not at all, not at all. Youre quite right, Mrs Pearce: I shall be particulary careful before the girl. Is that all?

MRS PEARCE: No, sir. Might she use some of those Japanese dresses you brought from abroad? I really cant put her back into her old things.

HIGGINS: Certainly. Anything you like. Is that all?

MRS PEARCE: Thank you, sir. Thats all. [*She goes out*]

HIGGINS: You know, Pickering, that woman has the most extraordinary ideas about me. Here I am, a shy, diffident sort of man. Ive never been able to feel really grown-up and tremendous, like other chaps. And yet she's firmly persuaded that I'm an arbitrary overbearing bossing kind of person. I cant account for it.

[Mrs Pearce *returns*]

MRS PEARCE: If you please, sir, the trouble's beginning already. Theres a dustman downstairs, Alfred Doolittle, wants to see you. He says you have his daughter here.

PICKERING: [*Rising*] Phew! I say! [*He retreats to the hearthrug*]

HIGGINS: [*Promptly*] Send the blackguard up.

MRS PEARCE: Oh, very well, sir. [*She goes out*]

PICKERING: He may not be a blackguard, Higgins.

HIGGINS: Nonsense. Of course he's a blackguard.

PICKERING: Whether he is or not, I'm afraid we shall have some trouble with him.

HIGGINS: [*Confidently*] Oh no: I think not. If theres any trouble he shall have it with me, not I with him. And we are sure to get something interesting out of him.

PICKERING: About the girl?

HIGGINS: No. I mean his dialect.

PICKERING: Oh!

MRS PEARCE: [*At the door*] Doolittle, sir. [*She admits Doolittle and retires*]

[Alfred Doolittle *is an elderly but vigorous dustman, clad in the costume of his profession, including a hat with a back brim covering his neck and shoulders. He has well marked and rather interesting features, and seems equally free from fear and conscience. He has a remarkably expressive voice, the result of a habit of giving vent to his feelings without reserve. His present pose is that of wounded honor and stern resolution*]

DOOLITTLE: [*At the door, uncertain which of the two gentlemen is his man*] Professor Higgins?

HIGGINS: Here. Good morning. Sit down.

DOOLITTLE: Morning, Governor. [*He sits down magisterially*] I come about a very serious matter, Governor.

HIGGINS: [To Pickering] Brought up in Hounslow. Mother Welsh, I should think. [Doolittle opens his mouth, amazed. Higgins continues] What do you want, Doolittle?

DOOLITTLE: [Menacingly] I want my daughter: thats what I want. See?

HIGGINS: Of course you do. Youre her father, arnt you? You dont suppose anyone else wants her, do you? I'm glad to see you have some spark of family feeling left. She's upstairs. Take her away at once.

DOOLITTLE: [Rising, fearfully taken aback] What!

HIGGINS: Take her away. Do you suppose I'm going to keep your daughter for you?

DOOLITTLE: [Remonstrating] Now, now, look here, Governor. Is this reasonable? Is it fairity to take advantage of a man like this? The girl belongs to me. You got her. Where do I come in? [He sits down again]

HIGGINS: Your daughter had the audacity to come to my house and ask me to teach her how to speak properly so that she could get a place in a flower-shop. This gentleman and my housekeeper have been here all the time. [Bullying him] How dare you come here and attempt to blackmail me? You sent her here on purpose.

DOOLITTLE: [Protesting] No, Governor.

HIGGINS: You must have. How else could you possibly know that she is here?

DOOLITTLE: Dont take a man up like that, Governor.

HIGGINS: The police shall take you up. That is a plant —a plot to extort money by threats. I shall telephone for the police. [He goes resolutely to the telephone and opens the directory]

DOOLITTLE: Have I asked you for a brass farthing? I leave it to the gentleman here: have I said a word about money?

HIGGINS: [Throwing the book aside and marching down on Doolittle with a poser] What else did you come for?

DOOLITTLE: [Sweetly] Well, what would a man come for? Be human, Governor.

HIGGINS: [Disarmed] Alfred: did you put her up to it?

DOOLITTLE: So help me, Governor, I never did. I take my Bible oath I aint seen the girl these two months past.

HIGGINS: Then how did you know she was here?

DOOLITTLE: ["Most musical, most melancholy"] I'll tell you, Governor, if youll only let me get a word in. I'm willing to tell you. I'm wanting to tell you. I'm waiting to tell you.

HIGGINS: Pickering: this chap has a certain natural gift of rhetoric. Observe the rhythm of his native woodnotes wild. "I'm willing to tell you: I'm wanting to tell you: I'm waiting to tell you." Sentimental rhetoric! thats the Welsh strain in him. It also accounts for his mendacity and dishonesty.

PICKERING: Oh, please, Higgins: I'm west country myself. [To Doolittle] How did you know the girl was here if you didnt send her?

DOOLITTLE: It was like this, Governor. The girl took a boy in the taxi to give him a jaunt. Son of her landlady, he is. He hung about on the chance of her giving him another ride home. Well, she sent him back for her luggage when she heard you was willing for her to stop here. I met the boy at the corner of Long Acre and Endell Street.

HIGGINS: Public house. Yes?

DOOLITTLE: The poor man's club, Governor: why shouldnt I?

PICKERING: Do let him tell his story, Higgins.

DOOLITTLE: He told me what was up. And I ask you, what was my feelings and my duty as a father? I says to the boy, "You bring me the luggage," I says—

PICKERING: Why didnt you go for it yourself?

DOOLITTLE: Landlady wouldnt have trusted me with it, Governor. She's that kind of woman: you know. I had to give the boy a penny afore he trusted me with it, the little swine. I brought it to her just to oblige you like, and make myself agreeable. Thats all.

HIGGINS: How much luggage?

DOOLITTLE: Musical instrument, Governor. A few pictures, a trifle of jewelry, and a bird-cage. She said she didnt want no clothes. What was I to think from that, Governor? I ask you as a parent what was I to think?

HIGGINS: So you came to rescue her from worse than death, eh?

DOOLITTLE: [Appreciatively: relieved at being so well understood] Just so, Governor. Thats right.

PICKERING: But why did you bring her luggage if you intended to take her away?

DOOLITTLE: Have I said a word about taking her away? Have I now?

HIGGINS: [Determinedly] Youre going to take her away, double quick. [He crosses to the hearth and rings the bell]

DOOLITTLE: [Rising] No, Governor. Dont say that. I'm not the man to stand in my girl's light. Heres a career opening for her, as you might say; and—

[Mrs Pearce opens the door and awaits orders]

HIGGINS: Mrs Pearce: this is Eliza's father. He has come to take her away. Give her to him. [He goes back to the piano, with an air of washing his hands of the whole affair]

DOOLITTLE: No. This is a misunderstanding. Listen here—

MRS PEARCE: He cant take her away, Mr Higgins: how can he? You told me to burn her clothes.

DOOLITTLE: Thats right. I cant carry the girl through the streets like a blooming monkey, can I? I put it to you.

HIGGINS: You have put it to me that you want your daughter. Take your daughter. If she has no clothes go out and buy her some.

DOOLITTLE: [Desperate] Wheres the clothes she

come in? Did I burn them or did your missus here?

MRS PEARCE: I am the housekeeper, if you please. I have sent for some clothes for your girl. When they come you can take her away. You can wait in the kitchen. This way, please.

[Doolittle, *much troubled, accompanies her to the door; then hesitates; finally turns confidentially to* Higgins]

DOOLITTLE: Listen here, Governor. You and me is men of the world, aint we?

HIGGINS: Oh! Men of the world, are we? Youd better go, Mrs Pearce.

MRS PEARCE: I think so, indeed, sir. [*She goes, with dignity*]

PICKERING: The floor is yours, Mr Doolittle.

DOOLITTLE: [*To* Pickering] I thank you, Governor. [*To* Higgins, *who takes refuge on the piano bench, a little overwhelmed by the proximity of his visitor; for* Doolittle *has a professional flavor of dust about him*] Well, the truth is, Ive taken a sort of fancy to you, Governor; and if you want the girl, I'm not so set on having her back home again but what I might be open to an arrangement. Regarded in the light of a young woman, she's a fine handsome girl. As a daughter she's not worth her keep; and so I tell you straight. All I ask is my rights as a father; and youre the last man alive to expect me to let her go for nothing; for I can see youre one of the straight sort, Governor. Well, whats a five-pound note to you? And whats Eliza to me? [*He returns to his chair and sits down judicially*]

PICKERING: I think you ought to know, Doolittle, that Mr Higgins's intentions are entirely honorable.

DOOLITTLE: Course they are, Governor. If I thought they wasnt, I'd ask fifty.

HIGGINS: [*Revolted*] Do you mean to say, you callous rascal, that you would sell your daughter for £50?

DOOLITTLE: Not in a general way I wouldnt; but to oblige a gentleman like you I'd do a good deal, I do assure you.

PICKERING: Have you no morals, man?

DOOLITTLE: [*Unabashed*] Cant afford them, Governor. Neither could you if you was as poor as me. Not that I mean any harm, you know. But if Liza is going to have a bit out of this, why not me too?

HIGGINS: [*Troubled*] I dont know what to do, Pickering. There can be no question that as a matter of morals it's a positive crime to give this chap a farthing. And yet I feel a sort of rough justice in his claim.

DOOLITTLE: Thats it, Governor. Thats all I say. A father's heart, as it were.

PICKERING: Well, I know the feeling; but really it seems hardly right—

DOOLITTLE: Dont say that, Governor. Dont look at it that way. What am I, Governors both? I ask you, what am I? I'm one of the undeserving poor: thats

what I am. Think of what that means to a man. It means that he's up agen middle class morality all the time. If theres anything going, and I put in for a bit of it, it's always the same story: "Youre undeserving; so you cant have it." But my needs is as great as the most deserving widow's that ever got money out of six different charities in one week for the death of the same husband. I dont need less than a deserving man: I need more. I dont eat less hearty than him; and I drink a lot more. I want a bit of amusement, cause I'm a thinking man. I want cheerfulness and a song and a band when I feel low. Well, they charge me just the same for everything as they charge the deserving. What is middle class morality? Just an excuse for never giving me anything. Therefore, I ask you, as two gentlemen, not to play that game on me. I'm playing straight with you. I aint pretending to be deserving. I'm undeserving; and I mean to go on being undeserving. I like it; and thats the truth. Will you take advantage of a man's nature to do him out of the price of his own daughter what he's brought up and fed and clothed by the sweat of his brow until she's growed big enough to be interesting to you two gentlemen? Is five pounds unreasonable? I put it to you; and I leave it to you.

HIGGINS: [*Rising, and going over to* Pickering] Pickering: if we were to take this man in hand for three months, he could choose between a seat in the Cabinet and a popular pulpit in Wales.

PICKERING: What do you say to that, Doolittle?

DOOLITTLE: Not me, Governor, thank you kindly. Ive heard all the preachers and all the prime ministers —for I'm a thinking man and game for politics or religion or social reform same as all the other amusements—and I tell you it's a dog's life any way you look at it. Undeserving poverty is my line. Taking one station in society with another, it's— it's—well, it's the only one that has any ginger in it, to my taste.

HIGGINS: I suppose we must give him a fiver.

PICKERING: He'll make a bad use of it, I'm afraid.

DOOLITTLE: Not me, Governor, so help me I wont. Dont you be afraid that I'll save it and spare it and live idle on it. There wont be a penny of it left by Monday: I'll have to go to work same as if I'd never had it. It wont pauperize me, you bet. Just one good spree for myself and the missus, giving pleasure to ourselves and employment to others, and satisfaction to you to think it's not been throwed away. You couldnt spend it better.

HIGGINS: [*Taking out his pocket book and coming between* Doolittle *and the piano*] This is irresistible. Lets give him ten. [*He offers two notes to the dustman*]

DOOLITTLE: No, Governor. She wouldnt have the heart to spend ten; and perhaps I shouldnt neither. Ten pounds is a lot of money: it makes a man feel prudent like; and then goodbye to happiness. You

give me what I ask you, Governor: not a penny
more, and not a penny less.

PICKERING: Why dont you marry that missus of
yours? I rather draw the line at encouraging that
sort of immorality.

DOOLITTLE: Tell her so, Governor: tell her so. I'm
willing. It's me that suffers by it. Ive no hold on
her. I got to be agreeable to her. I got to give her
presents. I got to buy her clothes something sinful.
I'm a slave to that woman, Governor, just because
I'm not her lawful husband. And she knows it too.
Catch her marrying me! Take my advice, Governor: marry Eliza while she's young and dont know
no better. If you dont youll be sorry for it after. If
you do, she'll be sorry for it after; but better her
than you, because youre a man, and she's only a
woman and dont know how to be happy anyhow.

HIGGINS: Pickering: if we listen to this man another
minute, we shall have no convictions left. [*To Doolittle*] Five pounds I think you said.

DOOLITTLE: Thank you kindly, Governor.

HIGGINS: Youre sure you wont take ten?

DOOLITTLE: Not now. Another time, Governor.

HIGGINS: [*Handing him a five-pound note*] Here you
are.

DOOLITTLE: Thank you, Governor. Good morning.
[*He hurries to the door, anxious to get away with
his booty. When he opens it he is confronted with
a dainty and exquisitely clean young Japanese lady
in a simple blue cotton kimono printed cunningly
with small white jasmine blossoms. Mrs Pearce is
with her. He gets out of her way deferentially and
apologizes*] Beg pardon, miss.

THE JAPANESE LADY: Garn! Dont you know your own
daughter?

DOOLITTLE: } *exclaiming* { Bly me! it's Eliza!
HIGGINS: } *simul-*   { Whats that! This!
PICKERING: } *taneously* { By Jove!

LIZA: Dont I look silly?

HIGGINS: Silly?

MRS PEARCE: [*At the door*] Now, Mr Higgins, please
dont say anything to make the girl conceited about
herself.

HIGGINS: [*Conscientiously*] Oh! Quite right, Mrs
Pearce. [*To Eliza*] Yes: damned silly.

MRS PEARCE: Please, sir.

HIGGINS: [*Correcting himself*] I mean extremely silly.

LIZA: I should look all right with my hat on. [*She
takes up her hat; puts it on; and walks across the
room to the fireplace with a fashionable air*]

HIGGINS: A new fashion, by George! And it ought to
look horrible!

DOOLITTLE: [*With fatherly pride*] Well, I never
thought she'd clean up as good looking as that,
Governor. She's a credit to me, aint she?

LIZA: I tell you, it's easy to clean up here. Hot and
cold water on tap, just as much as you like, there
is. Woolly towels, there is; and a towel horse so
hot, it burns your fingers. Soft brushes to scrub

yourself, and a wooden bowl of soap smelling like
primroses. Now I know why ladies is so clean.
Washing's a treat for them. Wish they saw what
it is for the like of me!

HIGGINS: I'm glad the bathroom met with your approval.

LIZA: It didnt: not all of it; and I dont care who hears
me say it. Mrs Pearce knows.

HIGGINS: What was wrong, Mrs Pearce?

MRS PEARCE: [*Blandly*] Oh, nothing, sir. It doesnt
matter.

LIZA: I had a good mind to break it. I didnt know
which way to look. But I hung a towel over it, I
did.

HIGGINS: Over what?

MRS PEARCE: Over the looking-glass, sir.

HIGGINS: Doolittle: you have brought your daughter
up too strictly.

DOOLITTLE: Me! I never brought her up at all, except
to give her a lick of a strap now and again. Dont
put it on me, Governor. She aint accustomed to it,
you see: thats all. But she'll soon pick up your free-
and-easy ways.

LIZA: I'm a good girl, I am; and I wont pick up no
free-and-easy ways.

HIGGINS: Eliza: if you say again that youre a good girl,
your father shall take you home.

LIZA: Not him. You dont know my father. All he
come here for was to touch you for some money to
get drunk on.

DOOLITTLE: Well, what else would I want money for?
To put into the plate in church, I suppose. [*She
puts out her tongue at him. He is so incensed by
this that* Pickering *presently finds it necessary to
step between them*] Dont you give me none of
your lip; and dont let me hear you giving this gentleman any of it neither, or youll hear from me
about it. See?

HIGGINS: Have you any further advice to give her before you go, Doolittle? Your blessing, for instance.

DOOLITTLE: No, Governor: I aint such a mug as to
put up my children to all I know myself. Hard
enough to hold them in without that. If you want
Eliza's mind improved, Governor, you do it yourself with a strap. So long, gentlemen. [*He turns to
go*]

HIGGINS: [*Impressively*] Stop. Youll come regularly to
see your daughter. It's your duty, you know. My
brother is a clergyman; and he could help you in
your talks with her.

DOOLITTLE: [*Evasively*] Certainly. I'll come, Governor. Not just this week, because I have a job at a
distance. But later on you may depend on me.
Afternoon, gentlemen. Afternoon, maam. [*He
takes off his hat to Mrs Pearce, who disdains the
salutation and goes out. He winks at Higgins,
thinking him probably a fellow-sufferer from Mrs
Pearce's difficult disposition, and follows her*]

LIZA: Dont you believe the old liar. He'd as soon you

set a bull-dog on him as a clergyman. You wont see him again in a hurry.

HIGGINS: I dont want to, Eliza. Do you?

LIZA: Not me. I dont want never to see him again, I dont. He's a disgrace to me, he is, collecting dust, instead of working at his trade.

PICKERING: What is his trade, Eliza?

LIZA: Taking money out of other people's pockets into his own. His proper trade's a navvy; and he works at it sometimes too—for exercise—and earns good money at it. Aint you going to call me Miss Doolittle any more?

PICKERING: I beg your pardon, Miss Doolittle. It was a slip of the tongue.

LIZA: Oh, I dont mind; only it sounded so genteel. I should just like to take a taxi to the corner of Tottenham Court Road and get out there and tell it to wait for me, just to put the girls in their place a bit. I wouldnt speak to them, you know.

PICKERING: Better wait til we get you something really fashionable.

HIGGINS: Besides, you shouldnt cut your old friends now that you have risen in the world. Thats what we call snobbery.

LIZA: You dont call the like of them my friends now, I should hope. Theyve took it out of me often enough with their ridicule when they had the chance; and now I mean to get a bit of my own back. But if I'm to have fashionable clothes, I'll wait. I should like to have some. Mrs Pearce says youre going to give me some to wear in bed at night different to what I wear in the daytime; but it do seem a waste of money when you could get something to shew. Besides, I never could fancy changing into cold things on a winter night.

MRS PEARCE: [Coming back] Now, Eliza. The new things have come for you to try on.

LIZA: Ah-ow-oo-ooh! [She rushes out]

MRS PEARCE: [Following her] Oh, dont rush about like that, girl. [She shuts the door behind her]

HIGGINS: Pickering: we have taken on a stiff job.

PICKERING: [With conviction] Higgins: we have.

Act III

It is Mrs Higgins's at-home day. Nobody has yet arrived. Her drawing room, in a flat on Chelsea Embankment, has three windows looking on the river; and the ceiling is not so lofty as it would be in an older house of the same pretension. The windows are open, giving access to a balcony with flowers in pots. If you stand with your face to the windows, you have the fireplace on your left and the door in the right-hand wall close to the corner nearest the windows.

Mrs Higgins was brought up on Morris and Burne Jones; and her room, which is very unlike her son's room in Wimpole Street, is not crowded with furniture and little tables and knickknacks. In the middle of the room there is a big ottoman; and this, with the carpet, the Morris wall-papers, and the Morris chintz window curtains and brocade covers of the ottoman and its cushions, supply all the ornament, and are much too handsome to be hidden by odds and ends of useless things. A few good oil-paintings from the exhibitions in the Grosvenor Gallery thirty years ago (the Burne Jones, not the Whistler side of them) are on the walls. The only landscape is a Cecil Lawson on the scale of a Rubens. There is a portrait of Mrs Higgins as she was when she defied fashion in her youth in one of the beautiful Rossettian costumes which, when caricatured by people who did not understand, led to the absurdities of popular estheticism in the eighteen-seventies.

In the corner diagonally opposite the door Mrs Higgins, now over sixty and long past taking the trouble to dress out of the fashion, sits writing at an elegantly simple writing-table with a bell button within reach of her hand. There is a Chippendale chair further back in the room between her and the window nearest her side. At the other side of the room, further forward, is an Elizabethan chair roughly carved in the taste of Inigo Jones. On the same side a piano in a decorated case. The corner between the fireplace and the window is occupied by a divan cushioned in Morris chintz.

It is between four and five in the afternoon.

The door is opened violently; and Higgins enters with his hat on.

MRS HIGGINS: [Dismayed] Henry! [Scolding him] What are you doing here to-day? It is my at-home day: you promised not to come. [As he bends to kiss her, she takes his hat off, and presents it to him]

HIGGINS: Oh bother! [He throws the hat down on the table]

MRS HIGGINS: Go home at once.

HIGGINS: [Kissing her] I know, mother. I came on purpose.

MRS HIGGINS: But you mustnt. I'm serious, Henry. You offend all my friends: they stop coming whenever they meet you.

HIGGINS: Nonsense! I know I have no small talk; but people dont mind. [He sits on the settee]

MRS HIGGINS: Oh! dont they? Small talk indeed! What about your large talk? Really, dear, you mustnt stay.

HIGGINS: I must. Ive a job for you. A phonetic job.

MRS HIGGINS: No use, dear. I'm sorry; but I cant get round your vowels; and though I like to get pretty postcards in your patent shorthand, I always have to read the copies in ordinary writing you so thoughtfully send me.

HIGGINS: Well, this isnt a phonetic job.

MRS HIGGINS: You said it was.

HIGGINS: Not your part of it. Ive picked up a girl.

MRS HIGGINS: Does that mean that some girl has picked you up?

HIGGINS: Not at all. I dont mean a love affair.

MRS HIGGINS: What a pity!

HIGGINS: Why?

MRS HIGGINS: Well, you never fall in love with anyone under forty-five. When will you discover that there are some rather nice-looking young women about?

HIGGINS: Oh, I cant be bothered with young women. My idea of a lovable woman is something as like you as possible. I shall never get into the way of seriously liking young women: some habits lie too deep to be changed. [*Rising abruptly and walking about, jingling his money and his keys in his trouser pockets*] Besides, theyre all idiots.

MRS HIGGINS: Do you know what you would do if you really loved me, Henry?

HIGGINS: Oh bother! What? Marry, I suppose?

MRS HIGGINS: No. Stop fidgeting and take your hands out of your pockets. [*With a gesture of despair, he obeys and sits down again*] Thats a good boy. Now tell me about the girl.

HIGGINS: She's coming to see you.

MRS HIGGINS: I dont remember asking her.

HIGGINS: You didnt. *I* asked her. If youd known her you wouldnt have asked her.

MRS HIGGINS: Indeed! Why?

HIGGINS: Well, it's like this. She's a common flower girl. I picked her off the kerbstone.

MRS HIGGINS: And invited her to my at-home!

HIGGINS: [*Rising and coming to her to coax her*] Oh, thatll be all right. Ive taught her to speak properly; and she has strict orders as to her behavior. She's to keep to two subjects: the weather and everybody's health—Fine day and How do you do, you know—and not to let herself go on things in general. That will be safe.

MRS HIGGINS: Safe! To talk about our health! about our insides! perhaps about our outsides! How could you be so silly, Henry?

HIGGINS: [*Impatiently*] Well, she must talk about something. [*He controls himself and sits down again*] Oh, she'll be all right: dont you fuss. Pickering is in it with me. Ive a sort of bet on that I'll pass her off as a duchess in six months. I started on her some months ago; and she's getting on like a house on fire. I shall win my bet. She has a quick ear; and she's been easier to teach than my middle-class pupils because she's had to learn a complete new language. She talks English almost as you talk French.

MRS HIGGINS: Thats satisfactory, at all events.

HIGGINS: Well, it is and it isnt.

MRS HIGGINS: What does that mean?

HIGGINS: You see, Ive got her pronunciation all right; but you have to consider not only how a girl pronounces, but what she pronounces; and thats where—

[*They are interrupted by the Parlor-Maid, announcing guests*]

THE PARLOR-MAID: Mrs and Miss Eynsford Hill.
[*She withdraws*]

HIGGINS: Oh Lord! [*He rises; snatches his hat from the table; and makes for the door; but before he reaches it his mother introduces him*]

[Mrs *and Miss Eynsford Hill are the mother and daughter who sheltered from the rain in Covent Garden. The mother is well bred, quiet, and has the habitual anxiety of straitened means. The daughter has acquired a gay air of being very much at home in society: the bravado of genteel poverty*]

MRS EYNSFORD HILL: [*To Mrs Higgins*] How do you do?
[*They shake hands*]

MISS EYNSFORD HILL: How d'you do? [*She shakes*]

MRS HIGGINS: [*Introducing*] My son Henry.

MRS EYNSFORD HILL: Your celebrated son! I have so longed to meet you, Professor Higgins.

HIGGINS: [*Glumly, making no movement in her direction*] Delighted. [*He backs against the piano and bows brusquely*]

MISS EYNSFORD HILL: [*Going to him with confident familiarity*] How do you do?

HIGGINS: [*Staring at her*] Ive seen you before somewhere. I havent the ghost of a notion where; but Ive heard your voice. [*Drearily*] It doesnt matter. Youd better sit down.

MRS HIGGINS: I'm sorry to say that my celebrated son has no manners. You mustnt mind him.

MISS EYNSFORD HILL: [*Gaily*] I dont. [*She sits in the Elizabethan chair*]

MRS EYNSFORD HILL: [*A little bewildered*] Not at all. [*She sits on the ottoman between her daughter and Mrs Higgins, who has turned her chair away from the writing-table*]

HIGGINS: Oh, have I been rude? I didnt mean to be. [*He goes to the central window, through which, with his back to the company, he contemplates the river and the flowers in Battersea Park on the opposite bank as if they were a frozen desert.*]

[*The Parlor-Maid returns, ushering in Pickering*]

THE PARLOR-MAID: Colonel Pickering.
[*She withdraws*]

PICKERING: How do you do, Mrs Higgins?

MRS HIGGINS: So glad youve come. Do you know Mrs Eynsford Hill—Miss Eynsford Hill?
[*Exchange of bows. The Colonel brings the Chippendale chair a little forward between Mrs Hill and Mrs Higgins, and sits down*]

PICKERING: Has Henry told you what weve come for?

HIGGINS: [*Over his shoulder*] We were interrupted: damn it!

MRS HIGGINS: Oh Henry, Henry, really!

MRS EYNSFORD HILL: [*Half rising*] Are we in the way?

MRS HIGGINS: [*Rising and making her sit down again*] No, no. You couldnt have come more fortunately: we want you to meet a friend of ours.

HIGGINS: [*Turning hopefully*] Yes, by George! We want two or three people. Youll do as well as anybody else.

[*The* Parlor-Maid *returns, ushering* Freddy]

THE PARLOR-MAID: Mr Eynsford Hill.

HIGGINS: [*Almost audibly, past endurance*] God of Heaven! another of them.

FREDDY: [*Shaking hands with* Mrs Higgins] Ahdedo?

MRS HIGGINS: Very good of you to come. [*Introducing*] Colonel Pickering.

FREDDY: [*Bowing*] Ahdedo?

MRS HIGGINS: I dont think you know my son, Professor Higgins.

FREDDY: [*Going to* Higgins] Ahdedo?

HIGGINS: [*Looking at him much as if he were a pickpocket*] I'll take my oath Ive met you before somewhere. Where was it?

FREDDY: I dont think so.

HIGGINS: [*Resignedly*] It dont matter, anyhow. Sit down.

> [*He shakes* Freddy's *hand, and almost slings him on the ottoman with his face to the windows; then comes round to the other side of it*]

HIGGINS: Well, here we are, anyhow! [*He sits down on the ottoman next* Mrs Eynsford Hill, *on her left*] And now, what the devil are we going to talk about until Eliza comes?

MRS HIGGINS: Henry: you are the life and soul of the Royal Society's soirées; but really youre rather trying on more commonplace occasions.

HIGGINS: Am I? Very sorry. [*Beaming suddenly*] I suppose I am, you know. [*Uproariously*] Ha, ha!

MISS EYNSFORD HILL: [*Who considers Higgins quite eligible matrimonially*] I sympathize. I havent any small talk. If people would only be frank and say what they really think!

HIGGINS: [*Relapsing into gloom*] Lord forbid!

MRS EYNSFORD HILL: [*Taking up her daughter's cue*] But why?

HIGGINS: What they think they ought to think is bad enough, Lord knows; but what they really think would break up the whole show. Do you suppose it would be really agreeable if I were to come out now with what *I* really think?

MISS EYNSFORD HILL: [*Gaily*] Is it so very cynical?

HIGGINS: Cynical! Who the dickens said it was cynical? I mean it wouldnt be decent.

MRS EYNSFORD HILL: [*Seriously*] Oh! I'm sure you dont mean that, Mr Higgins.

HIGGINS: You see, we're all savages, more or less. We're supposed to be civilized and cultured—to know all about poetry and philosophy and art and science, and so on; but how many of us know even the meanings of these names? [*To Miss Hill*] What do you know of poetry? [*To Mrs Hill*] What do you know of science? [*Indicating* Freddy] What does he know of art or science or anything else? What the devil do you imagine I know of philosophy?

MRS HIGGINS: [*Warningly*] Or of manners, Henry?

THE PARLOR-MAID: [*Opening the door*] Miss Doolittle. [*She withdraws*]

HIGGINS: [*Rising hastily and running to* Mrs Higgins] Here she is, mother. [*He stands on tiptoe and makes signs over his mother's head to* Eliza *to indicate to her which lady is her hostess*]

[Eliza, *who is exquisitely dressed, produces an impression of such remarkable distinction and beauty as she enters that they all rise, quite fluttered. Guided by* Higgins's *signals, she comes to* Mrs Higgins *with studied grace*]

LIZA: [*Speaking with pedantic correctness of pronunciation and great beauty of tone*] How do you do, Mrs Higgins? [*She gasps slightly in making sure of the H in Higgins, but is quite successful*] Mr Higgins told me I might come.

MRS HIGGINS: [*Cordially*] Quite right: I'm very glad indeed to see you.

PICKERING: How do you do, Miss Doolittle?

LIZA: [*Shaking hands with him*] Colonel Pickering, is it not?

MRS EYNSFORD HILL: I feel sure we have met before, Miss Doolittle. I remember your eyes.

LIZA: How do you do? [*She sits down on the ottoman gracefully in the place just left vacant by* Higgins]

MRS EYNSFORD HILL: [*Introducing*] My daughter Clara.

LIZA: How do you do?

CLARA: [*Impulsively*] How do you do? [*She sits down on the ottoman beside* Eliza, *devouring her with her eyes*]

FREDDY: [*Coming to their side of the ottoman*] Ive certainly had the pleasure.

MRS EYNSFORD HILL: [*Introducing*] My son Freddy.

LIZA: How do you do?

> [Freddy *bows and sits down in the Elizabethan chair, infatuated*]

HIGGINS: [*Suddenly*] By George, yes: it all comes back to me! [*They stare at him*] Covent Garden! [*Lamentably*] What a damned thing!

MRS HIGGINS: Henry, please! [*He is about to sit on the edge of the table*] Dont sit on my writing-table: youll break it.

HIGGINS: [*Sulkily*] Sorry.

> [*He goes to the divan, stumbling into the fender and over the fire-irons on his way; extricating himself with muttered imprecations; and finishing his disastrous journey by throwing himself so impatiently on the divan that he almost breaks it.* Mrs Higgins *looks at him, but controls herself and says nothing*]

[*A long and painful pause ensues*]

MRS HIGGINS: [*At last, conversationally*] Will it rain, do you think?

LIZA: The shallow depression in the west of these islands is likely to move slowly in an easterly direction. There are no indications of any great change in the barometrical situation.

FREDDY: Ha! ha! how awfully funny!

LIZA: What is wrong with that, young man? I bet I got it right.

FREDDY: Killing!

MRS EYNSFORD HILL: I'm sure I hope it wont turn cold. Theres so much influenza about. It runs right through our whole family regularly every spring.

LIZA: [*Darkly*] My aunt died of influenza: so they said.

MRS EYNSFORD HILL: [*Clicks her tongue sympathetically*]!!!

LIZA: [*In the same tragic tone*] But it's my belief they done the old woman in.

MRS HIGGINS: [*Puzzled*] Done her in?

LIZA: Y-e-e-e-es, Lord love you! Why should she die of influenza? She come through diphtheria right enough the year before. I saw her with my own eyes. Fairly blue with it, she was. They all thought she was dead; but my father he kept ladling gin down her throat til she came to so sudden that she bit the bowl off the spoon.

MRS EYNSFORD HILL: [*Startled*] Dear me!

LIZA: [*Piling up the indictment*] What call would a woman with that strength in her have to die of influenza? What become of her new straw hat that should have come to me? Somebody pinched it; and what I say is, them as pinched it done her in.

MRS EYNSFORD HILL: What does doing her in mean?

HIGGINS: [*Hastily*] Oh, thats the new small talk. To do a person in means to kill them.

MRS EYNSFORD HILL: [*To Eliza, horrified*] You surely dont believe that your aunt was killed?

LIZA: Do I not! Them she lived with would have killed her for a hat-pin, let alone a hat.

MRS EYNSFORD HILL: But it cant have been right for your father to pour spirits down her throat like that. It might have killed her.

LIZA: Not her. Gin was mother's milk to her. Besides, he'd poured so much down his own throat that he knew the good of it.

MRS. EYNSFORD HILL: Do you mean that he drank?

LIZA: Drank! My word! Something chronic.

MRS EYNSFORD HILL: How dreadful for you!

LIZA: Not a bit. It never did him no harm what I could see. But then he did not keep it up regular. [*Cheerfully*] On the burst, as you might say, from time to time. And always more agreeable when he had a drop in. When he was out of work, my mother used to give him fourpence and tell him to go out and not come back until he'd drunk himself cheerful and loving-like. Theres lots of women has to make their husbands drunk to make them fit to live with. [*Now quite at her ease*] You see, it's like this. If a man has a bit of a conscience, it always takes him when he's sober; and then it makes him low-spirited. A drop of booze just takes that off and makes him happy. [*To Freddy, who is in convulsions of suppressed laughter*] Here! what are you sniggering at?

FREDDY: The new small talk. You do it so awfully well.

LIZA: If I was doing it proper, what was you laughing at? [*To Higgins*] Have I said anything I oughtnt?

MRS HIGGINS: [*Interposing*] Not at all, Miss Doolittle.

LIZA: Well, thats a mercy, anyhow. [*Expansively*] What I always say is—

HIGGINS: [*Rising and looking at his watch*] Ahem!

LIZA: [*Looking round at him; taking the hint; and rising*] Well: I must go. [*They all rise. Freddy goes to the door*] So pleased to have met you. Goodbye. [*She shakes hands with Mrs Higgins*]

MRS HIGGINS: Goodbye.

LIZA: Goodbye, Colonel Pickering.

PICKERING: Goodbye, Miss Doolittle. [*They shake hands*]

LIZA: [*Nodding to the others*] Goodbye, all.

FREDDY: [*Opening the door for her*] Are you walking across the Park, Miss Doolittle? If so—

LIZA: Walk! Not bloody likely. [*Sensation*] I am going in a taxi. [*She goes out*]

[*Pickering gasps and sits down. Freddy goes out on the balcony to catch another glimpse of Eliza*]

MRS EYNSFORD HILL: [*Suffering from shock*] Well, I really cant get used to the new ways.

CLARA: [*Throwing herself discontentedly into the Elizabethan chair*] Oh, it's all right, mamma, quite right. People will think we never go anywhere or see anybody if you are so old-fashioned.

MRS EYNSFORD HILL: I daresay I am very old-fashioned; but I do hope you wont begin using that expression, Clara. I have got accustomed to hear you talking about men as rotters, and calling everything filthy and beastly; though I do think it horrible and unladylike. But this last is really too much. Dont you think so, Colonel Pickering?

PICKERING: Dont ask me. Ive been away in India for several years; and manners have changed so much that I sometimes dont know whether I'm at a respectable dinner-table or in a ship's forecastle.

CLARA: It's all a matter of habit. Theres no right or wrong in it. Nobody means anything by it. And it's so quaint, and gives such a smart emphasis to things that are not in themselves very witty. I find the new small talk delightful and quite innocent.

MRS EYNSFORD HILL: [*Rising*] Well, after that, I think it's time for us to go.

[*Pickering and Higgins rise*]

CLARA: [*Rising*] Oh yes: we have three at-homes to go to still. Goodbye, Mrs Higgins. Goodbye, Colonel Pickering. Goodbye, Professor Higgins.

HIGGINS: [*Coming grimly at her from the divan, and accompanying her to the door*] Goodbye. Be sure you try on that small talk at the three at-homes. Dont be nervous about it. Pitch it in strong.

CLARA: [*All smiles*] I will. Goodbye. Such nonsense, all this early Victorian prudery!

HIGGINS: [*Tempting her*] Such damned nonsense!

CLARA: Such bloody nonsense!

MRS EYNSFORD HILL: [*Convulsively*] Clara!

CLARA: Ha! ha! [*She goes out radiant, conscious of being thoroughly up to date, and is heard descending the stairs in a stream of silvery laughter*]

FREDDY: [*To the heavens at large*] Well, I ask you— [*He gives it up, and comes to* Mrs Higgins] Goodbye.

MRS HIGGINS: [*Shaking hands*] Goodbye. Would you like to meet Miss Doolittle again?

FREDDY: [*Eagerly*] Yes, I should, most awfully.

MRS HIGGINS: Well, you know my days.

FREDDY: Yes. Thanks awfully. Goodbye. [*He goes out*]

MRS EYNSFORD HILL: Goodbye, Mr Higgins.

HIGGINS: Goodbye. Goodbye.

MRS EYNSFORD HILL: [*To* Pickering] It's no use. I shall never be able to bring myself to use that word.

PICKERING: Dont. It's not compulsory, you know. Youll get on quite well without it.

MRS EYNSFORD HILL: Only, Clara is so down on me if I am not positively reeking with the latest slang. Goodbye.

PICKERING: Goodbye. [*They shake hands*]

MRS EYNSFORD HILL: [*To* Mrs Higgins] You mustnt mind Clara. [Pickering, *catching from her lowered tone that this is not meant for him to hear, discreetly joins* Higgins *at the window*] We're so poor! and she gets so few parties, poor child! She doesnt quite know. [Mrs. Higgins, *seeing that her eyes are moist, takes her hand sympathetically and goes with her to the door*] But the boy is nice. Dont you think so?

MRS HIGGINS: Oh, quite nice. I shall always be delighted to see him.

MRS EYNSFORD HILL: Thank you, dear. Goodbye.
[*She goes out*]

HIGGINS: [*Eagerly*] Well? Is Eliza presentable? [*He swoops on his mother and drags her to the ottoman, where she sits down in* Eliza's *place with her son on her left*]

[Pickering *returns to his chair on her right*]

MRS HIGGINS: You silly boy, of course she's not presentable. She's a triumph of your art and of her dressmaker's; but if you suppose for a moment that she doesnt give herself away in every sentence she utters, you must be perfectly cracked about her.

PICKERING: But dont you think something might be done? I mean something to eliminate the sanguinary element from her conversation.

MRS HIGGINS: Not as long as she is in Henry's hands.

HIGGINS: [*Aggrieved*] Do you mean that my language is improper?

MRS HIGGINS: No, dearest: it would be quite proper—say on a canal barge; but it would not be proper for her at a garden party.

HIGGINS: [*Deeply injured*] Well I must say—

PICKERING: [*Interrupting him*] Come, Higgins: you must learn to know yourself. I havent heard such language as yours since we used to review the volunteers in Hyde Park twenty years ago.

HIGGINS: [*Sulkily*] Oh, well, if you say so, I suppose I dont always talk like a bishop.

MRS HIGGINS: [*Quieting* Henry *with a touch*] Colonel Pickering: will you tell me what is the exact state of things in Wimpole Street?

PICKERING: [*Cheerfully: as if this completely changed the subject*] Well, I have come to live there with Henry. We work together at my Indian Dialects; and we think it more convenient—

MRS HIGGINS: Quite so. I know all about that: it's an excellent arrangement. But where does this girl live?

HIGGINS: With us, of course. Where should she live?

MRS HIGGINS: But on what terms? Is she a servant? If not, what is she?

PICKERING: [*Slowly*] I think I know what you mean, Mrs Higgins.

HIGGINS: Well, dash me if I do! Ive had to work at the girl every day for months to get her to her present pitch. Besides, she's useful. She knows where my things are, and remembers my appointments and so forth.

MRS HIGGINS: How does your housekeeper get on with her?

HIGGINS: Mrs Pearce? Oh, she's jolly glad to get so much taken off her hands; for before Eliza came, she used to have to find things and remind me of my appointments. But she's got some silly bee in her bonnet about Eliza. She keeps saying "You dont think, sir": doesnt she, Pick?

PICKERING: Yes: thats the formula. "You dont think, sir." Thats the end of every conversation about Eliza.

HIGGINS: As if I ever stop thinking about the girl and her confounded vowels and consonants. I'm worn out, thinking about her, and watching her lips and her teeth and her tongue, not to mention her soul, which is the quaintest of the lot.

MRS HIGGINS: You certainly are a pretty pair of babies, playing with your live doll.

HIGGINS: Playing! The hardest job I ever tackled: make no mistake about that, mother. But you have no idea how frightfully interesting it is to take a human being and change her into a quite different human being by creating a new speech for her. It's filling up the deepest gulf that separates class from class and soul from soul.

PICKERING: [*Drawing his chair closer to* Mrs Higgins *and bending over to her eagerly*] Yes: it's enormously interesting. I assure you, Mrs Higgins, we take Eliza very seriously. Every week—every day almost—there is some new change. [*Closer again*] We keep records of every stage—dozens of gramophone disks and photographs—

HIGGINS: [*Assailing her at the other ear*] Yes, by George: it's the most absorbing experiment I ever tackled. She regularly fills our lives up: doesnt she, Pick?

PICKERING: We're always talking Eliza.

HIGGINS: Teaching Eliza.

PICKERING: Dressing Eliza.

MRS HIGGINS: What!

HIGGINS: Inventing new Elizas.

[*Speaking together*]

HIGGINS: You know, she has the most extraordinary quickness of ear:

PICKERING: I assure you, my dear Mrs Higgins, that girl

HIGGINS: just like a parrot. Ive tried her with every

PICKERING: is a genius. She can play the piano quite beautifully.

HIGGINS: possible sort of sound that a human being can make—

PICKERING: We have taken her to classical concerts and to music

HIGGINS: Continental dialects, African dialects, Hottentot

PICKERING: halls; and it's all the same to her: she plays everything

HIGGINS: clicks, things it took me years to get hold of; and

PICKERING: she hears right off when she comes home, whether it's

HIGGINS: she picks them up like a shot, right away, as if she had

PICKERING: Beethoven and Brahms or Lehar and Lionel Monckton;

HIGGINS: been at it all her life.

PICKERING: though six months ago, she'd never as much as touched a piano—

MRS HIGGINS: [*Putting her fingers in her ears, as they are by this time shouting one another down with an intolerable noise*] Sh-sh-sh—sh! [*They stop*]

PICKERING: I beg your pardon. [*He draws his chair back apologetically*]

HIGGINS: Sorry. When Pickering starts shouting nobody can get a word in edgeways.

MRS HIGGINS: Be quiet, Henry. Colonel Pickering: dont you realize that when Eliza walked into Wimpole Street, something walked in with her?

PICKERING: Her father did. But Henry soon got rid of him.

MRS HIGGINS: It would have been more to the point if her mother had. But as her mother didnt something else did.

PICKERING: But what?

MRS HIGGINS: [*Unconsciously dating herself by the word*] A problem.

PICKERING: Oh, I see. The problem of how to pass her off as a lady.

HIGGINS: I'll solve that problem. Ive half solved it already.

MRS HIGGINS: No, you two infinitely stupid male creatures: the problem of what is to be done with her afterwards.

HIGGINS: I dont see anything in that. She can go her own way, with all the advantages I have given her.

MRS HIGGINS: The advantages of that poor woman who was here just now! The manners and habits that disqualify a fine lady from earning her own living without giving her a fine lady's income! Is that what you mean?

PICKERING: [*Indulgently, being rather bored*] Oh, that will be all right, Mrs Higgins. [*He rises to go*]

HIGGINS: [*Rising also*] We'll find her some light employment.

PICKERING: She's happy enough. Dont you worry about her. Goodbye. [*He shakes hands as if he were consoling a frightened child, and makes for the door*]

HIGGINS: Anyhow, theres no good bothering now. The thing's done. Goodbye, mother. [*He kisses her, and follows Pickering*]

PICKERING: [*Turning for a final consolation*] There are plenty of openings. We'll do whats right. Goodbye.

HIGGINS: [*To Pickering as they go out together*] Let's take her to the Shakespear exhibition at Earls Court.

PICKERING: Yes: lets. Her remarks will be delicious.

HIGGINS: She'll mimic all the people for us when we get home.

PICKERING: Ripping. [*Both are heard laughing as they go downstairs*]

MRS HIGGINS: [*Rises with an impatient bounce, and returns to her work at the writing-table. She sweeps a litter of disarranged papers out of her way; snatches a sheet of paper from her stationery case; and tries resolutely to write. At the third line she gives it up; flings down her pen; grips the table angrily and exclaims*] Oh, men! men!! men!!!

Act IV

The Wimpole Street laboratory. Midnight. Nobody in the room. The clock on the mantelpiece strikes twelve. The fire is not alight: it is a summer night.

Presently Higgins *and* Pickering *are heard on the stairs.*

HIGGINS: [*Calling down to Pickering*] I say, Pick: lock up, will you? I shant be going out again.

PICKERING: Right. Can Mrs Pearce go to bed? We dont want anything more, do we?

HIGGINS: Lord, no!

[Eliza *opens the door and is seen on the lighted landing in opera cloak, brilliant evening dress, and diamonds, with fan, flowers, and all accessories. She comes to the hearth, and switches on the electric lights there. She is tired: her pallor contrasts strongly with her dark eyes and hair; and her expression is almost tragic. She takes off her cloak; puts her fan and flowers on the piano; and sits down on the bench, brooding and silent. Higgins, in evening dress, with overcoat and hat, comes in, carrying a smoking jacket which he has picked up downstairs. He takes off the hat and overcoat; throws them carelessly on the newspaper stand; disposes of his coat in the same way; puts on the smoking jacket; and throws himself wearily into the easy-chair at the hearth. Pickering, similarly attired, comes in. He also takes off his hat and overcoat, and is about to throw them on Higgins's when he hesitates*]

PICKERING: I say: Mrs Pearce will row if we leave these things lying about in the drawing room.

HIGGINS: Oh, chuck them over the bannisters into the hall. She'll find them there in the morning and put them away all right. She'll think we were drunk.

PICKERING: We are, slightly. Are there any letters?

HIGGINS: I didnt look. [Pickering *takes the overcoats and hats and goes downstairs. Higgins begins half singing half yawning an air from La Fanciulla del Golden West. Suddenly he stops and exclaims*] I wonder where the devil my slippers are!

[Eliza *looks at him darkly; then rises suddenly and leaves the room*]
[Higgins *yawns again, and resumes his song*]

[Pickering *returns, with the contents of the letter-box in his hand*]

PICKERING: Only circulars, and this coroneted billet-doux for you. [He *throws the circulars into the fender, and posts himself on the hearthrug, with his back to the grate*]

HIGGINS: [Glancing *at the billet-doux*] Money-lender. [He *throws the letter after the circulars*]

[Eliza *returns with a pair of large down-at-heel slippers. She places them on the carpet before Higgins, and sits as before without a word*]

HIGGINS: [Yawning *again*] Oh Lord! What an evening! What a crew! What a silly tomfoolery! [He *raises his shoe to unlace it, and catches sight of the slippers. He stops unlacing and looks at them as if they had appeared there of their own accord*] Oh! theyre there, are they?

PICKERING: [Stretching *himself*] Well, I feel a bit tired. It's been a long day. The garden party, a dinner party, and the opera! Rather too much of a good thing. But youve won your bet, Higgins. Eliza did the trick, and something to spare, eh?

HIGGINS: [Fervently] Thank God it's over!

[Eliza *flinches violently; but they take no notice of her; and she recovers herself and sits stonily as before*]

PICKERING: Were you nervous at the garden party? I was. Eliza didnt seem a bit nervous.

HIGGINS: Oh, she wasnt nervous. I knew she'd be all right. No: it's the strain of putting the job through all these months that has told on me. It was interesting enough at first, while we were at the phonetics; but after that I got deadly sick of it. If I hadnt backed myself to do it I should have chucked the whole thing up two months ago. It was a silly notion: the whole thing has been a bore.

PICKERING: Oh come! the garden party was frightfully exciting. My heart began beating like anything.

HIGGINS: Yes, for the first three minutes. But when I saw we were going to win hands down, I felt like a bear in a cage, hanging about doing nothing. The dinner was worse: sitting gorging there for over an hour, with nobody but a damned fool of a fashionable woman to talk to! I tell you, Pickering, never again for me. No more artificial duchesses. The whole thing has been simple purgatory.

PICKERING: Youve never been broken in properly to the social routine. [Strolling *over to the piano*] I rather enjoy dipping into it occasionally myself: it makes me feel young again. Anyhow, it was a great success: an immense success. I was quite frightened once or twice because Eliza was doing it so well. You see, lots of the real people cant do it at all: theyre such fools that they think style comes by nature to people in their position; and so they never learn. Theres always something professional about doing a thing superlatively well.

HIGGINS: Yes: thats what drives me mad: the silly people dont know their own silly business. [Rising] However, it's over and done with; and now I can go to bed at last without dreading tomorrow.

[Eliza's *beauty becomes murderous*]

PICKERING: I think I shall turn in too. Still, it's been a great occasion: a triumph for you. Goodnight.
[He *goes*]

HIGGINS: [Following *him*] Goodnight. [Over *his shoulder, at the door*] Put out the lights, Eliza; and tell Mrs Pearce not to make coffee for me in the morning: I'll take tea. [He *goes out*]

[Eliza *tries to control herself and feel indifferent as she rises and walks across to the hearth to switch off the lights. By the time she gets there she is on the point of screaming. She sits down in Higgins's chair and holds on hard to the arms. Finally she gives way and flings herself furiously on the floor, raging*]

HIGGINS: [*In despairing wrath outside*] What the devil have I done with my slippers? [*He appears at the door*]

LIZA: [*Snatching up the slippers, and hurling them at him one after the other with all her force*] There are your slippers. And there. Take your slippers; and may you never have a day's luck with them!

HIGGINS: [*Astounded*] What on earth——! [*He comes to her*] Whats the matter? Get up. [*He pulls her up*] Anything wrong?

LIZA: [*Breathless*] Nothing wrong—with y o u. Ive won your bet for you, havnt I? Thats enough for you. *I* dont matter, I suppose.

HIGGINS: Y o u won my bet! You! Presumptuous insect! *I* won it. What did you throw those slippers at me for?

LIZA: Because I wanted to smash your face. I'd like to kill you, you selfish brute. Why didnt you leave me where you picked me out of—in the gutter? You thank God it's all over, and that now you can throw me back again there, do you? [*She crisps her fingers frantically*]

HIGGINS: [*Looking at her in cool wonder*] The creature is nervous, after all.

LIZA: [*Gives a suffocated scream of fury, and instinctively darts her nails at his face*]!!

HIGGINS: [*Catching her wrists*] Ah! would you? Claws in, you cat. How dare you shew your temper to me? Sit down and be quiet. [*He throws her roughly into the easy-chair*]

LIZA: [*Crushed by superior strength and weight*] Whats to become of me? Whats to become of me?

HIGGINS: How the devil do I know whats to become of you? What does it matter what becomes of you?

LIZA: You dont care. I know you dont care. You wouldnt care if I was dead. I'm nothing to you—not so much as them slippers.

HIGGINS: [*Thundering*] T h o s e slippers.

LIZA: [*With bitter submission*] Those slippers. I didnt think it made any difference now.

[*A pause. Eliza hopeless and crushed.
Higgins a little uneasy*]

HIGGINS: [*In his loftiest manner*] Why have you begun going on like this? May I ask whether you complain of your treatment here?

LIZA: No.

HIGGINS: Has anybody behaved badly to you? Colonel Pickering? Mrs Pearce? Any of the servants?

LIZA: No.

HIGGINS: I presume you dont pretend that *I* have treated you badly?

LIZA: No.

HIGGINS: I am glad to hear it. [*He moderates his tone*] Perhaps youre tired after the strain of the day. Will you have a glass of champagne? [*He moves towards the door*]

LIZA: No. [*Recollecting her manners*] Thank you.

HIGGINS: [*Good-humored again*] This has been coming on you for some days. I suppose it was natural for you to be anxious about the garden party. But thats all over now. [*He pats her kindly on the shoulder. She writhes*] Theres nothing more to worry about.

LIZA: No. Nothing more for you to worry about. [*She suddenly rises and gets away from him by going to the piano bench, where she sits and hides her face*] Oh God! I wish I was dead.

HIGGINS: [*Staring after her in sincere surprise*] Why? In heaven's name, why? [*Reasonably, going to her*] Listen to me, Eliza. All this irritation is purely subjective.

LIZA: I dont understand. I'm too ignorant.

HIGGINS: It's only imagination. Low spirits and nothing else. Nobody's hurting you. Nothing's wrong. You go to bed like a good girl and sleep it off. Have a little cry and say your prayers: that will make you comfortable.

LIZA: I heard your prayers. "Thank God it's all over!"

HIGGINS: [*Impatiently*] Well, dont you thank God it's all over? Now you are free and can do what you like.

LIZA: [*Pulling herself together in desperation*] What am I fit for? What have you left me fit for? Where am I to go? What am I to do? Whats to become of me?

HIGGINS: [*Enlightened, but not at all impressed*] Oh t h a t s whats worrying you, is it? [*He thrusts his hands into his pockets, and walks about in his usual manner, rattling the contents of his pockets, as if condescending to a trivial subject out of pure kindness*] I shouldnt bother about it if I were you. I should imagine you wont have much difficulty in settling yourself somewhere or other, though I hadnt quite realized that you were going away. [*She looks quickly at him: he does not look at her, but examines the dessert stand on the piano and decides that he will eat an apple*] You might marry, you know. [*He bites a large piece out of the apple and munches it noisily*] You see, Eliza, all men are not confirmed old bachelors like me and the Colonel. Most men are the marrying sort (poor devils!); and youre not bad-looking: it's quite a pleasure to look at you sometimes—not now, of course, because youre crying and looking as ugly as the very devil; but when youre all right and quite yourself, youre what I should call attractive. That is, to the people in the marrying line, you understand. You go to bed and have a good nice rest; and then get up and look at yourself in the glass; and you wont feel so cheap.

[*Eliza again looks at him, speechless,
and does not stir*]

[*The look is quite lost in him: he eats his apple with a dreamy expression of happiness, as it is quite a good one*]

HIGGINS: [*A genial afterthought occurring to him*] I daresay my mother could find some chap or other who would do very well.

LIZA: We were above that at the corner of Tottenham Court Road.

HIGGINS: [*Waking up*] What do you mean?

LIZA: I sold flowers. I didnt sell myself. Now youve made a lady of me I'm not fit to sell anything else. I wish youd left me where you found me.

HIGGINS: [*Slinging the core of the apple decisively into the grate*] Tosh, Eliza. Dont you insult human relations by dragging all this cant about buying and selling into it. You neednt marry the fellow if you dont like him.

LIZA: What else am I to do?

HIGGINS: Oh, lots of things. What about your old idea of a florist's shop? Pickering could set you up in one: he's lots of money. [*Chuckling*] He'll have to pay for all those togs you have been wearing today; and that, with the hire of the jewellery, will make a big hole in two hundred pounds. Why, six months ago you would have thought it the millennium to have a flower shop of your own. Come! youll be all right. I must clear off to bed: I'm devilish sleepy. By the way, I came down for something: I forget what it was.

LIZA: Your slippers.

HIGGINS: Oh yes, of course. You shied them at me. [*He picks them up, and is going out when she rises and speaks to him*]

LIZA: Before you go, sir—

HIGGINS: [*Dropping the slippers in his surprise at her calling him sir*] Eh?

LIZA: Do my clothes belong to me or to Colonel Pickering?

HIGGINS: [*Coming back into the room as if her question were the very climax of unreason*] What the devil use would they be to Pickering?

LIZA: He might want them for the next girl you pick up to experiment on.

HIGGINS: [*Shocked and hurt*] Is t h a t the way you feel towards us?

LIZA: I dont want to hear anything more about that. All I want to know is whether anything belongs to me. My own clothes were burnt.

HIGGINS: But what does it matter? Why need you start bothering about that in the middle of the night?

LIZA: I want to know what I may take away with me. I dont want to be accused of stealing.

HIGGINS: [*Now deeply wounded*] Stealing! You shouldnt have said that, Eliza. That shews a want of feeling.

LIZA: I'm sorry. I'm only a common ignorant girl; and in my station I have to be careful. There cant be any feelings between the like of you and the like of me. Please will you tell me what belongs to me and what doesnt?

HIGGINS: [*Very sulky*] You may take the whole damned houseful if you like. Except the jewels. Theyre hired. Will that satisfy you? [*He turns on his heel and is about to go in extreme dudgeon*]

LIZA: [*Drinking in his emotion like nectar, and nagging him to provoke a further supply*] Stop, please. [*She takes off her jewels*] Will you take these to your room and keep them safe? I dont want to run the risk of their being missing.

HIGGINS: [*Furious*] Hand them over. [*She puts them into his hands*] If these belonged to me instead of to the jeweller. I'd ram them down your ungrateful throat. [*He perfunctorily thrusts them into his pockets, unconsciously decorating himself with the protruding ends of the chains*]

LIZA: [*Taking a ring off*] This ring isnt the jeweller's: it's the one you bought me in Brighton. I dont want it now. [*Higgins dashes the ring violently into the fireplace, and turns on her so threateningly that she crouches over the piano with her hands over her face, and exclaims*] Dont you hit me.

HIGGINS: Hit you! You infamous creature, how dare you accuse me of such a thing? It is you who have hit me. You have wounded me to the heart.

LIZA: [*Thrilling with hidden joy*] I'm glad. Ive got a little of my own back, anyhow.

HIGGINS: [*With dignity, in his finest professional style*] You have caused me to lose my temper: a thing that has hardly ever happened to me before. I prefer to say nothing more tonight. I am going to bed.

LIZA: [*Pertly*] Youd better leave a note for Mrs Pearce about the coffee; for she wont be told by me.

HIGGINS: [*Formally*] Damn Mrs Pearce; and damn the coffee; and damn you; and damn my own folly in having lavished hard-earned knowledge and the treasure of my regard and intimacy on a heartless guttersnipe. [*He goes out with impressive decorum, and spoils it by slamming the door savagely*]

[*Eliza smiles for the first time; expresses her feelings by a wild pantomime in which an imitation of Higgins's exist is confused with her own triumph; and finally goes down on her knees on the hearthrug to look for the ring*]

Act V

Mrs. Higgins's *drawing room. She is at her writing-table as before. The* Parlor-Maid *comes in.*

THE PARLOR-MAID: [*At the door*] Mr Henry, maam, is downstairs with Colonel Pickering.

MRS HIGGINS: Well, shew them up.

THE PARLOR-MAID: Theyre using the telephone, maam. Telephoning to the police, I think.

MRS HIGGINS: What!

THE PARLOR-MAID: [*Coming further in and lowering*

her voice] Mr Henry is in a state, maam. I thought I'd better tell you.

MRS HIGGINS: If you had told me that Mr Henry was not in a state it would have been more surprising. Tell them to come up when theyve finished with the police. I suppose he's lost something.

THE PARLOR-MAID: Yes, maam. [*Going*]

MRS HIGGINS: Go upstairs and tell Miss Doolittle that Mr Henry and the Colonel are here. Ask her not to come down til I send for her.

THE PARLOR-MAID: Yes, maam.

[Higgins *bursts in. He is, as the* Parlor-Maid *has said, in a state*]

HIGGINS: Look here, mother: heres a confounded thing!

MRS HIGGINS: Yes, dear. Good morning. [*He checks his impatience and kisses her, whilst the* Parlor-Maid *goes out*] What is it?

HIGGINS: Eliza's bolted.

MRS HIGGINS: [*Calmly continuing her writing*] You must have frightened her.

HIGGINS: Frightened her! nonsense! She was left last night, as usual, to turn out the lights and all that; and instead of going to bed she changed her clothes and went right off: her bed wasnt slept in. She came in a cab for her things before seven this morning; and that fool Mrs. Pearce let her have them without telling me a word about it. What am I to do?

MRS HIGGINS: Do without, I'm afraid, Henry. The girl has a perfect right to leave if she chooses.

HIGGINS: [*Wandering distractedly across the room*] But I cant find anything. I dont know what appointments Ive got. I'm—

[Pickering *comes in. Mrs Higgins puts down her pen and turns away from the writing-table*]

PICKERING: [*Shaking hands*] Good morning, Mrs Higgins. Has Henry told you? [*He sits down on the ottoman*]

HIGGINS: What does that ass of an inspector say? Have you offered a reward?

MRS HIGGINS: [*Rising in indignant amazement*] You dont mean to say you have set the police after Eliza.

HIGGINS: Of course. What are the police for? What else could we do? [*He sits in the Elizabethan chair*]

PICKERING: The inspector made a lot of difficulties. I really think he suspected us of some improper purpose.

MRS HIGGINS: Well, of course he did. What right have you to go to the police and give the girl's name as if she were a thief, or a lost umbrella, or something? Really! [*She sits down again, deeply vexed*]

HIGGINS: But we want to find her.

PICKERING: We cant let her go like this, you know, Mrs Higgins. What were we to do?

MRS HIGGINS: You have no more sense, either of you, than two children. Why—

[*The* Parlor-Maid *comes in and breaks off the conversation*]

THE PARLOR-MAID: Mr Henry: a gentleman wants to see you very particular. He's been sent on from Wimpole Street.

HIGGINS: Oh, bother! I cant see anyone now. Who is it?

THE PARLOR-MAID: A Mr Doolittle, sir.

PICKERING: Doolittle! Do you mean the dustman?

THE PARLOR-MAID: Dustman! Oh no, sir: a gentleman.

HIGGINS: [*Springing up excitedly*] By George, Pick, it's some relative of hers that she's gone to. Somebody we know nothing about. [*To the* Parlor-Maid] Send him up, quick.

THE PARLOR-MAID: Yes, sir. [*She goes*]

HIGGINS: [*Eagerly, going to his mother*] Genteel relatives! now we shall hear something. [*He sits down in the Chippendale chair*]

MRS HIGGINS: Do you know any of her people?

PICKERING: Only her father: the fellow we told you about.

THE PARLOR-MAID: [*Announcing*] Mr Doolittle.

[*She withdraws*]

[Doolittle *enters. He is brilliantly dressed in a new fashionable frock-coat, with white waistcoat and grey trousers. A flower in his buttonhole, a dazzling silk hat, and patent leather shoes complete the effect. He is too concerned with the business he has come on to notice Mrs Higgins. He walks straight to Higgins, and accosts him with vehement reproach*]

DOOLITTLE: [*Indicating his own person*] See here! Do you see this? Y o u done this.

HIGGINS: Done what, man?

DOOLITTLE: This, I tell you. Look at it. Look at this hat. Look at this coat.

PICKERING: Has Eliza been buying you clothes?

DOOLITTLE: Eliza! not she. Not half. Why would she buy me clothes?

MRS HIGGINS: Good morning, Mr Doolittle. Wont you sit down?

DOOLITTLE: [*Taken aback as he becomes conscious that he has forgotten his hostess*] Asking your pardon, maam. [*He approaches her and shakes her proffered hand*] Thank you. [*He sits down on the ottoman, on Pickering's right*] I am that full of what has happened to me that I cant think of anything else.

HIGGINS: What the dickens h a s happened to you?

DOOLITTLE: I shouldnt mind if it had only h a p - p e n e d to me: anything might happen to anybody and nobody to blame but Providence, as you might say. But this is something that you done to me: yes, you, Henry Higgins.

HIGGINS: Have you found Eliza? Thats the point.

DOOLITTLE: Have you lost her?

HIGGINS: Yes.

DOOLITTLE: You have all the luck, you have. I aint found her; but she'll find me quick enough now after what you done to me.

MRS HIGGINS: But what has my son done to you, Mr Doolittle?

DOOLITTLE: Done to me! Ruined me. Destroyed my happiness. Tied me up and delivered me into the hands of middle class morality.

HIGGINS: [*Rising intolerantly and standing over* Doolittle] Youre raving. Youre drunk. Youre mad. I gave you five pounds. After that I had two conversations with you, at half-a-crown an hour. Ive never seen you since.

DOOLITTLE: Oh! Drunk! am I? Mad! am I? Tell me this. Did you or did you not write a letter to an old blighter in America that was giving five millions to found Moral Reform Societies all over the world, and that wanted you to invent a universal language for him?

HIGGINS: What! Ezra D. Wannafeller! He's dead. [*He sits down again carelessly*]

DOOLITTLE: Yes: he's dead; and I'm done for. Now did you or did you not write a letter to him to say that the most original moralist at present in England, to the best of your knowledge, was Alfred Doolittle, a common dustman.

HIGGINS: Oh, after your last visit I remember making some silly joke of the kind.

DOOLITTLE: Ah! you may well call it a silly joke. It put the lid on me right enough. Just give him the chance he wanted to shew that Americans is not like us: that they recognize and respect merit in every class of life, however humble. Them words is in his blooming will, in which, Henry Higgins, thanks to your silly joking, he leaves me a share in his Pre-digested Cheese Trust worth three thousand a year on condition that I lecture for his Wannafeller Moral Reform World League as often as they ask me up to six times a year.

HIGGINS: The devil he does! Whew! [*Brightening suddenly*] What a lark!

PICKERING: A safe thing for you, Doolittle. They wont ask you twice.

DOOLITTLE: It aint the lecturing I mind. I'll lecture them blue in the face, I will, and not turn a hair. It's making a gentleman of me that I object to. Who asked him to make a gentleman of me? I was happy. I was free. I touched pretty nigh everybody for money when I wanted it, same as I touched you, Henry Higgins. Now I am worried; tied neck and heels; and everybody touches me for money. It's a fine thing for you, says my solicitor. Is it? says I. You mean it's a good thing for you, I says. When I was a poor man and had a solicitor once when they found a pram in the dust cart, he got me off, and got shut of me and got me shut

of him as quick as he could. Same with the doctors: used to shove me out of the hospital before I could hardly stand on my legs, and nothing to pay. Now they finds out that I'm not a healthy man and cant live unless they looks after me twice a day. In the house I'm not let do a hand's turn for myself: somebody else must do it and touch me for it. A year ago I hadnt a relative in the world except two or three that wouldnt speak to me. Now Ive fifty, and not a decent week's wages among the lot of them. I have to live for others and not for myself: thats middle class morality. You talk of losing Eliza. Dont you be anxious: I bet she's on my doorstep by this: she that could support herself easy by selling flowers if I wasnt respectable. And the next one to touch me will be you, Henry Higgins. I'll have to learn to speak middle class language from you, instead of speaking proper English. Thats where y o u l l come in; and I daresay thats what you done it for.

MRS HIGGINS: But, my dear Mr Doolittle, you need not suffer all this if you are really in earnest. Nobody can force you to accept this bequest. You can repudiate it. Isnt that so, Colonel Pickering?

PICKERING: I believe so.

DOOLITTLE: [*Softening his manner in deference to her sex*] Thats the tragedy of it, maam. It's easy to say chuck it; but I havnt the nerve. Which of us has? We're all intimidated. Intimidated, maam: thats what we are. What is there for me if I chuck it but the workhouse in my old age? I have to dye my hair already to keep my job as a dustman. If I was one of the deserving poor, and had put by a bit, I could chuck it; but then why should I, acause the deserving poor might as well be millionaires for all the happiness they ever has. They dont know what happiness is. But I, as one of the undeserving poor, have nothing between me and the pauper's uniform but this here blasted three thousand a year that shoves me into the middle class. (Excuse the expression, maam: youd use it yourself if you had my provocation.) Theyve got you every way you turn: it's a choice between the Skilly of the workhouse and the Char Bydis of the middle class; and I havnt the nerve for the workhouse. Intimidated: thats what I am. Broke. Bought up. Happier men than me will call for my dust, and touch me for their tip; and I'll look on helpless, and envy them. And thats what your son has brought me to. [*He is overcome by emotion*]

MRS HIGGINS: Well, I'm very glad youre not going to do anything foolish, Mr Doolittle. For this solves the problem of Eliza's future. You can provide for her now.

DOOLITTLE: [*With melancholy resignation*] Yes, maam: I'm expected to provide for everyone now, out of three thousand a year.

HIGGINS: [*Jumping up*] Nonsense! he cant provide for her. He shant provide for her. She doesnt belong to him. I paid him five pounds for her. Doolittle: either youre an honest man or a rogue.

DOOLITTLE: [*Tolerantly*] A little of both, Henry, like the rest of us: a little of both.

HIGGINS: Well, you took that money for the girl; and you have no right to take her as well.

MRS HIGGINS: Henry: dont be absurd. If you want to know where Eliza is, she is upstairs.

HIGGINS: [*Amazed*] Upstairs!!! Then I shall jolly soon fetch her downstairs. [*He makes resolutely for the door*]

MRS HIGGINS: [*Rising and following him*] Be quiet, Henry. Sit down.

HIGGINS: I—

MRS HIGGINS: Sit down, dear; and listen to me.

HIGGINS: Oh very well, very well, very well. [*He throws himself ungraciously on the ottoman, with his face towards the windows*] But I think you might have told us this half an hour ago.

MRS HIGGINS: Eliza came to me this morning. She passed the night partly walking about in a rage, partly trying to throw herself into the river and being afraid to, and partly in the Carlton Hotel. She told me of the brutal way you two treated her.

HIGGINS: [*Bounding up again*] What!

PICKERING: [*Rising also*] My dear Mrs Higgins, she's been telling you stories. We didnt treat her brutally. We hardly said a word to her; and we parted on particularly good terms. [*Turning on Higgins*] Higgins: did you bully her after I went to bed?

HIGGINS: Just the other way about. She threw my slippers in my face. She behaved in the most outrageous way. I never gave her the slightest provocation. The slippers came bang into my face the moment I entered the room—before I had uttered a word. And used perfectly awful language.

PICKERING: [*Astonished*] But why? What did we do to her?

MRS HIGGINS: I think I know pretty well what you did. The girl is naturally rather affectionate, I think. Isnt she, Mr Doolittle?

DOOLITTLE: Very tender-hearted, maam. Takes after me.

MRS HIGGINS: Just so. She had become attached to you both. She worked very hard for you, Henry! I dont think you quite realize what anything in the nature of brain work means to a girl like that. Well, it seems that when the great day of trial came, and she did this wonderful thing for you without making a single mistake, you two sat there and never said a word to her, but talked together of how glad you were that it was all over and how you had been bored with the whole thing. And then you were surprised because she threw your slippers at you! *I* should have thrown the fire-irons at you.

HIGGINS: We said nothing except that we were tired and wanted to go to bed. Did we, Pick?

PICKERING: [*Shrugging his shoulders*] That was all.

MRS HIGGINS: [*Ironically*] Quite sure?

PICKERING: Absolutely. Really, that was all.

MRS HIGGINS: You didnt thank her, or pet her, or admire her, or tell her how splendid she'd been.

HIGGINS: [*Impatiently*] But she knew all about that. We didnt make speeches to her, if thats what you mean.

PICKERING: [*Conscience stricken*] Perhaps we were a little inconsiderate. Is she very angry?

MRS HIGGINS: [*Returning to her place at the writing-table*] Well, I'm afraid she wont go back to Wimpole Street, especially now that Mr Doolittle is able to keep up the position you have thrust on her; but she says she is quite willing to meet you on friendly terms and to let bygones be bygones.

HIGGINS: [*Furious*] Is she, by George? Ho!

MRS HIGGINS: If you promise to behave yourself, Henry, I'll ask her to come down. If not, go home; for you have taken up quite enough of my time.

HIGGINS: Oh, all right. Very well. Pick: you behave yourself. Let us put on our best Sunday manners for this creature that we picked out of the mud. [*He flings himself sulkily into the Elizabethan chair*]

DOOLITTLE: [*Remonstrating*] Now, now, Henry Higgins! have some consideration for my feelings as a middle class man.

MRS HIGGINS: Remember your promise, Henry. [*She presses the bell-button on the writing-table*] Mr Doolittle: will you be so good as to step out on the balcony for a moment. I dont want Eliza to have the shock of your news until she has made it up with these two gentlemen. Would you mind?

DOOLITTLE: As you wish, lady. Anything to help Henry to keep her off my hands. [*He disappears through the window*]

[*The* Parlor-Maid *answers the bell.* Pickering *sits down in* Doolittle's *place*]

MRS HIGGINS: Ask Miss Doolittle to come down, please.

THE PARLOR-MAID: Yes, maam.   [*She goes out*]

MRS HIGGINS: Now, Henry: be good.

HIGGINS: I am behaving myself perfectly.

PICKERING: He is doing his best, Mrs Higgins.

[*A pause.* Higgins *throws back his head; stretches out his legs; and begins to whistle*]

MRS HIGGINS: Henry, dearest, you dont look at all nice in that attitude.

HIGGINS: [*Pulling himself together*] I was not trying to look nice, mother.

MRS HIGGINS: It doesnt matter, dear. I only wanted to make you speak.

HIGGINS: Why?

MRS HIGGINS: Because you cant speak and whistle at the same time.

[Higgins *groans. Another very trying pause*]

HIGGINS: [*Springing up, out of patience*] Where the devil is that girl? Are we to wait here all day?

[Eliza *enters, sunny, self-possessed, and giving a staggeringly convincing exhibition of ease of manner. She carries a little work-basket, and is very much at home.* Pickering *is too much taken aback to rise*]

LIZA: How do you do, Professor Higgins? Are you quite well?

HIGGINS: [*Choking*] Am I—[*He can say no more*]

LIZA: But of course you are: you are never ill. So glad to see you again, Colonel Pickering. [*He rises hastily; and they shake hands*] Quite chilly this morning, isnt it? [*She sits down on his left. He sits beside her*]

HIGGINS: Dont you dare try this game on me. I taught it to you; and it doesnt take me in. Get up and come home; and dont be a fool.

[Eliza *takes a piece of needlework from her basket, and begins to stitch at it, without taking the least notice of this outburst*]

MRS HIGGINS: Very nicely put, indeed, Henry. No woman could resist such an invitation.

HIGGINS: You let her alone, mother. Let her speak for herself. You will jolly soon see whether she has an idea that I havnt put into her head or a word that I havnt put into her mouth. I tell you I have created this thing out of the squashed cabbage leaves of Covent Garden; and now she pretends to play the fine lady with me.

MRS HIGGINS: [*Placidly*] Yes, dear; but youll sit down, wont you?

[Higgins *sits down again, savagely*]

LIZA: [*To* Pickering, *taking no apparent notice of* Higgins, *and working away deftly*] Will y o u drop me altogether now that the experiment is over, Colonel Pickering?

PICKERING: Oh dont. You mustnt think of it as an experiment. It shocks me, somehow.

LIZA: Oh, I'm only a squashed cabbage leaf—

PICKERING: [*Impulsively*] No.

LIZA: [*Continuing quietly*]—but I owe so much to you that I should be very unhappy if you forgot me.

PICKERING: It's very kind of you to say so, Miss Doolittle.

LIZA: It's not because you paid for my dresses. I know you are generous to everybody with money. But it was from you that I learnt really nice manners; and that is what makes one a lady, isnt it? You see it was so very difficult for me with the example of Professor Higgins always before me. I was brought up to be just like him, unable to control myself, and using bad language on the slightest provocation. And I should never have known that ladies and gentlemen didnt behave like that if you hadnt been there.

HIGGINS: Well!!

PICKERING: Oh, thats only his way, you know. He doesnt mean it.

LIZA: Oh, *I* didnt mean it either, when I was a flower girl. It was only my way. But you see I did it; and thats what makes the difference after all.

PICKERING: No doubt. Still, he taught you to speak; and I couldnt have done that, you know.

LIZA: [*Trivially*] Of course: that is his profession.

HIGGINS: Damnation!

LIZA: [*Continuing*] It was just like learning to dance in the fashionable way: there was nothing more than that in it. But do you know what began my real education?

PICKERING: What?

LIZA: [*Stopping her work for a moment*] Your calling me Miss Doolittle that day when I first came to Wimpole Street. That was the beginning of self-respect for me. [*She resumes her stitching*] And there were a hundred little things you never noticed, because they came naturally to you. Things about standing up and taking off your hat and opening doors—

PICKERING: Oh, that was nothing.

LIZA: Yes: things that shewed you thought and felt about me as if I were something better than a scullery-maid; though of course I know you would have been just the same to a scullery-maid if she had been let into the drawing room. Y o u never took off your boots in the dining room when I was there.

PICKERING: You mustnt mind that. Higgins takes off his boots all over the place.

LIZA: I know. I am not blaming him. It is his way, isnt it? But it made such a difference to me that you didnt do it. You see, really and truly, apart from the things anyone can pick up (the dressing and the proper way of speaking, and so on), the difference between a lady and a flower girl is not how she behaves, but how she's treated. I shall always be a flower girl to Professor Higgins, because he always treats me as a flower girl, and always will; but I know I can be a lady to you, because you always treat me as a lady, and always will.

MRS HIGGINS: Please dont grind your teeth, Henry.

PICKERING: Well, this is really very nice of you, Miss Doolittle.

LIZA: I should like you to call me Eliza, now, if you would.

PICKERING: Thank you. Eliza, of course.

LIZA: And I should like Professor Higgins to call me Miss Doolittle.

HIGGINS: I'll see you damned first.

MRS HIGGINS: Henry! Henry!

PICKERING: [*Laughing*] Why dont you slang back at him? Dont stand it. It would do him a lot of good.

LIZA: I cant. I could have done it once; but now I cant go back to it. Last night, when I was wandering about, a girl spoke to me; and I tried to get back into the old way with her; but it was no use. You told me, you know, that when a child is brought to a foreign country, it picks up the language in a few weeks, and forgets its own. Well, I am a child in your country. I have forgotten my own language, and can speak nothing but yours. Thats the real break-off with the corner of Tottenham Court Road. Leaving Wimpole Street finishes it.

PICKERING: [*Much alarmed*] Oh! but youre coming back to Wimpole Street, arnt you? Youll forgive Higgins?

HIGGINS: [*Rising*] Forgive! Will she, by George! Let her go. Let her find out how she can get on without us. She will relapse into the gutter in three weeks without me at her elbow.

[Doolittle *appears at the centre window. With a look of dignified reproach at* Higgins, *he comes slowly and silently to his daughter, who, with her back to the window, is unconscious of his approach*]

PICKERING: He's incorrigible, Eliza. You wont relapse, will you?

LIZA: No: not now. Never again. I have learnt my lesson. I dont believe I could utter one of the old sounds if I tried. [Doolittle *touches her on her left shoulder. She drops her work, losing her self-possession utterly at the spectacle of her father's splendor*] A-a-a-a-a-ah-ow-ooh!

HIGGINS: [*With a crow of triumph*] Aha! Just so. A-a-a-a-ahowooh! A-a-a-a-ahowooh! A-a-a-a-ahowooh! Victory! Victory! [*He throws himself on the divan, folding his arms, and spraddling arrogantly*]

DOOLITTLE: Can you blame the girl? Dont look at me like that, Eliza. It aint my fault. Ive come into some money.

LIZA: You must have touched a millionaire this time, dad.

DOOLITTLE: I have. But I'm dressed something special today. I'm going to St George's, Hanover Square. Your stepmother is going to marry me.

LIZA: [*Angrily*] Youre going to let yourself down to marry that low common woman!

PICKERING: [*Quietly*] He ought to, Eliza. [*To Doolittle*] Why has she changed her mind?

DOOLITTLE: [*Sadly*] Intimidated, Governor. Intimidated. Middle class morality claims its victim. Wont you put on your hat, Liza, and come and see me turned off?

LIZA: If the Colonel says I must, I—I'll [*Almost sobbing*] I'll demean myself. And get insulted for my pains, like enough.

DOOLITTLE: Dont be afraid: she never comes to words with anyone now, poor woman! respectability has broke all the spirit out of her.

PICKERING: [*Squeezing Eliza's elbow gently*] Be kind to them, Eliza. Make the best of it.

LIZA: [*Forcing a little smile for him through her vexation*] Oh well, just to shew theres no ill feeling. I'll be back in a moment. [*She goes out*]

DOOLITTLE: [*Sitting down beside Pickering*] I feel uncommon nervous about the ceremony, Colonel. I wish youd come and see me through it.

PICKERING: But youve been through it before, man. You were married to Eliza's mother.

DOOLITTLE: Who told you that, Colonel?

PICKERING: Well, nobody told me. But I concluded —naturally—

DOOLITTLE: No: that aint the natural way, Colonel: it's only the middle class way. My way was always the undeserving way. But dont say nothing to Eliza. She dont know: I always had a delicacy about telling her.

PICKERING: Quite right. We'll leave it so, if you dont mind.

DOOLITTLE: And youll come to the church, Colonel, and put me through straight?

PICKERING: With pleasure. As far as a bachelor can.

MRS HIGGINS: May I come, Mr Doolittle? I should be very sorry to miss your wedding.

DOOLITTLE: I should indeed be honored by your condescension, maam; and my poor old woman would take it as a tremenjous compliment. She's been very low, thinking of the happy days that are no more.

MRS HIGGINS: [*Rising*] I'll order the carriage and get ready. [*The men rise, except* Higgins] I shant be more than fifteen minutes. [*As she goes to the door* Eliza *comes in, hatted and buttoning her gloves*] I'm going to the church to see your father married, Eliza. You had better come in the brougham with me. Colonel Pickering can go on with the bridegroom.

[Mrs Higgins *goes out.* Eliza *comes to the middle of the room between the centre window and the ottoman.* Pickering *joins her*]

DOOLITTLE: Bridegroom! What a word! It makes a man realize his position, somehow. [*He takes up his hat and goes towards the door*]

PICKERING: Before I go, Eliza, do forgive him and come back to us.

LIZA: I dont think papa would allow me. Would you, dad?

DOOLITTLE: [*Sad but magnanimous*] They played you off very cunning, Eliza, them two sportsmen. If it had been only one of them, you could have nailed him. But you see, there was two; and one of them chaperoned the other, as you might say. [*To Pickering*] It was artful of you, Colonel; but I bear no malice: I should have done the same myself. I been the victim of one woman after another all my life; and I dont grudge you two getting the better of Eliza. I shant interfere. It's time for us to go, Colonel. So long, Henry. See you in St George's, Eliza.   [*He goes out*]

PICKERING: [*Coaxing*] Do stay with us, Eliza.

[*He follows* Doolittle]

[Eliza *goes out on the balcony to avoid being alone with Higgins. He rises and joins her there. She immediately comes back into the room and makes for the door; but he goes along the balcony quickly and gets his back to the door before she reaches it]*

HIGGINS: Well, Eliza, youve had a bit of your own back, as you call it. Have you had enough? and are you going to be reasonable? Or do you want any more?

LIZA: You want me back only to pick up your slippers and put up with your tempers and fetch and carry for you.

HIGGINS: I havnt said I wanted you back at all.

LIZA: Oh, indeed. Then what are we talking about?

HIGGINS: About you, not about me. If you come back I shall treat you just as I have always treated you. I cant change my nature; and I dont intend to change my manners. My manners are exactly the same as Colonel Pickering's.

LIZA: Thats not true. He treats a flower girl as if she was a duchess.

HIGGINS: And I treat a duchess as if she was a flower girl.

LIZA: I see. *[She turns away composedly, and sits on the ottoman, facing the window]* The same to everybody.

HIGGINS: Just so.

LIZA: Like father.

HIGGINS: *[Grinning, a little taken down]* Without accepting the comparison at all points, Eliza, it's quite true that your father is not a snob, and that he will be quite at home in any station of life to which his eccentric destiny may call him. *[Seriously]* The great secret, Eliza, is not having bad manners or good manners or any other particular sort of manners, but having the same manner for all human souls: in short, behaving as if you were in Heaven, where there are no third-class carriages, and one soul is as good as another.

LIZA: Amen. You are a born preacher.

HIGGINS: *[Irritated]* The question is not whether I treat you rudely, but whether you ever heard me treat anyone else better.

LIZA: *[With sudden sincerity]* I dont care how you treat me. I dont mind your swearing at me. I dont mind a black eye: Ive had one before this. But *[Standing up and facing him]* I wont be passed over.

HIGGINS: Then get out of my way; for I wont stop for you. You talk about me as if I were a motor bus.

LIZA: So you are a motor bus: all bounce and go, and no consideration for anyone. But I can do without you: dont think I cant.

HIGGINS: I know you can. I told you you could.

LIZA: *[Wounded, getting away from him to the other side of the ottoman with her face to the hearth]* I know you did, you brute. You wanted to get rid of me.

HIGGINS: Liar.

LIZA: Thank you. *[She sits down with dignity]*

HIGGINS: You never asked yourself, I suppose, whether I could do without you.

LIZA: *[Earnestly]* Dont you try to get round me. Youll have to do without me.

HIGGINS: *[Arrogant]* I can do without anybody. I have my own soul: my own spark of divine fire. But *[With sudden humility]* I shall miss you, Eliza. *[He sits down near her on the ottoman]* I have learnt something from your idiotic notions: I confess that humbly and gratefully. And I have grown accustomed to your voice and appearance. I like them, rather.

LIZA: Well, you have both of them on your gramophone and in your book of photographs. When you feel lonely without me, you can turn the machine on. It's got no feelings to hurt.

HIGGINS: I cant turn your soul on. Leave me those feelings; and you can take away the voice and the face. They are not you.

LIZA: Oh, you are a devil. You can twist the heart in a girl as easy as some could twist her arms to hurt her. Mrs Pearce warned me. Time and again she has wanted to leave you; and you always got round her at the last minute. And you dont care a bit for her. And you dont care a bit for me.

HIGGINS: I care for life, for humanity; and you are a part of it that has come my way and been built into my house. What more can you or anyone ask?

LIZA: I wont care for anybody that doesnt care for me.

HIGGINS: Commercial principles, Eliza. Like *[Reproducing her Covent Garden pronunciation with professional exactness]* s'yollin voylets [selling violets], isnt it?

LIZA: Dont sneer at me. It's mean to sneer at me.

HIGGINS: I have never sneered in my life. Sneering doesnt become either the human face or the human soul. I am expressing my righteous contempt for Commercialism. I dont and wont trade in affection. You call me a brute because you couldnt buy a claim on me by fetching my slippers and finding my spectacles. You were a fool: I think a woman fetching a man's slippers is a disgusting sight: did I ever fetch your slippers? I think a good deal more of you for throwing them in my face. No use slaving for me and then saying you want to be cared for: who cares for a slave? If you come back, come back for the sake of good fellowship; for youll get nothing else. Youve had a thousand times as much out of me as I have out of you; and if you dare to set up your little dog's tricks of fetching and carrying slippers against my creation of a Duchess Eliza, I'll slam the door in your silly face.

LIZA: What did you do it for if you didnt care for me?

HIGGINS: *[Heartily]* Why, because it was my job.

LIZA: You never thought of the trouble it would make for me.

HIGGINS: Would the world ever have been made if its

maker had been afraid of making trouble? Making life means making trouble. Theres only one way of escaping trouble; and thats killing things. Cowards, you notice, are always shrieking to have troublesome people killed.

LIZA: I'm no preacher: I dont notice things like that. I notice that you dont notice me.

HIGGINS: [*Jumping up and walking about intolerantly*] Eliza: youre an idiot. I waste the treasures of my Miltonic mind by spreading them before you. Once for all, understand that I go my way and do my work without caring twopence what happens to either of us. I am not intimidated, like your father and your stepmother. So you can come back or go to the devil: which you please.

LIZA: What am I to come back for?

HIGGINS: [*Bouncing up on his knees on the ottoman and leaning over it to her*] For the fun of it. Thats why I took you on.

LIZA: [*With averted face*] And you may throw me out tomorrow if I dont do everything you want me to?

HIGGINS: Yes; and you may walk out tomorrow if I dont do everything you want me to.

LIZA: And live with my stepmother?

HIGGINS: Yes, or sell flowers.

LIZA: Oh! if I only could go back to my flower basket! I should be independent of both you and father and all the world! Why did you take my independence from me? Why did I give it up? I'm a slave now, for all my fine clothes.

HIGGINS: Not a bit. I'll adopt you as my daughter and settle money on you if you like. Or would you rather marry Pickering?

LIZA: [*Looking fiercely round at him*] I wouldnt marry you if you asked me; and youre nearer my age than what he is.

HIGGINS: [*Gently*] Than he is: not "than what he is."

LIZA: [*Losing her temper and rising*] I'll talk as I like. Youre not my teacher now.

HIGGINS: [*Reflectively*] I dont suppose Pickering would, though. He's as confirmed an old bachelor as I am.

LIZA: Thats not what I want; and dont you think it. Ive always had chaps enough wanting me that way. Freddy Hill writes to me twice and three times a day, sheets and sheets.

HIGGINS: [*Disagreeably surprised*] Damn his impudence! [*He recoils and finds himself sitting on his heels*]

LIZA: He has a right to if he likes, poor lad. And he does love me.

HIGGINS: [*Getting off the ottoman*] You have no right to encourage him.

LIZA: Every girl has a right to be loved.

HIGGINS: What! By fools like that?

LIZA: Freddy's not a fool. And if he's weak and poor and wants me, may be he'd make me happier than my betters that bully me and dont want me.

HIGGINS: Can he make anything of you? Thats the point.

LIZA: Perhaps I could make something of him. But I never thought of us making anything of one another; and you never think of anything else. I only want to be natural.

HIGGINS: In short, you want me to be as infatuated about you as Freddy? Is that it?

LIZA: No I dont. Thats not the sort of feeling I want from you. And dont you be too sure of yourself or of me. I could have been a bad girl if I'd liked. Ive seen more of some things than you, for all your learning. Girls like me can drag gentlemen down to make love to them easy enough. And they wish each other dead the next minute.

HIGGINS: Of course they do. Then what in thunder are we quarrelling about?

LIZA: [*Much troubled*] I want a little kindness. I know I'm a common ignorant girl, and you a book-learned gentleman; but I'm not dirt under your feet. What I done [*Correcting herself*] what I did was not for the dresses and the taxis: I did it because we were pleasant together and I come—came —to care for you; not to want you to make love to me, and not forgetting the difference between us, but more friendly like.

HIGGINS: Well, of course. Thats just how I feel. And how Pickering feels. Eliza: youre a fool.

LIZA: Thats not a proper answer to give me. [*She sinks on the chair at the writing-table in tears*]

HIGGINS: It's all youll get until you stop being a common idiot. If youre going to be a lady, youll have to give up feeling neglected if the men you know dont spend half their time snivelling over you and the other half giving you black eyes. If you cant stand the coldness of my sort of life, and the strain of it, go back to the gutter. Work til you are more a brute than a human being; and then cuddle and squabble and drink til you fall asleep. Oh, it's a fine life, the life of the gutter. It's real: it's warm: it's violent: you can feel it through the thickest skin: you can taste it and smell it without any training or any work. Not like Science and Literature and Classical Music and Philosophy and Art. You find me cold, unfeeling, selfish, dont you? Very well: be off with you to the sort of people you like. Marry some sentimental hog or other with lots of money, and a thick pair of lips to kiss you with and a thick pair of boots to kick you with. If you cant appreciate what youve got, youd better get what you can appreciate.

LIZA: [*Desperate*] Oh, you are a cruel tyrant. I cant talk to you: you turn everything against me: I'm always in the wrong. But you know very well all the time that youre nothing but a bully. You know I cant go back to the gutter, as you call it, and that I have no real friends in the world but you and the Colonel. You know well I couldnt bear to live with a low common man after you two; and it's wicked and cruel of you to insult me by pretending I could. You think I must go back to Wimpole Street because I have nowhere else to go but father's. But dont you be too sure that you have me under your feet to be trampled on and talked down. I'll marry Freddy, I will, as soon as he's able to support me.

HIGGINS: [Sitting down beside her] Rubbish! you shall marry an ambassador. You shall marry the Governor-General of India or the Lord-Lieutenant of Ireland, or somebody who wants a deputy-queen. I'm not going to have my masterpiece thrown away on Freddy.

LIZA: You think I like you to say that. But I havent forgot what you said a minute ago; and I wont be coaxed round as if I was a baby or a puppy. If I cant have kindness, I'll have independence.

HIGGINS: Independence? Thats middle class blasphemy. We are all dependent on one another, every soul of us on earth.

LIZA: [Rising determinedly] I'll let you see whether I'm dependent on you. If you can preach, I can teach. I'll go and be a teacher.

HIGGINS: Whatll you teach, in heaven's name?

LIZA: What you taught me. I'll teach phonetics.

HIGGINS: Ha! ha! ha!

LIZA: I'll offer myself as an assistant to Professor Nepean.

HIGGINS: [Rising in a fury] What! That impostor! that humbug! that toadying ignoramus! Teach him my methods! my discoveries! You take one step in his direction and I'll wring your neck. [He lays hands on her] Do you hear?

LIZA: [Defiantly non-resistant] Wring away. What do I care? I knew youd strike me some day. [He lets her go, stamping with rage at having forgotten himself, and recoils so hastily that he stumbles back into his seat on the ottoman] Aha! Now I know how to deal with you. What a fool I was not to think of it before! You cant take away the knowledge you gave me. You said I had a finer ear than you. And I can be civil and kind to people, which is more than you can. Aha! Thats done you, Henry Higgins, it has. Now I dont care that [Snapping her fingers] for your bullying and your big talk. I'll advertize it in the papers that your duchess is only a flower girl that you taught, and that she'll teach anybody to be a duchess just the same in six months for a thousand guineas. Oh, when I think of myself crawling under your feet and being trampled on and called names, when all the time I had only to lift up my finger to be as good as you, I could just kick myself.

HIGGINS: [Wondering at her] You damned impudent slut, you! But it's better than snivelling; better than fetching slippers and finding spectacles, isnt it? [Rising] By George, Eliza, I said I'd make a woman of you; and I have. I like you like this.

LIZA: Yes: you turn round and make up to me now

that I'm not afraid of you, and can do without you.

HIGGINS: Of course I do, you little fool. Five minutes ago you were like a millstone round my neck. Now youre a tower of strength: a consort battleship. You and I and Pickering will be three old bachelors together instead of only two men and a silly girl.

[Mrs Higgins returns, dressed for the wedding. Eliza instantly becomes cool and elegant]

MRS HIGGINS: The carriage is waiting, Eliza. Are you ready?

LIZA: Quite. Is the Professor coming?

MRS HIGGINS: Certainly not. He cant behave himself in church. He makes remarks out loud all the time on the clergyman's pronunciation.

LIZA: Then I shall not see you again, Professor. Good-bye.   [She goes to the door]

MRS HIGGINS: [Coming to Higgins] Goodbye, dear.

HIGGINS: Goodbye, mother. [He is about to kiss her, when he recollects something] Oh, by the way, Eliza, order a ham and a Stilton cheese, will you? And buy me a pair of reindeer gloves, number eights, and a tie to match that new suit of mine, at Eale & Binman's. You can choose the color. [His cheerful, careless, vigorous voice shows that he is incorrigible]

LIZA: [Disdainfully] Buy them yourself. [She sweeps out]

MRS HIGGINS: I'm afraid youve spoiled that girl, Henry. But never mind, dear: I'll buy you the tie and gloves.

HIGGINS: [Sunnily] Oh, dont bother. She'll buy em all right enough. Goodbye.

[They kiss. Mrs Higgins runs out. Higgins, left alone, rattles his cash in his pocket; chuckles; and disports himself in a highly self-satisfied manner]

The rest of the story need not be shewn in action, and indeed, would hardly need telling if our imaginations were not so enfeebled by their lazy dependence on the ready-mades and reach-me-downs of the rag-shop in which Romance keeps its stock of "happy endings" to misfit all stories. Now, the history of Eliza Doolittle, though called a romance because the transfiguration it records seems exceedingly improbable, is common enough. Such transfigurations have been achieved by hundreds of resolutely ambitious young women since Nell Gwynne set them the example by playing queens and fascinating kings in the theatre in which she began by selling oranges. Nevertheless, people in all directions have assumed, for no other reason than that she became the heroine of a romance, that she must have married the hero of it. This is unbearable, not only because her little drama, if acted on such a thoughtless assumption, must be spoiled, but because the true sequel is patent to anyone with a sense of human nature in general, and of feminine instinct in particular.

Eliza, in telling Higgins she would not marry him if he asked her, was not coquetting: she was announcing a well-considered decision. When a bachelor interests, and dominates, and teaches, and becomes important to a spinster, as Higgins with Eliza, she always, if she has character enough to be capable of it, considers very seriously indeed whether she will play for becoming that bachelor's wife, especially if he is so little interested in marriage that a determined and devoted woman might capture him if she set herself resolutely to do it. Her decision will depend a good deal on whether she is really free to choose; and that, again, will depend on her age and income. If she is at the end of her youth, and has no security for her livelihood, she will marry him because she must marry anybody who will provide for her. But at Eliza's age a good-looking girl does not feel that pressure: she feels free to pick and choose. She is therefore guided by her instinct in the matter. Eliza's instinct tells her not to marry Higgins. It does not tell her to give him up. It is not in the slightest doubt as to his remaining one of the strongest personal interests in her life. It would be very sorely strained if there was another woman likely to supplant her with him. But as she feels sure of him on that last point, she has no doubt at all as to her course, and would not have any, even if the difference of twenty years in age, which seems so great to youth, did not exist between them.

As our own instincts are not appealed to by her conclusion, let us see whether we cannot discover some reason in it. When Higgins excused his indifference to young women on the ground that they had an irresistible rival in his mother, he gave the clue to his inveterate old-bachelordom. The case is uncommon only to the extent that remarkable mothers are uncommon. If an imaginative boy has a sufficiently rich mother who has intelligence, personal grace, dignity of character without harshness, and a cultivated sense of the best art of her time to enable her to make her house beautiful, she sets a standard for him against which very few women can struggle, besides effecting for him a disengagement of his affections, his sense of beauty, and his idealism from his specifically sexual impulses. This makes him a standing puzzle to the huge number of uncultivated people who have been brought up in tasteless homes by commonplace or disagreeable parents, and to whom, consequently, literature, painting, sculpture, music, and affectionate personal relations come as modes of sex if they come at all. The word passion means nothing else to them; and that Higgins could have a passion for phonetics and idealize his mother instead of Eliza, would seem to them absurd and unnatural. Nevertheless, when we look round and see that hardly anyone is too ugly or disagreeable to find a wife or a husband if he or she wants one, whilst many old maids and bachelors are above the average in quality and culture, we cannot help suspecting that the disentanglement of sex from the associations with which it is so commonly confused, a disentanglement which persons of genius achieve by sheer intellectual analysis, is sometimes produced or aided by parental fascination.

Now, though Eliza was incapable of thus explaining to herself Higgins's formidable powers of resistance to the charm that prostrated Freddy at the first glance, she was instinctively aware that she could never obtain a complete grip of him, or come between him and his mother (the first necessity of the married woman). To put it shortly, she knew that for some mysterious reason he had not the makings of a married man in him, according to her conception of a husband as one to whom she would be his nearest and fondest and warmest interest. Even had there been no mother-rival, she would still have refused to accept an interest in herself that was secondary to philosophic interests. Had Mrs Higgins died, there would still have been Milton and the Universal Alphabet. Landor's remark that to those who have the greatest power of loving, love is a secondary affair, would not have recommended Landor to Eliza. Put that along with her resentment of Higgins's domineering superiority, and her mistrust of his coaxing cleverness in getting round her and evading her wrath when he had gone too far with his impetuous bullying, and you will see that Eliza's instinct had good grounds for warning her not to marry her Pygmalion.

And now, whom did Eliza marry? For if Higgins was a predestinate old bachelor, she was most certainly not a predestinate old maid. Well, that can be told very shortly to those who have not guessed it from the indications she has herself given them.

Almost immediately after Eliza is stung into proclaiming her considered determination not to marry Higgins, she mentions the fact that young Mr Frederick Eynsford Hill is pouring out his love for her daily through the post. Now Freddy is young, practically twenty years younger than Higgins: he is a gentleman (or, as Eliza would qualify him, a toff), and speaks like one; he is nicely dressed, is treated by the Colonel as an equal, loves her unaffectedly, and is not her master, nor ever likely to dominate her in spite of his advantage of social standing. Eliza has no use for the foolish romantic tradition that all women love to be mastered, if not actually bullied and beaten. "When you go to women," says Nietzsche, "take your whip with you." Sensible despots have never confined that precaution to women: they have taken their whips with them when they have dealt with men, and been slavishly idealized by the men over whom they have flourished the whip much more than by women. No doubt there are slavish women as well as slavish men: and women, like men, admire those that are stronger than themselves. But to admire a strong person and to live under that strong person's thumb are two different things. The weak may not be admired and hero-worshipped; but they are by no means disliked or shunned; and they never seem to have the least difficulty in marrying people who are too good for them. They may fail in emergencies; but life is not one long emergency: it is mostly a string of situations for which no exceptional strength is needed, and with which even rather weak people can cope if they have a stronger partner to help them out. Accordingly, it is a truth everywhere in evidence that strong people, masculine or feminine, not only do not marry stronger people, but do not shew any preference for them in selecting their friends. When a lion meets another with a louder roar "the first lion thinks the last a bore." The man or woman who feels strong enough for two, seeks for every other quality in a partner than strength.

The converse is also true. Weak people want to marry strong people who do not frighten them too much; and this often leads them to make the mistake we describe metaphorically as "biting off more than they can chew." They want too much for too little; and when the bargain is unreasonable beyond all bearing, the union becomes impossible: it ends in the weaker party being either discarded or borne as a cross, which is worse. People who are not only weak, but silly or obtuse as well, are often in these difficulties.

This being the state of human affairs, what is Eliza fairly sure to do when she is placed between Freddy and Higgins? Will she look forward to a lifetime of fetching Higgins's slippers or to a lifetime of Freddy fetching hers? There can be no doubt about the answer. Unless Freddy is biologically repulsive to her, and Higgins biologically attractive to a degree that overwhelms all her other instincts, she will, if she marries either of them, marry Freddy.

And that is just what Eliza did.

Complications ensued; but they were economic, not romantic. Freddy had no money and no occupation. His mother's jointure, a last relic of the opulence of Largelady Park, had enabled her to struggle along in Earlscourt with an air of gentility, but not to procure any serious secondary education for her children, much less give the boy a profession. A clerkship at thirty shillings a week was beneath Freddy's dignity, and extremely distasteful to him besides. His prospects consisted of a hope that if he kept up appearances somebody would do something for him. The something appeared vaguely to his imagination as a private secretaryship or a sinecure of some sort. To his mother it perhaps appeared as a marriage to some lady of means who could not resist her boy's niceness. Fancy her feelings when he married a flower girl who had become déclassée under extraordinary circumstances which were now notorious!

It is true that Eliza's situation did not seem wholly ineligible. Her father, though formerly a dustman, and now fantastically disclassed, had become extremely popular in the smartest society by a social talent which triumphed over every prejudice and every disadvantage. Rejected by the middle class, which he loathed, he had shot up at once into the highest circles by his wit, his dustmanship (which he carried like a banner), and his Nietzschean transcendence of good and evil. At intimate ducal dinners he sat on the right hand of the Duchess; and in country houses he smoked in the pantry and was made much of by the butler when he was not feeding in the dining room and being consulted by cabinet ministers. But he found it almost as hard to do all this on four thousand a year as Mrs Eynsford Hill to live in Earlscourt on an income so pitiably small that I have not the heart to disclose its exact figure. He absolutely refused to add the last straw to his burden by contributing to Eliza's support.

Thus Freddy and Eliza, now Mr and Mrs Eynsford Hill, would have spent a penniless honeymoon but for a wedding present of £500 from the Colonel to Eliza. It lasted a long time because Freddy did not know how to spend money, never having had any to spend, and Eliza, socially trained by a pair of old bachelors, wore her clothes as long as they held together and looked pretty, without the least regard to their being many months out of fashion. Still, £500 will not last two young people for ever; and they both knew, and Eliza felt as well, that they must shift for themselves in the end. She could quarter herself on Wimpole Street because it had come to be her home; but she was quite aware that she ought not to quarter Freddy there, and that it would not be good for his character if she did.

Not that the Wimpole Street bachelors objected. When she consulted them, Higgins declined to be bothered about her housing problem when that solution was so simple. Eliza's desire to have Freddy in the house with her seemed of no more importance than if she had wanted an extra piece of bedroom furniture. Pleas as to Freddy's character, and the moral obligation on him to earn his own living, were lost on Higgins. He denied that Freddy had any character, and declared that if he tried to do any useful work some competent person would have the trouble of undoing it: a procedure involving a net loss to the community, and great unhappiness to Freddy himself, who was obviously intended by Nature for such light work as amusing Eliza, which, Higgins declared, was a much more useful and honorable occupation than working in the city. When Eliza referred again to her project of teaching phonetics, Higgins abated not a jot of his violent opposition to it. He said she was not within ten years of being qualified to meddle with his pet subject; and as it was evident that the Colonel agreed with him, she felt she could not go against them in this grave matter, and that she had no right, without Higgins's consent, to exploit the knowledge he had given her; for his knowledge seemed to her as much his private property as his watch: Eliza was no communist. Besides, she was superstitiously devoted to them both, more entirely and frankly after her marriage than before it.

It was the Colonel who finally solved the problem, which had cost him much perplexed cogitation. He one day asked Eliza, rather shyly, whether she had quite given up her notion of keeping a flower shop. She replied that she had thought of it, but had put it out of her head, because the Colonel had said, that day at Mrs Higgins's, that it would never do. The Colonel confessed that when he said that, he had not quite recovered from the dazzling impression of the day before. They broke the matter to Higgins that evening. The sole comment vouchsafed by him very nearly led to a serious quarrel with Eliza. It was to the effect that she would have in Freddy an ideal errand boy.

Freddy himself was next sounded on the subject. He said he had been thinking of a shop himself; though it had presented itself to his pennilessness as a small place in which Eliza should sell tobacco at one counter whilst he sold newspapers at the opposite one. But he agreed that it would be extraordinarily jolly to go early every morning with Eliza to Covent Garden and buy flowers on the scene of their first meeting: a sentiment which earned him many kisses from his wife. He added that he had always been afraid to propose anything of the sort, because Clara would make an awful row about a step that must damage her matrimonial chances, and his mother could not be expected to like it after clinging for so many years to that step of the social ladder on which retail trade is impossible.

This difficulty was removed by an event highly unexpected by Freddy's mother. Clara, in the course of her incursions into those artistic circles which were the highest within her reach, discovered that her conversational qualifications were expected to include a grounding in the novels of Mr H. G. Wells. She borrowed them in various directions so energetically that she swallowed them all within two months. The result was a conversion of a kind quite common today. A modern Acts of the Apostles would fill fifty whole Bibles if anyone were capable of writing it.

Poor Clara, who appeared to Higgins and his mother as a disagreeable and ridiculous person, and to her own mother as in some inexplicable way a social failure, had never seen herself in either light; for, though to some extent ridiculed and mimicked in West Kensington like everybody else there, she was accepted as a rational and normal—or shall we say inevitable?—sort of human being. At worst they called her The Pusher; but to them no more than to herself had it ever occurred that she was pushing the air, and pushing it in a wrong direction. Still, she was not happy. She was growing desperate. Her one asset, the fact that her mother was what the Epsom

greengrocer called a carriage lady, had no exchange value, apparently. It had prevented her from getting educated, because the only education she could have afforded was education with the Earlscourt greengrocer's daughter. It had led her to seek the society of her mother's class; and that class simply would not have her, because she was much poorer than the greengrocer, and, far from being able to afford a maid, could not afford even a housemaid, and had to scrape along at home with an illiberally treated general servant. Under such circumstances nothing could give her an air of being a genuine product of Largelady Park. And yet its tradition made her regard a marriage with anyone within her reach as an unbearable humiliation. Commercial people and professional people in a small way were odious to her. She ran after painters and novelists; but she did not charm them; and her bold attempts to pick up and practice artistic and literary talk irritated them. She was, in short, an utter failure, an ignorant, incompetent, pretentious, unwelcome, penniless, useless little snob; and though she did not admit these disqualifications (for nobody ever faces unpleasant truths of this kind until the possibility of a way out dawns on them) she felt their effects too keenly to be satisfied with her position.

Clara had a startling eyeopener when, on being suddenly wakened to enthusiasm by a girl of her own age who dazzled her and produced in her a gushing desire to take her for a model, and gain her friendship, she discovered that this exquisite apparition had graduated from the gutter in a few months time. It shook her so violently, that when Mr H. G. Wells lifted her on the point of his puissant pen, and placed her at the angle of view from which the life she was leading and the society to which she clung appeared in its true relation to real human needs and worthy social structure, he effected a conversion and a conviction of sin comparable to the most sensational feats of General Booth or Gypsy Smith. Clara's snobbery went bang. Life suddenly began to move with her. Without knowing how or why, she began to make friends and enemies. Some of the acquaintances to whom she had been a tedious or indifferent or ridiculous affliction, dropped her: others became cordial. To her amazement she found that some "quite nice" people were saturated with Wells, and that this accessibility to ideas was the secret of their niceness. People she had thought deeply religious, and had tried to conciliate on that tack with disastrous results, suddenly took an interest in her, and revealed a hostility to conventional religion which she had never conceived possible except among the most desperate characters. They made her read Galsworthy; and Galsworthy exposed the vanity of Largelady Park and finished her. It exasperated her to think that the dungeon in which she had languished for so many unhappy years had been unlocked all the time, and that the impulses she had so carefully struggled with and stifled for the sake of keeping well with society, were precisely those by which alone she could have come into any sort of sincere human contact. In the radiance of these discoveries, and the tumult of their reaction, she made a fool of herself as freely and conspicuously as when she so rashly adopted Eliza's expletive in Mrs Higgins's drawing room; for the new-born Wellsian had to find her bearings almost as ridiculously as a baby; but nobody hates a baby for its ineptitudes, or thinks the worse of it for trying to eat the matches; and Clara lost no friends by her follies. They laughed at her to her face this time; and she had to defend herself and fight it out as best she could.

When Freddy paid a visit to Earlscourt (which he never did when he could possibly help it) to make the desolating announcement that he and his Eliza were thinking of blackening the Largelady scutcheon by opening a shop, he found the little household already convulsed by a prior announcement from Clara that she also was going to work in an old furniture shop in Dover Street, which had been started by a fellow Wellsian. This appointment Clara owed, after all, to her old social accomplishment of Push. She had made up her mind that, cost what it might, she would see Mr Wells in the flesh; and she had achieved her end at a garden party. She had better luck than so rash an enterprise deserved. Mr Wells came up to her expectations. Age had not withered him, nor could custom stale his infinite variety in half an hour. His pleasant neatness and compactness, his small hands and feet, his teeming ready brain, his unaffected accessibility, and a certain fine apprehensiveness which stamped him as susceptible, from his topmost hair to his tipmost toe, proved irresistible. Clara talked of nothing else for weeks and weeks afterwards. And as she happened to talk to the lady of the furniture shop, and that lady also desired above all things to know Mr Wells and sell pretty things to him, she offered Clara a job on the chance of achieving that end through her.

And so it came about that Eliza's luck held, and the expected opposition to the flower shop melted away. The shop is in the arcade of a railway station not very far from the Victoria and Albert Museum; and if you live in that neighborhood you may go there any day and buy a buttonhole from Eliza.

Now here is a last opportunity for romance. Would you not like to be assured that the shop was an immense success, thanks to Eliza's charms and her early business experience in Covent Garden? Alas! the truth is the truth: the shop did not pay for a long time, simply because Eliza and her Freddy did not know how to keep it. True, Eliza had not to begin at the very beginning: she knew the names and prices of the cheaper flowers; and her elation was unbounded when she found that Freddy, like all youths educated at cheap, pretentious, and thoroughly inefficient schools, knew a little Latin. It was very little,

but enough to make him appear to her a Porson or Bentley, and to put him at his ease with botanical nomenclature. Unfortunately he knew nothing else; and Eliza, though she could count money up to eighteen shillings or so, and had acquired a certain familiarity with the language of Milton from her struggles to qualify herself for winning Higgins's bet, could not write out a bill without utterly disgracing the establishment. Freddy's power of stating in Latin that Balbus built a wall and that Gaul was divided into three parts did not carry with it the slightest knowledge of accounts or business: Colonel Pickering had to explain to him what a cheque book and a bank account meant. And the pair were by no means easily teachable. Freddy backed up Eliza in her obstinate refusal to believe that they could save money by engaging a bookkeeper with some knowledge of the business. How, they argued, could you possibly save money by going to extra expense when you already could not make both ends meet? But the Colonel, after making the ends meet over and over again, at last gently insisted; and Eliza, humbled to the dust by having to beg from him so often, and stung by the uproarious derision of Higgins, to whom the notion of Freddy succeeding at anything was a joke that never palled, grasped the fact that business, like phonetics, has to be learned.

On the piteous spectacle of the pair spending their evenings in shorthand schools and polytechnic classes, learning bookkeeping and typewriting with incipient junior clerks, male and female, from the elementary schools, let me not dwell. There were even classes at the London School of Economics, and a humble personal appeal to the director of that institution to recommend a course bearing on the flower business. He, being a humorist, explained to them the method of the celebrated Dickensian essay on Chinese Metaphysics by the gentleman who read an article on China and an article on Metaphysics and combined the information. He suggested that they should combine the London School with Kew Gardens. Eliza, to whom the procedure of the Dickensian gentleman seemed perfectly correct (as in fact it was) and not in the least funny (which was only her ignorance), took his advice with entire gravity. But the effort that cost her the deepest humiliation was a request to Higgins, whose pet artistic fancy, next to Milton's verse, was calligraphy, and who himself wrote a most beautiful Italian hand, that he would teach her to write. He declared that she was congenitally incapable of forming a single letter worthy of the least of Milton's words; but she persisted; and again he suddenly threw himself into the task of teaching her with a combination of stormy intensity, concentrated patience, and occasional bursts of interesting disquisition on the beauty and nobility, the august mission and destiny, of human handwriting. Eliza ended by acquiring an extremely uncommercial script which was a positive extension of her personal beauty, and spending three times as much on stationery as anyone else because certain qualities and shapes of paper became indispensable to her. She could not even address an envelope in the usual way because it made the margins all wrong.

Their commercial schooldays were a period of disgrace and despair for the young couple. They seemed to be learning nothing about flower shops. At last they gave it up as hopeless, and shook the dust of the shorthand schools, and the polytechnics, and the London School of Economics from their feet for ever. Besides, the business was in some mysterious way beginning to take care of itself. They had somehow forgotten their objections to employing other people. They came to the conclusion that their own way was the best, and that they had really a remarkable talent for business. The Colonel, who had been compelled for some years to keep a sufficient sum on current account at his bankers to make up their deficits, found that the provision was unnecessary: the young people were prospering. It is true that there was not quite fair play between them and their competitors in trade. Their week-ends in the country cost them nothing, and saved them the price of their Sunday dinners; for the motor car was the Colonel's; and he and Higgins paid the hotel bills. Mr F. Hill, florist and greengrocer (they soon discovered that there was money in asparagus; and asparagus led to other vegetables), had an air which stamped the business as classy; and in private life he was still Frederick Eynsford Hill, Esquire. Not that there was any swank about him: nobody but Eliza knew that he had been christened Frederick Challoner. Eliza herself swanked like anything.

That is all. That is how it has turned out. It is astonishing how much Eliza still manages to meddle in the housekeeping at Wimpole Street in spite of the shop and her own family. And it is notable that

though she never nags her husband, and frankly loves the Colonel as if she were his favorite daughter, she has never got out of the habit of nagging Higgins that was established on the fatal night when she won his bet for him. She snaps his head off on the faintest provocation, or on none. He no longer dares to tease her by assuming an abysmal inferiority of Freddy's mind to his own. He storms and bullies and derides: but she stands up to him so ruthlessly that the Colonel has to ask her from time to time to be kinder to Higgins; and it is the only request of his that brings a mulish expression into her face. Nothing but some emergency or calamity great enough to break down all likes and dislikes, and throw them both back on their common humanity—and may they be spared any such trial!—will ever alter this. She knows that Higgins does not need her, just as her father did not need her. The very scrupulousness with which he told her that day that he had become used to having her there, and dependent on her for all sorts of little services, and that he should miss her if she went away (it would never have occurred to Freddy or the Colonel to say anything of the sort) deepens her inner certainty that she is "no more to him than them slippers"; yet she has a sense, too, that his indifference is deeper than the infatuation of commoner souls. She is immensely interested in him. She has even secret mischievous moments in which she wishes she could get him alone, on a desert island, away from all ties and with nobody else in the world to consider, and just drag him off his pedestal and see him making love like any common man. We all have private imaginations of that sort. But when it comes to business, to the life that she really leads as distinguished from the life of dreams and fancies, she likes Freddy and she likes the Colonel; and she does not like Higgins and Mr Doolittle. Galatea never does quite like Pygmalion: his relation to her is too godlike to be altogether agreeable.

The Playboy
of the Western World

by JOHN MILLINGTON SYNGE

   (1871–1909)

Synge follows Shaw as one more Irish playwright in a great procession. Yet he far from follows Shaw in any tradition of playwriting: rather he represents the break—as clean as it was conscious—with the whole theater reaching back from Shaw to Ibsen. For a good deal more than a generation, the problems of society rather than any picture of human life had inspired the main movement of drama; the main movement had become, indeed, a kind of Reform Movement; the drama's targets were the social evils, its tissue was the social dilemmas, of the age. As against an Ibsen, a Wilde might reduce the problem play to the merest problem playground; a Shaw, on occasion, might pretend a barrage of artillery while providing a display of fireworks; or Shaw might debate the affirmative side of a question in one comedy and the negative side in another. But he remained the debater, and his subject matter remained problematic and controversial. Underneath his satiric nonsense was always a core of bourgeois realism; and for all he might attack and even try to annihilate it, he clung fast to a bourgeois world.

From all this Synge, the great name in the Irish renascence begun by Lady Gregory and Yeats, turned sharply away; the only thing he wished to reform was a theater dehydrated by too many reformers. Like Shaw, Synge came away from Ireland in his youth; but unlike Shaw he went back to it and found, in the lore and language of its peasants, both the basis of his material and the key to his style. It is easy enough to call him a Romantic coming in the wake of Realism; but that extends only to his stage method and use of words: in truthfulness of observation, in unsparingness of presentation, he is much less romantic than realist. His peasants are not mere picturesque bumpkins; his Shadow of the Glen chronicles not a loutish prank but a brutal joke; his Tinker's Wedding is a good deal more "sordid" than a dozen Second Mrs. Tanquerays; and in the masterpiece before us, in The Playboy of the Western World, Synge is having his fun with romanticism every whit as much as he is having his fill. He is spoofing the romantic—whether in man's susceptibility to foolish hero worship, or in his way of turning small things into big, or in his capacity of endowing patricide with glamour; he is stressing our ability to swallow lies even where we know the truth. Turned by the townspeople into a hero, Christy Mahon struts about like one; while conversely, when he repeats at close range the deed that seemed to them so heroic at a distance, it leaves them not admiring but aghast.

So much in The Playboy is vivid and musical and Irish that we are apt to forget that this is not a poem but a satire; and a satire at the expense not simply of Irish peasants, or even of Ireland, or even of all mankind—but at the expense of all Art as well. The Playboy proclaims, along with the magic, the mendacity of words; the attempt of Synge, no less than of Christy, to hold people with a beguiling story; and just as they marvel at a distance but not in their own backyards, so do we respond one way in the theater and another way outside it. But meantime, since Synge himself was poet rather than preacher, one who preferred Art as a gay deceiver to Art as a governess or guide, he strove to make his writing as bright and lovely as he could, to give his jesting charm as well as point. No other comedy in the modern theater speaks with so lyrical a voice, or breaks into so melodious a laugh. None tells its lies more beautifully or uproariously. Yet none, thanks to the candor with which it admits and even admonishes the lying, is fundamentally more in league with truth.

JOHN MILLINGTON SYNGE

The Playboy of the Western World

THE PERSONS OF THE PLAY

CHRISTOPHER MAHON

OLD MAHON, *his father, a squatter*

MICHAEL JAMES FLAHERTY, called MICHAEL JAMES, *a publican*

MARGARET FLAHERTY, called PEGEEN MIKE, *his daughter*

WIDOW QUIN, *a woman of about thirty*

SHAWN KEOGH, *her cousin, a young farmer*

PHILLY CULLEN and JIMMY FARRELL, *small farmers*

SARA TANSEY, SUSAN BRADY, and HONOR BLAKE, *village girls*

A BELLMAN

SOME PEASANTS

The action takes place near a village, on a wild coast of Mayo. The first Act passes on an evening of autumn, the other two Acts on the following day.

Act I

SCENE: *Country public-house or shebeen, very rough and untidy. There is a sort of counter on the right with shelves, holding many bottles and jugs, just seen above it. Empty barrels stand near the counter. At back, a little to left of counter, there is a door into the open air, then, more to the left, there is a settle with shelves above it, with more jugs, and a table beneath a window. At the left there is a large open fire-place, with turf fire, and a small door into inner room. Pegeen, a wild-looking but fine girl, of about twenty, is writing at table. She is dressed in the usual peasant dress.*

PEGEEN: [*Slowly as she writes*] Six yards of stuff for to make a yellow gown. A pair of lace boots with lengthy heels on them and brassy eyes. A hat is suited for a wedding-day. A fine tooth comb. To be sent with three barrels of porter in Jimmy Farrell's creel cart on the evening of the coming Fair to Mister Michael James Flaherty. With the best compliments of this season. Margaret Flaherty.

SHAWN KEOGH: [*A fat and fair young man comes in as she signs, looks round awkwardly, when he sees she is alone*] Where's himself?

PEGEEN: [*Without looking at him*] He's coming. [*She directs the letter*] To Mister Sheamus Mulroy, Wine and Spirit Dealer, Castlebar.

SHAWN: [*Uneasily*] I didn't see him on the road.

PEGEEN: How would you see him [*Licks stamp and puts it on letter*] and it dark night this half hour gone by?

SHAWN: [*Turning towards the door again*] I stood a while outside wondering would I have a right to pass on or to walk in and see you, Pegeen Mike [*Comes to fire*], and I could hear the cows breathing, and sighing in the stillness of the air, and not a step moving any place from this gate to the bridge.

PEGEEN: [*Putting letter in envelope*] It's above at the cross-roads he is, meeting Philly Cullen; and a couple more are going along with him to Kate Cassidy's wake.

SHAWN: [*Looking at her blankly*] And he's going that length in the dark night?

PEGEEN: [*Impatiently*] He is surely, and leaving me lonesome on the scruff of the hill. [*She gets up and puts envelope on dresser, then winds clock*] Isn't it long the nights are now, Shawn Keogh, to be leaving a poor girl with her own self counting the hours to the dawn of day?

SHAWN: [*With awkward humour*] If it is, when we're wedded in a short while you'll have no call to complain, for I've little will to be walking off to wakes or weddings in the darkness of the night.

PEGEEN: [*With rather scornful good humour*] You're making mighty certain, Shaneen, that I'll wed you now.

SHAWN: Aren't we after making a good bargain, the way we're only waiting these days on Father Reilly's dispensation from the bishops, or the Court of Rome.

PEGEEN: [*Looking at him teasingly, washing up at

dresser] It's a wonder, Shaneen, the Holy Father'd be taking notice of the likes of you; for if I was him I wouldn't bother with this place where you'll meet none but Red Linahan, has a squint in his eye, and Patcheen is lame in his heel, or the mad Mulrannies were driven from California and they lost in their wits. We're a queer lot these times to go troubling the Holy Father on his sacred seat.

SHAWN: [Scandalized] If we are, we're as good this place as another, maybe, and as good these times as we were for ever.

PEGEEN: [With scorn] As good, is it? Where now will you meet the like of Daneen Sullivan knocked the eye from a peeler, or Marcus Quin, God rest him, got six months for maiming ewes, and he a great warrant to tell stories of holy Ireland till he'd have the old women shedding down tears about their feet. Where will you find the like of them, I'm saying?

SHAWN: [Timidly] If you don't, it's a good job, maybe; for [With peculiar emphasis on the words] Father Reilly has small conceit to have that kind walking around and talking to the girls.

PEGEEN: [Impatiently, throwing water from basin out of the door] Stop tormenting me with Father Reilly [Imitating his voice] when I'm asking only what way I'll pass these twelve hours of dark, and not take my death with the fear.

[Looking out of door]

SHAWN: [Timidly] Would I fetch you the Widow Quin, maybe?

PEGEEN: Is it the like of that murderer? You'll not, surely.

SHAWN: [Going to her, soothingly] Then I'm thinking himself will stop along with you when he sees you taking on, for it'll be a long night-time with great darkness, and I'm after feeling a kind of fellow above in the furzy ditch, groaning wicked like a maddening dog, the way it's good cause you have, maybe, to be fearing now.

PEGEEN: [Turning on him sharply] What's that? Is it a man you seen?

SHAWN: [Retreating] I couldn't see him at all; but I heard him groaning out, and breaking his heart. It should have been a young man from his words speaking.

PEGEEN: [Going after him] And you never went near to see was he hurted or what ailed him at all?

SHAWN: I did not, Pegeen Mike. It was a dark, lonesome place to be hearing the like of him.

PEGEEN: Well, you're a daring fellow, and if they find his corpse stretched above in the dews of dawn, what'll you say then to the peelers, or the Justice of the Peace?

SHAWN: [Thunderstruck] I wasn't thinking of that. For the love of God, Pegeen Mike, don't let on I was speaking of him. Don't tell your father and the men is coming above; for if they heard that story, they'd have great blabbing this night at the wake.

PEGEEN: I'll maybe tell them, and I'll maybe not.

SHAWN: They are coming at the door. Will you whisht, I'm saying?

PEGEEN: Whisht yourself.

[She goes behind counter. Michael James, fat jovial publican, comes in followed by Philly Cullen, who is thin and mistrusting, and Jimmy Farrell, who is fat and amorous, about forty-five]

MEN: [Together] God bless you. The blessing of God on this place.

PEGEEN: God bless you kindly.

MICHAEL: [To men who go to the counter] Sit down now, and take your rest. [Crosses to Shawn at the fire] And how is it you are, Shawn Keogh? Are you coming over the sands to Kate Cassidy's wake?

SHAWN: I am not, Michael James. I'm going home the short cut to my bed.

PEGEEN: [Speaking across the counter] He's right too, and have you no shame, Michael James, to be quitting off for the whole night, and leaving myself lonesome in the shop?

MICHAEL: [Good-humouredly] Isn't it the same whether I go for the whole night or a part only? and I'm thinking it's a queer daughter you are if you'd have me crossing backward through the Stooks of the Dead Women, with a drop taken.

PEGEEN: If I am a queer daughter, it's a queer father'd be leaving me lonesome these twelve hours of dark, and I piling the turf with the dogs barking, and the calves mooing, and my own teeth rattling with the fear.

JIMMY: [Flatteringly] What is there to hurt you, and you a fine, hardy girl would knock the head of any two men in the place?

PEGEEN: [Working herself up] Isn't there the harvest boys with their tongues red for drink, and the ten tinkers is camped in the east glen, and the thousand militia—bad cess to them!—walking idle through the land. There's lots surely to hurt me, and I won't stop alone in it, let himself do what he will.

MICHAEL: If you're that afeared, let Shawn Keogh stop along with you. It's the will of God, I'm thinking, himself should be seeing to you now.

[They all turn on Shawn]

SHAWN: [In horrified confusion] I would and welcome, Michael James, but I'm afeard of Father Reilly; and what at all would the Holy Father and the Cardinals of Rome be saying if they heard I did the like of that?

MICHAEL: [With contempt] God help you! Can't you sit in by the hearth with the light lit and herself beyond in the room? You'll do that surely, for I've heard tell there's a queer fellow above, going mad or getting his death, maybe, in the gripe of the ditch, so she'd be safer this night with a person here.

SHAWN: [With plaintive despair] I'm afeard of Father

Reilly, I'm saying. Let you not be tempting me, and we near married itself.

PHILLY: [*With cold contempt*] Lock him in the west room. He'll stay then and have no sin to be telling to the priest.

MICHAEL: [*To Shawn, getting between him and the door*] Go up now.

SHAWN: [*At the top of his voice*] Don't stop me, Michael James. Let me out of the door, I'm saying, for the love of the Almighty God. Let me out. [*Trying to dodge past him*] Let me out of it, and may God grant you His indulgence in the hour of need.

MICHAEL: [*Loudly*] Stop your noising, and sit down by the hearth.

[*Gives him a push and goes to counter laughing*]

SHAWN: [*Turning back, wringing his hands*] Oh, Father Reilly and the saints of God, where will I hide myself to-day? Oh, St. Joseph and St. Patrick and St. Brigid, and St. James, have mercy on me now!

[*Shawn turns round, sees door clear, and makes a rush for it*]

MICHAEL: [*Catching him by the coat-tail*] You'd be going, is it?

SHAWN: [*Screaming*] Leave me go, Michael James, leave me go, you old Pagan, leave me go, or I'll get the curse of the priests on you, and of the scarlet-coated bishops of the courts of Rome.

[*With a sudden movement he pulls himself out of his coat, and disappears out of the door, leaving his coat in* Michael's *hands*]

MICHAEL: [*Turning round, and holding up coat*] Well, there's the coat of a Christian man. Oh, there's sainted glory this day in the lonesome west; and by the will of God I've got you a decent man, Pegeen, you'll have no call to be spying after if you've a score of young girls, maybe, weeding in your fields.

PEGEEN: [*Taking up the defence of her property*] What right have you to be making game of a poor fellow for minding the priest, when it's your own the fault is, not paying a penny pot-boy to stand along with me and give me courage in the doing of my work?

[*She snaps the coat away from him, and goes behind counter with it*]

MICHAEL: [*Taken aback*] Where would I get a pot-boy? Would you have me send the bellman screaming in the streets of Castlebar?

SHAWN: [*Opening the door a chink and putting in his head, in a small voice*] Michael James!

MICHAEL: [*Imitating him*] What ails you?

SHAWN: The queer dying fellow's beyond looking over the ditch. He's come up, I'm thinking, stealing your hens. [*Looks over his shoulder*] God help me, he's following me now [*He runs into room*], and if he's heard what I said, he'll be having my

life, and I going home lonesome in the darkness of the night.

[*For a perceptible moment they watch the door with curiosity. Some one coughs outside. Then* Christy Mahon, *a slight young man, comes in very tired and frightened and dirty*]

CHRISTY: [*In a small voice*] God save all here!

MEN: God save you kindly.

CHRISTY: [*Going to the counter*] I'd trouble you for a glass of porter, woman of the house.

[*He puts down coin*]

PEGEEN: [*Serving him*] You're one of the tinkers, young fellow, is beyond camped in the glen?

CHRISTY: I am not; but I'm destroyed walking.

MICHAEL: [*Patronizingly*] Let you come up then to the fire. You're looking famished with the cold.

CHRISTY: God reward you. [*He takes up his glass and goes a little way across to the left, then stops and looks about him*] Is it often the police do be coming into this place, master of the house?

MICHAEL: If you'd come in better hours, you'd have seen "Licensed for the sale of Beer and Spirits, to be consumed on the premises," written in white letters above the door, and what would the polis want spying on me, and not a decent house within four miles, the way every living Christian is a bona fide, saving one widow alone?

CHRISTY: [*With relief*] It's a safe house, so.

[*He goes over to the fire, sighing and moaning. Then he sits down, putting his glass beside him and begins gnawing a turnip, too miserable to feel the others staring at him with curiosity*]

MICHAEL: [*Going after him*] Is it yourself is fearing the polis? You're wanting, maybe?

CHRISTY: There's many wanting.

MICHAEL: Many surely, with the broken harvest and the ended wars. [*He picks up some stockings, etc., that are near the fire, and carries them away furtively*] It should be larceny, I'm thinking.

CHRISTY: [*Dolefully*] I had it in my mind it was a different word and a bigger.

PEGEEN: There's a queer lad. Were you never slapped in school, young fellow, that you don't know the name of your deed?

CHRISTY: [*Bashfully*] I'm slow at learning, a middling scholar only.

MICHAEL: If you're a dunce itself, you'd have a right to know that larceny's robbing and stealing. Is it for the like of that you're wanting?

CHRISTY: [*With a flash of family pride*] And I the son of a strong farmer [*With a sudden qualm*], God rest his soul, could have bought up the whole of your old house a while since, from the butt of his tailpocket, and not have missed the weight of it gone.

MICHAEL: [*Impressed*] If it's not stealing, it's maybe something big.

CHRISTY: [*Flattered*] Aye; it's maybe something big.

JIMMY: He's a wicked-looking young fellow. Maybe he followed after a young woman on a lonesome night.

CHRISTY: [*Shocked*] Oh, the saints forbid, mister; I was all times a decent lad.

PHILLY: [*Turning on* Jimmy] You're a silly man, Jimmy Farrell. He said his father was a farmer a while since, and there's himself now in a poor state. Maybe the land was grabbed from him, and he did what any decent man would do.

MICHAEL: [*To Christy, mysteriously*] Was it bailiffs?

CHRISTY: The divil a one.

MICHAEL: Agents?

CHRISTY: The divil a one.

MICHAEL: Landlords?

CHRISTY: [*Peevishly*] Ah, not at all, I'm saying. You'd see the like of them stories on any little paper of a Munster town. But I'm not calling to mind any person, gentle, simple, judge or jury, did the like of me.

[*They all draw nearer with delighted curiosity*]

PHILLY: Well, that lad's a puzzle-the-world.

JIMMY: He'd beat Dan Davies' circus, or the holy missioners making sermons on the villainy of man. Try him again, Philly.

PHILLY: Did you strike golden guineas out of solder, young fellow, or shilling coins itself?

CHRISTY: I did not, mister, not sixpence nor a farthing coin.

JIMMY: Did you marry three wives maybe? I'm told there's a sprinkling have done that among the holy Luthers of the preaching north.

CHRISTY: [*Shyly*] I never married with one, let alone with a couple or three.

PHILLY: Maybe he went fighting for the Boers, the like of the man beyond, was judged to be hanged, quartered and drawn. Were you off east, young fellow, fighting bloody wars for Kruger and the freedom of the Boers?

CHRISTY: I never left my own parish till Tuesday was a week.

PEGEEN: [*Coming from counter*] He's done nothing, so. [*To Christy*] If you didn't commit murder or a bad, nasty thing, or false coining, or robbery, or butchery, or the like of them, there isn't anything that would be worth your troubling for to run from now. You did nothing at all.

CHRISTY: [*His feelings hurt*] That's an unkindly thing to be saying to a poor orphaned traveller, has a prison behind him, and hanging before, and hell's gap gaping below.

PEGEEN: [*With a sign to the men to be quiet*] You're only saying it. You did nothing at all. A soft lad the like of you wouldn't slit the windpipe of a screeching sow.

CHRISTY: [*Offended*] You're not speaking the truth.

PEGEEN: [*In mock rage*] Not speaking the truth, is it? Would you have me knock the head of you with the butt of the broom?

CHRISTY: [*Twisting round on her with a sharp cry of horror*] Don't strike me. I killed my poor father, Tuesday was a week, for doing the like of that.

PEGEEN: [*With blank amazement*] Is it killed your father?

CHRISTY: [*Subsiding*] With the help of God I did surely, and that the Holy Immaculate Mother may intercede for his soul.

PHILLY: [*Retreating with* Jimmy] There's a daring fellow.

JIMMY: Oh, glory be to God!

MICHAEL: [*With great respect*] That was a hanging crime, mister honey. You should have had good reason for doing the like of that.

CHRISTY: [*In a very reasonable tone*] He was a dirty man, God forgive him, and he getting old and crusty, the way I couldn't put up with him at all.

PEGEEN: And you shot him dead?

CHRISTY: [*Shaking his head*] I never used weapons. I've no license, and I'm a law-fearing man.

MICHAEL: It was with a hilted knife maybe? I'm told, in the big world it's bloody knives they use.

CHRISTY: [*Loudly, scandalized*] Do you take me for a slaughter-boy?

PEGEEN: You never hanged him, the way Jimmy Farrell hanged his dog from the license, and had it screeching and wriggling three hours at the butt of a string, and himself swearing it was a dead dog, and the peelers swearing it had life?

CHRISTY: I did not then. I just riz the loy and let fall the edge of it on the ridge of his skull, and he went down at my feet like an empty sack, and never let a grunt or groan from him at all.

MICHAEL: [*Making a sign to* Pegeen *to fill* Christy's *glass*] And what way weren't you hanged, mister? Did you bury him then?

CHRISTY: [*Considering*] Aye. I buried him then. Wasn't I digging spuds in the field?

MICHAEL: And the peelers never followed after you the eleven days that you're out?

CHRISTY: [*Shaking his head*] Never a one of them, and I walking forward facing hog, dog, or divil on the highway of the road.

PHILLY: [*Nodding wisely*] It's only with a common week-day kind of a murderer them lads would be trusting their carcase, and that man should be a great terror when his temper's roused.

MICHAEL: He should then. [*To Christy*] And where was it, mister honey, that you did the deed?

CHRISTY: [*Looking at him with suspicion*] Oh, a distant place, master of the house, a windy corner of high, distant hills.

PHILLY: [*Nodding with approval*] He's a close man, and he's right, surely.

PEGEEN: That'd be a lad with the sense of Solomon to have for a pot-boy, Michael James, if it's the truth you're seeking one at all.

PHILLY: The peelers is fearing him, and if you'd that lad in the house there isn't one of them would come smelling around if the dogs itself were lapping poteen from the dung-pit of the yard.

JIMMY: Bravery's a treasure in a lonesome place, and a lad would kill his father, I'm thinking, would face a foxy divil with a pitchpike on the flags of hell.

PEGEEN: It's the truth they're saying, and if I'd that lad in the house, I wouldn't be fearing the loosed kharki cut-throats, or the walking dead.

CHRISTY: [Swelling with surprise and triumph] Well, glory be to God!

MICHAEL: [With deference] Would you think well to stop here and be pot-boy, mister honey, if we gave you good wages, and didn't destroy you with the weight of work?

SHAWN: [Coming forward uneasily] That'd be a queer kind to bring into a decent quiet household with the like of Pegeen Mike.

PEGEEN: [Very sharply] Will you whisht? Who's speaking to you?

SHAWN: [Retreating] A bloody-handed murderer the like of . . .

PEGEEN: [Snapping at him] Whisht I am saying; we'll take no fooling from your like at all. [To Christy with a honeyed voice] And you, young fellow, you'd have a right to stop, I'm thinking, for we'd do our all and utmost to content your needs.

CHRISTY: [Overcome with wonder] And I'd be safe in this place from the searching law?

MICHAEL: You would, surely. If they're not fearing you, itself, the peelers in this place is decent droughty poor fellows, wouldn't touch a cur dog and not give warning in the dead of night.

PEGEEN: [Very kindly and persuasively] Let you stop a short while anyhow. Aren't you destroyed walking with your feet in bleeding blisters, and your whole skin needing washing like a Wicklow sheep.

CHRISTY: [Looking round with satisfaction] It's a nice room, and if it's not humbugging me you are, I'm thinking that I'll surely stay.

JIMMY: [Jumps up] Now, by the grace of God, herself will be safe this night, with a man killed his father holding danger from the door, and let you come on, Michael James, or they'll have the best stuff drunk at the wake.

MICHAEL: [Going to the door with men] And begging your pardon, mister, what name will we call you, for we'd like to know?

CHRISTY: Christopher Mahon.

MICHAEL: Well, God bless you, Christy, and a good rest till we meet again when the sun'll be rising to the noon of day.

CHRISTY: God bless you all.

MEN: God bless you.

[They go out except Shawn, who lingers at door]

SHAWN: [To Pegeen] Are you wanting me to stop along with you and keep you from harm?

PEGEEN: [Gruffly] Didn't you say you were fearing Father Reilly?

SHAWN: There'd be no harm staying now, I'm thinking, and himself in it too.

PEGEEN: You wouldn't stay when there was need for you, and let you step off nimble this time when there's none.

SHAWN: Didn't I say it was Father Reilly . . .

PEGEEN: Go on, then, to Father Reilly [In a jeering tone], and let him put you in the holy brotherhoods, and leave that lad to me.

SHAWN: If I meet the Widow Quin . . .

PEGEEN: Go on, I'm saying, and don't be waking this place with your noise. [She hustles him out and bolts the door] That lad would wear the spirits from the saints of peace. [Bustles about, then takes off her apron and pins it up in the window as a blind. Christy watching her timidly. Then she comes to him and speaks with bland good-humour] Let you stretch out now by the fire, young fellow. You should be destroyed travelling.

CHRISTY: [Shyly again, drawing off his boots] I'm tired, surely, walking wild eleven days, and waking fearful in the night.

[He holds up one of his feet, feeling his blisters, and looking at them with compassion]

PEGEEN: [Standing beside him, watching him with delight] You should have had great people in your family, I'm thinking, with the little, small feet you have, and you with a kind of a quality name, the like of what you'd find on the great powers and potentates of France and Spain.

CHRISTY: [With pride] We were great surely, with wide and windy acres of rich Munster land.

PEGEEN: Wasn't I telling you, and you a fine, handsome young fellow with a noble brow?

CHRISTY: [With a flash of delighted surprise] Is it me?

PEGEEN: Aye. Did you never hear that from the young girls where you come from in the west or south?

CHRISTY: [With venom] I did not then. Oh, they're bloody liars in the naked parish where I grew a man.

PEGEEN: If they are itself, you've heard it these days, I'm thinking, and you walking the world telling out your story to young girls or old.

CHRISTY: I've told my story no place till this night, Pegeen Mike, and it's foolish I was here, maybe, to be talking free, but you're decent people, I'm thinking, and yourself a kindly woman, the way I wasn't fearing you at all.

PEGEEN: [Filling a sack with straw] You've said the like of that, maybe, in every cot and cabin where you've met a young girl on your way.

CHRISTY: [Going over to her, gradually raising his voice] I've said it nowhere till this night, I'm telling you, for I've seen none the like of you the eleven long days I am walking the world, looking over a low ditch or a high ditch on my north or my south, into stony scattered fields, or scribes of bog, where you'd see young, limber girls, and fine prancing women making laughter with the men.

PEGEEN: If you weren't destroyed travelling, you'd have as much talk and streeleen, I'm thinking, as Owen Roe O'Sullivan or the poets of the Dingle Bay, and I've heard all times it's the poets are your like, fine fiery fellows with great rages when their temper's roused.

CHRISTY: [Drawing a little nearer to her] You've a power of rings, God bless you, and would there be any offence if I was asking are you single now?

PEGEEN: What would I want wedding so young?

CHRISTY: [With relief] We're alike, so.

PEGEEN: [She puts sack on settle and beats it up] I never killed my father. I'd be afeard to do that, except I was the like of yourself with blind rages tearing me within, for I'm thinking you should have had great tussling when the end was come.

CHRISTY: [Expanding with delight at the first confidential talk he has ever had with a woman] We had not then. It was a hard woman was come over the hill, and if he was always a crusty kind when he'd a hard woman setting him on, not the divil himself or his four fathers could put up with him at all.

PEGEEN: [With curiosity] And isn't it a great wonder that one wasn't fearing you?

CHRISTY: [Very confidentially] Up to the day I killed my father, there wasn't a person in Ireland knew the kind I was, and I there drinking, waking, eating, sleeping, a quiet, simple poor fellow with no man giving me heed.

PEGEEN: [Getting a quilt out of the cupboard and putting it on the sack] It was the girls were giving you heed maybe, and I'm thinking it's most conceit you'd have to be gaming with their like.

CHRISTY: [Shaking his head, with simplicity] Not the girls itself, and I won't tell you a lie. There wasn't anyone heeding me in that place saving only the dumb beasts of the field.

[He sits down at fire]

PEGEEN: [With disappointment] And I thinking you should have been living the like of a king of Norway or the Eastern world.

[She comes and sits beside him after placing bread and mug of milk on the table]

CHRISTY: [Laughing piteously] The like of a king, is it? And I after toiling, moiling, digging, dodging from the dawn till dusk with never a sight of joy or sport saving only when I'd be abroad in the dark night poaching rabbits on hills, for I was a devil to poach, God forgive me, [Very naïvely] and I near got six months for going with a dung fork and stabbing a fish.

PEGEEN: And it's that you'd call sport, is it, to be abroad in the darkness with yourself alone?

CHRISTY: I did, God help me, and there I'd be as happy as the sunshine of St. Martin's Day, watching the light passing the north or the patches of fog, till I'd hear a rabbit starting to screech and I'd go running in the furze. Then when I'd my full share I'd come walking down where you'd see the ducks and geese stretched sleeping on the highway of the road, and before I'd pass the dunghill, I'd hear himself snoring out, a loud lonesome snore he'd be making all times, the while he was sleeping, and he a man 'd be raging all times, the while he was waking, like a gaudy officer you'd hear cursing and damning and swearing oaths.

PEGEEN: Providence and Mercy, spare us all!

CHRISTY: It's that you'd say surely if you seen him and he after drinking for weeks, rising up in the red dawn, or before it maybe, and going out into the yard as naked as an ash tree in the moon of May, and shying clods against the visage of the stars till he'd put the fear of death into the banbhs and the screeching sows.

PEGEEN: I'd be well-nigh afeard of that lad myself, I'm thinking. And there was no one in it but the two of you alone?

CHRISTY: The divil a one, though he'd sons and daughters walking all great states and territories of the world, and not a one of them, to this day, but would say their seven curses on him, and they rousing up to let a cough or sneeze, maybe, in the deadness of the night.

PEGEEN: [Nodding her head] Well, you should have been a queer lot. I never cursed my father the like of that, though I'm twenty and more years of age.

CHRISTY: Then you'd have cursed mine, I'm telling you, and he a man never gave peace to any, saving when he'd get two months or three, or be locked in the asylums for battering peelers or assaulting men [With depression] the way it was a bitter life he led me till I did up a Tuesday and halve his skull.

PEGEEN: [Putting her hand on his shoulder] Well, you'll have peace in this place, Christy Mahon, and none to trouble you, and it's near time a fine lad like you should have your good share of the earth.

CHRISTY: It's time surely, and I a seemly fellow with great strength in me and bravery of . . .

[Someone knocks]

CHRISTY: [Clinging to Pegeen] Oh, glory! it's late for knocking, and this last while I'm in terror of the peelers, and the walking dead.

[Knocking again]

PEGEEN: Who's there?

VOICE: [Outside] Me.

PEGEEN: Who's me?

VOICE: The Widow Quin.

PEGEEN: [Jumping up and giving him the bread and milk] Go on now with your supper, and let on to be sleepy, for if she found you were such a warrant to talk, she'd be stringing gabble till the dawn of day.

[*He takes bread and sits shyly with his back to the door*]

PEGEEN: [*Opening door, with temper*] What ails you, or what is it you're wanting at this hour of the night?

WIDOW QUIN: [*Coming in a step and peering at Christy*] I'm after meeting Shawn Keogh and Father Reilly below, who told me of your curiosity man, and they fearing by this time he was maybe roaring, romping on your hands with drink.

PEGEEN: [*Pointing to Christy*] Look now is he roaring, and he stretched away drowsy with his supper and his mug of milk. Walk down and tell that to Father Reilly and to Shaneen Keogh.

WIDOW QUIN: [*Coming forward*] I'll not see them again, for I've their word to lead that lad forward for to lodge with me.

PEGEEN: [*In blank amazement*] This night, is it?

WIDOW QUIN: [*Going over*] This night. "It isn't fitting," says the priesteen, "to have his likeness lodging with an orphaned girl." [*To Christy*] God save you, mister!

CHRISTY: [*Shyly*] God save you kindly.

WIDOW QUIN: [*Looking at him with half-amazed curiosity*] Well, aren't you a little smiling fellow? It should have been great and bitter torments did rouse your spirits to a deed of blood.

CHRISTY: [*Doubtfully*] It should, maybe.

WIDOW QUIN: It's more than "maybe" I'm saying, and it'd soften my heart to see you sitting so simple with your cup and cake, and you fitter to be saying your catechism than slaying your da.

PEGEEN: [*At counter, washing glasses*] There's talking when any'd see he's fit to be holding his head high with the wonders of the world. Walk on from this, for I'll not have him tormented and he destroyed travelling since Tuesday was a week.

WIDOW QUIN: [*Peaceably*] We'll be walking surely when his supper's done, and you'll find we're great company, young fellow, when it's of the like of you and me you'd hear the penny poets singing in an August Fair.

CHRISTY: [*Innocently*] Did you kill your father?

PEGEEN: [*Contemptuously*] She did not. She hit himself with a worn pick, and the rusted poison did corrode his blood the way he never overed it, and died after. That was a sneaky kind of murder did win small glory with the boys itself.

[*She crosses to Christy's left*]

WIDOW QUIN: [*With good-humour*] If it didn't, maybe all knows a widow woman has buried her children and destroyed her man is a wiser comrade for a young lad than a girl, the like of you, who'd go helter-skeltering after any man would let you a wink upon the road.

PEGEEN: [*Breaking out into wild rage*] And you'll say

that, Widow Quin, and you gasping with the rage you had racing the hill beyond to look on his face.

WIDOW QUIN: [*Laughing derisively*] Me, is it? Well, Father Reilly has cuteness to divide you now. [*She pulls Christy up*] There's great temptation in a man did slay his da, and we'd best be going, young fellow; so rise up and come with me.

PEGEEN: [*Seizing his arm*] He'll not stir. He's pot-boy in this place, and I'll not have him stolen off and kidnabbed while himself's abroad.

WIDOW QUIN: It'd be a crazy pot-boy'd lodge him in the shebeen where he works by day, so you'd have a right to come on, young fellow, till you see my little houseen, a perch off on the rising hill.

PEGEEN: Wait till morning, Christy Mahon. Wait till you lay eyes on her leaky thatch is growing more pasture for her buck goat than her square of fields, and she without a tramp itself to keep in order her place at all.

WIDOW QUIN: When you see me contriving in my little gardens, Christy Mahon, you'll swear the Lord God formed me to be living lone, and that there isn't my match in Mayo for thatching, or mowing, or shearing a sheep.

PEGEEN: [*With noisy scorn*] It's true the Lord God formed you to contrive indeed. Doesn't the world know you reared a black lamb at your own breast, so that the Lord Bishop of Connaught felt the elements of a Christian, and he eating it after in a kidney stew? Doesn't the world know you've been seen shaving the foxy skipper from France for a threepenny bit and a sop of grass tobacco would wring the liver from a mountain goat you'd meet leaping the hills?

WIDOW QUIN: [*With amusement*] Do you hear her now, young fellow? Do you hear the way she'll be rating at your own self when a week is by?

PEGEEN: [*To Christy*] Don't heed her. Tell her to go into her pigsty and not plague us here.

WIDOW QUIN: I'm going; but he'll come with me.

PEGEEN: [*Shaking him*] Are you dumb, young fellow?

CHRISTY: [*Timidly, to Widow Quin*] God increase you; but I'm pot-boy in this place, and it's here I'd liefer stay.

PEGEEN: [*Triumphantly*] Now you have heard him, and go on from this.

WIDOW QUIN: [*Looking round the room*] It's lonesome this hour crossing the hill, and if he won't come along with me, I'd have a right maybe to stop this night with yourselves. Let me stretch out on the settle, Pegeen Mike; and himself can lie by the hearth.

PEGEEN: [*Short and fiercely*] Faith, I won't. Quit off or I will send you now.

WIDOW QUIN: [*Gathering her shawl up*] Well, it's a terror to be aged a score. [*To Christy*] God bless you now, young fellow, and let you be wary, or there's right torment will await you here if you go romancing with her like, and she waiting only, as they bade me say, on a sheepskin parchment to be wed with Shawn Keogh of Killakeen.

CHRISTY: [*Going to* Pegeen *as she bolts the door*] What's that she's after saying?

PEGEEN: Lies and blather, you've no call to mind. Well, isn't Shawn Keogh an impudent fellow to send up spying on me? Wait till I lay hands on him. Let him wait, I'm saying.

CHRISTY: And you're not wedding him at all?

PEGEEN: I wouldn't wed him if a bishop came walking for to join us here.

CHRISTY: That God in glory may be thanked for that.

PEGEEN: There's your bed now. I've put a quilt upon you I'm after quilting a while since with my own two hands, and you'd best stretch out now for your sleep, and may God give you a good rest till I call you in the morning when the cocks will crow.

CHRISTY: [*As she goes to inner room*] May God and Mary and St. Patrick bless you and reward you, for your kindly talk. [*She shuts the door behind her. He settles his bed slowly, feeling the quilt with immense satisfaction*] Well, it's a clean bed and soft with it, and it's great luck and company I've won me in the end of time—two fine women fighting for the likes of me—till I'm thinking this night wasn't I a foolish fellow not to kill my father in the years gone by.

Act II

SCENE: *As before. Brilliant morning light.* Christy, *looking bright and cheerful, is cleaning a girl's boots.*

CHRISTY: [*To himself, counting jugs on dresser*] Half a hundred beyond. Ten there. A score that's above. Eighty jugs. Six cups and a broken one. Two plates. A power of glasses. Bottles, a school-master'd be hard set to count, and enough in them, I'm thinking, to drunken all the wealth and wisdom of the County Clare. [*He puts down the boot carefully*] There's her boots now, nice and decent for her evening use, and isn't it grand brushes she has? [*He puts them down and goes by degrees to the looking-glass*] Well, this'd be a fine place to be my whole life talking out with swearing Christians, in place of my old dogs and cat, and I stalking around, smoking my pipe and drinking my fill, and never a day's work but drawing a cork an odd time, or wiping a glass, or rinsing out a shiny tumbler for a decent man. [*He takes the looking-glass from the wall and puts it on the back of a chair; then sits down in front of it and begins washing his face*] Didn't I know rightly I was handsome, though it was the divil's own mirror we had beyond, would twist a squint across an angel's brow; and I'll be growing fine from this

day, the way I'll have a soft lovely skin on me and won't be the like of the clumsy young fellows do be ploughing all times in the earth and dung. [*He starts*] Is she coming again? [*He looks out*] Stranger girls. God help me, where'll I hide myself away and my long neck naked to the world? [*He looks out*] I'd best go to the room maybe till I'm dressed again.

[*He gathers up his coat and the looking-glass, and runs into the inner room. The door is pushed open, and Susan Brady looks in, and knocks on door*]

SUSAN: There's nobody in it.

[*Knocks again*]

NELLY: [*Pushing her in and following her, with Honor Blake and Sara Tansey*] It'd be early for them both to be out walking the hill.

SUSAN: I'm thinking Shawn Keogh was making game of us and there's no such man in it at all.

HONOR: [*Pointing to straw and quilt*] Look at that. He's been sleeping there in the night. Well, it'll be a hard case if he's gone off now, the way we'll never set our eyes on a man killed his father, and we after rising early and destroying ourselves running fast on the hill.

NELLY: Are you thinking them's his boots?

SARA: [*Taking them up*] If they are, there should be his father's track on them. Did you never read in the papers the way murdered men do bleed and drip?

SUSAN: Is that blood there, Sara Tansey?

SARA: [*Smelling it*] That's bog water, I'm thinking, but it's his own they are surely, for I never seen the like of them for whity mud, and red mud, and turf on them, and the fine sands of the sea. That man's been walking, I'm telling you.

[*She goes down right, putting on one of his boots*]

SUSAN: [*Going to window*] Maybe he's stolen off to Belmullet with the boots of Michael James, and you'd have a right so to follow after him, Sara Tansey, and you the one yoked the ass cart and drove ten miles to set your eyes on the man bit the yellow lady's nostril on the northern shore.

[*She looks out*]

SARA: [*Running to window with one boot on*] Don't be talking, and we fooled to-day. [*Putting on other boot*] There's a pair do fit me well, and I'll be keeping them for walking to the priest, when you'd be ashamed this place, going up winter and summer with nothing worth while to confess at all.

HONOR: [*Who has been listening at the door*] Whisht! there's someone inside the room. [*She pushes door a chink open*] It's a man.

[*Sara kicks off boots and puts them where they were. They all stand in a line looking through chink*]

SARA: I'll call him. Mister! Mister! [*He puts in his head*] Is Pegeen within?

CHRISTY: [*Coming in as meek as a mouse, with the looking-glass held behind his back*] She's above on the cnuceen, seeking the nanny goats, the way she'd have a sup of goat's milk for to colour my tea.

SARA: And asking your pardon, is it you's the man killed his father?

CHRISTY: [*Sidling toward the nail where the glass was hanging*] I am, God help me!

SARA: [*Taking eggs she has brought*] Then my thousand welcomes to you, and I've run up with a brace of duck's eggs for your food to-day. Pegeen's ducks is no use, but these are the real rich sort. Hold out your hand and you'll see it's no lie I'm telling you.

CHRISTY: [*Coming forward shyly, and holding out his left hand*] They're a great and weighty size.

SUSAN: And I run up with a pat of butter, for it'd be a poor thing to have you eating your spuds dry, and you after running a great way since you did destroy your da.

CHRISTY: Thank you kindly.

HONOR: And I brought you a little cut of cake, for you should have a thin stomach on you, and you that length walking the world.

NELLY: And I brought you a little laying pullet—boiled and all she is—was crushed at the fall of night by the curate's car. Feel the fat of that breast, mister.

CHRISTY: It's bursting, surely.

[*He feels it with the back of his hand, in which he holds the presents*]

SARA: Will you pinch it? Is your right hand too sacred for to use at all? [*She slips round behind him*] It's a glass he has. Well, I never seen to this day a man with a looking-glass held to his back. Them that kills their fathers is a vain lot surely.

[*Girls giggle*]

CHRISTY: [*Smiling innocently and piling presents on glass*] I'm very thankful to you all to-day . . .

WIDOW QUIN: [*Coming in quickly, at door*] Sara Tansey, Susan Brady, Honor Blake! What in glory has you here at this hour of day?

GIRLS: [*Giggling*] That's the man killed his father.

WIDOW QUIN: [*Coming to them*] I know well it's the man; and I'm after putting him down in the sports below for racing, leaping, pitching, and the Lord knows what.

SARA: [*Exuberantly*] That's right, Widow Quin. I'll bet my dowry that he'll lick the world.

WIDOW QUIN: If you will, you'd have a right to have him fresh and nourished in place of nursing a feast. [*Taking presents*] Are you fasting or fed, young fellow?

CHRISTY: Fasting, if you please.

WIDOW QUIN: [*Loudly*] Well, you're the lot. Stir up now and give him his breakfast. [*To Christy*] Come here to me [*She puts him on bench beside her while the girls make tea and get his breakfast*]

and let you tell us your story before Pegeen will come, in place of grinning your ears off like the moon of May.

CHRISTY: [*Beginning to be pleased*] It's a long story; you'd be destroyed listening.

WIDOW QUIN: Don't be letting on to be shy, a fine, gamey, treacherous lad the like of you. Was it in your house beyond you cracked his skull?

CHRISTY: [*Shy but flattered*] It was not. We were digging spuds in his cold, sloping, stony, divil's patch of a field.

WIDOW QUIN: And you went asking money of him, or making talk of getting a wife would drive him from his farm?

CHRISTY: I did not, then; but there I was, digging and digging, and "You squinting idiot," says he, "let you walk down now and tell the priest you'll wed the Widow Casey in a score of days."

WIDOW QUIN: And what kind was she?

CHRISTY: [*With horror*] A walking terror from beyond the hills, and she two score and five years, and two hundredweights and five pounds in the weighing scales, with a limping leg on her, and a blinded eye, and she a woman of noted misbehaviour with the old and young.

GIRLS: [*Clustering round him, serving him*] Glory be.

WIDOW QUIN: And what did he want driving you to wed with her?

[*She takes a bit of the chicken*]

CHRISTY: [*Eating with growing satisfaction*] He was letting on I was wanting a protector from the harshness of the world, and he without a thought the whole while but how he'd have her hut to live in and her gold to drink.

WIDOW QUIN: There's maybe worse than a dry hearth and a widow woman and your glass at night. So you hit him then?

CHRISTY: [*Getting almost excited*] I did not. "I won't wed her," says I, "when all know she did suckle me for six weeks when I came into the world, and she a hag this day with a tongue on her has the crows and seabirds scattered, the way they wouldn't cast a shadow on her garden with the dread of her curse."

WIDOW QUIN: [*Teasingly*] That one should be right company.

SARA: [*Eagerly*] Don't mind her. Did you kill him then?

CHRISTY: "She's too good for the like of you," says he, "and go on now or I'll flatten you out like a crawling beast has passed under a dray." "You will not if I can help it," says I. "Go on," says he, "or I'll have the divil making garters of your limbs to-night." "You will not if I can help it," says I.

[*He sits up, brandishing his mug*]

SARA: You were right surely.

CHRISTY: [*Impressively*] With that the sun came out between the cloud and the hill, and it shining green in my face. "God have mercy on your soul," says he, lifting a scythe; "or on your own," says I, raising the loy.

SUSAN: That's a grand story.

HONOR: He tells it lovely.

CHRISTY: [*Flattered and confident, waving bone*] He gave a drive with the scythe, and I gave a lep to the east. Then I turned around with my back to the north, and I hit a blow on the ridge of his skull, laid him stretched out, and he split to the knob of his gullet.

[*He raises the chicken bone to his Adam's apple*]

GIRLS: [*Together*] Well, you're a marvel! Oh, God bless you! You're the lad surely!

SUSAN: I'm thinking the Lord God sent him this road to make a second husband to the Widow Quin, and she with a great yearning to be wedded, though all dread her here. Lift him on her knee, Sara Tansey.

WIDOW QUIN: Don't tease him.

SARA: [*Going over to dresser and counter very quickly, and getting two glasses and porter*] You're heroes surely, and let you drink a supeen with your arms linked like the outlandish lovers in the sailor's song. [*She links their arms and gives them the glasses*] There now. Drink a health to the wonders of the western world, the pirates, preachers, poteen-makers, with the jobbing jockies; parching peelers, and the juries fill their stomachs selling judgments of the English law.

[*Brandishing the bottle*]

WIDOW QUIN: That's a right toast, Sara Tansey. Now Christy.

[*They drink with their arms linked, he drinking with his left hand, she with her right. As they are drinking, Pegeen Mike comes in with a milk can and stands aghast. They all spring away from Christy. He goes down left. Widow Quin remains seated*]

PEGEEN: [*Angrily, to Sara*] What is it you're wanting?

SARA: [*Twisting her apron*] An ounce of tobacco.

PEGEEN: Have you tuppence?

SARA: I've forgotten my purse.

PEGEEN: Then you'd best be getting it and not fooling us here. [*To the Widow Quin, with more elaborate scorn*] And what is it you're wanting, Widow Quin?

WIDOW QUIN: [*Insolently*] A penn'orth of starch.

PEGEEN: [*Breaking out*] And you without a white shift or a shirt in your whole family since the drying of the flood. I've no starch for the like of you, and let you walk on now to Killamuck.

WIDOW QUIN: [*Turning to Christy, as she goes out with the girls*] Well, you're mighty huffy this day, Pegeen Mike, and, you young fellow, let you not forget the sports and racing when the noon is by.

[*They go out*]

PEGEEN: [*Imperiously*] Fling out that rubbish and put them cups away. [*Christy tidies away in great haste*] Shove in the bench by the wall. [*He does so*] And hang that glass on the nail. What disturbed it at all?

CHRISTY: [*Very meekly*] I was making myself decent only, and this a fine country for young lovely girls.

PEGEEN: [*Sharply*] Whisht your talking of girls.

[*Goes to counter—right*]

CHRISTY: Wouldn't any wish to be decent in a place . . .

PEGEEN: Whisht I'm saying.

CHRISTY: [*Looks at her face for a moment with great misgivings, then as a last effort, takes up a loy, and goes towards her, with feigned assurance*] It was with a loy the like of that I killed my father.

PEGEEN: [*Still sharply*] You've told me that story six times since the dawn of day.

CHRISTY: [*Reproachfully*] It's a queer thing you wouldn't care to be hearing it and them girls after walking four miles to be listening to me now.

PEGEEN: [*Turning round astonished*] Four miles.

CHRISTY: [*Apologetically*] Didn't himself say there were only four bona fides living in the place?

PEGEEN: It's bona fides by the road they are, but that lot came over the river lepping the stones. It's not three perches when you go like that, and I was down this morning looking on the papers the post-boy does have in his bag. [*With meaning and emphasis*] For there was great news this day, Christopher Mahon.

[*She goes into room left*]

CHRISTY: [*Suspiciously*] Is it news of my murder?

PEGEEN: [*Inside*] Murder, indeed.

CHRISTY: [*Loudly*] A murdered da?

PEGEEN: [*Coming in again and crossing right*] There was not, but a story filled half a page of the hanging of a man. Ah, that should be a fearful end, young fellow, and it worst of all for a man who destroyed his da, for the like of him would get small mercies, and when it's dead he is, they'd put him in a narrow grave, with cheap sacking wrapping him round, and pour down quicklime on his head, the way you'd see a woman pouring any frish-frash from a cup.

CHRISTY: [*Very miserably*] Oh, God help me. Are you thinking I'm safe? You were saying at the fall of night, I was shut of jeopardy and I here with yourselves.

PEGEEN: [*Severely*] You'll be shut of jeopardy no place if you go talking with a pack of wild girls the like of them do be walking abroad with the peelers, talking whispers at the fall of night.

CHRISTY: [*With terror*] And you're thinking they'd tell?

PEGEEN: [*With mock sympathy*] Who knows, God help you.

CHRISTY: [*Loudly*] What joy would they have to bring hanging to the likes of me?

PEGEEN: It's queer joys they have, and who knows

the thing they'd do, if it'd make the green stones cry itself to think of you swaying and swiggling at the butt of a rope, and you with a fine, stout neck, God bless you! the way you'd be a half an hour, in great anguish, getting your death.

CHRISTY: [*Getting his boots and putting them on*] If there's that terror of them, it'd be best, maybe, I went on wandering like Esau or Cain and Abel on the sides of Neifin or the Erris plain.

PEGEEN: [*Beginning to play with him*] It would, maybe, for I've heard the Circuit Judges this place is a heartless crew.

CHRISTY: [*Bitterly*] It's more than Judges this place is a heartless crew. [*Looking up at her*] And isn't it a poor thing to be starting again and I a lonesome fellow will be looking out on women and girls the way the needy fallen spirits do be looking on the Lord?

PEGEEN: What call have you to be that lonesome when there's poor girls walking Mayo in their thousands now?

CHRISTY: [*Grimly*] It's well you know what call I have. It's well you know it's a lonesome thing to be passing small towns with the lights shining sideways when the night is down, or going in strange places with a dog noising before you and a dog noising behind, or drawn to the cities where you'd hear a voice kissing and talking deep love in every shadow of the ditch, and you passing on with an empty, hungry stomach failing from your heart.

PEGEEN: I'm thinking you're an odd man, Christy Mahon. The oddest walking fellow I ever set my eyes on to this hour to-day.

CHRISTY: What would any be but odd men and they living lonesome in the world?

PEGEEN: I'm not odd, and I'm my whole life with my father only.

CHRISTY: [*With infinite admiration*] How would a lovely handsome woman the like of you be lonesome when all men should be thronging around to hear the sweetness of your voice, and the little infant children should be pestering your steps I'm thinking, and you walking the roads.

PEGEEN: I'm hard set to know what way a coaxing fellow the like of yourself should be lonesome either.

CHRISTY: Coaxing?

PEGEEN: Would you have me think a man never talked with the girls would have the words you've spoken to-day? It's only letting on you are to be lonesome, the way you'd get around me now.

CHRISTY: I wish to God I was letting on; but I was lonesome all times, and born lonesome, I'm thinking, as the moon of dawn.

[*Going to door*]

PEGEEN: [*Puzzled by his talk*] Well, it's a story I'm not understanding at all why you'd be worse than another, Christy Mahon, and you a fine lad with the great savagery to destroy your da.

CHRISTY: It's little I'm understanding myself, saving only that my heart's scalded this day, and I going off stretching out the earth between us, the way I'll not be waking near you another dawn of the year til the two of us do arise to hope or judgment with the saints of God, and now I'd best be going with my wattle in my hand, for hanging is a poor thing [*Turning to go*] and it's little welcome only is left me in this house to-day.

PEGEEN: [*Sharply*] Christy! [*He turns round*] Come here to me. [*He goes towards her*] Lay down that switch and throw some sods on the fire. You're pot-boy in this place, and I'll not have you mitch off from us now.

CHRISTY: You were saying I'd be hanged if I stay.

PEGEEN: [*Quite kindly at last*] I'm after going down and reading the fearful crimes of Ireland for two weeks or three, and there wasn't a word of your murder. [*Getting up and going over to the counter*] They've likely not found the body. You're safe so with ourselves.

CHRISTY: [*Astonished, slowly*] It's making game of me you were [*Following her with fearful joy*], and I can stay so, working at your side, and I not lonesome from this mortal day.

PEGEEN: What's to hinder you from staying, except the widow woman or the young girls would inveigle you off?

CHRISTY: [*With rapture*] And I'll have your words from this day filling my ears, and that look is come upon you meeting my two eyes, and I watching you loafing around in the warm sun, or rinsing your ankles when the night is come.

PEGEEN: [*Kindly, but a little embarrassed*] I'm thinking you'll be a loyal young lad to have working around, and if you vexed me a while since with your leaguing with the girls, I wouldn't give a thraneen for a lad hadn't a mighty spirit in him and a gamey heart.

[Shawn Keogh *runs in carrying a cleeve on his back, followed by the* Widow Quin]

SHAWN: [*To Pegeen*] I was passing below, and I seen your mountainy sheep eating cabbages in Jimmy's field. Run up or they'll be bursting surely.

PEGEEN: Oh, God mend them!

[*She puts a shawl over her head and runs out*]

CHRISTY: [*Looking from one to the other. Still in high spirits*] I'd best go to her aid maybe. I'm handy with ewes.

WIDOW QUIN: [*Closing the door*] She can do that much, and there is Shaneen has long speeches for to tell you now.

[*She sits down with an amused smile*]

SHAWN: [*Taking something from his pocket and offering it to Christy*] Do you see that, mister?

CHRISTY: [*Looking at it*] The half of a ticket to the Western States!

SHAWN: [*Trembling with anxiety*] I'll give it to you and my new hat [*Pulling it out of hamper*]; and my breeches with the double seat [*Pulling it off*]; and my new coat is woven from the blackest shearings for three miles around [*Giving him the coat*]; I'll give you the whole of them, and my blessing, and the blessing of Father Reilly itself, maybe, if you'll quit from this and leave us in the peace we had till last night at the fall of dark.

CHRISTY: [*With a new arrogance*] And for what is it you're wanting to get shut of me?

SHAWN: [*Looking to the* Widow *for help*] I'm a poor scholar with middling faculties to coin a lie, so I'll tell you the truth, Christy Mahon. I'm wedding with Pegeen beyond, and I don't think well of having a clever fearless man the like of you dwelling in her house.

CHRISTY: [*Almost pugnaciously*] And you'd be using bribery for to banish me?

SHAWN: [*In an imploring voice*] Let you not take it badly, mister honey, isn't beyond the best place for you where you'll have golden chains and shiny coats and you riding upon hunters with the ladies of the land.

[*He makes an eager sign to the* Widow Quin *to come to help him*]

WIDOW QUIN: [*Coming over*] It's true for him, and you'd best quit off and not have that poor girl setting her mind on you, for there's Shaneen thinks she wouldn't suit you though all is saying that she'll wed you now.

[Christy *beams with delight*]

SHAWN: [*In terrified earnest*] She wouldn't suit you, and she with the divil's own temper the way you'd be strangling one another in a score of days. [*He makes the movement of strangling with his hands*] It's the like of me only that she's fit for, a quiet simple fellow wouldn't raise a hand upon her if she scratched itself.

WIDOW QUIN: [*Putting* Shawn's *hat on* Christy] Fit them clothes on you anyhow, young fellow, and he'd maybe loan them to you for the sports. [*Pushing him towards inner door*] Fit them on and you can give your answer when you have them tried.

CHRISTY: [*Beaming, delighted with the clothes*] I will then. I'd like herself to see me in them tweeds and hat.

[*He goes into room and shuts the door*]

SHAWN: [*In great anxiety*] He'd like herself to see them. He'll not leave us, Widow Quin. He's a score of divils in him the way it's well nigh certain he will wed Pegeen.

WIDOW QUIN: [*Jeeringly*] It's true all girls are fond of courage and do hate the like of you.

SHAWN: [*Walking about in desperation*] Oh, Widow Quin, what'll I be doing now? I'd inform again him, but he'd burst from Kilmainham and he'd be sure and certain to destroy me. If I wasn't so God-fearing, I'd near have courage to come behind him and run a pike into his side. Oh, it's a hard case to be an orphan and not to have your father that

you're used to, and you'd easy kill and make yourself a hero in the sight of all. [*Coming up to her*] Oh, Widow Quin, will you find me some contrivance when I've promised you a ewe?

WIDOW QUIN: A ewe's a small thing, but what would you give me if I did wed him and did save you so?

SHAWN: [*With astonishment*] You?

WIDOW QUIN: Aye. Would you give me the red cow you have and the mountainy ram, and the right of way across your rye path, and a load of dung at Michaelmas, and turbary upon the western hill?

SHAWN: [*Radiant with hope*] I would surely, and I'd give you the wedding-ring I have, and the loan of a new suit, the way you'd have him decent on the wedding-day. I'd give you two kids for your dinner, and a gallon of poteen, and I'd call the piper on the long car to your wedding from Crossmolina or from Ballina. I'd give you . . .

WIDOW QUIN: That'll do so, and let you whisht, for he's coming now again.

[Christy *comes in very natty in the new clothes.* Widow Quin *goes to him admiringly*]

WIDOW QUIN: If you seen yourself now, I'm thinking you'd be too proud to speak to us at all, and it'd be a pity surely to have your like sailing from Mayo to the Western World.

CHRISTY: [*As proud as a peacock*] I'm not going. If this is a poor place itself, I'll make myself contented to be lodging here.

[Widow Quin *makes a sign to* Shawn *to leave them*]

SHAWN: Well, I'm going measuring the race-course while the tide is low, so I'll leave you the garments and my blessing for the sports to-day. God bless you! [*He wriggles out*]

WIDOW QUIN: [*Admiring* Christy] Well, you're mighty spruce, young fellow. Sit down now while you're quiet till you talk with me.

CHRISTY: [*Swaggering*] I'm going abroad on the hillside for to seek Pegeen.

WIDOW QUIN: You'll have time and plenty for to seek Pegeen, and you heard me saying at the fall of night the two of us should be great company.

CHRISTY: From this out I'll have no want of company when all sorts is bringing me their food and clothing [*He swaggers to the door, tightening his belt*], the way they'd set their eyes upon a gallant orphan cleft his father with one blow to the breeches belt. [*He opens door, then staggers back*] Saints of glory! Holy angels from the throne of light!

WIDOW QUIN: [*Going over*] What ails you?

CHRISTY: It's the walking spirit of my murdered da!

WIDOW QUIN: [*Looking out*] Is it that tramper?

CHRISTY: [*Wildly*] Where'll I hide my poor body from that ghost of hell?

[*The door is pushed open, and old* Mahon *appears on threshold.* Christy *darts in behind door*]

WIDOW QUIN: [*In great amusement*] God save you, my poor man.

MAHON: [*Gruffly*] Did you see a young lad passing this way in the early morning or the fall of night?

WIDOW QUIN: You're a queer kind to walk in not saluting at all.

MAHON: Did you see the young lad?

WIDOW QUIN: [*Stiffly*] What kind was he?

MAHON: An ugly young streeler with a murderous gob on him, and a little switch in his hand. I met a tramper seen him coming this way at the fall of night.

WIDOW QUIN: There's harvest hundreds do be passing these days for the Sligo boat. For what is it you're wanting him, my poor man?

MAHON: I want to destroy him for breaking the head on me with the clout of a loy. [*He takes off a big hat, and shows his head in a mass of bandages and plaster, with some pride*] It was he did that, and amn't I a great wonder to think I've traced him ten days with that rent in my crown?

WIDOW QUIN: [*Taking his head in both hands and examining it with extreme delight*] That was a great blow. And who hit you? A robber maybe?

MAHON: It was my own son hit me, and he the divil a robber, or anything else, but a dirty, stuttering lout.

WIDOW QUIN: [*Letting go his skull and wiping her hands in her apron*] You'd best be wary of a mortified scalp, I think they call it, lepping around with that wound in the splendour of the sun. It was a bad blow surely, and you should have vexed him fearful to make him strike that gash in his da.

MAHON: Is it me?

WIDOW QUIN: [*Amusing herself*] Aye. And isn't it a great shame when the old and hardened do torment the young?

MAHON: [*Raging*] Torment him is it? And I after holding out with the patience of a martyred saint till there's nothing but destruction on, and I'm driven out in my old age with none to aid me.

WIDOW QUIN: [*Greatly amused*] It's a sacred wonder the way that wickedness will spoil a man.

MAHON: My wickedness, is it? Amn't I after saying it is himself has me destroyed, and he a liar on walls, a talker of folly, a man you'd see stretched the half of the day in the brown ferns with his belly to the sun.

WIDOW QUIN: Not working at all?

MAHON: The divil a work, or if he did itself, you'd see him raising up a haystack like the stalk of a rush, or driving our last cow till he broke her leg at the hip, and when he wasn't at that he'd be fooling over little birds he had—finches and felts—or making mugs at his own self in the bit of a glass we had hung on the wall.

WIDOW QUIN: [*Looking at* Christy] What way was he so foolish? It was running wild after the girls may be?

MAHON: [*With a shout of derision*] Running wild, is it? If he seen a red petticoat coming swinging over the hill, he'd be off to hide in the sticks, and you'd see him shooting out his sheep's eyes between the little twigs and the leaves, and his two ears rising like a hare looking out through a gap. Girls, indeed!

WIDOW QUIN: It was drink maybe?

MAHON: And he a poor fellow would get drunk on the smell of a pint. He'd a queer rotten stomach, I'm telling you, and when I gave him three pulls from my pipe a while since, he was taken with contortions till I had to send him in the ass cart to the females' nurse.

WIDOW QUIN: [*Clasping her hands*] Well, I never till this day heard tell of a man the like of that!

MAHON: I'd take a mighty oath you didn't surely, and wasn't he the laughing joke of every female woman where four baronies meet, the way the girls would stop their weeding if they seen him coming the road to let a roar at him, and call him the looney of Mahon's.

WIDOW QUIN: I'd give the world and all to see the like of him. What kind was he?

MAHON: A small low fellow.

WIDOW QUIN: And dark?

MAHON: Dark and dirty.

WIDOW QUIN: [*Considering*] I'm thinking I seen him.

MAHON: [*Eagerly*] An ugly young blackguard.

WIDOW QUIN: A hideous, fearful villain, and the spit of you.

MAHON: What way is he fled?

WIDOW QUIN: Gone over the hills to catch a coasting steamer to the north or south.

MAHON: Could I pull up on him now?

WIDOW QUIN: If you'll cross the sands below where the tide is out, you'll be in it as soon as himself, for he had to go round ten miles by the top of the bay. [*She points to the door*] Strike down by the head beyond and then follow on the roadway to the north and east.

[Mahon *goes abruptly*]

WIDOW QUIN: [*Shouting after him*] Let you give him a good vengeance when you come up with him, but don't put yourself in the power of the law, for it'd be a poor thing to see a judge in his black cap reading out his sentence on a civil warrior the like of you.

[*She swings the door to and looks at* Christy, *who is cowering in terror, for a moment, then she bursts into a laugh*]

WIDOW QUIN: Well, you're the walking Playboy of the Western World, and that's the poor man you had divided to his breeches belt.

CHRISTY: [*Looking out: then, to her*] What'll Pegeen say when she hears that story? What'll she be saying to me now?

WIDOW QUIN: She'll knock the head of you, I'm thinking, and drive you from the door. God help her to be taking you for a wonder, and you a little schemer making up the story you destroyed your da.

CHRISTY: [*Turning to the door, nearly speechless with rage, half to himself*] To be letting on he was dead, and coming back to his life, and following after me like an old weazel tracing a rat, and coming in here laying desolation between my own self and the fine women of Ireland, and he a kind of carcase that you'd fling upon the sea . . .

WIDOW QUIN: [*More soberly*] There's talking for a man's one only son.

CHRISTY: [*Breaking out*] His one son, is it? May I meet him with one tooth and it aching, and one eye to be seeing seven and seventy divils in the twists of the road, and one old timber leg on him to limp into the scalding grave. [*Looking out*] There he is now crossing the strands, and that the Lord God would send a high wave to wash him from the world.

WIDOW QUIN: [*Scandalized*] Have you no shame? [*Putting her hand on his shoulder and turning him round*] What ails you? Near crying, is it?

CHRISTY: [*In despair and grief*] Amn't I after seeing the love-light of the star of knowledge shining from her brow, and hearing words would put you thinking on the holy Brigid speaking to the infant saints, and now she'll be turning again, and speaking hard words to me, like an old woman with a spavindy ass she'd have, urging on a hill.

WIDOW QUIN: There's poetry talk for a girl you'd see itching and scratching, and she with a stale stink of poteen on her from selling in the shop.

CHRISTY: [*Impatiently*] It's her like is fitted to be handling merchandise in the heavens above, and what'll I be doing now, I ask you, and I a kind of wonder was jilted by the heavens when a day was by.

[*There is a distant noise of girls' voices. Widow Quin looks from window and comes to him, hurriedly*]

WIDOW QUIN: You'll be doing like myself, I'm thinking, when I did destroy my man, for I'm above many's the day, odd times in great spirits, abroad in the sunshine, darning a stocking or stitching a shift; and odd times again looking out on the schooners, hookers, trawlers is sailing the sea, and I thinking on the gallant hairy fellows are drifting beyond, and myself long years living alone.

CHRISTY: [*Interested*] You're like me, so.

WIDOW QUIN: I am your like, and it's for that I'm taking a fancy to you, and I with my little houseen above where there'd be myself to tend you, and none to ask were you a murderer or what at all.

CHRISTY: And what would I be doing if I left Pegeen?

WIDOW QUIN: I've nice jobs you could be doing, gathering shells to make a whitewash for our hut within, building up a little goose-house, or stretching a new skin on an old currach I have, and if my hut is far from all sides, it's there you'll meet the wisest old men, I tell you, at the corner of my wheel, and it's there yourself and me will have great times whispering and hugging. . . .

VOICES: [*Outside, calling far away*] Christy! Christy Mahon! Christy!

CHRISTY: Is it Pegeen Mike?

WIDOW QUIN: It's the young girls, I'm thinking, coming to bring you to the sports below, and what is it you'll have me to tell them now?

CHRISTY: Aid me for to win Pegeen. It's herself only that I'm seeking now. [*Widow Quin gets up and goes to window*] Aid me for to win her, and I'll be asking God to stretch a hand to you in the hour of death, and lead you short cuts through the Meadows of Ease, and up the floor of Heaven to the Footstool of the Virgin's Son.

WIDOW QUIN: There's praying.

VOICES: [*Nearer*] Christy! Christy Mahon!

CHRISTY: [*With agitation*] They're coming. Will you swear to aid and save me for the love of Christ?

WIDOW QUIN: [*Looks at him for a moment*] If I aid you, will you swear to give me a right of way I want, and a mountainy ram, and a load of dung at Michaelmas, the time that you'll be master here?

CHRISTY: I will, by the elements and stars of night.

WIDOW QUIN: Then we'll not say a word of the old fellow, the way Pegeen won't know your story till the end of time.

CHRISTY: And if he chances to return again?

WIDOW QUIN: We'll swear he's a maniac and not your da. I could take an oath I seen him raving on the sands to-day.

[*Girls run in*]

SUSAN: Come on to the sports below. Pegeen says you're to come.

SARA: The lepping's beginning, and we've a jockey's suit to fit upon you for the mule race on the sands below.

HONOR: Come on, will you?

CHRISTY: I will then if Pegeen's beyond.

SARA: She's in the boreen making game of Shaneen Keogh.

CHRISTY: Then I'll be going to her now.

[*He runs out followed by the girls*]

WIDOW QUIN: Well, if the worst comes in the end of all, it'll be great game to see there's none to pity him but a widow woman, the like of me, has buried her children and destroyed her man.

[*She goes out*]

Act III

SCENE: *As before. Later in the day. Jimmy comes in, slightly drunk.*

JIMMY: [*Calls*] Pegeen! [*Crosses to inner door*] Pegeen Mike! [*Comes back again into the room*]

Pegeen! [Philly *comes in in the same state*] [*To* Philly] Did you see herself?

PHILLY: I did not; but I sent Shawn Keogh with the ass cart for to bear him home. [*Trying cupboards which are locked*] Well, isn't he a nasty man to get into such staggers at a morning wake? and isn't herself the divil's daughter for locking, and she so fussy after that young gaffer, you might take your death with drought and none to heed you?

JIMMY: It's little wonder she'd be fussy, and he after bringing bankrupt ruin on the roulette man, and the trick-o'-the-loop man, and breaking the nose of the cockshot-man, and winning all in the sports below, racing, lepping, dancing, and the Lord knows what! He's right luck, I'm telling you.

PHILLY: If he has, he'll be rightly hobbled yet, and he not able to say ten words without making a brag of the way he killed his father, and the great blow he hit with the loy.

JIMMY: A man can't hang by his own informing, and his father should be rotten by now.

[*Old* Mahon *passes window slowly*]

PHILLY: Supposing a man's digging spuds in that field with a long spade, and supposing he flings up the two halves of that skull, what'll be said then in the papers and the courts of law?

JIMMY: They'd say it was an old Dane, maybe, was drowned in the flood. [*Old* Mahon *comes in and sits down near door listening*] Did you never hear tell of the skulls they have in the city of Dublin, ranged out like blue jugs in a cabin of Connaught?

PHILLY: And you believe that?

JIMMY: [*Pugnaciously*] Didn't a lad see them and he after coming from harvesting in the Liverpool boat? "They have them there," says he, "making a show of the great people there was one time walking the world. White skulls and black skulls and yellow skulls, and some with full teeth, and some haven't only but one."

PHILLY: It was no lie, maybe, for when I was a young lad there was a graveyard beyond the house with the remnants of a man who had thighs as long as your arm. He was a horrid man, I'm telling you, and there was many a fine Sunday I'd put him together for fun, and he with shiny bones, you wouldn't meet the like of these days in the cities of the world.

MAHON: [*Getting up*] You wouldn't, is it? Lay your eyes on that skull, and tell me where and when there was another the like of it, is splintered only from the blow of a loy.

PHILLY: Glory be to God! And who hit you at all?

MAHON: [*Triumphantly*] It was my own son hit me. Would you believe that?

JIMMY: Well, there's wonders hidden in the heart of man!

PHILLY: [*Suspiciously*] And what way was it done?

MAHON: [*Wandering about the room*] I'm after walking hundreds and long scores of miles, winning clean beds and the fill of my belly four times in the day, and I doing nothing but telling stories of that naked truth. [*He comes to them a little aggressively*] Give me a supeen and I'll tell you now.

[Widow Quin *comes in and stands aghast behind him. He is facing* Jimmy *and* Philly, *who are on the left*]

JIMMY: Ask herself beyond. She's the stuff hidden in her shawl.

WIDOW QUIN: [*Coming to* Mahon *quickly*] You here, is it? You didn't go far at all?

MAHON: I seen the coasting steamer passing, and I got a drought upon me and a cramping leg, so I said, "The divil go along with him," and turned again. [*Looking under her shawl*] And let you give me a supeen, for I'm destroyed travelling since Tuesday was a week.

WIDOW QUIN: [*Getting a glass, in a cajoling tone*] Sit down then by the fire and take your ease for a space. You've a right to be destroyed indeed, with your walking, and fighting, and facing the sun. [*Giving him poteen from a stone jar she has brought in*] There now is a drink for you, and may it be to your happiness and length of life.

MAHON: [*Taking glass greedily and sitting down by fire*] God increase you!

WIDOW QUIN: [*Taking men to the right stealthily*] Do you know what? That man's raving from his wound to-day, for I met him a while since telling a rambling tale of a tinker had him destroyed. Then he heard of Christy's deed, and he up and says it was his son had cracked his skull. O isn't madness a fright, for he'll go killing someone yet, and he thinking it's the man has struck him so?

JIMMY: [*Entirely convinced*] It's a fright, surely. I knew a party was kicked in the head by a red mare, and he went killing horses a great while, till he eat the insides of a clock and died after.

PHILLY: [*With suspicion*] Did he see Christy?

WIDOW QUIN: He didn't. [*With a warning gesture*] Let you not be putting him in mind of him, or you'll be likely summoned if there's murder done. [*Looking round at* Mahon] Whisht! He's listening. Wait now till you hear me taking him easy and unravelling all. [*She goes to* Mahon] And what way are you feeling, mister? Are you in contentment now?

MAHON: [*Slightly emotional from his drink*] I'm poorly only, for it's a hard story the way I'm left to-day, when it was I did tend him from his hour of birth, and he a dunce never reached his second book, the way he'd come from school, many's the day, with his legs lamed under him, and he blackened with his beatings like a tinker's ass. It's a hard story, I'm saying, the way some do have their next and nighest raising up a hand of murder on them, and some is lonesome getting their death with lamentation in the dead of night.

WIDOW QUIN: [*Not knowing what to say*] To hear you talking so quiet, who'd know you were the same fellow we seen pass to-day?

MAHON: I'm the same surely. The wrack and ruin of three score years; and it's a terror to live that length, I tell you, and to have your sons going to the dogs against you, and you wore out scolding them, and skelping them, and God knows what.

PHILLY: [*To* Jimmy] He's not raving. [*To Widow Quin*] Will you ask him what kind was his son?

WIDOW QUIN: [*To Mahon, with a peculiar look*] Was your son that hit you a lad of one year and a score maybe, a great hand at racing and lepping and licking the world?

MAHON: [*Turning on her with a roar of rage*] Didn't you hear me say he was the fool of men, the way from this out he'll know the orphan's lot with old and young making game of him and they swearing, raging, kicking at him like a mangy cur.

[*A great burst of cheering outside, some way off*]

MAHON: [*Putting his hands to his ears*] What in the name of God do they want roaring below?

WIDOW QUIN: [*With the shade of a smile*] They're cheering a young lad, the champion Playboy of the Western World.

[*More cheering*]

MAHON: [*Going to window*] It'd split my heart to hear them, and I with pulses in my brain-pan for a week gone by. Is it racing they are?

JIMMY: [*Looking from door*] It is then. They are mounting him for the mule race will be run upon the sands. That's the playboy on the winkered mule.

MAHON: [*Puzzled*] That lad, is it? If you said it was a fool he was, I'd have laid a mighty oath he was the likeness of my wandering son. [*Uneasily, putting his hand to his head*] Faith, I'm thinking I'll go walking for to view the race.

WIDOW QUIN: [*Stopping him, sharply*] You will not. You'd best take the road to Belmullet, and not be dilly-dallying in this place where there isn't a spot you could sleep.

PHILLY: [*Coming forward*] Don't mind her. Mount there on the bench and you'll have a view of the whole. They're hurrying before the tide will rise, and it'd be near over if you went down the pathway through the crags below.

MAHON: [*Mounts on bench,* Widow Quin *beside him*] That's a right view again the edge of the sea. They're coming now from the point. He's leading. Who is he at all?

WIDOW QUIN: He's the champion of the world, I tell you, and there isn't a hop'orth isn't falling lucky to his hands to-day.

PHILLY: [*Looking out, interested in the race*] Look at that. They're pressing him now.

JIMMY: He'll win it yet.

PHILLY: Take your time, Jimmy Farrell. It's too soon to say.

WIDOW QUIN: [*Shouting*] Watch him taking the gate. There's riding.

JIMMY: [*Cheering*] More power to the young lad!

MAHON: He's passing the third.

JIMMY: He'll lick them yet!

WIDOW QUIN: He'd lick them if he was running races with a score itself.

MAHON: Look at the mule he has, kicking the stars.

WIDOW QUIN: There was a lep! [*Catching hold of* Mahon *in her excitement*] He's fallen! He's mounted again! Faith, he's passing them all!

JIMMY: Look at him skelping her!

PHILLY: And the mountain girls hooshing him on!

JIMMY: It's the last turn! The post's cleared for them now!

MAHON: Look at the narrow place. He'll be into the bogs! [*With a yell*] Good rider! He's through it again!

JIMMY: He neck and neck!

MAHON: Good boy to him! Flames, but he's in!

[*Great cheering, in which all join*]

MAHON: [*With hesitation*] What's that? They're raising him up. They're coming this way. [*With a roar of rage and astonishment*] It's Christy! by the stars of God! I'd know his way of spitting and he astride the moon.

[*He jumps down and makes for the door, but* Widow Quin *catches him and pulls him back*]

WIDOW QUIN: Stay quiet, will you. That's not your son. [*To* Jimmy] Stop him, or you'll get a month for the abetting of manslaughter and be fined as well.

JIMMY: I'll hold him.

MAHON: [*Struggling*] Let me out! Let me out, the lot of you! till I have my vengeance on his head to-day.

WIDOW QUIN: [*Shaking him, vehemently*] That's not your son. That's a man is going to make a marriage with the daughter of this house, a place with fine trade, with a license, and with poteen too.

MAHON: [*Amazed*] That man marrying a decent and a moneyed girl! Is it mad yous are? Is it in a crazy-house for females that I'm landed now?

WIDOW QUIN: It's mad yourself is with the blow upon your head. That lad is the wonder of the Western World.

MAHON: I seen it's my son.

WIDOW QUIN: You seen that you're mad. [*Cheering outside*] Do you hear them cheering him in the zig-zags of the road? Aren't you after saying that your son's a fool, and how would they be cheering a true idiot born?

MAHON: [*Getting distressed*] It's maybe out of reason that that man's himself. [*Cheering again*] There's none surely will go cheering him. Oh, I'm raving with a madness that would fright the world! [*He sits down with his hand to his head*] There was one time I seen ten scarlet divils letting on they'd cork my spirit in a gallon can; and one time I seen rats as big as badgers sucking the life blood from the butt of my lug; but I never till this day confused that dribbling idiot with a likely man. I'm destroyed surely.

WIDOW QUIN: And who'd wonder when it's your brain-pan that is gaping now?

MAHON: Then the blight of the sacred drought upon myself and him, for I never went mad to this day, and I not three weeks with the Limerick girls drinking myself silly, and parlatic from the dusk to dawn. [*To Widow Quin, suddenly*] Is my visage astray?

WIDOW QUIN: It is then. You're a sniggering maniac, a child could see.

MAHON: [*Getting up more cheerfully*] Then I'd best be going to the union beyond, and there'll be a welcome before me, I tell you [*With great pride*], and I a terrible and fearful case, the way that there I was one time, screeching in a straitened waistcoat, with seven doctors writing out my sayings in a printed book. Would you believe that?

WIDOW QUIN: If you're a wonder itself, you'd best be hasty, for them lads caught a maniac one time and pelted the poor creature till he ran out, raving and foaming, and was drowned in the sea.

MAHON: [*With philosophy*] It's true mankind is the divil when your head's astray. Let me out now and I'll slip down the boreen, and not see them so.

WIDOW QUIN: [*Showing him out*] That's it. Run to the right, and not a one will see.

[*He runs off*]

PHILLY: [*Wisely*] You're at some gaming, Widow Quin; but I'll walk after him and give him his dinner and a time to rest, and I'll see then if he's raving or as sane as you.

WIDOW QUIN: [*Annoyed*] If you go near that lad, let you be wary of your head, I'm saying. Didn't you hear him telling he was crazed at times?

PHILLY: I heard him telling a power; and I'm thinking we'll have right sport, before night will fall.

[*He goes out*]

JIMMY: Well, Philly's a conceited and foolish man. How could that madman have his senses and his brain-pan slit? I'll go after them and see him turn on Philly now.

[*He goes; Widow Quin hides poteen behind counter. Then hubbub outside*]

VOICES: There you are! Good jumper! Grand lepper! Darlint boy! He's the racer! Bear him on, will you!

[Christy *comes in, in Jockey's dress, with* Pegeen Mike, Sara, *and other girls, and men*]

PEGEEN: [*To crowd*] Go on now and don't destroy him and he drenching with sweat. Go along, I'm saying, and have your tug-of-warring till he's dried his skin.

CROWD: Here's his prizes! A bagpipes! A fiddle was played by a poet in the years gone by! A flat and three-thorned blackthorn would lick the scholars out of Dublin town!

CHRISTY: [*Taking prizes from the men*] Thank you kindly, the lot of you. But you'd say it was little only I did this day if you'd seen me a while since striking my one single blow.

TOWN CRIER: [*Outside, ringing a bell*] Take notice, last event of this day! Tug-of-warring on the green below! Come on, the lot of you! Great achievements for all Mayo men!

PEGEEN: Go on, and leave him for to rest and dry. Go on, I tell you, for he'll do no more. [*She hustles crowd out;* Widow Quin *following them*]

MEN: [*Going*] Come on then. Good luck for the while!

PEGEEN: [*Radiantly, wiping his face with her shawl*] Well, you're the lad, and you'll have great times from this out when you could win that wealth of prizes, and you sweating in the heat of noon!

CHRISTY: [*Looking at her with delight*] I'll have great times if I win the crowning prize I'm seeking now, and that's your promise that you'll wed me in a fortnight, when our banns is called.

PEGEEN: [*Backing away from him*] You've right daring to go ask me that, when all knows you'll be starting to some girl in your own townland, when your father's rotten in four months, or five.

CHRISTY: [*Indignantly*] Starting from you, is it? [*He follows her*] I will not, then, and when the airs is warming in four months, or five, it's then yourself and me should be pacing Neifin in the dews of night, the times sweet smells do be rising, and you'd see a little shiny new moon, maybe, sinking on the hills.

PEGEEN: [*Looking at him playfully*] And it's that kind of a poacher's love you'd make, Christy Mahon, on the sides of Neifin, when the night is down?

CHRISTY: It's little you'll think if my love's a poacher's, or an earl's itself, when you'll feel my two hands stretched around you, and I squeezing kisses on your puckered lips, till I'd feel a kind of pity for the Lord God is all ages sitting lonesome in his golden chair.

PEGEEN: That'll be right fun, Christy Mahon, and any girl would walk her heart out before she'd meet a young man was your like for eloquence, or talk, at all.

CHRISTY: [*Encouraged*] Let you wait, to hear me talking, till we're astray in Erris, when Good Friday's by, drinking a sup from a well, and making mighty kisses with our wetted mouths, or gaming in a gap or sunshine, with yourself stretched back unto your necklace, in the flowers of the earth.

PEGEEN: [*In a lower voice, moved by his tone*] I'd be nice so, is it?

CHRISTY: [*With rapture*] If the mitred bishops seen you that time, they'd be the like of the holy prophets, I'm thinking, do be straining the bars of Paradise to lay eyes on the Lady Helen of Troy, and she abroad, pacing back and forward, with a nosegay in her golden shawl.

PEGEEN: [*With real tenderness*] And what is it I have, Christy Mahon, to make me fitting entertainment for the like of you, that has such poet's talking, and such bravery of heart?

CHRISTY: [*In a low voice*] Isn't there the light of seven heavens in your heart alone, the way you'll be an angel's lamp to me from this out, and I abroad in the darkness, spearing salmons in the Owen, or the Carrowmore?

PEGEEN: If I was your wife, I'd be alone with you those nights, Christy Mahon, the way you'd see I was a great hand at coaxing bailiffs, or coining funny nick-names for the stars of night.

CHRISTY: You, is it? Taking your death in the hailstones, or in the fogs of dawn.

PEGEEN: Yourself and me would shelter easy in a narrow bush, [*With a qualm of dread*] but we're only talking, maybe, for this would be a poor, thatched place to hold a fine lad is the like of you.

CHRISTY: [*Putting his arm round her*] If I wasn't a good Christian, it's on my naked knees I'd be saying my prayers and paters to every jackstraw you have roofing your head, and every stony pebble is paving the laneway to your door.

PEGEEN: [*Radiantly*] If that's the truth, I'll be burning candles from this out to the miracles of God that have brought you from the south to-day, and I, with my gowns bought ready, the way that I can wed you, and not wait at all.

CHRISTY: It's miracles, and that's the truth. Me there toiling a long while, and walking a long while, not knowing at all I was drawing all times nearer to this holy day.

PEGEEN: And myself, a girl, was tempted often to go sailing the seas till I'd marry a Jew-man, with ten kegs of gold, and I not knowing at all there was the like of you drawing nearer, like the stars of God.

CHRISTY: And to think I'm long years hearing women talking that talk, to all bloody fools, and this the first time I've heard the like of your voice talking sweetly for my own delight.

PEGEEN: And to think it's me is talking sweetly, Christy Mahon, and I the fright of seven townlands for my biting tongue. Well, the heart's a wonder; and, I'm thinking, there won't be our like in Mayo, for gallant lovers, from this hour, to-day. [*Drunken singing is heard outside*] There's my father coming from the wake, and when he's had his sleep we'll tell him, for he's peaceful then.

[*They separate*]

MICHAEL: [*Singing outside*]
   The jailor and the turnkey
      They quickly ran us down,
   And brought us back as prisoners
      Once more to Cavan town.

[*He comes in supported by Shawn*]
   There we lay bewailing
      All in a prison bound. . . .

[*He sees* Christy. *Goes and shakes him drunkenly by the hand, while* Pegeen *and* Shawn *talk on the left*]

MICHAEL: [*To* Christy] The blessing of God and the holy angels on your head, young fellow. I hear tell you're after winning all in the sports below; and wasn't it a shame I didn't bear you along with me to Kate Cassidy's wake, a fine, stout lad, the like of you, for you'd never see the match of it for flows of drink, the way when we sunk her bones at noonday in her narrow grave, there were five men, aye, and six men, stretched out retching speechless on the holy stones.

CHRISTY: [*Uneasily, watching* Pegeen] Is that the truth?

MICHAEL: It is then, and aren't you a louty schemer to go burying your poor father unbeknownst when you'd a right to throw him on the crupper of a Kerry mule and drive him westwards, like holy Joseph in the days gone by, the way we could have given him a decent burial, and not have him rotting beyond, and not a Christian drinking a smart drop to the glory of his soul?

CHRISTY: [*Gruffly*] It's well enough he's lying, for the likes of him.

MICHAEL: [*Slapping him on the back*] Well, aren't you a hardened slayer? It'll be a poor thing for the household man where you go sniffing for a female wife; and [*Pointing to* Shawn] look beyond at that shy and decent Christian I have chosen for my daughter's hand, and I after getting the gilded dispensation this day for to wed them now.

CHRISTY: And you'll be wedding them this day, is it?

MICHAEL: [*Drawing himself up*] Aye. Are you thinking, if I'm drunk itself, I'd leave my daughter living single with a little frisky rascal is the like of you?

PEGEEN: [*Breaking away from* Shawn] Is it the truth the dispensation's come?

MICHAEL: [*Triumphantly*] Father Reilly's after reading it in gallous Latin, and "It's come in the nick of time," says he; "so I'll wed them in a hurry, dreading that young gaffer who'd capsize the stars."

PEGEEN: [*Fiercely*] He's missed his nick of time, for it's that lad, Christy Mahon, that I'm wedding now.

MICHAEL: [*Loudly with horror*] You'd be making him a son to me, and he wet and crusted with his father's blood?

PEGEEN: Aye. Wouldn't it be a bitter thing for a girl to go marrying the like of Shaneen, and he a middling kind of a scarecrow, with no savagery or fine words in him at all?

MICHAEL: [*Gasping and sinking on a chair*] Oh, aren't you a heathen daughter to go shaking the fat of my heart, and I swamped and drownded with the weight of drink? Would you have them turning on me the way that I'd be roaring to the dawn of day with the wind upon my heart? Have you not a word to aid me, Shaneen? Are you not jealous at all?

SHANEEN: [*In great misery*] I'd be afeard to be jealous of a man did slay his da.

PEGEEN: Well, it'd be a poor thing to go marrying your like. I'm seeing there's a world of peril for an orphan girl, and isn't it a great blessing I didn't wed you, before himself came walking from the west or south?

SHAWN: It's a queer story you'd go picking a dirty tramp up from the highways of the world.

PEGEEN: [*Playfully*] And you think you're a likely beau to go straying along with, the shiny Sundays of the opening year, when it's sooner on a bullock's liver you'd put a poor girl thinking than on the lily or the rose?

SHAWN: And have you no mind of my weight of passion, and the holy dispensation, and the drift of heifers I am giving, and the golden ring?

PEGEEN: I'm thinking you're too fine for the like of me, Shawn Keogh of Killakeen, and let you go off till you'd find a radiant lady with droves of bullocks on the plains of Meath, and herself bedizened in the diamond jewelleries of Pharaoh's ma. That'd be your match, Shaneen. So God save you now!

[*She retreats behind* Christy]

SHAWN: Won't you hear me telling you . . . ?

CHRISTY: [*With ferocity*] Take yourself from this, young fellow, or I'll maybe add a murder to my deeds to-day.

MICHAEL: [*Springing up with a shriek*] Murder is it? Is it mad yous are? Would you go making murder in this place, and it piled with poteen for our drink to-night? Go on to the foreshore if it's fighting you want, where the rising tide will wash all traces from the memory of man.

[*Pushing* Shawn *towards* Christy]

SHAWN: [*Shaking himself free, and getting behind* Michael] I'll not fight him, Michael James. I'd liefer live a bachelor, simmering in passions to the end of time, than face a lepping savage the like of him has descended from the Lord knows where. Strike him yourself, Michael James, or you'll lose my drift of heifers and my blue bull from Sneem.

MICHAEL: Is it me fight him, when it's father-slaying he's bred to now? [*Pushing* Shawn] Go on you fool and fight him now.

SHAWN: [*Coming forward a little*] Will I strike him with my hand?

MICHAEL: Take the loy is on your western side.

SHAWN: I'd be afeard of the gallows if I struck him with that.

CHRISTY: [*Taking up the loy*] Then I'll make you face the gallows or quit off from this.

[*Shawn flies out of the door*]

CHRISTY: Well, fine weather be after him, [*Going to* Michael, *coaxingly*] and I'm thinking you wouldn't wish to have that quaking blackguard in your house at all. Let you give us your blessing and hear her swear her faith to me, for I'm mounted on the springtide of the stars of luck, the way it'll be good for any to have me in the house.

PEGEEN: [*At the other side of* Michael] Bless us now, for I swear to God I'll wed him, and I'll not renege.

MICHAEL: [*Standing up in the centre, holding on to both of them*] It's the will of God, I'm thinking, that all should win an easy or a cruel end, and it's the will of God that all should rear up lengthy families for the nurture of the earth. What's a single man, I ask you, eating a bit in one house and drinking a sup in another, and he with no place of his own, like an old braying jackass strayed upon the rocks? [*To* Christy] It's many would be in dread to bring your like into their house for to end them, maybe, with a sudden end; but I'm a decent man of Ireland, and I liefer face the grave untimely and I seeing a score of grandsons growing up little gallant swearers by the name of God, than go peopling my bedside with puny weeds the like of what you'd breed, I'm thinking, out of Shaneen Keogh. [*He joins their hands*] A daring fellow is the jewel of the world, and a man did split his father's middle with a single clout, should have the bravery of ten, so may God and Mary and St. Patrick bless you, and increase you from this mortal day.

CHRISTY AND PEGEEN: Amen, O Lord!

[*Hubbub outside*]

[*Old* Mahon *rushes in, followed by all the crowd, and* Widow Quin. *He makes a rush at* Christy, *knocks him down, and begins to beat him*]

PEGEEN: [*Dragging back his arm*] Stop that, will you. Who are you at all?

MAHON: His father, God forgive me!

PEGEEN: [*Drawing back*] Is it rose from the dead?

MAHON: Do you think I look so easy quenched with the tap of a loy? [*Beats* Christy *again*]

PEGEEN: [*Glaring at* Christy] And it's lies you told, letting on you had him slitted, and you nothing at all.

CHRISTY: [*Catching* Mahon's *stick*] He's not my father. He's a raving maniac would scare the world. [*Pointing to* Widow Quin] Herself knows it is true.

CROWD: You're fooling Pegeen! The Widow Quin seen him this day, and you likely knew! You're a liar!

CHRISTY: [*Dumbfounded*] It's himself was a liar, lying stretched out with an open head on him, letting on he was dead.

MAHON: Weren't you off racing the hills before I got

my breath with the start I had seeing you turn on me at all?

PEGEEN: And to think of the coaxing glory we had given him, and he after doing nothing but hitting a soft blow and chasing northward in a sweat of fear. Quit off from this.

CHRISTY: [*Piteously*] You've seen my doings this day, and let you save me from the old man; for why would you be in such a scorch of haste to spur me to destruction now?

PEGEEN: It's there your treachery is spurring me, till I'm hard set to think you're the one I'm after lacing in my heart-strings half-an-hour gone by. [*To Mahon*] Take him on from this, for I think bad the world should see me raging for a Munster liar, and the fool of men.

MAHON: Rise up now to retribution, and come on with me.

CROWD: [*Jeeringly*] There's the playboy! There's the lad thought he'd rule the roost in Mayo. Slate him now, mister.

CHRISTY: [*Getting up in shy terror*] What is it drives you to torment me here, when I'd asked the thunders of the might of God to blast me if I ever did hurt to any saving only that one single blow.

MAHON: [*Loudly*] If you didn't, you're a poor good-for-nothing, and isn't it by the like of you the sins of the whole world are committed?

CHRISTY: [*Raising his hands*] In the name of the Almighty God. . . .

MAHON: Leave troubling the Lord God. Would you have him sending down droughts, and fevers, and the old hen and the cholera morbus?

CHRISTY: [*To* Widow Quin] Will you come between us and protect me now?

WIDOW QUIN: I've tried a lot, God help me, and my share is done.

CHRISTY: [*Looking round in desperation*] And I must go back into my torment is it, or run off like a vagabond straying through the Unions with the dusts of August making mudstains in the gullet of my throat, or the winds of March blowing on me till I'd take an oath I felt them making whistles of my ribs within?

SARA: Ask Pegeen to aid you. Her like does often change.

CHRISTY: I will not then, for there's torment in the splendour of her like, and she a girl any moon of midnight would take pride to meet, facing southwards on the heaths of Keel. But what did I want crawling forward to scorch my understanding at her flaming brow?

PEGEEN: [*To Mahon, vehemently, fearing she will break into tears*] Take him on from this or I'll set the young lads to destroy him here.

MAHON: [*Going to him, shaking his stick*] Come on now if you wouldn't have the company to see you skelped.

PEGEEN: [*Half laughing, through her tears*] That's it, now the world will see him pandied, and he an ugly liar was playing off the hero, and the fright of men.

CHRISTY: [*To Mahon, very sharply*] Leave me go!

CROWD: That's it. Now Christy. If them two set fighting, it will lick the world.

MAHON: [*Making a grab at* Christy] Come here to me.

CHRISTY: [*More threateningly*] Leave me go, I'm saying.

MAHON: I will maybe, when your legs is limping, and your back is blue.

CROWD: Keep it up, the two of you. I'll back the old one. Now the playboy.

CHRISTY: [*In low and intense voice*] Shut your yelling, for if you're after making a mighty man of me this day by the power of a lie, you're setting me now to think if it's a poor thing to be lonesome, it's worse maybe to go mixing with the fools of earth.

[Mahon *makes a movement towards him*]

CHRISTY: [*Almost shouting*] Keep off . . . lest I do show a blow unto the lot of you would set the guardian angels winking in the clouds above.

[*He swings round with a sudden rapid movement and picks up a loy*]

CROWD: [*Half frightened, half amused*] He's going mad! Mind yourselves! Run from the idiot!

CHRISTY: If I am an idiot, I'm after hearing my voice this day saying words would raise the topknot on a poet in a merchant's town. I've won your racing, and your lepping, and . . .

MAHON: Shut your gullet and come on with me.

CHRISTY: I'm going, but I'll stretch you first.

[*He runs at old* Mahon *with the loy, chases him out of the door, followed by crowd and* Widow Quin. *There is a great noise outside, then a yell, and dead silence for a moment.* Christy *comes in, half dazed, and goes to fire*]

WIDOW QUIN: [*Coming in, hurriedly, and going to him*] They're turning again you. Come on, or you'll be hanged, indeed.

CHRISTY: I'm thinking, from this out, Pegeen'll be giving me praises the same as in the hours gone by.

WIDOW QUIN: [*Impatiently*] Come by the back-door. I'd think bad to have you stifled on the gallows tree.

CHRISTY: [*Indignantly*] I will not, then. What good'd be my life-time, if I left Pegeen?

WIDOW QUIN: Come on, and you'll be no worse than you were last night; and you with a double murder this time to be telling to the girls.

CHRISTY: I'll not leave Pegeen Mike.

WIDOW QUIN: [*Impatiently*] Isn't there the match of her in every parish public, from Binghamstown unto the plain of Meath? Come on, I tell you, and I'll find you finer sweethearts at each waning moon.

CHRISTY: It's Pegeen I'm seeking only, and what'd I care if you brought me a drift of chosen females, standing in their shifts itself, maybe, from this place to the Eastern World?

SARA: [*Runs in, pulling off one of her petticoats*] They're going to hang him. [*Holding out petticoat and shawl*] Fit these upon him, and let him run off to the east.

WIDOW QUIN: He's raving now; but we'll fit them on him, and I'll take him, in the ferry, to the Achill boat.

CHRISTY: [*Struggling feebly*] Leave me go, will you? when I'm thinking of my luck to-day, for she will wed me surely, and I a proven hero in the end of all.

[*They try to fasten petticoat round him*]

WIDOW QUIN: Take his left hand, and we'll pull him now. Come on, young fellow.

CHRISTY: [*Suddenly starting up*] You'll be taking me from her? You're jealous, is it, of her wedding me? Go on from this.

[*He snatches up a stool, and threatens them with it*]

WIDOW QUIN: [*Going*] It's in the mad-house they should put him, not in jail, at all. We'll go by the back-door, to call the doctor, and we'll save him so.

[*She goes out, with* Sara, *through inner room. Men crowd in the doorway.* Christy *sits down again by the fire*]

MICHAEL: [*In a terrified whisper*] Is the old lad killed surely?

PHILLY: I'm after feeling the last gasps quitting his heart.

[*They peer in at* Christy]

MICHAEL: [*With a rope*] Look at the way he is. Twist a hangman's knot on it, and slip it over his head, while he's not minding at all.

PHILLY: Let you take it, Shaneen. You're the soberest of all that's here.

SHAWN: Is it me to go near him, and he the wickedest and worst with me? Let you take it, Pegeen Mike.

PEGEEN: Come on, so.

[*She goes forward with the others, and they drop the double hitch over his head*]

CHRISTY: What ails you?

SHAWN: [*Triumphantly, as they pull the rope tight on his arms*] Come on to the peelers, till they stretch you now.

CHRISTY: Me!

MICHAEL: If we took pity on you, the Lord God would, maybe, bring us ruin from the law to-day, so you'd best come easy, for hanging is an easy and a speedy end.

CHRISTY: I'll not stir. [*To* Pegeen] And what is it you'll say to me, and I after doing it this time in the face of all?

PEGEEN: I'll say, a strange man is a marvel, with his mighty talk; but what's a squabble in your back-yard, and the blow of a loy, have taught me that there's a great gap between a gallous story and a dirty deed. [*To Men*] Take him on from this, or the lot of us will be likely put on trial for his deed to-day.

CHRISTY: [*With horror in his voice*] And it's yourself will send me off, to have a horny-fingered hangman hitching his bloody slip-knots at the butt of my ear.

MEN: [*Pulling rope*] Come on, will you?

[*He is pulled down on the floor*]

CHRISTY: [*Twisting his legs round the table*] Cut the rope, Pegeen, and I'll quit the lot of you, and live from this out, like the madmen of Keel, eating muck and green weeds, on the faces of the cliffs.

PEGEEN: And leave us to hang, is it, for a saucy liar, the like of you? [*To Men*] Take him on, out from this.

SHAWN: Pull a twist on his neck, and squeeze him so.

PHILLY: Twist yourself. Sure he cannot hurt you, if you keep your distance from his teeth alone.

SHAWN: I'm afeard of him. [*To* Pegeen] Lift a lighted sod, will you, and scorch his leg.

PEGEEN: [*Blowing the fire, with a bellows*] Leave go now, young fellow, or I'll scorch your shins.

CHRISTY: You're blowing for to torture me. [*His voice rising and growing stronger*] That's your kind, is it? Then let the lot of you be wary, for, if I've to face the gallows, I'll have a gay march down, I tell you, and shed the blood of some of you before I die.

SHAWN: [*In terror*] Keep a good hold, Philly. Be wary, for the love of God. For I'm thinking he would liefest wreak his pains on me.

CHRISTY: [*Almost gaily*] If I do lay my hands on you, it's the way you'll be at the fall of night, hanging as a scarecrow for the fowls of hell. Ah, you'll have a gallous jaunt I'm saying, coaching out through Limbo with my father's ghost.

SHAWN: [*To* Pegeen] Make haste, will you? Oh, isn't he a holy terror, and isn't it true for Father Reilly, that all drink's a curse that has the lot of you so shaky and uncertain now?

CHRISTY: If I can wring a neck among you, I'll have a royal judgment looking on the trembling jury in the courts of law. And won't there be crying out in Mayo the day I'm stretched upon the rope with ladies in their silks and satins snivelling in their lacy kerchiefs, and they rhyming songs and ballads on the terror of my fate?

[*He squirms round on the floor and bites* Shawn's *leg*]

SHAWN: [*Shrieking*] My leg's bit on me. He's the like of a mad dog, I'm thinking, the way that I will surely die.

CHRISTY: [*Delighted with himself*] You will then, the way you can shake out hell's flags of welcome for my coming in two weeks or three, for I'm thinking

Satan hasn't many have killed their da in Kerry, and in Mayo too.

[Old Mahon *comes in behind on all fours and looks on unnoticed*]

MEN: [*To* Pegeen] Bring the sod, will you?

PEGEEN: [*Coming over*] God help him so. [*Burns his leg*]

CHRISTY: [*Kicking and screaming*] O, glory be to God!

[*He kicks loose from the table, and they all drag him towards the door*]

JIMMY: [*Seeing old* Mahon] Will you look what's come in?

[*They all drop* Christy *and run left*]

CHRISTY: [*Scrambling on his knees face to face with old* Mahon] Are you coming to be killed a third time, or what ails you now?

MAHON: For what is it they have you tied?

CHRISTY: They're taking me to the peelers to have me hanged for slaying you.

MICHAEL: [*Apologetically*] It is the will of God that all should guard their little cabins from the treachery of law, and what would my daughter be doing if I was ruined or was hanged itself?

MAHON: [*Grimly, loosening* Christy] It's little I care if you put a bag on her back, and went picking cockles till the hour of death; but my son and myself will be going our own way, and we'll have great times from this out telling stories of the villainy of Mayo, and the fools is here. [*To* Christy, *who is freed*] Come on now.

CHRISTY: Go with you, is it? I will then, like a gallant captain with his heathen slave. Go on now and I'll see you from this day stewing my oatmeal and washing my spuds, for I'm master of all fights from now. [*Pushing* Mahon] Go on, I'm saying.

MAHON: Is it me?

CHRISTY: Not a word out of you. Go on from this.

MAHON: [*Walking out and looking back at* Christy *over his shoulder*] Glory be to God! [*With a broad smile*] I am crazy again! [*Goes*]

CHRISTY: Ten thousand blessings upon all that's here, for you've turned me a likely gaffer in the end of all, the way I'll go romancing through a romping lifetime from this hour to the dawning of the judgment day. [*He goes out*]

MICHAEL: By the will of God, we'll have peace now for our drinks. Will you draw the porter, Pegeen?

SHAWN: [*Going up to her*] It's a miracle Father Reilly can wed us in the end of all, and we'll have none to trouble us when his vicious bite is healed.

PEGEEN: [*Hitting him a box on the ear*] Quit my sight. [*Putting her shawl over her head and breaking out into wild lamentations*] Oh my grief, I've lost him surely. I've lost the only Playboy of the Western World.

The Circle

by W. SOMERSET MAUGHAM
(1874–   )

The Circle is actually a matter of two triangles. Even so, it has strict geometrical form; it is put together with thorough respect for the best traditions of comedy, with, indeed, the respect that puts Maugham in the classical comedy-of-manners line of Etherege, Congreve, and Sheridan. That line conceivably ends with Maugham; after him, at any rate, it makes an abrupt turn; it is less pure, less artificial, less cold; it begins to admit the sentimental in place of the elegiac. No one since Maugham has given to drawing-room comedy so aphoristic a morality, or so aphoristic a conciseness. For all his greater fame in the novel and short story, Maugham comes off most happily in the theater, where his sense of form most helps what he wants to do, and where—from working in so artificial a medium—his tendency toward slickness least harms it.

There are perhaps more amusing Maugham plays than The Circle; but The Circle is superior to them from having affinities with high comedy no less than the comedy of manners. Thus, its characters are not people who sacrifice romance to position, but people who give up position for romance; not people who acquiesce in the way of the world but people who defy it. To be sure, Mr. Maugham—being himself an ironist and a worldling—cannot view what is romantic or defiant or exultant in their behavior as conclusive; he must exhibit, along with the romantic act, the realistic consequences. He must show—as Rupert Brooke did with Helen and Menelaus—what happened afterwards to such high romance. He must indicate that most people cannot live by love alone, particularly if they lived earlier in the greatest style and luxury; and that, anyway, love is seldom a match for the stings of ostracism and the ravages of time.

So Lady Kitty Champion-Cheney, in the flush of youthful ardor, had run off with Lord Porteous—she sacrificing great social, he great political position. And now, after thirty years of fading beauty and frustrated ambition and hole-in-corner romance, they lack distinction for the world and devotion for each other, they are commonplace people given to commonplace quarreling. Theirs is a tragicomedy of life turned sour and not even bittersweet; and Maugham has contrived that, having failed as an experience, their life together shall not even succeed as a Horrible Example. The final ironic twist is not what has happened to them, but that it cannot even deter others. In the full face of things, Lady Kitty's daughter-in-law, Elizabeth—sure that it will be different with her —runs off with Teddy Luton.

Doubtless the play is a little too aphoristic and pat. Irony, though by reputation a quiet fellow, at times can be awfully insistent. And it may also be asked, of course, whether the fate of the lovers—their snapping at trifles and bickering at the bridge table—is very different from the fate of most husbands and wives. Except that those who give up all for love are not, in the moment of ardor and affirmation, of common breed; and the tragic thing is that they must partake in the end of a common, and very disquieting, destiny.

461

W. SOMERSET MAUGHAM

The Circle

THE PERSONS OF THE PLAY

CLIVE CHAMPION-CHENEY
ARNOLD CHAMPION-CHENEY, M.P.
LORD PORTEOUS
EDWARD LUTON
LADY CATHERINE CHAMPION-CHENEY
ELIZABETH
MRS. SHENSTONE

The action takes place at Aston-Adey, Arnold Champion-Cheney's house in Dorset.

Act I

The Scene is a stately drawing-room at Aston-Adey, with fine pictures on the walls and Georgian furniture. Aston-Adey has been described, with many illustrations, in Country Life. *It is not a house, but a place. Its owner takes a great pride in it, and there is nothing in the room which is not of the period. Through the French windows at the back can be seen the beautiful gardens which are one of the features. It is a fine summer morning.*

Arnold *comes in. He is a man of about thirty-five, tall and good-looking, fair, with a clean-cut, sensitive face. He has a look that is intellectual, but somewhat bloodless. He is very well dressed.*

ARNOLD: [*Calling*] Elizabeth. [*He goes to the window and calls again*] Elizabeth! [*He rings the bell. While he is waiting he gives a look round the room. He slightly alters the position of one of the chairs. He takes an ornament from the chimney-piece and blows the dust from it. A Footman comes in*] Oh, George! See if you can find Mrs. Cheney, and ask her if she'd be good enough to come here.

FOOTMAN: Very good, sir.
[*The* Footman *turns to go*]
ARNOLD: Who is supposed to look after this room?

FOOTMAN: I don't know, sir.

ARNOLD: I wish when they dust they'd take care to replace the things exactly as they were before.

FOOTMAN: Yes, sir.

ARNOLD: [*Dismissing him*] All right.
[*The* Footman *goes out. Arnold goes again to the window and calls*]
ARNOLD: Elizabeth! [*He sees Mrs. Shenstone*] Oh, Anna, do you know where Elizabeth is?

[Mrs. Shenstone *comes in from the garden. She is a woman of forty, pleasant, and of elegant appearance*]

ANNA: Isn't she playing tennis?

ARNOLD: No, I've been down to the tennis court. Something very tiresome has happened.

ANNA: Oh?

ARNOLD: I wonder where the deuce she is.

ANNA: When do you expect Lord Porteous and Lady Kitty?

ARNOLD: They're motoring down in time for luncheon.

ANNA: Are you sure you want me to be here? It's not too late yet, you know. I can have my things packed and catch a train for somewhere or other.

ARNOLD: No, of course we want you. It'll make it so much easier if there are people here. It was exceedingly kind of you to come.

ANNA: Oh, nonsense!

ARNOLD: And I think it was a good thing to have Teddie Luton down.

ANNA: He is so breezy, isn't he?

ARNOLD: Yes, that's his great asset. I don't know that he's very intelligent, but, you know, there are occasions when you want a bull in a china shop. I sent one of the servants to find Elizabeth.

ANNA: I daresay she's putting on her shoes. She and Teddie were going to have a single.

ARNOLD: It can't take all this time to change one's shoes.

ANNA: [*With a smile*] One can't change one's shoes without powdering one's nose, you know.

[Elizabeth *comes in. She is a very pretty creature in the early twenties. She wears a light summer frock*]

ARNOLD: My dear, I've been hunting for you everywhere. What *have* you been doing?

ELIZABETH: Nothing! I've been standing on my head.

ARNOLD: My father's here.

ELIZABETH: [*Startled*] Where?

ARNOLD: At the cottage. He arrived last night.

ELIZABETH: Damn!

ARNOLD: [*Good-humoredly*] I wish you wouldn't say that, Elizabeth.

ELIZABETH: If you're not going to say "Damn" when a thing's damnable, when are you going to say "Damn"?

ARNOLD: I should have thought you could say, "Oh, bother!" or something like that.

ELIZABETH: But that wouldn't express my sentiments. Besides, at that speech day when you were giving away the prizes you said there were no synonyms in the English language.

ANNA: [*Smiling*] Oh, Elizabeth! It's very unfair to expect a politician to live in private up to the statements he makes in public.

ARNOLD: I'm always willing to stand by anything I've said. There *are* no synonyms in the English language.

ELIZABETH: In that case, I shall be regretfully forced to continue to say "Damn" whenever I feel like it.

[*Edward Luton shows himself at the window. He is an attractive youth in flannels*]

TEDDIE: I say, what about this tennis?

ELIZABETH: Come in. We're having a scene.

TEDDIE: [*Entering*] How splendid! What about?

ELIZABETH: The English language.

TEDDIE: Don't tell me you've been splitting your infinitives.

ARNOLD: [*With the shadow of a frown*] I wish you'd be serious, Elizabeth. The situation is none too pleasant.

ANNA: I think Teddie and I had better make ourselves scarce.

ELIZABETH: Nonsense! You're both in it. If there's going to be any unpleasantness we want your moral support. That's why we asked you to come.

TEDDIE: And I thought I'd been asked for my blue eyes.

ELIZABETH: Vain beast! And they happen to be brown.

TEDDIE: Is anything up?

ELIZABETH: Arnold's father arrived last night.

TEDDIE: Did he, by Jove! I thought he was in Paris.

ARNOLD: So did we all. He told me he'd be there for the next month.

ANNA: Have you seen him?

ARNOLD: No! He rang me up. It's a mercy he had a telephone put in the cottage. It would have been a pretty kettle of fish if he'd just walked in.

ELIZABETH: Did you tell him Lady Catherine was coming?

ARNOLD: Of course not. I was flabbergasted to know he was here. And then I thought we'd better talk it over first.

ELIZABETH: Is he coming along here?

ARNOLD: Yes. He suggested it, and I couldn't think of any excuse to prevent him.

TEDDIE: Couldn't you put the other people off?

ARNOLD: They're coming by car. They may be here any minute. It's too late to do that.

ELIZABETH: Besides, it would be beastly.

ARNOLD: I knew it was silly to have them here. Elizabeth insisted.

ELIZABETH: After all, she *is* your mother, Arnold.

ARNOLD: That meant precious little to her when she —went away. You can't imagine it means very much to me now.

ELIZABETH: It's thirty years ago. It seems so absurd to bear malice after all that time.

ARNOLD: I don't bear malice, but the fact remains that she did me the most irreparable harm. I can find no excuse for her.

ELIZABETH: Have you ever tried to?

ARNOLD: My dear Elizabeth, it's no good going over all that again. The facts are lamentably simple. She had a husband who adored her, a wonderful position, all the money she could want, and a child of five. And she ran away with a married man.

ELIZABETH: Lady Porteous is not a very attractive woman, Arnold. [*To Anna*] Do you know her?

ANNA: [*Smiling*] "Forbidding" is the word, I think.

ARNOLD: If you're going to make little jokes about it, I have nothing more to say.

ANNA: I'm sorry, Arnold.

ELIZABETH: Perhaps your mother couldn't help herself—if she was in love?

ARNOLD: And had no sense of honor, duty, or decency? Oh, yes, under those circumstances you can explain a great deal.

ELIZABETH: That's not a very pretty way to speak of your mother.

ARNOLD: I can't look on her as my mother.

ELIZABETH: What you can't get over is that she didn't think of you. Some of us are more mother and some of us more woman. It gives me a little thrill when I think that she loved that man so much. She sacrificed her name, her position, and her child to him.

ARNOLD: You really can't expect the said child to have any great affection for the mother who treated him like that.

ELIZABETH: No, I don't think I do. But I think it's a pity after all these years that you shouldn't be friends.

ARNOLD: I wonder if you realize what it was to grow up under the shadow of that horrible scandal. Everywhere, at school, and at Oxford, and afterward in London, I was always the son of Lady Kitty Cheney. Oh, it was cruel, cruel!

ELIZABETH: Yes, I know, Arnold. It was beastly for you.

ARNOLD: It would have been bad enough if it had been an ordinary case, but the position of the people made it ten times worse. My father was in the House then, and Porteous—he hadn't succeeded to the title—was in the House too; he was

Under-Secretary for Foreign Affairs, and he was very much in the public eye.

ANNA: My father always used to say he was the ablest man in the party. Everyone was expecting him to be Prime Minister.

ARNOLD: You can imagine what a boon it was to the British public. They hadn't had such a treat for a generation. The most popular song of the day was about my mother. Did you ever hear it? "Naughty Lady Kitty. Thought it such a pity . . ."

ELIZABETH: [*Interrupting*] Oh, Arnold, don't!

ARNOLD: And then they never let people forget them. If they'd lived quietly in Florence and not made a fuss the scandal would have died down. But those constant actions between Lord and Lady Porteous kept on reminding everyone.

TEDDIE: What were they having actions about?

ARNOLD: Of course my father divorced his wife, but Lady Porteous refused to divorce Porteous. He tried to force her by refusing to support her and turning her out of her house, and heaven knows what. They were constantly wrangling in the law courts.

ANNA: I think it was monstrous of Lady Porteous.

ARNOLD: She knew he wanted to marry my mother, and she hated my mother. You can't blame her.

ANNA: It must have been very difficult for them.

ARNOLD: That's why they've lived in Florence. Porteous has money. They found people there who were willing to accept the situation.

ELIZABETH: This is the first time they've ever come to England.

ARNOLD: My father will have to be told, Elizabeth.

ELIZABETH: Yes.

ANNA: [*To* Elizabeth] Has he ever spoken to you about Lady Kitty?

ELIZABETH: Never.

ARNOLD: I don't think her name has passed his lips since she ran away from this house thirty years ago.

TEDDIE: Oh, they lived here?

ARNOLD: Naturally. There was a houseparty, and one evening neither Porteous nor my mother came down to dinner. The rest of them waited. They couldn't make it out. My father sent up to my mother's room, and a note was found on the pincushion.

ELIZABETH: [*With a faint smile*] That's what they did in the Dark Ages.

ARNOLD: I think he took a dislike to this house from that horrible night. He never lived here again, and when I married he handed the place over to me. He just has a cottage now on the estate that he comes to when he feels inclined.

ELIZABETH: It's been very nice for us.

ARNOLD: I owe everything to my father. I don't think he'll ever forgive me for asking these people to come here.

ELIZABETH: I'm going to take all the blame on myself, Arnold.

ARNOLD: [*Irritably*] The situation was embarrassing enough anyhow. I don't know how I ought to treat them.

ELIZABETH: Don't you think that'll settle itself when you see them?

ARNOLD: After all, they're my guests. I shall try and behave like a gentleman.

ELIZABETH: I wouldn't. We haven't got central heating.

ARNOLD: [*Taking no notice*] Will she expect me to kiss her?

ELIZABETH: [*With a smile*] Surely.

ARNOLD: It always makes me uncomfortable when people are effusive.

ANNA: But I can't understand why you never saw her before.

ARNOLD: I believe she tried to see me when I was little, but my father thought it better she shouldn't.

ANNA: Yes, but when you were grown up?

ARNOLD: She was always in Italy. I never went to Italy.

ELIZABETH: It seems to me so pathetic that if you saw one another in the street you wouldn't recognize each other.

ARNOLD: Is it my fault?

ELIZABETH: You've promised to be very gentle with her and very kind.

ARNOLD: The mistake was asking Porteous to come too. It looks as though we condoned the whole thing. And how am I to treat him? Am I to shake him by the hand and slap him on the back? He absolutely ruined my father's life.

ELIZABETH: [*Smiling*] How much would you give for a nice motor accident that prevented them from coming?

ARNOLD: I let you persuade me against my better judgment, and I've regretted it ever since.

ELIZABETH: [*Good-humoredly*] I think it's very lucky that Anna and Teddie are here. I don't foresee a very successful party.

ARNOLD: I'm going to do my best. I gave you my promise and I shall keep it. But I can't answer for my father.

ANNA: Here is your father.

[Mr. Champion-Cheney *shows himself at one of the French windows*]

C.-C.: May I come in through the window, or shall I have myself announced by a supercilious flunkey?

ELIZABETH: Come in. We've been expecting you.

C.-C.: Impatiently, I hope, my dear child.

[Mr. Champion-Cheney *is a tall man in the early sixties, spare, with a fine head of gray hair and an intelligent, somewhat ascetic face. He is very carefully dressed. He is a man who makes the most of himself. He bears his years jauntily. He kisses* Elizabeth *and then holds out his hand to* Arnold]

ELIZABETH: We thought you'd be in Paris for another month.

c.-c.: How are you, Arnold? I always reserve to my-self the privilege of changing my mind. It's the only one elderly gentlemen share with pretty women.

ELIZABETH: You know Anna.

c.-c.: [Shaking hands with her] Of course I do. How very nice to see you here! Are you staying long?

ANNA: As long as I'm welcome.

ELIZABETH: And this is Mr. Luton.

c.-c.: How do you do? Do you play bridge?

LUTON: I do.

c.-c.: Capital. Do you declare without top honors?

LUTON: Never.

c.-c.: Of such is the kingdom of heaven. I see that you are a good young man.

LUTON: But, like the good in general, I am poor.

c.-c.: Never mind; if your principles are right, you can play ten shillings a hundred without danger. I never play less, and I never play more.

ARNOLD: And you—are going to stay long, Father?

c.-c.: To luncheon, if you'll have me.

[Arnold gives Elizabeth a harassed look]

ELIZABETH: That'll be jolly.

ARNOLD: I didn't mean that. Of course you're going to stay for luncheon. I meant, how long are you going to stay down here?

c.-c.: A week.

[There is a moment's pause. Every-one but Champion-Cheney is slightly embarrassed]

TEDDIE: I think we'd better chuck our tennis.

ELIZABETH: Yes. I want my father-in-law to tell me what they're wearing in Paris this week.

TEDDIE: I'll go and put the rackets away.

[Teddie goes out]

ARNOLD: It's nearly one o'clock, Elizabeth.

ELIZABETH: I didn't know it was so late.

ANNA: [To Arnold] I wonder if I can persuade you to take a turn in the garden before luncheon.

ARNOLD: [Jumping at the idea] I'd love it. [Anna goes out of the windows, and as he follows her he stops irresolutely] I want you to look at this chair I've just got. I think it's rather good.

c.-c.: Charming.

ARNOLD: About 1750, I should say. Good design, isn't it? It hasn't been restored or anything.

c.-c.: Very pretty.

ARNOLD: I think it was a good buy, don't you?

c.-c.: Oh, my dear boy! You know I'm entirely ignorant about these things.

ARNOLD: It's exactly my period . . . I shall see you at luncheon, then. [He follows Anna through the window]

c.-c.: Who is that young man?

ELIZABETH: Mr. Luton. He's only just been de-mobilized. He's the manager of a rubber estate in the F. M. S.

c.-c.: And what are the F. M. S. when they're at home?

ELIZABETH: The Federated Malay States. He joined up at the beginning of the war. He's just going back there.

c.-c.: And why have we been left alone in this very marked manner?

ELIZABETH: Have we? I didn't notice it.

c.-c.: I suppose it's difficult for the young to realize that one may be old without being a fool.

ELIZABETH: I never thought you that. Everyone knows you're very intelligent.

c.-c.: They certainly ought to by now. I've told them often enough. Are you a little nervous?

ELIZABETH: Let me feel my pulse. [She puts her finger on her wrist] It's perfectly regular.

c.-c.: When I suggested staying to luncheon Arnold looked exactly like a dose of castor oil.

ELIZABETH: I wish you'd sit down.

c.-c.: Will it make it easier for you? [He takes a chair] You have evidently something very disa-greeable to say to me.

ELIZABETH: You won't be cross with me?

c.-c.: How old are you?

ELIZABETH: Twenty-five.

c.-c.: I'm never cross with a woman under thirty.

ELIZABETH: Oh, then I've got ten years.

c.-c.: Mathematics?

ELIZABETH: No. Paint.

c.-c.: Well?

ELIZABETH: [Reflectively] I think it would be easier if I sat on your knees.

c.-c.: That is a pleasing taste of yours, but you must take care not to put on weight.

[She sits down on his knees]

ELIZABETH: Am I bony?

c.-c.: On the contrary. . . . I'm listening.

ELIZABETH: Lady Catherine's coming here.

c.-c.: Who's Lady Catherine?

ELIZABETH: Your—Arnold's mother.

c.-c.: Is she?

[He withdraws himself a little and Eliza-beth gets up]

ELIZABETH: You mustn't blame Arnold. It's my fault. I insisted. He was against it. I nagged till he gave way. And then I wrote and asked her to come.

c.-c.: I didn't know you knew her.

ELIZABETH: I don't. But I heard she was in London. She's staying at Claridge's. It seemed so heartless not to take the smallest notice of her.

c.-c.: When is she coming?

ELIZABETH: We're expecting her in time for luncheon.

c.-c.: As soon as that? I understand the embar-rassment.

ELIZABETH: You see, we never expected you to be here. You said you'd be in Paris for another month.

c.-c.: My dear child, this is your house. There's no reason why you shouldn't ask whom you please to stay with you.

ELIZABETH: After all, whatever her faults, she's Arnold's mother. It seemed so unnatural that they should never see one another. My heart ached for that poor lonely woman.

c.-c.: I never heard that she was lonely, and she certainly isn't poor.

ELIZABETH: And there's something else. I couldn't ask her by herself. It would have been so—so insulting. I asked Lord Porteous, too.

c.-c.: I see.

ELIZABETH: I daresay you'd rather not meet them.

c.-c.: I daresay they'd rather not meet me. I shall get a capital luncheon at the cottage. I've noticed you always get the best food if you come in unexpectedly and have the same as they're having in the servants' hall.

ELIZABETH: No one's ever talked to me about Lady Kitty. It's always been a subject that everyone has avoided. I've never even seen a photograph of her.

c.-c.: The house was full of them when she left. I think I told the butler to throw them in the dustbin. She was very much photographed.

ELIZABETH: Won't you tell me what she was like?

c.-c.: She was very like you, Elizabeth, only she had dark hair instead of red.

ELIZABETH: Poor dear! It must be quite white now.

c.-c.: I daresay. She was a pretty little thing.

ELIZABETH: But she was one of the great beauties of her day. They say she was lovely.

c.-c.: She had the most adorable little nose, like yours. . . .

ELIZABETH: D'you like my nose?

c.-c.: And she was very dainty, with a beautiful little figure; very light on her feet. She was like a *marquise* in an old French comedy. Yes, she was lovely.

ELIZABETH: And I'm sure she's lovely still.

c.-c.: She's no chicken, you know.

ELIZABETH: You can't expect me to look at it as you and Arnold do. When you've loved as she's loved you may grow old, but you grow old beautifully.

c.-c.: You're very romantic.

ELIZABETH: If everyone hadn't made such a mystery of it I daresay I shouldn't feel as I do. I know she did a great wrong to you and a great wrong to Arnold. I'm willing to acknowledge that.

c.-c.: I'm sure it's very kind of you.

ELIZABETH: But she loved and she dared. Romance is such an elusive thing. You read of it in books, but it's seldom you see it face to face. I can't help it if it thrills me.

c.-c.: I am painfully aware that the husband in these cases is not a romantic object.

ELIZABETH: She had the world at her feet. You were rich. She was a figure in society. And she gave up everything for love.

c.-c.: [*Dryly*] I'm beginning to suspect it wasn't only for her sake and for Arnold's that you asked her to come here.

ELIZABETH: I seem to know her already. I think her face is a little sad, for a love like that doesn't leave you gay, it leaves you grave, but I think her pale face is unlined. It's like a child's.

c.-c.: My dear, how you let your imagination run away with you!

ELIZABETH: I imagine her slight and frail.

c.-c.: Frail, certainly.

ELIZABETH: With beautiful thin hands and white hair. I've pictured her so often in that Renaissance Palace that they live in, with old Masters on the walls and lovely carved things all round, sitting in a black silk dress with old lace round her neck and old-fashioned diamonds. You see, I never knew my mother; she died when I was a baby. You can't confide in aunts with huge families of their own. I want Arnold's mother to be a mother to me. I've got so much to say to her.

c.-c.: Are you happy with Arnold?

ELIZABETH: Why shouldn't I be?

c.-c.: Why haven't you got any babies?

ELIZABETH: Give us a little time. We've only been married three years.

c.-c.: I wonder what Hughie is like now!

ELIZABETH: Lord Porteous?

c.-c.: He wore his clothes better than any man in London. You know he'd have been Prime Minister if he'd remained in politics.

ELIZABETH: What was he like then?

c.-c.: He was a nice-looking fellow. Fine horseman. I suppose there was something very fascinating about him. Yellow hair and blue eyes, you know. He had a very good figure. I liked him. I was his parliamentary secretary. He was Arnold's godfather.

ELIZABETH: I know.

c.-c.: I wonder if he ever regrets!

ELIZABETH: I wouldn't.

c.-c.: Well, I must be strolling back to my cottage.

ELIZABETH: You're not angry with me?

c.-c.: Not a bit.

[*She puts up her face for him to kiss. He kisses her on both cheeks and then goes out. In a moment* Teddie *is seen at the window*]

TEDDIE: I saw the old blighter go.

ELIZABETH: Come in.

TEDDIE: Everything all right?

ELIZABETH: Oh, quite, as far as he's concerned. He's going to keep out of the way.

TEDDIE: Was it beastly?

ELIZABETH: No, he made it very easy for me. He's a nice old thing.

TEDDIE: You were rather scared.

ELIZABETH: A little. I am still. I don't know why.

TEDDIE: I guessed you were. I thought I'd come and give you a little moral support. It's ripping here, isn't it?

ELIZABETH: It is rather nice.

TEDDIE: It'll be jolly to think of it when I'm back in the F. M. S.

ELIZABETH: Aren't you homesick sometimes?

TEDDIE: Oh, everyone is now and then, you know.

ELIZABETH: You could have got a job in England if you'd wanted to, couldn't you?

TEDDIE: Oh, but I love it out there. England's ripping to come back to, but I couldn't live here now. It's like a woman you're desperately in love with as long as you don't see her, but when you're with her she maddens you so that you can't bear her.

ELIZABETH: [Smiling] What's wrong with England?

TEDDIE: I don't think anything's wrong with England. I expect something's wrong with me. I've been away too long. England seems to me full of people doing things they don't want to because other people expect it of them.

ELIZABETH: Isn't that what you call a high degree of civilization?

TEDDIE: People seem to me so insincere. When you go to parties in London they're all babbling about art, and you feel that in their hearts they don't care two-pence about it. They read the books that everybody is talking about because they don't want to be out of it. In the F. M. S. we don't get very many books, and we read those we have over and over again. They mean so much to us. I don't think the people over there are half so clever as the people at home, but one gets to know them better. You see, there are so few of us that we have to make the best of one another.

ELIZABETH: I imagine that frills are not much worn in the F. M. S. It must be a comfort.

TEDDIE: It's not much good being pretentious where everyone knows exactly who you are and what your income is.

ELIZABETH: I don't think you want too much sincerity in society. It would be like an iron girder in a house of cards.

TEDDIE: And then, you know, the place is ripping. You get used to a blue sky and you miss it in England.

ELIZABETH: What do you do with yourself all the time?

TEDDIE: Oh, one works like blazes. You have to be a pretty hefty fellow to be a planter. And then there's ripping bathing. You know, it's lovely, with palm trees all along the beach. And there's shooting. And now and then we have a little dance to a gramophone.

ELIZABETH: [Pretending to tease him] I think you've got a young woman out there, Teddie.

TEDDIE: [Vehemently] Oh, no!

[She is a little taken aback by the earnestness of his disclaimer. There is a moment's silence, then she recovers herself]

ELIZABETH: But you'll have to marry and settle down one of these days, you know.

TEDDIE: I want to, but it's not a thing you can do lightly.

ELIZABETH: I don't know why there more than elsewhere.

TEDDIE: In England if people don't get on they go their own ways and jog along after a fashion. In a place like that you're thrown a great deal on your own resources.

ELIZABETH: Of course.

TEDDIE: Lots of girls come out because they think they're going to have a good time. But if they're empty-headed, then they're just faced with their own emptiness and they're done. If their husbands can afford it they go home and settle down as grass-widows.

ELIZABETH: I've met them. They seem to find it a very pleasant occupation.

TEDDIE: It's rotten for their husbands, though.

ELIZABETH: And if the husbands can't afford it?

TEDDIE: Oh, then they tipple.

ELIZABETH: It's not a very alluring prospect.

TEDDIE: But if the woman's the right sort she wouldn't exchange it for any life in the world. When all's said and done it's we who've made the Empire.

ELIZABETH: What sort is the right sort?

TEDDIE: A woman of courage and endurance and sincerity. Of course, it's hopeless unless she's in love with her husband.

[He is looking at her earnestly and she, raising her eyes, gives him a long look. There is silence between them]

TEDDIE: My house stands on the side of a hill, and the coconut trees wind down to the shore. Azaleas grow in my garden, and camellias, and all sorts of ripping flowers. And in front of me is the winding coast line, and then the blue sea. [A pause] Do you know that I'm awfully in love with you?

ELIZABETH: [Gravely] I wasn't quite sure. I wondered.

TEDDIE: And you? [She nods slowly] I've never kissed you.

ELIZABETH: I don't want you to.

[They look at one another steadily. They are both grave. Arnold comes in hurriedly]

ARNOLD: They're coming, Elizabeth.

ELIZABETH: [As though returning from a distant world] Who?

ARNOLD: [Impatiently] My dear! My mother, of course. The car is just coming up the drive.

TEDDIE: Would you like me to clear out?

ARNOLD: No, no! For goodness' sake stay.

ELIZABETH: We'd better go and meet them, Arnold.

ARNOLD: No, no; I think they'd much better be shown in. I feel simply sick with nervousness.

[Anna comes in from the garden]

ANNA: Your guests have arrived.

ELIZABETH: Yes, I know.

ARNOLD: I've given orders that luncheon should be served at once.

ELIZABETH: Why? It's not half-past one already, is it?

ARNOLD: I thought it would help. When you don't know exactly what to say you can always eat.

[*The* Butler *comes in and announces*]

BUTLER: Lady Catherine Champion-Cheney! Lord Porteous!

[*Lady Kitty comes in followed by* Porteous, *and the* Butler *goes out. Lady Kitty is a gay little lady, with dyed red hair and painted cheeks. She is somewhat outrageously dressed. She never forgets that she has been a pretty woman and she still behaves as if she were twenty-five.* Lord Porteous *is a very bald, elderly gentleman in loose, rather eccentric clothes. He is snappy and gruff. This is not at all the couple that* Elizabeth *expected, and for a moment she stares at them with round, startled eyes.* Lady Kitty *goes up to her with outstretched hands*]

LADY KITTY: Elizabeth! Elizabeth! [*She kisses her effusively*] What an adorable creature. [*Turning to* Porteous] Hughie, isn't she adorable?

PORTEOUS: [*With a grunt*] Ugh!

[Elizabeth, *smiling now, turns to him and gives him her hand*]

ELIZABETH: How d'you do?

PORTEOUS: Damnable road you've got down here. How d'you do, my dear? Why d'you have such damnable roads in England?

[*Lady Kitty's eyes fall on* Teddie *and she goes up to him with her arms thrown back, prepared to throw them round him*]

LADY KITTY: My boy, my boy! I should have known you anywhere!

ELIZABETH: [*Hastily*] That's Arnold.

LADY KITTY: [*Without a moment's hesitation*] The image of his father! I should have known him anywhere! [*She throws her arms round his neck*] My boy, my boy!

PORTEOUS: [*With a grunt*] Ugh!

LADY KITTY: Tell me, would you have known me again? Have I changed?

ARNOLD: I was only five, you know, when——when you . . .

LADY KITTY: [*Emotionally*] I remember as if it was yesterday. I went up into your room. [*With a sudden change of manner*] By the way, I always thought that nurse drank. Did you ever find out if she really did?

PORTEOUS: How the devil can you expect him to know that, Kitty?

LADY KITTY: You've never had a child, Hughie; how can you tell what they know and what they don't?

ELIZABETH: [*Coming to the rescue*] This is Arnold, Lord Porteous.

PORTEOUS: [*Shaking hands with him*] How d'you do? I knew your father.

ARNOLD: Yes.

PORTEOUS: Alive still?

ARNOLD: Yes.

PORTEOUS: He must be getting on. Is he well?

ARNOLD: Very.

PORTEOUS: Ugh! Takes care of himself, I suppose. I'm not at all well. This damned climate doesn't agree with me.

ELIZABETH: [*To Lady Kitty*] This is Mrs. Shenstone. And this is Mr. Luton. I hope you don't mind a very small party.

LADY KITTY: [*Shaking hands with* Anna *and* Teddie] Oh, no, I shall enjoy it. I used to give enormous parties here. Political, you know. How nice you've made this room!

ELIZABETH: Oh, that's Arnold.

ARNOLD: [*Nervously*] D'you like this chair? I've just bought it. It's exactly my period.

PORTEOUS: [*Bluntly*] It's a fake.

ARNOLD: [*Indignantly*] I don't think it is for a minute.

PORTEOUS: The legs are not right.

ARNOLD: I don't know how you can say that. If there is anything right about it, it's the legs.

LADY KITTY: I'm sure they're right.

PORTEOUS: You know nothing whatever about it, Kitty.

LADY KITTY: That's what you think. I think it's a beautiful chair. Hepplewhite?

ARNOLD: No, Sheraton.

LADY KITTY: Oh, I know. "The School for Scandal."

PORTEOUS: Sheraton, my dear. Sheraton.

LADY KITTY: Yes, that's what I say. I acted the screen scene at some amateur theatricals in Florence, and Ermeto Novelli, the great Italian tragedian, told me he'd never seen a Lady Teazle like me.

PORTEOUS: Ugh!

LADY KITTY: [*To Elizabeth*] Do you act?

ELIZABETH: Oh, I couldn't. I should be too nervous.

LADY KITTY: I'm never nervous. I'm a born actress. Of course, if I had my time over again I'd go on the stage. You know, it's extraordinary how they keep young. Actresses, I mean. I think it's because they're always playing different parts. Hughie, do you think Arnold takes after me or after his father? Of course I think he's the very image of me. Arnold, I think I ought to tell you that I was received into the Catholic Church last winter. I've been thinking about it for years, and the last time we were at Monte Carlo I met such a nice monsignore. I told him what my difficulties were and he was too wonderful. I knew Hughie wouldn't approve, so I kept it a secret. [*To Elizabeth*] Are you interested in religion? I think it's too wonderful. We must have a long talk about it one of these days. [*Pointing to her frock*] Callot?

ELIZABETH: No, Worth.

LADY KITTY: I knew it was either Worth or Callot. Of course, it's line that's the important thing. I go to Worth myself, and I always say to him, "Line, my dear Worth, line." What *is* the matter, Hughie?

PORTEOUS: These new teeth of mine are so damned uncomfortable.

LADY KITTY: Men are extraordinary. They can't stand the smallest discomfort. Why, a woman's life is uncomfortable from the moment she gets up in the morning till the moment she goes to bed at night. And d'you think it's comfortable to sleep with a mask on your face?

PORTEOUS: They don't seem to hold up properly.

LADY KITTY: Well, that's not the fault of your teeth. That's the fault of your gums.

PORTEOUS: Damned rotten dentist. That's what's the matter.

LADY KITTY: I thought he was a very nice dentist. He told me *my* teeth would last till I was fifty. He has a Chinese room. It's so interesting; while he scrapes your teeth he tells you all about the dear Empress Dowager. Are you interested in China? I think it's too wonderful. You know they've cut off their pigtails. I think it's such a pity. They were so picturesque.

[*The Butler comes in*]

BUTLER: Luncheon is served, sir.

ELIZABETH: Would you like to see your rooms?

PORTEOUS: We can see our rooms after luncheon.

LADY KITTY: I must powder my nose, Hughie.

PORTEOUS: Powder it down here.

LADY KITTY: I never saw anyone so inconsiderate.

PORTEOUS: You'll keep us waiting half an hour. I know you.

LADY KITTY: [*Fumbling in her bag*] Oh, well, peace at any price, as Lord Beaconsfield said.

PORTEOUS: He said a lot of damned silly things, Kitty, but he never said that.

[*Lady Kitty's face changes. Perplexity is followed by dismay, and dismay by consternation*]

LADY KITTY: Oh!

ELIZABETH: What is the matter?

LADY KITTY: [*With anguish*] My lip-stick!

ELIZABETH: Can't you find it?

LADY KITTY: I had it in the car. Hughie, you remember that I had it in the car.

PORTEOUS: I don't remember anything about it.

LADY KITTY: Don't be so stupid, Hughie. Why, when we came through the gates I said: "My home, my home!" and I took it out and put some on my lips.

ELIZABETH: Perhaps you dropped it in the car.

LADY KITTY: For heaven's sake send some one to look for it.

ARNOLD: I'll ring.

LADY KITTY: I'm absolutely lost without my lip-stick. Lend me yours, darling, will you?

ELIZABETH: I'm awfully sorry. I'm afraid I haven't got one.

LADY KITTY: Do you mean to say you don't use a lip-stick?

ELIZABETH: Never.

PORTEOUS: Look at her lips. What the devil d'you think she wants muck like that for?

LADY KITTY: Oh, my dear, what a mistake you make! You *must* use a lip-stick. It's so good for the lips. Men like it, you know. I couldn't *live* without a lip-stick.

[*Champion-Cheney appears at the window holding in his upstretched hand a little gold case*]

c.-c.: [*As he comes in*] Has anyone here lost a diminutive utensil containing, unless I am mistaken, a favorite preparation for the toilet?

[*Arnold and Elizabeth are thunderstruck at his appearance and even Teddie and Anna are taken aback. But Lady Kitty is overjoyed*]

LADY KITTY: My lip-stick!

c.-c.: I found it in the drive and I ventured to bring it in.

LADY KITTY: It's Saint Anthony. I said a little prayer to him when I was hunting in my bag.

PORTEOUS: Saint Anthony be blowed! It's Clive, by God!

LADY KITTY: [*Startled, her attention suddenly turning from the lip-stick*] Clive!

c.-c.: You didn't recognize me. It's many years since we met.

LADY KITTY: My poor Clive, your hair has gone quite white!

c.-c.: [*Holding out his hand*] I hope you had a pleasant journey down from London.

LADY KITTY: [*Offering him her cheek*] You may kiss me, Clive.

c.-c.: [*Kissing her*] You don't mind, Hughie?

PORTEOUS: [*With a grunt*] Ugh!

c.-c.: [*Going up to him cordially*] And how are you, my dear Hughie?

PORTEOUS: Damned rheumatic if you want to know. Filthy climate you have in this country.

c.-c.: Aren't you going to shake hands with me, Hughie?

PORTEOUS: I have no objection to shaking hands with you.

c.-c.: You've aged, my poor Hughie.

PORTEOUS: Some one was asking me how old you were the other day.

c.-c.: Were they surprised when you told them?

PORTEOUS: Surprised! They wondered you weren't dead.

[*The Butler comes in*]

BUTLER: Did you ring, sir?

ARNOLD: No. Oh, yes, I did. It doesn't matter now.

c.-c.: [*As the Butler is going*] One moment. My dear Elizabeth, I've come to throw myself on your mercy. My servants are busy with their own affairs. There's not a thing for me to eat in my cottage.

ELIZABETH: Oh, but we shall be delighted if you'll lunch with us.

C.-C.: It either means that or my immediate death from starvation. You don't mind, Arnold?

ARNOLD: My dear father!

ELIZABETH: [To the Butler] Mr. Cheney will lunch here.

BUTLER: Very good, ma'am.

C.-C.: [To Lady Kitty] And what do you think of Arnold?

LADY KITTY: I adore him.

C.-C.: He's grown, hasn't he? But then you'd expect him to do that in thirty years.

ARNOLD: For God's sake let's go in to lunch, Elizabeth!

Act II

The Scene is the same as in the preceding act. It is afternoon. When the curtain rises Porteous *and* Lady Kitty, Anna *and* Teddie *are playing bridge.* Elizabeth *and* Champion-Cheney *are watching.* Porteous *and* Lady Kitty *are partners.*

C.-C.: When will Arnold be back, Elizabeth?

ELIZABETH: Soon, I think.

C.-C.: Is he addressing a meeting?

ELIZABETH: No, it's only a conference with his agent and one or two constituents.

PORTEOUS: [Irritably] How anyone can be expected to play bridge when people are shouting at the top of their voices all round them, I for one cannot understand.

ELIZABETH: [Smiling] I'm so sorry.

ANNA: I can see your hand, Lord Porteous.

PORTEOUS: It may help you.

LADY KITTY: I've told you over and over again to hold your cards up. It ruins one's game when one can't help seeing one's opponent's hand.

PORTEOUS: One isn't obliged to look.

LADY KITTY: What was Arnold's majority at the last election?

ELIZABETH: Seven hundred and something.

C.-C.: He'll have to fight for it if he wants to keep his seat next time.

PORTEOUS: Are we playing bridge, or talking politics?

LADY KITTY: I never find that conversation interferes with my game.

PORTEOUS: You certainly play no worse when you talk than when you hold your tongue.

LADY KITTY: I think that's a very offensive thing to say, Hughie. Just because I don't play the same game as you do you think I can't play.

PORTEOUS: I'm glad you acknowledge it's not the same game as I play. But why in God's name do you call it bridge?

C.-C.: I agree with Kitty. I hate people who play bridge as though they were at a funeral and knew their feet were getting wet.

PORTEOUS: Of course you take Kitty's part.

LADY KITTY: That's the least he can do.

C.-C.: I have a naturally cheerful disposition.

PORTEOUS: You've never had anything to sour it.

LADY KITTY: I don't know what you mean by that, Hughie.

PORTEOUS: [Trying to contain himself] Must you trump my ace?

LADY KITTY: [Innocently] Oh, was that your ace, darling?

PORTEOUS: [Furiously] Yes, it was my ace.

LADY KITTY: Oh, well, it was the only trump I had. I shouldn't have made it anyway.

PORTEOUS: You needn't have told them that. Now she knows exactly what I've got.

LADY KITTY: She knew before.

PORTEOUS: How could she know?

LADY KITTY: She said she'd seen your hand.

ANNA: Oh, I didn't. I said I could see it.

LADY KITTY: Well, I naturally supposed that if she could see it she did.

PORTEOUS: Really, Kitty, you have the most extraordinary ideas.

C.-C.: Not at all. If anyone is such a fool as to show me his hand, of course I look at it.

PORTEOUS: [Fuming] If you study the etiquette of bridge, you'll discover that onlookers are expected not to interfere with the game.

C.-C.: My dear Hughie, this is a matter of ethics, not of bridge.

ANNA: Anyhow, I get the game. And rubber.

TEDDIE: I claim a revoke.

PORTEOUS: Who revoked?

TEDDIE: You did.

PORTEOUS: Nonsense. I've never revoked in my life.

TEDDIE: I'll show you. [He turns over the tricks to show the faces of the cards] You threw away a club on the third heart trick and you had another heart.

PORTEOUS: I never had more than two hearts.

TEDDIE: Oh, yes, you had. Look here. That's the card you played on the last trick but one.

LADY KITTY: [Delighted to catch him out] There's no doubt about it, Hughie. You revoked.

PORTEOUS: I tell you I did not revoke. I never revoke.

C.-C.: You did, Hughie. I wondered what on earth you were doing.

PORTEOUS: I don't know how anyone can be expected not to revoke when there's this confounded chatter going on all the time.

TEDDIE: Well, that's another hundred to us.

PORTEOUS: [To Champion-Cheney] I wish you wouldn't breathe down my neck. I never can play bridge when there's somebody breathing down my neck.

[*The party have risen from the bridge-table, and they scatter about the room*]

ANNA: Well, I'm going to take a book and lie down in the hammock till it's time to dress.

TEDDIE: [*Who has been adding up*] I'll put it down in the book, shall I?

PORTEOUS: [*Who has not moved, setting out the cards for a patience*] Yes, yes, put it down. I never revoke.

[*Anna goes out*]

LADY KITTY: Would you like to come for a little stroll, Hughie?

PORTEOUS: What for?

LADY KITTY: Exercise.

PORTEOUS: I hate exercise.

C.-C.: [*Looking at the patience*] The seven goes on the eight.

[*Porteous takes no notice*]

LADY KITTY: The seven goes on the eight, Hughie.

PORTEOUS: I don't choose to put the seven on the eight.

C.-C.: That knave goes on the queen.

PORTEOUS: I'm not blind, thank you.

LADY KITTY: The three goes on the four.

C.-C.: All these go over.

PORTEOUS: [*Furiously*] Am I playing this patience, or are you playing it?

LADY KITTY: But you're missing everything.

PORTEOUS: That's my business.

C.-C.: It's no good losing your temper over it, Hughie.

PORTEOUS: Go away, both of you. You irritate me.

LADY KITTY: We were only trying to help you, Hughie.

PORTEOUS: I don't want to be helped. I want to do it by myself.

LADY KITTY: I think your manners are perfectly deplorable, Hughie.

PORTEOUS: It's simply maddening when you're playing patience and people won't leave you alone.

C.-C.: We won't say another word.

PORTEOUS: That three goes. I believe it's coming out. If I'd been such a fool as to put that seven up I shouldn't have been able to bring these down. [*He puts down several cards while they watch him silently*]

LADY KITTY AND C.-C.: [*Together*] The four goes on the five.

PORTEOUS: [*Throwing down the cards violently*] Damn you! Why don't you leave me alone? It's intolerable.

C.-C.: It was coming out, my dear fellow.

PORTEOUS: I know it was coming out. Confound you!

LADY KITTY: How petty you are, Hughie!

PORTEOUS: Petty, be damned! I've told you over and over again that I will not be interfered with when I'm playing patience.

LADY KITTY: Don't talk to me like that, Hughie.

PORTEOUS: I shall talk to you as I please.

LADY KITTY: [*Beginning to cry*] Oh, you brute! You brute! [*She flings out of the room*]

PORTEOUS: Oh, damn! Now she's going to cry.

[*He stumbles out into the garden,* Champion-Cheney, Elizabeth *and* Teddie *are left alone. There is a moment's pause.* Champion-Cheney *looks from* Teddie *to* Elizabeth, *with an ironical smile*]

C.-C.: Upon my soul, they might be married. They frip so much.

ELIZABETH: [*Frigidly*] It's been nice of you to come here so often since they arrived. It's helped to make things easy.

C.-C.: Irony? It's a rhetorical form not much favored in this blessed plot, this earth, this realm, this England.

ELIZABETH: What exactly are you getting at?

C.-C.: How slangy the young women of the present day are! I suppose the fact that Arnold is a purist leads you to the contrary extravagance.

ELIZABETH: Anyhow you know what I mean.

C.-C.: [*With a smile*] I have a dim, groping suspicion.

ELIZABETH: You promised to keep away. Why did you come back the moment they arrived?

C.-C.: Curiosity, my dear child. A surely pardonable curiosity.

ELIZABETH: And since then you've been here all the time. You don't generally favor us with so much of your company when you're down at your cottage.

C.-C.: I've been excessively amused.

ELIZABETH: It has struck me that whenever they started fripping you took a malicious pleasure in goading them on.

C.-C.: I don't think there's much love lost between them now, do you?

[*Teddie is making as though to leave the room*]

ELIZABETH: Don't go, Teddie.

C.-C.: No, please don't. I'm only staying a minute. We were talking about Lady Kitty just before she arrived. [*To* Elizabeth] Do you remember? The pale, frail lady in black satin and old lace.

ELIZABETH: [*With a chuckle*] You are a devil, you know.

C.-C.: Ah, well, he's always had the reputation of being a humorist and a gentleman.

ELIZABETH: Did you expect her to be like that, poor dear?

C.-C.: My dear child, I hadn't the vaguest idea. You were asking me the other day what she was like when she ran away. I didn't tell you half. She was so gay and so natural. Who would have thought that animation would turn into such frivolity, and that charming impulsiveness lead to such a ridiculous affectation?

ELIZABETH: It rather sets my nerves on edge to hear the way you talk of her.

C.-C.: It's the truth that sets your nerves on edge, not I.

ELIZABETH: You loved her once. Have you no feeling for her at all?

C.-C.: None. Why should I?

ELIZABETH: She's the mother of your son.

C.-C.: My dear child, you have a charming nature, as simple, frank, and artless as hers was. Don't let pure humbug obscure your common sense.

ELIZABETH: We have no right to judge. She's only been here two days. We know nothing about her.

C.-C.: My dear, her soul is as thickly rouged as her face. She hasn't an emotion that's sincere. She's tinsel. You think I'm a cruel, cynical old man. Why, when I think of what she was, if I didn't laugh at what she has become I should cry.

ELIZABETH: How do you know she wouldn't be just the same now if she'd remained your wife? Do you think your influence would have had such a salutary effect on her?

C.-C.: [Good-humoredly] I like you when you're bitter and rather insolent.

ELIZABETH: D'you like me enough to answer my question?

C.-C.: She was only twenty-seven when she went away. She might have become anything. She might have become the woman you expected her to be. There are very few of us who are strong enough to make circumstances serve us. We are the creatures of our environment. She's a silly, worthless woman because she's led a silly, worthless life.

ELIZABETH: [Disturbed] You're horrible today.

C.-C.: I don't say it's I who could have prevented her from becoming this ridiculous caricature of a pretty woman grown old. But life could. Here she would have had the friends fit to her station, and a decent activity, and worthy interests. Ask her what her life has been all these years among divorced women and kept women and the men who consort with them. There is no more lamentable pursuit than a life of pleasure.

ELIZABETH: At all events she loved and she loved greatly. I have only pity and affection for her.

C.-C.: And if she loved what d'you think she felt when she saw that she had ruined Hughie? Look at him. He was tight last night after dinner and tight the night before.

ELIZABETH: I know.

C.-C.: And she took it as a matter of course. How long do you suppose he's been getting tight every night? Do you think he was like that thirty years ago? Can you imagine that that was a brilliant young man, whom everyone expected to be Prime Minister? Look at him now. A grumpy sodden old fellow with false teeth.

ELIZABETH: You have false teeth, too.

C.-C.: Yes, but damn it all, they fit. She's ruined him and she knows she's ruined him.

ELIZABETH: [Looking at him suspiciously] Why are you saying all this to me?

C.-C.: Am I hurting your feelings?

ELIZABETH: I think I've had enough for the present.

C.-C.: I'll go and have a look at the goldfish. I want to see Arnold when he comes in. [Politely] I'm afraid we've been boring Mr. Luton.

TEDDIE: Not at all.

C.-C.: When are you going back to the F. M. S.?

TEDDIE: In about a month.

C.-C.: I see. [He goes out]

ELIZABETH: I wonder what he has at the back of his head.

TEDDIE: D'you think he was talking at you?

ELIZABETH: He's as clever as a bagful of monkeys.

[There is a moment's pause. Teddie hesitates a little and when he speaks it is in a different tone. He is grave and somewhat nervous]

TEDDIE: It seems very difficult to get a few minutes alone with you. I wonder if you've been making it difficult?

ELIZABETH: I wanted to think.

TEDDIE: I've made up my mind to go away tomorrow.

ELIZABETH: Why?

TEDDIE: I want you altogether or not at all.

ELIZABETH: You're so arbitrary.

TEDDIE: You said so—you said you cared for me.

ELIZABETH: I do.

TEDDIE: Do you mind if we talk it over now?

ELIZABETH: No.

TEDDIE: [Frowning] It makes me feel rather shy and awkward. I've repeated to myself over and over again exactly what I want to say to you, and now all I'd prepared seems rather footling.

ELIZABETH: I'm so afraid I'm going to cry.

TEDDIE: I feel it's all so tremendously serious and I think we ought to keep emotion out of it. You're rather emotional, aren't you?

ELIZABETH: [Half smiling and half in tears] So are you for the matter of that.

TEDDIE: That's why I wanted to have everything I meant to say to you cut and dried. I think it would be awfully unfair if I made love to you and all that sort of thing, and you were carried away. I wrote it all down and thought I'd send it you as a letter.

ELIZABETH: Why didn't you?

TEDDIE: I got the wind up. A letter seems so—so cold. You see, I love you so awfully.

ELIZABETH: For goodness' sake don't say that.

TEDDIE: You mustn't cry. Please don't, or I shall go all to pieces.

ELIZABETH: [Trying to smile] I'm sorry. It doesn't mean anything really. It's only tears running out of my eyes.

TEDDIE: Our only chance is to be awfully matter-of-fact. [He stops for a moment. He finds it quite difficult to control himself. He clears his throat. He frowns with annoyance at himself]

ELIZABETH: What's the matter?

TEDDIE: I've got a sort of lump in my throat. It is idiotic. I think I'll have a cigarette. [She watches *him in silence while he lights a cigarette*] You see, I've never been in love with anyone before, not really. It's knocked me endways. I don't know how I can live without you now. . . . Does that old fool know I'm in love with you?

ELIZABETH: I think so.

TEDDIE: When he was talking about Lady Kitty smashing up Lord Porteous' career I thought there was something at the back of it.

ELIZABETH: I think he was trying to persuade me not to smash up yours.

TEDDIE: I'm sure that's very considerate of him, but I don't happen to have one to smash. I wish I had. It's the only time in my life I've wished I were a hell of a swell so I could chuck it all and show you how much more you are to me than anything else in the world.

ELIZABETH: [*Affectionately*] You're a dear old thing, Teddie.

TEDDIE: You know, I don't really know how to make love, but if I did I couldn't do it now because I just want to be absolutely practical.

ELIZABETH: [*Chaffing him*] I'm glad you don't know how to make love. It would be almost more than I could bear.

TEDDIE: You see, I'm not at all romantic and that sort of thing. I'm just a common or garden business man. All this is so dreadfully serious and I think we ought to be sensible.

ELIZABETH: [*With a break in her voice*] You owl!

TEDDIE: No, Elizabeth, don't say things like that to me. I want you to consider all the *pros* and *cons*, and my heart's thumping against my chest, and you know I love you, I love you, I love you.

ELIZABETH: [*In a sigh of passion*] Oh, my precious!

TEDDIE: [*Impatiently, but with himself, rather than with* Elizabeth] Don't be idiotic, Elizabeth. I'm not going to tell you that I can't live without you and a lot of muck like that. You know that you mean everything in the world to me. [*Almost giving it up as a bad job*] Oh, my God!

ELIZABETH: [*Her voice faltering*] D'you think there's anything you can say to me that I don't know already?

TEDDIE: [*Desperately*] But I haven't said a single thing I wanted to. I'm a business man. I want to put it all in a business way, if you understand what I mean.

ELIZABETH: [*Smiling*] I don't believe you're a very good business man.

TEDDIE: [*Sharply*] You don't know what you're talking about. I'm a first rate business man, but somehow this is different. [*Hopelessly*] I don't know why it won't go right.

ELIZABETH: What are we going to do about it?

TEDDIE: You see, it's not just because you're awfully pretty that I love you. I'd love you just as much if you were old and ugly. It's you I love, not what you look like. And it's not only love; love be

blowed! It's that I *like* you so tremendously. I think you're such a ripping good sort. I just want to be with you. I feel so jolly and happy just to think you're there. I'm so awfully *fond* of you.

ELIZABETH: [*Laughing through her tears*] I don't know if this is your idea of introducing a business proposition.

TEDDIE: Damn you, you won't let me.

ELIZABETH: You said "Damn you."

TEDDIE: I meant it.

ELIZABETH: Your voice sounded as if you meant it, you perfect duck!

TEDDIE: Really, Elizabeth, you're intolerable.

ELIZABETH: I'm doing nothing.

TEDDIE: Yes, you are, you're putting me off my blow. What I want to say is perfectly simple. I'm a very ordinary business man.

ELIZABETH: You've said that before.

TEDDIE: [*Angrily*] Shut up. I haven't got a bob besides what I earn. I've got no position. I'm nothing. You're rich and you're a big pot and you've got everything that anyone can want. It's awful cheek my saying anything to you at all. But after all there's only one thing that really matters in the world, and that's love. I love you. Chuck all this, Elizabeth, and come to me.

ELIZABETH: Are you cross with me?

TEDDIE: Furious.

ELIZABETH: Darling!

TEDDIE: If you don't want me tell me so at once and let me get out quickly.

ELIZABETH: Teddie, nothing in the world matters anything to me but you. I'll go wherever you take me. I love you.

TEDDIE: [*All to pieces*] Oh, my God!

ELIZABETH: Does it mean as much to you as that? Oh, Teddie!

TEDDIE: [*Trying to control himself*] Don't be a fool, Elizabeth.

ELIZABETH: It's you're the fool. You're making me cry.

TEDDIE: You're so damned emotional.

ELIZABETH: Damned emotional yourself. I'm sure you're a rotten business man.

TEDDIE: I don't care what you think. You've made me so awfully happy. I say, what a lark life's going to be!

ELIZABETH: Teddie, you are an angel.

TEDDIE: Let's get out quick. It's no good wasting time. Elizabeth.

ELIZABETH: What?

TEDDIE: Nothing. I just like to say Elizabeth.

ELIZABETH: You fool!

TEDDIE: I say, can you shoot?

ELIZABETH: No.

TEDDIE: I'll teach you. You don't know how ripping it is to start out from your camp at dawn and travel through the jungle. And you're so tired at night and the sky's all starry. It's a fair treat. Of course I didn't want to say anything about all that till you'd decided. I'd made up my mind to be absolutely practical.

ELIZABETH: [*Chaffing him*] The only practical thing you said was that love is the only thing that really matters.

TEDDIE: [*Happily*] Pull the other leg next time, will you? I should hate to have one longer than the other.

ELIZABETH: Isn't it fun being in love with some one who's in love with you?

TEDDIE: I say, I think I'd better clear out at once, don't you? It seems rather rotten to stay on in—in this house.

ELIZABETH: You can't go tonight. There's no train.

TEDDIE: I'll go tomorrow. I'll wait in London till you're ready to join me.

ELIZABETH: I'm not going to leave a note on the pincushion like Lady Kitty, you know. I'm going to tell Arnold.

TEDDIE: Are you? Don't you think there'll be an awful bother?

ELIZABETH: I must face it. I should hate to be sly and deceitful.

TEDDIE: Well, then, let's face it together.

ELIZABETH: No, I'll talk to Arnold by myself.

TEDDIE: You won't let anyone influence you?

ELIZABETH: No.

[*He holds out his hand and she takes it. They look into one another's eyes with grave, almost solemn affection. There is the sound outside of a car driving up*]

ELIZABETH: There's the car. Arnold's come back. I must go and bathe my eyes. I don't want them to see I've been crying.

TEDDIE: All right. [*As she is going*] Elizabeth.

ELIZABETH: [*Stopping*] What?

TEDDIE: Bless you.

ELIZABETH: [*Affectionately*] Idiot!

[*She goes out of the door and* Teddie *through the French window into the garden. For an instant the room is empty.* Arnold *comes in. He sits down and takes some papers out of his despatch-case.* Lady Kitty *enters. He gets up*]

LADY KITTY: I saw you come in. Oh, my dear, don't get up. There's no reason why you should be so dreadfully polite to me.

ARNOLD: I've just rung for a cup of tea.

LADY KITTY: Perhaps we shall have the chance of a little talk. We don't seem to have had five minutes by ourselves. I want to make your acquaintance, you know.

ARNOLD: I should like you to know that it's not by my wish that my father is here.

LADY KITTY: But I'm so interested to see him.

ARNOLD: I was afraid that you and Lord Porteous must find it embarrassing.

LADY KITTY: Oh, no. Hughie was his greatest friend. They were at Eton and Oxford together. I think

your father has improved so much since I saw him last. He wasn't good-looking as a young man, but now he's quite handsome.

[*The* Footman *brings in a tray on which are tea-things*]

LADY KITTY: Shall I pour it out for you?

ARNOLD: Thank you very much.

LADY KITTY: Do you take sugar?

ARNOLD: No. I gave it up during the war.

LADY KITTY: So wise of you. It's so bad for the figure. Besides being patriotic, of course. Isn't it absurd that I should ask my son if he takes sugar or not? Life is really very quaint. Sad, of course, but oh, so quaint! Often I lie in bed at night and have a good laugh to myself as I think how quaint life is.

ARNOLD: I'm afraid I'm a very serious person.

LADY KITTY: How old are you now, Arnold?

ARNOLD: Thirty-five.

LADY KITTY: Are you really? Of course, I was a child when I married your father.

ARNOLD: Really. He always told me you were twenty-two.

LADY KITTY: Oh, what nonsense! Why, I was married out of the nursery. I put my hair up for the first time on my wedding-day.

ARNOLD: Where is Lord Porteous?

LADY KITTY: My dear, it sounds too absurd to hear you call him Lord Porteous. Why don't you call him—Uncle Hughie?

ARNOLD: He doesn't happen to be my uncle.

LADY KITTY: No, but he's your godfather. You know, I'm sure you'll like him when you know him better. I'm so hoping that you and Elizabeth will come and stay with us in Florence. I simply adore Elizabeth. She's too beautiful.

ARNOLD: Her hair is very pretty.

LADY KITTY: It's not touched up, is it?

ARNOLD: Oh, no.

LADY KITTY: I just wondered. It's rather a coincidence that her hair should be the same color as mine. I suppose it shows that your father and you are attracted by just the same thing. So interesting, heredity, isn't it?

ARNOLD: Very.

LADY KITTY: Of course, since I joined the Catholic Church I don't believe in it any more. Darwin and all that sort of thing. Too dreadful. Wicked, you know. Besides, it's not very good form, is it?

[*Champion-Cheney comes in from the garden*]

C.-C.: Do I intrude?

LADY KITTY: Come in, Clive. Arnold and I have been having such a wonderful heart-to-heart talk.

C.-C.: Very nice.

ARNOLD: Father, I stepped in for a moment at the Harveys' on my way back. It's simply criminal what they're doing with that house.

C.-C.: What are they doing?

ARNOLD: It's an almost perfect Georgian house and they've got a lot of dreadful Victorian furniture. I gave them my ideas on the subject, but it's quite hopeless. They said they were attached to their furniture.

C.-C.: Arnold should have been an interior decorator.

LADY KITTY: He has wonderful taste. He gets that from me.

ARNOLD: I suppose I have a certain *flair*. I have a passion for decorating houses.

LADY KITTY: You've made this one charming.

C.-C.: D'you remember, we just had chintzes and comfortable chairs when we lived here, Kitty.

LADY KITTY: Perfectly hideous, wasn't it?

C.-C.: In those days gentlemen and ladies were not expected to have taste.

ARNOLD: You know, I've been looking at this chair again. Since Lord Porteous said the legs weren't right I've been very uneasy.

LADY KITTY: He only said that because he was in a bad temper.

C.-C.: His temper seems to me very short these days, Kitty.

LADY KITTY: Oh, it is.

ARNOLD: You feel he knows what he's talking about. I gave seventy-five pounds for that chair. I'm very seldom taken in. I always think if a thing's right you feel it.

C.-C.: Well, don't let it disturb your night's rest.

ARNOLD: But, my dear father, that's just what it does. I had a most horrible dream about it last night.

LADY KITTY: Here is Hughie.

ARNOLD: I'm going to fetch a book I have on Old English furniture. There's an illustration of a chair which is almost identical with this one.

[Porteous *comes in*]

PORTEOUS: Quite a family gathering, by George!

C.-C.: I was thinking just now we'd make a very pleasing picture of a typical English home.

ARNOLD: I'll be back in five minutes. There's something I want to show you, Lord Porteous. [*He goes out*]

C.-C.: Would you like to play piquet with me, Hughie?

PORTEOUS: Not particularly.

C.-C.: You were never much of a piquet player, were you?

PORTEOUS: My dear Clive, you people don't know what piquet is in England.

C.-C.: Let's have a game then. You may make money.

PORTEOUS: I don't want to play with you.

LADY KITTY: I don't know why not, Hughie.

PORTEOUS: Let me tell you that I don't like your manner.

C.-C.: I'm sorry for that. I'm afraid I can't offer to change it at my age.

PORTEOUS: I don't know what you want to be hanging around here for.

C.-C.: A natural attachment to my home.

PORTEOUS: If you'd had any tact you'd have kept out of the way while we were here.

C.-C.: My dear Hughie. I don't understand your attitude at all. If I'm willing to let bygones be bygones why should you object?

PORTEOUS: Damn it all, they're not bygones.

C.-C.: After all, I am the injured party.

PORTEOUS: How the devil are you the injured party?

C.-C.: Well, you did run away with my wife, didn't you?

LADY KITTY: Now, don't let's go into ancient history. I can't see why we shouldn't all be friends.

PORTEOUS: I beg you not to interfere, Kitty.

LADY KITTY: I'm very fond of Clive.

PORTEOUS: You never cared two straws for Clive. You only say that to irritate me.

LADY KITTY: Not at all. I don't see why he shouldn't come and stay with us.

C.-C.: I'd love to. I think Florence in spring-time is delightful. Have you central heating?

PORTEOUS: I never liked you, I don't like you now, and I never shall like you.

C.-C.: How very unfortunate! Because I liked you, I like you now, and I shall continue to like you.

LADY KITTY: There's something very nice about you, Clive.

PORTEOUS: If you think that, why the devil did you leave him?

LADY KITTY: Are you going to reproach me because I loved you? How utterly, utterly, utterly detestable you are!

C.-C.: Now, now, don't quarrel with one another.

LADY KITTY: It's all his fault. I'm the easiest person in the world to live with. But really he'd try the patience of a saint.

C.-C.: Come, come, don't get upset, Kitty. When two people live together there must be a certain amount of give and take.

PORTEOUS: I don't know what the devil you're talking about.

C.-C.: It hasn't escaped my observation that you are a little inclined to frip. Many couples are. I think it's a pity.

PORTEOUS: Would you have the very great kindness to mind your own business?

LADY KITTY: It is his business. He naturally wants me to be happy.

C.-C.: I have the very greatest affection for Kitty.

PORTEOUS: Then why the devil didn't you look after her properly?

C.-C.: My dear Hughie, you were my greatest friend. I trusted you. It may have been rash.

PORTEOUS: It was inexcusable.

LADY KITTY: I don't know what you mean by that, Hughie.

PORTEOUS: Don't, don't, don't try and bully me, Kitty.

LADY KITTY: Oh, I know what you mean.

PORTEOUS: They why the devil did you say you didn't?

LADY KITTY: When I think that I sacrificed everything for that man! And for thirty years I've had to live in a filthy marble palace with no sanitary conveniences.

C.-C.: D'you mean to say you haven't got a bathroom?

LADY KITTY: I've had to wash in a tub.

C.-C.: My poor Kitty, how you've suffered!

PORTEOUS: Really, Kitty, I'm sick of hearing of the sacrifices you made. I suppose you think I sacrificed nothing. I should have been Prime Minister by now if it hadn't been for you.

LADY KITTY: Nonsense!

PORTEOUS: What do you mean by that? Everyone said I should be Prime Minister. Shouldn't I have been Prime Minister, Clive?

C.-C.: It was certainly the general expectation.

PORTEOUS: I was the most promising young man of my day. I was bound to get a seat in the Cabinet at the next election.

LADY KITTY: They'd have found you out just as I've found you out. I'm sick of hearing that I ruined your career. You never had a career to ruin. Prime Minister! You haven't the brain. You haven't the character.

C.-C.: Cheek, push, and a gift of the gab will serve very well instead, you know.

LADY KITTY: Besides, in politics it's not the men that matter. It's the women at the back of them. I could have made Clive a Cabinet Minister if I'd wanted to.

PORTEOUS: Clive?

LADY KITTY: With my beauty, my charm, my force of character, my wit, I could have done anything.

PORTEOUS: Clive was nothing but my political secretary. When I was Prime Minister I might have made him Governor of some Colony or other. Western Australia, say. Out of pure kindness.

LADY KITTY: [With flashing eyes] D'you think I would have buried myself in Western Australia? With my beauty? My charm?

PORTEOUS: Or Barbados, perhaps.

LADY KITTY: [Furiously] Barbados! Barbados can go to—Barbados.

PORTEOUS: That's all you'd have got.

LADY KITTY: Nonsense! I'd have India.

PORTEOUS: I would never have given you India.

LADY KITTY: You would have given me India.

PORTEOUS: I tell you I wouldn't.

LADY KITTY: The King would have given me India. The nation would have insisted on my having India. I would have been a vice-reine or nothing.

PORTEOUS: I tell you that as long as the interests of the British Empire—damn it all, my teeth are coming out! [He hurries from the room]

LADY KITTY: It's too much. I can't bear it any more.

I've put up with him for thirty years and now I'm at the end of my tether.

C.-C.: Calm yourself, my dear Kitty.

LADY KITTY: I won't listen to a word. I've quite made up my mind. It's finished, finished, finished. [With a change of tone] I was so touched when I heard that you never lived in this house again after I left it.

C.-C.: The cuckoos have always been very plentiful. Their note has a personal application which, I must say, I have found extremely offensive.

LADY KITTY: When I saw that you didn't marry again I couldn't help thinking that you still loved me.

C.-C.: I am one of the few men I know who is able to profit by experience.

LADY KITTY: In the eyes of the Church I am still your wife. The Church is so wise. It knows that in the end a woman always comes back to her first love. Clive, I am willing to return to you.

C.-C.: My dear Kitty, I couldn't take advantage of your momentary vexation with Hughie to let you take a step which I know you would bitterly regret.

LADY KITTY: You've waited for me a long time. For Arnold's sake.

C.-C.: Do you think we really need bother about Arnold? In the last thirty years he's had time to grow used to the situation.

LADY KITTY: [With a little smile] I think I've sown my wild oats, Clive.

C.-C.: I haven't. I was a good young man, Kitty.

LADY KITTY: I know.

C.-C.: And I'm very glad, because it has enabled me to be a wicked old one.

LADY KITTY: I beg your pardon.

[Arnold comes in with a large book in his hand]

ARNOLD: I say, I've found the book I was hunting for. Oh. Isn't Lord Porteous here?

LADY KITTY: One moment, Arnold. Your father and I are busy.

ARNOLD: I'm so sorry. [He goes out into the garden]

LADY KITTY: Explain yourself, Clive.

C.-C.: When you ran away from me, Kitty, I was sore and angry and miserable. But above all I felt a fool.

LADY KITTY: Men are so vain.

C.-C.: But I was a student of history, and presently I reflected that I shared my misfortune with very nearly all the greatest men.

LADY KITTY: I'm a great reader myself. It has always struck me as peculiar.

C.-C.: The explanation is very simple. Women dislike intelligence, and when they find it in their husbands they revenge themselves on them in the only way they can, by making them—well, what you made me.

LADY KITTY: It's ingenious. It may be true.

C.-C.: I felt I had done my duty by society and I determined to devote the rest of my life to my own entertainment. The House of Commons had always bored me excessively and the scandal of our divorce gave me an opportunity to resign my seat. I have been relieved to find that the country got on perfectly well without me.

LADY KITTY: But has love never entered your life?

C.-C.: Tell me frankly, Kitty, don't you think people make a lot of unnecessary fuss about love?

LADY KITTY: It's the most wonderful thing in the world.

C.-C.: You're incorrigible. Do you really think it was worth sacrificing so much for?

LADY KITTY: My dear Clive, I don't mind telling you that if I had my time over again I should be unfaithful to you, but I should not leave you.

C.-C.: For some years I was notoriously the prey of a secret sorrow. But I found so many charming creatures who were anxious to console that in the end it grew rather fatiguing. Out of regard to my health I ceased to frequent the drawing-rooms of Mayfair.

LADY KITTY: And since then?

C.-C.: Since then I have allowed myself the luxury of assisting financially a succession of dear little things, in a somewhat humble sphere, between the ages of twenty and twenty-five.

LADY KITTY: I cannot understand the infatuation of men for young girls. I think they're so dull.

C.-C.: It's a matter of taste. I love old wine, old friends, and old books, but I like young women. On their twenty-fifth birthday I give them a diamond ring and tell them they must no longer waste their youth and beauty on an old fogey like me. We have a most affecting scene, my technique on these occasions is perfect, and then I start all over again.

LADY KITTY: You're a wicked old man, Clive.

C.-C.: That's what I told you. But, by George! I'm a happy one.

LADY KITTY: There's only one course open to me now.

C.-C.: What is that?

LADY KITTY: [With a flashing smile] To go and dress for dinner.

C.-C.: Capital. I will follow your example.

[As Lady Kitty goes out Elizabeth comes in]

ELIZABETH: Where is Arnold?

C.-C.: He's on the terrace. I'll call him.

ELIZABETH: Don't bother.

C.-C.: I was just strolling along to my cottage to put on a dinner jacket. [As he goes out] Arnold.

[Exit C.-C.]

ARNOLD: Hulloa! [He comes in] Oh, Elizabeth, I've found an illustration here of a chair which is almost identical with mine. It's dated 1750. Look!

ELIZABETH: That's very interesting.

ARNOLD: I want to show it to Porteous. [Moving a chair which has been misplaced] You know, it does exasperate me the way people will not leave

things alone. I no sooner put a thing in its place than somebody moves it.

ELIZABETH: It must be maddening for you.

ARNOLD: It is. You are the worst offender. I can't think why you don't take the pride that I do in the house. After all, it's one of the show places in the country.

ELIZABETH: I'm afraid you find me very unsatisfactory.

ARNOLD: [Good-humoredly] I don't know about that. But my two subjects are politics and decoration. I should be a perfect fool if I didn't see that you don't care two straws about either.

ELIZABETH: We haven't very much in common, Arnold, have we?

ARNOLD: I don't think you can blame me for that.

ELIZABETH: I don't. I blame you for nothing. I have no fault to find with you.

ARNOLD: [Surprised at her significant tone] Good gracious me! What's the meaning of all this?

ELIZABETH: Well, I don't think there's any object in beating about the bush. I want you to let me go.

ARNOLD: Go where?

ELIZABETH: Away. For always.

ARNOLD: My dear child, what are you talking about?

ELIZABETH: I want to be free.

ARNOLD: [Amused rather than disconcerted] Don't be ridiculous, darling. I daresay you're run down and want a change. I'll take you over to Paris for a fortnight if you like.

ELIZABETH: I shouldn't have spoken to you if I hadn't quite made up my mind. We've been married for three years and I don't think it's been a great success. I'm frankly bored by the life you want me to lead.

ARNOLD: Well, if you'll allow me to say so, the fault is yours. We lead a very distinguished, useful life. We know a lot of extremely nice people.

ELIZABETH: I'm quite willing to allow that the fault is mine. But how does that make it any better? I'm only twenty-five. If I've made a mistake I have time to correct it.

ARNOLD: I can't bring myself to take you very seriously.

ELIZABETH: You see, I don't love you.

ARNOLD: Well, I'm awfully sorry. But you weren't obliged to marry me. You've made your bed and I'm afraid you must lie on it.

ELIZABETH: That's one of the falsest proverbs in the English language. Why should you lie on the bed you've made if you don't want to? There's always the floor.

ARNOLD: For goodness' sake, don't be funny, Elizabeth.

ELIZABETH: I've quite made up my mind to leave you, Arnold.

ARNOLD: Come, come, Elizabeth, you must be sensible. You haven't any reason to leave me.

ELIZABETH: Why should you wish to keep a woman tied to you who wants to be free?

ARNOLD: I happen to be in love with you.

ELIZABETH: You might have said that before.

ARNOLD: I thought you'd take it for granted. You can't expect a man to go on making love to his wife after three years. I'm very busy. I'm awfully keen on politics and I've worked like a dog to make this house a thing of beauty. After all, a man marries to have a home, but also because he doesn't want to be bothered with sex and all that sort of thing. I fell in love with you the first time I saw you and I've been in love ever since.

ELIZABETH: I'm sorry, but if you're not in love with a man his love doesn't mean very much to you.

ARNOLD: It's so ungrateful. I've done everything in the world for you.

ELIZABETH: You've been very kind to me. But you've asked me to lead a life I don't like and that I'm not suited for. I'm awfully sorry to cause you pain, but now you must let me go.

ARNOLD: Nonsense! I'm a good deal older than you are and I think I have a little more sense. In your interests as well as in mine I'm not going to do anything of the sort.

ELIZABETH: [With a smile] How can you prevent me? You can't keep me under lock and key.

ARNOLD: Please don't talk to me as if I were a foolish child. You're my wife and you're going to remain my wife.

ELIZABETH: What sort of a life do you think we should lead? Do you think there'd be any more happiness for you than for me?

ARNOLD: But what is it precisely that you suggest?

ELIZABETH: Well, I want you to let me divorce you.

ARNOLD: [Astounded] Me? Thank you very much. Are you under the impression I'm going to sacrifice my career for a whim of yours?

ELIZABETH: How will it do that?

ARNOLD: My seat's wobbly enough as it is. Do you think I'd be able to hold it if I were in a divorce case? Even if it were a put-up job, as most divorces are nowadays, it would damn me.

ELIZABETH: It's rather hard on a woman to be divorced.

ARNOLD: [With sudden suspicion] What do you mean by that? Are you in love with some one?

ELIZABETH: Yes.

ARNOLD: Who?

ELIZABETH: Teddie Luton.

[He is astonished for a moment, then bursts into a laugh]

ARNOLD: My poor child, how can you be so ridiculous? Why, he hasn't a bob. He's a perfectly commonplace young man. It's so absurd I can't even be angry with you.

ELIZABETH: I've fallen desperately in love with him, Arnold.

ARNOLD: Well, you'd better fall desperately out.

ELIZABETH: He wants to marry me.

ARNOLD: I daresay he does. He can go to hell.

ELIZABETH: It's no good talking like that.

ARNOLD: Is he your lover?

ELIZABETH: No, certainly not.

ARNOLD: It shows that he's a mean skunk to take advantage of my hospitality to make love to you.

ELIZABETH: He's never even kissed me.

ARNOLD: I'd try telling that to the horse marines if I were you.

ELIZABETH: It's because I wanted to do nothing shabby that I told you straight out how things were.

ARNOLD: How long have you been thinking of this?

ELIZABETH: I've been in love with Teddie ever since I knew him.

ARNOLD: And you never thought of me at all, I suppose.

ELIZABETH: Oh, yes, I did. I was miserable. But I can't help myself. I wish I loved you, but I don't.

ARNOLD: I recommend you to think very carefully before you do anything foolish.

ELIZABETH: I have thought very carefully.

ARNOLD: By God! I don't know why I don't give you a sound hiding. I'm not sure if that wouldn't be the best thing to bring you to your senses.

ELIZABETH: Oh, Arnold, don't take it like that.

ARNOLD: How do you expect me to take it? You come to me quite calmly and say: "I've had enough of you. We've been married three years and I think I'd like to marry somebody else now. Shall I break up your home? What a bore for you! Do you mind my divorcing you? It'll smash up your career, will it? What a pity!" Oh, no, my girl, I may be a fool, but I'm not a damned fool.

ELIZABETH: Teddie is leaving here by the first train tomorrow. I warn you that I mean to join him as soon as he can make the necessary arrangements.

ARNOLD: Where is he?

ELIZABETH: I don't know. I suppose he's in his room.

[Arnold goes to the door and calls]

ARNOLD: George!

[For a moment he walks up and down the room impatiently. Elizabeth watches him. The Footman comes in]

FOOTMAN: Yes, sir.

ARNOLD: Tell Mr. Luton to come here at once.

ELIZABETH: Ask Mr. Luton if he wouldn't mind coming here for a moment.

FOOTMAN: Very good, madam.

[Exit Footman]

ELIZABETH: What are you going to say to him?

ARNOLD: That's my business.

ELIZABETH: I wouldn't make a scene if I were you.

ARNOLD: I'm not going to make a scene. [They wait in silence] Why did you insist on my mother coming here?

ELIZABETH: It seemed to me rather absurd to take

up the attitude that I should be contaminated by her when . . .

ARNOLD: [*Interrupting*] When you were proposing to do exactly the same thing. Well, now you've seen her what do you think of her? Do you think it's been a success? Is that the sort of woman a man would like his mother to be?

ELIZABETH: I've been ashamed. I've been so sorry. It all seemed dreadful and horrible. This morning I happened to notice a rose in the garden. It was all over-blown and bedraggled. It looked like a painted old woman. And I remembered that I'd looked at it a day or two ago. It was lovely then, fresh and blooming and fragrant. It may be hideous now, but that doesn't take away from the beauty it had once. That was real.

ARNOLD: Poetry, by God! As if this were the moment for poetry!

[*Teddie comes in. He has changed into a dinner jacket*]

TEDDIE: [*To Elizabeth*] Did you want me?

ARNOLD: I sent for you. [*Teddie looks from Arnold to Elizabeth. He sees that something has happened*] When would it be convenient for you to leave this house?

TEDDIE: I was proposing to go tomorrow morning. But I can very well go at once if you like.

ARNOLD: I do like.

TEDDIE: Very well. Is there anything else you wish to say to me?

ARNOLD: Do you think it was a very honorable thing to come down here and make love to my wife?

TEDDIE: No, I don't. I haven't been very happy about it. That's why I wanted to go away.

ARNOLD: Upon my word, you're cool.

TEDDIE: I'm afraid it's no good saying I'm sorry and that sort of thing. You know what the situation is.

ARNOLD: Is it true that you want to marry Elizabeth?

TEDDIE: Yes. I should like to marry her as soon as ever I can.

ARNOLD: Have you thought of me at all? Has it struck you that you're destroying my home and breaking up my happiness?

TEDDIE: I don't see how there could be much happiness for you if Elizabeth doesn't care for you.

ARNOLD: Let me tell you that I refuse to have my home broken up by a twopenny-halfpenny adventurer who takes advantage of a foolish woman. I refuse to allow myself to be divorced. I can't prevent my wife from going off with you if she's determined to make a damned fool of herself, but this I tell you: nothing will induce me to divorce her.

ELIZABETH: Arnold, that would be monstrous.

TEDDIE: We could force you.

ARNOLD: How?

TEDDIE: If we went away together openly you'd have to bring an action.

ARNOLD: Twenty-four hours after you leave this house I shall go down to Brighton with a chorus-girl. And neither you nor I will be able to get a divorce. We've had enough divorces in our family. And now get out, get out, get out!

[*Teddie looks uncertainly at* Elizabeth]

ELIZABETH: [*With a little smile*] Don't bother about me. I shall be all right.

ARNOLD: Get out! Get out!

Act III

The Scene is the same as in the preceding acts. It is the night of the same day as that on which takes place the action of the second act.

Champion-Cheney *and* Arnold, *both in dinner jackets, are discovered.* Champion-Cheney *is seated.* Arnold *walks restlessly up and down the room.*

C.-C.: I think, if you'll follow my advice to the letter, you'll probably work the trick.

ARNOLD: I don't like it, you know. It's against all my principles.

C.-C.: My dear Arnold, we all hope that you have before you a distinguished political career. You can't learn too soon that the most useful thing about a principle is that it can always be sacrificed to expediency.

ARNOLD: But supposing it doesn't come off? Women are incalculable.

C.-C.: Nonsense! Men are romantic. A woman will always sacrifice herself if you give her the opportunity. It is her favorite form of self-indulgence.

ARNOLD: I never know whether you're a humorist or a cynic, Father.

C.-C.: I'm neither, my dear boy; I'm merely a very truthful man. But people are so unused to the truth that they're apt to mistake it for a joke or a sneer.

ARNOLD: [*Irritably*] It seems so unfair that this should happen to me.

C.-C.: Keep your head, my boy, and do what I tell you.

[*Lady Kitty and* Elizabeth *come in. Lady Kitty is in a gorgeous evening gown*]

ELIZABETH: Where is Lord Porteous?

C.-C.: He's on the terrace. He's smoking a cigar. [*Going to window*] Hughie!

[*Porteous comes in*]

PORTEOUS: [*With a grunt*] Yes? Where's Mrs. Shenstone?

ELIZABETH: Oh, she had a headache. She's gone to bed.

[*When* Porteous *comes in* Lady Kitty *with a very haughty air purses her lips and takes up an illustrated paper.* Porteous *gives her an irritated look, takes another illustrated paper and sits himself down at the other end of the room. They are not on speaking terms*]

C.-C.: Arnold and I have just been down to my cottage.

ELIZABETH: I wondered where you'd gone.

C.-C.: I came across an old photograph album this afternoon. I meant to bring it along before dinner, but I forgot, so we went and fetched it.

ELIZABETH: Oh, do let me see it! I love old photographs.

[*He gives her the album, and she, sitting down, puts it on her knees and begins to turn over the pages. He stands over her.* Lady Kitty *and* Porteous *take surreptitious glances at one another*]

C.-C.: I thought it might amuse you to see what pretty women looked like five-and-thirty years ago. That was the day of beautiful women.

ELIZABETH: Do you think they were more beautiful then than they are now?

C.-C.: Oh, much. Now you see lots of pretty little things, but very few beautiful women.

ELIZABETH: Aren't their clothes funny?

C.-C.: [*Pointing to a photograph*] That's Mrs. Langtry.

ELIZABETH: She has a lovely nose.

C.-C.: She was the most wonderful thing you ever saw. Dowagers used to jump on chairs in order to get a good look at her when she came into a drawing-room. I was riding with her once, and we had to have the gates of the livery-stable closed when she was getting on her horse because the crowd was so great.

ELIZABETH: And who's that?

C.-C.: Lady Lonsdale. That's Lady Dudley.

ELIZABETH: This is an actress, isn't it?

C.-C.: It is, indeed. Ellen Terry. By George! How I loved that woman!

ELIZABETH: [*With a smile*] Dear Ellen Terry!

C.-C.: That's Bwabs. I never saw a smarter man in my life. And Oliver Montagu. Henry Manners with his eye-glass.

ELIZABETH: Nice-looking, isn't he? And this?

C.-C.: That's Mary Anderson. I wish you could have seen her in "A Winter's Tale." Her beauty just took your breath away. And look! There's Lady Randolph. Bernal Osborne—the wittiest man I ever knew.

ELIZABETH: I think it's too sweet. I love their absurd bustles and those tight sleeves.

C.-C.: What figures they had! In those days a woman wasn't supposed to be as thin as a rail and as flat as a pancake.

ELIZABETH: Oh, but aren't they laced in? How could they bear it?

C.-C.: They didn't play golf then, and nonsense like

that, you know. They hunted, in a tall hat and a long black habit, and they were very gracious and charitable to the poor in the village.

ELIZABETH: Did the poor like it?

C.-C.: They had a very thin time if they didn't. When they were in London they drove in the Park every afternoon, and they went to ten-course dinners, where they never met anybody they didn't know. And they had their box at the opera when Patti was singing or Madam Albani.

ELIZABETH: Oh, what a lovely little thing! Who on earth is that?

C.-C.: That?

ELIZABETH: She looks so fragile, like a piece of exquisite china, with all those furs on and her face up against her muff, and the snow falling.

C.-C.: Yes, there was quite a rage at that time for being taken in an artificial snowstorm.

ELIZABETH: What a sweet smile, so roguish and frank, and debonair! Oh, I wish I looked like that! Do tell me who it is!

C.-C.: Don't you know?

ELIZABETH: No.

C.-C.: Why—it's Kitty.

ELIZABETH: Lady Kitty. [*To* Lady Kitty] Oh, my dear, do look! It's too ravishing. [*She takes the album over to her impulsively*] Why didn't you tell me you looked like that? Everybody must have been in love with you.

[Lady Kitty *takes the album and looks at it. Then she lets it slip from her hands and covers her face with her hands. She is crying*]

[*In consternation*] My dear, what's the matter? Oh, what have I done? I'm so sorry.

LADY KITTY: Don't, don't talk to me. Leave me alone. It's stupid of me.

[Elizabeth *looks at her for a moment perplexed, then, turning round, slips her arm in* Champion-Cheney's *and leads him out on to the terrace*]

ELIZABETH: [*As they are going, in a whisper*] Did you do that on purpose?

[Porteous *gets up and goes over to* Lady Kitty. *He puts his hand on her shoulder. They remain thus for a little while*]

PORTEOUS: I'm afraid I was very rude to you before dinner, Kitty.

LADY KITTY: [*Taking his hand which is on her shoulder*] It doesn't matter. I'm sure I was very exasperating.

PORTEOUS: I didn't mean what I said, you know.

LADY KITTY: Neither did I.

PORTEOUS: Of course I know that I'd never have been Prime Minister.

LADY KITTY: How can you talk such nonsense, Hughie? No one would have had a chance if you'd remained in politics.

PORTEOUS: I haven't the character.

LADY KITTY: You have more character than anyone I've ever met.

PORTEOUS: Besides, I don't know that I much wanted to be Prime Minister.

LADY KITTY: Oh, but I should have been so proud of you. Of course you'd have been Prime Minister.

PORTEOUS: I'd have given you India, you know. I think it would have been a very popular appointment.

LADY KITTY: I don't care twopence about India. I'd have been quite content with Western Australia.

PORTEOUS: My dear, you don't think I'd have let you bury yourself in Western Australia?

LADY KITTY: Or Barbados.

PORTEOUS: Never. It sounds like a cure for flat feet. I'd have kept you in London.

[*He picks up the album and is about to look at the photograph of* Lady Kitty. *She puts her hands over it*]

LADY KITTY: No, don't look.

[*He takes her hand away*]

PORTEOUS: Don't be so silly.

LADY KITTY: Isn't it hateful to grow old?

PORTEOUS: You know, you haven't changed much.

LADY KITTY: [*Enchanted*] Oh, Hughie, how can you talk such nonsense?

PORTEOUS: Of course you're a little more mature, but that's all. A woman's all the better for being rather mature.

LADY KITTY: Do you really think that?

PORTEOUS: Upon my soul I do.

LADY KITTY: You're not saying it just to please me?

PORTEOUS: No, no.

LADY KITTY: Let me look at the photograph again. [*She takes the album and looks at the photograph complacently*] The fact is, if your bones are good, age doesn't really matter. You'll always be beautiful.

PORTEOUS: [*With a little smile, almost as if he were talking to a child*] It was silly of you to cry.

LADY KITTY: It hasn't made my eyelashes run, has it?

PORTEOUS: Not a bit.

LADY KITTY: It's very good stuff I use now. They don't stick together either.

PORTEOUS: Look here, Kitty, how much longer do you want to stay here?

LADY KITTY: Oh, I'm quite ready to go whenever you like.

PORTEOUS: Clive gets on my nerves. I don't like the way he keeps hanging about you.

LADY KITTY: [*Surprised, rather amused, and delighted*] Hughie, you don't mean to say you're jealous of poor Clive?

PORTEOUS: Of course I'm not jealous of him, but he does look at you in a way that I can't help thinking rather objectionable.

LADY KITTY: Hughie, you may throw me downstairs like Amy Robsart; you may drag me about the floor by the hair of my head; I don't care, you're jealous. I shall never grow old.

PORTEOUS: Damn it all, the man was your husband.

LADY KITTY: My dear Hughie, he never had your style. Why, the moment you come into a room everyone looks and says: "Who the devil is that?"

PORTEOUS: What? You think that, do you? Well, I daresay there's something in what you say. These damned Radicals can say what they like, but, by God, Kitty! When a man's a gentleman—well, damn it all, you know what I mean.

LADY KITTY: I think Clive has degenerated dreadfully since we left him.

PORTEOUS: What do you say to making a bee-line for Italy and going to San Michele?

LADY KITTY: Oh, Hughie! It's years since we were there.

PORTEOUS: Wouldn't you like to see it again—just once more?

LADY KITTY: Do you remember the first time we went? It was the most heavenly place I'd ever seen. We'd only left England a month, and I said I'd like to spend all my life there.

PORTEOUS: Of course I remember. And in a fortnight it was yours, lock, stock, and barrel.

LADY KITTY: We were very happy there, Hughie.

PORTEOUS: Let's go back once more.

LADY KITTY: I daren't. It must be all peopled with the ghosts of our past. One should never go again to a place where one has been happy. It would break my heart.

PORTEOUS: Do you remember how we used to sit on the terrace of the old castle and look at the Adriatic? We might have been the only people in the world, you and I, Kitty.

LADY KITTY: [*Tragically*] And we thought our love would last forever.

[*Enter* Champion-Cheney]

PORTEOUS: Is there any chance of bridge this evening?

C.-C.: I don't think we can make up a four.

PORTEOUS: What a nuisance that boy went away like that! He wasn't a bad player.

C.-C.: Teddie Luton?

LADY KITTY: I think it was very funny his going without saying good-by to anyone.

C.-C.: The young men of the present day are very casual.

PORTEOUS: I thought there was no train in the evening.

C.-C.: There isn't. The last train leaves at 5.45.

PORTEOUS: How did he go then?

C.-C.: He went.

PORTEOUS: Damned selfish I call it.

LADY KITTY: [*Intrigued*] Why did he go, Clive?

[Champion-Cheney *looks at her for a moment reflectively*]

C.-C.: I have something very grave to say to you. Elizabeth wants to leave Arnold.

LADY KITTY: Clive! What on earth for?

C.-C.: She's in love with Teddie Luton. That's why

he went. The men of my family are really very unfortunate. Does she want to run away with him?

PORTEOUS: Does she want to run away with him?

LADY KITTY: [With consternation] My dear, what's to be done?

c.-c.: I think you can do a great deal.

LADY KITTY: I? What?

c.-c.: Tell her, tell her what it means.

[He looks at her fixedly. She stares at him]

LADY KITTY: Oh, no, no!

c.-c.: She's a child. Not for Arnold's sake. For her sake. You must.

LADY KITTY: You don't know what you're asking.

c.-c.: Yes, I do.

LADY KITTY: Hughie, what shall I do?

PORTEOUS: Do what you like. I shall never blame you for anything.

[The Footman comes in with a letter on a salver. He hesitates on seeing that Elizabeth is not in the room]

c.-c.: What is it?

FOOTMAN: I was looking for Mrs. Champion-Cheney, sir.

c.-c.: She's not here. Is that a letter?

FOOTMAN: Yes, sir. It's just been sent up from the "Champion Arms."

c.-c.: Leave it. I'll give it to Mrs. Cheney.

FOOTMAN: Very good, sir. [He brings the tray to Clive, who takes the letter. The Footman goes out]

PORTEOUS: Is the "Champion Arms" the local pub?

c.-c.: [Looking at the letter] It's by way of being a hotel, but I never heard of anyone staying there.

LADY KITTY: If there was no train I suppose he had to go there.

c.-c.: Great minds. I wonder what he has to write about! [He goes to the door leading on to the garden] Elizabeth!

ELIZABETH: [Outside] Yes.

c.-c.: Here's a note for you.

[There is silence. They wait for Elizabeth to come]

[She enters]

ELIZABETH: It's lovely in the garden tonight.

c.-c.: They've just sent this up from the "Champion Arms."

ELIZABETH: Thank you.

[Without embarrassment she opens the letter. They watch her while she reads it. It covers three pages. She puts it away in her bag]

LADY KITTY: Hughie, I wish you'd fetch me a cloak. I'd like to take a little stroll in the garden, but after thirty years in Italy I find these English summers rather chilly. [Without a word Porteous goes out. Elizabeth is lost in thought] I want to talk to Elizabeth, Clive.

c.-c.: I'll leave you.   [He goes out]

LADY KITTY: What does he say?

ELIZABETH: Who?

LADY KITTY: Mr. Luton.

ELIZABETH: [Gives a little start. Then she looks at Lady Kitty] They've told you?

LADY KITTY: Yes. And now they have, I think I knew it all along.

ELIZABETH: I don't expect you to have much sympathy for me. Arnold is your son.

LADY KITTY: So pitifully little.

ELIZABETH: I'm not suited for this sort of existence. Arnold wants me to take what he calls my place in Society. Oh, I get so bored with those parties in London. All those middle-aged painted women, in beautiful clothes, lolloping round ballrooms with rather old young men. And the endless luncheons where they gossip about so-and-so's love affairs.

LADY KITTY: Are you very much in love with Mr. Luton?

ELIZABETH: I love him with all my heart.

LADY KITTY: And he?

ELIZABETH: He's never cared for anyone but me. He never will.

LADY KITTY: Will Arnold let you divorce him?

ELIZABETH: No, he won't hear of it. He refuses even to divorce me.

LADY KITTY: Why?

ELIZABETH: He thinks a scandal will revive all the old gossip.

LADY KITTY: Oh, my poor child!

ELIZABETH: It can't be helped. I'm quite willing to accept the consequences.

LADY KITTY: You don't know what it is to have a man tied to you only by his honor. When married people don't get on they can separate, but if they're not married it's impossible. It's a tie that only death can sever.

ELIZABETH: If Teddie stopped caring for me I shouldn't want him to stay with me for five minutes.

LADY KITTY: One says that when one's sure of a man's love, but when one isn't any more—oh, it's so different. In those circumstances one's got to keep a man's love. It's the only thing one has.

ELIZABETH: I'm a human being. I can stand on my own feet.

LADY KITTY: Have you any money of your own?

ELIZABETH: None.

LADY KITTY: Then how can you stand on your own feet? You think I'm a silly, frivolous woman, but I've learned something in a bitter school. They can make what laws they like, they can give us the suffrage, but when you come down to bedrock it's the man who pays the piper who calls the tune. Woman will only be the equal of man when she earns her living in the same way that he does.

ELIZABETH: [Smiling] It sounds rather funny to hear you talk like that.

LADY KITTY: A cook who marries a butler can snap her fingers in his face because she can earn just as much as he can. But a woman in your position and a woman in mine will always be dependent on the men who keep them.

ELIZABETH: I don't want luxury. You don't know how sick I am of all this beautiful furniture. These over-decorated houses are like a prison in which I can't breathe. When I drive about in a Callot frock and a Rolls-Royce I envy the shop-girl in a coat and skirt whom I see jumping on the tail-board of a bus.

LADY KITTY: You mean that if need be you could earn your own living?

ELIZABETH: Yes.

LADY KITTY: What could you be? A nurse or a typist. It's nonsense. Luxury saps a woman's nerve. And when she's known it once it becomes a necessity.

ELIZABETH: That depends on the woman.

LADY KITTY: When we're young we think we're different from everyone else, but when we grow a little older we discover we're all very much of a muchness.

ELIZABETH: You're very kind to take so much trouble about me.

LADY KITTY: It breaks my heart to think that you're going to make the same pitiful mistake that I made.

ELIZABETH: Oh, don't say it was that, don't, don't.

LADY KITTY: Look at me, Elizabeth, and look at Hughie. Do you think it's been a success? If I had my time over again do you think I'd do it again? Do you think he would?

ELIZABETH: You see, you don't know how much I love Teddie.

LADY KITTY: And do you think I didn't love Hughie? Do you think he didn't love me?

ELIZABETH: I'm sure he did.

LADY KITTY: Oh, of course in the beginning it was heavenly. We felt so brave and adventurous and we were so much in love. The first two years were wonderful. People cut me, you know, but I didn't mind. I thought love was everything. It *is* a little uncomfortable when you come upon an old friend and go towards her eagerly, so glad to see her, and are met with an icy stare.

ELIZABETH: Do you think friends like that are worth having?

LADY KITTY: Perhaps they're not very sure of themselves. Perhaps they're honestly shocked. It's a test one had better not put one's friends to if one can help it. It's rather bitter to find how few one has.

ELIZABETH: But one has some.

LADY KITTY: Yes, they ask you to come and see them when they're quite certain no one will be there who might object to meeting you. Or else they say to you: "My dear, you know I'm devoted to you, and I wouldn't mind at all, but my girl's growing up—I'm sure you understand; you won't think it unkind of me if I don't ask you to the house?"

ELIZABETH: [*Smiling*] That doesn't seem to me very serious.

LADY KITTY: At first I thought it rather a relief, because it threw Hughie and me together more. But you know, men are very funny. Even when they are in love they're not in love all day long. They want change and recreation.

ELIZABETH: I'm not inclined to blame them for that, poor dears.

LADY KITTY: Then we settled in Florence. And because we couldn't get the society we'd been used to we became used to the society we could get. Loose women and vicious men. Snobs who liked to patronize people with a handle to their names. Vague Italian Princes who were glad to borrow a few francs from Hughie and seedy countesses who liked to drive with me in the Cascine. And then Hughie began to hanker after his old life. He wanted to go big game shooting, but I dared not let him go. I was afraid he'd never come back.

ELIZABETH: But you knew he loved you.

LADY KITTY: Oh, my dear, what a blessed institution marriage is—for women, and what fools they are to meddle with it! The Church is so wise to take its stand on the indi—indi——

ELIZABETH: Solu——

LADY KITTY: Bility of marriage. Believe me, it's no joke when you have to rely only on yourself to keep a man. I could never afford to grow old. My dear, I'll tell you a secret that I've never told a living soul.

ELIZABETH: What is that?

LADY KITTY: My hair is not naturally this color.

ELIZABETH: Really.

LADY KITTY: I touch it up. You would never have guessed, would you?

ELIZABETH: Never.

LADY KITTY: Nobody does. My dear, it's white, premature of course, but white. I always think it's a symbol of my life. Are you interested in symbolism? I think it's too wonderful.

ELIZABETH: I don't think I know very much about it.

LADY KITTY: However tired I've been I've had to be brilliant and gay. I've never let Hughie see the aching heart behind my smiling eyes.

ELIZABETH: [*Amused and touched*] You poor dear.

LADY KITTY: And when I saw he was attracted by some one else the fear and the jealousy that seized me! You see, I didn't dare make a scene as I should have done if I'd been married—I had to pretend not to notice.

ELIZABETH: [*Taken aback*] But do you mean to say he fell in love with anyone else?

LADY KITTY: Of course he did eventually.

ELIZABETH: [*Hardly knowing what to say*] You must have been very unhappy.

LADY KITTY: Oh, I was dreadfully. Night after night I sobbed my heart out when Hughie told me he was going to play cards at the club and I knew he was with that odious woman. Of course, it wasn't as if there weren't plenty of men who were only too anxious to console me. Men have always been attracted by me, you know.

ELIZABETH: Oh, of course, I can quite understand it.

LADY KITTY: But I had my self-respect to think of. I felt that whatever Hughie did I would do nothing that I should regret.

ELIZABETH: You must be very glad now.

LADY KITTY: Oh, yes. Notwithstanding all my temptations I've been absolutely faithful to Hughie in spirit.

ELIZABETH: I don't think I quite understand what you mean.

LADY KITTY: Well, there was a poor Italian boy, young Count Castel Giovanni, who was so desperately in love with me that his mother begged me not to be too cruel. She was afraid he'd go into a consumption. What could I do? And then, oh, years later, there was Antonio Melita. He said he'd shoot himself unless I——well, you understand I couldn't let the poor boy shoot himself.

ELIZABETH: D'you think he really would have shot himself?

LADY KITTY: Oh, one never knows, you know. Those Italians are so passionate. He was really rather a lamb. He had such beautiful eyes.

[Elizabeth *looks at her for a long time and a certain horror seizes her of this dissolute, painted old woman*]

ELIZABETH: [*Hoarsely*] Oh, but I think that's——dreadful.

LADY KITTY: Are you shocked? One sacrifices one's life for love and then one finds that love doesn't last. The tragedy of love isn't death or separation. One gets over them. The tragedy of love is indifference.

[Arnold *comes in*]

ARNOLD: Can I have a little talk with you, Elizabeth?

ELIZABETH: Of course.

ARNOLD: Shall we go for a stroll in the garden?

ELIZABETH: If you like.

LADY KITTY: No, stay here. I'm going out anyway.
[*Exit* Lady Kitty]

ARNOLD: I want you to listen to me for a few minutes, Elizabeth. I was so taken aback by what you told me just now that I lost my head. I was rather absurd and I beg your pardon. I said things I regret.

ELIZABETH: Oh, don't blame yourself. I'm sorry that I should have given you occasion to say them.

ARNOLD: I want to ask you if you've quite made up your mind to go.

ELIZABETH: Quite.

ARNOLD: Just now I seem to have said all that I didn't want to say and nothing that I did. I'm stupid and tongue-tied. I never told you how deeply I loved you.

ELIZABETH: Oh, Arnold!

ARNOLD: Please let me speak now. It's so very difficult. If I seemed absorbed in politics and the house, and so on, to the exclusion of my interest in you, I'm dreadfully sorry. I suppose it was absurd of me to think you would take my great love for granted.

ELIZABETH: But, Arnold, I'm not reproaching you.

ARNOLD: I'm reproaching myself. I've been tactless and neglectful. But I do ask you to believe that it hasn't been because I didn't love you. Can you forgive me?

ELIZABETH: I don't think that there's anything to forgive.

ARNOLD: It wasn't till today when you talked of leaving me that I realized how desperately in love with you I was.

ELIZABETH: After three years?

ARNOLD: I'm so proud of you. I admire you so much. When I see you at a party, so fresh and lovely, and everybody wondering at you, I have a sort of little thrill because you're mine, and afterwards I shall take you home.

ELIZABETH: Oh, Arnold, you're exaggerating.

ARNOLD: I can't imagine this house without you. Life seems on a sudden all empty and meaningless. Oh, Elizabeth, don't you love me at all?

ELIZABETH: It's much better to be honest. No.

ARNOLD: Doesn't my love mean anything to you?

ELIZABETH: I'm very grateful to you. I'm sorry to cause you pain. What would be the good of my staying with you when I should be wretched all the time?

ARNOLD: Do you love that man as much as all that? Does my unhappiness mean nothing to you?

ELIZABETH: Of course it does. It breaks my heart. You see, I never knew I meant so much to you. I'm so touched. And I'm so sorry, Arnold, really sorry. But I can't help myself.

ARNOLD: Poor child, it's cruel of me to torture you.

ELIZABETH: Oh, Arnold, believe me, I have tried to make the best of it. I've tried to love you, but I can't. After all, one either loves or one doesn't. Trying is no help. And now I'm at the end of my tether. I can't help the consequences—I must do what my whole self yearns for.

ARNOLD: My poor child, I'm so afraid you'll be unhappy. I'm so afraid you'll regret.

ELIZABETH: You must leave me to my fate. I hope you'll forget me and all the unhappiness I've caused you.

ARNOLD: [*There is a pause. Arnold walks up and down the room reflectively. He stops and faces her*] If you love this man and want to go to him I'll do nothing to prevent you. My only wish is to do what is best for you.

ELIZABETH: Arnold, that's awfully kind of you. If I'm treating you badly at least I want you to know that I'm grateful for all your kindness to me.

ARNOLD: But there's one favor I should like you to do me. Will you?

ELIZABETH: Oh, Arnold, of course I'll do anything I can.

ARNOLD: Teddie hasn't very much money. You've been used to a certain amount of luxury, and I can't bear to think that you should do without anything you've had. It would kill me to think that you were suffering any hardship or privation.

ELIZABETH: Oh, but Teddie can earn enough for our needs. After all, we don't want much money.

ARNOLD: I'm afraid my mother's life hasn't been easy, but it's obvious that the only thing that's made it possible is that Porteous was rich. I want you to let me make you an allowance of two thousand a year.

ELIZABETH: Oh, no, I couldn't think of it. It's absurd.

ARNOLD: I beg you to accept it. You don't know what a difference it will make.

ELIZABETH: It's awfully kind of you, Arnold. It humiliates me to speak about it. Nothing would induce me to take a penny from you.

ARNOLD: Well, you can't prevent me from opening an account at my bank in your name. The money shall be paid in every quarter whether you touch it or not, and if you happen to want it, it will be there waiting for you.

ELIZABETH: You overwhelm me, Arnold. There's only one thing I want you to do for me. I should be very grateful if you would divorce me as soon as you possibly can.

ARNOLD: No, I won't do that. But I'll give you cause to divorce me.

ELIZABETH: You!

ARNOLD: Yes. But of course you'll have to be very careful for a bit. I'll put it through as quickly as possible, but I'm afraid you can't hope to be free for over six months.

ELIZABETH: But, Arnold, your seat and your political career!

ARNOLD: Oh, well, my father gave up his seat under very similar circumstances. He's got along very comfortably without politics.

ELIZABETH: But they're your whole life.

ARNOLD: After all one can't have it both ways. You can't serve God and Mammon. If you want to do the decent thing you have to be prepared to suffer for it.

ELIZABETH: But I don't want you to suffer for it.

ARNOLD: At first I rather hesitated at the scandal. But I daresay that was only weakness on my part. Under the circumstances I should have liked to keep out of the Divorce Court if I could.

ELIZABETH: Arnold, you're making me absolutely miserable.

ARNOLD: What you said before dinner was quite right. It's nothing for a man, but it makes so much difference to a woman. Naturally I must think of you first.

ELIZABETH: That's absurd. It's out of the question. Whatever there's to pay I must pay it.

ARNOLD: It's not very much I'm asking you, Elizabeth.

ELIZABETH: I'm taking everything from you.

ARNOLD: It's the only condition I make. My mind is absolutely made up. I will never divorce you, but I will enable you to divorce me.

ELIZABETH: Oh, Arnold, it's cruel to be so generous.

ARNOLD: It's not generous at all. It's the only way I have of showing you how deep and passionate and sincere my love is for you. [*There is a silence. He holds out his hand*] Good night. I have a great deal of work to do before I go to bed.

ELIZABETH: Good night.

ARNOLD: Do you mind if I kiss you?

ELIZABETH: [*With agony*] Oh, Arnold!

[*He gravely kisses her on the forehead and then goes out. Elizabeth stands lost in thought. She is shattered. Lady Kitty and Porteous come in. Lady Kitty wears a cloak*]

LADY KITTY: You're alone, Elizabeth?

ELIZABETH: That note you asked me about, Lady Kitty, from Teddie . . .

LADY KITTY: Yes?

ELIZABETH: He wanted to have a talk with me before he went away. He's waiting for me in the summer house by the tennis court. Would Lord Porteous mind going down and asking him to come here?

PORTEOUS: Certainly. Certainly.

ELIZABETH: Forgive me for troubling you. But it's very important.

PORTEOUS: No trouble at all.   [*He goes out*]

LADY KITTY: Hughie and I will leave you alone.

ELIZABETH: But I don't want to be left alone. I want you to stay.

LADY KITTY: What are you going to say to him?

ELIZABETH: [*Desperately*] Please don't ask me questions. I'm so frightfully unhappy.

LADY KITTY: My poor child!

ELIZABETH: Oh, isn't life rotten? Why can't one be happy without making other people unhappy?

LADY KITTY: I wish I knew how to help you. I'm simply devoted to you. [*She hunts about in her mind for something to do or say*] Would you like my lip-stick?

ELIZABETH: [*Smiling through her tears*] Thanks. I never use one.

LADY KITTY: Oh, but just try. It's such a comfort when you're in trouble.

[*Enter* Porteous *and* Teddie]

PORTEOUS: I brought him. He said he'd be damned if he'd come.

LADY KITTY: When a lady sent for him? Are these the manners of the young men of today?

TEDDIE: When you've been solemnly kicked out of a house once I think it seems rather pushing to come back again as though nothing had happened.

ELIZABETH: Teddie, I want you to be serious.

TEDDIE: Darling, I had such a rotten dinner at that pub. If you ask me to be serious on the top of that I shall cry.

ELIZABETH: Don't be idiotic, Teddie. [*Her voice faltering*] I'm so utterly wretched.

[*He looks at her for a moment gravely*]

TEDDIE: What is it?

ELIZABETH: I can't come away with you, Teddie.

TEDDIE: Why not?

ELIZABETH: [*Looking away in embarrassment*] I don't love you enough.

TEDDIE: Fiddle!

ELIZABETH: [*With a flash of anger*] Don't say "Fiddle" to me.

TEDDIE: I shall say exactly what I like to you.

ELIZABETH: I won't be bullied.

TEDDIE: Now look here, Elizabeth, you know perfectly well that I'm in love with you, and I know perfectly well that you're in love with me. So what are you talking nonsense for?

ELIZABETH: [*Her voice breaking*] I can't say it if you're cross with me.

TEDDIE: [*Smiling very tenderly*] I'm not cross with you, silly.

ELIZABETH: It's harder still when you're being rather an owl.

TEDDIE: [*With a chuckle*] Am I mistaken in thinking you're not very easy to please?

ELIZABETH: Oh, it's monstrous. I was all wrought up and ready to do anything, and now you've thoroughly put me out. I feel like a great big fat balloon that some one has put a long pin into. [*With a sudden look at him*] Have you done it on purpose?

TEDDIE: Upon my soul I don't know what you're talking about.

ELIZABETH: I wonder if you're really much cleverer than I think you are.

TEDDIE: [*Taking her hands and making her sit down*] Now tell me exactly what you want to say. By the way, do you want Lady Kitty and Lord Porteous to be here?

ELIZABETH: Yes.

LADY KITTY: Elizabeth asked us to stay.

TEDDIE: Oh, I don't mind, bless you. I only thought you might feel rather in the way.

LADY KITTY: [*Frigidly*] A gentlewoman never feels in the way, Mr. Luton.

TEDDIE: Won't you call me Teddie? Everybody does, you know.

[*Lady Kitty tries to give him a withering look, but she finds it very difficult to prevent herself from smiling. Teddie strokes Elizabeth's hands. She draws them away*]

ELIZABETH: No, don't do that. Teddie, it wasn't true when I said I didn't love you. Of course I love you. But Arnold loves me, too. I didn't know how much.

TEDDIE: What has he been saying to you?

ELIZABETH: He's been very good to me, and so kind. I didn't know he could be so kind. He offered to let me divorce him.

TEDDIE: That's very decent of him.

ELIZABETH: But don't you see, it ties my hands. How can I accept such a sacrifice? I should never forgive myself if I profited by his generosity.

TEDDIE: If another man and I were devilish hungry and there was only one mutton chop between us, and he said, "You eat it," I wouldn't waste a lot of time arguing. I'd wolf it before he changed his mind.

ELIZABETH: Don't talk like that. It maddens me. I'm trying to do the right thing.

TEDDIE: You're not in love with Arnold; you're in love with me. It's idiotic to sacrifice your life for a slushy sentiment.

ELIZABETH: After all, I did marry him.

TEDDIE: Well, you made a mistake. A marriage without love is no marriage at all.

ELIZABETH: *I* made the mistake. Why should he suffer for it? If anyone has to suffer it's only right that I should.

TEDDIE: What sort of a life do you think it would be with him? When two people are married it's very difficult for one of them to be unhappy without making the other unhappy too.

ELIZABETH: I can't take advantage of his generosity.

TEDDIE: I daresay he'll get a lot of satisfaction out of it.

ELIZABETH: You're being beastly, Teddie. He was simply wonderful. I never knew he had it in him. He was really noble.

TEDDIE: You are talking rot, Elizabeth.

ELIZABETH: I wonder if you'd be capable of acting like that.

TEDDIE: Acting like what?

ELIZABETH: What would you do if I were married to you and came and told you I loved somebody else and wanted to leave you?

TEDDIE: You have very pretty blue eyes, Elizabeth. I'd black first one and then the other. And after that we'd see.

ELIZABETH: You damned brute!

TEDDIE: I've often thought I wasn't quite a gentleman. Had it ever struck you?

[*They look at one another for a while*]

ELIZABETH: You know, you are taking an unfair advantage of me. I feel as if I came to you quite unsuspectingly and when I wasn't looking you kicked me on the shins.

TEDDIE: Don't you think we'd get on rather well together?

PORTEOUS: Elizabeth's a fool if she don't stick to her husband. It's bad enough for the man, but for the woman—it's damnable. I hold no brief for Arnold. He plays bridge like a foot. Saving your presence, Kitty, I think he's a prig.

LADY KITTY: Poor dear, his father was at his age. I daresay he'll grow out of it.

PORTEOUS: But you stick to him, Elizabeth, stick to him. Man is a gregarious animal. We're members of a herd. If we break the herd's laws we suffer for it. And we suffer damnably.

LADY KITTY: Oh, Elizabeth, my dear child, don't go. It's not worth it. It's not worth it. I tell you that, and I've sacrificed everything to love.

[*A pause*]

ELIZABETH: I'm afraid.

TEDDIE: [*In a whisper*] Elizabeth.

ELIZABETH: I can't face it. It's asking too much of me. Let's say good-by to one another, Teddie. It's the only thing to do. And have pity on me. I'm giving up all my hope of happiness.

[*He goes up to her and looks into her eyes*]

TEDDIE: But I wasn't offering you happiness. I don't think my sort of love tends to happiness. I'm jealous. I'm not a very easy man to get on with. I'm often out of temper and irritable. I should be fed to the teeth with you sometimes, and so would you be with me. I daresay we'd fight like cat and dog, and sometimes we'd hate each other. Often you'd be wretched and bored stiff and lonely, and often you'd be frightfully homesick, and then you'd regret all you'd lost. Stupid women would be rude to you because we'd run away together. And some of them would cut you. I don't offer you peace and quietness. I offer you unrest and anxiety. I don't offer you happiness. I offer you love.

ELIZABETH: [*Stretching out her arms*] You hateful creature. I absolutely adore you!

[*He throws his arms round her and kisses her passionately on the lips*]

LADY KITTY: Of course the moment he said he'd give her a black eye I knew it was finished.

PORTEOUS: [*Good-humoredly*] You are a fool, Kitty.

LADY KITTY: I know I am, but I can't help it.

TEDDIE: Let's make a bolt for it now.

ELIZABETH: Shall we?

TEDDIE: This minute.

PORTEOUS: You're damned fools, both of you, damned fools! If you like you can have my car.

TEDDIE: That's awfully kind of you. As a matter of fact I got it out of the garage. It's just along the drive.

PORTEOUS: [*Indignantly*] How do you mean, you got it out of the garage?

TEDDIE: Well, I thought there'd be a lot of bother, and it seemed to me the best thing would be for Elizabeth and me not to stand upon the order of our going, you know. Do it now. An excellent motto for a business man.

PORTEOUS: Do you mean to say you were going to steal my car?

TEDDIE: Not exactly. I was only going to bolshevize it, so to speak.

PORTEOUS: I'm speechless. I'm absolutely speechless.

TEDDIE: Hang it all, I couldn't carry Elizabeth all the way to London. She's so damned plump.

ELIZABETH: You dirty dog!

PORTEOUS: [*Spluttering*] Well, well, well! . . . [*Helplessly*] I like him, Kitty, it's no good pretending I don't. I like him.

TEDDIE: The moon's shining, Elizabeth. We'll drive all through the night.

PORTEOUS: They'd better go to San Michele. I'll wire to have it got ready for them.

LADY KITTY: That's where we went when Hughie and I . . . [*Faltering*] Oh, you dear things, how I envy you!

PORTEOUS: [*Mopping his eyes*] Now don't cry, Kitty. Confound you, don't cry.

TEDDIE: Come, darling.

ELIZABETH: But I can't go like this.

TEDDIE: Nonsense! Lady Kitty will lend you her cloak. Won't you?

LADY KITTY: [*Taking it off*] You're capable of tearing it off my back if I don't.

TEDDIE: [*Putting the cloak on* Elizabeth] And we'll buy you a tooth-brush in London in the morning.

LADY KITTY: She must write a note for Arnold. I'll put it on her pin-cushion.

TEDDIE: Pin-cushion be blowed! Come, darling. We'll drive through the dawn and through the sunrise.

ELIZABETH: [*Kissing* Lady Kitty *and* Porteous] Good-by. Good-by.

[*Teddie stretches out his hand and she takes it. Hand in hand they go out into the night*]

LADY KITTY: Oh, Hughie, how it all comes back to me! Will they suffer all we suffered? And have we suffered all in vain?

PORTEOUS: My dear, I don't know that in life it matters so much what you do as what you are. No one can learn by the experience of another because no circumstances are quite the same. If we made rather a hash of things perhaps it was because we were rather trivial people. You can do anything in this world if you're prepared to take the consequences, and consequences depend on character.

[*Enter* Champion-Cheney, *rubbing his hands. He is as pleased as Punch*]

c.-c.: Well, I think I've settled the hash of that young man.

LADY KITTY: Oh!

c.-c.: You have to get up very early in the morning to get the better of your humble servant.

[*There is the sound of a car starting*]

LADY KITTY: What is that?

c.-c.: It sounds like a car. I expect it's your chauffeur taking one of the maids for a joy-ride.

PORTEOUS: Whose hash are you talking about?

c.-c.: Mr. Edward Luton's, my dear Hughie. I told Arnold exactly what to do and he's done it. What makes a prison? Why, bars and bolts. Remove them and a prisoner won't want to escape. Clever, I flatter myself.

PORTEOUS: You were always that, Clive, but at the moment you're obscure.

C.-C.: I told Arnold to go to Elizabeth and tell her she could have her freedom. I told him to sacrifice himself all along the line. I know what women are. The moment every obstacle was removed to

her marriage with Teddie Luton, half the allurement was gone.

LADY KITTY: Arnold did that?

C.-C.: He followed my instructions to the letter. I've just seen him. She's shaken. I'm willing to bet five hundred pounds to a penny that she won't bolt. A downy old bird, eh? Downy's the word. Downy.

[He begins to laugh. They laugh too. Presently they are all three in fits of laughter]

The Show-Off

by GEORGE KELLY

(1887–   )

Though George Kelly is not particularly old, and still gives us plays from time to time, he harks back to a period when all that was obvious, average, orthodox in American middle-class life was everywhere being held up to view—and, in most cases, to scorn. Suddenly and insistently America developed a satirical ear and eye, a sense of what could be seen from a suburban front porch, or heard in a summer hotel, or overheard in a dentist's waiting room. Suddenly and insistently, the small, eloquent, significant detail— often as matter-of-fact as a flyswatter, or as grubby as the ring around the bathtub—replaced the old, glib romantic symbols of middle-class dreaming. At the same time, and in the same way, the American language became part of the motive-power of an emerging American literature.

On the one hand, there was all our slang to exploit; on the other, there were all our genteelisms to expose. Beyond both, there were the ubiquitous clichés, the unending wisecracks, the Chamber of Commerce pomposities; and with all these things for props and counters, there quickly developed a whole literature of the close-to-home and the near-at-hand; of the surfaces of American life that sometimes revealed the depths. Much of it was conceived in satire and dedicated to the proposition that almost all men are created dismally alike. The classic locale for this conformity became the title of one book, Main Street; the classic symbol became the title of another by the same author—Babbitt.

But Sinclair Lewis was simply the most famous of many such satirists and social observers: soon Ring Lardner, Mencken, the Zona Gale of Miss Lulu Bett, and dozens of others had all Suburbia from Maine to Oregon, all Philistia from Boston to Spokane, living in glass houses and ceaselessly pelted with stones.

George Kelly's The Show-Off takes us back to that era; it was among the first plays that applied a sharply satiric method to a flatly realistic milieu. But most of all, of course—and most triumphantly of all—it impaled, or rather perhaps empedestaled, one of the great American types, one of the chief products of our smoking-car civilization; one to be encountered, in a haze of cigar smoke, along with the Rotarian, the live-wire salesman, the practical-joking "card," the whistle-stop Don Juan. Mr. Kelly's Aubrey Piper, the big bluff, the would-be bigshot, the guy with a carnation in his buttonhole whether or not he has a buck in his pocket, is at once in the great line of noisy braggarts, extending from the Miles Gloriosus of Plautus, the Braggadocio of Spenser, the Bobadil of Jonson, straight on to Bob Acres and O'Casey's Paycock; and in the forefront of classic American types. At any rate, plumped down in the lower-middle-class household of the Fishers, tricked out with the wisecracks and commonplaces of the period, he is wonderfully possible and reminiscent, while yet being gloriously farcical and unfettered.

With equal ease he can invent success or account for failure, improve on what exists or improvise what doesn't. He will lie about anything, to anyone, in front of anyone else; and no matter how badly he is thrown, he dusts himself off and mounts an even higher horse. He is a natural liar, but the nature of his lying is connected with the nature of his life; one can't help turning sociological and speculating how much Aubrey's mania to seem a big shot is tied up with the American gospel of success and worship of the successful. We might even wonder whether he is not a comic victim of the same pressures that Willy Loman, in Death of a Salesman, is a tragic victim of. But I think not. Willy Loman's is a peculiarly American tragedy, an involvement with American values: Willy is a desperate conformist who swallows the myths, who follows the methods, of others; Aubrey, with a grandly flatulent individualism, creates his own fantasies. Willy talks money as though it were arithmetic, where to Aubrey it is more like astronomy.

In any case, Mr. Kelly has kept Aubrey comic; has saved this clown who means no harm, and only does it, from the realistic penalties of his clowning. We glimpse, we more than glimpse, what trouble and grief Aubrey can cause others; but Mr. Kelly, whose way thereafter was to be decidedly more harsh, has been merciful toward his hero and suggested, at the end, that even with Aubrey in the household, all's right with the world. The Show-Off is just faintly "popularized": we could wish for a little more bite, as we could wish for somewhat less padding. But then Aubrey began life in a one-act sketch, a sort of solo *flight or solo spill, in which he had, really, his greatest triumph; and what with being enlarged into three acts, and with the passage of thirty years, The Show-Off has its weaknesses. But its very virtue now lies* *partly in its being a period piece, of which our stage furnishes few better; and partly in its remaining, at so many important points, both sound criticism and excellent fun.*

GEORGE KELLY

The Show-Off

CAST OF CHARACTERS

CLARA

MRS. FISHER

AMY

FRANK HYLAND

MR. FISHER

JOE

AUBREY PIPER

MR. GILL

MR. ROGERS

Act I

[*After a slight pause a door out at the left is heard to close, and then* Clara *comes in carrying a fancy box of candy. She glances about the room and crosses to the kitchen-door at the right*]

CLARA: Anybody out there? [*She crosses back again towards the left, laying the box of candy on the center-table as she passes. Upon reaching the parlor-doors, at the left, she opens them and calls into the parlor*] You in there, Mom? [Mrs. Fisher *can be heard coming down the stairs.* Clara *turns, with a glance toward the hall-door, and moves over to the mirror above the mantelpiece.* Mrs. Fisher *appears in the hall-door and glances in at* Clara]

MRS. FISHER: Oh, it's *you*, Clara. [*She peers out into the hall*]

CLARA: Where is everybody?

MRS. FISHER: I thought I heard that front-door open.

CLARA: Where are they all?

MRS. FISHER: [*Moving towards the parlor-door*] Your Pop's gone over to Gillespie's for some tobacco: I don't know where Joe is. [*She glances into the parlor, then turns and kisses* Clara. Clara *moves down to the chair at the left of the center-table and* Mrs. Fisher *moves over to the kitchen-door at the right*] I don't know how you can stand that fur on you, Clara, a night like this.

CLARA: It's rather cool out.

MRS. FISHER: [*Calling out through the kitchen-door*] You out there, Joe?

CLARA: [*Sitting down*] He isn't out there.

MRS. FISHER: [*Turning around to the cellar-door at her left*] He must be around here somewhere; he was here not two minutes ago, when I went upstairs. [*Opening the cellar-door and calling down*] You down there, Joey?

JOE: [*From the cellar*] Yes.

MRS. FISHER: All right. [*Closes the cellar-door*]

JOE: What do you want?

MRS. FISHER: [*Turning to the cellar-door again*] What?

[Joe *and* Clara, *speaking together*]

JOE: What do you want?

CLARA: He sez, "What do you want?"

MRS. FISHER: [*Opening the cellar-door again*] I don't want anything; I was just wonderin' where you were. [*She closes the cellar-door and comes a step or two forward, fastening an old-fashioned brooch that she wears on the front of her dress*] He spends half his time down in that cellar foolin' with that old radio thing. He sez he can make one himself, but I sez, "I'll believe it when I see it."

CLARA: There's some of that candy you like.

MRS. FISHER: [*Crossing to the center-table*] Oh, did you bring me some more of that nice candy? [*Beginning to untie the ribbon around the candy*] I never got a taste of that last you brought.

CLARA: Why not?

MRS. FISHER: Why,—Lady Jane took it away with her down to the office, and never brought it back. She sez the girls down there et it. I sez, "I guess you're the girl that et it." She sez she didn't, but I know she did.

CLARA: Well, I hope you'll keep that out of sight, and don't let her take that too.

MRS. FISHER: [*Opening the candy*] Oh, she won't get her hands on this, I can promise you that. Let her buy her own candy if she's so fond of it.

CLARA: [*Opening the "Delineator"*] She won't *buy* much of *anything*, if she can get hold of it any other way.

MRS. FISHER: Oh, isn't that lovely! Look Clara— [*Tilting the box of candy towards* Clara] Don't that look nice?

CLARA: Yes, they do their candy up nice.

MRS. FISHER: [*Gingerly picking up the cover of lace paper*] That looks just like Irish point lace, don't it? [Clara *nods yes*] I think I'll put that away somewhere,—in a book or something. My, look at all the colors—look Clara—did you ever see so many colors?

CLARA: It's pretty, isn't it?

MRS. FISHER: It's beautiful—seems a pity to spoil it. Do you want a bit of it, Clara?

CLARA: Not now, Mom.

MRS. FISHER: I think I'll take this pink one here. I *like* the pink ones. [*She picks up the box and the lid and moves around to the chair at the right of the table*] Mind how they all have this little fancy paper around them. You'd wonder they'd bother, wouldn't you?—just for a bit of candy. [*She tastes the candy and chews, critically*] That's nice candy, isn't it?

CLARA: Yes, I like bonbons.

MRS. FISHER: [*Sitting down*] I do too—I think I like them better than most anything. [*Putting the box of candy down on the table*] I'm sorry these are not all bonbons.

CLARA: [*Looking up from the "Delineator"*] They *are* all bonbons—[*Her Mother looks at her*] There's nothing else in there.

MRS. FISHER: Oh, are they!—I thought only the pink ones were the bonbons.

CLARA: No, they're all bonbons.

MRS. FISHER: Well, that's lovely. I can eat any one of them I like, then, can't I? [*She sits back in her chair and rocks and chews*] How is it you're not home to-night, Clara?

CLARA: Frank had to go to a dinner of some kind at the Glenwood Club; so I thought I'd stay in town and get something. He said he might call for me here around eight o'clock. I was in anyway about my lamp.

MRS. FISHER: [*Rocking*] Men are always going to dinners somewhere. Seems to me they can't talk about anything unless they've got a dinner in front of them. It's no wonder so many of them are fat.

CLARA: [*Turning a page of the "Delineator"*] Where's Amy,—upstairs?

MRS. FISHER: Yes, she's gettin' dressed. I was just hookin' her when you came in.

CLARA: Is she going out?

MRS. FISHER: I don't know whether she is or not,—I didn't hear her say. [*Leaning a bit towards Clara, and lowering her voice*] But it's Wednesday night, you know.

CLARA: Is that fellow still coming here?

MRS. FISHER: Oh, right on the dot—such as he is. Sunday nights too now, as well as Wednesdays. It looks like a steady thing. And you never in your life heard anybody talk so much, Clara—I don't know how she stands him. Your Pop can hardly stay in the room where he is. I believe in my heart that's the reason he went over to Gillespie's to-night—so he wouldn't be listenin' to him.

CLARA: Doesn't she take him into the parlor?

MRS. FISHER: She does, yes; but she might just as well leave him out here; for he's not in there five minutes till he's out here again—talkin' about Socialism. That's all you hear,—Socialism—and capital and labor. You'd think he knew somethin' about it. And the Pennsylvania Railroad. He's always talkin' about that, too. That's where he works, you know. I don't know what he does down there. He sez himself he's head of the freight department; but as I sez to our Joe, I sez, "I don't know how *he* can be head of *anything*, from the talk of him." Joe sez he thinks he's a nut. And your Pop told him right to his face here last Sunday night—that he didn't know the meanin' of the *word* Socialism. [*She checks herself and gets up*] I'd better not be talkin' so loud,—he's apt to walk in on us. [*She moves up towards the hall-door and glances out*] He's a great joker, you know—That's what he did last Sunday night. [*Coming forward again to a point above the center-table*] I never got such a fright in my life. Your Pop and me was sittin' here talkin', just the way we are now, when, all of a sudden, I glanced up, and there he was,—standin' in the doorway there, doin' this [*She points her forefinger and thumb at Clara and wiggles her thumb. Clara laughs faintly*]—as though he was a bandit, you know. Well,—I thought the breath'd leave my body. Then he sez, "Haha!—that's the time I fooled you!" I don't know how long he'd been standin' there. But, as luck'd have it, we wasn't talkin' about him at the time: altho we *had* been talkin' about him not five minutes before. I don't know whether he heard us or not, for I don't know how long he'd been standin' there. I hope he did: it'd just be the price of him, for bein' so smart. [*With a glance toward the hall-door, and speaking very confidentially*] But, you know, what'd kill you, Clara, you can't say a *word* about him in front of her. [*Clara moves*] Oh, not a word. No matter what he sez, she thinks it's lovely. When Joe told her here the other night he thought he was a nut, she just laughed, and said that Joe was jealous of him—because *he* could express himself and *he* couldn't. [*Clara smiles*] You never *heard* such talk. And, you know, Clara, *I* think he wears a wig. [*Clara laughs*] I do, honestly. And our Joe sez he thinks he does too. But when I asked *her* about it here one mornin', I thought she'd take the head right off me. You never *seen* anybody get themselves into such a temper. She sez, "It's a lie," she sez, "he *don't* wear a wig." She sez, "People always say somethin' like that about a fellow that makes a good appearance." But, *I* think he does, just the same; and the first chance I get I'm goin' to take a good look. [*She moves around to her chair again, at the right of the table*] He often sits right here, you know, under this light, while he's talkin'; [*Selecting another piece of candy*] and I'm goin' to look close the very first chance I get. [*She sits down] I can tell a wig as good as anybody. [*She rocks and looks straight out, chewing*] She won't make a liar out of me.

AMY: [*From the head of the stairs*] Mom, did you see anything of that blue bar-pin of mine?

MRS. FISHER: [*Calling back to her*] Which blue bar-pin?

AMY: Well now, how many blue bar-pins have I got?

MRS. FISHER: I don't know how many you've got, and I don't care! [*Turning back again and speaking rather to herself*] So don't be botherin' me about it. [*Calling up to Amy again*] If you can't find it, go look for it. [*She resumes her rocking and her chewing*] She thinks all she's got to do is come to the head of them stairs and holler and everybody'll jump.—But she'll get sadly left.—I've got somethin' else to do besides waitin' on her. [*She takes another bite of candy, and turns casually to Clara*] Did you get your lamp yet?

CLARA: No, that's what I was in town to-day about. The girl sez they haven't been able to match the silk till yesterday.

MRS. FISHER: I wish I could get somethin' done to that one of mine there in the parlor; the wire's right out through the silk in two places.

CLARA: Why doesn't Amy take it in some day [Mrs. Fisher *makes a sound of amusement*]—when she's going to work?

MRS. FISHER: Why don't she! It's all Amy can do to take *herself* into work these days. I've almost got to *push* her out the door every morning.

CLARA: Couldn't she take it over at lunch-time?

MRS. FISHER: She sez she hasn't time at lunch-time.

CLARA: Oh, she has so time.

MRS. FISHER: Of course she has.

CLARA: It's only at Ninth and Chestnut, and she's at Eighth.

MRS. FISHER: That's what I told her. I sez, "I bet if it was somethin' for yourself you'd have plenty of time." [*Leaning towards* Clara] But, you know,—what I think, Clara—I think she's meetin' this fellow at lunch-time. Because in the mornin's here she stands fixin' herself there in front of that glass till it's a wonder to me she don't drop on the floor. And whenever you see them gettin' very particular that way all of a sudden—there's somethin' in the wind. I sez to her the other mornin', when she was settlin' herself there till I got tired lookin' at her, I sez, "You must be goin' to see him to-day, ain't you?" And she sez, "He must be on your mind, isn't he?" "No," I sez, "but by the looks of things, I think he's on yours. And," I sez, "maybe after you get him you won't think he was worth all the bother you went to." Because, you know, Clara, she don't know a *thing* about him; except that he works in the Pennsylvania freight office—I believe he *did* tell her that much. But *she* don't know whether he works there or not. He could tell her anything; and she'd be-

lieve it [*Taking another bite of candy and settling herself in her chair*]—before she'd believe me.

CLARA: That's where he works [*Her Mother looks at her sharply*]—at the Pennsylvania freight office.

MRS. FISHER: How do you know?

CLARA: Frank knows him.

MRS. FISHER: Frank Hyland?

CLARA: Yes,—he sez he eats his lunch at the same place, there at Fifteenth and Arch.

MRS. FISHER: And, does he say he knows him?

CLARA: Yes. He sez he's seen him around there for a long time. I've often heard him speak of him, but I didn't know it was the same fellow. Frank always called him Carnation Charlie. He sez he's always got a big carnation in his buttonhole.

MRS. FISHER: [*Tapping the table conclusively*] That's the one; he's always got it on when he comes here, too.

CLARA: Frank sez he's never seen him without it.

MRS. FISHER: I haven't either. And I believe in my heart, Clara, that's what's turned her head. [Clara *smiles*] You often see things like that, you know. The worst fool of a man can put a carnation in his coat or his hat over one eye, and half a dozen sensible women'll be dyin' about him.

CLARA: Well, Frank sez this fellow's absolutely *crazy*.

MRS. FISHER: That's what your Father sez.

CLARA: He sez they kid the life out of him down around the restaurant there.

MRS. FISHER: Well, he don't know who Frank Hyland *is*, does he?

CLARA: No, Frank didn't tell him. He sez he just happened to get talking to him the other day and he mentioned that he was calling on a girl up this way named Fisher. So then Frank found out what his right name was, and when he came home he asked me about him.

MRS. FISHER: Well, is he sure it's the same fellow?

CLARA: He told him his name was Piper.

MRS. FISHER: [*With finality*] That's the name— Aubrey Piper. I don't know where he got the Aubrey from; I never heard of such a name before, did you?

CLARA: Yes, I've heard the name of Aubrey.

MRS. FISHER: [*Rocking*] Well, I never did. Sounds to me more like a place than a name. [Amy *can be heard coming down the stairs*] Here she comes. [*She snatches up the box of candy and puts it under her apron*]

CLARA: Don't say anything, now.

MRS. FISHER: It'd be no use. [*Trying to be casual*] What color are you havin' your lamp-shade made, Clara?

AMY: [*Hurrying in at the hall-door*] Mom, you *must* have seen something of that bar-pin of mine; I can't find it anywhere. [*She tosses a beaded bag onto the center-table and turns to the mantel-piece and looks for the bar-pin*]

MRS. FISHER: [*Abstractedly*] I saw a pin of yours in

one of the drawers in the buffet there a few days ago, I don't know whether it's there yet or not.

AMY: [*Hurrying across to the buffet at the right*] How's it *you're* not home to-night, Clara? [*She starts to rummage in the buffet-drawers*]

CLARA: [*Casually*] I had my dinner in town.

AMY: Is that parlor all right, Mom?

MRS. FISHER: Certainly it's all right.

AMY: Well, did you side it?

MRS. FISHER: [*Sharply*] Certainly I sided it.

AMY: All right, Mom, don't make a speech about it.

MRS. FISHER: [*Considerably ruffled*] No, but you'd think the way she sez it that I sat here all day with my two hands as long as each other. [*Amy finds the pin and slams the drawer shut, leaving various ends of tape and pieces of lace hanging out. Then she starts back towards the mirror over the mantelpiece*] Did you find it?

AMY: [*Disrespectfully*] Yes.

MRS. FISHER: [*Rising, still holding the candy under her apron, and stepping over to the buffet*] It's a wonder you wouldn't leave these drawers the way you found them. She does that every time she goes near this buffet. [*She puts the various odds and ends back into the drawers and closes them*] She's in such a great rush lately.

AMY: [*Settling herself at the mirror*] Isn't that a new dress on you, Clara?

CLARA: Yes.

MRS. FISHER: [*Coming back to her chair*] I'd like to see the kind of house you'll keep.

AMY: Well, I hope it won't be anything like this one, I'll tell you that.

MRS. FISHER: [*Stopping halfway to her chair*] Oh, go easy, lady! You might be very glad to have half as good, if you live long enough. [*Continuing to her chair, and looking keenly at Clara's dress*] I thought I hadn't seen that dress on you before. [*She sits down*]

CLARA: No, I only got it last week.

MRS. FISHER: Stand up there till I see it.

[*Clara gets up and takes a couple of steps towards the left, pulling down her skirt, then turns around to her left and faces her Mother. Amy comes down to the center-table, looking sharply at Clara's dress*]

CLARA: I got it at a sale in Strawbridge's.

[*Amy opens her beaded purse on the table and looks at herself critically in the little inside mirror; then adds a touch of powder*]

MRS. FISHER: It's a nice length.

CLARA: I didn't have to have a thing touched on it.

MRS. FISHER: That's what I was tellin' you about the other day, Amy.—Do you see the way that dress hangs?

AMY: Yeh.

MRS. FISHER: [*Speaking directly to Clara*] There was a dress on Queen Mary in last Sunday's Ledger

that I was sayin' to Amy I thought'd look good on me. And it had all buttons up and down the front, the way that has.

CLARA: [*Coming back to her chair*] A lot of the new dresses are made that way.

MRS. FISHER: How much was it?

CLARA: [*Sitting down*] Forty-two seventy-five.

[*Amy starts to polish her nails*]

MRS. FISHER: [*Turning away, with a lift of her eyes to Heaven*] You must have plenty of money.

AMY: Mom, where'd you put those roses I brought home?

MRS. FISHER: They're out there in the dining-room. [*Amy starts towards the right*] I put them in some water. [*Amy goes out; and Mrs. Fisher rocks for a second or two; then she turns and calls after Amy*] I think it's time you lit the light in that parlor, Amy, if that fellow of yours is comin' here to-night. [*She rocks a little bit more, then turns casually to Clara*] What time is it by your watch there, Clara? [*With a glance toward the mantelpiece at the back*] That old clock of ours is stopped again.

CLARA: [*Looking at her wrist-watch*] Quarter past eight.

MRS. FISHER: [*Getting up suddenly*] I must tell her. [*The box of candy lands on the floor*] My God, there goes the candy! Pick that up, Clara, I can't stoop; and put it out of sight. [*Going towards the door up at the right*] It's a wonder I didn't do that while she was in here. [*Calling out after Amy*] Amy!

AMY: Yes?

MRS. FISHER: Clara sez it's a quarter past eight by her watch;—you'd better get some kind of a light in that parlor if that fellow's comin'. [*She moves back towards her chair, then speaks in a very sub-dued tone to Clara*] She brings flowers home with her from the city now, every night he's coming. She must have flowers for him in the parlor. [*She sits down*] I told her, I sez, "I bet it'd be a long time before you'd bring any flowers home from the city to me."

CLARA: That's another new dress on *her* to-night, isn't it?

MRS. FISHER: [*Straightening the magazines on the table*] She's had it about a week.

CLARA: What's she getting so many new dresses for lately?

MRS. FISHER: Heaven knows, I don't.

CLARA: That's the fourth I've seen on her since Easter.

MRS. FISHER: Tryin' to make him think she's rich, I guess. I told her the other night she might not get so many after she gets him.

AMY: [*Entering from the right, carrying a vase of roses, and crossing directly to the parlor-doors at the left*] You need another box of matches out there, Mom.

MRS. FISHER: Is that box of matches gone already?

AMY: Pretty near. [*She goes into the parlor*]

MRS. FISHER: I swear I don't know where all the matches go to;—seems to me all I do is buy matches. [Amy *strikes a match in the parlor*] Be careful of them lace curtains there, now, Amy, if you're goin' to light that lamp. [*The lamp is lit in the parlor; and* Amy *closes the parlor-doors*]

CLARA: [*Rising and handing her Mother the box of candy, which she has been holding since she picked it up from the floor*] I think I'll go, before he comes.

MRS. FISHER: [*Rising*] You'd better, unless you want to be here all night. [Clara *moves up to the looking-glass over the mantelpiece, and* Mrs. Fisher *crosses to the buffet with the candy*] For if he ever starts talkin', you'll never get out. [*She puts the candy into one of the drawers, then starts across towards the hall-door, up at the left*] You wouldn't mind, you know, if he'd stay in there in the parlor;—but the minute ever he hears a voice out here, he's out like a jumpin'-jack. [Amy *can be heard coughing out in the hallway, and, as* Mrs. Fisher *passes back of* Clara, Clara *half turns and suggests with a movement of her hand that* Amy *might overhear her*] Oh, he's not here yet; you'd know it if he was. [*She peers keenly out into the hallway, then turns and tiptoes back to* Clara, *and speaks in a very low tone*] She stands out there in the vestibule until she sees him get off the trolley, then she comes in and lets him ring, so he won't think she's been waitin' for him. [*She tiptoes back and peers out into the hallway again, and* Clara *moves over to the right, adjusting her neck-piece.* Mrs. Fisher *comes back to the center-table*] You never seen anybody so crazy about a fellow.

CLARA: Well, I think somebody ought to tell her about him, Mom.

MRS. FISHER: [*Folding the ribbon and the paper from the candy-box*] What's the good of tellin' her;—she'd only give you a look if you said anything about him.

CLARA: Well, I'd say it anyway, whether she gave me a look or not; for, remember what I'm telling you, Mom, it's *you* that'll have them on your hands if she takes him. [*Her Mother looks at her sharply*]

MRS. FISHER: *I'll* have them on my hands?

CLARA: [*Turning to her Mother*] Well now, who else *will*, Mom? You couldn't leave her out on the street; and that's exactly where she'll land if she takes *him*; for you know how long Amy could get along on a hundred and fifty dollars a month.

MRS. FISHER: Takes more than that to keep herself, never name a house and a husband.

CLARA: Well, that's exactly what he gets, for he's only a clerk down there.

MRS. FISHER: He told her he was the head of the department.

CLARA: He's a clerk, Mom,—like a hundred others down there: Frank knows what he does.

MRS. FISHER: [*Moving a step or two nearer to* Clara] Well, why don't *you* say something to her, Clara?

CLARA: Now, you know how much attention she'd pay to anything I'd say.

MRS. FISHER: [*With measured definiteness*] She won't pay any attention to what anybody sez.

CLARA: Especially if she knew it was Frank Hyland that said it.

MRS. FISHER: She thinks everybody's jealous of him; and jealous of *her* because she's gettin' him. So let her get him. If she makes her bed, let her lie in it.

CLARA: [*Looking straight out*] Well, that's the trouble, Mom; it isn't always the person that makes the bed that lies *in* it.—Very often somebody else has to lie in it.

MRS. FISHER: [*Turning back to the table*] Well, it'll be nobody around here, I can promise you that.

CLARA: [*Turning to the buffet-mirror*] Maybe not.

MRS. FISHER: No maybe about it.

CLARA: But you know what *you* are, Mom, where Amy's concerned.

MRS. FISHER: [*Taking a step towards* Clara] Why, don't be silly, Clara. Do you think your Father'd be listenin' to that rattle-brain here every night?

CLARA: [*Turning and speaking directly to her Mother*] He has to listen to him now, doesn't he— or go out, as he did tonight. [*The front-door closes. They both turn and glance in the direction of the hallway*] Maybe this is Frank now. [*There is a slight pause, then* Frank Hyland *comes in, and comes forward to the center-table*]

MRS. FISHER: Hello, Frank.

HYLAND: Hello, Mother. Hello, Clara. [*He puts his hat down on the table*]

CLARA: I was just going; I thought maybe you weren't coming.

HYLAND: [*Looking at his watch*] I couldn't get away from there until nearly eight o'clock.

MRS. FISHER: Frank,—Clara sez you know this fellow that's comin' to see our Amy.

HYLAND: Who, Piper?

MRS. FISHER: Yes—the one that does so much talkin'.

HYLAND: Yes, I know him. [*He moves to the left and sits down on the arm of the Morris-chair*]

MRS. FISHER: I think he's crazy, Frank; [Hyland *makes a sound of amusement*] I do, honestly; and Pop and Joe sez they think he is, too.

CLARA: Mom sez he told Amy he was head of the freight department, Frank.

MRS. FISHER: He did, honestly, Frank; and she believes him. But Clara sez *you* say he's only a clerk down there.

CLARA: That's all he is, Mom.

MRS. FISHER: He isn't head of the freight department, is he, Frank?

[Frank *sits looking away off, dreamily*]

CLARA: Frank—

HYLAND: [*Turning*] I beg your pardon, what did you say, dear?

MRS. FISHER: He isn't head of the freight department down there, is he?

HYLAND: No, he's just one of the clerks.

MRS. FISHER: [*Turning to* Clara] Now, you see that —and she'd only laugh at you if you told *her* that. [*Turning back to* Hyland] How much do them freight-clerks get a month, Frank?
[Hyland *is gazing out of the window at the left*]

CLARA: Frank, Mom is talking to you.

HYLAND: [*Turning*] Oh, I beg your pardon, what did you say, Mother?

MRS. FISHER: I say, how much do them freight-clerks get a month?

HYLAND: Why,—about a hundred and forty or fifty dollars,—I don't know exactly; but not any more than that. [*His eyes wander to the window again*]

MRS. FISHER: What are we goin' to do about it, Frank?—It looks like a steady thing. He comes Wednesday and Sunday nights now—and if she ever takes him, she'll be the poorest woman in the city. You know how our Amy spends money. [*Turning to* Clara] She's got seven pairs of shoes up in that hall-closet.

HYLAND: [*Abstractedly*] Amy certainly does let her money fly. [Mrs. Fisher *gives him a stony look*]

MRS. FISHER: Well, if she does she earns it. She might as well have a good time now while she's young;—God knows what's ahead of her. [*The front door-bell rings,—a series of funny little taps*] Here he is now, I know his ring. [*She steps up to the mantelpiece and glances out into the hallway*]

CLARA: [*Turning towards the kitchen-door*] We'll go out the side-door. Come on, Frank.
[Hyland *rises and picks up his hat from the table, as he crosses below it*]

HYLAND: Good-night, Mother. [Mrs. Fisher *is too occupied with her interests out in the hallway*] Do you want to go to a picture, Clara?

CLARA: [*Going out at the right*] I don't care.

HYLAND: [*Following her*] It's only about twenty after eight. [*He glances at his watch*]

CLARA: We can get the second show at Broad and Columbia Avenue.

MRS. FISHER: [*Following them out*] Frank, I wish you'd talk to Amy some time, and tell her what you told me; she won't believe *me*.

HYLAND: I don't suppose she'd believe me, either, Mother.

AUBREY: [*Out at the front-door*] Right on the job!

AMY: Hello!

AUBREY: The pride of old West Philly! [*He laughs a bit, boisterously*]

AMY: I'll take your hat, Aubrey.

AUBREY: Anything to please the ladies. [*The front-door closes*] The boy rode off with many thanks, and many a backward bow. [*He laughs again,*

rather wildly. Mrs. Fisher *tiptoes into the room from the right and stands listening, keenly*] Do you know, I think I'll have to get hold of an air-ship somewhere, Amy, to come out here to see you.

AMY: It *is* quite a trip for you, isn't it?

AUBREY: Just one shining hour and a half, if you say it quick; by the little old Brill special. And how is the Mother? [Mrs. Fisher's *face hardens, and a door closes. Then she tiptoes over to the double-doors at the left and listens.* Aubrey's *voice can be heard fairly distinctly from beyond the doors*] Say, Amy—wasn't that hold-up in last night's paper somewhere out this way?

AMY: Yes, it was right over here on Erie Avenue.

[Mr. Fisher *appears in the hall-door and stands, looking with amusement at his wife. He takes an old pipe and tobacco-pouch from the pocket of his knit-jacket and starts to fill the pipe*]

AUBREY: A doctor's house, wasn't it?

AMY: Yes, Doctor Donnelly's. They got nearly two thousand dollars.

AUBREY: I don't believe that, Amy.

AMY: Why not?

AUBREY: I don't believe there's that much money *in* North Philadelphia. [*He roars with laughter.* Mr. Fisher *gives his wife a little dig in the ribs and makes a sound like a startled cat. She starts violently, smothering a little shriek*]

MRS. FISHER: Oh, you frightened me!
[Mr. Fisher *continues to the center-table and sets his newspaper down*]

MR. FISHER: You ought to be pretty nearly frightened to death by this time, oughtn't you? [*He replaces the tobacco-pouch in his pocket*]

MRS. FISHER: Well, it's no wonder I'd be.

MR. FISHER: You've been jumpin' that way ever since I knew you.

MRS. FISHER: Well, what do you come pussy-footin' in that way for, when you know how nervous I am?

MR. FISHER: I didn't come pussy-footin' in at all.

MRS. FISHER: You did so, or I'd have heard you.

MR. FISHER: You *would* have heard me, if you weren't so busy listenin' to somethin' that's none of your business.

MRS. FISHER: Well, it'll be somethin' of my business if you go spillin' any of that dirty old tobacco on my nice new table-cloth, I tell you that. [*She resumes her listening at the door, and* Mr. Fisher *brushes the tobacco from the table-cloth*]

MR. FISHER: I'm not spillin' any of it. [*There's a burst of laughter from* Aubrey *in the parlor, and* Mr. Fisher *looks toward the parlor-door*] Who's in there—Windy? [Mrs. Fisher *nods, yes, and the old man moves down at the right of the center-table, picking up the newspaper and reaching into his vest-pocket for his spectacles.*] What's he doin', laughin' at some more of them West Philadelphia jokes of his? [*He sits down to read, in the chair at the right of the table, and Mrs. Fisher comes tiptoeing towards the chair at the left of the table*]

MRS. FISHER: [*In a lowered tone*] He was astin' Amy about that robbery over at Doctor Donnelly's yesterday mornin'; and when she told him the bandits got away with nearly two thousand dollars, he said it couldn't be true, because there wasn't that much money *in* North Philadelphia.

MR. FISHER: [*With mock laughter*] Ha! Ha! Ha!

MRS. FISHER: [*Returning to the parlor-doors to listen*] Shush!

[*There's a Ha! Ha! Ha! from the parlor from* Aubrey, *and the old man looks quickly and distrustfully in that direction.* Aubrey *continues to laugh*]

MR. FISHER: [*Settling himself to read*] I'll bet there wouldn't have to be much money up this way to be more than *he's* got.

[*There's a sound of hammering in the cellar.* Mrs. Fisher *hurries across to the cellar-door*]

AUBREY: [*In the parlor*] You know, I discovered tonight, Amy, that I can save a full fifteen minutes on this trip over here, by transferring up Twenty-ninth to the Lehigh Avenue car, instead of going on in and up Nineteenth.

MRS. FISHER: [*Opening the cellar-door and calling down, in a subdued voice*] Joe! Stop that hammering down there, we can't hear our ears up here. [*The old man gives a hard chuckle.* Mrs. Fisher *tip-toes back towards the parlor-doors, looking at her husband stonily*] What ails *you*?

AMY: [*In the parlor*] It *is* hard to get out here, unless you use the Park trolley. I hear some people say that's a great deal quicker.

[Mrs. Fisher *listens keenly again with her ear against the parlor-door*]

AUBREY: I don't know how they ever found this place.

AMY: I don't know how *you* ever found *West* Philadelphia.

AUBREY: Lot of people think they haven't found it *yet*. [*He bursts into violent laughter*] Lost somewhere between the Schuylkill River and Darby. [*He laughs some more. The old man looks piercingly over his spectacles at his wife*]

MR. FISHER: [*Almost shouting*] Come away from there, Josie! [Mrs. Fisher *is startled almost to death. She places her hand on her bosom and moves away from the door towards the center of the room*] Don't be listenin' to that damned blatherskite.

MRS. FISHER: [*Trying to be casual*] I wasn't listenin' to him;—I was just seein' what he was sayin'. [*She moves up to the little stand between the hall-door and the mantelpiece and picks up her knitting-bag.* Amy *is very much amused at something* Aubrey *has just said in the parlor.* Mrs. Fisher

glances toward the parlor-doors, then comes down to her husband's right, and, with another glance toward the door, speaks very confidentially] He was astin' Amy how she ever found this part of town to live in; and she was astin' him how *he* ever found *West* Philadelphia. He sez West Philadelphia ain't *been* found yet,—that it's lost somewhere between the Schuylkill River and Darby. [*She moves over to the arm-chair at the right, in front of the window, and sits down*]

MR. FISHER: I wish to God *he'd* get lost some night, somewhere between here and the Schuylkill River.

MRS. FISHER: [*Taking the needles and the pink wool out of the knitting-bag*] What'd kill you, too, you know, he always dies laughin' whenever he gets off one of them bum jokes.

MR. FISHER: Somebody's got to laugh.

AUBREY: [*From the parlor*] Ha! Ha! That's the time I fooled you, Amy! Leave it to me to put it right over the plate.

[Amy *has quite a laughing fit in the parlor. Her Mother looks narrowly toward the parlor-doors until* Amy *has finished laughing*]

MRS. FISHER: He's got Amy laughin' now, too. [*She commences to knit; and there is a slight pause. Then she glances at the clock on the mantelpiece*] That old clock has stopped again, Neil.

MR. FISHER: [*Without moving*] Needs fixin'.

MRS. FISHER: It's *been* fixed twice,—don't do no good. [*There is a pause, and* Mrs. Fisher *sighs*] I think it's terrible lonesome not to hear the clock —it's too still in a room.—It always sounds to me like soap-bubbles meltin'.

MR. FISHER: H'm—here's a fellow here's been left a quarter of a million dollars, and he won't take it.

MRS. FISHER: [*Sharply*] What's the matter with him?

MR. FISHER: Nothin' at all's the matter with him— he just won't take it.

MRS. FISHER: [*Resuming her knitting*] He mustn't be in his right mind, poor boy. I wisht somebody'd leave *me* a quarter of a million dollars.

MR. FISHER: You wouldn't know what to do with it if they did.

MRS. FISHER: Well, I know *one* thing I'd do with it; and that'd be to have somethin' done to that old heater of ours downstairs, and not be freezin' to death all *next* winter, the way I was last. [Aubrey *laughs in the parlor.* Mrs. Fisher *glances toward the parlor-doors; then shifts her knitting*] Every sweater I start I swear it'll be the last—and then I start right in on another. [*She gives a faint little laugh and looks at her husband; but he's reading; so she subsides and continues to knit. Suddenly she stops and rests her knitting in her lap, and thinks; then turns to* Mr. Fisher] Well now, what becomes of money like that, Neil, that people won't take?

MR. FISHER: [*Squinting at her over his glasses*] What'd you say?

MRS. FISHER: I say, what becomes of money that people won't take that way?

MR. FISHER: [Resuming his paper] Why, nothing at all becomes of it;—they just come and get it. [She looks at him steadily]

MRS. FISHER: Who does?

MR. FISHER: The people that won't take it.

[Mrs. Fisher is puzzled for a second]

MRS. FISHER: [Resuming her knitting] Well, I'll bet if they left it to me they wouldn't have to come and take it.

MR. FISHER: [Looking at her again with a shade of irritation] Who wouldn't have to come and take it?

MRS. FISHER: [Losing her temper] Why, the people that won't take it!

MR. FISHER: What are you talkin' about, Josie, do you know?

MRS. FISHER: Yes, I do know very well what I'm talkin' about!—but I don't think you do.

MR. FISHER: Let me read this paper, will you?

MRS. FISHER: [Knitting rapidly] Go ahead and read it!—I'm sure I don't want to talk to you. It was you that started talkin' to me—readin' about that young man that took the money. [Joe comes up from the cellar, carrying some kind of a radio-arrangement on a flat base-board and a screwdriver] Joe, I'm goin' to have that light took out of that cellar, if you don't stop spendin' all your time down there.

JOE: [Holding his work under the table-lamp to look at it closely] You don't want me hammerin' up here, do you?

MRS. FISHER: I don't want you hammerin' anywhere. I want you to go out at night and get some air, and not be cooped up in that dusty old cellar.

[There's a violent burst of laughter from Aubrey in the parlor. Joe glances toward the parlor-doors, then turns, with something of distress in his expression, to his Mother]

JOE: Who's in there—the Pennsylvania Railroad?

MRS. FISHER: Yes, and he's got about as much sense as yourself.

JOE: [Moving around to the chair at the left of the center-table and sitting down] You won't say that when you're sittin' here listenin' to the Grand Opera. [He starts to tighten the small screws in the base-board]

MRS. FISHER: I won't be listenin' to it, don't fret—I got somethin' else to do besides listenin' to a lot of dagoes singin'.

MR. FISHER: [Looking over at Joe's radio-arrangement] What is it?

MRS. FISHER: He sez when he gets that radio-thing finished, I can sit here and listen to the Grand Opera.

MR. FISHER: [Resuming his paper] What's that, them singin' people?

MRS. FISHER: Yes—them that goes away up high, you know—that Clara has on her victrola.

[The parlor-door opens, and Amy comes out, walking on air]

AMY: Oh, it's all right if you let it run for a minute. [She crosses to the right to the kitchen-door, glancing at herself in the mantelpiece-mirror as she pauses]

MRS. FISHER: What's the matter?

AMY: Nothing; Aubrey wants a drink of water. [She goes out at the right]

MRS. FISHER: [With a significant sound] Oh.

AUBREY: [Coming out of the parlor] Stay right where you are, folks, right where you are. [He moves to the mirror over the mantelpiece] Just a little social attention,—going right out again on the next train. [He surveys himself critically in the mirror, touching his tie and toupé gingerly. Mrs. Fisher gives him a smouldering look, and Joe looks at his Father. Aubrey turns from the mirror, and indicates his reflection with a wide gesture] There you are, Mother! Any woman's fancy, what do you say? Even to the little old carnation. [He gives the table a double tap with his knuckles, then laughs, and moves up towards the kitchen-door, and calls out to Amy] Come on, Amy, step on the United Gas out there; customer in here waiting for the old aqua pura. [Moving down to Mr. Fisher's right] Man's got to have something to drink—how about it, Pop? [He gives Mr. Fisher a slap on the right shoulder] You'll stay with me on that, won't you? [He laughs and moves up to the mirror again. Old man Fisher is very much annoyed] Yes, sir. [Coming forward again at the right] I want to tell those of you who have ventured out this evening, that this is a very pretty little picture of domestic felicity. [He laughs a little and looks from one to the other, patronizingly; but nobody pays the slightest attention to him] Father reading,—Mother knitting; [Mrs. Fisher withers him with a quick look] But then, Mama, is always knitting. [She knits rapidly and Aubrey laughs, and moves up and across back of the table] And little old Tommy Edison over here, working eighteen hours a day to make the rich man richer and the poor man poorer. [He gives Joe a tap on the back, then moves back again towards Mr. Fisher] What about it, Popcorn? [Slaps him on the back] Shake it up! Right or raving?

MR. FISHER: [Starting to his feet violently] God damn it, let me alone! And keep your hands to yourself. [He crosses below the center-table and up to the hall-door] I never saw such a damn pest in my life! [He goes up the stairs bristling with rage, and muttering to himself. Aubrey is vastly amused. He leans on the back of Mr. Fisher's chair and roars with laughter]

AUBREY: Sign on the dotted line! And little old

Popsy-Wopsy getting sore and going to leave us flat. [*He laughs again considerably; then turns to* Mrs. Fisher] Nevertheless, and notwithstanding, Mrs. Fisher, I'd like to mention that the kid from West Philadelphia is giving the growing boy the said and done. [*He indicates* Joe *with a waving gesture.* Amy *comes in from the right with a glass of water. He turns and acknowledges her with even a wider gesture*] And there she is herself, and not a moving picture. [Amy *extends the glass of water, laughing, and with a touch of self-consciousness*] Blushing as she gave it, looking down—at her feet so bare, and her tattered gown. [Amy *giggles, and her Mother looks sharply at* Amy's *shoes.* Aubrey *takes the glass of water and turns to* Mrs. Fisher] How's that, Mother Fisher? Can't beat that little old Willie Shakespeare, can you? No, sir,—I'd like to tell the brothers that that little old Shakespeare party shook a wicked spear. [*He laughs at his own comedy, and* Amy *is immeasurably delighted*] Well, here's laughter, ladies! and, [*Turning to* Joe] Mr. Marconi,—my best regards to you. [*He drinks*]

AMY: I'm afraid it's not very cold.

[*He just raises his hand, signifying that it's perfectly satisfactory*]

MRS. FISHER: Why didn't you let it run?

AMY: I did, but it doesn't seem to get any colder.

AUBREY: [*Handing the glass back to* Amy] Very nice indeed. And a sweeter draught, from a fairer hand was never quaffed.

AMY: [*Flipping her hand at him*] Oh, you! [*She goes out at the right again with the empty glass*]

AUBREY: [*Laughing a bit*] Thank you very much. [*He turns and moves across above the table towards* Joe, *drawing a gaily-bordered handkerchief from his breast-pocket and touching it to his lips*] Yes, sir, Mr. Joseph, I want to tell you you're wasting time; for when you're all through, they'll offer you twenty cents for it, and sell it for twenty million. [*He punctuates this last remark with a series of patronizing taps on* Joe's *back*]—Take it or leave it—sign on the dotted line. [*He taps his knuckles on the table, and moves back again to* Mrs. Fisher's *left*] Yes, sir,—that's exactly what they did to little old yours truly here. Twenty Lincoln Anacondas, for a formula that would have solved the greatest problem before the Industrial Chemical world to-day. [Amy *comes in from the right, and, looking at* Aubrey *wonderingly, moves across towards the left.* Aubrey *moves forward and across in front of the table towards* Joe] A formula to prevent the rusting of iron and steel. [Joe *gets up and moves up and around above the table towards the kitchen-door at the right*] A solution of Vanadium and Manganese, to be added to the metal in its molten state; [Joe *stops and looks back at him*] instead of applied externally as they have been doing.

JOE: What did you say, Aubrey?

AUBREY: I said, a simple combination of chemical elements, to be added to the metal in its *molten* state, instead of applied externally as they have been doing.

[Joe *and* Aubrey, *speaking together*]

JOE: [*Speaking to his Mother*] Mom, do you know anything about that little screw-driver with the black handle?

AUBREY: But,—simply because it was discovered by a working-man—that they saw they couldn't buy—

MRS. FISHER: Do you mean the one you fixed the sewing machine with?

[Joe *and* Aubrey, *speaking together*]

JOE: Yes, that little short one with the black handle.

AUBREY: They gave it the swinging door.

[Amy *moves over to the parlor-doors*]
[Mrs. Fisher *and* Aubrey, *speaking together*]

MRS. FISHER: I think I saw it on that shelf out there, over the sink. And now, don't go upsettin' everything out there.

AUBREY: They'd rather go on paying a million dollars a year [Joe *goes out, and* Aubrey *follows him to the kitchen-door*]—to paint their steel and iron structures throughout the country, than pay *me*.

MRS. FISHER: Do you see it, Joe?

AUBREY: [*Coming down to* Mrs. Fisher's *left*] And do you know *why*, Mrs. Fisher?

JOE: [*Answering his Mother from the kitchen*] No!

AUBREY: Then, I'll tell you. Because I work for my living. That's the said and done on the whole business. [Mrs. Fisher *starts to put her things into the knitting-bag, preparatory to getting up*] Keep them poor and get them married; and then, [*He looks away off*] as my darling old Mother used to say, "You've got them on their beams and hinges."

MRS. FISHER: [*Getting up*] I don't see that anybody's tryin' to make anybody get married if they don't want to. [*She passes up to the kitchen-door, putting her knitting-bag on the buffet as she goes*]

AUBREY: [*Following her up*] But they *do* want to, Mrs. Fisher,—but the capitalist wants to stop them.

MRS. FISHER: [*Turning at the kitchen-door and speaking directly to him*] Well, I guess it'd be just as well to stop *some* of 'em. [*She goes out*]

AUBREY: [*Calling after her through the kitchen-door*] Ah, don't go back on little old William Jennings Bryan, Mother Fisher. Life, liberty and the pursuit of happiness, you know. [*He turns and comes forward at the right again, laughing a little*] Sign on the dotted line.

AMY: [*Trying to conceal her temper*] Come on in here, Aubrey.

AUBREY: [*Starting towards her*] Yes, sir, Amy, I want to tell you it's the poor man that gets it every time. I put a question up to Secretary Mellon, in a letter six weeks ago—that absolutely stumped him, because I haven't had a line from him since. [Amy *is smiling into his eyes. He passes in front of her and goes into the parlor. The curtain commences* to descend slowly. Amy *looks darkly toward the kitchen-door, and stamps her foot with temper; then follows* Aubrey *into the parlor*] I simply asked him to what extent his proposed program of Income Tax Revision would affect the great American Railroad Employe. [*The curtain is down*]

Three hours pass

The curtain rises again

Mrs. Fisher *is sitting at the right of the table asleep, her knitting lying in her lap; and* Joe, *sitting at the left of the table, is endeavoring to pass the tip of a wire through a small eyelet on the base-board.* Amy *starts to play the piano in the parlor; and, after the usual introduction,* Aubrey *begins to sing,* "Rocked In the Cradle Of The Deep," *in a heavy bass voice.*

AUBREY: [*Singing*]
    "Rocked in the cradle of the deep,
    I lay me down,—in peace to sleep—
    Secure I rest upon the wave,
    For Thou alone—
            [Mrs. Fisher *starts slightly and wakens.* Joe *glances at her.* Aubrey *continues*]
    has the power to save."
MRS. FISHER: Where'd you put it? What? Did you say something?
            [Aubrey *continues to sing*]
JOE: Not a thing, Mom.
MRS. FISHER: [*Brushing back her hair*] I must have been dozin'.
JOE: You've been dead.
MRS. FISHER: What?
JOE: Since half-past nine.
    [Mrs. Fisher *becomes conscious of* Aubrey *singing*]
MRS. FISHER: What time is it now, Joe? [*The singing becomes louder, and* Mrs. Fisher *rises, with her eyes fastened on the parlor-door*] Is that him singin' in there?
JOE: [*Reaching into his belt-pocket for an Ingersoll watch*] The old Scientific American himself. A quarter of twelve.
MRS. FISHER: My God! what's he startin' to sing at this hour for! [*She steps to the buffet at the right and puts her knitting-bag into one of the drawers*]
JOE: Talent should never be suppressed at any time, Mother.
MRS. FISHER: It's a wonder Amy wouldn't have sense enough to stop him. [*She slams the buffet-drawer shut, and starts across towards the parlor-doors*] I never saw a man yet that didn't think he could sing. Put that thing away, now, Joe, you've been at it long enough. And see that that back is locked. I don't think Amy has any idea what time it is or she'd shut him up.
JOE: Let the young man express himself. [*He gets

up and crosses below the table towards the right, and up to the kitchen-door*]
MRS. FISHER: Oh, I wouldn't care if he bawled his head off, as far as I'm concerned—I'd be glad if he did; but I don't want him to waken your Father. [*She steps up to the hall-door and listens, at the foot of the stairs*] And that's what he'll be doin' the first thing you know, and then the fat'll be in the fire for sure. [Aubrey *reaches a high note, and* Joe *and his Mother stand looking at each other. Then* Joe *bursts out laughing*] Ain't that terrible, Joe? Do you think I ought to tell Amy what time it is?
JOE: No, give the boy a chance. [Aubrey *finishes on a high note and holds it*] Hurray!
        [Aubrey *can be heard applauding himself.* Joe *applauds, also*]
MRS. FISHER: [*Frantically, and going towards* Joe] Shush, Joe!
JOE: [*Going out through the door at the right*] Sign on the dotted line!
MRS. FISHER: Don't encourage him, for God's sake, Joe, he's bad enough as it is.
MR. FISHER: [*Shouting from the head of the stairs*] Josie!
MRS. FISHER: [*Rushing back towards the hall-door on her tiptoes*] Yes?
MR. FISHER: What the devil's goin' on down there! Do you know what time it is?
MRS. FISHER: [*Trying to pacify him*] Why, Joe was just cuttin' up here a minute ago.
MR. FISHER: What's Amy playin' the piano for, at this time of the night?
MRS. FISHER: [*Trying not to be heard in the parlor*] Why, her and Joe was just foolin'—
MR. FISHER: Damn funny kind of foolin', at this time of night! The neighbors'll be wonderin' what kind of a house we're keepin' here!
MRS. FISHER: Well, they've stopped it now, Neil.
MR. FISHER: Well, tell them to see that it's *kept* stopped! And get them lights out down there and go to bed! It's nearly twelve o'clock.
    [Mrs. Fisher *turns and looks at the parlor-doors. Then there's a burst of wild laughter from* Aubrey. *This decides* Mrs. Fisher. *She steps resolutely towards the doors with the ostensible purpose of opening them, but, before she can reach the knob, the door is yanked open from the inside and* Amy *steps out, looking resentfully at her*]
AMY: What's the matter?
MRS. FISHER: [*A trifle disconcerted*] Why,—a—I was just comin' to tell you to be sure and put them lights out; I'm just goin' up—it's nearly twelve o'clock.
AUBREY: [*Thrusting his head and shoulders out through the door*] I am also just about to take my reluctant leave, Mrs. Fisher.
MRS. FISHER: [*Trying to be polite*] Well, I don't want to hurry you, but—
AUBREY: In fact, the recent outburst was in the nature

of a farewell concert. [*He breaks into a wild laugh and draws back into the parlor; and Mrs. Fisher, with a series of frantic gestures, intended to convey to Amy the imminence of her Father at the head of the stairs, steps back out of the range of the parlor-door. Amy makes an impatient movement of her body, and stamps her foot, then flounces into the parlor and slams the door*] The little old song at twilight, you know, Mother Fisher—to soothe the savage breast. [*He gives vent to another gale of laughter; and Mrs. Fisher stands petrified, expecting to hear her husband again*]

MRS. FISHER: [*As Aubrey's laugh subsides*] The damn fool! [*She crosses to the right to the kitchen-door and calls out to Joe*] Joe!

JOE: Yeh?

MRS. FISHER: You'd better bring Gypsy Queen in and put her in the laundry there; she was shiverin' when I opened the door this mornin'. I think it's too cold for her on that back porch yet a while. [*She moves a little back towards the center of the room*]

JOE: [*Out at the right*] Come on in here, Gypsy! Come on. [*He whistles*]

MRS. FISHER: [*Turning around to her left and looking back toward the kitchen-door*] Ain't she there?

JOE: I don't see her.

MRS. FISHER: [*Calling in a high voice*] Where are you, Gypsy?

JOE: Here she is. Come on in here, Gypsy! Come on! That's the old gypsy kid. [*The door out at the right closes*]

MRS. FISHER: [*Going a step nearer the kitchen-door*] Go into that laundry there, Gypsy.

JOE: Come back here, Gypsy!

MRS. FISHER: Make her go in there, Joe.

JOE: [*Stamping his foot*] Gypsy!

MRS. FISHER: [*Stamping her foot at the kitchen-door*] Go back there, Gypsy! You bad girl! And go into that laundry this minute—

JOE: There she goes.

MRS. FISHER: And don't let me hear a sound out of you when you get in there either, or I'll come right straight out and give you what I gave you last Sunday afternoon. [*A door closes*] You better put the ketch on that door, Joe, or she'll be pushin' it open again; she wants to lay out here on this rug. [*Going nearer to the door again, and calling*] Now, you remember what I told you, Gypsy; and don't let me have to speak to you again. [*Turning and moving across the room to the left*] Your Father has her spoiled. [*A door out in the hallway at the left opens, and Amy can be heard laughing. Mrs. Fisher stops dead in the middle of the room and listens*]

AUBREY: [*Calling from the hallway*] Good-night, Mrs. Fisher.

[*Mrs. Fisher turns and darts back into the cellar-alcove at the right*]

AMY: [*In the hallway*] I guess she's gone up, Aubrey.

AUBREY: [*Coming in at the hall-door, poising on one toe, hat and cane in hand, and looking about the room*] Montreal, Mother.

[*Mrs. Fisher flattens herself against the wall at the head of the cellar-stairs, and listens with a stony expression*]

AMY: I don't think she's in there, Aubrey.

AUBREY: And silence was her answer. [*He laughs wildly, turns, and starts out into the hallway again*] Right you are, Amy—[*Glancing up the stairs*] On the right side she is sleeping. [*He goes laughing out into the hallway*]

JOE: [*Coming in from the kitchen, mimicking Aubrey's laugh*] Ha! Ha! Ha! [*He passes his Mother without seeing her*]

MRS. FISHER: [*Coming out of the alcove*] Shush! Don't let him hear you, Joe.

[*Joe turns and looks at his Mother, then continues across to the left to the hall-door*]

JOE: Is he goin'?

MRS. FISHER: [*Following Joe to the center of the room*] At last! [*Joe glances out into the hallway*] Don't let him see you, now, Joe, or we'll have him here for another hour.

JOE: [*Starting up the stairs*] I'm goin' to bed.

MRS. FISHER: Joe!

JOE: [*Leaning back and looking*] What?

MRS. FISHER: Come here!

[*Amy can be heard giggling in the hallway. Joe comes back to his Mother*]

JOE: What?

MRS. FISHER: [*Very confidentially*] What was that he was sayin' here to-night, about discoverin' something to keep rust out of iron and steel?

JOE: [*Very much amused*] Wasn't that a scream?

MRS. FISHER: That's what *you're* always talkin' about, ain't it?

JOE: Yes, I was talkin' to *him* about it one night here, while he was waitin' for Amy to come down; and he's forgot where he heard it.

MRS. FISHER: Can you imagine!

JOE: I was wonderin' if you were gettin' that tonight.

MRS. FISHER: No, it never struck me till afterwards.

JOE: [*With a shade of seriousness*] Did you get what he said tonight, Mom?

MRS. FISHER: Now, you know I never pay any attention to what *he* sez.

JOE: [*Turning away laughing*] He's a bird. [*He goes to the hall-door and looks out into the hall*]

MRS. FISHER: Don't let him see you now, Joe.

JOE: The vestibule-door's shut. [*He goes up the stairs. His Mother follows him to the hall-door*]

MRS. FISHER: You'd better close that window at the head of your bed, Joe, and not have it blowin' in on you all night. [*She glances out into the hallway, then steps to the parlor-door, opens it quietly and glances in, and starts across towards the right. The front-door closes out in the hallway, then the vestibule-door. Mrs. Fisher glances over her right shoulder toward the hallway, then continues to the kitchen-door. Just as she reaches the kitchen-door and glances out, the parlor-door is flung open and Amy comes in. She takes a couple of steps towards the middle of the room, then stands still, looking bitterly at her Mother. Mrs. Fisher speaks without looking at her]* Did you put that light out in there?

AMY: [*In a quiet rage*] That was a *nice* trick you people did tonight!

> [*Her Mother turns and looks at her*]

MRS. FISHER: What?

AMY: Everybody walking out of the room, while Aubrey was talking.

MRS. FISHER: What did you *want* us to do, sit here all night listenin' to him?

AMY: You wouldn't have *had* to sit here all night listening to him; he was only in here five minutes.

MRS. FISHER: [*Moving back towards the center-table*] That's no thanks to him; he'd have been here till mornin' if somebody didn't do somethin'.

AMY: [*Swinging to the mirror over the mantelpiece*] I was never so mortified in my life.

MRS. FISHER: [*Standing above the center-table*] Oh, don't waste your sympathy, Amy! He don't have to have anybody listen to him; he'd talk to the wall if there wasn't anybody else around.

AMY: [*Coming forward at her Mother's right*] What did Pop get into such a temper about?

MRS. FISHER: [*Getting mad*] Because he hit him on the back!

AMY: That was a lot to get mad about.

MRS. FISHER: Well, he's always hittin' *somebody!*—on the back—or the shoulder—or someplace else. And your Father *said* the next time he did it he'd walk out of the room!—He can't say two words *together* without *hittin'* somebody someplace.

AMY: Well, I'll bet you won't get a chance to insult him *again*, Mom, I'll tell you that. [*She flounces down to the arm-chair at the extreme right*]

MRS. FISHER: Then, let him stop his silly talk! and he won't get insulted. Sign on the dotted line! every two minutes. And talkin' about Shakespeare. [*She crosses to the parlor-door*] What kind of goin' on is that for a sensible man. [*She slams the parlor-door shut, and moves up to the hall-door to listen for Mr. Fisher*] It's no wonder our Joe sez he's a nut!

AMY: Oh, everybody's a nut with the people around here!

MRS. FISHER: [*Coming back towards the center-table*] Oh, it ain't only the people around here that sez it; everybody that knows him sez it. [*Amy makes a sound of derisive amusement*] You needn't laugh, for it's true.

AMY: [*Turning sharply to her Mother*] Who do *you* know that knows him?

MRS. FISHER: I know Frank Hyland.

> [*Amy is puzzled for the fraction of a second*]

AMY: You mean Clara's *husband?*

MRS. FISHER: Yes, I mean Clara's *husband.*

AMY: Oh, don't make up a lie, Mom! Frank Hyland never saw Aubrey Piper.

MRS. FISHER: Oh, didn't he!

AMY: No, he didn't.

MRS. FISHER: Well now, my lady, you're so smart, he knows him better than you do.

AMY: I don't believe it.

MRS. FISHER: Doesn't matter whether you believe it or not, he knows him just the same; he's been lookin' at him for years, down at that restaurant at Fifteenth and Arch, where he eats his lunch. And he sez he's as crazy as a *bass*-singer.

AMY: [*Whirling on her Mother*] I suppose that's what Clara was here to tell you, was it?

MRS. FISHER: What does it matter *who* was here to tell it, Amy, if it's true.

AMY: [*Stepping up close to her Mother*] Well now, listen, Mom, I want to tell you something right now! You tell our Clara for me the next time you see her, to mind her own damn business—[*She taps the back of the chair twice with her knuckles, emphasizing the words "damn" and "business"*] as far as Aubrey Piper is concerned.

MRS. FISHER: [*Before Amy has finished speaking*] Oh, don't fly into a temper, if anybody speaks to you! [*She turns and crosses hurriedly to the hall-door to listen*]

AMY: [*Stamping her foot*] Well then, don't speak to me about things that *put* me in a temper!

MRS. FISHER: You're not frightenin' anybody around here. [*She looks up the stairs and listens*]

AMY: No, and nobody around here is frightening *me*, either— Our Clara took who *she* wanted. And I guess you took who *you* wanted. [*Mrs. Fisher moves steadily forward at the left to a point in front of the lower left-hand corner of the center-table*] And if I want Aubrey Piper I'll take *him!*

MRS. FISHER: [*Taking Amy's tone*] Well, take him then!—and the sooner the better; for it's a pity to spoil two houses with you. [*She leans forward a little on the table and speaks with a steady precision*] Only remember this, Amy,—if you *do* take him,—be sure that you keep him—and that—he—keeps—you. [*Amy looks at her keenly*] And don't be comin' around here cryin' for your *Pop* to keep you.

AMY: [*With a sound of amused derision, and flouncing down to the arm-chair at the right*] Don't make me laugh.

MRS. FISHER: You can laugh all you like; there's a lot of that kind of laughin' goin' on these days. But they change their tune as soon as the rent begins to come due; and it's the Mothers and Fathers that has to listen to the changed tune. But nothin'll do but they'll get married.

AMY: [*Pinning her Mother with a quick look*] You got married, didn't you?

MRS. FISHER: Yes I did.

AMY: [*Turning away again*] Well—

MRS. FISHER: To a man that was able to keep me.

AMY: [*Back to her Mother again*] And how do *you* know that Aubrey Piper wouldn't be able to keep *his* wife?

MRS. FISHER: Because I know what he *earns*;—[*She strikes the table with her fist*] and it isn't enough.

AMY: [*Stamping her foot*] Oh, don't go making up things, Mom!—You don't know anything *about* what he earns.

MRS. FISHER: [*With measured emphasis*] He earns a hundred and fifty dollars a month and not a penny more, for Frank Hyland sez so.

AMY: What does Frank Hyland know about it?

MRS. FISHER: He knows what he *does!*—His business takes him in there all the time.

AMY: And what does he say he does?

MRS. FISHER: Why, he sez he's a clerk, of course,— [*Amy makes a sound of amusement*] like a hundred others down there.

AMY: That shows how much he knows about it.

MRS. FISHER: But I suppose he told you he *owns* the Pennsylvania Railroad.

AMY: Well, I'd take his word before I'd take Frank Hyland's.

[*Her Mother looks at her narrowly, and there is a pause*]

MRS. FISHER: [*Significantly*] Why would you take *his* word before you would take Frank Hyland's?

AMY: Well, why shouldn't I?

MRS. FISHER: [*Losing her temper*] Because he's a fool!—of a blatherskite.

AMY: That's only your opinion, Mom.

MRS. FISHER: It's the opinion of everybody that ever listened to him. But you'd believe *him* before you'd believe the word of a steady sensible man.

AMY: I don't know anything about Frank Hyland.

MRS. FISHER: You know he's been your brother-in-law for five years; and what do you know about this other clown?

AMY: Well, what do you *want* to know about him?

MRS. FISHER: *I* don't want to know *anything* about him; I *know* all I want to know about him. But before I'd get the name of havin' a fellow comin' to see *me* steady, there's a few things I'd want to know about him, I'll tell you that. [*She turns away and takes a step towards the back of the room*]

AMY: I've told you where he lives and where he works,—what else do you want to know about him?

MRS. FISHER: There's no use talkin' to you, Amy.

AMY: No, and there's no use talking to you, either.

MRS. FISHER: [*Turning to her sharply*] This fellow's got you so crazy mad about him, that I believe you'd take him if you knew he had a wife and family somewhere, and not two cents in his pocket. [*She moves towards the mantelpiece at the back, removing her spectacles*]

AMY: Well, I guess we'd get along some way even if I did.

MRS. FISHER: All right.

AMY: Everybody else does.

MRS. FISHER: [*Turning upon Amy in a rage, and wiping the glasses in her apron*] That's the kind of talk that leaves them livin' in garrets! And back at their jobs ten days after the weddin'.

AMY: Oh, you talk as though everybody that was married was starving to death.

MRS. FISHER: [*Lifting the glasses towards Amy with a quiet, knowing gesture*] There are ways of starvin' to death, Amy, besides not gettin' enough to eat. [*With a change to great shrewdness of tone and manner*] And the funny part of it is, Amy,—like a lot of others, you're very shrewd about money while you're at home, as far as what you give your Mother and Father is concerned; but the minute some clown, with a flower in his coat and patent-leather shoes, winks at you, you seem to forget there's such a thing in the world as a ton of coal. [*Crossing suddenly above the table towards Amy in quite a surge of temper*] And then it's just as Clara sez, it's your *people* that has to come to the rescue.

AMY: [*Furiously*] I wish I'd been here while she was talking! I bet I'd a told her a thing or two!

MRS. FISHER: Oh, you needn't try to turn it onto Clara;—she wasn't talkin' at all.

AMY: [*Stamping her foot*] She *must* have been talking!

MRS. FISHER: She simply asked me where you were! —and I told her you were gettin' dressed—that this fellow was comin' here to-night: so then she told me that Frank Hyland knew him, and where he worked, and what he got and all about him. [*She turns away and moves to the left. There is a slight pause*]

AMY: [*Half crying*] I'd just take him for *spite* now.
[*Mrs. Fisher comes to a stop, and turns slowly—and looks at her*]

MRS. FISHER: Well, let me tell *you*, Amy—the day a girl that's used to spendin' money the way you do, takes a thirty-five-dollar-a-week man,—the only one she's spitin' is herself. [*She moves slowly to the mantelpiece at the back and puts her glasses down definitely, then turns and starts to remove her apron*] There'll be no more permanent waves after that—[*She rolls her apron up*] you can make up your mind to that. [*She flings the rolled apron onto the sofa at the right of the mantelpiece, and commences to unfasten the old-fashioned brooch in the front of her house-dress*] Nor fifty-five dollar beaded dresses, neither.

AMY: [*In a crying temper*] Well, I'd never bother anybody around here if I needed anything, I'll tell you that.

MRS. FISHER: Maybe you won't.

AMY: I won't,—you needn't worry.

MRS. FISHER: [*With a bitter levelness*] Time'll *tell* that, Lady Jane; I've heard the likes of you before. [*She detaches the brooch and goes to the hall-door, glances out into the hallway, then turns and looks back at Amy*] Put out that light and go to bed, it's twelve o'clock. [*She goes up the stairs. Amy stands for a second, fuming, over at the right; then she swings suddenly to the middle of the room and stops, with her hands on her hips, irresolute. Then she comes forward and stands above the table, thinking. As she clasps her hands together she becomes conscious of the ring in her hand. She tiptoes to the hall-door, stands listening for a second, then looks up. Then she hurries back to the center-table, looks at the ring, slides it onto the third finger of her left hand and holds it so that the diamond will catch the light from the chandelier. But, the reflection is evidently unsatisfactory; so, with a furtive glance toward the hall-door, she shifts her position to a point nearer the table-lamp and holds her hand so that the ring will reflect that light. The curtain commences to descend slowly; and she stands, holding her hand at arm's length, lost in the melting wonder of her engagement ring*]

Act II

SCENE: *Same as preceding Act, six months later, about five-thirty on a Monday afternoon. Mrs. Fisher is sitting in the arm-chair below the buffet, over at the right, listening in on the radio. Suddenly the front-door closes with a bang, and she starts, and looks in the direction of the hall-door. Aubrey bounces into the room, very much done up, with the traditional carnation, as usual, and comes forward, putting his hat down on the table.*

AUBREY: Hello, Mother—Amy here? [*He steps to the mirror at the back and gives himself a critical touch here and there*]

MRS. FISHER: [*Commencing to remove the listeners*] Our Amy?

AUBREY: Yes, have you seen anything of her?

MRS. FISHER: [*Rising*] No, I haven't seen anything of her. [*She places the listeners on the buffet, and signs off*]

AUBREY: [*Turning from the glass*] Wonder where she is?

MRS. FISHER: Isn't she home?

AUBREY: No, I just came by there.

MRS. FISHER: [*Picking up her knitting-bag from the buffet*] She hasn't been here today.

AUBREY: She was saying this morning she thought she'd go out looking for a house today; I suppose she hasn't got back yet. [*He gives the chair at the left of the center-table a double tap with his cane as he crosses down to the window at the left*] I wanted to take her out to the Automobile Show tonight; I got the loan of Harry Albright's car.

MRS. FISHER: [*Moving to the chair at the right of the center-table*] Did you say she was out lookin' for a house?

AUBREY: [*Moving back, towards her*] Yes, we've got to get out of that place we're in. The LePage printing people have bought the whole block: they're going to put up a new building there.

MRS. FISHER: [*Standing with her hand on the back of the chair*] How soon do you have to get out?

AUBREY: Soon as we can find a place, I suppose. I understand they want to begin tearing down there about the first of the year.

MRS. FISHER: I'm afraid you won't find it so easy to get a place as reasonable as that again in a hurry. [*She sits down*]

AUBREY: I don't *want* a place as reasonable as that, if I can get something better. [*He plants himself at the left of the table and looks away off, with a dreamy narrowing of his eyes, and balancing himself on his toes*] I want a home—something with a bit of ground around it—where I can do a bit of tennis in the evening—[*He makes a couple of leisurely passes at an imaginary tennis-ball*] if I feel like it.

MRS. FISHER: [*Beginning to knit on a green sweater*] Well, if you do you'll pay for it.

AUBREY: That is exactly what I expect to do, Mother Fisher, not giving you a short answer,—that is exactly what I expect to do. [*He gives the table a double tap with the cane*] But, I want what I'm paying for, I'll tell you that. No more of the old first-of-the-month business for this bambino. He's all washed-up, and signed on the dotted line. [*He moves up to the mirror at the back*]

MRS. FISHER: They're not puttin' *up* any more houses, from what I can hear.

AUBREY: Be yourself, now, Mother Fisher, be yourself.

MRS. FISHER: Well, where *are* they?

AUBREY: You ought to go out along the Boulevard some Sunday,—see what they're doing out there.

MRS. FISHER: Well, there's no danger of you goin' out along the Boulevard, except for a walk.

AUBREY: [*Moving to the hall-door and glancing out into the hallway*] Lot of people out that way, Mother.

MRS. FISHER: Well, if there is they're payin' more than you're able to pay.

AUBREY: Man's got to live somewhere, Mother. [*He swings forward to the window down at the left, and stands whistling to the canary*]

MRS. FISHER: Well, if he's wise, he'll live where he's able to pay for it;—unless he wants to be breakin' up half a dozen times a year—like a lot of them are doin'. Makin' a big show. Buyin' ten thousand dollar houses, and puttin' fifty dollars down on them. [*He turns to her*] Besides, you haven't got any furniture for a house, even if you got one—unless you want to be sittin' on the floor.

AUBREY: The matter of furniture nowadays, Little Mother, is a very inconsequential item, from what I can gather.

MRS. FISHER: You ought to price it sometime when you're in the city, and see how unconsequent it is.

AUBREY: [*Settling himself for a golf shot, using his cane for a club*] I've investigated the matter very thoroughly, Mrs. Fisher, and I find that there are at least fifteen first-class establishments right here in this city that will furnish a man's house from garret to garage, and give him the rest of his life to pay for it. [*He hits the imaginary golf-ball, and pretends to follow it straight out with his eyes*]

MRS. FISHER: They'd need to give some of them the rest of their lives, at the rate they're goin' now.

AUBREY: Give the growing boy a chance, Mrs. Fisher, give the growing boy a chance. You know what Mr. L. D. Brophy of the American Can Company said in the September number of the American Magazine, don't you?

MRS. FISHER: No, I don't.

AUBREY: Well, I'll tell you. [Mrs. Fisher *shifts her knitting, giving him a wearied glance*] He said, "I would say, to that innumerable host of young men, standing on the threshold of life, uncertain, and, mayhap, dismayed—as they contemplate the stress of modern industrial competition, 'Rome was not built in a day'." Those were his very words, I wouldn't kid you, and I think the old boy's got it right, if you ask me. [*He moves up to the hall-door again and glances out*]

MRS. FISHER: What are *you* goin' out to the Automobile Show for?

AUBREY: [*Turning and coming forward again*] Repeat the question, Mrs. Fisher, if you please.

MRS. FISHER: I say, what are you goin' out to the *Automobile* Show for?

AUBREY: [*Coming to a point above the center-table*] Ha! Married five months ago today, Mother; got to celebrate the happy event. Besides, one never knows what a day will bring, in the way of an opportunity to satisfy a long-felt want. And since she knocks but once—[*He taps his cane on the table, causing* Mrs. Fisher *to start slightly*] at each man's door, the kid here doesn't want to miss his chance by any uncertainty as to just what choo-choo he prefers. [Mrs. Fisher *turns with an annoyed expression, to find him pointing at her with his forefinger and thumb. He laughs at her annoyance*] Well, got to run along now, Mother, and see if Amy's back at the house yet. [*He picks up his hat from the table and starts for the hall-door*]

MRS. FISHER: What'll I tell her if she comes here after you're gone?

AUBREY: [*Stopping at the door*] Why, tell her I've got the loan of Harry Albright's car, and I want her to see that new Jordan Six that I was telling her about, out at the Show. And that I'll be at Childs' at Fifteenth and Chestnut until eight o'clock. [*He looks at his Ingersoll*]

MRS. FISHER: Fifteenth and Chestnut?

AUBREY: That's the said and done, Mother. [*He laughs boisterously*] The old Café Infanté. [*He laughs again*] Olive oil, Mother. [*He goes out the hall-door, breaking into another laugh, and in a second the front-door closes with a bang, causing* Mrs. Fisher *to start again, and look irritatedly toward the hall-door. Then she resumes her knitting. The parlor-door opens and* Amy *drifts in, and starts across towards the chair at the left of the table*]

AMY: Hello!

[Mrs. Fisher *starts again*]

MRS. FISHER: Oh, you frightened me, Amy—walkin' in that way like a ghost! When did you come in?

AMY: [*Sitting down, with a wearied air*] A couple of minutes ago—I've been in the parlor.

MRS. FISHER: Why, your man just left here, didn't you see him?

AMY: No, I heard him when I came in—I went in the parlor.

MRS. FISHER: He's lookin' for you— He sez he wants you to go to some kind of an Automobile Show with him.

AMY: I know; I don't want to go; I'm too tired.

MRS. FISHER: What's he doin' about his supper?

AMY: I told him this morning to get something in town; I knew I wouldn't be home till late.

[Mrs. Fisher *resumes her knitting; and there is a slight pause*]

MRS. FISHER: He sez you've got to get out of that place you're in.

AMY: Yes, they're going to tear those houses down. That's what I was doing today—looking around for someplace.

MRS. FISHER: Did you see anything?

AMY: I saw a couple of places that were fair, but they want too much money.

MRS. FISHER: I'm afraid that's what you'll find, Amy, wherever you go.

AMY: Thirty-eight dollars a month—for a little two-story house—that didn't even have a front porch.

MRS. FISHER: Well, you're surely not lookin' for a house, Amy, are you?

AMY: Yes, if I can find one.

MRS. FISHER: And have you any idea what they're askin' for houses these days?

AMY: Well, Aubrey sez he *will* not live in rooms any longer.

MRS. FISHER: What the devil does it matter *what he* sez! He don't know what he's sayin' half the time, anyway. It's *you* that has to stretch the money, and it'll only go so far; and the money that *he* gets won't cover any forty-dollar rents, you can make up your mind to that right now, before you go any further. And that's what you'll be asked to pay, Amy, remember I'm tellin' you.

AMY: He doesn't want to pay rent—he wants to buy.

MRS. FISHER: What on, thirty-two dollars a week?

AMY: He sez he can put it into a new building society that he heard about, over in Frankford.

MRS. FISHER: Wouldn't he have to pay the building society?

AMY: Well, he wouldn't have to pay it all at once.

MRS. FISHER: There'd be more onces than he'd be able to meet. I thought *you* had a *little* sense, but you're nearly as bad as him.

AMY: No, but you talk awfully silly, Mother; you'd think everybody that was married was living out in the street.

MRS. FISHER: That's where a good many of them would be livin', Amy, only that somebody belongin' to them is givin' them a hand. Money'll only go so far, and I've been keepin' house too long not to know just how far that far is. Nobody can tell *me*.

AMY: There was a girl down in our office that was married, just before I was married, and the fellow she married didn't even get as much money as Aubrey gets; he got about twenty-five a week—he was a guard in the Corn Exchange Bank; and *they* bought a house, out in Kensington, and they say it's beautiful.

MRS. FISHER: She's back at her job, though, isn't she?

AMY: [*With reluctant admission*] She never left her job.

MRS. FISHER: Well,—that's how she's doin' it. You told me yourself there were five girls in your office that have married within the last two years. Do you think they're hanging over books nine hours a day because they *like* it? And you haven't got any furniture even if you got a house.

AMY: Oh, you can always get furniture.

MRS. FISHER: You can if you pay for it. And I don't know how you expect to do all these wonders later on, when you find it so hard to make ends meet now, with only the rent of two rooms to pay for. You're everlastin' borrowin' from me as it is.

AMY: I always pay you, don't I?

MRS. FISHER: You do when you get it. But, that's not the point, Amy; it's that what you get one week don't last you till the next.

AMY: The reason I was short last week, Aubrey bought that new overcoat.

MRS. FISHER: And next week it'll be something else.

AMY: Well, a man can't be shabby, Mom, in a position like Aubrey's. He sez he's got nearly eighty clerks down there in his department; and he sez unless he sets some kind of an example of personal appearance, he sez there are some of them down there that'd come in in overalls.

MRS. FISHER: [*Laying her knitting on the table and looking keenly at* Amy] How is it, Amy, that a girl like you—that was smart enough to keep books, has so little sense when it comes to what some man tells you?

[Amy *looks at her Mother steadily*]

AMY: Who do you mean, Aubrey?

MRS. FISHER: Yes.

AMY: Why, what does he tell me that I have so little sense about?

MRS. FISHER: That he has eighty clerks under him.

AMY: So he has.

MRS. FISHER: And gets thirty-two dollars a week?

AMY: He gets thirty-two fifty. [Mrs. Fisher *resumes her knitting, shaking her head hopelessly*] Well now, Mom, you know yourself what the Pennsylvania Railroad pays its men.

MRS. FISHER: I don't know what anybody pays anybody.

AMY: Well, the Pennsylvania Railroad is notorious. Aubrey sez that only that a couple of things haven't panned out just right with him, he'd have left them *long* ago. He sez they just try to break your spirit. He sez that's one of the main reasons why he pays so much attention to his clothes.—He sez he just wouldn't *please* them.

MRS. FISHER: How much did he pay for that overcoat?

AMY: Twenty-eight dollars. [Mrs. Fisher *raises her eyes to Heaven*] Oh, he didn't have to pay it all at once; the man said on account of it being so near Christmas he could let it go till the first of February.

MRS. FISHER: I guess he'll be wantin' a suit, now, the first you know, to go with the overcoat.

AMY: No, his suit's all right,—yet a while. But this suit of mine is beginning to go; I've worn it till I'm tired looking at it.

MRS. FISHER: People can't *get* things so handy once they're married.

AMY: I thought I'd be able to put something away out of this week, toward a suit; but I don't know where the money went to:—it just seemed to go. Honestly, I had exactly *twelve cents* in my purse when Aubrey gave me his pay.

MRS. FISHER: I don't know what'll become of you, Amy, if ever you have a houseful of children to keep. [Amy *sits looking at nothing, with a rather troubled expression about the eyes, and her Mother continues to knit. Suddenly* Amy *bursts into tears.* Mrs. Fisher *looks at her: then she gets up quietly, laying her knitting on the table, and crosses in front of the table to her—and lays her hand on her arm*] Now, there's no use a startin' that kind a thing, now, Amy; for it won't do you a bit of good. [*She continues across*]

AMY: I don't know what I'm going to do, Mom—I'm nearly crazy.

MRS. FISHER: [*Turning*] I'll tell you what you're goin' to do, Amy, if you're a wise woman—You're goin' to realize that you're married; and that you've got some kind of a house to keep up; and just how much money you're goin' to get each week to keep it up *on*; and then suit your ideas accordin'. And if you don't, you'll have plenty of cryin' to do. And you'll have nobody to thank but yourself, for you had nothing but impudence for them that tried to tell you—how many beans made five. [*The front-door is heard to close*] I guess this is your Father. Go into the parlor there, and don't let him see you cryin'.

[*Amy rises and steps quickly across and thru the parlor-doors at the left into the parlor; and* Mrs. Fisher *crosses above the center-table to the buffet and puts her knitting into one of the drawers.* Clara *appears in the hall-door*]

CLARA: What's the matter?

[Mrs. Fisher *turns and looks at her*]

MRS. FISHER: There's nothing at all the matter.

CLARA: What did Joe telephone me for?

MRS. FISHER: *Our* Joe, do you mean?

CLARA: Yes; Bertha said he telephoned the house about four o'clock and told her to tell me to come right over home as soon as I came in.

MRS. FISHER: Well, I'm sure *I* don't know what he'd want you for, Clara; he didn't leave any word with me for you this morning.

CLARA: [*Coming forward towards the center-table*] I was over paying my Electric, and just got back; so I came right over; I thought maybe something was wrong here, and he was calling from next door.

MRS. FISHER: No, he hasn't been home here today.

[Clara *puzzles for a second, then tosses her purse onto the table*]

CLARA: I wonder what he wanted me for. [*She turns to the mirror at the back and touches her hat*]

MRS. FISHER: Is that girl at your house sure it was our Joe?

CLARA: [*Coming back to the table*] She said it was; and I suppose she knows his voice,—she's often answered the 'phone when he's called. [*She picks up a book from the table and glances casually at it*]

MRS. FISHER: Well, maybe he wants to see you about something; I'd wait a while; he'll be here at six.

CLARA: [*Looking suddenly at her Mother*] Maybe he's heard some news about that formula that those people are interested in.

MRS. FISHER: [*Coming over to the table*] Oh, I guess he'll be an old man before he ever hears anything from that. [*She folds and settles various things on the table, and* Clara *glances through the book. Then, as she moves over to settle the upper left-hand corner of the table-cover, she gives* Clara *a little push*] Look out of my way, Clara, till I fix this cloth. [Clara *just moves without looking up from the book*] That's a book Joe brought home last night: about that woman that was left up on the North Pole. He sez it's very nice. I've got to put those potatoes on, for your Father's supper; he'll be here around six. [*She moves to the door at the right*]

CLARA: [*Standing at the left of the table, still looking at the book*] Did you know that Amy's got to get out of those rooms she's in?

MRS. FISHER: [*From the kitchen*] Yes.

CLARA: They're going to tear those houses down.

MRS. FISHER: [*Coming back into the room*] So she was telling me.

CLARA: [*Moving to the chair at the left of the table*] What's she going to do, [*Tossing the book onto the table*] come in here to live? [*She sits down*]

MRS. FISHER: Now, that's a sensible question for you to ask, Clara;—you know how much she's comin' in here to live.

CLARA: [*Commencing to remove her gloves*] I don't know where else she'll go,—with rents the way they are now;—unless she goes back to work.

MRS. FISHER: She'll have to look around.

CLARA: What good will it do her to look around—she certainly won't find anything as reasonable as where she is now: and when she's not able to pay that, how does she expect to pay any more?

[*The parlor-door is whipped open and* Amy *is standing between the curtains looking tight-lipped at* Clara]

AMY: How do *you* know I'm not able to pay my rent where I am?

MRS. FISHER: [*Moving towards the hall-door*] Now, don't start a fight, Amy, your Pop'll be in here any minute. [*She looks out into the hallway*]

AMY: [*Speaking to her Mother, and indicating* Clara *with a gesture*] No, but I'd like to know what business it is of hers whether I can pay my rent or not. I don't see that anybody's asking *her* to pay it for me.

CLARA: [*Very sure of her ground*] It's a bit late in the day to talk that way, Amy; your husband's been to Frank Hyland *twice* already to pay it for you. [Amy *looks at her aghast, and* Mrs. Fisher *comes forward between them*] It's time you quit this posing in front of me; *I* know how you're fixed better than you do yourself. [*She turns sharply away and flings her gloves onto the table*]

AMY: [*Almost crying*] Now, do you hear that, Mom!

MRS. FISHER: Stop your talk, Amy! Do you want your Father to walk in and hear you?

AMY: [*Lowering her voice, but still speaking with angry rapidity*] She sez that Aubrey Piper's been to Frank Hyland twice, for the loan of *our* rent.

CLARA: So he has.

AMY: You're a liar!

[Mrs. Fisher *gives her a slap on the back; and there is a vibrant pause. Then* Amy *moves down towards the window at the left and bursts out crying*]

MRS. FISHER: [*With controlled excitement*] Will you stop when I speak to *you!* [*There is a pause*] What kind of talk do you call that! [*She steps to the hall-door again and glances out into the hallway*]

AMY: [*Whirling again upon* Clara] Well, that's what

she is! Aubrey Piper never asked Frank Hyland for a cent in his life.

CLARA: He's asked him a dozen times, and got it, too; till I put a stop to it.

MRS. FISHER: [*Coming forward again, and speaking with authority*] Now, that'll do, Clara!—I don't want to hear another word—out of either one of you—I had enough of that when the two of you were at home.

AMY: Well, I'll make her prove what she sez about Aubrey Piper, just the same!

CLARA: It's very easily proved. Just come over to the house some night and I'll show you a few of his letters.

AMY: What do you do, open them?

CLARA: I do now, yes,—since I found out who they're from.

MRS. FISHER: [*Keenly*] Do you mean to tell me, Clara, that he's writin' to Frank Hyland for money?

AMY: No, he doesn't do anything of the kind, Mom, that's another of her lies!

MRS. FISHER: [*Before* Amy *has finished speaking*] I'm not talkin' to you, Amy.

AMY: She just makes those things up.

CLARA: I make them *up*!

AMY: [*Crying*] Yes!

CLARA: And I've got at least twelve letters right in my bureau-drawer this minute that he's written within the last two months.

MRS. FISHER: What does he write letters for?

CLARA: For money—so he can pay seven dollars for a seat out at the football game—as he did Thanksgiving afternoon,—Frank saw him there.

MRS. FISHER: Why don't he just ast Frank Hyland for the money when he sees him, instead of writin' to him?

CLARA: I suppose he thinks a written request is more appropriate, coming from one of the heads of the Pennsylvania Railroad.

MRS. FISHER: How much does he ast for, when he asts him?

CLARA: There was one a couple of weeks ago, for three hundred.

[Amy *makes a sound of bitter amusement, and turns away*]

MRS. FISHER: [*Aghast*] Three hundred dollars?

CLARA: That's what the letter said.

[Mrs. Fisher *turns and looks at* Amy]

MRS. FISHER: What would he have wanted three hundred dollars for, Amy?

AMY: Oh, ask her, Mom; she's good at making things up. [*She sweeps towards the parlor-doors*]

MRS. FISHER: [*Taking a step or two after her*] Oh, you wouldn't believe it, even if it was true, if it was against him.

AMY: Well, I wouldn't believe *her*, anyway. [Amy *slams the parlor-door with a bang*]

MRS. FISHER: [*Raising her voice*] You wouldn't be-

lieve your own Mother,—never name your sister. [*She turns to* Clara] She flew at *me* like a wild-cat, when I told her he wore a wig. I guess she knows it herself by this time.

CLARA: She's for *him*, Mom; and the sooner you get that into your head the better.

MRS. FISHER: [*Moving towards the right, above the table*] I know very well she is, you needn't tell me. And she'd turn on everyone belongin' to her for him. The idea of askin' anybody for three hundred dollars. [*She continues towards the kitchen-door, fuming; then turns*] I suppose he wanted to buy an automobile or something. That's where he is tonight, out at the Automobile Show—and not two cents in his pocket—like a lot of others that'll be out there I guess— And I'll bet he'll be doin' more talk out there than them that'll buy a dozen cars.

CLARA: I think that's what he *did* want the money for.

MRS. FISHER: It wouldn't surprise me,—the damned fool. [*She steps to the mantelpiece and glances out into the hallway*] It'd be fitter for him to be thinkin' about gettin' a house to live in.

CLARA: He doesn't think he *needs* to think about that; he thinks he's coming in here.

MRS. FISHER: [*Turning sharply, on her way back to the kitchen-door*] Comin' in here *to live*, do you mean?

CLARA: That's what he told Frank, the day before yesterday.

MRS. FISHER: Well, he's very much mistaken if he does, I can tell you that. I'd like to be listenin' to that fellow seven days in the week. I'd rather go over and live with your Aunt Ellie in Newark.

CLARA: [*Rising, and picking up her gloves from the table*] Well, that's about what you'll have to do, Mom, if you ever let them in on you. [*She stands looking straight out, unfastening her neck-piece*]

MRS. FISHER: I won't let them in on me, don't fret. Your Father 'ud have something to say about that.

CLARA: [*Slipping off her neck-piece*] Pop may not always *be* here, Mom. [*She turns around to her left and moves to a point above the table, and puts her fur and gloves down*]

MRS. FISHER: Well, I'll be here, if he isn't; and the furniture is mine. And there's very little danger of my walkin' off and leavin' it to any son-in-law. [*The front-door closes*] I guess this is your Pop now, and I haven't even got the kettle on. [*She hurries out at the right.* Clara *glances at the hall-door, and* Joe *appears in it, and stands for the fraction of a second, irresolute*]

JOE: Where's Mom?

CLARA: Out in the kitchen,—why?

JOE: [*Motioning to her, causing the paper to drop from his hand*] Come here,—don't let her hear you. [Clara *steps towards him with a shade of apprehension in her face and manner*] Listen, Clara

—Pop had some kind of a stroke this afternoon at his work.

CLARA: *Pop* did?

JOE: They found him layin' in front of one of the boilers.

CLARA: Oh, my God!

JOE: I tried to get you on the 'phone about four o'clock.

CLARA: I know—I came right over as soon as I came in.

JOE: *You* better tell Mom. [*He starts for the stairs, and* Clara *turns towards the kitchen-door*]

CLARA: [*Turning sharply back again*] Joe!

JOE: [*Stopping abruptly on the first step of the stairs*] What?

CLARA: Where's Pop now?

JOE: They took him to the Samaritan Hospital. I just came from there—they telephoned me to the office.

CLARA: Well, is he very bad?

JOE: *I* think he's done.

CLARA: Oh, don't say that, Joe!

JOE: That's what the Doctor at the Hospital sez.— He hasn't regained consciousness since three o'clock. So you'd better tell Mom to get her things on and go right down there. I've got to change my clothes; I went right up there from work. [*He starts up the stairs; and* Clara *moves vaguely towards the kitchen-door. She stops and stands looking toward the kitchen in a controlled panic of indecision. Then, abruptly she whirls round and steps quickly back to the hall-door*]

CLARA: [*In a subdued voice*] Joe!

JOE: What?

CLARA: That Samaritan Hospital's at Broad and Ontario, isn't it?

JOE: Yes.

[*She turns slowly and looks out, irresolute. Then she stoops down abstractedly and picks up the newspaper that* Joe *dropped. The parlor-door opens sharply and* Amy *stands looking at her apprehensively. Their eyes meet*]

AMY: What is it?

[Mrs. Fisher *appears in the door at the right, drying an agate-ware plate*]

MRS. FISHER: Wasn't that your Pop that came in, Clara?

[Clara *makes a deft, silencing gesture with her left hand to* Amy, *and moves towards the center-table*]

CLARA: No, it wasn't, Mom, it was the boy with the paper.

MRS. FISHER: [*Coming further into the room to see the clock*] I wonder what's keepin' him; he's late to-night. [Clara *leans against the center-table, keeping her face averted from her Mother*] He's nearly always here before this. [*She moves back again towards the kitchen*]

AMY: [*Crossing quickly down to* Clara's *left*] What is it, Clara?

MRS. FISHER: [*Turning and looking at* Clara] What's the matter with her?

[Clara *tries to control her feelings*]

AMY: I don't know what's the matter with her, Mom! Something *Joe* just told her—he's just gone upstairs.

MRS. FISHER: [*Coming forward apprehensively at* Clara's *right*] What is it, Clara,—somethin' about your Father? Is that what you're cryin' for?

AMY: Why don't you tell her, Clara?

MRS. FISHER: Go to the foot of the stairs, Amy, and call Joe. [Amy *steps towards the foot of the stairs*] Something's happened to your Father, I know it.

CLARA: [*Moving a step or two towards her Mother*] Now, it's nothing to get upset about, Mom; he just took a little spell of some kind at his work this afternoon, and they had to take him to the hospital. [Amy *comes forward eagerly, and crosses to a point below the table*] Joe just came from there, and he sez we'd better get our things on right away and go down there.

[Mrs. Fisher *sways a step forward, letting the agate-ware plate slide from her hands to the floor.* Amy *steps towards her Mother, lifting the chair from the right of the table and guiding her Mother into it*]

AMY: Here, sit down here, Mom.

MRS. FISHER: [*Slightly dazed*] What is it she's sayin' happened to your Father, Amy?

[Amy *passes back of the chair to her Mother's right, and* Clara *comes to her left*]

CLARA: Now, it's nothing to get excited about, Mom; it might be just a little heart-attack or something that he took. [*She takes the towel from her Mother's hand and hands it to* Amy] Put this over there.

[Amy *turns to the buffet*]

MRS. FISHER: There was never anything the matter with your Father's heart, Clara.

CLARA: Well, it's pretty hot in there where he works, you know that. [Mrs. Fisher *shakes her head up and down, knowingly*] And men at Pop's age are always taking little spells of some kind.

MRS. FISHER: [*With a long, heavy sigh*] Ah, I guess it's a stroke, Clara.

CLARA: It might not be, Mom, you can't tell.

MRS. FISHER: That's how his two brothers went, you know.

CLARA: Amy, you'd better go to the telephone next door and tell Frank Hyland I won't be home. [Amy *hurries across towards the hall-door, and* Clara *follows her, continuing her instructions*] If he isn't home yet, tell Bertha to tell him to come right down to the Samaritan Hospital as soon as he comes. And tell Johnny Harbison to go to the corner for a taxi.

[*The front-door closes after* Amy, *and* Clara *steps back to her Mother's side*]

MRS. FISHER: Is that where your Father is, Clara, the Samaritan Hospital?

CLARA: Yes; it's right down there near where he works, at Broad and Ontario.

MRS. FISHER: [*Starting to cry*] Your poor Father— I wonder what happened to him.

[*Clara reflects her Mother's sentiment*]

CLARA: [*Picking up the plate*] Now, there's no use looking on the dark side of it already, Mom.

MRS. FISHER: No, but me gettin' his supper out there, and him not comin' home to it at all. And maybe *never* comin' home to it again, Clara, for all we know.

CLARA: He'll be home again, Mom—Pop is a strong man. [*She puts the plate on the buffet*]

MRS. FISHER: [*Suddenly*] I guess he's dead, now, and you're not tellin' me.

CLARA: [*Coming to her Mother's left*] He isn't dead, Mom; I'd have told you if he was.

MRS. FISHER: What did Joe say?

CLARA: Just what I told you; that he'd had a spell of some kind.

MRS. FISHER: Well, why didn't he tell me! What's he doin' upstairs, anyway?

CLARA: He's changing his clothes; he's got to go right back down there again.

MRS. FISHER: He's cryin' I guess. You know, it'll kill our poor Joe, Clara, if anything happens to your Father.

CLARA: He sez we'd better go right down there, too, Mom; so you'd better go upstairs and fix yourself up a bit. Give me your apron.

MRS. FISHER: [*Rising and commencing to remove her apron*] I don't know whether I'll be able to dress myself now or not; my hands are like lead.

CLARA: You don't need to get all dressed up, Mom— just put on your black-silk waist; that skirt's good enough. [*She goes towards the door at the right with the apron and goes out*]

MRS. FISHER: [*Taking the comb from the back of her head and commencing to comb her hair*] Well, I'm not goin' down there lookin' like a dago woman.

CLARA: [*Coming quickly in again*] Nobody'll see you in the dark. [*She picks up the plate and towel from the buffet and straightens the runner*]

MRS. FISHER: [*Moving aimlessly about in front of the mantelpiece*] It won't be dark in the *hospital*; unless somethin' happens to the lights. [*Clara goes out again*] Put that gas out under them potatoes, Clara, I just lit it. And you'd better pick up this room a bit while I'm upstairs, you don't know who might be comin' here if they hear about your Father. [*She stops and looks helplessly about the room*] Oh, dear, Oh, dear, Oh, dear! I don't know what I'm doin'. [*Clara comes in again*] Take all them papers off that table, Clara, and put them in the kitchen.

CLARA: [*Crossing to the table and folding and gather-*

ing up the various papers] You'd better bring your umbrella down with you, Mom, when you go up, —it looked like rain when I came in.

MRS. FISHER: Oh, and I let our Amy take my rubbers the last day she was here, and she *never* brings anything back.

CLARA: [*Taking the papers out into the kitchen*] You won't need rubbers.

MRS. FISHER: Oh, I get my feet all wet, when I don't have rubbers. [*She is facing the hall-door, fastening the old-fashioned brooch at her throat. Aubrey frames himself in the door, with a bandage around his head, and looking a bit battered*] My God, what happened to *you*, now!

AUBREY: [*Coming forward at the left, removing his hat*] It's beginning to rain. [*He places his hat and cane on the table, and stands in front of the table removing his gloves*]

MRS. FISHER: [*Following him with her eyes*] Never mind the rain, the rain didn't do that to you. [*She comes forward at his left. Clara comes in and stands over near the door at the right, looking at him*] I guess you ran into somebody, didn't you?

AUBREY: [*With a shade of nonchalance*] Don't get excited, Mother,—just a little misunderstanding on the part of the traffic-officer.

MRS. FISHER: You don't mean to tell me that you ran into a traffic-officer!

[*Clara comes forward at the right*]

AUBREY: Control, now, Little Mother, I assure there is no occasion for undue solicitation. [*He turns and sees Clara*] Good evening, Mrs. Hyland.

CLARA: Hello! What happened to your head?

MRS. FISHER: You look like a bandit.

AUBREY: The veriest trifle, Mrs. Hyland—just a little spray from the wind-shield.

MRS. FISHER: Where's the car you borrowed? Smashed, I guess, ain't it?

AUBREY: The car I borrowed, Mrs. Fisher, is now in the hands of the bandits of the law. The judicial gentlemen, who have entered into a conspiracy with the regulators of traffic—to collect fines from motorists—by ordering them to go one way—and then swearing that they told them to go another.

MRS. FISHER: Never mind your fancy talk, we've heard too much of that already! I want to know who you killed,—or what you did run into; for I know you ran into somethin'. And where's the automobile that someone was fool enough to lend you?

AUBREY: The automobile, Little Mother, is perfectly safe—parked and pasturing—in the courtyard of the Twenty-second and Hunting Park Avenue Police Station.

MRS. FISHER: Did you get arrested, too?

AUBREY: I accompanied the officer as far as the

station-house, yes; and I told them a few things while I was there, too, about the condition of traffic in this city.

MRS. FISHER: I guess they told you a few things, too, didn't they?

AUBREY: Beg pardon?

MRS. FISHER: [*Starting abruptly for the hall-door*] Never mind; you're welcome.

CLARA: You'd better change your shoes, Mom; you can't go down there with those.

MRS. FISHER: [*Pointing toward the cellar-door*] See if my long black coat's in the cellar-way there. [*Clara goes quickly to the cellar-door, opens it, and looks for the coat*] That fellow's got me so upset I don't know what I'm doin'. [*She goes out the hall-door and to her left, up the stairs. Aubrey moves over to the chair at the right, where Mrs. Fisher collapsed, and sits down,—quite ruffled in his dignity. Clara closes the cellar-door and, with a glance toward the hall-door, comes quickly forward at Aubrey's left*]

CLARA: What did they do, fine you, Aubrey?

AUBREY: They were all set to fine me; but when I got through with them they didn't have a leg to stand on. So they tried to cover themselves up as gracefully as possible, by trumping up a charge against me of driving an automobile without a license.

CLARA: What did they do, take the automobile *away* from you?

AUBREY: Nothing of the sort; they simply complied with the usual procedure in a case of this kind— which is to release the defendant on bond, pending the extent of the victim's injuries.

CLARA: Was there somebody injured?

AUBREY: The traffic-cop that ran into me, yes.

CLARA: For God's sake, couldn't you find anybody but the traffic-cop to run into!

AUBREY: I did not run into him, Mrs. Hyland—you don't understand the circumstances of the case.

CLARA: Well, I understand this much about them— that they can give you ten years for a thing like that. And it'd just serve you right if they did, too. Borrowin' people's automobiles, and knowing no more about running them than I do. [*She turns away to her right and moves across above the table towards the hall-door*]

AUBREY: No time like the present to learn, Mrs. Hyland.

CLARA: [*Turning to him sharply*] Well, you'll very likely have plenty of time, from now on,—if that officer is seriously injured. [*She continues over and down to the window at the left, where she draws the drape aside and looks anxiously down the street for the taxi*]

AUBREY: He was faking a broken arm around there when I left—But it's a wonder to me the poor straw-ride wasn't signed on the dotted line; for he ran head on right into me.

CLARA: [*Crossing back towards him, in front of the Morris-chair*] Was *he* in a car, too?

AUBREY: No, he was jay-walking—trying to beat me to the crossing, after giving me the right of way.

CLARA: Where did this thing happen?

AUBREY: Broad and Erie Avenue, I wouldn't kid you.

CLARA: Did they take the cop to the hospital?

AUBREY: Yes, we took him over there in the car.

CLARA: Did they let *you* run it?

AUBREY: Repeat the question, Mrs. Hyland.

CLARA: You heard me,—I don't need to repeat it. And take that silly-looking bandage off your head, before Amy sees you; and don't frighten the life out of her. [*She steps up to the hall-door and glances out*] She's got enough to worry her now without looking at you.

[*Aubrey rises, and, detaching the handkerchief from around his head, moves across to a point above the center-table*]

AUBREY: Is my wife here?

CLARA: She's next door, telephoning, yes; and she'll be back in a minute. [*Coming forward a step or two at the left*] Pop just had a stroke of some kind at his work this afternoon, Joe just told us.

AUBREY: What are you doing, kidding me?

CLARA: [*Starting to cry*] No, of course I'm not kidding you! What would I be kidding you about a thing like that for? [*She crosses down and across in front of the center-table. The front-door closes*]

AUBREY: Where is he now?

CLARA: They took him to the Samaritan Hospital; we're just going down there.

[*Amy appears in the hall-door, and stands looking questioningly at Aubrey*]

AMY: What's the matter, Aubrey?

[*He turns and looks at her*]

AUBREY: [*Extending his arm and hand in a magnificent gesture*] Well! [*Amy comes forward to her husband*] The old kid herself!

AMY: What is it, Aubrey?

AUBREY: [*Taking her in his arms*] Nothing in the world but this, Baby. [*He kisses her affectionately*]

CLARA: Did you get Frank on the 'phone, Amy?

[*Mrs. Fisher can be heard hurrying down the stairs*]

AMY: [*Crossing above Aubrey and speaking directly to Clara*] He wasn't home yet; I told the girl to tell him as soon as he came in.

MRS. FISHER: [*Coming through the hall-door, and tossing her little knit-jacket onto the small stand at the left of the mantelpiece*] Clara, is that automobile-cab here yet?

CLARA: It'll be here in a minute, Mom.

MRS. FISHER: What do you think of this fellow, Amy,—runnin' wild through the city breakin' policemen's bones! We didn't have enough trouble without that—with your poor Father layin' dead for all we know,—down in the Jewish hospital.

[*She starts to cry and steps down to the window at the left to look out for the taxicab*] It's enough to make a body light-headed.

CLARA: Where's your coat, Mom?

MRS. FISHER: [*Turning to her*] Isn't it there in the cellar-way?

CLARA: No, I just looked.

MRS. FISHER: [*Going up to the hall-door*] It must be upstairs. Joe!

AMY: [*At Aubrey's right*] I thought you were out at the Automobile Show, Aubrey.

MRS. FISHER: [*At the foot of the stairs*] Listen, Joe—

AUBREY: I had a little mix-up at Broad and Erie Avenue.

AMY: You didn't get hurt, did you?

[Mrs. Fisher *and* Aubrey, *speaking together*]

MRS. FISHER:—Throw down my long black coat; you'll find it on a hook there in the hall-closet. [*She starts for the buffet*]

AUBREY:—Nothing but a scratch or two, here on my forehead, from the glass in the wind-shield. Just a little shake-up.

MRS. FISHER: [*Stopping and turning sharply at the right of the center-table*] He nearly killed a traffic-officer!—That's how much of a little shake-up it was. [*She continues to the buffet, where Clara is standing*] Get out of my way, Clara, till I get a clean handkerchief out of here. [*She pushes Clara out of her way and opens the left-hand drawer of the buffet and rummages for a handkerchief. Clara passes across in front of the center-table to the window at the left*]

AMY: You *didn't*, Aubrey, did you?

AUBREY: Certainly not, Amy—your Mother's raving.

[Mrs. Fisher *finds the handkerchief, slams the drawer shut and turns*]

MRS. FISHER: The man's in the hospital!—I don't know what more you want.

[*The big black coat lands at the foot of the stairs with a thud, causing Mrs. Fisher to start nervously; then she hurries across at the back towards the hall-door, tucking the folded handkerchief at her waist*]

AMY: Is he, Aubrey?

AUBREY: Do you think I'd be here, Kid, if he was?

MRS. FISHER: [*On the way over*] You wouldn't be here, only that someone was fool enough to bail you out; instead of lettin' you stay in where you couldn't be killin' people. [Clara *has stepped up to the foot of the stairs and picked the coat up immediately it fell, and now stands holding it for her Mother to put on; but* Mrs. Fisher *disregards her, going straight out to the foot of the stairs and calling shrilly up to* Joe] Joe, why don't you tell a body when you're goin' to throw a thing down that way, and not be frightenin' the life out of people! [*She comes back into the room again and* Clara *assists her.* Amy *stands above the center-table looking wide-eyed at* Aubrey, *who*

sways forward at the left, and, crossing below the center-table to the chair at the right, where he has been previously seated, sits down*]

CLARA: Aren't you going to put on another waist, Mom?

MRS. FISHER: No, this one is good enough—I'll keep the coat buttoned up. Put that collar inside.

AMY: [*In a lowered tone*] Are you out on bail, Aubrey?

AUBREY: They always bail a man in a case like this, Amy; they've got my car on their hands.

MRS. FISHER: [*Buttoning the coat, and moving to the mirror over the mantelpiece*] Get my hat, will you, Clara?

CLARA: [*Starting for the hall-door*] Where is it, upstairs?

MRS. FISHER: No, it's in the parlor there, inside the top of the Victrola.

[Clara *comes back and goes into the parlor*]

AMY: Why didn't you bring the car back with you, Aubrey?—That fellow might want it tomorrow.

AUBREY: I'll have it for him all right; I've got to call around there for it Monday morning at ten o'clock.

[Mrs. Fisher *turns sharply from her primping at the mirror*]

MRS. FISHER: I guess you've got to go down there to a hearing Monday morning at ten o'clock,— [Amy *turns and looks at her Mother*] and pay your fine! [*Speaking directly to* Amy] I guess that's the automobile he's got to call for.

[Clara *hurries out of the parlor brushing the dust off an old black hat, with a bunch of cherries on it*]

CLARA: I'd better go out and get a whisk-broom and dust this, Mom.

MRS. FISHER: [*Turning to her nervously*] No, never mind, it's good enough, give it to me.

CLARA: [*Crossing below her Mother, to the right*] Your coat needs dusting. [*She takes a whisk-broom from a hook just inside the kitchen-door*]

AMY: How much did they fine you, Aubrey?

AUBREY: They didn't fine me at all.

MRS. FISHER: [*Settling her hat*] They'll do that Monday.

AUBREY: Time'll tell that, Mother Fisher.

[Clara *hurries back and starts brushing her Mother's coat*]

MRS. FISHER: And you'll pay it, too, or go to jail; and it'ud just be the price of you.

AUBREY: They didn't seem very anxious to do any fining today, after I got through telling it to them.

MRS. FISHER: Am I all right, Clara?

AUBREY: I took a slam at the Pennsylvania Railroad, too, while I was at it.

MRS. FISHER: You're always takin' slams at somethin'; that's what's leavin' you under bail right now. Are you ready, Clara?

[*She hurries to the foot of the stairs*]

CLARA: [*Hurrying back to the kitchen with the whisk-broom*] Yes, I'm ready.

AUBREY: Never mind about that, Mother Fisher.

MRS. FISHER: [*Calling up the stairs*] Are you goin' down there with us, Joe?

JOE: [*From upstairs*] Comin' right down.

[*Mrs. Fisher comes in to the mantel-piece and picks up her gloves. Clara hurries in from the kitchen again to the center-table and picks up her neck-piece and gloves*]

AUBREY: Only don't be surprised if you hear of a very quiet little shake-up very soon—in the Department of Public Safety.

MRS. FISHER: Are you warm enough with that coat, Clara?

CLARA: Yes, I'm all right. How about the umbrella?

MRS. FISHER: I think it's out there in the hall-rack; look and see.

[*Clara hurries out into the hallway, and Mrs. Fisher stands putting on her gloves. Amy crosses to* Aubrey's *left*]

AMY: [*Very quietly*] How much bail did they put you under, Aubrey?

AUBREY: One thousand berries, Amy.

[*Mrs. Fisher looks over at them keenly*]

AMY: A thousand dollars!

AUBREY: That's regulation—[*Amy turns and gives her Mother a troubled look, and* Mrs. Fisher *moves forward at the left to a point where she can see* Aubrey] A little chicken-feed for the stool-pigeons.

MRS. FISHER: Did *he* say they put him under a thousand dollars' bail?

AUBREY: That's what I said, Mrs. Fisher, one thousand trifles—I wouldn't kid you.

MRS. FISHER: You wouldn't kid anybody that'd listen to you for five minutes. And who did you get to go a thousand dollars bail *for* you?

AUBREY: Don't be alarmed, Little Mother,—I saw that the affair was kept strictly within the family.

MRS. FISHER: What do you mean?

AUBREY: Your other son-in-law—was kind enough to come forward.

[*Clara hurries in from the hallway with the umbrella, and comes forward at the extreme left*]

MRS. FISHER: Clara's husband!

AUBREY: That's the gentleman, Mrs. Fisher,—Mr. Francis X. Hyland.

MRS. FISHER: [*Helplessly*] My God! [*She turns around to her right till she locates* Clara] Do you hear that, Clara?

CLARA: What?

MRS. FISHER: He got Frank Hyland to go his bail for a thousand dollars.

CLARA: [*Looking bitterly at* Aubrey] What did you do, write him another letter?

AUBREY: That was not necessary, Mrs. Hyland, not giving you a short answer. I simply called your husband at his office, and he came right up. But too late, of course, to be a witness to the fact that it was the trolley-car that ran into *me*.

MRS. FISHER: How many more things ran into you,—besides traffic-cops and trolley-cars! I suppose a couple of the buildin's ran into you too, didn't they?

[*Joe hurries in from the hall-door buttoning his overcoat*]

JOE: Are you ready, Mom?

CLARA: [*Going up to the hall-door*] Yes, we're ready.

[*Joe comes forward at the extreme left, looking questioningly from one to the other. Clara goes out into the hall*]

AUBREY: You'll find out all about that Monday morning, Mrs. Fisher.

MRS. FISHER: [*Moving up towards the hall-door*] Well, see that nothin' else runs into you between now and Monday.

JOE: What's the matter?

MRS. FISHER: We don't want Frank Hyland losin' any thousand-dollar bills on account of you.

JOE: What's happened, Mom?

MRS. FISHER: [*Turning to Joe, and pointing at Aubrey with a wide gesture*] Why, this crazy Jack here's been runnin' into everything in the city but ourselves; and he got himself arrested; and Frank Hyland had to bail him out for a thousand dollars.

[*She starts to cry*]

JOE: What were you doin', Aubrey, joy-ridin'?

MRS. FISHER: No!—he was trolley-ridin',—and traffic-cop-ridin',—and every other kind of ridin',—in an automobile that he borrowed.

CLARA: [*Hurrying in from the hallway*] I think I see that taxi coming, Mom.

MRS. FISHER: [*Starting towards the hall-door*] Come on here, Joe. [*Joe crosses up at the left of the center-table to the mirror over the mantelpiece, looking disapprovingly at* Aubrey. Aubrey *rises and strolls over to a point in front of the center-table*] How do we get down there, Clara?

CLARA: Right down Erie Ave.

AUBREY: Too bad I left that car down there at the Station House, I could have run you down there.

[*They all turn and look at him; and* Mrs. Fisher, *with poison in her right eye, moves forward at the left of the center-table, with a level ominous slowness*]

MRS. FISHER: You wouldn't run *me* down there,—don't fret—not if you had a thousand cars. There's enough of us in the hospital as it is. [*Aubrey simply regards her from a great height*] And don't you come down there neither;—for you'd only start talkin', and that'd finish Pop quicker than a stroke.

[*There's a startling hoot from the taxicab horn outside, which almost throws* Mrs. Fisher *from her balance*]

CLARA: [*Going out*] Come on, Joe.

JOE: [*Following her out*] Ain't you comin' down to the hospital, Amy?

MRS. FISHER: [*Going out*] No, you'd better stay here, Amy,—there'd better be some one of us here—or that fellow'll be runnin' into somethin' else. You ought to have somethin' heavier on you than that fur, Clara.

[*Aubrey sits down at the left of the center-table*]

CLARA: [*In the hallway*] I'm all right, we'll be down there in a few minutes.

MRS. FISHER: Have you got your coat buttoned up good, Joe?

[*The front-door closes after them. Amy turns from the hall-door, where she has been standing, seeing them out, and comes forward to the back of the chair at the left of the center-table, where* Aubrey *is sitting*]

AMY: Where's your toupé, Aubrey? [*Touching the sticking-plasters on his forehead*]

AUBREY: In my pocket here.

AMY: [*Stroking his hair*] Is your head hurting you?

AUBREY: [*Reaching for her hand and drawing it down over his left shoulder*] Not a bit, Honey—just a couple of little scratches. [*He kisses her hand. She raises her eyes and looks straight ahead, with a troubled expression*]

AMY: Aubrey, what do you think they'll do to you down there Monday?

AUBREY: Now, don't you worry about that, Sweetheart; I'll be right there if they try to pull anything.

[*She moves over thoughtfully towards the upper right-hand corner of the center-table. Then a new thought occurs to her, and she turns her head and looks at him narrowly*]

AMY: You hadn't had anything to drink, had you, Aubrey?

AUBREY: [*Looking at her quickly*] Who, me?

AMY: I mean I thought somebody might have treated you or something.

AUBREY: [*Making a statement*] I had a glass of Champagne six months ago with a friend of mine in his suite at the Ritz-Carlton Hotel, and I haven't had a drink of anything since.

AMY: You better take off your overcoat, Aubrey; we'll have to stay here till they get back.

[*He gets up and commences to remove the overcoat*]

AUBREY: Yes, I guess we will.—I wonder how your Father is.

AMY: [*Taking the overcoat from him*] Pretty bad I guess,—or they wouldn't have sent for Joe. [*She takes the coat up to the sofa at the right of the mantelpiece, and Aubrey takes a huge cigar from his vest-pocket and feels for a match*] I'll get you a match, Aubrey. [*She goes out into the kitchen, and Aubrey moves to a point above the center-table, biting the tip of his cigar*]

AUBREY: I thought I had some here, but I guess I haven't. Did they send for Joe?

AMY: Yes, they telephoned for him, to the place where he works.

AUBREY: Your Mother said it was a stroke.

AMY: [*Entering with some matches*] I guess that's what it is, too; his two brothers died that way.

AUBREY: [*Taking the matches from her*] I'm sorry to hear that, Amy. But, you mustn't worry, now, Kid.

AMY: It isn't only that I'm worried about, Aubrey;—I'm thinking about you—Monday. [*She takes hold of the lapels of his coat and almost cries*]

AUBREY: [*Putting his arm around her*] Now, listen to me, Baby—you know I'd tell you, don't you, if there was anything to worry about.

AMY: But, they're getting awfully strict in this city; there's been so many automobile accidents lately.

AUBREY: They're only strict, Honey, when a man's driving under the influence of liquor.

[*There's a slight pause, and* Amy *thinks hard*]

AMY: What if that traffic-cop is hurt bad, Aubrey?

AUBREY: It'd only be a fine for reckless driving, even if they could prove it *was* reckless driving; and I can prove it was the copper's fault. [*Detaching himself from her*] So they'll very likely be *apologizing* to me around there Monday morning, instead of fining me. [*He moves across and down to the window at the left,—with ever so slight a touch of swagger*]

AMY: Oh, I wouldn't care if they only fined you, Aubrey; because I could go back to work until it was paid.

AUBREY: [*Looking out the window*] You'll never go back to work, Kid, while I'm on the boat.

AMY: I wouldn't mind it, Aubrey.

AUBREY: Not while you're *my* wife, Amy. [*He half turns to her, with considerable consequence*] I'd rather leave the Pennsylvania Railroad *flat*; and go out and take one of the jobs that have been offered me where they pay a man what he's worth.

AMY: You don't think they might do anything else to you, do you, Aubrey?

AUBREY: [*Turning to her*] Oh, they might try to take away my license.

AMY: You haven't *got* a license, have you?

AUBREY: [*Turning back to the window*] No, I neglected to attend to it this year.

AMY: They can fine you for that, can't they?

AUBREY: Driving an automobile without a license, you mean?

AMY: Yes.

AUBREY: Sure—they can fine you for anything unless you know how to beat them to it. [*He strikes the match on the arm of the Morris-chair at his right. Amy rests her hands on the center-table, and looks straight out, wretchedly*]

AMY: [*Tonelessly*] What is it they send them to prison for, Aubrey? [*He is just holding the lighted match to the cigar, and, consequently, is unable to answer her immediately. The front door-bell rings. She glances apprehensively in the direction of the hall-door, then meets his eyes]* I wonder who that is.

AUBREY: [*Tossing the burnt match into the window at his left*] Do you want me to answer it?

AMY: I wish you would, Aubrey; it might be something about Pop.

[*He crosses in front of the Morris-chair and up at the left of the center-table to the mirror over the mantelpiece, where he stands settling his tie and vest. Amy turns to the couch and gathers up his coat, then steps forward to the center-table and picks up his hat and the bandage that he took off his head*]

AUBREY: [*Touching the plasters on his forehead*] Does my head look all right?

AMY: [*Glancing at him, as she goes towards the hooks at the head of the cellar-stairs*] Yes, it's all right, Aubrey.

AUBREY: Wait a minute—[*He steps to her side and takes the carnation from the buttonhole of his overcoat, then steps back to the mirror and fixes it in his sack-coat*]

AMY: Hurry up, Aubrey.

[*The door-bell rings again*]

AUBREY: [*Going out into the hallway*] All right—all right.

[*Amy hangs the overcoat and hat up, then turns the cellar-door, and tosses the bandage down the cellar-stairs. Then she crosses quickly to a point in front of the mantelpiece and listens intently*]

GILL: [*At the front-door*] Good evenin'.

AUBREY: Good evening, sir.

GILL: Is this where Mr. Fisher lives?

AUBREY: This is Mr. Fisher's residence, yes, sir. What can I do for you?

GILL: Why, I got some things of his here that the boss ast me to leave.

AUBREY: Oh, just step inside for a minute. Getting a little colder I think.

[*The front-door closes*]

GILL: Well, we can look for it any time, now.

AUBREY: Will you just step in this way, please? [*Aubrey enters from the hallway*] There's a gentleman here, Amy, with some things belonging to your Father. Just come right in.

[*Aubrey comes forward a few steps at the left; and Gill enters*]

GILL: Good evenin'.

AMY: Good evening.

AUBREY: This is my wife, Mrs. Piper.

GILL: [*Nodding*] How do you do.

[*Amy nods*]

AUBREY: Mrs. Piper is Mr. Fisher's daughter. The rest of the folks have gone down to the hospital.

GILL: I see. [*Turning to Amy*] Have you *heard* anything from the hospital yet?

AMY: Not yet, no.

AUBREY: We didn't know anything about it at all, till fifteen minutes ago.

GILL: It's too bad.

AUBREY: Those hospitals won't tell you anything.

AMY: Do you work with my Father?

GILL: No, ma'am, I'm a twister on the second floor. But, one of the machinist's-helpers that works with your Father knows I live out this way, so he ast me to stop by with these things on me way home. [*He crosses towards Amy, with a hat and overcoat, and a more or less discolored lunch-box*]

AMY: [*Taking the things*] Thanks ever so much.

GILL: There's just the overcoat and hat, and his lunch-box.

AMY: Thanks.

GILL: McMahon sez if he comes across anything else he'll let me know.

AMY: [*Crossing to the sofa with the things*] No, I don't imagine there's anything else.

GILL: If there is, I'll bring it up.

AMY: Well, that's very nice of you; I'm ever so much obliged to you. [*She comes back towards Gill*]

AUBREY: Who is this McMahon?

GILL: He's one of the machinist's-helpers down there.

AUBREY: I see.

AMY: Were you there when my Father was taken sick?

GILL: No, ma'am, I wasn't. I don't think there was anybody there, to tell you the truth. McMahon sez he was talkin' to him at a quarter of three, and he sez when he came back from the annex at three o'clock, he found Mr. Fisher layin' in front of number five.

AUBREY: [*With a suggestion of professionalism*] Very likely a little touch of Angina Pectoria.

[*Gill looks at him*]

GILL: The doctor down there sez he thought it was a stroke.

AUBREY: Same thing.

AMY: Won't you sit down, Mr. —a—

GILL: No, thank you, ma'am, I can't stay; I've got to get along out home.

[*There's a rapping out at the right. They all look in the direction of the kitchen*]

AMY: Oh, I guess it's Mrs. Harbison—I'll go.

[*She goes out at the right*]

AUBREY: [*Crossing above Gill towards the right*] Don't stand out there talking, now, Amy, with nothing around you. [*Surveying himself in the buffet-mirror at the right*] Do you live up this way, Governor?

GILL: No, sir, I live out Richmond way.

AUBREY: I see.

GILL: I take number thirty-two over Allegheny Avenue.

AUBREY: [*Turning and moving over towards the center-table*] Too bad my car's laid up, I could run you out there.

GILL: Oh, that's all right; the trolley takes me right to the door.

AUBREY: I had to turn it in Thursday to have the valves ground.

AMY: [*Appearing in the kitchen-door*] I'm wanted on the telephone, Aubrey; I'll be right in. Will you excuse me for a minute?

GILL: That's all right, ma'am; I'm goin' right along meself.

AUBREY: Very likely some word from the Hospital.

GILL: I hope it ain't any bad news.

AUBREY: Well, you've got to be prepared for most anything, Governor, when a man gets up around the old three-score mark.

GILL: That's true, a lot of them push off about that age.

AUBREY: Especially when a man's worked hard all his life.

GILL: Yes, I guess Mr. Fisher's worked pretty hard.

AUBREY: Not an excuse in the world for it, either.— I've said to him a thousand times if I've said to him once, "Well, Pop, when are you going to take the big rest?" "Oh," he'd say, "I'll have lots of time to rest when I'm through." "All right," I'd say, "go ahead; only let me tell you, Pop, you're going to be through ahead of schedule if you don't take it soon."

GILL: Well, I guess it comes pretty hard on a man that's been active all his life to quit all of a sudden.

AUBREY: Well, he wouldn't have to quit exactly.—I mean, he's a handy man; he could putter around the house. There are lots of little things here and there that I'm not any too well satisfied with. [*He glances around the room*]

GILL: Is Mr. Fisher's wife livin'?

AUBREY: Yes, she's here with us too.

GILL: Well, that makes it nice.

AUBREY: Well, it's a pretty big house here; so when I married last June, I said, "Come ahead, the more the merrier." [*He laughs a little*]

GILL: 'Tis a pretty big house this.

AUBREY: Yes, they don't make them like this anymore, Governor. Put up by the McNeil people out here in Jenkintown.

GILL: Oh, yes.

AUBREY: They just put up the twenty of them—kind of sample houses—ten on that side and ten on this. Of course, these on this side have the southern exposure,—so a man's got to do quite a bit of wire-pulling to get hold of one of these.

GILL: You've got to do some wire-pullin' to get hold of *any* kind of a house these days.

AUBREY: Well, I have a friend here in town that's very close to the city architect, and he was able to fix it for me.

GILL: [*Glancing toward the window, at the left*] It's a nice street.

AUBREY: Nice in summer.

GILL: I was surprised when I saw it, because when I ast a taxicab-driver down here where it was, he said he never heard of it.

AUBREY: [*Looking at him keenly*] Never heard of Cresson Street?

GILL: He said not.

AUBREY: [*With pitying amusement*] He must be an awful straw-ride.

GILL: I had to ast a police officer.

AUBREY: Well, I'll tell you, Governor,—I don't suppose they have many *calls* for taxicabs out this way. You see, most everybody in through here has his own *car*.

GILL: I see.

AUBREY: Some of them have a half dozen, for that matter. [*He laughs, a bit consequentially*]

GILL: [*Starting for the parlor-doors*] There certainly is plenty of them knockin' around.

AUBREY: All over the ice. [Aubrey *indicates the hall-door*] This way, Governor.

GILL: [*Turning towards the hall-door*] Oh, excuse me.

AUBREY: [*Moving towards the hall-door*] Those doors go into the parlor.

GILL: I see. [*He turns at the hall-door*] A fellow was tellin' me over here in the cigar store that there was quite a smash-up about a half hour ago down here at Broad and Erie Avenue.

AUBREY: That so?

GILL: He sez there was some *nut* down there runnin' into everything in sight. He sez he even ran into the traffic-cop; and broke his arm. Can you imagine what they'll *do* to that guy, knockin' the traffic-cop down!

AUBREY: What was the matter with him, was he stewed?

GILL: No,—the fellow in the cigar store sez he was just a *nut*. He sez they didn't know where he got hold of this car; he sez it didn't belong to him. I guess he picked it up somewhere. They took it away from him and pinched him. [*Starting to go out*] So I guess he won't be runnin' into anything else for a while.

AUBREY: [*Following him out*] Traffic's in pretty bad shape in this town right now.

GILL: Certainly is. Why, a man's not safe walkin' along the sidewalk, these days. I hope your wife'll hear some good news.

AUBREY: Well, while there's life there's hope, you know.

GILL: That's right. No use lookin' on the dark side of things.

[Amy *enters from the right, with a wide-eyed, wan expression, and comes slowly down to the center-table*]

AUBREY: Where do you get your car, Governor?

GILL: Why, I can get one right at the corner here, and transfer.

AUBREY: Oh, that's right, so you can. Well, we're ever so much obliged to you.

GILL: Don't mention it.

AUBREY: Good-night, sir.

GILL: Good-night. [*The door closes*]

AUBREY: [*Coming in from the hall-door*] When did *you* come in, Amy? [*He stops to look at himself in the mantelpiece-mirror*]

AMY: [*Without turning*] I came in the side-door; I thought that man'd be still here.

AUBREY: [*Coming down to her*] Well, Kid, what's the good word?

AMY: [*Breaking down*] Aubrey, Pop is dead. [*She buries her face in the lapel of his coat. He takes her in his arms, looks straight ahead, and there is a long pause—during which Amy cries hard*]

AUBREY: Don't let it get you, Honey—you have nothing to regret; and nothing to fear. The Kid from West Philly'll never go back on you,—you know that, don't you, Baby? [*She continues to cry*] You know that, don't you, Amy? [*She doesn't answer him*] Amy.

AMY: What?

AUBREY: You know I'm with you, don't you?

AMY: Yes.

[*He kisses her hair affectionately*]

AUBREY: Don't cry, Honey; the old man's better off than we are. He knows all about it now. [*He kisses her again; then detaches himself and moves over and down at the left of the center-table*]

AMY: What do you think we ought to do, Aubrey?

AUBREY: There's nothing at all that you can do that I can see, Sweetheart; except to sit tight till the folks get back. They'll be down there themselves in a few minutes, and they'll know all about it.

AMY: They said that Pop died at a quarter of six.

AUBREY: Was that the Hospital on the telephone?

AMY: Yes.

AUBREY: [*Moving up to a point above the center-table again*] Something we ought to have in here, Amy; a telephone—not be letting the whole neighborhood in on our business. [*Amy leans on the back of the chair at the right and cries softly*] Now, pull yourself together, Sweetheart. [*He crosses to her and puts his arm around her shoulders*]

AMY: This is where Pop always used to sit in the evening.—It'll seem funny not to see him here anymore. [*She breaks down again*]

AUBREY: [*After a slight pause*] The old gent had to go sometime. [*He passes back of her, comes forward at the right and stands, looking at the tip of his cigar*] Your Mother'll have you and me to comfort her now. [*He strolls across below the center-table and stops, thinking profoundly. Amy sinks down on the chair dejectedly*]

AMY: I don't know how Mom'll keep this house going now, just on Joe's pay.

AUBREY: Why don't you say something to your Mother about letting *us* come in here? She'll need a man in the house. And my salary 'ud cover the rent.

AMY: Mom doesn't have to pay rent, Aubrey,—she owns this house. Pop left it to her. He made his will out the week after we were married. [*Aubrey looks at her keenly*] Clara got him to do it.

AUBREY: Who's the executor, do you know?

AMY: Clara is.

[*Aubrey nods comprehendingly*]

AUBREY: [*Looking away off*] Too bad your Father didn't make *me* the executor of that will;—I could have saved him a lot of money. [*He replaces the cigar in his mouth*]

AMY: I suppose he thought on account of Clara being the oldest.

AUBREY: I wonder why your Father never *liked* me.

AMY: Pop never said he didn't like you, Aubrey.

AUBREY: I always tried to be clubby with him. I used to slap him on the back whenever I spoke to him.

AMY: Pop was always very quiet.

AUBREY: And the Kid from West Philly had too much to say. Well,—forgive and forget.—It's all over now.—And the old man can be as quiet as he likes.

[*Amy cries again, and there is a pause. Aubrey stands smoking*]

AMY: [*Pulling herself together and getting up*] You haven't had anything to eat tonight yet, have you, Aubrey?

AUBREY: [*Coming out of his abstraction, and sauntering up at the left of the center-table*] Don't worry about me, Sweetheart.

AMY: [*Going to the buffet-drawer at the right for an apron*] I'll get you something.

AUBREY: It'll be all the same at the finish,—whether I've had my dinner or not. [*He rests his fist on the table, throws his head back, and looks to the stars*] "Sic transit gloria mundi." And we never get used to it. [*He moves across to the upper right-hand corner of the center-table*] The paths of glory lead but to the grave. [*He stops again, leans on the table and looks out and away off*] And yet we go on,—building up big fortunes—only to leave them to the generations yet unborn. Well, [*He moves forward to the chair at the right*]—so it goes. [*He sits down, throws one leg across his knee, and shakes his head up and down slowly*] And so it will always go, I suppose. "Sic transit gloria mundi."

AMY: [*Standing at his right*] What does that mean, Aubrey, "Sic transit gloria mundi"?

AUBREY: [*Casually*] It's an old saying from the French—meaning, "we're here to-day, and gone tomorrow."

AMY: [*Looking out, wretchedly*] I'm worried about tomorrow, Aubrey. [*He looks at her*]

AUBREY: What are you worried about, Sweetheart?

AMY: I mean Monday.

AUBREY: [*Extending his hand towards her*] Now,—

"sufficient unto the day is the evil thereof,"—you know that, don't you, Baby?

[*She takes his hand and moves over to the back of his chair*]

AMY: But, you didn't have a license, Aubrey. And if that traffic-officer should be seriously injured——

AUBREY: Don't you worry about that, Sweetheart;— we're here today; and if he's seriously injured,— we'll know all about it Monday. [*The curtain commences to descend slowly*] "Sic transit gloria mundi."

Act III

SCENE: *Same as preceding Act—the following Monday, about four o'clock in the afternoon. Mrs. Fisher is seated at the right of the center-table, in black, watching* Mr. Rogers, *the insurance agent, opposite her, writing on various papers.* Clara, *also in mourning, is standing back of her Mother's chair, watching* Mr. Rogers.

ROGERS: [*Handing* Mrs. Fisher *an insurance receipt*] Now, will you just sign that, Mrs. Fisher. Right on that line there. [*He hands her his fountain-pen*]

MRS. FISHER: [*After a sincere attempt to write with the fountain-pen*] It won't write.

CLARA: Press on it a bit, Mom.

MRS. FISHER: I *am* pressin' on it.

ROGERS: Just let me have it a second, Mrs. Fisher.
[*She hands him the pen*]

MRS. FISHER: I never saw one of them fountain-pens yet that'd write.

ROGERS: [*Holding the pen out and shaking it, in an attempt to force the ink forward*] They cut up a little once in a while.

[Mrs. Fisher *looks keenly to see if her carpet is being stained*]

MRS. FISHER: I gave one to my son the Christmas before last, and it's been in that drawer there from that day to this.

ROGERS: [*Handing her the pen again*] There we are. I think you'll find that all right.

MRS. FISHER: Right here?

ROGERS: That's right. [*He commences to collect his papers*]

MRS. FISHER: [*Writing*] It's writin' now all right.

ROGERS: It's usually pretty satisfactory. [*She hands him the receipt, and he hands her another*] And that one also, Mrs. Fisher, if you please.

MRS. FISHER: In the same place?

ROGERS: Yes; right on the dotted line. It's just a duplicate.

[*She looks at him sharply; then signs it and hands it back to him; and he puts it into his wallet.* Mrs. Fisher *looks distrustfully at the point of the fountain-pen*]

MRS. FISHER: Here's the pen.

ROGERS: Thank you. [*He signs a check and looks at it*]

MRS. FISHER: [*Half-turning towards the cellar-door*] See if that cellar-door is closed, Clara, I feel a draught from somewhere.

[Clara *goes and sees that the door is closed*]

ROGERS: [*Handing a check*] There you are, Mrs. Fisher, one thousand dollars.

MRS. FISHER: Thank you.
[Clara *comes forward again*]

ROGERS: [*Collecting his things*] That's money we like to pay, Mrs. Fisher, and money we don't like to pay.

MRS. FISHER: No, things are never very pleasant when this kind of money is bein' paid.

ROGERS: [*Rising, and putting his wallet into his inside-pocket*] Well, at least, it doesn't make things any less pleasant, Mrs. Fisher.

MRS. FISHER: [*Rising*] No, I'm sure I don't know what a lot of folks'ud do without it.

ROGERS: Pretty hard to make a good many of them see it that way, Mrs. Fisher.

MRS. FISHER: [*Moving around to a point above the table*] Yes, I guess we don't think much about trouble when we're not havin' it.

ROGERS: Lot of people think they're never going to have trouble; [Mrs. Fisher *shakes her head knowingly*] and never going to need a dollar.

MRS. FISHER: They're very foolish.

ROGERS: Very foolish indeed.

MRS. FISHER: Everybody'll have trouble if they live long enough.

ROGERS: Yes, indeed.

MRS. FISHER: Well now, what do I do with this check, Mr. Rogers?

ROGERS: Why, you can deposit it if you like, Mrs. Fisher, or have it cashed—just whatever you like.

CLARA: Frank'll get it cashed for you, Mom, downtown.

MRS. FISHER: I'm not used to thousand-dollar checks, you know, Mr. Rogers.

ROGERS: I'm not very used to them myself, Mrs. Fisher, except to pay them out to somebody else. [*He laughs a little*]

MRS. FISHER: Well, will you take this, then, Clara, and give it to Frank Hyland?

CLARA: [*Advancing*] Yes; I'll give it to him tonight, Mom.

[Rogers *moves to the window at the left and takes a paper from his pocket*]

MRS. FISHER: Don't go layin' it down somewhere, now, and forgettin' where you left it,—the way you're always doin' with your gloves.

CLARA: [*Crossing to the buffet where her purse is lying*] I'll put it in my purse here.

[Mrs. Fisher *comes forward at the right of the Morris-chair*]

ROGERS: [*Turning and coming back a little from the*

window] Oh, by the way, Mrs. Fisher—would you give this to your son-in-law, Mr. Piper? [*He hands her the paper*]

MRS. FISHER: What is it?

ROGERS: Why, it's a little explanation of some of the features of a very attractive *accident* policy that our company has brought out recently;—and I was talking to Mr. Piper about it the day I called for Mr. Fisher's policy. He seemed to be very much interested. In fact, I find that people are usually a little more susceptible to the advantages of a good insurance policy, when they actually see it being paid to somebody else. Now, that particular policy there—is a kind of combination of accident and life-insurance policy,—as well as disability and dividend features. In fact, we contend that there is no investment on the market today [*Clara sits down in the arm-chair at the right window*] that offers the security or return that that particular policy described there does. The thing is really almost benevolent.

MRS. FISHER: How much is it for?

ROGERS: Why, we *have* them as low as ten thousand dollars; but the policy that Mr. *Piper* was most interested in, was one of our fifty-*thousand* dollar policies.

[*Clara laughs faintly, and her Mother looks over at her*]

MRS. FISHER: [*Turning back to* Rogers] It's no wonder she's laughin', Mr. Rogers; for if you knew Mr. Piper as well as she knows him, you'd laugh too. He has just about as much notion of takin' out a fifty-thousand-dollar insurance policy as I have. And just about as much chance of payin' for it.

ROGERS: Why, he seemed very much interested, Mrs. Fisher.

MRS. FISHER: He was showin' off, Mr. Rogers, what he's always doin'. Why, that fellow don't make enough salary in six months—to pay one year's premium on a policy like this. So, if I was you, I'd just put this paper right back in my pocket, for you're only wastin' it to be givin' it to him.

ROGERS: [*Taking the paper*] Seems rather funny that he'd talk about it at all,—I mean, if he had no idea of taking it.

MRS. FISHER: He never has any idea when *he* talks, Mr. Rogers—that's the reason he talks so much; it's no effort. That's the reason he's gettin' thirty-two dollars a week, down here in the Pennsylvania Freight Office. And it's a wonder to me they give him *that* much, after listenin' to him for five minutes.

ROGERS: It's particularly funny, because I spoke to Mr. Piper first about one of our ten-thousand-dollar policies; but he didn't seem to be interested in anything but the *fifty*-thousand-dollar life and *accident* policy.

MRS. FISHER: Well, I can understand him being in-terested in the accident part of it, after last Monday. I suppose you heard about him runnin' into everything here last Monday evening, didn't you? Down here at Broad and Erie Avenue.

ROGERS: Oh, was that Mr. Piper?

MRS. FISHER: That was him. He ran into a traffic-cop, and broke his arm.

ROGERS: Yes, I saw that in the paper; but the name was spelled Pepper in my paper.

MRS. FISHER: Well, it was spelled Piper in our paper.

ROGERS: Well, what did they do about that, Mrs. Fisher?

MRS. FISHER: Why, he's down there today, at the Magistrate's, gettin' his hearin'. God knows what they'll do with him; for he didn't own the car he was drivin', and didn't have a license to drive it.

ROGERS: Well, that's very unfortunate.

MRS. FISHER: But, he'll very likely tire the magistrate out so with his talk, that the man'll discharge him just to get rid of him.

ROGERS: [*Laughing*] I'm afraid Mr. Piper won't want to see *me* today when he comes back.

MRS. FISHER: He may not *be* back, for six months.

ROGERS: [*Starting for the hall-door*] Oh, well, let's hope it won't be anything like that. Good afternoon, Mrs. Hyland.

CLARA: [*Rising*] Good afternoon, Mr. Rogers.

[*He goes out into hallway*]

ROGERS: Good afternoon, Mrs. Fisher.

MRS. FISHER: Good afternoon, Mr. Rogers. [*Calling after him from the hall-door*] Will you close that vestibule-door tight after you, Mr. Rogers——

ROGERS: Yes, I will, Mrs. Fisher.

MRS. FISHER: This hallway gets awful cold when that vestibule-door isn't shut tight. [*A door closes in the hallway, then another door. And then* Mrs. Fisher *turns, removing her glasses, and moves towards the mantelpiece*] I'm glad you were here; I don't understand them insurance papers. [*She puts her glasses on the mantelpiece*]

CLARA: [*Moving to the chair at the right of the center-table*] What do you think you'll do with that money, Mom?

MRS. FISHER: Why, I think I'll just put it into a bank somewhere; everything is paid. And then I'll have something in my old days. [*She comes forward to the chair at the left of the center-table*]

CLARA: Do you want me to put the check right into the bank?

MRS. FISHER: No,—I want to see the money first. [*She sits down*] But, can you imagine that clown, Clara, takin' up that man's time talkin' about a fifty-thousand-dollar policy; and him in debt to his eyes.

CLARA: [*Sitting down*] What does it matter, Mom; you can never change a man like Piper.

MRS. FISHER: No, but I hate to see him makin' such a fool of Amy; and of all of us,—with his name in all the papers, and the whole city laughin' at him.

CLARA: He doesn't mind that, he likes it.

MRS. FISHER: But, Amy's married to him, Clara,—that's the trouble.

CLARA: Amy doesn't mind it either, Mom, as long as it's Aubrey.

MRS. FISHER: Well, she ought to mind it, if she's got any pride.

CLARA: [Looking straight ahead, wistfully] She's in love with him, Mom—she doesn't see him through the same eyes that other people do.

MRS. FISHER: You're always talkin' about love; you give me a pain.

CLARA: Well, don't you think she is?

MRS. FISHER: How do I know whether she is or not? I don't know anything about when people are in love; except that they act silly—most everybody that I ever knew that was. I'm sure she acted silly enough when she took him.

CLARA: She might have taken worse, Mom. [Mrs. Fisher looks at her; and Clara meets the look] He does his best. He works every day, and he gives her his money; and nobody ever heard of him looking at another woman.

MRS. FISHER: But, he's such a rattle-brain, Clara.

CLARA: Oh, there are lots of things that are harder to put up with in a man than that, Mom. I know he's terribly silly, and has too much to say, and all that, but,—I don't know, I feel kind of sorry for him sometimes. He'd so love to be important; and, of course, he never will be.

MRS. FISHER: Well, I swear I don't know how Amy stands the everlastin' talk of him. He's been here now only a week, and I'm tellin' you, Clara, I'm nearly light-headed. I'll be glad when they go.

CLARA: I'd rather have a man that talked too much than one of those silent ones. Honestly, Mom, I think sometimes if Frank Hyland doesn't say something I'll go out of my mind.

MRS. FISHER: What do you want him to say?

CLARA: Anything; just so I'd know he had a voice.

MRS. FISHER: He's too sensible a man, Clara, to be talkin' when he has nothin' to say.

CLARA: I don't think it's so sensible, Mom, never to have anything to say.

MRS. FISHER: Well, lots of men are that way in the house.

CLARA: But there are usually children there,—it isn't so bad.

MRS. FISHER: Well, if Amy ever has any children, and they have as much to say as their Father, I don't know what'll become of her.

CLARA: She'll get along some way; people always do.

MRS. FISHER: Leanin' on somebody else,—that's how they get along.

CLARA: There are always the Leaners and the Bearers, Mom. But, if she's in love with the man she's married to,—and he's in love with her,—and there are children——

MRS. FISHER: I never saw a married woman so full of love.

CLARA: I suppose that's because I never had any of it, Mom.

[Her Mother looks over at her]

MRS. FISHER: Don't your man love you?

[Clara looks straight out, shaking her head slowly]

CLARA: He loved someone else before he met me.

MRS. FISHER: How do you know?

CLARA: The way he talks sometimes.

MRS. FISHER: Why didn't he marry her?

CLARA: I think he lost her. I remember he said to me one time—"Always be kind, Clara, to anybody that loves you; for," he said, "a person always loses what he doesn't appreciate. And," he said, "it's a terrible thing to lose love." He said, "You never realize what it was worth until you've lost it." I think that's the reason he gives Piper a hand once in a while,—because he sees Amy's in love with him, and he wants to make it easy for her; because I have an idea he made it pretty hard for the woman that loved him.

[Mrs. Fisher leans back and rocks slowly]

MRS. FISHER: Well, a body can't have everything in this world, Clara. [There is a pause: and Clara touches her handkerchief to her eyes. Then the front-door closes softly, and Mrs. Fisher gets up] Maybe this is them now. [She moves up to the hall-door. Amy comes in, looking wearied. She is in mourning] What happened, Amy? [Amy wanders down to the chair at left of table and sits down, and her Mother follows her down at the left] Where's Aubrey Piper?

AMY: He's coming.

CLARA: Is Frank with him?

AMY: Yes.

MRS. FISHER: Where are they?

AMY: Aubrey stopped at the corner to get some cigars.

CLARA: What happened down there?

AMY: Oh, a lot of talk.

MRS. FISHER: [Leaning towards her, solicitously] Are you sick?

AMY: No.

MRS. FISHER: Well, you look sick.

AMY: I have a headache; we had to wait there so long.

CLARA: Why don't you take off your hat?

[Amy starts to remove her hat]

MRS. FISHER: Will I make you a cup of tea?

AMY: No, don't bother, Mom; I can get it myself.

MRS. FISHER: [Going towards the right door] It won't take a minute.

[Amy takes her handkerchief from her bag. Clara glances toward the right door]

CLARA: [In a subdued tone] What did they do to Aubrey?

AMY: [Confidentially] Fined him—a thousand dollars. Don't let Mom know. Recklessness, and driving without a license.

CLARA: Did Frank pay it?

AMY: Yes; I told him I'd be responsible for it.

CLARA: How can *you* ever pay him a thousand dollars, Amy?

AMY: I can go back to work for a while. I can always go back to the office. [Clara *moves*] Well, it was either that or six months in jail. And Frank said we couldn't have that.

CLARA: Was there anybody there that we know?

AMY: I didn't see anybody.

CLARA: Was the traffic-cop there?

AMY: Yes, there were fourteen witnesses. The traffic-cop's arm was broken. The fellow that owned the car was there, too.

CLARA: When do you think you'll go back to work?

AMY: [*After a troubled pause*] As soon as I get settled. There's no use in my going back now; I'd only have to be leaving again pretty soon.

[*Clara looks at her*]

CLARA: Does Mom know?

AMY: No, I haven't told her.

[*There is a pause. Clara gets up; and, with a glance toward the kitchen-door, moves around and crosses towards the left, above the center-table. She stops back of Amy's chair and looks at her for a second compassionately; then she steps forward and lays her hand on her shoulder*]

CLARA: Don't worry about it, Amy. [*She moves towards the window at the left*] I wish to God it was me.

[*There is a murmur of voices at the front-door; then Aubrey's laugh rings through the house. Amy rises quickly, picks up her hat from the table, and signifies to Clara, with a gesture, that she will go into the parlor. Clara moves across in front of the center-table*]

AUBREY: [*Entering, all dressed up, and with a little flourish of his cane to Clara*] Hello, Clara!

CLARA: Hello.

AUBREY: [*Hanging up his hat and cane on the hooks at the head of the cellar-stairs*] Where's Amy?

CLARA: She's just gone in the parlor there.

[*Frank Hyland appears in the hall-door and comes forward to the chair at the left of the table*]

HYLAND: Hello!

[*Aubrey crosses to the parlor, removing his gloves*]

AUBREY: You in there, Amy?

AMY: Yes.

[*He goes into the parlor; and Clara moves across above the center-table to Hyland's left*]

CLARA: How it is you didn't go back to the office, Frank?

[*Aubrey hurries out of the parlor again and across to the hooks, removing his overcoat. Mrs. Fisher appears in the kitchen-door, and stands, looking at him*]

HYLAND: It was so late when we got through down there I didn't think it was worth while.

AUBREY: Hello, Mother.

MRS. FISHER: I see you're back again.

[*He hangs up his overcoat*]

AUBREY: Right on the job, Mother,—doing business at the old stand. [*He takes the carnation from the overcoat and fastens it in the sack-coat. Mrs. Fisher comes forward at the right*]

HYLAND: Hello, Mother!

MRS. FISHER: Hello, Frank.

HYLAND: You're lookin' good, Mother.

MRS. FISHER: Well, I'm not feelin' good, Frank, I can tell you that.

HYLAND: What's the trouble?

MRS. FISHER: Why, I'm troubled to think of all the bother you've been put to in this business.

HYLAND: Don't worry about that, Mother—we've got to have a little bother once in a while.

MRS. FISHER: What did they do down there today, Frank?

HYLAND: Why,—they——

AUBREY: [*Coming forward, adjusting the carnation*] I'll tell you what they *tried* to do.

MRS. FISHER: Oh, shut up, you! Nobody wants to hear what you've got to say about it at all.

[*Clara crosses above the Morris-chair and looks out the window at the left*]

AUBREY: Well, I *told* them down there what I had to say about it, whether they wanted to hear it or not. [*He goes up to the mirror at the back*]

MRS. FISHER: I guess they let you go just to get rid of you.

[*He turns to his left and looks at her; then starts for the parlor-doors*]

CLARA: Why don't you take your coat off, Frank?

[*Aubrey goes into the parlor, looking back over his shoulder at his Mother-in-law, who has not taken her eyes off him*]

HYLAND: [*Looking at his watch*] I've got to meet that fellow at North Philadelphia Station at four o'clock.

MRS. FISHER: [*Coming a step or two nearer to the table*] What did they say to that fellow down there today, Frank?

HYLAND: Why, nothing very much, Mother—just a little reprimand, for driving without a license.

MRS. FISHER: Didn't they fine him at all, for breakin' that man's arm?

HYLAND: A little bit, not very much.—You see, that was more or less in the nature of an accident.

MRS. FISHER: How much was it?

HYLAND: Now, Mrs. Fisher, as Aubrey says, "It's all washed up, and signed on the dotted line." [*He laughs*]

MRS. FISHER: How much was it, Clara, do *you* know?

CLARA: He hasn't told me, Mom.

MRS. FISHER: Well, I'll bet you paid it, **Frank**, whatever it was; for I know he didn't have it. [*She sits at the right of the table*]

HYLAND: [*Rising*] Well, you know, it's getting near Christmas, Mother—got to give some kind of a little present here and there.

MRS. FISHER: Well, I don't think it's right that you should have to be goin' around payin' for that fellow's mistakes.

HYLAND: [*Standing up a bit toward the hall-door, putting on his gloves*] That's about all any of us is doin' in this world, Mother—payin' for somebody's mistakes—and somebody payin' for ours, I suppose.

MRS. FISHER: Well, it don't seem right to me.

HYLAND: Well, I'll tell you, Mother—when you've made a couple of mistakes that *can't* be paid for, why, then you try to forget about them by payin' for the kind that can. [*He makes a little pallid sound of amusement. And there is a pause.* Mrs. Fisher *rocks back and forth*]

CLARA: Will you be home for dinner tonight, Frank?

HYLAND: [*Coming suddenly out of an abstraction*] What'd you say?

CLARA: I say, will you be home for dinner tonight?

HYLAND: [*Picking up his hat from the table*] I don't think so; I'll very likely have to go to dinner with *him*. [*He goes towards the hall-door*] Good-bye, Mother.

MRS. FISHER: Good-bye, Frank.

HYLAND: [*Going out into the hallway*] Good-bye, dear.

[*Clara wanders up to the hall-door and looks out after him*]

CLARA: Good-bye.

[*The vestibule-door is heard to close. And there is a significant pause; during which* Clara *stands looking wistfully out into the hallway*]

MRS. FISHER: [*Rising, and moving to a point above the table*] Listen, Clara.

[*Clara comes towards her*]

CLARA: What?

MRS. FISHER: Didn't he tell you how much they fined Aubrey?

CLARA: No, he didn't, Mom, really.

MRS. FISHER: Didn't *she* tell you, while I was out puttin' the tea on?

CLARA: [*Moving forward to the chair at the left of the table*] Well now, what does it matter, Mom? You won't have to pay it. [*She sits down*]

MRS. FISHER: Well, I'll find out; it'll very likely be in the evening paper.

CLARA: Well, I wouldn't say anything to Amy about it, even if it is; she has enough to bother her now.

MRS. FISHER: Well, she brought it on herself if she has:—nobody could tell her anything.

CLARA: Well, there's nothing can be done by fighting with her, Mom.

MRS. FISHER: [*With conviction*] There's nothing can

be done by *anything*, Clara,—when once the *main* thing is done. And that's the marriage. That's where all the trouble starts—gettin' married.

CLARA: If there were no marriages, Mom, there'd be no world.

MRS. FISHER: [*Moving around to the chair at the right of the table again*] Oh, everybody sez that!—if there were no marriages there'd be no world.

CLARA: Well, would there?

MRS. FISHER: Well, what if there wouldn't? [*She sits down*] Do you think it'd be any worse than it is now? I think there'll be no world pretty soon, anyway, the way things are goin'. A lot of whiffets gettin' married, and not two cents to their names, and then throwin' themselves on their people to keep them. They're so full of love before they're married. You're about the only one I've *heard* talkin' about love *after* they were married. It's a wonder to me you have a roof over you; for they never have, with that kind of talk. Like the two in the parlor there—that has to *kiss* each other, every time they meet on the floor. [*She bristles for a second or two; and then there is a silence*]

CLARA: [*Quietly*] Amy's going to have a child, Mom.

[*Her Mother looks at her*]

MRS. FISHER: How do you know?

CLARA: She told me so.

MRS. FISHER: [*Softening a bit*] Why didn't she tell me?

CLARA: I suppose she thought it'd start a fight.

MRS. FISHER: [*Indignant again*] I don't know why it'd start a fight; *I* never fight with anybody; except him: and I wouldn't fight with *him* only for his impudence.

CLARA: Has Amy said anything to you about coming in here to live?

MRS. FISHER: She said something to me the night your Father was laid out, but I wasn't payin' much attention to her.

CLARA: I think you ought to let her come in here, Mom. [*Her Mother looks at her*] She'd be company for you, now that Pop is gone. And you don't know what day Joe might take a notion to get married.

MRS. FISHER: What's changed *your* ideas so much about lettin' her come in here? You were very much against it when she was married.

CLARA: I'd be against it now, if things around here were the way they were then. You didn't even own this house, Mom, when Amy was married: it was Pop's; and I knew if anything ever happened to him, and there was no will,—you might not find it so easy to order anybody out of it.

MRS. FISHER: It isn't that I'd mind lettin' Amy come in here, Clara,—but I wouldn't like to please him; for I know the first thing *I'd* know, he'd very likely be tellin' somebody that he'd let *me* come in. [*Clara smiles faintly*] Oh, I wouldn't put it past him; he's told bigger lies than that. And if I ever found out that he said *that,*—he'd go out of here inside of five minutes, bag and baggage. [*The front door-bell rings*] See who that is, Clara. [*They rise; and Clara goes out—into the hallway, and Mrs. Fisher crosses below the table to the parlor-doors*] Are you in there, Amy? [*She opens the door*]

AMY: Yes; what is it, Mom?

MRS. FISHER: This kettle's boilin' out here, if you want a cup of tea.

AMY: All right, Mom, I'll be right out.

MRS. FISHER: [*Crossing to the kitchen-door*] I'm goin' to make it right away, so you'd better come out if you want it hot. [*She goes out at the right*]

AMY: [*Coming out of parlor*] Do you want a cup of tea, Aubrey? [*She crosses to the mirror over the mantelpiece and touches her hair*]

AUBREY: [*Coming out of the parlor*] No, thanks, Honey, I don't care for any just now. [*He strolls to the hall-door, glances out, then moves to Amy's side and puts his hands on her shoulders and kisses her affectionately. Then he pats her on the shoulder. She moves towards the kitchen-door*]

AUBREY: [*Patting her hand*] Everything'll be all right, Kid. You know me.

[*She goes out into the kitchen, and he settles himself at the mirror over the buffet at the right*]

CLARA: [*In the hallway*] Yes, I think it is myself. [*Appearing in the hall-door*] Just come right in, I'll call my Mother. Is she out in the kitchen, Aubrey?

AUBREY: [*Turning*] Yes, she's getting some tea.

[*Gill appears in the hall-door*]

GILL: Well, you needn't bother, Ma'am, if she's busy. I just wanted to leave this watch.

AUBREY: How do you do.

GILL: How do you do.

[*Clara stops and looks back at the watch*]

AUBREY: And how is the young man?

GILL: I can't complain.

CLARA: Is that my Father's watch?

GILL: Yes, Ma'am. Are you Mr. Fisher's daughter?

CLARA: Yes. Close that door, Aubrey, will you?—I don't want Mom to see it. [*To Gill*] I'd rather my Mother wouldn't see it. [*She takes the watch, and Aubrey closes the kitchen-door*]

GILL: That's right.

CLARA: I believe she gave him this watch when they were married.

[*Aubrey comes forward again, at the right*]

GILL: Yes, it'd make her feel bad.

CLARA: Thanks ever so much.

GILL: McMahon didn't notice it when he was gettin' the rest of Mr. Fisher's things together.

CLARA: I see.

GILL: He said it was hangin' under the time-chart, back of number five.

AUBREY: This is the gentleman that brought Pop's lunch-box home.

CLARA: Oh, is that so?

GILL: I stopped by the day Mr. Fisher died.

CLARA: Did you work with my father?

GILL: No, Ma'am; I'm a twister; but I live out this way.

AUBREY: How is it you're not working today, Governor?

GILL: Mondays and Tuesdays is my earlies as a rule.

AUBREY: I see.

GILL: But the hunkies don't always get the stuff up to us. You got to keep right after them. Well, I guess I'll be gettin' along. [*He starts for the parlor-doors, then remembers that that is not the way out, and turns to his left towards the hall-door*]

CLARA: I'm ever so much obliged to you, for bringing this watch up.

GILL: [*Turning to her, at the hall-door*] Oh, that's all right. I'm only sorry for the reason I have to do it.

CLARA: Yes, it was very sad.

GILL: Mr. Fisher was a hard-workin' man.

CLARA: I suppose he worked *too* hard, for his age.

GILL: Yes, I guess he did.

CLARA: You couldn't stop him, though.

GILL: No, that's what your brother-in-law here was sayin' the day I was here. He was tellin' me about all the times *he* tried to get him to quit, and take a rest. [*Aubrey turns to the buffet-mirror*] But, I guess when a man's worked as hard all his life as Mr. Fisher did, it ain't so easy for him to quit.

CLARA: No, I guess not.

GILL: [*Stepping a little forward again*] I didn't know that was you, Mr. Piper, that was in that automobile smash-up that I was tellin' you about the day I was here.

AUBREY: [*Turning*] That so?

GILL: I didn't know it till I saw your picture in the paper the next day.

AUBREY: What paper did you see it in?

GILL: I saw it in the Record.

AUBREY: Wasn't a very good picture of me, was it?

GILL: I knew it was you, though, the minute I saw it.

AUBREY: A friend of mine loaned me his car while mine was laid up, and something went wrong with the steering-gear.

GILL: How did you make out about that traffic-cop?

AUBREY: Oh, I squared that up all right.

CLARA: Where do you live up here, Mr. a—

GILL: I live out Richmond way. I'd like to get a house over this way more, on account of bein' a little nearer my work, but I don't see much chance.

CLARA: No, I don't know of any vacant houses around here right now.

GILL: No, your brother-in-law was tellin' me about the time *he* had gettin' hold of *this* one. [*Aubrey turns to the buffet-mirror again and smooths his toupé with considerable precision*] Well, I'll be gettin' along. [*He starts out into the hallway*]

CLARA: [*With a bitter look over her shoulder at Aubrey, and following Gill out into the hallway*]

Well, thanks, ever so much, Mr. a— [*She puts the watch back of the statuette on the little stand at the left of the Mantelpiece*]

GILL: Don't mention it.

CLARA: I'm sure Mother'll be glad to have this watch. [*Aubrey turns and looks after them. Then, with a glance toward the kitchen-door, he moves carefully to the mantelpiece and tries to see what is going on at the front-door*]

GILL: Yes; she might as well have it as one of them hunkies down there.

CLARA: Can you open it?

GILL: Yes, I got it. Good-bye.

CLARA: Good-bye; and thank you.

GILL: You're welcome.

[*The front-door closes; and* Aubrey *glides hastily for the parlor-doors, in an attempt to avoid* Clara;—*but just as he reaches the parlor-doors, she appears in the hall-door, and, with a quick glance toward the kitchen-door, comes forward to the back of the Morris-chair*]

CLARA: Come here, Aubrey, I want to talk to you. [*He turns towards her, with an attempt at non-chalance*] What do you mean by telling people that this is your house?

AUBREY: I didn't tell anybody it was my house.

CLARA: You *must* have told this man, or he wouldn't have said so.

AUBREY: What do you think I am, a liar?

CLARA: Yes, I do; one of the best I know.

AUBREY: Well, ask Amy what I said to him, she was here when I was talking to him.

CLARA: [*Before he has finished speaking*] I don't have to ask anybody anything!—you were lying to him here to-day, right in front of me.

AUBREY: [*With a shade of challenge in his manner*] What'd I say?

CLARA: That you'd fixed the automobile thing up.

AUBREY: It's fixed up, isn't it?

CLARA: You didn't fix it up. [*There is a slight pause, during which* Aubrey, *his dignity considerably outraged, moves forward and crosses in front of her to the front of the center-table, where he stops.* Clara *moves down at the right of the Morris-chair to a point near him*] You'd have gone to jail for six months only for Frank Hyland. And telling this man that you tried to persuade Pop to stop working.

AUBREY: [*Over his left shoulder*] So I did.

CLARA: When?

AUBREY: I didn't say it to him. But I told Amy he ought to stop. And I think he'd be right here to-day if he'd taken my advice.

CLARA: He wouldn't be right here to-day if he'd stopped expecting *you* to keep him. [*He moves further over to the right; and she follows him*] And now, listen to me, Aubrey; I want to talk seriously to you. You've made a lot of trouble for us since you've been in this family; and I want you to stop it. There's no reason my husband, because he hap-

pens to have a few dollars, should be going around paying *your* bills.

AUBREY: [*Half-turning to her*] What do you want me to do?

CLARA: I want you to stop telling *lies*; for that's about all everything you do amounts to. Trying to make people believe you're something that you're not;—when if you'd just stop your talking and your showing-off, you *might* be the thing that you're trying to make them believe you are. [*She glances toward the kitchen-door, and then speaks to him again, in a slightly lower tone*] Your wife's going to have a child one of these days, Aubrey, and you want to pull yourself together and try to be sensible, like the man of a family *should* be. You're smart enough;—there's no reason why a fellow like you should be living in two rooms over a barber shop. I should think you'd have more respect for your wife. [*She turns and moves a few steps up towards the kitchen-door*]

AUBREY: A man doesn't stand much chance of getting ahead, Clara, when the boss has got a grudge against him.

CLARA: [*Turning sharply to her right, and moving to the upper right-hand corner of the center-table*] Well, stop your silly talk, and get rid of that carnation, and the boss might get rid of his grudge. [*She glances toward the kitchen-door again, leans across the table towards him, and lowers her voice*] But, what I wanted to tell you was this, Aubrey,—I've asked Mom to let you and Amy come in here; and she sez she wouldn't mind it only that she knows that the first thing she'd *hear* is that you'd told someone that you'd taken *her* in. And, you see, that's exactly what you've done already,—to this man that brought the watch. If I told Mom that there'd be war.

AUBREY: Are you going to tell her?

CLARA: [*With authoritative levelness*] I'm going to put that up to you. And the very first time I hear that you've told anybody that this is *your* house,—I'll see to it that you'll get a house that *will* be your own.

[Aubrey *smiles, a bit smugly, and looks at her out of the sides of his eyes*]

AUBREY: I guess your Mother'ud have something to say about that, Clara.

CLARA: [*With a measured evenness*] Well, the only thing that needs to worry you, is what *I'll* have to say about it. [Aubrey's *smugness begins to fade—into a questioning narrowness*] This is my house—Pop left it to me; so that Mom'ud always have a roof over her. For he knew how long she'd have it if Amy ever got round her. And if Amy ever got hold of it, he knew what she'd do if it ever came to a choice between you and Mom.

AUBREY: What are you doing, kidding me?

[Clara *holds his eyes steadily for a fraction of a second*]

CLARA: I'm giving you a tip;—see that you keep it to yourself. [*Aubrey withdraws his eyes slowly and looks straight out, weighing this new bit of intelligence carefully in his mind*] Be wise, now, Aubrey —you've got a chance to sit *in* here and live like a human being; and if you throw it away, you'll have nobody to blame but yourself. [*There is a sound at the front-door of a newspaper being thrown into the vestibule, and a man's voice says,"Paper!" Then the front-door is heard to close*] Open that door there, Mom'll be wondering what it's doing shut. [*She crosses up to the hall-door and goes out for the newspaper. Aubrey stands for a second thinking; and then Amy opens the kitchen-door and comes in. She glances about the room*]

AMY: Where's Clara, Aubrey?

AUBREY: I think she's out on the front porch. [*Amy glances toward the hall-door, then turns to her husband*] How are you feeling?

AMY: All right, I just had some tea. Listen, Aubrey, —[*She takes hold of the lapels of his coat*] Mom said we could come in here to live.

AUBREY: Yes, I got Clara to fix it up.

AMY: She said we could have *my* room.

AUBREY: Is it a front room?

AMY: No, it's that one at the head of the stairs.

AUBREY: Will we put that bureau of ours in there?

AMY: I think the one that's in there is better-looking. Let's go up and see. [*She starts up towards the hall-door*]

AUBREY: [*Following her*] You look nice in black, Amy.

AMY: [*Glancing in the mantelpiece-mirror as she passes it*] This is the dress that Clara gave me.

[*Clara appears in the hall-door with the evening paper in her hand*]

CLARA: It's in the paper here about that trial today. [*Amy takes the paper*] Keep it out of sight and don't let Mom see it.

AMY: [*Going out the hall-door and to her left up the stairs*] I'll take it upstairs.

[*Clara moves down towards the center-table, and Aubrey crosses above her towards the hall-door. As he passes her he excludes her with a look*]

AUBREY: [*Calling after Amy as he starts up the stairs*] Has it got my picture in it?

[*Clara looks after him, rather hopelessly. Mrs. Fisher comes in from the kitchen and moves down to the buffet at the right for her knitting-bag*]

MRS. FISHER: You goin' to stay here for supper to-night, Clara?

CLARA: Yes, I might as well, Mom; Frank won't be home. I think I'll run in next door and tell Bertha I won't be home. [*She starts towards the kitchen-door*]

MRS. FISHER: [*Crossing up to the mantelpiece for her spectacles*] Yes, you'd better; she'll be expectin' you. Put somethin' around you.

CLARA: [*Stopping at the hooks at the head of the cellar-stairs*] Is there something here?

MRS. FISHER: Put that old raincoat of Joe's around you; it's good enough. [*She moves forward to the chair at the right of the center-table*] And go to the side-door, Clara; and don't be bringin' Mrs. Harbison to the front. [*She sits down and puts on her spectacles; and Clara shakes the old raincoat out and puts it around her shoulders*] I told Amy she could have that side room upstairs.

CLARA: She might as well be using it, Mom.

MRS. FISHER: But I know I'm not goin' to hit it with him.

CLARA: Well, it's better to be fighting than lonesome, Mom. [*She goes out at the right, and Mrs. Fisher takes a purple sweater that she's working on, out of the knitting-bag. A door out at the right closes after Clara. Mrs. Fisher commences to knit, when suddenly there is a shout of laughter from Aubrey upstairs. Mrs. Fisher freezes instantly into a stony stillness, and listens narrowly. There is another gale of laughter from Aubrey, and this decides Mrs. Fisher. She puts her knitting back into the bag, very definitely, puts the bag on the table, gets up and marches resolutely across in front of the table and up to the hall-door. Just as she reaches the hall-door, with the ostensible purpose of reminding Aubrey that this is not his house, there is another roar from him. Amy can be heard laughing this time, also. Mrs. Fisher subsides, and thinks. She appears to suddenly realize the futility of all remonstrances against the irresponsibility of Aubrey; and, after a thoughtful pause, to accept the situation. And as she moves back across the room, in front of the mantelpiece, to resume her chair at the right of the table, she seems a little older. Just as she reaches a point above the center-table, the front-door closes, with a bang. She starts nervously, and steps back to the mantelpiece to peer out into the hallway*]

MRS. FISHER: Is that you, Joe?

JOE: [*From the hallway*] Yes.

MRS. FISHER: [*Continuing to her chair at the right of the table*] It's a wonder you wouldn't take the door off the hinges, and be done with it.

[*Joe hurries in from the hallway*]

JOE: How did they make out down there to-day, Mom?

[*He tosses the evening paper onto the center-table, and continues on over and up to the hooks at the head of the cellar-stairs, to hang up his hat and overcoat*]

MRS. FISHER: [*Sitting down*] Who do you mean, Aubrey Piper?

JOE: Yes. Are they back yet?

MRS. FISHER: They're upstairs.

JOE: What'd they do to him?

MRS. FISHER: They fined him.

JOE: How much?

MRS. FISHER: [*Taking her knitting out of the bag*] I don't know; they wouldn't tell me. Frank paid it. But, I'll find out; it'll very likely be in the evening paper.

[*Joe comes forward to the center-table*]

JOE: [*Picking up the paper from the table*] It isn't in this paper, I looked.

MRS. FISHER: I'll find out.

JOE: But, there's something else in to-night's paper, Mom.

MRS. FISHER: [*Knitting*] What?

JOE: [*Indicating a certain point on the paper*] Just cast your eyes on this, right here.

MRS. FISHER: [*Looking casually*] What is it?

JOE: [*Reading*] "Philadelphia Youth Makes Important Chemical Discovery. Mr. Joseph Fisher of North Philadelphia Perfects Rust-Preventive Solution." [*He gives his Mother a squeeze and a kiss*]

MRS. FISHER: [*Startled, and giving him a little slap*] Stop it, Joe! [*He laughs exultantly, strikes the palms of his hands together, and strides across above the table towards the left*] Did they buy the thing from you, Joe?

JOE: [*Turning to her, at the left of the center-table*] One hundred thousand dollars, Mother! They signed for it this afternoon in the lawyer's office. [*He becomes aware that the shoe-lace of his right shoe is untied, and puts his foot up on the chair to tie it*]

MRS. FISHER: [*Leaning towards him*] The Meyers and Stevens people?

JOE: Yeh. They sent for me to come over there this afternoon about two o'clock, so I knocked off and got hold of Farley right away, and we went over there. And they had the contracts all drawn up and everything.

MRS. FISHER: What did you say about a hundred thousand dollars, Joe?

JOE: That's what they paid for it this afternoon, on account;—[*He starts across above the center-table and up to the hooks again at the right, removing his coat*] then they're to market it for me from their laboratories, and give *me* half the net.

MRS. FISHER: [*Talking over her right shoulder*] What's the net?

JOE: [*Hanging his coat up*] Whatever's left after all expenses are paid.

[*Mrs. Fisher tries to encompass the situation*]

MRS. FISHER: I guess they'll see that there ain't much left, won't they?

JOE: [*Coming forward again to the center-table*] Why, there'll be a fortune out of this thing, Mom. Have you any idea what a rust-preventive means as an industrial chemical problem? Why, they'll make a million dollars out of this, within the next five years. [*He moves over to the left, removing his tie*]

MRS. FISHER: Well, how much of that are you goin' to get, Joe?

JOE: I'll get the same as they get, that's the contract.

MRS. FISHER: A million dollars?

JOE: Easy, I got a hundred thousand today.

[*Mrs. Fisher shifts her eyes and tries to concentrate*]

MRS. FISHER: How many noughts is a hundred thousand?

JOE: [*Coming back to her left, taking a pencil from his vest-pocket*] It's a one, [*He leans over the table and writes it on the margin of the newspaper*] and two noughts, and three more noughts. [*Mrs. Fisher looks at it closely. Joe replaces the pencil in his pocket and moves across again towards the left*] They paid that today on account. I knew it was coming, though; their head chemist out at Bristol told me six weeks ago it was all set. I've got to go over there to their offices right away; they made an appointment for the newspaper and magazine people over there at five o'clock. [*He starts for the hall-door*] I've got to talk to them.

MRS. FISHER: Did they give you any of the money, Joe?

JOE: [*Stopping at the hall-door*] A hundred thousand dollars, sure.

MRS. FISHER: Not in money, though?

JOE: [*Laughing, and coming back towards the center-table*] Not in dollar bills, no; they gave me a check for it.

MRS. FISHER: Where is it?

JOE: Farley has it in his safe, down in the office.

MRS. FISHER: How much do you have to give *him*, half of it?

JOE: No, he's not a partner, he's just my lawyer. I give him five per cent of all monies received. [*He moves forward at the left of the center-table*]

MRS. FISHER: How much will that be?

JOE: Well, that was five thousand dollars right off the bat, today. Pretty soft for that bird. When I first talked to him he wanted to stick me for ten per cent; but I nailed that quick; I knew what this was goin' to be worth.

MRS. FISHER: What are you goin' to do now, Joe, stop workin'?

JOE: No, of course not, I'm not goin' to stop working! I've got that oil-paint thing on the carpet, now.

MRS. FISHER: Well, won't you have to go to Washington or someplace?

JOE: [*Rolling his tie up on his finger, and stuffing it into his vest-pocket*] No, that's all been attended to. But I'll tell you, Mom—I might go to Trenton.

MRS. FISHER: New Jersey?

JOE: Yes.

MRS. FISHER: Not to live, surely?

JOE: I might—till I put this oil-paint thing through.

MRS. FISHER: Well, I think you'd be very foolish, Joe, to go to Trenton at *your* age.

JOE: [*Removing his cuff-links and dropping them*

into his vest-pocket] Well, the Meyers and Stevens people made me a proposition this afternoon that looks pretty good. They've got one of the most perfectly equipped experimenting laboratories in the world, just outside of Trenton; and it's open day and night; and that's what I want. I'd have had this rust-preventive through six months sooner, if I could have had the use of a laboratory somewhere at night. So they want me to go up there on a salary, with a first look at anything I strike; but I didn't want to say anything till I talked to *you*.

MRS. FISHER: What do you mean?

JOE: I mean, I wouldn't like the idea of goin' away, and leavin' you alone in the house.

MRS. FISHER: [*Resuming her knitting*] Oh, you go ahead, Joe,—if it's for your good. Never mind me, —I'll get along some way.

JOE: I don't like the idea of leavin' you here alone.

MRS. FISHER: Nearly every Mother is left alone, Joe, if she lives long enough.

[Joe *looks straight out and thinks*]

JOE: I was wonderin', Mom,—why Amy couldn't come in here: she seems to be havin' a pretty tough time of it.

[*There is a slight pause, during which Mrs. Fisher knits*]

MRS. FISHER: She's *in* here already; and her man with her.

JOE: I mean, to stay.

MRS. FISHER: They're goin' to stay;—she can have that room at the head of the stairs. [*She stops knitting and thinks, looking steadily at the floor in front of her*] They'll have to live somewhere; and I guess it'll have to be here. It's just as our Clara said here one night,—I remember it as if it was yesterday. She said, "Remember what I'm telling, you, Mom,—it's *you* that'll have them on your hands if she takes him." And I suppose that's true. She made her bed,—and I guess it's me that'll have to lie in it.

JOE: [*Starting up and across towards the hooks at the head of the cellar-stairs, to get a paper out of his coat-pocket*] They want me to go to Trenton right away.

MRS. FISHER: What would you do, Joe, come home over Sundays?

JOE: Sure, it's only thirty-eight miles from here.

MRS. FISHER: [*Astonished*] Is that all the further Trenton is from Philadelphia?

JOE: [*Starting across towards the left to the hall-door, removing his vest*] That's all.

MRS. FISHER: It always seemed very far away to me. I guess it's the name.

JOE: I'm goin' up to get fixed up a bit before I go over to that office.

MRS. FISHER: [*Suddenly putting her knitting on the table, preparatory to getting up*] Well, listen, Joe!

JOE: [*Stopping, with his foot on the first step of the stairs*] What?

MRS. FISHER: [*Getting up and moving across in front of the center-table*] Come here. [Joe *comes down to her left*] Don't say anything about this to him, Joe, or he'll be wantin' to go up and talk to the newspaper men, too.

[Joe *laughs faintly, then looks away off and thinks*].

JOE: You know, Mom,—I kinda feel that there's somethin' comin' to that nut out of this thing.

MRS. FISHER: How do you mean?

JOE: *He* gave me an idea here one night.

MRS. FISHER: [*Seizing him suddenly by both arms*] Well, for God's sake, don't tell *him* that, Joe!— or, as sure as you live, he'll be tellin' everybody that he done the whole thing.

JOE: You remember the night he was sayin' here about bein' at work on a solution for the prevention of rust in iron and steel?

MRS. FISHER: Yes.

JOE: Well, you know, I'd been tellin' him somethin' about it a week or so before—

MRS. FISHER: Yes, you told me.

JOE: While he was waitin' here for Amy one night.

MRS. FISHER: Yes.

JOE: Well, he forgot that night he was tellin' *me* about it that it was me that had been tellin' *him* about it; and he got it mixed.

MRS. FISHER: That's the way he does with everything.

JOE: And it was the way he got it mixed, Mom, that gave me the idea. *He* said,—that it was a combination of chemical elements to be added to the metal in its *molten state*, instead of applied *externally*, as they *had* been doin'. And I *landed* on it—the way Howe did when he dreamed of puttin' the eye in the point of the needle instead of the other end. That was exactly what *I'd* been doin'—applying the solution *externally*—in a mixture of paint. But the next day, I tried adding parts of it to the molten state of the metal, and it did the trick. Of course, he didn't know what he was sayin' when he said it—

MRS. FISHER: He never does.

JOE: And he didn't know anything about the solution-formula—But it was the way he got what I'd been tellin' him *twisted*, Mom,—that put the thing over.

MRS. FISHER: Well, that's no credit to him, Joe.

JOE: I know.

MRS. FISHER: He was only blowin' when he said it.

JOE: Sure.

MRS. FISHER: He don't know what a formala means. And I'd have told him where he heard it, too, if I'd been you.

JOE: [*Thoughtfully*] I'd like to give him a little present of some kind.

[*His Mother looks at him sharply*]

MRS. FISHER: What would you give him a present for?

JOE: [*Breaking into a little laugh*] For makin' a mistake.

MRS. FISHER: That's all everybody's doin' around here,—givin' that fellow presents for makin' mistakes. That's what Frank Hyland said here to-day, when I ast him why he paid his fine. He said, "Oh, you've got to give a little present here and there once in a while." There's no use tryin' to be sensible anymore.

JOE: I'd like to give him *somethin'*.

[*She looks at him again keenly, and thinks for a second*]

MRS. FISHER: I'll tell you what you can do, Joe, if you're so anxious to *give* him somethin'.—Find out what fine Frank Hyland paid for him this afternoon, and tell him you're goin' to give him that. But don't tell him what you're givin' it to him *for*, Joe, or we won't be able to live in the house with him. And don't give him money, Joe; for he'd only be goin' from one room to another here in an automobile. And don't give it to her neither, Joe; for she'll only hand it right over to him.—Give it to me. [*Joe looks at her*] And I'll give it to them when I think they need it. [*A door closes out at the right; and* Joe *steps up towards the mantelpiece to look off*] That's Clara; she's been next door telephonin'. [*She turns to her left and picks up her knitting from the table and sits down again.* Clara *comes in, slipping off the raincoat*]

JOE: Hello!

CLARA: [*Hanging the raincoat up on the hook*] How's it you're home so early, Joe?

[Aubrey *enters from the hall-door, smoking a cigar*]

JOE: The long threatening has come at last!

CLARA: [*Coming forward, looking at him seriously*] What?

JOE: The big news.

CLARA: The steel thing? [*Joe laughs*] Did they buy it, Joe?

JOE: One hundred thousand dollars!—first payment—they gave me the check this afternoon.

CLARA: Joe, you're not telling me the truth!

AUBREY: [*Coming forward*] Something about the invention, Joe?

JOE: Hello, Aubrey!

CLARA: [*Coming down to her Mother's right*] Did they, Mom?

JOE *and* MRS. FISHER, *speaking together.*

MRS. FISHER: ——So he sez.

JOE: —They bought it this afternoon.

CLARA: Isn't that wonderful!

AUBREY: [*Extending his hand to* Joe] Congratulations!

JOE: [*Laughing*] Thanks.

AUBREY: So we put it over!

[Mrs. Fisher *poisons him with a look*]

JOE: To the tune of one hundred thousand clackers.

[*He swings above* Aubrey *towards the hall-door*]

AUBREY: [*Turning and following him*] No kidding?

JOE: [*Running up the stairs*] The check's in the safe, down in the lawyer's office.

AUBREY: [*Calling up the stairs after him*] Well, Kid, you know what I always told you!

JOE *and* CLARA, *speaking together.*

JOE: —Leave it to you to call the turn, Aubrey.

CLARA: [*Running up to the hall-door*] Joe! Come here and tell us something about it.

JOE: [*Calling back*] I've got to get dressed, Clara, I'll tell you about it later.

[Aubrey *comes forward at the left, laughing; but suddenly he becomes conscious of Mrs. Fisher's left eye, and his laugh freezes into a detached gaze out the window at the left*]

MRS. FISHER: [*Speaking to* Clara] He's got to go down to see them people that bought the thing from him.

CLARA: [*Coming forward to the center-table*] Why, what will Joe *do* with all that money, Mom?

MRS. FISHER: [*Knitting*] Heaven knows, I don't.

CLARA: Have you any idea how much a hundred thousand dollars is?

MRS. FISHER: Joe sez it's a one and two noughts, and then three more noughts.

CLARA: Why, it's a fortune!

MRS. FISHER: Well, he brought it on himself; he'll have to tend to it; I'm sure I won't.

AUBREY: [*Coming towards the center-table from the left*] If he's a *wise bird*, he'll let *me* handle that money for him. [*Mrs. Fisher pins him with a look, and her knitting slides to her lap*] I could give him a couple of very fly tips on that.

MRS. FISHER: [*With dangerous steadiness*] He don't want *your* tips; nor your *taps* neither. We *know* about one tip *you* gave a man, and his arm has been in a sling ever since.

[Clara *picks up the "Delineator" from the table and moves over to the right to the buffet, to look at the styles*]

AUBREY: That's all right, Mrs. Fisher; but if he's a wise Bimbo,—he'll take the drooping left, [*He lowers the lid of his left eye, very mysteriously*] and I'll *double* that money for him, within the next two weeks; [*Mrs. Fisher resumes her knitting*] and give him an extra pair of trousers.

MRS. FISHER: I guess he'd *need* an extra pair of trousers, if he was sittin' around waitin' for *you* to double his money for him.

AUBREY: Well, I'm telling you, Mother,—he's an awful straw-ride if he doesn't get in on some of that copper-clipping that those people are writing me about.

[*She looks at him, hard*]

MRS. FISHER: What is it, a copper mine this time?

AUBREY: 'Tain't a mine at all,—it's a mint.

MRS. FISHER: What are they writin' to *you* about it for?

AUBREY: They're writing to everybody.

MRS. FISHER: They must be. [*She resumes her knitting*]

AUBREY: Prospective Investors—They hear a man's got a few dollars laying around idle, and they get in touch with him.

MRS. FISHER: Well, nobody's heard that you have any dollars layin' around idle, have they?

AUBREY: [*With a touch of consequence*] Oh,—I don't know,—they may have.

[Mrs. Fisher *stops knitting and leans towards him, stonily,—her left elbow resting on the table*]

MRS. FISHER: Listen, Boy,—if you've got any dollars layin' around idle, it'd be better for you to pay Frank Hyland the money he paid to keep you out of jail, than to be lookin' around for an investment for it—in some old copper mine, out in God-Knows-Where—that you don't know no more about than them that's writin' to you about it. [*She knits again, indignantly*]

AUBREY: I know a whole lot about this proposition, Mrs. Fisher; and so do a lot of other people. Why, —they say they can see enough copper in those rocks, right now, to keep this thing going for the next ten years.

MRS. FISHER: [*Almost violently*] They *shoot* that in there.

AUBREY: Shoot copper into solid rocks, eh?

MRS. FISHER: [*Putting her knitting down on the table and picking up the newspaper that* Joe *has left there*] That's what I said. [Aubrey *turns away, with a gesture of helplessness, and moves across in front of the Morris-chair to the window at the left*] I read all about just how they do it, in a magazine not two weeks ago. [*Looking at the paper*] Then they shoot a lot of letters to the likes of you, and you *shoot off* about it.

AMY: [*Entering hurriedly from the hall-door and coming forward to the center-table*] Mom, is it true what Joe sez about the invention?

MRS. FISHER: [*Looking sharply at something in the paper*] Here it is in the paper.

[Aubrey *moves across above the Morris-chair towards the center-table*]

AMY: Isn't that wonderful, Aubrey?

[Aubrey *nods and smiles*]

MRS. FISHER: [*To Clara*] I thought our Joe said it wasn't *in* here.

CLARA: [*Moving a step or two from the buffet*] What is it?

AMY: [*Leaning over her Mother's left shoulder, looking at the paper*] What does it say, Mom?

MRS. FISHER: [*Reading*] Mad Motorist Fined One Thousand Dollars for Reckless Driving. [Aubrey *glides forward and crosses in front of the Morris-chair to the window at the left again. Amy straightens up and gives a distressed look at Clara, who suggests, with a nod, that she go into the kitchen*] Mr. Aubrey Piper, of 903 Lehigh Avenue, was arraigned today before Magistrate Lister of the 22nd and Huntington Park Avenue Police Station, to answer to the charge of having disregarded traffic-signals at Broad Street and Erie Avenue last Monday evening; resulting in rather serious injuries to Mr. Joseph Hart, a traffic-officer. The defendant was fined one thousand dollars for recklessness, disregard of traffic-signals, and operating an automobile without a license. [*She lowers the paper to her lap and looks at* Aubrey]

AUBREY: [*Turning from the window, and with a magnificent gesture*] That's the law for you. [*He folds his arms and leans on the back of the Morris-chair, looking straight out*]

MRS. FISHER: What do you think of that, Clara?

CLARA: [*Moving to the arm-chair below the buffet at the right*] Well, it's all over now, Mom—Frank paid it.

MRS. FISHER: What did he pay it *for*?

CLARA: [*Sitting down*] Well, it was either that or go to jail, Mom; and you wouldn't want that, on account of Amy. [*She opens the "Delineator"*]

MRS. FISHER: Well, Frank Hyland didn't have to pay it— [*She sits looking straight out, fuming*] Amy's got a Mother. [*Turning sharply to* Clara] And you take that thousand-dollar insurance check that I gave you and give it to him as soon as ever you see him. I don't want Frank Hyland goin' around payin' out thousand-dollar bills on account of this clown. [*She looks bitterly at* Aubrey, *who looks at her with an expression as though he were trying to come to some conclusion as to the most effectual means of putting her in her place*] It's bad enough for *me* to have to do it.

CLARA: [*Calling to* Amy] Amy.

AMY: [*From the kitchen*] What?

CLARA: Come here a minute.

[Mrs. Fisher *puts the newspaper back onto the table and resumes her knitting. Aubrey strolls over and sits down at the left of the center-table, reaching for the newspaper which* Mrs. Fisher *has just put down. Amy comes in from the kitchen*]

AMY: What?

CLARA: Here's that skirt I was telling you about.

[Amy *comes forward to* Clara's *left and they look at a certain skirt in the "Delineator."* Aubrey *deposits some ashes from his cigar on the little tray on the table, then sits back, takes a pair of tortoise-shell rimmed glasses, with a black-tape attachment for over the ear, from his vest-pocket, and settles them on his nose. His Mother-in-law gives him a look*]

AUBREY: Was that Insurance man here today?

[Amy *opens the left-hand drawer of the buffet and takes out a package of Life-Savers. She takes one herself, then offers* Clara *one;* Clara *takes it; and the two continue their discussion of the styles in the "Delineator"*]

MRS. FISHER: What do you want to know for?

AUBREY: [*Glancing over the evening paper*] Nothing,

—I was just wondering if he got around this way today.—Did he leave a paper here for me?

MRS. FISHER: [Knitting] He *wanted* to; but I told him not to waste his time—[Aubrey *looks at her narrowly*] talkin' to *you* about fifty-thousand-dollar policies.

AUBREY: Well, what about it?

MRS. FISHER: [Looking at him] Nothin' at *all* about it; only the man was laughin' up his sleeve at you.

AUBREY: Is that so?

MRS. FISHER: What else *could* he do? He knows you haven't the faintest idea of takin' out any such policy.

AUBREY: How do you know he does?

MRS. FISHER: Because he knows you're only a clerk; and that you don't get enough salary in *six months* —to pay one year's premium on a policy like that.

AUBREY: What were you doing, handing out a line of gab about my business?

MRS. FISHER: [Quietly knitting again] You haven't got any business for anybody to hand out a line of gab about—that I ever heard of.

[Amy *moves slowly across above the center-table towards the left, picking up a newspaper*]

AUBREY: Well, whether I have any line of business or not, it isn't necessary for you to be gabbing to perfect strangers about it.

MRS. FISHER: [Getting mad] Then, you stop gabbin' to people about fifty-thousand-dollar policies!—On your thirty-two dollars a week. [Turning to him furiously] I told him *that,* too.

AMY: [Touching Aubrey on the left shoulder, as she passes back of him] Keep quiet, Aubrey.

MRS. FISHER: So he'd know how much attention to pay to you the *next* time you start.

[Amy *moves forward to the Morris-chair at the left and sits down*]

AUBREY: What else did you tell him?

MRS. FISHER: I told him the truth!—whatever I told him.—And I guess that's more than can be said for a whole lot *you* told him. [She knits again]

AUBREY: [Resuming his paper] A man'ud certainly have a swell chance trying to make anything of himself around *this hut.*

[Mrs. Fisher *stops knitting, and leans her elbow on the table*]

MRS. FISHER: Listen, Boy,—any time you don't like this *hut,* you go right straight back to Lehigh Avenue to your two rooms over the dago barber shop. And I'll be glad to see your heels.

CLARA: Stop talking, Mom.

MRS. FISHER: Nobody around here's tryin' to stop you from makin' somethin' of yourself.

AUBREY: No, and nobody's trying to help me any, either; only trying to make me look like a *pin-head* —every chance they get.

MRS. FISHER: Nobody'll have to try very hard to make

you look like a *pin-head*; your own silly talk'll do that for you, any time at all.

AUBREY: I suppose it's silly talk to try to make a good impression.

MRS. FISHER: [Turning to him and speaking definitely] Yes; it's silly to try to make an impression of any kind; for the only one that'll be made'll be the right one,—and that'll make itself.

AUBREY: Well, if you were out in the world as much as *I* am, you'd very soon see how much easier it is for a fellow to get along—if people think he's got something.

MRS. FISHER: Well, anybody that'ud listen to *you* very long'ud know you *couldn't* have very much.

AUBREY: Is that so.

MRS. FISHER: [Tersely] You heard me.

[Clara *rises and moves towards her Mother*]

AUBREY: [Reaching over to dispose of some more cigar-ashes] People that are smart enough to be able to make it easier for you——

CLARA: Aubrey,—that'll do. [He is silenced; and resumes his paper. Clara shows her Mother a particular pattern in the "Delineator"] Mom, that'd look good for that new black crepe de chine of yours, No. 18, there in the middle.

MRS. FISHER: But, I wouldn't want that bunch of fullness like that right there, Clara.

[Joe *enters hurriedly from the hall-door, wearing a clean shirt and collar, and with his face washed and hair combed*]

CLARA: Well, you're always saying you look too thin; and I think—Joe, tell me something about the invention.

JOE: [Crossing quickly to the hooks at the right for his coat] They telephoned for me this afternoon about two o'clock, and I got hold of Farley and we went right over there. And they had the contracts all drawn up and everything.

CLARA: [Having moved up towards the hooks with him] Well, did they really give you a hundred thousand dollars for it?

[Aubrey *gets up and moves around and up to the upper left-hand corner of the table*]

JOE: [Coming forward, putting on his coat] Check's in the safe, down in Farley's office.

AUBREY: [Flicking some ashes from his cigar] Joe!— what do you think we ought to do with that money?

[Joe *tries to hide his laughter, and steps down to his Mother's right; and Clara comes forward and leans on the buffet*]

JOE: You know, it was a funny thing, Mom,—when I first talked to the Meyers and Stevens people, I was only to get *fifty* thousand dollars advance; and when I went up there to-day they had the contracts all made out for a *hundred* thousand.

AUBREY: And they're getting away with murder at that.

MRS. FISHER: [*Turning to him impatiently*] Oh, keep still, you!—You don't know anything about this at all.

AUBREY: I made *them* think I knew something about it.

MRS. FISHER: You made *who* think?

AUBREY: The Meyers and Stevens people.

JOE: What are you talkin' about, Aubrey, do you know?

AUBREY: Certainly, I know what I'm talking about. *I* went to see those people, last Saturday afternoon, after you told me they'd talked to you.

JOE: [*Crossing towards him, to a point above the center-table*] And, what'd you do up there?

AUBREY: Why, I told them,—that they'd have to double the advance, if they wanted to do business with us.

MRS. FISHER: And, what business was it of yours?

AUBREY: Well,—I'm Joe's guardian, ain't I?

MRS. FISHER: Who told you you were?

AUBREY: Well,—he's got to have somebody tend to his business, doesn't he?—He's only a lad.

MRS. FISHER: Well, he doesn't need *you* to tend to his business for him—He tended to his business long before he ever saw *you*.

AUBREY: He never landed a hundred thousand dollars, though, till he saw me, did he?

JOE: Well, what did you say to them, Aubrey?

AUBREY: Why,—I simply told them that your Father was dead,—and that I was acting in the capacity of *business*-adviser to you: and that, if this discovery of yours was as important as you had led me to believe it was, they were simply taking advantage of your youth by offering you fifty thousand dollars for it. And that I refused to allow you to negotiate further—unless they doubled the advance, market it at their expense, and one half the net—*sign* on the dotted line. [*He flicks more ashes from his cigar*]

JOE: Well, did they know who you were?

AUBREY: I told them—that I was head of the house here; [Mrs. Fisher *grips the edge of the table, threateningly*] *and* that I was also connected with the Pennsylvania Railroad.

MRS. FISHER: It's too bad they didn't know what you do down there; and call your bluff.

AUBREY: I beat them to it; I called theirs first. [*He strolls towards the left, with a bit of swagger*]

JOE: Well, I certainly have to give you credit, Aubrey; that's the way the contract reads.

AUBREY: [*Strolling back again*] I told it to them; and I told it to your lawyer, too.

JOE: I'll have to give you a little present of some kind out of this, Aubrey.

AUBREY: [*Dismissing the suggestion with a touch of ceremony*] You'll not give *me* any present, Joe;—give it to your Mother. [*He strolls over to the left again*] She'll need it more than I will. [*He comes forward at the left of the Morris-chair*] Amy,—have you got the financial page there?

AMY: [*Handing him the newspaper*] Is this it, Aubrey?

AUBREY: [*Taking it*] Thank you. [*He crosses in front of her to the chair at the left of the center-table and sits down. Amy gets up, looking at him wonderingly*]

AMY: Aubrey, you're wonderful!

AUBREY: [*Settling himself to look over the bond market*] A little bit of bluff goes a long way sometimes, Amy.

AMY: Isn't he wonderful, Mom?

[Mrs. Fisher *prepares to resume her knitting*]

MRS. FISHER: [*After a long sigh*] God help *me*, from now on.

[*The curtain descends slowly, with Amy standing lost in admiration of the wonder of Aubrey. When the curtain rises again Aubrey is reading, Mrs. Fisher is knitting, Clara is sitting reading the "Delineator," over on the arm of the arm-chair at the right, Joe is putting on his overcoat and hat at the mantelpiece-mirror, and Amy is sitting in the Morris-chair at the left, just looking at Aubrey*]

Juno and the Paycock

by SEAN O'CASEY

(1884–   )

Sean O'Casey completes the list of Irish playwrights—Congreve, Goldsmith, Sheridan, Wilde, Shaw, Synge—in whom, in so many forms, from the glassiest wit to the most volcanic and belching humor, the Spirit of Comedy has declared itself. Like certain of the others, perhaps more than any of the others, O'Casey is associated at times with other modes than comedy; indeed, of his two best and best-known plays, one—Juno—is only intermittently a comedy, and the other—The Plough and the Stars—is not comedy at all. Indeed, many people might contend that nothing written in English since, can equal The Plough and the Stars for tragic force. And much in Juno, too, is shaped for tragedy. But it is because I feel that nothing written in English since Juno can match the vigor of its comic scenes that I have preferred it to any of O'Casey's outright comedies, for inclusion here. What, to me, gives Juno its special distinction—as what gives special distinction to so many of Dickens' novels—is the comedy side.

Where so many writers—comedy-writers in particular—work in a general tradition far superior to their specific talent, in Juno it is the other way round: the tradition is debatable, but the talent distinguished. Reduced to category, Juno is hardly more than a naturalistic slice of life. The slum milieu as a whole; the Paycock's moleskin trousers, the beer bottles and dishes of tea; even the famous alarm clock lying on its face, suggest an all too familiar sort of design, an all too recognizable kind of detail. (This is indeed the type of play where, if the scene designer is expert and evocative enough, there is almost no need for the playwright.)

But, of course, O'Casey stands apart for being at least as much poet as photographer, as much concerned with the unique life of the Doyle household as with the typical life of the Dublin slums: he would achieve both the smell common to all vestibules and the smell peculiar to a single home. In the same way, his people must talk like Dubliners of a certain class; but yet like themselves, and again with a gift of language great enough to bring particular pleasure to whoever shall hear them in the theater. The mean and humdrum effects of routine naturalism O'Casey will have none of: his people shall not be tired phonograph records, but spontaneous, self-willed musical instruments. And as with the instrument, so with

the tune: O'Casey rejects the onomatopoeia of naturalism, the moans and monotones: Juno is no cheerless, drab composition but lusty and in many places bold and drunken and outrageously gay. As angry and fiercely fuming as Dickens, as indignant over the world's poverty and as resentful over his early own, O'Casey no more than Dickens can set forth life's black sufferings in straight realism's gray dust. Like Dickens, what with the sheer joy of creating, what with the wild, impenitent, incorrigible folly of human beings, he must infuse comedy into his story, release comedy into the air. And the comedy gives Juno its essential strength, its occasional magnificence.

Juno and the Paycock cannot be summed up. It is social commentary; it is racial criticism; it is comedy of character, tragedy of character, tragedy of circumstance—in it, heredity and environment are made co-defendants. That it cannot be summed up testifies to its remarkable richness and fullness, but no less to its lack of unity, to the failure of its picture and its plot to coalesce. As sound tragedy, in my opinion it quite fails: toward the end, ill fortune seems to crash down too fast and from too many sides: for any such concatenation of woe, we need far more careful planning. Some of the woes have, moreover, an old-fashioned and stagy air, so that what was meant for tragedy of a kind seems more like melodrama of a kind; and though we are given, at the end, a Juno summoning up her bare-knuckled and brokenhearted strength in the moment of family defeat, there falls even on her a slightly too emphatic and theatrical light. The plot, furthermore, not only rather weakens belief, it spoils the essential effect: for, assuming that Jack Boyle would come into an inheritance, the point shouldn't be his losing it through someone else's blunder, but rather his foolishly and flashily squandering the money himself, his coming to grief through his own weak character. For weakness like Jack Boyle's is the real villain of this play and of the society it mirrors; not conventional stage wickedness, like Charlie Bentham's.

The creation and comprehension of character is what gives to Juno its vigor and stature and bitter humor. In Juno, in the Paycock, in Johnny, in Joxer, we have vivid human beings; we have the Irish; we have the poor; we have the family; we have a complex of things that we can reduce to no single form of causation. Here are people as God made them, as Ireland made them, as poverty made them; as, finally, drink made them—only, of course, it was the other things that helped make them drink. And in that complex we find that comedy—and tragedy—of character which are interpenetrating and even indissoluble, and which are what we mean by human life. Jack Boyle, with his lies, his loafing, his pretensions and evasions and boozy makeshifts, has about him, in exuberant form, so much of human weakness and male showing off and Irish brag as to be immensely comic, as to be part of that tall-windowed world—Falstaffian, Bobadilian, Micawberish—of the timeless loafers and braggarts and scamps. The great scenes of the play are those between the Paycock and Juno, the Paycock and Joxer, or involving all three: here, while exposing character, O'Casey invests his play with a kind of poetry, enlarges it with humor. It is lifelike and yet more than lifelike, with the aeration and leverage of heroic comedy. The picture here doesn't quite constitute universal life, but it does provide universal laughter. And we somehow sense the truer horror of Jack Boyle and Joxer in the very midst of hilarity: their triumph as comedians is the measure of their tragic bankruptcy as human beings. As we laugh at them, we realize how much they make others suffer: somehow they set far greater vibrations going in their cups than Johnny ever does in his coffin.

SEAN O'CASEY

Juno and the Paycock

CHARACTERS IN THE PLAY

"CAPTAIN" JACK BOYLE
JUNO BOYLE, *his wife*
JOHNNY BOYLE } *their children* } Residents in
MARY BOYLE   the Tenement
"JOXER" DALY
MRS. MAISIE MADIGAN
"NEEDLE" NUGENT, *a tailor*
MRS. TANCRED
JERRY DEVINE
CHARLES BENTHAM, *a school teacher*
AN IRREGULAR MOBILIZER
TWO IRREGULARS
A COAL-BLOCK VENDOR
A SEWING MACHINE MAN
TWO FURNITURE REMOVAL MEN
TWO NEIGHBOURS

SCENE

ACT I: *The living apartment of a two-roomed tenancy of the Boyle family, in a tenement house in Dublin*

ACT II: *The same*

ACT III: *The same*

A few days elapse between Acts I and II, and two months between Acts II and III

During Act III the curtain is lowered for a few minutes to denote the lapse of one hour

PERIOD OF THE PLAY: 1922

Act I

The living-room of a two-room tenancy occupied by the Boyle family in a tenement house in Dublin. Left, a door leading to another part of the house; left of door a window looking into the street; at back a dresser; farther to right at back, a window looking into the back of the house. Between the window and the dresser is a picture of the Virgin; below the picture, on a bracket, is a crimson bowl in which a floating votive light is burning. Farther to the right is a small bed partly concealed by cretonne hangings strung on a twine. To the right is the fireplace; near the fireplace is a door leading to the other room. Beside the fireplace is a box containing coal. On the mantelshelf is an alarm clock lying on its face. In a corner near the window looking into the back is a galvanized bath. A table and some chairs. On the table are breakfast things for one. A teapot is on the hob and a frying-pan stands inside the fender. There are a few books on the dresser and one on the table. Leaning against the dresser is a long-handled shovel—the kind invariably used by labourers when turning concrete or mixing mortar. Johnny Boyle is sitting crouched beside the fire. Mary with her jumper off—it is lying on the back of a chair—is arranging her hair before a tiny mirror perched on the table. Beside the mirror is stretched out the morning paper, which she looks at when she isn't gazing into the mirror. She is a well-made and good-looking girl of twenty-two. Two forces are working in her mind—one, through the circumstances of her life, pulling her back; the other, through the influence of books she has read, pushing her forward. The opposing forces are apparent in her speech and her manners, both of which are degraded by her environment, and improved by her acquaintance—slight though it be—with literature. The time is early forenoon.

MARY: [*Looking at the paper*] On a little bye-road, out beyant Finglas, he was found.

[*Mrs. Boyle enters by door on right; she has been shopping and carries a small parcel in her hand. She is forty-five years of age, and twenty years ago she must have been a pretty woman; but her face has now assumed that look which ultimately settles down upon the faces of the women of the working-class; a look of listless monotony and harassed anxiety, blending with an expression of mechanical resistance. Were circumstances favourable, she would probably be a handsome, active and clever woman*]

MRS. BOYLE: Isn't he come in yet?

MARY: No, mother.

MRS. BOYLE: Oh, he'll come in when he likes; struttin' about the town like a paycock with Joxer, I suppose. I hear all about Mrs. Tancred's son is in this mornin's paper.

MARY: The full details are in it this mornin'; seven wounds he had—one entherin' the neck, with an exit wound beneath the left shoulder-blade; another in the left breast penethratin' the heart, an' . . .

JOHNNY: [*Springing up from the fire*] Oh, quit that readin', for God's sake! Are yous losin' all your feelin's? It'll soon be that none of you'll read anythin' that's not about butcherin'!

[*He goes quickly into the room on left*]

MARY: He's gettin' very sensitive, all of a sudden!

MRS. BOYLE: I'll read it myself, Mary, by an' by, when I come home. Everybody's sayin' that he was a Diehard—thanks be to God that Johnny had nothin' to do with him this long time. . . . [*Opening the parcel and taking out some sausages, which she places on a plate*] Ah, then, if that father o' yours doesn't come in soon for his breakfast, he may go without any; I'll not wait much longer for him.

MARY: Can't you let him get it himself when he comes in?

MRS. BOYLE: Yes, an' let him bring in Joxer Daly along with him? Ay, that's what he'd like, an' that's what he's waitin' for—till he thinks I'm gone to work, an' then sail in with the boul' Joxer, to burn all the coal an' dhrink all the tea in the place, to show them what a good Samaritan he is! But I'll stop here till he comes in, if I have to wait till to-morrow mornin'.

VOICE OF JOHNNY INSIDE: Mother!

MRS. BOYLE: Yis?

VOICE OF JOHNNY: Bring us in a dhrink o' wather.

MRS. BOYLE: Bring in that fella a dhrink o' wather, for God's sake, Mary.

MARY: Isn't he big an' able enough to come out an' get it himself?

MRS. BOYLE: If you weren't well yourself you'd like somebody to bring you in a dhrink o' wather.

[*She brings in drink and returns*]

MRS. BOYLE: Isn't it terrible to have to be waitin' this way! You'd think he was bringin' twenty poun's a week into the house the way he's going on. He wore out the Health Insurance long ago, he's afther wearin' out the unemployment dole, an', now, he's thryin' to wear out me! An' constantly singin', no less, when he ought always to be on his knees offerin' up a Novena for a job!

MARY: [*Tying a ribbon fillet-wise around her head*] I don't like this ribbon, ma; I think I'll wear the green—it looks betther than the blue.

MRS. BOYLE: Ah, wear whatever ribbon you like, girl, only don't be botherin' me. I don't know what a girl on strike wants to be wearin' a ribbon round her head for, or silk stockins on her legs either; it's wearin' them things that make the employers think they're givin' yous too much money.

MARY: The hour is past now when we'll ask the employers' permission to wear what we like.

MRS. BOYLE: I don't know why you wanted to walk out for Jennie Claffey; up to this you never had a good word for her.

MARY: What's the use of belongin' to a Trades Union if you won't stand up for your principles? Why did they sack her? It was a clear case of victimization. We couldn't let her walk the streets, could we?

MRS. BOYLE: No, of course yous couldn't—yous wanted to keep her company. Wan victim wasn't enough. When the employers sacrifice wan victim, the Trades Unions go wan betther be sacrificin' a hundred.

MARY: It doesn't matther what you say, ma—a principle's a principle.

MRS. BOYLE: Yis; an' when I go into oul' Murphy's tomorrow, an' he gets to know that, instead o' payin' all, I'm goin' to borry more, what'll he say when I tell him a principle's a principle? What'll we do if he refuses to give us any more on tick?

MARY: He daren't refuse—if he does, can't you tell him he's paid?

MRS. BOYLE: It's lookin' as if he was paid, whether he refuses or no.

[Johnny *appears at the door on left. He can be plainly seen now; he is a thin, delicate fellow, something younger than Mary. He has evidently gone through a rough time. His face is pale and drawn; there is a tremulous look of indefinite fear in his eyes. The left sleeve of his coat is empty, and he walks with a slight halt*]

JOHNNY: I was lyin' down; I thought yous were gone. Oul' Simon Mackay is thrampin' about like a horse over me head, an' I can't sleep with him—they're like thunder-claps in me brain! The curse o'—God forgive me for goin' to curse!

MRS. BOYLE: There, now; go back an' lie down again, an' I'll bring you in a nice cup o' tay.

JOHNNY: Tay, tay, tay! You're always thinkin' o' tay. If a man was dyin', you'd thry to make him swally a cup o' tay!   [*He goes back*]

MRS. BOYLE: I don't know what's goin' to be done with him. The bullet he got in the hip in Easter Week was bad enough, but the bomb that shatthered his arm in the fight in O'Connell Street put the finishin' touch on him. I knew he was makin' a fool of himself. God knows I went down on me bended knees to him not to go agen the Free State.

MARY: He stuck to his principles, an', no matther how you may argue, ma, a principle's a principle.

VOICE OF JOHNNY: Is Mary goin' to stay here?

MARY: No, I'm not goin' to stay here; you can't expect me to be always at your beck an' call, can you?

VOICE OF JOHNNY: I won't stop here be meself!

MRS. BOYLE: Amn't I nicely handicapped with the whole o' yous! I don't know what any o' yous ud do without your ma. [*To Johnny*] Your father'll be here in a minute, an' if you want anythin', he'll get it for you.

JOHNNY: I hate assin' him for anythin'. . . . He hates to be assed to stir. . . . Is the light lightin' before the picture o' the Virgin?

MRS. BOYLE: Yis, yis! The wan inside to St. Anthony isn't enough, but he must have another wan to the Virgin here!

[*Jerry Devine enters hastily. He is about twenty-five, well set, active and earnest. He is a type, becoming very common now in the Labour Movement, of a mind knowing enough to make the mass of his associates, who know less, a power, and too little to broaden that power for the benefit of all. Mary seizes her jumper and runs hastily into room left*]

JERRY: [*Breathless*] Where's the Captain, Mrs. Boyle, where's the Captain?

MRS. BOYLE: You may well ass a body that: he's wherever Joxer Daly is—dhrinkin' in some snug or another.

JERRY: Father Farrell is just afther stoppin' to tell me to run up an' get him to go to the new job that's goin' on in Rathmines; his cousin is foreman o' the job, an' Father Farrell was speakin' to him about poor Johnny an' his father bein' idle so long, an' the foreman told Father Farrell to send the Captain up an' he'd give him a start—I wondher where I'd find him?

MRS. BOYLE: You'll find he's ayther in Ryan's or Foley's.

JERRY: I'll run round to Ryan's—I know it's a great house o' Joxer's.   [*He rushes out*]

MRS. BOYLE: [*Piteously*] There now, he'll miss that job, or I know for what! If he gets win' o' the word, he'll not come back till evenin', so that it'll be too late. There'll never be any good got out o' him so long as he goes with that shouldher-shruggin' Joxer. I killin' meself workin', an' he sthruttin' about from mornin' till night like a pay-cock!

[*The steps of two persons are heard coming up a flight of stairs. They are the footsteps of Captain Boyle and Joxer. Captain Boyle is singing in a deep, sonorous, self-honouring voice*]

THE CAPTAIN: Sweet Spirit, hear me prayer! Hear . . . oh . . . hear . . . me prayer . . . hear, oh, hear . . . Oh, he . . . ar . . . oh, he . . . ar . . . me . . . pray . . . er!

JOXER: [*Outside*] Ah, that's a darlin' song, a daaarlin' song!

MRS. BOYLE: [*Viciously*] Sweet spirit hear his prayer! Ah, then, I'll take me solemn affeydavey, it's not for a job he's prayin'!

[*She sits down on the bed so that the cretonne hangings hide her from the view of those entering*]

[*The Captain comes slowly in. He is a man of about sixty; stout, grey-haired and stocky. His neck is short, and his head looks like a stone ball that one sometimes sees on top of a gate-post. His cheeks, reddish-purple, are puffed out, as if he were always repressing an almost irrepressible ejaculation. On his upper lip is a crisp, tightly cropped moustache; he carries himself with the upper part of his body slightly thrown back, and his stomach slightly thrust forward. His walk is a slow, consequential strut. His clothes are dingy, and he wears a faded seaman's-cap with a glazed peak*]

BOYLE: [*To Joxer, who is still outside*] Come on, come on in, Joxer; she's gone out long ago, man. If there's nothing else to be got, we'll furrage out a cup o' tay, anyway. It's the only bit I get in comfort when she's away. 'Tisn't Juno should be her pet name at all, but Deirdre of the Sorras, for she's always grousin'.

[*Joxer steps cautiously into the room. He may be younger than the Captain but he looks a lot older. His face is like a bundle of crinkled paper; his eyes have a cunning twinkle; he is spare and loosely built; he has a habit of constantly shrugging his shoulders with a peculiar twitching movement, meant to be ingratiating. His face is invariably ornamented with a grin*]

JOXER: It's a terrible thing to be tied to a woman that's always grousin'. I don't know how you stick it—it ud put years on me. It's a good job she has to be so ofen away, for [*with a shrug*] when the cat's away, the mice can play!

BOYLE: [*With a commanding and complacent gesture*] Pull over to the fire, Joxer, an' we'll have a cup o' tay in a minute.

JOXER: Ah, a cup o' tay's a darlin' thing, a daaarlin' thing—the cup that cheers but doesn't . . .

[*Joxer's rhapsody is cut short by the sight of Juno coming forward and confronting the two cronies. Both are stupefied*]

MRS. BOYLE: [*With sweet irony—poking the fire, and turning her head to glare at Joxer*] Pull over to the fire, Joxer Daly, an' we'll have a cup o' tay in a minute! Are you sure, now, you wouldn't like an egg?

JOXER: I can't stop, Mrs. Boyle; I'm in a desperate hurry, a desperate hurry.

MRS. BOYLE: Pull over to the fire, Joxer Daly; people is always far more comfortabler here than they are in their own place.

[Joxer *makes hastily for the door.* Boyle *stirs to follow him; thinks of something to relieve the situation—stops, and says suddenly:*]
Joxer!

JOXER: [*At door ready to bolt*] Yis?

BOYLE: You know the foreman o' that job that's goin' on down in Killesther, don't you, Joxer?

JOXER: [*Puzzled*] Foreman—Killesther?

BOYLE: [*With a meaning look*] He's a butty o' yours, isn't he?

JOXER: [*The truth dawning on him*] The foreman at Killesther—oh yis, yis. He's an oul' butty o' mine —oh, he's a darlin' man, a daarlin' man.

BOYLE: Oh, then, it's a sure thing. It's a pity we didn't go down at breakfast first thing this mornin' —we might ha' been working now; but you didn't know it then.

JOXER: [*With a shrug*] It's betther late than never.

BOYLE: It's nearly time we got a start, anyhow; I'm fed up knockin' round, doin' nothin'. He promised you—gave you the straight tip?

JOXER: Yis. "Come down on the blow o' dinner," says he, "an' I'll start you, an' any friend you like to brin' with you." "Ah," says I, "you're a darlin' man, a daaarlin' man."

BOYLE: Well, it couldn't come at a betther time— we're a long time waitin' for it.

JOXER: Indeed we were; but it's a long lane that has no turnin'.

BOYLE: The blow up for dinner is at one—wait till I see what time it 'tis.

[*He goes over to the mantelpiece, and gingerly lifts the clock*]

MRS. BOYLE: Min' now, how you go on fiddlin' with that clock—you know the least little thing sets it asthray.

BOYLE: The job couldn't come at a betther time; I'm feelin' in great fettle, Joxer. I'd hardly believe I ever had a pain in me legs, an' last week I was nearly crippled with them.

JOXER: That's betther an' betther; ah, God never shut wan door but He opened another!

BOYLE: It's only eleven o'clock; we've lashins o' time. I'll slip on me oul' moleskins afther breakfast, an' we can saunter down at our ayse. [*Putting his hand on the shovel*] I think, Joxer, we'd betther bring our shovels?

JOXER: Yis, Captain, yis; it's betther to go fully pre-pared an' ready for all eventualities. You bring your long-tailed shovel, an' I'll bring me navvy. We mighten' want them, an', then agen, we might: for want of a nail the shoe was lost, for want of a shoe the horse was lost, an' for want of a horse the man was lost—aw, that's a darlin' proverb, a daarlin' . . .

[*As Joxer is finishing his sentence.* Mrs. Boyle *approaches the door and* Joxer *retreats hurriedly. She shuts the door with a bang*]

BOYLE: [*Suggestively*] We won't be long pullin' our-selves together agen when I'm working for a few weeks.

[Mrs. Boyle *takes no notice*]

BOYLE: The foreman on the job is an oul' butty o' Joxer's; I have an idea that I know him meself. [*Silence*] . . . There's a button off the back o' me moleskin trousers. . . . If you leave out a needle an' thread I'll sew it on meself. . . . Thanks be to God, the pains in me legs is gone, anyhow!

MRS. BOYLE: [*With a burst*] Look here, Mr. Jacky Boyle, them yarns won't go down with Juno. I know you an' Joxer Daly of an oul' date, an' if you think you're able to come it over me with them fairy tales, you're in the wrong shop.

BOYLE: [*Coughing subduedly to relieve the tenseness of the situation*] U-u-u-ugh!

MRS. BOYLE: Butty o' Joxer's! Oh, you'll do a lot o' good as long as you continue to be a butty o' Joxer's!

BOYLE: U-u-u-ugh!

MRS. BOYLE: Shovel! Ah, then, me boyo, you'd do far more work with a knife an' fork than ever you'll do with a shovel! If there was e'er a genuine job goin' you'd be dh'other way about—not able to lift your arms with the pains in your legs! Your poor wife slavin' to keep the bit in your mouth, an' you gallivantin' about all the day like a pay-cock!

BOYLE: It ud be betther for a man to be dead, betther for a man to be dead.

MRS. BOYLE: [*Ignoring the interruption*] Everybody callin' you "Captain," an' you only wanst on the wather, in an oul' collier from here to Liverpool, when anybody, to listen or look at you, ud take you for a second Christo For Columbus!

BOYLE: Are you never goin' to give us a rest?

MRS. BOYLE: Oh, you're never tired o' lookin' for a rest.

BOYLE: D'ye want to dhrive me out o' the house?

MRS. BOYLE: It ud be easier to dhrive you out o' the house than to dhrive you into a job. Here, sit down an' take your breakfast—it may be the last you'll get, for I don't know where the next is goin' to come from.

BOYLE: If I get this job we'll be all right.

MRS. BOYLE: Did ye see Jerry Devine?

BOYLE: [*Testily*] No, I didn't see him.

MRS. BOYLE: No, but you seen Joxer. Well, he was here lookin' for you.

BOYLE: Well, let him look!

MRS. BOYLE: Oh, indeed, he may well look, for it ud be hard for him to see you, an' you stuck in Ryan's snug.

BOYLE: I wasn't in Ryan's snug—I don't go into Ryan's.

MRS. BOYLE: Oh, is there a mad dog there? Well, if you weren't in Ryan's you were in Foley's.

BOYLE: I'm telling you for the last three weeks I haven't tasted a dhrop of intoxicatin' liquor. I wasn't in ayther wan snug or dh'other—I could swear that on a prayer-book—I'm as innocent as the child unborn!

MRS. BOYLE: Well, if you'd been in for your breakfast you'd ha' seen him.

BOYLE: [Suspiciously] What does he want me for?

MRS. BOYLE: He'll be back any minute an' then you'll soon know.

BOYLE: I'll dhrop out an' see if I can meet him.

MRS. BOYLE: You'll sit down an' take your breakfast, an' let me go to me work, for I'm an hour late already waitin' for you.

BOYLE: You needn't ha' waited, for I'll take no breakfast—I've a little spirit left in me still!

MRS. BOYLE: Are you goin' to have your breakfast—yes or no?

BOYLE: [Too proud to yield] I'll have no breakfast—yous can keep your breakfast. [Plaintively] I'll knock out a bit somewhere, never fear.

MRS. BOYLE: Nobody's goin' to coax you—don't think that.

[She vigorously replaces the pan and the sausages in the press]

BOYLE: I've a little spirit left in me still.

[Jerry Devine enters hastily]

JERRY: Oh, here you are at last! I've been searchin' for you everywhere. The foreman in Foley's told me you hadn't left the snug with Joxer ten minutes before I went in.

MRS. BOYLE: An' he swearin' on the holy prayer-book that he wasn't in no snug!

BOYLE: [To Jerry] What business is it o' yours whether I was in a snug or no? What do you want to be gallopin' about afther me for? Is a man not to be allowed to leave his house for a minute without havin' a pack o' spies, pimps an' informers cantherin' at his heels?

JERRY: Oh, you're takin' a wrong view of it, Mr. Boyle; I simply was anxious to do you a good turn. I have a message for you from Father Farrell: he says that if you go to the job that's on in Rathmines, an' ask for Foreman Managan, you'll get a start.

BOYLE: That's all right, but I don't want the motions of me body to be watched the way an asthronomer ud watch a star. If you're folleyin' Mary aself, you've no pereeogative to be folleyin' me. [Suddenly catching his thigh] U-ugh, I'm afther gettin' a terrible twinge in me right leg!

MRS. BOYLE: Oh, it won't be very long now till it travels into your left wan. It's miraculous that whenever he scents a job in front of him, his legs begin to fail him! Then, me bucko, if you lose this chance, you may go an' furrage for yourself!

JERRY: This job'll last for some time too, Captain, an' as soon as the foundations are in, it'll be cushy enough.

BOYLE: Won't it be a climbin' job? How d'ye expect me to be able to go up a ladder with these legs? An', if I get up aself, how am I goin' to get down agen?

MRS. BOYLE: [Viciously] Get wan o' the labourers to carry you down in a hod! You can't climb a laddher, but you can skip like a goat into a snug!

JERRY: I wouldn't let myself be let down that easy, Mr. Boyle; a little exercise, now, might do you all the good in the world.

BOYLE: It's a docthor you should have been, Devine—maybe you know more about the pains in me legs than meself that has them?

JERRY: [Irritated] Oh, I know nothin' about the pains in your legs; I've brought the message that Father Farrell gave me, an' that's all I can do.

MRS. BOYLE: Here, sit down an' take your breakfast, an' go an' get ready; an' don't be actin' as if you couldn't pull a wing out of a dead bee.

BOYLE: I want no breakfast, I tell you; it ud choke me afther all that's been said. I've a little spirit left in me still.

MRS. BOYLE: Well, let's see your spirit, then, an' go in at wanst an' put on your moleskin trousers!

BOYLE: [Moving towards the door on left] It ud be betther for a man to be dead! U-ugh! There's another twinge in me other leg! Nobody but meself knows the sufferin' I'm goin' through with the pains in these legs o' mine!

[He goes into the room on the left as Mary comes out with her hat in her hand]

MRS. BOYLE: I'll have to push off now, for I'm terrible late already, but I was determined to stay an' hunt that Joxer this time.   [She goes off]

JERRY: Are you going out, Mary?

MARY: It looks like it when I'm putting on my hat, doesn't it?

JERRY: The bitther word agen, Mary.

MARY: You won't allow me to be friendly with you; if I thry, you deliberately misundherstand it.

JERRY: I didn't always misundherstand it; you were often delighted to have the arms of Jerry around you.

MARY: If you go on talkin' like this, Jerry Devine, you'll make me hate you!

JERRY: Well, let it be either a weddin' or a wake! Listen, Mary, I'm standin' for the Secretaryship of our Union. There's only one opposin' me; I'm popular with all the men, an' a good speaker—all are sayin' that I'll get elected.

MARY: Well?

JERRY: The job's worth three hundred an' fifty pounds a year, Mary. You an' I could live nice an' cosily on that; it would lift you out o' this place an' . . .

MARY: I haven't time to listen to you now—I have to go.

[She is going out, when Jerry bars the way]

JERRY: [Appealingly] Mary, what's come over you with me for the last few weeks? You hardly speak to me, an' then only a word with a face o' bitherness on it. Have you forgotten, Mary, all the happy evenins that were as sweet as the scented hawthorn that sheltered the sides o' the road as we saunthered through the country?

MARY: That's all over now. When you get your new job, Jerry, you won't be long findin' a girl far better than I am for your sweetheart.

JERRY: Never, never, Mary! No matther what happens, you'll always be the same to me.

MARY: I must be off; please let me go, Jerry.

JERRY: I'll go a bit o' the way with you.

MARY: You needn't, thanks; I want to be by meself.

JERRY: [Catching her arm] You're goin' to meet another fella; you've clicked with someone else, me lady!

MARY: That's no concern o' yours, Jerry Devine; let me go!

JERRY: I saw yous comin' out o' the Cornflower Dance Class, an' you hangin' on his arm—a thin, lanky strip of a Micky Dazzler, with a walkin'-stick an' gloves!

VOICE OF JOHNNY: [Loudly] What are you doin' there—pullin' about everything!

VOICE OF BOYLE: [Loudly and viciously] I'm puttin' on me moleskin trousers!

MARY: You're hurtin' me arm! Let me go, or I'll scream, an' then you'll have the oul' fella out on top of us!

JERRY: Don't be so hard on a fella, Mary, don't be so hard.

BOYLE: [Appearing at the door] What's the meanin' of all this hillabaloo?

MARY: Let me go, let me go!

BOYLE: D'ye hear me—what's all this hillabaloo about?

JERRY: [Plaintively] Will you not give us one kind word, one kind word, Mary?

BOYLE: D'ye hear me talkin' to yous? What's all this hillabaloo for?

JERRY: Let me kiss your hand, your little, tiny, white hand!

BOYLE: Your little, tiny, white hand—are you takin' leave o' your senses, man?

[Mary breaks away and rushes out]

BOYLE: This is nice goins on in front of her father!

JERRY: Ah, dhry up, for God's sake!

[He follows Mary]

BOYLE: Chiselurs don't care a damn now about their parents, they're bringin' their fathers' grey hairs down with sorra to the grave, an' laughin' at it, laughin' at it. Ah, I suppose it's just the same everywhere—the whole worl's in a state o' chassis! [He sits by the fire] Breakfast! Well, they can keep their breakfast for me. Not if they were down on their bended knees would I take it—I'll show them I've a little spirit left in me still! [He goes over to the press, and takes out a plate and looks at it]

Sassige! Well, let her keep her sassige. [He returns to the fire, takes up the teapot and gives it a gentle shake] The tea's wet right enough.

[A pause; he rises, goes to the press, takes out the sausage, puts it on the pan, and puts both on the fire. He attends the sausage with a fork]

BOYLE: [Singing]
When the robins nest agen,
And the flowers are in bloom,
When the Springtime's sunny smile seems to banish all sorrow an' gloom;
Then me bonny blue-ey'd lad, if me heart be true till then—
He's promised he'll come back to me,
When the robins nest agen!

[He lifts his head at the high note, and then drops his eyes to the pan]

BOYLE: [Singing]
When the . . .

[Steps are heard approaching; he whips the pan off the fire and puts it under the bed, then sits down at the fire. The door opens and a bearded man looking in says:]

You don't happen to want a sewin' machine?

BOYLE: [Furiously] No, I don't want e'er a sewin' machine!

[He returns the pan to the fire, and commences to sing again]

BOYLE: [Singing]
When the robins nest agen,
And the flowers they are in bloom,
He's . . .

[A thundering knock is heard at the street door]

BOYLE: There's a terrible tatheraraa—that's a stranger—that's nobody belongin' to the house.

[Another loud knock]

JOXER: [Sticking his head in at the door] Did ye hear them tatherarahs?

BOYLE: Well, Joxer, I'm not deaf.

JOHNNY: [Appearing in his shirt and trousers at the door on left; his face is anxious and his voice is tremulous] Who's that at the door; who's that at the door? Who gave that knock—d'ye yous hear me—are yous deaf or dhrunk or what?

BOYLE: [To Johnny] How the hell do I know who 'tis? Joxer, stick your head out o' the window an' see.

JOXER: An' mebbe get a bullet in the kisser? Ah, none o' them thricks for Joxer! It's betther to be a coward than a corpse!

BOYLE: [Looking cautiously out of the window] It's a fella in a thrench coat.

JOHNNY: Holy Mary, Mother o' God, I . . .

BOYLE: He's goin' away—he must ha' got tired knockin'.

[Johnny returns to the room on left]

BOYLE: Sit down an' have a cup o' tay, Joxer.

JOXER: I'm afraid the missus ud pop in on us agen

before we'd know where we are. Somethin's tellin' me to go at wanst.

BOYLE: Don't be superstitious, man; we're Dublin men, an' not boyos that's only afther comin' up from the bog o' Allen—though if she did come in, right enough, we'd be caught like rats in a thrap.

JOXER: An' you know the sort she is—she wouldn't listen to reason—an' wanse bitten twice shy.

BOYLE: [Going over to the window at back] If the worst came to the worst, you could dart out here, Joxer; it's only a dhrop of a few feet to the roof of the return room, an' the first minute she goes into dh'other room I'll give you the bend, an' you can slip in an' away.

JOXER: [Yielding to the temptation] Ah, I won't stop very long anyhow. [Picking up a book from the table] Whose is the buk?

BOYLE: Aw, one o' Mary's; she's always readin' lately—nothin' but thrash, too. There's one I was lookin' at dh'other day: three stories. The Doll's House, Ghosts, an' The Wild Duck—buks only fit for chiselurs!

JOXER: Didja ever rade Elizabeth, or Th' Exile o' Sibayria? . . . Ah, it's a darlin' story, a daarlin' story!

BOYLE: You eat your sassige, an' never min' Th' Exile o' Sibayria.

[Both sit down; Boyle fills out tea, pours gravy on Joxer's plate, and keeps the sausage for himself]

JOXER: What are you wearin' your moleskin trousers for?

BOYLE: I have to go to a job, Joxer. Just afther you'd gone, Devine kem runnin' in to tell us that Father Farrell said if I went down to the job that's goin' on in Rathmines I'd get a start.

JOXER: Be the holy, that's good news!

BOYLE: How is it good news? I wondher if you were in my condition, would you call it good news?

JOXER: I thought . . .

BOYLE: You thought! You think too sudden sometimes, Joxer. D'ye know, I'm hardly able to crawl with the pains in me legs!

JOXER: Yis, yis; I forgot the pains in your legs. I know you can do nothin' while they're at you.

BOYLE: You forgot; I don't think any of yous realize the state I'm in with the pains in me legs. What ud happen if I had to carry a bag o' cement?

JOXER: Ah, any man havin' the like of them pains id be down an' out, down an' out.

BOYLE: I wouldn't mind if he had said it to meself; but, no, oh no, he rushes in an' shouts it out in front o' Juno, an' you know what Juno is, Joxer. We all know Devine knows a little more than the rest of us, but he doesn't act as if he did; he's a good boy, sober, able to talk an' all that, but still . . .

JOXER: Oh ay; able to argufy, but still . . .

BOYLE: If he's runnin' afther Mary, aself, he's not goin' to be runnin' afther me. Captain Boyle's able to take care of himself. Afther all, I'm not gettin' brought up on Virol. I never heard him usin' a curse; I don't believe he was ever dhrunk in his life—sure he's not like a Christian at all!

JOXER: You're afther takin' the word out o' me mouth—afther all, a Christian's natural, but he's unnatural.

BOYLE: His oul' fella was just the same—a Wicklow man.

JOXER: A Wicklow man! That explains the whole thing. I've met many a Wicklow man in me time, but I never met wan that was any good.

BOYLE: "Father Farrell," says he, "sent me down to tell you." Father Farrell! . . . D'ye know, Joxer, I never like to be beholden to any o' the clergy.

JOXER: It's dangerous, right enough.

BOYLE: If they do anything for you, they'd want you to be livin' in the Chapel. . . . I'm goin' to tell you somethin', Joxer, that I wouldn't tell to anybody else—the clergy always had too much power over the people in this unfortunate country.

JOXER: You could sing that if you had an air to it!

BOYLE: [Becoming enthusiastic] Didn't they prevent the people in "47" from seizin' the corn, an' they starvin'; didn't they down Parnell; didn't they say that hell wasn't hot enough nor eternity long enough to punish the Fenians? We don't forget, we don't forget them things, Joxer. If they've taken everything else from us, Joxer, they've left us our memory.

JOXER: [Emotionally] For mem'ry's the only friend that grief can call its own, that grief . . . can . . . call . . . its own!

BOYLE: Father Farrell's beginnin' to take a great intherest in Captain Boyle; because of what Johnny did for his country, says he to me wan day. It's a curious way to reward Johnny be makin' his poor oul' father work. But that's what the clergy want, Joxer—work, work, work for me an' you; havin' us mulin' from mornin' till night, so that they may be in betther fettle when they come hoppin' round for their dues! Job! Well, let him give his job to wan of his hymn-singin', prayer-spoutin', crawthumpin' Confraternity men!

[The voice of a coal-block vendor is heard chanting in the street]

VOICE OF COAL VENDOR: Blocks . . . coal-blocks! Blocks . . . coal-blocks!

JOXER: God be with the young days when you were steppin' the deck of a manly ship, with the win' blowin' a hurricane through the masts, an' the only sound you'd hear was, "Port your helm!" an' the only answer, "Port it is, sir!"

BOYLE: Them was days, Joxer, them was days. Nothin' was too hot or too heavy for me then. Sailin' from the Gulf o' Mexico to the Antanartic Ocean. I seen things, I seen things, Joxer, that no mortal man should speak about that knows his Catechism. Ofen, an' ofen, when I was fixed to the wheel with a marlin-spike, an' the wins blowin' fierce an' the waves lashin' an' lashin', till you'd think every minute was goin' to be your last, an' it blowed, an' blowed—blew is the right word, Joxer, but blowed is what the sailors use. . . .

JOXER: Aw, it's a darlin' word, a daarlin' word.

BOYLE: An', as it blowed an' blowed, I ofen looked up at the sky an' assed meself the question—what is the stars, what is the stars?

VOICE OF COAL VENDOR: Any blocks, coal-blocks; blocks, coal-blocks!

JOXER: Ah, that's the question, that's the question—what is the stars?

BOYLE: An' then, I'd have another look, an' I'd ass meself—what is the moon?

JOXER: Ah, that's the question—what is the moon, what is the moon?

[*Rapid steps are heard coming towards the door. Boyle makes desperate efforts to hide everything; Joxer rushes to the window in a frantic effort to get out; Boyle begins to innocently lilt "Oh, me darlin' Jennie, I will be thrue to thee," when the door is opened, and the black face of the* Coal Vendor *appears*]

THE COAL VENDOR: D'yes want any blocks?

BOYLE: [*With a roar*] No, we don't want any blocks!

JOXER: [*Coming back with a sigh of relief*] That's afther puttin' the heart across me—I could ha' sworn it was Juno. I'd betther be goin', Captain; you couldn't tell the minute Juno'd hop in on us.

BOYLE: Let her hop in; we may as well have it out first as at last. I've made up me mind—I'm not goin' to do only what she damn well likes.

JOXER: Them sentiments does you credit, Captain; I don't like to say anything as between man an' wife, but I say as a butty, as a butty, Captain, that you've stuck it too long, an' that it's about time you showed a little spunk.

How can a man die betther than facin' fearful
    odds,
For th' ashes of his fathers an' the temples of
    his gods?

BOYLE: She has her rights—there's no one denyin' it, but haven't I me rights too?

JOXER: Of course you have—the sacred rights o' man!

BOYLE: Today, Joxer, there's goin' to be issued a proclamation be me, establishin' an independent Republic, an' Juno'll have to take an oath of allegiance.

JOXER: Be firm, be firm, Captain; the first few minutes'll be the worst:—if you gently touch a nettle it'll sting you for your pains; grasp it like a lad of mettle, an' as soft as silk remains!

VOICE OF JUNO outside: Can't stop, Mrs. Madigan—I haven't a minute!

JOXER: [*Flying out of the window*] Holy God, here she is!

BOYLE: [*Packing the things away with a rush in the press*] I knew that fella ud stop till she was in on top of us!   [*He sits down by the fire*]

[*Juno enters hastily; she is flurried and exited*]

JUNO: Oh, you're in—you must have been only afther comin' in?

BOYLE: No, I never went out.

JUNO: It's curious, then, you never heard the knockin'.
            [*She puts her coat and hat on bed*]

BOYLE: Knockin'? Of course I heard the knockin'.

JUNO: An' why didn't you open the door, then? I suppose you were so busy with Joxer that you hadn't time.

BOYLE: I haven't seen Joxer since I seen him before. Joxer! What ud bring Joxer here?

JUNO: D'ye mean to tell me that the pair of yous wasn't collogin' together here when me back was turned?

BOYLE: What ud we be collogin' together about? I have somethin' else to think of besides collogin' with Joxer. I can swear on all the holy prayer-books . . .

MRS. BOYLE: That you weren't in no snug! Go on in at wanst now, an' take off that moleskin trousers o' yours, an' put on a collar an' tie to smarten yourself up a bit. There's a visitor comin' with Mary in a minute, an' he has great news for you.

BOYLE: A job, I suppose; let us get wan first before we start lookin' for another.

MRS. BOYLE: That's the thing that's able to put the win' up you. Well, it's no job, but news that'll give you the chance o' your life.

BOYLE: What's all the mystery about?

MRS. BOYLE: G'win an' take off the moleskin trousers when you're told!

[*Boyle goes into room on left*] [*Mrs. Boyle tidies up the room, puts the shovel under the bed, and goes to the press*]

MRS. BOYLE: Oh, God bless us, looka the way everything's thrun about! Oh, Joxer was here, Joxer was here!

[*Mary enters with Charlie Bentham; he is a young man of twenty-five, tall, good-looking, with a very high opinion of himself generally. He is dressed in a brown coat, brown knee-breeches, grey stockings, a brown sweater, with a deep blue tie; he carries gloves and a walking-stick*]

MRS. BOYLE: [*Fussing round*] Come in, Mr. Bentham; sit down, Mr. Bentham, in this chair; it's more comfortabler than that, Mr. Bentham. Himself'll be here in a minute; he's just takin' off his trousers.

MARY: Mother!

BENTHAM: Please don't put yourself to any trouble, Mrs. Boyle—I'm quite all right here, thank you.

MRS. BOYLE: An' to think of you knowin' Mary, an' she knowin' the news you had for us, an' wouldn't let on; but it's all the more welcomer now, for we were on our last lap!

VOICE OF JOHNNY *inside:* What are you kickin' up all the racket for?

BOYLE: [*Roughly*] I'm takin' off me moleskin trousers!

JOHNNY: Can't you do it, then, without lettin' th' whole house know you're takin' off your trousers? What d'ye want puttin' them on an' takin' them off again?

BOYLE: Will you let me alone, will you let me alone? Am I never goin' to be done thryin' to please th' whole o' yous?

MRS. BOYLE: [*To Bentham*] You must excuse th' state o' th' place, Mr. Bentham; th' minute I turn me back that man o' mine always makes a litther o' th' place, a litther o' th' place.

BENTHAM: Don't worry, Mrs. Boyle; it's all right, I assure . . .

BOYLE: [*Inside*] Where's me braces; where in th' name o' God did I leave me braces? . . . Ay, did you see where I put me braces?

JOHNNY: [*Inside, calling out*] Ma, will you come in here an' take da away ou' o' this or he'll dhrive me mad.

MRS. BOYLE: [*Going towards the door*] Dear, dear, dear, that man'll be lookin' for somethin' on th' day o' Judgment. [*Looking into room and calling to* Boyle] Look at your braces, man, hangin' round your neck!

BOYLE: [*Inside*] Aw, Holy God!

MRS. BOYLE: [*Calling*] Johnny, Johnny, come out here for a minute.

JOHNNY: Ah, leave Johnny alone, an' don't be annoyin' him!

MRS. BOYLE: Come on, Johnny, till I inthroduce you to Mr. Bentham. [*To Bentham*] My son, Mr. Bentham; he's afther goin' through the mill. He was only a chiselur of a Boy Scout in Easter Week, when he got hit in the hip; and his arm was blew off in the fight in O'Connell Street. [*Johnny comes in*] Here he is, Mr. Bentham; Mr. Bentham, Johnny. None can deny he done his bit for Irelan', if that's goin' to do him any good.

JOHNNY: [*Boastfully*] I'd do it agen, ma, I'd do it agen; for a principle's a principle.

MRS. BOYLE: Ah, you lost your best principle, me boy, when you lost your arm; them's the only sort o' principles that's any good to a workin' man.

JOHNNY: Ireland only half free'll never be at peace while she has a son left to pull a trigger.

MRS. BOYLE: To be sure, to be sure—no bread's a lot betther than half a loaf. [*Calling loudly in to* Boyle] Will you hurry up there?

[Boyle *enters in his best trousers, which aren't too good, and looks very uncomfortable in his collar and tie*]

MRS. BOYLE: This is me husband; Mr. Boyle, Mr. Bentham.

BENTHAM: Ah, very glad to know you, Mr. Boyle. How are you?

BOYLE: Ah, I'm not too well at all; I suffer terrible with pains in me legs. Juno can tell you there what . . .

MRS. BOYLE: You won't have many pains in your legs when you hear what Mr. Bentham has to tell you.

BENTHAM: Juno! What an interesting name! It reminds one of Homer's glorious story of ancient gods and heroes.

BOYLE: Yis, doesn't it? You see, Juno was born an' christened in June; I met her in June; we were married in June, an' Johnny was born in June, so wan day I says to her, "You should ha' been called Juno," an' the name stuck to her ever since.

MRS. BOYLE: Here, we can talk o' them things agen; let Mr. Bentham say what he has to say now.

BENTHAM: Well, Mr. Boyle, I suppose you'll remember a Mr. Ellison of Santry—he's a relative of yours, I think.

BOYLE: [*Viciously*] Is it that prognosticator an' procrastinator! Of course I remember him.

BENTHAM: Well, he's dead, Mr. Boyle . . .

BOYLE: Sorra many'll go into mournin' for him.

MRS. BOYLE: Wait till you hear what Mr. Bentham has to say, an' then, maybe, you'll change your opinion.

BENTHAM: A week before he died he sent for me to write his will for him. He told me that there were two only that he wished to leave his property to: his second cousin, Michael Finnegan of Santry, and John Boyle, his first cousin, of Dublin.

BOYLE: [*Excitedly*] Me, is it me, me?

BENTHAM: You, Mr. Boyle; I'll read a copy of the will that I have here with me, which has been duly filed in the Court of Probate.

[*He takes a paper from his pocket and reads*]

6th February 1922

This is the last Will and Testament of William Ellison, of Santry, in the County of Dublin. I hereby order and wish my property to be sold and divided as follows:—

£20 to the St. Vincent de Paul Society.

£60 for Masses for the repose of my soul (5s. for each Mass).

The rest of my property to be divided between my first and second cousins.

I hereby appoint Timothy Buckly, of Santry, and Hugh Brierly, of Coolock, to be my Executors.

(*Signed*) WILLIAM ELLISON.
HUGH BRIERLY.
TIMOTHY BUCKLY.
CHARLES BENTHAM, N.T.

BOYLE: [*Eagerly*] An' how much'll be comin' out of it, Mr. Bentham?

BENTHAM: The Executors told me that half of the property would be anything between £1500 and £2000.

MARY: A fortune, father, a fortune!

JOHNNY: We'll be able to get out o' this place now, an' go somewhere we're not known.

MRS. BOYLE: You won't have to trouble about a job for awhile, Jack.

BOYLE: [*Fervently*] I'll never doubt the goodness o' God agen.

BENTHAM: I congratulate you, Mr. Boyle.
                                    [*They shake hands*]

BOYLE: An' now, Mr. Bentham, you'll have to have a wet.

BENTHAM: A wet?

BOYLE: A wet—a jar—a boul!

MRS. BOYLE: Jack, you're speakin' to Mr. Bentham, an' not to Joxer.

BOYLE: [*Solemnly*] Juno . . . Mary . . . Johnny . . . we'll have to go into mournin' at wanst. . . . I never expected that poor Bill ud die so sudden. . . . Well, we all have to die some day . . . you, Juno, to-day . . . an' me, maybe, to-morrow. . . . It's sad, but it can't be helped. . . . Requiescat in pace . . . or, usin' our oul' tongue like St. Patrick or St. Bridget, Guh sayeree jeea ayera!

MARY: Oh, father, that's not Rest in Peace; that's God save Ireland.

BOYLE: U-u-ugh, it's all the same—isn't it a prayer? . . . Juno, I'm done with Joxer; he's nothin' but a prognosticator an' a . . .

JOXER: [*Climbing angrily through the window and bounding into the room*] You're done with Joxer, are you? Maybe you thought I'd stop on the roof all the night for you! Joxer out on the roof with the win' blowin' through him was nothin' to you an' your friend with the collar an' tie!

MRS. BOYLE: What in the name o' God brought you out on the roof; what were you doin' there?

JOXER: [*Ironically*] I was dhreamin' I was standin' on the bridge of a ship, an' she sailin' the Antartic Ocean, an' it blowed, an' blowed, an' I lookin' up at the sky an' sayin', what is the stars, what is the stars?

MRS. BOYLE: [*Opening the door and standing at it*] Here, get ou' o' this, Joxer Daly; I was always thinkin' you had a slate off.

JOXER: [*Moving to the door*] I have to laugh every time I look at the deep-sea sailor; an' a row on a river ud make him sea-sick!

BOYLE: Get ou' o' this before I take the law into me own hands!

JOXER: [*Going out*] Say aw rewaeawr, but not good-bye. Lookin' for work, an' prayin' to God he won't get it!   [*He goes*]

MRS. BOYLE: I'm tired tellin' you what Joxer was; maybe now you see yourself the kind he is.

BOYLE: He'll never blow the froth off a pint o' mine agen, that's a sure thing. Johnny . . . Mary . . .

you're to keep yourselves to yourselves for the future. Juno, I'm done with Joxer. . . . I'm a new man from this out. . . .
[*Clasping Juno's hand, and singing emotionally*]

> O, me darlin' Juno, I will be thrue to thee;
> Me own, me darlin' Juno, you're all the world to me.

Act II

The same, but the furniture is more plentiful, and of a vulgar nature. A glaringly upholstered arm-chair and lounge; cheap pictures and photos every-where. Every available spot is ornamented with huge vases filled with artificial flowers. Crossed festoons of coloured paper chains stretch from end to end of ceiling. On the table is an old attaché case. It is about six in the evening, and two days after the First Act. Boyle, in his shirt-sleeves, is voluptuously stretched on the sofa; he is smoking a clay pipe. He is half asleep. A lamp is lighting on the table. After a few moments' pause the voice of Joxer is heard singing softly outside at the door—"Me pipe I'll smoke, as I dhrive me moke—are you there, Mor . . . ee . . . ar . . . i . . . teee!"

BOYLE: [*Leaping up, takes a pen in his hand and busies himself with papers*] Come along, Joxer, me son, come along.

JOXER: [*Putting his head in*] Are you be yourself?

BOYLE: Come on, come on; that doesn't matther; I'm masther now, an' I'm goin' to remain masther.

[*Joxer comes in*]

JOXER: How d'ye feel now, as a man o' money?

BOYLE: [*Solemnly*] It's a responsibility, Joxer, a great responsibility.

JOXER: I suppose 'tis now, though you wouldn't think it.

BOYLE: Joxer, han' me over that attackey case on the table there. [*Joxer hands the case*] Ever since the Will was passed I've run hundreds o' docky-ments through me hans—I tell you, you have to keep your wits about you.
                          [*He busies himself with papers*]

JOXER: Well, I won't disturb you; I'll dhrop in when . . .

BOYLE: [*Hastily*] It's all right, Joxer, this is the last one to be signed to-day. [*He signs a paper, puts it into the case, which he shuts with a snap, and sits back pompously in the chair*] Now, Joxer, you want to see me; I'm at your service—what can I do for you, me man?

JOXER: I've just dhropped in with the £3:5s. that Mrs. Madigan riz on the blankets an' table for you, an' she says you're to be in no hurry payin' it back.

BOYLE: She won't be long without it; I expect the first cheque for a couple o' hundhred any day. There's the five bob for yourself—go on, take it, man; it'll not be the last you'll get from the Captain. Now an' agen we have our differ, but we're there together all the time.

JOXER: Me for you, an' you for me, like the two Musketeers.

BOYLE: Father Farrell stopped me to-day an' tole me how glad he was I fell in for the money.

JOXER: He'll be stoppin' you ofen enough now; I suppose it was "Mr." Boyle with him?

BOYLE: He shuk me be the han' . . .

JOXER: [Ironically] I met with Napper Tandy, an' he shuk me be the han'!

BOYLE: You're seldom asthray, Joxer, but you're wrong shipped this time. What you're sayin' of Father Farrell is very near to blasfeemey. I don't like any one to talk disrespectful of Father Farrell.

JOXER: You're takin' me up wrong, Captain; I wouldn't let a word be said agen Father Farrell—the heart o' the rowl, that's what he is; I always said he was a darlin' man, a daarlin' man.

BOYLE: Comin' up the stairs who did I meet but that bummer, Nugent. "I seen you talkin' to Father Farrell," says he, with a grin on him. "He'll be folleyin' you," says he, "like a Guardian Angel from this out"—all the time the oul' grin on him, Joxer.

JOXER: I never seen him yet but he had that oul' grin on him!

BOYLE: "Mr. Nugent," says I, "Father Farrell is a man o' the people, an', as far as I know the History o' me country, the priests was always in the van of the fight for Irelan's freedom."

JOXER: [Fervently]
Who was it led the van, Soggart Aroon?
Since the fight first began, Soggart Aroon?

BOYLE: "Who are you tellin'?" says he. "Didn't they let down the Fenians, an' didn't they do in Parnell? An' now . . ." "You ought to be ashamed o' yourself," says I, interruptin' him, "not to know the History o' your country." An' I left him gawkin' where he was.

JOXER: Where ignorance 's bliss 'tis folly to be wise; I wondher did he ever read the Story o' Irelan'.

BOYLE: Be J. L. Sullivan? Don't you know he didn't.

JOXER: Ah, it's a darlin' buk, a daarlin' buk!

BOYLE: You'd betther be goin', now, Joxer; his Majesty, Bentham, 'll be here any minute, now.

JOXER: Be the way things is lookin', it'll be a match between him an' Mary. She's thrun over Jerry altogether. Well, I hope it will, for he's a darlin' man.

BOYLE: I'm glad you think so—I don't. [Irritably] What's darlin' about him?

JOXER: [Nonplussed] I only seen him twiced; if you want to know me, come an' live with me.

BOYLE: He's too dignified for me—to hear him talk you'd think he knew as much as a Boney's Oraculum. He's given up his job as teacher, an' is goin' to become a solicitor in Dublin—he's been studyin' law. I suppose he thinks I'll set him up, but he's wrong shipped. An' th' other fella—Jerry's as bad. The two o' them ud give you a pain in your face, listenin' to them; Jerry believin' in nothin', an' Bentham believin' in everythin'. One that says all is God an' no man; an' th' other that says all is man an' no God!

JOXER: Well, I'll be off now.

BOYLE: Don't forget to dhrop down afther awhile; we'll have a quiet jar, an' a song or two.

JOXER: Never fear.

BOYLE: An' tell Mrs. Madigan that I hope we'll have the pleasure of her organization at our little enthertainment.

JOXER: Righto; we'll come down together.

[He goes out]

[Johnny comes from room on left, and sits down moodily at the fire. Boyle looks at him for a few moments, and shakes his head. He fills his pipe]

VOICE OF JUNO at the door: Open the door, Jack, this thing has me nearly kilt with the weight.

[Boyle opens the door. Juno enters carrying the box of a gramophone, followed by Mary carrying the horn and some parcels. Juno leaves the box on the table and flops into a chair]

JUNO: Carryin' that from Henry Street was no joke.

BOYLE: U-u-ugh, that's a grand-lookin' insthrument—how much was it?

JUNO: Pound down, an' five to be paid at two shillins a week.

BOYLE: That's reasonable enough.

JUNO: I'm afraid we're runnin' into too much debt; first the furniture, an' now this.

BOYLE: The whole lot won't be much out of £2000.

MARY: I don't know what you wanted a gramophone for—I know Charlie hates them; he says they're destructive of real music.

BOYLE: Desthructive of music—that fella ud give you a pain in your face. All a gramophone wants is to be properly played; its thrue wondher is only felt when everythin's quiet—what a gramophone wants is dead silence!

MARY: But, father, Jerry says the same; afther all, you can only appreciate music when your ear is properly trained.

BOYLE: That's another fella ud give you a pain in your face. Properly thrained! I suppose you couldn't appreciate football unless your fut was properly thrained.

MRS. BOYLE: [To Mary] Go on in ower that an' dress, or Charlie'll be in on you, an' tea nor nothing'll be ready.

[Mary goes into room left]

MRS. BOYLE: [*Arranging table for tea*] You didn't look at our new gramophone, Johnny?

JOHNNY: 'Tisn't gramophones I'm thinking of.

MRS. BOYLE: An' what is it you're thinkin' of, allanna?

JOHNNY: Nothin', nothin', nothin'.

MRS. BOYLE: Sure, you must be thinkin' of somethin'; it's yourself that has yourself the way y'are; sleepin' wan night in me sisther's, an' the nex' in your father's brother's—you'll get no rest goin' on that way.

JOHNNY: I can rest nowhere, nowhere, nowhere.

MRS. BOYLE: Sure, you're not thryin' to rest anywhere.

JOHNNY: Let me alone, let me alone, let me alone, for God's sake.

[*A knock at street door*]

MRS. BOYLE: [*In a flutter*] Here he is; here's Mr. Bentham!

BOYLE: Well, there's room for him; it's a pity there's not a brass band to play him in.

MRS. BOYLE: We'll han' the tea round, an' not be clusthered round the table, as if we never seen nothin'.

[*Steps are heard approaching, and* Juno, *opening the door, allows* Bentham *to enter*]

JUNO: Give your hat an' stick to Jack, there . . . sit down, Mr. Bentham . . . no, not there . . . in th' easy chair be the fire . . . there, that's betther. Mary'll be out to you in a minute.

BOYLE: [*Solemnly*] I seen be the paper this mornin' that Consols was down half per cent. That's serious, min' you, an' shows the whole counthry's in a state o' chassis.

MRS. BOYLE: What's Consols, Jack?

BOYLE: Consols? Oh, Consols is—oh, there's no use tellin' women what Consols is—th' wouldn't undherstand.

BENTHAM: It's just as you were saying, Mr. Boyle . . .

[Mary *enters, charmingly dressed*]

BENTHAM: Oh, good evening, Mary; how pretty you're looking!

MARY: [*Archly*] Am I?

BOYLE: We were just talkin' when you kem in, Mary; I was tellin' Mr. Bentham that the whole counthry's in a state o' chassis.

MARY: [*To Bentham*] Would you prefer the green or the blue ribbon round me hair, Charlie?

MRS. BOYLE: Mary, your father's speakin'.

BOYLE: [*Rapidly*] I was jus' tellin' Mr. Bentham that the whole counthry's in a state o' chassis.

MARY: I'm sure you're frettin', da, whether it is or no.

MRS. BOYLE: With all our churches an' religions, the worl's not a bit the betther.

BOYLE: [*With a commanding gesture*] Tay!

[Mary *and* Mrs. Boyle *dispense the tea*]

MRS. BOYLE: An' Irelan's takin' a leaf out o' the worl's buk; when we got the makin' of our own laws I thought we'd never stop to look behind us, but instead of that we never stopped to look before us! If the people ud folley up their religion betther there'd be a betther chance for us—what do you think, Mr. Bentham?

BENTHAM: I'm afraid I can't venture to express an opinion on that point, Mrs. Boyle; dogma has no attraction for me.

MRS. BOYLE: I forgot you didn't hold with us: what's this you said you were?

BENTHAM: A Theosophist, Mrs. Boyle.

MRS. BOYLE: An' what in the name o' God's a Theosophist?

BOYLE: A Theosophist, Juno, 's a—tell her, Mr. Bentham, tell her.

BENTHAM: It's hard to explain in a few words: Theosophy's founded on The Vedas, the religious books of the East. Its central theme is the existence of an all-pervading Spirit—the Life-Breath. Nothing really exists but this one Universal Life-Breath. And whatever even seems to exist separately from this Life-Breath, doesn't really exist at all. It is all vital force in man, in all animals, and in all vegetation. This Life-Breath is called the Prawna.

MRS. BOYLE: The Prawna! What a comical name!

BOYLE: Prawna; yis, the Prawna. [*Blowing gently through his lips*] That's the Prawna!

MRS. BOYLE: Whist, whist, Jack.

BENTHAM: The happiness of man depends upon his sympathy with this Spirit. Men who have reached a high state of excellence are called Yogi. Some men become Yogi in a short time, it may take others millions of years.

BOYLE: Yogi! I seen hundreds of them in the streets o' San Francisco.

BENTHAM: It is said by these Yogi that if we practise certain mental exercises that we would have powers denied to others—for instance, the faculty of seeing things that happen miles and miles away.

MRS. BOYLE: I wouldn't care to meddle with that sort o' belief; it's a very curious religion, altogether.

BOYLE: What's curious about it? Isn't all religions curious?—if they weren't, you wouldn't get any one to believe them. But religions is passin' away—they've had their day like everything else. Take the real Dublin people, f'rinstance: they know more about Charlie Chaplin an' Tommy Mix than they do about SS. Peter an' Paul!

MRS. BOYLE: You don't believe in ghosts, Mr. Bentham?

MARY: Don't you know he doesn't, mother?

BENTHAM: I don't know that, Mary. Scientists are beginning to think that what we call ghosts are sometimes seen by persons of a certain nature. They say that sensational actions, such as the killing of a person, demand great energy, and that that energy lingers in the place where the action occurred. People may live in the place and see nothing, when someone may come along whose personality has some peculiar connection with the energy of the place, and, in a flash, the person sees the whole affair.

JOHNNY: [*Rising swiftly, pale and affected*] What sort o' talk is this to be goin' on with? Is there nothin' betther to be talkin' about but the killin' o' people? My God, isn't it bad enough for these things to happen without talkin' about them!

[*He hurriedly goes into the room on left*]

BENTHAM: Oh, I'm very sorry, Mrs. Boyle; I never thought . . .

MRS. BOYLE: [*Apologetically*] Never mind, Mr. Bentham, he's very touchy.

[*A frightened scream is heard from* Johnny *inside*]

MRS. BOYLE: Mother of God, what's that?

[*He rushes out again, his face pale, his lips twitching, his limbs trembling*]

JOHNNY: Shut the door, shut the door, quick, for God's sake! Great God, have mercy on me! Blessed Mother o' God, shelter me, shelther your son!

MRS. BOYLE: [*Catching him in her arms*] What's wrong with you? What ails you? Sit down, sit down, here, on the bed . . . there now . . . there now.

MARY: Johnny, Johnny, what ails you?

JOHNNY: I seen him, I seen him . . . kneelin' in front o' the statue . . . merciful Jesus, have pity on me!

MRS. BOYLE: [*To Boyle*] Get him a glass o' whisky . . . quick, man, an' don't stand gawkin'.

[*Boyle gets the whisky*]

JOHNNY: Sit here, sit here, mother . . . between me an' the door.

MRS. BOYLE: I'll sit beside you as long as you like, only tell me what was it came across you at all?

JOHNNY: [*After taking some drink*] I seen him. . . . I seen Robbie Tancred kneelin' down before the statue . . . an' the red light shinin' on him . . . an' when I went in . . . he turned an' looked at me . . . an' I seen the wouns bleedin' in his breast. . . . Oh, why did he look at me like that? . . . it wasn't my fault that he was done in. . . . Mother o' God, keep him away from me!

MRS. BOYLE: There, there, child, you've imagined it all. There was nothin' there at all—it was the red light you seen, an' the talk we had put all the rest into your head. Here, dhrink more o' this—it'll do you good. . . . An', now, stretch yourself down on the bed for a little. [*To Boyle*] Go in, Jack, an' show him it was only in his own head it was.

BOYLE: [*Making no move*] E-e-e-e-eh; it's all nonsense; it was only a shadda he saw.

MARY: Mother o' God, he made me heart lep!

BENTHAM: It was simply due to an over-wrought imagination—we all get that way at times.

MRS. BOYLE: There, dear, lie doun in the bed, an' I'll put the quilt across you . . . e-c-e-eh, that's it . . .

you'll be as right as the mail in a few minutes.

JOHNNY: Mother, go into the room an' see if the light's lightin' before the statue.

MRS. BOYLE: [*To Boyle*] Jack, run in an' see if the light's lightin' before the statue.

BOYLE: [*To Mary*] Mary, slip in an' see if the light's lightin' before the statue.

[*Mary hesitates to go in*]

BENTHAM: It's all right; Mary, I'll go.

[*He goes into the room; remains for a few moments, and returns*]

BENTHAM: Everything's just as it was—the light burning bravely before the statue.

BOYLE: Of course; I knew it was all nonsense.

[*A knock at the door*]

BOYLE: [*Going to open the door*] E-e-e-e-eh.

[*He opens it, and* Joxer, *followed by* Mrs. Madigan, *enters.* Mrs. Madigan *is a strong, dapper little woman of about forty-five; her face is almost always a widespread smile of complacency. She is a woman who, in manner at least, can mourn with them that mourn, and rejoice with them that do rejoice. When she is feeling comfortable, she is inclined to be reminiscent; when others say anything, or following a statement made by herself, she has a habit of putting her head a little to one side, and nodding it rapidly several times in succession, like a bird pecking at a hard berry. Indeed, she has a good deal of the bird in her, but the bird instinct is by no means a melodious one. She is ignorant, vulgar and forward, but her heart is generous withal. For instance, she would help a neighbour's sick child; she would probably kill the child, but her intention would be to cure it; she would be more at home helping a drayman to lift a fallen horse. She is dressed in a rather soiled grey dress and a vivid purple blouse; in her hair is a huge comb, ornamented with huge coloured beads. She enters with a gliding step, beaming smile and nodding head.* Boyle *receives them effusively*]

BOYLE: Come on in, Mrs. Madigan; come on in; I was afraid you weren't comin'. . . . [*Slyly*] There's some people able to dhress, ay, Joxer?

JOXER: Fair as the blossoms that bloom in the May, an' sweet as the scent of the new-mown hay. . . . Ah, well she may wear them.

MRS. MADIGAN: [*Looking at* Mary] I know some as are as sweet as the blossoms that bloom in the May—oh, no names, no pack dhrill!

BOYLE: An' now I'll inthroduce the pair o' yous to Mary's intended: Mr. Bentham, this is Mrs. Madigan, an oul' back-parlour neighbour, that, if she could help it at all, ud never see a body shuk!

BENTHAM: [*Rising, and tentatively shaking the hand of* Mrs. Madigan] I'm sure, it's a great pleasure to know you, Mrs. Madigan.

MRS. MADIGAN: An' I'm goin' to tell you, Mr. Bentham, you're goin' to get as nice a bit o' skirt in Mary, there, as ever you seen in your puff. Not like some of the dhressed-up dolls that's knockin' about lookin' for men when it's a skelpin' they want. I remember, as well as I remember yestherday, the day she was born—of a Tuesday, the 25th o' June, in the year 1901, at thirty-three minutes past wan in the day be Foley's clock, the pub at the corner o' the street. A cowld day it was too, for the season o' the year, an' I remember sayin' to Joxer, there, who I met comin' up th' stairs, that the new arrival in Boyle's ud grow up a hardy chiselur if it lived, an' that she'd be somethin' one o' these days that nobody suspected, an' so signs on it, here she is to-day, goin' to be married to a young man lookin' as if he'd be fit to commensurate in any position in life it ud please God to call him!

BOYLE: [Effusively] Sit down, Mrs. Madigan, sit down, me oul' sport. [To Bentham] This is Joxer Daly, Past Chief Ranger of the Dear Little Shamrock Branch of the Irish National Foresters, an oul' front-top neighbour, that never despaired, even in the darkest days of Ireland's sorra.

JOXER: Nil desperandum, Captain, nil desperandum.

BOYLE: Sit down, Joxer, sit down. The two of us was ofen in a tight corner.

MRS. BOYLE: Ay, in Foley's snug!

JOXER: An' we kem out of it flyin', we kem out of it flyin', Captain.

BOYLE: An' now for a dhrink—I know yous won't refuse an oul' friend.

MRS. MADIGAN: [To Juno] Is Johnny not well, Mrs. . . .

MRS. BOYLE: [Warningly] S-s-s-sh.

MRS. MADIGAN: Oh, the poor darlin'.

BOYLE: Well, Mrs. Madigan, is it tea or what?

MRS. MADIGAN: Well, speakin' for meself, I jus' had me tea a minute ago, an' I'm afraid to dhrink any more—I'm never the same when I dhrink too much tay. Thanks, all the same, Mr. Boyle.

BOYLE: Well, what about a bottle o' stout or a dhrop o' whisky?

MRS. MADIGAN: A bottle o' stout ud be a little too heavy for me stummock afther me tay. . . . A-a-ah, I'll thry the ball o' malt.

[Boyle prepares the whisky]

MRS. MADIGAN: There's nothin' like a ball o' malt occasional like—too much of it isn't good. [To Boyle, who is adding water] Ah, God, Johnny, don't put too much wather on it! [She drinks] I suppose yous'll be lavin' this place.

BOYLE: I'm looking for a place near the sea; I'd like the place that you might say was me cradle, to be me grave as well. The sea is always callin' me.

JOXER: She is callin', callin', callin', in the win' an' on the sea.

BOYLE: Another dhrop o' whisky, Mrs. Madigan?

MRS. MADIGAN: Well, now, it ut be hard t[...] seein' the suspicious times that's in it.

BOYLE: [With a commanding gesture] Song! [...] Juno . . . Mary . . . "Home to Our Mountains[...]

MRS. MADIGAN: [Enthusiastically] Hear, hear!

JOXER: Oh, tha's a darlin' song, a daarlin' song!

MARY: [Bashfully] Ah no, da; I'm not in a singin' humour.

MRS. MADIGAN: Gawn with you, child, an' you only goin' to be marrid; I remember as well as I remember yestherday,—it was on a lovely August evenin', exactly, accordin' to date, fifteen years ago, come the Tuesday folleyin' the nex' that's comin' on, when me own man—the Lord be good to him—an' me was sittin' shy together in a doty little nook on a counthry road, adjacent to The Stiles. "That'll scratch your lovely, little white neck," says he, ketchin' hould of a danglin' bramble branch, holdin' clusters of the loveliest flowers you ever seen, an' breakin' it off, so that his arm fell, accidental like, roun' me waist, an' as I felt it tightenin', an' tightenin', an' tightenin', I thought me buzzom was every minute goin' to burst out into a roystherin' song about

The little green leaves that were shakin' on the threes,
The gallivantin' butherflies, an' buzzin' o' the bees!

BOYLE: Ordher for the song!

JUNO: Come on, Mary—we'll do our best.

[Juno and Mary stand up, and choosing a suitable position, sing simply "Home to Our Mountains"]

[They bow to company, and return to their places]

BOYLE: [Emotionally, at the end of song] Lull . . . me . . . to . . . rest!

JOXER: [Clapping his hands] Bravo, bravo! Darlin' girulls, darlin' girulls!

MRS. MADIGAN: Juno, I never seen you in betther form.

BENTHAM: Very nicely rendered indeed.

MRS. MADIGAN: A noble call, a noble call!

MRS. BOYLE: What about yourself, Mrs. Madigan?

[After some coaxing, Mrs. Madigan rises and in a quavering voice sings the following verse]

If I were a blackbird I'd whistle and sing;
I'd follow the ship that my thrue love was in;
An' on the top riggin', I'd there build me nest,
An' at night I would sleep on me Willie's white breast!

[Becoming husky, amid applause, she sits down]

MRS. MADIGAN: Ah, me voice is too husky now, Juno; though I remember the time when Maisie Madigan could sing like a nightingale at matin' time. I remember as well as I remember yestherday, at a party given to celebrate the comin' of the first

nnie an' Benny Jimeson—who was
548, yous may remember, in Henrietta
at, afther Easter Week, hung out a green,
n' orange pole, an', then, when the Tans
their Jazz dancin', whipped it in agen, an'
out a red, white an' blue wan instead, givin'
an excuse that a barber's pole was strictly non-
olitical—singin' "An' You'll Remember Me,"
with the top notes quiverin' in a dead hush of
pethrified attention, folleyed be a clappin' o' hans
that shuk the tumblers on the table, an' capped by
Jimeson, the barber, sayin' that it was the best
rendherin' of "You'll Remember Me" he ever
heard in his natural!

BOYLE: [Peremptorily] Ordher for Joxer's song!

JOXER: Ah no, I couldn't; don't ass me, Captain.

BOYLE: Joxer's song, Joxer's song—give us wan of
your shut-eyed wans.

      [Joxer settles himself in his chair;
takes a drink; clears his throat; solemnly closes his
eyes, and begins to sing in a very querulous voice]

    She is far from the lan' where her young hero
      sleeps,
    An' lovers around her are sighing [He hesitates]
    An' lovers around her are sighin' . . . sighin' . . .
    sighin' . . .

                        [A pause]

BOYLE: [Imitating Joxer]

    And lovers around her are sighing!

What's the use of you thryin' to sing the song if
you don't know it?

MARY: Thry another one, Mr. Daly—maybe you'd
be more fortunate.

MRS. MADIGAN: Gawn, Joxer; thry another wan.

JOXER: [Starting again]

    I have heard the mavis singin' his love song to
      the morn;
    I have seen the dew-dhrop clingin' to the rose
      jus' newly born; but . . . but . . . [Frantically]
    To the rose jus' newly born . . . newly born
    . . . born.

JOHNNY: Mother, put on the gramophone, for God's
sake, an' stop Joxer's bawlin'.

BOYLE: [Commandingly] Gramophone! . . . I hate to
see fellas thryin' to do what they're not able to do.
    [Boyle arranges the gramophone, and is
about to start it, when voices are heard of persons
descending the stairs]

MRS. BOYLE: [Warningly] Whisht, Jack, don't put it
on, don't put it on yet; this must be poor Mrs.
Tancred comin' down to go to the hospital—I forgot all about them bringin' the body to the church
to-night. Open the door, Mary, an' give them a bit
o' light.

[Mary opens the door, and Mrs. Tancred—a very
old woman, obviously shaken by the death of her
son—appears, accompanied by several neighbours. The first few phrases are spoken before
they appear]

FIRST NEIGHBOUR: It's a sad journey we're goin' on,
but God's good, an' the Republicans won't be always down.

MRS. TANCRED: Ah, what good is that to me now?
Whether they're up or down—it won't bring me
darlin' boy from the grave.

MRS. BOYLE: Come in an' have a hot cup o' tay, Mrs.
Tancred, before you go.

MRS. TANCRED: Ah, I can take nothin' now, Mrs.
Boyle—I won't be long afther him.

FIRST NEIGHBOUR: Still an' all, he died a noble death,
an' we'll bury him like a king.

MRS. TANCRED: An' I'll go on livin' like a pauper. Ah,
what's the pains I suffered bringin' him into the
world to carry him to his cradle, to the pains I'm
sufferin' now, carryin' him out o' the world to
bring him to his grave!

MARY: It would be better for you not to go at all,
Mrs. Tancred, but to stay at home beside the fire
with some o' the neighbours.

MRS. TANCRED: I seen the first of him, an' I'll see the
last of him.

MRS. BOYLE: You'd want a shawl, Mrs. Tancred; it's
a cowld night, an' the win's blowin' sharp.

MRS. MADIGAN: [Rushing out] I've a shawl above.

MRS. TANCRED: Me home is gone now; he was me
only child, an' to think that he was lyin' for a
whole night stretched out on the side of a lonely
counthry lane, with his head, his darlin' head, that
I often kissed an' fondled, half hidden in the
wather of a runnin' brook. An' I'm told he was the
leadher of the ambush where me nex' door neighbour, Mrs. Mannin', lost her Free State soldier son.
An' now here's the two of us oul' women, standin'
one on each side of a scales o' sorra, balanced be
the bodies of our two dead darlin' sons. [Mrs.
Madigan returns, and wraps a shawl around her]
God bless you, Mrs. Madigan. . . . [She moves
slowly towards the door] Mother o' God, Mother
o' God, have pity on the pair of us! . . . O Blessed
Virgin, where were you when me darlin' son was
riddled with bullets, when me darlin' son was
riddled with bullets! . . . Sacred Heart of the Crucified Jesus, take away our hearts o' stone . . . an' give
us hearts o' flesh! . . . Take away this murdherin'
hate . . . an' give us Thine own eternal love!
              [They pass out of the room]

MRS. BOYLE: [Explanatorily to Bentham] That was
Mrs. Tancred of the two-pair back; her son was
found, e'er yesterday, lyin' out beyant Finglas
riddled with bullets. A Die-hard he was, be all accounts. He was a nice quiet boy, but latherly he
went to hell, with his Republic first, an' Republic
last an' Republic over all. He often took tea with

us here, in the oul' days, an' Johnny, there, an' him used to be always together.

JOHNNY: Am I always to be havin' to tell you that he was no friend o' mine? I never cared for him, an' he could never stick me. It's not because he was Commandant of the Battalion that I was Quarther-Masther of, that we were friends.

MRS. BOYLE: He's gone now—the Lord be good to him! God help his poor oul' creature of a mother, for no matther whose friend or enemy he was, he was her poor son.

BENTHAM: The whole thing is terrible, Mrs. Boyle; but the only way to deal with a mad dog is to destroy him.

MRS. BOYLE: An' to think of me forgettin' about him bein' brought to the church to-night, an' we singin' an' all, but it was well we hadn't the gramophone goin', anyhow.

BOYLE: Even if we had aself. We've nothin' to do with these things, one way or t'other. That's the Government's business, an' let them do what we're payin' them for doin'.

MRS. BOYLE: I'd like to know how a body's not to mind these things; look at the way they're afther leavin' the people in this very house. Hasn't the whole house, nearly, been massacreed? There's young Dougherty's husband with his leg off; Mrs. Travers that had her son blew up be a mine in Inchegeela, in Co. Cork; Mrs. Mannin' that lost wan of her sons in ambush a few weeks ago, an' now, poor Mrs. Tancred's only child gone west with his body made a collandher of. Sure, if it's not our business, I don't know whose business it is.

BOYLE: Here, there, that's enough about them things; they don't affect us, an' we needn't give a damn. If they want a wake, well, let them have a wake. When I was a sailor, I was always resigned to meet with a wathery grave; an' if they want to be soldiers, well, there's no use o' them squealin' when they meet a soldier's fate.

JOXER: Let me like a soldier fall—me breast expandin' to th' ball!

MRS. BOYLE: In wan way, she deserves all she got; for lately, she let th' Die-hards make an open house of th' place; an' for th' last couple of months, either when th' sun was risin' or when th' sun was settin', you had C.I.D. men burstin' into your room, assin' you where were you born, where were you christened, where were you married, an' where would you be buried!

JOHNNY: For God's sake, let us have no more o' this talk.

MRS. MADIGAN: What about Mr. Boyle's song before we start th' gramophone?

MARY: [Getting her hat, and putting it on] Mother, Charlie and I are goin' out for a little sthroll.

MRS. BOYLE: All right, darlin'.

BENTHAM: [Going out with Mary] We won't be long away, Mrs. Boyle.

MRS. MADIGAN: Gwan, Captain, gwan.

BOYLE: E-e-e-e-eh, I'd want to have a few more [me, before I'd be in fettle for singin'.

JOXER: Give us that poem you writ t'other day. [the rest] Aw, it's a darlin' poem, a daarlin' poem.

MRS. BOYLE: God bless us, is he startin' to write poetry!

BOYLE: [Rising to his feet] E-e-e-e-eh.
[He recites in an emotional, consequential manner the following verses]

Shawn an' I were friends, sir, to me he was all in all.
His work was very heavy and his wages were very small.
None betther on th' beach as Docker, I'll go bail,
'Tis now I'm feelin' lonely, for to-day he lies in jail.
He was not what some call pious—seldom at church or prayer;
For the greatest scoundrels I know, sir, goes every Sunday there.
Fond of his pint—well, rather, but hated the Boss by creed
But never refused a copper to comfort a pal in need.

E-e-e-e-eh.   [He sits down]

MRS. MADIGAN: Grand, grand; you should folly that up, you should folly that up.

JOXER: It's a daarlin' poem!

BOYLE: [Delightedly] E-e-e-e-eh.

JOHNNY: Are yous goin' to put on th' gramophone to-night, or are yous not?

MRS. BOYLE: Gwan, Jack, put on a record.

MRS. MADIGAN: Gwan, Captain, gwan.

BOYLE: Well, yous'll want to keep a dead silence.
[He sets a record, starts the machine, and it begins to play "If you're Irish, come into the Parlour." As the tune is in full blare, the door is suddenly opened by a brisk, little bald-headed man, dressed circumspectly in a black suit; he glares fiercely at all in the room; he is Needle Nugent, a tailor. He carries his hat in his hand]

NUGENT: [Loudly, above the noise of the gramophone] Are yous goin' to have that thing bawlin' an' the funeral of Mrs. Tancred's son passin' the house? Have none of yous any respect for the Irish people's National regard for the dead?
[Boyle stops the gramophone]

MRS. BOYLE: Maybe, Needle Nugent, it's nearly time we had a little less respect for the dead, an' a little more regard for the livin'.

MRS. MADIGAN: We don't want you, Mr. Nugent, to teach us what we learned at our mother's knee. You don't look yourself as if you were dyin' of grief; if y'ass Maisie Madigan anything, I'd call you a real thrue Die-hard an' live-soft Republican,

epublican funerals in the day, an'
55 half the night makin' suits for the
ards!

[*Persons are heard running down to the
, some saying, "Here it is, here it is." Nugent
draws, and the rest, except* Johnny, *go to the
ndow looking into the street, and look out.
ounds of a crowd coming nearer are heard; portion are singing*]

To Jesus' Heart all burning
With fervent love for men,
My heart with fondest yearning
Shall raise its joyful strain.
While ages course along,
Blest be with loudest song
The Sacred Heart of Jesus
By every heart and tongue.

MRS. BOYLE: Here's the hearse, here's the hearse!

BOYLE: There's t'oul' mother walkin' behin' the coffin.

MRS. MADIGAN: You can hardly see the coffin with the wreaths.

JOXER: Oh, it's a darlin' funeral, a daarlin' funeral!

MRS. MADIGAN: We'd have a betther view from the street.

BOYLE: Yes—this place ud give you a crick in your neck.

[*They leave the room, and go down.*
Johnny *sits moodily by the fire*]

[*A young man enters; he looks at* Johnny *for a moment*]

THE YOUNG MAN: Quarther-Masther Boyle.

JOHNNY: [*With a start*] The Mobilizer!

THE YOUNG MAN: You're not at the funeral?

JOHNNY: I'm not well.

THE YOUNG MAN: I'm glad I've found you; you were stoppin' at your aunt's; I called there but you'd gone. I've to give you an ordher to attend a Battalion Staff meetin' the night afther to-morrow.

JOHNNY: Where?

THE YOUNG MAN: I don't know; you're to meet me at the Pillar at eight o'clock; then we're to go to a place I'll be told of to-night; there we'll meet a mothor that'll bring us to the meeting. They think you might be able to know somethin' about them that gave the bend where Commandant Tancred was shelterin'.

JOHNNY: I'm not goin', then. I know nothing about Tancred.

THE YOUNG MAN: [*At the door*] You'd betther come for your own sake—remember your oath.

JOHNNY: [*Passionately*] I won't go! Haven't I done enough for Ireland! I've lost me arm, an' me hip's desthroyed so that I'll never be able to walk right agen! Good God, haven't I done enough for Ireland?

THE YOUNG MAN: Boyle, no man can do enough for Ireland!   [*He goes*]
[*Faintly in the distance the crowd is heard saying*]

Hail, Mary, full of grace, the Lord is with Thee;
Blessed art Thou amongst women, and blessed,
etc.

Act III

The same as Act II. It is about half-past six on a November evening; a bright fire burns in the grate; Mary, *dressed to go out, is sitting on a chair by the fire, leaning forward, her hands under her chin, her elbows on her knees. A look of dejection, mingled with uncertain anxiety, is on her face. A lamp, turned low, is lighting on the table. The votive light under the picture of the Virgin gleams more redly than ever.* Mrs. Boyle *is putting on her hat and coat. It is two months later.*

MRS. BOYLE: An' has Bentham never even written to you since—not one line for the past month?

MARY: [*Tonelessly*] Not even a line, mother.

MRS. BOYLE: That's very curious. . . . What came between the two of yous at all? To leave you so sudden, an' yous so great together. . . . To go away t' England, an' not to even leave you his address. . . . The way he was always bringin' you to dances, I thought he was mad afther you. Are you sure you said nothin' to him?

MARY: No, mother—at least nothing that could possibly explain his givin' me up.

MRS. BOYLE: You know you're a bit hasty at times, Mary, an' say things you shouldn't say.

MARY: I never said to him what I shouldn't say, I'm sure of that.

MRS. BOYLE: How are you sure of it?

MARY: Because I love him with all my heart and soul, mother. Why, I don't know; I often thought to myself that he wasn't the man poor Jerry was, but I couldn't help loving him, all the same.

MRS. BOYLE: But you shouldn't be frettin' the way you are; when a woman loses a man, she never knows what she's afther losin', to be sure, but, then, she never knows what she's afther gainin', either. You're not the one girl of a month ago—you look like one pinin' away. It's long ago I had a right to bring you to the doctor, instead of waitin' till to-night.

MARY: There's no necessity, really, mother, to go to the doctor; nothing serious is wrong with me—I'm run down and disappointed, that's all.

MRS. BOYLE: I'll not wait another minute; I don't like the look of you at all. . . . I'm afraid we made a mistake in throwin' over poor Jerry. . . . He'd have been betther for you than that Bentham.

MARY: Mother, the best man for a woman is the one for whom she has the most love, and Charlie had it all.

MRS. BOYLE: Well, there's one thing to be said for him—he couldn't have been thinkin' of the money, or he wouldn't ha' left you . . . it must ha' been somethin' else.

MARY: [*Wearily*] I don't know . . . I don't know, mother . . . only I think . . .

MRS. BOYLE: What d'ye think?

MARY: I imagine . . . he thought . . . we weren't . . . good enough for him.

MRS. BOYLE: An' what was he himself, only a school teacher? Though I don't blame him for fightin' shy of people like that Joxer fella an' that oul' Madigan wan—nice sort o' people for your father to introduce to a man like Mr. Bentham. You might have told me all about this before now, Mary; I don't know why you like to hide everything from your mother; you knew Bentham, an' I'd ha' known nothin' about it if it hadn't bin for the Will; an' it was only to-day, afther long coaxin', that you let out that he's left you.

MARY: It would have been useless to tell you—you wouldn't understand.

MRS. BOYLE: [*Hurt*] Maybe not. . . . Maybe I wouldn't understand. . . . Well, we'll be off now.
[*She goes over to door left, and speaks to Boyle inside*]

MRS. BOYLE: We're goin' now to the doctor's. Are you goin' to get up this evenin'?

BOYLE: [*From inside*] The pains in me legs is terrible! It's me should be poppin' off to the doctor instead o' Mary, the way I feel.

MRS. BOYLE: Sorra mend you! A nice way you were in last night—carried in in a frog's march, dead to the world. If that's the way you'll go on when you get the money it'll be the grave for you, an asylum for me and the Poorhouse for Johnny.

BOYLE: I thought you were goin'?

MRS. BOYLE: That's what has you as you are—you can't bear to be spoken to. Knowin' the way we are, up to our ears in debt, it's a wondher you wouldn't ha' got up to go to th' solicitor's an' see if we could ha' gotten a little o' the money even.

BOYLE: [*Shouting*] I can't be goin' up there night, noon an' mornin', can I? He can't give the money till he gets it, can he? I can't get blood out of a turnip, can I?

MRS. BOYLE: It's nearly two months since we heard of the Will, an' the money seems as far off as ever. . . . I suppose you know we owe twenty pouns to oul' Murphy?

BOYLE: I've a faint recollection of you tellin' me that before.

MRS. BOYLE: Well, you'll go over to the shop yourself for the things in future—I'll face him no more.

BOYLE: I thought you said you were goin'?

MRS. BOYLE: I'm goin' now; come on, Mary.

BOYLE: Ey, Juno, ey!

MRS. BOYLE: Well, what d'ye want now?

BOYLE: Is there e'er a bottle o' stout left?

MRS. BOYLE: There's two o' them here still.

BOYLE: Show us in one o' them an' leave t'other there till I get up. An' throw us in the paper that's on the table, an' the bottle o' Sloan's Liniment that's in th' drawer.

MRS. BOYLE: [*Getting the liniment and the stout*] What paper is it you want—the *Messenger*?

BOYLE: *Messenger*! The *News o' the World*!
[*Mrs. Boyle brings in the things asked for, and comes out again*]

MRS. BOYLE: [*At door*] Mind the candle, now, an' don't burn the house over our heads. I left t'other bottle o' stout on the table.
[*She puts bottle of stout on table. She goes out with Mary. A cork is heard popping inside*]

[*A pause; then outside the door is heard the voice of Joxer lilting softly: "Me pipe I'll smoke, as I dhrive me moke . . . are you . . . there . . . Mor . . . ee . . . ar . . . i . . . teee!" A gentle knock is heard, and after a pause the door opens, and Joxer, followed by Nugent, enters*]

JOXER: Be God, they must be all out; I was thinkin' there was somethin' up when he didn't answer the signal. We seen Juno an' Mary goin', but I didn't see him, an' it's very seldom he escapes me.

NUGENT: He's not goin' to escape me—he's not goin' to be let go to the fair altogether.

JOXER: Sure, the house couldn't hould them lately; an' he goin' about like a mastherpiece of the Free State counthry; forgettin' their friends; forgettin' God—wouldn't even lift his hat passin' a chapel! Sure they were bound to get a dhrop! An' you really think there's no money comin' to him afther all?

NUGENT: Not as much as a red rex, man; I've been a bit anxious this long time over me money, an' I went up to the solicitor's to find out all I could—ah, man, they were goin' to throw me down the stairs. They toul' me that the oul' cock himself had the stairs worn away comin' up afther it, an' they black in the face tellin' him he'd get nothin'. Some way or another that the Will is writ he won't be entitled to get as much as a make!

JOXER: Ah, I thought there was somethin' curious about the whole thing; I've bin havin' sthrange dhreams for the last couple o' weeks. An' I notice that that Bentham fella doesn't be comin' here now—there must be somethin' on the mat there too. Anyhow, who, in the name o' God, ud leave anythin' to that oul' bummer? Sure it ud be unnatural. An' the way Juno an' him's been throwin' their weight about for the last few months! Ah, him that goes a borrowin' goes a sorrowin'!

NUGENT: Well, he's not goin' to throw his weight

about in the suit I made for him much longer. I'm
tellin' you seven pouns aren't to be found growin'
on the bushes these days.

JOXER: An' there isn't hardly a neighbour in the
whole street that hasn't lent him money on the
strength of what he was goin' to get, but they're
after backing the wrong horse. Wasn't it a mercy
o' God that I'd nothin' to give him! The softy I
am, you know, I'd ha' lent him me last juice! I
must have had somebody's good prayers. Ah, afther
all, an honest man's the noblest work o' God!

                                    [Boyle coughs inside]

JOXER: Whisht, damn it, he must be inside in bed.

NUGENT: Inside o' bed or outside of it, he's goin' to
pay me for that suit, or give it back—he'll not
climb up my back as easily as he thinks.

JOXER: Gwan in at wanst, man, an' get it off him,
an' don't be a fool.

NUGENT: [Going to door left, opening it and looking
in] Ah, don't disturb yourself, Mr. Boyle; I hope
you're not sick?

BOYLE: Th' oul' legs, Mr. Nugent, the oul' legs.

NUGENT: I just called over to see if you could let me
have anything off the suit.

BOYLE: E-e-e-eh, how much is this it is?

NUGENT: It's the same as it was at the start—seven
pouns.

BOYLE: I'm glad you kem, Mr. Nugent; I want a good
heavy top-coat—Irish frieze, if you have it. How
much would a top-coat like that be, now?

NUGENT: About six pouns.

BOYLE: Six pouns—six an' seven, six an' seven is
thirteen—that'll be thirteen pouns I'll owe you.
[Joxer slips the bottle of stout that is on the table
into his pocket. Nugent rushes into the room, and
returns with suit on his arm; he pauses at the door]

NUGENT: You'll owe me no thirteen pouns. Maybe
you think you're betther able to owe it than pay it!

BOYLE: [Frantically] Here, come back to hell ower
that—where're you goin' with them clothes o'
mine?

NUGENT: Where am I goin' with them clothes o'
yours? Well, I like your damn cheek!

BOYLE: Here, what am I goin' to dhress meself in
when I'm goin' out?

NUGENT: What do I care what you dhress yourself in!
You can put yourself in a bolsther cover, if you
like.
[He goes towards the other door, followed by Joxer]

JOXER: What'll he dhress himself in! Gentleman
Jack an' his frieze coat!   [They go out]

BOYLE: [Inside] Ey, Nugent; ey, Mr. Nugent, Mr.
Nugent!

[After a pause Boyle enters hastily, buttoning the
braces of his moleskin trousers; his coat and vest
are on his arm; he throws these on a chair and
hurries to the door on right]

BOYLE: Ey, Mr. Nugent, Mr. Nugent!

JOXER: [Meeting him at the door] What's up, what's
wrong, Captain?

BOYLE: Nugent's been here an' took away me suit—
the only things I had to go out in!

JOXER: Tuk your suit—for God's sake! An' what were
you doin' while he was takin' them?

BOYLE: I was in bed when he stole in like a thief in
the night, an' before I knew even what he was
thinkin' of, he whipped them from the chair an'
was off like a redshank!

JOXER: An' what, in the name o' God, did he do that
for?

BOYLE: What did he do it for? How the hell do I
know what he done it for?—jealousy an' spite, I
suppose.

JOXER: Did he not say what he done it for?

BOYLE: Amn't I afther tellin' you that he had them
whipped up an' was gone before I could open me
mouth?

JOXER: That was a very sudden thing to do; there
mus' be somethin' behin' it. Did he hear anythin',
I wondher?

BOYLE: Did he hear anythin'?—you talk very queer,
Joxer—what could he hear?

JOXER: About you not gettin' the money, in some
way or t'other?

BOYLE: An' what ud prevent me from gettin' th'
money?

JOXER: That's jus' what I was thinkin'—what ud prevent you from gettin' the money—nothin', as far
as I can see.

BOYLE: [Looking round for bottle of stout, with an
exclamation] Aw, holy God!

JOXER: What's up, Jack?

BOYLE: He must have afther lifted the bottle o' stout
that Juno left on the table!

JOXER: [Horrified] Ah no, ah no; he wouldn't be
afther doin' that now.

BOYLE: An' who done it then? Juno left a bottle o'
stout here, an' it's gone—it didn't walk, did it?

JOXER: Oh, that's shockin'; ah, man's inhumanity to
man makes countless thousands mourn!

MRS. MADIGAN: [Appearing at the door] I hope I'm
not disturbin' you in any discussion on your forth-
comin' legacy—if I may use the word—an' that
you'll let me have a barny for a minute or two with
you, Mr. Boyle.

BOYLE: [Uneasily] To be sure, Mrs. Madigan—an
oul' friend's always welcome.

JOXER: Come in the evenin', come in th' mornin';
come when you're assed, or come without warnin',
Mrs. Madigan.

BOYLE: Sit down, Mrs. Madigan.

MRS. MADIGAN: [Ominously] Th' few words I have to
say can be said standin'. Puttin' aside all formu-
laries, I suppose you remember me lendin' you
some time ago three pouns that I raised on blankets
an' furniture in me uncle's?

BOYLE: I remember it well. I have it recorded in

me book—three pouns five shillins from Maisie Madigan, raised on articles pawned; an', item: fourpence, given to make up the price of a pint, on th' principle that no bird ever flew on wan wing; all to be repaid at par, when the ship comes home.

MRS. MADIGAN: Well, ever since I shoved in the blankets I've been perishing with th' cowld, an' I've decided, if I'll be too hot in th' nex' world aself, I'm not goin' to be too cowld in this wan; an' consequently, I want me three pouns, if you please.

BOYLE: This is a very sudden demand, Mrs. Madigan, an' can't be met; but I'm willin' to give you a receipt in full, in full.

MRS. MADIGAN: Come on, out with th' money, an' don't be jack-actin'.

BOYLE: You can't get blood out of a turnip, can you?

MRS. MADIGAN: [Rushing over and shaking him] Gimme me money, y'oul' reprobate, or I'll shake the worth of it out of you!

BOYLE: Ey, houl' on, there; houl' on, there! You'll wait for your money now, me lassie!

MRS. MADIGAN: [Looking around the room and seeing the gramophone] I'll wait for it, will I? Well, I'll not wait long; if I can't get th' cash, I'll get th' worth of it.   [She catches up the gramophone]

BOYLE: Ey, ey, there, wher'r you goin' with that?

MRS. MADIGAN: I'm goin' to th' pawn to get me three quid five shillins; I'll brin' you th' ticket, an' then you can do what you like, me bucko.

BOYLE: You can't touch that, you can't touch that! It's not my property, an' it's not ped for yet!

MRS. MADIGAN: So much th' betther. It'll be an ayse to me conscience, for I'm takin' what doesn't belong to you. You're not goin' to be swankin' it like a paycock with Maisie Madigan's money—I'll pull some o' th' gorgeous feathers out o' your tail!
          [She goes off with the gramophone]

BOYLE: What's th' world comin' to at all? I ass you, Joxer Daly, is there any morality left anywhere?

JOXER: I wouldn't ha' believed it, only I seen it with me own two eyes. I didn't think Maisie Madigan was that sort of woman; she has either a sup taken, or she's heard somethin'.

BOYLE: Heard somethin'—about what, if it's not any harm to ass you?

JOXER: She must ha' heard some rumour or other that you weren't goin' to get th' money.

BOYLE: Who says I'm not goin' to get th' money?

JOXER: Sure, I don't know—I was only sayin'.

BOYLE: Only sayin' what?

JOXER: Nothin'.

BOYLE: You were goin' to say somethin'—don't be a twisther.

JOXER: [Angrily] Who's a twisther?

BOYLE: Why don't you speak your mind, then?

JOXER: You never twisted yourself—no, you wouldn't know how!

BOYLE: Did you ever know me to twist; did you ever know me to twist?

JOXER: [Fiercely] Did you ever do anythin' else! Sure, you can't believe a word that comes out o' your mouth.

BOYLE: Here, get out, ower o' this; I always knew you were a prognosticator an' a procrastinator!

JOXER: [Going out as Johnny comes in] The anchor's weighed, farewell, ree . . . mem . . . ber . . . me. Jacky Boyle, Esquire, infernal rogue an' damned liar.

JOHNNY: Joxer an' you at it agen?—when are you goin' to have a little respect for yourself, an' not be always makin' a show of us all?

BOYLE: Are you goin' to lecture me now?

JOHNNY: Is mother back from the doctor yet, with Mary?

[Mrs. Boyle enters; it is apparent from the serious look on her face that something has happened. She takes off her hat and coat without a word and puts them by. She then sits down near the fire, and there is a few moments' pause]

BOYLE: Well, what did the doctor say about Mary?

MRS. BOYLE: [In an earnest manner and with suppressed agitation] Sit down here, Jack; I've something to say to you . . . about Mary.

BOYLE: [Awed by her manner] About . . . Mary?

MRS. BOYLE: Close that door there and sit down here.

BOYLE: [Closing the door] More throuble in our native land, is it? [He sits down] Well, what is it?

MRS. BOYLE: It's about Mary.

BOYLE: Well, what about Mary—there's nothin' wrong with her, is there?

MRS. BOYLE: I'm sorry to say there's a gradle wrong with her.

BOYLE: A gradle wrong with her! [Peevishly] First Johnny an' now Mary; is the whole house goin' to become an hospital! It's not consumption, is it?

MRS. BOYLE: No . . . it's not consumption . . . it's worse.

JOHNNY: Worse! Well, we'll have to get her into some place ower this, there's no one here to mind her.

MRS. BOYLE: We'll all have to mind her now. You might as well know now, Johnny, as another time. [To Boyle] D'ye know what the doctor said to me about her, Jack?

BOYLE: How ud I know—I wasn't there, was I?

MRS. BOYLE: He told me to get her married at wanst.

BOYLE: Married at wanst! An' why did he say the like o' that?

MRS. BOYLE: Because Mary's goin' to have a baby in a short time.

BOYLE: Goin' to have a baby!—my God, what'll Bentham say when he hears that?

MRS. BOYLE: Are you blind, man, that you can't see that it was Bentham that has done this wrong to her?

BOYLE: [*Passionately*] Then he'll marry her, he'll have to marry her!

MRS. BOYLE: You know he's gone to England, an' God knows where he is now.

BOYLE: I'll folly him, I'll folly him, an' bring him back, an' make him do her justice. The scoundrel, I might ha' known what he was, with his yogees an' his prawna!

MRS. BOYLE: We'll have to keep it quiet till we see what we can do.

BOYLE: Oh, isn't this a nice thing to come on top o' me, an' the state I'm in! A pretty show I'll be to Joxer an' to that oul' wan, Madigan! Amn't I afther goin' through enough without havin' to go through this!

MRS. BOYLE: What you an' I'll have to go through'll be nothin' to what poor Mary'll have to go through; for you an' me is middlin' old, an' most of our years is spent; but Mary'll have maybe forty years to face an' handle, an' every wan of them'll be tainted with a bitther memory.

BOYLE: Where is she? Where is she till I tell her off? I'm tellin' you when I'm done with her she'll be a sorry girl!

MRS. BOYLE: I left her in me sister's till I came to speak to you. You'll say nothin' to her, Jack; ever since she left school she's earned her livin', an' your fatherly care never throubled the poor girl.

BOYLE: Gwan, take her part agen her father! But I'll let you see whether I'll say nothin' to her or no! Her an' her readin'! That's more o' th' blasted nonsense that has the house fallin' down on top of us! What did th' likes of her, born in a tenement house, want with readin'? Her readin's afther bringin' her to a nice pass—oh, it's madnin', madnin', madnin'!

MRS. BOYLE: When she comes back say nothin' to her, Jack, or she'll leave this place.

BOYLE: Leave this place! Ay, she'll leave this place, an' quick too!

MRS. BOYLE: If Mary goes, I'll go with her.

BOYLE: Well, go with her! Well, go, th' pair o' yous! I lived before I seen yous, an' I can live when yous are gone. Isn't this a nice thing to come rollin' in on top o' me afther all your prayin' to St. Anthony an' The Little Flower! An' she's a Child o' Mary, too—I wonder what'll the nuns think of her now? An' it'll be bellows'd all over th' disthrict before you could say Jack Robinson; an' whenever I'm seen they'll whisper, "That's th' father of Mary Boyle that had th' kid be th' swank she used to go with; d'ye know, d'ye know?" To be sure they'll know—more about it than I will meself!

JOHNNY: She should be dhriven out o' th' house she's brought disgrace on!

MRS. BOYLE: Hush, you, Johnny. We needn't let it be bellows'd all over the place; all we've got to do is to leave this place quietly an' go somewhere where we're not known, an' nobody'll be th' wiser.

BOYLE: You're talkin' like a two-year-oul', woman. Where'll we get a place ou' o' this?—places aren't that easily got.

MRS. BOYLE: But, Jack, when we get the money . . .

BOYLE: Money—what money?

MRS. BOYLE: Why, oul' Ellison's money, of course.

BOYLE: There's no money comin' from oul' Ellison, or any one else. Since you've heard of wan throuble, you might as well hear of another. There's no money comin' to us at all—the Will's a wash-out!

MRS. BOYLE: What are you sayin', man—no money?

JOHNNY: How could it be a wash-out?

BOYLE: The boyo that's afther doin' it to Mary done it to me as well. The thick made out the Will wrong; he said in th' Will, only first cousin an' second cousin, instead of mentionin' our names, an' now any one that thinks he's a first cousin or second cousin t'oul' Ellison can claim the money as well as me, an' they're springin' up in hundreds, an' comin' from America an' Australia, thinkin' to get their whack out of it, while all the time the lawyers is gobblin' it up, till there's not as much as ud buy a stockin' for your lovely daughter's baby!

MRS. BOYLE: I don't believe it, I don't believe it, I don't believe it!

JOHNNY: Why did you say nothin' about this before?

MRS. BOYLE: You're not serious, Jack; you're not serious!

BOYLE: I'm tellin' you the scholar, Bentham, made a banjax o' th' Will; instead o' sayin', "th' rest o' me property to be divided between me first cousin, Jack Boyle, an' me second cousin, Mick Finnegan, o' Santhry," he writ down only, "me first an' second cousins," an' the world an' his wife are afther th' property now.

MRS. BOYLE: Now I know why Bentham left poor Mary in th' lurch; I can see it all now—oh, is there not even a middlin' honest man left in th' world?

JOHNNY: [*To Boyle*] An' you let us run into debt, an' you borreyed money from everybody to fill yourself with beer! An' now you tell us the whole thing's a washout! Oh, if it's thrue, I'm done with you, for you're worse than me sisther Mary!

BOYLE: You hole your tongue, d'ye hear? I'll not take any lip from you. Go an' get Bentham if you want satisfaction for all that's afther happenin' us.

JOHNNY: I won't hole me tongue, I won't hole me tongue! I'll tell you what I think of you, father an' all as you are . . . you . . .

MRS. BOYLE: Johnny, Johnny, Johnny, for God's sake, be quiet!

JOHNNY: I'll not be quiet, I'll not be quiet; he's a nice father, isn't he? Is it any wondher Mary went asthray, when . . .

MRS. BOYLE: Johnny, Johnny, for my sake be quiet—for your mother's sake!

BOYLE: I'm goin' out now to have a few dhrinks with th' last few makes I have, an' tell that lassie o' yours not to be here when I come back; for if I lay me eyes on her, I'll lay me hans on her, an' if I lay me hans on her, I won't be accountable for me actions!

JOHNNY: Take care somebody doesn't lay his hands on you—y'oul' . . .

MRS. BOYLE: Johnny, Johnny!

BOYLE: [*At door, about to go out*] Oh, a nice son, an' a nicer daughter, I have. [*Calling loudly upstairs*] Joxer, Joxer, are you there?

JOXER: [*From a distance*] I'm here, More . . . ee . . . aar . . . i . . . tee!

BOYLE: I'm goin' down to Foley's—are you comin'?

JOXER: Come with you? With that sweet call me heart is stirred; I'm only waiting for the word, an' I'll be with you, like a bird!

[*Boyle and* Joxer *pass the door going out*]

JOHNNY: [*Throwing himself on the bed*] I've a nice sisther, an' a nice father, there's no bettin' on it. I wish to God a bullet or a bomb had whipped me ou' o' this long ago! Not one o' yous, not one o' yous, have any thought for me!

MRS. BOYLE: [*With passionate remonstrance*] If you don't whisht, Johnny, you'll drive me mad. Who has kep' th' home together for the past few years —only me? An' who'll have to bear th' biggest part o' this throuble but me?—but whinin' an' whingin' isn't goin' to do any good.

JOHNNY: You're to blame yourself for a gradle of it —givin' him his own way in everything, an' never assin' to check him, no matther what he done. Why didn't you look afther th' money? why . . .

[*There is a knock at the door;* Mrs. Boyle *opens it;* Johnny *rises on his elbow to look and listen; two men enter*]

FIRST MAN: We've been sent up be th' Manager of the Hibernian Furnishing Co., Mrs. Boyle, to take back the furniture that was got a while ago.

MRS. BOYLE: Yous'll touch nothin' here—how do I know who yous are?

FIRST MAN: [*Showing a paper*] There's the ordher, ma'am. [*Reading*] A chest o' drawers, a table, wan easy an' two ordinary chairs; wan mirror; wan chesterfield divan, an' a wardrobe an' two vases. [*To his comrade*] Come on, Bill, it's afther knockin'-off time already.

JOHNNY: For God's sake, mother, run down to Foley's an' bring father back, or we'll be left without a stick.

[*The men carry out the table*]

MRS. BOYLE: What good would it be?—you heard what he said before he went out.

JOHNNY: Can't you thry? He ought to be here, an' the like of this goin' on.

[Mrs. Boyle *puts a shawl around her, as* Mary *enters*]

MARY: What's up, mother? I met men carryin' away the table, an' everybody's talking about us not gettin' the money after all.

MRS. BOYLE: Everythin's gone wrong, Mary, everythin'. We're not gettin' a penny out o' the Will, not a penny—I'll tell you all when I come back; I'm goin' for your father.   [*She runs out*]

JOHNNY: [*To* Mary, *who has sat down by the fire*] It's a wondher you're not ashamed to show your face here, afther what has happened.

[Jerry *enters slowly; there is a look of earnest hope on his face. He looks at* Mary *for a few moments*[

JERRY: [*Softly*] Mary!

[Mary *does not answer*]

JERRY: Mary, I want to speak to you for a few moments, may I?

[Mary *remains silent;* Johnny *goes slowly into room on left*]

JERRY: Your mother has told me everything, Mary, and I have come to you. . . . I have come to tell you, Mary, that my love for you is greater and deeper than ever. . . .

MARY: [*With a sob*] Oh, Jerry, Jerry, say no more; all that is over now; anything like that is impossible now!

JERRY: Impossible? Why do you talk like that, Mary?

MARY: After all that has happened.

JERRY: What does it matter what has happened? We are young enough to be able to forget all those things. [*He catches her hand*] Mary, Mary, I am pleading for your love. With Labour, Mary, humanity is above everything; we are the Leaders in the fight for a new life. I want to forget Bentham, I want to forget that you left me—even for a while.

MARY: Oh, Jerry, Jerry, you haven't the bitter word of scorn for me after all.

JERRY: [*Passionately*] Scorn! I love you, love you, Mary!

MARY: [*Rising, and looking him in the eyes*] Even though . . .

JERRY: Even though you threw me over for another man; even though you gave me many a bitter word!

MARY: Yes, yes, I know; but you love me, even though . . . even though . . . I'm . . . goin' . . . goin' . . . [*He looks at her questioningly, and fear gathers in his eyes*] Ah, I was thinkin' so. . . . You don't know everything!

JERRY: [*Poignantly*] Surely to God, Mary, you don't mean that . . . that . . . that . . .

MARY: Now you know all, Jerry; now you know all!

JERRY: My God, Mary, have you fallen as low as that?

MARY: Yes, Jerry, as you say, I have fallen as low as that.

JERRY: I didn't mean it that way, Mary . . . it came on me so sudden, that I didn't mind what I was sayin'. . . . I never expected this—your mother

never told me. . . . I'm sorry . . . God knows,
I'm sorry for you, Mary.

MARY: Let us say no more, Jerry; I don't blame you
for thinkin' it's terrible. . . . I suppose it is. . . .
Everybody'll think the same . . . it's only as I expected—your humanity is just as narrow as the
humanity of the others.

JERRY: I'm sorry, all the same. . . . I shouldn't have
troubled you. . . . I wouldn't if I'd known. . . .
If I can do anything for you . . . Mary . . . I
will.

[He turns to go, and halts at the door]

MARY: Do you remember, Jerry, the verses you read
when you gave the lecture in the Socialist Rooms
some time ago, on Humanity's Strife with Nature?

JERRY: The verses—no; I don't remember them.

MARY: I do. They're runnin' in me head now—

An' we felt the power that fashion'd
All the lovely things we saw,
That created all the murmur
Of an everlasting law,
Was a hand of force an' beauty,
With an eagle's tearin' claw.

Then we saw our globe of beauty
Was an ugly thing as well,
A hymn divine whose chorus
Was an agonizin' yell;
Like the story of a demon,
That an angel had to tell;

Like a glowin' picture by a
Hand unsteady, brought to ruin;
Like her craters, if their deadness
Could give life unto the moon;
Like the agonizing horror
Of a violin out of tune.

[There is a pause, and Devine goes slowly out]

JOHNNY: [Returning] Is he gone?

MARY: Yes.

[The two men re-enter]

FIRST MAN: We can't wait any longer for t'oul' fella
—sorry, Miss, but we have to live as well as th'
nex' man.   [They carry out some things]

JOHNNY: Oh, isn't this terrible! . . . I suppose you
told him everything . . . couldn't you have waited
for a few days? . . . he'd have stopped th' takin'
of the things, if you'd kep' your mouth shut. Are
you burnin' to tell every one of the shame you've
brought on us?

MARY: [Snatching up her hat and coat] Oh, this is
unbearable!   [She rushes out]

FIRST MAN: [Re-entering] We'll take the chest o'
drawers next—it's the heaviest.

[The votive light flickers for a moment,
and goes out]

JOHNNY: [In a cry of fear] Mother o' God, the light's
afther goin' out!

FIRST MAN: You put the win' up me the way you
bawled that time. The oil's all gone, that's all.

JOHNNY: [With an agonizing cry] Mother o' God,
there's a shot I'm afther gettin'!

FIRST MAN: What's wrong with you, man? Is it a fit
you're takin'?

JOHNNY: I'm afther feelin' a pain in me breast, like
the tearin' by of a bullet!

FIRST MAN: He's goin' mad—it's a wondher they'd
leave a chap like that here by himself.

[Two Irregulars enter swiftly; they carry revolvers;
one goes over to Johnny; the other covers the
two furniture men]

FIRST IRREGULAR: [To the men, quietly and inci-
sively] Who are you?—what are yous doin' here?
—quick!

FIRST MAN: Removin' furniture that's not paid for.

IRREGULAR: Get over to the other end of the room
an' turn your faces to the wall—quick!

[The two men turn their faces to the
wall, with their hands up]

SECOND IRREGULAR: [To Johnny] Come on, Sean
Boyle, you're wanted; some of us have a word to
say to you.

JOHNNY: I'm sick, I can't—what do you want with
me?

SECOND IRREGULAR: Come on, come on; we've a distance to go, an' haven't much time—come on.

JOHNNY: I'm an oul' comrade—yous wouldn't shoot
an oul' comrade.

SECOND IRREGULAR: Poor Tancred was an oul' comrade o' yours, but you didn't think o' that when
you gave him away to the gang that sent him to his
grave. But we've no time to waste; come on—here,
Dermot, ketch his arm. [To Johnny] Have you
your beads?

JOHNNY: Me beads! Why do you ass me that, why
do you ass me that?

SECOND IRREGULAR: Go on, go on, march!

JOHNNY: Are yous goin' to do in a comrade?—look
at me arm, I lost it for Ireland.

SECOND IRREGULAR: Commandant Tancred lost his
life for Ireland.

JOHNNY: Sacred Heart of Jesus, have mercy on me!
Mother o' God, pray for me—be with me now in
the agonies o' death! . . . Hail, Mary, full o'
grace . . . the Lord is . . . with Thee.

[They drag out Johnny Boyle, and the
curtain falls. When it rises again the most of the
furniture is gone. Mary and Mrs. Boyle, one on
each side, are sitting in a darkened room, by the
fire; it is an hour later]

MRS. BOYLE: I'll not wait much longer . . . what
did they bring him away in the mothor for?
Nugent says he thinks they had guns . . . is me
throubles never goin' to be over? . . . If anything

ud happen to poor Johnny, I think I'd lose me mind. . . . I'll go to the Police Station, surely they ought to be able to do somethin'.

[*Below is heard the sound of voices*]

MRS. BOYLE: Whisht, is that something? Maybe, it's your father, though when I left him in Foley's he was hardly able to lift his head. Whisht!

[*A knock at the door, and the voice of* Mrs. Madigan, *speaking very softly*] Mrs. Boyle, Mrs. Boyle.

[Mrs. Boyle *opens the door*]

MRS. MADIGAN: Oh, Mrs. Boyle, God an' His Blessed Mother be with you this night!

MRS. BOYLE: [*Calmly*] What is it, Mrs. Madigan? It's Johnny—something about Johnny.

MRS. MADIGAN: God send it's not, God send it's not Johnny!

MRS. BOYLE: Don't keep me waitin', Mrs. Madigan; I've gone through so much lately that I feel able for anything.

MRS. MADIGAN: Two polismen below wantin' you.

MRS. BOYLE: Wantin' me; an' why do they want me?

MRS. MADIGAN: Some poor fella's been found, an' they think it's, it's . . .

MRS. BOYLE: Johnny, Johnny!

MARY: [*With her arms round her mother*] Oh, mother, mother, me poor, darlin' mother.

MRS. BOYLE: Hush, hush, darlin'; you'll shortly have your own throuble to bear. [*To Mrs. Madigan*] An' why do the polis think it's Johnny, Mrs. Madigan?

MRS. MADIGAN: Because one o' the doctors knew him when he was attendin' with his poor arm.

MRS. BOYLE: Oh, it's thrue, then; it's Johnny, it's me son, me own son!

MARY: Oh, it's thrue, it's thrue what Jerry Devine says—there isn't a God, there isn't a God; if there was He wouldn't let these things happen!

MRS. BOYLE: Mary, Mary, you musn't say them things. We'll want all the help we can get from God an' His Blessed Mother now! These things have nothin' to do with the Will o' God. Ah, what can God do agen the stupidity o' men!

MRS. MADIGAN: The polis want you to go with them to the hospital to see the poor body—they're waitin' below.

MRS. BOYLE: We'll go. Come, Mary, an' we'll never come back here agen. Let your father furrage for himself now; I've done all I could an' it was all no use—he'll be hopeless till the end of his days. I've got a little room in me sisther's where we'll stop till your throuble is over, an' then we'll work together for the sake of the baby.

MARY: My poor little child that'll have no father!

MRS. BOYLE: It'll have what's far betther—it'll have two mothers.

A ROUGH VOICE *shouting from below*: Are yous goin' to keep us waitin' for yous all night?

MRS. MADIGAN: [*Going to the door, and shouting down*] Take your hour, there, take your hour! If

yous are in such a hurry, skip off, then, for nobody wants you here—if they did yous wouldn't be found. For you're the same as yous were undher the British Government—never where yous are wanted! As far as I can see, the Polis as Polis, in this city, is Null an' Void!

MRS. BOYLE: We'll go, Mary, we'll go; you to see your poor dead brother, an' me to see me poor dead son!

MARY: I dhread it, mother, I dhread it!

MRS. BOYLE: I forgot, Mary, I forgot; your poor oul' selfish mother was only thinkin' of herself. No, no, you mustn't come—it wouldn't be good for you. You go on to me sisther's an' I'll face th' ordeal meself. Maybe I didn't feel sorry enough for Mrs. Tancred when her poor son was found as Johnny's been found now—because he was a Die-hard! Ah, why didn't I remember that then he wasn't a Die-hard or a Stater, but only a poor dead son! It's well I remember all that she said—an' it's my turn to say it now: What was the pain I suffered, Johnny, bringin' you into the world to carry you to your cradle, to the pains I'll suffer carryin' you out o' the world to bring you to your grave! Mother o' God, Mother o' God, have pity on us all! Blessed Virgin, where were you when me darlin' son was riddled with bullets, when me darlin' son was riddled with bullets? Sacred Heart o' Jesus, take away our hearts o' stone, and give us hearts o' flesh! Take away this murdherin' hate, an' give us Thine own eternal love! [*They all go slowly out*]

[*There is a pause; then a sound of shuffling steps on the stairs outside. The door opens and* Boyle *and* Joxer, *both of them very drunk, enter*]

BOYLE: I'm able to go no farther. . . . Two polis, ey . . . what were they doin' here, I wondher? . . . Up to no good, anyhow . . . an' Juno an' that lovely daughter o' mine with them. [*Taking a sixpence from his pocket and looking at it*] Wan single, solitary tanner left out of all I borreyed. . . . [*He lets it fall*] The last o' the Mohicans. . . . The blinds is down, Joxer, the blinds is down!

JOXER: [*Walking unsteadily across the room, and anchoring at the bed*] Put all . . . your throubles . . . in your oul' kit-bag . . . an' smile . . . smile . . . smile!

BOYLE: The counthry'll have to steady itself . . . it's goin' . . . to hell. . . . Where'r all . . . the chairs . . . gone to . . . steady itself, Joxer. . . . Chairs'll . . . have to . . . steady themselves. . . . No matther . . . what any one may . . . say. . . . Irelan' sober . . . is Irelan' . . . free.

JOXER: [*Stretching himself on the bed*] Chains . . . an' . . . slaveree . . . that's a darlin' motto . . . a daaarlin' . . . motto!

BOYLE: If th' worst comes . . . to th' worse . . . I can join a . . . flyin' . . . column. . . . I done

. . . me bit . . . in Easther Week . . . had no business . . . to . . . be . . . there . . . but Captain Boyle's Captain Boyle!

JOXER: Breathes there a man with soul . . . so . . . de . . ad . . . this . . . me . . . o . . . wn, me nat . . . ive l . . . an'!

BOYLE: [*Subsiding into a sitting posture on the floor*] Commandant Kelly died . . . in them . . . arms

. . . Joxer. . . . Tell me Volunteer Butties . . . says he . . . that . . . I died for . . . Irelan'!

JOXER: D'jever rade Willie . . . Reilly . . . an' his own . . . Colleen . . . Bawn? It's a darlin' story, a daarlin' story!

BOYLE: I'm telling you . . . Joxer . . . th' whole worl's . . . in a terr . . . ible state o' . . . chassis!

Children of Darkness

by EDWIN JUSTUS MAYER
(1896–   )

Though Edwin Justus Mayer is chiefly known for The Firebrand, his entertaining costume play of the twenties about Benvenuto Cellini, he is chiefly notable for Children of Darkness. Children of Darkness was not, like The Firebrand, a popular success; but then, unlike The Firebrand, it was not essentially popular playwriting. To be sure, its lugubrious title, somehow suggesting the world of a Gorki, must have added to its problems at the box office: the original title, Jailer's Wench, though perhaps going too far in the opposite direction, at least went in the right one. But the fact remains that Children of Darkness must always, which is part of its cachet, have been a special case for Broadway, making of an audience a double demand that the usual Broadway audience cannot meet. It demands, first, the ability to appreciate its wit, tone, ironic flavor, elaborate artifice; it demands further the ability to accept its harsh, inhuman premise; to shed all one's moral sensibility and watch evil and villainy disporting themselves without reserve, and malignity taking its pleasure.

Mr. Mayer's comedy, in other words, is as acrid as it is artificial. It takes place in early eighteenth-century England, when language was both fulsome and starched; it is laid in a sort of annex to Newgate Prison, where behavior was both stealthy and vicious; and it is strewn with characters as untouched by morality as anyone in Congreve and as greedy for money as anyone in Jonson. It is thus a kind of crossing of the two most cold-blooded strains in English comedy; but a kind of crossing, also, of the two most distinguished. On this score it is perhaps unique in the modern English-speaking theater. Somerset Maugham, Noel Coward, and others have caught at times the brutal want of morals, the brittle tone of mockery of Restoration writers: but their people are not outright villains nor their ways necessarily wicked. Lillian Hellman in such plays as The Little Foxes and Another Part of the Forest offers villains with a diamond-cut-diamond sharpness, an almost gloating malevolence; but so far from merging with this the artificial comedy of the Restoration, her plays are much less comedies of any kind than sardonic melodramas: they as fully exploit our emotions as Children of Darkness outlaws them. There is no heat of any kind in Children of Darkness: rather, to the acrid-tasting juice of Jonson has been added the ice

of Congreve, to contrive a theatrical absinthe frappé.

For part of his play Mr. Mayer has leaned a little on history: at any rate, one of his characters, Jonathan Wild, is grimly historical; and the action of the play covers the twenty-four hours before that great highwayman was hanged. Wild, who was a good deal more formidable, if less romantic, than a highwayman—who was really the coldhearted head of a great gang of London thugs and thieves, and as ruthless toward them as toward society at large—is well suited to Mr. Mayer's gallery of rogues and knaves. But though, in Children of Darkness, Wild's imminent fate always forces us to keep an eye on the clock, our eye is not too often on Wild himself; for our particular study and delight, Mr. Mayer has invented several equally inhuman but generally more interesting exhibits. There is, for one, Mr. Snap, in whose apartments the prisoners of the play are lodged: a fellow in the established tradition of Jacobean and Restoration comedy—briskly heartless, jauntily conscienceless, genteelly fiendish. Again, there is the highborn poisoner, Lord Wainwright, who has, along with a Borgia's tastes, a Chesterfield's aplomb, and a Dr. Johnson's hatred of cant. Into this menagerie of tigresses and jackals and wolves he brings the coiled glossiness of a snake. Not entering, moreover, till the last act, he provides the play with just the breath of fresh carbon monoxide that it needs.

The last act does not, however, entirely crown the play. For two acts and a half Mr. Mayer, with great ingenuity and considerable wit, has permitted his villains to plot and counterplot, betray and outfox one another: never characters so blackhearted, never any more bland. But now Mr. Mayer must put an end to his story. This means, among other things, that he must put an end to Jonathan Wild, and elects to show us Wild led cursing and screaming and whimpering to the gallows. And here, I think, both from the imminency of the event and the intensity of Wild's emotion, we come too close to sheer primitive horror, to the awful animal cry of a living thing face to face with extinction, for even the most grisly comedy to operate. For here we no longer have Wild the highwayman or Wild the thief or Wild the double-crosser; we no longer have Wild indeed at all, but anyone, any human being, dragged away to die. And so we no longer have even sardonic or sinister comedy, but only the most primitive drama. And as Mr. Mayer is too horrifying over Wild, he is perhaps too sentimental over La Ruse—over his first setting Cartwright free with the money from the faked reprieve, and then committing suicide. What is needed is some invincibly worldly, imperturbably knavish ending, which would at the same time manage to give Cartwright his freedom. What we get, dredging down into La Ruse's father-feelings and carrying him to suicide on a wave of realizations better suited to Elizabethan drama or modern psychological realism, seems excessive and wrong—though the final curtain itself, with the ineffable Wainwright craving access to Laetitia's chamber, is brilliantly right.

The problem of how to end any work that trades so freely in human depravity is always ticklish; it remained to plague Volpone. But Mr. Mayer's third-act offenses are not capital ones, are blemishes rather than great blunders, blemishes on a play that has consistent fascination and, as such things go, distinction

as well. Children of Darkness is decidedly, at times, too florid and overliterary; and certain of its longer scenes need greater wit and cut and bounce. But on the whole this kind of artificial play needs this kind of artificial writing: without it, there can be no elegance, and so no atmosphere, and so—in a sense—no joke. For the joke, at bottom, is the great joke of almost all comedy—the difference between appearance and reality, the thing said and the thing done, the fawning lie and the appalling truth. Our enjoyment here must rest on such things as that Mr. Snap seems as sanctimonious as an undertaker; that Lord Wainwright seems as stately as a prime minister; that insults are offered as though they were compliments; that injuries are inflicted as though they were kindnesses; that the amenities of a death house suggest those of a salon. Our enjoyment proceeds, indeed, from our entering a world where, as it were, every prospect pleases and only man is vile.

EDWIN JUSTUS MAYER

Children of Darkness

CAST OF CHARACTERS

MR. SNAP, *Under-Sheriff of London and Middlesex*
FIRST BAILIFF
MR. CARTWRIGHT
MR. FIERCE
JONATHAN WILD, THE GREAT
COUNT LA RUSE
LAETITIA
LORD WAINWRIGHT
BAILIFFS

ACTS I, II AND III: *Room in the house of Mr. Snap, adjoining Newgate Prison, London*

Act I

A room on the top floor of Mr. Snap's *house, close by Newgate Prison.*

There is a barred window Right Center at back and another in Left wall of hall off Center. The city can be seen lying vaguely away.

At the Left rear corner is a fireplace, but as the season is late spring, it is not in use. A fine old tall clock in Right rear corner that strikes the hour and the half hour; a sofa under Right Center window. A door Center. A door at the Right front leads into a hall. A door Left.

The room has been designed for living, but latterly someone has been using it as an office; for a table at the Left Center, where the clearest light falls, is covered with a disorderly array of ledgers, papers, an ink-pot, quill pens, etc. Chairs Right, Left and back of table; also Right Center and below fireplace.

Mr. Snap, old and myopic, walks up and down the room. He looks at the clock, then at the door, as if expecting someone. At length, a Bailiff enters.

BAILIFF: We've brought the boy from the jail, sir.
MR. SNAP: Never mind the boy, knave! Are the gallows prepared for Mr. Wild, sir?

BAILIFF: Aye, sir.
MR. SNAP: Even if Wild don't swing—there will always be a rogue to take his place.
BAILIFF: Aye, sir—so there will.
MR. SNAP: You said you'd brought the boy from the jail. Where is he?
BAILIFF: He's in the hall.
MR. SNAP: Fetch him to me! But wait. You know all the rogues in London. You must know Mr. Fierce.
BAILIFF: Aye, one of Wild's gang. He tumbled me downstairs—when we took Wild.
MR. SNAP: 'Tis your chance to tumble him, for he comes this morning to visit Wild. You will seize him at the door and bring him here—but not before you've put the irons on him, knave. Now let me see the boy. [*Bailiff goes out. Mr. Snap whistles cheerily. The Bailiff returns, with a comrade. Cartwright walks between them; he is young, straight, clear-eyed, but obviously depressed*] Your servant, Mr. Cartwright. [*Dismisses Bailiff*] I am Mr. Snap of the jail.
CARTWRIGHT: [*Wearily*] Why am I brought here, Mr. Snap?
MR. SNAP: You'll be delighted to hear, Mr. Cartwright. [*The Bailiff goes*] Sit down, Mr. Cartwright, sit down! That is, if you can on such a morning! I had my walk this morning—I would not have missed my walk on such a morning!
CARTWRIGHT: I would have missed mine gladly.
MR. SNAP: [*Chuckling unpleasantly*] Would you? Would you? Because they walked you to Newgate? You're in the doldrums, Mr. Cartwright. Because you're jailed? At your age I had been jailed a dozen times. Why, 'tis only the effeminate and useless young who keep out of jail completely; the young who have never been in jail are a disgrace to their youth, sir.
CARTWRIGHT: Perhaps. [*Points towards prison*] But 'tis monstrous that men should treat men so—
MR. SNAP: I guessed at once you were held for debt! It takes a rogue to pay his bills honestly; a gentleman is much too busy accumulating more such, to pay such as he has accumulated.
CARTWRIGHT: I was gulled into signing a paper. But why have you brought me here, Mr. Snap?
MR. SNAP: Why, sir, because I guessed you would far rather be held here than down in the jail.

CARTWRIGHT: But I was consigned to the jail, by writ.

MR. SNAP: Yes, but I've power there, Mr. Cartwright. I'd not have you here were you not a gentleman. I've a daughter, a daughter I prize, a daughter who, I may say, possesses all the domestic virtues! I'd not expose her to the riff-raff—no, not for any sum. You shall be held here, sir.

CARTWRIGHT: [Overjoyed] This is more than kind of you, Mr. Snap.

MR. SNAP: Of course, you have some small fees to disburse through me.

CARTWRIGHT: [Dismayed] Fees!

MR. SNAP: What did you expect, sir? You've said yourself the King's Writ consigned you to Newgate—not to my house!

CARTWRIGHT: I thought you brought me here from kindness—not to be fee'd!

MR. SNAP: [Mistakes Cartwright's innocence for impudence] Do not put me out of temper with such remarks, Mr. Cartwright. What! Must kindness be divorced from profit? I will have you know, Mr. Cartwright, your remark has lowered my spirits—they droop, they droop perceptibly! Perhaps after all you were best returned to the jail.

CARTWRIGHT: [Terrified] Anywhere but there! How much is requisite?

MR. SNAP: For ten guineas you may enjoy the entire privacy of this floor.

CARTWRIGHT: I have but five pounds to my name. [Takes out money]

MR. SNAP: But you can procure five pounds additional? [Cartwright shakes his head hopelessly] Have you no friend? No mistress?

CARTWRIGHT: No.

MR. SNAP: Pray, what is your means of livelihood, then?

CARTWRIGHT: [Defiantly, for he has learned that his proud avowal often brings derision] I am a poet.

MR. SNAP: [Sadly disillusioned] What, a poet! I thought you were a gentleman. On my word, sir, you have a better air than the vulgarity of your trade allows. But hold—you say you are a poet—and have no mistress?

CARTWRIGHT: [Quietly, resentful] Every poet has the same mistress.

MR. SNAP: [Jeeringly] Is she beautiful, poet?

CARTWRIGHT: So beautiful—that she destroys my own ugliness.

MR. SNAP: Is she rich, poet?

CARTWRIGHT: She owns all seed—all harvests.

MR. SNAP: And yet she cannot provide you with five pounds more! On my word, your fol-de-rol-dol has put me in a mood to do the handsome thing. I will sell you the privacy of the floor for what money you have. [He takes the money]

[A loud hubbub of blows, cries and oaths is heard in the hall. Mr. Fierce, a muscular ruffian, bare-headed, bare-throated and coatless, is dragged in by two Bailiffs. Although he is manacled, they have a difficult time holding him]

MR. FIERCE: [Bellowing at Mr. Snap] Call off your terriers—your male wenches!

MR. SNAP: Mr. Fierce, I believe. I have had the pleasure before, have I not? [He takes a document from his pocket] We have a warrant for your arrest.

MR. FIERCE: Damn your eyes for a lying cuckold!

MR. SNAP: [Merrily] My wife is dead, sir.

MR. FIERCE: She's cuckolding you then in hell!

MR. SNAP: [Amiably] It is my duty to warn you, Mr. Fierce, that anything you say may be used against you. You are charged with the grand larceny of a silver locket from one Lady Margaret Stebbins, since deceased.

MR. FIERCE: Silver locket. [The words have stunned him; he asks in a curious voice] Who swore to the complaint? [Mr. Snap offers him the warrant. Sullenly] I can't read.

MR. SNAP: [Reads from the document] Jonathan Wild made the complaint.

MR. FIERCE: [Quivering] Jonathan Wild!

MR. SNAP: He is witness that you offered him the stolen property, which he declined.

MR. FIERCE: Declined! 'Twas he who told me of the locket—where to filch it—

MR. SNAP: Aye, Mr. Wild usually knows where other people's valuables lie.

MR. FIERCE: And that he'd get rid of it for me! He has it now, for disposal!

MR. SNAP: I doubt if you can prove that. [He hands the warrant to one of the Bailiffs] Take him to the jail.

MR. FIERCE: [Awakening from his stupor—fighting savagely] He's here in this house— By God, I'll kill him—the double-cheating bastard—of a French dancing-master— I'll chew him to pieces— I'll bathe in his blood—[A murderous blow subdues Fierce; he is dragged away]

CARTWRIGHT: Horrible. Wild has used this unfortunate man and then betrayed him.

MR. SNAP: And betrayed a thousand other tools—and yet he sniffles, prates of his honour and the principle of the thing. Let me warn you against Mr. Wild, and against a precious friend of his, also held here, who calls himself Count La Ruse. Put your faith in me, sir.

CARTWRIGHT: 'Twas published Wild was sentenced to death.

MR. SNAP: He'll swing any day, now. There is no crime so low he hasn't had a hand in it, and here, where his talents are somewhat circumscribed, he robs La Ruse, La Ruse robs him—

CARTWRIGHT: And you rob both of them.

MR. SNAP: I, sir? I, sir! Be more careful, sir.

CARTWRIGHT: Which is my room, Mr. Snap?

MR. SNAP: I will show you. 'Tis in the best of taste. I furnished it myself. [They exit. And as they do *so*, Cartwright *in the lead*, Wild, *a burly, boisterous man of forty, enters*] Ah! Mr. Wild.

JONATHAN: My locket—my silver locket—— Have they seized that villain Fierce?

MR. SNAP: We've just jailed him.

JONATHAN: Well, speed his trial, for if they hang me before they hang him, I'll never collect my bounty.

MR. SNAP: Then I'll collect it for you—— [Mr. Snap *exits.* Jonathan *looks on table for locket—goes to chimney and peers up it.* La Ruse, *a polished, cynical, middle-aged man, enters; watches* Jonathan *in amusement; takes snuff*]

LA RUSE: You have missed something, Jonathan?

JONATHAN: My locket's gone.

LA RUSE: You are irritated, what! You should use snuff—there is nothing so good for an irritation as snuff.

JONATHAN: [*Crossing to table*] Damn your snuff, sir! You know how I hate it. The thing is not here —it is not to be found—'tis incomprehensible. [*Sits at table, searching*]

LA RUSE: You have the fault of all great men—you permit yourself to be absorbed by a single business. Yes, greatness is narrowness, preoccupation; second rate men like myself must take refuge in the variation of clouds, images, women.

JONATHAN: A pox on your women! I am sure I made an entry of it.

LA RUSE: [*Looking into the sky; dreamily*] There are birds in the air, Jonathan, white birds! They are crying something to me which I do not understand. [*Affects to listen to the birds*] What are you telling me—you free things? [*He is joyful*] You are crying, one of your kind will soon fly to me—with wings for myself! Wings—wings to bear me far away! Yes, yes. It will be a bird who nests in the sun—a white bird! [*Suddenly*] What? It will not be a white bird? [*He becomes sorrowful*] It will be a black bird. [*He shivers*] My wings will be black.

JONATHAN: [*Convulsively*] A thousand hells! La Ruse! This is no time for your coloured words.

LA RUSE: Your obedient servant, Jonathan.

JONATHAN: [*Striking the table for emphasis*] Mr. Fierce, sir, is dishonest.

LA RUSE: This is appalling. You are sure?

JONATHAN: Mr. Fierce had scarcely brought me the locket—I had scarcely entered it on my records, when I missed it again.

LA RUSE: But pray, why should he bring you the locket and then take it away again?

JONATHAN: Because he knew he wouldn't have lived long if he hadn't apparently given it to me. La Ruse, do you know what the rogue did further? While I had left the room for a few moments he obliterated the records, wiped it from my books. I did not credit him with so much wit.

LA RUSE: We have been fooled, then, by a damnable sharper, what! By my honour, I'll call him out— I'll run him through with dispatch——

JONATHAN: [*Rises*] My dear Count, long before I missed the locket I swore out a warrant against Mr. Fierce.

LA RUSE: A warrant?

JONATHAN: 'Tis the principle of the thing!

LA RUSE: You have delivered him to the hangman?

JONATHAN: Candidly, my dear Count, I thought my delivering him up might favorably affect my fate.

LA RUSE: [*Bowing*] To me you will always be the great Jonathan, whatever your fate.

JONATHAN: You've heard? They've set the date for my hanging?

LA RUSE: No.

JONATHAN: Bah. What is it to be hanged? 'Tis but a dance—without music.

LA RUSE: They'll never hang you, Jonathan.

JONATHAN: Yet consider my position, La Ruse. Why should I hang when the Prime Minister is spared? He is the leader of a party, I am the leader of a gang; but both are primarily organized for spoils. And I am to be hanged, not because I differ from those who make and maintain the Law, but because I am too much like them for their own liking. It is declared that I have sacrificed my tools! Can you name me the statesman who has sacrificed his career for a friend? Then why am I to be garroted—rather than received at Court? Because, my fallen aristocratic friend, I was not born an aristocrat. But whatever my fate, your rotten aristocracy will not long survive me. The future belongs to men like myself—self-made men, if I may coin a phrase—the powers of government will yet pass into the hands of men who know how to build an organization, and make it profitable.

LA RUSE: Yes, yes, you are concentrated; we are diverted. A stray tune—a pretty face—a lyrical line, illusions us. You are not illusioned. Life—

MR. SNAP: [*Enters*] Life! Did you say life, Count? And what could be better than life on such a morning? The air! The balmy air! What! You haven't been out in the balmy air?

LA RUSE: Our spirits have wandered abroad, sir.

MR. SNAP: Spirits indeed! Did you say spirits? They've no lungs, sir—you must have lungs for the enjoyment of the air! Why, the streets are packed with knaves. What could have kept you here on such a fragrant morning, gentlemen?

JONATHAN: Do not answer him, Count. He but mocks us.

MR. SNAP: Come, sir, let the Count answer for himself.

LA RUSE: You are easily answered. Our spirits have wandered abroad, but our bodies, detained by locks, bolts, bars and judicial process, have necessarily languished where you see them now.

MR. SNAP: Spoken like a scholar, sir. I vow 'tis the very essence of an education to keep you jailed by me. You must pardon my little joke at your expense, but I am in high spirits. I have just jailed a poet.

JONATHAN: Truth to tell, Mr. Snap, I thought your joke in exceeding bad taste—twitting us with our lack of liberty.

MR. SNAP: [Visibly incensed] Bad taste! Did you say bad taste? What! Shall the taste of a jailer be questioned by his felons? What! I am not to have my little joke—simply because you are condemned?

JONATHAN: [Starting—ashen-faced] You have heard —they've set the date for my hanging?

MR. SNAP: I have heard nothing. You have set me out of temper with your impertinence, sir! I am no longer in high spirits. I am in exceeding low spirits—and your fault, Mr. Wild. [Jonathan finds the world too much for him] What! Does he sniffle!

LA RUSE: He has had a troublous morning, Mr. Snap. [Sympathetically] Jonathan, pray retire to your room.

MR. SNAP: Does he forget that it is only by my grace that he continues to carry on his nefarious business, in jail, as out?

LA RUSE: You accept a certain percentage of the transactions, I believe.

MR. SNAP: I do, I do, and I won't deny it for my soul's sake—except under oath.

LA RUSE: I honour you for owning you are not squeamish, Mr. Snap.

MR. SNAP: I will tell you what, Sir Fop; I am not squeamish—there's not a man in London will say I am squeamish—distinctly, I am not! But as for your friend here—I am squeamish. What! Weeping! Sensitive! This father of bridle-culls—millkens — buttocks-and-files — assassins! [Jonathan groans] This thieving pimp and pimping thief! This fence—who has taught men to steal and then delivered 'em up for the bloody bounty? You may lay to what I have said, sir, as Jack Ketch will presently lay to Mr. Wild.

LA RUSE: [Smiling; taking snuff] You are a gentleman, Mr. Snap—

MR. SNAP: [Thumpingly] I am obliged to you for the notification, sir.

JONATHAN: [Leaping to his feet] Sir, as you can see, I can scarcely articulate— I am distraught—a wronged man—but your words shall not go unanswered—my spirit cries out in rebuttal! You are a fool, Mr. Snap—you pervert the truth of my life—which a man of your mean stature must misunderstand. Know, then, sir, that I have an awkward pride in my nature, which is better pleased with being at the head of the lowest class than at the botton of the highest. [He pauses for breath. Count La Ruse lays his snuff-box on the table and places a strengthening hand on his friend's shoulder] Permit me to say, though the idea may be somewhat coarse, I had rather stand on the sum-

mit of a dung-hill than at the bottom of a hill in Paradise! [He collapses into chair]

LA RUSE: Your words, Jonathan, are like those pebbles which in the mouth of another Demosthenes turned into jewels. [Jonathan's anguished fingers happen on the snuff-box] Ah, Mr. Snap, you do not understand Mr. Wild [Jonathan pinches snuff-box] I, Count La Ruse, an exile from my country, a stranger in your country, alone understand his true greatness.

[The snuff-box disappears up Jonathan's capacious sleeve]

JONATHAN: [Rising unsteadily] Alone—alone—I ask only to be alone. [He makes for the door] 'Tis the principle of the thing—

MR. SNAP: [Rushing between him and the exit] Hold! Do you dare complain?

JONATHAN: [Piteously] Let me leave, Mr. Snap. I have every reason to leave immediately.

LA RUSE: Mr. Wild complains of nothing—but that you stand between him and the door.

MR. SNAP: [Whirling on him] Complain, sir! Do you not both eat at my table?

LA RUSE: A man of my position honours your table, Mr. Snap. But do not let us quarrel. Let me admit that I will never forget the way you have treated me—never.

MR. SNAP: That's a better tune than you have been singing, sir.

JONATHAN: [Darting by him] Alone—alone—all things conspire against me.   [He exits]

MR. SNAP: [Grumbling] Ay, twelve good men and true have conspired to hang him by the neck— [Jonathan slams door] until dead. Bad taste, indeed! What do you do at the door, sir?

LA RUSE: [Shuts door] A keyhole is like a woman, Mr. Snap; it tells secrets to the world. [He goes to the fireplace, reaches up the flue and finds something there; he gives it to Mr. Snap] Mr. Wild's silver locket as I promised. He blames its loss on the unfortunate Fierce.

MR. SNAP: [Examining it with delight] Sound, shining silver. By everything holy, a valuable ornament for some fat Duke's slim mistress.

LA RUSE: [Watching Mr. Snap's avarice with a peculiar disdain] I doubt not such will be its fate. Beauty the world over is born in silence, and dies in carnival.

MR. SNAP: We shall profit by this, never fear. I have yet to see a more desirable trinket.

LA RUSE: I hold there are still more desirable trinkets to be had, sir.

MR. SNAP: [Reverently] And if you can't lay your hands on them, there's no thief in London can.

LA RUSE: Thank you, Mr. Snap. Nothing's so pleasing to the ear of man as flattery. But the things to which I had reference have no pawnable substance—they lie safely hidden in the silver locket of the spirit.

MR. SNAP: Well, I suppose you must talk so. But it puzzles me why so many of the gentry should be of a melancholic frame of mind. They seem to drink bitterness from their mother's rich breasts. [Laetitia appears in the door. She is twenty-nine, a ravishing woman; vital to the excess of carnality] Good morning, daughter. 'Tis Laetitia, Count.

LA RUSE: [With an elaborate gesture] The enchanting Mistress Laetitia.

LAETITIA: [With one of her own] The noble Count Ruse.

MR. SNAP: Daughter, I have business. You must cheer the Count— Aye, cheer him, but not to the point where you might lose your maidenly reserve— I would not have that. [He goes, with a final admonition of his head]

LAETITIA: [Laughs—throws her arms wide] Take me, La Ruse.

LA RUSE: [Studying the manufacture of a chair] I am not in a mood.

LAETITIA: [Undiscomfited] I adore you, La Ruse. I do. Show me the lover who knows how to renounce me—ay, and how to denounce me—and he shall be surfeited with my fidelity.

LA RUSE: Liar!

LAETITIA: [Approaching him] I am mad about you, La Ruse. Are you not mad about me?

LA RUSE: I abominate you.

LAETITIA: And yet you make love to me.

LA RUSE: Because I abominate you.

LAETITIA: 'Tis your one drawback as a lover that your reasoning is always original.

LA RUSE: And true. The surrender of a woman one adores is but tepid compared to the subjection of a woman one abominates. Therefore— [He clasps and kisses her]

LAETITIA: [Sparkling] For a prisoner, sir, you take more liberties than a free man dares.

LA RUSE: [Coldly leaving her] Pray remember, Madam, you have granted me greater liberties than any I now implore.

LAETITIA: It is the privilege of a lady to remember, sir, as it is the duty of a gentleman to forget. But alas! When a gentleman becomes a lover, he ceases to be a gentleman; the one is killed in the other. Yet I adore you, La Ruse, and would not willingly be without you.

LA RUSE: I shall be free of you yet.

LAETITIA: I shall do my best to hold you here. Yet you are foolish, sir—imagining you can escape me merely by leaving me.

LA RUSE: Out of this jail, and I am out of your life.

LAETITIA: Leave these prison walls, and your days shall still be spent in matching your mind against my mind—your nights, [Sits on his knee] in matching your strength against my strength—your time, always, in matching your malice against my malice. [Kisses him] You desire me, La Ruse.

LA RUSE: I desire no woman. I have found too many

hairs—of too many colours—on my shoulder. [Surveying her hair; critically] Your own is far from the most attractive shade I have found on my shoulder.

LAETITIA: But it is the final shade you will find there. [Rises] You and I can no more escape from each other than from the reflection we must see if we look in the glass, or from the shadow we must see if we walk in the sun.

LA RUSE: But you forget—one may easily walk out of the sun.

LAETITIA: [Lightly] You will not kill yourself yet, La Ruse.

LA RUSE: [Intensely] Not while there is still a chance I may be free of you. But if the day should come—

LAETITIA: Egoist! Do you think yourself alone in resenting the tie which binds us? Do you never think I have my own moods when I would be free of you?

LA RUSE: Would that they came more often!

LAETITIA: What if I should tell you—I had yielded to such a mood?

LA RUSE: I should be indifferent.

LAETITIA: I have yielded to such a mood.

LA RUSE: [Instantly jealous] You lie.

LAETITIA: No.

LA RUSE: Come here to me, hussy.

LAETITIA: [Studying the manufacture of chair] I am not in a mood.

LA RUSE: You are simply revengeful.

LAETITIA: And perhaps—I may yield to another such mood!

LA RUSE: Do so, and be damned.

LAETITIA: This is not indifference. This is love!

LA RUSE: Why? And what if it were proved anew what everyone knows: that a woman like yourself has many mouths—all of them lying?

LAETITIA: Does it mean something to you—that I have been lying?

LA RUSE: Yes. Is it not absurd? I cannot bear the thought of another embracing you with love, although I embrace you with loathing!

LAETITIA: Reassure yourself, La Ruse. I adore you. Yet, what if I had deceived you? 'Twould be no more on my part than the closing of my eyes in an amorous day-dream. The dream would pass quickly, my eyes would open—and your enduring image would be still in the glass before me.

LA RUSE: I am unworthy of such chaste fidelity. But since you are so sure of me, why do you deny the favour I have petitioned a thousand times?

LAETITIA: [Insolently] To slip the great lock for you? Why should I?

LA RUSE: Because I go mad in my confinement here.

LAETITIA: [Amazed] But, La Ruse, La Ruse! 'Twas what you said to me when I first saw you in the jail! When I persuaded Papa to bring you here! This is ungracious of you, sir.

LA RUSE: I tell you, minx, I go mad here! Why will

you not slip the lock for me? If all you have spoken is true, I shall still be yours while in full flight from you.

LAETITIA: But in an abstraction not wholly satisfactory to the warmth of my nature!

LA RUSE: What if I were to give you my word to return when I had paid the debt which sent me here?

LAETITIA: Poor Papa is fond of observing you were well-born. Alas, Count La Ruse! We ladies who were not well-born have learned to our cost that the word of a gentleman is not always sacred when given to a lady of another class.

LA RUSE: You wrong yourself, Laetitia. You do belong to my class.

LAETITIA: [*Not without a trace of bitterness*] I am a jailer's wench—and past time I was married.

LA RUSE: No matter, you belong to my class: The devil has elevated you to his submerged party. You talk like no jailer's wench; you have been given an infernal gift of tongues. You act like no jailer's wench; you do as you please, and it is your present pleasure to torture me by holding me here.

LAETITIA: I have heard there is no happier state than to be the prisoner of love.

LA RUSE: There is no happier state—when one is the jailer.

LAETITIA: [*Clapping her hands*] Was ever a woman so fortunate as myself—to have her lover under lock and key? I vow, sir, half the great love tragedies would have been comedies had the ladies been placed in my position.

LA RUSE: This may yet prove more of a comedy than you think, Madam.

LAETITIA: You mean, La Ruse, that you have been tampering with the great lock.

LA RUSE: [*Casually*] Among others.

LAETITIA: Yes. You have also been tampering with the locks of Papa's arms-chest.

LA RUSE: Nothing is so easily beaten into shape of a key—as a pistol or knife.

LAETITIA: The locks are strong everywhere to hold you.

LA RUSE: [*Fiercely*] My spirit is strong everywhere to be free.

LAETITIA: Then our repulsions shall lend an intense piquance to our emotions. We shall spend delicious hours hating one another. You will visit me later, La Ruse?

LA RUSE: [*Studying the manufacture of chair*] I am not in a mood.

LAETITIA: [*Dangerously*] Take care, sir! There is always a refuge for a neglected woman! There is always—

[*She is interrupted by the entrance of* Cartwright]

CARTWRIGHT: [*Very much abashed*] I beg your pardon. I thought— [*He makes a motion to withdraw*]

LAETITIA: [*Lyrically*] Stay, young gentleman! [*She flashes a mischievous glance at* La Ruse] You are a stranger, sir? I do not remember seeing you.

CARTWRIGHT: I was taken only this morning. [*He feels that—somehow—he has spoken too freely, and again attempts to withdraw*]

LAETITIA: [*Persuasively*] Do not run away, young gentleman. [*She repeats her mischievous glance at* La Ruse]

LA RUSE: [*Exploding*] Get out, you young fool.
            [Cartwright's *face darkens; he takes a
                          step toward* La Ruse]

LAETITIA: [*Lays a restraining hand on the boy*] You must not mind Count La Ruse. He is not in a mood—or in a mood—I really forget which it is! Devote yourself rather to me.

CARTWRIGHT: I could not help but do that. I did not expect in such a place—

LAETITIA: Yes?

CARTWRIGHT: [*Colouring*] To find such loveliness.

LAETITIA: [*Delighted*] For shame, young gentleman! I vow not even the Count vies with you as a gallant.

CARTWRIGHT: [*Anxiously*] I would not have you think I was being merely a gallant.
            [La Ruse *yawns audibly*]

LAETITIA: I would not think that, sir, for I hold there's no more pleasing charm than sincerity. [*Sits on table.* La Ruse *yawns—audibly*]

CARTWRIGHT: [*Looks at* La Ruse] Though they are the fashion of the town, yet I despise these gallants—who make a mask of something better than a mask, a disguise of something real.

LA RUSE: [*Vigorously*] And I admire those gallants immensely, sir—because I am one myself. [*He goes closer to the couple*] I perceive from the nature of your eloquence you are hopelessly young.

LAETITIA: Divinely young, La Ruse.

CARTWRIGHT: [*Smarting at both references*] I was not arrested for the crime of youth, sir.

LA RUSE: You should have been. At your age every man should be arrested and jailed until thirty. In this way, folly would be ended for all time.

CARTWRIGHT: [*Lashing back*] There is proverbially no fool like an old fool, sir.

LAETITIA: You mind Count La Ruse without cause; he is by way of being a misanthrope; they say his mistress would be untrue to him.

LA RUSE: [*Sky-rocketing*] What is your name, sir?

CARTWRIGHT: [*Steps toward* La Ruse] Mr. Cartwright.

LAETITIA: [*Applauding his tone. Rises*] I see you are as valiant as you are quick, Mr. Cartwright. But I pray you, gentlemen, for my sake—let your wits be your weapons.

CARTWRIGHT: Do you think I would fight him? I would not follow his code while I have courage to follow a better code: I have sworn never to lay my hands on a human being, except in love.

LAETITIA: [Laughs] Except in love?—You've been rude, La Ruse.

LA RUSE: [Interested by the boy's naive declaration] I meant no offense, sir. Last night's wine has left me on edge.

CARTWRIGHT: I regret the words passed.

[They bow to each other]

LAETITIA: [Vastly entertained by the proceedings] You were discussing the gallants, gentlemen; it promised to be most edifying to the ignorance of my female ears.

CARTWRIGHT: You were defending the beaux, Count La Ruse.

LA RUSE: Your servant, Mr. Cartwright. I will prove my case. What is it, sir, to fall in love with a woman? 'Tis a most involuntary gesture; for a woman to be flattered when a man falls in love with her were as if she were to be flattered when a man catches the measles. He can no more help the one than the other. But gallantry, sir—gallantry is the deliberate wisdom of men who do choicely what fools must do willy-nilly; and a woman of perception must always prefer your mature gentleman to your young idiot. I see that you take me amiss, Mr. Cartwright; you must permit me the license of a general remark. It follows, from what I have said, that the very spice of affectation is to appear more sincere than sincerity itself. I must blame my art when people think me insincere—because I so manifestly am.

CARTWRIGHT: [Radically] Count La Ruse: Your gallants have bravado, without bravery; courtesy, without sacrifice; honour, without a cause to die for.

LAETITIA: I vow, sir, but you talk beyond your years! You must be a collegian.

CARTWRIGHT: [Proudly] I was expelled.

LAETITIA: Expelled?

LA RUSE: 'Tis a special form of graduation, designed for the more original of the students.

CARTWRIGHT: [With the same self-conscious defiance as when he admitted his talent to Mr. Snap] I wrote a tract against God.

LAETITIA: That was wicked, sir. I am High Church, and devout. You look as if you were of good family, and sure, one of good family should not be atheistic.

CARTWRIGHT: [The note of the born zealot kindling in his voice] I am not atheistic. I believe in love.

LAETITIA: [Excited] We shall all be blasted! You are young; you have been led astray by books. You must let me convert you again.

CARTWRIGHT: I must convert you.

LA RUSE: Would you leave me out in the wintry cold? What are the articles of your belief?

CARTWRIGHT: [With the full note of the zealot] That the Paradise which men have lost is to be found again on earth. Is the air given us, only that we may stifle? Is the sea given us, only that we may drown? Are the flowers given us, only that we may faint? No. While we dream of a distant Heaven, Heaven is at hand for us to storm. I believe everything is forbidden by men, yet the wise are passionate; that nothing is forbidden by nature, yet the wise are austere. I believe that fear adds only to fear, hate adds only to hate, but that beauty—beauty adds to everything. [He has been looking at Laetitia] And you— [To her] you who are so radiant in my eyes, I believe you will take my hand, you will walk with me into shadowy, holy places.

LAETITIA: I know not whether to be flattered—or frightened—or attracted by your presumption! Your talk is strange.

CARTWRIGHT: Truth is strange.

LA RUSE: [Extends his hand in the ancient Roman salute] Hail, Pilate!

LAETITIA: Why do you talk so? Are you a poet?

CARTWRIGHT: Yes.

LAETITIA: Why did you not say as much before? 'Tis in his nature, then—such incoherence! [Recovers her coquetry; as if thrilled] A poet! But how charming!

LA RUSE: I am not surprised to find you jailed; the law and the muses have ever played ill together. They are like Mistress Laetitia's spinet—out of tune, the music jars.

LAETITIA: [Winningly] And will you write a poem to me, Mr. Cartwright? Will you dedicate a poem to me?

CARTWRIGHT: My heart is doing so now.

LAETITIA: [Away a little] La Ruse, the pattern of your conceits was never so taking as this.

LA RUSE: [Bitingly] Romantic vein! The inspiration of your muse is Mistress Laetitia, daughter of your jailer.

CARTWRIGHT: You are Mr. Snap's daughter?

LAETITIA: Do you hate me, now—since my father is your jailer?

CARTWRIGHT: You have set me free.

LA RUSE: [Agonized] Free! [Rises] Free! Never blaspheme with that word, sir.

CARTWRIGHT: I did not use it as a word, but as a mystery.

LA RUSE: [Roughly] You have another mystery to explain—your bursting in here without a by-your-leave.

CARTWRIGHT: I meant no disrespect. Mr. Snap has sold me the privacy of this floor.

LA RUSE: [Warmly] Oh! Indeed, Mr. Snap has sold me the privacy of this floor. 'Tis not the first time— [The clock strikes twelve]

LAETITIA: Noon! I must look to the cook; we shall be at table directly. I shall persuade Papa to let you sit at table with us, Mr. Cartwright.

CARTWRIGHT: You make me very happy, Mistress Laetitia. [Bows]

LAETITIA: You shall sit by my side.

LA RUSE: [As she passes, aside] Minx!

CARTWRIGHT: You make me very happy!

LAETITIA: 'Twill be my aim to make you happier while you are lodged here. I must acquaint you afterwards with the more intimate ways of the place. [Smiles enigmatically at La Ruse, ravishingly at the poet, and exits]

LA RUSE: [Sits on sofa. Oblivious of Cartwright's enchantment] I must ask you never to degrade the name of freedom by uttering it before that woman —before any woman. Yes, you will find monarchies are ruled by women, republics by men: for liberty bears a fiercer cut than Fashion permits. Mr. Cartwright—I grieve to note you have heard not one of my priceless words.

CARTWRIGHT: I beg your pardon.

LA RUSE: You have heard the sirens' song, and are lost. How old are you, sir?

CARTWRIGHT: Twenty-one.

LA RUSE: Twenty-one! Are people still twenty-one? For what are you held?

CARTWRIGHT: For a debt of two hundred pounds.

LA RUSE: Odd! I am held for the precise amount.

CARTWRIGHT: How long have you been held?

LA RUSE: I was taken the year of the flood. Do you know, I have gambled away as much as fifty thousand pounds at a sitting; I have thrice been held for murder, each time justly—and each time been released within the week; and yet for a beggarly two hundred pounds I have been caged here these three long years?

CARTWRIGHT: [Envisioning a like fate] Three years!

LA RUSE: Two in the jail, and one here. Have you hope for a speedier release?

CARTWRIGHT: None.

LA RUSE: No parents?

CARTWRIGHT: I have an uncle.

LA RUSE: Won't he help you?

CARTWRIGHT: He sent me here.

LA RUSE: You may console yourself with the thought that the malice of a relative is still more endurable than his affection. You borrowed from your uncle?

CARTWRIGHT: No, he sued me for my inheritance.

LA RUSE: And you lost your suit. I myself have several times been defended by eminent counsel, and each time been eminently convicted; for the fame of lawyers appears founded on the number of cases they lose, famously.

CARTWRIGHT: I won my suit.

LA RUSE: My rhetoric has gone astray. Then why are you here?

CARTWRIGHT: My lawyers had me arrested—perceiving as they did that I owed them more than the value of the property—which they seized.

LA RUSE: It is not the meek who will inherit the earth: it is the lawyers. Such is the testament of Count La Ruse.

CARTWRIGHT: Manifestly, you adopted that as a nom de plume.

LA RUSE: Say rather as a nom de crime. I was born— but no matter. The blood of kings flows in my veins.

CARTWRIGHT: [With pride] And in mine.

LA RUSE: The Homeric strain: a noble lineage. Beware, sir, lest you cross it with the treason of another Helen.

CARTWRIGHT: [Resentfully] Mistress Laetitia?

LA RUSE: You are acute. Yes, I meant Mistress Laetitia. But did I? Who knows what anyone means any more? The world threatens to be a garment which has gone out of style, while I still must wear it. This is death, to me, for I long ago took a sense of pleasure in place of my soul.

CARTWRIGHT: I am sorry for you, Count La Ruse.

LA RUSE: Damn your impudence! Keep your sorrow for yourself; you will need it, here. When you have been detained as long as I have been, you will learn there is only one reality, and a bitter one.

CARTWRIGHT: There is another reality—and I think I have found it.

LA RUSE: [Shrugs his shoulders] After all, what would it avail you if you desired freedom as passionately as I do?

CARTWRIGHT: [Hesitantly] I should find a way.

LA RUSE: [Skeptical. Laughs] What way, sir?

CARTWRIGHT: [Uncertain if he is being wise] This way. [He reveals a knife. Rises]

LA RUSE: [Snatches it from him] A knife!

CARTWRIGHT: [Sure he has not been wise] I have never carried a blade. A prisoner slipped it to me when we were searched.

LA RUSE: [Feeling the blade; with mounting excitement] Keen—keen! But why am I surprised? Liberty is keen. [He radiates the knife in the light] Bright—bright! But why am I surprised? Freedom is bright. [His exaltation approaches ecstasy] Mouth about your women, you son of Homer! Will they glitter like this? A knife—I have a knife —a knife!

CARTWRIGHT: Let me have the knife back. You grow over-excited.

LA RUSE: Over-excited? You are a poet—and have no more perception? [Closes his eyes in rapture; runs his fingers over the sharp edge] I am calm and at peace with the world at last. Life—my sense of pleasure returns to me; already I am walking the streets, frequenting the tables, dining tete-a-tete with the King's mistress! What hour, think you, will be best?

CARTWRIGHT: Best—

LA RUSE: Midnight—

CARTWRIGHT: For what?

LA RUSE: [Impatiently] Why, when we shall excellently cut the throat of Mr. Snap—seize his keys —and escape.

CARTWRIGHT: Mr. Snap! Laetitia's father!

LA RUSE: [Too engrossed by the future to notice the

poet's horror] Hell's father, sir! [*He radiates the blade again*]

CARTWRIGHT: [*Snatches vainly*] The knife is mine.

LA RUSE: Yours, sir? You are mistaken. The blade has been in my family for generations, and sentiment forbids me let it go. [*Puts knife in pocket*]

CARTWRIGHT: [*Impotently*] I'll not be responsible for the cutting of any throats!

LA RUSE: [*Dismissing the subject*] You will never make a great poet, sir, for I see you are a moral man.

CARTWRIGHT: I will not harm Mistress Laetitia.

LA RUSE: [*Solemnly*] She will harm you—

CARTWRIGHT: You have some cause to be malicious.

LA RUSE: I will tell you, Mr. Cartwright: it would profit you more in Heaven to cut the throat of Mr. Snap—than to kiss the throat of his daughter.

CARTWRIGHT: Doubtless Mistress Laetitia has repelled your advances.

LA RUSE: [*Sadly*] There is only one possible explanation of this world, Mr. Cartwright: the Gods themselves are stupid. Yes. For that reason it is said we were made in their image. They have had one brilliant idea, sir: snuff. [*He feels for his snuff-box; finds it gone; recalls that he left it on the table, and looks there*] Gone! My snuff-box gone! Your precious Mr. Snap—or that other damnable rogue—

CARTWRIGHT: Jonathan Wild?

LA RUSE: [*Searching frantically*] The identical villain! I would have parted with my bowels, before that box. It was given me by—a lady! You are new here, Mr. Cartwright; let me warn you against Mr. Wild—and Mr. Snap; two of the consummate thieves of the age. [*Cartwright crosses to table*] 'Tis not to be found! Wild was here—Snap was here—is it possible that that minx—? 'Twas while Wild was here—I was comforting him. By God, I'll have it back or I'll demolish the house.

[*Cartwright surveys the room. He sees some paper at table, sits back of table and begins writing a lyric. He has scarcely begun, however, when Laetitia enters*]

LAETITIA: Oh, La Ruse! Pray, leave the house stand at least for dinner, which is ready.

LA RUSE: Damn dinner! I couldn't digest nectar at the moment!

LAETITIA: What's happened to him?

CARTWRIGHT: He's lost his snuff-box.

LAETITIA: What a pity. If he had it now he might sneeze out his temper.

LA RUSE: If I had it now I wouldn't be in a temper.

LAETITIA: 'Tis the oddest matter [*La Ruse looks round sofa*] but one is forever losing things in this charming house.

CARTWRIGHT: For myself I have found much more here than I could ever lose—

LAETITIA: I vow, Mr. Cartwright, you are a sweet young man.

LA RUSE: When you hear that purring—look out for claws, Mr. Cartwright.

LAETITIA: You're in need of food. [*Wild appears*] Ah! Mr. Wild— Dinner waits—

LA RUSE: [*Glares at Wild*] Let it wait, Madam. I've been robbed of my appetite by the scoundrel who robbed me of my snuff-box—a treasured piece of mine.

JONATHAN: Sir, you look palpably at me when you say that! Sir, do you dare imply—

LA RUSE: Sir, I imply I want my snuff-box back at once!

LAETITIA: [*Nervously*] Stand aside from them, Mr. Cartwright.

JONATHAN: Sir, I'll not have you talk to me in this manner; 'tis the principle of the thing! [*Coolly*] Yes. As a principled man, have I asked you for the return of my silver locket?

LA RUSE: [*To Jonathan*] Do you dare imply—

LAETITIA: [*Firmly*] Enough. We shall have no more of your joint ill-manners! La Ruse, you must look for your box later—and you, Mr. Wild, for your locket.

LA RUSE: [*Fuming*] By Heaven, Madam, you may depend that I will!

MR. SNAP: [*Bustles in*] I am in high spirits again; they bubble over.

LAETITIA: Stop your nonsense, Papa, and come along. [*She takes the poet by the arm*] I'll show you, as we pass, how the rooms lie, sir. [*Notices La Ruse*] Come along, La Ruse.

LA RUSE: [*Vaguely; to himself*] White birds—

LAETITIA: Awaken La Ruse, Papa. [*Goes out with Cartwright*]

MR. SNAP: Come along, Count. [*Wild exits*] Wild hangs tomorrow. [*Chuckles*]

LA RUSE: Tomorrow? You say Wild hangs tomorrow?

LAETITIA'S VOICE: [*Vexed*] Come along, Papa.

MR. SNAP: Coming, Daughter. You are ready, Count?

LA RUSE: [*Looks at the knife behind Mr. Snap's back*] Quite ready, dear Mr. Snap.

Act II

The same, that night. The room is lighted by an adequate number of candles; the window remains open. The papers, etc., have been removed from the table.

La Ruse *discovered on sofa, looking out of window.*

MR. SNAP: [*Enters*] Ah! La Ruse, I'm belching affluently.

LA RUSE: That was a most excellent supper, Mr. Snap. [*Musing*] I believe I shall never sup better in your house—never.

MR. SNAP: [Sardonic] Did you say never? You are not thinking of trying to leave us through your window again, Count?

LA RUSE: No. This time I shall leave through your front door. When the clock strikes twelve I shall vanish like the maid with the glass slipper.

MR. SNAP: [Pleasantly entertained] And if you do, sir, Cinderella'll find a coach awaiting her at the door —a police-coach! I am delighted, Count. You have recovered your good humour.

LA RUSE: I protest, Mr. Snap. You never saw me in better humour than today at noon.

MR. SNAP: You'll not deny you grew sulky during afternoon.

LA RUSE: I was bored. I was resentful at being left alone.

MR. SNAP: It was plain to see you were in a rage against yourself.

LA RUSE: [With sudden vehemence] Not against myself.

MR. SNAP: [Always prepared to take umbrage] Against me, sir? Against me? Had you the audacity to resent me at my own table?

LA RUSE: [His anger dying away in soul-weariness] Not against you, Mr. Snap.

MR. SNAP: Then against who—or what, sir?

LA RUSE: Who can tell? One has memories, Mr. Snap —or better, one has not. Perhaps I was in a rage against the sun which rises. Perhaps against my first love—or my last. Strange, that one should forget one's last love before one's first!

MR. SNAP: By the bye, while you were vexed with Laetitia's absence this afternoon then, she was in her room.

LA RUSE: Yes. Did you notice Mr. Cartwright at supper? He was singularly animated.

MR. SNAP: He is odd, sir, like all of his kind. He spent the afternoon in his room with his metrical ruminations.

LA RUSE: Yes, I had thundered on his door, without arousing him.

MR. SNAP: Pray, Count, you have said naught of Mr. Wild and his fate.

LA RUSE: You've not told him he hangs tomorrow?

MR. SNAP: [Considerate] It seemed a pity to spoil his supper.

LA RUSE: [Unforgiving] Damn him. He has spoiled my after-supper.

MR. SNAP: [Craftily] I have been thinking of telling him—but I have been thinking more of not telling him.

LA RUSE: [Pricks up his ears] How now? What is in your agile mind?

MR. SNAP: Mr. Wild is a man of wealth.

LA RUSE: [With conviction] He is certainly the possessor of a valuable snuff-box.

MR. SNAP: He has money.

LA RUSE: Everybody's money.

MR. SNAP: He is about to die.

LA RUSE: Has he relatives?

MR. SNAP: Relatives? Did you say relatives? He has seven wives.

LA RUSE: What do you propose?

MR. SNAP: What if we tell him that a reprieve is possible—if he acts wisely and quickly?

LA RUSE: You would delude him into the belief he could be saved—when he must surely hang in the morning?

MR. SNAP: [His little eyes dancing] 'Tis the very point, that. He will be on his way to the gallows ere he's aware of his duping! 'Twill be choking late then for a hue and a cry over what money we get from him!

LA RUSE: Mr. Snap, forgive me. I had failed to perceive the sublime heights of your imagination.

MR. SNAP: [Beams] I'll admit, I think the plot neatly contrived.

LA RUSE: Yes, but why only a reprieve? Why not a full pardon—

MR. SNAP: For that we can easily garner a hundred pounds from the unfeeling villain!

LA RUSE: One hundred pounds. That's but fifty for each of us! Why not more, Mr. Snap?

MR. SNAP: Why, we cannot gouge him of more; he would not pay more, not for his very life, sir!

LA RUSE: [Soliloquises] The plot is neat— Jonathan is close, he parts unwilling from a bad farthing, but he fears death—how he fears death! Mr. Snap, do you fear death?

MR. SNAP: [Upset] Death? Did you say death? 'Tis a word as chilling as a cold sheet.

LA RUSE: There may always be a hot brick for your feet, Mr. Snap.

MR. SNAP: Do not say death, sir! I've no use for the word—no use at all!

LA RUSE: [Encouragingly] You are in good health, Mr. Snap.

MR. SNAP: [Brightens] I've never a day of sickness.

LA RUSE: [Thoughtfully] And still, you can never be sure. Health is no sign we shall not die. Death comes like a thief in the night—like a stab in the dark. Yes, I hear a beating of dark wings, now.

MR. SNAP: [Terrified] If you continue to rave on, I'll leave you! 'Tis my heart you hear beating; you have set shivers like lice running down my spine. Were the wind to blow a candle out, I'd think my life blown out!

LA RUSE: [Blows out a candle] There, sir, 'tis the candle's flame gone out, not yours! [Lights candle at fireplace]

MR. SNAP: Be done with your cursed fancies—done, I say!

LA RUSE: [Acquiesces] Think you he could procure the money tonight?

MR. SNAP: I don't know. I've tapped the walls of his room, sounded the floor and all to no effect, yet I could swear he must have coin o' the realm where he could lay his hand on't.

LA RUSE: But why not bell the cat yourself and keep all the profits?

MR. SNAP: I am not enough of an actor for the role, sir. Mr. Wild, being a knave, would see through to my native honesty. [Laetitia *sings and plays spinet off stage*] Now, with your refined ability—
[*Voices are heard, passing through the hall*]

LA RUSE: [*Listens; becomes intense*] 'Tis Laetitia and her poet.
[*The voices are heard in the adjoining room*]

MR. SNAP: Call him now!

LA RUSE: [*Looks gloomily toward the voices*] No, later. I have somewhat to say to Laetitia.

MR. SNAP: [*Authoritative*] No, no, 'tis not Laetitia hangs tomorrow. We must first dispose of Mr. Wild. [*Calling*] Mr. Wild! Mr. Wild!

JONATHAN: [*Heard off stage*] Yes, Mr. Snap.

MR. SNAP: He's coming—Remember, one hundred pounds.

JONATHAN: [*Enters*] Yes, Mr. Snap.

MR. SNAP: [*As he exits*] Count La Ruse has something to say to you, Mr. Wild.

JONATHAN: You are disturbed, La Ruse: pray, why?

LA RUSE: I am disturbed, sir: I'll not permit myself to be disturbed. What! Shall the stars be obscured by a slut?

JONATHAN: I sympathize with your tender emotion, Count.

LA RUSE: Jonathan! Mr. Snap has asked me to speak to you for him—to give you good news!

JONATHAN: [*Gasps*] I am not to hang?

LA RUSE: Not quite.

JONATHAN: How, not quite? They will hang me a few feet lower? There's something uncommon in this, La Ruse. Why should you speak for Mr. Snap?

LA RUSE: Mr. Snap feared his inflammable nature—feared that with the best of wills you would come to words again.

JONATHAN: 'Tis still no reason he should not speak for himself.

LA RUSE: You are right, Jonathan. 'Tis but the reason he gave me. He asked me to speak, because he knew me to be your loyal friend—but mostly because he fears to be seen in what must remain, after all, a hanging matter.

JONATHAN: Fears to be seen! Your reasoning grows sounder; Mr. Snap is not the soul of courage.

LA RUSE: [*Grows animated*] Courage, Jonathan? You have not heard the extent of his cowardice. Not only will he not speak—he'll not accept your money himself! No, sir! It must be passed him through me.

JONATHAN: [*Upset*] Money? Money for what?

LA RUSE: You know Mr. Snap.

JONATHAN: I know Mr. Snap.

LA RUSE: He has been feeling his way—

JONATHAN: In my room. I have watched him through a crack. There's not a board hasn't felt the soft caress of his fingers.

LA RUSE: Nevertheless, Mr. Snap has been feeling his way towards a full pardon for you, Jonathan. I see you do not believe it.

JONATHAN: Pity is not in Mr. Snap's nature as in yours or mine, Count.

LA RUSE: You forget there are moments when even pity may be combined with profit.

JONATHAN: There's truth in that: it had not struck me before. Mr. Snap would not willingly lose my board, for I am vilely over-charged. There's no tavern in London charges what Mr. Snap charges me for the privilege of being speeded forth some morning on a terrible journey. Though I feign otherwise, Count, I dread that journey of all things.

LA RUSE: You will never make that journey, Jonathan, if you listen well. Of all people, you should be aware that men in office are—men in office.

JONATHAN: Well—to the terms. What am I asked to slip from the halter?

LA RUSE: [*Dismissing it as a bagatelle*] Three hundred pounds.

JONATHAN: [*Appalled*] Three hundred pounds!

LA RUSE: There are many to be bribed. If you pay me the money, you may believe me, Mr. Snap will see but little of it.
[*Laetitia is heard singing and playing spinet off stage*]

JONATHAN: I'll not pay it! What! Pay three hundred pounds to a set of rogues who should be in my place? Let them do it—let it come! By Heaven, they'll not have three hundred pounds from me—not for my life! 'Tis not worth it—

LA RUSE: [*Shrugs his shoulders*] For myself, I should think a thousand pounds cheap. 'Tis likely, as you choke, you'll wish you'd not been so covetous.

JONATHAN: Covetous, sir? 'Tis the principle of the thing!—What shall I do? [*Hopefully*] They'll take less.

LA RUSE: [*Decisively*] No. Your reprieve will bring a clamour on their—[*Music stops*]—heads. You must let them have a fat umbrella for the storm. 'Tis three hundred pounds or your life.

JONATHAN: [*Groans*] My money or my life! How do I know, sir, if I pay this money I'll get the pardon?

LA RUSE: You must take the chance, Jonathan. I am convinced the offer is authentic. Mr. Snap is not enough of an actor to have deceived me.

JONATHAN: Very well—I'll pay—but after the pardon is signed.

LA RUSE: Do you think you deal with infants, sir? Why, they have made it a point the money be delivered at once—tonight.

JONATHAN: [*His suspicions re-awakened*] Tonight? Why so quickly?

LA RUSE: You force me to be unsparing, Jonathan. Those in power say you are such a monstrous villain they are not anxious to do't, not even for the money. You must pin them down at once.

JONATHAN: Three hundred pounds! [Laetitia *and* Cartwright *are heard laughing off stage*] 'Tis Laetitia and Cartwright. They're coming.

LA RUSE: [*Rising*] Damn Laetitia. I never want to see her again as long as I live. But by God I'll see her once before the night is over when I'm through with you, Mr. Wild—[*They exit. Laetitia enters with* Cartwright. *She carries an elegant fan, which she uses well*]

LAETITIA: [*With a shade of disappointment*] I thought I heard voices. [Cartwright *kisses her*] La Ruse usually repairs here [*Crosses to light lamps*] at this time.

CARTWRIGHT: We are fortunate, then.

LAETITIA: Yes, we are fortunate. [*Crosses; lights candles. They cross to the sofa*] 'Tis more pleasant in this room. Let us sit by the window. [*Taps him with her fan*] The night is warm for the spring.

CARTWRIGHT: I could not keep my eyes from you, at table. I wished only we were alone together in your room again.

LAETITIA: I noticed you, sir.

CARTWRIGHT: Why would you not meet my glance?

LAETITIA: You were injudicious enough.

CARTWRIGHT: Can love be injudicious?

LAETITIA: Can love be anything else?

CARTWRIGHT: I have had a dream—a dream of spring-madness!

LAETITIA: Madness sufficient to set up a flock of hatters shops! We were strangers this morning.

CARTWRIGHT: And now—we are not strangers.

LAETITIA: A single day has sufficed to change the years. I had always known it would be thus—when love at last came into my life—when at last I permitted the sweet and dangerous intimacy of a man! Comfort me, sir, with the assurance I have not yielded to one who took me lightly; let me hear you say, I love you.

CARTWRIGHT: I love you.

LAETITIA: I would believe you did I not know there are three things a man says with equal ease: "I love you—" "I regret, Madam, I can see you no more—" "By Gad, sir, she was as pretty a wench as ever I bedded!"

CARTWRIGHT: I love you!   [*Kisses hand. Kneels*]

LAETITIA: My naive heart would believe you—

CARTWRIGHT: Did I not tell you, this afternoon, I had saved myself for you—as you had saved yourself for me! I was waiting—waiting for someone who would share with me the immense burden of being. Often it seemed to me I was a fool. Spring came tenderly everywhere—so tenderly. Only to me it came like a sword. Laetitia, Laetitia, you have healed my wound of spring! My wound of life!

LAETITIA: I believe that you love me. And you must believe that I love you. [*Kiss*] Come, sir, let go of me—we shall be seen by the world.

CARTWRIGHT: The world will not like us? So much the worse for the world!

LAETITIA: So much the worse for us—nay, for me! Your arm—remove your arm, sir! My good name —'tis nothing to you?

CARTWRIGHT: [*Upset*] I meant no harm.

LAETITIA: No, only to hold me where we might be discovered! Alas, am I betrayed already? Is this the stuff of your oath, on the threshold of my room?

CARTWRIGHT: Forgive me.

LAETITIA: [*To him*] You will remember your promise. You will be discreet.

CARTWRIGHT: I will do always whatever you ask me.

LAETITIA: [*Relents further*] Come, sir, you have a face like Mr. Wild at the sight of a rope! My temper is out of me. [*Capriciously kisses him*] There, sir, you see! World or no world! [*Takes his hands. Kisses hand*]

CARTWRIGHT: [*Lifted from the depths*] Laetitia! You are kind.

LAETITIA: [*Gaily. Lets go hand*] Now you are like Papa—in high spirits!

CARTWRIGHT: In Heaven!

LAETITIA: Where the cherubim sing, like the poets, always of the Spring? Tell me why poets must sing always of the Spring?

CARTWRIGHT: [*Carries the happy mood*] Because they are boys who must run to a fire. April's their fire. They stand too close and catch the flame.

LAETITIA: [*Sententious*] Wise children soon learn to stand away from the fire.

CARTWRIGHT: [*Mystical*] Is it a part of wisdom—to stand away from the fire?

LAETITIA: For all that, I do not like your Spring as I like my Autumn. The skies flame and meadows are cool, but your cool April love is crossed then by some hot wind sweeping back from summer, by an unseasonable heat burning life to a delicious decay. I could gallop, or swoon: the yellow on a leaf has curious power to make me desire. [*Laughs strangely and draws* Cartwright *close*] I must teach you the joy of things yellow-tinged, overripe, sir.

CARTWRIGHT: [*Impulsively*] Let me come to your room again tonight.

LAETITIA: It would be too dangerous. I vow you will prove an eager lover. [*Restive, she walks here and there*] I must warn you, be neither too importunate nor too negligent; for one or t'other is the death of love—I have read. Where can La Ruse be, tonight?

CARTWRIGHT: [*Saddened*] I could almost believe you wished him with us. I dislike La Ruse.

LAETITIA: Would you be jealous of an impoverished rake? I have as little to do with him as possible— although I will confess he amuses me.

CARTWRIGHT: He is malicious. Why should he amuse you?

LAETITIA: Perhaps because he is malicious. Pray—

there was something in your tone—has La Ruse warned you against me?

CARTWRIGHT: [*Hesitant*] Yes.

LAETITIA: [*Smiles*] It was like La Ruse. Truth to tell he made certain advances, and found me inaccessible.

CARTWRIGHT: [*Triumphant*] I guessed as much. And told him so.

LAETITIA: You shall have a kiss for that—[*He crosses to her*] presently, Mr. Cartwright.

CARTWRIGHT: Must you still call me Mr. Cartwright?

LAETITIA: More than ever, sir. [*Severely*] If our intimacy teaches you nothing else, let it teach you this—that discretion is the first talent of a lover. For the last time, I charge you to remember your promise to me—Mr. Cartwright.

CARTWRIGHT: [*Subdued*] I will do always—

LAETITIA: Whatever I ask! Pray, how will you address me before others? Like this: Mistress Laetitia.

CARTWRIGHT: [*In her formal accents*] Mistress Laetitia. But O! Vile and obscene! We must be formal: we must bow correctly for fear that our pure emotions will be weighed—checked—and found wanting, in the foul balance of the world! Young as I am, Laetitia, I believe love will redeem men when men have redeemed love. Dare with me, Laetitia! Let us cry of the world we are true: we are lovers: our lips have met: our bodies have burned with the clear fire of our spirits: the sky is serene, the wind is tender, because we are lovers! Let us heap flowers under a white heaven on the green earth.

LAETITIA: [*Gasps*] 'Tis breath-taking to hear you go on! 'Tis a parliamentary wind of words!

CARTWRIGHT: [*Obsessed*] Will you dare with me?

LAETITIA: Let me think awhile. Yes, 'tis a pretty picture you have conjured for me! Two lovers, hand in hand, walk desolate ways in defiance of the conventions.

CARTWRIGHT: [*Prophetic: fierce*] Their desolation shall bloom.

LAETITIA: The fashionable world stands agape and offended—but what of that? They have each other. They are not received—but what of that? They have each other. They are pilloried, they are stoned—but what of that? They have each other. Always and always, each other.

CARTWRIGHT: [*Exalted*] And love, and victory.

LAETITIA: Always and always, each other. [*Starts from her visionary posture; with sudden dismay*] Yes—but what then?

CARTWRIGHT: [*Stupidly*] Then? When?

LAETITIA: [*In a torrent*] When they have had each other for an eternity? When he tires of her beauty and she of his oratory? When he cannot abide her friends, and she deceives him with his best friend? When, in short, they have had each other to the point of wishing they had never had each other?

CARTWRIGHT: [*Stricken*] You have been mocking me.

LAETITIA: [*Sweetly*] I would not have you think that. I was but measuring your ideal against the reality of things. Come, sir. You must first convert me, as you promised this morning.

CARTWRIGHT: [*Revived*] The grace of your spirit will make you understand.

LAETITIA: You shall have that promised kiss now. Tell me; how much do you love me?

CARTWRIGHT: [*Trembles*] Let me tell you in your room tonight.

LAETITIA: [*Agitated*] No, no—'Twould be too dangerous! And yet—perhaps! Ask me again, sir. Not another word now! I will see— [*La Ruse enters. She becomes mildly petulant*] Where have you been, La Ruse? You are later than usual.

LA RUSE: [*Coldly*] I doubted not but Mr. Cartwright was capable of amusing you.

LAETITIA: He has been reading me his verses; they are pretty verses. [*Roguishly, to Cartwright*] Are they not?

CARTWRIGHT: Pretty?

LA RUSE: If naught else damns you, Madam, your choice of adjectives will. I respect your gift, Mr. Cartwright. 'Twas a pity you were not here during the afternoon: the sunlight fell through the windows for a poet! Did I say poet? For more, sir: for lovers. [*Cartwright starts*] Yes, 'twas a pity you weren't here.

CARTWRIGHT: [*Shortly*] I was writing in my room.

LA RUSE: [*Smiles*] Of love?

CARTWRIGHT: [*Sullen*] Perhaps.

LA RUSE: Youth, sir—youth is not thus to be served! [*He studies the boy's face*] Why, sir, because on such a day you should not have written of love—you should have enjoyed love!

CARTWRIGHT: You desire to affront me, La Ruse!
                [*Laetitia sends him a frightened glance*]

LA RUSE: Why should I desire to affront you, Mr. Cartwright?

CARTWRIGHT: Because you do not like me, and because I do not like you.

LAETITIA: [*Very uneasy*] Gentlemen, gentlemen! Pray, what causes this sudden heat between you?

LA RUSE: We fight over truth and beauty, Madam. Perhaps more beauty than truth, since you are present.

LAETITIA: [*Angrily*] You are possessed, La Ruse! Mr. Cartwright: pray, leave us—you'll find me here when you return!

CARTWRIGHT: [*Unwilling*] Would you have me withdraw—now?

LAETITIA: [*Firmly*] Now—now!—Until La Ruse is himself again!

                [*Cartwright goes out*]

LA RUSE: Harlot!

LAETITIA: Your language, La Ruse! I am not in a mood for these profane terms of endearment.

LA RUSE: Where were you this afternoon?

LAETITIA: Pray, if you've nothing better to say than this, say nothing.

LA RUSE: Where were you this afternoon? And where was Cartwright?

LAETITIA: Your silence will at the least be more genteel.

LA RUSE: [To her] You were both missing, all the afternoon! I cannot believe it possible, minx! Were you really with the boy?

LAETITIA: I was alone this afternoon, but what if I had not been alone, this or any other afternoon? Did you not tell me you should watch such a procedure with magnificent indifference?

LA RUSE: [Characterised by the same sudden weariness which overcame him when with Mr. Snap] I am not concerned for you.

LAETITIA: Your concern is not for me! La Ruse, you begin to lose your singular force when you are thus obvious: like a common lover, whose jaundiced eyes stain all things yellow, but mostly, those things which are not.

LA RUSE: [Rather to himself] The yellow merges into black; the shadow of a bird I saw. I am like an actor whose perfection in a role has forced him to play the part until it has become odious to him. My delight was the comedy of repetition; to say the same word, to make the same gesture, in separate delicate moments. And now——

LAETITIA: [Spurs him] And now, pray?

LA RUSE: I say the word, I make the gesture without the delight. I am resolved Mr. Cartwright shall be saved from a like fate. I discern in the poet's youth a talent more than mere youth. I would not have his quality debased by your merciless instincts. I would protect the shadow of my former self from your attractive ferocity.

LAETITIA: Your name, sir, your name? 'Tis highly improper for me to converse with a gallant whose name is unknown to me—although I perceive he is excellent, virtuous, angelic! One who protects widows, orphans, curates! Your name, your seraphic name, sir!

LA RUSE: Silence, trollop!

LAETITIA: La Ruse: you of a thousand crimes, thief, blackguard, ravisher! 'Tis a new penny-whistle you play me! 'Tis a new pamphlet by Mr. DeFoe cried on the streets: The Pope turns Protestant! The King preaches sedition! La Ruse turns evangelist!

LA RUSE: [Controls himself] Yes: the last lock I pick shall be on the gates of Paradise. I shall pick one or two before that, however.

LAETITIA: It seems that the creed of the church is lamentably insufficient. Pray, sir, will you not convert me to your peculiar creed? Your rival——in conversion——is Mr. Cartwright. He has promised to save me: my desolation shall bloom. We are to make love on the highways, which I learn is a far more marked virtuous way of making love than in private——

LA RUSE: [Catches her up] Ah! You have been making less virtuous love in private!

LAETITIA: 'Twas a mere figure of speech, such as you use often, and Mr. Cartwright.

LA RUSE: [Viciously] I would have wrung his juvenile neck for him, this afternoon.

[Takes her in his arms]

LAETITIA: [Trills a few high notes] I adore you, La Ruse. You were concerned with wringing his neck for him: not with saving his soul from me.

LA RUSE: I could not bear the thought of the cub in your arms. [Despairingly] I could not bear the thought! Yet why? What have I to do with what women do! Who are you—what are you, that your bawdiness causes my blood to choke my brain?

LAETITIA: [Impatiently] 'Tis the moment when your strict grammatical rule requires that you say you do not love me—though you do.

LA RUSE: Yes; in this chemical reality we must kiss evil on the mouth even as our spirits take flight from evil. [Kisses her] Like two wild horses, released by birth, body and soul strain different ways and tear us to pieces. 'Tis your pleasure—Madam, to whip the steeds o' myself until sense careens, but God be praised! your power is but the power of matter lacerating matter in a small confine, and I shall soon be out of that, I promise you. [Looks at knife]

LAETITIA: I have a secret may keep you here longer than you think.

LA RUSE: Mr. Cartwright is no secret, and will not keep me here.

LAETITIA: Perhaps 'tis a new lock, of a special sort, designed to keep you here! I will reveal my secret to you tomorrow—La Ruse.

LA RUSE: Tomorrow? I'll not be the sort of guest who's always leaving tomorrow. I shall make a more graceful exit—who knows—perhaps tonight.

LAETITIA: You talk as if you had some plan.

LA RUSE: Plan?—Never a day or a night goes by but I have some plan——

LAETITIA: You talk now—as if——

LA RUSE: As if?—Pray finish your sentence, Madam!

LAETITIA: [Rises] I vow, La Ruse, because I was not to be found—because Mr. Cartwright was not to be found——

LA RUSE: [Wryly] Singular coincidence!

LAETITIA: You indulge in this wild talking of fleeing tonight! When you know 'tis but talk! Do you think the bolts will be weakened by your jealousy? For shame, sir! Would you be jealous of an impoverished poet?

LA RUSE: No: of an amorous day-dream.

LAETITIA: Believe whatever you will, I adore you. La Ruse, you will confess that even though you are a Count——

LA RUSE: I am not a Count: I am a Marquis.

LAETITIA: [The snob in her responding] A Marquis! But, La Ruse! You are the strangest of men: you have withheld this from me all the while. Marquis! And one were your wife, she would be a Marquise —only to think of that!

LA RUSE: You manage to seem a lady, until your veneration for a trumpery thus reveals you. I lowered my title, Madam, when I lowered my standards; an old family custom. My line, which began in a palace, ends in a jail.

LAETITIA: You are still a young man. 'Tis far from impossible—

LA RUSE: Shall I add another mouth to the pack? I have had one child—a bastard. Yes, I have withheld that also. He's a boy of ten by now, and thinks himself the son of an English lord, who is himself deceived, since he was deceived. I shall leave no issue with my name, and for this, much will be forgiven me on high.

LAETITIA: [*Earnestly*] 'Tis strange, La Ruse, you should talk thus at this jointure—'tis most strange! For 'twas in my thoughts to observe, when you interrupted, that although a Count—a Marquis, you are not much of a match today.

LA RUSE: What do you get at, Madam? 'Tis true, mothers with frumpish daughters no longer leer into my face.

LAETITIA: No: you are not much of a match today. Yet—if you were to ask me to marry you—

LA RUSE: Ask you to marry me!

LAETITIA: [*Quickly*] I should say yes, and force Papa's consent. Ah! That was an unmannerly noise, La Ruse.

LA RUSE: [*Dazed*] Marry you! Marry you! Do you think because you have been my mistress you shall be my familiar? What! Are our bedfellows to answer us back? Monstrous presumption! What is your crest, Madam? Does it show bolts and bars against a field of human misery? Marry you! Marry you! Infamous affront to the blood royal in my veins!

LAETITIA: [*Serenely*] Truth to tell, you have taken the suggestion less violently than I thought you would.

LA RUSE: There was a sovereign, Madam, once offered me the hand of his niece. I refused her, although the refusal must cause my downfall, as it did. I was fastidious: her ankles were confused with her leg. I am still fastidious, Madam; if in more elementary respects. Besides—

LAETITIA: [*Unflinching*] Besides, you think me untrue. I am not, La Ruse, and will prove it. Will you visit me tonight? Is't my fault if you force me to play the man in our courtship? I vow you regard me as something seen late at night in a cemetery!

LA RUSE: [*Horrified*] This afternoon—

LAETITIA: [*Exasperated*] This afternoon! I tell you 'twas no different from a thousand afternoons: dishes clattered and were still, the hot sun shone, a drowsiness filled the blue air, and I slept—as I always do.

LA RUSE: [*Vastly surprised*] As you always do? I thought you never slept, Madam! For I have noticed this peculiarity about you—your eyes are always open. You should see an oculist—one with a number of lenses: he will fit you with spectacles made for a wealthy tiger who failed to call back for them. The price is excessive, but the relief cosmological.

LAETITIA: [*Impatiently*] You are like the Prince in the play you will read me so often, though it bores me: words, words, words! Answer me, La Ruse, one way or t'other.

LA RUSE: Why should you desire me to visit you? I am like the Prince again: I have bad dreams.

LAETITIA: [*Softening*] I would dispel them.

LA RUSE: Yet 'tis whispered by mothers—you are the mother of nightmares.

LAETITIA: [*Clipping her words*] I grow weary of your reviling me.

LA RUSE: I have ever thought it strange myself that men should derive their refreshment from the weariness of women.

LAETITIA: [*In cold rage*] 'Tis too much! La Ruse, you shall learn I can repay far more than I am loaned!

LA RUSE: Rare creditor! I will have you done in oils and present the portrait to my banker.

LAETITIA: Hearken, La Ruse: you have imagined the poet in my arms; he shall be there. The lips you have tasted, he shall taste; the joy you have known, he shall know! I'll not have you sent back to the prison! I'll keep you here, where you shall see only that which you have cried, "I cannot bear!"—myself in the arms of another.

LA RUSE: [*Struggles fiercely*] It matters not! My spirit is strong to be free.

LAETITIA: [*As the clock strikes the hour*] The torment of the night begins for you!

LA RUSE: [*Ringingly*] You are late, Madam, by the clock which strikes in Heaven! The hour of my deliverance is at hand.

LAETITIA: [*Malefic*] You are white already, La Ruse; you shall be grey with the grey dawn!

LA RUSE: [*Exorcises her*] Back to your inferno, devil!

LAETITIA: [*Throws her fan on the table*] 'Tis you return to the inferno—not I! Enough! You have set my course.   [*Exits rapidly*]

LA RUSE: [*Breaking*] Set her course!—'Fore God she'll do as she swears! Laetitia!

CARTWRIGHT: [*Enters*] What new malice have you inflicted on her? And where is she gone?

LA RUSE: [*Flicks a spot of dust from his coat*] She has taken a fancy to Pluto, and is over the Styx by now.

CARTWRIGHT: Count La Ruse.

LA RUSE: Mr. Cartwright?

CARTWRIGHT: You are a scoundrel.

LA RUSE: Your opinion has had judicial recognition, sir.

CARTWRIGHT: You have lied—

LA RUSE: Of Laetitia? To lie of Laetitia is as if one

were to speak the truth of another—the same affect is achieved.

CARTWRIGHT: [*Homicidal*] I'll blood you.

LA RUSE: [*Laughs*] You have sworn never to lay your hands on a human being, except in love. I would advise you not to lay your hands upon me, Mr. Cartwright. I am much the stronger of the two—and I may be armed.

CARTWRIGHT: [*Quietly, after a pause*] I never thought I should want to kill a man, but had I had my knife—

LA RUSE: Then I am obliged to the gentleman who took your knife.

CARTWRIGHT: And so am I, Count La Ruse.

LA RUSE: Besides, he has a use for it—tonight.

CARTWRIGHT: What would it profit me to throw myself at you? Mr. Wild is wicked; he can be killed. But you are evil, Count La Ruse, and evil must be killed by itself, or it does not die.

LA RUSE: The young rhetorician to the old rhetorician! [*Suddenly grave*] I know not why, Mr. Cartwright, but you make me speak not what I feel towards you, but the cutting opposite.

CARTWRIGHT: You are envious of me, sir.

LA RUSE: [*Sadly*] I am envious of you, not because of a woman, as you think, but because I was myself denied any special gift, and have, perhaps, too high a regard for the gifts of others. In my heart, Mr. Cartwright, I would be your friend.

CARTWRIGHT: Friend!

LA RUSE: Yes. 'Tis a sudden weakness of my past, an outbreak of paternity which ill-becomes my smile, I'll allow. I've a son, somewhere; I speak to you now as I would speak to him, were he your age.

CARTWRIGHT: You speak as a discredited rival.

LA RUSE: [*Loses his temper*] Rival? *You* my rival? With Laetitia? You! Is the pup in her lap my rival? You are still in your high-chair—pray, tighten your bib, the gruel spills on your flannel!

CARTWRIGHT: [*Laughs*] 'Tis as you said: you speak as a friend, as father to son.

LA RUSE: [*Checks himself*] I do, sir, but you goad me damnably. I'd not give much for the young man who succumbs to the ordinary hurt of first love, which is a sort of new teething we must all suffer. But you are in danger of a wound far more perverse, and therefore far more delicate! Heal yourself, before the fester penetrates beyond the heart and becomes permanent in the spirit.

CARTWRIGHT: Is not the very spice of affectation to appear more sincere than sincerity itself?

LA RUSE: Would you ham-string me on my own idle words? I implore you to heed me, lest you learn to your sorrow that there are women in whom the mother has been completely omitted, and that Laetitia is such a woman.

CARTWRIGHT: I have felt the mother in Laetitia comfort me.

LA RUSE: She could bear a kingdom, and never feel a maternal thrill! Take your light elsewhere, or 'twill go out like my own.

CARTWRIGHT: I have found that my light grows in her radiance, La Ruse.

LA RUSE: Mr. Cartwright: we are all of us defenseless when we love a good woman; how much more so when we love the implacable itself! But 'tis no use. A man, young or old, will as soon admit his secret body-odours as that the perfume of all creation is not in his new mistress! [*Cartwright starts*] You started at the word: damme, but you did! Death-in-Hell! You confirm my suspicions! Is't really so?

CARTWRIGHT: I must know, before I reply, how you speak—as friend, as father to son, or—

LA RUSE: I stepped out of character for your sake, but I speak as the Count La Ruse, lover of Laetitia!

CARTWRIGHT: And you speak to the poet Cartwright, lover of Laetitia!

LA RUSE: Whippersnapper!

CARTWRIGHT: Now I am a blackguard, but I feel better. [*Taunting him*] La Ruse: she loves me, she loves me, she loves me!

LA RUSE: Add she loves me not; that ends the rhyme always. You elephantine gods! where is your ancient nimbleness? Naught's divine, all's clownish, Mr. Cartwright: you do not believe I have been her lover?

CARTWRIGHT: Were I to believe that, I must believe—

LA RUSE: Laetitia has asked me to visit her tonight.

CARTWRIGHT: Your malice undoes you! She—

LA RUSE: Your silence undoes you: she's hinted you may visit her tonight. Well, I'll offer you this challenge for your soul: that Laetitia loves me, that we mirror each other, are bound to each other; that if I knock on her door tonight, she'll admit me! Do you take my challenge?

CARTWRIGHT: Do you think I would stoop to it?

LA RUSE: She'll admit me, I say, and where will you be? You'll be on the landing, outside her door: you'll be there with cold hands and a burning throat when your knock goes unanswered! Do you take my challenge?

CARTWRIGHT: No!

LA RUSE: I warned you once it would profit you more to cut the throat of Mr. Snap than to kiss the throat of his daughter. Well, poet and sweet-singer, tonight I shall do both! Yes, this shall be my final folly! I will risk my chance of freedom to prove a point of vanity.

CARTWRIGHT: Your point of vanity is my whole faith!

LA RUSE: Vanity or faith, there's a fire abroad which only your tears will put out! Do you take my challenge?

CARTWRIGHT: I take nothing, and I give nothing, but I hold fast to what I know.

LA RUSE: You do take my challenge. It must lie between us as men of honour.

CARTWRIGHT: As blackguards.

LA RUSE: Amen.

LAETITIA: [*Enters*] Ah, gentlemen, conversing most amiably, are you?

LA RUSE: Yes, we've been discussing the astronomical position of Venus tonight.

CARTWRIGHT: And of Lucifer.

LAETITIA: Leave him alone in his dark thoughts.

JONATHAN: [*Enters*] La Ruse! La Ruse!

LA RUSE: Well, Mr. Wild, what's on your mind?

JONATHAN: What's on my mind? Don't you know?

LA RUSE: Of course. You've decided?

JONATHAN: I'll take the risk. [*Mr. Snap enters*] Pay the full three hundred pounds. We'll stop in my room later—three hundred pounds.

MR. SNAP: What did he say?

LA RUSE: He'll pay the full one hundred pounds. Whispering, Mr. Cartwright? I don't like whispering.

CARTWRIGHT: Then I'll whisper the whole night through.

LA RUSE: Better go to sleep in your narrow bed.

MR. SNAP: Well, gentlemen—An amiable round of cards? Will you join us—[*Jonathan takes cards*] Mr. Cartwright?

CARTWRIGHT: Thank you. I don't play.

MR. SNAP: Incredible, La Ruse—he doesn't play.

LAETITIA: My fan—I'm sure I left it on the table before—

[*Cartwright crosses to card table*]

LA RUSE: I'll visit you tonight, wench. [*Crossing to card table—sits*] Really, Mr. Cartwright, you should have some amusement, and cards are your only chance.

CARTWRIGHT: I might be tricked by the knave in the pack.

MR. SNAP: Oh, come, sir, we are all honest. That was a bad card you threw, La Ruse. I'll wager you hold a bad hand.

LA RUSE: Yes, but I've a wager I hold a better hand before the night is over.

CARTWRIGHT: The cards may not fall as you think, La Ruse.

[*La Ruse looks at Laetitia, who is singing lightly*]

LA RUSE: [*Beams*] A mislaid fan, a daughter singing, the men at the cards! They may say what they want of felons and jailers, but where in all Merrie England will you find a more domestic scene than this?

[*Laetitia resumes her singing*]

Act III

The same, next morning

Mr. Snap *enters with* Lord Wainwright, *a nobleman whose face is a chronic deadly white. His teeth are his most prominent feature; they pro-*trude *over his lip. His eyes are his least prominent feature; they are of that peculiar grey which seems to diffuse itself, the better to see. In his bearing, he has the genuine distinction of his class; and his speech is tinged with a hesitancy which is contradicted by the decisiveness of his thoughts.*

MR. SNAP: [*Cheerily*] Sit down, my lord, sit down! [*Dusting sofa*] You will stand? As you please. Is't not a fine morning, Lord Wainwright? I had my walk this morning. I wouldn't miss my walk on such a morning, my lord.

LORD WAINWRIGHT: I find myself totally uninterested in your pedestrian habits. [*Feels in his pockets*] Damn me, if some rascal in the jail hasn't relieved me of my snuff-box! Plague on him! The box was a masterpiece. I shall miss it.

MR. SNAP: 'Tis a pity, your lordship. You are well out of the jail, I'll warrant you. I marked you out of the mob at once— I saw at once you were a gentleman.

LORD WAINWRIGHT: [*Impatiently*] It is just as obvious that I am a gentleman as that you are not.

MR. SNAP: Your lordship!

LORD WAINWRIGHT: I must insist you abandon the cant of your kind, Mr. Snap. I have had enough of the cant of my own kind, since the day my mother told me a lying story of a stork and a chimney. I am here because I finally took extreme measures to stop the flow of unmeaning talk around me. If you will not affect social compliments, but level your conversation to the mean quality of your nature, as 'tis apparent, you will find we will get along a great deal better. I trust I have made myself plain.

MR. SNAP: Plain, my lord? Plain, did you say? I confess, I do not understand you.

LORD WAINWRIGHT: You found me in the jail; you offered me the privilege of being locked up in your home, instead.

MR. SNAP: Yes, I could not have offered you lodging yesterday; but fortunately Mr. Wild [*Coughs*] vacates his room today.

LORD WAINWRIGHT: As your house could not possibly stink worse than the jail, I accepted your suggestion. Now, sir, what will you gouge me?

MR. SNAP: Gouge you, my lord! Did you say gouge you? You will find, Lord Wainwright, I am not avaricious.

LORD WAINWRIGHT: I see every evidence of avarice in your person. You brought me here to be well paid for your trouble.

MR. SNAP: [*Smarting*] And why not, my lord? Is't wrong I should be well paid for breaking the law? For chancing my official position? Is't wrong, my lord?

LORD WAINWRIGHT: 'Tis confoundedly right. Why do you not talk thus always? You would find me more amicable. I am well provided with money, Mr. Snap.

MR. SNAP: [*A little overcome by his honesty*] My lord!

LORD WAINWRIGHT: What privilege will my money buy for me?

MR. SNAP: For a reasonable sum you may buy the entire privacy of this floor.

LORD WAINWRIGHT: The sum will not be reasonable, and the floor will not be private, but I will buy it. The furnishings here are in the worst of taste; pray, is my bedroom of the same order?

MR. SNAP: 'Tis an exquisite room, your lordship. I furnished it myself, and I am—whatever rogues may say—a man of taste.

LORD WAINWRIGHT: I suspect our tastes differ. I am exceedingly fond of small objects, carved precisely —knick-knacks on which the eye may rest with pleasure. There is a want of them in this room, for instance.

MR. SNAP: My lord, we dare not leave them about. We have lodgers here not to be trusted. I should warn you against Mr. Wild, but he leaves [*Coughs*] this morning. Beware, however, of a scamp calling himself Count La Ruse. As for your knick-knacks, sir, chance has put one or two in my way; I hope to interest you in them.

LORD WAINWRIGHT: I'll have a look at them. I'll try to make myself as comfortable as possible until my trial.

MR. SNAP: Pray, my lord, may I inquire for what you are held?

LORD WAINWRIGHT: I thought I heard you inquire of the clerk in the prison?

MR. SNAP: I did, my lord, but I failed to catch his reply.

LORD WAINWRIGHT: [*Indifferently*] I poisoned my wife—and a few of her intimate friends.

MR. SNAP: [*Covers the shock with a silly laugh*] Dear me! Why did you do that?

LORD WAINWRIGHT: A gentleman does not discuss his family affairs with a vulgar stranger.

MR. SNAP: [*Not quite recovered*] Gentleman! 'Tis true—you seem such a gentleman.

LORD WAINWRIGHT: I am a lord, Mr. Snap, and would have you know that all the eminent poisoners were of good family; 'twas a symptom of their subtle breeding. You will do me the justice of not derogating my rank because I rid the world of a few useless people; a fact which, in any competent civilization, would indubitably raise my rank.

MR. SNAP: As for that, my lord, a lord is a lord to me, no matter what he's done. I hope I know the deference due to a man like yourself.

LA RUSE: [*Enters and stops short at sight of* Lord Wainwright] Lord Wainwright!

LORD WAINWRIGHT: I am equally astonished. Why, 'tis—

LA RUSE: [*Quickly*] Count La Ruse. I have long for-

gotten I had any other name, and must beg your lordship the favour of forgetting with me.

LORD WAINWRIGHT: Count La Ruse. [*Turns to Mr. Snap; in a peculiar tone*] So this is your Count La Ruse! We are old acquaintances—are we not, Count?

MR. SNAP: A happy coincidence! You gentlemen will have the past to discuss. I'll go down below and see if there's a trace of some callers I'm expecting. [*Winks at* La Ruse] Callers for Mr. Wild.

[*He exits*]

LORD WAINWRIGHT: Pray, would you loan me your snuff, Count? My box was filched from me in the jail.

LA RUSE: And mine here. I'm starved for the powder. Take heed you leave nothing of value where Mr. Snap can reach it. He's as unprincipled as a fox on the run.

LORD WAINWRIGHT: [*Permits himself a smile*] I am obliged for the warning. Mr. Snap has been so good as to tender me a similar warning against yourself. I find myself amused.

LA RUSE: [*Unabashed*] I have been derelict in asking —how is your dear lady?

LORD WAINWRIGHT: [*Without emotion*] Dead.

LA RUSE: [*Shaken*] Dead!

LORD WAINWRIGHT: Quite dead. In fact, will never rise again. Did you think her ladyship would live forever? The expression of your face leads me to think you did.

LA RUSE: The news was unexpected. I remember her ladyship as an example of your fine English beauty, in which health is so much of the beauty. 'Tis hard to think of her dead. I tender you my deepest sympathy, Lord Wainwright.

LORD WAINWRIGHT: [*Passively*] Your sympathy is wasted: her ladyship's passing was a blessing, to me.

LA RUSE: I cannot believe you; there were not many like Lady Wainwright. With all respect, I was attached to her.

LORD WAINWRIGHT: You should be consoled by the knowledge, my dear Marquis, she was much attached to you.

LA RUSE: Yes, she did her best to save me from my many follies. May she rest in peace; she was a wise and charming lady.

LORD WAINWRIGHT: To her lovers. At home she was a bitch.

LA RUSE: [*Flares*] You make too free with your lady's memory!

LORD WAINWRIGHT: On my word, for a mere acquaintance, you are most concerned for my wife's good name! Is't possible you were more than a mere acquaintance of Lady Wainwright?

LA RUSE: I have not been unaware of your insinuations, sir; to answer them would be to dignify them. I have still some of the instincts of my breeding.

LORD WAINWRIGHT: Cant! We have all the same instincts. Answer what you will, without cant.

LA RUSE: I will say this: you have a son, and when you degrade his mother, you degrade your heir. Sir, the passing of her ladyship may have been a blessing to you, but what a loss it must be to the boy! Do you not think of that? I glimpsed him in the park, not so many years ago; a golden-haired, rollicking boy.

LORD WAINWRIGHT: He will rollick no more.

LA RUSE: [After a pause] He is dead, also.

LORD WAINWRIGHT: Of the same distemper which removed his mother. By my honour, my dear Count—you have believed my family immortal. A boy dies, and there's such an expression on your face—

LA RUSE: And you—have you no regret for your son's passing?

LORD WAINWRIGHT: None at all. I never believed him to be my son.

LA RUSE: Not your son! But you brought him up.

LORD WAINWRIGHT: I played the father for a while, but the jest wearied me. It became intolerable a bastard should inherit my name and acres. The boy did not resemble me, not in the slightest.

LA RUSE: It scarcely becomes a man thus to slander his dead wife and her child.

LORD WAINWRIGHT: 'Tis exquisitely fitting I should meet you here and break the news; for a thought had often occurred to me; the boy was altogether of your type; had your head, eyes, mouth, gait and insufferable habit of talk, talk, talk.

LA RUSE: You knew—all the while— You knew— Why are you held, Lord Wainwright?—You spoke of a distemper; what was this distemper?

LORD WAINWRIGHT: [Brutally] Arsenic.

LA RUSE: You— O! monster!

LORD WAINWRIGHT: And now the jest wearies you. I made little effort to conceal what I had done; to do so would have meant so much more of cant— hypocritical heavings of the breast, streaming tears, and lying eulogies. The funerals delighted me, and I let it be known.

LA RUSE: You are mad—stark mad, I perceive!

LORD WAINWRIGHT: So my lawyers say, but 'tis they who are mad, or they would not be lawyers. Pray, do me the favour of not intruding overmuch on my privacy here. I've a dislike for your company —always had, but at length can tell you so.

LA RUSE: [Mechanically] I leave this house forever this morning.

LORD WAINWRIGHT: One offense removed from my sight without my going to extremes.

MR. SNAP: [Comes in from the hall] What a day! What a day! Life's up and coming, gentlemen! You should see the gallants: they're winning the ladies everywhere, with insults; and the children, the happy children, are rollicking in the streets! What a day!

LA RUSE: [Stabbed] Rollicking!

MR. SNAP: I see you've been affected by your recollections with his lordship. There's nothing so pleasant as talking of old times. But you must accompany me now, La Ruse; the crowd gathers below already, and we must discuss, when Mr. Wild discovers— Pray, make yourself at your ease, my lord.

[Laetitia has entered]

LORD WAINWRIGHT: A wench! A pretty wench!

MR. SNAP: 'Tis my daughter, Laetitia. Daughter, this is Lord Wainwright, a new lodger in the house. His lordship's a real lord, and not one of your nobles born in a deck of cards and glass of whisky.

LAETITIA: [Ingratiatingly] 'Tis most pleasant to have you in the house, my lord. Good morning, La Ruse.

MR. SNAP: [To La Ruse] Let us go. The moment arrives, and we've no plan—

LAETITIA: [Piqued by La Ruse's silence] Do you set a new fashion, sir? Do you not say good morning? [He makes a slight response] I vow, if 'tis a good morning, you should admit the fact more graciously, I think.

MR. SNAP: By chance, Laetitia, Lord Wainwright's a great friend of Count La Ruse.

[Wainwright puts his hands over his ears and walks away]

LAETITIA: [Gets a fuller view of La Ruse] Why, what ails you? You seem ill?

LA RUSE: [Musters up a little of his usual manner] Ill, Madam? Ill? I am well enough.

LAETITIA: Will you have a glass of spirits?

LA RUSE: [Resenting her sympathy] Thank you. There's no necessity.

MR. SNAP: [Has been waiting; irritably] But there's necessity for haste for both of us, sir! Are you rooted in the floor?

LAETITIA: Stay, Papa. I must know—what have you done further with Mr. Cartwright?

MR. SNAP: Further? Did you say further? The young rascal is locked in his room, and 'tis likely still feels the butt of my pistol on his face. In truth, I hope he does.

LAETITIA: 'Tis likely he meant less harm than we thought, Papa. I've forgiven him, this bright morning. I'm sure he's had nought to eat nor drink.

MR. SNAP: 'Twas you cried most "whip him! Scourge him! Lock him in his room! Send him back to the jail!"

LAETITIA: The early hour—the noise—the fighting —I was frightened. Since 'twas Love made him act thus, I owe him the duty of kindness.

LA RUSE: [Strangely] He may kill you.

LAETITIA: He's a boy, and easily handled.

MR. SNAP: [Peremptorily] La Ruse! You've wasted enough time. We must look to Mr. Wild, sir! [La Ruse goes out like a blind man who knows the *way.* Mr. Snap *whispers to* Laetitia, *indicating* Wainwright] A poisoner!   [*Exits*]

LAETITIA: [*A spring released by the words*] Lord Wainwright! Pray, why is one of your station in such a place as this? [*Bows*]

LORD WAINWRIGHT: Cant! Your father's whisper had all the discretion of a thunderclap. Do you find me repulsive, now?

LAETITIA: 'Twould be presumptuous indeed for me to find one of your station repulsive, my lord. [*Bows*]

LORD WAINWRIGHT: We have our ugly faces.

LAETITIA: No; far from finding you repulsive, I'll confess that for me there's a titillating distinction in the thought you have poisoned people. I am no ordinary woman, my lord; I've lived so long in the atmosphere of a jail that I've come to measure my respect for men by the quality of their misdeeds; and yours would seem to belong in the very aristocracy of crime. Perhaps some day you will excite my ears with the history of your exploits. I should be ravished to hear them.

LORD WAINWRIGHT: [*Displeased*] For a wench you have a loathsome flow of words.

LAETITIA: I have listened much to the conversation of your friend, Count La Ruse.

LORD WAINWRIGHT: I might have guessed.

LAETITIA: Is he not your friend?

LORD WAINWRIGHT: Certainly not.

LAETITIA: But Papa said—

LORD WAINWRIGHT: Your father is a knave and a fool.

LAETITIA: You are plain-spoken.

LORD WAINWRIGHT: You will find me increasingly so, wench.

LAETITIA: For myself, I greatly admire Count La Ruse.

LORD WAINWRIGHT: I greatly despise him. A word-monger, I have had the courage to use a vial, and not a phrase.

LAETITIA: He has killed men and done worse with women— Papa has told me.

LORD WAINWRIGHT: He has had his moments—has aspired to be what I am; but there was a flaw in him he could not overcome; a belief in words—in cant! The world knows him as a villain. I know him as a sentimentalist.

LAETITIA: I thought all men were sentimentalists.

LORD WAINWRIGHT: All men but myself. I fight naked.

LAETITIA: You are a man with a mind of your own. And perhaps will find me a woman with a mind of her own.

LORD WAINWRIGHT: A plague on your mind! Do you think me interested in a woman's mind? I am not twenty, wench.

LAETITIA: Your lordship has called me so a number of times; my name is Laetitia, Mistress Laetitia.

LORD WAINWRIGHT: Your name is Laetitia, and you are still a wench.

LAETITIA: It pleases your lordship to affect an uncouthness which the refinement of your thought denies. [*Bows*]

LORD WAINWRIGHT: Cant! Nothing but cant! I foresee I must undo the harm La Ruse has done you before I find your presence bearable.

LAETITIA: Your lordship flatters me with your courteous interest.

LORD WAINWRIGHT: My interest is always in myself. [*Casually*] I propose to enjoy your favours, wench.

LAETITIA: [*Left breathless*] My lord!

LORD WAINWRIGHT: Pray, spare me the cant of a lying outburst of your virtue. I can see in your eyes—

LAETITIA: [*His gaze forces hers to drop*] Did I ask you to look there, my lord—but not my master?

LORD WAINWRIGHT: It must be as patent to yourself as 'tis to me; you have been placed here for my convenience.

LAETITIA: And you think a woman like myself is to be won thus—by being told she is to be a convenience?

LORD WAINWRIGHT: What do you wish of me? Repartee? Shall I speak like the world, of your eyes and the blue skies; your cheeks and the red rose— when all the while, like the world, I am thinking of a bed? I tell you, wench, I would live a celibate all of my days before a word of such cant should pass my lips to a woman.

LAETITIA: Your words have sealed your celibacy here inviolate, my lord—but not my master!

LORD WAINWRIGHT: I suppose you have some entanglement of a low order with one of the wardens of the prison, or stableboys there.

LAETITIA: Stableboy!

LORD WAINWRIGHT: No? Ah! You greatly admire Count La Ruse. 'Tis he, without a doubt. I'm lucky. He's told me he leaves the house this morning, not to return.

LAETITIA: A favorite notion of La Ruse's—without substance, my lord—but not my master.

LORD WAINWRIGHT: Then we will buy him off. He's threadbare, and will welcome the money.

LAETITIA: [*Her fingers drumming on the table*] Is this the sum of your courtship?

LORD WAINWRIGHT: No. For yourself—I promise you shall have more money than you have ever had.

LAETITIA: [*Slaps his face*] Filthy beast!

LORD WAINWRIGHT: [*Wipes his face thoroughly*] I thought you a woman of sense.

LAETITIA: Of too much sense—to sell what can never be bought back.

LORD WAINWRIGHT: Cant! You have nothing to sell of the nature. Where is your room? I'll visit you this very night.

LAETITIA: [*Rising. Passionately*] On the first floor of the moon! Seek it there. You'll not come closer, Lord Wainwright!

LORD WAINWRIGHT: Where is your room, wench? You'll not say? Then I must bribe your father to give me ingress.

LAETITIA: I promise, nay I swear; if ever you so much as gain ingress over my threshold—I'll recant all I have said, I'll own you for my lord and master.

LORD WAINWRIGHT: A dangerous promise, wench.

LAETITIA: A safe promise. What your crimes could not do, your manners have done. I find you repulsive. I hate you! I hate you!

LORD WAINWRIGHT: [Smiles] Then I have accomplished the beginning of my end. Pray, don't run because of me. I'm content for the moment and will seek my own room. Perhaps you'll tell me where it lies, wench?

LAETITIA: I am not your servant.

LORD WAINWRIGHT: You shall be more. Adieu, from your lord—and master. [He exits]

LAETITIA: [Her fists clenched] Turk! Mohammedan!

[Cartwright comes in. There is a large bruise on his forehead, and in his eyes the look of a man who has seen things clear, too suddenly, and is a little strange as a result. He stops short at sight of Laetitia, then bows with exaggerated deference]

CARTWRIGHT: [With a peculiar purring softness] Good morning, Mistress Laetitia.

LAETITIA: You! And now you must plague me! It has not been enough—

CARTWRIGHT: It makes me most happy to see you, dear lady, charming as always. I trust you slept well?

LAETITIA: Impudence! If I did not sleep well 'twas because of your infant outburst.

CARTWRIGHT: [Smoothly] I greatly regret having incommoded you, Mistress Laetitia. Is it not a delicious day? May I hope, presently, to have your hand in the dance? I've been told your minuet is as irreproachable as my own.

LAETITIA: Pray, what is this nonsense you babble? I am not in a mood for it, I warn you.

CARTWRIGHT: 'Tis not nonsense, but an event of world-shaking importance. I have become a very discreet gentleman; my manners now are exquisite.

LAETITIA: Cant! [Amazed at her use of the word, and put further out of temper by it] And now you have the audacity to make game of me. I'll speak with you, Mr. Cartwright, when you've apologized for your behaviour.

CARTWRIGHT: I do not make game of you, Madam. We play a game together. Pray, would you leave me when the game's just begun?

LAETITIA: You're inexcusably young. I'll humour you.

CARTWRIGHT: The game's called cat-and-mouse; and as you played cat before, you must play mouse now —as is only fair, you'll be the first to admit.

LAETITIA: You played cat enough last night—clawing

La Ruse as you did! You—you who swore—"I will do, always, whatever you ask me!"

CARTWRIGHT: And so I will, dear lady.

LAETITIA: Pray, were you demented? What was your reason—nay, where was your reason? Falling on La Ruse at three o'clock in the morning—

CARTWRIGHT: [Punctilious] At three-seventeen.

LAETITIA: Falling on him in the hall—

CARTWRIGHT: [More intensely] As he left your room—

LAETITIA: Causing a hullabaloo—bringing Papa out with a whip and pistol— When you knocked, I persuaded you to return to your room. Why did you leave it again?

CARTWRIGHT: I did not leave my room. My room left me. Pray, Madam, have you ever had the floor drop from under you? The sensation is unique.

LAETITIA: Your talk was always bizarre, but I vow 'tis now altogether lacking in sense, Mr. Cartwright.

CARTWRIGHT: 'Tis sense that your father believes I would have ravished you but for the heroic interference of Count La Ruse. Yes, 'tis sense, but is't not also most bizarre?

LAETITIA: Do you think I'm unaware how hard it must be to forgive me for that lie? But what else could I do?

CARTWRIGHT: [With sudden plaintiveness] But you cried, "Whip him! Scourge him!" Why did you want me beaten harder than I was beaten?

LAETITIA: I was fearful lest you should cry out— what you knew. Shame and grief consume me— Why should you listen to me now—though I speak the truth at last?

CARTWRIGHT: [Impulsively] Tell me only this: when we were alone together, and I felt your softness— was it true then?

LAETITIA: I'll not deceive you; 'twas partly true. Pray, do not despise me too much. Why should you believe that La Ruse forced his way into my room—That he was never my lover before, and will never be again? Even now, when I speak the truth at last, you are right to put no faith in me.

CARTWRIGHT: I should not have looked into your eyes—

LAETITIA: Have you forgotten so soon—drawn shades, and open lips? Were you to lie in my arms now, my softness should all be true, and lasting, and still.

CARTWRIGHT: Hearts loud, and life still. [Bends over her proffered mouth, and bursts into laughter] Cat-and-mouse! Who's cat now? Who's mouse?

LAETITIA: [Stupefied] You'll not kiss me?

CARTWRIGHT: Kiss you! In broad daylight? We might be seen, Madam.

LAETITIA: This is witchcraft— You speak no longer like yourself, but like La Ruse.

CARTWRIGHT: [Cunningly] Because I'm no longer a cat. 'Tis said, there are no more wolves in England, but most ignorantly, Madam; there are no more men; we are all wolves.

LAETITIA: Your eyes burn me, I vow, like a wild animal's! Pray, recollect—I'm a female—your gentility—

CARTWRIGHT: Do you but let down your hair, dear lady, and you'll see me eat it, ravenously.

LAETITIA: I'll call for help—

CARTWRIGHT: [Laughs] You will only call in more wolves. [Prosaically] 'Tis strange, dear lady, how lovely you are. I've seen all beasts, clear or striped, but you are the most beautiful beast I have ever seen.

LAETITIA: [Has the courage of one at bay] You'll be whipped for these insults! [Pushes him]

CARTWRIGHT: [With melancholy wonder] Why should your eyes seem different from other eyes? You are loved madly, Madam.

LAETITIA: Aye, madly! Think of what you do, Mr. Cartwright—you'll regret later—

CARTWRIGHT: You have brought love to my heart, tears to my eyes, and a great rage to my brain. Where's peace, now? What death must I live— and you die?

LAETITIA: No more—let me pass at once—at once— [Laetitia tries to escape]

CARTWRIGHT: [Pushes her on sofa] I will do, always, whatever you ask me. [Strokes her hair] Shall I twist this around your throat, tightly—in the charming Italian fashion? I will do, always, whatever you ask me. Will you ask me to whip you, scourge you? Pray, ask me to kill you, Madam. I will do, always, whatever you ask me.

[The terrified Laetitia sees La Ruse enter]

LAETITIA: [Imploringly] La Ruse! La Ruse!

LA RUSE: [Hastens] What's this?

CARTWRIGHT: [Turns] La Ruse?

LAETITIA: [Runs by him] He would have killed me!

CARTWRIGHT: [Laughs] Saved again, by your nocturnal hero!

LAETITIA: He would have killed me!

LA RUSE: Alas! I am punctual only when 'twould have been better never to have arrived.

LAETITIA: I'll have him flayed alive.

LA RUSE: Do you not see, the boy's in travail? [Takes her hand] Hearken to me, Madam. You'll not say a word; the boy has suffered enough.

LAETITIA: [In utter caprice, smiles at the poet] Of course I'll not say a word! Do you know, Mr. Cartwright, I begin to like you. I begin to like you very much, since feeling your violent hand.

LA RUSE: You hear this woman, Mr. Cartwright? Why did you let me distract you?

[Mr. Snap enters]

LAETITIA: [Quickly] No more, now.

MR. SNAP: [Jubilant] 'Tis done, La Ruse! 'Tis well done! 'Tis all prepared, sir!

LAETITIA: What's all prepared, Papa? The money you've promised me for my new bonnet?

MR. SNAP: She'll have her money; won't she, La Ruse?

LA RUSE: The bailiffs have come for Mr. Wild. He hangs directly.

MR. SNAP: He's left you a legacy, daughter: your new bonnet, and a kerchief or two for myself as well. The payment's over and done with already. [To La Ruse] They'll seize him as he comes down the hall.

[Wild comes in. The appalled Snap darts behind La Ruse's back]

JONATHAN: [Is in a state of perspiring agitation] Mr. Snap! Mr. Snap! Where's Mr. Snap?

MR. SNAP: [Emerges haltingly] Your servant, Mr. Wild. What can I do for you? Pray, command me.

JONATHAN: I've been talking with Lord Wainwright —says you said I'm to vacate my room at once— I'm pardoned, am I not? The money's passed and I'm pardoned?

MR. SNAP: [Obeys La Ruse's nod] Aye, you're pardoned, Mr. Wild.

JONATHAN: [Gasps] Why didn't you tell me?

MR. SNAP: The pardon's but here— I was on the point of rushing to your room—

JONATHAN: Is't a complete pardon?

MR. SNAP: Aye, a complete pardon.

JONATHAN: O, God! They're not going to hang me— they're not going to hang me. They're not going to hang me!

MR. SNAP: Let us adjourn to my office. Some few minor details of the pardon still must be settled between us.

JONATHAN: Details, sir? Details in your mouth mean money. If 'tis more money you want, you'll not have it— I've paid all that I will pay, and more.

MR. SNAP: 'Tis not money, sir. But in a case like your own, there's this and that must be settled before all's concluded according to the law's niceties—

LORD WAINWRIGHT: [Enters carrying fan. Speaks as Mr. Snap speaks] This is not a prison but a bazaar of the arts. I've a gift for you, wench. [Crosses to her; shows the fan. Wild and Mr. Snap depart]

LAETITIA: [Snatches the fan] My fan! I missed it last night!

LORD WAINWRIGHT: Mr. Wild sold me the fan for his wife's. I find myself amused!

[A horrible cry is heard in the hall—the cry of a beast who has stumbled into a trap. Mr. Snap runs in]

MR. SNAP: Lord, he's a bulky fellow, and tussles arrantly! [The sound of the fight passes from the hall to the adjoining room] They don't dare use their pistols on him; he'd rather be shot than hanged.

JONATHAN: [*Straining against the two Bailiffs who hold him, is seen at the door, where they get him in hand. Wildly*] Gulled! Gulled! Villains! Assassins! Curse you! Curse you! My money! My money! My life! My life!

MR. SNAP: [*Merrily*] Taste! Did you say I'd no taste, sir? You'll get your walk in the air today, sir!

JONATHAN: [*Half fainting, as he is led away*] O, God! They're going to hang me—someone stop them— someone help me— O, God! Someone help me.
[*Laetitia exits*]

MR. SNAP: Aye, help him for the rogue of rogues! I must attend him to the gallows; 'tis not the hardest duty I've done. [*Exits*]

CARTWRIGHT: Wild is an odious man, but I pity him.

LORD WAINWRIGHT: Pray, who is this warm-hearted young man? Must I endure his charitable impulses, with all the rest?

LA RUSE: Mr. Cartwright, a poet. Lord Wainwright, a poisoner.

LORD WAINWRIGHT: I detest poets.

CARTWRIGHT: And I detest poisoners. [*Crosses to window and watches. The catcalls of a crowd below rise thickly*]

LORD WAINWRIGHT: Interminable cant! Well, I've one comfort; I've a snuff-box again. [*Takes a pinch*]

LA RUSE: [*Tries to see the box*] A snuff-box again! Pray, my lord, I'm dying for a pinch. [*Wainwright hands him the box*] My snuff-box!

LORD WAINWRIGHT: Yours! Am I swindled again?

LA RUSE: Yes. Who sold you the article? Mr. Snap?

LORD WAINWRIGHT: Mr. Wild! You must prove this, sir, for you're as great a thief as the others.

LA RUSE: [*Traces the lines*] My monogram. You must look close—'tis hidden in the design.

LORD WAINWRIGHT: Cunningly: I never noticed. This fails to amuse me.

CARTWRIGHT: [*As another shower of catcalls rises*] He's in the cart now, and the cart starts—

LA RUSE: God speed!

CARTWRIGHT: The mob follows—

LA RUSE: 'Tis a pity they do not follow Wild as far as he goes! I'll paraphrase one of your potentates, sir: "O! That the world had but one neck, that I might hang it!"

LORD WAINWRIGHT: [*Glares at La Ruse*] One must envy Mr. Wild: he'll soon be stone-deaf! [*Exits*]

CARTWRIGHT: Count La Ruse.

LA RUSE: Mr. Cartwright?

CARTWRIGHT: I owe you an apology, sir.

LA RUSE: [*Surprised*] For what, pray?

CARTWRIGHT: For attacking you.

LA RUSE: You were belaboured enough for that.

CARTWRIGHT: And for my behaviour in general.

LA RUSE: We must all apologize for that.

CARTWRIGHT: You are generous.

LA RUSE: I am sad—sad at the thought that you must remain here while I have at last found a way to freedom: I leave this morning. Have you no possible means of imitating me soon?

CARTWRIGHT: [*Looks into the sky*] Can I fly on the wings of those white birds?

LA RUSE: White birds! Do they fly again? Then you are safe. I have discovered they are the true omens of hope.

CARTWRIGHT: [*Cries out*] Their talons tear me.

LA RUSE: You are torn by your own talons. My friend, my son—more than you guess, my son now —you must not give way. No matter how often we are born, it is always in pain. You have become a man, and must prepare to act as a man!

CARTWRIGHT: [*Passionately*] Act as a man! I know what you mean, and my heart tells me 'tis a lie. Because I must lean a little awry, be a little dirty, I am a man! Do you think because a woman has smiled or not smiled I'll throw acid on the world? Have I been burned terribly? I'll thrust my hand deeper into the flame.

LA RUSE: I rejoice, for I perceive in you a strength which I lacked.

CARTWRIGHT: [*With sudden gloom*] My strength will die, for here the flame is infernal. To be held here—

LA RUSE: Ah, here! Yes—

CARTWRIGHT: There's a witch in this house; she's sworn to teach me the joy of yellow-tinged things.

LA RUSE: You must not permit—

CARTWRIGHT: The inevitable! Do you think, because I am a poet, I am less than a man?

LA RUSE: I think, because you are a poet, you should be more than a man.

CARTWRIGHT: Time and loneliness will make me less —here. I'll shut myself in my room. I'll work. And always I'll hear light feet passing in the hall.

LA RUSE: [*Excitedly*] I forbid you to hear them.

CARTWRIGHT: I'll hear them, always. One day, or one night, I'll fling my pen aside—I'll run, I'll throw myself into her open arms—

LA RUSE: [*Anguished*] They'll not release you until you've taken her very mold! You are right: the rest is too awful. 'Tis rankly unfair. Could I but do something for you—

CARTWRIGHT: I am lost for two hundred pounds.

LA RUSE: [*Starts*] Two hundred pounds! I'll— [*Lays his hand on his pocket and removes it angrily*] Why the devil do you tell me your woes? Because a life is ruined, a talent despoiled, shall I be troubled? Take your own medicine, sir; what's your sickness to do with me? I am well again! Pray, take yourself where I won't pity you for the brief moments I remain: I despise myself for my pity.

CARTWRIGHT: [*Mildly*] I'll trouble you no further. You have tried to be my friend in a friendless place. Will I see you again?

LA RUSE: I'll make it a point. But stay— Yes, I can do something for you. I've a little token of hope you shall have of me now. [*Hands* Cartwright *his knife*]

CARTWRIGHT: The knife!

LA RUSE: 'Tis the most I can do for you.

CARTWRIGHT: You have given me a brave testimonial of friendship, and I shall thank you—by using it bravely.

LA RUSE: But not rashly. If the moment comes—when you fling your pen aside—I would have you strike clean. 'Twould be the last honour you could pay to life.

CARTWRIGHT: I will aim for my heart.

LA RUSE: The thought pierces my own, but you will do well. [*The clock strikes the hour.* Cartwright *puts knife in pocket*] And now, I must look to my luggage.

CARTWRIGHT: I'll await your call in my room.
[*Goes out.* La Ruse, *with an effort, puts him from mind; is attracted to the window*]

LA RUSE: [*Tenderly*] White birds! I shall fly with you after all.

LAETITIA: [*Enters*] La Ruse.

LA RUSE: Madam?

LAETITIA: You've been most ungallant this morning. You'd scarcely greet me, when you should have thanked me.

LA RUSE: [*Raising his eyebrows*] Thanked you?

LAETITIA: For last night. Of late you have grown obtuse, my lover.

LA RUSE: Of late I have grown wise, Madam.

LAETITIA: If weariness is wisdom.

LA RUSE: It may well be.

LAETITIA: I promised you should hear my secret this morning, La Ruse.

LA RUSE: [*Enjoying himself to the full*] You may keep it forever now. Your business is no longer my business. You'll not scoff when you hear my secret: I've money to pay my debt. You still scoff? Madam, can you count beyond your fingers? [*Shows her the money*]

LAETITIA: [*Thunderstruck*] How did you get this money?

LA RUSE: 'Twas like your new bonnet: an unwitting legacy from the lamented Great Jonathan. Two hundred pounds for my debt, and fifty for a nest-egg. When your father hears this he'll double up with a belly-ache, but he can do naught. I have the honour, Mistress Snap, to bid you an eternal farewell.

LAETITIA: [*Bites her lips*] You can't leave, La Ruse! You must first hear what I say.

LA RUSE: I have given thought to your remarkable words of yesterday, and have guessed your secret, Madam.
[*They look at each other. She sees that he has*]

LAETITIA: Have you no feeling? Would you desert me—

LA RUSE: Your secret will speed me on my way.

LAETITIA: [*Flares*] Not when Papa knows—

LA RUSE: I am down on the books for debt, Madam. When that debt is paid, I'll laugh at your papa for the father of a strumpet. I am free of you until the North Star turns South for warmth.

LAETITIA: Cant!

LA RUSE: [*Struck by this*] Cant! Did you say cant? The monster Wainwright has made an impression. I foresee my successor.

LAETITIA: [*Shivers*] No, never that horrible man! He terrifies me, La Ruse. I have never met such a man.

LA RUSE: Have you at last met a man who terrifies you? I may yet be revenged.

LAETITIA: Do not say that! The cold passion of that man has made me feel, for the first time in my life, as if I need a protector. I beseech you, La Ruse, do not depart now.

LA RUSE: I am not in a mood—to stay. Goodbye, Laetitia.

LAETITIA: Go, then! Do you think I'll not be consoled for your loss? There are means at hand—

LA RUSE: Lord Wainwright?

LAETITIA: Do not name him! But the poet—

LA RUSE: He terrified you, also.

LAETITIA: Only for an instant. Do you forget, you once made the same gesture? 'Tis over with him as quickly as 'twas with you. Cartwright is but a doll with your features, and I'm not a woman of my mind if I can't dress him in your clothes—lend him your peculiar charm—paint your smile on his face! Already, he begins babbling like yourself.

LA RUSE: [*Loses his composure*] Infernal woman!

LAETITIA: Within a week, or a fortnight, I'll think I talk to you when I talk to him. Oh, I can draw your pattern, La Ruse—cut the pretty doll to your elegant vile shape; for 'tis the shape, alas, I adore.

LA RUSE: Infernal woman! If I thought you'd succeed—

LAETITIA: You'll be far away. I vow, La Ruse, you haven't told me where you go.

LA RUSE: I go nowhere. When I leave this house—Count La Ruse is no more. I take ship at once for the colonies. There—

LAETITIA: There—you will be what you are here.

LA RUSE: [*Violently*] No.

LAETITIA: [*Pityingly*] Do you think you can kill La Ruse in yourself? 'Tis late, my lover, for a new marriage of the elements.

LA RUSE: You lie.

LAETITIA: 'Tis to be seen. Take ship for the colonies! What will you do? Work in the Carolina rice-fields with the slaves? But you'll never reach the dock. No. I'll describe your route for you from the prison door. You'll pause at a tavern for a bumper of liberty; 'twill lead to another bumper. A wench will catch your eye; you'll toy with her and have half a mind to do more; you'll have another bumper, and you'll do more. This will lead to a bumper of repentance; and as by this time your funds are depleted, you must try your luck at the tables. There you'll be stripped, and as your ship sails you'll be meditating some purse-cutting expedition. From this meditation 'tis but a short step to your return here. Yes, you're old to play a new part; you'll find it easier to don a costume which fits, and speak lines you know.

LA RUSE: Devil, I could almost believe you! What if I should be returned here? What if I should find an echo of myself—where I had left a poet?

LAETITIA: You will, La Ruse, I promise you.

LA RUSE: Infernal woman! You've put thoughts into my head—

LAETITIA: 'Tis palpable someone must.

LA RUSE: Damn you for a lying harlot! I'm off when your father returns.

LAETITIA: You can't leave before, and perhaps not then. I'll downstairs and tell him—what I have to tell him. I'll wager, debt or no debt, he keeps you here.

LA RUSE: [Savagely] Let him try!

LAETITIA: You're a fool, sir, but I love you—more than the poet who'll sing my praises if you do leave; the poet whom I'll cut to your pattern! [She laughs; exits]

LA RUSE: [Stares after her] Cut to my pattern! She'll do't, by God, she'll do't! [He comes to a dozen decisions in as many moments: he suffers his passion] Too old to play a new part! [His passion grows, and reaches a climax; he accepts his fate, goes to door and calls] Mr. Cartwright! Mr. Cartwright!

[Cartwright comes in. La Ruse faces him with an air of amazed joy]

CARTWRIGHT: You are leaving?

LA RUSE: You are leaving, sir!

CARTWRIGHT: [Incredulous] I am leaving?

LA RUSE: We are both leaving. I've had the most extraordinary communication, within the minute.

CARTWRIGHT: But tell me—

LA RUSE: [Pirouettes] Shout! Laugh! Sing! The world is ours again.

CARTWRIGHT: But tell me—

LA RUSE: True, I must tell you. I've mentioned my son: we've been parted by my escapades. I've just heard from his guardians: they've come to my rescue. Yes, I'm about to be everlastingly reconciled to my son: he's come into a vast and beautiful estate, is rich without measure! And I'm to share in his new wealth. You're held for a beggarly two hundred pounds: here's the sum, and fifty pounds additional for your needs. Now, sir, will you believe at last in white birds?

CARTWRIGHT: [Dazed] 'Tis perhaps the difference to me between life and death, fame and infamy—I'll not be coy over taking the money—

LA RUSE: I was not coy over taking the money myself!

CARTWRIGHT: I rejoice at your own good fortune, Count La Ruse.

LA RUSE: I rejoice at it myself. I would have you have a token of mine for remembrance. Will you accept this snuff-box?

CARTWRIGHT: [Overwhelmed] I've nothing to give in return.

LA RUSE: No? I would like a token. The knife! You'll not need it now, and 'twas yours when first we met; 'twill be a lively memento of our time together. Will you let me have it back?

CARTWRIGHT: [Gives him knife] Of course. 'Tis likely I can never repay you; but were I able, where should I reach you?

LA RUSE: Write me—damn me if I know my new address! I've forgotten—'tis a strange one. Write me care of Mr. Snap: I delay to fee him to forward my letters. Run, sir! Joy awaits you.

CARTWRIGHT: And you?

LA RUSE: I am a little too old for joy, but peace will perhaps serve me better.

CARTWRIGHT: You have truly been a father to me, Count La Ruse.

LA RUSE: Would you greatly mind if I gave you a father's parting benediction? [He kisses him]

CARTWRIGHT: There are tears in your eyes.

LA RUSE: The tears of reconciliation with my son—and with parting from you. I've grown overly fond of you, sir. And now, like a true father who's never been wise in his own life, I'll instruct you how to be wise. Take no man's advice, love no woman too much. When you come to the shade, as you will, do not disparage it because you have seen the sun: there may be wonders in the darkness. Farewell.

CARTWRIGHT: Farewell!—If I could say something more—to show my gratitude! I shall write a sonnet to you, if I may.   [Exits]

LA RUSE: Sonnet to me! 'Twill be my fate, 'tis one of his minor works. [But with this his mask perishes; he walks to the window and stands as he stood a short while before] It must be a black bird, after all—

LAETITIA: [Enters. Wide-eyed] O, fool! fool! Given him your money—freed him in your place—O, fool! O, fool! sentimental fool!

LA RUSE: [Walks to the door heavily] 'Tis the only wise thing I have ever done. There have been too many hairs on my shoulder—

LAETITIA: [With an evil smile] Now you belong to me—forever.

LA RUSE: Now I am free forever. [He goes out. Laetitia wonders. The thud of a body falling is heard in the hall. She runs, sees, retreats into the room, incapable of an outcry]

MR. SNAP: [Enters. Chuckling] 'Twas an expeditious hanging. What is it, Daughter? [She points; he exits into the fall and returns, awed] Stabbed himself—clean through the heart.

LAETITIA: [*Finds voice; beats hysterically on her father's breast*] I'll strangle his child— I'll strangle his child in my womb—

MR. SNAP: [*Seizes her hands; looks up at her, a great fear in his face*] His child!

[*Wainwright appears. Laetitia collapses in her father's arms*]

WAINWRIGHT: [*Assists him in picking up her limp form*] Pray, Mr. Snap, show me into her room—I must have ingress into her room.

Morning's at Seven

by PAUL OSBORN
(1901–   )

Paul Osborn has been one of the most skillful and successful adapters of books into play form— *On Borrowed Time, The Innocent Voyage, A Bell For Adano, Point of No Return.* That, despite all his skill, the plays have seldom proved the equal of the books, simply indicates the difficulty of transferring something from a commodious medium to a constricted one, of converting, as it were, a sofa into a chair. Yet where several of Mr. Osborn's adaptations had great success, a play quite his own, *Morning's at Seven,* though far superior to the things he adapted and indeed to most American comedies of the past twenty years, had a shortish run and even a lukewarm critical reception. *Morning's at Seven* has had, however, from the outset its very strong admirers. We may perhaps set down its lack of popular success to the fact that it dealt overwhelmingly with old people, who are no source of glamour to ordinary theater audiences; we may perhaps set down its lack of critical esteem, when first produced, to a production that stressed its farce elements at the expense of its comedy ones, and hence caused it to be judged as something less than it was.

Certainly, there is farce in *Morning's at Seven;* but it is farce having a bearing on human character and human values rather than just being a species of theater. For the play has a solid human base, and penetrates below what constitutes domestic or family comedy to comedy of character: ultimately, that is to say, Mr. Osborn makes us care about his people in terms of themselves rather than of the situations they create, or even the social or satiric comment they engender. *Morning's at Seven* has something in common with certain plays of George Kelly: if one were to use the cliché word that differentiates it, it would be that it is more compassionate; but it seems sounder to call *Morning's at Seven* the work of a humorist. Which is to say that, right in the midst of Mr. Osborn's exposing and satirizing of his very limited people, there is yet a vast amount of fellow-feeling: he brings us to see at last how in terms of essential fate, of fundamental desire and frustration, our lives can be as petty as theirs, and theirs every bit as poignant as our own.

And Mr. Osborn does this, I think, without over-forcing the note. There are moments when he does seem to force it, when he cannot quite find, in the voices or the vocabularies of his people, the leverage needed to deepen or transform them. Mostly, however, Mr. Osborn is content with doing justice to the surface, and letting what lies beneath it take care of itself. There is a great deal of surface, and with a great many sides to it. There is domestic comedy, with all the immemorial frictions of family life, and with the seeming moral that not even two houses are big enough to hold one family. There is social comedy, the capturing of middle-class existence at its most circumscribed and parrotlike. And there is a comedy of old age, which is where *Morning's at Seven* achieves its high-pitched petulant squeaks but also its occasional momentary cello notes: a comedy of age that has its touch of tragedy not because its people stand so near to death but because they have been immersed so weakly in life. And yet, even now, they are warm with life—still kicking their heels, still raising their voices and cocking their ears. They talk ridiculous bromides, but with passion; they make absurd gestures, but with feeling. They seem, indeed, so much unlike us and yet can become so disconcertingly the same; and never more, perhaps, than when they insist on being dramatic about their plights and grievances, and turn farcical instead. But here, most of all, it is the humorist in Mr. Osborn, and not the farceur, that counts.

Mr. Osborn drops into mere broad theater-writing in places: Homer and Myrtle, for example, are never quite up to the company they keep, nor is the baby they suddenly expect quite in keeping. The play, too, winds up by winding down a little; there might better be a more ironic, more pleasantly melancholy note at the end. But this is a play that, with subject matter that seems banal and looks drab and promises to be trivial, can in places be as amusing as the broadest farce, and as touching and resonant as life itself.

PAUL OSBORN

Morning's at Seven

Act I

SCENE: *The back porches and back yards of two houses in a middle-western town*

On the stage right is a neatly kept lawn with a few trees and under them a wicker chair. At back is seen the rear of the house, with windows on two levels. There are steps leading up to the porch. The lawn is bordered at extreme right by a hedge. This house and lawn take up four-fifths of the stage on the right.

Stage center is a path which extends back, separating the two lawns and the two houses and leading to the street beyond.

On stage left is practically a duplication of stage right except that the house is not in as good repair, the grass is not as neatly clipped and there are more trees and bushes, giving it a somewhat wilder appearance. It is bordered at extreme left by a hedge.

Exits and entrances can be made from either house through the back doors, from the drive between the houses and through the hedges extreme right and left.

Although it is not yet dusk it is evidently toward the close of a summer's day. Before the act is over it is dark.

As the curtain rises, Thor, Cora, and Arry are discovered sitting in the back yard of the house at stage right. Thor is sitting on the tree stump center, smoking. Cora sits on the porch ledge by the steps. Apart from them on the porch near the drive center sits Arry. She is looking down the drive between the houses toward the street beyond. She seldom takes her eyes from the street.

THOR: Then he listened to my heart. With one of those ear things. Listened quite awhile. Didn't say a word. Scared me to death. Then he began to thump me. Chest, sides, back—all over. Still didn't say a word. Took my blood pressure. Wound a little sack around my arm, pumped a little machine, watched a needle, oh, he did everything you could think of! Examination lasted over an hour. Then you know what he said?

CORA: What?

THOR: He says, "Mr. Swanson, there's not a thing in the world the matter with you. You've got a good heart, sound lungs, fine stomach—I don't know when I've seen a man of your age as well off as you are." Now what do you know about that? He's just a lousy doctor, that's all.

CORA: Did you tell him about your neck?

THOR: Of course I did! Said it wasn't anything to worry about! By God, I don't know how a doctor like that gets the reputation he has! Didn't even say I had to give up smoking!

CORA: Well, that's silly. Everybody knows you ought to give up smoking.

THOR: [*Disgusted*] Of course they do! I smoke much too much. Look at that. [*Refers to his cigarette*] It stands to reason when a man gets along in his late sixties he's got to cut down on things like that! Well, I'll see old Doc Brooks tomorrow. He may be old but I bet he knows enough to tell me to quit smoking.

CORA: You didn't say anything to the doctor about my side, did you?

THOR: By God, Cora, I didn't! I forgot all about it.

CORA: It doesn't matter.

THOR: I was so damned mad. I'll speak to Doc Brooks about it tomorrow. Does it hurt you? [*He rises—crosses to* Cora]

CORA: Just when I lean over.

THOR: Want me to rub it for you?

CORA: It'll be all right.

THOR: Well, you want to watch those things. Can't be too careful. [*He crosses to chair—sits*]

CORA: [*Whispering*] Thanks for asking to rub it, though.

ARRY: [*From up on porch*] What's that? What did you say?

THOR: Nothing!

ARRY: Cora did. I heard her. She was whispering.

THOR: Well, she told me she didn't want me to rub her back for her.

ARRY: I don't see what there is to whisper about. When your own sister talks behind your back—

THOR: [*After slight pause*] See anything yet, Arry? Aaronetta?

ARRY: [*Still looking down the street*] What?

THOR: See anything yet?

ARRY: The Davises just drove by.

THOR: Which way they going?

ARRY: Toward town.

[Cora *produces a banana and begins to strip it*]

THOR: Going to have supper down there and going to a movie— No sign of Homer and Myrtle?

ARRY: Not yet. [*Rises and comes to head of porch steps*] Dear, I wonder why they don't come. Wouldn't it be awful if he didn't bring her after all?

CORA: Maybe her train's late.

ARRY: My, I bet Ida's excited! [*Crosses and takes a piece of banana just as* Cora *is about to eat it*] I wonder if I shouldn't go over there and see if there's anything I can do.

CORA: No, you stay away from there. Ida's got that Allen girl in to help her. If she wants us for anything she'll call us.

ARRY: Do you think we'll meet her? Myrtle, I mean?

THOR: Meet her? I guess Homer won't be bringing any girl of his home without introducing her to his old aunts and uncle.

ARRY: Well, there's something awful funny about it, if you ask me. How long has Homer been engaged to Myrtle now, Cora?

CORA: It must be nearly seven years. Of course they were going together four or five years before that.

ARRY: Well, don't you think it's funny, Homer's going with a girl for twelve years and none of us has ever seen her? Not even his own mother?

THOR: Well, Homer's shy. He can't be rushed into anything. Anyway, he's bringing her home now.

ARRY: Well, that's just because of that movie Ida saw the other day about the old bachelor. She said she felt so sorry for that old bachelor she came right home and gave Homer a terrible talking to. Said if he didn't bring Myrtle home she'd make him eat his dinners down town for a whole month.

CORA: Oh, she didn't either, Arry!

ARRY: [*To* Cora] She told me she did! [*To* Thor] She said she wasn't going to have any son of hers end up the way that old bachelor in the movie did.

THOR: Why? How'd he end up?

ARRY: He shot himself. [*They all giggle.* Arry *crosses center and takes last piece of banana as she goes*] Anyway, Ida's right about that old bachelor business. Homer's forty years old his last birthday, remember. If he's going to marry Myrtle he'd better do it pretty soon. [*Sits stump*]

THOR: Well, I don't think Ida ought to rush him. You got to let a man work out those things for himself.

CORA: Homer likes his *home*. He likes it here with his mother.

ARRY: Well, I just wonder what Myrtle thinks. I see myself waiting twelve years for any man.

THOR: You been waiting sixty-five years for one! [*He laughs heartily*]

ARRY: [*Flaring up*] Don't you worry, Theodore Swanson! I could have had plenty of men if I'd wanted them!

THOR: [*Suddenly placating*] Sure you could, Arry.

ARRY: And they're plenty I could have right now too! Don't fool yourself about that!

THOR: Sure there are.

ARRY: Don't think I don't see the way men look at me on the street. I know what they're thinking. I could have a home of my own in two minutes if I wanted one.

THOR: Don't doubt it for a second, Arry.

ARRY: I was the prettiest of all us four sisters, wasn't I, Cora?

CORA: No. You weren't as pretty as Esty.

ARRY: Well, I was prettier than you or Ida. And look at what Esty got. Do you think I'd be married to a man like David?

THOR: Of course you wouldn't, Arry.

ARRY: [*Crosses to porch steps*] Trouble with me is I never saw a man who was worth the powder to blow him up with. Pretty poor specimens on the whole. [*She is now half way up the steps. Puts her hand out for banana and finds it gone*] Where'd that banana go? [Cora *holds up the empty skins.* Arry *giggles*] For goodness' sakes, did I eat all that?

CORA: No, I had a bite.

ARRY: Want me to get you another one?

CORA: No, I've had enough.

[Arry *returns to her post on the porch*]

THOR: You know what I hate most about this Myrtle-Homer situation?

CORA: What?

THOR: That nice house up there on Sycamore Drive that his father built for them.

CORA: You certainly do like that house, don't you, Thor?

THOR: Five years that house's been standing there empty. All nicely furnished. I said to Carl just the other day, "Why don't you rent that house until Homer's ready for it, Carl?"

CORA: You did! What'd he say?

THOR: He says "No, Thor, no. That's Homer's house. I want it to be all new and ready for him any time he wants to move in." By God, if I was a young fellow I'd get married just to live in that nice house!

[*Pause. Arry rises and comes to top step. In a confidential tone*]

ARRY: Thor, you know what I've been wondering about Homer and Myrtle?

THOR: What?

ARRY: I wonder if there isn't something going on there.

CORA: Oh, Arry!

ARRY: Oh, you can be as innocent as you like but I know what men are. Something could be going on there every night for all we know.

THOR: Nope! Couldn't be going on every night! She lives in North Lyons. They don't see each other every night.

CORA: Well, I think that's a terrible thought to have about your own nephew!

ARRY: Well, it certainly could be true, couldn't it, Thor?

THOR: [*Expanding*] Well, it's hard to say. If it was anybody but Homer I'd be inclined to say it could be. But Homer—I don't know.

CORA: Well, I know it isn't! Homer has never spent a night away from his home in his whole life as far as I know. He's always here in the mornings.

ARRY: Well, my goodness, he wouldn't have to spend the whole night, would he?

[*Suddenly the door of the house at left is thrown open and Ida comes out hurriedly onto the porch and motions to Cora*]

IDA: Cora! Cora!

CORA: [*Rising and starting toward her on a run*] What's the matter, Ida?

IDA: Come here a minute.

[*Cora hurries to her and the two step inside the screen door and stand there whispering excitedly. Ida's sudden burst out of the door has brought Thor and Arry out of their lethargy. Thor leans forward in his chair, and Arry crosses center. They both watch with curiosity and excitement. Pause. The whispering goes on. Arry can stand it no longer*]

ARRY: [*Suddenly*] Yap, yap, yap, yap, yap! When those two get together they're like a couple of old hens.

THOR: What's the matter with her?

ARRY: How do I know? Does anybody ever tell *me* anything?

THOR: [*Rising*] Gee, Ida seems excited.

ARRY: It's "Cora, Cora, Cora" all the time! They just like to keep me out of things. She's probably burned her roast and I hope she has! And another thing, Theodore Swanson, the next time Cora starts any more of this business about me getting a man and having a home of my own like she did this morning—

THOR: [*Uncomfortable*] Oh, Arry, Cora didn't mean anything.

ARRY: Well, I don't know. Cora's made a couple of awful funny remarks lately about me living by myself. She's got some bee in her bonnet. She's up to something.

THOR: Oh, she isn't either.

ARRY: Well, she hadn't better be, that's all I say.

THOR: Now your home's right here with us, Arry. Just as long as you want it.

ARRY: Well, don't you forget it either. I guess I'm entitled to some consideration around here.

THOR: All right. All right. Now keep still. Here comes Cora.

[*Ida has gone back into house. Cora joins Arry and Thor*]

ARRY: Well, did you have your little conference?

CORA: Oh, my goodness, it's Carl! Ida says he's acting funny.

ARRY: [*Quickly*] He's not going to have a spell, is he?

CORA: That's what she's afraid of. He's got his forehead leaned up against the kitchen wall and he won't move. Everybody's having to walk around him.

ARRY: Oh, that's it, all right! No doubt about it!

CORA: That poor Allen girl doesn't know what's the matter. She's scared stiff. And Ida's nearly frantic. With Homer and Myrtle coming—

ARRY: And that's just what brought it on! Myrtle! Don't you see? He can't face her. That's the way it always used to be. Any new person he wanted to make an impression on— Oh, I bet he's going to have a terrible spell! I'd better go over and see what I can do. [*She starts over*]

CORA: [*Grabbing her*] You do no such thing!

ARRY: Oh, my goodness!

CORA: You stay right where you are!

[*At this point Arry is looking up the drive. She turns suddenly and calls in a hoarse voice*]

ARRY: Thor!

THOR: [*Jumping*] Huh? What?

ARRY: [*Running up on the porch—Thor and Cora following*] They're here! They're here! [*Cora and Thor are back—Arry way out in view*] Oh, my goodness, he really brought her! Look! Look! [*She dances in excitement*]

CORA: [*Pulling her back out of view*] Now be careful, Arry. Go up closer to the house.

[*They station themselves right in front of the door, and all huddle together, looking down the drive toward the front of the house opposite. Arry is nearest the corner,* Thor *behind her,* Cora *behind him*]

ARRY: Look! Look! They're getting out! That's her! That's Myrtle! Oh, Lord, he's helping her out of the car!

THOR: Yes sir, by God, he certainly is!

ARRY: Look! He's got hold of her arm!

THOR: By God, he has! Imagine that!

ARRY: You don't think she's a cripple or something?

CORA: Oh, Arry, he's just helping her.

ARRY: Well, he's certainly doing a good job of it—. My goodness, look how he's got hold of her arm! You can't tell me there isn't something going on there!

CORA: We'd better go in. We can see better from the dining room anyway.

[Carl *enters from the other house.* Thor *sees him, but* Arry *and* Cora *don't.* Thor *tries to draw* Arry's *attention by nudging her*]

ARRY: Look! Look! Stop pushing, Thor. There they go.—Stop it, Thor.

THOR: [*Taking the bull by the horns*] Good afternoon, Carl.

[Arry *and* Cora *look up guiltily and look over at* Carl *with a mixture of curiosity and embarrassment. They start moving away nonchalantly from their posts*]

CARL: [*Quietly*] Good afternoon, Thor.

CORA: Oh, good afternoon, Carl.

CARL: Good afternoon, Cora.

ARRY: [*With an embarrassed laugh*] Well, I see you've got company.

CARL: Yes. Homer brought Myrtle for over Sunday.

ARRY: Oh, is that it? Isn't that nice.

[*Pause.* Carl *stands there quietly. The others don't know what to do*]

THOR: [*Heartily*] Well, begins to look as if you're going to have that house occupied pretty soon, Carl. Up there on Sycamore Drive.

CARL: [*Trying to force a laugh*] Yes. Yes, it does, doesn't it?

THOR: [*Encouraged*] Well, I'll be glad to see it happen. I always say all you have to do is to leave young people alone and pretty soon things will take care of themselves. Guess that's about the size of it.

[*Pause.* Carl *hasn't been listening. He has been staring past them. Now he looks up quickly, noticing the silence*]

CARL: What's that?

THOR: [*Lamely*] I say I guess that's about the size of it.

CARL: Oh!

[*He crosses to tree and puts his hand against it and then leans his head on his hand. Pause.* Cora,

Arry *and* Thor *all stand watching him a minute*]

THOR: [*In an awed whisper*] By God, he's having a spell all right!

CORA: Poor Ida! I'd better telephone her he's out of the kitchen. [*She goes in house right*]

ARRY: [*Following up the steps*] I think we ought to 'phone Esty about it all, too. It's only fair. Goodness knows she doesn't have much in her life any more. Come on, Thor. [*She stands with screen door open*]

THOR: All right. I kind of hate to leave Carl. [*Phone rings*] There! There's Cora talking to her now.

[*They exit into house.* Carl *is still leaning against the tree.* Ida *enters—doesn't see* Carl]

IDA: Carl! [*He makes no sign*] Carl! [*Still makes no sign. She sees him. Crosses to him*] Carl! What *is* the matter? You're not really going to have a spell, are you? Answer me, Carl! [*She shakes his arm*] Now you've got to stop this. Right away! Before it gets hold of you! You've got to shake it off and come right into the house with me and see Myrtle and Homer. They want you to come in.

CARL: They don't want to see me.

IDA: They do, Carl! They do! Myrtle asked for you especially. She wants to meet you.

CARL: Why should she want to meet *me?*

IDA: Stop talking that way, Carl!

CARL: Why should anybody want to meet a failure like me?

IDA: Oh, Carl, you're just giving in to it! Now stop it! Myrtle is here. You've got to help entertain her. You know how hard it is for Homer to talk in front of strangers. You're the host, Carl. You just *can't* have a spell now!

CARL: [*Straightens up—faces front*] I never asked much out of life! Never made many demands! All I wanted to be was just a dentist!

IDA: Oh, my goodness! Never mind about that now, Carl!

CARL: That's not so much to ask! Just to be a dentist. Charlie Watson went on and became a dentist! But I wasn't up to it!

IDA: Of course you were, Carl! It just didn't work out that way.

CARL: I had a lofty ideal but I never achieved it.

IDA: You're just as good as anybody else, Carl.

CARL: I failed!

[*He leans on the tree again.* Homer *and* Myrtle *come out onto the porch.* Homer *speaks*]

HOMER: This's the back yard.

IDA: [*Pushing* Carl *off left—they both exit*] Oh, my goodness! They're coming out! Carl! Carl!

MYRTLE: The back yard! Oh, isn't it lovely!

HOMER: [*At head of steps—points stage left*] That's the garage.

MYRTLE: Oh, yes! Isn't it nice!

HOMER: That one's my father's and mine and that one's Uncle Thor's. My father built them both.

MYRTLE: He must be terribly clever.

HOMER: He's a good builder. [*Pause—Homer points right*] That's the hedge.

MYRTLE: Oh, yes.

HOMER: That's where Aunt Cora thinks she heard a man hiding a couple of times.

MYRTLE: Oh, that's right. I remember.

HOMER: She says she heard him cough once just about dark.

MYRTLE: Well, does she think it's somebody watching the house?

HOMER: I guess so. Guess she just imagined it though.

MYRTLE: Oh!

HOMER: Uncle Thor says it's probably just one of Aunt Arry's men hanging around to check up on her.

MYRTLE: Oh, maybe that's it.

HOMER: No, that's a joke.

MYRTLE: Oh, I see. [*She laughs at the joke, nervously. Sees* Ida *who is backing on stage left—looking off after* Carl. Myrtle *steps toward her*] Oh, there you are! Did you find Mr. Bolton?

IDA: [*A bit flustered*] I—I guess he must have gone for a little walk.

MYRTLE: Oh, dear. I do so want to meet him.

IDA: [*Blanking her view*] Oh, he'll be back in time for supper. He often takes a little walk about this time.

MYRTLE: [*In her best social manner*] I love your back yard, Mrs. Bolton. It looks so cool. It's simply heavenly.

IDA: Yes, we like it very much.

MYRTLE: All the trees and everything. I bet you sit out here all the time.

IDA: We sit out here a good deal of the time.

MYRTLE: Well, I should think you would. It's simply heavenly. I don't know when I've seen a more attractive back yard.

IDA: Yes, we're very fond of it.

MYRTLE: Well, I should think so. It's so nice and wild, too. Like being in a forest.

IDA: I'm glad you like it.

MYRTLE: Well, I certainly do. It's simply—heavenly, that's all there is to it.

IDA: Well, it's nice of you to say so.

MYRTLE: Well, I mean it.

[*Pause. Conversation comes to an end abruptly*]

HOMER: [*Suddenly*] Have mosquitoes sometimes.

IDA: Yes, there are mosquitoes sometimes.

MYRTLE: How dreadful!

IDA: But I don't think we've had quite so many this year as usual. Have you noticed that, Homer?

HOMER: [*In a loud voice*] Not so many. That's right.

MYRTLE: Isn't it interesting the way those things go? [*To Homer*] One year you'll have a lot of mosquitoes and the next year not so many mosquitoes. [*To Ida*] Or a lot of caterpillars one year and the next year not so many caterpillars. I wonder why that is.

IDA: I don't know why that is. Do you, Homer?

HOMER: No. I don't know why it is.

MYRTLE: It's very interesting, isn't it? Anyway I suppose the mosquitoes and caterpillars and all those things have some purpose. They wouldn't have been put here if they hadn't.

IDA: No, I don't suppose they would have.

HOMER: Don't suppose so.

MYRTLE: It's all a part of some big plan. Some big—plan of some kind.

[*Pause. Conversation ends abruptly*]

HOMER: [*Suddenly*] Want to sit down?

MYRTLE: All right. [*Crosses to stump*] I'll take this cozy little place over here. Won't you sit down too, Mrs. Bolton?

IDA: [*Starting up steps*] No, I really should be about supper.

MYRTLE: Oh, do sit down for just a minute.

IDA: Well, for just a minute then. [*In silence they sit. Homer squats down and starts cutting weeds with his pen knife. Myrtle and Ida smile at each other. Ida on the edge of her chair. Short pause. Ida rises*] And now I really must go in. [*Crosses to head of steps. Homer rises*] I'll leave you two youngsters out here by yourselves. I guess you can attend to yourselves all right.

MYRTLE: [*Rises—giggling, embarrassed*] Well—maybe we can.

IDA: You probably have a lot to talk over.

HOMER: We haven't got anything to talk over.

IDA: Of course you have! I know! I'll come out again as soon as I can— If you should see your father tell him I want to see him, Homer.

HOMER: All right, Mother. [*She goes into house left*]

MYRTLE: [*Sits on stump*] Oh, I think your mother's too wonderful!

HOMER: She's pretty nice, all right.

MYRTLE: She's so *friendly!* She's just what a mother should be!

HOMER: She's pretty nice. [*He sits in chair left center*]

MYRTLE: Oh, she's more than that. She's so—*human!* [*Pause. Homer sits staring before him. Myrtle looking at the house right*] And that's where your Uncle Thor and Aunt Cora live.

HOMER: And Aunt Arry.

MYRTLE: Oh, yes. She's the maiden aunt, isn't she?

HOMER: She's the old maid.

[*Myrtle gives a little nervous laugh*]

MYRTLE: How long has she been living with them?

HOMER: About forty-five to fifty years.

MYRTLE: My goodness, that must be pretty hard on your Aunt Cora.

HOMER: Why? They're sisters.

MYRTLE: Yes, but wouldn't you think a woman would want to live alone—I mean just alone with her husband?

HOMER: Aunt Arry didn't have any other place to go when her mother died so Aunt Cora took her in.

MYRTLE: Aunt Cora must be pretty nice, I think, to share her home like that.

HOMER: Aunt Cora's nice. Not as nice as mother.

MYRTLE: Oh, of course not! Of course not. My goodness——. Anyway it must be awfully pleasant for all of them to live so close together now that they're getting older. They must be a lot of company for each other.

HOMER: Then there's Aunt Esther, too.

MYRTLE: Oh, yes, Aunt Esther.

HOMER: She lives up the street about a block and a half.

MYRTLE: And she's married to——?

HOMER: Uncle David.

MYRTLE: That's right. He's the one who studies all the time.

HOMER: He's a very highly educated man. He doesn't like us.

MYRTLE: Why not?

HOMER: He thinks we're morons.

MYRTLE: Morons? Why does he think that?

HOMER: I don't know. He says we don't think about important enough things.

MYRTLE: Does he think about important things?

HOMER: Practically all of the time.

MYRTLE: What does he do?

HOMER: Doesn't do anything now. He used to be a college professor. But he couldn't get along with the President.

MYRTLE: Oh.

HOMER: He said the President was a moron too!

MYRTLE: Well, he doesn't think *you're* a moron, Homer?

HOMER: He thinks we all are except my father.

MYRTLE: Why, what's the matter with your father?

HOMER: He says my father has something more than the rest of us. Something that makes him question life sometimes.

MYRTLE: Oh, I see.

HOMER: But the rest of us are all morons. That's why he never comes down here and never lets any of us come up there.

MYRTLE: He sounds awfully odd to me.

HOMER: He doesn't let Aunt Esther come down either. He's afraid we'll pull her down to our level.

MYRTLE: So she never comes down.

HOMER: Just when he doesn't know it. She hasn't been down now for over a week though.

MYRTLE: I'm afraid I wouldn't like your Uncle David very well.

HOMER: Oh, I think you would. He's awfully nice. I've always sort of liked Uncle David.

[*Pause. Myrtle turns to* Homer]

MYRTLE: Homer—do you think your mother liked me?

HOMER: She didn't say anything—I guess so though.

MYRTLE: Dear, I hope she did. I tried to make a good impression on her. I liked her so much.

HOMER: She's pretty nice all right.

MYRTLE: It was terribly sweet of her to ask me to come. [*Pause. She takes a quick look at him. Steps toward him*] Of course I couldn't help but wonder why it just happened that this time you decided to bring me. Because she has asked you to before, hasn't she?

HOMER: [*Uncomfortable*] Uh-huh.

[*Pause*]

MYRTLE: I mean I wondered if anything happened to change your mind about bringing me.

[*Slight pause*]

HOMER: [*Suddenly*] My mother saw a movie.

MYRTLE: A movie?

HOMER: Uh-huh.

MYRTLE: Oh! [*Pause*] I guess she wouldn't think very much of me if she knew about us, would she?

HOMER: Well, there's no reason for her to know.

MYRTLE: She'd think I wasn't very nice.

HOMER: Older people don't understand things like that very well, Myrtle. Maybe we'd better not talk about it here.

MYRTLE: Oh, all right. Of course your mother must think it's rather funny about you and me though. Being engaged so long. [*Pause*] Hasn't she ever asked you anything about it? About when we're going to get married, I mean?

HOMER: Uh-huh.

MYRTLE: What did you say to her?

HOMER: I told her you had a job.

MYRTLE: Oh!—Well, I was thinking about my job the other day. I was wondering whether I oughtn't to give it up.

HOMER: I thought you liked it.

MYRTLE: Oh, I do! It's a good job. But—well, I get awfully sick of it sometimes. And after all, I am thirty-nine years old, you know.

[*Pause. Myrtle stares at* Homer. *Nervously, he looks off left*]

HOMER: [*Pointing off left*] My father set out most of these trees himself. Transplanted some of them. That one there I remember when it was just a twig he brought over from a house he was building on Maple Street. It must have been fifteen years ago.

MYRTLE: My, you wouldn't think it would get that big in fifteen years.

HOMER: They grow awfully fast.

[*Pause. Homer is staring before him. Myrtle looks at him, nervously*]

MYRTLE: There isn't anything the matter, is there, Homer?

HOMER: [*Shaking his head*] Un-uh——.

MYRTLE: You're not mad at me about anything, are you?

HOMER: No.

MYRTLE: You act so funny here. Are you sorry you brought me after all?

HOMER: No, I guess not.

[*Myrtle smiles at him and suddenly takes his arm and snuggles to him*]

MYRTLE: You silly!

HOMER: [*Pulling away*] They'll see you from the other house, Myrtle.

MYRTLE: Oh! [*She drops his arm. Pause. Then she rises and moves over by the trees left—stands looking off*] I get awfully lonesome sometimes about this time of day. Or maybe a little later. I guess it's really not so bad at the office. I'm usually pretty busy. But when I get through and have to go to my room.—And then when it starts getting dark— [*Turns to* Homer] Often when I know you're not going to be coming down I don't bother to get myself any supper. I just go right to bed. [*They laugh —embarrassed. Pause*] Sometimes I wonder how I ever happened to get stuck with that job. It doesn't seem natural. I guess when you come right down to it what a woman really wants is a home of her own.

[*Pause.* Homer *makes no answer.* Arry *wanders out from the porch at right, casually, as though she were not aware of the others. They watch her for a time without speaking. She fans herself energetically*]

HOMER: That's Aunt Arry. [*Pause as* Arry *looks off right*] She knows we're here.

MYRTLE: Oh!

[*They watch her as she wanders down center pretending not to notice them. Sees a weed and makes a great fuss over picking it up. Then notices* Homer *and* Myrtle, *with much surprise*]

ARRY: Oh! Oh, hello, Homer.

HOMER: Hello, Aunt Arry.

ARRY: [*Throwing the weed over the hedge*] When did you get home?

HOMER: Little while ago.

ARRY: Well! [*Pause.* Arry *waits expectantly. As there is no move toward an introduction she bows politely to* Myrtle] How do you do?

MYRTLE: How do you do?

ARRY: It has been a pleasant day, hasn't it?

MYRTLE: Hasn't it?

[*Pause. Nothing more to say*]

HOMER: [*Suddenly—rising*] This's Myrtle Brown.

ARRY: Oh! Oh, how do you do, Myrtle?

MYRTLE: How do you do?

ARRY: I'm Homer's aunt.

MYRTLE: Well, I guess I know that. You're Aunt Arry. You're the one that sent me that handsome linen luncheon set for my hope chest.

ARRY: [*Confused*] Oh, my goodness, that wasn't anything.

MYRTLE: Well, I just guess it *was* something! That's about the most handsome linen luncheon set *I've* ever seen.

ARRY: [*Laughs, embarrassed*] Did you really like it?

MYRTLE: I certainly did. You'd be surprised how often I take that luncheon set out and look at it. Sometimes those flowers on the napkins seem to me to be absolutely real.

ARRY: [*Flattered—turns away a bit, laughs*] They're appliquéd, you know.

MYRTLE: I know they are. You must have used your eyes altogether too much doing that.

ARRY: Oh, my goodness! I don't have very much to do. I'm working on a quilt. It's appliquéd, too. Perhaps you'd like to see it while you're here.

MYRTLE: I'd simply love to.

HOMER: [*Suddenly*] Myrtle knits.

[Cora *is seen passing the screen door, house right*]

ARRY: [*Bowing pleasantly*] Oh?—Haven't seen your father yet, have you, Homer?

[Cora *listens in door*]

HOMER: No.

ARRY: [*Crossing to steps*] Dear, I hope he's going to be all right.

[Homer *looks up suddenly, startled. At the same moment* Cora *sticks her head out of the door*]

CORA: [*Hissing*] Arry!

ARRY: [*Crossing to* Cora] Oh, all right, Cora. [*Sweetly to others as she starts in*] I guess I have to help with supper. I just came out for a breath of air.

HOMER: [*Rising abruptly*] Where *is* Father?

ARRY: I don't know, Homer. He and Ida were out there in the yard when you came out. I just happened to notice them from the house. He must have gone off through the hedge.

[Homer *turns suddenly and goes off to the house.* Myrtle *watches him, startled*]

MYRTLE: Well, Homer, what—?

HOMER: [*At the door*] Mother!

[Myrtle *turns back to* Arry *who is nearly in the house again*]

MYRTLE: Mr. Bolton isn't ill, is he?

ARRY: [*Confidentially*] Well, no, he isn't ill exactly but you see sometimes he has these awful sp—

[*This time* Cora *comes right out onto the back porch*]

CORA: Arry!

ARRY: Oh, my goodness!

CORA: It's time to set table.

ARRY: [*Giving* Cora *a cross look—turns back to* Myrtle *sweetly*] Well, I'm very glad to have met you, Myrtle. Perhaps we'll see you after supper.

MYRTLE: I hope so.

[Arry *bows politely to* Myrtle *and starts in door*]

ARRY: [*In an undertone to* Cora] I wasn't going to tell her a thing!

[*She exits—*Cora *has been staring curiously at* Myrtle]

CORA: [*Stepping forward—embarrassed*] How do you do, Myrtle?

MYRTLE: How do you do?

CORA: I expect we'll meet each other after supper.

MYRTLE: I expect so.

CORA: Well, excuse me. I've got to go in now. [*Starts in*]

MYRTLE: All right.

[Cora *turns back*]

CORA: I'm Aunt Cora.

MYRTLE: Yes, I know. [Cora *bows politely and goes in quickly.* Ida *and* Homer *come out of house left, and start down the steps.* Homer *acts very moody*] Is there anything wrong with Mr. Bolton?

IDA: No, no, he just had a little headache is all. He'll walk it off and be all right when he gets back.

MYRTLE: [*Sits stump*] Oh!

IDA: And I guess I can sit down for a little while now. Supper's nearly ready.

[*Sits chair*—Homer *sits on porch step by* Ida]

MYRTLE: It is? I had no idea it was so late. [*Rises—crosses to porch left*] I think I'd better go in and wash up then.

IDA: Oh, all right. Just ask the Allen girl in there and she'll show you where to go. The little towel with the escalloped border is for you.

MYRTLE: Oh, all right, thank you. I won't be long.

[Myrtle *exits.* Homer *rises—crosses center*]

IDA: Now, Homer!

HOMER: I don't care, Mother! If he started talking about going back to the fork again.

IDA: But I tell you he didn't. He didn't say anything about the fork at all.

HOMER: Are you sure?

IDA: It hadn't got to that.

HOMER: Well, it hadn't better! If he starts talking about going back to the fork again—

IDA: Well, he didn't. I felt kind of sorry for him this time. It was one of those dentist spells. Now stop acting up and sit down. I want to tell you how much I like Myrtle. I think she's just as nice as she can be.

HOMER: Well, I wish you wouldn't leave me alone with her all the time.

IDA: Now Homer—!

HOMER: I don't care, it's embarrassing. I don't know what to say to her.

IDA: Well, aren't you the limit. What do you say to her when you go down to visit her in North Lyons?

HOMER: That's different.

IDA: You are a goose, aren't you?

HOMER: Well, I just wish you wouldn't leave us alone. She keeps hinting things when you're not with us.

IDA: What things?

HOMER: Oh, she wants to know why I brought her home.

IDA: Well, I should think she'd know that. When a man brings a girl home to meet his mother—

HOMER: Now, Mother, you know I haven't made up my mind about anything yet!

IDA: Now Homer—!

HOMER: [*Shaking his head obstinately*] Haven't made up my mind.

IDA: Well, when are you going to?

HOMER: Well, I like it living here at home.

IDA: But that's no excuse. And it isn't as though you'd

be going way off somewhere. After all, Sycamore Drive is only half a mile away. You can come down here every night if you want to at first.

HOMER: It wouldn't be the same.

IDA: You'll be surprised how quickly you'll feel at home in that new house, Homer.

HOMER: But I've got all my things here and everything.

IDA: Well, I just wish you'd seen that movie I saw, Homer. That movie actor even looked a little like you.

HOMER: Who was it?

IDA: Oh, nobody important.

HOMER: Oh!

IDA: But he certainly gave you a very clear picture of just how lonely an old bachelor can be.

[*Pause*]

HOMER: [*Turns to* Ida] You'd be awfully lonesome.

IDA: [*Turning away from him*] Oh, I don't say it's going to be easy for me either.

HOMER: Of course it isn't.

IDA: It'll seem strange not to have you coming home after your day's work. But I've had you a long time. Longer than most mothers.

HOMER: I don't know what you'd do with my little room up there.

IDA: I've thought of that too. I think I'll keep it just as it is. And you'll know that it'll be ready for you any time you want it. Perhaps you'll want to spend a night down here sometime—you and Myrtle.

HOMER: [*Gloomily*] My room's too small for two people.

IDA: We might move in a double bed.

HOMER: [*Embarrassed*] Oh, Mother! [*Pause. They are both rather embarrassed*] And Myrtle gets so personal sometimes.

IDA: What do you mean?

HOMER: Oh, she wants to know all sorts of things. The other day she asked me what size underwear I wore.

IDA: She did? What for?

HOMER: I guess she wanted to buy me some.

IDA: Well, that does seem odd.

HOMER: She wrote it down in a little book she's got.

[*Pause. They are both depressed*]

IDA: Of course after you're married she'll be buying your underwear.

[*Pause*]

HOMER: There's something awful nice about Myrtle though.

IDA: Of course there is.

HOMER: She's awfully good-hearted and she does nice little things for you all the time.

IDA: Does she?

HOMER: She's awfully lonesome down there in North Lyons too. It isn't that I'm not awfully fond of her, Mother.

IDA: Do you love her, Homer?

HOMER: Well, I wouldn't want never to see her again. [*Pause*] Mother.

IDA: Yes, Homer?

HOMER: If I was to marry Myrtle do you think I'd— get used to it?

IDA: [*Faintly*] I guess so—

HOMER: I don't know. Maybe I would. And you want me to do it so bad— [Ida *is crying*] Mother, what's the matter!

IDA: Never mind me, Homer!

HOMER: Mother, you're crying!

IDA: I never thought of that! That she'd be buying your underwear! [*She has a fresh burst of crying and gets up and starts toward the house*]

HOMER: Mother—.

IDA: [*As she exits into house left*] Never mind me, Homer. I'll be all right. I'm just a silly old goose! [Homer *pushes the chair back. Kicks the ground, disgusted with himself for upsetting his mother. He wanders down to the tree left and leans against it much as his father did. It has become quite dark.* Thor *comes out of the door at right and stands on the porch. Suddenly he sees* Homer *and stares at him in amazement*]

THOR: [*Softly*] By God! [*He puts his head into the door*] Arry! Cora! Come here! [Homer *starts up guiltily, having heard* Thor. Thor *comes back out and looks over at* Homer. *He sees that* Homer *has heard him. Casually*] Oh, that you, Homer?

HOMER: Yes.

[Cora *and* Arry *rush out of the house and stop abruptly at a signal from* Thor. *They stare at* Homer]

THOR: What you doing out there all by yourself?

HOMER: Nothing—I—I was just going in.

THOR: Anything the matter with you?

HOMER: No—no— [*He goes into the house, hurriedly*]

ARRY: What is it? What's the matter?

THOR: Homer, by God! He was having a spell! I damn near thought it was Carl!

CORA: [*Excited*] What do you mean, Thor?

THOR: Had his head leaned up on that tree just like Carl does!

CORA: No!

THOR: Yes!

ARRY: Heredity!

THOR: By God, it is! It's heredity!

[Esther *is seen hurrying down between the houses*]

CORA: No, no, it can't be!

THOR: He was standing just like this! [*He turns suddenly and leans his forehead against the back of the house, his rear facing the audience*]

ARRY: That's it! That's it! Just the way Carl does!

[Esther *appears*]

CORA: Here's Esty!

ESTHER: Good gracious! What's happened to Thor?

ARRY: Esty! Esty! Now Homer's got 'em!

ESTHER: Got what?

ARRY: Spells! Like Carl's!

ESTHER: [*Pointing to* Thor] You mean Thor!

THOR: [*Disgusted*] Naw, naw.—Homer!

ARRY: Thor saw him standing right against that tree over there. [Esther *laughs suddenly*] Well, I don't see what there is to laugh at!

ESTHER: [*Sitting on the stump*] Now, Arry, you don't really think Homer's going to have spells too?

ARRY: I certainly do!

ESTHER: Well, I don't! I don't think Homer's got the gumption to have a spell. He's too lazy.

CORA: [*Giggling*] Of course he is.

[Esther *laughs with her*]

ARRY: Of course you two smarties would know it all! And Thor saw him with his own eyes! Didn't you, Thor?

THOR: Well, you know it was kind of dark— I just thought for a minute it looked funny—

ARRY: [*Angry*] Well, Theodore Swanson! How can you back down like that?

THOR: You know how it is, Arry—I got kind of excited—

ARRY: You mean to stand there and say Homer's not going to have spells? After bringing us all the way out here?

THOR: [*Apologetically*] No, I guess not, Arry—. Maybe he was just kind of resting.

ARRY: [*Crossing up the stairs*] Well, if I couldn't live up to my convictions better than that— Men have no more courage than—.   [*Exits into house*]

THOR: Oh, Arry! [*He starts after her*] I'll just go in and— I guess I shouldn't have said anything about it at all.

CORA: Oh, let her alone, Thor. Don't pamper her so!

THOR: No, I don't want her to be mad at me. Poor Arry! She's all alone in the world.

[*He goes in.* Esther *rises and crosses to porch steps by* Cora]

CORA: [*Disgusted*] All alone in the world! The way Arry can always take Thor in—. [*Turns to Esty— they smile at each other—both sit on porch steps*] It's good to see you, Esty. You don't have to get right back, do you?

ESTHER: David'll be back from his walk in a little while. I want to be there before he is. Carl hasn't come back yet, has he?

CORA: Not yet.

ESTHER: Ida phoned me. She wants me to talk to him if he's acting bad.

CORA: Oh, I think he'll be all right. It's just one of those dentist spells.

ESTHER: Well, I've seen those dentist spells when they got pretty bad sometimes. It's only one step from a dentist spell to a "Where am I" spell, you know.

CORA: Now, Esty! Carl's not going to have a "Where am I" spell!

ESTHER: I certainly hope not.

CORA: Why, he hasn't had one of those in years and years.

ESTHER: Well, we can't do anything until he gets back. I'll talk to him. Maybe if he isn't too far gone it might help some—. Now tell me. Have you met Myrtle yet?

CORA: I haven't really met her. I just talked to her a second.

ESTHER: [Controlling a giggle] What's she like?

CORA: [Giggling nervously] Now, Esty! She's very nice! Not the way we imagined at all!

ESTHER: She has got teeth like this though, hasn't she?

CORA: Now, Esty, she has no such thing!

ESTHER: And she talks like this to Homer.

[They both giggle]

CORA: She doesn't either! She's perfectly all right! And we shouldn't sit here and giggle about it!

ESTHER: I can't help it! Somehow the idea of Homer's having a girl—

CORA: You know what Arry thinks? Well, Arry thinks that maybe everything isn't as straight there as it might be.

ESTHER: Well, maybe it isn't. Wonderful things can happen.

CORA: Esty!

[This sends them into a mild case of hysterics]

ESTHER: [She wipes her eyes] My goodness, I haven't laughed so much for a long time.

CORA: That's right. How is David behaving?

ESTHER: Oh, I don't know, Cora. This last week I've hardly been out of the house.

CORA: I think it's a shame.

ESTHER: He made me promise I'd never come down again without his permission.

CORA: You didn't promise him—?

ESTHER: Well—I—I really had to. He said— [She gives a nervous giggle] He said if I ever came down again I'd—I'd have to live on the second floor the rest of my life.

CORA: Live on the second floor?

ESTHER: Upstairs. And he'd live downstairs.

CORA: But that's silly, Esty! You couldn't live on the second floor.

ESTHER: I guess I'd have to. The house divided, you know.

CORA: How would you get your meals?

ESTHER: He says I can come down the backstairs and use the kitchen when I want it.

CORA: If that isn't just like David! Why doesn't he live on the second floor?

ESTHER: He thought it would be easier for me on account of the bathroom.

CORA: Oh! Well, what would he do for a bathroom?

ESTHER: He'd have another put in. In that little closet off the kitchen.

CORA: But that would cost money, Esty!

ESTHER: I know it would. That's the one thing that worries me. Of course he'd only put in a seat and a basin. He says maybe I'd let him use the bath now and then.

CORA: [Sharply] Well, I wouldn't!

ESTHER: Oh, I'd have to.—He says he'll put up a bell that will ring when he wants to use it. So we wouldn't bump into each other.

CORA: And you wouldn't see each other at all?

ESTHER: I guess not. He says if we're going to be independent we might as well be independent. Of course if we should meet in the hall we'd bow to each other, like two acquaintances.

CORA: Well, he's just trying to scare you, Esty. And I think you ought to take a stand against him! You ought to be able to come down here any time you want to. David's just jealous!

ESTHER: I know it, Cora. He gets more so all the time. If he'd only stop talking about his Crystal Fortress.

CORA: You know, Esty, I always thought that Crystal Fortress was rather a lovely idea.

ESTHER: You wouldn't if you'd lived in it fifty-five years.

CORA: No, I think it's lovely. Your friends or anybody can come up to the fortress and look in through the door—and you can see them and talk to them and everything—but no one can ever really come into it except just the two of you. Just you two all alone there by yourselves. It must be nice sometimes to be all alone with—the person you live with. [Pause. Esther sits watching Cora. Suddenly Cora turns on her and says with surprising viciousness] Esty! I hope Homer doesn't marry Myrtle!

ESTHER: What!

CORA: Oh, I know it's selfish of me! But I hope he doesn't!

ESTHER: But why, Cora?

CORA: Because if he doesn't, Carl has promised to let me have that house up on Sycamore Drive, to lease it to me for as long as I want.

ESTHER: But what would you want with that house?

CORA: I want to live in it! I want for Thor and me to live in it! All by ourselves.

ESTHER: And this house?

CORA: Arry can have it! She can have everything that's in it!

ESTHER: I see.

CORA: Wouldn't it be wonderful, Esty?

ESTHER: Yes, I suppose it would, Cora.

CORA: [Pause. Cora feels Esther staring at her] Of course, I suppose it would make Arry good and mad.

ESTHER: Do you think Thor will do it?

CORA: Well, I—I don't know. I haven't asked him yet, of course.

ESTHER: When is Carl going to let you know?

CORA: Well, Carl says that if Homer doesn't say definitely that he's going to get married while Myrtle's here—that is, set an actual date and all—well, Carl thinks Homer never will marry her and then I can have the house. I've got the lease all drawn up, right here. All he's got to do is sign it.

[*She shows the lease in front of her waist.* Esther *looks at her sharply*]

ESTHER: [*Rising*] Well, I just hope it goes through without making any trouble for anyone.

CORA: [*Rising—suspicious*] What do you mean? Who could it make any trouble for?

ESTHER: Oh, I didn't mean anybody in particular— I just meant—

CORA: I don't understand, Esty—.

ESTHER: Shhh—!

CORA: What is it?

ESTHER: Carl.

CORA: Dear, I hope he's all right. How does he look to you?

ESTHER: I can't tell yet. Let's see what he'll do.

[Carl *has entered from stage left. The lights have gone on in the house and he stops in the patch of light from the window. Puts foot on step, and then decides not to go in. Stands there*]

CORA: [*In a whisper*] Dear, he looks kind of sad standing there, doesn't he?

ESTHER: Yes, he does.

CORA: He's afraid to go in.

ESTHER: I guess I'd better go over.

CORA: You're not scared, are you?

ESTHER: No, I guess not.

CORA: I'll be in the kitchen watching if you want me.

ESTHER: All right. [Cora *exits into house right.* Esther *starts across to Carl. He is so absorbed staring at the house he doesn't hear* Esther *until she is on him*] Good evening, Carl.

[Carl *turns on her quickly and stands staring at her. Pause*]

CARL: Oh!

ESTHER: It's Esty.

CARL: Oh, yes—.

ESTHER: I'm sorry I startled you.

CARL: [*Confused*] Well, that's—that's all right, Esty —I was just—standing here—. [*He becomes self-conscious and ashamed and to cover it very jovial*] Well, well, how are you, Esty? How are you?

ESTHER: I'm all right, Carl.

CARL: Well, it's nice to see you. Haven't seen you for several days.

ESTHER: No, I've been pretty busy with my garden.

CARL: [*Pulling chair up by porch steps*] Well, come and sit down. How's David?

ESTHER: [*She sits—Carl sits by her on steps*] David's fine.

CARL: Glad to hear it! Glad to hear it! Wonderful man, David. Wonderful man.

ESTHER: Yes, there're some fine things about David.

CARL: Fine things? No! He's a wonderful man, Esty! [Carl *suddenly realizes* Esther *has been staring at him. Pause. He becomes self-conscious and embarrassed*] Well—er—Myrtle's here.

ESTHER: Yes, I know.

CARL: Haven't met her yet. Guess I will at supper.

ESTHER: I want to meet her too.

CARL: [*Eagerly*] You do? Well now, see here, Esty, you can go right in with me and we'll meet her together. [*He rubs his hands happily*] Yes, sir, that's just what we'll do!

ESTHER: All right, Carl. Come on. Let's go in. [*She starts to rise*]

CARL: [*Quickly stopping her*] No, no. Not just yet. Let's wait a minute. [*Pause. He is ashamed*] Fact is, I sort of had one of my old—spells come on me, Esty.

ESTHER: Yes, Ida told me.

CARL: Guess I'm all right now.

ESTHER: Yes, you seem all right, Carl . . .

CARL: Yes. All right now. [*Pause—he suddenly drops his pose of joviality and turns on* Esther *intensely*] It's just that—! Just that—! I'm not a stupid man, Esty!

ESTHER: I know you're not, Carl.

CARL: I'm not an educated man like David, but I'm not a stupid one!

ESTHER: Of course you're not.

CARL: [*Rising*] Then WHERE AM I, Esty? WHERE AM I?

ESTHER: [*Rising—sharply*] Now, Carl!

CARL: [*Excited*] That's what I say, "Where am I in life." I'm caught, Esty!

ESTHER: Now listen to me, Carl—.

CARL: I'm not where I should be at all! There's some other place in life where I should be! I'm *Carl Bolton*, Esty!

ESTHER: Yes, yes, now be quiet—

CARL: The same Carl Bolton I was when I was a boy!

ESTHER: Yes, Carl, but—

CARL: But now I'm sixty-eight years old and WHERE AM I?

ESTHER: Now stop this, Carl!

CARL: Maybe I'm not Carl Bolton any more at all!

ESTHER: Well, maybe you're not!

[*Sudden pause.* Carl *stares at her slowly*]

CARL: What's that, Esty?

ESTHER: I say maybe you're not Carl Bolton any more.

CARL: I don't understand. How could that be?

[Esty *pats his arm reassuringly*]

ESTHER: Carl, you don't think you're the only one who feels this way about things, do you?

CARL: Why—I don't know, Esty—

ESTHER: Well, I think lots of people feel exactly the same way as you do, only they don't go around having spells about it. You know, Carl, I don't think it's been any harder on you than on any of the others. Just think of all that Cora's been through. Never having a real home of her own . . . And Thor—Arry having the whip hand over him all these years . . . I bet sometimes he wishes he were somewhere else in life, too.

CARL: Yes, that's true, Esty, but—

ESTHER: Even if it only meant living alone with Cora in another house.

[*Pause. Carl looks up*]

CARL: Did Cora tell you about that?

ESTHER: Yes. She said you might lease her the house.

CARL: Well, I—I did promise her, Esty. She kept at me so about it—. I guess I shouldn't have, though—

ESTHER: Why not? If Homer isn't going to use it there's no reason to just go on keeping it empty.

CARL: [*After slight pause*] But, there's another thing about letting Cora have the house, though, you know, Esty—. I mean—well, what do you think?

ESTHER: You mean—Arry?

CARL: [*Nods*] What do you think? Do you think Arry would—let Thor go?

ESTHER: Well, we've never been sure about Arry and Thor, Carl.

CARL: You girls have always been pretty sure. Gee, Esty, I'd hate for Arry to start anything.

ESTHER: I know. I thought of that when Cora was telling me. But I think you ought to do it, Carl. I think you ought to do it.

[*Pause. Carl watches Esty for a minute*]

CARL: All right, Esty. [*Pause*] I wonder if Cora ever knew about Arry and Thor?

ESTHER: If she did she's kept it to herself pretty well—. Oh, well, I think Arry really loved Thor. I think she probably still does. Anyway, it's the closest thing to a husband she'll ever know. Come to think of it, Carl, I guess Arry doesn't quite know where she is either.

[*Pause*]

CARL: Well, things get tangled up, don't they, Esty?

ESTHER: Don't they, though.

CARL: For everybody, I guess. [*Pause*] I feel better. Lots better.

ESTHER: That's good. Shall we go in and see Myrtle then?

CARL: All right. [*They start toward the house*] I always feel better talking to you, Esty.

ESTHER: Well, I'm the oldest.

[*They exit into house left. The stage is empty for a minute. A Man is seen to come from behind the hedge at right and approach the house at left, cautiously. He goes up to it and stands peering through the lighted window. Cora comes into dining room of house right and starts to set table. Sees* Man *and calls* Thor *and* Arry]

CORA: [*In an excited whisper. All three come out on the porch*] There he is! See! I knew it was someone!

THOR: [*Calling*] What do you want?

[*He switches on the porch light. Then crosses down.* Man *turns—there is a sudden shocked pause—then a frenzied fear seizes them all. They all speak at once*]

CORA: It's David! My goodness, it's David!

ARRY: [*Yelling frantically*] Esty! Esty!

THOR: [*In a loud voice*] Now look here, David! Esty's not here!

ARRY: [*Yelling*] Get out the front door, Esty!

CORA: Arry!

ARRY: [*Coming to head of steps*] Well, he was looking in the window! He must have seen her.

THOR: I've been in the house, David. She might have slipped in when—

CORA: She was only going to stay a second, David. She was just going home—.

[*Esther comes out of the house at left, hurriedly. The others freeze. David stands center, watching Esther. She comes down left center, followed by Ida and Carl. Homer and Myrtle stay on the porch left*]

ESTHER: [*Nervously*] Why, David, what are you doing here? I was just coming home. I really was. Myrtle is here, you see, and I just ran down to—

IDA: She's only been here a minute—.

ESTHER: You see, Ida phoned me Carl was having a spell—.

CARL: That's right, David. I had a spell.

ESTHER: But I'm all ready to go now. Come on, let's—.

[*David has not moved. Esther stops suddenly and watches him. He is looking at her. The others watch in silence. Suddenly he looks at the group containing Thor, Cora and Arry. They shrink back as he eyes them. He looks them over slowly, from head to foot, giving each a thorough inspection. Then he looks at the other group. He gives them the same individual, critical inspection. He stands a moment, throwing his head back in a puzzled way. He speaks to himself as though he were trying to reason something out*]

DAVID: [*Softly*] "And God created man in his own image; male and female created he them." [*After a moment's thought, he gives a sudden shrug, as though the entire problem were beyond him. He turns suddenly to* Thor, *as though seeing him for the first time*] Good evening, Theodore.

THOR: [*Taken aback*] Good—evening, David—.

DAVID: [*Bowing pleasantly*] Cora—Aaronetta—.

CORA: [*As David turns to the others*] Good—evening, David—.

DAVID: [*More genuine*] Good evening, Carl.

CARL: [*Eagerly*] Good evening, David.

DAVID: Ida—Homer—. [*He hesitates before* Myrtle]

HOMER: This's Myrtle Brown.

DAVID: Ah! This is Myrtle Brown. Good evening, Myrtle.

MYRTLE: Good evening. I'm very pleased to—

[*He turns to* Esther. *Formally as to the others*]

DAVID: Good evening, Esther.

ESTHER: [*Bewildered*] Good evening, David—.

[*He bows to her formally and then surveys them all, smiling*]

DAVID: Well, well, here we all are together again. Our own little circle. I must say, you all seem to me very much the same as you always did.

[*He beams on them. There is a rustling in the groups. They look at one another, bewildered*]

CORA: That's—very nice of you, David.

DAVID: Yes, just about the same. A little older, perhaps. Grayer. Pulses all a trifle slower, probably. But I can still see the same bright, intelligent expressions on your faces that I remember so well. [*Slight pause as he beams on them*] And now before I leave you there is just one thing more. You have all been in my home at one time or another. You all know how the entry hall leads into the living room and so is the entrance to the lower floor. And from the entry hall the staircase leads to the second floor. Well, now since Esther has decided it will be better for us to live apart from each other—.

ESTHER: [*Steps toward him*] David—.

DAVID: From now on, I will be living on the lower floor; Esther on the second.

ARRY: What's he mean, Esty?

ESTHER: Why, you know David. He didn't mean—

IDA: [*Following Esty*] What's he mean?

CORA: He told Esty if she came down here again she'd have to live on the second floor. } *Ad lib.*

ARRY: He what? He did not.

IDA: I don't believe it.

CORA: S'fact!

THOR: By God, what d'ye know about that!

DAVID: [*Raising his hand for silence*] Esther is a free agent now. She has a perfect right to come and go as she pleases and to have anyone she wishes visit her. Doubtless you will be there a great deal. Now none of you would come into the lower floor, of course. But may I suggest that as you pass through the entry hall and on up the stairs to be as—silent as possible?

[*Pause*]

ESTHER: But David, you don't really mean it?

DAVID: [*Surprised*] That was our understanding, was it not, Esther? It seems to me it was.

ESTHER: But, David, these are my *sisters!* They're all I have! I've got to have something in my life!

DAVID: And now you have your sisters. Who am I to deprive you of that?

ARRY: That's what I say! Who are you to—

CORA: Arry!

ARRY: I don't care! He hasn't got any right to treat Esty like that!

IDA: I don't think he has either!

ARRY: Esty ought to be able to come down and see us any time she wants to.

CORA: After all, we are her sisters, David. It's only natural.

ESTHER: [*Encouraged*] We don't do any harm, David. We just talk. I have a good time with my sisters. I don't care how ignorant they are!

ARRY: Of course she don't. Give it to him, Esty!

IDA: We're behind you, Esty.

ESTHER: I want to be able to come down here any time I want to!

ARRY: That's the ticket, Esty!

ESTHER: And I don't want to live on the second floor either! } *Ad lib.*

IDA: 'Course she don't!

ARRY: Good for you, Esty!

CORA: She's got to have something in her life!

ARRY: Give it to him, Esty!

[*They are all clustered around* Esther, *facing David, excited and angry. Sudden pause*]

DAVID: [*Bowing courteously*] Goodnight, Cora.

CORA: [*Taken aback*] Well—goodnight—David—.

DAVID: [*Bowing*] Theodore—Ida—Aaronetta—.

THOR: Goodnight, David—.

[*They all watch him, bewildered. He turns to* Carl]

DAVID: Goodnight, Carl.—By the way, Carl, in the houses you have built you have also installed the plumbing, haven't you?

CARL: Why, yes, I have, David.

DAVID: I am turning the little closet near my kitchen into a bathroom. Do you suppose you could do it?

CARL: Why, I guess so—.

DAVID: Would it be much of an undertaking?

CARL: That all depends on the bathroom upstairs. Is it right over the closet?

DAVID: Ah, that I'm afraid I wouldn't know.

CARL: If it is it would be easy.

DAVID: Perhaps you would come up and look at it in the morning.

CARL: Well, I'd be glad to, David.

DAVID: Thank you, Carl. Goodnight, Carl.—Homer. —Myrtle—.

MYRTLE: Goodnight. I'm delighted to have—

[*David has started out. He stops, turns*]

DAVID: [*Gently*] You won't forget my little reminder, will you? About being quiet when you visit Esther? I say it out of the utmost kindness. You know, of course, without my telling you, how much you all depress me? [*He looks from one to another, smiling*] Yes.—Well, goodnight, then. Goodnight. [*He bows and exits between houses*]

THOR: By God! David can be awful nice when he wants to be.

ESTHER: Oh, dear. I never should have come down here. It's all my fault.

ARRY: It's not your fault at all! David's an old fool, if you want my opinion.

CARL: [*Suddenly*] David's no fool! [*Quick silence. They all look at* Carl, *sharply*] David lives straight ahead the way he was meant to. *He knows where he is. He didn't branch off.*

IDA: [*Crossing to him*] Oh, my goodness!

HOMER: [*Pushing* Myrtle *in house*] Come in to supper, Myrtle.

IDA: It's time to come in to supper, Carl. Come along.

CORA: Go in to supper, Carl.

HOMER: Come in to supper, Father.

CARL: David thought it all out way back there at the crossroads. Then he went straight ahead.

IDA: Now stop it, Carl.—Homer!

HOMER: [*Joining them*] I'm coming, Mother.

CARL: He lived his life just the way he planned it. But *I* branched off.

IDA: [*Taking his arm*] Come on now, Carl.

CARL: [*To* Ida] Don't you see? I took the wrong turn. I got lost.

HOMER: Now get hold of yourself, Father.

CARL: [*Suddenly*] I've got to go back to the fork!

IDA: [*Distressed*] Oh, Carl, Carl! Don't say that!

CARL: I've got to take the other way.

HOMER: [*Trying to shake him*] Father!

CARL: I've got to go back to the fork.

IDA: [*Her hands over her ears*] Don't say that, Carl.

HOMER: Father, stop it! You're hurting my mother. You stop it now.

[*He shakes him.* Carl *stops suddenly. They have all been watching, breathless. Suddenly* Carl *seems to come to himself. He sees* Homer's *attitude, sees all the others watching, sees* Ida *crying, sees* Myrtle *staring in amazement*]

CARL: [*Trying to explain*] I—I—. I didn't mean—. [*Starts left—speaks to* Myrtle *on porch steps*] I didn't mean—. [*Turns to all of them*] I just meant that I got to go back to the fork. [*Exits through hedge left*] I've got to take the other way. I've got to—

IDA: [*Taking a step toward him*] Carl.

HOMER: [*His arms around her*] Never mind, Mother.

IDA: Carl!

HOMER: [*Comforting her*] Come in the house, Mother.

[Ida *drops her head on* Homer's *shoulder*]

IDA: [*Sobbing*] It came so quick—.

HOMER: I knew it would. I knew he was working up to it.

IDA: And he's always going back to that fork—. I never know what that means.

HOMER: That's all right, Mother. I'll be here. I won't leave you, Mother.

IDA: Oh, Homer, Homer—.

HOMER: Come in the house, Mother. Don't you worry. I'll take care of you. There, there, Mother, there, there.

[*As he leads the sobbing* Ida *into the house left,* Myrtle *crosses down left from the steps and watches them bewildered. The others have been watching and after* Homer *and* Ida *have gone*

in, all eyes center on Myrtle. Myrtle *eyes them, helplessly. She gives a nervous laugh and falteringly walks up the steps. Again she gives a little laugh.* Homer *has switched porch light off*]

MYRTLE: I guess I better—

ARRY: [Arry, *deeply touched, takes a few steps toward her, wanting to do something but not knowing what*] I—I—. Myrtle?

MYRTLE: [*Stopping*] Yes?

ARRY: I—. I've just been thinking—. I wondered—. Well, if supper isn't quite ready I thought maybe —maybe you'd have time to see that quilt I'm making—.

MYRTLE: [*Grateful, relieved*] I'd *love* to see it.

ARRY: [*Taking her arm and leading her toward the house right*] It isn't finished, you know—. There's more to be done on it—.

MYRTLE: I'm sure it's beautiful—.

ARRY: I hope you think so. You see—. I didn't mean to tell you—. But I'm making it for you—. To go with the luncheon set—.

MYRTLE: Oh, no!

ARRY: Yes, it's the same pattern.

MYRTLE: Oh, but, I couldn't accept it—. A *quilt!*

ARRY: [*They are going up the steps*] You won't have to take it if you don't like it—.

MYRTLE: I know I'll like it but—.

ARRY: [*They are inside now*] Well, it's yours then. My goodness, I certainly wouldn't have any use for it—.

[*They exit out of sight. Pause.* Cora *has been watching where* Homer *and* Ida *left*]

CORA: Esty, Homer will never marry Myrtle now, will he?

ESTHER: Looks pretty bad.

THOR: Damn shame. Myrtle's a nice girl, too.

CORA: Well—. [*Light goes on in* Arry's *room*] Esty, you just stay down here with us tonight and David'll come to his senses by morning. You can have the bedroom downstairs.

ESTHER: [*Rising*] I'm tired.

CORA: Of course you are.

ESTHER: It takes it out of you.

[*They start up the porch steps and around center*]

CORA: You're not as young as you were, Esty.

ESTHER: I guess that's it.

CORA: Besides, it's been a busy day.

ESTHER: Busy! It's been the busiest day I've had for a long time!

[*They exit into side door. Pause.* Arry *comes out and looks around, suspicious*]

ARRY: Where's Cora and Esty?

THOR: Just went in.

ARRY: [*Crossing to porch edge, sitting*] Oh!— Myrtle's lying down in my room. I think she wanted to be alone.

THOR: Uh-huh.

ARRY: She's real nice, Myrtle.

THOR: Yup.

ARRY: Well, guess we better go in. [*Rises—switches porch light off*]

THOR: [*Rising—crossing to porch step*] Yup.

ARRY: [*Moving back to front of porch. Stands looking at the sky a minute*] 'S going to be a nice night, Thor.

THOR: [*Turns and looks*] Yup.

[*Pause*]

ARRY: [*Dreamily*] Remember how bright it was that night we took the boat to—.

THOR: [*Quickly*] Shh! Arry! [*He glances over shoulder toward the house*]

ARRY: [*Resigned*] All right! [*Suddenly bursting out*] I get awful sick of having to keep still all the time! Sometimes I wish Cora would die!

THOR: [*Shocked*] Arry!

ARRY: [*Suddenly frightened*] I didn't mean that, Thor! I didn't mean that!

THOR: I should hope not! [*Crosses up to porch*]

ARRY: I really didn't, Thor!

THOR: I don't like that, Arry.

[*Thor goes in abruptly. Arry stands a moment, alone, frightened. She looks up at the sky*]

ARRY: [*Frightened*] I didn't mean that! Honest! [*She hurries into the house*]

Act II

SCENE: *The same. Seven-fifteen the next morning. Bright sun. Thor comes out of the house at right. Is eating an apple, contentedly. Suddenly throws it from him.*

THOR: God, how I hate apples! [*He moves down to his chair and sits*] Cora! I wonder where the hell she's got to? Arry!

ESTHER: [*Enters from the center porch door. Crosses down steps*] Good morning, Thor.

THOR: Oh, morning, Esty.

ESTHER: What time is it?

THOR: About quarter past seven.

ESTHER: My goodness, isn't that awful. I never stay in bed that late. Is everybody else up?

THOR: [*Sleepily*] Dunno, Esty. Haven't seen anybody. Just got up myself— Still, Cora must be up. She wasn't in bed.—By God, the way she kicked around last night—you'd thought she had the measles or something.

ESTHER: Thor, what happened last night after I went to bed? Ida came over, didn't she?

THOR: Yes, she did, Esty.

ESTHER: What did she say?

THOR: Well, seems Homer broke off with Myrtle.

ESTHER: Oh, my goodness, I was afraid that was it.

THOR: Yup. Told her it was all off. Couldn't leave his mother now that Carl was having spells again.

ESTHER: [*Furious*] Oh, that makes me so mad! I was afraid that would happen. Did Myrtle go back to North Lyons?

THOR: Nope. Can't get a train till this afternoon.

ESTHER: Oh, poor girl. Where is she?

THOR: Over at Ida's in bed, probably.

ESTHER: Poor thing. What an awful position for her to be in. [*Arry comes out of Ida's house*] Oh, there's Arry. Good morning, Arry.

ARRY: Good morning, Esty. [*To Thor*] Where's Cora?

THOR: I haven't seen her, Arry.

ARRY: Well, she isn't at Ida's and she isn't in bed.

THOR: Did you look on the roof?

ARRY: What would Cora be doing on the roof?

THOR: Dunno. She just might suddenly have gone crazy or something. [*He chuckles*]

ARRY: [*Peeved*] All right, you're so smart, listen to this. Carl didn't come home last night.

ESTHER: What?

ARRY: He didn't come home last night, and he hasn't been home this morning.

THOR: The hell you say!

ESTHER: How do you know?

ARRY: [*Impatiently*] How do you think I know? Ida just told me. She's nearly frantic. She wants to get out the Boy Scouts, but Homer won't let her.

ESTHER: Why won't he?

ARRY: Oh, you know how Homer is. He says it's embarrassing. It might get around.

THOR: It's a hell of a time for Homer to get embarrassed.

ESTHER: Hasn't Ida any idea where he is?

ARRY: Of course she hasn't. He's probably wandering around the streets having a spell with everyone he meets.

THOR: [*Getting up*] By God, we ought to do something.

ARRY: And another thing. Cora's gone, too.

THOR: What do you mean, "gone"?

ARRY: Well, where is she?

THOR: I don't know, but— [*Suddenly accusing*] Now, look here, Arry, Cora hasn't got anything to do with Carl being gone. Cora was right in that bed with me all night—

ARRY: I didn't say anything about—

THOR: She kicked me every five minutes—

ARRY: [*Shouting*] I didn't say Cora had gone with Carl—

THOR: Well, don't go making any cracks about Cora —[*Crosses right—sits chair*]

ARRY: I'm not making any cracks about her. But Cora went over to Ida's to talk to Carl. She was all excited about something. Said she had to see him right away. And when she found out Carl hadn't been home she ran out without saying a word. That was twenty minutes ago and she hasn't been seen or heard of since.

THOR: [*Uneasily*] What did she want to talk to Carl about?

ARRY: That's what I'd like to know. Cora's up to something, you mark my words. Last night when she found out Homer wasn't going to marry Myrtle she got as nervous as a monkey. She's got some bee in her bonnet and if it's what I think it is—. [Esther *suddenly puts her hand up to her mouth. Arry catches her and eyes her, sharply*] What do *you* think she wants to see Carl about, Esty?

ESTHER: [*Innocently*] Me?

ARRY: [*Imitating her*] Yes, me!

ESTHER: How would I know, Arry?

ARRY: Oh, you make me sick. But I'll tell you one thing! If Cora is up to something—and if it's what I think it is—well, some people around here had just better watch out, that's all I say.

[*She looks significantly at* Thor *who squirms uneasily.* Ida *comes out of house at left*]

IDA: [*Mournfully crossing down steps—sits ledge left*] Esty, Esty, have you heard—?

ESTHER: Yes, Ida—.

IDA: Poor Carl!

ESTHER: Now nothing's happened to him, Ida.

IDA: If we could only drag the river or something—

ESTHER: Now, Ida, there's no river anywhere around here.

IDA: He was always such a good husband to me. Never a cross word. [*Calling to* Thor] Have you heard about Carl, Thor?

THOR: [*Calling back*] Yeah! Terrible thing, Ida.

IDA: He was such a good man.

THOR: By God, he was, Ida! That's a fact!

IDA: What do you think I ought to do?

THOR: Well, if it was me, I think I'd begin to look around a little—.

IDA: That's what I think. But Homer says we don't want the whole neighborhood to know.

THOR: [*Rises*] Tell you what I'll do. I know a fellow down at the police station—Jim—

IDA: [*Horrified*] Police!

THOR: Sure. They're the ones to handle things like this. I could call Jim up sort of casually—not giving anything away—you know, and ask him what you're supposed to do in a case like this.

ESTHER: That's just the thing to do, Ida.

IDA: [*Hesitantly*] But Homer says if anything had happened we'd have heard—.

ARRY: Not necessarily. Just suppose Carl took it into his head last night to walk up on Randall's hill where he goes. And suppose he fell off that bad drop there. He was having a spell, remember. And suppose he knocked himself unconscious on one of those rocks—or even just broke a leg—why, he could lie there for weeks before—

ESTHER: Oh, Carl wouldn't fall off that drop!

ARRY: In the dark he wouldn't?

ESTHER: No, he wouldn't. Carl's no fool.

ARRY: Esty, sometimes you are the most exasperating woman I ever knew!

THOR: [*To* Ida] What do you say, Ida? I won't give

away a thing. I'll just say, "Hello, Jim. How are you? How're the kids?"

ESTHER: You might mention something about Carl.

THOR: Sure, I'll sneak Carl in.

IDA: Well, all right. But if it comes out all over the paper tomorrow—?

ARRY: [*Crosses right—starts in*] Come on, Ida. It's not going to get in the paper.

IDA: [*Rises—follows* Thor *up steps*] Well, all right. But you be careful what you say, Thor.

THOR: By God, Ida, if Jim gets any idea of what I called him for I'll eat my hat.

[Thor *and* Ida *go in house right.* Arry *is still on the porch—*Esther *sits stump*]

ARRY: All over the paper! Anybody'd think Carl was running for Mayor or something— [*Notices that* Esty *has sat down*] Aren't you coming in, Esty?

ESTHER: I don't think so. They don't need me.

ARRY: [*Hesitantly*] I don't suppose they *need* me either but— [*She takes one step down*] You're not angry, are you?

ESTHER: [*Surprised*] Why should I be angry?

ARRY: Well, I thought maybe I—spoke to you kind of sharp.

ESTHER: [*Smiling*] Oh! Oh, that's all right, Arry.

ARRY: I didn't mean to be—. You know how I talk sometimes.

ESTHER: Yes, I know.

ARRY: I've just been all on edge the last few days.

ESTHER: Really? Why?

ARRY: Well, I don't know exactly. But there's something going on around here I don't know about. And if there's one thing I hate it's to have things going on behind my back.

ESTHER: Yes, you always hated that, Arry.

ARRY: For one thing it isn't polite. I like people to be open and above board. When people start to sneak and— [Cora *enters hurriedly from between the houses. She is excited.* Arry *turns on her sharply*] Well, it's about time! Where have you been?

CORA: [*Anxiously*] Has Carl come back?

ARRY: What do you want to know for?

ESTHER: No, he hasn't, Cora.

CORA: Nobody's heard anything?

ESTHER: Not a thing.

ARRY: [*Who has been eyeing her*] What are you so excited about it for?

CORA: [*Flustered*] Who wouldn't be excited about it?

ARRY: And where have you been?

[*Pause.* Cora *gets over being flustered. She becomes rather superior, as though possessed of some secret knowledge*]

CORA: Well, I'll tell you, Arry. I've been for a little walk.

ARRY: You haven't either. You've been looking for Carl.

CORA: Well, my goodness, we've all got to do everything we can. I went over to Ida's—

ARRY: That's right. To see Carl.

CORA: Yes. And when I found he wasn't there I thought he might have gone up to Homer's house. But when I got up there, there wasn't any sign of him.

ARRY: But what did you want to see him for?

CORA: [*Suddenly impatient*] Oh, Arry, if I wanted to tell you that I would.

ARRY: [*Suddenly very dignified*] Oh! Well, I certainly crave your pardon, Cora. I assure you I had no intentions of prying. [*She starts toward the house*]

CORA: [*Sorry*] Oh, it—it isn't anything, Arry—. Don't get hurt.

ARRY: Please, Cora. I certainly wouldn't want you to tell me anything you didn't want to. I'll just go in and you can tell it to Esther. [*Arry goes in*]

CORA: Oh, dear, now Arry's angry—. Well, I can't help it! [*She turns to* Esther, *excited*] Oh, Esty, I'm so upset I don't know what to do! The first thing this morning I go over to see Carl—the lease all ready to sign—and he's gone. [*She takes the lease from her blouse*] I've put in here forty-five dollars a month. Twenty-year lease. I think he'll agree to that, don't you, Esty?

ESTHER: That seems fair enough.

CORA: Oh, Esty, isn't it wonderful?

ESTHER: It isn't wonderful yet. Thor hasn't agreed to it yet, you know.

CORA: [*Crossing to steps right—sitting*] Oh, he *will*! He's *got* to! He loves that house! Oh, Esty, I've never been so happy in my whole life as I am right this minute!

ESTHER: [*Rises—crosses to* Cora—*hesitantly*] Thor may not take this just the way you think, you know. [*Hurriedly*] I mean—. Well, remember it isn't so easy to pick up and leave a house you've lived in so long—leave all the furniture and everything you're used to—. So you know what I think?

CORA: What?

ESTHER: I think it might be a good idea to talk it over first with—Arry.

[*Quick pause.* Cora *draws back*]

CORA: Arry! [*She looks suspiciously at* Esty]

ESTHER: Yes.

CORA: [*In a hard voice*] Why? What business is it of hers?

ESTHER: It is her business in a way.

CORA: I don't see how.

ESTHER: Well, she's always lived with you. You're the only home she's ever known. You can't say she's not concerned.

CORA: I don't care if she is concerned. Thor is *my* husband, Esty.

ESTHER: Of course, Cora—I just thought—.

CORA: [*With a slight sneer*] You just thought nothing—.

ESTHER: But, Cora—

[Thor *comes out, followed by* Ida *and* Arry. Cora

hurriedly slips the lease into her waist although a small part of it shows]

IDA: But what's the next step for us to take, Thor?

THOR: [*Coming down the steps, followed by* Ida. Arry *stays on the porch*] By God, Ida, you got me. If you won't let me tell the police who Carl is—. They can't very well start looking for somebody they don't know.

[Esty *sits*]

ESTHER: What did they tell you, Thor?

THOR: They said to give a description of him.

ESTHER: I should think you could do that.

THOR: Ida says I can't.

IDA: [*Nervously—crosses to* Esty] Well, Esty, Homer says—.

CORA: [*Sweetly*] Good morning, Thor.

THOR: What've you been up to this morning?

CORA: Me? Nothing at all.

IDA: Did you see anything of Carl?

CORA: Not a thing, Ida.

THOR: What'd you want to see Carl in such a hurry about?

CORA: I just wanted to find him for Ida.

ARRY: [*On porch just above* Cora—*laughing*] That's very funny. Very funny. [*She changes to a matter-of-fact voice*] And what's this sticking out of your waist? [*Pulls the lease*]

CORA: [*Slapping her hand*] You keep your hands to yourself.

ARRY: Well, what is it?

CORA: None of your business.

ARRY: Hoity-toity!

[Arry *moves up on the porch—but during the following scene eyes* Cora *intently*]

IDA: Maybe if we just gave a description without giving his name—.

THOR: Sure! No use giving his name. Just his description. Sixty-six years old—.

IDA: Sixty-eight, Thor.

THOR: Sixty-*eight*? Are you sure?

IDA: Well, I—I thought I was. Sixty-eight, isn't it, Esty?

ESTHER: Let's see. I'm seventy-two. And Cora's two years younger than I—.

CORA: That's right. And Ida's four years younger than me.

IDA: Sixty-six, that's right. And Carl's two years older—.

ESTHER: Sixty-eight.

THOR: Well, what the hell do you know about that! I wouldn't have said Carl was a day over sixty-six. By God, we're certainly getting along, this crowd.

[*Hearty laugh*]

IDA: [*Crosses porch ledge, left—sits*] Yes, sir, we certainly are.

THOR: We're certainly not getting any younger. And by God, I'm glad we're not. When I think how I used to go to that office every day at eight o'clock—

CORA: You never used to mind that so much, Thor.

THOR: Well, I'd mind it now.

ESTHER: Still, if you were getting younger you'd get back to the age where you wouldn't mind it.

THOR: What's that, Esty?

ESTHER: I say if you were forty again you wouldn't mind going to the office.

THOR: I'm not forty though.

ESTHER: But if you were getting younger you'd get back to forty.

THOR: [Looking at her] What the hell are you talking about, Esty?

ESTHER: Never mind.—Anyway, blue eyes.

[Arry gets down off the porch and starts slowly toward Cora]

IDA: What's that, Esty?

ESTHER: Carl.

IDA: Oh, yes, Carl.

ESTHER: He's got blue eyes.

IDA: Oh!—Yes, that's right. Blue eyes.

THOR: Bald. [Slight pause. He looks up at Ida, puzzled] Carl's bald, isn't he?

IDA: He's got kind of a fringe.

THOR: You sure? I would have said Carl was pretty damn near completely bald.

CORA: No, he had quite a bit of hair in back, Thor.

THOR: Really? Well, that just goes to show. You look at a thing and you look at it and still you don't see it. I'm going to get a good square look at Carl the next time I see him.

IDA: [Tearfully] If you ever have a chance to see him.

THOR: Oh, by God, Ida, I'm sorry, I forgot.

[Arry has been circling closer and closer. At this point she is near enough to Cora to make a quick dive for the paper. She gets it and starts racing across the lawn as fast as she can go. Cora is on her feet in an instant and after her, shrieking. Thor sits up, startled]

CORA: Arry! You give that back! You come back here with that paper. Arry! [A race ensues in which Arry, running as hard as she can, tries to get the paper out of the envelope and read it] Catch her, Ida! Hurry! Head her off that way!

[Ida heads her off from going in the house]

ESTHER: Give her back that paper, Arry!

THOR: What the hell's going on here?

CORA: You dare read that paper and I'll fix you, Aaronetta Gibbs!

ESTHER: You stop, Arry! Stop!

IDA: [Suddenly entering into the spirit of the thing] Look out, Arry, Cora's gaining on you.

THOR: What are they doing?

IDA: [Laughing] I don't know. Arry's got something of Cora's. [Shouting] Look out, Arry.

[They are all shrieking, ad lib. Arry races right and gets cornered by Ida right—Esty center—and Cora coming after her from the left—. They are at the height of their shrieking and pulling at each other as David enters left. The noise subsides.

Even Arry *quiets down and with a final jerk,* Cora *gets the paper.* Esther, *in utter confusion, faces* David, *weakly.* David *surveys them, smiling.*]

DAVID: [Pleasantly] Playing tag?

ESTHER: No, no—. We were just—.

DAVID: But don't apologize, Esther. You are a free agent now. You can amuse yourself any way you wish.

ESTHER: But you don't understand, David—.

DAVID: Please go on with the game. Don't let me interrupt you—.

ESTHER: But we weren't playing a game. We were—.

DAVID: [Calling off left] I'll go in and wait for you in your room, Carl. [Starts up steps of house left]

CARL: [Off stage] All right, David.

EVERYBODY: Carl!

ESTHER: David!

[She follows him into house. Carl, loaded down with tools, enters left. Ida crosses to him]

IDA: Carl!

CARL: [Puts down bags] Oh, Ida—I hope you haven't been worried, Ida.

IDA: Worried! My goodness, Carl, I've been nearly frantic! Where have you been? What's the matter? Are you all right? Are you hurt?

CARL: [Surprised] Hurt?

IDA: But where have you been, Carl? You stayed out all night. I've been nearly frantic. We even called the police.

CARL: Police?

IDA: We thought you might be dead!

CARL: Dead? No.

IDA: You didn't come home all night. I've been nearly frantic. Where have you been, Carl?

CARL: [Surprised she doesn't know] Why, I've been up at David's.

IDA: But where did you sleep?

CARL: Well, we didn't sleep, Ida—. We talked. David's going to help me find out where I am. We're right in the middle of it now. We just stopped long enough to come down and get my tools and pack my clothes—.

IDA: Pack your clothes?

CARL: Yes, I— [Realizes she doesn't understand] Oh! You see, I'm moving, Ida.

IDA: What do you mean?

CARL: Well, David has invited me to live with him. He wants me to.

IDA: Live with David?

CARL: Yes. You see, we're going to live on the lower floor. We're going to put in a real bath instead of just a seat and a basin and we're going to use the side entrance and—

IDA: What are you talking about, Carl?

CARL: [Turns to her—as to a child] I'm going to live with David for awhile.

IDA: But what about me?

CARL: [Blankly] You?

IDA: Yes, me, Carl.

CARL: Oh, that's right. Well, you can live here just the way you do now.

IDA: You don't mean you're going to leave me, Carl?

CARL: But, I've lived here a long time, Ida. I want to live somewhere else for a while. You'll be all right. You've got Homer.

IDA: I just don't understand—.

CARL: [Crossing to pick up tools] I'll explain it to you sometime, Ida. I'll come down and see you—.
                    [David calls from inside house]

DAVID: We're wasting valuable time, Carl.

CARL: [Briskly—going in] Be right there, David. Be right there.

IDA: Carl! I've got to talk to you, Carl—
    [Follows him—Arry, Thor and Cora are watching]

THOR: Well, what the hell do you know about that.

ARRY: I always knew that marriage wouldn't last.— Anyway, Carl has got hair on the back of his head. Quite a bit of it.

THOR: There you are! Damn it all, I forgot to look again!   [Sits]

CORA: [Starting left] Well, I've got to run over and see him.

ARRY: [Suddenly pulling Cora around] Oh, you do, eh! What for?
    [Sudden pause. They revert to their old tension]

CORA: If you ask me that again, Arry, I'll—

THOR: That's right. What the hell's the matter with you two?

ARRY: What's in the paper, is what I want to know.

THOR: Whose paper is it?

ARRY: Cora's. She's been hiding it.

THOR: What business is it of yours then?

ARRY: Cora's up to something and I know it.

CORA: [Hard] You want to know what's in this paper, Arry?

ARRY: Yes, I do!
    [Pause. Cora glares at Arry. She hands her the paper]

CORA: [In a hard voice] All right, look for yourself.
    [She gives Arry the paper. Arry reads it and looks up slowly. They eye each other in silence]

THOR: [Impatiently] Well, what is it? [Cora takes the paper and gives it to Thor. He reads it as Arry watches Cora, trying to figure out exactly what it means. Thor looks up, puzzled] This here's a twenty-year lease on Homer's house.

CORA: [Steadily] Yes.

THOR: It's made out to you.

CORA: Yes.

THOR: What's it for?

ARRY: That's what I want to know.

THOR: Look here, Cora, what's the big idea?

CORA: [After a moment] I'm going to rent it for us, Thor.

THOR: Us? What do we want with it?

CORA: You like that house, don't you, Thor?

THOR: Of course I like it but—

CORA: You like it better than this one, don't you?

THOR: What if I do? That's no reason to rent it.

CORA: Listen, Thor. We haven't got many years left ahead of us, have we?

THOR: What's that got to do with it?

CORA: Everything. I want for the rest of the years we *have* got for you and me to move up there and live together in that nice house. Have a real home of our own.

THOR: [Frightened] Now, look here, Cora, I don't know what you're getting at.

ARRY: I know what she's getting at.

CORA: There's no reason in the world that I can see why we can't do it. Carl has promised to sign the lease. We can afford it. And we'd love it. Just you and me—alone.

THOR: [Rises] Good Lord, Cora, now look here—

CORA: [Steadily] I've thought it all out, Thor. We can give this house to Arry. We can make out some kind of transfer and she can own it in her own name. She won't be lonesome with Ida and Esty here. And we can have what's left of the years together—alone—as we should always have had them in the past.

THOR: [Horrified] Cora! [Slight pause. Arry turns quickly and runs into the house] Arry—. [He takes a step toward her and then turns back. Cora is watching him] By God, Cora, how could you say a thing like that?

CORA: [Crosses center a step—steadily] It's the truth, isn't it?

THOR: But right in front of Arry.

CORA: She had it coming to her.

THOR: But think how she must feel.

CORA: I know how she feels.—Well, what about it, Thor? Shall we do it?

THOR: [Uneasily] But we can't do a thing like that—

CORA: Why not?

THOR: We just couldn't. It wouldn't be fair to Arry. Poor Arry, she's all alone in the world.

CORA: So am I. You can be alone a lot of different ways, Thor.

THOR: And Carl isn't going to rent that house—.

CORA: If he doesn't then we can't do it. But if he does, are you willing?

THOR: But Cora—

CORA: You're not afraid, are you, Thor?

THOR: Afraid? Afraid of what?

CORA: Of anything.

THOR: [Uneasily] I don't know what you mean.

CORA: All right. Then you think it over, Thor, will you?

THOR: [Same] I guess—I can think it over—.

CORA: [Crossing left to Ida's house] Thank you.— Now I'm going over to Ida's and talk to Carl. I think we can get that house, Thor.

THOR: [Crossing center—afraid] Don't do it now, Cora. Wait till we talk it over.

CORA: [On steps] No, Carl may get away again. We don't want to take any chances.

[She exits into house]

THOR: *[Desperate]* But—. *[Arry enters from house right. Thor turns]* Gee, Arry, I'm so sorry about that. Cora didn't mean anything—.

ARRY: She meant it all right.

THOR: She was just mad. I'm sorry as I can be.

ARRY: No use being sorry. The point is what are you going to do about it? If Cora gets that house are you going to move up there?

THOR: Of course not, Arry—.

ARRY: How will you get out of it?

THOR: I'll talk to Cora and—

ARRY: What will you tell her?

THOR: *[Sits stump]* I'll fix it up some way.

ARRY: She's over seeing Carl now. Why didn't you stop her?

THOR: I couldn't just then—

ARRY: You listened to Cora. Now you listen to me, Thor. Cora can talk about having what's left of her life alone with you. Well, what about me? How many years do you think I've got left?

THOR: I know, Arry, I know—.

ARRY: And whose fault is it that *I* haven't got a home of my own?

THOR: All right, Arry. Now your home's right here with us—.

ARRY: I've got just as much right here as Cora.

THOR: Now be quiet, Arry. I'll think of something.

ARRY: You'd better. Because I'm not going to spend the rest of my life alone. After all I've given up.

THOR: I don't think Carl'll give her the house anyway.

ARRY: Well, if he does, and you leave me now, Thor, don't think I won't tell what's happened. I'm not ashamed. I'd *like* to have Cora know.

THOR: *[Sharply]* Now keep still, Arry.

ARRY: All right. But don't think Cora's going to make it easy for you. You'd better think up something pretty good, Thor. *[She starts in—stops on top step]* You didn't have much breakfast this morning, did you?

THOR: *[Abused]* I had an apple.

ARRY: Well, come in. I'll fix you something.

[She goes in. Thor starts in, gloomily]

THOR: Doggone it all! *[As he starts in, Homer comes out of house left, furious—he slams porch door—starts around center on porch—then sees Thor. Thor speaks gloomily]* 'Morning, Homer.

HOMER: *[Stops pacing]* 'Morning, Uncle Thor. *[Continues pacing—suddenly stops and looks up, furious]* Aunt Cora got my house away from me!

THOR: *[Quickly]* What's that?

HOMER: While I was shaving!

THOR: What do you mean, Homer?

HOMER: I was upstairs shaving and when I came down my father had rented my house to Aunt Cora.

THOR: You mean he signed the lease?

HOMER: Just as I was coming downstairs.

THOR: Oh, my God!

[Thor exits into house right—Ida comes out of house left—follows Homer down center]

IDA: Homer—. Oh, Homer, I'm so sorry about it!

HOMER: *[Moving away]* I don't want to talk about it, Mother. I've got to think.

IDA: Do you feel awfully bad?

HOMER: How do you think I feel? How would you feel if you suddenly found out you didn't have a house any more? That was *my* house. Myrtle's and mine.

IDA: Yes, it was, Homer, but—

HOMER: *[Sits]* And now it's not my house any more. Now Myrtle and I haven't got a house any more.

IDA: I don't suppose Carl thought you'd care—. You and Myrtle weren't going to use it—

HOMER: We go up and look at it, don't we? We talk to each other about it. Now what are we going to talk about?

IDA: But you said you weren't going to get married and—

HOMER: I didn't say we weren't engaged.

IDA: Oh, dear, I'd do anything to get it back for you. I've never seen Cora so stubborn about anything. She won't even talk about it. She's calling up the electric company right now to have the lights turned on.

HOMER: What I'm going to say to Myrtle when she gets up, I don't know. It'll just about break her heart. She makes plans about that house all the time. She's told all her friends down in North Lyons about her beautiful house. Well, now she hasn't got one any more. We just took it away from her. Pretty small business, I must say! Invite a girl to stay over night and then take her house away from her when she's asleep. Pretty small business! *I* don't know what the world's coming to.

IDA: Well, I'll talk to Carl about it just as soon as I can. He and David have locked themselves in the bedroom until they're finished packing and won't talk to us but as soon as they come out I'll—

HOMER: That won't do any good. He can't do anything. No, my house is gone, Mother. It's just gone.

IDA: *[Distressed—sits stump]* Oh, Homer, I'm so sorry—

HOMER: *[Suddenly—rising]* What's it all about, that's what I ask myself!

IDA: What's what all about, Homer?

HOMER: *[Turning to Ida]* All of it. Why hasn't Myrtle a home and been living up there in my house all this time? What's it all about that I'm forty years old and still living here and not having a home of my own?

IDA: But that's what you've always wanted, Homer.

HOMER: *[Accusingly]* *Why* have I wanted it? I'm a man.

IDA: Of course, Homer.

HOMER: Then what's it all about? Myrtle cried half

the night last night. I heard her. And then my father leaves home. And then they take our beautiful house away from us. So what's it all about?

IDA: [*Rising*] I'm so sorry, Homer.

HOMER: [*Crossing to left exit*] I've got to think these things out. That's what I've got to do. I've got to think these things out. [*Exits*]

IDA: [*Following—and off*] Oh, dear. Oh, dear—.

[David *and* Carl *come out of house left. They are loaded with suitcases, tools, etc.* Carl *eagerly listens to* David]

CARL: Of course, it's just a supposition, David.

DAVID: That's right, Carl, just a supposition. [*Puts bags down left center—*Carl *does same*] Let us suppose that right now, at this moment, you *are* a dentist. Let's assume that.

CARL: [*Eagerly*] All right, David, all right.

DAVID: You have your office. All your instruments, your chair, your tools—

CARL: X-ray machine.

DAVID: X-ray machine. Everything. And you're working on a patient. And suddenly do you know what you're going to say to yourself?

CARL: What?

DAVID: WHERE AM I? What am I doing here? I'm caught! I'm *Carl Bolton!* Where am I? Just as you do now—And how are you going to answer yourself? You can't say: Where am I? I'm a dentist. *What* am I, yes. But that's not what you ask yourself, Carl. You ask yourself: *Where* am I? Where am I in *life?* What's the meaning of it? And that's a very natural question, Carl. It's a question that a man like you must inevitably ask himself. The only reason that you think it strange, that anyone thinks it's strange, is because the people you have been in contact with have never let that problem worry them. They are content to answer the question: "Where am I?" by: "I'm a dentist." And why shouldn't they? After all, it doesn't much matter where they are, does it?

CARL: [*Eagerly*] But the answer, David. What's the answer?

DAVID: Ah, that's another thing. That's what we must find out.

CARL: If I could only find out that answer—

DAVID: We'll talk about it, Carl. We'll talk about it. Well, shall we get loaded?

[Ida *enters left—*Esther *comes out of house and down steps*]

CARL: Yes, yes.

[*They start to load each other with the bags and tools*]

IDA: [*Tearfully*] Carl, I've always been a good wife to you. I've always been faithful and— [*Turning to* Esty] Esty, what are we going to do?

ESTHER: [*Crossing down steps—sitting porch ledge*] I don't know what *you're* going to do, Ida. But I know what *I'm* going to do.

IDA: What?

ESTHER: I'm going to sit right here and sort of bask in the sun.

[David *looks up, surprised*]

IDA: But they're going to leave us, Esty.

ESTHER: Well, let them! For heaven's sakes let them go and find out where they are once and for all. If they got to be as old as they are without knowing the Lord knows it's high time for them to find out.

DAVID: You see, Carl, as I was saying, there are some people who never ask themselves the question: Where am I?

ESTHER: There's some people who don't have to. I *know* where I am. I'm on the second floor. And to tell the truth, I'm beginning to like the idea pretty well.

DAVID: Well, I'm glad if the arrangement pleases you, Esther.

ESTHER: It does. I've had more fun last night and today than I've had for a long time.

DAVID: Ah, yes. Your games and so forth—

ESTHER: That's right. I like games. With lots of people on both sides.

DAVID: Ah, yes. Well, you're a free agent now, Esther.

ESTHER: I know I am. When I sat outside that locked door a few minutes ago waiting for you two to come out, I suddenly said to myself: "There's no fool like an old fool," and I was thinking of you and Carl. And then I said it again and it suddenly meant *me.* For fifty years I've washed and cooked and brought up children and now suddenly I've got a chance to be free. I can come down here any time I want to, can go to the movies with the girls—do anything. [*She stretches*] It's nice!

[*Pause.* David *stands looking at her. Suddenly he turns to* Carl]

DAVID: Well, Carl, we'd better get back to the bathroom.

CARL: [*Picking up tools*] All right, David. I'll come down and see you, Ida.

IDA: I never thought you'd leave me, Carl.

CARL: I never thought I would either, Ida, but—
[*They exit up center*]

DAVID: [*Starts out—then turns back to* Esther] You'll be occupying the second floor tonight?

ESTHER: I haven't decided yet. I may stay down here. Thor says I can stay as long as I like.

DAVID: Ah!

ESTHER: But I'll be quiet if I come in late.

[*He stands looking at her for a second*]

DAVID: Well, pleasant dreams, Esther.

ESTHER: Thank you.

[*He starts out—stops and turns*]

DAVID: I meant to say, if you prefer the lower floor to the upper—

ESTHER: No, I think I prefer the upper.

DAVID: I thought perhaps the stairs—

ESTHER: The stairs won't bother me any.

DAVID: That's fine. [*He hesitates a minute*] If there

is any rearrangement of furniture you wish done, Carl and I will be glad to help you.

ESTHER: Thank you, David.

DAVID: There's no use straining yourself.

ESTHER: No.

DAVID: Well, good morning, Esther.

ESTHER: Good morning, David. [David *exits up path.* Esther *watches him go, amused. Suddenly she starts to sing softly*] Oh, sole mio.—. Ti-di-di-di-di—. Ti-di-di-di-di—.

[Cora *comes out of* Ida's *house. She crosses down the steps and walks center to the path, waving the lease at* Esty *as she goes*]

CORA: Hello, Esty. All signed!

ESTHER: Where are you going?

CORA: [*Stopping*] I'm going down the street to see Harold Blake. To see if we can use his truck. Maybe he can move us up there after work to-morrow or the next day. [*Slightly malicious*] You see, Esty, I've decided you're right. It *is* hard to go away and leave a house you've lived in so long—all the furniture and all—. So I've decided to take some furniture along. Just Thor's chair so he won't be lonesome—and a couple of pieces out of the bedroom—. Arry won't miss those. My goodness, Arry's got the whole house to live in. Isn't that right, Esty? [Esther *has been looking at her steadily. She doesn't reply*] Well, goodbye, Esty, and if anybody wants to make trouble, they can. [*She starts out between the houses—airily—and meets* Ida *coming in. She greets her effusively*] Hello, Ida.

[*She exits—Ida crosses to* Esty]

IDA: Well, I must say you didn't do much to—.

ESTHER: [*Rises—grabs* Ida *tensely*] Ida!

IDA: What's the matter, Esty?

ESTHER: Cora! I'm kind of scared. She's going through with this house thing, Ida. Cora means business.

IDA: Do you really think so?

ESTHER: Yes, I do. And you know what's going to happen, don't you?

IDA: [*Uneasily*] Oh, I don't think if it comes right down to it Arry will really stir up anything.

ESTHER: You don't, eh? Well, I do! Arry's mad enough to do anything. She'll tell all there is to tell and more too.

IDA: Well, what can we do about it?

ESTHER: What do you suppose Arry would do if we told her we knew about her and Thor?

IDA: [*Shocked*] We couldn't do that!

ESTHER: Now, wait a minute, Ida. The only thing that Arry's got over Thor is that she thinks none of us know about it.

IDA: She's hinted it in front of us often enough.

ESTHER: I know, but she hasn't any idea we ever caught on. She thought she was so smart about it. So if we tell her that all of us—even Cora—have

known all along—. Well, there wouldn't be much point in her telling. Anyway, it would take some wind out of her sails, wouldn't it?

IDA: It would be awfully hard on Arry.

ESTHER: Not as hard as it will be on everybody if she starts to make trouble. [*Suddenly*] Let's go in and talk to Arry before Cora gets back. [*She starts drawing* Ida *toward the house*]

IDA: But Thor's in there.

ESTHER: We'll get her out here then. We'll get her out if we have to drag her out.

IDA: All right.—Oh, dear! It never rains but it pours. [*They start in.* Myrtle *comes out house left*]

MYRTLE: Oh, good morning, Mrs. Bolton.

IDA: [*Stops—comes down steps*] Oh! Oh, good morning, Myrtle. Are you up?

MYRTLE: Yes, I am.

ESTHER: Good morning, Myrtle.

MYRTLE: Good morning. Isn't it lovely out?

ESTHER: Yes, isn't it? [*To* Ida] I'll go in. Come in as soon as you can.

IDA: All right. [Esther *goes in*] Well, you had a pretty good sleep, didn't you?

MYRTLE: I guess you think I'm a dreadful laggard, staying in bed so long?

IDA: Not at all. I'm glad you did.

MYRTLE: I don't always do it!

IDA: I bet you don't. And I'll bet you're good and hungry, too.

MYRTLE: No. I helped myself to some coffee and a little toast.

IDA: But you'll want more than that.

MYRTLE: I couldn't, really. That was just what I wanted.

IDA: Are you sure?

MYRTLE: Yes, really.

IDA: Well, if you're sure. [Ida *makes a move to start in*]

MYRTLE: Oh, is Homer—around?

IDA: Why, I wonder where he got to— Homer?

[Homer *enters*]

HOMER: Here I am.

IDA: Oh! I thought you'd gone in.

MYRTLE: Good morning, Homer.

HOMER: Good morning, Myrtle.

MYRTLE: Isn't it a lovely day?

HOMER: Sure is.

MYRTLE: My, you can feel the sun on you as warm as toast. I thought maybe you'd like to take a little walk?

HOMER: I'd like to.

MYRTLE: That's the first thing I thought of when I woke this morning, and saw the sunshine. I thought, Homer and I will take a nice walk this morning, till train time. Maybe we'll go up and look at our new house even.

[*Embarrassed pause*]

HOMER: Well—

MYRTLE: Of course if you don't want to—

HOMER: [Stepping toward her] No, it isn't that. I—. All right.

IDA: That's right. Now you take a nice walk and be back for lunch. Now I've got to run over to Cora's for a minute if you'll excuse me.

MYRTLE: Oh, of course.

IDA: You're sure you don't want any more breakfast?

MYRTLE: [Brightly] Honest Injun! [Ida enters house right— Pause. Homer waits awkwardly. Myrtle turns to him with a bright smile] Hello.

HOMER: Hello.

MYRTLE: Did you have a good sleep?

HOMER: Not very.

MYRTLE: Oh, what a shame. I slept ever so nicely.

HOMER: Did you?

MYRTLE: That's the softest bed I think I ever slept on.

HOMER: I thought about things all night.

MYRTLE: Now you shouldn't have done that. I told you when you went to bed that you were to go right to sleep and not think about anything.

HOMER: [Turns away] I couldn't help it.

MYRTLE: That was bad of you.

HOMER: [Turns toward her] Myrtle.

MYRTLE: [Stopping him] Now don't you feel bad about anything, Homer. I thought it all out last night. I see just what you mean about not leaving your mother. And I think it's nice of you. We can go on just the way we have been. It's been wonderful this way and—

HOMER: No, it's not that. It's something else.

MYRTLE: What?

HOMER: It's—something I've got to tell you before we go. It wouldn't be fair not to.

MYRTLE: What is it?

[She waits—Homer hesitates]

HOMER: It's not very nice.

MYRTLE: My goodness, it can't be so very bad. Now out with it.

HOMER: It's about our house.

MYRTLE: [Suddenly alarmed] Nothing's happened to it, Homer! It hasn't burned down or anything—?

HOMER: No, it's—all right.

MYRTLE: [Her hand to her heart] My goodness, you scared me. You shouldn't say things like that.

HOMER: It's just that—. It isn't our house any more.
[Pause. Myrtle looks at him, puzzled]

MYRTLE: Our house—isn't our house any more?

HOMER: My father just rented it to Aunt Cora. She's got a twenty-year lease on it.

MYRTLE: On our house?

HOMER: Uh-huh. I guess he thought we weren't going to be using it. [Myrtle, bewildered, puts her hand to her head. She turns away slightly, too stunned to understand it yet. Homer watches her. Anguished] Gee, Myrtle, I'm so sorry!

MYRTLE: [In a dazed voice] It's all right. Of course, it's all right—. It really wasn't our house, was it? Not really. It was your father's house. You couldn't expect him to just keep it empty until— He has kept it empty for five years—. You couldn't expect—. [She turns away from him—trying to reason it out—and to keep back the tears]

HOMER: [Stepping toward her] I'll build you one myself, Myrtle. I'll build you a house that'll make that house look like a garage.

MYRTLE: Don't be silly! [She moves over by stump]

HOMER: [Crossing to chair left—sitting] Myrtle— I've been thinking things out.

MYRTLE: [Wearily] Yes, you said you had. [Sits stump]

HOMER: Not just last night. Today, too. I ought to have got married and had a home of my own a long time ago. I ought to have done it.

MYRTLE: [Faintly] Why didn't you, Homer?

HOMER: I got caught. Somehow or other I got caught. But I'd do it now, Myrtle. I'd do it now except—

MYRTLE: Except what?

HOMER: Except now I really have to stay here with my mother.

MYRTLE: What do you mean?

HOMER: My father's going away. He said to my mother, "You'll be all right. You've got Homer."

MYRTLE: What did he mean?

HOMER: He meant she had me to take care of her. She didn't need him.

MYRTLE: [Slightly bitter] She's always depended on you, Homer. You told me that last night.

HOMER: Yes, that's what I mean. She's always had me to take care of her. Maybe that's the trouble.

MYRTLE: [Pause—then suddenly turns to him] Homer! Do you mean you really want to marry me now—? [Rising and crossing to him—rapidly] Because if you do—if you really want to—it doesn't matter about our house—and you could be with your mother too. I could come and live here with you in this house. And we could have your little room. It's a darling little room. I looked at it on the way down. And we could all be together. [Homer turns to her— She pauses] That is, if you wanted to, of course.

HOMER: You mean, you'd live here—with everybody?

MYRTLE: Of course I would. I'd just love it.

HOMER: You always said a woman wanted a home of her own.

MYRTLE: Well, I'd be having it. It'd be even nicer in one way than being up there on Sycamore Drive. We'd never be lonesome here.

[Pause. Homer rises]

HOMER: [Suddenly] I'm awfully fond of you, Myrtle.

MYRTLE: Are you, Homer?

HOMER: I'm fonder of you than anything I could think of. [Pauses, he stands looking at her] I think you're wonderful.

[They stand looking at each other a minute]

MYRTLE: Thank you, Homer. [Myrtle *looks away a minute—starts to say something—then changes her mind—looks back*] Shall we take our walk? [Homer *comes to her. He starts to put his arm around her. Hesitates. Looks over at the other house. Puts his arm around her anyway. They exit up center.—The door of the house at right opens and* Esther *comes out. She has hold of Arry's hand and is pulling her.* Arry *is drawing back*]

ARRY: What do you want to talk to me about?

ESTHER: Oh, come on, Arry. We're not going to hurt you.

ARRY: [*Drawing back*] I don't trust you, Esty. When you start talking—. [*She suddenly comes out with a rush.* Ida, *who has given her a push, appears in the door behind her—steps to the right of her*] Hey! Quit that! What'd you push me for?

IDA: I didn't push you.

ARRY: You did too.

IDA: I just wanted to come out and you were blocking the way.

ARRY: What's going on here anyway? [*They are at each side of her—she looks from one to the other*] I'm going back in. [*She starts to duck into the house.* Ida *grabs one arm—*Esther *the other*]

ESTHER: Oh, no, you're not.

IDA: You're coming right along with us.

ARRY: [*Struggling*] You let go of me. Let go of me!

ESTHER: Oh, be quiet, Arry.

ARRY: Let go of me! [*Screaming*] Let go of me!

ESTHER: Oh, my goodness. Let go of her, Ida. [*They let go of* Arry]

ARRY: Thank you. Thank you so much. [*She starts up steps*]

ESTHER: Go on back in. If you don't want to hear what we have to say, you don't need to.

ARRY: [*Stops—turns slowly*] I didn't say I wouldn't like to hear what you had to say, Esty, but when one person wishes to talk to another, there are certain rules of nice behavior they try to observe.

ESTHER: [*Trying not to giggle*] I'm sorry, Arry.

ARRY: I doubt very much whether in the best society you would find one person approaching the back of another person and pushing them from behind.

IDA: I'm sorry, Arry. We just wanted to have a little talk with you. Of course, if you don't care to—

ARRY: I'd be very glad to. [*She walks over to the stump, sits. Faces* Esther *and* Ida] Well, Esther!

ESTHER: Well, Arry, I'll tell you. It's about Thor and Cora moving up to Homer's house—. [Arry *jumps up and starts to run in*]

ARRY: Oh, no, you don't! I know you, Esty!

ESTHER: [*As she and* Ida *stop* Arry] Now wait a minute, Arry.

ARRY: [*Between them*] I don't want to talk about it.

IDA: You *got* to talk about it.

ARRY: I knew I shouldn't have trusted you—.

ESTHER: Why? What do you think we're going to say?

ARRY: You're going to say Thor and Cora ought to move up there.

ESTHER: Well, don't you think they should?

ARRY: No, I don't.

IDA: Why not?

ARRY: Just because I don't, that's all.

ESTHER: But if Cora wants to—and Thor wants to—.

ARRY: Thor doesn't want to.

IDA: How do you know?

ARRY: [*Hesitating*] Well, I—. I don't think he does—.

ESTHER: Why, have you talked to him?

ARRY: Well, I—. Not much.

ESTHER: Then you're not sure, are you?

ARRY: No, I'm not sure—.

IDA: Then if he does want to and Cora wants to—why, it would be pretty nice for them, don't you think?

[Arry, *trapped, moves back to the stump. They watch her*]

ARRY: [*Sullenly—sits*] I don't know what business it is of yours anyway.

ESTHER: Strictly speaking, I don't suppose it is. But after all, we're sisters. And it means so much to Cora. . . . I'm just thinking of her happiness.

ARRY: And what about *my* happiness?

ESTHER: Well, in this case, certainly Cora's happiness is the one to consider.

ARRY: I don't see why.

ESTHER: Don't you? Cora wants to live alone with Thor, Arry.

ARRY: [*Suddenly vicious*] Well, she's not going to!

IDA: Oh, isn't she?

ARRY: Over my dead body she is. If they try anything there's a few things I can tell—.

IDA: You've made that threat a lot of times, Arry—.

ARRY: I mean it.

ESTHER: What could you tell, Arry?

ARRY: Plenty.

ESTHER: What could you tell that all of us don't already know? That we haven't all known for years?

[*Sudden pause.* Arry *looks up at* Esther, *startled*]

ARRY: [*Softly*] What do you mean, Esty? [*She looks at* Ida, *frightened, and back at* Esther. *In a whisper*] What do you mean?

IDA: Do you think we're all blind, Arry?

ESTHER: Don't you think all of us know by this time about you and Thor?

[*Pause*]

ARRY: [*Frightened*] No—no—Esty—.

IDA: We've all known for years. All of us.

ARRY: No—no—.

ESTHER: But we've all kept our mouths shut for Cora's sake. If you want to make a nasty business out of it go on and do it. But it won't get you anywhere, Arry. And you won't look so nice, carrying on for years with the husband of your own sister right under her very nose—.

ARRY: [Shocked—rises] Esty! Esty, what do you mean? You don't think—Ida, you don't think—that Thor and me—all this time— Oh, my God! [She buries her face in her hands. Ida and Esther watch uneasily]

IDA: What do you mean, Arry?

ARRY: [Moaning—sits stump] Oh, my God! Oh, my God!

ESTHER: [Uneasily] But you've always hinted in front of everyone, Arry—.

ARRY: You've all thought that Thor and me—all these years— Does Cora think that?

ESTHER: I don't know, Arry. Nobody's ever said anything to Cora. I guess Cora doesn't think anything.

ARRY: [Suddenly she turns toward the house. Rises, and yells with a sudden frenzied frightenedness] Thor! Thor! Thor!

ESTHER: [She and Ida move down right] Arry—. Wait—.

ARRY: Thor! Thor!

THOR: [Hurries out of the house right] What's the matter? What's the matter, Arry?

ARRY: They say that—. They think that—.

[Cora has entered between the houses. She stops, frozen, watching the scene]

CORA: Why, Arry, what's the matter?

                    [Arry hesitates a minute—looks at Cora
—then suddenly runs into the house, weeping]

THOR: What's the matter with her?

ESTHER: [Starting into house] I don't quite know. I'll find out.

THOR: What did you say to her, Esty?

CORA: [Hard] Yes. What did you say to her?

ESTHER: [Looking at Cora] We just had a little fuss, Cora.

CORA: About what?

                    [Pause. Esty looks at Cora]

ESTHER: I'll tell you later. [She exits]

CORA: Thor! [He turns and sees her watching him] I wonder what she could have said to Arry?

THOR: I don't know, Cora. Maybe she said something Arry didn't like so much.

CORA: Yes, she must have. I wonder what it could have been?

THOR: I don't know, Cora.

                    [Pause. Cora turns to Ida brightly]

CORA: Ida, has Carl still got those packing cases he used to have in his garage?

IDA: [Mystified] Why—I don't know, Cora—.

CORA: Harold Blake hasn't got any. He says he can move Thor and me up day after tomorrow, but he just hasn't got any packing cases.

                    [Thor looks at her startled]

THOR: [Hesitantly] Day after tomorrow?

CORA: Uh-huh! [To Ida] Can we go over and see if they're still there? [She has started off left]

IDA: [Following] Yes—of course—.

THOR: But Cora—. But Cora—. [They go off left—Thor watches them. He sits on ledge—depressed] The day after tomorrow! Good God!

[Homer and Myrtle enter from between the houses. They see Thor but he doesn't see them. Myrtle goes quickly into Ida's house and Homer crosses to Thor]

HOMER: Uncle Thor.

THOR: [Startled] Oh, hello, Homer.

HOMER: I've got to talk to you, Uncle Thor.

THOR: Well, go ahead, Homer.

HOMER: It's about my house. I've got to have it back.

THOR: Well, by God, Homer, nobody wishes you had it back more than I do.

HOMER: But I've got to have it back.

THOR: Well, there's no use talking to me about it. You'll have to talk to your Aunt Cora.

HOMER: No, I've got to talk to you about it. You see, last night when I thought my father was going to start having spells again—I felt I shouldn't leave my mother—and I told that to Myrtle and—

THOR: Yeah, I see the predicament, Homer, but—

HOMER: But this morning Myrtle said we could get married and live here with my mother and—.

THOR: I know, Homer. That's kinda tough but—

HOMER: It isn't that so much but, you see—Myrtle just told me. She's going to have a—baby.

                    [Pause. There is a complete, dead silence.
Thor looks at Homer in complete and utter be-
wilderment]

THOR: [In a ghostly whisper] What?

HOMER: Uh-huh.

THOR: A—baby—?

HOMER: Uh-huh.

THOR: You mean—a—[He gestures with his hands] —baby—.

HOMER: Uh-huh.

THOR: [In a whisper, slowly looking Homer over] Well, for God's sakes! [He rises and walks around Homer, staring at him from all angles. Homer stands, head down in embarrassment] Well, what the hell do you know about that! [Homer's head sinks lower] Well, I'll be God damned! [Suddenly Thor's face lights up with a great glow. He beams at Homer. He shouts—] Well! Well! [He rubs his hands together, beaming at Homer] Well, well! Well, well! What the hell do you know about that! [Slaps Homer on the back] That's a pretty good one! Yes sir, by God, you certainly had your old Uncle Thor fooled!

HOMER: [Suddenly smiling, modestly] Just one of those things, you know.

THOR: Sure, sure!

HOMER: Don't really know how it happened.

THOR: By God, ain't it the truth.

HOMER: Kinda lose your head sometimes—.

THOR: [Clapping him on the back] Ain't it the truth.

By God! Well, what the hell do you know about that!

Act III

SCENE: *The same. A short time later. As the curtain rises,* Cora *is eagerly watching the expression on* Esther's *face, which is one of sheer blankness. Both are seated, on steps house right, and chair left of steps.*

ESTHER: Homer?

CORA: That's what he told Thor.

ESTHER: But it's not possible, Cora.

CORA: Seems it is.

ESTHER: A baby!

CORA: [*Nervously*] Shh! For goodness' sakes, Esty, don't keep saying it. If Arry ever got hold of it Ida would find out in a minute.

ESTHER: But I just don't understand. How did it happen?

CORA: How does it usually happen?

ESTHER: But Homer must have—must have—

CORA: Of course he must have. That's the point.

ESTHER: Must have been all this time—

CORA: Seven years—

ESTHER: Well, I give up. I've seen a lot of things in my time, Cora. First the telephone. Everybody said it wouldn't work.

CORA: [*Giggling*] Now stop it, Esty! Somebody'll hear you. Besides, it's an awful thing.

ESTHER: Of course it's an awful thing.

CORA: If Arry should ever find out—

ESTHER: What are they going to do about it?

CORA: Well, they're going to get married—

ESTHER: I know, but even so—

CORA: Oh, they'll take a trip somewhere when the time comes. There's no hurry. Now for goodness' sakes, you mustn't let on to Thor that I told you. I promised him I wouldn't.

ESTHER: Does Homer know you know?

CORA: *Nobody* knows, Esty! *Nobody!* Thor promised Homer he wouldn't breathe it to a soul.

ESTHER: But why *did* Homer tell Thor?

CORA: Well— [*She rises—crosses down right—hesitates. Suddenly she reverts to the grim atttitude she had in the previous act*] He wants his house back.

ESTHER: [*Looking at her quickly*] Oh! I see.

CORA: I've just had a talk with Thor. He says I've got to let them have it.

ESTHER: Well, I suppose he feels if they're going to have a baby—.

CORA: [*Turns to* Esty] That's not the reason Thor wants me to give it back. Is it, Esty?

ESTHER: What do you mean, Cora?

CORA: You know what I mean. Thor's afraid to move up there with me.

ESTHER: [*Rises—crosses to* Cora] Cora, I'd like to ask you something.

CORA: What?

ESTHER: Have you ever doubted that Thor loved you?

[Cora *is not prepared for this. She is rather surprised. She thinks it over*]

CORA: Why—no—.

ESTHER: Have you ever doubted that you came first—always—with Thor?

CORA: [*After a moment*] No—I've never doubted that—

ESTHER: And you know you always will come first?

CORA: Yes.—

ESTHER: Well, that's something to be able to say after fifty years of marriage, isn't it?

CORA: [*Slowly*] Yes, it's something. It's a *lot*. If that's all you can get. [*She turns away.* Esther *watches her*] Well, I better go in. Now for goodness' sakes, Esty, don't let on to Thor.

ESTHER: Let on what? Oh, about the baby!

CORA: [*Motioning her to be quiet*] Esty! Esty!

ESTHER: [*In a whisper—sitting*] All right. All right.

[Cora *stands quietly a moment*]

CORA: Anyway, it'll be nice to have a baby in the family again, won't it?

ESTHER: Real nice.

[Cora *starts in as* Thor *comes out of the house at left, followed by* Ida, Myrtle *and* Homer. Esther *and* Cora *watch* Myrtle]

THOR: [*As he comes down the steps*] What you want to do, Homer, is to take a nice long honeymoon. To hell with these picky little two, three week affairs. Months, I say, even if you have to wait a few months before you can get away.

HOMER: That sounds like a good idea, Uncle Thor.

THOR: You bet it's a good idea. Pick some nice quiet place and just settle down and live there awhile. Get to know each other. Come on, we'll dig up that atlas and have a look— Oop! Watch out there! Take it easy! [*He catches* Myrtle *by the arm and helps her down the steps*]

MYRTLE: Oh, thank you.

THOR: [*Carefully walking her center*] Bad step there —Well, Esty, old girl, have you heard the news?

ESTHER: [*Startled*] Why—I—I thought it was a se—

[*She glances at* Cora]

CORA: [*Quickly*] Homer and Myrtle are going to be married.

THOR: [*Chuckling—standing between* Homer *and* Myrtle] Yes, sir, gonna tie them up tighter'n a drumstick.

ESTHER: Congratulations, Homer.

HOMER: Thank you, Aunt Esther.

ESTHER: I'm sure you'll be very happy, Myrtle.

MYRTLE: Well, I just guess I will be. My goodness, I'm about as happy right now as a girl has any right to be. Everybody's being so nice it just— hurts.

THOR: Well, they better be nice! Aren't you going to congratulate them, Cora?

CORA: [*Who has been absorbed looking over* Myrtle *for evidence*] Of course I am. Congratulations, Homer.

[*There is a slight pause.* Homer *looks at her sullenly. Then turns away*]

HOMER: [*Gruffly*] Thank you.

[Cora *is disturbed. The others watch her*]

CORA: [*Flustered—after pause*] Well, well, I know you're going to be very happy, Myrtle.

MYRTLE: Well, I do, too. I just guess I will be. My goodness, I'm almost as happy right this minute as any girl——. It isn't every day a girl gets a proposal of marriage. I just guess we'll be happy, won't we, Homer?

HOMER: Might be happy if we had a house to live in. [*There is a dead pause. All eyes are focussed on* Cora. *She becomes very flustered and turns away*]

MYRTLE: Now you stop talking about that, Homer. My goodness, we can get along without that house. We'll be so happy right here in this house that you're going to be astounded.

HOMER: I don't want to live in this house.

MYRTLE: Well, we're going to. Now you stop striking discordant notes, Homer. We're just going to change the subject and not revert to it again. We'll just change the subject—er— [*Pause. They all wait for her to do it*] Did you hear what Mother Ida said? [*She crosses to stump*]

ESTHER: No. What did Mother Ida say?

MYRTLE: She said she didn't feel so much as if she was losing a son but more like she was gaining a daughter.

ESTHER: Did she say that!

MYRTLE: Yes, she did. [*Sits stump*]

IDA: [*Sadly*] It isn't going to be so easy though—

HOMER: [*Firmly*] Now, Mother, none of that. I've made up my mind.

IDA: [*Timidly*] Oh, I know you have, Homer. And I'm so glad. I just meant if you shouldn't live here it isn't going to be so easy—with your father gone—

HOMER: I'll speak to my father, but it isn't going to influence me. I've made up my mind. Myrtle and I are going to be married and we're going to live alone. If we can find some old house. Just us two.

THOR: By God, that's all right for a while, Homer, but you can't keep a marriage down to two forever, you know.

MYRTLE: [*Giggling nervously*] Oh, you!

IDA: Well, there's plenty of time to think of that later.

THOR: [*Roaring*] By God, that's a fact, Ida. Plenty of time for that later. [*He nudges* Homer *and gives him a knowing wink*]

MYRTLE: Well, my goodness, we're certainly crossing our bridges—

HOMER: [*Firmly*] If I should ever have a son I won't let him stay around the house after he's nineteen.

IDA: Homer!

HOMER: I won't, Mother. There's no use arguing. At nineteen he gets out.

MYRTLE: Homer!

HOMER: Animals, too. You don't see an animal hanging around home after it's grown up, do you?

THOR: No sir, you don't, Homer. That's a fact.

HOMER: [*To* Esther] Did you ever hear of a grown male dog who wouldn't leave his mother?

ESTHER: I don't think I ever did, Homer.

HOMER: [*To* Ida] Did you ever hear of *any* animal that wouldn't get out when he grew up?

IDA: I—I don't know, Homer.

HOMER: Even pigs. The mother pushes them out right away. And that's the way it ought to be.

MYRTLE: [*To them all*] It's very interesting, isn't it?

IDA: [*Tearfully*] I'm sure I never tried to do anything to hold Homer—

MYRTLE: [*Crossing to her quickly*] Well, I should just guess you didn't either—

IDA: I always tried to push him out—

MYRTLE: Of course you did. Now we won't have any more talk like this! Don't you say anything more, Homer. My goodness, I guess I can realize how your mother feels!

HOMER: Well, every animal *I* ever heard of—

MYRTLE: Homer!

IDA: [*Tearfully*] Oh! [*She runs into house left*]

MYRTLE: Oh, Mother Ida— He didn't mean— [*She turns to* Homer] My goodness, Homer, I just don't know what's got into you! You used to always be so nice to your mother. You just seem to be striking discordant notes all the time. Pigs, indeed! You're getting just terrible, Homer!

THOR: Well, come on. Let's get this honeymoon figured out. Where do you suppose that atlas is, Cora?

[*They all look at* Cora]

CORA: [*Crossing center—strangely grim*] I don't know.

THOR: [*Uneasily*] Well, come on. We'll find it. [*As they start in* Arry *comes out. They all stop suddenly and look at her.* Cora *watches her. Tentatively*] Hello, Arry. Headache gone?

ARRY: I want to talk to you a minute, Thor.

THOR: [*Uneasily*] Well, we were just going in and—

ARRY: I guess you can spare me a few minutes.

[*Slight pause.* Thor *is uneasy.* Arry *starts down the steps*]

THOR: Well, all right, Arry.

ARRY: Thank you. [*She crosses down to* Esty]

THOR: Look in the bottom of the victrola, Homer. I think the atlas's in there. I'll be in in a minute.

[Myrtle *and* Homer *exit.* Arry *reaches* Esther. *There is a feeling of tension.* Arry *hands* Esther *a letter*]

ARRY: I want you to read this sometime, Esty.

ESTHER: What is it?

ARRY: You'll find out.

ESTHER: All right, Arry. [*She eyes her a moment sharply*] Is your head better?

ARRY: My head's all right.

ESTHER: Good.

[Arry *turns to* Cora, *who has been watching her*]

ARRY: [*Suddenly*] Don't you worry. You won't have to bother with me any more. Just don't you worry.

[*A moment's pause. They stand looking at each other*]

CORA: [*After a moment, quietly*] Arry wants to talk to Thor, Esty. Would you take a little walk with me?

[Esther *and* Cora *go out between the houses in silence.* Thor *looks after them a moment, uneasily, and then he goes to* Arry *who has seated herself and sits looking quietly into space*]

THOR: [*Uneasily*] You oughtn't to say things like that to Cora, Arry. No use getting her any madder than she is. [*He looks at her. She is paying no attention*] And what did you mean by she won't have to bother with you any more? [*She doesn't answer.* Thor *looks at her, uneasy. With fake cheerfulness*] Anyway, I think everything's going to turn out fine. [*He sits by her on the lower step— Pause.* Arry *has not moved—*Thor *still uneasy*] All of us got a little excited—but, hell, what's the difference? Nobody meant what they said. [*Pause. He eyes her*] Anything the matter, Arry?

ARRY: [*After a moment*] What does it mean to you to grow old, Thor?

[Thor *looks at her in surprise*]

THOR: What do you mean, Arry?

ARRY: Doesn't getting old mean that—well, that things don't trouble you so much any more? That everything's more peaceful and quiet—.

THOR: Peaceful and quiet! I guess that must be when you get *real* old, Arry. Say in your late eighties.

ARRY: I always thought of getting old sort of like going to bed when you're nice and drowsy—and yet you know you won't fall to sleep for a little while yet—and you just lie there sort of comfortably—and enjoy it—. But it isn't that way at all.

THOR: I don't know what you're getting at, Arry.

ARRY: Well, I've been lying down thinking. [*She turns to him suddenly*] You've been real good to me, Thor. You're a real good man.

THOR: [*Embarrassed*] Oh, hell, Arry.

ARRY: I mean it. Cora too. I want you to know I appreciate the way you've had me in your home all these years.

THOR: It was your home too, Arry.

ARRY: Nope. That's what I found out. It wasn't ever my home. I haven't got a home. That's what I mean about getting old. I guess it's nice and peaceful if you got a home. If you got a husband. If you got somebody to get old with—. But I haven't. So you know what I'm going to do, Thor?

THOR: What, Arry?

ARRY: I'm going to go away.

THOR: What do you mean?

ARRY: I'm leaving. I'm leaving you and Cora to have a home together.

THOR: But, Arry—

ARRY: No, Thor, I'm going to do it. I should have done it years ago, but I didn't. I'm going to try to forget you, Thor.

THOR: Gee, Arry, I don't know what to say.

ARRY: There's nothing to say. [Arry *rises and crosses to steps*] Thor.

THOR: Yeah?

ARRY: When I die—you know what I want on my stone?

THOR: What?

ARRY: "Home is the sailor, home from the sea
And the hunter, home from the hill."

THOR: All right, Arry.

ARRY: Mama used to say that.—Now I'll go in and pack. [*Goes up stairs—at top—turns*] Thor. [*He turns*] I'm not sorry about anything.

THOR: All right, Arry.

ARRY: Not sorry at all.

[*She exits.* Thor *looks after her, sadly*]

THOR: [*Rising—going up steps*] Poor Arry! All alone in the world.

[Thor *stands looking after her a moment. He stops as* David *and* Carl *enter, loaded down with* Carl's *luggage and tools as they were when they left.* Thor, *unnoticed, watches them.* David *puts bags on the porch—*Carl *leaves his down left*]

DAVID: For example, if you were taken blindfolded to some part of the city and the blindfold were taken off, how would you find out where you were?

CARL: I'd look to see what street I was on.

DAVID: Exactly. Now say there wasn't any sign.—Or say you were lost in a woods. At night. How would you find out where you were?

[Thor *shakes his head, and exits*]

CARL: Well, I know the North star. And I could wander around until I found some landmark I knew and get my location that way—.

DAVID: All right. Now to find your location in life, Carl, you do the same thing. Just wander around until you find a few landmarks. A man like you has got to make it his business to find his own location among the concepts that we know. He has got to search himself, search all the knowledge that he has, all the knowledge that others have until the last blade of grass in that lawn, or the last pebble in that road bears some relation to him, takes on some meaning, becomes a landmark so he knows just where he is. Only then is a man like you safe; when you can say, "I am eight miles north of water; I am three thoughts under love; I am ten beats past despair," then you'll know where you are, Carl. [David *pauses and looks at* Carl] Do you understand what I mean, Carl?

CARL: Well—I don't *quite* understand, David.

DAVID: [*Thoughtfully*] Well, there's an *idea* there, Carl.

CARL: [*Eagerly*] I know there is, David.

DAVID: [*Turning to* Carl] Yes, there's an idea there *somewhere*, if we can pin it down. Well, let's pin it down, Carl. Let's pin it down.

CARL: All right, David. Let's!

[Esther *comes in between the houses center to stump—*David *breaks off*]

DAVID: Ah, Esther.

ESTHER: I thought it was you, David.

DAVID: Yes, Esther, it is I.

CARL: We're—we're bringing my things back.

ESTHER: Yes, I see. There's nothing wrong, is there?

CARL: Well, it's that little closet we were going to make into a bath. It's not very well located. It's not under the upstairs bathroom.

ESTHER: Yes, I could have told you that.

CARL: Well, it would cost nearly three hundred dollars to put it in shape.

ESTHER: As much as that? Oh, dear, dear!

CARL: We'd practically have to tear the whole house down.

ESTHER: I see. I see.

CARL: And as David says you haven't the three hundred dollars—the idea doesn't seem very practical.

ESTHER: Well, no, it certainly doesn't, does it?

CARL: And so—we're bringing my things back. [*Embarrassed pause*] Well, I'll just take these out.

[*He exits left with tools.* Esther *stands watching* David]

ESTHER: Poor Carl. He seems upset.

DAVID: Upset? No.—Fundamentally I should say Carl's a very sound person, Esther.

ESTHER: [*Smiling*] Really?

DAVID: Yes. He thinks things out very clearly—very logically. [*Pause. She stands regarding him, smiling. He is embarrassed. Starts to pick up bags*] Well—.

ESTHER: [*Sits*] David, I'd like to read you something.

DAVID: [*Hesitating with bags in hand*] Well, Esty, I—

ESTHER: You know what we've all suspected about Arry and Thor all these years, don't you, David?

DAVID: [*Turning*] Oh, I've heard the talk, Esther. I never paid much attention to it.

ESTHER: Arry just gave me this letter. [*Shows the letter.* David *puts down bags and crosses to stump and sits*] Do you remember—oh, it must have been all of forty years ago—after Arry had been living with them about a year—Cora had to go to the hospital for a couple of weeks?

DAVID: I think I do—vaguely—

ESTHER: Thor and Arry were alone. She was about seventeen. She didn't know much about anything. Right off the farm. She was pretty, full of life. You remember how Arry was. And— [*She reads*] ". . . and I don't know how it happened, Esty. I

just don't. I loved Thor so much. I didn't realize it. I should have gone away but I couldn't. We were both so miserable and scared. We didn't know what to do. But never after that time, Esty. Never. If Cora should ever know I'd just die." [Esther *puts the letter down. They both sit thinking a moment*] And so she just went on—living with them—because there wasn't any other place for her to go after that. [*Pause*] Well, I feel kind of sorry for Arry. I guess she feels her life hasn't been to much purpose. [*She reads*] "When you and Ida told me what all of you had been thinking all this time—it seems to me I'd never be able to hold up my head again. It doesn't much matter about the years ahead—but it suddenly seemed as if all the years I've already lived didn't make much sense. I might just as well not have lived them." [*Pause. She puts the letter down*]

DAVID: [*Rises*] In the eyes of the world—I'm a failure —but we've kept our lives clear, Esther, and intelligent.

ESTHER: Yes, David, we have, haven't we?

DAVID: We've never let that other third element ever come in. We've kept ourselves to ourselves.

ESTHER: [*Smiling*] Yes, I know what you mean by a Crystal Fortress, David.

[*He turns away. There is a moment's pause.* Esther *watches him, smiling*]

DAVID: It's a tragic line Aaronetta says about the years behind her, "I might just as well not have lived them."

ESTHER: Yes.

DAVID: [*He turns to her, hesitating*] Did you ever feel like that, Esther?

ESTHER: No, David.

DAVID: [*Eagerly*] That's good.

ESTHER: But, you see, I always had you, David.

[David *is touched, embarrassed*]

DAVID: Thank you, Esther. [*He turns to her with a smile and a short bow*] Thank you. I'll take these in.

[David *goes in house left with bags.* Esther *rises and puts letter away as she sees* Cora *come down the path.* Cora *stops at the stump and stands looking ahead of her in silence*]

ESTHER: Well, Cora?

CORA: [*Quietly*] I'm going to give Homer back his house.

ESTHER: [*Surprised*] You are?

CORA: Yes. I've just been looking at it. I walked up there after you left me. It's a beautiful house and Thor loves it—. But as I stood there looking at it I suddenly realized something. Living up there alone with Thor is not what I'm after. *That's* not the important thing. But there *is* something that's important and I'm going to have it. [*She turns away*] I hate Arry!

ESTHER: No, Cora.

CORA: I hate her. But she can go on living with us.

There's no other place for her. But she's not going on living with us the way she has been. Because I'm going to find out where I stand, Esty. And I'm going to live alone with Thor in that very house—even with Arry there. [*After a moment*] You remember that poem Papa used to say about us girls, Esty?

"Esty's smartest,
Arry's wildest,
Ida's slowest,
Cora's mildest."

And then he always used to look at me and say, "Poor Cora." You remember that?

ESTHER: Yes.

CORA: [*Tensely*] Well, I'm not "Poor Cora" any more! There's such a thing as being too mild!

[*Carl enters from the house left. Comes down porch steps*]

CARL: [*Hesitantly*] Oh, Cora! I sort of hate to say anything to you about it but—.

CORA: I'm giving Homer back his house, Carl.

CARL: [*Relieved*] You are? Well, now that's awfully nice of you, Cora. Somehow I just knew you would.

[*Thor, Myrtle and Homer come out from the house at right. Cora watches them. Esther watches Cora*]

THOR: [*Crossing down steps*] By God, that's just the place for you. Now why the hell do you suppose I didn't think of that sooner?

MYRTLE: My goodness, it sounds simply heavenly.

THOR: You wait till you see that water coming down. And there's a little boat that goes right out under the falls. Cora and I spent a whole week there once.

[*David and Ida enter from house left*]

HOMER: What do you think, Myrtle?

MYRTLE: I think it sounds simply—divine!

HOMER: Then that settles it. That's where we'll go.

THOR: Hello, David. Heard the news?

DAVID: Ah, yes. My congratulations, Homer.

HOMER: Thank you, Uncle David.

DAVID: I hope you're not being too impetuous. [*Bowing to Myrtle*] Myrtle, I hope—

MYRTLE: My goodness, I just guess I will be. I'm just about as happy this minute as any girl has a right to be—.

CARL: Homer.

HOMER: Yes, Father?

CARL: Aunt Cora is giving you your house back.

HOMER: What?

MYRTLE: Our house!

[*They both look at Cora*]

CORA: [*Flustered*] Yes, I—. Of course, I guess I meant all along for you to have it back—. I—.

MYRTLE: Oh, I just think you are all the nicest people

I ever met. I just have never met so many nice people before. Aren't you going to say anything, Homer?

HOMER: [*Crossing to Cora—kissing her*] Well, thank you, Aunt Cora. Thank you ever so much.

CORA: Well—that's all right, Homer—.

MYRTLE: I just feel like crying—.

[*Arry comes out with hatbox and suitcase. She has on a large picture hat and looks very pretty. They all look at her. She poses at the top of steps for them. You see Cora stiffen and turn away. Esther watches her*]

THOR: By God, don't you look pretty, Arry.

ARRY: [*The great lady*] Thank you, Thor.

[*Esty rises*]

IDA: Where are you going, Arry?

[*Pause. Arry comes down a step*]

ARRY: I'm moving out. [*She looks around at them all*]

IDA: Moving?

ESTHER: Where are you going?

CARL: What do you mean, Arry?

MYRTLE: Why, Aunt Arry—?

ARRY: Yes, I'm leaving. I should have left years ago, of course, but I didn't realize all the things I know now—.

ESTHER: Now, look here, Arry—.

ARRY: Don't try to stop me, Esty. Please. It's a little upsetting, of course, when you get to be my age to suddenly find out you're not wanted any more.

THOR: [*Sorry*] Ah, Arry—!

CORA: [*Evenly*] Let her finish, Thor.

ARRY: That all the years you thought you were a part of a home you were really just sort of a—servant in it—and you could be dismissed when your services were no longer needed—.

THOR: By God, don't say that, Arry. You don't have to go anywhere.

[*As Arry goes on Esty moves nearer Cora*]

ARRY: [*With a little smile*] But, Thor, I'm not wanted here.

THOR: You are, too. By God, this is your home, Arry. Isn't that so, Cora?

ARRY: Oh, don't ask Cora, Thor. Cora wants to live alone—. She doesn't want any sister of hers—.

CORA: [*Starting toward Arry, furious*] All right, Arry—. I've stood—.

ESTHER: [*Grabbing Cora*] Wait a minute, Cora.

CORA: Arry—!

ESTHER: Cora!

[*Cora turns and Esther hands her Arry's letter and motions for her to read it. Cora does so during the following scene. Arry turns to Myrtle*]

ARRY: I haven't had the opportunity to felicitate you on your approaching nuptials, Myrtle. I know you'll be very happy.

MYRTLE: Thank you, Aunt Arry.

ARRY: Homer too, of course.

HOMER: Thank you, Aunt Arry.

ARRY: But when you come right down to it, it's the woman that ought to be the happiest.

MYRTLE: I just guess that's the truth.

ARRY: She's the one who makes the home and looks after things and keeps it together.

MYRTLE: That's just the woman's function, I should think.

[Cora *has finished half the letter. She turns swiftly to* Esther—Esty *motions her to finish the letter*—Cora *moves to* Thor's *chair—sits*]

ARRY: And marriage gives a woman dignity, Myrtle. It gives her dignity and companionship and a place to be when she gets old. I know you'll be very happy, Myrtle.

MYRTLE: I know I will be.

ARRY: That's right. [*She turns.* Cora *has finished the letter and you see it has softened her.* Arry *and she look at each other.* Arry *is terrified and looks accusingly at* Esty] Esty!

[Esty *nods admittal that she gave* Cora *the letter. A moment's pause.* Cora *rises slowly. Crumples the letter and goes to* Arry]

CORA: You're going away, Arry.

ARRY: Yes, Cora.

CORA: [*Touched*] I'll—I'll miss you, Arry—.

[Arry *looks at her slowly*]

THOR: By God, you don't have to go, Arry.

ARRY: Yes, Thor, I must go. We'll see each other now and then but I'm not going to live here any more.

THOR: But where are you going to go?

ARRY: Well, I'm going to move over to Ida's.—Ida told me years ago if I ever wanted to move over to her I could. Didn't you, Ida?

IDA: Of course, Arry.

CARL: Anytime you want to, Arry.

ARRY: [*Crossing between* Ida *and* Carl] Well, now I want to. I want to spend the rest of the years with you. [*Pause*]

HOMER: Well, if we're going to see our house we'd better go.

MYRTLE: Our house! My goodness! I've just never had so many people so nice to me all at once.—

THOR: By God, Myrtle, if anybody isn't nice to you just come to your old Uncle Thor.

MYRTLE: [*Crossing to* Thor] Well, I certainly will. I'll just look on you as—well, as my—protector.

[*They laugh together*]

HOMER: [*Taking hold of* Myrtle, *gruffly*] All right. That's enough. We better go now.

MYRTLE: Yes, Homer.

[*They exit up center between houses.* Arry *hands* Carl *her bags and starts toward* Ida's *house as—*

the curtain falls]

The Male Animal

by JAMES THURBER

(1894–   )

and ELLIOTT NUGENT

(1900–   )

The Male Animal *is not a robust or large-scaled play; there are those—myself among them, the first time I saw it—who might insist that it is no play at all. But as it is much easier, in the theater, to find well-trained carpenters than true writers of comedy,* The Male Animal *seems a good deal better than many things a good deal better made. There is something rather civilized about its very casualness—that is to say, there is an attitude toward life implicit in it that goes beyond, say, its attitude toward Sacco and Vanzetti. Nor is the play slick, like so painfully much contemporary comedy. And in addition to its virtues as a collaboration, it catches, periodically, the specific sense of Mr. Thurber. Or, better yet, the nonsense. Whether seen or read,* The Male Animal *keeps something engaging about it.*

Mr. Thurber, of course, is an established and rueful expert on the male animal. There is—as scores of drawings bear witness—no one more authoritative about the male animal in relation to the female; or in relation, again, to his secret self, whereby Caspar Milquetoast keeps re-emerging as Walter Mitty, or—in the present case—as an alcohol-aerated Tommy Turner. Indeed, in their story of the academic and domestic woes of the mild-mannered Professor Turner, Mr. Thurber and Mr. Nugent have gone farcically but cogently at all the representative things —male animal, man of good will, homme moyen sensuel—that Tommy embodies, and embodies American-style. Tommy's world, when we first glimpse it, has a kind of educated placidity, of cultured ordinariness, about it. It seems creditable and self-respecting, but far from vivid or adventurous; it seems so safe, in fact, as to suggest a rut. And then, in a trice, there blows up a row. Two rows. Because, for literary reasons, Turner wants to read a Vanzetti letter to his class, a reactionary trustee sniffs redness in his politics. And because an old beau of Tommy's wife's—a former football star—turns up for a game, Tommy feels compelled to prove the redness of his blood.

In doing battle, Tommy's first weapon is neither pen nor sword, for there are two battles, really— Tommy must slay the inhibited professor in himself before taking on his he-man adversary. So, in advance of drawing the sword, Tommy drains the bottle; and what ensues is one of the funniest drinking scenes, and eventual drunken scenes, in a theater deluged with them. The besotted professor elects to hold his mate—as swans do, and bull elephants—by fighting for her. And he does hold her, for the very good if not altogether heroic reason that her old beau couldn't be more anxious to give her up.

The drinking scene is the brightest spot in a play that otherwise—and quite properly—depends for effect on more prosaically reminiscent touches of domestic comedy. But it is the brightest spot, not for being under the influence of alcohol, but for constituting the full emergence of Thurber. Here, for a spell, an artist in nonsense can indulge himself. And what this scene, and scattered bits throughout, go to prove is that, more even than Mr. Thurber is an expert on the male animal in relation to the female, he is an authority on it as a leading specimen in the cosmic zoo.

JAMES THURBER and ELLIOTT NUGENT

The Male Animal

CAST OF CHARACTERS

CLEOTA

ELLEN TURNER

TOMMY TURNER

PATRICIA STANLEY

WALLY MYERS

DEAN FREDERICK DAMON

MICHAEL BARNES

JOE FERGUSON

MRS. BLANCHE DAMON

ED KELLER

MYRTLE KELLER

"NUTSY" MILLER

NEWSPAPER REPORTER

TIME: *The present.* SCENE: *The living room in the house of Professor Thomas Turner, in a mid-western university town.*

ACT I: *Late Fall. A Friday evening*

ACT II: Scene 1. *The following day, after lunch*
    Scene 2. *Three hours later*

ACT III: *Two days later, noon*

Act I

SCENE: *The living room of a pleasant, inexpensive little house. There is no distinction of architectural design, but someone with natural good taste has managed to make it look attractive and liveable on a very modest budget. There are some good prints on the walls. The hangings are cheerful, and the furniture, picked up through various bargains and inheritances, goes together to make a pleasing, informal atmosphere.*

The front door opens onto a porch. The wall is lined with book-shelves which continue around the corner to the fireplace. Below this fireplace is a stand with a radio-phonograph. In the center of the rear wall, a bay window with window seat. This corner is used by the Turner family as a casual de-

pository for visitors' hats and coats, although they have also a coat-rail just inside the front door. In front of the bay window, a long table backs a comfortable sofa facing front. To the right of the bay window are more book-shelves, a small landing, and a stairway running up and off right. In the corner below the stair near the dining room door, a table up right against stairs has been prepared today to serve as a temporary bar, with a tray, cocktail shaker, and two or three bottles and glasses. In the right wall, two doors, the upper one leading to the dining room, the lower one to another porch and back yard. Two small settees, an arm-chair, a couple of small end or coffee tables, and one or two straight chairs complete the furnishings of the room. There are two or three vases of flowers, and the books and magazines which frequently litter this room have been put tidily away.*

At the rise of the curtain, the phone on table behind the sofa is ringing. Cleota, a colored maid, enters from the dining room and answers it.

CLEOTA: Professah Turner's res-i-dence—Who?— You got de wrong numbah—Who?— What you say?— Oh, Mistah *Turner!* No, he ain't heah. He jus' went out to buy some likkah— Who is dis callin'? Yessuh. Yessuh. Ah doan' get dat, but Ah'll tell him Doctah Damon. Ah say Ah'll tell him. [*Hangs up; starts for dining room*]

ELLEN'S VOICE: [*Off upstairs*] Who was it, Cleota?

CLEOTA: It was Doctah Damon. He say he comin' ovah to see Mistah Turner or Mistah Turner come over to see him, or sumpin'. [*Turns on lights from wall switch*]

ELLEN: [*Appearing on stairs*] What was that again, Cleota?

[*She is an extremely pretty young woman about twenty-nine or thirty. Quick of speech and movement she has a ready smile and a sweetness of personality that warms the room. She is completely feminine and acts always from an emotional, not an intellectual stimulus*]

CLEOTA: Doctah Damon doan talk up. He kinda muffles.

ELLEN: [*Picks up magazines on table. Crossing to bookcase with them*] I'm afraid it's you that kind of muffles.

CLEOTA: Yessum. Miz Turner, Ah'm fixin' them hor

doves for the pahty. Did you say put dem black seed ones in de oven?

ELLEN: Black seed ones? Oh, heavens, Cleota, you're not heating the caviar?

CLEOTA: No'm, ah ain't heatin' it, but taste lak' sumpin' oughtta be done to it.

ELLEN: It's to be served cold. Here, you pick up the rest of the magazines. I'll take a look at the canapés.   [Exits to dining room]

CLEOTA: Yessum. Ah ain't no hand at 'em. People where Ah worked last jus' drank without eatin' anything. [Sound of whistling; Tommy Turner enters left. He is a young associate professor, thirty-three years old. He wears glasses, is rather more charming than handsome. His clothes are a little baggy. He has a way of disarranging his hair with his hands, so that he looks like a puzzled spaniel at times. He is carrying chrysanthemums and two bottles of liquor, wrapped in paper and tied with string] Oh, hello, Mr. Turner!

TOMMY: [Putting flowers and bottles on sofa] Hello, Cleota! [Removes and hangs up coat and hat]

CLEOTA: You bettah not mess up dis room, 'cause dey is guess comin'.

TOMMY: All right, Cleota. I'll be good.

[Cleota exits to dining room. Tommy picks up bundles—looks for place to put down bottles —puts them on chair—unwraps flowers, throwing paper on floor—throws string down—sticks flowers in vase in middle of other flowers; sees book, picks it up, looks at it disapprovingly, looks upstairs and makes a gesture of disgust, throws it in waste-basket—crosses to pick up liquor]

ELLEN: [Enters from dining room] Hello, dear!

TOMMY: Hello, Ellen! Those are for you. [Indicates his flowers]

ELLEN: Oh, thank you, Tommy. They're lovely. [Surveys the flowers]

TOMMY: The ones in the middle.

ELLEN: Yes—

TOMMY: I got the liquor, too.

ELLEN: [Taking flowers out of vase] Did you get the right kind?

TOMMY: I got both kinds.
                    [Ellen picks up litter he has made]

ELLEN: Tommy, you're a house-wrecker, but you're nice. [Kisses him]

TOMMY: Did I do something right?

ELLEN: Cleota—Cleota, will you fill this vase with water, please? [Hands it to Cleota in doorway— Cleota goes out] What became of the book that was on this table?

TOMMY: That? Oh, I threw it in the waste-basket. It's trash.

ELLEN: [Rescuing book] But you can't throw it away. Wally gave it to Patricia.

TOMMY: Oh, he did?

ELLEN: Besides, it's just the right color for this room. [Voices off-scene]

PAT'S VOICE: Oh, Wally, quit arguing! [Door is opened, and Pat backs into room] I'm going to dinner with Mike, and then to the rally with you. You can't feed me at the training table. [Hangs coat up on wall hooks. She is a pretty, lively girl of 19 or 20]

WALLY: [Appears in doorway. He is six-feet-one, and weighs 190 pounds, mostly muscle. He is full of energy and health, and not without a good deal of naive charm] Aw, that guy Barnes! I don't see why you have to— Oh, how do you do, Mrs. Turner— Professor Turner?

TOMMY: Hello, Butch!

ELLEN: That's Wally Myers.

TOMMY: Oh, hello!

WALLY: Oh, has Butch been coming here, too?
                              [Tommy crosses down right]

PATRICIA: [Pushing Wally] Go on, get out of here, half-back. I have to get dressed. Hey, Ellen, excited about seeing the great Ferguson, again? He just drove up to the Beta House in a Deusenberg!

[Cleota re-enters with vase; Ellen takes it; Cleota exits]

ELLEN: Did you see him?

PATRICIA: No, the kids were telling me. Has he still got his hair?

ELLEN: I haven't seen him in ten years. We'll soon find out.

WALLY: Say, is he coming here?

ELLEN: Yes. Why don't you come back and meet him, Wally? You can tell him all about the game tomorrow.

WALLY: Gee, thanks! But nobody could tell Joe Ferguson anything about a football game. He's all-time All-American, you know. Well, thanks, Mrs. Turner. I'll be back. See you later, Pat. [Exits]

PATRICIA: [Closes door; then opens it and sticks head into room] So long! [Takes bottle of nail-polish from her pocket book and starts to fix run in stocking]

TOMMY: Does he mean that now Joe belongs to the ages, like Lincoln?

ELLEN: Um-hum, in a way.

TOMMY: [Crossing to bookcase] Well, I suppose he has passed into legend. I used to admire him myself—almost.

ELLEN: Pat, why don't you and Michael stay here for dinner? Supper, rather. It's just a bite. We're all going out to eat after the rally.

PATRICIA: No, thanks. You know how Mike feels about Mr. Keller. He'd spit in his eye.

TOMMY: Why do we have to have Ed Keller to this party?

ELLEN: Oh, Joe has to have someone to talk football with. Ed's his closest friend here. He practically paid Joe's way through college. You can stand the Kellers one night.

TOMMY: Just barely. I don't know how to entertain trustees.

PATRICIA: Well, you'd better be entertaining tonight with the great Ferguson coming. [Rises] Weren't you engaged to him once, Ellen?

ELLEN: Not officially. Just for fun.

PATRICIA: [Starting up stairs] Baby, that can be dangerous, too! [Exits] [Tommy has found an article in "Harper's" and is reading]

ELLEN: Oh, Dean Damon phoned, Tommy.

TOMMY: What'd he want?

ELLEN: I don't know. Cleota answered the phone.

TOMMY: Oh—I see— Oh, I'll bet I know. I saw the Dean this morning. What do you think?

ELLEN: Oh, I don't know— Oh, Tommy, you don't mean—?

TOMMY: Yes, I do.

ELLEN: Oh Tommy, that's wonderful! It's three hundred and fifty more a year, isn't it?

TOMMY: Five hundred! I'm no piker.

ELLEN: Well, you certainly deserve it.

TOMMY: Now I can get you that fur coat next February. People must think I let you freeze in the winter.

ELLEN: No, they don't. And, don't worry about me— You need some new things, yourself.—I love the flowers, Tommy. And this promotion couldn't have come on a better day for me. Do you know what day it is?

TOMMY: Friday, isn't it? Why?

ELLEN: Oh, nothing—never mind. [Glances around room] What became of all the match-boxes? I had one in each ash tray.

TOMMY: [She is digging in his pockets] I haven't seen any match-boxes. [She finds two. He smiles guiltily] Say, you look very pretty tonight. That's a new dress, isn't it?

ELLEN: No— It's my hair that's bothering you. It's done a new way—

TOMMY: Doesn't bother me. I like it.

ELLEN: [Looking around] One more.

TOMMY: Oh, you exaggerate this match-box thing. Oh! [Hands her one] I ought to take you out to dinner more and show you off.

ELLEN: [Redistributing match-boxes] Well, we're going out tonight after the rally.

TOMMY: I mean just the two of us. Tonight will be like old times. Remember how Joe was always horning in on our dinner dates? I don't believe we ever had one that he didn't come over and diagram the Washington Monument play or something on the tablecloth with a pencil.

ELLEN: Statue of Liberty play, darling.

TOMMY: He was always coming. I never saw him going.

ELLEN: There's still one missing.

TOMMY: I haven't got it— [Finds match-box] I'll bet Joe does something to get his wife down. Probably cleans his guns with doilies. Clumsy guy. Always knocking knives and forks on the floor.

ELLEN: He wasn't clumsy. He was very graceful. [Crossing to bookcase, fixes books] He was a swell dancer.

TOMMY: I remember he got the first and the last dance with you, the last time we all went to a dance together.

ELLEN: Phi Psi Christmas dance, wasn't it?

TOMMY: No, the May Dance. Out at the Trowbridge Farm. Remember how it rained?

ELLEN: I remember I had the last dance with Joe because you disappeared somewhere.

TOMMY: No, I was watching—from behind some ferns.

ELLEN: They played "Three O'Clock in the Morning" and "Who?" It was a lovely night, wasn't it?

TOMMY: No, it poured down. You and Joe were dancing out on the terrace when it started. You both got soaked, but you kept right on dancing.

ELLEN: Oh, yes, I remember. My dress was ruined.

TOMMY: You were shining wet—like Venus and Triton.

ELLEN: Why didn't you cut in?

TOMMY: I had a cold. Besides, my feet hurt. [He starts toward stairs] I'll dress. [Doorbell rings] I hope he isn't here already.

[Ellen admits Damon and Michael. Damon, the head of the English Department, is a tall, thin distinguished-looking man of some 65 years. He has gray hair, eyes capable of twinkling through glasses whose rims he has a habit of peering over. He talks slowly, selecting his words, in a voice at once compelling and humorous. He often hesitates, peers over his glasses before saying the last word of a phrase or a sentence. Michael Barnes is a Senior in the Arts College, an intensely serious young man and a fine literary student. The older people who surround him find his youthful grimness about life's problems sometimes amusing, but more frequently alarming]

ELLEN: Oh, come in, Doctor Damon.

MICHAEL: How do you do, sir?

DAMON: Hello, Thomas!

ELLEN: Where's Mrs. Damon?

DAMON: I shall pick her up and bring her along shortly for the festivities. This is in the nature of an unofficial call.

TOMMY: Hello, Michael! You both look a little grim. Has anything happened?

DAMON: [Showing paper] Michael has written another of his fiery editorials.

PATRICIA: [Runs down the stairs] Ellen, did you see my—oh! How do you do, Doctor Damon? Hi, Michael!

MICHAEL: H'lo!

DAMON: Sit down, my dear. I have here an editorial written by Michael for The Lit, which comes out tomorrow. Perhaps, to save time, one of us should read it aloud— [*Reading*] "When this so-called University forces such men out of its faculty as Professor Kennedy, Professor Sykes, and Professor Chapman, because they have been ignorantly called Reds, it surrenders its right to be called a seat of learning. It admits that it is nothing more nor less than a training school—you will recognize the voice of our good friend, Hutchins, of Chicago —a training school for bond salesmen, farmers, real-estate dealers, and ambulance chasers. It announces to the world that its faculty is subservient—" [Damon *peers over glasses at* Michael]

MICHAEL: Oh, I didn't mean you, of course, Doctor Damon.

DAMON: "—that its faculty is subservient to its trustees, and that its trustees represent a political viewpoint which must finally emerge under its proper name, which is—Fascism."

PATRICIA: Oh, Michael! There you go again!

DAMON: Wait till you hear where he has actually gone.

PATRICIA: Isn't that all?

DAMON: Unhappily, there is more.

PATRICIA: Oh, Lord!

DAMON: "These professors were not Reds. They were distinguished liberals. Let us thank God that we still have one man left who is going ahead teaching what he believes should be taught."

TOMMY: Who's that?

DAMON: "He is not afraid to bring up even the Sacco-Vanzetti case. He has read to his classes on the same day Vanzetti's last statement and Lincoln's letter to Mrs. Bixby." I hope we are not alienating the many friends of Abraham Lincoln. "The hounds of bigotry and [Tommy *rises and glances at* Michael *questioningly*] reaction will, of course, be set upon the trail of this courageous teacher, but, if they think they are merely on the spoor of a lamb they are destined to the same disappointment as the hunters who in chasing the wild boar, came accidently upon a tigress and her cubs. Our hats are off to Professor Thomas Turner of the English Department." That's all.

ELLEN: Tommy?

TOMMY: Michael, I think you might have consulted me about this.

PATRICIA: Michael, you fool! They'll kick you out of school for this—and Tommy too!

ELLEN: You never told me you had brought up the Sacco-Vanzetti case in your classes, Tommy.

DAMON: Yes, just what is this Vanzetti letter you have read?

TOMMY: I haven't read it yet.

MICHAEL: When you told me the other day you were going to read it, I thought you meant that day.

TOMMY: No, Michael. I just meant some day. But I was talking to you as a friend, I was not giving an interview to an editor.

ELLEN: But why were you going to read this letter, Tommy?

TOMMY: Because it's a fine piece of English composition, and I'm teaching a class in English composition. An obscure little class. I don't want any publicity, Michael. I just want to be left alone.

ELLEN: But nobody thinks of Vanzetti as a writer, Tommy.

TOMMY: It happens that he developed into an extraordinary writer. I don't think you could help being interested in the letter yourself, Doctor Damon.

DAMON: You would be surprised at my strength of will in these matters, Thomas. What I am interested in is preserving some air of academic calm here at Midwestern—

PATRICIA: You don't want to get Tommy kicked out of school, do you, Michael?

MICHAEL: No. I didn't think of that. I thought Mr. Turner was about the only man we had left who would read whatever he wanted to to his classes. I thought he was the one man who would stand up to these stadium builders.

TOMMY: I'm not standing up to anyone, Michael. I'm not challenging anyone. This is just an innocent little piece I wanted to read.

[Michael *turns away*]

ELLEN: [*Rises*] I'm sure this piece must be fine, Tommy, but you can't read it now. Keller and the other trustees kicked Don Chapman out last month for doing things just as harmless as this. [*Turning to* Michael] You'll have to change that editorial, Michael.

MICHAEL: I can't. The magazines were run off the presses last night. They've already been delivered to the news stands.

DAMON: They go on sale in the morning. [*To Ellen*] I think that our—er—tigress here may have to issue a denial tomorrow. After all, he hasn't read it yet.

ELLEN: [*To Tommy*] Yes, and you mustn't read it now.

PATRICIA: Will Michael be kicked out of school, Doctor Damon?

DAMON: Sufficient unto the day is the evil thereof, my dear.

PATRICIA: [*To Michael*] There! You see—

DAMON: [*Crossing down to* Tommy] Of course I quite understand how you meant to present this letter, Thomas; but our good friend Mr. Keller would not. Do not underestimate Mr. Edward K. Keller. He rolls like the juggernaut over the careers of young professors.

TOMMY: I know.

DAMON: [*Starting to door*] Since he must be with us tonight let us confine our conversation to the— woeful inadequacies of the Illinois team.

TOMMY: [*Rising*] It isn't Illinois we're playing—it's Michigan.

DAMON: Oh, I must remember that.   [*Exits*]

PATRICIA: There, you see! You will be kicked out.

MICHAEL: He didn't say that.

PATRICIA: Yes, he did. You needn't bother to come back for me, Michael. I'm staying here for supper. [*Runs up stairs*]

MICHAEL: I see. I'm sorry, Mr. Turner. I guess I got —well—carried away.

TOMMY: [*Crossing*] I know, Michael. Sometimes, when I see that light in your eye I wish I could be carried away too.

MICHAEL: Yes, sir. [*He goes out grimly. Slight pause*]

TOMMY: Well—

ELLEN: I'm sorry, Tommy.

TOMMY: Oh it's all right. Maybe I can read this thing later on, after all the fuss quiets down—say next spring.

ELLEN: It would still be dangerous.

TOMMY: Yes, I guess it would. I know I'm not a tiger, but I don't like to be thought of as a pussy-cat either.

ELLEN: It's getting late. You'd better go and put on that gray suit I laid out for you. And be sure your socks are right side out, and Tommy—don't try to be a tiger in front of Ed Keller.

TOMMY: [*At stair landing*] I won't. I'm scared of those Neanderthal men. I'll talk about football.

ELLEN: Thank you, darling. That's swell. You know how Joe is—always cheerful. And we do want it to be a good party.

TOMMY: I'll be cheerful. I'll be merry and bright. I'll be the most cheerful son-of-a-gun in this part of the country. [*He sings as he exits up the stairs*]

"Who's afraid of the Big Bad Wolf?
The Big Bad Wolf?
The Big Bad Wolf?
Who's afraid tum-tee-ump—"

[Ellen *looks after him doubtfully. Doorbell rings*]

ELLEN: [*Calling upstairs*] Hurry, Tommy! They're here! [*Crosses to door; admits* Joe Ferguson, *followed by* Wally Myers] Hello, Joe!

JOE: Ellen, darling! How are you? Gosh, you look great! Why, you're younger and prettier than ever! If I were a braver man, I'd kiss you. Doggone it, I *will* kiss you! [*Kisses her on cheek, hugs her, lifts her off the floor—whirls her around.* Joe *is big, handsome, successful, and pleasing, about* 35]
                                    [Wally *closes door*]

ELLEN: It's terribly nice to see you again, Joe. If I were a younger woman, I'd say it's been all of ten years.

JOE: [*Crossing up to sofa; puts box of flowers down*] Gosh, this is swell! Where's the great Thomas?

ELLEN: Tommy will be right down. I see Wally found you—so you've met?

JOE: Yeh. We joined forces outside.

ELLEN: [*At settee*] Come on over here and sit down.

JOE: I forgot to ask you Wally, who's going in at the **other** half tomorrow? Stalenkiwiecz?

WALLY: No, sir. Wierasocka.

JOE: Oh, is he?

WALLY: Yeh. He's a Beta. From Oregon.

JOE: Oh, yeh—yeh, I know him.

WALLY: [*Sits in center of settee beside* Ellen] Stalenkiwiecz is laid up. They think he's got whooping cough.

JOE: That's bad! I've got a thousand fish on that game. [*Sits on settee. It is very crowded*]

WALLY: I think it's safe, all right, Mr. Ferguson, but I wish we had you. Stalenkiwiecz, Wierasocka, Myers and Whirling Joe Ferguson.

ELLEN: Do they still call you that, Joe?

JOE: Oh, sure, remember how—

WALLY: Say, he was the greatest open-field runner there ever was.

ELLEN: Yes, Joe. How does it happen you've never even—

WALLY: Why, you made Red Grange look like a cripple.

JOE: Aw, they say you're not so bad yourself. Say, Ellen, how's—

WALLY: Aw, I'm just fair, that's all. [*Produces a clipping from coat pocket*] This is what Grantland Rice said about me. [*Hands it to* Joe]

JOE: Yeh.—Too bad this is Wally's last year. We're going to miss him—eh, Ellen?

ELLEN: Have you got anything to do, Wally?

WALLY: Well—the Coach wants me to help him with the back-field next season. Not much money in it, of course.

JOE: [*Hands clipping back to* Wally] Well, if you want my advice, don't go in for coaching. I had a sweet offer from Cincinnati in 'Twenty-nine. Remember that, Ellen?

ELLEN: I remember very well. Do you remember when—

WALLY: Nineteen twenty-nine! [*Leaning forward meditatively*] —I was only twelve years old then—

TOMMY: [*Comes downstairs*] Hello, Joe! It's nice to see you again!

JOE: [*Rises and shakes hands*] Tommy, old man, how are you? Ten years! Teaching must be good for you. And Ellen, here, looks like a million bucks! That reminds me—I came laden with gifts. [*Turns and almost runs into* Wally. *He goes and gets flowers*] These are a few flowering weeds—

ELLEN: Thank you, Joe. They're lovely. Tommy, will you call Cleota?

TOMMY: Sure! [*Goes into dining room, calls*] Cleota!

ELLEN: It's fun to get flowers. Very festive.

JOE: Oh, it's nothing much, but I wanted you to know I remembered the great day. Think I'd forget it was your birthday?

ELLEN: You never used to. [Tommy *re-enters*] Tommy gave me some flowering weeds, too—for my birthday.

TOMMY: For your—oh—yes— Not such nice ones, I'm afraid. [*To* Ellen] I'm a lucky man.

[Cleota *enters*]

ELLEN: Will you find something to put these in, Cleota?

CLEOTA: [*Sighs*] Yassum. Ah guess Ah'll hafta put 'em in de sink wit dat ice. [*Exits to dining room*]

JOE: Boy, it's sure great to be here!

TOMMY: It's nice to have you.—Staying long?

JOE: Got to be in Washington next week. [*Noticing bookcases*] Well, Tommy, I see you've still got a lot of books.

TOMMY: Oh, yes.

JOE: You know I never get a chance to read books. [*He sits on settee again*]

WALLY: Say, you must have a swell job! [*Sits on bench front of fireplace*]

JOE: By the time I get through at night, I'm lucky if I can keep up with what's going on in the world. Way things are changing, you gotta do that. I take fifteen magazines. That keeps me busy.

ELLEN: [*Linking an arm through* Tommy's] Tommy had several articles in *Harper's* and the *Atlantic*.

JOE: No! Say, that's fine! But you'll have to boil them down to *The Reader's Digest* to reach me, Tommy. You know, that's a great little magazine.

TOMMY: Do you like bouillon cubes?

ELLEN: [*Hurrying him out*] Tommy, you'd better make a drink.

TOMMY: Yes. We have a lot of celebrating to do. [*Crosses into dining room calling "Cleota"*]

ELLEN: How've you been, Joe? [*Sits next to* Joe]

JOE: Fine, except for a little sinus trouble.

WALLY: You know, Mrs. Turner, I recognized him right away from that big picture in the gym.

[Tommy *re-enters with bowl of ice, mixes drinks*]

ELLEN: That's fine. How's Brenda? I meant to ask before.

JOE: Fine! Great! Little heavier, maybe. We're being divorced, you know.

ELLEN: But I didn't know. Oh, Joe, I'm sorry.

JOE: Nothing to be sorry about. It's just one of those things.

TOMMY: What's the matter?

ELLEN: Joe and his wife are breaking up.

TOMMY: Oh, that's too bad.

JOE: No, it's all fine. We're both taking it in our stride. Took her out to dinner last week—along with her new boy friend.

TOMMY: Wasn't that rather complicated?

ELLEN: Oh, you're not up to date, Tommy. That's the modern way of doing things.

JOE: Sure! Take it in your stride. Gosh, Ellen, I can't take my eyes off you. [*This is cute so* Wally *laughs.* Joe *notices* Tommy *watching*] Nice little place you got here. [*Rises*] Need any help, Tommy? I'm a demon on Manhattans. [*Doorbell rings*]

TOMMY: I'm all right, thanks.

JOE: I hope that's Ed, the old scoundrel.

ELLEN: [*Goes to the door and admits the* Damons] I'm so glad— Hello, Mrs. Damon!

BLANCHE: [*Entering*] Hello, Ellen dear! How do you do, Mr. Turner?

ELLEN: You must know Joe Ferguson.

BLANCHE: Oh, of course!

ELLEN: This is Mrs. Damon, Joe. You remember Dean Damon?

JOE: Yes indeed! Nice to see you again, sir.

DAMON: [*Crossing to him and shaking hands*] Back for the slaughter of the—uh—Michigan innocents, eh?

JOE: That's right.

[Ellen and Blanche *have turned to* Wally]

ELLEN: Mrs. Damon, may I present Mr. Myers?

BLANCHE: Oh, yes of course we all know about our great fullback.

[Tommy *gives away cocktails.* Joe *gets cocktail from* Tommy]

WALLY: How do you do?

ELLEN: Let me help you with your coat.

BLANCHE: Thank you, dear. [*To* Wally] Tell me, are you nervous about the game?

WALLY: No, ma'am.

BLANCHE: Not the least little bit?

WALLY: No, ma'am.

BLANCHE: That's nice. [*Sits down*]

DAMON: I remember you not only from the gridiron but from my Shakespeare class. You slept very quietly.

JOE: You know, I never did finish reading *Hamlet*. I always wondered how that came out. [*He laughs heartily.* Damon *laughs politely*]

TOMMY: [*Crossing with two cocktails*] Does anybody mind a Manhattan?

BLANCHE: Oh, Ellen! Could we have sherry?

ELLEN: Certainly. Tommy—

TOMMY: Sherry coming right up. Here, Wally. [*Gives him cocktail*]

WALLY: No, thanks. I'm in training.

TOMMY: Well, just hold it. Sherry for you too, Doctor Damon?

DAMON: When Mrs. Damon says we, she means me. Sherry, thanks.

BLANCHE: [*Drinking other cocktail*] A little sherry is such fun. [*Wally* offers her cigarette from box on coffee table] No thanks, I'll smoke my "Spuds"! [*Wally* lights Blanche's cigarette]

PATRICIA: [*Coming downstairs*] Hello, everybody!

ELLEN: [*Brings her down to* Joe] This is my sister Patricia.

PATRICIA: How do you do?

JOE: [*Admiring her*] How do you *do?* My goodness! Why, you're as big and pretty as your sister. How about a drink?

PATRICIA: No, thanks. [*To* Ellen] Still has his hair. Hello, Wally!

[Tommy *pours sherry for* Damons]

WALLY: Hi, Pat! Look, can I pick you up at Hennick's a little earlier?

PATRICIA: I'm not going to Hennick's. I'm eating here. That date's off.

WALLY: With Barnes? Say, that's swell. [*Smacks* Patricia *on the back, almost knocking her down. Crosses to* Ellen] I got to run along, Mrs. Turner. Nice party. [*Shakes* Ellen's *hand heartily. Crosses to* Joe] Glad I met you, Joe—I mean, Mr. Ferguson. [*They shake hands*] I'll be seeing you. Goodbye, everybody! I'll go out the back way. [*Exits*]

JOE: Take it easy, old man. Don't break a leg on me. Remember, I've got a thousand fish on that game. [*Follows* Wally *out*]

WALLY: I won't.

BLANCHE: He's a handsome boy, Patricia. [*Doorbell rings*] And seems very healthy.

PATRICIA: I have to keep in training for him. [Patricia *and* Damon *sit down on bench before the fireplace*]

TOMMY: I'll get it.

[*The Kellers come into the room. Ed Keller is a big, loud, slightly bald man of about thirty-eight, heavy around the middle. He is a prosperous real-estate man, owns the Keller Building, is a trustee and as such, the biggest voice and strongest hand on the Board. Myrtle Keller, also in her late thirties, dresses well and is not bad-looking, was once pretty, but is now a slightly faded blonde*]

ED: Hello, Ellen! Hi, Turner! Where is *he*? [*Passes* Tommy *fast, without handshake:* Joe *reappears;* Ed *comes down and meets* Joe. *This is a typical meeting between two old friends of the hale-and-hearty, back-slapping variety who haven't met for years*] Hiya, you old rascal! Hahya, boy?

JOE: [*Running to meet him, so that they clinch in the middle of the room, hugging, slapping backs, etc.*] Hello, you old son-of-a-gun! How are you, Ed? [*He goes to* Myrtle] Hello, Myrtle! Gosh, I'm glad to see you! [*Hugs her*]

MYRTLE: [*Screams*] I'm glad to see you, too! Ellen—

JOE: [*Back to* Ed] Gee, you're looking swell, Ed, old boy, old boy!

ED: Judas Priest, this is swell! How are you anyway, Joe? [*The men's voices predominate during the following*]

JOE: Fine! Swell! Never better. You've put on a little weight, eh, Eddie? And what's happened to the crowning glory?

ED: Worry: real-estate, Roosevelt. Wonder I got any left.

MYRTLE: How do you do, Doctor Damon? How do you do, Mrs. Damon? Haven't seen you in a long, long time. Hello, Patricia—Oh, quiet down! Ed! [*Sits down*] Are we late, Ellen?

ELLEN: Not at all. Just in time for the canapés.

JOE: How long's it been, Ed? Seven, eight years, isn't it?

ED: Eight, anyway.

ELLEN: Look, you two, will you break it up and say hello to people?

ED: All right, Ellen, but it sure is fine to see The Whirler again. How do you do, Doctor Damon? Not drinking straight Scotch, I hope?

DAMON: [*Rising*] If I did that, my stomach—and Mrs. Damon—would punish me severely.

ELLEN: Won't you have a cocktail, Ed? [*Crosses to* Ed *with drink*]

ED: Thanks.

JOE: Say, this is Ellen's birthday. How about a little toast?

TOMMY: Well, fill 'em up. [*Pours drinks, one for himself*]

ED: Well, happy birthday, Ellen!
      [*They drink;* Ed *starts the "Happy Birthday to You" song, and they all sing. It is obvious* Tommy *is bored; he takes a drink—then noticing everybody standing, he rises, sings the last line very off key. Cleota enters, comes up behind* Damon *with plate of canapés*]

CLEOTA: [*After song dies*] Hor doves?

DAMON: I beg your pardon—oh! Thank you. [*Takes one*]

JOE: [*As Tommy pours another round*] Let's drink one toast to The Big Red Team. What do you say?
[Tommy *starts humming "The Big Bad Wolf."*]

ED: The Big Red Team.

TOMMY: [*Singing softly to himself*]

"The Big Red Team—
   Big Red Team.
   Who's afraid of The Big Red Team—"

ED: What's that?

TOMMY: Huh? [*Ed glares at him. To* Ellen] What did I do?

ELLEN: Tommy! You'd better eat something. Those cocktails are strong.

TOMMY: I'm doing all right, honey. How's everything in Detroit, Joe?

JOE: [*Taking a canapé* Ellen *is serving*] I don't know. All right, I guess.

ELLEN: Tommy means Pittsburgh. The Bryson Steel Company is in Pittsburgh, Tommy.
      [Cleota *gives* Ellen *tray and exits dining room*]

TOMMY: Oh, yes, sure. Well, how's everything in Pittsburgh?

JOE: Well, it might be worse.

ED: [*Stuffing caviar into his mouth*] Couldn't be much worse out here.

TOMMY: Have a drink.

ELLEN: [*Crossing to* Myrtle—*serving canapés*] How are the kids, Myrtle?

MYRTLE: They're all right. The baby has some kind

of rash on her little hips, but it's nothing, really. Makes her cross, though.

ED: [*To Joe*] Time sure does fly. Now Buster wants to go to Princeton. No matter how you watch 'em, they get in with the wrong kids.

[*The women's voices predominate*]

BLANCHE: How's your sister?

MYRTLE: They took a stone out of her as big as a walnut. She can't weigh more than ninety pounds.

BLANCHE: They cut old Mrs. Wilmot open for the same trouble, and didn't find a thing!

JOE: [*Spreading this*] I remember when I actually got along with only one car, and thought it was plenty. Now I've got three, and the bills are terrific— Do you know what my gas bill was last month?

[*Damon rises, bored, picks out book and glances through it*]

MYRTLE: Ed, when was it I had that impacted tooth out?

ED: Seven years ago. Year the banks closed. 'Thirty-three.

TOMMY: Fill 'em up. [*Pours himself another*]

ELLEN: Tommy! [*She takes shaker away from him*] Dividend for the women folks. Give me your glass, Myrtle.

MYRTLE: Thanks.

BLANCHE: No more for us. Mercy, we'll be light-headed.

TOMMY: [*Follows Ellen over, takes shaker, pours himself another*] But we're celebrating the homecoming game. Banks closing and everything.

JOE: How's building out here now, Ed?

TOMMY: Yeh, how's building?

ED: Lousy. Whatta ya expect with that man in the White House? You know what *I* think? I think he's crazy.

JOE: You know what I heard? [*The women stop their talk to listen, but Joe whispers in Ed's ear*]

ED: I wouldn't be a damn bit surprised. [*Ed's voice predominates in the following*]

ED: Only hope for business I see is some big new industry. And he'll probably do something to ruin that.

BLANCHE: [*Sotto voce*] Patricia, may I see the little girls' room?

MYRTLE: Me, too.

PATRICIA: Yes, I'll show you. [*They start toward stairs*]

MYRTLE: [*As they start upstairs*] Is it serious?

BLANCHE: [*Disappearing upstairs*] They took a pint of pus out of her!

[*Damon slams book shut and looks after them*]

ED: Well, Doctor Damon, we men on the Board of Trustees are certainly glad that this Red scare is over.

DAMON: No doubt you are.

ED: Now maybe the new stadium project will get somewhere.

DAMON: And the Endowment Fund?

ED: Yeh, sure—that's important too. I'm working to convince the substantial alumni that we've got all this Parlor Pink business over and done with. Got 'em all weeded out.

JOE: Yeah—all that newspaper stuff was pretty bad.

ED: Sure! Nobody felt like coming through for anything when they read about men like Kennedy and Sykes and Chapman being in the faculty. That Chapman was nothing but a damn Red.

TOMMY: No, he wasn't, Mr. Keller. Don Chapman was a humanist.

ELLEN: We knew him very well.

JOE: How do you know he wasn't a Red, Tommy?

ED: He went to Soviet Russia for his vacation once, didn't he?

TOMMY: He just went to see the Drama Festival.

ED: [*Suspiciously*] Well, it's a mighty long way to go to see a show.

CLEOTA: [*Who has just entered*] Suppah is se'ved.
[*Exits*]

ELLEN: [*Quickly*] Shall we go into the dining room? It's only a salad. We're going out to eat afterwards. Come along, Ed, we don't want to miss that rally. [*She links her arm through* Ed's *and they exit*]

ED: Say, that's right. I haven't missed a Michigan rally in seventeen years.

ELLEN: [*Re-enters; goes to stairs; calls up*] Supper's ready.

[*Patricia, Blanche, and* Myrtle *come downstairs*]

BLANCHE: Come, Frederick. [*Takes* Damon's *arm and follows into dining room*]

ELLEN: Patricia, you get a plate for Mr. Ferguson. He's the guest of honor you know.

JOE: And I'll get a plate for you, Ellen. Come on.
[*Joe and* Patricia *exit*]

MYRTLE: [*As she goes into dining room*] Oh, what a lovely table, Ellen!

[*During the following scene until* Ed's *re-entrance, there is the general conversation in the dining room, as everybody is finding his supper and beginning to eat*]

ELLEN: [*Crossing to Tommy*] Tommy, don't say any more about Don Chapman tonight, please.

TOMMY: All right, I won't. Let's get something to eat. [*Ellen takes his arm. They start for dining room*] Joe looks better, doesn't he?

ELLEN: Better?

TOMMY: Well, bigger anyway.   [*They exit*]

[*Cleota has entered with cleanup tray. She puts dirty glasses on her tray. She is singing "I Can't Give You Anything But Love" during all this. She finds one glass with some liquor in it. After a long scrutiny she raises it to her lips, is just about to drink when she hears*]

ED: [*Off-stage*] Come on, Myrtle! Hurry up! Joe's got to speak at this rally.

[Cleota *drinks and quickly puts glass on tray and resumes song as* Ed *enters and sits down.* Blanche *and* Myrtle *enter with* Damon *following them and carrying two plates*]

BLANCHE: Frederick, put it down there on the table.

MYRTLE: [*As they cross the room*] What makes you think there was something suspicious about it?

BLANCHE: [*Sitting down*] Well, his family won't allow a post mortem. Thank you, Frederick, that's fine.

[Cleota *has gone out.* Ellen *enters with* Joe. Joe *sits sofa*]

ELLEN: I hope you can all find a place to sit.

JOE: What's the matter with this? Come on, Ellen.

ELLEN: [*Smiles and sits beside him, speaking to* Patricia, *who appears in dining room door*] Pat, is Tommy getting some food?

PATRICIA: Yeh, he's all right. [*Sits on fireplace bench*]

TOMMY: [*Entering*] Sure, I'm fine. [*Looks around for a place to settle*]

ELLEN: Bring in the coffee, please, Cleota.

ED: There's room here for somebody.

TOMMY: I'll sit— [*Looks around for a place away from* Ed—*only vacant space is chair beside* Ed's *settee*] here.

MYRTLE: Eat your vegetables, Ed.

ED: Aw, this is a party.

BLANCHE: Where's Michael Barnes this evening, Patricia? Frederick tells me he's written a remarkable editorial. [Damon *drops his fork on plate*] Be careful, Frederick!

ED: Barnes—Barnes? I haven't read a decent editorial since Brisbane died.

PATRICIA: Michael couldn't come. He doesn't like Mr.—er—

MYRTLE: Doesn't like what?

PATRICIA: Doesn't like parties.

BLANCHE: I'm always so interested in *The Literary Magazine.* What was the editorial, Patricia?

DAMON: Eat your dinner, my dear. Remember, Mr. Keller—wants to get to the rally.

ED: Huh?

BLANCHE: What's the matter with you? [*To* Patricia] I hope I haven't said anything, dear.

[Patricia *shakes her head*]

ED: What's going on over there? Who is this Barnes?

TOMMY: One of Patricia's beaux.

ED: Some writer!

TOMMY: He's a student. Editor on *The Literary Magazine.*

ED: Oh, yeah, I've heard of him. What's he done now?

ELLEN: Oh, it's nothing really.

TOMMY: Well, since it's come up, Ellen, we might as well tell Mr. Keller. He'll read about it tomorrow— [Ellen *rises*] I told Michael I was going to

read something to one of my English classes and he got a mistaken idea about it and wrote a sort of—

[Cleota *serving coffee*]

ELLEN: [*Breaking in quickly*] Just a silly little editorial—that's all.

ED: I see.

PATRICIA: Because Tommy isn't really going to read it at all.

[Myrtle *rises. Exits carrying plate of food*]

ED: What was it this kid said, you were going to read? Anything important?

TOMMY: [*After a moment*] It's a short, but beautifully written piece of English by Bartolomeo Vanzetti.

ED: Never heard of him. [*Takes coffee from* Cleota. *Pause*] Hey, you don't mean Vanzetti of Sacco and Vanzetti!

TOMMY: Yes, the same man.

ED: You mean you're going to read something *he* wrote?

TOMMY: Yes, I was going to.

ELLEN: [*Quickly*] But now he's not—Michael didn't understand.

ED: Why would you ever think of such a dumb thing in the first place?

TOMMY: It's part of a series. I read many such letters to my class.

ED: You mean letters by anarchists?

TOMMY: [*Restrains himself*] No, letters by men who were not professional writers—like Lincoln, General Sherman—

ED: Well, it's a good thing you changed your mind. Putting Lincoln and General Sherman in a class with Vanzetti! Wouldn't look very good.

JOE: What's this?

ED: [*To* Joe] Wait a minute. [*To* Tommy] Is this thing going to be printed? This editorial?

DAMON: We discovered it too late to stop it.

ED: And this kid didn't submit it to the Publications Committee?

DAMON: Unfortunately, he did not. Ellen dear, Mrs. Damon and I must be running along.

ELLEN: Oh, I'm sorry.

DAMON: I have a committee meeting.

BLANCHE: What committee?

DAMON: Come, Blanche.

BLANCHE: [*Rising*] Oh, yes, that little committee.

ED: Well, I hope this thing's not too bad. You better deny it quick, Turner. I tell you. I'll call the papers in the morning.

TOMMY: No, I'll take care of it.

JOE: [*Rises*] What's going on here?

MYRTLE: [*Enters from dining room with two dishes of sherbet*] Here's some sherbet, Ed.

ED: Put it down there. I'm just telling Turner here we've had enough of this Red business among the students and the faculty. Don't want any more.

TOMMY: [*Sits sofa*] This isn't Red, Mr. Keller.

ED: Maybe not, but it looks bad. We don't want anything Red—or even Pink—taught here.

TOMMY: But who's to decide what is Red or what is Pink?

ED: We are! Somebody's got to decide what's fit to teach. If we don't, who would.

DAMON: I thought the faculty had—

ED: No sir. You fellows are too wishy-washy. We saw that in the Chapman case. Americanism is what we want taught here.

JOE: Americanism is a fine thing.

TOMMY: Fine! But how would you define Americanism?

ED: Why—er—everybody knows what Americanism is. What do you believe in?

TOMMY: I believe that a college should be concerned with ideas. Not just your ideas or my ideas, but all ideas.

ED: No, sir! That's the *trouble*—too many ideas floating around—You put ideas of any kind into young people's heads, and the first thing you know, they start believing them.

DAMON: On the contrary. I have been putting ideas into young people's heads for forty-two years with no [*Twinkles slyly at* Joe] —visible—results whatever. [*There is a dubious laugh from* Ed *and* Joe *until* Joe *gets* Damon's *meaning*]

BLANCHE: Come, Frederick. Good night, Ellen! Lovely party! [*She bustles* Damon *out the door*]

ED: [*Rises*] Turner, you better think twice before you read anything. I can promise you the trustees will clamp down on any professor who tries anything funny. I'm telling you that for your own good.

JOE: Say, I thought we were going to have some fun. Let's break this up. How about some music? [*Crosses to Victrola. He puts on a record which starts to play Wayne King's recording of "Cornsilk."*]

ED: That's right. We're celebrating tonight. Just wanted to get that out of my system. [*He picks up the dish of ice*] Oh, I didn't want this—I wanted some of that ice cream. [*He starts for the dining room*]

MYRTLE: He means he wants both. Here, I'll show you. [*She follows him into the dining room*]

PATRICIA: [*At a sign from* Ellen] I'll bet you'd like some ice cream, too, Mr. Ferguson.

JOE: No, I— [Patricia *winks at him; he glances at* Tommy] Oh, sure! Sure, I would. [*He follows* Patricia *into dining room*]

PATRICIA: [*As they exit*] Can you still skip?

JOE: No—not at my age.

ELLEN: Tommy, have you had too much to drink?

TOMMY: No. Not enough.

ELLEN: Your eyes have that funny look.

TOMMY: Did you hear what Mr. Keller said to me? I don't like to be talked to like that.

ELLEN: [*Crossing to him*] Just because he was nasty and you've had a few drinks. Tommy, you're not going to go ahead and read that letter.

TOMMY: Yes, Ellen, I think I have to.

ELLEN: Tommy, try to be practical for once. At least wait until you're not so mad. Try to think of this the way any other man would think of it.

TOMMY: I'm not any other man.

ELLEN: Well, try to be. Do you think Joe would do something that would get him into trouble just because somebody irritated him?

TOMMY: *Joe!* I don't see why you don't try to understand how *I* feel about this.

ELLEN: I'm simply trying to keep you out of a lot of trouble. I don't see why—

TOMMY: But you see how Joe would feel. That's very plain to you, isn't it?

ELLEN: Yes, it is. Joe wouldn't get all mixed up.

TOMMY: I'm not mixed up. I'm trying to understand what goes on in your mind. It *can't* be like Joe Ferguson's mind!

ELLEN: Oh, you and your mind! I have to go through such a lot with your mind!

TOMMY: Maybe you wouldn't if you understood it better.

ELLEN: Oh, I know, I know! I'm too dumb for you!

TOMMY: Now, Ellen, I didn't say that.

ELLEN: You said Joe and I were stupid.

TOMMY: I said he was.

ELLEN: But he isn't. He's a big man. In some ways he's smarter than you.

TOMMY: Well, you ought to know. [*He turns away from her*]

ELLEN: Oh, look, Tommy—what are we fighting about?

TOMMY: [*Turns*] You said I was dumb.

ELLEN: Tommy, you've had too many drinks or you wouldn't say that.

TOMMY: No, I haven't, but I don't feel very well. I feel very unhappy and slightly sick.

ELLEN: I'll get you some bicarbonate of soda.

TOMMY: No, you won't. I'll go upstairs and lie down for a few minutes myself. I can do that much. Let's not bring this down to the level of bicarbonate of soda. [*Crosses to stairway—starts up slowly. Suddenly can contain himself no longer—makes a mad dash for it*]

ELLEN: [*Hesitates for a minute at the foot of the stairs—calls after him*] Tommy! Tommy, I didn't—

JOE: [*Enters*] Anything the matter?

[Cleota *enters, straightens up the room*]

ELLEN: Oh—no. Tommy's not feeling well. He got sick once before at a party. He's not used to drinking, and he's very sensitive about it. Cleota. Will you get Mr. Turner some bicarbonate of soda from the kitchen? [Cleota *nods—exits.* Joe *crosses to* Victrola] Cleota will get him some bicarbonate of soda from the kitchen. He'd never find it upstairs.

JOE: [*Turns off the music and takes off the record*] Why wouldn't he? Where do you keep it?

ELLEN: In the medicine chest.

JOE: [*Smiles*] What was that stuff between him and Ed?

ELLEN: Oh, it's nothing, really. I'll tell you about it tomorrow.

JOE: [*Finds another record*] Fine— Say, look what I found! "Who?" Remember that, Ellen? [*He puts the record on, starts it. Ellen moves closer to the Victrola and listens as it plays:*]

"Who-o-o stole my heart away?
Who-o-o makes me dream all day?
Dreams I know can never come true.
Seems as though I'd ever be blue.
Who-o-o means my happiness—"

[*As naturally as if they were always dancing to this song, they both begin to dance*] Gee, this takes me back— The May Dance. Remember?

ELLEN: Um-huh—it rained.

JOE: You said you didn't know it was raining. I know I didn't. [*Holds her closer*]

ELLEN: [*Breaks away*] I'm a little rusty, Joe. I haven't danced in—oh, I don't remember when. Makes me feel young.

JOE: Then what are we stopping for? Come on.

ELLEN: Well—all right.
[*They go back into the dance. They stand looking at each other, he ardently, she caught up in the music*]

JOE: I can answer all those questions—[*As the music goes into the instrumental reprise, Joe kisses her, and she kisses back for a long moment, then tries to pull away*] No one but you—

ELLEN: [*As he tries to kiss her again*] Oh, no, Joe, please, I—Say, how many cocktails did I have?
[*They stand for an instant, looking at each other. Offstage we hear:*]

MYRTLE: Ed, get away from that ice cream. You've had enough.
[*Joe and Ellen quietly start dancing again*]

ED: Oh—all right.

[*Tommy has come down the stairs—sees them dancing there as Myrtle and Ed enter*]

MYRTLE: [*Nudging Ed*] Look, Ed! Just like the old days, isn't it? Seeing them dancing together?

ED: I'll say. [*Then loudly*] They make a darn handsome couple, don't they?
[*Tommy, although he has not seen the kiss, has sensed the whole intimacy of the scene and the meaning of Ed's remark*]

JOE: She dances like a dream.

ED: [*Chuckling*] Like a "dream can never come true," eh, Joe? You look mighty sweet in there, boy.
[*Ellen sees Tommy. Following her glance, Ed and Myrtle and Joe turn and look at Tommy*]

ELLEN: [*Breaking away*] Oh—Tommy—are you all right?

TOMMY: [*Coming down*] Yes, thanks.—Don't—let me spoil the party.

ED: Party's breaking up anyway, Tommy.
[*Turns off Victrola*]

TOMMY: I just thought I'd get some more air—
[*Crosses to door which leads out to garden*]

ED: I don't want to miss any of that rally. [*A band is heard in the distance, approaching. Holds out Myrtle's coat*] Myrtle! [*Myrtle crosses to him*]

PATRICIA: [*Enters from dining room with bicarbonate of soda in glass*] Who's this for, Ellen?

ELLEN: Tommy! [*To Tommy, as he stands with his back turned, breathing the fresh air*] Tommy, will you take this bicarbonate?

TOMMY: Just—put it by for a moment. You go to the rally, Ellen— I'm going to walk around out here—and cool off. Good night, everybody— You're coming to lunch tomorrow, aren't you, Joe?

JOE: Yes, sir!

TOMMY: That's what I thought. [*He goes out, closing the screen door*]
[*Ellen puts soda on table*]

PATRICIA: [*Looks out the window; the band is heard louder, coming down*] Ellen! It's the team and the band and a lot of the kids! They must be going in the Neil Avenue gate!

ED: Come on, let's step on it!

JOE: Yeh. [*Listens to music coming closer*] Boy, that sounds good! Gosh, doesn't that take you back?

MYRTLE: Where'll we go after the rally?

JOE: I'll take you all to the Dixie Club! Whatta ya say, Ellen?

ELLEN: Oh, I haven't been there in years! It would be fun— But, no, I'm not going. [*Calls*] I'm going to stay here and get you to bed, Tommy.

TOMMY'S VOICE: [*Off*] No, I'd rather you didn't— really.

PATRICIA: [*As music gets much louder*] Hey! They're stopping in front of the house!

WALLY: [*Entering*] Ready, Pat?

PATRICIA: Sure!

WALLY: [*Crossing to Joe. He is breathless and excited*] Look, Mr. Ferguson, we brought the band over to escort you to the chapel. You're going to ride in the Axline Buggy! We hauled it out of the trophy rooms!

ED: The Axline Buggy! Wow!

WALLY: Yes! We got two horses—not the old black ones, but we got two horses! Whatta ya say?

ED: Fine! Fine!

NUTSY: [*Runs in, dressed in band-leader's uniform and carrying his glistening stick*] Hey come on! Let's get going! The carriage waits, Mr. Ferguson!
[*Does drum major's salute and clicks heels*]

WALLY: This is Nutsy Miller, the leader of the band.

JOE: Hiya, Nutsy?

NUTSY: Hiya, Joe?

JOE: Okay, fellas! Whatta ya say, Ellen—you ride with me.—Some fun, huh?

ELLEN: [*In the spirit of it*] Oh—all right. Hurray!

JOE: Hit her, Ed!

[*Ed, Joe, Wally, Ellen, Patricia, Nutsy sing*]

> "And if we win the game,
> We'll buy a keg of booze,
> And we'll drink to old Midwestern
> Till we wobble in our shoes."

[*They all go out, Joe and Ellen the center of the gay, excited group, arm in arm. A shout goes up as Joe appears outside*]

VOICES: [*Outside*]

> "Oh, we don't give a damn
> For the whole state of Michigan
> The whole state of Michigan
> The whole state of Michigan
> Oh, we don't give a damn
> For the whole state of Michigan
> Now or ever more."

Rah-rah-rah-rah. Ferguson—Ferguson—Ferguson. [*The band starts another march. Tommy has reappeared in the lower door a moment after the general exit. He crosses slowly, absently picking up soda on the way, looks out after them, then closes the door. The cheers for Ferguson and the band music slowly die away as Tommy comes down, muttering: "Rah. Rah. Rah." He looks at the soda in distaste; distaste for himself. Glances at Victrola, switches it on, dropping needle about twelve bars from the end of the chorus. Victrola plays:*]

> "Dreams I know can never come true.
> Seems as though I'll always be blue.
> Who-o-o means my happiness?
> Who-o-o? Shall I answer yes?
> Who-o-o? Well, you ought to guess.
> Who? Who? No one but you."

[*Tommy listens for a moment, then makes awkwardly, solemnly, a couple of dance steps, frowns, shakes his head, and drops into settee giving it up. He drinks the bitter cup of soda as the music ends and the curtain falls*]

Act II

SCENE 1: *Same as Act One. About 1:00 P.M., the following day.*

At rise, Joe, *with coat off, is center, arranging plates, knives, forks, etc., on the floor in the form of a football team's backfield. The end table* has evidently been used for serving luncheon as there are still a plate, cup, etc. Ellen *is seated center, finishing her coffee and watching* Joe. Patricia *is down on her knees on the floor, studying the array of dishes, napkins, salt cellars and glasses which are ankle-deep around* Joe *in football formation.* Cleota *enters from the dining room, carrying an empty tray. She crosses to the end table, begins clearing away the dishes.*

JOE: Now here—it's a balanced line. Move those two men out a little more. [*Patricia moves men out*] This is a wonderful play. [*Jumps downstage facing up. Puts downstage "backfield" in position*]

ELLEN: Cleota, did you phone Mr. Turner's office again?

CLEOTA: [*At end table clearing away dishes*] Yessum. Dey ain' no answeh.

PATRICIA: I saw Tommy, Ellen—about an hour ago.

ELLEN: Where?

PATRICIA: He was walking out on the little road back of the Ag buildings. Just moping along. I yelled at him, but he didn't hear me.

ELLEN: I'm getting worried.

JOE: [*Intent on his own activity*] Everything's going to be okay. Nothing to worry about—— Now, study this play, girls, or you won't know it when you see it this afternoon. This is Michigan. And this is Midwestern. —Now! From the balanced line, we shift. Hup! [*He executes a Notre Dame shift*] Wally takes the left end's place, but he plays out a little.

PATRICIA: Isn't Wally going to carry the ball?

JOE: Shh! Michigan spreads out. They're watching that wide end, but it's too obvious. They're watching the other side of the line, too.

CLEOTA: [*Moving down, wide-eyed*] What's goin' on heah?

ELLEN: Shh! It's a football game.

JOE: The ball is snapped back. Now look, here we go! Both of us. [*Carrying a plate and a napkin*] Close together. Fading back but threatening a left end run as well as a pass.

PATRICIA: But who are you?

JOE: I'm both of them—Lindstrom and Wierasocka.— [*Comes forward*] Skolsky cuts down the left side line deep and takes out Wupperman— that's the jam pot. [*Picks up "Wally."*] Wally is running wide around right end, [*Runs around end*] faking as though he had the ball but hasn't really got it—apparently! Now, then, just as Michigan is charging in on Lindstrom and Wierasocka, trying to decide which one has the ball, Wally lets himself out! He's *really* got it!

PATRICIA: Hooray!

JOE: It's a fake fake. It's an old play, so corny only a football genius like Coach Sprague would use it. With no interference at all, Wally cuts over and goes straight down the right side of the field! He stiff-arms the safety man— [*Running with the cream pitcher*] Touchdown!

PATRICIA: Whoopee! [*She knocks over the jam pot*] Oh, Lord, there goes Wupperman!

[*During Joe's "touchdown," Tommy has appeared quietly in door to the back yard. He watches Joe with distaste. No one notices him in the confusion*]

CLEOTA: Um-hm. You through playin' now?
    [*Pat and Joe help her pick up dishes, working with backs to Tommy*]

PATRICIA: I'm sorry, Ellen.

ELLEN: It's all right. You can take the teams to the showers now, Cleota. Can't she, Joe?

JOE: Sure! How do you like it?

ELLEN: I think it's nice.

JOE: Nice?! It's marvelous! That play is going to put us in the Rose Bowl. [*To Patricia*] Did I ever tell you about how we used the Statue of Liberty play? [*Assumes attitude*] I would go back for a pass, and Jonesy would take it out of my hand and cut around to the left.
    [*Cleota picks up tray of dishes and exits. Suddenly Joe realizes that, not the imaginary ball but the cup, has been taken out of his hand and that there is no Jonesy. He looks around slowly, puzzled, too late to have seen Tommy quietly returning to the outdoors with the cup. Doorbell rings*]

ELLEN: I'll answer it.

[*Admits Damon. Joe looks to see where he might have dropped the cup; he is still puzzled*]

PATRICIA: [*Starting for the stairs*] It's a wonderful play, Mr. Ferguson. If it works. [*Exits up stairs*]

JOE: The coach gave it to me in strictest confidence.
    [*Gives another look for cup—repeats gesture with right arm drawn back and lifted, trying to re-live the scene*]

ELLEN: Can you come in and wait, Doctor Damon? Tommy is out somewhere, but I'm expecting him back.
    [*Cleota exits with tray and dishes, leaving coffee things on table*]

DAMON: I can't wait very long. [*Indicates magazine in pocket*]

ELLEN: Is that *The Literary Magazine?*

DAMON: It's a powder magazine. Bombs are bursting all around. [*Sees Joe, who has been putting on coat and looking in drapes for cup*] Oh—good afternoon.

JOE: Good afternoon, Doctor Damon.
    [*Phone rings*]

ELLEN: Excuse me, I'll— [*She goes to phone*] Hello— Yes, thank you. [*Hangs up*] That was Ed Keller's office, Joe. He's on his way over here.

JOE: Oh, yeah. He called me this morning. He's fit to be tied about this *Literary Magazine* thing. Have you seen it?

DAMON: Yes. This is it.

JOE: May I take a look at it? Gosh, I didn't realize what this thing was— [*He takes magazine and scans editorial*] Calls the trustees Fascists! This kid's dangerous—un-American.

DAMON: Oh, no!

ELLEN: Oh, no, not really. He's from an old Chillicothe family.

JOE: This is bad stuff for the university. I'm afraid all hell's going to break loose. Of course, it's none of my business, but—

DAMON: [*Taking the magazine out of Joe's hand*] You take the words right out of my mouth. I haven't had such a day since poor Doctor Prendergast shot his secretary.

JOE: Well, I'm not a trustee, but I know how they feel.

ELLEN: I know.

JOE: Tommy'd better deny this, pretty fast, and get himself out in the clear. I'm telling you. I'm sorry about this, Ellen— Where is Tommy?

ELLEN: I don't know.

JOE: You don't think— [*Lowers voice to whisper*] You don't think he may be a little sore about your going out with me last night?

ELLEN: I don't know. Oh, Joe, I'm all upset.
    [*Doorbell rings*]

JOE: Shall I answer it?

ELLEN: Would you?

JOE: [*He opens door*] Hi, Ed!

ED: [*In doorway*] Turner here?

ELLEN: No, he isn't.

ED: Well, I want to see him before the game. Tell him to call my office. Coming, Joe?

ELLEN: [*Quickly*] I don't know just when he'll— Won't you come in? Dean Damon is here.

ED: Oh! [*He comes into the room a few steps. Joe closes the door*] Well, I'm glad somebody's here. How do you do, sir? Do you know where I could find President Cartwright?

DAMON: His secretary informed me that he is at the barber shop, having his beard trimmed.

ED: That'll be a big help! [*To Ellen, then Joe*] I thought Turner was going to deny this story. Papers keep calling *me*—they say he hasn't. Here I am, bearing the brunt of this damn disgraceful attack. "Fascists!" You oughta heard Si McMillan! And do you know Kressinger's in town from Detroit?

ELLEN: Is he a trustee, too?

DAMON: Oh, yes, young Michael certainly exploded his dynamite at a moment when the concentration of trustees is at its thickest.

ED: Yeh. There goes the new stadium. There goes your Endowment Fund! Unless something is done, and done quick! [*Crossing to Ellen*] Ellen, you tell your husband what I said!

JOE: [*Moving in*] Look, Ed, it isn't Ellen's fault.

ED: [*Crossing to Joe*] It isn't my fault, either. Here,

I kept this whole week-end free. I've got my office full of eighteen-year-old Bourbon so we fellows could cut loose a little. And look what happens! All we need now is for Wierasocka to fumble a punt! [*Stomps out*]

JOE: I'll—see you later.

       [*Takes overcoat and hat; follows* Ed *out*]

DAMON: I didn't like the way Mr. Keller said "There goes your Endowment Fund." [*Phone rings*] If that's the newspapers I'm not here.

ELLEN: Oh, I don't want to talk to them either. [*Goes to dining-room door. Calls:*] Cleota—

                 [*Phone rings again*]

PATRICIA: [*Runs down the stairs*] I'm going out to talk to Michael. I got him on the phone but he hung up on me! [*Phone rings*] Good afternoon, Doctor Damon. [*Gets coat*] I'll knock his ears off. [*Slams out the door*]

                   [*Phone rings*]

DAMON: Good afternoon, Patricia.

[Cleota *enters from the dining room*]

ELLEN: Answer the phone, Cleota.

CLEOTA: [*Crosses to phone*] Hello— Says what?— Says he is?—Ah didn' say you said he was, I say what is it?—No, he ain' heah— No, dis ain' Miz Turner.

ELLEN: [*Prompting her*] Who is calling, please.

CLEOTA: Who's dis?—Wait a minute—[*Puts hand over mouthpiece—to* Ellen] It's de *Daily* sump'n.

ELLEN: Hang up, Cleota.

CLEOTA: G'bye.   [*Hangs up and exits*]

ELLEN: Oh, Lord, see what's happened already! Doctor Damon, suppose Tommy didn't read this letter?

DAMON: Let us not take refuge in conditional clauses, my dear.

ELLEN: Would you read it if you were Tommy?

DAMON: Now we go into the subjunctive. My dear, for forty-two years I have read nothing to my classes which was written later than the first half of the seventeenth century.

ELLEN: There must be some way—some compromise—that wouldn't be too humiliating.

DAMON: The policy of appeasement? Yes, it has its merits, and I'm afraid it's all I have to offer. [*Rises*] I can't wait any longer for Thomas. Tell him that if he decides not to read the letter, I shall feel easier in my mind. Much easier. [*Picks up hat. Comes back*] And—slightly disappointed— Good afternoon, my dear— [*He opens the door, and in flies* Patricia. *They collide*] Wup, wup, *wup!*

PATRICIA: Don't let Michael in! I don't want to talk to him any more!

DAMON: Did you—uh—knock his ears off?

PATRICIA: I got him told. But he wants to tell me his side of it. He thinks *he* has a side.

DAMON: A common failing, my dear—Good afternoon.   [*He goes out*]

PATRICIA: [*Bolts the door after him*] There, I've bolted that young genius out! [*Crossing to* Ellen] Oh, Ellen! Give me a football player any time. Give me a guy without so much intellect or whatever it is. Somebody that doesn't want to be bawling the world out all the time—always doing something brave or fine or something. [*Turns as* Michael *comes in slamming door*] Go away!

ELLEN: Quiet down, Patricia— Come in, Michael.

MICHAEL: [*To* Patricia] You're being very silly.

ELLEN: [*Noticing* Michael's *distraught look*] Can I give you a glass of milk?

MICHAEL: No, thank you. She won't listen to me, Mrs. Turner. I'm not trying to ruin your husband's life or my life or anybody's life. It's the principle of the thing she won't see.

PATRICIA: Oh, the principle! I'll bet nobody else would make a fool of himself and his friends and —my brother-in-law—over a principle.

     [Ellen, *taking the dishes with her, quietly slips out toward the kitchen, unnoticed by* Michael]

MICHAEL: [*With the enormous gravity of the young man in love*] All right, Pat. I'm glad to know the qualities you admire in a man. They are certainly noble virtues, and I'm sure Wally is lousy with them.

PATRICIA: Oh, make up your mind who you're imitating, Ralph Waldo Emerson or Hemingway! You—you *writer!*

MICHAEL: Now who's imitating Hemingway?

PATRICIA: I wish you'd go away!

MICHAEL: [*Rushing to the front door*] I'm going! I'm going for good! I'm going out of your life! [*On the last word he jerks at door to make a dramatic exit, but it won't open, since* Pat *bolted it. Doorknob comes off in his hand*]

PATRICIA: [*With a smile of complete victory*] It's bolted, you dope!

[Michael *inserts knob and gets the door open finally. In walks* Tommy *with the other doorknob in his hand. The two stand and look at each other. The knob has again come out in* Michael's *hand*]

MICHAEL: [*A little guiltily*] Sorry, Mr. Turner!

TOMMY: What's going on here?

          [Michael *puts the knob in.* Tommy *screws the other knob on*]

MICHAEL: I was just going.

TOMMY: That's all right. Come in if you want to.

MICHAEL: Say, you look terrible.

TOMMY: Me? Why, what's the matter?

MICHAEL: I've got to get out of here.

TOMMY: [*Shuts door*] Oh, it's all right, Michael. Come in. Did somebody do something to you?

MICHAEL: Patricia. She did plenty. I suppose it's just as well I've found out what she wants in life: a handsome, half-witted half-back.

TOMMY: Yes, I know how that feels.

MICHAEL: Yes, sir. Well, you can't get anywhere with

a woman who doesn't understand what you have to do.

TOMMY: No. No, you can't, Michael. You'd like to, but you can't— Well— Good-bye, Michael— Come back in about an hour, will you? I want to give you a piece of my mind.

MICHAEL: [*Puzzled*] Yes, sir.

[*Exits. Tommy looks around—takes cup out of pocket and puts it on table; hangs up coat and hat, then crosses to settee and sits thinking*]

ELLEN: [*Enters*] Oh, hello, darling!

TOMMY: Hello.

ELLEN: [*Uneasily*] Well, I'm glad you remembered where you live. I was beginning to be worried. We phoned your office three times, but nobody knew where you were.

TOMMY: [*Looking up slowly*] Huh?

ELLEN: I say nobody knew where you were—since early this morning.

TOMMY: I was walking.

ELLEN: Without any breakfast? All this time?

TOMMY: Well, I—came around to the back door a while ago, but Joe was doing the Statue of Liberty or something again, so I went away.

ELLEN: You were right here and you went away?

TOMMY: Yes, I couldn't face that right now. Not the Statue of Liberty.

ELLEN: Oh! Well, Doctor Damon's been here—and Ed Keller, and the newspapers have been calling up. There's going to be a lot of trouble if you don't hurry up and deny that story of Michael's—or have you done it?

TOMMY: No—I haven't denied it.

ELLEN: [*Troubled*] You mean you've made up your mind to read it? Is that what you've been—walking around for? Tommy, I don't know what to say to you.

TOMMY: I think maybe you've said enough already.

ELLEN: That isn't very kind.

TOMMY: None of this is going to sound very kind but I've figured out exactly what I want to say, and I have to get it out before I get all mixed up.

ELLEN: I don't see why you are being so mean.

TOMMY: It's just that last night I began to see you, and myself, clearly for the first time.

ELLEN: If this is a story you're writing, and you're trying it out on me, it isn't very good.

TOMMY: Oh, I saw you and Joe clearly, too.

ELLEN: [*Relieved. Crossing to* Tommy] Oh, you saw him kiss me— I thought that was it—

TOMMY: No— No, I didn't— Did he kiss you? Well, that's fine—I've been meaning to ask you, what became of Housman's "Last Poems"? [*Turns to bookcase*]

ELLEN: Tommy, [*Puts her hand on his shoulder*] listen to me—I wanted to have a good time last night, and you spoiled it—

TOMMY: Didn't you enjoy it at all?

ELLEN: [*Piqued*] Yes, I did. I'm not a hundred years old—yet. I just decided to quit worrying about you, and have a little fun. For about an hour I felt like a girl again—wearing flowers at a Spring Dance—when I was young and silly—

TOMMY: Young and happy.

ELLEN: All right, he—kissed me. I kissed him, too. We didn't go out in the dark to do it.

TOMMY: [*Piling books he is taking from book shelves on settee*] I hope you didn't lend that book to anybody; it was a first edition.

ELLEN: Did *you* hear what *I* said?

TOMMY: Sure, I heard you. I'm listening—You said you went out in the dark and kissed Joe.

ELLEN: I said no such thing, and you know it.

TOMMY: I wish we had had separate book-plates.

ELLEN: [*Turns to him*] So that when you really make me mad and I get out of here, I can find my own books quickly?

TOMMY: [*At bookcase*] I hate sentimental pawing over things by a couple breaking up. We're not living in the days of Henry James Meredith. Look at Joe and his wife.

ELLEN: Tommy, I want you to stop this. If you're going to be jealous *be* jealous, rave or throw things, but don't act like the lead in a Senior Class play!

[*This thrust gets home*]

TOMMY: I'm trying to tell you that I don't care what you and Joe do. I'm trying to tell you that it's fine. It's very lucky that he came back just now.

ELLEN: What do you mean?

TOMMY: I mean on the money *I* make, I can go on fine alone, reading whatever I want to to my classes. That's what I want. And that's what I'm going to do.

ELLEN: Oh, that's what you want! Suddenly that's what you want. More than me?

TOMMY: It isn't so sudden. Not any more sudden than your feeling for Joe. It's logical. We get in each other's way. You wear yourself out picking up after me. Taking matches out of my pockets. [*Finds matches in pockets and throws them on table*] Disarranging my whole way of life.

ELLEN: Why haven't you said all this before?

TOMMY: I couldn't very well.

ELLEN: Why couldn't you? If you felt this way?

TOMMY: Well, we hadn't split up on this letter issue, for one thing—and then there was no place for you to go. I didn't want you to have to go back to Cleveland, or to work in some tea shoppe.

ELLEN: Oh, I see. Some tea shoppe! That's what you think I'd have to do! Well, you needn't have spared my feelings. I can make as much money as you.

TOMMY: You don't have to, now.

ELLEN: [*Turns*] Oh, you mean you waited to tell me this till Joe came along! I thought you were jealous of Joe. I could understand that. You aren't the least bit aroused at the idea of his kissing me— *out in the dark—for hours!*

TOMMY: No, I'm not.

ELLEN: So that's why you've been wandering around! That's what you've been figuring out! How nice it would be if he would take me off your hands, so you could be left alone with your books and match-boxes and *litter!* I suppose any man would do as well as Joe. [*Crosses back to* Tommy]

TOMMY: [*Crossing to her*] He's not just any man, and you know that. He's always been in love with you, and you've always been in love with him! [*He is angry and jealous now*]

ELLEN: That's ridiculous!

TOMMY: [*Moving toward her*] I felt it when I saw you dancing together. It was unmistakable. You've just admitted it.

ELLEN: Oh, you can't do that now! You can't be jealous now just because you think I want you to be!

TOMMY: I saw you dancing together—like angels! I saw you go out in that carriage together! I saw you together years ago, when I was young enough and dumb enough to believe that I really took you away from him. There's something that happens when you two dance together that doesn't happen when we dance together!

ELLEN: All right—have it your way. If you want to be free, then I want to be free—and I've gone around for ten years mooning about Joe— Well, maybe I have—maybe I have, because I'm certainly sick of you right now! [*Whirls away from him*]

TOMMY: [*Shaking her*] Ellen—Ellen, listen—

ELLEN: Never mind—all right—*all right*—ALL RIGHT! [*She breaks away—suddenly stops short as* Joe *enters brightly*]

JOE: Oh, I'm sorry—if I— [*He stops in embarrassment. There is a pause. He has caught only the tone; but he sees and feels the tension. He is carrying a wrapped bottle and a newspaper*]

TOMMY: Hello, Joe!

JOE: Hello! [*Pause*] I brought the rum. [*Holds up bottle, sees only their backs. Crosses down to coffee table. Puts bottle on table; holds up newspaper*] Big picture of Wally all over the front page. [*Silence*] Good picture, isn't it?

TOMMY: You and Ellen have some rum.

JOE: The rum's for the punch—later.

ELLEN: Could I have some—now?

                                        [Tommy *exits*]

JOE: [*Surprised*] Right now?—Sure.

TOMMY: [*From dining room*] I'll get you some glasses. [*Re-enters with two glasses*]

JOE: [*Unscrewing the top*] Tommy, old man, I just left Ed Keller and Si McMillan. This thing your young friend wrote in the magazine. [*Pours drink*] I read the piece over again. He's got you on a spot, Tommy. [*Crosses to* Ellen—*gives her drink*]

ELLEN: Want to drink a toast, Joe?—To Tommy's happiness?

JOE: [*Looks at both of them*] Sure— [*Pours himself drink—crosses up—offers toast*] Your happiness, Tommy. [*They drink amid a long silence, Joe nervously finishing his;* Ellen *taking a long drink, grimacing as the drink burns her throat*] What's the matter? What's it about? Maybe I could talk to Ed—

TOMMY: No. I don't want that. I'll run my own life my own way.

ELLEN: That's what it's about. Tommy wants to—live alone.

JOE: What?

ELLEN: He wants to be left alone—

JOE: I beg your pardon?

ELLEN: Us! Tommy and me! We're breaking up!

JOE: [*Awed, puzzled*] Just before the game—? You're both crazy! Maybe I better go.

TOMMY: Not at all! You're not exactly a stranger around here. You knew Ellen as long ago as I did.

JOE: I knew her a long time before you did—and this is a fine way to be treating her.

TOMMY: [*Baiting a hook*] Yes, I know. I was just saying I barged in and took her away from you.

JOE: Oh, no, you didn't. You had nothing to do with it. She got sore at me on account of another girl.

TOMMY: Oh, that's where I came in?

JOE: Sure! If you think you took her away from me, you're crazy. Here, you better have some rum.

ELLEN: He can't drink this early.

TOMMY: I don't *need* any rum. Go on, Joe.

JOE: [*Sits on sofa*] Well, Ellen and I had a fight. You weren't in on it. You came in later—

ELLEN: Joe, do we have to—

TOMMY: It's all right. It's his turn.

JOE: She said she hated me and never wanted to see me again. She threw something at me. She thought I went away with this girl—I mean—

TOMMY: Never mind—I know what you mean—

ELLEN: I never said you went. I never said that.

JOE: Oh, yes, you did—you intimated it.

ELLEN: No, that was your idea. I thought you were bragging about it.

JOE: Well, you got awfully mad. I thought you never did want to see me again. I guess I was dumb. Brenda says it shows you liked me. [*From* Ellen's *expression,* Joe *is reminded of* Tommy's *presence; he turns*] Oh—sorry!

TOMMY: Oh, don't mind me. Who's Brenda? Another girl?

JOE: My wife.

TOMMY: Oh, sorry!

JOE: Ellen knows her. She's from Cleveland. Brenda's always been jealous of Ellen. She found a picture of you.

TOMMY: What picture?

ELLEN: I gave him a picture. He wouldn't give it back.

JOE: It's a swell picture. You were wearing that floppy hat. Red.

ELLEN: Blue.

JOE: It had ribbons. Made you look like you were sixteen.

TOMMY: I've never seen it.

ELLEN: It was a silly hat. This was ages ago.

TOMMY: I mean, I've never seen the picture.

ELLEN: [Angrily] I threw them all away.

JOE: [Remembering] It kind of went down over one eye.

TOMMY: She looks nice in hats like that.

[Ellen suddenly begins to cry; collapses on sofa]

JOE: [Rising] Now look what you've done!

TOMMY: [Rising] Look what you've done! Bringing up old floppy blue hats! [Joe moves to Ellen] Don't touch her! She doesn't like to be touched when she's crying.

JOE: I've seen her cry. I know what to do.

TOMMY: Oh, you do?

JOE: She cried when we had that fight about the girl. She was lying on the floor and kicking and crying —on her stomach.

ELLEN: I was not!

TOMMY: Be careful what you say!

JOE: Well, I mean I knew what to do. [Crosses to other end of sofa] I picked her up then.

TOMMY: Well, you're not going to pick her up now.

ELLEN: Will you both please let me alone?! Will you please go away!

JOE: There! She wants you to go away. And I don't blame her, if this is the way you treat her. I wouldn't have stood for it ten years ago, and I'm not going to stand for it now.

TOMMY: But what are you going to do?

JOE: I'm going to get her away from all this! It isn't nice!

TOMMY: It isn't exactly to my taste, either. I didn't want it to turn out this way, but it did: me feeling like a cad, Ellen crying, and you acting like a fool.

JOE: Me acting like a fool?

ELLEN: Everybody's acting like a fool.

JOE: You've certainly messed things up, brother.

TOMMY: Don't call me brother! I can't stand that, now!

JOE: If Ellen weren't here, I'd call you worse than brother.

ELLEN: Well, I'm not going to be here! Please, please, stop—both of you! Nobody has said a word about what I want to do. You're going to settle that between yourselves. Bandying me back and forth!

TOMMY: Nobody's bandying you, Ellen.

ELLEN: [Sniffling] I know when I'm being bandied! [Rises—looks at them] I don't want either of you! You can both go to hell! [Runs upstairs, crying]

TOMMY: [Up to stairs. Joe also crosses to stairs. Both look up, then each looks away] She means me.

JOE: She said both of us.

TOMMY: She was looking at me.

JOE: How did we get into this anyway?

TOMMY: You two-stepped into it. You kissed your way into it.

JOE: I'm sorry about that. Sorry it happened.

TOMMY: You're not sorry it happened. You're sorry I found it out. Do you know anything about women? Didn't you know what she was thinking about when she was dancing with you?

JOE: No. I don't think when I'm dancing.

TOMMY: I know. You think in your office. Well, you'll have to think in your home after this. She likes to be thought about.

JOE: I thought about her. I remembered her birthday. I brought her flowers.

TOMMY: Well, you'll have to keep on bringing her things—fur coats and things—She's still young and pretty.

JOE: I don't get you.

TOMMY: I'm being broadminded. I'm takings things in my stride. It's the modern way of doing things. You ought to know that.

JOE: [Shrewdly] What makes me think you're still crazy about her and are up to some damn something or other?

TOMMY: Don't be acute. I couldn't stand you being acute.

JOE: I'm not dumb.

TOMMY: Yes, you are. It isn't what I feel that counts. It's what she feels. I think she's always been in love with you. Why, I don't know. It's supposed to be beyond reason. I guess it is.

JOE: You just think that because of last night?

TOMMY: No. Because of what lay behind last night. That wasn't just a kiss. That's nothing. This thing is too deep for jealousy or for anything but honesty. A woman must not go on living with a man when she dances better with another man.

JOE: That's silly. That's the silliest— Dancing doesn't mean everything.

TOMMY: The way you do it does. The things that happen to you. The light you give off.

JOE: Light?!

TOMMY: Oh, these things are too subtle for you, Joe. I've made some study of them. [Turns away]

JOE: Maybe all this studying's bad for you.

TOMMY: All I want to know is whether you felt the same thing she felt last night.

JOE: I felt fine. This is embarrassing! A man makes love to a woman. He doesn't talk it over with her husband!

TOMMY: I'm just trying to be honest.

JOE: You're a funny guy. Conscientious. What does it get you? Like this letter you're going to read— Say, is that what started the trouble?

TOMMY: Yes, it's an integral part of the trouble— things like that.

JOE: Well, what are we going to do? I mean now? I mean from now on?

TOMMY: From now on will work itself out. Right now you'd better go upstairs and comfort her. She'll be expecting you.

JOE: Oh, no. Not me! You ought to know more what to do right now. It's your house. She's still your wife.

TOMMY: She doesn't want to talk to me. She's just done that. But she oughtn't to be left alone right now. Well, don't be a big baby!!

JOE: It doesn't seem right somehow for me to go upstairs.

TOMMY: This is not a moment for cheap moralizing!

JOE: Well—good God Almighty! [*Goes upstairs*]

MICHAEL: [*Comes in door as* Tommy *sighs deeply*] What's the matter?

TOMMY: [*Sees him*] Oh! Why don't you knock? Never mind— [*Rises. Crosses down and paces; he glares upstairs, still has his glare when he turns back to* Michael]

MICHAEL: Well, I came back like you said.

TOMMY: *As* you said. Oh—never mind!

MICHAEL: Before you start in on me, Mr. Turner, please remember that I've been through a lot today. I can't stand much more.

TOMMY: [*Pats him on shoulder*] Thanks.

MICHAEL: [*Gloomily*] They'll probably do something to you—especially if we lose to Michigan. You know what Keller did the last time they beat us in a Homecoming Game? He ran the flag on his office building down to half mast.

TOMMY: [*Looking upstairs—distracted*] Don't worry about me.

MICHAEL: Well, I'm feeling better. I've put her out of my mind. It's ended as simply as that. [*Drops into chair*] There's a girl who could sit with you and talk about Shelley. Well, I'm glad I found out about women. [*Crash upstairs*] What was that?

TOMMY: I'm sure I don't know. What were you saying?

MICHAEL: I say Patricia knew things. She knew odd things like, "A Sonnet on Political Greatness": she quoted that one night. Wouldn't you think a girl like that had some social consciousness?

TOMMY: That's the sonnet that ends:
"Quelling the anarchy of hopes and fears,
    Being himself alone."

MICHAEL: Yes, but when an issue comes up and a man has to be himself alone, she reveals the true stature of her character and goes off to Hennick's with that football player. I saw them—right in the front window—drinking Seven-Up—he uses a straw.

TOMMY: Yes, but he's handsome. What is more, he whirls. He's a hunter. He comes home at night with meat slung over his shoulders, and you sit there drawing pictures on the wall of your cave.

MICHAEL: I see. Maybe I ought to sock him with a ball bat.

TOMMY: No. You are a civilized man, Michael. If the male animal in you doesn't like the full implications of that, he must nevertheless be swayed by Reason. You are not living in the days of King Arthur when you fought for your woman. Nowadays, the man and his wife and the other man talk it over. Quietly and calmly. They all go out to dinner together.

MICHAEL: Intellectually, Patricia is sleeping with that guy. I feel like going out tonight with the Hot Cha-cha.

TOMMY: With the what?

MICHAEL: It's a girl. They call her that. What if she was kicked out of the Pi Phi House? She's honest! She does what she believes in! And—well, Hot Cha-cha doesn't argue all the time anyway.

TOMMY: Look, Michael, hasn't she got a name? You don't call her *that*, do you?

MICHAEL: Marcia Gardner. They just call her—

TOMMY: Yes, you told me what they call her.

[*Slight pause*]

MICHAEL: [*Transformed*] Patricia's not coming to class when you read that letter. She's gone over to the Philistines— Oh, Mr. Turner, I wish I were like you! Middle-aged, settled down, happily married— [Tommy *takes off his glasses and peers across at* Michael] and through with all this hell you feel when you're young and in love.

TOMMY: [*Nettled*] Middle-aged?

MICHAEL: Yes, you know what Rupert Brooke says:
"That time when all is over,

[Tommy *writhes, turns his back*]

And love has turned to kindliness."
Is kindliness peaceful?

TOMMY: Don't ask me. [*Two quick crashes from upstairs bring* Tommy *to his feet as* Joe *enters down the stairs, looking worn and worried, his hair slightly disarranged. Sharply*] You look ruffled!

JOE: [*Just as sharply, but a bit absently*] What?
[*The two men look each other over*]

TOMMY: I say—what ruffled you?

JOE: Do we have to discuss these things in front of this boy?

MICHAEL: [*Rising*] I am not a boy.

TOMMY: This is Michael Barnes.

JOE: Oh, so you're the little boy that started all this! I want to tell you that you write too much, you have too much to say, you get too many people into too much trouble. You've not only got Tommy and Ellen involved, but me.

MICHAEL: I don't see how this concerns you, do you, Mr. Turner?

TOMMY: Yes.

MICHAEL: What?

JOE: [*Waving* Michael *out*] Goodbye!

MICHAEL: [*In wordless wrath at being treated like a child*] Oh!

[*Exits to garden*]

JOE: Oh, God, I wish I was in Pittsburgh!

TOMMY: [*Eagerly*] What happened?

JOE: Well, old man, I guess you're right. She was pretty bitter—about you. She picked up something you'd given her and threw it against the wall and broke it into a thousand pieces.

TOMMY: What was it?

JOE: I didn't see it till after she threw it.

TOMMY: Oh!

JOE: Every time she mentioned your name, she threw something. Kept me ducking.

TOMMY: [*Sadly*] I see. You want to marry Ellen, don't you?

JOE: Well, I always liked her, but I don't like to go through so much. [*Pause*] Are you sure you understand women?

TOMMY: Yes.

JOE: Well, when Ellen and I had that fight about the girl, she threw things on account of me, and Brenda thinks that meant she was in love with me. Now she throws things on account of *you*.

TOMMY: [*After an instant of hope*] In both instances, she threw them at *you*, didn't she?

JOE: [*Glumly*] Yeh, I guess so.

TOMMY: Well, there you are. What did she say when you left? What was she doing?

JOE: She was in a terrible state. I don't think she'll be able to go to the game. She may have a sick headache for days. What do you do then?

TOMMY: Get her a hot water bottle. [*Rises. Crossing to dining room*] Cleota!—Cleota!

CLEOTA: [*Off*] Yes, suh?

TOMMY: There's a hot water bottle out there in the—somewhere. [*Returning*] Fill it and bring it in, please.

CLEOTA: [*Off*] Yes, suh.

[*Tommy crosses and sits on sofa*]

JOE: [*Rises. Glances at wrist-watch*] I don't want to miss this game. I sort of wish Stalenkiwiecz wasn't laid up, don't you?

TOMMY: I haven't given it much thought one way or another.

JOE: Of course, Wierasocka's all right, but Stalenkiwiecz is a better pass-receiver.

TOMMY: Is he? Why?

JOE: I don't know why. He just is. "Why!" [*His pacing has carried him to door leading to garden. He remembers the vanishing cup and takes one more look*] 'Course they may not give Brenda a divorce.

TOMMY: I think they will.

JOE: I don't know.

CLEOTA: [*Enters with hot water bottle and folded towel. She hands them to* Tommy] Is you gotta pain?

TOMMY: No:—Oh, thank you.

[*Cleota exits*]

JOE: I don't suppose we ought to go and leave her.

TOMMY: [*Going to him with bottle*] Oh, I'm not going. Here. [*Hands him bottle and towel*]

JOE: [*Taking it. It burns his hand*] Ow!

TOMMY: Hold it by the end.

JOE: Won't this thing burn her?

TOMMY: [*Impatiently*] You wrap the towel around it.

JOE: You shouldn't stay here in the house alone with her, things being the way they are, should you?

TOMMY: Please don't worry about that!

JOE: [*Looking at the bottle*] I thought these things were different now than they used to be.

TOMMY: What do you mean, different?

JOE: I mean better looking—somehow.

[*There is a pause during which* Joe *tries to wrap the towel around the hot water bottle but various parts of it insist on remaining exposed. Finally* Tommy *crosses down to* Joe *angrily*]

TOMMY: Well, why don't you take it up to her?

ELLEN: [*Coming down the stairs*] It's time to get started, isn't it? [*The two men turn and stare at her,* Joe *still holding the hot water bottle. Ellen is utterly serene, with no sign of tears or hysterics. Washed and powdered, with her hat on, she stands at the foot of the stairs, putting on her gloves*] Do you realize what time it is? The Kellers will be waiting for us at Esther Baker's. We'll leave the car there and walk to the stadium. It's only a block. [*The men are still staring*] What are you doing with that thing, Joe?

TOMMY: He was going to lie down with it for a while.

JOE: I was not! Here! [*Tries to hand it to* Tommy]

TOMMY: I don't want it.

ELLEN: We've got to hurry, Joe. [*Takes the bottle from* Joe *and puts it on sofa*] Have you got the tickets?

JOE: Yeh, I've got them. [*Goes to radio*] Say, what number is the game on?

ELLEN: It's around 1210 on the dial. [*As* Joe *turns on radio and fiddles with dial—to* Tommy] Sure you won't go to the game?

TOMMY: Oh, no— [*With shy politeness*] How are you?

[*Dance music is heard on the radio.* Joe *keeps fiddling with dials trying to find the right station*]

ELLEN: Me? I'm fine.

[*Band music is heard on the radio*]

TOMMY: That's good.

JOE: [*After listening to music*] Well, it hasn't started yet—just music. Let's go. [*Gets Ellen's coat from hook*] This yours?

ELLEN: [*As he helps her into coat*] Yes.

JOE: Well, is it warm enough?

ELLEN: Yes. Oh, it's very warm.

TOMMY: No, it isn't.

CLEOTA: [*Enters with thermos. Gives it to* Tommy] Here's your thermos bottle, Mr. Turner.

TOMMY: Thank you. [*Takes it. Cleota exits*]

ELLEN: It's a very warm day, anyway, and we'll have the laprobe from the car.

TOMMY: Ellen. [*She crosses to him eagerly*] You forgot your thermos bottle— You'd better make a note of this, Joe. It gets cold in stadiums late in the afternoon. Ellen gets chilly sometimes, so she likes hot coffee.

[Joe *nods.* Ellen *who has been staring at* Tommy, *suddenly throws the thermos bottle on the floor, then rushes out, passing* Joe. Joe *looks after her, then comes back to face* Tommy *threateningly*]

JOE: Did you slap her?

TOMMY: No, I kicked her.

JOE: Well, you must have done something!

[*The radio, which has been playing band music changes to an* Announcer's Voice]

JOE: [*picks thermos bottle up from floor, puts it on table, listens to radio for a moment*] Here I get her all calmed down and you make her cry again. I see now what kind of a life she has here. I'm going to take her away from this and keep her away!

TOMMY: [*Shouting*] All right! Why don't you get started?

ANNOUNCER'S VOICE: [*Over band*] Well, here we are on Midwestern field on a mighty fine afternoon for a football game. [*Voice quieter*] It looks like the Big Day of the year, folks. Neither one of these great teams has lost a game. The Michigan squad is out on the field, warming up. They look even bigger than last year.—

JOE: [*Topping him*] Because I've got a few more things to say to you. First! [*As he takes a breath, the* Announcer's *voice comes through clearly*]

ANNOUNCER'S VOICE: Here comes the Scarlet Stampede now! [*There is a roar of cheering and the* Band's *music swells*]

JOE: [*Turns to radio, then in an agonized voice to* Tommy] My God, they're coming out on the field! We'll miss the kick-off! [*Turns and dashes out the door*]

[Tommy *stands looking after them as the curtain falls*]

SCENE 2: *The Turner living room, two hours later. It is growing dark outside*

Tommy *on settee and* Michael *in chair, wide apart, facing the audience, so that they have to turn their heads to see each other. Each has a glass in his hand, and they are sprawled in their seats, silent, brooding. The room shows indications of quite a bout: a bottle here, a few magazines flung there, a cushion on the floor.* Tommy *gets the Scotch bottle, pours a little into* Michael's *glass, emptying the bottle. He starts to pour some into his own glass, finds the bottle empty so pours some from* Michael's *glass into his own.*

Throws the bottle into waste-basket. There is a pause.

MICHAEL: He is probably still running with that ball—

TOMMY: [*Pause*] Quiet—quiet!— What time is it?

MICHAEL: [*Looks at wrist-watch, has trouble seeing it*] It's getting dark.

TOMMY: [*Pause*] Do you know the first law of human nature?

MICHAEL: Yes. Self-propagation.

TOMMY: Not any more. That's gone with last year's nightingale.

MICHAEL: Gone with last year's rose.

TOMMY: [*Slight pause*] Yes— Defense of the home— against prowlers and predatory—prowlers— Do you know what the tiger does when the sanctity of his home is jeopardized?

MICHAEL: I know. You told me. He talks it over with the other man, quietly and calmly.

TOMMY: He does not. I'm ashamed of you.

MICHAEL: I think we must have another drink— possibly.

TOMMY: All right. Hey! *Hey!* [*He is pleased with this shouting*] That's the way to talk to 'em. [*He puts back his head and yells*] Heyyy!!

[Cleota *enters: she turns on the lights*]

CLEOTA: Mistah Turner, what is it?

TOMMY: What do you want?—Oh, we should like to have something more to drink.

CLEOTA: [*Disgusted*] Dey ain' no more to drink. I'll make you all some black coffee.   [*Exits*]

TOMMY: [*Pause*] What'd she say?

MICHAEL: Nothing.

TOMMY: Where was I?

MICHAEL: Let's see—you were talking about tigers.

TOMMY: Oh, yes. But let us take the wolf. What does he do? I mean, when they come for his mate. He tears 'em to pieces. [*Illustrates*]

MICHAEL: But we are civilized men. Aren't we?

TOMMY: And so does the leopard, and the lion, and the hawk. They tear 'em to pieces. Without a word.

MICHAEL: You had it figured out the other way around a while ago. You said we should give up our women. [Tommy *stands, falters*] It's better sitting down.

[Tommy *sits*]

TOMMY: Let us say that the tiger wakes up one morning and finds that the wolf has come down on the fold. What does he—? Before I tell you what he does, I will tell you what he does not do.

MICHAEL: Yes, sir.

TOMMY: He does not expose everyone to a humiliating intellectual analysis. He comes out of his corner like this— [*Assumes awkward fighting pose, fists up—rises—sits quickly*] The bull elephant in him is aroused.

MICHAEL: [*Holds up forefinger*] Can't you stick to one animal?

TOMMY: No, that's my point. All animals are the same, including the human being. We are male animals, too.

MICHAEL: [*Stares at him, bewildered*] You said—

TOMMY: [*With emotion*] Even the penguin. He stands for no monkey-business where his mate is concerned. Swans have been known to drown Scotties who threatened their nests.

MICHAEL: [*After some thought*] I don't think so.

TOMMY: There it is, in us always, though it may be asleep. The male animal. The mate. When you are married long enough, you become a mate— Think of the sea lion for a minute.

MICHAEL: All right.

TOMMY: His mate is lying there in a corner of the cave on a bed of tender boughs or something. [*Turns to* Michael *for confirmation*] Is that all right, "tender boughs"?

MICHAEL: Yeah!

TOMMY: [*Imitating fish swimming with hand gestures*] Now, who comes swimming quietly in through the early morning mist, sleek and powerful, dancing and whirling and throwing kisses?

MICHAEL: Joe Ferguson.

TOMMY: And what do I do?

MICHAEL: You say, "Hello."

TOMMY: The sea lion knows better. He snarls. He gores. He roars with his antlers. He knows that love is a thing you do something about. He knows it is a thing that words can kill. You do something. You don't just sit there. [Michael *rises*] I don't mean you. [Michael *sits*] A woman likes a man who does something. All the male animals fight for the female, from the land crab to the bird of paradise. They don't just sit and talk. [Michael *is almost asleep*] They act. [*He has run down, now stops, almost asleep. His head jerks and wakens him. He removes glasses and blinks owlishly around*] I hope I have made all this clear to you. Are there any questions?

MICHAEL: [*Rousing*] No, sir.

[Ellen *and* Joe *enter.* Ellen *sees the disordered room, bottles on the floor,* Tommy's *and* Michael's *condition.* Michael *and* Tommy *rise*]

ELLEN: Tommy! What in the world have you been doing.

TOMMY: Drinking.

ELLEN: What for?

TOMMY: I was celebrating. Ellen, I have found myself. [*Sways for a second. Surveys* Joe] I know now what I have to do.

ELLEN: Yes, I know. We've been through all that.

TOMMY: I think perhaps you had better go away for a little while. [*Waves toward upstairs*]

ELLEN: I'm going. I'll be down in a minute, Joe. [*She slams upstairs*]

JOE: Boy, wasn't that some football game? I'm running Wally Myers for President.

TOMMY: [*Beckoning to* Michael] Come on.
[*He and* Michael *begin moving furniture to the sides of the room*]

JOE: [*Watches, slightly puzzled, making talk*] Yes, sir, some game, wasn't it? What did you think of Michigan going into the lead like that? If Wally hadn't snared that pass—

MICHAEL: We didn't listen to the game.

JOE: You didn't listen to the game?

MICHAEL: No, we turned it off. [*Gesture of turning off radio*]

TOMMY: The game didn't last all this time. Where have you been?

JOE: Well, we stopped in at President Cartwright's house.

TOMMY: What for?

JOE: 'Cause Ellen and I were making one last effort to get you out of this mess.

TOMMY: Ellen and you. You would know exactly what to do, wouldn't you?

JOE: You guys are pie-eyed!

TOMMY: [*To* Michael] Did you hear that?

MICHAEL: Yes.

JOE: What's the idea of moving all the furniture around like this?

TOMMY: I don't want you to break anything when you fall.

JOE: I'm not going to fall.

TOMMY: Yes, you are. [*Crosses to* Joe, *rolling up his sleeves*] I am going to knock you cold.
[Michael *sits arm of settee*]

JOE: [*Kindly*] Now, Tommy—let's sit down and talk this over.

TOMMY: [*Turning to* Michael] "Talk," he says, to a man of action. "Sit down," he says, to a tigress and her cubs!

JOE: How in the—? How did you guys get so cock-eyed? I wish Ellen'd hurry up. [*Crossing to dining-room door*] Cleota!

TOMMY: Don't call for help. I could take Cleota and you in the same ring!

JOE: Well, what's this all about?

TOMMY: You crept into this house to take Ellen away, didn't you? You thought it was the house of a professor who would talk and talk and talk—

JOE: And so you have! I came here to see a football game—

MICHAEL: That's a lie.

JOE: Why don't you go home?

MICHAEL: 'Cause I want to watch.

JOE: Well, there isn't going to be anything to watch.

TOMMY: [*Assuming fighter's pose*] Come on, put up your fists.

JOE: Get away from me, Tommy. [*Pushes* Tommy's *arm which pivots* Tommy *around so he faces* Michael] I'd break you in two, and I don't want to do that.

TOMMY: [*At first to* Michael, *then realizing he is facing the wrong way he turns to* Joe] Why don't you want to do that?

JOE: 'Cause how would it look if I came here and took Ellen and knocked you down on the way out?

MICHAEL: Maybe he's right. That's a point of honor, Mr. Turner.

TOMMY: Is it?

MICHAEL: But we could fight him about something else.

TOMMY: About what?

MICHAEL: He doesn't want you to read that letter.

TOMMY: [*To* Michael] That has nothing to do with this [*Realizes it has*] —oh, yes! Going to President Cartwright's house. Trying to make me lose my job.

JOE: Why would I?

TOMMY: So you could get Ellen.

JOE: Now, Tommy, listen—

TOMMY: Oh, yes! Now I see I'm going to have to knock you further than I had previously decided upon. Come out in the back yard. [*Pulls* Joe *who breaks away from* Tommy. Michael *pushes* Joe]

JOE: [*Turns and strides back to* Michael] Don't push me!

TOMMY: Hey!! [*He lunges at* Joe *with a badly aimed "haymaker"*]

JOE: [*Ducks and catches* Tommy *to keep him from falling*] Now look, if you do ever get in a fight, Tommy, don't lead with your right. It leaves you wide open.

TOMMY: Oh, does it?

ELLEN: [*Enters from stairs with suitcase, which she drops when she sees odd positions of belligerents*] Tommy! What's happened? What are you doing now?

TOMMY: Fighting.

[*The music of the band is heard in the distance. Through the following scene it grows louder to* Ellen's *exit, then dies away as the band goes around the corner and comes up again to medium for the end of the Scene*]

ELLEN: Fighting! What about?

MICHAEL: Penguins.

ELLEN: What!

JOE: [*Trying to explain*] Oh, it was all mixed up—about a lot of tigers and a cub. Tommy doesn't care what you and I are trying to do! He wants us to stay out of it!

ELLEN: [*To* Tommy] Oh, I see. That's what you were fighting about.

TOMMY: It wasn't about you.—Point of honor.

ELLEN: Oh yes, I see. You don't want me mixed up with anything. All right. You can pull the house down on top of you with your birds and letters and whiskey. Just let me get out of—what is all that racket?

JOE: [*Opens the door a crack—then closes it*] Oh, they're having a victory parade and they want me

to ride in that carriage with Wally Myers and the band.

TOMMY: You attract bands like flies, don't you!

ELLEN: [*As she starts for door*] Goodbye, Tommy! I'll be out in the car, Joe. Bring my bag, please! [*She slams out*]

[*The men look after her.* Joe *goes up to stair landing and gets bag and crosses to* Tommy]

JOE: You're getting me in deeper and deeper. I should'a taken a poke at you when I had the chance!

TOMMY: [*Rising. Mad*] Fine! Come out in the back yard!

JOE: I'm not coming out in the back yard! [Michael *pushes him. Very mad, he turns on* Michael] "Don't push me!" I said, I don't like to be pushed!

TOMMY: You said, "Don't lead with your right." [*He hits* Joe *on the nose with his left fist*]

JOE: [*Pinching bridge of nose and dropping suitcase on settee*] Ow-w-w! Now you've started my sinus trouble! All right, if you want a fight, you've got a fight! [*He pushes* Tommy *outside*]

MICHAEL: [*Pulls a chair up in front of the door and sits watching the fight off stage. He applauds its progress of blows*] Hit him! Hit him! [*Quotes softly*]
"And all the summer afternoon
    They hunted us and slew!
    But tomorrow—by the living God!"
Don't forget to lead with your right, Mr. Turner!—
That's right! Right in the eye!

[Cleota *enters to dining room door.* Wally *and* Patricia *come in laughing—see what's happening*]

PATRICIA: Michael!!

WALLY: What's going on here?

CLEOTA: Godamighty!

PATRICIA: Oh—Michael, stop them! Wally, stop them!

MICHAEL: [*Spreading arms wide across door*] No, don't stop them! Let Mr. Turner alone and he'll tear him to pieces!

[*Crash outside*]

WALLY: Get away from that door! [*He hurls* Michael *aside*]

PATRICIA: [*Runs and kneels beside* Michael] Michael! Michael!

ELLEN: [*Re-enters front door, calling*] Joe, are you coming? [*She sees* Michael *and* Patricia, *and looks around the room for* Tommy *and* Joe]

MICHAEL: [*With rapid fervor*]
"And many-a broken heart is here,"

ELLEN: What is it?

MICHAEL:
"And many-a broken head,
    But tomorrow—by the living God!—
    We'll try the game again!"

[*He tries to rise but collapses*]

[Joe *and* Wally *enter carrying the unconscious* Tommy. *They carry him to sofa*]
PATRICIA: [*Drops* Michael *in disgust*] Oh, Michael!
ELLEN: [*Screaming as she sees* Tommy *being carried in, out cold*] Tommy!!

[*The phone rings insistently*]

CLEOTA: [*Goes to the phone, picks up the receiver and in her usual way says*] Professah Turner's res-i-dence!

[*The curtain falls swiftly*]

Act III

SCENE: *The* Turner *living room. Same as Acts One and Two*
About noon, Monday.
The room is neat and orderly, but the flowers and other signs of festivity have been removed.
The stage is empty, but the phone bell is ringing. A moment later, the doorbell also begins to sound insistently. Cleota *enters from the dining room, wiping her hands on her apron, scuttles for an instant between the bells, picks up phone.*

CLEOTA: [*Into phone*] Stop ringin' dis thing both at once—Who?—Ah cain' heah you foh de ringin'. Hol' on— [*Putting down the receiver, she hurries to the front door and opens it cautiously, bracing herself to prevent a forced entrance. She speaks through the crack of the door*] Ah tol' you stop ringin' eve'ything. Ah'm heah, ain' I?
REPORTER'S VOICE: [*Off*] I'd like to see Mr. Turner.
CLEOTA: Is you a newspapah?
REPORTER'S VOICE: Yeh, I'm from the *Daily Journal.*
CLEOTA: He cain' see nobody—he's sick.
REPORTER: I know—but will he be up today? Is he going to his class?
CLEOTA: He ain' goin' nowheah. His haid huhts him. He's sick. Go 'way. [*She forces the door shut, bolts it, returns to the telephone*] Professah Turner's res-i-dence— *Daily* what?—You jus' *was* heah —No, Professah Turner ain' talkin' to nobody. He's sick in bed with his haid— No, he ain' goin' an' you ain' comin'. He ain't not talkin' 'cause he don' wanta talk. He jus' ain't talkin' cause he cain' talk. Goodbye. [*The bolted door is rattled from outside, then the doorbell begins to ring insistently.* Cleota *looks at the door angrily and starts for it. Looks back at the phone and mutters*] What's the matter with dis house? Will you please stop ringin' dat bell? [*As she opens door— sees* Patricia *and laughs, embarrassed*] Oh! It's YOU!
PATRICIA: [*Entering*] What's the matter?
CLEOTA: I thought it was that newspapah again. He just left.

PATRICIA: He didn't go—he's outside picketing. Where's my sister, Cleota?
CLEOTA: Upstairs. Miss Patricia, Ah wish Ah knew bettah what's goin' on heah.
PATRICIA: Never mind.
CLEOTA: Mr. Michael jus' left.
PATRICIA: Oh. Well, if Mr. Michael Barnes comes here again, *don't let him in!*
CLEOTA: No, ma'am.   [*Exits*]

[Ellen *comes from upstairs; she looks depressed*]
PATRICIA: Hello, Ellen! How's Tommy? Is he still asleep?
ELLEN: Yes, but he tosses around and mutters. The doctor says he can get up this afternoon.
PATRICIA: No concussion, then?
ELLEN: Yes, a little.
PATRICIA: [*Sits on settee*] I guess when anybody's as crazy as Tommy or Michael, a little concussion doesn't make any difference.
ELLEN: Did you get the butter?
PATRICIA: Oh, Lord, no—I'll go back.
ELLEN: Never mind. I need a little air.
PATRICIA: How's *your* head?
ELLEN: Oh, all right.
PATRICIA: Is it? Say, what is this second springtime you're all going through, anyway?
ELLEN: Tommy won't let me in on what he's really thinking about. He thinks I'm not smart enough to understand it—that's what it comes down to.
PATRICIA: Oh, a mental problem! I haven't been exactly listening at key-holes, but isn't there a Joe Something-or-other mixed up in this?
ELLEN: Oh, there's more to it than a fight about Joe.
PATRICIA: Pretty good one round here Saturday about Joe. You know Tommy was fighting for you in his mid-Victorian way, don't you?
ELLEN: Oh, but he was drunk. When he's sober he despises me. He thinks I'm a dimwit.
PATRICIA: But he wouldn't want you any other way than you are.
ELLEN: Thanks.
PATRICIA: [*Laughing*] I mean you're smart enough for Tommy and you know it, and he knows it.
ELLEN: I'm all mixed up. I want to go away some place where I can think.
PATRICIA: Look, this is a new century. You're not Diana of the Crossways or somebody.
ELLEN: Well, what do you want me to do—stay here when he doesn't want me?
PATRICIA: No, but if you're going away, go away with Joe. Tommy's certainly been throwing you at him. Why don't you take him up on it? See what happens.
ELLEN: Is this advice to the lovelorn? Do you think he would come running after me?
PATRICIA: Well, you've got to quit moping around and do something. I thought we Stanley women were supposed to have some resources. [*Rises;*

crossing to Ellen] Look, your great-grandmother chased her man all the way to Nebraska in a covered wagon.

ELLEN: Well, I'm not going to chase anybody anywhere! I'm going to talk this over with Tommy, fairly and squarely, face to face. [*Crosses to front door and opens it*]

PATRICIA: "Fairly and squarely!" How did your generation ever get through the 1920's?

ELLEN: [*Sadly*] We didn't.   [*She exits*]
                                         [*Patricia sits on sofa; sighs*]

TOMMY: [*Comes slowly down stairs. He wears terrycloth bathrobe, and has a wet turkish towel twisted about his head*] Hello, Pat!

PATRICIA: [*Rises. Worried*] Tommy—you shouldn't be up!

TOMMY: I'm all right. What day is this?

PATRICIA: Monday.

TOMMY: Cleota—Cleota! [*To Patricia*] Can I take this thing off?

PATRICIA: You're not supposed to. You ought to lie down.

TOMMY: [*Sits chair*] I'll just lean back. [*Does so. Winces*] No—I guess I won't.

CLEOTA: [*Appears in dining-room door. Sees Tommy*] Mistah Turner—is you up?

TOMMY: Yes, I'm up. Cleota, don't let anyone in this house except Mr. Michael Barnes.
                [*Patricia shakes her head violently "No" to Cleota from above Tommy*]

CLEOTA: Yessuh—Ah do de best Ah can. [*Exits*]

TOMMY: Where's Ellen?

PATRICIA: She went out to [*Teasing*]— to get the transfer man—for her trunk.

TOMMY: She's going away?

PATRICIA: Oh, no. She just likes to call on transfer men. Didn't you know that?

TOMMY: I can't stand irony so early in the day, Patricia.

PATRICIA: You're all right now, you see. She wouldn't go before. I don't know why.

TOMMY: You ought to know why. Your sister wouldn't walk out on anybody when he's down—even when he's down with delirium tremens.

PATRICIA: You didn't have D.T.'s. You had concussion.

TOMMY: Seemed more like D.T.'s.

PATRICIA: You don't know very much about my little sister, do you?

TOMMY: I know a lot more than I did last Friday. [*Rises. Crossing to sofa*] I think I will lie down.

PATRICIA: Why do you have to make everything as hard as you can? [*Tommy winces with pain*] Do you want another cold towel?

TOMMY: No, thanks. [*Phone rings. Lies back on sofa*] Oh, those bells!!

PATRICIA: [*Answering phone*] Yes?—Who? No, Michael Barnes isn't here.

TOMMY: He was here and he's coming back.

PATRICIA: This is Patricia Stanley— Yes— Yes— I'll be very glad to tell him to call you—if I see him. Goodbye! [*Slams receiver down*] That was Hot Cha-cha Gardner.

TOMMY: Oh-oh! Why did she call here?

PATRICIA: She said they told her Michael was on his way here, but obviously she just called for my benefit— So that's where he went Saturday night! You had that Hot—that Miss Gardner in some of your classes; do you remember her?

TOMMY: [*Reflectively*] I don't know. What does she look like?

PATRICIA: Well, she—doesn't wear any— [*Gestures*]

TOMMY: I only had her in Wordsworth.

PATRICIA: Calling up here! [*There is a knock at the door; Patricia smiles grimly. She goes and opens the door. Michael steps in; he is taken aback at seeing Patricia*] Good-morning, Michael! Come in.

TOMMY: Yes, come in, Michael. [*Pantomimes "telephone" for Michael's benefit*]

MICHAEL: [*Comes down a little nervously and stands near Tommy*] I got the car for you— Feel better now that you're up? [*Doesn't get the pantomime*]

TOMMY: [*Pantomiming*] Yes, much better. How do you feel?

MICHAEL: I feel all right.

TOMMY: That's good. [*Mimics Patricia's gesture*]
                [*Michael doesn't get it. Looks inside his coat to see what's wrong. Patricia turns and catches pantomime*]

PATRICIA: If you'll excuse me—

MICHAEL: Oh, Pat, wait!—I—could I talk to you for a minute? Couldn't we go outside there and—

PATRICIA: [*Proud and angry*] No, we couldn't go outside there. Is it anything you're ashamed to say in front of Tommy?

MICHAEL: [*Stiffening*] No. No, I'm not. Only— Well, I don't want to get off on the wrong foot again. I'm sorry I got so mad Saturday. I said things and did things that—

PATRICIA: You certainly did.

MICHAEL: [*Shouting*] Well, I'm sorry, and— [*Then, reasonably*] Oh, Pat, you ought to be able to see this my way. We just lost our tempers and—well— Mr. Turner and I are in a jam. I think you ought to—well—make an effort to understand what we're trying to do and stand by us—that is, if you care anything about me at all.

PATRICIA: [*With false sweetness*] Oh, I certainly do. I've been standing by—taking messages for you— phone calls. I'm so glad we had this nice talk. [*Shakes his hand*] And before you go, be sure to call [*Dropping her sweetness, she yells:*] Maple 4307. [*Patricia flounces out door*]

MICHAEL: [*Looking after her*] Maple 430— [*Crossing to Tommy*] Did The Cha-cha call here?

TOMMY: That's what I was trying to tell you. Patricia answered the phone. The—Chow-chow—snapped right in her face.

MICHAEL: And I didn't even *do* anything. [*Sits on sofa*] I hope. [*Looks up miserably*]

TOMMY: Michael, you're making me nervous.

MICHAEL: Will you be able to go to the faculty meeting tonight?

TOMMY: I'll be there.

MICHAEL: They'll be out to get you—I know this is all my fault, Mr. Turner.

TOMMY: Yes, you're certainly the man that lighted the match.

MICHAEL: I just came from the President's office; he flayed me alive.

TOMMY: Are you kicked out?

MICHAEL: Suspended.

TOMMY: Michael, tell me— Are you really a Communist?

MICHAEL: Me?—No—I only know one guy who is. I'm—well, I guess I'm an unconfused liberal. I think I'll go to Stringfellow Barr's school in Annapolis and read the classics.

TOMMY: I wonder where I'll go?

[Ellen *enters front door with parcel*]

ELLEN: Good morning, Michael.

MICHAEL: [*Rises*] Hello, Mrs. Turner!

ELLEN: [*Sees* Tommy] Good morning, Tommy— [*Crossing to dining-room door. Calls*] Cleota—

TOMMY: Good morning.

[Cleota *enters*]

ELLEN: Here's the butter, Cleota. Will you make Mr. Turner a cup of tea? [*Turns back to him*] Would you like a hard-boiled egg?

TOMMY: No, thanks. Nothing hard. My teeth hurt.
[*Cleota exits*]

ELLEN: Are you waiting for Patricia, Michael?

MICHAEL: I saw her. I'm leaving town, Mrs. Turner.

ELLEN: I'm awfully sorry, Michael.

WALLY'S VOICE: [*Off-stage*] Pat! Oh, Pat!

ELLEN: Come in, Wally. [Wally *comes in from garden*] Patricia's gone out somewhere.

WALLY: Oh, I see. [*To* Michael] You waiting for her?

MICHAEL: That's none of your business. Why?

WALLY: [*Lowers his voice*] I know what you did Saturday night, that's why. Well, thanks, Mrs. Turner. I just cut across the back way. I'll walk on down to the house. [*Starts out*]

MICHAEL: [*Stops him*] I think I'll walk along. I want to talk to you.

WALLY: You don't have to.

MICHAEL: If I didn't have to, I wouldn't do it. I'm no masochist.

WALLY: [*Stares after him blankly, then follows, furious*] You don't have to use words like that in front of ladies.

MICHAEL: I'll be back in time to drive you to class, Mr. Turner. [*Turns and* Wally *bumps into him.* Michael *pushes* Wally *out*]

TOMMY: Thanks.

ELLEN: [*Takes tea from* Cleota *who has entered with cup on tray*] Here's your tea.
[Cleota *goes out*]

TOMMY: Thanks.

ELLEN: [*With some constraint*] How do you feel?

TOMMY: Very strange.

ELLEN: Is everything clear to you now?

TOMMY: [*Stirs tea*] Clear in the center. It's kind of fuzzy around the edges.

ELLEN: I hope it's clear enough to give me a chance to say something without your going off on one of your literary tangents.

TOMMY: I don't do that.

ELLEN: I know you think I'm not very bright or something, [Tommy *tries to demur, but she continues*] but you must realize that you got me all mixed up Friday and that you were even less helpful Saturday.

TOMMY: That wasn't me, Saturday. That was a drunken sea lion.

ELLEN: I rather liked you as a sea lion.

TOMMY: Yes, I must have been very funny. Did you ever read Hodgson's poem, "The Bull"?

ELLEN: Oh, Tommy!

TOMMY: It's the story of the defeated male. There is no defeat that can be quite so complete.

ELLEN: You wouldn't admit that this defeat was on account of— No, it has to be something out of a book.

TOMMY: When the bull's head is in the dust, life goes on and leaves him there; it's a psychological fact. The poets understand these things.

ELLEN: And all the cows react the same way? As if they were reading instructions from a blackboard? Oh, Tommy, listen to me—
[*Doorbell rings*]

TOMMY: The point is, I don't want any pity.

CLEOTA: [*Entering from dining room*] Miz Turner; Miz Turner! It's dat prize-fightah. I seen him from de windah.

[Ellen *admits* Joe, *who comes in without his old bounce; he is worried and restless*]

ELLEN: Hello, Joe!

JOE: Hello. [*Awkwardly to* Tommy] Hello.

TOMMY: Hello!

JOE: I'm sorry, Tommy. I didn't hit you hard. You slipped and hit your head on a bench.

TOMMY: Yeh, I know. What's the matter with your hand?

JOE: You kinda bit me. Ed's out in the car. We just chased a reporter away hanging around out there.

ELLEN: Well, don't let any reporters in, Cleota.

TOMMY: And don't let Keller in.
[Cleota *nods and exits*]

JOE: [*Indicating wet towel*] Do you have to keep that thing on?

TOMMY: No, I just do it because I like it.
[*Throws down towel*]

JOE: Could I have a little slug of something? I—

ELLEN: Certainly! Scotch?

JOE: Yeh, fine. [Ellen *exits. There is a pause. Joe still wonders about the vanished cup*] I got the galloping jumps. I can use a little drink. Haven't slept for two nights.

TOMMY: Worrying about something?

JOE: [*Turns to Tommy*] Yeh, worrying about something— And my cold's worse.

TOMMY: Want some Kleenex.

JOE: [*Irritated*] No, I don't want some Kleenex. Darn reporters been bothering me, too.

TOMMY: What do they want with you?

JOE: Oh, they wanted me to pick an All-American team.

TOMMY: [*Incredulously—almost*] Did you?

JOE: Yeh. Kinda took my mind off things.

TOMMY: [*Sarcastically*] Who'd you pick for right guard?

JOE: Shulig—Kansas State Teachers'. [*Crossing to Tommy*] Look, Tommy, where the hell do we all stand now? [Tommy *picks up towel, presses it to his head again*] Does that kinda throb?

TOMMY: No.

JOE: Well, I wanta know where we all stand.

TOMMY: Oh, let it alone, Joe. It'll work out. You and I can handle this. I don't want Ellen worried about details now. She's got enough trouble with me— sitting around the house looking like a hot-oil shampoo—

ELLEN: [*Enters with bottle of Scotch. She pours a drink of straight Scotch at table*] There's been more drinking in this house in the last two days than we've done in ten years.

[Joe *takes off coat, puts it on chair; sits down*]

TOMMY: [*After a pause*] Ellen, Joe picked Shulig of Kansas State Teachers' for right guard, on his All-American. Isn't that nice?

JOE: [*Reminiscently*] It was kinda hard choosing between him and Feldkamp of Western Reserve. Both big and fast.

ELLEN: [*Crossing with drink*] Here you are, dear— [*She is coolly oblivious of* Tommy's *hand which he puts out for drink; goes on to* Joe, *who doesn't realize she means him*] Dear. [*He looks up at her with a start—looks at* Tommy—*takes drink*]

TOMMY: I don't want any.

JOE: Say, have you got a Pennsylvania time-table around?

ELLEN: Where are you going, Joe?

JOE: Well, I've got to be in Washington tomorrow.

ELLEN: That's going to rush me.

JOE: What do you mean?

ELLEN: [*Crossing above settee*] Well, Joe, I thought you and I might start out late this afternoon and go as far as that little Inn at Granville tonight. Just for a start.

TOMMY: [*Rises*] What did you say?

ELLEN: [*To* Joe] I think it's the nicest place around here. Don't you?

JOE: I—I—eh— Could I have a little more Scotch? [*Rises; crosses and gets another drink*]

ELLEN: I don't want you to get drunk, Joe.

JOE: I'll be all right—I'll be all right. What time is it?

TOMMY: Never mind what time it is. [*Crossing to* Ellen] Would you mind explaining this a little better.

ELLEN: I'll try to make it as clear as I can for both of you. I simply have to make a fresh start now, Tommy. You understand women; you must see that. I can't stay here now. You've made your plans, and now I have to make mine.

TOMMY: Yes—but not like this—not running off to Granville!

ELLEN: All right, if you're afraid of a scandal, we'll go farther away. Put Granville out of your mind, then. We'll go directly to Pittsburgh.

JOE: Huh?

ELLEN: It's a very big town. Nobody need know anything about it.

JOE: About what?

ELLEN: About us. About our eloping together.

[*Both men stop cold*]

TOMMY: Ellen!

JOE: [*Desperately*] But you see—I don't live in Pittsburgh. [*He makes a large circular gesture*] I live in Sewickley. [*Gesture—small*] And my boss lives there too. And my mother. My mother's not very well. My mother—

TOMMY: Oh, you and your mother!

JOE: Besides, it's a Presbyterian town.

ELLEN: You're not being very gallant, Joe.

TOMMY: No. Are you trying to get out of this?

JOE: No, but I come from a long line of married people! And besides, I'm not going to Pittsburgh directly. I've got to go to Washington, and that's one place I couldn't take you, Ellen!

TOMMY: You'll take her any place she wants to go, but she's not going any place!

ELLEN: Oh, yes, I am!

ED: [*There is a loud knock, and Ed Keller enters*] I can't sit out in that car all day, you know.

JOE: Oh, I'm sorry, Ed, but—jees, I forgot all about you. [Joe *turns to* Tommy] I persuaded Ed to come over and talk to you before this thing gets too bad. [*Leads Ed to* Tommy]

TOMMY: It couldn't get any worse!

JOE: I mean about the trustees.

TOMMY: Let the trustees take care of themselves. We have troubles of our own.

ED: You'll find out this is your trouble. Is he able to talk?

JOE: Lord, yes!

ED: [*To* Tommy] Well, then, listen. We just had a trustees' meeting in the President's office. Michael

Barnes is out, and you're on your way out. You'll be asked to resign tonight.

ELLEN: [*Rising*] Oh, Tommy!

JOE: Ed's trying to help him while there's still time. After tonight, it will be too late.

TOMMY: What do you care what happens tonight? You won't be here. You'll be in Granville or somewhere.

ED: What're you going to be doing in Granville?

TOMMY: Please don't ask personal questions.

ELLEN: Do you mind if I stay a little while, Tommy?

TOMMY: [*Angrily*] Why shouldn't you stay? It's your house.

ED: Sit down, Ellen. [*She sits down. To Tommy*] There's just one thing you can do: come out with a statement to the papers quick. Say you were sick. Say you didn't know anything about Barnes' editorial. You think it's an outrage. You're not going to read this Vanzetti thing, and you think Barnes is getting what he deserves. That's the only thing that'll save your neck.

ELLEN: [*Rises*] Tommy wouldn't say that about Michael, Ed, and you shouldn't ask him to.

TOMMY: Thank you.

ED: All right, then! That's all I had to say. Goodbye! This is on your own head.

ELLEN: Ed! Just a minute, please. [*Crossing to Tommy*] I know that reading this letter must mean something to you, Tommy. Something none of us can quite understand. I wish I could. It might help me to understand a lot of other things, when I can get away where I can think.

TOMMY: Such as what?

ELLEN: Such as what is important to you. What you've been fighting for. Whether it's something you really believe in and love, or just your own selfish pride. I think you got into this just because you were mad at me. And that's ridiculous, because now you don't care what I do or say about it. You're out of that.

ED: [*To Joe*] I don't see what she's talking about. [*Joe motions him to be quiet*]

TOMMY: All right, I'll try to explain what it means to me. Perhaps originally pride had something to do with this. And jealousy.

ELLEN: And stubbornness—

TOMMY: And—please. I am trying to say that—now —I am not fighting about you and me at all. This is bigger than you and me or any of us.

ELLEN: Is it?

ED: [*Ironically*] It must be a masterpiece. That letter must be quite a nice piece of propaganda.

TOMMY: Why don't you read it and find out?

ED: I don't read things like that.

TOMMY: You don't even know what you're objecting to.

JOE: Well, Tommy, why don't you read the letter to us, and let us see what it is?

TOMMY: I'll be glad to read it to you, but I'll read it to my class too. [*Crosses to bookcase*]

ED: You don't have to read it to me. I know what kind of stuff it is.

[*The front door bursts open, and* Patricia *backs in, leaving the door open.* Wally *is outside. They talk in excited undertones*]

PATRICIA: But I can't go with you now! I told you I've got to wait here and see what Tommy's going to do.

WALLY: But you're not going to the class! You said you're not going!

PATRICIA: I'm not! I just want to know!

WALLY: I'll bet you *are* going! You're waiting here for Michael to go with you!

PATRICIA: Oh, go away! [*Sees others*] Oh—I'm sorry.

ED: What's this now?

JOE: [*Grinning*] Hey, Pat, you better think twice before you scrap with Wally here. [*Tommy goes upstairs for book*] He's coming in with me at Pittsburgh next year.

WALLY: A lot she cares about Pittsburgh! I run sixty-two yards through Michigan and all she wants is to listen to Mike Barnes talk about his love life.

ED: She does?

ELLEN: [*Trying to stop him*] Wally, how's Stalenkiwiecz?

WALLY: He's much better. [*Crossing to* Patricia] If you knew what I know about that guy Barnes—

PATRICIA: I know what you're hinting at! And what if he did? It only shows what an intense person Michael is. I know that no matter what he did, he was thinking of me.

WALLY: That's disgusting!

PATRICIA: And aren't you a little bit disgusting to mention it? I thought *men* had some loyalty! [*She goes out*]

WALLY: [*Following her out*] Now, listen here— Do you know what he did?—I'll tell you what he did.

ED: What kind of a house is this?

[*As they go out the lower door,* Damon, *carrying an umbrella, walks quietly in the open front door and looks around, as* Tommy *comes downstairs with an open book in his hand*]

TOMMY: All right, here it is. Now sit down—or stand up—but listen!—Oh, come in, Doctor Damon. You're just in time.

DAMON: In time for what? [*Sees them*] Has the Inquisition moved its headquarters?

TOMMY: I'm just going to read the Inquisition a letter from one of its victims.

ED: That's about enough of that.

DAMON: Gentlemen, gentlemen— This may not be wise, Thomas.

TOMMY: It may not be wise, but it's necessary. I think you'll have to take a stand, too, Doctor Damon.

DAMON: I hope not. [*Sits on settee*]

[*Ellen sits at opposite side of room*]

TOMMY: So did I hope not. I didn't start out to lead a crusade. I simply mentioned one day that I meant to read to my class three letters by men whose profession was not literature, but who had something sincere to say. Once I had declared that very harmless intention, the world began to shake, great institutions trembled, and football players descended upon me and my wife. I realized then that I was doing something important.

ED: [*Sarcastically*] You make it sound mighty innocent. Reading Lincoln and General Sherman—and Vanzetti. What was the reason you gave for picking out Vanzetti?

TOMMY: [*Crosses to Ed*] Originally I chose him to show that broken English can sometimes be very moving and eloquent, but now—

ED: We wouldn't object if this was just a case of broken English—it's more than that.

TOMMY: Yes, you've made it more than that.

ED: Vanzetti was an anarchist! He was executed for murder.

TOMMY: He was accused of murder, but thousands of people believe he was executed simply because of the ideas he believed in.

ED: That's a dangerous thing to bring up.

TOMMY: [*Getting really mad*] No, it's a dangerous thing to keep down. I'm fighting for a teacher's rights. But if you want to make it political, all right! You can't suppress ideas because you don't like them—not in this country—not yet. [*Crossing to Damon*] This is a university! It's our business to bring what light we can into this muddled world—to try to follow truth!

DAMON: You may be right, Thomas, but I wish you would make an effort not to—uh—uh—intone.

TOMMY: I'm not intoning—I'm yelling! Don't you see this isn't about Vanzetti. This is about us! If I can't read this letter today, tomorrow none of us will be able to teach anything except what Mr. Keller here and the Legislature permit us to teach. Can't you see what that leads to—what it has led to in other places? We're holding the last fortress of free thought, and if we surrender to prejudice and dictation, we're cowards.

ELLEN: Tommy, no matter how deeply you feel about this, what can you *do*? What can any one man do? Except to lose everything—

TOMMY: I have very little more to lose. And I can't tell you what I hope to gain. I can't answer that. I only know that I have to do it.

[*Patricia appears in doorway, stops and listens*]

DAMON: May we hear the letter—in a slightly calmer mood, perhaps?

TOMMY: Yes, sir— This may disappoint you a little, Mr. Keller. It isn't inflammatory, so it may make you feel a little silly. At least, I hope so— [*He holds up the book, pauses. Ed and Joe get set in their seats*] Vanzetti wrote this in April, 1927, after he was sentenced to die. It has been printed in many newspapers. It appears in this book. You could destroy every printed copy of it, but it would not die out of the language, because a great many people know it by heart. [*He reads, hardly referring to the book, watching them*] "If it had not been for these thing, I might have live out my life talking at street corners to scorning men. I might have die, unmarked, unknown, a failure. Now we are not a failure. Never in our full life could we hope to do so much work for tolerance, for Justice, for man's understanding of man, as now we do by accident. Our words—our lives—our pain—nothing! The taking of our lives—the lives of a good shoemaker and a poor fish-peddler—all! That last moment belongs to us—that agony is our triumph!" [*He closes the book. There is silence for a moment*] Well, that's it— [*Crosses and puts book on table*]

[*Keller is puzzled; Ellen, who has been moved by the letter, looks up in surprise, meets Tommy's eyes, then drops hers*]

JOE: [*Uncomfortably*] Well, that isn't so bad! That isn't a bad letter.

ED: Is that all of it?

TOMMY: Yes, that's all.

JOE: [*Rises*] Maybe Tommy's right. I don't see that it would do so much harm.

ED: [*Slowly*] Yes, it will. If he reads this letter to his class he'll get a lot of those kids worried about that man. Make socialists out of 'em.

JOE: It's got me worried already.

ED: [*Rises*] No— I won't have it— You fellows are trying to defy the authority of the trustees. You say you're going to take a stand. Well, we've *taken* a stand. I wouldn't care if that letter were by Alexander Hamilton.

TOMMY: [*Crossing to Ed*] Neither would I. The principle is exactly the same.

JOE: [*Speaking hopefully*] Well, then, read something else. Why can't you read Hoover?

ED: Yeah.

JOE: He writes a lot of stuff—a lot of good stuff in his book.

TOMMY: Hoover can't write as well as Vanzetti.

ED: [*Winces*] That's a terrible thing to say. You'll get in trouble saying things like that.

TOMMY: Very likely.

JOE: Ed, look—can't we compromise somehow? Seems a shame that a little thing like this should—

ELLEN: [*Rises*] It isn't little! Joe, you have some influence around here.

TOMMY: I can fight my own battles, Ellen.

ELLEN: Can't I say anything any more—not even on your side?

ED: All right, Turner, I've heard the letter and—

TOMMY: [*Answering* Ellen] Not out of a sense of self-sacrifice or something.

ED: What?

ELLEN: Oh, yes, you always know—

ED: [*To* Joe] Do we always have to have women butting into this?

JOE: Ellen isn't women. She's Tommy's wife.

ELLEN: No, I'm not—

ED: No, Turner, it comes to this— [*Turns to* Ellen] You're not what? Do you mean to stand there and tell me you two are not—

TOMMY: Will you please not ask personal questions?

ED: [*Turns to* Tommy] No. *We can't have that in this school!*

ELLEN: It's Joe and I who are going away together.

ED: [*To* Tommy] Yeh, will you let me— [*Turns to* Ellen] You and Joe are going to what! [*Crosses to* Joe] What the—what is going on here anyway?

JOE: Now don't look at me!

ED: You can't go away with Ellen!

JOE: I didn't say—

ELLEN: [*Sits down*] We might as well tell him now. I'm going to Pittsburgh with Joe.

ED: [*Crossing back to* Ellen] Why, you can't do that! Why, the newspapers would make Midwestern University look like some kind of a honkytonk or something. This is worse than that damn letter!

TOMMY: Aren't you getting off the subject?

ED: No! What kind of a woman are you?

TOMMY: [*Crossing to* Ed] You come out in the back yard! Right out in the back yard!

JOE: Be careful, Ed!

ELLEN: No more fights please!

DAMON: [*Rises*] I think I shall get a breath of fresh air. [*Goes to front door, opens it*]

ELLEN: Well, I can't stay *here* now.

JOE: Look, Ed, you don't understand. You got things all mixed up.

ED: Well, I've got this much straight—if we can keep sex out of this for a minute. I came here to say to you that if you read this letter today you're out of this university tomorrow! You take this stand and you stand alone!

DAMON: [*Crossing to* Ed] Mr. Keller, for forty-two years I have followed a policy of appeasement. I might say I have been kicked around in this institution by one Edward K. Keller after another—

ED: There is only one Edward K. Keller.

DAMON: There has always been at least one. But there is an increasing element in the faculty which resents your attitude toward any teacher who raises his voice or so much as clears his throat. I warn you that if you persist in persecuting Thomas Turner, you will have a fight on your hands, my friend.

ED: Do you think that Bryson and Kressinger and I are afraid of a few dissatisfied book-worms who work for twenty-five hundred a year?

DAMON: [*Furious*] These men are not malcontents! Some of them are distinguished scholars who have made this University what it is!

ED: They've made it what it is! What about me? Who's getting this new stadium? Who brought Coach Sprague here from Southern Methodist?

JOE: He means that this thing is bigger than stadiums and coaches.

ED: Nothing's bigger than the new stadium.

JOE: Now we've all had a bad week-end around here, and you're not helping any.

ED: Do you think I've had a good week-end!

[Michael *and* Nutsy *enter front door with petition*]

MICHAEL: Come in, Nutsy.

ED: Now what!

MICHAEL: We're circulating petitions for Mr. Turner. Show 'em, Nutsy.

NUTSY: This one's just from 14th Avenue and the Athletic house. [*Turns to* Tommy] We've got three hundred and fifty-seven names.

DAMON: We want no student insurrections!

JOE: Let me see that thing: [*Takes petition from* Nutsy]

ED: You're wasting your time with that handful of names. Turner will be out tomorrow and Barnes is on his way home now.

MICHAEL: I'm not on my way home yet, sir.

ED: *Ohhh!* So you're Barnes! So you're the little puppy that called me a Fascist!

PATRICIA: [*Rises; comes between* Ed *and* Michael. *To* Ed] Well, the way you're treating everybody, I think you *are* a Fascist!

ELLEN: Patricia!

TOMMY: Let her alone.

ELLEN: Oh, she can stand up for Michael, but I can't stand up for you! Is that it?

TOMMY: This is—ah—different.

ED: Do I have to stand here and be insulted by every sixteen-year-old child that comes into this room?

PATRICIA: I'm not sixteen, I'm nineteen!

MICHAEL: She'll soon be twenty.

ED: [*To* Michael] Why don't *you* get packing?

MICHAEL: You don't need to worry about me. I'll be far away from here by tomorrow. Come on, Nutsy!
[Nutsy *starts out*, Michael *following*]

PATRICIA: [*Starts after him*] If you throw him out, I'm going with him! Wait, Michael!

ED: Are you married to this little radical?

PATRICIA: You don't have to be married to somebody to go away with him—do you, Ellen?   [*Exits*]
[Michael *follows her out*]

DAMON: I think I shall go home, have my Ovaltine and lie down. [*Exit, closing door*]

ED: He'll need his Ovaltine.

JOE: [*Crossing to* Ed] Say, Ed, look! This thing has been signed by Stalenkiwiecz and Wierasocka.

ED: [*Crossing to* Joe] What! I don't believe it. [*Takes petition, looks at it*]

JOE: Ed, you ought to have some respect for men like Dean Damon and Stalenkiwiecz and Wierasocka.

ED: They can't do this to me! Two of the biggest men in the university signing the Red petition! You, the greatest half-back we ever had, running away with a woman! Why—they'll never ask us to the Rose Bowl now!

TOMMY: What is the Rose Bowl?

ED: [Thrusts petition into Joe's hand] I'm getting out of this house! Coming, Joe?

JOE: No.

ED: You can't depend on anybody! I've a damn good notion to resign from the board of trustees. [To Tommy] But I'll kick you out if it's the last thing I do.

TOMMY: Just to make things even—I'll kick you out. Here's your hat. [Gives him Joe's derby]

ED: We'll see! [Puts on hat and stomps out]

JOE: Hey, that's my hat!

TOMMY: Well, get another one. [Closes door] Well, that's that.

[They look at each other]

JOE: Yeh, that's that. [Pause] Well, I s'pose Ed will never speak to me again.

TOMMY: I have to go to class. I'll be late. [Starts for stairs]

ELLEN: [Appealingly to Tommy] Tommy—I—

TOMMY: I know. I know.

ELLEN: You know what?

TOMMY: I know what you're going to say—but I don't want substitutes. I don't want loyalty.

[Ellen turns away]

JOE: What's the matter with that?

TOMMY: I just don't want Ellen standing by like a Red Cross nurse because she knows I'm in trouble.

JOE: I don't know whether you need a nurse or a psychoanalyst!

ELLEN: I think he's analyzed it very well himself. It isn't because you think I don't care, it's because you don't.

TOMMY: [Almost bursting] I thought we could settle this quietly and calmly.

ELLEN: Quietly and calmly! Oh, Lord! [Picks up large ashtray—smashes it on floor]

TOMMY: Now, don't do that! I can throw things, too! [Picks up cup]

ELLEN: No, you can't—you haven't got enough blood in you!

[Tommy glares at her, puts cup down coldly—suddenly snatches it and crashes it into fireplace—reaches for saucer]

JOE: [Leaps for Tommy—grabs saucer from him] Now wait—let me handle this. I don't throw things— I just want to say that I came to this city to see a football game.

ELLEN: [Crossing to Joe] Oh, no, you didn't! You came for me. You haven't been here for a ball-game in ten years. You wait till Brenda and you are separated, then you come for me!

JOE: Oh, hell! [Throws saucer in fireplace then wilts as he realizes this household has affected him, too]

TOMMY: [Desperately insisting upon his own doom] That's very smart, Ellen. That's very penetrating. That's all I wanted to know. [To Joe] Subconsciously, you came here for Ellen, so don't try to deny it.

JOE: I don't do things subconsciously! You're full of childish explanations of everything that comes up!

TOMMY: And you're full of psychological evasions!

ELLEN: [Screaming] Oh, shut up! Both of you! I am not going to listen to any more of this! [Runs upstairs]

[Tommy sits sofa—there is a long pause]

JOE: Well I'll tell you one thing! I'm not going upstairs this time! If you'd explained what you were standing for on Saturday, things would have cleared up around here and I'd be in Washington now, talking to Ickes.

TOMMY: Are you still in love with Norma?

JOE: Norma who?

TOMMY: Your wife.

JOE: My wife's name is Brenda. And you're not going to talk her over with me. I can't be alone with you two minutes and have any private life left!

ELLEN'S VOICE: [Off upstairs] Tommy! What did you do with my nail file???!

JOE: Oh, Lord—she sounds worse than last Saturday.

TOMMY: I haven't got it. [He absently goes through a pocket, finds it, brings it out] Oh! Yeh, I've got it. [He starts filing a nail]

JOE: I've gone through more hell here in three days than I've had with Phyllis in three years.

TOMMY: Yeh! [Rising] Phyllis? Who is Phyllis? Are you carrying on with some other woman in Pittsburgh? You can't do this.

JOE: [Springing to his feet] I'm not carrying on with anybody. Phyllis is my secretary and there's nothing between us!

TOMMY: Then why did you say you've been going through hell for three years?

JOE: [Yelling] 'Cause you get me all balled up.

[Ellen comes downstairs with bag—sets it down]

TOMMY: Here— [Hands her nail file] You didn't pack anything!

ELLEN: [Puts file in purse] I've been packed for three days!

TOMMY: Well, you can't go with just one suitcase— There isn't much here, but—there're the books. They're yours. Most of them I gave to you. [Turns away]

ELLEN: Can I have "The Shropshire Lad"? Isn't that the one that has: [Quotes]
    "And now the fancy passes by—"

TOMMY: [Finds book; brings it to her]
    "And nothing will remain—"

MICHAEL: [Sticks his head in front door] You've just five minutes to get to your class, Mr. Turner. We'll wait for you in the car.

TOMMY: Thanks! [Michael exits, closing door] Well, so long, Joe. I know you'll get Ellen a place of her own for a while anyway. Ellen, you can take that four-poster money with you. I'll have one more check coming, too. [Starts upstairs]

JOE: What's "four-poster money"?

ELLEN: We were saving up to buy a new bed. [Cries. Sits on settee]

JOE: Oh, my Lord, here we go again!

TOMMY: [Crossing to Joe] Why did you have to ask what four-poster money is? [To Ellen] Ellen, please.

ELLEN: Oh, go on! Go on! Put on your coat and comb your hair! If you're going to be kicked out of school, you can't go over there looking like a tramp.

TOMMY: All right. [Goes upstairs]

JOE: [Pause] Look, Ellen, everything's gonna be all right.

ELLEN: Is it?

JOE: [Looking upstairs] I wouldn't worry about that guy.

ELLEN: I don't.

JOE: I mean he's sure to get another job. He's had more publicity than Wally Myers.

ELLEN: I don't care what becomes of him.

JOE: [Watches her for a moment] Come here. [Crossing to her pulls her to her feet] You're still crazy about that guy, aren't you?

ELLEN: I'm kind of scared of him. He used to be just—nice, but now he's wonderful!

[Tommy appears on stairs in time to catch the end of this. Very slowly a light begins to dawn upon him. Joe sees him but Ellen doesn't]

JOE: [Looks around, sees Victrola, gets idea, pulls Ellen to it] I don't think he's so wonderful!

ELLEN: Yes, he is! That letter's wonderful. What he's trying to do is wonderful. He wouldn't let me or you or anyone stop him. Even Ed.

JOE: He's a scrapper all right, but he can't dance. [Puts needle on]

[Tommy comes downstairs. Joe turns on Victrola which plays "Who?"]

ELLEN: Oh, who wants to dance now?

JOE: [They are dancing] This is important. It's all in the light you give off.

ELLEN: Light? What are you talking about?

JOE: The important thing about dancing is that the man has got to lead. [Beckons to Tommy who comes on into room from stairs]

TOMMY: May I cut in? [Takes Ellen and dances with her]

ELLEN: Tommy! Let me go!

TOMMY: [Shouting] No, I think you're wonderful too!

ELLEN: You think I'm dumb! Were you listening?

TOMMY: No.

JOE: [Near door; out-yelling them] Hey—don't start that again!

TOMMY: [Still dancing, gets his hat from table and jams it on his head] Joe—why don't you go back to your wife? We can send her a wire.

JOE: Don't worry about me, brother. I sent her a wire this morning. [Goes out]

TOMMY: [Dances with Ellen] Quit leading!

ELLEN: I'm not leading. You were listening!

TOMMY: You were yelling. Well, turn!

ELLEN: Make me turn. [He does] Don't be so rough—and put your hat on straight. You look terrible. [She throws her arms around Tommy and they kiss as the curtain falls]

Blithe Spirit

by NOEL COWARD
(1899–   )

There is something extraordinary, something sui generis about Noel Coward, not because of any single quality in him but because he is so curious a mixture. He possesses a number of virtues—a natural gift for being funny; a kind of cultivated one for being shocking; a wackiness in the best English style; a cleverness all his own. As a chronicler of outrageous bad manners, he is perhaps more than just entertaining; he has caught something of the spirit of the age. His brittleness, too—even certain aspects of his naughtiness—have a connection with the twenties, and with the society he has done more than parody if less than pulverize.

Yet almost no one so truly witty and clever as Coward can, on occasion, be so vulgar; or, in another vein, so sentimental. Coward, among other things, belongs with those who make a great to-do over not making a great to-do about sex and the like; in this he is not just good box office because he is a "smart" playwright, but equally because he is a shrewd one, well aware that the faintly scandalous makes good box office. With Mr. Coward there is, besides, the question of taste. He is not the first man to unite an uncommon wit with a trashy mind, or to turn tawdry in treating of tawdriness. What is singular, what makes him a special case, is that a man who can be so amazing in the good sense can yet be so appalling in the bad. He has much the same virtues as the Restoration playwrights; but quite different, quite contradictory rather than complementary, faults.

His best work is that which is most disinfected of reality; which, so to speak, has been twice filtered, by artifice and absurdity alike. This can be in the brief satirical nonsense of ditties like Mad Dogs and Englishmen or in the sustained high-farce fantasy of Blithe Spirit. In Blithe Spirit, indeed, Mr. Coward is remarkably free from his usual faults, and remarkably full of his particular virtues. The play concerns one of the most refreshing ménages à trois in the modern theater; and it proves what a fillip can be given to an ordinary situation by putting it to new and quite out-of-the-ordinary use. A man with two women on his hands is an essentially funny but by now all too familiar object; a man with two wives on his hands is funnier; a man with two wives on his hands, one in spectral form, turns out to be funnier still: though, perhaps oddly, a man with two wives on his hands, both of them spectral, is somewhat less funny.

The souffléd madness, the blend of the urbane and the fantastic is the large, pervasive merit of Blithe Spirit: the play, in this sense, is one of the very few creditable descendants of The Importance of Being Earnest. A character like Madame Arcati, however, is all Mr. Coward's own. It was altogether out of him that there sprang this conductor of séances with the character of a Girl Scout leader, this medium who is even more chin-up than starry-eyed. Madame Arcati, as portrayed by Mildred Natwick, remains one of the great comedy memories of theater-going; but she is in her own right one of the gayest comedy creations of the modern stage.

Blithe Spirit

CHARACTERS

EDITH, *a maid*

RUTH

CHARLES

DR. BRADMAN

MRS. BRADMAN

MADAME ARCATI

ELVIRA

The action of the play takes place in the living-room of Charles Condomine's house in Kent.

ACT I
Scene 1: *Before dinner on a summer evening*
Scene 2: *After dinner*

ACT II
Scene 1: *The next morning*
Scene 2: *Late the following afternoon*
Scene 3: *Early evening. A few days later*

ACT III
Scene 1: *After dinner. A few days later*
Scene 2: *Several hours later*

Act I

SCENE 1: *The scene is the living-room of the Condomines' house in Kent. The room is light, attractive and comfortably furnished. On the right there are French windows opening on to the garden. On the left there is an open fireplace. At the back, on the left, there are double doors leading into the dining-room. Up left, on an angle, there are double doors leading to the hall, the stairs, and the servants' quarters. When the curtain rises it is about eight o'clock on a summer evening. There is a wood fire burning because it is an English summer evening. Edith comes to table with tray of drinks. Ruth comes in. She is a smart-looking woman in the middle thirties. She is dressed for dinner but not elaborately.*

RUTH: That's right, Edith.

EDITH: Yes'm.

RUTH: Now you'd better fetch me the ice bucket.

EDITH: Yes'm.

RUTH: Did you manage to get the ice out of those little tin trays?

EDITH: Yes'm—I 'ad a bit of a struggle though—but it's all right.

RUTH: And you filled the little trays up again with water?

EDITH: Yes'm.

RUTH: Very good, Edith—you're making giant strides.

EDITH: Yes'm.

RUTH: Madame Arcati, Mrs. Bradman and I will have our coffee in here after dinner and Mr. Condomine and Dr. Bradman will have theirs in the dining-room—is that quite clear?

EDITH: Yes'm.

RUTH: And when you're serving dinner, Edith, try to remember to do it calmly and methodically.

EDITH: Yes'm.

RUTH: As you are not in the Navy it is unnecessary to do everything at the double.

EDITH: Very good, 'm.

RUTH: Now go and get the ice.

EDITH: [*Straining at the leash*] Yes'm. [*She starts off at full speed*]

RUTH: *Not* at a run, Edith.

EDITH: [*Slowing down*] Yes'm. [*Edith goes*]

[*Charles comes in. He is a nice-looking man of about forty wearing a loose-fitting velvet smoking jacket*]

CHARLES: No sign of the advancing hordes?

RUTH: Not yet.

CHARLES: [*Going to the cocktail tray*] No ice.

RUTH: It's coming. I've been trying to discourage Edith from being quite so fleet of foot. You mustn't mind if everything is a little slow motion tonight.

CHARLES: I shall welcome it. The last few days have been extremely agitating. What do you suppose induced Agnes to leave us and go and get married?

RUTH: The reason was becoming increasingly obvious, dear.

CHARLES: Yes, but in these days nobody thinks anything of that sort of thing—she could have popped into the cottage hospital, had it, and popped out again.

RUTH: Her social life would have been seriously undermined.

CHARLES: We must keep Edith in the house more.

[Edith *comes in slowly with the ice bucket*]

RUTH: That's right, Edith—put it down on the table.

EDITH: Yes'm. [*She does so*]

CHARLES: I left my cigarette case on my dressing table, Edith—would you get it for me?

EDITH: Yes, sir. [*She runs out of the room*]

CHARLES: There now!

RUTH: You took her by surprise.

CHARLES: [*At the cocktail table*] A dry Martini I think, don't you?

RUTH: Yes, darling—I expect Madame Arcati will want something sweeter.

CHARLES: We'll have this one for ourselves anyhow.

RUTH: [*Taking a cigarette and sitting down*] Oh dear!

CHARLES: What's the matter?

RUTH: I have a feeling that this evening's going to be awful.

CHARLES: It'll probably be funny, but not awful.

RUTH: You must promise not to catch my eye—if I giggle—and I'm very likely to—it will ruin everything.

CHARLES: You mustn't—you must be dead serious and if possible a little intense. We can't hurt the old girl's feelings however funny she is.

RUTH: But why the Bradmans, darling? He's as skeptical as we are—he'll probably say the most dreadful things.

CHARLES: I've warned him. There must be more than three people and we couldn't have the Vicar and his wife because (a) they're dreary, and (b) they probably wouldn't have approved at all. It had to be the Bradmans. [Edith *rushes into the room with* Charles' *cigarette case. Taking it*] Thank you, Edith. Steady does it.

EDITH: [*Breathlessly*] Yes, sir. [Edith, *with an obvious effort, goes out slowly*]

CHARLES: We might even make her walk about with a book on her head like they do in deportment lessons. [Charles *gives* Ruth *cocktail*] Here, try this.

RUTH: [*Sipping it*] Lovely—dry as a bone.

CHARLES: [*Raising his glass to her*] To *The Unseen!*

RUTH: I must say that's a wonderful title.

CHARLES: If this evening's a success I shall start on the first draft tomorrow.

RUTH: How extraordinary it is.

CHARLES: What?

RUTH: Oh, I don't know—being in right at the beginning of something—it gives one an odd feeling.

CHARLES: Do you remember how I got the idea for *The Light Goes Out?*

RUTH: Suddenly seeing that haggard, raddled woman in the hotel at Biarritz—of course I remember—we sat up half the night talking about it—

CHARLES: She certainly came in very handy—I wonder who she was.

RUTH: And if she ever knew, I mean ever recognized, that description of herself—poor thing . . . here's to her, anyhow . . . [*She finishes her drink*]

CHARLES: [*Takes her glass and goes to drinks table*] Have another.

RUTH: Darling—it's most awfully strong.

CHARLES: [*Pouring it*] Never mind.

RUTH: Used Elvira to be a help to you—when you were thinking something out, I mean?

CHARLES: [*Pouring out another cocktail for himself*] Every now and then—when she concentrated—but she didn't concentrate very often.

RUTH: I do wish I'd known her.

CHARLES: I wonder if you'd have liked her.

RUTH: I'm sure I should—as you talk of her she sounds enchanting—yes, I'm sure I should have liked her because you know I have never for an instant felt in the least jealous of her—that's a good sign.

CHARLES: Poor Elvira.

RUTH: Does it still hurt—when you think of her?

CHARLES: No, not really—sometimes I almost wish it did— I feel rather guilty—

RUTH: I wonder if I died before you'd grown tired of me if you'd forget me so soon?

CHARLES: What a horrible thing to say . . .

RUTH: No—I think it's interesting.

CHARLES: Well to begin with I *haven't* forgotten Elvira— I *remember* her very distinctly indeed—I remember how fascinating she was, and how maddening—[*Sits*] I remember how badly she played all games and how cross she got when she didn't win—I remember her gay charm when she had achieved her own way over something and her extreme acidity when she didn't—I remember her physical attractiveness, which was tremendous—and her spiritual integrity which was nil . . .

RUTH: You can't remember something that was nil.

CHARLES: I remember how morally untidy she was . . .

RUTH: Was she more physically attractive than I am?

CHARLES: That was a very tiresome question, dear, and fully deserves the wrong answer.

RUTH: You really are very sweet.

CHARLES: Thank you.

RUTH: And a little naïve, too.

CHARLES: Why?

RUTH: Because you imagine that I mind about Elvira being more physically attractive than I am.

CHARLES: I should have thought any woman would mind—if it were true. Or perhaps I'm old-fashioned in my views of female psychology. . . .

RUTH: Not exactly old-fashioned, darling, just a bit didactic.

CHARLES: How do you mean?

RUTH: It's didactic to attribute to one type the defects of another type—for instance, because you know perfectly well that Elvira would mind terribly if you found another woman more attractive physically than she was, it doesn't necessarily follow that I should. Elvira was a more physical person than I—I'm certain of that—it's all a question of degree.

CHARLES: [*Smiling*] I love you, my love.

RUTH: I know you do—but not the wildest stretch of imagination could describe it as the first fine careless rapture.

CHARLES: Would you like it to be?

RUTH: Good God, no!

CHARLES: Wasn't that a shade too vehement?

RUTH: We're neither of us adolescent, Charles, we've neither of us led exactly prim lives, have we? And we've both been married before—careless rapture at this stage would be incongruous and embarrassing.

CHARLES: I hope I haven't been in any way a disappointment, dear.

RUTH: Don't be so idiotic.

CHARLES: After all your first husband was a great deal older than you, wasn't he? I shouldn't like to think that you'd missed out all along the line.

RUTH: There are moments, Charles, when you go too far.

CHARLES: Sorry, darling.

RUTH: As far as waspish female psychology goes, there's a strong vein of it in you.

CHARLES: I've heard that said about Julius Caesar.

RUTH: Julius Caesar is neither here nor there.

CHARLES: He may be for all we know—we'll ask Madame Arcati.

RUTH: You're awfully irritating when you're determined to be witty at all costs—almost supercilious.

CHARLES: That's exactly what Elvira used to say.

RUTH: I'm not at all surprised—I never imagined—physically triumphant as she was—that she was entirely lacking in perception.

CHARLES: Darling Ruth!

RUTH: There you go again . . .

CHARLES: [*Kissing her lightly*] As I think I mentioned before—I love you, my love.

RUTH: Poor Elvira.

CHARLES: Didn't that light, comradely kiss mollify you at all?

RUTH: You're very annoying, you know you are—when I said "Poor Elvira" it came from the heart—you must have bewildered her so horribly.

CHARLES: Don't I ever bewilder you at all?

RUTH: Never for an instant—I know every trick.

CHARLES: Well, all I can say is that we'd better get a divorce immediately . . .

RUTH: Put my glass down, there's a darling.

CHARLES: [*Taking it*] She certainly had a great talent for living—it was a pity that she died so young.

RUTH: Poor Elvira.

CHARLES: That remark is getting monotonous.

RUTH: Poor Charles, then.

CHARLES: That's better.

RUTH: And later on, poor Ruth, I expect.

CHARLES: You have no faith, Ruth. I really do think you should try to have a little faith.

RUTH: I shall strain every nerve.

CHARLES: Life without faith is an arid business.

RUTH: How beautifully you put things, dear.

CHARLES: I *aim* to please.

RUTH: If I died, I wonder how long it would be before you married again.

CHARLES: You won't die—you're not the dying sort.

RUTH: Neither was Elvira.

CHARLES: Oh yes, she was, now that I look back on it—she had a certain ethereal, not quite of this world quality—nobody could call you even remotely ethereal.

RUTH: Nonsense—she was of the earth earthy.

CHARLES: Well, she is now, anyhow.

RUTH: You know that's the kind of observation that shocks people.

CHARLES: It's discouraging to think how many people are shocked by honesty and how few by deceit.

RUTH: Write that down, you might forget it.

CHARLES: You underrate me.

RUTH: Anyhow it was a question of bad taste more than honesty.

CHARLES: I was devoted to Elvira. We were married for five years. She died. I missed her very much. That was seven years ago. I have now, with your help, my love, risen above the whole thing.

RUTH: Admirable. But if tragedy should darken our lives, I still say—with prophetic foreboding—poor Ruth! [*Bell*]

CHARLES: That's probably the Bradmans.

RUTH: It might be Madame Arcati.

CHARLES: No, she'll come on her bicycle—she always goes everywhere on her bicycle.

RUTH: It really is very spirited of the old girl.

CHARLES: Shall I go, or shall we let Edith have her fling?

RUTH: Wait a minute and see what happens.

[*There is a slight pause*]

CHARLES: Perhaps she didn't hear.

RUTH: She's probably on one knee in a pre-sprinting position waiting for cook to open the kitchen door.

[*There is the sound of a door banging and* Edith *is seen scampering across the hall*]

CHARLES: Steady, Edith.

EDITH: [*Dropping to a walk*] Yes, sir.

[Mrs. Bradman *comes to* Ruth—*shakes hands.* Dr. Bradman *shakes hands with* Charles. Dr. Bradman *is a pleasant-looking middle-aged man.* Mrs. Bradman *is fair and rather faded*]

EDITH: Dr. and Mrs. Bradman.

DR. BRADMAN: We're not late, are we? I only got back from the hospital about half an hour ago.

CHARLES: Of course not—Madame Arcati isn't here yet.

MRS. BRADMAN: That must have been her we passed coming down the hill—I said I thought it was.

RUTH: Then she won't be long. I'm so glad you were able to come.

MRS. BRADMAN: We've been looking forward to it—I feel really quite excited . . .

DR. BRADMAN: [Shaking hands with Ruth] I guarantee that Violet will be good—I made her promise.

MRS. BRADMAN: There wasn't any need—I'm absolutely thrilled. I've only seen Madame Arcati two or three times in the village—I mean I've never seen her do anything at all peculiar, if you know what I mean.

CHARLES: Dry Martini?

DR. BRADMAN: By all means.

CHARLES: She certainly is a strange woman. It was only a chance remark of the Vicar's about seeing her up on the Knoll on Midsummer Eve dressed in sort of Indian robes that made me realize that she was psychic at all. Then I began to make inquiries—apparently she's been a professional in London for years.

MRS. BRADMAN: It is funny, isn't it? I mean anybody doing it as a profession.

DR. BRADMAN: I believe it's very lucrative.

MRS. BRADMAN: Do you believe in it, Mrs. Condomine—do you think there's anything really genuine about it at all?

RUTH: I'm afraid not—but I do think it's interesting how easily people allow themselves to be deceived . . .

MRS. BRADMAN: But she must believe in herself, mustn't she—or is the whole business a fake?

CHARLES: I suspect the worst. A real professional charlatan. That's what I am hoping for anyhow—the character I am planning for my book must be a complete impostor, that's one of the most important factors of the whole story.

DR. BRADMAN: What exactly are you hoping to get from her?

CHARLES: [Handing Dr. and Mrs. Bradman cocktails] Jargon, principally—a few of the tricks of the trade—it's many years since I went to a séance. I want to refresh my memory.

DR. BRADMAN: Then it's not entirely new to you?

CHARLES: Oh no—when I was a little boy an aunt of mine used to come and stay with us—she imagined that she was a medium and used to go off into the most elaborate trances after dinner. My mother was fascinated by it.

MRS. BRADMAN: Was she convinced?

CHARLES: [Gets cocktail for himself] Good heavens, no—she just naturally disliked my aunt and loved making a fool of her.

DR. BRADMAN: [Laughing] I gather that there were never any tangible results?

CHARLES: Oh sometimes she didn't do so badly. On one occasion when we were all sitting round in the pitch dark with my mother groping her way through Chaminade at the piano, my aunt suddenly gave a shrill scream and said that she saw a small black dog by my chair, then someone switched on the lights and sure enough there was.

MRS. BRADMAN: But how extraordinary.

CHARLES: It was obviously a stray that had come in from the street. But I must say I took off my hat to Auntie for producing it, or rather for utilizing—even Mother was a bit shaken.

MRS. BRADMAN: What happened to it?

CHARLES: It lived with us for years.

RUTH: I sincerely hope Madame Arcati won't produce any livestock—we have so very little room in this house.

MRS. BRADMAN: Do you think she tells fortunes? I love having my fortune told.

CHARLES: I expect so—

RUTH: I was told once on the pier at Southsea that I was surrounded by lilies and a golden seven—it worried me for days.

[All laugh]

CHARLES: We really must all be serious, you know, and pretend that we believe implicitly, otherwise she won't play.

RUTH: Also, she might really mind—it would be cruel to upset her.

DR. BRADMAN: I shall be as good as gold.

RUTH: Have you ever attended her, Doctor—professionally, I mean?

DR. BRADMAN: Yes—she had influenza in January—she's only been here just over a year, you know. I must say she was singularly unpsychic then—I always understood that she was an authoress.

CHARLES: Oh yes, we originally met as colleagues at one of Mrs. Wilmot's Sunday evenings in Sandgate . . .

MRS. BRADMAN: What sort of books does she write?

CHARLES: Two sorts. Rather whimsical children's stories about enchanted woods filled with highly conversational flora and fauna, and enthusiastic biographies of minor royalties. Very sentimental, reverent and extremely funny.

[There is the sound of the front door bell]

RUTH: Here she is.

DR. BRADMAN: She knows, doesn't she, about to-night? You're not going to spring it on her.

CHARLES: Of course—it was all arranged last week—I told her how profoundly interested I was in anything to do with the occult, and she blossomed like a rose.

RUTH: I really feel quite nervous—as though I were going to make a speech.

[Edith is seen sedately going towards the door]

CHARLES: You go and meet her, darling.

[Edith has opened the door, and Madame Arcati's voice very high and clear, is heard]

MADAME ARCATI: I've leant my bike up against that little bush, it will be *perfectly* all right if no one touches it.

EDITH: Madame Arcati.

RUTH: How nice of you to have come all this way.

[Ruth *and* Charles *greet her simultaneously. Madame Arcati enters. She is a striking woman, dressed not too extravagantly but with a decided bias towards the barbaric. She might be any age between forty-five and sixty-five.* Ruth *ushers her in*]

CHARLES: [*Advancing*] My dear Madame Arcati!

MADAME ARCATI: I'm afraid I'm rather late, but I had a sudden presentiment that I was going to have a puncture so I went back to fetch my pump, and then of course I didn't have a puncture at all.
[Madame Arcati *takes off cloak and hands it to* Ruth]

CHARLES: Perhaps you will on the way home.

MADAME ARCATI: Doctor Bradman—the man with the gentle hands!

DR. BRADMAN: I'm delighted to see you looking so well. This is my wife.

MADAME ARCATI: We are old friends— [*Shakes hands with* Mrs. Bradman] We meet coming out of shops.

CHARLES: Would you like a cocktail?

MADAME ARCATI: [*Peeling off some rather strange-looking gloves*] If it's a dry Martini, yes—if it's a concoction, no. Experience has taught me to be wary of concoctions.

CHARLES: It is a dry Martini.

MADAME ARCATI: How delicious. It was wonderful cycling through the woods this evening—I was deafened with bird-song.

RUTH: It's been lovely all day.

MADAME ARCATI: But the evening's the time—mark my words. [*She takes the cocktail* Charles *gives her. To others*] Thank you. Cheers! Cheers!

RUTH: Don't you find it very tiring bicycling everywhere?

MADAME ARCATI: On the contrary—it stimulates me —I was getting far too sedentary in London, that horrid little flat with the dim lights—they had to be dim, you know, the clients expect it.

MRS. BRADMAN: I must say I find bicycling very exhausting.

MADAME ARCATI: Steady rhythm—that's what counts. Once you get the knack of it you need never look back—on you get and away you go.

MRS. BRADMAN: But the hills, Madame Arcati— pushing up those awful hills—

MADAME ARCATI: Just knack again—down with your head, up with your heart, and you're over the top like a flash and skimming down the other side like a dragon-fly. This is the best dry Martini I've had for years.

CHARLES: Will you have another?

MADAME ARCATI: [*Holding out her glass*] Certainly. [Charles *takes her glass and refills it at drinks table*] You're a very clever man. Anybody can write books, but it takes an artist to make a dry Martini that's dry enough.

RUTH: Are you writing anything nowadays, Madame Arcati?

MADAME ARCATI: Every morning regular as clock-work, seven till one.

CHARLES: [*Gives* Madame Arcati *cocktail*] Is it a novel or a memoir?

MADAME ARCATI: It's a children's book—I have to finish it by the end of October to catch the Christmas sales. It's mostly about very small animals, the hero is a moss beetle. [Mrs. Bradman *laughs nervously*] I had to give up my memoir of Princess Palliatini because she died in April—I talked to her about it the other day and she implored me to go on with it, but I really hadn't the heart.

MRS. BRADMAN: [*Incredulously*] You *talked* to her about it the other day?

MADAME ARCATI: Yes, through my control, of course. She sounded very irritable.

MRS. BRADMAN: It's funny to think of people in the spirit world being irritable, isn't it? I mean, one can hardly imagine it, can one?

CHARLES: We have no reliable guarantee that the after life will be any less exasperating than this one, have we?

MRS. BRADMAN: [*Laughing*] Oh, Mr. Condomine, how *can* you!

RUTH: I expect it's dreadfully ignorant of me not to know—but who was Princess Palliatini?

MADAME ARCATI: She was originally a Jewess from Odessa of quite remarkable beauty. It was an accepted fact that people used to stand on the seats of railway stations to watch her whizz by.

CHARLES: She was a keen traveler?

MADAME ARCATI: In her younger days, yes—later on she married a Mr. Clarke in the Consular Service and settled down for a while . . .

RUTH: How did she become Princess Palliatini?

MADAME ARCATI: That was years later. Mr. Clarke passed over and left her penniless with two strapping girls—

RUTH: How unpleasant.

MADAME ARCATI: And so there was nothing for it but to obey the beckoning finger of adventure and take to the road again—so off she went, bag and baggage, to Vladivostok.

CHARLES: What an extraordinary place to go!

MADAME ARCATI: She had cousins there. Some years later she met old Palliatini who was returning from a secret mission in Japan. He was immediately staggered by her beauty and very shortly afterwards married her. From then on her life became really interesting.

DR. BRADMAN: I should hardly have described it as dull before.

RUTH: What happened to the girls?

MADAME ARCATI: She neither saw them nor spoke to them for twenty-three years.

MRS. BRADMAN: How extraordinary.

MADAME ARCATI: Not at all. She was always very erratic emotionally.

[*The double doors of the dining-room open and Edith comes in*]

EDITH: [*Nervously*] Dinner is served, Mum.

RUTH: Thank you, Edith. Shall we?

[*Edith retires backwards into the dining-room*]

MADAME ARCATI: No red meat, I hope?

RUTH: There's meat, but I don't think it will be very red—would you rather have an egg or something?

MADAME ARCATI: [*She and Ruth rise*] No, thank you—it's just that I make it a rule never to eat red meat before I work—it sometimes has an odd effect . . .

CHARLES: What sort of effect?

MADAME ARCATI: Oh, nothing of the least importance—if it isn't very red it won't matter much—anyhow, we'll risk it.

RUTH: [*Mrs. Bradman rises. Madame Arcati goes out first with Ruth followed by Mrs. Bradman, Dr. Bradman and Charles*] Come along, then—Mrs. Bradman—Madame Arcati—you're on Charles's right . . .

[*They all move into the dining-room as the lights fade on the scene*]

SCENE 2: *When the lights go up again, dinner is over, and Ruth, Mrs. Bradman and Madame Arcati are sitting having their coffee.*

MADAME ARCATI: . . . on her mother's side she went right back to the Borgias which I think accounted for a lot one way and another—even as a child she was given to the most violent destructive tempers—very inbred, you know.

MRS. BRADMAN: Yes, she must have been.

MADAME ARCATI: My control was quite scared the other day when we were talking—I could hear it in her voice—after all, she's only a child . . .

RUTH: Do you always have a child as a control?

MADAME ARCATI: Yes, they're generally the best—some mediums prefer Indians, of course, but personally I've always found them unreliable.

RUTH: In what way unreliable?

MADAME ARCATI: Well, for one thing they're frightfully lazy and also, when faced with any sort of difficulty, they're rather apt to go off into their own tribal language which is naturally unintelligible—that generally spoils everything and wastes a great deal of time. No, children are undoubtedly more satisfactory, particularly when they get to know you and understand your ways. Daphne has worked for me for years.

MRS. BRADMAN: And she still goes on being a child—I mean, she doesn't show signs of growing any older?

MADAME ARCATI: [*Patiently*] Time values on the "Other Side" are utterly different from ours.

MRS. BRADMAN: Do you feel funny when you go off into a trance?

MADAME ARCATI: In what way funny?

RUTH: [*Hastily*] Mrs. Bradman doesn't mean funny in its comic implication, I think she meant odd or strange—

MADAME ARCATI: The word was an unfortunate choice.

MRS. BRADMAN: I'm sure I'm very sorry.

MADAME ARCATI: It doesn't matter in the least—please don't apologize.

RUTH: When did you first discover that you had these extraordinary powers?

MADAME ARCATI: When I was quite tiny. My mother was a medium before me, you know, and so I had every opportunity of starting on the ground floor as you might say. I had my first trance when I was four years old and my first protoplasmic manifestation when I was five and a half—what an exciting day that was, I shall never forget it—of course the manifestation itself was quite small and of very short duration, but, for a child of my tender years, it was most gratifying.

MRS. BRADMAN: Your mother must have been so pleased.

MADAME ARCATI: [*Modestly*] She was.

MRS. BRADMAN: Can you foretell the future?

MADAME ARCATI: Certainly not. I disapprove of fortune tellers most strongly.

MRS. BRADMAN: [*Disappointed*] Oh really—why?

MADAME ARCATI: Too much guesswork and fake mixed up with it—even when the gift is genuine—and it only very occasionally is—you can't count on it.

RUTH: Why not?

MADAME ARCATI: Time again—time is the reef upon which all our frail mystic ships are wrecked.

RUTH: You mean because it has never yet been proved that the past and the present and the future are not one and the same thing.

MADAME ARCATI: I long ago came to the conclusion that nothing has ever been definitely proved about anything.

RUTH: How very wise.

[*Edith comes in with a tray of drinks. This she brings over to the table by Ruth. Ruth moves a coffee cup and a vase to make room for it*]

RUTH: Edith, we don't want to be disturbed for the next hour or so for any reason whatsoever—is that clear?

EDITH: Yes'm.

RUTH: And if anyone should telephone, just say we are out and take a message.

MRS. BRADMAN: Unless it's an urgent call for George.

RUTH: Unless it's an urgent call for Dr. Bradman.

EDITH: Yes'm. [Edith *goes out swiftly*]

RUTH: There's not likely to be one, is there?

MRS. BRADMAN: No, I don't think so.

MADAME ARCATI: Once I am off it won't matter, but an interruption during the preliminary stages might be disastrous.

MRS. BRADMAN: I wish the men would hurry up—I'm terribly excited.

MADAME ARCATI: Please don't be—it makes everything very much more difficult.

[Charles *and* Dr. Bradman *come out of the dining-room. They are smoking cigars*]

CHARLES: [*Cheerfully*] Well, Madame Arcati—the time is drawing near.

MADAME ARCATI: Who knows? It may be receding!

CHARLES: How very true.

DR. BRADMAN: I hope you feel in the mood, Madame Arcati.

MADAME ARCATI: It isn't a question of mood—it's a question of concentration.

RUTH: You must forgive us being impatient. We can perfectly easily wait though, if you're not quite ready to start . . .

MADAME ARCATI: Nonsense, my dear, I'm absolutely ready— [*She rises*] Heigho, heigho, to work we go!

CHARLES: Is there anything you'd like us to do?

MADAME ARCATI: Do?

CHARLES: Yes—hold hands or anything?

MADAME ARCATI: All that will come later— [*She goes to the window*] First a few deep, deep breaths of fresh air— [*Over her shoulder*] You may talk if you wish, it will not disturb me in the least. [*She flings open the windows wide and inhales deeply and a trifle noisily*]

RUTH: [*With a quizzical glance at* Charles] Oh dear!

CHARLES: [*Putting his finger to his lips warningly*] An excellent dinner, darling—I congratulate you.

RUTH: The mousse wasn't quite right.

CHARLES: It looked a bit hysterical but it tasted delicious.

MADAME ARCATI: That cuckoo is very angry.

CHARLES: I beg your pardon?

MADAME ARCATI: I said that cuckoo is very angry . . . listen . . .

[*They all listen obediently*]

CHARLES: How can you tell?

MADAME ARCATI: Timbre . . . No moon—that's as well, I think—there's mist rising from the marshes— [*A thought strikes her*] There's no need for me to light my bicycle lamp, is there? I mean, nobody is likely to fall over it?

RUTH: No, we're not expecting anybody else.

MADAME ARCATI: Good-night, you foolish bird. You have a table?

CHARLES: Yes. We thought that one would do.

MADAME ARCATI: [*Closing the window, she comes over to the table and touches it lightly with her finger*] I think the one that has the drinks on it would be better.

DR. BRADMAN: [*Lifting off the tray*] Change over.

CHARLES: [*To Ruth*] You told Edith we didn't want to be disturbed?

RUTH: Yes, darling.

MADAME ARCATI: [*Walking about the room—twisting and untwisting her hands*] This is a moment I always hate.

RUTH: Are you nervous?

MADAME ARCATI: Yes. When I was a girl I always used to be sick.

DR. BRADMAN: How fortunate that you grew out of it.

RUTH: [*Hurriedly*] Children are always much more prone to be sick than grown-ups, though, aren't they? I know I could never travel in a train with any degree of safety until I was fourteen.

MADAME ARCATI: [*Still walking*] Little Tommy Tucker sings for his supper, what shall he have but brown bread and butter? I despise that because it doesn't rhyme at all—but Daphne loves it.

DR. BRADMAN: Who's Daphne?

RUTH: Daphne is Madame Arcati's control—she's a little girl.

DR. BRADMAN: Oh, I see—yes, of course.

CHARLES: How old is she?

MADAME ARCATI: Rising seven when she died.

MRS. BRADMAN: And when was that?

MADAME ARCATI: February the sixth, 1884.

MRS. BRADMAN: Poor little thing.

DR. BRADMAN: She must be a bit long in the tooth by now, I should think.

MADAME ARCATI: You should think, Dr. Bradman, but I fear you don't—at least, not profoundly enough.

MRS. BRADMAN: Do be quiet, George—you'll put Madame Arcati off.

MADAME ARCATI: [Charles *brings piano chair down to table*] Don't worry, my dear—I am quite used to skeptics—they generally turn out to be the most vulnerable and receptive in the long run.

RUTH: You'd better take that warning to heart, Dr. Bradman.

DR. BRADMAN: Please forgive me, Madame Arcati— I assure you I am most deeply interested.

MADAME ARCATI: It is of no consequence—will you all sit round the table please and place your hands downwards on it?

[Ruth, Mrs. Bradman *and* Dr. Bradman *are seated at table*]

CHARLES: What about the lights?

MADAME ARCATI: All in good time, Mr. Condomine. [*The four of them sit down at each side of a small square table.* Madame Arcati *surveys them critically, her head on one side. She is whistling a little tune*] The fingers should be touching . . . that's right . . . I presume that that is the gramophone, Mr. Condomine?

CHARLES: Yes—would you like me to start it? It's an electric one.

MADAME ARCATI: Please stay where you are—I can manage— [*She goes over to the gramophone and looks over the records*] Now let me see—what have we here—Brahms—oh dear me, no—Rachmaninoff—too florid—where is the dance music?

RUTH: They're the loose ones on the left.

MADAME ARCATI: I see. [*She stoops down and produces a pile of dance records—these she sorts rapidly on the piano*]

CHARLES: I'm afraid they're none of them very new.

MADAME ARCATI: Daphne is really more attached to Irving Berlin than anybody else—she likes a tune she can hum—ah, here's one—"Always"—

CHARLES: [*Half jumping up again*] "Always"!

RUTH: Do sit down, Charles—what is the matter?

CHARLES: [*Subsiding*] Nothing—nothing at all.

MADAME ARCATI: The light switch is by the door?

RUTH: Yes, all except the small one on the desk, and the gramophone.

MADAME ARCATI: Very well—I understand.

RUTH: Charles, do keep still.

MRS. BRADMAN: Fingers touching, George—remember what Madame Arcati said.

MADAME ARCATI: Now there are one or two things I should like to explain, so will you all listen attentively?

RUTH: Of course.

MADAME ARCATI: Presently, when the music begins, I am going to switch out the lights. I may then either walk about the room for a little or lie down flat—in due course I shall draw up this dear little stool and join you at the table—I shall place myself between you and your wife, Mr. Condomine, and rest my hands lightly upon yours—I must ask you not to address me or move or do anything in the least distracting—is that quite, quite clear?

CHARLES: Perfectly.

MADAME ARCATI: Of course I cannot guarantee that anything will happen at all—Daphne may be unavailable—she had a head cold very recently, and was rather under the weather, poor child. On the other hand, a great many things might occur—one of you might have an emanation, for instance, or we might contact a poltergeist which would be extremely destructive and noisy . . .

RUTH: [*Anxiously*] In what way destructive?

MADAME ARCATI: They throw things, you know.

RUTH: No—I didn't know.

MADAME ARCATI: But we must cross that bridge when we come to it, mustn't we?

CHARLES: Certainly—by all means.

MADAME ARCATI: Fortunately an Elemental at this time of the year is most unlikely . . .

RUTH: What do Elementals do?

MADAME ARCATI: Oh, my dear, one can never tell—they're dreadfully unpredictable—usually they take the form of a very cold wind . . .

MRS. BRADMAN: I don't think I shall like that—

MADAME ARCATI: Occasionally reaching almost hurricane velocity—

RUTH: You don't think it would be a good idea to take the more breakable ornaments off the mantelpiece before we start?

MADAME ARCATI: [*Indulgently*] That really is not necessary, Mrs. Condomine—I assure you I have my own methods of dealing with Elementals.

RUTH: I'm so glad.

MADAME ARCATI: Now then—are you ready to empty your minds?

DR. BRADMAN: Do you mean we're to try to think of nothing?

MADAME ARCATI: Absolutely nothing, Dr. Bradman. Concentrate on a space or a nondescript colour, that's really the best way . . .

DR. BRADMAN: I'll do my damnedest.

MADAME ARCATI: Good work!—I will now start the music. [*She goes to the gramophone, puts on the record of "Always," and begins to walk about the room; occasionally she moves into an abortive little dance step, and once, on passing a mirror on the mantelpiece, she surveys herself critically for a moment and adjusts her hair. Then, with sudden speed, she runs across the room and switches off the lights*]

MRS. BRADMAN: Oh dear!

MADAME ARCATI: Quiet—please . . . [*Presently in the gloom* Madame Arcati, *after wandering about a little, draws up a stool and sits at the table between* Charles *and* Ruth. *The gramophone record comes to an end. There is dead silence*] Is there anyone there? . . . [*A long pause*] Is there anyone there? [*Another long pause*] One rap for yes—two raps for no—now then—is there anyone there? . . . [*After a shorter pause the table gives a little bump*]

MRS. BRADMAN: [*Involuntarily*] Oh!

MADAME ARCATI: Shhhh! . . . Is that you, Daphne? [*The table gives a louder bump*] Is your cold better, dear? [*The table gives two loud bumps very quickly*] Oh, I'm so sorry—are you doing anything for it? [*The table bumps several times*] I'm afraid she's rather fretful . . . [*There is a silence*] Is there anyone there who wishes to speak to anyone here? [*After a pause the table gives one bump*] Ah! Now we're getting somewhere. No. Daphne, don't do that, dear, you're hurting me . . . Daphne, dear, please . . . Oh, oh, oh! . . . be good, there's a dear child . . . You say there is someone there who wishes to speak to someone here? [*One bump*] Is it I? [*Two bumps*] Is it Dr. Bradman? [*Two bumps*] Is it Mrs. Bradman? [*Two bumps*] Is it Mrs. Condomine? [*Several very loud bumps, which continue until* Madame Arcati *shouts it down*] Stop it! Behave yourself! Is it Mr. Condomine? [*There is a dead silence for a moment, and then a very loud single bump*] There's someone who wishes to speak to you, Mr. Condomine.

CHARLES: Tell them to leave a message.

[*The table bangs about loudly*]

MADAME ARCATI: I really must ask you not to be flippant, Mr. Condomine . . .

RUTH: Charles, how can you be so idiotic? You'll spoil everything.

CHARLES: I'm sorry—it slipped out.

MADAME ARCATI: Do you know anybody who has passed over recently?

CHARLES: Not recently, except my cousin in the Civil Service, and he wouldn't be likely to want to communicate with me—we haven't spoken for years.

MADAME ARCATI: [*Mystically*] Are you Mr. Condomine's cousin in the Civil Service? [*The table bumps violently several times*] I'm afraid we've drawn a blank . . . Can't you think of anyone else? Rack your brains . . .

RUTH: [*Helpfully*] It might be old Mrs. Plummet, you know—she died on Whit Monday . . .

CHARLES: I can't imagine why old Mrs. Plummet should wish to talk to me—we had very little in common.

RUTH: It's worth trying, anyhow.

MADAME ARCATI: Are you old Mrs. Plummet? [*The table remains still*]

RUTH: She was very deaf—perhaps you'd better shout—

MADAME ARCATI: [*Shouting*] Are you old Mrs. Plummet? [*Nothing happens*] There's nobody there at all.

MRS. BRADMAN: How disappointing—just as we were getting on so nicely.

DR. BRADMAN: Violet, be quiet.

MADAME ARCATI: [*Rising*] Well, I'm afraid there's nothing for it but for me to go into a trance. I had hoped to avoid it because it's so exhausting—however, what must be must be. Excuse me a moment while I start the gramophone again.

CHARLES: [*In a strained voice*] Not "Always"—don't play "Always"—

RUTH: Why ever not, Charles? Don't be absurd.

MADAME ARCATI: [*Gently*] I'm afraid I must—it would be unwise to change horses in midstream if you know what I mean . . . [*She restarts the gramophone*]

CHARLES: Have it your own way.

[*Madame Arcati comes slowly back toward the table and sits down again. After a few moments she begins to moan—then in the darkness a child's voice is heard reciting rather breathily "Little Tommy Tucker"*]

DR. BRADMAN: That would be Daphne—she ought to have had her adenoids out.

MRS. BRADMAN: George—please—

[*Madame Arcati suddenly gives a loud scream and falls off the stool on to the floor*]

CHARLES: Good God!

RUTH: Keep still, Charles . . .

[*Charles subsides. Everyone sits in silence for a moment, then the table starts bouncing about*]

MRS. BRADMAN: It's trying to get away . . . I can't hold it . . .

RUTH: Press down hard.

[*The table falls over with a crash*]

RUTH: There now!

MRS. BRADMAN: Ought we to pick it up or leave it where it is?

DR. BRADMAN: How the hell do I know?

MRS. BRADMAN: There's no need to snap at me.

[*A perfectly strange and very charming voice says, "Leave it where it is!"*]

CHARLES: Who said that?

RUTH: Who said what?

CHARLES: Somebody said, "Leave it where it is."

RUTH: Nonsense, dear.

CHARLES: I heard it distinctly.

RUTH: Well, nobody else did—did they?

MRS. BRADMAN: I never heard a sound.

CHARLES: It was you, Ruth—you're playing tricks.

RUTH: I'm not doing anything of the sort. I haven't uttered.

[*There is another pause, and then the voice says, "Good evening, Charles"*]

CHARLES: [*Very agitated*] Ventriloquism—that's what it is—ventriloquism . . .

RUTH: [*Irritably*] What is the matter with you?

CHARLES: You must have heard *that*—one of you must have heard *that!*

RUTH: Heard *what?*

CHARLES: You mean to sit there solemnly and tell me that none of you heard anything at all?

DR. BRADMAN: I certainly didn't.

MRS. BRADMAN: Neither did I—I wish I had. I should love to hear something.

RUTH: It's you who are playing the tricks, Charles—you're acting to try to frighten us . . .

CHARLES: [*Breathlessly*] I'm not—I swear I'm not. [*The voice speaks again. It says, "It's difficult to think of what to say after seven years, but I suppose good evening is as good as anything else"*]

CHARLES: [*Intensely*] Who are you? [*The voice says, "Elvira, of course—don't be so silly"*] I can't bear this for another minute . . . [*He rises violently*] Get up, everybody—the entertainment's over . . .

RUTH: Oh, Charles, how tiresome you are—just as we were beginning to enjoy ourselves. What on earth is the matter with you?

CHARLES: Nothing's the matter with me—I'm just sick of the whole business, that's all.

DR. BRADMAN: Did you hear anything that we didn't hear really?

CHARLES: [*With a forced laugh*] Of course not—I was only pretending . . .

RUTH: I knew you were . . .

MRS. BRADMAN: Oh dear . . . look at Madame Arcati! [*Madame Arcati is lying on the floor with her feet up on the stool from which she fell. She is obviously quite unconscious*]

RUTH: What are we to do with her?

CHARLES: Bring her round—bring her round as soon as possible.

DR. BRADMAN: [*Going over and kneeling down beside her*] I think we'd better leave her alone.

RUTH: But she might stay like that for hours.

DR. BRADMAN: [*After feeling her pulse and examining her eye*] She's out all right.

CHARLES: [*Almost hysterically*] Bring her around! It's dangerous to leave her like that . . .

RUTH: Really, Charles, you are behaving most peculiarly.

CHARLES: [*Going to* Madame Arcati *and shaking her violently*] Wake up, Madame Arcati—wake up—it's time to go home!

DR. BRADMAN: Here—go easy, old man . . .

CHARLES: Get some brandy—give her some brandy—lift her into the chair—help me, Bradman . . . [Ruth *pours out some brandy while* Charles *and* Dr. Bradman *lift* Madame Arcati *laboriously into an armchair. Leaning over her*] Wake up, Madame Arcati—Little Tommy Tucker, Madame Arcati!

RUTH: Here's the brandy.

[*Madame Arcati gives a slight moan and a shiver*]

CHARLES: [*Forcing some brandy between her lips*] Wake up!—

[*Madame Arcati gives a prolonged shiver and chokes slightly over the brandy*]

MRS. BRADMAN: She's coming round.

RUTH: Be careful, Charles—you're spilling it all down her dress.

MADAME ARCATI: [*Opening her eyes*] Well, that's that.

RUTH: [*Solicitously*] Are you all right?

MADAME ARCATI: Certainly I am—never felt better in my life.

CHARLES: Would you like some more brandy?

MADAME ARCATI: So that's the funny taste in my mouth—well, really! Fancy allowing them to give me brandy! Doctor Bradman, you ought to have known better—brandy on top of trance might have been catastrophic. Take it away, please—I probably shan't sleep a wink tonight as it is.

CHARLES: I know I shan't.

RUTH: Why on earth not?

CHARLES: The whole experience has unhinged me.

MADAME ARCATI: Well, what happened—was it satisfactory?

RUTH: Nothing much happened, Madame Arcati, after you went off.

MADAME ARCATI: Something happened all right. I can feel it. [*She rises and sniffs*] No poltergeist, at any rate—that's a good thing. Any apparitions?

DR. BRADMAN: Not a thing.

MADAME ARCATI: No protoplasm?

RUTH: I'm not quite sure what it is, but I don't think so.

MADAME ARCATI: Very curious. I feel as though something tremendous had taken place.

RUTH: Charles pretended he heard a voice, in order to frighten us.

CHARLES: It was only a joke.

MADAME ARCATI: A very poor one, if I may say so— [*She walks about a little more*] Nevertheless, I am prepared to swear that there is someone else psychic in this room apart from myself.

RUTH: I don't see how there can be really, Madame Arcati.

MADAME ARCATI: I do hope I haven't gone and released something—however, we are bound to find out within a day or two—if any manifestation should occur or you hear any unexpected noises—you might let me know at once.

RUTH: Of course we will—we'll telephone immediately.

MADAME ARCATI: I think I really must be on my way now.

RUTH: Wouldn't you like anything before you go?

MADAME ARCATI: No, thank you—I have some Ovaltine all ready in a saucepan at home—it only needs hotting up.

DR. BRADMAN: Wouldn't you like to leave your bicycle here and let us drive you?

MRS. BRADMAN: I honestly do think you should, Madame Arcati, after that trance and everything—you can't be feeling quite yourself.

MADAME ARCATI: Nonsense, my dear, I'm as fit as a fiddle—always feel capital after a trance—rejuvenates me. Good night, Mrs. Condomine.

RUTH: It was awfully sweet of you to take so much trouble.

MADAME ARCATI: I'm sorry so little occurred—it's that cold of Daphne's, I expect—you know what children are when they have anything wrong with them. We must try again some other evening.

RUTH: That would be lovely.

MADAME ARCATI: Good night, Mrs. Bradman—

MRS. BRADMAN: It was thrilling, it really was—I felt the table absolutely shaking under my hands.

MADAME ARCATI: Good night, Doctor.

DR. BRADMAN: Congratulations, Madame Arcati.

MADAME ARCATI: I am fully aware of the irony in your voice, Doctor Bradman. As a matter of fact you'd be an admirable subject for telepathic hypnosis—a great chum of mine is an expert—I should like her to look you over.

DR. BRADMAN: I'm sure I should be charmed.

MADAME ARCATI: Good night, everyone—next time we must really put our backs into it!

[*With a comprehensive smile and a wave of the hand, she goes out followed by* Charles. Ruth *sinks down into a chair, laughing helplessly*]

RUTH: Oh dear! . . . Oh dear! . . .

MRS. BRADMAN: [*Beginning to laugh too*] Be careful, Mrs. Condomine—she might hear you.

RUTH: I can't help it—I really can't—I've been holding this in for ages.

MRS. BRADMAN: She certainly put you in your place, George, and serves you right.

RUTH: She's raving mad, of course—mad as a hatter.

MRS. BRADMAN: But do you really think she *believes*?

DR. BRADMAN: Of course not—the whole thing's a put-up job—I must say, though, she shoots a more original line than they generally do.

RUTH: I should think that she's probably half convinced herself by now.

DR. BRADMAN: Possibly—the trance was genuine enough—but that, of course, is easily accounted for.

RUTH: Hysteria?

DR. BRADMAN: Yes—a form of hysteria, I should imagine.

MRS. BRADMAN: I do hope Mr. Condomine got all the atmosphere he wanted for his book.

RUTH: He might have got a great deal more if he hadn't spoiled everything by showing off . . . I'm really very cross with him. [*At this moment* Elvira *comes in through the closed French windows. She is charmingly dressed in a sort of negligee. Everything about her is grey: hair, skin, dress, hands, so we must accept the fact that she is not quite of this world. She passes between* Dr. *and* Mrs. Bradman *and* Ruth *while they are talking. None of them sees her. She goes upstage and sits soundlessly on a chair. She regards them with interest, a slight smile on her face*] I suddenly felt a draught—there must be a window open.

DR. BRADMAN: [*Looking*] No—they're shut.

MRS. BRADMAN: [*Laughing*] Perhaps it was one of those what you may call 'ems that Madame Arcati was talking about.

DR. BRADMAN: Elementals.

RUTH: [*Also laughing again*] Oh no, it couldn't be—she distinctly said that it was the wrong time of the year for Elementals.

[Charles *comes in again*]

CHARLES: Well, the old girl's gone pedalling off down the drive at the hell of a speed—we had a bit of trouble lighting her lamp.

MRS. BRADMAN: Poor thing.

CHARLES: I've got a theory about her, you know—I believe she is completely sincere.

RUTH: Charles! How could she be?

CHARLES: Wouldn't it be possible, Doctor? Some form of self-hypnotism?

DR. BRADMAN: It might be . . . as I was explaining to your wife just now, there are certain types of hysterical subjects . . .

MRS. BRADMAN: George dear—it's getting terribly late, we really must go home—you have to get up so early in the morning.

DR. BRADMAN: You see? The moment I begin to talk about anything that really interests me, my wife interrupts me . . .

MRS. BRADMAN: You know I'm right, darling—it's past eleven.

DR. BRADMAN: [*To Charles*] I'll do a little reading up on the whole business—just for the fun of it.

CHARLES: You must have a drink before you go.

DR. BRADMAN: No, really, thank you—Violet's quite right, I'm afraid. I have got to get up abominably early tomorrow—I have a patient being operated on in Canterbury.

MRS. BRADMAN: [*To Ruth*] It has been a thrilling evening—I shall never forget—it was sweet of you to include us.

DR. BRADMAN: Good night, Mrs. Condomine—thank you so much.

CHARLES: You're sure about the drink!

DR. BRADMAN: Quite sure, thanks.

RUTH: We'll let you know if we find any poltergeists whirling about.

DR. BRADMAN: I should never forgive you if you didn't.

MRS. BRADMAN: Come along, darling . . .

[Charles *leads the* Bradmans *out into the hall.* Ruth, *passing close to* Elvira, *goes over to the fire and turns over a log with her foot. Then she takes a cigarette and is lighting it as* Charles *comes back into the room*]

RUTH: Well, darling?

CHARLES: [*Absently*] Well?

RUTH: Would you say the evening had been profitable?

CHARLES: Yes—I suppose so.

RUTH: I must say it was extremely funny at moments.

CHARLES: Yes—it certainly was.

RUTH: What's the matter?

CHARLES: The matter?

RUTH: Yes—you seem odd somehow—do you feel quite well?

CHARLES: Perfectly. I think I'll have a drink. Do you want one?

RUTH: No, thank you, dear.

CHARLES: [*Pouring himself out a drink*] It's rather chilly in this room.

RUTH: Come over by the fire.

CHARLES: I don't think I'll make any notes tonight—I'll start fresh in the morning. [*He is bringing his drink over to the fire when he sees* Elvira] My God! [*He drops the drink on the floor.* Ruth *jumps up*]

RUTH: Charles!

ELVIRA: That was very clumsy, Charles dear.

CHARLES: Elvira!—then it's true—it was you!

ELVIRA: Of course it was.

RUTH: [*Coming to him*] Charles—darling Charles—what are you talking about?

CHARLES: [*To Elvira*] Are you a ghost?

ELVIRA: I suppose I must be—it's all very confusing.

RUTH: [*Becoming agitated*] Charles—what do you keep looking over there for? Look at me—what's happened?

CHARLES: Don't you see?

RUTH: See what?

CHARLES: Elvira.

RUTH: [*Staring at him incredulously*] Elvira!!

CHARLES: [*With an effort at social grace*] Yes—Elvira dear, this is Ruth—Ruth, this is Elvira.

RUTH: [*With forced calmness*] Come and sit down, darling.

CHARLES: Do you mean to say you can't see her?

RUTH: Listen, Charles—you just sit down quietly by the fire and I'll mix you another drink. Don't worry about the mess on the carpet—Edith can clean it up in the morning. [*She takes him by the arm*]

CHARLES: [*Breaking away*] But you must be able to see her—she's there—look—right in front of you—there—

RUTH: Are you mad? What's happened to you?

CHARLES: You can't see her?

RUTH: If this is a joke, dear, it's gone quite far enough. Sit down for God's sake and don't be idiotic.

CHARLES: [*Clutching his head*] What am I to do—what the hell am I to do!

ELVIRA: I think you might at least be a little more pleased to see me—after all, you conjured me up.

CHARLES: I didn't do any such thing. I did nothing of the sort.

ELVIRA: Nonsense, of course you did. That awful child with the cold came and told me you wanted to see me urgently.

CHARLES: It was all a mistake—a horrible mistake.

RUTH: Stop talking like that, Charles—as I told you before, the *joke's* gone far enough.

CHARLES: [*Aside*] I've gone mad, that's what it is—I've just gone raving mad.

RUTH: [*Going to the table and quickly pouring him out some neat brandy*] Here—let me get you a drink.

CHARLES: [*Mechanically—taking it*] This is appalling!

RUTH: Relax.

CHARLES: How can I relax? I shall never be able to relax again as long as I live.

RUTH: Drink some brandy.

CHARLES: [*Drinking it at a gulp*] There now—are you satisfied?

RUTH: Now sit down.

CHARLES: Why are you so anxious for me to sit down—what good will that do?

RUTH: I want you to relax—you can't relax standing up.

ELVIRA: African natives can—they can stand on one leg for hours.

CHARLES: I don't happen to be an African native.

RUTH: You don't happen to be a *what*?

CHARLES: [*Savagely*] An African native!

RUTH: What's that got to do with it?

CHARLES: It doesn't matter, Ruth—really it doesn't matter—we'll say no more about it. [*He sits down*] See, I've sat down.

RUTH: Would you like some more brandy?

CHARLES: Yes, please.

ELVIRA: Very unwise—you always had a weak head.

CHARLES: I could drink you under the table.

RUTH: There's no need to be aggressive, Charles—I'm doing my best to help you.

CHARLES: I'm sorry.

RUTH: [*Bringing him some more brandy*] Here—drink this—and then we'll go to bed.

ELVIRA: Get rid of her, Charles—then we can talk in peace.

CHARLES: That's a thoroughly immoral suggestion, you ought to be ashamed of yourself.

RUTH: What is there immoral in that?

CHARLES: I wasn't talking to you.

RUTH: Who were you talking to, then?

CHARLES: Elvira, of course.

RUTH: To hell with Elvira!

ELVIRA: There now—she's getting cross.

CHARLES: I don't blame her.

RUTH: What don't you blame her for?

CHARLES: Oh, God!

RUTH: Now look here, Charles— I gather you've got some sort of plan behind all this. I'm not quite a fool. I suspected you when we were doing that idiotic séance.

CHARLES: Don't be so silly—what plan could I have?

RUTH: I don't know—it's probably something to do with the characters in your book—how they, or one of them would react to a certain situation—I refuse to be used as a guinea pig unless I'm warned beforehand what it's all about.

CHARLES: [*Patiently*] Ruth, Elvira is here—she's standing a few yards away from you.

RUTH: [*Sarcastically*] Yes, dear, I can see her distinctly—under the piano with a horse.

CHARLES: But, Ruth . . .

RUTH: I am not going to stay here arguing any longer . . .

ELVIRA: Hurray!

CHARLES: Shut up.

RUTH: [*Incensed*] How dare you speak to me like that!

CHARLES: Listen, Ruth—please listen—

RUTH: I will not listen to any more of this nonsense—I am going up to bed now. I'll leave you to turn out the lights. I shan't be asleep—I'm too upset so you can come in and say good night to me if you feel like it.

ELVIRA: That's big of her, I must say.

CHARLES: Be quiet—you're behaving like a gutter-snipe.

RUTH: [*Icily—at door*] That is all I have to say.

Good night, Charles. [Ruth *walks swiftly out of the room without looking at him again*]

CHARLES: Ruth . . .

ELVIRA: That was one of the most enjoyable half-hours I have ever spent.

CHARLES: Oh, Elvira—how could you!

ELVIRA: Poor Ruth.

CHARLES: [*Staring at her*] This is obviously an hallucination, isn't it?

ELVIRA: I'm afraid I don't know the technical term for it.

CHARLES: [*Rising and walking about the room*] What am I to do?

ELVIRA: What Ruth suggested—relax.

CHARLES: Where have you come from?

ELVIRA: Do you know, it's very peculiar, but I've sort of forgotten.

CHARLES: Are you here to stay indefinitely?

ELVIRA: I don't know that either.

CHARLES: Oh, my God!

ELVIRA: Why, would you hate it so much if I did?

CHARLES: Well, you must admit it would be embarrassing.

ELVIRA: I don't see why, really—it's all a question of adjusting yourself—anyhow I think it's horrid of you to be so unwelcoming and disagreeable.

CHARLES: Now look here, Elvira . . .

ELVIRA: [*Near tears*] I do—I think you're mean.

CHARLES: Try to see my point, dear—I've been married to Ruth for five years, and you've been dead for seven . . .

ELVIRA: Not dead, Charles—"passed over." It's considered vulgar to say "dead" where I come from.

CHARLES: Passed over, then.

ELVIRA: At any rate, now that I'm here, the least you can do is to make a pretense of being amiable about it . . .

CHARLES: Of course, my dear, I'm delighted in one way . . .

ELVIRA: I don't believe you love me any more.

CHARLES: I shall always love the memory of you.

ELVIRA: [*Rising and walking about*] You mustn't think me unreasonable, but I really am a little hurt. You called me back—and at great inconvenience I came—and you've been thoroughly churlish ever since I arrived.

CHARLES: [*Gently*] Believe me, Elvira, I most emphatically did not send for you—there's been some mistake.

ELVIRA: [*Irritably*] Well, somebody did—and that child said it was you—I remember I was playing backgammon with a very sweet old Oriental gentleman—I think his name was Genghis Khan—and I'd just thrown double sixes, and then that child paged me and the next thing I knew I was in this room . . . perhaps it was your subconscious.

CHARLES: Well, you must find out whether you are going to stay or not, and we can make arrangements accordingly.

ELVIRA: I don't see how I can.

CHARLES: Well, try to think—isn't there anyone that you know, that you can get in touch with over there—on the other side, or whatever it's called—who could advise you?

ELVIRA: I can't think—it seems so far away—as though I'd dreamed it . . .

CHARLES: You must know somebody else beside Genghis Khan.

ELVIRA: Oh, Charles . . .

CHARLES: What is it?

ELVIRA: I want to cry, but I don't think I'm able to . . .

CHARLES: What do you want to cry for?

ELVIRA: It's seeing you again—and you being so irascible like you always used to be . . .

CHARLES: I don't mean to be irascible, Elvira . . .

ELVIRA: Darling—I don't mind really—I never did.

CHARLES: Is it cold—being a ghost?

ELVIRA: No—I don't think so.

CHARLES: What happens if I touch you?

ELVIRA: I doubt if you can. Do you want to?

CHARLES: Oh, Elvira . . . [*He buries his face in his hands*]

ELVIRA: What is it, darling?

CHARLES: I really do feel strange, seeing you again . . .

ELVIRA: That's better.

CHARLES: [*Looking up*] What's better?

ELVIRA: Your voice was kinder.

CHARLES: Was I ever unkind to you when you were alive?

ELVIRA: Often . . .

CHARLES: Oh, how can you! I'm sure that's an exaggeration.

ELVIRA: Not at all—you were an absolute pig that time we went to Cornwall and stayed in that awful hotel—you hit me with a billiard cue.

CHARLES: Only very, very gently . . .

ELVIRA: I loved you very much.

CHARLES: I loved you too . . . [*He puts out his hand to her and then draws it away*] No, I can't touch you—isn't that horrible?

ELVIRA: Perhaps it's as well if I'm going to stay for any length of time . . .

CHARLES: I feel strangely peaceful—I suppose I shall wake up eventually . . .

ELVIRA: Put your head back.

CHARLES: [*Doing so*] Like that?

ELVIRA: [*Stroking his hair*] Can you feel anything . . . ?

CHARLES: Only a very little breeze through my hair. . . .

ELVIRA: Well, that's better than nothing.

CHARLES: [*Drowsily*] I suppose if I'm really out of my mind they'll put me in an asylum.

ELVIRA: Don't worry about that—just relax—

CHARLES: [*Very drowsily indeed*] Poor Ruth . . .

ELVIRA: [*Gently and sweetly*] To hell with Ruth.

Act II

SCENE 1: *It is about nine-thirty the next morning. The sun is pouring in through the open French windows. Ruth is sitting at the breakfast table, drinking coffee and reading the* Times. *After a few moments* Charles *comes in. He kisses her.*

CHARLES: Good morning, darling.

RUTH: [*With a certain stiffness*] Good morning, Charles.

CHARLES: [*Going to the open window and taking a deep breath*] It certainly is.

RUTH: What certainly is what?

CHARLES: A good morning—a tremendously good morning—there isn't a cloud in the sky and everything looks newly washed.

RUTH: [*Turning a page of the* Times] Edith's keeping your breakfast hot—you'd better ring.

CHARLES: [*Pressing the bell by the fireplace*] Anything interesting in the *Times*?

RUTH: Don't be silly, Charles.

CHARLES: [*Coming to the table*] I intend to work all day.

RUTH: Good.

CHARLES: It's extraordinary about daylight, isn't it?

RUTH: How do you mean?

CHARLES: The way it reduces everything to normal.

RUTH: Does it?

CHARLES: [*Sits. Firmly*] Yes—it does.

RUTH: I'm sure I'm very glad to hear it.

CHARLES: You're very glacial this morning.

RUTH: Are you surprised?

CHARLES: Frankly—yes. I expected more of *you*.

RUTH: Well, really!

CHARLES: I've always looked upon you as a woman of perception and understanding.

RUTH: Perhaps this is one of my off days.

[Edith *comes in with some bacon and eggs and toast*]

CHARLES: [*Cheerfully*] Good morning, Edith.

EDITH: Good morning, sir.

CHARLES: Feeling fit?

EDITH: Yes, sir—thank you, sir.

CHARLES: How's cook?

EDITH: I don't know, sir—I haven't asked her.

CHARLES: You should. You should begin every day by asking everyone how they are—it oils the wheels.

EDITH: Yes, sir.

CHARLES: Greet her for me, will you?

EDITH: Yes, sir.

RUTH: That will be all for the moment, Edith.

EDITH: Yes'm.   [Edith *goes out*]

RUTH: I wish you wouldn't be facetious with the servants, Charles—it confuses them and undermines their morale.

CHARLES: I consider that point of view retrogressive, if not downright feudal.

RUTH: I don't care what you consider it, I have to run the house and you don't.

CHARLES: Are you implying that I couldn't?

RUTH: You're at liberty to try.

CHARLES: I take back what I said about it being a good morning—it's a dreadful morning.

RUTH: You'd better eat your breakfast while it's hot.

CHARLES: It isn't.

RUTH: [*Putting down the* Times] Now look here, Charles—in your younger days this display of roguish flippancy might have been alluring—in a middle-aged novelist it's nauseating.

CHARLES: Would you like me to writhe at your feet in a frenzy of self-abasement?

RUTH: That would be equally nauseating but certainly more appropriate.

CHARLES: I really don't see what I've done that's so awful.

RUTH: You behaved abominably last night. You wounded me and insulted me.

CHARLES: I was the victim of an aberration.

RUTH: Nonsense—you were drunk.

CHARLES: Drunk?

RUTH: You had four strong dry Martinis before dinner—a great deal too much burgundy at dinner—heaven knows how much port and kümmel with Doctor Bradman while I was doing my best to entertain that madwoman—and then two double brandies later—I gave them to you myself—of course you were drunk.

CHARLES: So that's your story, is it?

RUTH: You refused to come to bed and finally when I came down at three in the morning to see what had happened to you I found you in an alcoholic coma on the sofa with the fire out and your hair all over your face.

CHARLES: I was not in the least drunk, Ruth. Something happened to me—you really must believe that—something very peculiar happened to me.

RUTH: Nonsense.

CHARLES: It isn't nonsense—I know it looks like nonsense now in the clear, remorseless light of day, but last night it was far from being nonsense—I honestly had some sort of hallucination—

RUTH: I would really rather not discuss it any further.

CHARLES: But you must discuss it—it's very disturbing.

RUTH: There I agree with you. It showed you up in a most unpleasant light—I find that extremely disturbing.

CHARLES: I swear to you that during the séance I was convinced that I heard Elvira's voice—

RUTH: Nobody else did.

CHARLES: I can't help that—I did.

RUTH: You couldn't have.

CHARLES: And later on I was equally convinced that she was in this room—I saw her distinctly and talked to her. After you'd gone up to bed we had quite a cosy little chat.

RUTH: And you seriously expect me to believe that you weren't drunk?

CHARLES: I *know* I wasn't drunk. If I'd been all that drunk I should have a dreadful hangover now, shouldn't I?

RUTH: I'm not at all sure that you haven't.

CHARLES: I haven't got a trace of a headache—my tongue's not coated—look at it. [*He puts out his tongue*]

RUTH: I've not the least desire to look at your tongue; kindly put it in again.

CHARLES: I know what it is—you're frightened.

RUTH: Frightened? Rubbish! What is there to be frightened of?

CHARLES: Elvira. You wouldn't have minded all that much even if I had been drunk—it's only because it was all mixed up with Elvira.

RUTH: I seem to remember last night before dinner telling you that your views of female psychology were rather didactic. I was right. I should have added that they were puerile.

CHARLES: That was when it all began.

RUTH: When what all began?

CHARLES: We were talking too much about Elvira—it's dangerous to have somebody very strongly in your mind when you start dabbling with the occult.

RUTH: She certainly wasn't strongly in my mind.

CHARLES: She was in mine.

RUTH: Oh, she was, was she?

CHARLES: You tried to make me say that she was more physically attractive than you, so that you could hold it over me.

RUTH: I did not. I don't give a hoot how physically attractive she was.

CHARLES: Oh yes, you do—your whole being is devoured with jealousy.

RUTH: [*Rises and starts to clear table*] This is *too* much!

CHARLES: Women! My God, what I think of women!

RUTH: Your view of women is academic to say the least of it—just because you've always been dominated by them it doesn't necessarily follow that you know anything about them.

CHARLES: I've never been dominated by anyone.

RUTH: You were hag-ridden by your mother until you were twenty-three—then you got into the clutches of that awful Mrs. Whatever-her-name-was—

CHARLES: Mrs. Winthrop-Lewellyn.

RUTH: I'm not interested. Then there was Elvira—she ruled you with a rod of iron.

CHARLES: Elvira never ruled anyone, she was much too elusive—that was one of her greatest charms. [*Sits*]

RUTH: Then there was Maud Charteris—

CHARLES: My affair with Maud Charteris lasted exactly seven and a half weeks and she cried all the time.

RUTH: The tyranny of tears! Then there was—

CHARLES: If you wish to make an inventory of my sex life, dear, I think it only fair to tell you that you've missed out several episodes—I'll consult my diary and give you the complete list after lunch.

RUTH: It's no use trying to impress me with your routine amorous exploits—

CHARLES: The only woman in my whole life who's ever attempted to dominate me is you—you've been at it for years.

RUTH: That is completely untrue.

CHARLES: Oh, no, it isn't. You boss me and bully me and order me about—you won't even allow me to have an hallucination if I want to.

RUTH: Alcohol will ruin your whole life if you allow it to get a hold on you, you know.

CHARLES: Once and for all, Ruth, I would like you to understand that what happened last night has nothing whatever to do with alcohol. You've very adroitly rationalized the whole affair to your own satisfaction, but your deductions are based on complete fallacy. I am willing to grant you that it was an aberration, some sort of odd psychic delusion brought on by suggestion or hypnosis. I was stone cold sober from first to last and extremely upset into the bargain.

RUTH: *You* were upset indeed! What about me?

CHARLES: You behaved with a stolid, obtuse lack of comprehension that frankly shocked me!

RUTH: I consider that I was remarkably patient. I shall know better next time.

CHARLES: Instead of putting out a gentle, comradely hand to guide me you shouted staccato orders at me like a sergeant-major.

RUTH: You seem to forget that you gratuitously insulted me.

CHARLES: I did not.

RUTH: You called me a guttersnipe—you told me to shut up—and when I quietly suggested that we should go up to bed you said, with the most disgusting leer, that it was an immoral suggestion.

CHARLES: [*Exasperated*] I was talking to Elvira!

RUTH: If you were I can only say that it conjures up a fragrant picture of your first marriage.

CHARLES: My first marriage was perfectly charming and I think it's in the worst possible taste for you to sneer at it.

RUTH: I am not nearly so interested in your first marriage as you think I am. It's your second marriage that is absorbing me at the moment—it seems to me to be on the rocks.

CHARLES: Only because you persist in taking up this ridiculous attitude.

RUTH: My attitude is that of any normal woman whose husband gets drunk and hurls abuse at her.

CHARLES: [*Shouting*] I was not drunk!

RUTH: Be quiet, they'll hear you in the kitchen.

CHARLES: I don't care if they hear me in the Folkestone Town Hall—I was not drunk!

RUTH: Control yourself, Charles.

CHARLES: How can I control myself in the face of your idiotic damned stubbornness? It's giving me claustrophobia.

RUTH: [*Quietly*] You'd better ring up Doctor Bradman.

[Edith *comes in with a tray to clear away the breakfast things*]

EDITH: Can I clear, please'm?

RUTH: Yes, Edith.

EDITH: Cook wants to know about lunch, mum.

RUTH: [*Coldly*] Will you be in to lunch, Charles?

CHARLES: Please don't worry about me—I shall be perfectly happy with a bottle of gin in my bedroom.

RUTH: Don't be silly, dear. [*To* Edith] Tell cook we shall both be in.

EDITH: Yes'm.

RUTH: [*Conversationally—after a long pause*] I'm going into Hythe this morning—is there anything you want?

CHARLES: Yes—a great deal—but I doubt if you could get it in Hythe.

RUTH: Tell cook to put Alka-Seltzer down on my list, will you, Edith?

EDITH: Yes'm.

RUTH: [*At the window—after another long pause*] It's clouding over.

CHARLES: You have a genius for understatement.
[*In silence, but breathing heavily,* Edith *staggers out with the tray*]

RUTH: [*As she goes*] Don't worry about the table, Edith—I'll put it away.

EDITH: Yes'm.
[*When* Edith *has gone* Charles *goes over to* Ruth]

CHARLES: Please, Ruth—be reasonable.

RUTH: I'm perfectly reasonable.

CHARLES: I wasn't pretending—I really did believe that I saw Elvira and when I heard her voice I was appalled.

RUTH: You put up with it for five years. [*Puts chair by gramophone*]

CHARLES: [*Puts table in hall*] Naturally when I saw her I had the shock of my life—that's why I dropped the glass.

RUTH: But you *couldn't* have seen her.

CHARLES: I know I couldn't have but I *did!*

RUTH: I'm willing to concede then that you imagined you did.

CHARLES: That's what I've been trying to explain to you for hours.

RUTH: Well, then, there's obviously something wrong with you.

CHARLES: Exactly—there is something wrong with me—something fundamentally wrong with me—

that's why I've been imploring your sympathy and all I got was a sterile temperance lecture.

RUTH: You had been drinking, Charles—there's no denying that.

CHARLES: No more than usual.

RUTH: Well, how do you account for it then?

CHARLES: [*Frantically*] I can't account for it—that's what's so awful.

RUTH: [*Practically*] Did you feel quite well yesterday—during the day, I mean?

CHARLES: Of course I did.

RUTH: What did you have for lunch?

CHARLES: You ought to know, you had it with me.

RUTH: [*Thinking*] Let me see now, there was lemon sole and that cheese thing—

CHARLES: Why should having a cheese thing for lunch make me see my deceased wife after dinner?

RUTH: You never know—it was rather rich.

CHARLES: Why didn't you see your dead husband then? You had just as much of it as I did.

RUTH: This is not getting us anywhere at all.

CHARLES: Of course it isn't, and it won't as long as you insist on ascribing supernatural phenomena to colonic irritation.

RUTH: Supernatural grandmother!

CHARLES: I admit she'd have been much less agitating.

RUTH: [*Sits*] Perhaps you ought to see a nerve specialist.

CHARLES: I am not in the least neurotic and never have been.

RUTH: A psychoanalyst then.

CHARLES: I refuse to endure months of expensive humiliation only to be told at the end of it that at the age of four I was in love with my rocking horse.

RUTH: What do you suggest then?

CHARLES: I don't suggest anything—I'm profoundly uneasy.

RUTH: Perhaps there's something pressing on your brain.

CHARLES: If there were something pressing on my brain I should have violent headaches, shouldn't I?

RUTH: Not necessarily. An uncle of mine had a lump the size of a cricket ball pressing on his brain for years and he never felt a thing.

CHARLES: [*Rises*] I know I should know if I had anything like that.

RUTH: He didn't.

CHARLES: What happened to him?

RUTH: He had it taken out and he's been as bright as a button ever since.

CHARLES: Did he have any sort of delusions—did he think he saw things that weren't there?

RUTH: No, I don't think so.

CHARLES: Well, what the hell are we talking about him for then? It's sheer waste of valuable time.

RUTH: I only brought him up as an example.

CHARLES: I think I'm going mad.

RUTH: How do you feel now?

CHARLES: Physically do you mean?

RUTH: Altogether.

CHARLES: [*After due reflection*] Apart from being worried I feel quite normal.

RUTH: Good. You're not hearing or seeing anything in the least unusual?

CHARLES: Not a thing.

[*At this moment* Elvira *comes in from the garden, carrying an armful of roses. The roses are as grey as the rest of her*]

ELVIRA: You've absolutely ruined that border by the sundial—it looks like a mixed salad.

CHARLES: O my God!

RUTH: What's the matter now?

CHARLES: She's here again!

RUTH: What do you mean? Who's here again?

CHARLES: Elvira.

RUTH: Pull yourself together and don't be absurd.

ELVIRA: It's all those nasturtiums—they're so vulgar.

CHARLES: I like nasturtiums.

RUTH: You like what?

ELVIRA: [*Putting her grey roses into a vase*] They're all right in moderation but in a mass like that they look beastly.

CHARLES: Help me, Ruth—you've got to help me—

RUTH: [*Rises*] What did you mean about nasturtiums?

CHARLES: Never mind about that now—I tell you she's here again.

ELVIRA: You have been having a nice scene, haven't you? I could hear you right down the garden.

CHARLES: Please mind your own business.

RUTH: If your behaving like a lunatic isn't my business nothing is.

ELVIRA: I expect it was about me, wasn't it? I know I ought to feel sorry but I'm not—I'm delighted.

CHARLES: How can you be so inconsiderate?

RUTH: [*Shrilly*] Inconsiderate!—I like that, I must say—

CHARLES: Ruth—darling—please . . .

RUTH: I've done everything I can to help—I've controlled myself admirably—and I should like to say here and now that I don't believe a word about your damned hallucinations—you're up to something, Charles—there's been a certain furtiveness in your manner for weeks— Why don't you be honest and tell me what it is?

CHARLES: You're wrong—you're dead wrong—I haven't been in the least furtive—I—

RUTH: You're trying to upset me—for some obscure reason you're trying to goad me into doing something that I might regret—I won't stand for it any more— You're making me utterly miserable— [*She bursts into tears and collapses on sofa*]

CHARLES: Ruth—please— [*Sits on sofa beside* Ruth]

RUTH: Don't come near me——

ELVIRA: Let her have a nice cry—it'll do her good.

CHARLES: You're utterly heartless!

RUTH: Heartless!

CHARLES: [*Wildly*] I was not talking to you—I was talking to Elvira.

RUTH: Go on talking to her then, talk to her until you're blue in the face but don't talk to me—

CHARLES: Help me, Elvira—

ELVIRA: How?

CHARLES: Make her see you or something.

ELVIRA: I'm afraid I couldn't manage that—it's technically the most difficult business—frightfully complicated, you know—it takes years of study—

CHARLES: You are here, aren't you? You're not an illusion?

ELVIRA: I may be an illusion but I'm most definitely here.

CHARLES: How did you get here?

ELVIRA: I told you last night—I don't exactly know—

CHARLES: Well, you must make me a promise that in future you only come and talk to me when I'm alone—

ELVIRA: [*Pouting*] How unkind you are—making me feel so unwanted—I've never been treated so rudely—

CHARLES: I don't mean to be rude, but you must see—

ELVIRA: It's all your own fault for having married a woman who is incapable of seeing beyond the nose on her face—if she had a grain of real sympathy or affection for you she'd believe what you tell her.

CHARLES: How could you expect anybody to believe this?

ELVIRA: You'd be surprised how gullible people are —we often laugh about it on the other side.

[Ruth, *who has stopped crying and been staring at* Charles *in horror, suddenly gets up*]

RUTH: [*Gently*] Charles—

CHARLES: [*Surprised at her tone*] Yes, dear—

RUTH: I'm awfully sorry I was cross—

CHARLES: But, my dear—

RUTH: I understand everything now, I do really—

CHARLES: You do?

RUTH: [*Patting his arm reassuringly*] Of course I do.

ELVIRA: Look out—she's up to something—

CHARLES: Will you please be quiet?

RUTH: Of course, darling—we'll all be quiet, won't we? We'll be as quiet as little mice.

CHARLES: Ruth dear, listen—

RUTH: I want you to come upstairs with me and go to bed—

ELVIRA: The way that woman harps on bed is nothing short of erotic.

CHARLES: I'll deal with you later—

RUTH: Whenever you like, darling. Come along.

CHARLES: Ruth dear—I'd really rather not go to bed in the middle of the morning—

ELVIRA: How you've changed, darling!

CHARLES: Don't be disgusting.

RUTH: [*Sweetly*] I'm sorry, dear—I didn't mean to be.

CHARLES: What are you up to?

RUTH: I'm not up to anything—I just want you to go quietly to bed and wait there until Doctor Bradman comes—

CHARLES: No, Ruth—you're wrong—

RUTH: [Firmly] Come, dear—

ELVIRA: She'll have you in a strait jacket before you know where you are.

CHARLES: [Frantically] Help me—you must help me—

ELVIRA: [Enjoying herself] My dear, I would with pleasure, but I can't think how—

CHARLES: I can—listen, Ruth—

RUTH: Yes, dear?

CHARLES: If I promise to go to bed will you let me stay here for five minutes longer?

RUTH: I really think it would be better—

CHARLES: Bear with me—however mad it may seem —bear with me for just five minutes longer—

RUTH: [Letting go of him] Very well—what is it?

CHARLES: Sit down then.

RUTH: [Sitting down] All right—there.

CHARLES: Now listen—listen carefully—

ELVIRA: Have a cigarette, it will soothe your nerves.

CHARLES: I don't want a cigarette.

RUTH: [Indulgently] Then you shan't have one, darling.

CHARLES: Ruth, I want to explain to you clearly and without emotion that beyond any shadow of doubt the ghost or shade or whatever you like to call it of my first wife Elvira is in this room now.

RUTH: Yes, dear.

CHARLES: I know you don't believe it and are trying valiantly to humour me but I intend to prove it to you.

RUTH: Why not lie down and have a nice rest and you can prove anything you want to later on?

CHARLES: She may not be here later on.

ELVIRA: Don't worry—she will!

CHARLES: O God!

RUTH: Hush, dear.

CHARLES: [To Elvira] Promise you'll do what I ask?

ELVIRA: That all depends what it is.

CHARLES: Ruth—you see that bowl of flowers on the piano?

RUTH: Yes, dear—I did it myself this morning.

ELVIRA: Very untidily if I may say so.

CHARLES: You may not.

RUTH: Very well—I never will again—I promise.

CHARLES: Elvira will now carry that bowl of flowers to the mantelpiece and back again. You will, Elvira, won't you—just to please me?

ELVIRA: I don't really see why I should—you've been quite insufferable to me ever since I materialized.

CHARLES: Please.

ELVIRA: All right, I will just this once—not that I approve of all these Herman The Great carryings on. [She goes over to the piano]

CHARLES: Now, Ruth—watch carefully.

RUTH: [Patiently] Very well, dear.

CHARLES: Go on, Elvira—bring it to the mantelpiece and back again.

[Elvira does so, taking obvious pleasure in doing it in a very roundabout way. At one moment she brings it up to within an inch of Ruth's face. Ruth shrinks back with a scream and then jumps to her feet]

RUTH: [Furiously] How dare you, Charles! You ought to be ashamed of yourself!

CHARLES: What on earth for?

RUTH: [Hysterically] It's a trick—I know perfectly well it's a trick—you've been working up to this— it's all part of some horrible plan—

CHARLES: It isn't—I swear it isn't—Elvira—do something else for God's sake—

ELVIRA: Certainly—anything to oblige.

RUTH: [Becoming really frightened] You want to get rid of me—you're trying to drive me out of my mind—

CHARLES: Don't be so silly.

RUTH: You're cruel and sadistic and I'll never forgive you—[Elvira lifts up a light chair and waltzes solemnly round the room with it, then she puts it down with a bang. Making a dive for the door] I'm not going to put up with this any more.

CHARLES: [Holding her] You must believe it—you must—

RUTH: Let me go immediately—

CHARLES: That was Elvira—I swear it was—

RUTH: [Struggling] Let me go—

CHARLES: Ruth—please—

[Ruth breaks away from him and runs towards the windows. Elvira gets there just before her and shuts them in her face. Ruth starts back, appalled]

RUTH: [Looking at Charles with eyes of horror] Charles—this is madness—sheer madness! it's some sort of auto-suggestion, isn't it—some form of hypnotism, swear to me it's only that? Swear to me it's only that.

ELVIRA: [Taking an expensive vase from the mantelpiece and crashing it into the grate] Hypnotism my foot!

[Ruth gives a scream and goes into violent hysterics as the curtain falls]

SCENE 2:   *The time is late on the following afternoon. When the curtain rises Ruth is sitting alone at the tea table, which is set in front of the fire. After a moment or two she gets up and, frowning thoughtfully, goes over to the piano and takes a cigarette out of a box. As she returns to the table the front door bell rings. She hears it and straightens herself as though preparing for a difficult interview. Edith enters.*

EDITH: Madame Arcati.

[Edith steps aside and

Madame Arcati comes in. Edith goes out. Madame Arcati is wearing a tweed coat and skirt and a great many amber beads and, possibly, a beret]

MADAME ARCATI: My dear Mrs. Condomine, I came directly I got your message.

RUTH: That was very kind of you.

MADAME ARCATI: [*Briskly*] Kind? Nonsense! Nothing kind about it—I look upon it as an outing.

RUTH: I'm so glad—will you have some tea?

MADAME ARCATI: China or Indian?

RUTH: China.

MADAME ARCATI: Good. I never touch Indian, it upsets my vibrations.

RUTH: Do sit down.

MADAME ARCATI: [*Turning her head and sniffing*] I find this room very interesting—very interesting indeed. I noticed it the other night.

RUTH: I'm not entirely surprised. [*She proceeds to pour out tea*]

MADAME ARCATI: [*Sitting down and pulling off her gloves*] Have you ever been to Cowden Manor?

RUTH: No, I'm afraid I haven't.

MADAME ARCATI: That's very interesting too—strikes you like a blow between the eyes the moment you walk into the drawing-room. Two lumps of sugar, please, and no milk at all.

RUTH: I am profoundly disturbed, Madame Arcati, and I want your help.

MADAME ARCATI: Aha! I thought as much. What's in these sandwiches?

RUTH: Cucumber.

MADAME ARCATI: Couldn't be better. [*She takes one*] Fire away.

RUTH: It's most awfully difficult to explain.

MADAME ARCATI: Facts first—explanations afterwards.

RUTH: It's the facts that are difficult to explain—they're so fantastic.

MADAME ARCATI: Facts very often are. Take creative talent for instance, how do you account for that? Look at Shakespeare and Michael Angelo! Try to explain Mozart snatching sounds out of the air and putting them down on paper when he was practically a baby—facts—plain facts. I know it's the fashion nowadays to ascribe it all to glands but my reply to that is fiddlededee.

RUTH: Yes, I'm sure you're quite right.

MADAME ARCATI: There are more things in heaven and earth than are dreamt of in your philosophy, Mrs. Condomine.

RUTH: There certainly are.

MADAME ARCATI: Come now—take the plunge—out with it. You've heard strange noises in the night no doubt—boards creaking—doors slamming—subdued moaning in the passages—is that it?

RUTH: No—I'm afraid it isn't.

MADAME ARCATI: No sudden gusts of cold wind, I hope.

RUTH: No, it's worse than that.

MADAME ARCATI: I'm all attention.

RUTH: [*With an effort*] I know it sounds idiotic but the other night—during the séance—something happened—

MADAME ARCATI: I knew it! Probably a poltergeist, they're enormously cunning, you know, they sometimes lie doggo for days—

RUTH: You know that my husband was married before?

MADAME ARCATI: Yes—I have heard it mentioned.

RUTH: His first wife, Elvira, died comparatively young—

MADAME ARCATI: [*Sharply*] Where?

RUTH: Here—in this house—in this very room.

MADAME ARCATI: [*Whistling*] Whew! I'm beginning to see daylight!

RUTH: She was convalescing after pneumonia and one evening she started to laugh helplessly at one of the B.B.C. musical programmes and died of a heart attack.

MADAME ARCATI: And she materialized the other evening—after I had gone?

RUTH: Not to me, but to my husband.

MADAME ARCATI: [*Rising impulsively*] Capital—capital! Oh, but that's splendid!

RUTH: [*Coldly*] From your own professional standpoint I can see that it might be regarded as a major achievement!

MADAME ARCATI: [*Delighted*] A triumph, my dear! Nothing more nor less than a triumph!

RUTH: But from my own personal point of view you must see that, to say the least of it, it's embarrassing.

MADAME ARCATI: [*Walking about the room*] At last—at last—a genuine materialization!

RUTH: Please sit down again, Madame Arcati.

MADAME ARCATI: How could anyone sit down at a moment like this? It's tremendous! I haven't had such a success since the Sudbury case.

RUTH: [*Sharply*] Nevertheless I must insist upon you sitting down and controlling your natural exuberance. I appreciate fully your pride in your achievement but I would like to point out that it has made my position in this house untenable and that I hold you entirely responsible.

MADAME ARCATI: [*Contrite*] Forgive me, Mrs. Condomine—I am being abominably selfish—[*She sits down*] How can I help you?

RUTH: How? By sending her back immediately to where she came from, of course.

MADAME ARCATI: I'm afraid that that is easier said than done.

RUTH: Do you mean to tell me that she is liable to stay here indefinitely?

MADAME ARCATI: It's difficult to say—I fear it depends largely on her.

RUTH: But my dear Madame Arcati—

MADAME ARCATI: Where is she now?

RUTH: My husband has driven her into Folkestone

—apparently she was anxious to see an old friend of hers who is staying at the Grand.

MADAME ARCATI: [*Producing a notebook*] Forgive this formality, but I shall have to make a report to the Psychical Research people—

RUTH: I would be very much obliged if there were no names mentioned.

MADAME ARCATI: The report will be confidential.

RUTH: This is a small village you know and gossip would be most undesirable.

MADAME ARCATI: I quite understand. You say she is visible only to your husband?

RUTH: Yes.

MADAME ARCATI: "Visible only to husband." Audible too I presume?

RUTH: Extremely audible.

MADAME ARCATI: "Extremely audible." Your husband was devoted to her?

RUTH: [*With slight irritation*] I believe so—

MADAME ARCATI: "Husband devoted."

RUTH: It was apparently a reasonably happy marriage—

MADAME ARCATI: Tut, tut, Mrs. Condomine.

RUTH: I beg your pardon?

MADAME ARCATI: When did she pass over?

RUTH: Seven years ago.

MADAME ARCATI: Aha! That means she must have been on the waiting list.

RUTH: Waiting list?

MADAME ARCATI: Yes, otherwise she would have got beyond the materialization stage by now. She must have marked herself down for a return visit and she'd never have been able to manage it unless there were a strong influence at work.

RUTH: Do you mean that Charles—my husband—wanted her back all that much?

MADAME ARCATI: Possibly, or it might have been her own determination—

RUTH: That sounds much more likely.

MADAME ARCATI: Would you say that she was a woman of strong character?

RUTH: [*With rising annoyance*] I really don't know, Madame Arcati. I never met her. Nor am I particularly interested in how and why she got here. I am solely concerned with the question of how to get her away again as soon as possible.

MADAME ARCATI: I fully sympathize with you, Mrs. Condomine, and I assure you I will do anything in my power to help—but at the moment I fear I cannot offer any great hopes.

RUTH: But I always understood that there was a way of exorcising ghosts—some sort of ritual?

MADAME ARCATI: You mean the old Bell and Book method?

RUTH: Yes—I suppose I do.

MADAME ARCATI: Poppycock, Mrs. Condomine. It was quite effective in the days of genuine religious belief but that's all changed now. I believe the de-cline of faith in the Spirit World has been causing grave concern.

RUTH: [*Impatiently*] Has it indeed?

MADAME ARCATI: There was a time of course when a drop of holy water could send even a poltergeist scampering for cover, but not any more—"*Où sont les neiges d'antan?*"

RUTH: Be that as it may, Madame Arcati, I must beg of you to do your utmost to dematerialize my husband's first wife as soon as possible.

MADAME ARCATI: The time has come for me to admit to you frankly, Mrs. Condomine, that I haven't the faintest idea how to set about it.

RUTH: [*Rises*] Do you mean to sit there and tell me that having mischievously conjured up this ghost or spirit or whatever she is and placed me in a hideous position you are unable to do anything about it at all?

MADAME ARCATI: Honesty is the best policy.

RUTH: But it's outrageous! I ought to hand you over to the police.

MADAME ARCATI: [*Rising*] You go too far, Mrs. Condomine.

RUTH: [*Furiously*] I go too far indeed? Do you realize what your insane amateur muddling has done?

MADAME ARCATI: I have been a professional since I was a child, Mrs. Condomine—"Amateur" is a word I cannot tolerate.

RUTH: It seems to me to be the height of amateurishness to evoke malignant spirits and not be able to get rid of them again.

MADAME ARCATI: [*With dignity*] I was in a trance. Anything might happen when I am in a trance.

RUTH: Well, all I can suggest is that you go into another one immediately and get this damned woman out of my house.

MADAME ARCATI: I can't go into trances at a moment's notice—it takes hours of preparation—in addition to which I have to be extremely careful of my diet for days beforehand. Today, for instance, I happened to lunch with friends and had pigeon pie which, plus these cucumber sandwiches, would make a trance out of the question.

RUTH: Well, you'll have to do something.

MADAME ARCATI: I will report the whole matter to the Society for Psychical Research at the earliest possible moment.

RUTH: Will they be able to do anything?

MADAME ARCATI: I doubt it. They'd send an investigating committee, I expect, and do a lot of questioning and wall tapping and mumbo jumbo and then they'd have a conference and you would probably have to go up to London to testify—

RUTH: [*Near tears*] It's too humiliating—it really is.

MADAME ARCATI: Please try not to upset yourself—nothing can be achieved by upsetting yourself.

RUTH: It's all very fine for you to talk like that, Madame Arcati—you don't seem to have the faintest realization of my position.

MADAME ARCATI: Try to look on the bright side.

RUTH: Bright side indeed! If your husband's first wife suddenly appeared from the grave and came to live in the house with you, do you suppose you'd be able to look on the bright side?

MADAME ARCATI: I resent your tone, Mrs. Condomine, I really do.

RUTH: You most decidedly have no right to—you are entirely to blame for the whole horrible situation.

MADAME ARCATI: Kindly remember that I came here the other night on your own invitation.

RUTH: On my husband's invitation.

MADAME ARCATI: I did what I was requested to do, which was to give a séance and establish contact with the other side—I had no idea that there was any ulterior motive mixed up with it.

RUTH: Ulterior motive?

MADAME ARCATI: Your husband was obviously eager to get in touch with his former wife. If I had been aware of that at the time I should naturally have consulted you beforehand—after all *"Noblesse oblige"*!

RUTH: He had no intention of trying to get in touch with anyone—the whole thing was planned in order for him to get material for a mystery story he is writing about a homicidal medium.

MADAME ARCATI: [*Drawing herself up*] Am I to understand that I was only invited in a spirit of mockery?

RUTH: Not at all—he merely wanted to make notes of some of the tricks of the trade.

MADAME ARCATI: [*Incensed*] Tricks of the trade! Insufferable! I've never been so insulted in my life. I feel we have nothing more to say to one another, Mrs. Condomine. Good-bye—[*She goes towards the door*]

RUTH: Please don't go—please—

MADAME ARCATI: Your attitude from the outset has been most unpleasant, Mrs. Condomine. Some of your remarks have been discourteous in the extreme and I should like to say without umbrage that if you and your husband were foolish enough to tamper with the unseen for paltry motives and in a spirit of ribaldry, whatever has happened to you is your own fault, and, to coin a phrase, as far as I'm concerned you can stew in your own juice! [Madame Arcati *goes majestically from the room*]

RUTH: [*Left alone, walks about the room*] Damn—damn—damn!

[*After a moment or two* Charles *comes in with* Elvira]

CHARLES: What on earth was Madame Arcati doing here?

RUTH: She came to tea.

CHARLES: Did you ask her?

RUTH: Of course I did.

CHARLES: You never told me you were going to.

RUTH: You never told me you were going to ask Elvira to live with us.

CHARLES: I didn't.

ELVIRA: [*Sauntering over to the tea table*] Oh, yes, you did, darling—it was your subconscious.

CHARLES: What was the old girl so cross about?—she practically cut me dead.

RUTH: I told her the truth about why we invited her the other night.

CHARLES: That was quite unnecessary and most unkind.

RUTH: She needed taking down a bit, she was blowing herself out like a pouter pigeon.

CHARLES: Why did you ask her to tea?

ELVIRA: To get me exorcised, of course. Oh dear, I wish I could have a cucumber sandwich—I did love them so.

CHARLES: Is that true, Ruth?

RUTH: Is what true?

CHARLES: What Elvira said.

RUTH: You know perfectly well I can't hear what Elvira says.

CHARLES: She said that you got Madame Arcati here to try to get her exorcised. Is that true?

RUTH: We discussed the possibilities.

ELVIRA: There's a snake in the grass for you.

CHARLES: You had no right to do such a thing without consulting me.

RUTH: I have every right—this situation is absolutely impossible and you know it.

CHARLES: If only you'd make an effort and try to be a little more friendly to Elvira we might all have quite a jolly time.

RUTH: I have no wish to have a jolly time with Elvira.

ELVIRA: She's certainly very bad tempered, isn't she? I can't think why you married her.

CHARLES: She's naturally a bit upset—we must make allowances.

ELVIRA: I was never bad tempered though, was I, darling? Not even when you were beastly to me—

CHARLES: I was never beastly to you.

RUTH: [*Exasperated*] Where is Elvira at the moment?

CHARLES: In the chair, by the table.

RUTH: Now look here, Elvira—I shall have to call you Elvira, shan't I? I can't very well go on saying Mrs. Condomine all the time, it would sound too silly—

ELVIRA: I don't see why not.

RUTH: Did she say anything?

CHARLES: She said she'd like nothing better.

ELVIRA: [*Giggling*] You really are sweet, Charles darling—I worship you.

RUTH: I wish to be absolutely honest with you, Elvira—

ELVIRA: Hold on to your hats, boys!

RUTH: I admit I did ask Madame Arcati here with a view to getting you exorcised and I think that if you were in my position you'd have done exactly the same thing—wouldn't you?

ELVIRA: I shouldn't have done it so obviously.

RUTH: What did she say?

CHARLES: Nothing—she just nodded and smiled.

RUTH: [*With a forced smile*] Thank you, Elvira—that's generous of you. I really would so much rather that there were no misunderstandings between us—

CHARLES: That's very sensible, Ruth—I agree entirely.

RUTH: [*To Elvira*] I want, before we go any further, to ask you a frank question. Why did you really come here? I don't see that you could have hoped to have achieved anything by it beyond the immediate joke of making Charles into a sort of astral bigamist.

ELVIRA: I came because the power of Charles's love tugged and tugged and tugged at me. Didn't it, my sweet?

RUTH: What did she say?

CHARLES: She said that she came because she wanted to see me again.

RUTH: Well, she's done that now, hasn't she?

CHARLES: We can't be inhospitable, Ruth.

RUTH: I have no wish to be inhospitable, but I should like to have just an idea of how long you intend to stay, Elvira?

ELVIRA: I don't know—I really don't know! [*She giggles*] Isn't it awful?

CHARLES: She says she doesn't know.

RUTH: Surely that's a little inconsiderate?

ELVIRA: Didn't the old spiritualist have any constructive ideas about getting rid of me?

CHARLES: What did Madame Arcati say?

RUTH: She said she couldn't do a thing.

ELVIRA: [*Moving gaily over to the window*] Hurray!

CHARLES: Don't be upset, Ruth dear—we shall soon adjust ourselves, you know—you must admit it's a unique experience—I can see no valid reason why we shouldn't get a great deal of fun out of it.

RUTH: Fun? Charles, how can you—you must be out of your mind!

CHARLES: Not at all—I thought I was at first—but now I must say I'm beginning to enjoy myself.

RUTH: [*Bursting into tears*] Oh, Charles—Charles—

ELVIRA: She's off again.

CHARLES: You really must not be so callous, Elvira —try to see her point a little—

RUTH: I suppose she said something insulting—

CHARLES: No, dear, she didn't do anything of the sort.

RUTH: Now look here, Elvira—

CHARLES: She's over by the window now.

RUTH: Why the hell can't she stay in the same place!

ELVIRA: Temper again—my poor Charles, what a terrible life you must lead.

CHARLES: Do shut up, darling, you'll only make everything worse.

RUTH: Who was that "darling" addressed to—her or me?

CHARLES: Both of you.

RUTH: [*Rises. Stamping her foot*] This is intolerable!

CHARLES: For heaven's sake don't get into another state—

RUTH: [*Furiously*] I've been doing my level best to control myself ever since yesterday morning and I'm damned if I'm going to try any more, the strain is too much. She has the advantage of being able to say whatever she pleases without me being able to hear her, but she can hear me all right, can't she, without any modified interpreting?

CHARLES: Modified interpreting? I don't know what you mean.

RUTH: Oh yes, you do—you haven't told me once what she really said—you wouldn't dare. Judging from her photograph she's the type who would use most unpleasant language—

CHARLES: Ruth—you're not to talk like that.

RUTH: I've been making polite conversation all through dinner last night and breakfast and lunch today—and it's been a nightmare—and I am not going to do it any more. I don't like Elvira any more than she likes me and what's more I'm certain that I never could have, dead or alive. If, since her untimely arrival here the other evening, she had shown the slightest sign of good manners, the slightest sign of breeding, I might have felt differently towards her, but all she has done is try to make mischief between us and have private jokes with you against me. I am now going up to my room and I shall have my dinner on a tray. You and she can have the house to yourselves and joke and gossip with each other to your heart's content. The first thing in the morning I am going up to London to interview the Psychical Research Society and if they fail me I shall go straight to the Archbishop of Canterbury—   [*She goes out*]

CHARLES: [*Making a movement to follow her*] Ruth—

ELVIRA: Let her go—she'll calm down later on.

CHARLES: It's unlike her to behave like this—she's generally so equable.

ELVIRA: No, she isn't, not really, her mouth gives her away—it's a hard mouth, Charles.

CHARLES: Her mouth's got nothing to do with it—I resent you discussing Ruth as though she were a horse.

ELVIRA: Do you love her?

CHARLES: Of course I do.

ELVIRA: As much as you loved me?

CHARLES: Don't be silly—it's all entirely different.

ELVIRA: I'm so glad. Nothing could ever have been quite the same, could it?

CHARLES: You always behaved very badly.

ELVIRA: Oh, Charles!

CHARLES: I'm grieved to see that your sojourn in the other world hasn't improved you in the least.

ELVIRA: [*Curling up in sofa*] Go on, darling—I love it when you pretend to be cross with me—

CHARLES: I'm now going up to talk to Ruth.

ELVIRA: Cowardly custard.

CHARLES: Don't be so idiotic. I can't let her go like that—I must be a little nice and sympathetic to her.

ELVIRA: I don't see why! If she's set on being disagreeable I should just let her get on with it.

CHARLES: The whole business is very difficult for her—we must be fair.

ELVIRA: She should learn to be more adaptable.

CHARLES: She probably will in time—it's been a shock—

ELVIRA: Has it been a shock for you too, darling?

CHARLES: Of course—what did you expect?

ELVIRA: A nice shock?

CHARLES: What do you want, Elvira?

ELVIRA: Want? I don't know what you mean.

CHARLES: I remember that whenever you were overpoweringly demure like that it usually meant that you wanted something.

ELVIRA: It's horrid of you to be so suspicious. All I want is to be with you.

CHARLES: Well, you are.

ELVIRA: I mean alone, darling. If you go and pamper Ruth and smalm her over, she'll probably come flouncing down again and our lovely quiet evening together will be spoilt.

CHARLES: You're incorrigibly selfish.

ELVIRA: Well, I haven't seen you for seven years—it's only natural that I should want a little time alone with you—to talk over old times. I'll let you go up just for a little while if you really think it's your duty.

CHARLES: Of course it is.

ELVIRA: [Smiling] Then I don't mind.

CHARLES: [Rises] You're disgraceful, Elvira.

ELVIRA: You won't be long, will you? You'll come down again very soon?

CHARLES: I shall most likely dress for dinner while I'm upstairs—you can read the *Tatler* or something.

ELVIRA: Darling, you don't have to dress—for me.

CHARLES: I always dress for dinner.

ELVIRA: What are you going to have? I should like to watch you eat something really delicious—

CHARLES: [Smiling and kissing his hand to her] Be a good girl now—you can play the gramophone if you like.

ELVIRA: [Demurely] Thank you, Charles.

[Charles *goes out. Elvira gets up, looks in the gramophone cupboard, finds the record of "Always" and puts it on. She starts to waltz lightly round the room to it. Edith comes in to fetch the tea tray. She sees the gramophone playing by itself so she turns it off and puts the record back in the cupboard. While she is picking up the tray Elvira takes the record out and puts it on again. Edith gives a shriek, drops the tray and rushes out of the room. Elvira continues to waltz gaily*]

SCENE 3: *The time is evening several days later. When the curtain rises Mrs. Bradman is sitting in an armchair. Ruth is standing by the window drumming on the pane with her fingers.*

MRS. BRADMAN: [*In armchair*] Does it show any signs of clearing?

RUTH: [*At window—looking out*] No, it's still pouring.

MRS. BRADMAN: I do sympathize with you, really I do—it's really been quite a chapter of accidents, hasn't it?

RUTH: It certainly has.

MRS. BRADMAN: That happens sometimes, you know—everything seems to go wrong at once—exactly as though there were some evil forces at work. I remember once when George and I went away for a fortnight's holiday not long after we were married—we were dogged by bad luck from beginning to end—the weather was vile—George sprained his ankle—I caught a terrible cold and had to stay in bed for two days—and to crown everything the lamp fell over in the sitting-room and set fire to the treatise George had written on hyperplasia of the abdominal glands.

RUTH: [*Absently*] How dreadful.

MRS. BRADMAN: He had to write it all over again—every single word.

RUTH: You're sure you wouldn't like a cocktail or some sherry or anything?

MRS. BRADMAN: No, thank you—really not—George will be down in a minute and we've got to go like lightning—we were supposed to be at the Wilmots' at seven and it's nearly that now.

RUTH: I think I'll have a little sherry—I feel I need it. [*She goes to the side table and pours herself some sherry*]

MRS. BRADMAN: Don't worry about your husband's arm, Mrs. Condomine—I'm sure it's only a sprain.

RUTH: It's not his arm I'm worried about.

MRS. BRADMAN: And I'm sure Edith will be up and about again in a few days—

RUTH: My cook gave notice this morning.

MRS. BRADMAN: Well, really! Servants are awful, aren't they? Not a shred of gratitude—at the first sign of trouble they run out on you—like rats leaving a sinking ship.

RUTH: I can't feel that your simile was entirely fortunate, Mrs. Bradman.

MRS. BRADMAN: [*Flustered*] Oh, I didn't mean that, really I didn't!

[Dr. Bradman *comes in*]

DR. BRADMAN: Nothing to worry about, Mrs. Condomine—it's only a slight sprain—

RUTH: I'm so relieved.

DR. BRADMAN: He made a good deal of fuss when I examined it—men are much worse patients than women, you know—particularly highly strung men like your husband.

RUTH: Is he so highly strung, do you think?

DR. BRADMAN: Yes, as a matter of fact I wanted to talk to you about that. I'm afraid he's been overworking lately.

RUTH: [*Frowning*] Overworking?

DR. BRADMAN: He's in rather a nervous condition—nothing serious, you understand—

RUTH: What makes you think so?

DR. BRADMAN: I know the symptoms. Of course the shock of his fall might have something to do with it, but I certainly should advise a complete rest for a couple of weeks—

RUTH: You mean he ought to go away?

DR. BRADMAN: I do. In cases like that a change of atmosphere can work wonders.

RUTH: What symptoms did you notice?

DR. BRADMAN: Oh, nothing to be unduly alarmed about—a certain air of strain—an inability to focus his eyes on the person he is talking to—a few rather marked irrelevancies in his conversation.

RUTH: I see. Can you remember any specific example?

DR. BRADMAN: Oh, he suddenly shouted "What are you doing in the bathroom?" and then, a little later, while I was writing him a prescription, he suddenly said "For God's sake behave yourself!"

MRS. BRADMAN: How extraordinary.

RUTH: [*Nervously*] He often goes on like that—particularly when he's immersed in writing a book—

DR. BRADMAN: Oh, I am not in the least perturbed about it really—but I do think a rest and a change would be a good idea.

RUTH: Thank you so much, Doctor. Would you like some sherry?

DR. BRADMAN: No, thank you—we really must be off.

RUTH: How is poor Edith?

DR. BRADMAN: She'll be all right in a few days—she's still recovering from the concussion.

MRS. BRADMAN: It's funny, isn't it, that both your housemaid and your husband should fall down on the same day, isn't it?

RUTH: Yes, if that sort of thing amuses you.

MRS. BRADMAN: [*Giggling nervously*] Of course I didn't mean it like that, Mrs. Condomine—

DR. BRADMAN: Come along, my dear—you're talking too much as usual.

MRS. BRADMAN: You are horrid, George. Good-bye, Mrs. Condomine—[*Rises*]

RUTH: [*Shaking hands*] Good-bye.

DR. BRADMAN: [*Also shaking hands*] I'll pop in and have a look at both patients sometime tomorrow morning.

RUTH: Thank you so much.

[Charles *comes in. His left arm is in a sling. Elvira follows him and sits down by the fire*]

DR. BRADMAN: Well—how does it feel?

CHARLES: All right.

DR. BRADMAN: It's only a slight sprain, you know.

CHARLES: Is this damned sling really essential?

DR. BRADMAN: It's a wise precaution—it will prevent you using your left hand except when it's really necessary.

CHARLES: I had intended to drive into Folkestone this evening—

DR. BRADMAN: It would be much better if you didn't.

CHARLES: It's extremely inconvenient—

RUTH: You can easily wait and go tomorrow, Charles—

ELVIRA: I can't stand another of those dreary evenings at home. Charles—it'll drive me dotty—and I haven't seen a movie for seven years—

CHARLES: Let me be the first to congratulate you.

DR. BRADMAN: [*Kindly*] What's that, old man?

RUTH: [*With intense meaning*] Charles dear—try to be sensible, I implore you.

CHARLES: Sorry—I forgot.

DR. BRADMAN: You can drive the car if you promise to go very slowly and carefully. Your gear shift is on the right, isn't it?

CHARLES: Yes.

DR. BRADMAN: Well, use your left hand as little as possible.

CHARLES: All right.

RUTH: You'd much better stay at home.

DR. BRADMAN: Couldn't you drive him in?

RUTH: [*Stiffly*] I'm afraid not—I have lots to do in the house and there's Edith to be attended to.

DR. BRADMAN: Well, I'll leave you to fight it out among yourselves—[*To Charles*] But remember if you do insist on going—carefully does it—the roads are very slippery anyhow. Come along, Violet.

MRS. BRADMAN: Good-bye again— Good-bye, Mr. Condomine.

CHARLES: Good-bye.

[*He goes into the hall with the* Bradmans. Ruth, *left alone, puts her sherry glass down on the table irritably*]

RUTH: You really are infuriating, Elvira—surely you could wait and go to the movies another night— [Elvira *gives a little laugh and, taking a rose out of a vase, throws it at* Ruth *and vanishes through the French windows. Picking up the rose and putting it back in the vase*] And stop behaving like a schoolgirl—you're old enough to know better.

CHARLES: [*Coming in*] What?

RUTH: I was talking to Elvira.

CHARLES: She isn't here.

RUTH: She was a moment ago—she threw a rose at me.

CHARLES: She's been very high-spirited all day. I know this mood of old. It usually meant that she was up to something.

RUTH: You're sure she isn't here?

CHARLES: Quite sure.

RUTH: I want to talk with you.

CHARLES: O God!

RUTH: I must—it's important.

CHARLES: You've behaved very well for the last few days, Ruth—you're not going to start making scenes again, are you?

RUTH: I resent that air of patronage, Charles. I have behaved well, as you call it, because there was nothing else to do, but I think it only fair to warn you that I offer no guarantee for the future. My patience is being stretched to its uttermost.

CHARLES: As far as I can see the position is just as difficult for Elvira as it is for you—if not more so. The poor little thing comes back trustingly after all those years in the other world and what is she faced with? Nothing but brawling and hostility?

RUTH: What did she expect?

CHARLES: Surely even a protoplasmic manifestation has the right to expect a little of the milk of human kindness?

RUTH: Milk of human fiddlesticks.

CHARLES: That just doesn't make sense, dear.

RUTH: Elvira is about as trusting as a puff adder.

CHARLES: You're granite, Ruth—sheer, unyielding granite.

RUTH: And a good deal more dangerous into the bargain.

CHARLES: Dangerous? I never heard anything so ridiculous. How could a poor lonely, wistful little spirit like Elvira be dangerous?

RUTH: Quite easily—and she is. She's beginning to show her hand.

CHARLES: How do you mean—in what way?

RUTH: [Sits on sofa] This is a fight, Charles—a bloody battle—a duel to the death between Elvira and me. Don't you realize that?

CHARLES: Melodramatic hysteria.

RUTH: It isn't melodramatic hysteria—it's true. Can't you see?

CHARLES: No, I can't. You're imagining things—jealousy causes people to have the most curious delusions.

RUTH: I am making every effort not to lose my temper with you, Charles, but I must say you are making it increasingly difficult for me.

CHARLES: All this talk of battles and duels—

RUTH: She came here with one purpose and one purpose only—and if you can't see it you're a bigger fool than I thought you.

CHARLES: What purpose could she have had beyond a natural desire to see me again? After all, you must remember that she was extremely attached to me, poor child.

RUTH: Her purpose is perfectly obvious. It is to get you to herself forever.

CHARLES: That's absurd—how could she?

RUTH: By killing you off of course.

CHARLES: Killing me off? You're mad!

RUTH: Why do you suppose Edith fell down the stairs and nearly cracked her skull?

CHARLES: What's Edith got to do with it?

RUTH: Because the whole of the top stair was covered with axle grease. Cook discovered it afterwards.

CHARLES: You're making this up, Ruth—

RUTH: I'm not. I swear I'm not. Why do you suppose when you were lopping that dead branch off the pear tree that the ladder broke? Because it had been practically sawn through on both sides.

CHARLES: But why should she want to kill me? I could understand her wanting to kill you, but why me?

RUTH: If you were dead it would be her final triumph over me. She'd have you with her forever on her damned astral plane and I'd be left high and dry. She's probably planning a sort of spiritual remarriage. I wouldn't put anything past her.

CHARLES: [Rises. Really shocked] Ruth!

RUTH: Don't you see now?

CHARLES: [Walking about the room] She couldn't be so sly, so wicked—she couldn't.

RUTH: Couldn't she just!

CHARLES: I grant you that as a character she was always rather light and irresponsible but I would never have believed her capable of low cunning—

RUTH: Perhaps the spirit world has deteriorated her.

CHARLES: Oh, Ruth!

RUTH: For heaven's sake stop looking like a wounded spaniel and concentrate—this is serious.

CHARLES: What are we to do?

RUTH: You're not to let her know that we suspect a thing—behave perfectly ordinarily—as though nothing had happened. I'm going to Madame Arcati immediately—I don't care how cross she is she's got to help us—even if she can't get rid of Elvira she must know some technical method of rendering her harmless. If a trance is necessary she shall go into a trance if I have to beat her into it. I'll be back in a half an hour—tell Elvira I've gone to see the Vicar—

CHARLES: This is appalling—

RUTH: Never mind about that—remember now, don't give yourself away by so much as a flick of an eyelid—

[Elvira comes in from the garden]

CHARLES: Look out—

RUTH: What?

CHARLES: I merely said it's a nice lookout.

ELVIRA: What's a nice lookout?

CHARLES: The weather, Elvira—the glass is going down and down and down—it's positively macabre.

ELVIRA: I find it difficult to believe that you and Ruth, at this particular moment, can't think of anything more interesting to talk about than the weather.

RUTH: [Rises] I can't stand this any more. I really can't.

CHARLES: Ruth dear—please—

ELVIRA: Has she broken out again?

RUTH: What did she say?

CHARLES: She asked if you had broken out again.

RUTH: How dare you talk like that, Elvira!

CHARLES: Now then, Ruth—

RUTH: [*With dignity*] Charles and I were not talking about the weather, Elvira, as you so very shrewdly suspected. I should loathe you to think *that we had any secrets from you* and so I will explain exactly what we were talking about. I was trying to persuade him *not* to drive you into Folkestone this evening. It will be bad for his arm and you can perfectly easily wait until tomorrow. However, as he seems to be determined to place your wishes before mine in everything, I have nothing further to say. I'm sure I hope you both enjoy yourselves. [*She goes out and slams the door*]

CHARLES: There now.

ELVIRA: Oh, Charles—have you been beastly to her?

CHARLES: No—Ruth doesn't like being thwarted any more than you do.

ELVIRA: She's a woman of sterling character. It's a pity she's so unforgiving.

CHARLES: As I told you before—I would rather not discuss Ruth with you—it makes me uncomfortable.

ELVIRA: I won't mention her again. Are you ready?

CHARLES: What for?

ELVIRA: To go to Folkestone of course.

CHARLES: [*Rises from pouffe*] I want a glass of sherry first.

ELVIRA: I don't believe you want to take me at all.

CHARLES: Of course I want to take you, but I still think it would be more sensible to wait until tomorrow—it's a filthy night.

ELVIRA: [*Crossly*] How familiar this is.

CHARLES: In what way familiar?

ELVIRA: All through our married life I only had to suggest something for you immediately to start hedging me off—

CHARLES: I'm not hedging you off, I merely said—

ELVIRA: All right—all right—we'll spend another cosy, intimate evening at home with Ruth sewing away at that hideous table centre and snapping at us like a terrier.

CHARLES: Ruth is perfectly aware that the table centre is hideous. It happens to be a birthday present for her mother—

ELVIRA: It's no use trying to defend Ruth's taste to me—it's thoroughly artsy craftsy and you know it.

CHARLES: It is not artsy craftsy.

ELVIRA: She's ruined this room—look at those curtains and that awful shawl on the piano—

CHARLES: Lady Mackinley sent it to us from Burma.

ELVIRA: Obviously because it had been sent to her from Birmingham.

CHARLES: If you don't behave yourself I shan't take you into Folkestone ever.

ELVIRA: [*Coaxingly*] Please, Charles—don't be elderly and grand with me! Please let's go now.

CHARLES: Not until I've had my sherry.

ELVIRA: You are tiresome, darling—I've been waiting about for hours—

CHARLES: A few more minutes won't make any difference then. [*He pours himself out some sherry*]

ELVIRA: [*Petulantly, flinging herself into a chair*] Oh, very well.

CHARLES: Besides, the car won't be back for a half an hour at least.

ELVIRA: [*Sharply*] What do you mean?

CHARLES: [*Sipping his sherry nonchalantly*] Ruth's taken it—she had to go and see the Vicar—

ELVIRA: [*Jumping up—in extreme agitation*] What!!

CHARLES: What on earth's the matter?

ELVIRA: You say *Ruth's* taken the ear?

CHARLES: Yes—to go and see the Vicar—but she won't be long.

ELVIRA: [*Wildly*] O, my God! O, my God!

CHARLES: Elvira!—

ELVIRA: Stop her! You must stop her at once—

CHARLES: Why—what for?—

ELVIRA: [*Jumping up and down*] Stop her—go out and stop her immediately!

CHARLES: It's too late now—she's gone already.

ELVIRA: [*Backs away towards window*] Oh! Oh! Oh! Oh!!!

CHARLES: What are you going on like this for? What have you done?

ELVIRA: [*Frightened*] Done?—I haven't done anything—

CHARLES: Elvira—you're lying—

ELVIRA: [*Backing away from him*] I'm not lying. What is there to lie about?

CHARLES: What are you in such a state for?

ELVIRA: [*Almost hysterical*] I'm not in a state—I don't know what you mean—

CHARLES: You've done something dreadful—

ELVIRA: [*Backs away*] Don't look at me like that, Charles—I haven't—I swear I haven't—

CHARLES: [*Striking his forehead*] My God, the car!

ELVIRA: No, Charles—no—

CHARLES: Ruth was right—you did want to kill me —you've done something to the car—

ELVIRA: [*Howling like a banshee*] Oh—oh—oh— oh!—

CHARLES: What did you do—answer me?

[*At this moment the telephone rings.* Charles *stops dead; then with slow steps goes to it*]

CHARLES: [*At telephone*] Hallo—hallo—yes, speaking—I see—the bridge at the bottom of the hill— thank you. No, I'll come at once— [*He slowly puts back the receiver. As he does so the door bursts open*]

ELVIRA: [*Obviously retreating from someone*] Well, of all the filthy, low-down tricks— [*She shields her head with her hands and screams*] Ow—stop it—Ruth—let go—

[*She runs out of the room and slams the door. It opens again immediately and slams again.*
Charles *stares, aghast*]

Act III

SCENE 1:   *The time is evening a few days later. Charles is standing before the fire drinking his after-dinner coffee. He is in deep mourning. He finishes his coffee, puts the cup down on the mantelpiece, lights a cigarette and settles himself comfortably in an armchair. He adjusts a reading lamp and with a sigh of well-being opens a novel and begins to read it. There is a ring at the front doorbell. With an exlamation of annoyance he puts down the book, gets up and goes out into the hall. After a moment or so Madame Arcati comes in. Charles follows her and shuts the door. Madame Arcati is wearing the strange, rather barbaric evening clothes that she wore in Act One.*

MADAME ARCATI: I hope you will not consider this an intrusion, Mr. Condomine.

CHARLES: Not at all—please sit down, won't you?

MADAME ARCATI: Thank you. [*She does so*]

CHARLES: Would you like some coffee—or a liqueur?

MADAME ARCATI: No, thank you. I had to come, Mr. Condomine.

CHARLES: [*Politely*] Yes?

MADAME ARCATI: I felt a tremendous urge—like a rushing wind, and so I hopped on my bike and here I am.

CHARLES: It was very kind of you.

MADAME ARCATI: No, no, no—not kind at all—it was my duty—I know it strongly.

CHARLES: Duty?

MADAME ARCATI: I reproach myself bitterly, you know.

CHARLES: Please don't—there is no necessity for that. [*Sits in armchair*]

MADAME ARCATI: I allowed myself to get into a huff the other day with your late wife. I rode all the way home in the grip of temper, Mr. Condomine. —I have regretted it ever since.

CHARLES: My dear Madame Arcati . . .

MADAME ARCATI: [*Holding up her hand*] Please let me go on. Mine is the shame, mine is the blame—I shall never forgive myself. Had I not been so impetuous—had I listened to the cool voice of reason—much might have been averted. . . .

CHARLES: You told my wife distinctly that you were unable to help her—you were perfectly honest. Over and above the original unfortunate mistake I see no reason for you to reproach yourself.

MADAME ARCATI: I threw up the sponge—in a mo-ment of crisis I threw up the sponge instead of throwing down the gauntlet . . .

CHARLES: Whatever you threw, Madame Arcati, I very much fear nothing could have been done—it seems that circumstances have been a little too strong for all of us.

MADAME ARCATI: I cannot bring myself to admit defeat so easily—it is gall and wormwood to me—I could have at least concentrated—made an effort.

CHARLES: Never mind.

MADAME ARCATI: I do mind. I cannot help it. I mind with every fibre of my being. I have been thinking very carefully, I have also been reading up a good deal during the last few dreadful days . . . I gather that we are alone?

CHARLES: [*Looking round*] My first wife is not in the room, she is upstairs lying down, the funeral exhausted her. I imagine that my second wife is with her but of course I have no way of knowing for certain.

MADAME ARCATI: You have remarked no difference in the texture of your first wife since the accident?

CHARLES: No, she seems much as usual, a little under the weather perhaps, a trifle low-spirited, but that's all.

MADAME ARCATI: Well, that washes that out.

CHARLES: I'm afraid I don't understand.

MADAME ARCATI: Just a little theory I had. In the nineteenth century there was a pretty widespread belief that a ghost who participated in the death of a human being disintegrated automatically—

CHARLES: How do you know that Elvira was in any way responsible for Ruth's death?

MADAME ARCATI: Elvira—such a pretty name—it has a definite lilt to it, hasn't it? [*She hums for a moment singing the Elvi-i-ira*] Elvira—Elvi-ira . . .

CHARLES: [*Rather agitated*] You haven't answered my question. How did you know?

MADAME ARCATI: It came to me last night, Mr. Condomine—it came to me in a blinding flash—I had just finished my Ovaltine and turned the light out when I suddenly started up in bed with a loud cry —"Great Scott. I've got it!" I said—after that I began to put two and two together. At three in the morning—with my brain fairly seething—I went to work on my crystal for a little but it wasn't very satisfactory—cloudy, you know—

CHARLES: [*Moving about uneasily*] I would be very much obliged if you would keep any theories you have regarding my wife's death to yourself, Madame Arcati . . .

MADAME ARCATI: My one desire is to help you. I feel I have been dreadfully remiss over the whole affair—not only remiss but untidy.

CHARLES: I am afraid there is nothing whatever to be done.

MADAME ARCATI: [*Triumphantly*] But there is—there is! [*She produces a piece of paper from her bag and brandishes it*] I have found a formula—here it is!

I copied it out of Edmondson's *Witchcraft and Its Byways.*

CHARLES: [*Irritably*] What the hell are you talking about?

MADAME ARCATI: [*Rises*] Pluck up your heart, Mr. Condomine . . . all is not lost!

CHARLES: [*Rises*] Now look here, Madame Arcati—

MADAME ARCATI: You are still anxious to dematerialize your first wife, I suppose?

CHARLES: [*In a lower voice, with a cautious look towards the door*] Of course I am—I'm perfectly furious with her, but—

MADAME ARCATI: But what?

CHARLES: Well—she's been very upset for the last few days—you see apart from me being angry with her which she always hated even when she was alive, Ruth, my second wife, has hardly left her side for a moment—you must see that she's been having a pretty bad time what with one thing and another . . .

MADAME ARCATI: Your delicacy of feeling does you credit but I must say, if you will forgive my bluntness, that you are a damned fool, Mr. Condomine.

CHARLES: [*Stiffly*] You are at liberty to think whatever you please.

MADAME ARCATI: Now, now, now—don't get on your high horse—there's no sense in that, is there? I have a formula here that I think will be able to get rid of her without hurting her feelings in the least. It's extremely simple and requires nothing more than complete concentration from you and minor trance from me—I may even be able to manage it without lying down.

CHARLES: Honestly I would rather—

[*At this moment the door opens and* Elvira *enters, coming quickly into the room. She is obviously very upset*]

ELVIRA: Charles—

CHARLES: What on earth's the matter?

ELVIRA: [*Seeing* Madame Arcati] Oh! What's she doing here?

CHARLES: She came to offer me her condolences.

ELVIRA: They should have been congratulations.

CHARLES: Please don't say things like that, Elvira—it is in the worst possible taste. Madame Arcati—allow me to introduce my first wife Elvira—

MADAME ARCATI: How do you do?

ELVIRA: What does she want, Charles? Send her away—[*She walks about the room*]

MADAME ARCATI: In what part of the room is she at the moment?

CHARLES: She's moving about rather rapidly. I'll tell you when and where she settles.

ELVIRA: She's the one who got me here in the first place, isn't she?

CHARLES: Yes.

ELVIRA: Well, please tell her to get me away again as soon as possible—I can't stand this house another minute.

CHARLES: Really, Elvira—I'm surprised at you.

ELVIRA: [*Nearly in tears*] I don't care how surprised you are—I want to go home—I'm sick of the whole thing.

CHARLES: Don't be childish, Elvira.

ELVIRA: I'm not being childish—I mean it.

MADAME ARCATI: [*Sniffling*] Very interesting—very interesting—I smell protoplasm strongly!

ELVIRA: What a disgusting thing to say.

MADAME ARCATI: [*Very excited*] Where is she now?

CHARLES: Here—close to me.

MADAME ARCATI: [*Mystically—stretching out her hands*] Are you happy, my dear—?

ELVIRA: [*Stamping her foot*] Tell the silly old bitch to mind her own business.

MADAME ARCATI: [*In a sing-song voice*] Was the journey difficult? Are you weary?

ELVIRA: She's dotty.

CHARLES: Just a moment, Madame Arcati .

MADAME ARCATI: [*With her eyes shut*] This is wonderful—wonderful—

ELVIRA: For God's sake tell her to go into the other room, Charles. I've got to talk to you.

CHARLES: Madame Arcati . . .

MADAME ARCATI: Just a moment. I almost have contact—I can sense the vibrations—this is magnificent . . .

CHARLES: Go on, Elvira—don't be a spoilsport—give her a bit of encouragement.

ELVIRA: If you'll promise to get her into the other room.

CHARLES: All right.

[Elvira *goes up to* Madame Arcati *and blows gently into her ear*]

MADAME ARCATI: [*Jumping*] Yes, yes—again—again—

ELVIRA: [*Blowing in the other ear behind* Madame Arcati] How's that?

MADAME ARCATI: [*Clasping and unclasping her hands in a frenzy of excitement*] This is first rate—it really is first rate. Absolutely stunning!

CHARLES: I'm so glad you're pleased.

ELVIRA: Please get rid of her. Ruth will be in in a minute.

CHARLES: Madame Arcati, would you think it most frightfully rude if I asked you to go into the dining-room for a moment? My first wife wishes to speak to me alone.

MADAME ARCATI: Oh, must I? It's so lovely being actually in the room with her.

CHARLES: Only for a few minutes—I promise she'll be here when you come back.

MADAME ARCATI: Very well. Hand me my bag, will you?—it's on the sofa.

ELVIRA: [*Picking it up and handing it to her*] Here you are.

MADAME ARCATI: [*Taking it and blowing her a kiss*]

Oh, you darling—you little darling. [Madame Arcati, *humming ecstatically, goes into the dining-room and shuts the door*]

ELVIRA: How good is she really?

CHARLES: I don't know.

ELVIRA: Do you think she really could get me back again?

CHARLES: But my dear child . . .

ELVIRA: And don't call me your dear child—it's smug and supercilious.

CHARLES: There's no need to be rude.

ELVIRA: [*Turning away*] The whole thing's been a failure—a miserable, dreary failure—and oh! what *high hopes* I started out with.

CHARLES: You can't expect much sympathy from me, you know. I am perfectly aware that your highest hope was to murder me.

ELVIRA: Don't put it like that, it sounds so beastly.

CHARLES: It is beastly. It's one of the beastliest ideas I've ever heard.

ELVIRA: There was a time when you'd have welcomed the chance of being with me forever.

CHARLES: Your behaviour has shocked me immeasurably, Elvira, I had no idea you were so unscrupulous.

ELVIRA: [*Bursting into tears*] Oh, Charles.

CHARLES: Stop crying.

ELVIRA: They're only ghost tears—they don't mean anything really—but they're very painful.

CHARLES: You've brought all this on yourself, you know. [*Sits on sofa*]

ELVIRA: That's right—rub it in. Anyhow, it was only because I loved you—the silliest thing I ever did in my whole life was to love you—you were always unworthy of me.

CHARLES: That remark comes perilously near impertinence, Elvira.

ELVIRA: I sat there, on the other side, just longing for you day after day. I did really—all through your affair with that brassy-looking woman in the South of France I went on loving you and thinking truly of you—then you married Ruth and even then I forgave you and tried to understand because all the time I believed deep inside that you really loved me best . . . that's why I put myself down for a return visit and had to fill in all those forms and wait about in draughty passages for hours—if only you'd died before you met Ruth everything might have been all right—she's absolutely ruined you—I hadn't been in the house a day before I realized that. Your books aren't a quarter as good as they used to be either.

CHARLES: [*Incensed. Rises*] That is entirely untrue . . . Ruth helped me and encouraged me with my work which is a damned sight more than you ever did.

ELVIRA: That's probably what's wrong with it.

CHARLES: All you ever thought of was going to parties and enjoying yourself.

ELVIRA: Why shouldn't I have fun? I died young, didn't I?

CHARLES: You needn't have died at all if you hadn't been idiotic enough to go out on the river with Guy Henderson and get soaked to the skin—

ELVIRA: So we're back at Guy Henderson again, are we?

CHARLES: You behaved abominably over Guy Henderson and it's no use pretending that you didn't.

ELVIRA: [*Sits on arm of chair*] Guy adored me—and anyhow he was very attractive.

CHARLES: You told me distinctly that he didn't attract you in the least.

ELVIRA: You'd have gone through the roof if I'd told you that he did.

CHARLES: Did you have an affair with Guy Henderson?

ELVIRA: I would rather not discuss it if you don't mind.

CHARLES: Answer me—did you or didn't you?

ELVIRA: Of course I didn't.

CHARLES: You let him kiss you though, didn't you?

ELVIRA: How could I stop him? He was bigger than I was.

CHARLES: [*Furiously*] And you swore to me—

ELVIRA: Of course I did. You were always making scenes over nothing at all.

CHARLES: Nothing at all.

ELVIRA: You never loved me a bit really—it was only your beastly vanity.

CHARLES: You seriously believe that it was only vanity that upset me when you went out in the punt with Guy Henderson?

ELVIRA: It was not a punt—it was a little launch.

CHARLES: I don't care if it was a three-masted schooner you had no right to go!

ELVIRA: You seem to forget *why* I went! You seem to forget that you had spent the entire evening making sheep's eyes at that overblown looking harridan with the false pearls.

CHARLES: A woman in Cynthia Cheviot's position would hardly wear false pearls.

ELVIRA: They were practically all she was wearing.

CHARLES: I am pained to observe that seven years in the echoing vaults of eternity have in no way impaired your native vulgarity.

ELVIRA: That was the remark of a pompous ass.

CHARLES: There is nothing to be gained by continuing this discussion.

ELVIRA: You always used to say that when you were thoroughly worsted.

CHARLES: On looking back on our married years, Elvira, I see now, with horrid clarity, that they were nothing but a mockery.

ELVIRA: You invite mockery, Charles—it's something to do with your personality, I think, a certain seedy grandeur.

CHARLES: Once and for all, Elvira—

ELVIRA: You never suspected it but I laughed at you

steadily from the altar to the grave—all your ridiculous petty jealousies and your fussings and fumings—

CHARLES: You were feckless and irresponsible and morally unstable—I realized that before we left Budleigh Salterton.

ELVIRA: Nobody but a monumental bore would have thought of having a honeymoon at Budleigh Salterton.

CHARLES: What's the matter with Budleigh Salterton?

ELVIRA: I was an eager young bride, Charles—I wanted glamour and music and romance—all I got was potted palms, seven hours of every day on a damp golf course and a three-piece orchestra playing "Merrie England."

CHARLES: It's a pity you didn't tell me so at the time.

ELVIRA: I did—but you wouldn't listen—that's why I went out on the moors that day with Captain Bracegirdle. I was desperate.

CHARLES: You swore to me that you'd gone over to see your aunt in Exmouth!

ELVIRA: It was the moors.

CHARLES: With Captain Bracegirdle?

ELVIRA: With Captain Bracegirdle.

CHARLES: [Furiously] I might have known it—what a fool I was—what a blind fool! Did he make love to you?

ELVIRA: [Sucking her finger and regarding it thoughtfully] Of course.

CHARLES: Oh, Elvira!

ELVIRA: Only very discreetly—he was in the cavalry, you know—

CHARLES: Well, all I can say is that I'm well rid of you.

ELVIRA: Unfortunately you're not.

CHARLES: Oh yes, I am—you're dead and Ruth's dead—I shall sell this house lock, stock and barrel and go away.

ELVIRA: I shall follow you.

CHARLES: I shall go a long way away—I shall go to South America—you'll hate that, you were always a bad traveller.

ELVIRA: [At piano] That can't be helped—I shall have to follow you—you called me back.

CHARLES: I did not call you back!

ELVIRA: Well somebody did—and it's hardly likely to have been Ruth.

CHARLES: Nothing in the world was further from my thoughts.

ELVIRA: You were talking about me before dinner that evening.

CHARLES: I might just as easily have been talking about Joan of Arc but that wouldn't necessarily mean that I wanted her to come and live with me.

ELVIRA: As a matter of fact she's rather fun.

CHARLES: Stick to the point.

ELVIRA: When I think of what might have happened if I'd succeeded in getting you to the other world after all—it makes me shudder, it does honestly . . . it would be nothing but bickering and squabbling forever and ever and ever . . . I swear I'll be better off with Ruth—at least she'll find her own set and not get in my way.

CHARLES: So I get in your way, do I?

ELVIRA: Only because I was idiotic enough to imagine that you loved me, and I sort of felt sorry for you.

CHARLES: I'm sick of these insults—please go away.

ELVIRA: There's nothing I should like better—I've always believed in cutting my losses. That's why I died.

CHARLES: [Rises] Of all the brazen sophistry—

ELVIRA: Call that old girl in again—set her to work—I won't tolerate this any longer—I want to go home. [She starts to cry]

CHARLES: For heaven's sake don't snivel.

ELVIRA: [Stamping her foot] Call her in—she's got to get me out of this.

CHARLES: [Going to the dining-room door] I quite agree—and the sooner the better. [He opens the door] Madame Arcati—would you please come in now?

[Madame Arcati comes in eagerly]

MADAME ARCATI: Is the darling still here?

CHARLES: [Grimly] Yes, she is.

MADAME ARCATI: Where—tell me where?

CHARLES: Over by the piano—blowing her nose.

MADAME ARCATI: [Approaching the piano] My dear—oh, my dear—

ELVIRA: Stop her fawning on me, Charles, or I shall break something.

CHARLES: Elvira and I have discussed the whole situation, Madame Arcati, and she wishes to go home immediately.

MADAME ARCATI: Home?

CHARLES: Wherever she came from.

MADAME ARCATI: You don't think she would like to stay a few days longer—while I try to get things a little more organized?

ELVIRA: No—no—I want to go now.

MADAME ARCATI: I could come and be here with her—I could bring my crystal—

ELVIRA: God forbid!

CHARLES: We are both agreed that she must go as soon as possible. Please strain every nerve, Madame Arcati—make every effort—you said something about a formula—what is it?

MADAME ARCATI: [Reluctantly] Well—if you insist.

CHARLES: I most emphatically do insist.

ELVIRA: [Wailing] Oh, Charles. . . .

CHARLES: Shut up.

MADAME ARCATI: I can't guarantee anything, you know—I'll do my best but it may not work.

CHARLES: What is the formula?

MADAME ARCATI: Nothing more than a little verse

really—it fell into disuse after the seventeenth century—I shall need some pepper and salt—

CHARLES: There's pepper and salt in the dining-room —I'll get it. [He goes]

MADAME ARCATI: We ought of course to have some Shepherd's Wort and a frog or two but I think I can manage without. You won't be frightened, dear, will you? It's absolutely painless.

CHARLES: [Coming back with the cruet] Will this be enough?

MADAME ARCATI: Oh yes—I only need a little—put it on the table please. Now then, let me see— [She fumbles in her bag for the paper and her glasses] Ah yes—[To Charles] Sprinkle it, will you —just a soupçon—there, right in the middle— [Charles does so]

ELVIRA: This is going to be a flop—I can tell you that here and now.

MADAME ARCATI: Now a few snapdragons out of that vase, there's a good chap.

ELVIRA: [Contemptuously] Merlin does all this sort of thing at parties and bores us all stiff with it, only he always uses blackthorn and a great deal of whimsy!

CHARLES: Here you are.

MADAME ARCATI: Now then—the gramophone—in the old days of course they used a zither or reed pipes—[She goes to the gramophone] We'd better have the same record we had before, I think.

ELVIRA: I'll get it. [She takes out the record and puts it on the gramophone]

MADAME ARCATI: [Watching, fascinated] Oh, if only that Mr. Emsworth of the Psychical Research Society could see this—he'd have a fit, he would really! Don't start it yet, dear. Now then—[Charles gets piano chair and brings it down to table] Sit down, please, Mr. Condomine, rest your hands on the table but don't put your fingers in the pepper —I shall turn out the lights myself. Oh, shucks, I'd nearly forgotten—[She goes to the table and makes designs in the sprinkled pepper and salt with her forefinger] One triangle—[She consults the paper] One half circle and one little dot— there!

ELVIRA: This is waste of time—she's a complete fake.

CHARLES: Anything's worth trying.

ELVIRA: I'm as eager for it to succeed as you are— don't make any mistake about that. But I'll lay you ten to one it's a dead failure.

MADAME ARCATI: Now, if your wife would be kind enough to lie down on the sofa—

CHARLES: Go on, Elvira.

ELVIRA: [Lies down on sofa] This is sheer nonsense —don't blame me if I get the giggles.

CHARLES: Concentrate—think of nothing.

MADAME ARCATI: That's right—quite right—hands at the sides—legs extended—breathe steadily— one two—one two—one two—is she comfortable?

CHARLES: Are you comfortable, Elvira?

ELVIRA: No.

CHARLES: She's quite comfortable.

MADAME ARCATI: I shall join you in a moment, Mr. Condomine—I may have to go into a slight trance but if I do pay no attention—Now first the music and away we go! [Madame Arcati turns on the gramophone and stands quite still by the side of it with her hands behind her head for a little— then suddenly, with great swiftness, she runs to the door and switches out the lights. Her form can dimly be discerned moving about in the darkness. Charles gives a loud sneeze]

ELVIRA: [Giggling] Oh, dear—it's the pepper.

CHARLES: Damn!

MADAME ARCATI: Hold on to yourself—concentrate —[Madame Arcati recites in a sing-song voice]
  "Ghostly spectre—ghoul or fiend
  Never more be thou convened
  Shepherd's Wort and Holy Rite
  Banish thee into the night."

ELVIRA: What a disagreeable little verse.

CHARLES: Be quiet, Elvira.

MADAME ARCATI: Shhh! [There is silence] Is there anyone there? . . . Is there anyone there?—one rap for yes—two raps for no. Is there anyone there? . . . [The table gives a loud bump] Aha! Good stuff! Is it Daphne? . . . [The table gives another bump] I'm sorry to bother you, dear, but Mrs. Condomine wants to return. [The table bumps several times very quickly] Now then, Daphne . . . Did you hear what I said? [After a pause the table gives one bump] Can you help us? . . . [There is another pause, then the table begins to bump violently without stopping] Hold tight, Mr. Condomine—it's trying to break away. Oh! Oh! Oh— [The table falls over with a crash]

CHARLES: What's the matter, Madame Arcati? Are you hurt?

MADAME ARCATI: [Wailing] Oh! Oh! Oh—

CHARLES: [Turns on lights] What on earth's happening? [Madame Arcati is lying on the floor with the table upside down on her back. Charles hurriedly lifts it off. Shaking her] Are you hurt, Madame Arcati?

ELVIRA: She's in one of her damned trances again and I'm here as much as ever I was.

CHARLES: [Shaking Madame Arcati] For God's sake wake up.

MADAME ARCATI: [Moaning] Oh! Oh! Oh—

ELVIRA: Leave her alone—she's having a whale of a time. If I ever do get back I'll strangle that bloody little Daphne. . . .

CHARLES: Wake up!

MADAME ARCATI: [Sitting up suddenly] What happened?

CHARLES: Nothing—nothing at all.

MADAME ARCATI: [Rising and dusting herself] Oh yes, it did—I know something happened.

CHARLES: You fell over—that's all that happened.

MADAME ARCATI: Is she still here?

CHARLES: Of course she is.

MADAME ARCATI: Something must have gone wrong.

ELVIRA: Make her do it properly. I'm sick of being messed about like this.

CHARLES: She's doing her best. Be quiet, Elvira.

MADAME ARCATI: Something happened—I sensed it in my trance—I felt it—it shivered through me.

[*Suddenly the window curtains blow out almost straight and Ruth walks into the room. She is still wearing the brightly colored clothes in which we last saw her but now they are entirely grey. So is her hair and her skin*]

RUTH: Once and for all, Charles, what the hell does this mean?

[*The lights fade*]

SCENE 2:   *When the lights go up again several hours have elapsed. The whole room is in slight disarray. There are birch branches and evergreens laid on the floor in front of the doors and crossed birch branches pinned rather untidily onto the curtains. The furniture has been moved about a bit. On the bridge table there is a pile of playing cards, Madame Arcati's crystal and a Ouija board. Also a plate of sandwiches and two empty beer mugs. Madame Arcati is stretched out on the sofa with her eyes shut. Elvira is seated at the bridge table looking despondently at the debris. Ruth is by the fireplace. Charles is walking irritably about the room.*

RUTH: Well—we've done all we can—I must say I couldn't be more exhausted.

ELVIRA: It will be daylight soon.

[*The clock strikes five, very slowly*]

RUTH: That clock's always irritated me—it strikes far too slowly.

CHARLES: It was a wedding present from Uncle Walter.

RUTH: Whose Uncle Walter?

CHARLES: Elvira's.

RUTH: Well, all I can say is he might have chosen something a little more decorative.

ELVIRA: If that really were all you could say, Ruth, I'm sure it would be a great comfort to us all.

RUTH: [*Grandly*] You can be as rude as you like, Elvira, I don't mind a bit—as a matter of fact I should be extremely surprised if you weren't.

ELVIRA: [*Truculently*] Why?

RUTH: The reply to that is really too obvious.

CHARLES: I wish you two would stop bickering for one minute.

RUTH: This is quite definitely one of the most frustrating nights I have ever spent.

ELVIRA: The reply to that is pretty obvious too.

RUTH: I'm sure I don't know what you mean.

ELVIRA: Skip it.

RUTH: Now listen to me, Elvira. If you and I have got to stay together indefinitely in this house— and it looks unpleasantly—[*Turns to Madame Arcati*]—likely—we had better come to some sort of an arrangement.

ELVIRA: What sort of an arrangement?

CHARLES: You're *not* going to stay indefinitely in this house.

RUTH: With you then—we shall have to be with you.

CHARLES: I don't see why—why don't you take a cottage somewhere?

RUTH: You called us back.

CHARLES: I've already explained until I'm black in the face that I did nothing of the sort.

RUTH: Madame Arcati said you did.

CHARLES: Madame Arcati's a muddling old fool.

ELVIRA: I could have told you that in the first place.

RUTH: I think you're behaving very shabbily, Charles.

CHARLES: I don't see what I've done.

RUTH: We have all agreed that as Elvira and I are dead that it would be both right and proper for us to dematerialize again as soon as possible. That, I admit. We have allowed ourselves to be subjected to the most humiliating hocus-pocus for hours and hours without complaining—

CHARLES: Without complaining?

RUTH: We've stood up—we've lain down—we've concentrated. We've sat interminably while that tiresome old woman recited extremely unflattering verses at us. We've endured five séances—we've watched her fling herself in and out of trances until we're dizzy and at the end of it all we find ourselves exactly where we were at the beginning. . . .

CHARLES: Well, it's not my fault.

RUTH: Be that as it may, the least you could do is to admit failure gracefully and try to make the best of it—your manners are boorish to a degree.

CHARLES: I'm just as exhausted as you are. I've had to do all the damned table tapping, remember.

RUTH: If she can't get us back, she can't and that's that. We shall have to think of something else.

CHARLES: She *must* get you back—anything else is unthinkable.

ELVIRA: There's gratitude for you!

CHARLES: Gratitude?

ELVIRA: Yes, for all the years we've both devoted to you—you ought to be ashamed.

CHARLES: What about all the years I've devoted to you?

ELVIRA: Nonsense—we've waited on you hand and foot—haven't we, Ruth? You're exceedingly selfish and always were.

CHARLES: In that case I fail to see why you were both so anxious to get back to me.

RUTH: You called us back. And you've done nothing but try to get rid of us ever since we came—hasn't he, Elvira?

ELVIRA: He certainly has.

RUTH: And now, owing to your idiotic inefficiency, we find ourselves in the most mortifying position—we're neither fish, flesh nor fowl nor whatever it is.

ELVIRA: Good red herring.

RUTH: It can't be.

CHARLES: Well, why don't you do something about it? Why don't you go back on your own?

RUTH: We can't—you know perfectly well we can't.

CHARLES: Isn't there anybody on the other side who can help?

RUTH: How do I know? I've only been there a few days . . . ask Elvira.

ELVIRA: I've already told you, that's no good—if we got Cagliostro, Mesmer, Merlin, Gil de Retz and the Black Douglas in a row they couldn't do a thing—the impetus has got to come from here. . . . Perhaps darling Charles doesn't want us to go quite enough.

CHARLES: I certainly do.

ELVIRA: Well, you must have a very weak will then. I always suspected it.

RUTH: It's no use arguing any more—wake up Madame Arcati.

ELVIRA: Oh, not another séance—please, not another séance!

CHARLES: [Loudly—bending over Madame Arcati] Please wake up, Madame Arcati . . .

RUTH: Shake her.

CHARLES: It might upset her.

RUTH: I don't care if it kills her.

CHARLES: Please wake up, Madame Arcati. . . .

MADAME ARCATI: [Waking] What time is it?

CHARLES: Ten past five!

MADAME ARCATI: What time did I go off? [She sits up]

CHARLES: Over an hour ago.

MADAME ARCATI: [Reaching for her bag] Curious . . . very curious. Forgive me for a moment, I must just make a note of that for my diary. [She takes a book out of her bag and scribbles in it] Are they still here?

CHARLES: Yes.

MADAME ARCATI: How disappointing.

CHARLES: Have you any suggestions?

MADAME ARCATI: [Rising briskly] We mustn't give up hope. Chin up—never give in—that's my motto.

RUTH: This schoolgirl phraseology's driving me mad.

MADAME ARCATI: Now then . . .

CHARLES: Now then what?

MADAME ARCATI: What do you say we have another séance and really put our shoulders to the wheel? —Make it a real rouser!

ELVIRA: For God's sake not another séance.

MADAME ARCATI: I might be able to materialize a trumpet if I tried hard enough—better than nothing, you know—I feel as fit as a fiddle after my rest.

ELVIRA: I don't care if she materializes a whole symphony orchestra—I implore you not to let her have another séance.

CHARLES: Don't you think, Madame Arcati, that perhaps we've had enough séances? After all they haven't achieved much, have they?

MADAME ARCATI: Rome wasn't built in a day, you know.

CHARLES: I know it wasn't, but. . . .

MADAME ARCATI: Well then—cheer up—away with melancholy.

CHARLES: Now listen, Madame Arcati . . . before you go off into any further trances I really think we ought to discuss the situation a little.

MADAME ARCATI: Good—an excellent idea—and while we're doing it I shall have another of these delicious sandwiches—I'm as hungry as a hunter.

CHARLES: Would you like some more beer?

MADAME ARCATI: No, thank you—better not.

CHARLES: Very well—I think I'll have a small whisky and soda.

MADAME ARCATI: Make it a double and enjoy yourself.

[Charles goes to the drinks table and mixes himself a whisky and soda]

RUTH: One day I intend to give myself the pleasure of telling Madame Arcati exactly what I think of her.

CHARLES: She's been doing her best.

MADAME ARCATI: Are the girls getting despondent?

CHARLES: I'm afraid they are rather.

MADAME ARCATI: We'll win through yet—don't be downhearted.

RUTH: If we're not very careful she'll materialize a hockey team.

MADAME ARCATI: Now then, Mr. Condomine—the discussion—fire away.

CHARLES: Well, my wives and I have been talking it over and they are both absolutely convinced that I somehow or other called them back.

MADAME ARCATI: Very natural.

CHARLES: I am equally convinced that I did not.

MADAME ARCATI: Love is a strong psychic force, Mr. Condomine—it can work untold miracles. A true love call can encompass the universe—

CHARLES: [Hastily] I'm sure it can, but I must confess to you frankly that although my affection for both Elvira and Ruth is of the warmest I cannot truthfully feel that it would come under the heading that you describe.

ELVIRA: I should just think not indeed.

MADAME ARCATI: You may not know your own strength, Mr. Condomine.

CHARLES: [Firmly] I did not call them back—either consciously or subconsciously.

MADAME ARCATI: But, Mr. Condomine . . .

CHARLES: That is my final word on the subject.

MADAME ARCATI: Neither of them could have appeared unless there had been somebody—a psychic subject—in the house, who wished for them . . .

CHARLES: Well, it wasn't me.

ELVIRA: Perhaps it was Doctor Bradman—I never knew he cared.

MADAME ARCATI: Are you sure?—Are you really sure?

CHARLES: Absolutely positive.

MADAME ARCATI: [*Snapping her fingers*] Great Scott, I believe we've been barking up the wrong tree!

CHARLES: How do you mean?

MADAME ARCATI: The Sudbury case!

CHARLES: I don't understand.

MADAME ARCATI: There's no reason why you should —it was before your day—I wonder—oh, I wonder. . . .

CHARLES: What was the Sudbury case? I wish you'd explain.

MADAME ARCATI: It was the case that made me famous, Mr. Condomine—it was what you might describe in theatrical parlance as my first smash hit! I had letters from all over the world about it— especially India.

CHARLES: What did you do?

MADAME ARCATI: I dematerialized old Lady Sudbury after she'd been firmly entrenched in the private chapel for over seventeen years.

CHARLES: [*Rises*] How?—Can't you remember how?

MADAME ARCATI: Chance—a fluke—I happened on it by the merest coincidence.

CHARLES: What fluke—what was it?

MADAME ARCATI: Wait—all in good time. [*She begins to walk about the room*] Now let me see— who was in the house during our first séance?

CHARLES: Only the Bradmans, Ruth and me and yourself.

MADAME ARCATI: Ah, yes—yes—to be sure—but the Bradmans weren't here last night, were they?

CHARLES: No.

MADAME ARCATI: Quickly . . . my crystal—

CHARLES: [*Handing it to her*] Here. . . .

MADAME ARCATI: [*Shaking it crossly*] Damn the thing, it's cloudy again—[*She looks again*] Ah!— that's better—it's there again—it's there again— I'm beginning to understand.

CHARLES: I wish I was. What's there again?

MADAME ARCATI: A bandage—a white bandage— hold on to a white bandage. . . .

CHARLES: I haven't got a white bandage.

MADAME ARCATI: Shhh! [*She puts the crystal down and stands silent for a moment*]

ELVIRA: She's too good, you know—she ought to be in a circus.

[*Madame Arcati advances to the middle of the room and raises her arms slowly—she begins to intone*]

MADAME ARCATI:

Be you in nook or cranny answer me
Do you in Still-room or closet answer me
Do you behind the panel, above the stairs
Beneath the eaves—waking or sleeping

Answer me!
That ought to do it or I'm a Dutchman.

CHARLES: Do what?

MADAME ARCATI: Hush—wait— [*She picks up one of the birch branches and waves it solemnly to and fro*]

RUTH: For God's sake don't let her throw any more of that garlic about. It nearly made me sick last time.

CHARLES: Would you like the gramophone on or the lights out or anything?

MADAME ARCATI: No, no—it's near—it's very near—

ELVIRA: If it's a ghost I shall scream.

RUTH: I hope it's nobody we know—I shall feel so silly.

[*Suddenly the door opens and* Edith *comes into the room. She is wearing a pink flannel dressing gown and bedroom slippers. Her head is bandaged*]

EDITH: Did you ring, sir?

MADAME ARCATI: The bandage! The white bandage!

CHARLES: No, Edith.

EDITH: I'm sorry, sir—I could have sworn I heard the bell—or somebody calling—I was asleep—I don't rightly know which it was. . . .

MADAME ARCATI: Come here, child.

EDITH: Oh! [*She looks anxiously at* Charles]

CHARLES: Go on—go to Madame Arcati—it's quite all right.

MADAME ARCATI: Who do you see in this room, child?

EDITH: Oh, dear. . . .

MADAME ARCATI: Answer please.

EDITH: [*Falteringly*] You; madame—[*She stops*]

MADAME ARCATI: Go on.

EDITH: The Master.

MADAME ARCATI: Anyone else?

EDITH: Oh no, madame. . . .

MADAME ARCATI: [*Inflexibly*] Look again.

EDITH: [*Imploringly, to* Charles] I don't understand, sir—I—

MADAME ARCATI: Come, child—don't beat about the bush—look again.

[Elvira *begins to move about the room almost as though she were being pulled.* Edith *follows with her eyes*]

RUTH: Do concentrate, Elvira, and keep still.

ELVIRA: I can't.

MADAME ARCATI: Do you see anyone else now?

EDITH: [*Slyly*] Oh no, madame.

MADAME ARCATI: She's lying.

EDITH: Oh, madame!

MADAME ARCATI: They always do.

CHARLES: They?

MADAME ARCATI: [*Sharply*] Where are they now?

EDITH: By the fireplace. Oh!

CHARLES: She can see them—do you mean she can see them?

MADAME ARCATI: Probably not very clearly—but enough—

EDITH: [*Bursting into tears*] Let me go—I haven't done nothing nor seen nobody—let me go back to bed.

MADAME ARCATI: Give her a sandwich.

EDITH: [*Drawing away*] I don't want a sandwich. I want to go back to bed. . . .

CHARLES: [*Handing* Edith *the plate*] Here, Edith.

MADAME ARCATI: Nonsense—a big healthy girl like you saying no to a delicious sandwich—I never heard of such a thing—sit down.

EDITH: [*To Charles*] Please, sir, I . . .

CHARLES: Please do as Madame Arcati says, Edith.

EDITH: [*Sitting down and sniffing*] I haven't done nothing wrong.

CHARLES: It's all right—nobody said you had.

RUTH: If she's been the cause of all this unpleasantness I'll give her a week's notice tomorrow.

ELVIRA: You may not be here tomorrow—

MADAME ARCATI: Look at me, Edith. [Edith *obediently does so*] Cuckoo—cuckoo—cuckoo—

EDITH: [*Jumping*] Oh, dear—what's the matter with her? Is she barmy?

MADAME ARCATI: Here, Edith—this is my finger—look—[*She waggles it*] Have you ever seen such a long, long, long finger? Look now it's on the right—now it's on the left—backwards and forwards it goes—see—very quietly backwards and forwards—tic-toc—tic—toc—tic-toc.

ELVIRA: The mouse ran up the clock.

RUTH: Be quiet—*you'll* ruin everything.

[Madame Arcati *whistles a little tune close to* Edith's *face—then she snaps her fingers.* Edith *looks stolidly in front of her without flinching.* Madame Arcati *stands back*]

MADAME ARCATI: Well—so far so good—she's off all right.

CHARLES: Off?

MADAME ARCATI: She's a Natural—just the same as the Sudbury case—it really is the most amusing coincidence. Now then—would you ask your wives to stand close together please?

CHARLES: Where?

MADAME ARCATI: Over there by you.

CHARLES: Elvira—Ruth—

RUTH: I resent being ordered about like this.

ELVIRA: I don't like this at all—I don't like any of it—I feel peculiar.

CHARLES: I'm afraid I must insist.

ELVIRA: It would serve you right if we flatly refused to do anything at all.

MADAME ARCATI: Are you sorry for having been so mischievous, Edith?

EDITH: [*Cheerfully*] Oh yes, madame.

MADAME ARCATI: You know what you have to do now, don't you, Edith?

EDITH: Oh yes, madame.

RUTH: I believe it's going to work whatever it is. Oh, Charles.

CHARLES: Shhh!

RUTH: This is good-bye, Charles.

ELVIRA: Tell her to stop for a minute—there's something I want to say before I go.

CHARLES: You should have thought of that before—it's too late now.

ELVIRA: Of all the mean, ungracious—

RUTH: Charles, listen a moment . . .

MADAME ARCATI: [*In a shrill voice*] Lights! [Madame Arcati *rushes to the door and switches off the lights. In the dark* Edith *is singing "Always" in a very high cockney voice*]

ELVIRA: [*In the dark*] I saw Captain Bracegirdle again, Charles—several times—I went to the Four Hundred with him twice when you were in Nottingham. And I must say I couldn't have enjoyed it more.

RUTH: Don't think you're getting rid of us quite so easily, my dear—you may not be able to see us but we shall be here all right—I consider that you have behaved atrociously over the whole miserable business. And I should like to say here and now—

[*Her voice fades into a whisper and then disappears altogether*]

MADAME ARCATI: [*Exultantly*] Splendid! Hurrah! We've done it! That's quite enough singing for the moment, Edith.

CHARLES: [*After a pause*] Shall I put on the lights?

MADAME ARCATI: No—I will.

[Charles *pulls the curtains and daylight floods into the room.* Ruth *and* Elvira *have disappeared.* Edith *is still sitting on the chair*]

CHARLES: They've gone—they've really gone.

MADAME ARCATI: Yes—I think we've really pulled it off this time.

CHARLES: You'd better wake her up, hadn't you? She might bring them back again.

MADAME ARCATI: [*Clapping her hands in* Edith's *face*] Wake up, child!

EDITH: [*Nearly jumping out of the chair*] Good 'eavens! Where am I?

CHARLES: It's all right, Edith—you can go back to bed now.

EDITH: Why, it's morning.

CHARLES: Yes—I know it is.

EDITH: But I was in bed—how did I get down 'ere?

CHARLES: I rang, Edith—I rang the bell and you answered it—didn't I, Madame Arcati?

EDITH: Did I drop off? Do you think it's my concussion again? Oh, dear!

CHARLES: Off you go, Edith, and thank you very much. [*He presses a pound note into her hand*] Thank you very much indeed.

EDITH: Oh, sir, whatever for? [*She looks at him in sudden horror*] Oh, sir!! [*She bolts from the room*]

CHARLES: [*Surprised*] What on earth did she mean by that?

MADAME ARCATI: Golly, what a night! I'm ready to drop in my tracks.

CHARLES: Would you like to stay here?—there's the spare room, you know.

MADAME ARCATI: No, thank you—each to his own nest—I'll pedal home in a jiffy—it's only seven miles.

CHARLES: I'm deeply grateful to you, Madame Arcati. I don't know what arrangements you generally make but I trust you will send in your account in due course.

MADAME ARCATI: Good heavens, Mr. Condomine—it was a pleasure—I wouldn't dream of such a thing.

CHARLES: But really I feel that all those trances. . . .

MADAME ARCATI: I enjoy them, Mr. Condomine, thoroughly. I always have since a child.

CHARLES: Perhaps you'd give me the pleasure of lunching with me one day soon?

MADAME ARCATI: When you come back—I should be delighted.

CHARLES: Come back?

MADAME ARCATI: [Lowering her voice] Take my advice, Mr. Condomine, and go away immediately.

CHARLES: But, Madame Arcati! You don't mean that . . . ?

MADAME ARCATI: [Clearing her stuff from table] This must be an unhappy house for you—there must be memories both grave and gay in every corner of it—also—[She pauses]

CHARLES: Also what?

MADAME ARCATI: [Thinking better of it] There are more things in heaven and earth, Mr. Condomine. [She places her finger to her lips] Just go—pack your traps and go as soon as possible.

CHARLES: [Also in lowered tones] Do you mean that they may still be here?

MADAME ARCATI: [She nods and then nonchalantly whistles a little tune] Quien sabe, as the Spanish say. [She collects her bag and her crystal]

CHARLES: [Looking furtively round the room] I wonder—I wonder. I'll follow your advice, Madame Arcati. Thank you again.

MADAME ARCATI: Well, good-bye, Mr. Condomine—it's been fascinating—from first to last—fascinating. Do you mind if I take just one more sandwich to munch on my way home? [Comes down to table for sandwich]

CHARLES: By all means.

[Madame Arcati goes to the door. Charles follows her to see her safely out]

MADAME ARCATI: [As they go] Don't trouble—I can find my way. Cheerio once more and good hunting!

[Charles watches her into the hall and then comes back into the room. He prowls about for a moment as though he were not sure that he was alone]

CHARLES: [Softly] Ruth—Elvira—are you there? [A pause] Ruth—Elvira—I know damn well you're there—[Another pause] I just want to tell you that I'm going away so there's no point in your hanging about any longer—I'm going a long way away—somewhere where I don't believe you'll be able to follow me. In spite of what Elvira said I don't think spirits can travel over water. Is that quite clear, my darlings? You said in one of your more acid moments, Ruth, that I had been hag-ridden all my life! How right you were—but now I'm free, Ruth dear, not only of Mother and Elvira and Mrs. Winthrop-Lewellyn, but free of you too, and I should like to take this farewell opportunity of saying I'm enjoying it immensely —[A vase crashes into the fireplace] Aha—I thought so—you were very silly, Elvira, to imagine that I didn't know all about you and Captain Bracegirdle—I did. But what you didn't know was that I was extremely attached to Paula West-lake at the time! [The clock strikes sixteen viciously and very quickly] I was reasonably faithful to you, Ruth, but I doubt if it would have lasted much longer—you were becoming increasingly domineering, you know, and there's nothing more off putting than that, is there? [A large picture falls down with a crash] Good-bye for the moment, my dears. I expect we are bound to meet again one day, but until we do I'm going to enjoy myself as I've never enjoyed myself before. You can break up the house as much as you like—I'm leaving it anyhow. Think kindly of me and send out good thoughts—[The overmantel begins to shake and tremble as though someone were tugging at it] Nice work, Elvira—persevere. Good-bye again—parting is such sweet sorrow! [He goes out of the room just as the overmantel crashes to the floor and the curtain pole comes tumbling down. The curtain falls]

The Voice of the Turtle

by JOHN VAN DRUTEN

(1901–   )

In the contemporary theater, John van Druten has been one of the more successful—and consistent—writers of what is best described generically as light comedy, since his are almost equally comedies of manners and comedies of mating. Indeed, the celebrated stage set of The Voice of the Turtle, containing (and requiring) both living room and bedroom, symbolizes the sort of double appeal that Mr. van Druten commonly aims at, the blend of manners and romance. But it is from being so much at home in the comedy-of-manners tradition, from displaying in his work a sense of social ease, that Mr. van Druten stands superior to other playwrights whose talents are perhaps no less than his, and whose plots are perhaps no more conventional. Mr. van Druten brings no great insight into life, but rather a proper tolerance, intelligence, and fund of experience; and though he has written creditably in a more serious vein, he comes off best at skillful light comedy.

The presence of skill very often, indeed, must make up for a certain not just lightness but actual thinness of treatment. In such a play as Bell, Book and Candle—a drawing-room fantasy based on the amusing idea that witches exist in modern society—Mr. van Druten cannot, after a while, quite sustain the fantasy, and lets it fizzle out as mere Boy-Meets-Witchgirl formula. But the play itself remains workmanlike and tidy to the end.

On the other hand, in what is certainly the best of his recent plays, in The Voice of the Turtle, he gained immensely from the straightforward, self-contained, thoroughly human nature of his material. Here was a tale whose very charm lay in all absence of bulky plot machinery—a tale that passed up all the cut-and-dried obstacles of the usual stage romance to become, in effect, a realistic idyl: Boy Meets Girl, Mates Girl, Very Probably Marries Girl, with few of the orthodox setbacks. At the same time, the play was not to be idyllic at the cost of being insipid; Mr. van Druten quite appreciated its comic values. Part of the comedy lay in how seriously the young heroine took herself, just as part of the romance lay in how determined she was not to be romantic. But the comedy sprang even more out of the nature of Sally's relationship with Bill, out of his being wiser and worldlier at every turn, down-to-earth where she is always breathless: it is a comedy of contrasts, a comedy—on its own terms—of sense and sensibility.

The special fillip it seemed to have when first produced—its strictly wartime setting, the fact that Bill Page was a sergeant as well as a suitor—has now rather vanished, despite the fact that war has not. But I don't think it has much harmed the play, because it was less, perhaps, the moment of war that gives The Voice of the Turtle its real fillip than it was the generation of the Sally Middletons. In romantic comedy, from time immemorial, the heroine role has been an ingénue role: the young girl, that is to say, remains a virgin until she is married. No doubt one of the advantages, for Shakespeare, in having Rosalind and Viola put on boys' clothes was that they need not be lured into taking them off. In Restoration comedy, though the heroine may remain chaste only from prudential or worldly motives—or, now and then, to stress how dissolute are the other women in the play—chaste she does remain. After the Restoration, of course, the heroine becomes pure ingénue; and by Victorian times, far from having improper relations with the hero himself, is apt to break off with him because of his misconduct with other women. After the twentieth-century breakup, sex came to be more and more realistically and honestly treated; we had the New Woman and the Modern Bohemian Girl, we had all sorts of plays blending sex with "sophistication"; but down to our own time, the heroine of a well-bred romantic comedy remained an ingénue. In violating this convention, Sally Middleton may not have been the first of her kind in the theater, but she was, I think, the first full-length portrait of her kind—the thoroughly girlish, romantic, unsophisticated heroine, who is not a virgin at the outset, is mated at the end of the second act, and is not conclusively married at the end of the third. The circumstances, to be sure, are a little special: Sally, in giving herself to Bill, is making a soldier happy; and Sally herself, however well born and well mannered and romantic, is yet by profession an actress.

The point of all this is that it makes possible the kind of realistic idyll—common enough in Continental literature—that, on our stage, the older taboo prevented. And it equally makes possible a kind of worldly comedy that the older taboo prevented. The relationship between Sally and Bill can be realistic in a new way, while Sally herself can be a new and amusing kind of "romantic" heroine. When, at the second-act curtain, Bill murmurs, "I love you," Sally says, "No. No, don't say that. We must keep this gay." The line would be out of the question if they had also to keep it respectable.

For the rest, The Voice of the Turtle is full of shrewd and entertaining detail. The play may lack all depth, but it exploits every square inch of the surface. If essentially a romance, it is also a play about New York, even about Broadway and show people. In human terms, The Voice of the Turtle profits from not being overclever or witty; from hardly differing, except for its so-to-speak softer lighting, from real

life. In stage terms, The Voice of the Turtle has of course just the cleverness that in human terms it rejects, being built around a story that has only three characters, and on a set that has all of three rooms. And with plays like this, it is perhaps not a writer's general talent that is decisive, but his special touch. The problem here was to be pleasantly sophisticated without turning hard; to be pleasantly romantic, again, without turning soft; to be realistic enough to offer a hundred enjoyable recognitions, and yet escapist enough to guarantee a sense of release. There are doubtless many things that, in the final sense, are better worth doing: but not too many that are harder to do.

JOHN VAN DRUTEN

The Voice of the Turtle

CAST OF CHARACTERS

SALLY MIDDLETON
OLIVE LASHBROOKE
BILL PAGE

ACT I
Scene 1: *Friday afternoon*
Scene 2: *Friday evening*

ACT II
Scene 1: *Saturday morning*
Scene 2: *Late Saturday night*

ACT III
Scene 1: *Sunday morning*
Scene 2: *Late Sunday afternoon*

The action, throughout, takes place over a week-end in early April in an apartment in the East Sixties, near Third Avenue, New York City.

Act I

THE SCENE *throughout is a smallish apartment in New York, in the East Sixties, near Third Avenue. The set comprises the entire apartment, with the exception of the bathroom. We see the bedroom, with double bed, to the right of the stage; living room center; kitchen, through a swing-door, left. The kitchen has an icebox, stove and sink in a combined unit in the left wall. The front door to the apartment is in the back wall, center, opening into the living room, which is down two steps. The windows are in the right wall of the bedroom, back wall of living room, and back wall of kitchen. Under the living-room window is a day-bed, disguised as a couch. The telephone is below the bed in the bedroom. The bathroom and dressing room are off right of the back wall of the bedroom.*

SCENE 1: *The apartment, late in the afternoon of a Friday at the beginning of April.*

When the curtain rises, Sally Middleton *is dis-covered in the kitchen, fixing a tray of drinks which she carries into the living room through the swing-door. She sets the tray down on a table, muttering to herself as she does so. Actually, she is running over the words of the Potion Scene from* Romeo and Juliet, *but only becomes audible as she reaches the end.* Sally *is twenty-two, small, direct, naïve and very pretty.*

SALLY: [*Finishing the speech aloud*] Stay, Tybalt, stay! Romeo, I come!
            [*She pushes open the swing-door again, returning to the kitchen*]
This do I drink to thee!
            [*Then in her own voice*]
There, I know it!
[*She opens the icebox and gets out the tray of ice cubes. During the ensuing business, she starts the Potion Scene again, acting it to herself, and not overdoing it; the only thing that makes it ridiculous is the business that punctuates it*]
Farewell!
            [*Slams icebox door*]
God knows when we shall meet again!
I have a faint, cold fear thrills through my veins—
[*Turns on the hot faucet to run over the ice tray*]
That almost freezes up the heat of life.
I'll call them back again to comfort me.
            [*Ice breaks into sink. She turns off tap*]
Nurse! What should she do here?
My dismal scene I needs must act alone.
Come, vial.
[*Takes up ice-bucket, and starts to pick up ice*]
What if this mixture do not work at all?
Shall I be married then tomorrow morning?
No, no, this shall forbid it.
            [*Looks around for a prop, sees mixing spoon and uses it*]
Lie thou there!
            [*She places the spoon on the drain-board, then takes the ice-bucket into the living room, where she puts it on the drink-table, still reciting*]
What if it be a poison which the friar
Subtly have ministered to have me dead . . .
            [*She dries up*]
Have me dead . . . have me dead . . .
[*She crosses to the couch where a Temple Shake-speare is lying open, and refreshes her memory*]

Lest in this marriage he should be dishonor'd,
Because he married me before to Romeo.
　　　　　　　　[*Front-door buzzer rings.*
She goes to answer it, gabbling the next lines]
I fear it is, and yet methinks it should not,
For he hath still been tried a holy . . .

[*She opens the door. Olive Lashbrooke is standing outside. She is about twenty-eight, smart and attractive, without being good-looking, and rather gay*]
Olive!

OLIVE: Sally! Darling!
　　　　　　　　　　　　　　[*They kiss*]

SALLY: Come in. How are you?

OLIVE: Couldn't be better. [*Looks around*] So this is it! It's very grand.

SALLY: [*Pleased*] Do you think so?

OLIVE: Very. How long have you had it?

SALLY: Six weeks.

OLIVE: [*Inspecting; impressed*] Um!

SALLY: [*Naïvely excited*] Do you want to see it all?

OLIVE: Sure.

SALLY: Well, this is the living room. It's sunken. Kitchen's in here. [*Opens door. They go through*]

OLIVE: Darling, it's enormous! You could feed the whole army. Do you have a maid?

SALLY: Colored. Daily. *When* she comes. Which isn't very often. I think she's got a complicated love life.

OLIVE: Don't we all? [*They return to living room*] How did you find this?

SALLY: It's Claire Henley's. Claire's on the road with the Lunts.

OLIVE: [*As they re-cross living room*] I don't know how that girl gets the break she does. I was sick about *your* show. Did you get my message, opening night?

SALLY: Yes, I didn't know where to thank you. You were jumping around so.

OLIVE: Darling, I *know*. Split weeks and one-night stands. It's heaven to be through. How long did you run, actually?

SALLY: Five days.

OLIVE: Did you get any notices?

SALLY: A couple of mentions. [*Opening bedroom door*] Here's the bedroom.

OLIVE: [*Going in*] Very saucy. [*Flippantly*] Luxe.

SALLY: What?

OLIVE: [*As before*] Luxe. French, darling. One of those untranslatable expressions. It means luxury. And beds like that!

SALLY: [*Pointing off*] Bathroom and dressing room in there.

OLIVE: [*Impressed*] Dressing room! [*She peeps in*]

SALLY: [*Excusing it*] Well . . .

OLIVE: Darling, it's the cutest place I ever saw in all my life. [*Going to the window*] Where do you look out?

SALLY: Onto the summer garden of the "Bonne Chanson." That French restaurant next door.

OLIVE: What's that like?

SALLY: Lovely. But terribly expensive. You know, no menu. The man just comes and *suggests*.

OLIVE: Put yourself right next door to temptation, eh? Or is it for the boy-friends when they come to take you out? [*Acting*] "Where shall we eat?" "Wherever you say." "How about the place next door?" "Okay." [*Back to her own voice*] I know. I once thought of taking an apartment over the Colony, myself. What are you paying Claire for this?

SALLY: [*Slightly embarrassed*] A hundred and a quarter.

OLIVE: Have you got another job?

SALLY: No.

OLIVE: No! And there's nothing in the offing, this late in the season, for any of us.

SALLY: I know. But I still have a little money left over from that radio serial I did. And it's when you're out of work you *need* a nice place to live. When you're *in* work . . .

OLIVE: You live at Sardi's—if you can get in. Yes, but all the same! What did you want to move for, anyway?

SALLY: I was tired of a hotel room. And there were reasons.

OLIVE: [*Eagerly*] What?

SALLY: [*Evasively*] Not now. Come and have a drink.

OLIVE: Lovely.

　　　　　　　　[*They return to the living room*]

SALLY: [*As they go*] What'll you have?

OLIVE: What have you got?

SALLY: Whatever you want. Gin . . . rum . . . Scotch . . .

OLIVE: Scotch? You *have* been on a bust. [*Flippantly*] Or is all this . . . guilty splendor?

SALLY: Don't be silly. Scotch?

OLIVE: Sure. [*Sally pours two Scotches. A large one for Olive, and a smaller one for herself. Olive picks up the Shakespeare*] What on earth are you studying Juliet for?

SALLY: [*Pouring*] Practice.

OLIVE: Darling, you're out of your mind. You know, you take the theatre too seriously. You'll be going to Madame Pushkin's school next, studying "de free body," and learning how to act *milk!* [*Breaking off*] I had the greatest success telling about Madame Pushkin in the company, by the way. Henry Atherton adored her. I gave you credit for inventing her.

SALLY: [*Bringing her the drink*] Was it wonderful playing with Henry Atherton? I've always had the most terrific thing about him. You used to have, too.

OLIVE: Did I? Well, it's gone now, if I did. He isn't interested in anything a day over twenty. There was a little ingenue in the company—she couldn't have been more than eighteen. You've never seen such carryings-on . . . holding hands and giggling in the wings, all through my one decent scene.

SALLY: [Disappointed] Oh!

OLIVE: [Drinking] It's good to be back in New York. By the way, I've asked someone to call for me here. Is that all right?

SALLY: Of course. Who is it?

OLIVE: A man called Bill Page.

SALLY: An actor?

OLIVE: No, just a man. At least, he used to be. He's a soldier now. He's at Camp Something-or-Other up the Hudson. Got a week-end pass, starting this afternoon. I left a message at my hotel telling him to come on here and pick me up.

SALLY: What's he like?

OLIVE: He's sweet. And he's mine!

SALLY: I didn't mean . . .

OLIVE: I know, darling, but I thought I'd tell you. I've known him for ages. He used to live in Pittsburgh, and whenever I played there we always had a "gay little something." Though when I say "whenever," I think actually it was only twice. I'd lost sight of him for years, and then when we were in Detroit about six weeks ago, he turned up again. He was stationed somewhere near, and came to see the show. Now, he's moved up here.

SALLY: [Smiling] And are you still having a "gay little something"?

OLIVE: Well, we did in Detroit.

SALLY: Are you in love with him?

OLIVE: No, darling, not a bit. But he's attractive. Only he's sort of the . . . reserved kind. You never know what he's thinking, or get any further with him.

SALLY: It doesn't sound as though there was much further left for you to get. [Rises] By the way, what's happened to the Commander?

OLIVE: Ned Burling? Ah, darling, now you're talking! He's at sea somewhere . . . I guess. What makes you ask about him?

SALLY: I was just remembering that "gay little something" of yours.

OLIVE: And it was something!

SALLY: Do you ever hear from him?

OLIVE: No, he's not the writing kind. He was . . . you know . . . just "Butch." Besides, that was one of those . . . [Mocking] "lovely things that isn't meant to last. A little Intermezzo, or a wild, brief gypsy Czardas." Ah, me! Quel goings-on!

SALLY: [Moving away, repeating the phrase, reflectively] "One of those lovely things that isn't meant to last."

OLIVE: [Catching her tone, crosses to her] Sally, what's the matter? You're unhappy about something. What is it? Is it . . . love?

SALLY: I guess so. If you can call it that.

OLIVE: You can always call it that. Come on. Tell Auntie Olive all about it. Well?

SALLY: Well, you've heard of Kenneth Bartlett—the producer?

OLIVE: Yes. Darling, it isn't him? [Sally nods] Sally, how simply sensational! And he's putting on Romeo and Juliet for you!

SALLY: Don't be silly. You know he only does musicals.

OLIVE: Yes, the new one opened last night. It's a smash, from the notices. Where did you meet him?

SALLY: At a cocktail party. [She stops]

OLIVE: [Eagerly] Well, go on. Tell.

SALLY: [Slowly] Well, he's terribly nice. And young, and attractive. At least, I guess he's around forty, but he seemed young. And we talked . . . about the theatre, of course . . . and then he took me on to dinner. We went next door. That was the first time I'd been there.

OLIVE: But not the last.

SALLY: [Shyly] No. It sort of became . . . "our" place.

OLIVE: How long ago was all this?

SALLY: Two months. His show was in rehearsal, then. He told me all about it . . . sang me some of the songs. He made me feel wonderful . . . like being starred, and getting the star dressing room. Do you know?

OLIVE: I know.

SALLY: Well, then I found that Claire was going away, and had this place right next door to . . .

OLIVE: "Your" place . . .

SALLY: So I took it. You know, it was funny . . . when I came to see it, Claire had the radio on, and it was playing the Londonderry Air. That's always been my lucky tune. I thought it meant the apartment would be lucky.

OLIVE: So you let her soak you a hundred and a quarter.

SALLY: Well, it was nice to have. And . . . [Timidly] just occasionally he stayed all night . . . and I got breakfast, and . . . oh, I don't know . . . but it was nice. I love having someone to do for. Even in that tiny hotel room . . . that time you stayed with me, because of the snow, do you remember? . . . It was sort of exciting, like having "Cousin Olive" to stay overnight when one was little. [Pointing below window] By the way, if you ever want it, that's a day-bed.

OLIVE: Lovely. But what happened with "Cousin Bartlett"? What went wrong?

SALLY: [Grimly] I did.

OLIVE: Yes, I know, dear. But what went wrong?

SALLY: Well, he talked a lot about keeping it gay . . . not bringing love into it . . . or getting serious about each other . . .

OLIVE: And you did, and he didn't like that?

SALLY: He said I made scenes.

OLIVE: Did you?

SALLY: I guess I did. At least, they wouldn't be scenes

if they were in a play, but . . . yes, I guess I made scenes. Little ones. You see, he's married.

OLIVE: Did you know that?

SALLY: Yes, he told me that the first evening. But they don't get on, and she's a lot older than he is. Oh, *he* didn't tell me that. He didn't say anything about her, except to let me know he *had* a wife. And they've two children, so you see, it couldn't be anything serious for *him*. Oh, he was very sweet about it . . . really he was. Only he said that it couldn't go on like that . . . for *my* sake. So, it's all over. We said good-bye a month ago. [*Rising and starting to pace*] I've been so miserable ever since. We've had the most awful weather. I don't think spring's *ever* coming, this year. I've just stayed home, and studied *Juliet* and read Dorothy Parker's poems. I never used to mind being by myself, but now . . . since Ken . . . Well, it's the first time I've had an apartment of my own, and it seems such waste.

OLIVE: I know. I feel the same way whenever I go to a hotel, and they give me a big double room all to myself.

SALLY: Oh, what did I have to go and fall in love for? Or, if I did, why did I have to go and show it? Or, worse still, talk about it? I believe there's nothing men hate so much as talking about it.

OLIVE: There's nothing they hate so much as *your* talking about it.

SALLY: Well, it's not going to happen again. Sex, I mean. Not for a long, long time. Not till I'm thirty. It should never have started in the first place. Father was quite right about the theatre.

OLIVE: Oh, darling, you're not going to start blaming it on the theatre?

SALLY: If I'd stayed home in Joplin, none of this would have happened.

OLIVE: Don't they . . . in Joplin?

SALLY: Olive, tell me something. Something I want to know.

OLIVE: What?

SALLY: Well, *do* ordinary girls? I was raised to think they didn't. Didn't even want to. And what I want to know is—don't they? They don't in movies. Oh, I know that's censorship . . . but . . . the people who go and *see* the movies . . . are they like that too? Or else don't they notice that it's all false?

OLIVE: I've wondered about that, myself.

SALLY: Even in Shakespeare, his heroines don't. Ever. Juliet carries on like crazy about not. I don't know whether what Mother and Father taught me was right, or true, or anything. Were you raised like that?

OLIVE: Oh, sure. And I wasn't even legitimate. But Mama raised me just as strict as if I was.

SALLY: Did you have qualms when you started?

OLIVE: Never.

SALLY: What did you feel?

OLIVE: I just felt—"So, this is it! I like it!" [*Then,*

kindly] Oh, Sally, darling, you're not starting a conscience, or thinking you're promiscuous, because you've had one affair, are you?

SALLY: [*Unhappily*] I've had two. There was that boy in the company at Skowhegan last summer that I was so unhappy about. I told you.

OLIVE: Well, two, then.

SALLY: No, I . . . don't think I'm promiscuous . . . yet. Though I don't imagine anyone ever does think that about themselves. Do . . . [*She stops*]

OLIVE: Do I . . . were you going to say?

SALLY: Well, I was, only I suddenly realized how awful it sounded.

OLIVE: No, I don't. Maybe you're right, and no one does, but I just think for a gal with a funny face, I've really done rather well. *You're* pretty. You can afford to be choosey. [*Walking away*] I wonder what's happened to Bill. I hope they gave him the message. Would you mind if I called up the hotel to ask?

SALLY: No, do. It's in the bedroom. Can I fix you another drink?

OLIVE: [*Nodding*] A tiny one. [*She goes into bedroom, where she dials a number on the telephone*]

SALLY: I'll just get a glass for *him*. [*She goes into kitchen, and gets a third glass, then comes back and fixes a drink for* Olive]

OLIVE: [*In bedroom, on phone*] Give me the desk, please. Hello, desk? This is Miss Lashbrooke. Has a Sergeant Page called for me? I left a note . . . Oh, he did? How long ago? Oh, thank you. By the way, you might just see if there are any messages for me. I'll hold on. [*Sally comes into the bedroom. To* Sally] He's on his way here.

SALLY: Good. [*Hands* Olive *her glass*]

OLIVE: Thanks. [*Drinks. Then, into phone*] Hello . . . yes . . . yes . . . I see . . . all right, just leave it in my box. Anything else? Who called? [*Her voice rising in excitement*] Lieutenant Comm . . . *what* number? Wait a minute, I'll get a pencil. [*She gets one from the telephone table, scribbling on a pad*] Give me that number again. Eldorado . . . yes . . . What time was that? Thanks. [*She hangs up, and sits staring*]

SALLY: Was that *the* Commander?

OLIVE: [*A little dazed and excited. Nods*] He's in town. He called at five o'clock. I must call him. [*Sally starts to leave*] Don't go. [*Lifts receiver and dials*] Wouldn't you know it would happen like this? Well, at least he called me. That's something.

SALLY: [*Sits on bed, staring at her*] You're still crazy about him, aren't you?

OLIVE: Yes, damn it. In the worst way.

SALLY: Well, don't let him know it.

OLIVE: [*Laughing with slight bitterness*] You—giving *me* advice now! [*Into phone*] Hello . . . is Commander Burling there? Ned? This is Olive. Yes, I just called the hotel and they told me. When did you get into town? You did? You are? When? You mean, you're just here till . . . Well, I never got it. I've been on the road with a play, and I guess the mail got . . . Oh, I can't. I'm terribly sorry, but I can't. How about lunch tomorrow? [*Disappointed*] Oh. No, I'm tied up the whole week-end. I've got someone to look after. Yes, I know. Darling, I know. I know, but . . . [*She is growing agonized*] Oh, hell, I will! Yes, yes, I will. I don't know how I . . . but I will. What's the time now? Oh, my God, no, no, make it eight, will you? Eight at my hotel. Yes . . . lovely to talk to *you*. Good-bye now. [*She hangs up, and looks at* Sally] There. There's an object lesson in how not to act with a man.

SALLY: You're seeing him tonight?

OLIVE: It's his last leave. He's got till Sunday afternoon. And he called *me* right away. He wrote to me! I'm going to dinner with him. [*She rises*]

SALLY: But . . . What about . . . *this* one? [*Pointing to front door*]

OLIVE: I don't know. I must think. What am I going to do? Bill's on his way here. Sally, what am I going to say?

SALLY: [*Unhelpfully*] I don't know.

OLIVE: No, but be some help.

SALLY: I can't. Why did you have to have dinner with him? You could have met him later . . . say, for supper.

OLIVE: And let Bill spend the whole evening . . . "expecting"? That's the kind of thing men never forgive. No, this way, he'll at least have a chance to fix up something else for himself. Could I say that my family . . . ? No, he knows I haven't any. Besides, one can always ditch one's family after midnight. Who *can't* one ditch? That's what it comes down to. Who can't one ditch? Mother . . . father . . . brother . . . grandmother. [*Suddenly*] I've got it. Husband!

SALLY: Whose husband?

OLIVE: Mine!

SALLY: Doesn't he know you haven't a husband?

OLIVE: He hasn't seen me for about two years. Except that flash in Detroit . . . and that wasn't the kind of occasion when one would mention being married. And now my husband's turned up on his last leave. . . .

SALLY: [*Slightly shocked*] Olive, you can't!

OLIVE: I've got to tell him *something*. Oh, darling, I know it's awful of me, but you've not seen Ned. It's nearly a year since I have, and he's so divine. [*Front-door buzzer sounds*] There *is* Bill. Listen, you'll help me?

SALLY: How?

OLIVE: With the husband story.

SALLY: I'll slip out, and let you talk to him.

OLIVE: No, don't do that. Stay and back me up.

SALLY: I couldn't.

OLIVE: *I* would . . . for you.

[*Buzzer again*]

SALLY: I *must* answer the door.

OLIVE: [*As they go into living room*] What's the time?

SALLY: A quarter of seven.

OLIVE: Oh, my God, and I've got to be dressed by eight. Why do things like this always have to happen to me?

SALLY: Shall I let him in?

OLIVE: I guess you'll have to.

[*Sally goes to the front door, and admits* Bill Page. *He is about thirty-two, adult, quiet and attractive. He wears a Sergeant's stripes, and carries an evening paper and a tiny week-end toilet-case*]

BILL: Miss Sally Middleton?

SALLY: Yes, won't you come in? Olive's here.

OLIVE: [*Coming into view—brightly*] Bill—darling!

BILL: [*Coming in*] Hello.

[*They kiss*]

OLIVE: Sally, this is Bill Page. Sally Middleton.

SALLY: How do you do?

BILL: How do you do?

SALLY: May I take your things? [*She takes his cap and bag and puts them on desk*] Let me give you a drink.

BILL: Thanks.

SALLY: Scotch?

BILL: Swell. [*Looking around*] This is very pleasant. I haven't been in an apartment like this for quite a time. It's two years since I was in New York.

OLIVE: How does it look to you?

BILL: Like every other place these days . . . a lot too full of soldiers. But it's still good. *You're* looking blooming.

OLIVE: [*Uncomfortably bright*] Oh, yes, I'm fine.

BILL: I don't know whether you've made any plans for this week-end, but I've got a lot.

OLIVE: [*Miserably*] You have?

BILL: I thought tonight, we'd just have a quiet dinner . . . not go anywhere afterwards . . . just concentrate on good food, good drink and good . . . [*Sally hands him his glass*] Thank you so much. [*Then, turning back to* Olive] Then I thought tomorrow we might take in a theatre. There was a notice in the evening paper of a new musical that opened last night. I imagine it will be all sold out, but I thought that, being in the theatre, you might know some way of getting tickets. [*Pause*] How about it? Have you got any strings you can pull?

OLIVE: [*Nerving herself*] Bill . . . I've got something to tell you. [*Sally edges to the bedroom door*] Don't go, Sally.

SALLY: You left your glass in the bedroom.

OLIVE: I don't want another drink.

SALLY: I'll just get it.

[*She goes into the bedroom, closing the door behind her.* Bill *notices this with slight surprise, as he turns back to Olive. In the bedroom, Sally goes over to the window, looks out, draws the curtains and then sits, doing nothing, unwilling to return to the living room]*

BILL: Well, what is it?

OLIVE: Bill, darling, I don't know how to tell you, but . . . I'm afraid our week-end's off.

BILL: How do you mean?

OLIVE: Darling, I can't come out with you. I . . . Listen, you didn't know I was married, did you?

[Olive *plays this scene with all the conviction possible. There must be no sense that she is lying, or doing it badly. Whether or not Bill is deceived is another question]*

BILL: No—when?

OLIVE: About eighteen months ago. It didn't take. That's why I didn't tell you in Detroit.

BILL: Well?

OLIVE: Well, just this afternoon, he called me up. He's in the Navy. It's his last leave, and . . . he wanted to see me.

BILL: Yes?

OLIVE: I've got to have dinner with him.

BILL: Oh, that's tough for you. And for me.

OLIVE: I know.

BILL: Well, we'll meet later.

OLIVE: [*Quickly*] Oh, darling, I can't. I . . .

BILL: What?

OLIVE: [*Very uncomfortable*] Well, he . . . he *is* my husband. I mean, we're not divorced, or anything.

BILL: You mean—you're going back to him?

OLIVE: [*Not altogether liking this*] Well, I . . . I don't know about permanently, but . . . it's his last leave, and . . .

BILL: [*Sparing her more*] I see.

OLIVE: You're not mad at me?

BILL: No. But you can't expect me not to be a little disappointed. It's all right, though. These things happen. Not often, I guess, but . . .

OLIVE: I'll see you next time you get leave.

BILL: [*Smiling*] Okay.

OLIVE: You do understand?

BILL: [*Smiling and patting her hand*] Sure. Everything.

OLIVE: [*Not liking this, either*] Bill, you're sweet. You always were. And, look, I've got to go. It's so late.

BILL: [*Rising*] Right now?

OLIVE: I'm meeting Ned at eight.

BILL: What's his other name?

OLIVE: [*After a slight pause*] Burling.

BILL: [*Looking at her*] Mrs. Ned Burling! Who'd have thought it?

OLIVE: [*Very uncomfortable now*] He's a Commander. I *must* go. [*Calls*] Sally! Sally!

BILL: Do you want me to take you anywhere?

OLIVE: [*Hurriedly*] No . . . no . . . you stay here, and have your drink in peace. [*Sally returns*]

I've broken it to him, Sally, and he's been sweet.

SALLY: [*Smiling politely*] Oh?

OLIVE: And now I've got to fly.

SALLY: It's started to rain.

OLIVE: Oh, hell, can you get a taxi anywhere around here?

SALLY: Sometimes on Third Avenue. But not when it's raining.

OLIVE: I'll find one. Good-bye, Bill, and do forgive me. I'll call you. Where are you staying?

BILL: I don't know yet. I went straight from the station to your hotel. I asked if they'd a room there, but they were all full up. So I just came on here.

OLIVE: [*Abashed*] Oh, Bill . . . I should have gotten you a room. New York's so full, only . . .

BILL: Don't worry. I'll find something.

OLIVE: I'll call you too, Sally. Bless you, and . . . [*She breaks off, floundering, kisses her and goes to the door*] Good-bye, Bill.

BILL: Good-bye. Have fun.

OLIVE: [*Turning, reproachfully*] Oh, Bill, that's not kind.

BILL: I'm sorry.

OLIVE: [*As before*] No, it's not kind at all!

[*She goes*]

BILL: [*Turning to Sally, with a slightly rueful grin*] Well . . .

SALLY: [*Smiling*] Well?

BILL: Give her a minute to get clear, and then I'll go along.

SALLY: There's no hurry.

BILL: Aren't you going out?

SALLY: No.

BILL: Well, all the same . . . I wonder if I might use your telephone.

SALLY: [*Going to the bedroom door*] Yes, of course. It's in there.

BILL: Thank you so much.

[*He goes into the bedroom. Sally closes the door on him, to give him privacy, and then draws the curtains, lights the lamps and settles down with the evening paper on the couch. In the bedroom, Bill takes out a small notebook from his pocket, looks up a number, dials it, sitting on the bed*]

BILL: Hello? Can I speak to Miss Westbury, please? Miss Joan Westbury. Isn't that . . . [*Referring to his book again*] Butterfield 8-1747? Don't Mr. and Mrs. Arthur Westbury live there? Oh, I see. Can you tell me where they're living now? I see. Thank you. [*Hangs up, gets notebook out again, and looks up another number, dialing it*] Hello . . . Is Miss Van Huysen there, please? Oh, are you expecting her in? Oh, I see. Well, will you tell her, Monday, that Mr. Page called, Friday? Mr. Bill Page, of Pittsburgh. No, no number. [*Hangs up again, and then dials another number after a moment's reflection and search*] Hello, is Mr. Frank Archer there? Frank? This is Bill Page. Yes.

Oh, I'm in town for the week-end. Say, you don't happen to know Joan's number, do you? Joan Westbury. I called her old number, but . . . no kidding? I hadn't heard. How does she look in her uniform? Say, whatever happened to Alice . . . what was her other name? That's right . . . Alice Hopewell. She *is?* When did she *get* married? What—Phyllis, too? Well, that's about all the old gang, isn't it? Frank, could *we* have some dinner tonight? Oh, you are? That's all right. It was just that I got stood up, that's all. Oh, I don't know. I'll probably go to the Stage Door Canteen, or something. I'm not stopping *anywhere* at the moment. I'll call *you.* Sure. Good-bye. [*Hangs up again. Looks in book again, thumbing leaves . . . is about to dial another number, then mutters, "Oh, the hell with it. She's probably dead." Rises, looks out of window, says, "Oh, damn the rain!" and returns to the other room*]

SALLY: [*Looking up with a polite smile*] Did you get your number?

BILL: Yes, thanks. Well . . .

SALLY: Won't you have another drink?

BILL: You're sure you're in no hurry?

SALLY: None at all.

BILL: Well, then, thanks. I'd like to.

SALLY: Help yourself, won't you?

BILL: [*Going to drink-table*] Will *you?*

SALLY: I don't think so, thanks.

[*She watches him, commiseratingly, but unable to think of anything to talk about*]

BILL: [*Making conversation*] Are you and Olive old friends?

SALLY: We are, rather. She was in the first play I was ever in.

BILL: Oh. I ought to know, of course, but I haven't been around. Are you a well-known actress?

SALLY: [*Laughing*] Me? I've never been in anything but flops. My longest run was three weeks.

BILL: You're not in anything now?

SALLY: No, nor likely to be, for months.

BILL: [*Coming back with his drink*] What do actresses do between jobs?

SALLY: Well, *I* just sit and think about how I'm going to act all the parts I'll never get a chance to act. Like Juliet, or Nina in *The Sea Gull.* That's a Russian play.

BILL: I know.

SALLY: Oh, I'm sorry. I didn't mean to be patronizing. Only not a lot of people do know, and I didn't know if you knew anything about the theatre. *I* don't know anything about real life.

BILL: [*Amused*] Real life?

SALLY: I always think of it like that. I mean, all of us . . . actors, and authors, too . . . we aren't really living in the real world at all. We're giving our whole lives to . . . make-believe.

BILL: [*Sitting*] Why do you do it, then?

SALLY: I guess because I'm made that way. And in the hope of . . .

BILL: Of some day seeing your name in lights?

SALLY: Oh, I hope it isn't that. Of course, it's part of it. It would be silly to pretend it wasn't. But the hope . . . of one day being able to express . . . well, that thing one feels one's got to express . . .

BILL: "That one Talent which is death to hide?"

SALLY: [*Struck*] Oh . . . what's that?

BILL: Milton. The sonnet on his blindness.

SALLY: Oh . . . it's lovely. Say it again. Say it all.

BILL: I don't think I can remember it all. It's years since I've looked at it. But . . . [*Quietly*]
"When I consider how my light is spent
   Ere half my days in this dark world and wide,
   And that one Talent which is death to hide,
   Lodged with me useless . . ."
I don't remember any more.

SALLY: [*Savoring it*] Oh . . . yes.

BILL: Well, that's wonderful . . . if you *have* the talent.

SALLY: Have *you?* I mean . . . do you do anything creative?

BILL: No, I'm afraid the only talent *I've* ever had is a talent for appreciation.

SALLY: What *did* you do before the war?

BILL: I didn't do anything at all till I was twenty-five, except have a very good time.

SALLY: Were you a . . . playboy?

BILL: Well, that's not a thing one would ever think of oneself as being . . . but, I suppose—by present-day standards, anyway—that's what I was. My family had a lot of money . . . and I went to Princeton, and Europe and . . . appreciated things. Very much indeed.

SALLY: And then?

BILL: Well, then things went wrong with the family, and the business went smash, and I had to come back and buckle down to . . . "real life."

SALLY: Was that awful for you?

BILL: A little. I told myself it was good for me. I guess maybe it was.

SALLY: And then the Army?

BILL: Yes.

SALLY: And . . . afterwards?

BILL: I haven't any plans for afterwards. I just hope there'll still be things left to appreciate.

SALLY: There'll always be. So long as there are people. Free people. That's what it's all about, isn't it? The war, I mean?

BILL: You mustn't ask a soldier what the war's about.

SALLY: [*After a pause, tasting the phrase again*] "That one Talent which is death to hide . . ."

BILL: [*Smiling at her*] That sums you up, does it?

SALLY: Oh, no. Milton could say that. I'm not that conceited. But it's what it *feels* like, when you're out of work, or doing something second-rate. It's like having something *entrusted* to you . . . for the benefit of others . . . that you're wasting.

[*Breaking off*] Oh, no . . . that sounds awful! Phony and arty, like Madame Pushkin.

BILL: Who's she?

SALLY: Madame Pushkin? Oh, she's an imaginary character that Olive and I invented. An old Russian actress who runs a school where she teaches the Pushkin method. Her husband, Dr. Pushkin, is a very great director, and every morning he chases her around the bedroom for one hour in her nightgown to "giff her de free body." Didn't Olive ever tell you about her?

BILL: Olive and I have never talked like this.

SALLY: [*Abashed*] I'm sorry.

BILL: What for?

SALLY: Going on about myself.

BILL: I've liked it. And *I've* gone on about myself, too . . . which is something I haven't done for years. Will you have dinner with me?

SALLY: [*After a second*] Oh . . . no, thanks.

BILL: Why not?

SALLY: You don't have to ask me.

BILL: I know I don't. But will you?

SALLY: Well . . . we go Dutch.

BILL: No, I asked you.

SALLY: Only because Olive let you down.

BILL: Only because if she hadn't, I wouldn't have had the chance.

SALLY: [*Embarrassed by the compliment*] Well, thank you very much, then.

BILL: Where shall we go?

SALLY: Wherever you say.

BILL: What's the place next door like?

SALLY: [*After a half-second's pause, with an echo in her ears*] Very expensive.

BILL: But good?

SALLY: Yes, but . . .

BILL: Let's go there. [*He notices a hesitation about her*] Have you anything against it?

SALLY: N-no . . . But it's . . . *very* expensive.

BILL: All the same. Besides, it's raining quite hard now, so *let's* go next door. There was a restaurant of the same name in Paris that I used to go to quite a lot, once upon a time. Did you know Paris?

SALLY: No. I never went to Europe. I was only eighteen when the war broke out.

BILL: My God. That hurts.

SALLY: What?

BILL: That that's possible, already. [*He looks at her*]

SALLY: [*After an embarrassed pause*] I'll just get my coat. [*She starts into the bedroom. Bill stands looking after her*]

SCENE 2: *The same. About 10:30 the same night.*

The stage is as we left it. Then the sound of a key is heard in the front door. Bill and Sally come in.

BILL: What a night! [*Closes the door behind him*] Did you get wet?

SALLY: Running from next door? No. Come in and sit down, won't you?
[*Bill shakes out his cap, and puts it down. He helps Sally off with her coat. She switches on the lamps*]

SALLY: Would you like a drink?

BILL: Not after all that brandy. I must have had five, waiting for the rain to stop.

SALLY: [*After a moment's pause, going to the radio*] Would you like the news?

BILL: I don't think so. Unless *you* would.

SALLY: I don't think . . . really. [*She starts to wander purposely*] Have a candy? [*Offers box*]

BILL: No, thanks. You don't have to entertain me, you know. Relax. What are you fussing about?

SALLY: Was I fussing? I didn't mean to. [*Pause*] That was a lovely dinner. Thank you.

BILL: You were right. It's a good place.

SALLY: It was better even than usual tonight. That was your remembering the proprietor from Paris. And he you. You must have gone there a lot.

BILL: I did. I used to go with . . . a girl I used to go with. Almost every evening, at one time, for weeks on end.

SALLY: Was it a famous place?

BILL: No, just tiny. But we used to think of it as "our" place. We were very young.

SALLY: Were you in love with her?

BILL: I used to think I was.

SALLY: What happened to her?

BILL: She got married. Women do, you know.

SALLY: Yes. This isn't being a very amusing evening for you. Going to that restaurant . . . sort of upset you, didn't it?

BILL: Did that show?

SALLY: I *thought* . . .

BILL: I'm sorry. But "upset" is too strong a word. It was just . . . seeing it all done up exactly like the place in Paris, the same pictures on the walls, the same lamps on the tables, the same tablecloths . . . Well, it brought things back.

SALLY: The girl, you mean? Was she a French girl?

BILL: No, she was an American. I wasn't having an affair with Mimi, the little Midinette. But I didn't only mean the girl. I meant everything. Those were happy years. I was very happy then.

SALLY: And you're not now?

BILL: Is anyone?

SALLY: It's awful, but *I* am. Quite often.

BILL: It's not at all awful. It's wonderful. But I'm afraid I infected you at dinner. You were a bit low, too, I thought.

SALLY: [*Moving away*] Well, strangely, that place has memories for *me*, too. More recent ones than yours, but . . .

BILL: Why didn't you tell me?

SALLY: [*Vaguely*] Oh . . .

BILL: I'm afraid it wasn't a very good choice, for either of us.

SALLY: I *am* sorry. You're having a miserable time.

BILL: No, I'm having a grand time. [*Yawns*] Oh, I'm sorry.

SALLY: You see!

BILL: That wasn't misery . . . or boredom. It was too much dinner, and not enough sleep.

SALLY: Don't you get enough?

BILL: I haven't had enough for months. Tomorrow morning, I shall stay in bed till lunchtime. Sunday, I probably shan't get up at all . . . till it's time to go back.

SALLY: Is that how you want to spend your leave?

BILL: Well, there are worse ways.

SALLY: But it wasn't what you'd planned.

BILL: [*Putting out his cigarette*] No! [*Then, after a second*] Did you know Olive was going to tell me all that story?

SALLY: [*Startled*] What do you mean?

BILL: You don't think I believed it, do you? You didn't think I *would* believe it? [*Sally stares at him*] Olive's far too . . . well, too frank and free a person, not to have mentioned a husband if she had one.

SALLY: But you haven't seen each other.

BILL: We saw each other in Detroit, six weeks ago.

SALLY: Yes, but then you . . .

BILL: What?

SALLY: [*Unable to go on, without giving away too much*] Nothing.

BILL: Oh, she told you about it, did she? I guess girls always do.

SALLY: [*After just too long a pause*] I don't know what you're talking about.

BILL: [*Smiling*] Okay.

SALLY: [*Rising*] Are you in love with Olive?

BILL: Is that your favorite question?

SALLY: [*Blushing and subsiding*] I'm sorry.

BILL: I'm not in the least in love with her. So don't worry. I guess I'm a little sore at her for letting me down. But I'll get over that, by tomorrow.

SALLY: [*Slightly shocked*] As quickly as that?

BILL: Oh, I think so. [*He yawns again*] Oh, I am sorry. I should be going.

SALLY: [*Rising*] Well, if you're sleepy. Has the rain stopped?

BILL: I don't know. [*Goes to window and looks out*] No, I think it's worse.

SALLY: [*Following him to window*] You can't go out in that.

BILL: If it doesn't let up soon, I'll have to.

SALLY: Well, don't go yet. It's sure to stop.

BILL: [*Returning to the couch*] Tell me some more about Madame Pushkin.

SALLY: [*Laughing*] Oh, it's silly.

BILL: No, I like the sound of her. What is the Pushkin method?

SALLY: Well, to begin with, she believes that you must never play a part the way it's written. That's too easy. [*Assuming a mock-Russian accent and personality*] Always you must look for de *odder* side of a character. Ven I play Lady Macbess, I concentrate on her . . . her *child-like* qvalities. Ven ve com to de scene from de sleep-valking, I skip! [*And does so*]

BILL: [*Laughing*] You're a fool!

SALLY: [*Laughing, too*] I know. There's heaps more. Her parents were on the stage, too, you know. She was conceived during an intermission of *The Cherry Orchard*.

BILL: Are you making all this up as you go along?

SALLY: Certainly. Olive and I do it for hours on end. We call it "How to be ham though high-brow." Olive . . . [*She stops a little self-consciously on the mention of* Olive's *name*]

BILL: Look, you needn't get self-conscious about mentioning Olive's name to me. She hasn't broken my heart.

SALLY: Has anyone, ever? Did the girl in Paris?

BILL: At it again?

SALLY: Oh, dear, it's an obsession.

BILL: Why's it an obsession?

SALLY: I don't know. Because I'm a fool, I guess. I always think that everyone ought to be in love with *someone*.

BILL: Are *you*?

SALLY: I . . . I think I am.

BILL: Not sure? Have you been in love often?

SALLY: [*Seriously, considering it*] No . . . not often.

BILL: [*Kidding her a little*] I suppose actresses need to fall in love a lot . . . to be good actresses?

SALLY: [*Becoming Madame Pushkin instantly*] Oh, yes, Meester Payche! Alvays ven I play a rôle I must be in lof. Sometimes I valk de streets for hours, to find someone to fall in lof viz! [*Telephone rings. She continues in the accent*] De telephone. Excuse please. I go.

[*She goes into the bedroom, and turns on the light, answering the telephone very gaily, in Pushkin accents. Bill sits alone, amused, for a moment, then returns to the window, looks out again, then throws himself on the divan, below it, playing with the radio. He turns it on very softly to some gentle instrumental music, lights a cigarette, and stretches out full length on his back, listening to it*]

SALLY: [*On the telephone*] Hillo . . . [*Then, remembering, in her own voice*] I mean—hello. [*Then, recognizing* Olive's *voice, she resumes the accent*] Is Madame Pushkin speakink, Miss Lashbrooke. [*Then, back to her own voice again*] I was just telling about her . . . To Bill . . . Yes, he's still here . . . No, we went out to dinner. . . . No, I've had a very *nice* evening. He wasn't a bit miserable. Where are you? . . . Well, it was a good thing you didn't, because that *was* where we went. . . . Oh, we had the most wonderful Vichyssoise, and duck with oranges, salad with a lot of garlic. . . . What? Yes, I guess we do . . . and Crêpes Suzettes . . . Olive, you don't *mind* our having gone to dinner, do you? It was just that he asked me, and he hadn't any other place to go . . . No, I don't think he has. I don't think he's tried. . . . Well, it's raining. Hard . . . Are *you* having fun? What did *you* have to eat? . . . Oh, lovely. Yes, of course he's all right. Why not? . . . Well, I won't tell him if you don't want me to. Good-bye, Olive.

[*She hangs up, a little bothered and puzzled. Then she returns to the other room, where she stops at the sight of Bill, who has fallen asleep, with the cigarette burning between his fingers. She takes it gently from his hand, and he wakes*]

BILL: [*Sitting up*] What . . . ? Oh, I'm sorry. I've been asleep.

SALLY: I'm sorry I woke you, but you might have set yourself on fire.

[*She gives him the cigarette back*]

BILL: [*Rising*] I might have set the place on fire. I'd better get along and look for a hotel room.

SALLY: Yes, you'll have awful trouble, finding one. The hotels are all full up.

BILL: Are they?

SALLY: Ol . . . [*She checks herself*] The friend who just called up said they were.

BILL: [*Registering her change of phrase*] Well, I'll dig up something. This is liable to keep up all night. So . . .

[*He crosses to Sally, extending his hand*]

SALLY: [*As they shake hands, with a sudden thought*] Would you want to stay here? That's a day-bed. It's quite comfortable.

BILL: I know it is. But . . . I don't think I should do that.

SALLY: I can give you a toothbrush.

BILL: I've got that with me.

SALLY: It seems silly to go out in all that rain. You'll get so wet looking for a taxi. You haven't any change of clothes. You're tired. I'll give you breakfast in the morning.

BILL: Oh, you needn't do that.

SALLY: I'd like to.

BILL: Well, it's very good of you . . .

SALLY: Then you will?

BILL: Yes, thank you. [*Yawns again*] Oh . . .

SALLY: [*Commiseratingly*] Ah, look at you! Why don't you go to bed, right away? It's all made up. I've only got to take the cover off.

BILL: Let me help you.

SALLY: Oh, thank you.

[*She takes the cushions from the day-bed, while Bill strips off the cover*]

SALLY: [*After a moment*] Would you like some pajamas?

BILL: I couldn't wear your pajamas.

SALLY: They aren't mine. They're men's pajamas. My . . . brother stays here sometimes.

BILL: Oh . . . well, then, thank you very much. That would be a luxury.

SALLY: I'll get them for you.

[*She goes to the bedroom, taking her coat with her, and gets a pair of men's pajamas and bedroom slippers from a drawer. Meanwhile, Bill takes off his coat, hanging it over the back of a chair in the living room. Sally returns*]

SALLY: [*Handing him the pajamas*] Here . . .

BILL: [*After the tiniest pause—taking them*] Thanks. These are very resplendent.

SALLY: I brought you some slippers, too.

BILL: All the comforts of home. [*There is a tiny movement of embarrassment. Then he slumps onto the bed.*] Gee, I'm tired. [*He starts to unlace his shoes*]

SALLY: I'll just empty the ashtrays.

[*She starts emptying them into the largest, while he continues to unlace his shoes. The radio starts playing the Londonderry Air, and she pauses, raising her head to listen to it*]

BILL: [*Noticing*] What is it?

[*She crosses to the radio, and turns it louder, to hear better. She smiles*]

SALLY: That's my lucky tune.

BILL: The Londonderry Air?

SALLY: It's silly, but whenever I hear that, nice things always seem to happen to me. [*Collecting herself*] I'll just take these out. The bathroom's through there.

[*She goes into the kitchen. Bill takes his toilet case and the pajamas and goes into the bathroom. In the kitchen, Sally empties the ashtrays and washes them. Then she gets a tray with a Thermos set from the shelves, and fills the jug with ice-water from the icebox, taking the tray into the living room and setting it on the desk. She clears the drink-table of its tray, which she takes to the kitchen. Back in the living room again, she tidies the room, turning down the day-bed, and arranging the ottoman footrest of the armchair as a night-table, with the Thermos tray, cigarettes, matches, and ashtray, beside the bed. Throughout this business, the radio continues. Then she goes into the bedroom*]

SALLY: [*Calling to the closed bathroom door*] Have you everything you want?

BILL: [*Putting his head around the door, toothbrush in hand*] Did you call?

SALLY: I said, have you everything you want?

BILL: Oh, sure, thanks. Everything.

[*She smiles at him, and he shuts the door again. She strips the cover from her own bed, folds it and lays it on top of the chest of drawers. Then she goes back to the living room, switching off lights. Bill returns in pajamas, carrying his folded clothes. He looks around*]

BILL: [*Indicating a chair*] This all right?

SALLY: Sure.

[He lays his clothes neatly across the chair]

BILL: *[Coming to the bed]* You don't know how good that looks. *[Sits on it]* And feels. *[He kicks off the slippers, and gets into bed]* And is. *[He sits up, smiling]*

SALLY: What are you smiling at?

BILL: I was just remembering a novel I once read about life in 1910 . . . where the heroine was compromised because she was seen coming out of a man's apartment, after dark.

SALLY: I guess things *have* changed.

BILL: You're not kidding.

SALLY: *[Dubiously]* Although I don't know that my mother would . . . *quite* understand this. It's silly, because it couldn't be more sensible. But there are a lot of people still who wouldn't believe in it.

BILL: Well, don't tell 'em.

SALLY: I don't intend to. *[Pause]* Well . . . good night.

BILL: Good night, Sally.

[He switches out the bed light]

SALLY: Good night, Cousin Bill.

BILL: Huh?

SALLY: Nothing. Oh, I left the kitchen light on. *[She goes back to the kitchen, talking from there, over her shoulder]* I'll just leave a note for Verona, to tell her not to disturb you. If she comes. *[She starts to scribble a note on a pad hanging on a nail]* Verona's the colored maid. I don't expect she'll show up, but I'll be on the safe side. *[She finishes the note, tears off the sheet and places it prominently. Then she switches off the kitchen light. The only remaining light is now in the bedroom. She returns to the dark living room]*

SALLY: Are you all right?

[There is no answer. Bill is asleep. Sally tiptoes on into the bedroom, closing the door behind her. She sits on the bed, takes off her shoes, and is starting on her stockings as the curtain falls]

Act II

SCENE 1: *The same. Around noon, the next day.*

When the curtain rises, Bill is in the kitchen, squeezing orange juice at the sink. A coffee percolator is bubbling on the stove. A tray is set with cup aud saucer and cream pitcher. The day-bed in the living room has been made, and in the bedroom Sally's bed has also been made, and the room tidied.

After a moment, Sally lets herself in at the front door. She is in outdoor things, and carries some marketing bags, and a manuscript. Her manner is gay, and ever so lightly "high." Bill hears the door, and comes into the living room.

BILL: Good morning.

SALLY: *[Dumping her packages on the couch]* Good morning.

BILL: *[Smiling]* How are you this morning?

SALLY: I'm fine. *[She looks around]* Is Verona here?

BILL: I haven't seen her.

SALLY: Did *you* make your bed?

BILL: Sure.

SALLY: You shouldn't have.

BILL: Why not?

SALLY: Because . . . it's not a man's thing to do.

BILL: You'd be surprised what a lot of men are doing it, nowadays.

SALLY: Yes, but this is your vacation. Have you had breakfast?

BILL: I've just put on some coffee, as you said in your note I might.

SALLY: I was *afraid* Verona wasn't going to show up. I meant to get your breakfast myself, but I had to go out.

BILL: Did *you* have breakfast?

SALLY: No. I had a cocktail.

BILL: A what?

SALLY: A cocktail.

BILL: When?

SALLY: Oh, about half an hour ago. It's made me a little heady.

BILL: Didn't you have any breakfast *before* the cocktail?

SALLY: No, there wasn't time. I thought if you were still here, and hadn't a date, we might have lunch. I did some marketing.

BILL: You seem to have done a lot.

SALLY: I can never resist a delicatessen. I hate eating alone, except things you can sort of cuddle up on the couch with . . . like potato salad. *[She pats the package, indicating it]*

BILL: I should never have thought of cuddling up with potato salad.

SALLY: I'd better take these in the kitchen. *[She starts to do so, talking as she goes]* I wish I'd started housekeeping before rationing. It must have been so easy, then. I always do everything too late. *[She returns to the living room]* It's the loveliest spring morning out. The weather's changed at last. In more ways than one, I think.

BILL: What do you mean by that?

SALLY: I think *my* weather's changed, too. I've got a job.

BILL: You have?

SALLY: That's what I went out about. That's what I had the cocktail about, too. They called me at half-past nine. I didn't disturb you, did I? I tried not to.

BILL: I didn't know a thing till half-past eleven.

SALLY: I was afraid the telephone might have woken you. *[Correcting herself]* Wakened you. But you were still sleeping when I left.

BILL: Not snoring, I hope?

SALLY: No, you were very peaceful. [*Turning to him with her characteristic sudden directness*] Don't you think there's something rather . . . frightening about people asleep? They look so unlike themselves, and sort of . . . vulnerable. I always feel one oughtn't to look.

BILL: When you have to sleep with fifty other men every night, you get over feeling like that.

SALLY: Do you hate it all?

BILL: [*Briefly*] No.

SALLY: Like it?

BILL: That would be going a little far. I don't think you're expected to *like* it.

SALLY: A job to be done?

BILL: You do like to talk about things, don't you?

SALLY: Yes, it's my besetting sin. I always hope if I talk about things, it will help me know what I feel about them. But it never does. It only muddles me more. [*Looking at him*] You're depressed this morning.

BILL: No, I just haven't had my coffee yet. It should be ready by now. You'd better have some, too.

SALLY: *I'm* not depressed.

BILL: [*With meaning*] No, I know . . .

SALLY: You think I'm tight.

BILL: [*Unconvincingly*] No, I don't.

SALLY: I am. A little. And I'm happy, too.

BILL: [*As they go into kitchen*] Tell me about the job.

SALLY: Oh, it's a lovely job. Only . . . may I tell you when we sit down? I hate telling a story in bits . . . if it's a good story.

BILL: All right. [*He gets another cup and saucer from the shelves, and puts it on the tray. Sally starts putting her packages in the icebox*] By the way, your telephone rang while you were out. It rang twice.

SALLY: Oh, who was it?

BILL: I don't know.

SALLY: Didn't you answer?

BILL: No.

SALLY: Why not?

BILL: I didn't think it would sound very well to have a man's voice answering your telephone.

SALLY: I wouldn't have thought of that.

BILL: Suppose it had been your Aunt Minnie from Duluth? Or . . . your brother, for that matter?

SALLY: My . . . ?

BILL: [*Quickly*] Whose very handsome pajamas I wore last night.

SALLY: Oh . . . yes. [*He takes the tray and goes into the living room. Sally follows with the percolator*] You mean you just let it ring? I don't think I could do that, even in someone else's house. It always sounds to me as if it was going crazy when I don't answer. Besides, it might be something lovely.

BILL: [*Setting the tray down and sitting down to it with her*] For instance?

SALLY: [*Pouring coffee*] Well . . . a long-lost uncle with a lot of money, or a lovely party, or a job.

BILL: How often has it been one of those?

SALLY: It was a job this morning.

BILL: Yes, you win on that. [*Takes his cup*] Now do you feel settled enough to tell about it?

SALLY: [*Taking hers*] Yes, I think so. Well, as I say, it's really a lovely job. It's a play that's in rehearsal already. I knew about it from a friend of mine who was going to be in it. Well, yesterday was the fifth day. Oh, I don't guess you know about that. You can fire actors up to the fifth day, if they're no good.

BILL: No, I didn't know. What happens *after* the fifth day?

SALLY: You have to keep them, or pay them two weeks' salary. It's a rule of Equity. Well, it seems they fired her yesterday.

BILL: Your friend?

SALLY: Yes. I feel sort of badly about that . . . getting her part, I mean . . . though, actually, she couldn't have been in it very long, if it had run, because she's going to have a baby, only she didn't tell them that. And I don't think it was quite honorable. I mean, it may be an act of God, but not if it's already started, I should think.

BILL: [*Bewildered*] What *are* you talking about? What may be an act of God?

SALLY: Having a baby. It is, in the theatre.

BILL: I never knew the theatre was that different. I see now what you mean about real life! Well, go on . . . They fired her, and sent for you?

SALLY: Yes. I'm starting rehearsals Monday. The author took me next door for a cocktail, and I didn't like to tell him I hadn't had any breakfast. It sounded too pathetic. And then he told me something really thrilling.

BILL: What was that?

SALLY: Well, I'm not supposed to tell. But . . . well, you don't know anyone in the theatre, do you?

BILL: Only Olive.

SALLY: Well, I don't guess you'll be seeing her.

BILL: I guess not.

SALLY: I think I can tell you. You see, the leading man isn't very good, but he was all they could get, because of the draft.

BILL: You mean—he's a 4-F?

SALLY: I guess so. Anyway, his acting's 4-F. Well, now, with Olive's tour closing, there's a chance they might get Henry Atherton. And that'd be wonderful. I've always had the most terrific crush on him.

BILL: [*Surprised*] That wizened, whimsy little man with dyed gold hair?

SALLY: Oh, he's sweet. And it's not dyed. Is it?

BILL: Olive said it was. And she said he used to make passes at all the kids in the company.

SALLY: Yes, she told me. But he's a great star, and

it would be a big chance for me. I told you last night that was my lucky tune.

BILL: What kind of a part have you got in this play?

SALLY: Oh, a lovely part. I have to go mad in one act. Do you know anything about insanity?

BILL: Not a thing. Why?

SALLY: I thought you might give me some pointers. Although, as a matter of fact, I know just how I want to do it, if I can.

BILL: How is that?

SALLY: I want to play it very quietly, and as if I thought I were quite sane, myself. I mean, I don't imagine mad people ever *think* they're mad. They probably think everyone else is.

BILL: [*In Pushkin accents*] You are qvite right. Dat is how I teach my vife, Madame Pushkin, to play Ophelia.

SALLY: I don't go *very* mad. I mean, not straws and things.

BILL: I'm glad of that. I don't like plays where people go *very* mad.

SALLY: Nor do I. Though they're fun to do. What other kinds of plays don't you like?

BILL: Plays about men who are paralyzed from the waist down. Plays where a lot of people all get caught together in a catastrophe—a flood, or an earthquake, or an air raid—and all face death in a lump. There's always a prostitute in those plays, have you noticed? Usually a clergyman, too. That's what's called "taking a cross-section of humanity." I don't like plays about prostitutes.

SALLY: They're lovely to act. Olive's played lots. I haven't been one since I was in high school. And then they called it a courtesan.

BILL: [*Laughing*] I bet you were immense.

[*He rises to get cigarettes from the pocket of his coat which is hanging over a chair. Sally rises, too, taking the percolator back to the kitchen*]

BILL: Well, things *are* looking up for you. I guess you're right, and the weather *has* changed. The rain is over, the winter is past, and the voice of the turtle is heard in our land.

SALLY: [*Arrested in the doorway*] What did you say?

BILL: I was quoting from the Bible.

SALLY: Oh. [*She comes back for the tray, and then stops again, worriedly*] But turtles don't *have* voices . . . do they?

BILL: Turtle *dove*.

SALLY: Oh. [*As she goes back to the kitchen with the tray*] I never could understand the Bible. I don't see why they give it to children to read. [*She returns to the living room*]

BILL: You know, we ought to do something to celebrate this job of yours. Will you have dinner with me?

SALLY: You took me to dinner last night.

BILL: So what?

SALLY: So you shouldn't do it again.

BILL: But I want to do it again. Very much. And

what do you say we go to a theatre? That new musical. Do you like musicals?

SALLY: I adore them. If they're good.

BILL: Well, this is supposed to be very good.

SALLY: Yes, it is. I've heard some of the songs.

BILL: Well, let's go, then.

SALLY: We'd never get seats.

BILL: Not even through a broker?

SALLY: I don't think so. After those notices . . . and the first Saturday.

BILL: I wondered whether Olive mightn't have some pull. I started to ask her yesterday.

SALLY: I know. But I don't think she has. And I wouldn't want to ask her now, anyway.

BILL: Why not?

SALLY: Well, you're *her* friend, and Olive's rather hot against that kind of thing. Beau-snatching. I don't know that I really ought to come at all.

BILL: Now you listen to me. In the first place, you haven't snatched me. Any snatching that's been going on, *I've* been doing. And in the second, I'm not her beau . . . any more. She gave me the good, old-fashioned gate last night, even though I did suspect she was trying to leave it on the latch. The point is, we're going to that musical. How *does* one get tickets for a show like that, at the last moment? People do.

SALLY: Well, there are things called house seats.

BILL: What are they?

SALLY: They're tickets that the management keeps up its sleeve for friends, and influential people.

BILL: Who is the management?

SALLY: Kenneth Bartlett's putting it on.

BILL: Do you know him?

SALLY: [*Remotely*] Yes, I . . . know him.

BILL: Well, then call him up. Tell him a friend of yours . . . a service man . . . is in town . . . you can say it's his last furlough . . .

SALLY: [*Faintly alarmed*] Is it?

BILL: No, but it makes a better story. And can he please buy two of the house seats for tonight? [*Sally sits dumbly*] What's the matter?

SALLY: I can't ask him.

BILL: Don't you know him well enough?

SALLY: It isn't that.

BILL: What then?

SALLY: It's just that . . . I can't. There are reasons. Really, there are. I can't.

BILL: Well, then, I'll go foraging this afternoon when I look for a hotel room, and you can stay here and study how to go slightly mad.

SALLY: I'm afraid you won't get anything.

BILL: Well, don't be so worried about it.

SALLY: But you wanted to see it. You're having an awful leave. You're not doing any of the things you planned to do.

BILL: I'm enjoying the things I'm doing, instead.

SALLY: [*Suddenly, as always*] Do you believe in pride?

BILL: Now what do you mean by that?

SALLY: Suppose someone had . . . not treated you badly, it's not that . . . suppose you'd behaved badly to someone . . . do you think you ought to ask them for a favor?

BILL: I should hardly think so. What's this about? The theatre tickets?

SALLY: [Quickly] No. Oh, no. Just general principles.

BILL: Have you behaved badly to someone?

SALLY: Well, not badly in the ordinary sense. But . . . well . . . What's the difference between true pride and false?

BILL: I really wouldn't know.

SALLY: I'm sure you oughtn't to.

BILL: Oughtn't to what?

SALLY: Ask the favor.

BILL: [After a moment] Well, let's stop this abstract speculation and get lunch.

SALLY: [Coming out of her reverie] Oh . . . yes. [She rises]

BILL: Sally.

SALLY: What?

BILL: You're very sweet. [She looks up at him with surprise. He takes her hands] I haven't the faintest idea what goes on in that funny little head of yours, but you're very sweet.

[He leans forward and kisses her, gently. They hold the kiss for a moment, then he releases her]

SALLY: Oh . . . that was a surprise.

BILL: Do you mind?

SALLY: No, it was nice.

BILL: I thought so, too. Come and show me where things are. [He goes into the kitchen. She follows him, more disturbed than ever] What are we going to have? Not potato salad, I hope?

SALLY: [Still in a slight trance] No, I thought maybe . . . scrambled eggs.

BILL: Good.

SALLY: [Reaching down below stove] I'll get the frying pan.

BILL: Do you have a double boiler? I think they're better in a double boiler.

SALLY: [Bringing one out, abstractedly] Are they? I've never used one.

BILL: Do you like them wet or dry?

SALLY: What?

BILL: Your eggs.

SALLY: Oh . . . wet, I think.

BILL: Good. So do I. And how about coming out of that trance?

SALLY: I'm sorry. [Then, suddenly] Will you excuse me a minute? [She leaves quickly and goes to the bedroom, closing the door firmly behind her. She looks at the telephone hesitantly for a moment, then sits, grasps it with determination, and dials. Meanwhile Bill is collecting things for the meal in the kitchen—eggs, milk, pepper, salt, etc., filling the base of the double boiler and putting it on the stove. Into phone] Hello? Is Mr. Bartlett there? Miss Middleton. Miss Sally Middleton. Thanks. [She holds on nervously] Hello . . . Ken? Yes. I'm fine. Ken, I wonder if I can ask you a favor? . . . Well, a friend of mine . . . a soldier . . . is in town on leave, and he wanted terribly to go to your show tonight. I wondered if you had any seats left he could buy . . . Well, two . . . yes, yes, I was going with him . . . You could? Oh, that's wonderful. It was the only thing he wanted to see and . . . it's terribly nice of you . . . Oh, are you going to be there? Good. Yes, yes, of course, we'd like to . . . Page. Sergeant Page . . . Oh, that's sweet of you. I do appreciate it. . . . Ken, I read the notices. I'm so glad it's such a hit. Well, thank you again . . . so much. Good-bye, Ken. [She hangs up with a little exhausted "Phew" from the strain, then returns to the kitchen]

BILL: [Breaking eggs into a bowl] Now come and learn how to make scrambled eggs properly.

SALLY: All right.

BILL: First you break the eggs.

SALLY: Yes, I do know that.

BILL: Oh . . . do you have an egg-beater?

SALLY: [Getting it] Yes. It's always scared me to death.

BILL: They're better if you beat them.

SALLY: [As Bill breaks the last egg] Bill . . .

BILL: [Pausing] What?

SALLY: It's all right about tonight. I've got the tickets.

BILL: You have? How?

SALLY: I called up Kenneth Bartlett. They're at the theatre, in your name. You're to pick them up by seven o'clock. He wants us to have a drink with him in the intermission.

BILL: Good. What's he like?

SALLY: He's nice. Very nice.

BILL: What made you suddenly change your mind?

SALLY: I don't know. Yes, I do.

BILL: What was it?

SALLY: Your kissing me.

BILL: I don't quite see the connection.

SALLY: I don't think I could explain.

BILL: May I kiss you again for getting them?

SALLY: If you want to.

BILL: I do. [He kisses her again] Thank you.

SALLY: [Smiling] Thank you.

BILL: We're going to have a nice evening. Now then . . . [He starts beating the eggs as the curtain falls]

SCENE 2:   The same. Two A.M.

When the curtain rises, the stage is in darkness. The radio is playing. The announcer's voice is heard.

ANNOUNCER: W.O.T.C. New York. Two A.M., Saturn Watch time. We bring you now an electrically transcribed program of the latest dance rhythms.

[*Music starts. After it has been playing a moment the telephone begins to ring. After three or four rings, the front door opens.* Bill *and* Sally *come in. She wears a dinner dress under a day coat*]

SALLY: It is! I told you it was! [*She starts for the bedroom*]

BILL: Wait a minute. You don't want to answer that.

SALLY: [*Arrested*] Why not?

BILL: Because you know perfectly well who it is.

SALLY: [*Whispering*] Olive?

BILL: Sure. And I don't know what you're whispering for. She can't possibly hear you. [Sally *stands irresolute, looking at him pleadingly. The bell continues*] Do you want to talk to her . . . now?

SALLY: Not really.

BILL: [*Takes her hand and pulls her toward sofa*] Well, then this is your chance for a first lesson in self-control with the telephone. Sit down, and let it ring.

[Sally *sits down. The telephone continues. It is obviously an effort to her to stay where she is.* Bill *switches on the lamps and stands watching her with amusement. Silence for a moment. Then she leaps up*]

SALLY: It's no good. I can't stand it.

[*The telephone stops*]

BILL: There. It's all over. It's stopped.

SALLY: I feel as if it had died. And *I'd* killed it. [*She now notices the radio*] Did you turn the radio on?

BILL: No.

SALLY: Then it must have *been* on. We must have left it on. [*She goes to radio and turns it off*] It must have been playing all evening . . . all by itself.

BILL: [*Amused*] Does that bother you, too?

SALLY: Yes, it does. Sort of hurting its feelings . . . no one listening.

BILL: You're crazy.

SALLY: [*Taking off her coat*] It's sort of spooky, too. The telephone and the radio, both going, and no one paying any attention. It's like . . . like a world where everyone's dead, and *they're* still going on.

BILL: [*Taking the coat from her*] You have pretty fancies, don't you? I hate to spoil it, but if everyone *were* dead, there wouldn't be any telephone and radio to go on.

SALLY: Why not?

BILL: Because they don't work without human agency . . . yet.

SALLY: I don't think of things like that. Isn't it funny, to think that all those things, like electricity, were there all the time . . . just waiting to be discovered?

BILL: I bet they got awfully impatient. Thought Benjamin Franklin and Marconi were just *never* coming along.

SALLY: [*Looking worried*] Oh . . .

BILL: Stop it.

SALLY: What?

BILL: Getting sorry for electricity.

SALLY: [*Laughing*] Oh . . . I was, too. [*She rises*] Do you want a drink?

BILL: I could do with a nightcap. Are you going to have one?

SALLY: I think I'll have a glass of milk . . . if you don't mind.

BILL: Why should I mind?

SALLY: Men do . . . sometimes.

BILL: I wish you'd stop thinking that *I'm* "men." As a matter of fact, I'll have a glass of milk, too.

SALLY: [*As they go through to the kitchen*] Good. Would you like some cookies? My mother made them. She sent them to me.

BILL: [*Taking the cookie jar*] Where does your mother live?

SALLY: [*Getting the milk from the icebox*] At home. Joplin, Missouri.

BILL: I've never been to Joplin.

SALLY: [*Pouring two glasses*] Why should you?

BILL: Have you a large family?

SALLY: Um. Rather.

BILL: Are you fond of them?

SALLY: Yes, very. Only I can't stand them for more than two weeks at a time, any more. That's sad, don't you think?

BILL: I think it's natural.

SALLY: I hate myself for it. But it's no good, trying. That's another reason why I'm so happy about this job coming now. I was afraid I'd have to go back home for the summer.

[*They return to the living room, settling on the couch, with the milk and cookies*]

SALLY: [*As they go*] I guess a family's really only good when you're sick . . . once you're grown up. And I'm never sick. So . . . [*Sitting and taking up her milk*] I wonder if that *was* Olive on the telephone?

BILL: She's probably been calling ever since we left the theatre.

SALLY: It was too bad we had to run into her. We should have seen her in the intermission. Or afterwards. She'll think we were avoiding her.

BILL: Sure. That's why she's calling.

SALLY: But we weren't. We couldn't help it.

BILL: [*Eating, calmly*] I know.

SALLY: Doesn't that worry you?

BILL: [*As before*] Not a bit. I didn't think the guy looked so hot, did you? Of course, I may be prejudiced, but I don't think *I'd* have turned down *me* for him.

SALLY: I was a *little* disappointed.

BILL: [*After a pause, watching her*] I liked your friend, Kenneth Bartlett.

SALLY: [*Eagerly*] He *is* nice, isn't he?

BILL: I thought he was grand. He likes you, too.

SALLY: How do you know?

BILL: He said so. Told me what a grand kid you were, and a good little actress . . . and generally tops.

SALLY: [*Wondering a little*] Did he? When?

BILL: In the men's room at the Plaza. That's where men always tell each other things like that.

SALLY: You didn't *mind* our going on with his party, did you?

BILL: No, it was a good party. I've had a grand evening. And a grand day. Except that I've not seen much of *you*.

SALLY: [*Laughing*] You've seen me steadily for the last thirty hours!

BILL: I haven't. I slept ten of them, damn it. Spent three alone this afternoon getting a hotel room . . . sat beside you in a crowded theatre all evening, and shared you with a party of ten ever since. Will you spend tomorrow with me, to make up?

SALLY: I'd love to.

BILL: Good. [*There is a small pause. He rises, walking away and looking into his milk*] Did you notice the girl at the Persian Room that I went over to talk to?

SALLY: Yes.

BILL: Do you know who that was?

SALLY: No. Not . . . ?

BILL: [*Nodding*] That was the girl from Paris.

SALLY: It's been that kind of an evening! How . . . how long since you'd seen her?

BILL: Seven years.

SALLY: Not *since* Paris?

BILL: We said good-bye at the Gare du Nord, on May the second, 1936.

SALLY: Were you engaged, or anything?

BILL: We were engaged, and *everything*. We were going to be married that summer. But that was the summer that things busted up for me. She couldn't see herself living in Pittsburgh, with no money.

SALLY: She married someone else, you said. Was that her husband with her tonight?

BILL: Yes. This *is* my evening for running into my successors, isn't it?

SALLY: What was he like?

BILL: Well, there again I guess I'm prejudiced.

SALLY: Was it *awful* . . . seeing her again?

BILL: No. Not after the first moment. And that was funny, because . . . last night at the restaurant it did get me down, remembering it all. And then the minute we'd said hello, the corner of my mouth suddenly stopped twitching, and I found myself looking at her and wondering what the hell it had all been about. I don't know *when* I stopped loving her—I just stopped thinking of her, I guess, and didn't realize I had . . . until tonight. Last night must have been just a . . . sort of reflex action.

SALLY: Haven't you been in love since?

BILL: [*Briefly*] No. Nor wanted to. That was quite enough.

SALLY: You don't believe in love?

BILL: I don't believe in being unhappily in love, and I'm not taking chances.

SALLY: I know what you mean. Does it feel . . . good, to be over it?

BILL: Good, but a little shocking, if you've been cherishing the illusion that you weren't.

SALLY: Yes. [*Then looking away from him, after a pause*] I was in love with Kenneth Bartlett. At least, I thought I was.

BILL: [*Quietly*] I know.

SALLY: How do you know?

BILL: [*Quickly*] Oh, he didn't tell me. I guessed. [*Gently*] Did *you* find you were over it tonight?

SALLY: [*Nodding*] I was dreading seeing him at the theatre. And then he came up to us, and it was all right. I just thought how nice he was.

BILL: That's wonderful. I wish *I'd* been able to think that . . . about *her*.

SALLY: I'm sorry you couldn't. It's a good feeling. But you're right. It *is* a little shocking.

BILL: I think it's only one's vanity that's shocked. One likes to think one's the kind that *doesn't* get over things.

SALLY: But you do think one *ought* to . . . get over them, I mean?

BILL: Good God, yes. [*He sits beside her on the couch*]

SALLY: [*After a pause*] It's funny our being in the same boat.

BILL: It's a good boat. [*Taking her hand*] Sally . . .

SALLY: What?

BILL: You don't think . . . my coming along had anything to do with helping to set you free, do you?

SALLY: I . . . don't know.

BILL: I'd like to think it did.

SALLY: I think it did.

BILL: I'm glad.

SALLY: So am I . . . Did . . . [*She stops*] No, I won't ask that.

BILL: Why not?

SALLY: No, I won't.

BILL: Were you going to ask whether *your* coming along helped to set *me* free?

SALLY: You don't have to answer that. And I *didn't* ask it.

BILL: If I say I think I was free already . . . let me say, too, that I think it was your coming along that helped me *know* I was, and that I'm very grateful.

SALLY: I'm glad.

BILL: So am I. [*He draws her to him and kisses her*] You're very sweet.

SALLY: You're very nice.

BILL: I couldn't have imagined . . . possibly . . . having so nice a time as this.

SALLY: Me, too. I've had such miserable week-ends here alone.

[*Silence for a moment. He continues to fondle her, his lips against her hair and cheek, moving toward her lips again. Again they kiss.*

Then, suddenly, she thrusts him aside, and rises abruptly and agitatedly]

BILL: What's the matter?

SALLY: We mustn't go on like this.

BILL: Why not?

SALLY: Because I've given it up!

BILL: What?

SALLY: That sort of thing.

BILL: For Lent?

SALLY: No . . . permanently.

BILL: [*Protesting, laughing*] Oh, Sally . . . darling . . .

SALLY: I have. I'm sorry, but I have.

BILL: Why have you?

SALLY: I *can't* go on doing it with every man I meet.

BILL: [*Amused*] Do you?

SALLY: I *did*. No, I didn't, *really*, but . . . I've got to draw the line somewhere.

BILL: So you draw it at me?

SALLY: There's nothing personal about it. I do *like* you, but . . . we mustn't go on like that.

BILL: I'm sorry. Do you want me to go?

SALLY: No, but, well, maybe you'd rather.

BILL: Because you won't let me make love to you?

SALLY: Yes.

BILL: Is this another of your theories about "men"?

SALLY: It's a true one. If you start something like that . . . well you've no right to start it, if you don't mean to go through with it. And I *don't* mean to . . . and I *shouldn't* have started it. And you've every right to be mad at me.

BILL: I'm not mad at you.

SALLY: Aren't you?

BILL: No, I think you're absurd, but sweet.

SALLY: I'm terribly sorry.

BILL: It's all right . . . so long as you like me.

SALLY: I do.

BILL: And you'll see me tomorrow?

SALLY: If you still want to.

BILL: Sure, I want to. I want to see you *all* tomorrow.

SALLY: I thought you were going to sleep all day.

BILL: That was in another life. What shall we do?

SALLY: Do you want to come to breakfast?

BILL: Yes, please. What time?

SALLY: What time would you like it?

BILL: Any time. Nine o'clock?

SALLY: Certainly.

BILL: And then?

SALLY: Well, if it's fine, and it really looked tonight as if it might be . . . we can . . . walk in the Park . . . go to the Zoo . . . take a bus some place. Up to the Cloisters, maybe.

BILL: That sounds swell. Well, if we're breakfasting at nine . . . [*He makes a move*]

SALLY: We don't have to. Why don't you call me when you wake up?

BILL: I might not wake up. And I don't want to waste any of tomorrow with you. I'll leave a call for eight o'clock.

SALLY: Oh, but that's awful for you. Eight o'clock on Sunday morning when you're on leave.

BILL: I don't mind. Would *you* like to call me when *you* wake up?

SALLY: No, I don't mind waking at eight.

BILL: You won't have to. You can sleep till half-past.

SALLY: I don't see that *either* of us has to. Why don't you stay here again?

BILL: Do you mean that?

SALLY: If you weren't too uncomfortable.

BILL: What sort of places do you think I've *been* sleeping in this last year?

SALLY: Well, then, please do. Then you can sleep as late as you want in the morning, and we'll just do whatever we feel like. I like days like that.

BILL: So do I.

SALLY: [*Worried again*] Of course, it does waste your hotel room.

BILL: And disappoints the Hotel Taft. But I think it can take that.

SALLY: Well, then, will you?

BILL: [*After a tiny pause*] Sure. Thanks.

SALLY: Do you want to turn in now?

BILL: Well, it's almost three. I should think I might. [*Goes to divan, and strips cover*] This is where I came in!

SALLY: You haven't got your bag this time. You'll want a toothbrush. I'll get it for you.

BILL: Why don't you go ahead, and get yourself to bed first? You were up hours earlier than I was.

SALLY: I'm all right.

BILL: No, do. You don't have to play hostess to me tonight. [*He gives her her coat*] I'll tidy up, and empty the ashtrays . . . Go on.

SALLY: All right, then. I won't be long. [*She goes into the bedroom, taking her coat, strips her bed cover, and takes off her shoes. Bill performs the night ritual with the ashtrays, drinks the last of his milk, and takes the glasses, cookie jar and ashtrays into the kitchen. Meanwhile Sally tries to get out of her dress, but the zipper catches. She tugs at it for quite a while, despairingly. Then she calls*] Bill! Bill! [*But Bill is in the kitchen and does not hear. She comes into the living room and calls again*] Bill! Where are you, Bill!

[*Bill emerges from the kitchen*]

BILL: Were you calling?

SALLY: Yes, my zipper's stuck.

BILL: Oh. Let me see. [*He examines it*]

SALLY: I've pulled and pulled. [*He fidgets with it*] It's never done this, before.

BILL: Yes, it's good and stuck. It's a good thing I'm here, or you'd have had to sleep in it. You still may, of course. Have you a pair of pliers?

SALLY: There are some tools in the kitchen in a box under the sink. [*Bill goes for them*] I don't really know what's there. I'm the kind who's no use with tools. Even keys won't work for me, and then someone else comes along, and it turns as easily as anything. [*She fidgets again with her zipper*] You know, this is one of my nightmares, having this happen to me in the theatre . . . during a quick change.

BILL: [*In kitchen*] Here we are.

SALLY: [*Calling*] Find it?

BILL: [*Returning*] Found it. Now then, hold still, take a deep breath, and I'll try not to hurt. [*He applies the pliers, missing the first time*] Damn. That's better . . . now it's coming . . . there! [*The zipper unzips, and her dress falls to the floor, leaving her in her slip*] Oh, I'm sorry. I'm afraid that was rather overdoing it.

SALLY: [*Stooping and picking up her dress*] Thank you so much.

BILL: [*Embarrassed*] Girls who wear zippers shouldn't live alone. Modern proverb.

SALLY: Well . . . thank you.
                    [*She is about to go. He catches her*]
BILL: Sally . . .
        [*He kisses her, and she responds. As the kiss threatens to grow more passionate, she pulls herself away*]
SALLY: [*Releasing herself, as he tries to hold her*] Don't, Bill . . . please don't.
                [*He lets her go. She goes back to the bedroom, where she stands a moment, fighting tears. Then she hangs her dress in the closet, with her coat, and goes through to the bathroom*]
[*Bill stands looking after her. Then he shrugs, turns down the day-bed, removes his coat, sits and unlaces one shoe and takes it off. He is about to start the second shoe, when he stops, looking first at his bed and then at the bedroom door*]
BILL: [*To himself*] No, this is all too god-damned silly!
        [*He puts his shoe on again, and also his coat. Then he goes to the desk, takes paper and pencil and starts to write a note*]

[*Sally comes back into the bedroom, wearing pajamas, and looking very small and young. Her mood is still melancholy, and she is near tears. She switches out the lights, except for the bed lamp, and gets into bed*]
[*During the above Bill has finished his note. He lays it on the day-bed, switches off the lamps and takes his cap, going to the door, as Sally calls*]
SALLY: [*In a muffled voice*] Bathroom's all clear.
[*He hears her, and stands with his hand on the knob of the front door*] Bill! I said the bathroom's all clear.
            [*He goes over, cap in hand, and opens the bedroom door*]
BILL: Sally, I'm not staying.
                    [*He comes into the room*]
SALLY: Why not?
BILL: Because it's silly.
SALLY: Why?

BILL: Well, because . . . as they'd say in one of those plays we both hate . . . because I'm a man, and you're a woman.

SALLY: [*After a tiny pause—gravely, but with quote marks*] And I . . . rouse the beast in you?

BILL: Exactly . . . So . . . I'll see you tomorrow.
                            [*He starts to go*]
SALLY: Bill . . . there's a beast in me, too! [*He stands looking at her, and then comes slowly to the bed*] I'm sorry, Bill, for being such a fool.

BILL: [*Tenderly*] Sally . . . [*He sits on the bed and takes her in his arms. She melts into them. In the kiss*] Oh, Sally, sweet . . .

SALLY: Oh, Bill . . .
            [*The telephone rings. She starts, disengages herself, stretching out her hand, automatically, to answer it*]
BILL: [*Slapping her hand*] Uh huh. No, no!

SALLY: [*Looking stricken*] Oh . . . [*He draws her into his arms again. She remains pressed against him, her cheek against his, looking at the telephone with scared eyes. Whispering*] You shouldn't be here.

BILL: Ssh.

SALLY: She'll come around in the morning.

BILL: Let the morning look after itself. [*He kisses her again and, without breaking the embrace, switches out the bed light. The telephone goes on ringing. In the dark*] I love you, Sally.

SALLY: No. No, don't say that. You mustn't. We must keep this gay!
                    [*The telephone goes on ringing*]

Act III

SCENE 1:   *The same. Noon. Sunday*

   When the curtain rises, a card-table has been set up and laid for breakfast for two. Sally's bed has been made; the day-bed is still turned down and unslept in, as it was left. In the bedroom, Bill's coat and cap are on the back of a chair.

   In the kitchen, breakfast is cooking—coffee on the stove, and water boiling in a saucepan. Sally comes through into the living room with two glasses of orange juice, which she puts on the table, attending to the toaster and starting to pour the coffee which she also fetches from the kitchen. Bill comes into the bedroom from the bathroom, fully dressed, except for his coat.

BILL: [*Calling*] How's everything coming?

SALLY: [*Calling back*] Everything's ready!
            [*Bill puts on his coat, tossing his cap onto the bed, and goes into the living room*]

BILL: Oh, boy, sump'n smells good!

SALLY: It's the coffee. I wish coffee tasted as good as it smells.

BILL: I think if I were a woman, I'd *wear* coffee as a perfume.

[*He kisses her and then, feeling thoroughly at home, removes his coat and throws it across the back of the couch*]

SALLY: [*Rising*] I'll just see if the water's boiling for the eggs.

BILL: No, don't. Sit down. Be still. There's lots of time for the eggs.

SALLY: But the water will boil over.

BILL: No, it won't. Unless you've overfilled the saucepan. It'll just boil away. And I suppose that'll worry you. Mustn't leave the water alone. It'll get hurt.

SALLY: [*Smiling*] I'd better turn it off. [*Goes into kitchen*] Don't you *want* eggs? I can just as easily put them on.

BILL: And then keep hopping up and down, watching the time? No, let's have our coffee in peace.

SALLY: All right.

[*She turns off the stove and comes back to living room, where she takes the toast from the toaster, bringing it to the table*]

BILL: [*Rising*] One thing *I'll* do before we really settle.

SALLY: What's that?

BILL: Cover up the day-bed. Don't you think it looks kind of deserted and reproachful . . . all unslept in?

SALLY: [*Helping him with the cover*] Yes, I do. I always think a bed that hasn't been slept in looks sort of forlorn in the morning. If ever I come in very late at night, and my bed's been turned down, I always want to say to it, "It's all right. Here I am."

BILL: [*Straightening the cover*] Do you have a Sunday paper?

SALLY: [*Returning to the table*] No, we'll have to go out for one. We should have thought of it last night.

BILL: I'll go and get it, later. I must have my funnies.

SALLY: Me, too. It wouldn't be Sunday to me, without Dick Tracy.

BILL: Let's get *all* the Sunday papers, and really mess up the apartment. [*Comes back to the table and sits*] This is so pleasant, Sally *dear*. Our second breakfast together. Quite an old married couple. You're nice to have breakfast with.

SALLY: So are you. Have you . . . have you had breakfast with a lot of girls?

BILL: [*Putting down his cup*] Sally, that is not a question to ask *now*. If ever.

SALLY: I wasn't being curious . . . about your life, I mean. I was just wondering whether there was a lot of difference between girls at breakfast.

BILL: Yes. Quite a lot.

SALLY: Do some of them . . . bother you . . . *talking* about things?

BILL: Sally, stop it.

SALLY: I'm asking quite impersonally.

BILL: You can't. It's an extremely personal question.

SALLY: I'm sorry. There ought to be a book of rules for conversation on occasions like this.

BILL: There oughtn't to be a book at all. Just be natural, and yourself.

SALLY: I *was* being myself.

BILL: Well, then, *don't* be yourself. Think of the other fellow for a change.

SALLY: I didn't mean . . .

BILL: Sally, I said "stop."

SALLY: I'm sorry. Shall I start some more toast?

BILL: Yes, please, unless it means fetching it from the kitchen.

SALLY: No, I've got it right here.

BILL: Then, yes, please.

[*She rises. The front-door buzzer goes. They both start*]

SALLY: [*In a stricken whisper*] Olive!

BILL: [*Also whispering*] Don't answer it.

SALLY: [*Whispering*] Oh, but I must!

BILL: [*Whispering*] Let her think you've gone out. She'll go away.

SALLY: [*Still whispering*] She'll ask the elevator man, and he'll tell her I haven't. She'll come back.

BILL: Let her.

SALLY: I can't. I'll get rid of her. You go into the bathroom. [*She starts him toward the bathroom*]

BILL: And suppose *she* wants to go to the bathroom?

SALLY: Then go into the kitchen. Take all that with you. [*Indicating table*]

BILL: Really!

[*The buzzer sounds again*]

SALLY: [*Whispering feverishly*] Please!

[*Bill unwillingly takes the table and carries it through to the kitchen. Sally follows with the toaster. Then she looks around, straightening the chairs. The buzzer goes again*]

SALLY: [*Calling*] I'm just coming!

[*She starts for the door, and then remembers Bill's coat, lying over the back of the couch. She gets that, too, and thrusts it at him in the kitchen. Then, in a wild scramble, she opens the door. Olive is outside*]

SALLY: [*With creditable surprise*] Olive!

OLIVE: I've been ringing and ringing.

SALLY: I'm sorry. I was in the bathroom. I *thought* I heard the buzzer.

[*Throughout the ensuing scene, Bill is in the kitchen, listening and pantomiming reactions to what goes on, while he puts on his coat and drinks the remainder of his coffee*]

OLIVE: Well, how are you this morning?

SALLY: [*Wandering around, looking for traces of Bill to cover*] I'm fine.

OLIVE: You were out very late last night.

SALLY: I know. [*Then, quickly*] How do *you* know?

OLIVE: I called you until three o'clock. What time did you get in?

SALLY: Oh, about . . . a quarter past, I think.

OLIVE: Where did you go?

SALLY: [*Still wandering*] To the Persian Room with Ken.

OLIVE: Ken? Bartlett? Are you and he on again?

SALLY: Oh, no. We met at the theatre. What did you call up for?

OLIVE: I wanted to talk to you. Why did you and Bill cut me last night?

SALLY: [*Indignant and stopping her walk*] We didn't. We waved and waved. You saw us. You waved back.

OLIVE: I mean in the intermission. I looked for you everywhere.

SALLY: We went next door for a drink with Ken.
[*She starts to prowl again, tidying things*]

OLIVE: How did you get tickets? Ned had to pay $17.60 each for the twenty-seventh row or something. You were way down front.

SALLY: [*Straightening the cover on the day-bed*] Ken gave us the house seats.

OLIVE: What *are* you fidgeting around like that for? Come and sit down, for goodness' sake.

SALLY: I'm sorry.

[*She picks up the evening paper lying on the desk, and suddenly remembers that this is where* Bill's *cap has formerly been. She wonders where it is and then, with a glance at the bedroom, remembers with a gasp*]

OLIVE: [*Noticing the gasp*] What's the matter?

SALLY: Nothing. Why?

OLIVE: The way you jumped.

SALLY: [*Innocently*] I just remembered something.

OLIVE: What?

SALLY: Something I've got to do. Listen, is that the telephone?

OLIVE: I don't hear anything.

SALLY: I think it is. I'll just go see. [*She goes into the bedroom, picks the cap up quickly, goes to the night table, stuffs it into the drawer, looks around again and then picks up the telephone*] Hello? Hello? No, I guess it wasn't.

[*She returns to the living room*]

OLIVE: Well, then, now will you sit down and relax?

SALLY: Yes, now I'll sit down and relax.
[*She does so*]

OLIVE: You and Bill have certainly been seeing a lot of each other!

SALLY: Well, I don't think he knows many people in New York.

OLIVE: [*Sarcastically*] So you thought you'd be kind to him.

SALLY: [*Sharply*] It wasn't a question of being kind. He's very nice. Very nice indeed.

[*She turns her head slightly toward kitchen, where* Bill *pantomimes his reaction to this*]

OLIVE: I know he is. I introduced him to you. Where did he finally end up staying?

SALLY: He got a room at the Hotel Taft.

OLIVE: Is he there now, do you know?

SALLY: How should I know?

OLIVE: Would you mind if I called him up?

SALLY: No, of course not.

OLIVE: [*Starting across to bedroom. Stops in doorway*] Come and talk to me.

[Sally, *who has made a small start toward kitchen, follows her.* Bill *applies his eye to the door crack and sees them go. He waits a moment, and then takes the opportunity to slip out. He makes for the front door, looks around for his cap, remembers where it is, gives a panic-stricken look at the bedroom, and then shrugs his shoulders and slips out. In the meantime, in the bedroom, the following scene takes place*]

OLIVE: Where's the book? [*She puts her hand to the night-table drawer*]

SALLY: [*Hastily*] It's underneath . . . on the floor.

OLIVE: Oh, yes. You are nervous this morning.

SALLY: [*Sitting on bed*] I'm sorry.

OLIVE: [*Hunting for the number*] What did you think of the show last night?

SALLY: I thought it was lovely.

OLIVE: I thought it stank.

SALLY: Oh . . . why?

OLIVE: What do you mean—why?

SALLY: I mean—why?

OLIVE: [*Crossly*] I don't know why. I thought it did. If I tell you a piece of fish stinks, you don't ask me why, do you?

[*Dials number*]

SALLY: It's a big hit.

OLIVE: Anything's a hit in war time.

SALLY: Not the plays I'm in. Oh . . .

OLIVE: [*Into phone*] I want to speak to Sergeant Page, please. Oh, all right. [*To Sally*] What were you going to say?

SALLY: I've got a job.

OLIVE: You haven't! What? [*Into phone*] I want to speak to Sergeant Page, please. Sergeant William Page. Yes, he's registered there. [*To Sally*] What's the job?

SALLY: They've let Myra Foley out of *The Dark Dreamer*. They sent for me yesterday.

OLIVE: Darling, how exciting! I hear it's a wonderful part. [*Flatly*] I had an offer yesterday, too.

SALLY: Oh, what was it?

OLIVE: [*Grimly*] They want me to go out with *Tobacco Road*!

SALLY: Are you going?

OLIVE: Darling . . . all those turnips? [*Into phone*] Oh . . . well will you say Miss Lashbrooke called? Lashbrooke. L-A-S—No, S as in . . . Oh, hell, say Olive. Yes, Olive. [*Hangs up*] Not there.

SALLY: He's probably gone out.

OLIVE: Aren't you smart?

SALLY: Olive, don't be that way. What's the matter?

OLIVE: [*Turning on her*] The matter is that I don't like the way you've acted over Bill. He was my beau, and . . .

SALLY: And you left him on my hands.

OLIVE: Not for you to take over.

SALLY: I haven't "taken him over."

OLIVE: I thought I was safe with *you.*

SALLY: Well, I like that. Why?

OLIVE: I thought you were all broken up about Kenneth Bartlett. I should have known that was just the dangerous time.

[*She goes into the living room*]

SALLY: [*Following her*] What was I to do? Leave him alone all week-end?

OLIVE: That wasn't your business.

SALLY: You turned him down for your Commander friend. What's happened to him, by the way?

OLIVE: He had to go call on his grandmother in Gramercy Park. We're meeting for lunch at the Brevoort.

SALLY: *You've* been having fun this week-end. Why shouldn't I?

OLIVE: Did you say *fun?*

SALLY: Hasn't it been?

OLIVE: *You* went to the Persian Room last night. What do you think *we* did?

SALLY: What?

OLIVE: Played gin rummy at the 1-2-3 until four o'clock, when he practically passed out from Cuba Libres. He's only just *discovered* gin rummy. That's the kind of a guy he is. I think the real reason I hated the show so much last night was that he worshipped it. And so noisily.

SALLY: Yes, I heard his laugh.

OLIVE: It stopped the show in one place. The whole audience turned around. Of course, I know he's good-looking. . . .

SALLY: [*Involuntarily*] Oh . . . [*She stops*]

OLIVE: What were you going to say?

SALLY: I was sort of . . . disappointed in his looks.

OLIVE: Oh, no, he's *terribly* good-looking. Although the hairline did seem to me to have receded a little since last year. And to think I passed up Bill for that! What time's Bill going back tonight— do you know?

SALLY: No, I don't.

OLIVE: Maybe we could dine together. If not, let's you and me. Dutch.

SALLY: I . . . I don't think I can.

OLIVE: Why? What are you doing?

SALLY: I've got to work on the part.

OLIVE: Just an early dinner. I'd like to get to bed early, anyway.

SALLY: [*Rising*] We'll see, but I don't think so. Thank you very much.

OLIVE: Now *you're* mad at *me!*

SALLY: Well, I don't think you've any right . . .

OLIVE: [*Rising*] I have a perfect right. Bill was *my* gink.

SALLY: [*Courageously for a second*] Well, he isn't any more!

OLIVE: You know, I'm a fool. That's what's the matter with me. Trusting everyone! Gullible Gertie! You . . . who were so worried about yourself the other afternoon . . . who were going to "give it all up" . . .

SALLY: Well, I meant that . . .

OLIVE: [*Rising*] Only Bill came along, and you couldn't keep your hands off him.

SALLY: [*Angry, and also agonized, imagining that Bill can hear*] Olive . . . I think you'd better go!

OLIVE: Oh, I'll go fast enough, only . . . [*The telephone rings. They both start*] There's your telephone.

[*Sally goes into the bedroom and answers it*]

SALLY: Hello . . . yes . . . Who's that? [*Her mouth opens in astonishment. She looks involuntarily toward the kitchen*] Where are you? How did you . . . ? [*She smiles*] Yes . . . yes, of course you can come around. Olive's here. She's just been calling you at the Taft.

OLIVE: [*Coming into the room*] Let me talk to him.

SALLY: She wants to talk to you. . . . Yes, as soon as you like. Yes, I know. I've got it. No! All right. Here. Here's Olive.

[*She hands the phone to* Olive]

OLIVE: [*Cooing a little*] Bill? How are you? I've been calling and calling you. What are you doing? How soon? [*Looks at her watch*] Well, don't make it any more. I've got to run. I'll see you. [*She hangs up*] Where was he?

SALLY: At a drug store.

OLIVE: Where—did he say?

SALLY: He said quite near.

OLIVE: I'll just wait and say hello to him.

SALLY: What time is your lunch?

OLIVE: One.

SALLY: It must be almost that now.

OLIVE: He can wait. [*Honeyedly*] What were we talking about?

SALLY: [*Primly*] I think I'd asked you to go, and you said you would.

OLIVE: Oh, darling, you didn't mean that. Nor did I. [*She kisses her*]

SALLY: [*With distaste*] Let's go in the other room. Oh . . . [*She pauses*]

OLIVE: What is it?

SALLY: Just . . . the thing I remembered before. Something I have to give the elevator man. You go on. I'll be right after you.

[*She moves toward the dressing room, as though she were going in, to deceive* Olive. *Olive goes on into the living room, where she sees the manuscript on a table, and picks it up to read.*]

Sally *takes Bill's cap from the drawer of the night table and looks around for something to wrap it in. All there is is a copy of* Vogue. *She thrusts it between the pages, and goes out to the front door*]

OLIVE: What have you got there?

SALLY: Just a copy of Vogue.

OLIVE: What does the elevator man want a copy of Vogue for?

SALLY: [*Opening the door*] For his wife.

OLIVE: Really! You don't mind my looking at your script?

SALLY: [*As she goes*] No, of course not.
[*She goes out, leaving the door open. Olive sits puzzledly with the script, not looking at it. Sally returns from the elevator, smiling contentedly*]

OLIVE: [*Suspiciously*] You're very pleased with yourself about something.

SALLY: [*Airily*] No, no. I'm just happy.

OLIVE: What about?

SALLY: [*Vaguely*] Oh . . . everything.

OLIVE: [*After a moment's scrutiny of her*] Sally . . . you wouldn't be going and getting silly and sentimental over Bill, would you? Because, if you do, you'll lose him even quicker than you lost Kenneth Bartlett.

SALLY: I've no intention of getting sentimental.

OLIVE: [*Sweetly*] No, darling, no intention—but you're the kind who can't sew a button on for a man without thinking it's for life. And Bill's told me, over and over again, that he's no place for sentiment in his scheme of things.

SALLY: [*After a silence, rising*] Well, I've told you before, neither have I . . . any more. So that's all right. [*Doorbell rings*] There he is.

OLIVE: He's got here quick.

[*Sally opens door. Enter Bill. He wears his cap, carries the Sunday newspaper, and some flowers in paper*]

BILL: [*Gesturing with his cap*] Hello.

SALLY: [*Smiling broadly*] Hello.

OLIVE: Hello, Bill.

BILL: [*Pleasantly, but perfunctorily*] Hello. [*To Sally*] I was afraid I might be calling too early for you, but I had to go out to get my Sunday paper, so I brought you these. [*He hands her the flowers*]

SALLY: Oh . . . how lovely! [*She looks at them*] "Daffodils . . . that come before the swallow dares . . ."

BILL: [*Finishing the quotation*] "And take the winds of March with beauty."

OLIVE: What a cute saying!

BILL: He was a cute sayer.

OLIVE: Who?

BILL: Shakespeare.

SALLY: I love spring flowers. Thank you so much. I'll just put them in water.
[*She takes them to the kitchen*]

BILL: Well, what sort of a time have *you* been having?

OLIVE: Not a lot of fun. What time do you have to go back tonight?

BILL: Around ten.

OLIVE: Well, Ned's train goes at four. I wonder . . . could we dine together?

BILL: I'm afraid I have a dinner date.

OLIVE: Oh, that's too bad. Well, maybe a cocktail?

BILL: I'm afraid that's gone, too.

OLIVE: [*Defeated*] Oh. Oh, well, I'm sorry. [*Telephone rings*] There's the telephone. Sally! Sally! Telephone!

SALLY: [*Coming from kitchen*] I know. I heard it.
[*She goes through to the bedroom, leaving the door open*]

OLIVE: I have to go. I'll just wait until Sally's through.
[*She starts to put on her gloves*]

SALLY: [*Into telephone*] Hello? Yes . . . Well, I . . . You have? Oh, how wonderful! Where? Yes . . . yes, of course. Right away.
[*She hangs up, stands a moment, bothered, and then returns to the living room*]

SALLY: I've got to go out.

BILL: [*Disappointed*] Oh . . . where?

SALLY: That was the producer calling. They've made another change in the cast. The leading man's out, and they've got Henry Atherton! [*Olive pulls a face*] He was the star of Olive's show that just closed.

BILL: Yes, I know. He was the one with the . . . [*He indicates his hair*] Yes, I remember.

SALLY: They want me to go and work with him this afternoon.

BILL: Could you lunch with me first?

SALLY: I'm afraid I can't. I've got to go right away. They've all had big breakfasts.

BILL: Well, can I take you there?

SALLY: [*Nodding*] I'll just go and change.
[*She runs back to the bedroom, closing the door behind her, and disappears into the dressing-room*]

OLIVE: [*Sugaredly*] Sally's sweet, isn't she?

BILL: She certainly is.

OLIVE: But, you know, playing with Henry Atherton, I'm afraid she's headed for trouble. She's just about the age he likes them.

BILL: Oh, I should think Sally could take care of herself.

OLIVE: Oh, yes, she can . . . if she wants to. But a star's a star, and she's always had a crush on him. [*Collecting herself to go*] Can you still not manage cocktails, by the way?

BILL: I'm afraid I can't.

OLIVE: Well, you'll let me know next time you're coming, won't you? And . . . [*Seductively*] I won't let *anything* interfere.

BILL: Olive, I'm afraid I don't play around with married women.

OLIVE: [*After a defeated second*] Oh, but that's all over. We talked it out thoroughly. I'm not seeing him again.

BILL: You mean—you're divorcing?

OLIVE: Yes.

BILL: Do you think that looks well—to divorce a service man?

OLIVE: Just what are you trying to say?

BILL: Just . . . very tactfully, and with no hard feelings . . . that I think we'd better . . . leave things as they are.

OLIVE: [*Rallying after a moment*] I guess I bought that all right! Well, I've got to lunch with my ex. Good-bye, Bill.

BILL: Good-bye, Olive.

[*They shake hands*]

OLIVE: Say good-bye to Sally for me. [*She turns at the door*] By the way, did Sally *tell* you anything about Ned?

BILL: No. But I saw him with you last night. And, Olive, you'd never have married that—not in a million years.

OLIVE: [*Looking at him*] I never knew men could be such bitches! [*She goes*]

[*Bill laughs, takes a cigarette. Sally returns in a hurry, having changed her dress and carrying her hat, bag, gloves and shoes*]

SALLY: Has she gone?

BILL: She's gone. I'm afraid that's the end of a beautiful friendship.

SALLY: [*Putting on her shoes*] I'm afraid . . . for me, too.

BILL: Well, it can't be helped. Where are you rehearsing?

SALLY: At Henry Atherton's apartment. It's on 90th Street.

BILL: Is that usual?

SALLY: What?

BILL: Rehearsing in actors' apartments?

SALLY: Oh . . . yes . . . quite. If they're stars.

BILL: Is anyone else going to be there?

SALLY: I guess so. Why—what's the matter?

BILL: [*Briefly*] Nothing. [*Changing his mood*] How long will it go on?

SALLY: All afternoon, I'm afraid.

BILL: [*Lightly*] What am *I* going to do?

SALLY: Would you like to come back here? I'll give you the key, and you can . . . use the apartment as if it were your own.

BILL: I thought that's what I *had* been doing. You'll have dinner with me?

SALLY: Yes.

BILL: Promise?

SALLY: I promise. Now I must go.

BILL: [*Stopping her and holding her*] Sally, I don't see anything of you . . . at all! I want to talk to you . . . about so many things.

SALLY: [*Shyly*] No—why? We don't need to talk. There's nothing to talk about. We've had a lovely time, and . . . well, we don't want to get . . . sentimental about it. Do we?

BILL: [*Quietly—disappointed*] I guess not.

SALLY: Well, then. Come along. I'm late. [*She goes to the door. He stands still. She looks back at him*] Aren't you coming?

BILL: [*After a second*] Sure.

SALLY: I'll just ring for the elevator.

[*She goes out. He looks after her a moment, putting out his cigarette, his face puzzled and unhappy. Then he picks up his cap, shrugs, and follows her out*]

SCENE 2: *The same. About six-thirty*

The card-table is set up again, laid now for supper. The whole room has been made to look as attractive as possible. The daffodils are in a vase, and there are a number of other vases of spring flowers, including some sprays of white lilac.

Bill is kneeling on the day-bed, a book in his hand, dividing his attention between it and the window from which he is watching for Sally's return. After a moment, he sees her coming, goes into the kitchen, opens the icebox and takes out a bottle of champagne, which he brings to the living room, setting it on a side-table, where two champagne glasses are waiting. Then the buzzer sounds, and he goes to the door and opens it. Sally is outside.

SALLY: [*Subduedly*] Hi!

BILL: Hi!

SALLY: [*Seeing the table*] Why, what's all this?

BILL: I thought we'd have dinner home tonight.

SALLY: It'll be rather a picnic one.

BILL: Well . . .

SALLY: Lunch sausage and marinated herring, I'm afraid.

BILL: That's all right.

SALLY: Where did these flowers come from? [*She turns, looking around*] Oh, but all these . . . Bill, you shouldn't!

BILL: You said you liked spring flowers, and the streets were full of them.

SALLY: Oh, but they're beautiful. [*She goes from vase to vase*] The whole room smells of them. I've never had so many. Bill, you darling . . . [*She goes to him impulsively and kisses him. Then she retreats, subduedly*] Thank you *so* much.

BILL: [*Slightly constrained, too*] How about a drink?

SALLY: [*Seeing the tray*] Champagne? Where did you find that?

BILL: [*Opening the bottle*] I found it.

SALLY: Not in *my* wine cellar!

BILL: Like some?

SALLY: Yes, please! Oh, Bill, this is very nice.

BILL: I'm glad you're pleased.

SALLY: [Sitting on the couch] It's the loveliest spring evening out.

BILL: I know. I've been looking at it, watching for you to come back.

SALLY: You know, two days ago . . . the day you got here . . . it was still all grim and wintry . . . and suddenly since then it's come with a rush. Sometimes I feel that I can't bear the spring, it's so exciting!

BILL: [Handing her a glass] I know. I walked in the Park after I left you, and it's bursting all over it. All the trees and shrubs in a kind of young green haze, and all the flowers on the corner stands looked as if they were growing there, and you wanted to buy great armfuls . . .

SALLY: You did buy great armfuls.

BILL: I bought all I could carry. [Lifting his glass] Well . . . to the spring.

SALLY: The spring.

[They drink]

BILL: [Affecting casualness] How was the rehearsal?

SALLY: That was exciting, too.

BILL: And Henry Atherton?

SALLY: He was good. You're right, though. It is dyed. But he's going to be wonderful in it. I don't know . . . I daren't say it yet . . . but I really think that this may be what I've been waiting for all these years.

BILL: [With slight double meaning] This . . . play, you mean?

SALLY: [Not getting it] Yes. Perhaps that's part of the spring, too.

BILL: [In a new voice] Sally . . .

SALLY: What?

BILL: [Sitting beside her] This is . . . our spring, isn't it? We'll have it together?

SALLY: [A little evasive] Of course . . . if you're going to be here.

BILL: I think I am. I think I can count on the spring and summer . . . if I'm lucky. I've been thinking of it all afternoon. Things that we can do together.

SALLY: [Smiling nervously and taking a cigarette] Give me a light.

BILL: [Taking the cigarette from her] Sally, don't do that.

SALLY: What?

BILL: Hold out on me.

SALLY: I don't know what you mean.

BILL: I wanted us to have dinner here tonight, because . . . well, partly because I wanted to talk to you . . .

SALLY: I wish you wouldn't.

BILL: Sally . . . if I told you that . . . given the least possible encouragement from you . . . I think I could be . . . very much in love with you . . . what would you say?

SALLY: [After a second] I wouldn't give it to you.

BILL: Why not?

SALLY: Because I don't want you to be in love with me . . . or think you are.

BILL: Why don't you?

SALLY: Because . . . that isn't how we started this.

BILL: Sally, you don't go into a love affair deliberately . . .

SALLY: I know, but . . . I don't want it to be like that. This way it's . . . fun.

BILL: Will it be any less fun if I'm in love with you?

SALLY: [Positively] Oh . . . yes! Bill, we don't have to talk about it. It has been fun . . . it is fun . . . it can go on being fun, if you won't spoil it.

BILL: That is a remark I seem to have heard before . . . but not from anyone like you.

SALLY: What do you mean?

BILL: It's the kind of thing old-fashioned women used to say . . . the older, married women . . . when they wanted to keep you hanging around.

SALLY: But I do want to keep you . . . well, not hanging around . . . but around if you want to be.

BILL: I do.

SALLY: Well, then . . . [She moves away]

BILL: [After a moment] I can't be so crazy as to have got you all wrong, but . . . you baffle me, Sally.

SALLY: I don't see why.

BILL: I guess it's the times.

SALLY: [Puzzled] The Times?

BILL: I don't mean the newspaper. I mean . . . the times . . . the war, or something. Or perhaps it's the theatre.

SALLY: I still don't know what you're talking about.

BILL: [Rising and going to her] Sally, you're not the kind of girl who has affairs . . . promiscuously . . . Or are you?

SALLY: I don't know.

BILL: What do you mean?

SALLY: I mean, I don't know what constitutes "promiscuously." I have affairs. I mean, I've had affairs.

BILL: [Quietly] Many affairs?

SALLY: You told me that was a question that one shouldn't ask.

BILL: I was quite right. One shouldn't. But, Sally, if I said that rather than keep this . . . just an affair . . . I'd sooner . . . call the whole thing off—what would you say?

SALLY: [After a long pause] I think I'd say . . . we'd better call it off.

BILL: Are you afraid of getting hurt?

SALLY: Maybe.

BILL: Sally, I wouldn't hurt you.

SALLY: That's something that I don't see how anyone can promise anyone . . . ever. And I wish you wouldn't talk about it.

BILL: There was a book of poems by your bed . . . [Fetching it from the day-bed] Poems by Dorothy Parker. You had a whole lot of them marked. Why did you have them marked?

SALLY: I guess . . . because I liked them.

BILL: This one . . . [He finds it and reads]

"I will not make you songs of hearts denied,
And you, being man, would have no tears of me,
And should I offer you fidelity
You'd be, I think, a little terrified."

[He closes the book] That one's *double*-marked. You must have liked it a lot.

SALLY: I do.

BILL: Was that, by any chance, your experience with Kenneth Bartlett?

SALLY: Perhaps . . . a little.

BILL: And you're afraid of it happening again?

SALLY: It always happens . . . doesn't it?

BILL: I don't think so.

SALLY: Well, it always does to me.

BILL: Always?

SALLY: Yes, always.

BILL: [Gently] How *often* has it happened to you?

SALLY: Twice. So far.

BILL: [Smiling, relieved] Is that all?

SALLY: What do you mean?

BILL: Is that all the affairs you've had? Two?

SALLY: [Turning to him—with naïve pleasure] You don't think that a lot?

BILL: No. Though I think it's two too many . . . for *you*.

SALLY: How many have *you* had?

BILL: I've never counted. And if I had, I wouldn't tell you.

SALLY: I told *you*.

BILL: I know.

SALLY: [With tiny sarcasm] You think it's different for a man?

BILL: I think the permissible *number* is different for a man.

SALLY: You knew about me, didn't you? You didn't believe that story about the pajamas?

BILL: No.

SALLY: Well, then . . .

BILL: Yes . . . but, Sally, I want this to have *meant* something to you.

SALLY: It did. It was terribly sweet . . .

BILL: But that's all? You won't let it mean more? Not even if I tell you that . . . if you offered me fidelity, I'd be . . . I think . . . a little *gratified*? In fact, that if you *don't* offer it to me, I'd feel as if I'd had a door slammed right bang in my face.

SALLY: [Moved, protesting] Oh, Bill!

BILL: As if the spring had suddenly turned around and said, "That's all there is. Now you can go back to winter."

SALLY: Not winter. We can keep it spring.

BILL: Nothing *stays* spring. And I wouldn't want it. There'd be something stultified and horrible about the spring, if it always stayed like that. It's *got* to become summer, and fall, and . . .

SALLY: [Bitterly] Winter.

BILL: Yes, one day. But for both of us . . . at the same time. Sally, I *am* in love with you. There's still time to turn back . . . for me to turn back, I mean . . . without its hurting too much. I told you I didn't believe in being unhappily in love. I don't. And I'm not going to be. I'm not having an awfully happy time right now. None of us are. That's not a bid for pity. It's just telling you why I feel this way. I gave up looking forward to anything seven years ago, and I've got along all right that way. With . . . Olive . . . and taking what came. That's how I wanted it. And I can go on like that. But I can't begin again . . . hoping . . . and wanting . . . and planning . . . unless there is *some* chance of those plans working out. You're scared of getting hurt again. Well, so am I. *Bitterly* scared.

SALLY: [Almost in tears] What do you *want*?

BILL: [Beside her now] I want you to let yourself love me . . . if you *can*. Because I think you can. I think you've a great talent for love, Sally, and that you're trying to fritter it and dissipate it . . . because it's been trodden on before. And if you go on like that, you'll kill it. And . . . [Slowly] I think that's one talent that *is* death to hide. [Sally *bursts into tears*] Yes, cry, if you want to. Please, please cry. Only . . . don't shut me out . . . and don't shut yourself out.

SALLY: [Sobbing] Oh, Bill . . .

BILL: I'm not asking such a great deal. I think I'd like to marry you, but we won't talk of *that*, yet. I want you to love me . . . *terribly*, but I'm not even asking *that* of you, yet.

SALLY: [Between tears] I do love you! I love you terribly! That's the hell of it! [Scrambling to her knees on the couch beside him] I won't make scenes, Bill. I won't be troublesome. . . .

BILL: [Taking her face in his hands] Ssh. You've said all I wanted you to say now. [He kisses her gently] Drink up your drink. It's getting warm.

SALLY: [Gulping it and tears at the same time] I shall be tight again. I haven't had any food.

BILL: What—not all day? Well, then, you must have dinner right away. Come and sit down.

SALLY: It'll take a little while to fix.

BILL: It's all fixed. They're sending it up from next door. From . . . "our" place. It's coming up at seven. The first course is in the icebox. Vichyssoise. I'll get it right now. [He starts to the kitchen]

SALLY: Bill . . . [She moves toward him]

BILL: [At kitchen door] You pour yourself another drink and sit down. Pour me one, too. [He goes into kitchen and takes two cups of soup from the icebox. Sally, moving a little as if in a dream, refills the glasses and bring them to the table, where she sits. Bill returns and places the soup] There. [He bends and kisses her lightly on the top of her *head. Then, standing waiter-like, with his napkin over his arm]* Madame est servie. *[He sits. Sally is still blinking away tears. She dips a spoon, and tastes]*

SALLY: Oh, Bill, this is heaven

BILL: *[Who hasn't touched his—looking at her]* Isn't it? *[He puts out his hand, and holds hers. They look at each other and smile, and then, still holding hands, dip their spoons and begin to eat as the curtain falls]*